AMERICAN
FOREIGN RELATIONS

AMERICAN FOREIGN RELATIONS

Volume 2

A History · Since 1895

FIFTH EDITION

THOMAS G. PATERSON

J. GARRY CLIFFORD

KENNETH J. HAGAN

HOUGHTON MIFFLIN COMPANY
Boston   New York

Editor-in-Chief: Jean L. Woy
Associate Editor: Leah Strauss
Project Editor: Aileen Mason
Editorial Assistant: Jane Lee
Associate Production/Design Coordinator: Jodi O'Rourke
Assistant Manufacturing Coordinator: Andrea Wagner
Senior Marketing Manager: Sandra McGuire
Senior Cover Design Coordinator: Deborah Azerrad Savona
Cover Design: Diana Coe/ko Design
Cover Art: *New York Celebrates the End of World War II,* 1945 e.t. archive, London

Printed in the U.S.A.

Library of Congress Catalog Card Number: 99-71941

ISBN: 0–395–93887–2

1 2 3 4 5 6 7 8 9-FFG-03 02 01 00 99

for

Colin Graham Paterson

Carol Davidge

Vera Low Hagan

Thomas G. Paterson is professor of history emeritus at the University of Connecticut. Born in Oregon, he earned his B.A. from the University of New Hampshire (1963) and his Ph.D. from the University of California, Berkeley (1968). He has written *Contesting Castro* (1994), *On Every Front* (1992), *Meeting the Communist Threat* (1988), and *Soviet-American Confrontation* (1973), and he is co-author of *A People and a Nation* (1998, with Mary Beth Norton et al.). Tom has edited three books of original essays: *Explaining the History of American Foreign Relations* (1991, with Michael J. Hogan), *Kennedy's Quest for Victory* (1989), and *Cold War Critics* (1971). He has also edited *Major Problems in American Foreign Relations* (2000, with Dennis Merrill), *The Origins of the Cold War* (1999, with Robert J. McMahon), and *Imperial Surge* (1992, with Stephen G. Rabe). With Bruce Jentleson, Tom was senior editor for the four-volume *Encyclopedia of American Foreign Relations* (1997). A microfilm edition of *The United States and Castro's Cuba, 1950s–1970s: The Paterson Collection* appeared in 1999. He has served on the editorial boards of *Diplomatic History* and the *Journal of American History,* and he is a past president of the Society for Historians of American Foreign Relations. Recipient of a Guggenheim fellowship, Tom has also directed National Endowment for the Humanities Summer Seminars for College Teachers. A frequent speaker on American college campuses, he has also lectured in Canada, China, Colombia, Cuba, New Zealand, Puerto Rico, Russia, and Venezuela.

J. Garry Clifford teaches at the University of Connecticut, where he is a professor of political science and director of its graduate program. Born in Massachusetts, he earned his B.A. from Williams College (1964) and his Ph.D. in history from Indiana University. He has also taught at the University of Tennessee and Dartmouth College and has directed a National Endowment for the Humanities Seminar for High School Teachers at the Franklin D. Roosevelt Presidential Library. For his book *The Citizen Soldiers* (1972), he won the Frederick Jackson Turner Award of the Organization of American Historians. With Norman Cousins, he has edited *Memoir of a Man: Grenville Clark* (1975), and with Samuel R. Spencer, Jr., he has written *The First Peacetime Draft* (1986). Garry's articles have appeared in Gordon Martel, ed., *American Foreign Relations Reconsidered* (1994), Michael J. Hogan and Thomas G. Paterson, eds., *Explaining the History of American Foreign Relations* (1991), and in such journals as the *Journal of American History, Review of Politics, Mid-America, American Neptune,* and *Diplomatic History.* He has served on the editorial board of *Diplomatic History* and also on the editorial board of the Modern War Series published by the University Press of Kansas. He frequently participates in American professional conferences and has also lectured in Russia.

Kenneth J. Hagan is an adjunct professor on the faculties of the U.S. Naval War College and the Naval Postgraduate School and professor of history and museum director emeritus at the U.S. Naval Academy in Annapolis. He previously taught at Claremont McKenna College, Kansas State University, and the U.S. Army Command and General Staff College. A native of California, he received his A.B. from the University of California, Berkeley (1958) and his Ph.D. from Claremont Graduate School (1970). Ken is the author of *This People's Navy: The Making of American Sea Power* (1991), a comprehensive history of American naval strategy and policy since the Revolution, and of *American Gunboat Diplomacy and the Old Navy, 1877–1889* (1973). His scholarship also includes two edited collections of original essays: *In Peace and War: Interpretations of American Naval History, 1775–1984* (1984) and *Against All Enemies: Interpretations of American Military History from Colonial Times to the Present* (1986). He frequently contributes articles to the journal *Naval History* and lectures annually at the Canadian Forces College in Toronto. Besides regularly participating in panels at conferences in the United States, he has given papers on the history of naval strategy in Sweden, Greece, Turkey, France, and Spain. A retired captain in the naval reserve, he served on active duty with the Pacific Fleet from 1958 to 1963 and currently advises the Naval ROTC college program on its history curriculum.

Contents

Chapter 5
Asia, Latin America, and the Vagaries of Power,
1920–1939 **141**

Chapter 6
Survival and Spheres: The Allies and the Second World War,
1939–1945 **173**

Chapter 7
All-Embracing Struggle: The Cold War Begins, 1945–1950   222

Chapter 8
Global Watch: The Korean War and Eisenhower Foreign Relations, 1950–1961   266

Chapter 9
Passing the Torch: The Vietnam Years, 1961–1969   **315**

Chapter 10
Détente and Disequilibrium, 1969–1977   **361**

Chapter 11
To Begin the World Over Again: Carter, Reagan, and Revivalism, 1977–1989   **406**

Chapter 12
Sheriff of the Posse: Americans and the World Since 1989   **460**

Maps and Graphs

Preface

Once again the advance of scholarly literature, the encouraging comments of instructors and students in history, political science, and international relations, and the passage of time have prompted us to revise *American Foreign Relations*. As before, in this fifth edition we engage influential approaches and interpretations, especially those articulated by younger scholars. We seek to explain foreign relations in the broadest manner as the many ways that peoples, organizations, states, and systems interact—economic, cultural, strategic, environmental, political, and more.

We continue to emphasize the theme of expansionism, explaining its many manifestations. We also show that on almost every issue in the history of American foreign relations, alternative voices unfailingly sounded among and against official policymakers. Americans have always debated their place in the world, their wars, their overseas commitments, and the status of their principles and power, and they have always debated the people of other nations about the spread of U.S. influence. We try to capture with vivid description and quotation the drama of the many debates.

A historical overview such as this one necessarily draws on the copious work of scholars in the United States and abroad. Their expertise informs this book throughout and helps lend it the authority instructors and students expect. Our "Further Reading" and "Notes" sections are one way to thank them for their books, articles, and conference papers. We have also appreciated their recommendations for text revisions and their suggestions for teaching the courses for which this book is intended. We thank them, too, for challenging us to consider the many different approaches and theories that have commanded attention in this field: world systems, corporatism, dependency, culture, psychology and personality, medical biography, lessons from the past ("thinking in time"), bureaucratic politics, public opinion, executive-legislative competition, gender, national security and power, impact on recipients of foreign aid, the natural environment, and ideology among them. This book also presents the findings of our own ongoing archival research and writing as we discover and rediscover the past.

The traditional topics of diplomacy, war, economic intercourse, and politics remain central to our presentation of the foreign-relations story, but we have made this edition more comprehensive by extending our discussion of the cultural dimensions of foreign relations: race-based and gender-based images of other peoples that condition the decisionmaking environment; the proliferation abroad of American mass culture (such as films and sports); the foreign response to "Americanization"; travel and tourism that help create a pool of knowledge about foreign places that promotes an expansionist consciousness; and "public diplomacy"—the presentation of a positive image of the United States abroad through propaganda, radio and television, and trade fairs. We have also expanded our coverage of relations with Native Americans and the frontier experience in the eighteenth and nineteenth centuries. Issues that spring from human interaction with the natural environment and the international conferences convened to deal with damage to the environment also receive more space in this edition. The post–Cold War declassification of documents in foreign archives—Russian, East German,

Cuban, and Chinese among them—has helped us rewrite our treatment of the Korean War, Sino-American relations, the Cuban missile crisis, and the failure of détente in the 1970s. Because scholars have increasingly explored medical health as a factor in decisionmaking, we have integrated this subject—as in the lives of Woodrow Wilson, Franklin D. Roosevelt, John F. Kennedy, and Ronald Reagan.

In preparing this edition, we once again immersed ourselves in the memoirs, diaries, letters, speeches, recorded tapes, and oral histories of U.S. and international leaders. We often let them speak for themselves in the frankest terms, guarded and unguarded. We have sought to capture their anger and their humor, their cooperation and their competitiveness, their truths and their lies, their moments of doubt and times of confidence, their triumphs and setbacks. *American Foreign Relations,* in short, strives to capture the erratic pulse of international relations through peoples' struggles to plan, decide, and administer. We study not only the leaders who made influential decisions, but also the world's peoples who welcomed, resisted, or endured the decisions that profoundly influenced their lives. In this regard, we have drawn on the growing scholarship that studies non-state actors, including peace groups, African Americans, and international bodies such as the World Health Organization.

Each chapter opens with a significant and dramatic event—a "Diplomatic Crossroad"—that helps illustrate the chief characteristics and issues of the era. The introductory and concluding sections of each chapter set the themes. Illustrations from collections around the world—many of them new to this edition—are closely tied to the narrative in image and caption description. The revised maps, graphs, and "Makers of American Foreign Relations" tables in each chapter provide essential information. The updated chapter bibliographies guide further reading and serve as a starting point for term or research papers. The "General Bibliography" at the end of the book is also a place to begin research or seek more information. The "General Bibliography" consists of three parts: first, general reference works, such as biographical dictionaries, atlases, statistics, encyclopedias, and bibliographies; second, overviews of U.S. relations with countries and regions, from Afghanistan to Zimbabwe; and, third, overviews of subjects, such as Air Force and air power, CIA and covert action, Congress, cultural relations, ethnic conflict, human rights, isolationism, Manifest Destiny, Monroe Doctrine, oil, refugees, slave trade and slavery, terrorism, and United Nations.

In the late 1970s, the People's Republic of China adopted a new system for rendering Chinese phonetic characters into the Roman alphabet. Called the Pinyin method, it replaced the Wade-Giles technique, which had long been used in English. Use of the Pinyin method is now common, and we use it in *American Foreign Relations.* Many changes are minor—Shantung has become Shandong and Mao Tse-tung has become Mao Zedong, for example. But when we have a possibly confusing Pinyin spelling, we have placed the Wade-Giles spelling in parentheses—for example, Beijing (Peking) or Jiang Jieshi (Chiang Kai-shek).

Instructors and students interested in the study of foreign-relations history are invited to join the Society for Historians of American Foreign Relations (SHAFR). This organization publishes a superb journal, *Diplomatic History,* and a newsletter; offers book, article, and lecture prizes and dissertation research grants; and holds an annual conference where scholars present their views and research results. Dues are very reasonable. For information, contact the SHAFR Business Office, Department of History, Wright State University, Dayton, OH 45435, or see SHAFR's web site at www.ohiou.edu/~shafr/shafr.htm. At this home page you will also find links to other sites related to American foreign relations.

Another informative web site is H-Diplo: Diplomatic History, found at www.h-net.msu.edu/~diplo. Besides presenting provocative online discussions on foreign-relations history, this site also provides research and bibliographic aids and an extensive list of links to other useful resources, including journals, newspapers, archives and presidential libraries, research organizations such as the National Security Archive, and government agencies such as the Central Intelligence Agency and Department of State.

Many colleagues, friends, students, and editors contributed to this edition of *American Foreign Relations* by providing research leads, correction of errors, reviews of the text, library searches, documents and essays, and editorial assistance. We give our heartiest thanks to John Burns, Alejandro Corbacho, Frank Costigliola, Michael Donoghue, Elizabeth Mahan, Elizabeth McKillen, Dennis Merrill, Marc O'Reilly, Chester Pach, Kenneth E. Shewmaker, Mark A. Stoler, Thomas Walker, Wang Li, and Imanuel Wexler. Jake Kawatski expertly prepared the comprehensive index. Houghton Mifflin's talented team merits the highest of praise: Jean L. Woy, editor-in-chief; Leah Strauss, associate editor; Aileen Mason, project editor; Jodi O'Rourke, production/design coordinator; Andrea Wagner, manufacturing coordinator; Pembroke Herbert, photo researcher; Patricia Herbst, copyeditor; and Deborah Karacozian, proofreader.

We are also eager to thank the many people who helped us in previous editions: Philip J. Avillo, Jr., Richard Baker, Ann Balcolm, Michael A. Barnhart, Kenneth J. Blume, Robert Beisner, R. Christian Berg, Richard Bradford, Kinley J. Brauer, Richard Dean Burns, Charles Conrad Campbell, Chen Jian, John Coogan, Carol Davidge, Mark Del Vecchio, Ralph Di Carpio, Justus Doenecke, Xavier Franco, Irwin Gellman, Paul Goodwin, James Gormly, Eric Hafter, Hope M. Harrison, Alan Henrikson, Gregg Herken, George Herring, Ted Hitchcock, Joan Hoff, Reginald Horsman, Michael Hunt, Edythe Izard, Holly Izard, Richard Izard, Leith Johnson, Burton Kaufman, Melville T. Kennedy, Jr., Thomas Lairson, Lester Langley, Thomas M. Leonard, Li Yan, Terrence J. Lindell, Martha McCoy, David McFadden, Charles McGraw, Matt McMahon, Robert McMahon, Shane Maddock, Elizabeth Mahan, Paul Manning, Herman Mast, Dennis Merrill, Jean-Donald Miller, Carl Murdock, Brian Murphy, R. Kent Newmyer, Arnold Offner, John Offner, Jerry Padula, Carol Petillo, David Pletcher, Salvadore Prisco, Stephen G. Rabe, Carol S. Repass, Wayne Repeta, Barney J. Rickman III, Michael Roskin, John Rourke, Kent M. Schofield, David Sheinin, Anna Lou Smethurst, Elbert B. Smith, Thomas G. Smith, Kenneth R. Stevens, Mark A. Stoler, William W. Stueck, Jr., Duane Tananbaum, George Turner, Jonathan G. Utley, Wang Li, Kathryn Weathersby, Ralph E. Weber, Edmund S. Wehrle, Lawrence Wittner, Sol Woolman, and Thomas Zoumaras.

We welcome comments and suggestions from students and instructors.

T. G. P.
J. G. C.
K. J. H.

AMERICAN FOREIGN RELATIONS

Imperialist Leap, 1895–1900

"If There Must Be War."   Lord Salisbury and President Grover Cleveland slug it out during the Venezuelan crisis of 1895. According to the historian Richard E. Welch, Jr., Cleveland's "innate talent to identify his personal judgment with righteousness and truth encouraged him to confuse compromise with surrender." (Life, 1896)

DIPLOMATIC CROSSROAD

The Venezuelan Crisis, 1895

Grover Cleveland felt pleased. On July 7, 1895, the day his third daughter was born, he wrote an enthusiastic note to Secretary of State Richard Olney. Just a few days before, Olney had personally delivered a 12,000-word draft document to the president on the Venezuelan boundary dispute. A successful corporate lawyer and former attorney general, Olney fretted and fidgeted. He knew that Cleveland wanted the dispute cleared up, and Olney himself liked to keep his desk tidy. The president's note arrived bearing laudatory words: "It's the best thing of the kind I ever read." Cleveland suggested "a little more softened verbiage here and there," and he directed Olney to send the document to London, which he did on July 20, 1895. Cleveland later christened it Olney's "twenty-inch gun." It was as much Cleveland's weapon as Olney's.[1]

They aimed the gun at Great Britain, which for decades had haggled with Venezuela over the boundary separating that country and British Guiana. A Britisher, Robert Schomburgk, had drawn a line in the 1840s, but nobody liked it. Both sides made claims that went deep into the other's territory. In the 1880s, the discovery of gold in the disputed region—including the largest nugget ever found, 509 ounces—heightened competition. At stake, too, was control of the mouth of the Orinoco River, gateway to the potential trade of northern South America, which U.S. entrepreneurs were beginnning to turn into a "commercial battle-ground."[2] In the 1870s Venezuela had begun to appeal to the United States for help, arguing that the poaching British violated the Monroe Doctrine. Washington repeatedly asked the British to submit the issue to arbitration but met constant rebuff. In December 1894, Cleveland renewed the call for arbitration. After another British refusal, the impatient president ordered the State Department to prepare a report on the boundary question. The "twenty-inch gun" sounded Olney's memorable answer.

Why did Cleveland and Olney become so agitated about the Venezuelan boundary question? First, the political dimension: In the early 1890s the Venezuelan government hired William L. Scruggs, a former U.S. minister to Caracas, to propagandize its case before the American public. His widely circulated pamphlet, *British Aggressions in Venezuela, or the Monroe Doctrine on Trial* (1895), aroused considerable sympathy for the South American nation. Olney himself read it before preparing his blast of July 20. American sentiment soon congealed: The land-grabbing British were robbing a poor hemispheric friend of the United States. A unanimous congressional resolution of February 1895, calling for arbitration, reflected growing U.S. concern. Cleveland listened attentively to such expressions, because his Democratic party had lost badly in the 1894 congressional elections and Republicans were attacking his administration as pusillanimous for not annexing

Hawai'i and for doing nothing when the British briefly landed troops in Nicaragua in April 1895. Cleveland could deflect criticism and recoup Democratic losses by bold action. As one Democrat advised the president: "Turn this Venezuela question up or down, North, South, East or West, and it is a 'winner.'"[3]

The president did not need such partisan inducements. He leaned toward action anyway because of momentous events in the 1890s, the golden age of European imperialism, when the powers were carving up territories in Asia, the Near East, and Africa. The British, already holding large stakes in Latin America, seemed intent on enlarging them. Their recent intervention in Nicaragua looked ominous, like the French intervention in Mexico a generation earlier. "Palpably unjust," as Olney's predecessor Walter Q. Gresham described it, Britain's claim against Venezuela became a symbol of European intrusion into the Western Hemisphere.[4]

The American depression of the 1890s also helped fix attention on Venezuela. Many, including Cleveland, thought that overproduction had caused the slump and expanding foreign trade could cure it. Might the British close off the Orinoco River and hence the markets of the area? At that time, American economic activity in Venezuela was ripening. For example, the National Association of Manufacturers, organized in 1895 to expand exports, chose Caracas as the site for its first permanent overseas display of American products. In short, international competition and economic woes suggested that Venezuela's dispute with Britain threatened U.S. interests.

Cleveland's own character and style colored his response. He did not like bullies. He had already rejected Hawaiian annexation in part because he thought that Americans had bullied the Hawaiians. Now Britain seemed to be arrogantly manhandling the Venezuelans. Seeking an intellectual peg on which to hang their case, the president and Olney found it in a refurbished Monroe Doctrine. Olney's "twenty-inch gun" of July 20, 1895, invoked that venerable principle in bumptious and unvarnished language. The brash message noted that the British claim had grown larger and larger, cutting deeper and deeper into Venezuela, possibly leading to political control. Olney warned that the European partition of Africa might repeat itself in Latin America. The "safety," "honor," and "welfare" of the United States were at stake, and the Monroe Doctrine forbade European intervention leading to control in the Western Hemisphere. He asserted that "any permanent political union between a European and an American state [was] unnatural and inexpedient."

Driven by its national interest, the United States had to intervene in the dispute. "The states of America, South as well as North, by geographical proximity, by natural sympathy, by similarity of governmental constitutions, are friends and allies, commercially and politically, of the United States. To allow the subjugation of any one of them by a European power is, of course, to completely reverse that situation and signifies the loss of all the advantages incident to their natural relations with us." The forceful overriding theme of Olney's proclamation addressed an international audience: "To-day the United States is practically sovereign on this continent, and its fiat is law upon the subjects to which it confines its interposition." And more: The United States's "infinite resources combined with its isolated position render it master of the situation and practically invulnerable as against any or

"The Real British Lion." A popular American depiction of the British global presence during the crisis over Venezuela. A few years later, President Cleveland himself recalled British behavior as "mean and hoggish." (*New York Evening World,* 1895)

all other powers."[5] Olney, finally, demanded arbitration, vaguely threatened U.S. intervention, and requested a British answer before the president's annual message to Congress in December.

Ambassador to England Thomas Bayard delivered the document to the giant of European diplomats, Lord Salisbury, then doubling as the British prime minister and foreign secretary. The bearded sixty-five-year-old Salisbury struck an imposing figure—intelligent, aristocratic, cautious, well read. He received the missive with some surprise and sent it to the Foreign Office for study. Distracted by crises elsewhere (especially in Africa), Salisbury saw no urgency. In the late nineteenth century American Anglophobic bombast was not unusual. The issue, he thought, would probably fizzle out once American politics calmed down. Nor did he relish arbitrating any question that might weaken the British Empire. The British reply did not arrive until after Cleveland's annual message (actually tame on the Venezuelan controversy). Salisbury's note, which smacked of "the peremptory schoolmaster trying—with faded patience—to correct the ignorance of dullards in Washington," denied the applicability of the Monroe Doctrine and dismissed any U.S. interest in the dispute.[6]

Cleveland, all 250 pounds of him, was duck-hunting in North Carolina when the British response reached Washington. On his return he read it and became "mad clean through."[7] Now what? War? Retreat? Olney struggled for alternatives and finally selected one that left some maneuvering room, kept diplomacy in the hands of the executive branch, and avoided war or backstepping: an American study commission appointed by the president. Cleveland's special message to Congress on December 17 rang the alarm bell. England must arbitrate; the United States would create an investigating commission to set the true boundary line; and then American action would follow. Most observers labeled the message an ultimatum, with the possibility of war lurking throughout.

The nation buzzed in anticipation. Congress appropriated funds for the investigating commission. Irish-Americans volunteered to fight the hated British. Both Republicans and Democrats lined up behind the president, and Senator Henry Cabot Lodge noted with approval that "Jingoes are plenty enough now."[8] New York City police commissioner Theodore Roosevelt boomed: "Let the fight come if it must; I don't care whether our sea coast cities are bombarded or not; we would take Canada."[9] Many business leaders rallied behind the administration, with Whitelaw Reid, editor of the *New York Tribune,* hyperbolically declaring that "this is the golden opportunity of our merchants to extend our trade to every quarter of Central and South America."[10] British ambassador Sir Julian Pauncefote reported: "Nothing is heard but the voice of the Jingo bellowing defiance to England."[11]

Jingo fevers subsided rapidly in early 1896. Many bankers and business people became alarmed when the stock market plummeted, in large part because British investors were pulling out. Joseph Pulitzer's *New York World* put out a special Christmas issue with portraits of the Prince of Wales and Lord Salisbury under the headline "PEACE AND GOOD WILL," implying that a war was unconscionable with Britain, a country so close in race, language, and culture.[12] Critics such as E. L. Godkin, editor of *The Nation,* and respected international law specialist John Bassett Moore pointed out how haughtily Cleveland and Olney had acted. Even Ambassador Bayard feared that the president had been "too *precipitate,* for I do not see why he should abandon suddenly his attitude of conservatism and go apparently into the camp of aggressiveness."[13] But Cleveland never wanted war. He wanted peace on U.S. terms.

What followed seemed anticlimactic. The British cabinet, on January 11, 1896, instructed Salisbury to seek an "honourable settlement" with the United States.[14] A new dispute with Germany over South Africa necessitated retreat. England needed friends now, not enemies. British troops could not defend Canada, and the Admiralty thought that the Royal Navy was outgunned in the North Atlantic and Caribbean. Formal talks continued until November 1896, when Britain and the United States agreed to set up a five-person arbitral board to define the boundary, with each to name two members, who would in turn select the fifth. Finally, in October 1899, the tribunal reached a decision that rejected the extreme claims of each party and generally followed the Schomburgk line. The pivotal Point Barima at the mouth of the Orinoco went to Venezuela, which came out of the dispute pretty well, considering that neither the United States nor Great Britain cared much about *Venezuela*'s national interest.

In fact, the United States negotiated directly with Britain without ever consulting Venezuela. Both parties excluded Venezuela's duly accredited minister in Washington from the talks. Olney never even gave the Venezuelans a copy of his "twenty-inch gun" (they eventually read it in the newspapers); and when they balked over the 1896 Anglo-American agreement, he curtly made one concession: Venezuela could name one of the five members of the arbitration board—so long as that person was not a Venezuelan. Lobbyist William Scruggs complained that the

United States sought to "*bull-doze* Venezuela."[15] He had it right, but Washington's vigorous diplomacy targeted others besides that South American nation. The overweening theme of Olney's "twenty-inch gun" merits repeating: "To-day the United States is practically sovereign on this continent, and its fiat is law upon the subjects to which it confines its interposition."

Men of Empire in the 1890s

The Venezuelan crisis punctuated an era of imperialist competition when, as one senator grandly put it: "The great nations are rapidly absorbing . . . all the waste areas of the earth. It is a moment which makes for civilization and the advancement of the race."[16] Cleveland and Olney helped move the United States toward world-power status. As an example of forceful, even aggressive, American diplomacy, the Venezuelan controversy accelerated important trends. Besides ignoring the rights and sensibilities of small nations, it revealed a United States more sure of itself, more certain about the components of its "policy," and willing to lecture others. The episode stimulated what critics at the time called "jingoism." The Monroe Doctrine gained new stature as a warning to European nations to curb their activities in the Western Hemisphere. The executive branch kept the Venezuelan issue in *its* hands, thereby strengthening the foreign-policy power of the president by going to the brink of war without consulting Congress.

Other ramifications became evident. Latin Americans learned once again that the United States intended to establish supremacy in the Western Hemisphere and would intervene when it saw fit. The United States had always kept an eye on the Caribbean, but the Venezuelan crisis and the outbreak of revolution in Cuba in 1895 intensified North American interest, a significant dimension of which was economic. The Venezuelan issue and the disposition of the Orinoco River also brought more attention to the theory of overproduction as a cause of depression, which exports could allegedly cure. Commercial expansion, always a trend in American history, received another boost.

The discord with Britain over Venezuela helped foster Anglo-American rapprochement. Cooperation and mutual interest increasingly characterized relations between Washington and London. British diplomats sought U.S. friendship as a possible counterweight to growing German power, and Britain's willingness to permit the United States to govern Caribbean affairs facilitated the emerging entente.

One way, the chief way, the United States could manage events in that area was through naval power. The Venezuelan crisis, joined by crises in Asia and the belief that naval construction would employ those idled by depression, stimulated additional American naval expansion. The Navy Act of 1896, for example, provided for three new battleships and ten new torpedo boats. All told, then, the Venezuelan boundary dispute advanced the United States along the path of expansion.

That path, by the end of the decade, led to new U.S. colonies in the Pacific, Asia, and the Caribbean, a firm hold on independent Cuba, and Europe's recognition of U.S. hegemony in the Caribbean. By 1900, too, the United States had pledged itself to preserve the "Open Door" in China; it had built a navy that had

"Either Caesar or Nothing!"   Uncle Sam protests against imperialism but refuses to return to his cramped log cabin now that he has taken up "skyscraper" diplomacy, according to this German cartoon. (*Kladderadatsch,* 1899)

just annihilated the Spanish fleet and ranked sixth in the world; and it had developed an export trade amounting to $1.5 billion. Steel and iron production exemplified its industrial might, which almost equaled that of Britain and Germany combined. U.S. acquisition of new colonies after the Spanish-American-Cuban-Filipino War suggests that *only then,* about 1898, did the United States become an imperialist world power. But what actually happened, one scholar writes, was a "culmination" not an "aberration."[17] Having taken halting steps toward a larger empire before the depression of the 1890s, the United States then took the leap.

Assistant Secretary of the Navy Theodore Roosevelt described the anti-imperialists in 1897 as "men of a by-gone age" and "provincials."[18] Indeed, anti-imperialism waned through the late nineteenth century. Increasing numbers of educated, economically comfortable Americans made the case for formal empire (colonies or protectorates) or informal empire (commercial domination). Naval officers, diplomats, politicians, farmers, skilled artisans, business leaders, and clergy made up what political scientists call the "foreign-policy public." Better read than

Grover Cleveland (1837–1908).
This portrait of the two-term president, overweight from frequenting saloons as a young man, exhibits the gruff American attitude toward Britain during the Venezuelan crisis. The historian Dexter Perkins wrote that Cleveland was "so honest, so brave, so independent . . . , but also so rigid and inflexible in his thinking, so unimaginative, so dogmatic." (Library of Congress)

most Americans and having access to lecterns to disperse their ideas, this "elite" helped move America to war and empire. Neither "public opinion," nor the jingoistic "yellow press," nor the "people" in the 1890s compelled the United States to war. Rather, two key elements stand out: a McKinley administration very much in charge of its diplomacy through skillful maneuvering, and a majoritarian view within the articulate "foreign-policy public" in favor of a vigorous outward thrust.

Analysis of the phrase "public opinion" helps explain the *hows* as distinct from the *whys* of decisionmaking. One often hears that "public opinion" or "the man in the street" influenced a leader to follow a certain course of action. But "public opinion" did not comprise a unified, identifiable group speaking with one voice. Further, political leaders and other articulate, knowledgeable people often shaped the "public opinion" they wanted to hear by their very handling of events and their control over information—that is, leaders *led*. In trying to determine who the "people" are and what "public opinion" is, social-science studies demonstrate that in the 1890s the people who counted, the people who expressed their opinion publicly in order to influence policy, numbered no more than 1.5 million to 3 million, or between 10 and 20 percent of the voting public. This percentage—upper- and middle-income groups, educated, active politically—constituted the "foreign-policy public." As Secretary of State Walter Q. Gresham put it in 1893: "After all, public opinion is made and controlled by the thoughtful men of the country."[19] The "public opinion" the president heard in the 1890s did not come from the "people," but rather from a small, articulate segment of the American population alert to foreign-policy issues. Although this educated public counted anti-imperialists among them, including substantial numbers of women activists, the "foreign-policy public" leaned heavily toward the side of imperialism.

The president, as a consummate politician and good tactician, often dominates policymaking, even thwarting the advice of the "foreign-policy public" itself. President Cleveland, for example, successfully resisted pressure to annex Hawai'i and withdrew the treaty from the Senate, and he never let Congress or influential public opinion set the terms of his policy toward the Venezuelan crisis. Pressures from jingoes in Congress and a sensationalist press intruded in the 1890s, but the initiative in foreign affairs, unlike in the 1860s and 1870s, remained largely in the hands of the men in the executive branch. In most historical periods, the public *reacts* to *immediate* events; the executive *acts* and *manages* with *long-term* policy considerations.

Cleveland Confronts *Cuba Libre*, 1895–1897

The year 1895 brought momentous events. The Venezuelan crisis, Japan's defeat of China in the Sino-Japanese War, and the outbreak of revolution in Cuba—all carried profound meaning for U.S. foreign relations. The sugar-rich island of Cuba, since the close of its unsuccessful war for independence (1868–1878), suffered political repression and poverty. After that war Cuban nationalists prepared for a new assault on their Spanish overlords. From 1880 to 1895, Cuban national hero José Martí plotted from exile in the United States. In 1892 he organized the Cuban Revolutionary party, using U.S. territory to recruit men and money. Martí's op-

Makers of American Foreign Relations, 1895–1900

Presidents	Secretaries of State
Grover Cleveland, 1893–1897	Walter Q. Gresham, 1893–1895
	Richard Olney, 1895–1897
William McKinley, 1897–1901	John Sherman, 1897–1898
	William R. Day, 1898
	John Hay, 1898–1905

portunity came when Cuba's economy fell victim in 1894 to a new U.S. tariff, which raised duties on imported sugar and hence reduced Cuban sugar shipments to the United States. On February 24, 1895, with cries of "*Cuba Libre*," the rebels opened their drive for independence.

Cuban revolutionaries kept a cautious eye on the United States, well known for its relentless interest in the island, and thus feared an ultimate U.S. attempt to control their nation's destiny. José Martí's fifteen-year stay in the United States had turned him into a critic of what he called "the monster"—an "aggressive" and "avaricious" nation "full of hate" and "widespread spiritual coarseness." And he warned against a U.S. "conquering policy" that "arrogantly" treated Latin American countries as "dependencies."[20] On May 19 Martí died in action.

Cuban and Spanish military strategies produced destruction and death. Led by General Máximo Gómez, a veteran of the 1868–1878 war, the *insurrectos* burned cane fields, blew up mills, and disrupted railroads, with the goal of rendering Cuba an economic liability to Spain. "The chains of Cuba have been forged by her own richness," Gómez proclaimed, "and it is precisely this which I propose to do away with soon."[21] Although outnumbered (about 30,000 Cuban troops fought 200,000 Spanish) and lacking adequate supplies, the insurgents, with the sympathy of the populace, wore the Spanish down through guerrilla tactics. Journalists covering this phase of the war included the young Briton Winston S. Churchill, who reported the thrill of being "shot at without result."[22] By late 1896 rebels controlled about two-thirds of the island, with the Spanish concentrated in coastal and urban regions. That year, to break the rebel stronghold in the rural areas, Governor-General Valeriano y Nicolau Weyler instituted the brutal reconcentration program. He divided the island into districts and then herded a half-million Cubans into fortified camps, where frightful sanitation conditions, poor food, and disease contributed to the death of perhaps 200,000 people. Weyler's soldiers regarded any Cubans outside the camps as rebels and hence targets for death; they also killed livestock, destroyed crops, and polluted water sources. This effort to starve the insurgents and deprive them of physical and moral support, combined with the rebels' destructive behavior, made a shambles of Cuba's society and economy.

The Cleveland administration faced several alternatives. It could recognize Cuban belligerency. But such an act, Olney noted, would relieve Spain of any responsibility for paying claims filed by Americans for properties destroyed in Cuba.

Cleveland and Olney found recognition of Cuban independence even less appetizing, for they believed the Cubans incapable of self-government and feared anarchy and even racial war. That course might also arouse a Spanish declaration of war or force U.S. belligerency because, logically, a Spanish attempt to conquer an "independent" Cuba would constitute a violation of the Monroe Doctrine. Olney toyed with buying the island at one point. The Cleveland administration settled on a dual policy of hostility to the revolution and pressure on Spain to grant some autonomy. Diplomacy and lecturing to a foreign government seemed to work in the Venezuelan crisis; perhaps it would work with Cuba.

Prodded by a Republican Congress (it passed a resolution in April 1896, urging the president to recognize Cuban belligerency), by continued evidence of wholesale destruction, and by Spanish obstinacy in refusing reforms and adhering to force, Olney sent a note to Spain in April 1896. He urged a political solution that would leave "Spain her rights of sovereignty . . . yet secure to the [Cubans] all such rights and powers of local self-government as they [could] ask."[23] Spain should initiate reforms short of independence. Olney showed particular concern for the interests of Americans, not those of the Cubans. With American property estimated at $50 million, the decline in sugar production wrought disaster to Cuban-American trade relations. In 1892 Cuba had shipped to the United States goods worth $79 million; by 1898 that figure had slumped to $15 million.

When Spain rejected Olney's advice, the Cleveland administration seemed stymied. It did not desire war, but it meant to protect U.S. interests. Congress kept asking for firm action. And in Havana, hotheaded American consul-general Fitzhugh Lee clamored for U.S. annexation. Cleveland did not feel he could fire Lee, nephew of General Robert E. Lee, because the incumbent president needed political friends at a time when Democrats were dumping him in favor of William Jennings Bryan. Consul-General Lee also warned that "there may be a revolution within a revolution," noting that Cuban insurgents vowed to redistribute property, which U.S. officials (and Creole elites) would not tolerate.[24] It further nettled Cleveland and Olney that Spain had approached the courts of Europe for diplomatic support, with the argument that the Monroe Doctrine threatened all European powers. Spain's appeal went unheeded, but leaders in Washington still worried about possible European intrusion in Cuba.

British ambassador to Spain H. Drummond Wolff accurately claimed that for Cuba the United States wanted "peace with commerce."[25] In December 1896, Cleveland reported that neither the Spanish nor the Cuban rebels had established their authority over the island. Americans felt a humanitarian concern, he said, and their trade and investments ("pecuniary interest") faced destruction. Further, to maintain its neutrality, the United States had to police the coastline to intercept unlawful expeditions. Spain must grant autonomy or "home rule," but not independence, to "fertile and rich" Cuba to end the bloodshed and devastation. Otherwise, the United States, having thus far acted with "restraint," might abandon its "expectant attitude."[26]

But Cleveland had more bark than bite. Through Olney he successfully buried a Senate resolution urging recognition of Cuban independence and contented himself with some limited Spanish reforms of February 1897. Thereafter he let the Cuban issue fester, bequeathing it to the incoming McKinley administration.

McKinley's Road to War, 1897–1898

A veteran Republican politician and deft manager of people, President William McKinley had defeated William Jennings Bryan in the election of 1896. The tee-totaling Ohioan seemed a stable, dignified figure in a time of crisis. He projected deep religious conviction, personal warmth, sincerity, commitment to economic development and the revival of business, party loyalty, and support for expansion abroad. Yet McKinley often gave the appearance of being a pliant follower, a mindless flunky of the political bosses. One joke went: "Why is McKinley's mind like a bed?" Answer: "Because it has to be made up for him every time he wants to use it." Plucky Theodore Roosevelt allegedly remarked that McKinley had "no more backbone than a chocolate éclair."[27] Such an image was created in large part by bellicose imperialists who believed that McKinley was not moving fast enough and by critics of domestic policy such as Bryan who saw McKinley as clay in the hands of big business and party machines. Certainly a party regular and friend of large corporations, the president was no lackey. A manager of diplomacy, who wanted expansion and empire without war and a settlement of the Cuban question without U.S. military intervention, McKinley acted as his own man.

McKinley shared America's image of itself as an expanding, virile nation of superior institutions and as a major power in Latin America. He agreed that the United States must have a large navy, overseas commerce, and foreign bases. He believed strongly that America must export its surplus goods. As a tariff specialist, he favored high tariffs on manufactured goods, low tariffs on raw materials, and reciprocity agreements. Although McKinley uttered almost nothing about foreign issues in the campaign of 1896, the Republican party platform overflowed with expansionist rhetoric. It urged American control of Hawai'i, a Nicaraguan canal run by the United States, an enlarged navy, purchase of the Virgin Islands, and Cuban independence. Between election and inauguration, however, McKinley quietly joined Cleveland and Olney in sidetracking a Senate resolution for recognition of Cuba. He wanted a free hand, and he did not believe that Cubans could govern themselves. His appointment of the old and ailing Senator John Sherman as secretary of state suggested further that McKinley would take charge of his own diplomacy. His inaugural address vacuously urged peace, never mentioning the Cuban crisis.

McKinley's first tilt with Congress came in March 1897. Resolutions on Cuba sprang up repeatedly, but the president managed to kill them. He did satisfy imperialists by sending a Hawaiian annexation treaty to the Senate. The president was preparing for his own nonpublic diplomatic assault on Spain. In June, Madrid received an American reprimand for Weyler's uncivilized warfare and for his disruption of the Cuban economy. Spain, however, showed no signs of tempering its military response to the insurrection. American citizens languished in Spanish jails;

William McKinley (1843–1901). A Civil War veteran and long-time member of Congress, the twenty-fifth president displayed supreme political skills in his quest for empire. An aide wrote in his diary in 1898 that McKinley "is the strong man of the Cabinet, the dominating force; but with it all are such gentleness and graciousness." An assassin killed him in Buffalo, New York. (Library of Congress)

American property continued to be razed. Fitzhugh Lee, who remained at his post in Havana, bellowed for U.S. intervention. In July, McKinley instructed the new American minister to Spain, Stewart L. Woodford, to demand that the Spanish stop the fighting. Increasingly convinced that the Cuban *insurrectos* would not compromise, the president implored Spain to grant autonomy. A new Spanish government soon moderated policy by offering Cuba a substantial degree of self-government. Even more, it removed the hated Weyler and promised to end reconcentration. Never fully implemented, these reforms did not end the fighting, because the Cuban junta demanded full independence.

McKinley's December 6, 1897, annual message to Congress discussed the Cuban insurrection at great length. Voicing the "gravest apprehension," McKinley rejected annexation as "criminal aggression." He argued against recognition of belligerency, because the rebels hardly constituted a government worthy of recognition. And he ruled out intervention as premature at a time when the Spanish were traveling the "honorable paths" of reform. He asked for patience to see if Spanish changes would work, but he hinted that the United States would keep open all policy options, including intervention "with force."[28]

By mid-January evidence had poured into Washington proving that the reforms had not moderated the crisis; in fact, insurgents, conservatives, and the Spanish army all denounced them. Antireform Spaniards rioted in Havana. The United States ordered the warship *Maine* to Havana on January 24, 1898, to protect American citizens and demonstrate concern. On February 9, the State Department received a copy of a private letter written in late 1897 by Spanish minister to the United States Enrique Dupuy de Lôme and sent to a senior Spanish politician touring Cuba. Intercepted in Cuba by a rebel sympathizer who forwarded it to the Cuban junta in New York City. Not only did it reach the State Department, but William Randolph Hearst's flamboyant *New York Journal* published it that day with the banner headline: "Worst Insult to the United States in its History." De Lôme labeled McKinley "weak," a "bidder for the admiration of the crowd," and a "would-be politician."[29] McKinley, along with most Americans, found de Lôme's remarks infuriating. The administration particularly resented another statement that suggested that Spain did not take its reform proposals seriously and would persist in fighting to defeat the rebels. Spain, it appeared, had tricked the United States. De Lôme's hasty recall hardly salved the hurt.

Trying to avoid war, a restless McKinley nevertheless recognized the dangerous trend. On occasion in early 1898 he had to take drugs to sleep. The rush of events did not improve his demeanor. Less than a week after the de Lôme episode, on February 15, explosions ripped through the *Maine,* anchored conspicuously in Havana harbor. Two hundred sixty-six of 354 U.S. officers and crew died as the 6,700-ton vessel sank quickly. With no evidence but with considerable emotion many Americans assumed that Spain had committed the dastardly deed. McKinley ordered an official investigation and decided to try diplomacy and threat again. In early March, Woodford protested strongly to the Spanish government about the de Lôme incident and the *Maine.* The "grave" Cuban crisis had to be resolved. On March 6 the president met with Joe Cannon, chair of the House Committee on Appropriations, and urged him to present a bill providing $50 million for arms. "It

The U.S.S. *Maine* Before and After.
Part of the battleship was raised in 1911, investigated, and sunk at sea with flag flying. The investigators concluded that an external explosion of unknown origins destroyed the vessel. Notwithstanding a 1976 navy study by Admiral Hyman G. Rickover that blamed the sinking on an internal accident, the historians Harold and Peggy Samuels, in *Remembering the* Maine (1995), argue anew that the ship exploded because of an external mine, most likely planted by Spanish zealots. (Before—*Harper's Weekly,* 1888; after—National Archives)

seemed as though a hundred Fourths of July had been let loose in the House," a clerk noted, as Congress enthusiastically obliged three days later.[30] Spain, Woodford reported, was stunned by the appropriation.

In mid-March Senator Redfield Proctor of Vermont, a friend of McKinley reportedly opposed to war, graphically told his colleagues about his recent trip to Cuba. He recounted ugly stories about the reconcentration camps. "Torn from their homes, with foul earth, foul air, foul water, and foul food or none, what wonder that one-half died and that one-quarter of the living are so diseased that they cannot be saved?"[31] Shortly after this moving speech, which convinced many members of Congress and business leaders that Spain could not bring order to Cuba, the American court of inquiry on the *Maine* concluded that an external mine of unknown origins had destroyed the vessel. A Spanish commission at about the same time attributed the disaster to an internal explosion. In 1898 vocal Americans pinned the crime squarely on Spain. "Remember the *Maine,* to hell with Spain" became the popular chant.

Such events inexorably narrowed options. The president did explore the possibility of purchasing Cuba for $300 million—or some other means "by which Spain can part with Cuba without loss of respect and with certainty of American control."[32] But a jingo frenzy had seized the Congress. Following one stormy Senate session, Vice President Garrett Hobart warned McKinley: "They will act without you if you do not act at once." "Say no more," McKinley responded.[33] On March 27 Washington cabled the U.S. demands: an armistice, Cuban-Spanish negotiations to secure a peace, McKinley's arbitration of the conflict if there was no peace by October, termination of the reconcentration policy, and relief aid to the Cubans. Implicit was the demand that Spain grant Cuba its independence under U.S. supervision. As a last-ditch effort to avoid American military intervention, the ultimatum had little chance of success. Spain's national pride and interest precluded surrender. Madrid's answer showed promise: It had already terminated reconcentration, would launch reforms, and would accept an armistice if the rebels did so first. By refusing McKinley's mediation and Cuban independence, the Spanish reply did not satisfy the president or Congress. McKinley began to write a war message in early April. On the ninth, Spain made a new concession, declaring a unilateral suspension of hostilities "for such length of time" as the Spanish commander "may think prudent."[34] Too qualified, the declaration still sidestepped Cuban independence and U.S. mediation. Any chance of European intervention ended when the British told Washington that they would "be guided [on Cuban issues] by the wishes of the President."[35]

Why War: Exploiting Opportunity

On April 11 McKinley asked Congress for authority to use armed force to end the Cuban war. Since neither Cubans nor Spaniards could stem the flow of blood, Americans would do so because of the "cause of humanity" and the "very serious injury to the commerce, trade, and business of our people, and the wanton destruction of property." And, citing the *Maine,* McKinley described the conflict as "a constant menace to our peace." At the very end of the message, noting that Spain had recently offered an armistice, the president asked Congress to give this new information "your just and careful attention."[36]

As Congress debated an armistice that the Cubans themselves rejected, McKinley beat back a Senate attempt to recognize the rebels. He strongly believed that Cuba needed American tutelage to prepare for self-government. Indeed, as the historian Louis A. Pérez, Jr., has argued, McKinley's decision for war may have been "directed as much against Cuban independence as it was against Spanish sovereignty."[37] Congress did endorse the Teller Amendment, which disclaimed any U.S. intention of annexing the island. Some who voted for the amendment feared that annexation would commit the United States to assume Cuba's large bond debt. On April 19 Congress proclaimed Cuba's independence (but without recognizing the Cuban junta), demanded Spain's evacuation from the island, and directed the president to use force to ensure these results. Spain, on April 21, broke diplomatic relations. On the twenty-second, American ships began to blockade Cuba; two days later Spain declared war. On the twenty-fifth, Congress declared that a state of war had existed from the twenty-first.

Because of the Teller Amendment, the decision for war seemed selfless and humanitarian, and for many Americans it undoubtedly was. But the decision had more complex motives. Different people endorsed war for different reasons. McKinley himself cited humanitarian concern, property, commerce, and the removal of an annoyance. Politics also mattered. Senator Lodge, among others, told the White House that "if the war in Cuba drags on through the summer . . . we [Republicans] shall go down to the greatest defeat ever known."[38] Important business leaders, initially hesitant, shifted in March and April to demand an end to Cuban disorder. Farmers and business leaders interested in Asian and Latin American markets thought victory against Spain might open new trade doors by eliminating a colonial power. Many highly moralistic Americans simply felt compelled to end the bloodshed. Republican senator George F. Hoar of Massachusetts, later an anti-imperialist, could not "look idly on while hundreds of thousands of innocent human beings . . . die of hunger close to our doors. If there is ever to be a war it should be to prevent such things."[39] Lyman Abbott, well-known pastor of Plymouth Church in Brooklyn, thought war the "answer to America to the question of its own conscience: Am I my brother's keeper?"[40] Ending Spanish rule in Cuba, declared a Catholic priest, would get rid of all that "is old and vile and rotten and mean and cruel and false."[41] Church missionaries dreamed of new opportunities to convert the "uncivilized." Imperialists hoped war would add new territories to the United States and encourage the growth of a larger navy. "Warriors" differed from "imperialists" in that some people opposed empire and sincerely thought war would halt the long conflict in Cuba, whereas the imperialists seized on war as an opportunity to expand the American empire.

Emotional nationalism also mattered. The de Lôme and *Maine* incidents stimulated a national anger already infused with notions of American superiority, racial and otherwise. Imperialist senator Albert Beveridge waxed ebullient: "At last, God's hour has struck. The American people go forth in a warfare holier than liberty—holy as humanity."[42] The journalist Finley Peter Dunne's popular Irish-American characters provided a fitting summary: "'We're a gr-reat people,' said Mr. Hennessy, earnestly. 'We ar-re,' said Mr. Dooley. 'We ar-re that. An' th best iv it is, we know we ar-re.'"[43] Excited statements by people such as Roosevelt, who looked on war as he looked on horseback riding and cowboying in the Dakotas— a sport, a game, fun—aroused martial fevers. Newspapers of the "yellow press" variety, such as Hearst's *New York Journal* and Pulitzer's *New York World,* sensationalized stories of Spanish atrocities. Others proudly compared the Cuban and American revolutions. The American people, already steeped in a brash nationalism and prepared by earlier aggressive diplomatic triumphs, reacted favorably to this hyperbole.

"Cuba Reconciling the North and South."   Captain Fritz W. Guerin's 1898 photograph trumpeted nationalism in the Spanish-American-Cuban-Filipino War. Golden-haired Cuba, liberated from her chains by her North American heroes, oversees the reconciliation of the Union and Confederacy in a splashy display of patriotism. (Library of Congress)

Both Washington and Madrid had tried diplomacy, but their diplomatic paths never crossed. McKinley wanted "peace" and independence for Cuba under U.S. tutelage. The first Spain could not deliver because the Cuban rebels had become entrenched and bent on independence and Spanish forces remained weak. The second Spain could not grant immediately for fear that ultranationalists might overthrow the Bourbon constitutional monarchy. Spain said it would fight the war more humanely and grant autonomy, but McKinley and Congress wanted more, and they believed they had the right and duty to judge the affairs of Spain and Cuba.

Critics said America might have been less haughty, letting the Cubans and Spaniards settle their own affairs. McKinley's actions in dispatching the *Maine* and asking Congress for $50 million probably encouraged the Cuban rebels to resist any compromise. He might have given Spain a bit more breathing space. Spain, after all, did fire Weyler, terminate reconcentration, and approve an armistice; most important, Madrid did grant partial autonomy, which ultimately might have led to independence. Some critics said the president should have recognized the Cuban insurgents and covertly aided them, and then American soldiers would not necessarily have had to fight in Cuba, the Philippines, and Puerto Rico. American matériel, not men, in other words, might have liberated Cuba from Spanish rule. McKinley wanted to avoid war, and he only reluctantly chose it after trying other options. That he adamantly refused to recognize the insurgency or the republic suggests also that the president did not endorse outright Cuban independence. He probably had two goals in 1898: to remove Spain from Cuba and to control Cuba in some manner yet ill defined. When the Spanish balked at a sale and both belligerents rejected compromise, McKinley opted for war—the only means to oust Spain *and* to control Cuba.

The Spanish-American-Cuban-Filipino War

Americans flocked to recruiting stations and enlisted in what they trumpeted as a glorious expedition to demonstrate U.S. right and might. They were cocky. Young author Sherwood Anderson joked that fighting Spain would be "like robbing an old gypsy woman in a vacant lot at night after a fair."[44] U.S. ambassador to England John Hay called it a "splendid little war," and Theodore Roosevelt, who resigned as assistant secretary of the navy to lead the flashy but overrated Rough Riders, remarked that "it wasn't much of a war, but it was the best war we had."[45] It was a short war, ending August 12, but 5,462 Americans died in it—only 379 of them in combat. Most of the rest met death from malaria and yellow fever. As hundreds of disease-wracked men came home to be quarantined on the tip of Long Island, a surgeon wrote: "The pale faces, the sunken eyes, the staggering gait and the emaciated forms" marked some as "wrecks for life" and others as "candidates for a premature grave."[46]

Led by officers seasoned in the Civil War and in campaigns against Native Americans, the new imperial fighters embarked from Florida in mid-June. Seventeen thousand men, clutching their Krag-Jörgensen rifles, crammed into the flotilla for a week. They ate hardtack and tasteless canned beef, drank bitter coffee, waited anxiously, and got seasick. On June 22 they disembarked on Cuban soil, finding no Spanish resistance. Cuban insurgents met with American officers, and they agreed to help one another against Spanish forces.

Yet the big news had already arrived from the Philippine Islands, Spain's major colony in Asia. Only days after the American declaration of war, Commodore George Dewey sailed his Asiatic Squadron from Hong Kong to Manila Bay, where he smashed the Spanish fleet with the loss of one sailor. Slipping by the Spanish guns at Corregidor, Dewey entered the bay at night. Early in the morning of May 1 his flagship *Olympia* began to demolish the ten incompetently handled Spanish ships. With his laconic order, "You may fire when ready, Gridley," Dewey quickly became a first-line hero. Some people, ignorant of American interests in the Pacific, the beckoning China market, and the feebleness of Spanish rule over the Philippines, wondered how a war to liberate Cuba saw its first action in Asia. Although probably few Americans knew the location of the Philippines, naval officials had pinpointed them in contingency plans as early as 1896. Often credited alone with ordering Dewey on February 25, 1898, to attack Manila if war broke out, Assistant Secretary of the Navy Theodore Roosevelt actually set in motion preexisting war plans already known and approved by the president. After the war, when the Navy Department balked at revealing its advance preparations, Roosevelt was "naturally delighted at shouldering the responsibility."[47]

By late June, U.S. troops in Cuba had advanced toward Santiago, where dispirited Spanish soldiers manned antique guns. Joined by experienced Cuban rebels, the North Americans on July 1 battled for San Juan Hill. American forces, spearheaded by the Rough Riders and the black soldiers of the Ninth Cavalry, finally captured the strategic promontory overlooking Santiago after suffering heavy casualties. Two days later the Spanish fleet, penned in Santiago harbor for weeks by U.S. warships, made a desperate daylight break for open sea. Some U.S. vessels nearly collided as they hurried to sink the helpless Spanish craft, which went down with 323 dead. Its fleet destroyed, Spain entered its imperial death throes. Santiago soon surrendered.

U.S. troops also invaded another Spanish colony, Puerto Rico, which expansionists such as Roosevelt coveted as a Caribbean base for a "proper navy" and a strategic post that might help protect a Central American canal.[48] In nineteen days General Nelson A. Miles, losing only three soldiers, captured the sugar- and coffee-exporting island. At least at first, the Puerto Rican elite welcomed their new North American masters as an improvement over their Spanish rulers.

Manila capitulated in mid-August, after the Spanish put up token resistance in a deal with Dewey that salvaged Spanish pride and kept Filipino nationalist Emilio Aguinaldo from the walled city. Washington soon ordered Aguinaldo and other Filipino rebels, who had fought against the Spanish for independence since 1896 and had surrounded Manila for weeks, to remain outside the capital and to recognize the authority of the United States.

In July, to ensure uninterrupted reinforcement of Dewey, the United States officially absorbed Hawai'i, where ships took on coal en route to Manila. From 1893 to 1897, when Cleveland refused annexation, politics in Hawai'i had changed little. The white revolutionaries clung to power. Once elected, McKinley proclaimed: "We need Hawai'i . . . a good deal more than we did California. It is manifest destiny."[49] After negotiating a new treaty with the white-led Hawaiian government, he adopted the ploy of asking for a joint resolution. On July 7, 1898, Congress passed the resolution for annexation by a majority vote (290 to 91 in the House and 42 to 21 in the Senate), thereby formally attaching the strategically and commercially important islands to the United States.

Peace and Empire: The Debate in the United States

Spain sued for peace, and on August 12 the belligerents proclaimed an armistice. To negotiate with the Spanish in Paris, McKinley appointed a "peace commission" loaded with imperialists and headed by Secretary of State William R. Day, friend and follower of the president's wishes. As negotiations continued into autumn, and after McKinley tested public opinion by touring the Midwest, he chose to demand all of the Philippines, the island of Guam in the Marianas, and Puerto Rico, as well as to make Cuba independent. Articulate Filipinos pleaded for their country's freedom but met a stern U.S. rebuff. Spanish diplomats accepted this American land grab after the United States offered $20 million as compensation. In early December, U.S. delegates signed the treaty and walked out of the elegant French conference room with the Philippines, Puerto Rico, and Guam.

"Hurrah for Imperialism."
This anti-imperialist cartoon
expressed the fear that the
United States was walking
blindly along a disastrous path
of empire. Anti-imperialists lost
the debate in part because
Uncle Sam knew where he
was going in adding new territories to the U.S. domain.
(*Life,* 1898)

Anti-imperialists howled in protest. They had organized the Anti-Imperialist League in Boston in November 1898, but they never acted in unison. They counted among their number such unlikely bedfellows as steel magnate Andrew Carnegie, labor leader Samuel Gompers, agrarian spokesman William Jennings Bryan, Massachusetts senator George Hoar, Harvard president Charles W. Eliot, and the humorist Mark Twain—people who had often disagreed on domestic issues. Some anti-imperialists took inconsistent positions. Hoar, the most outspoken senator against the treaty, had voted for war and annexation of Hawai'i. An expansionist, Carnegie apparently would accept colonies if they could be taken without force. He even offered to write a personal check for $20 million to buy the independence of the Philippines. And the anti-imperialists could not overcome the *fait accompli,* possession and occupation of territory, handed them by McKinley. After all, argued the president, could America really let loose of this real estate so nobly taken in battle?

The anti-imperialists denounced the thesis that greatness lay in colonies. Some of them wanted trade too, but not at the cost of subjugating other peoples. The anti-imperialist David Starr Jordan, president of Stanford University, spoke of the "peaceful conquest" of Mexico by trade rather than by annexation.[50] Quoting the Declaration of Independence and Washington's Farewell Address, these critics recalled America's tradition of self-government and *continental* expansion. Some anti-imperialists insisted that serious domestic problems demanded attention and resources first. And one senator, opposed to annexation, depicted the Philippines as a racial "witches' cauldron" and chanted: "Black spirits and white,/Red spirits and gray,/Mingle, mingle, mingle,/You that mingle may."[51] Mark Twain wrote a scathing parody of the *Battle Hymn of the Republic*: "Mine eyes have seen the orgy of the launching of the Sword;/He is searching out the hoardings where the

George F. Hoar (1826–1904).
Graduate of Harvard, this Republican became a U.S. senator in 1877. He urged Cuban independence and opposed the annexation of the Philippines. He praised the Filipinos for their written constitution and ability to govern themselves. He compared the lynching of African Americans in the U.S. South to the "lynching" of the Filipino people. (Library of Congress)

strangers' wealth is stored;/ He has loosed his fateful lightning, and with woe and death has scored;/His lust is marching on."[52]

Prominent women also participated in the debate, hoping to build a distinct foreign-policy constituency out of existing networks of women's clubs and organizations. The New Hampshire pacifist Lucia True Ames Mead pronounced it immoral for "any nation . . . which buys or takes by conquest another people, and dominates them without promise of granting them independence."[53] The social reformer Jane Addams saw children playing war games in the streets of Chicago. The kids were *not freeing Cubans,* she protested, but rather *slaying Spaniards* in their not-so-innocent play. Although unsuccessful in the fight against empire, tens of thousands of women became activists over the next decade. "Never before," writes the historian Judith Papachristou, "had American women involved themselves in foreign affairs in such a way and to such an extent."[54]

The imperialists, led by Senators Henry Cabot Lodge and Nelson Aldrich, Roosevelt, and McKinley, and backed strongly by business leaders, engaged their opponents in vigorous debate in early 1899. These empire builders stressed pragmatic considerations, although they communicated common ideas of racial superiority and national destiny to civilize the savage world. "We are a conquering race," boasted Senator Albert Beveridge, and "we must obey our blood and occupy new markets, and, if necessary, new lands."[55] The Philippines provided stepping-stones to the rich China market and strategic ports for the expanding navy that protected American commerce and demonstrated U.S. prestige. International competition also dictated that the United States keep the fruits of victory, argued the imperialists; otherwise, a menacing Germany or expansionist Japan might pick up what America discarded. Few believed that the United States should relinquish territory acquired through blood. National honor demanded retention, or so the annexationists argued. Roosevelt, countering the charge that no one had asked the Filipinos if they desired annexation to the United States, delighted in telling Democratic anti-imperialists that President Thomas Jefferson took Louisiana without a vote by its inhabitants. McKinley put it simply: "Duty determines destiny."[56] Duty, destiny, defense, and dollars became the alliterative imperialist litany.

Pro-imperialist Senator Lodge described the treaty fight as the "closest, most bitter, and most exciting struggle I . . . ever expect to see in the Senate."[57] Shortly before the upper house took action, word reached Washington that Filipino insurrectionists and American soldiers had begun to fight. The news apparently stimulated support for the Treaty of Paris. Democrats tended to be anti-imperialists and Republicans imperialists, yet enough of the former endorsed the treaty on February 6, 1899, to pass it, just barely, by the necessary two-thirds vote, 57 to 27. William Jennings Bryan, believing that rejection of the treaty would prolong the war and that the Philippines could be freed after terminating the hostilities with Spain, urged an aye vote on his anti-imperialist friends. The Republicans probably had enough votes in reserve to pass the treaty even if Bryan had opposed it. Eight days later, the tie-breaking vote of the vice president killed a Senate resolution providing for Philippine independence as soon as the Filipinos established a stable government.

Imperial Collisions in Asia: The Philippine Insurrection and the Open Door in China

Controlling, protecting, and expanding the enlarged U.S. empire became a major chore. The Filipinos proved the most obstructionist. By the end of the war, Aguinaldo and rebel forces controlled most of the islands, having routed the Spanish and driven them into Manila. Aguinaldo had arrived from exile in a U.S. warship and believed that American leaders, including Dewey, had promised his country independence if he joined U.S. forces in defeating the Spanish. Ordered out of Manila by U.S. authorities after the Spanish-American armistice, he and his cohorts had to endure racial insults, including "nigger" and "goo goo." American soldiers considered the Filipinos inferior, the equivalent of Indians and blacks at home. Although one Methodist missionary boasted that the Americans had found Manila "a pesthole, and made it a health resort," critics claimed that imperialism exported the worst in American life.[58] The Treaty of Paris angered the Filipinos, as did McKinley's decree asserting the supreme authority of the United States in the Philippines. In open defiance of Washington, Aguinaldo and other prominent Filipinos organized a government at Malolos, wrote a constitution, and proclaimed the Philippine Republic in late January 1899.

Although American anti-imperialist critics did not err in calling the Filipino government as virtuous as that of Chicago, McKinley believed his new subjects to

Emilio Aguinaldo (1869–1964).   Of mixed Chinese and Tagalog ancestry, this Filipino nationalist was exiled by the Spanish from his country in 1897. He returned with American forces and later clashed with them when he declared independence for the Philippines. Captured in 1901, he then declared allegiance to the United States. During World War II, however, he favored the Japanese, who occupied the islands, and American authorities briefly imprisoned him in 1945 when they reestablished U.S. power over Manila. (Library of Congress)

be ill fitted for self-government. In February 1899 the Filipinos began fighting better-armed American troops. After bloody struggles, Aguinaldo was captured in March 1901. Before the insurrection collapsed in 1902, some 4,165 Americans and more than 200,000 Filipinos died. One hundred twenty-five thousand American troops quelled the insurrection, which cost the United States at least $160 million. In Batangas province south of Manila, General J. Franklin Bell drove insurrectionists into the hills and killed their livestock. Then malaria-transmitting mosquitoes "were forced to get their meals from people" instead of cattle. The result: an "epidemiological catastrophe" wherein the Batangas population declined by 90,000 (one-quarter of the people) over a six-year period.[59] Anti-imperialist William James, distinguished Harvard University philosopher, poignantly summarized the impact of U.S. intervention: "We are destroying the lives of these islanders by the thousands, their villages and their cities. . . . Civilization is, then, the big, hollow, resounding, corrupting, sophisticating, confusing torrent of mere brutal momentum and irrationality that brings forth fruits like this!"[60]

One of the ugliest wars in American history, this contest saw both sides commit atrocities. After Filipinos massacred an American regiment on Samar and stuffed molasses into disemboweled corpses to attract ants, General Jacob Smith told his officers: "I want no prisoners. I wish you to kill and burn, the more you kill and burn the better you will please me."[61] Americans burned *barrios* to the ground, placing villagers in reconcentration camps like those that had defaced Cuba. To get information, Americans administered the "water cure," forcing prisoners to swallow gallons of water and then punching the swollen stomach to empty it quickly. General Arthur MacArthur viewed his task as "conquering eight millions of recalcitrant, treacherous, and sullen people."[62] Racist notions of white superiority surfaced. Army captain Frank R. McCoy could not comprehend the Muslim Moros who refused American medical treatment. "You mention Cholera to them," he wrote, "and they throw up their hands [saying,] 'God has given and God has taken away.'"[63] For most soldiers, an army song had it right: "Civilize 'em with a Krag."[64] The civil governor of the Philippines from 1901 to 1904, William Howard Taft, put the question less crudely when he described the American mission as to "teach those people individual liberty, which shall lift them up to a point of civilization . . . , and which shall make them rise to call the name of the United States blessed."[65] In fact, Taft administered a sedition act that sought to suppress criticism of the United States. His authorities censored newspapers and jailed dissenters.

For years, the Moros would not submit to American rule. One military expert predicted that "the Moro question will eventually be settled in the same manner as the Indian question, that is by gradual extermination."[66] In a June 1913 battle on the island of Jolo, U.S. forces killed 500 Moros. The army's premier "guerrilla warrior," General John J. Pershing, called that bloody encounter "the fiercest [fighting] I have ever seen."[67] Until 1914, moreover, the followers of Artemio Ricarte harassed the U.S. military with their hit-and-run tactics. Ricarte himself, imprisoned from 1904 to 1910 and then deported to Hong Kong and Japan, refused allegiance to the United States and set up a government-in-exile that demanded "immediate and complete independence and the equalization of wealth."[68]

William Howard Taft (1857–1930) and Animal. The first U.S. civil governor of the Philippines, Taft weighed more than 300 pounds. He once proudly reported to Washington that he had ridden twenty-five miles to a high mountain spot. Secretary of War Elihu Root replied: "HOW IS HORSE?" (U.S. Army Military History Institute)

The carrot joined the stick to pacify the Philippines. Local self-government, social reforms, and American schools, which taught Filipinos of all social classes English and arithmetic, helped win over elites and key minorities. "We'll larn ye our language," said the inimitable Mr. Dooley, "because 'tis easier to larn ye ours thin to larn ourselves ye'ers."[69] A general amnesty proclaimed by President Theodore Roosevelt on July 4, 1902, also encouraged accommodation. By restricting suffrage at the outset to Filipinos with wealth, education, and previous government service, U.S. administrators successfully wooed Filipino elites, including former revolutionaries. American roads, bridges, port improvements, and sanitation projects soon followed. At the St. Louis World's Fair in 1904, a thousand Filipinos were put on display as "living exhibits," and photographs and dioramas depicted their "rapid social, educational and sanitary development" under "the kindly tutelage of the United States."[70] In 1916, the Jones Act promised Philippine independence but set no date. Thirty years later the Philippines became an independent nation allied with the United States.

Proximity to China made the Philippines especially valuable to U.S. leaders who predicted lucrative markets for American products. In early 1898 business

"The Metamorphosis of a Bontoc Igorot."   Dean Worcester, an American zoology professor who served as the U.S. secretary of the interior for the Philippines from 1900 to 1913, included these two photographs of "Pit-a-pit," a Bontoc Igorot, in his 1914 book to illustrate his conclusion that U.S. policies and programs had a civilizing effect on Filipinos. The two pictures were taken nine years apart. Worcester classified the islands' population of 8 million into eighty-four tribes, including the Bontoc Igorot. At the 1904 St. Louis World's Fair, the village of three Igorot tribes (Bontoc, Syoc, and Benguet) became one of the most popular exhibits, to which visitors flocked because of the popularized image of the Igorot as head-hunters and dog-eaters. As the scholar Eric Breitbart writes in his book, *A World on Display 1904* (1997), this image "symbolized the gulf between 'savagery' and 'civilization'" and between "clothed and naked," confirming the "otherness" of native peoples abroad. (Dean Worcester, *The Philippines Past and Present* [New York: Macmillan Company, 1914], vol. 2, frontispiece)

leaders organized the American Asiatic Association to stimulate public and governmental concern to protect and enlarge U.S. interests in China. Treasury official Frank Vanderlip typically lauded the Philippines as the "pickets of the Pacific, standing guard at the entrances to trade with the millions of China."[71] Although China attracted only 2 percent of U.S. foreign commerce, American traders had long dreamed of an unbounded China market, and missionaries romanticized a Christian kingdom. These ambitions remained dreams more than reality. Yet dreams spurred action, and during the 1890s the United States, despite limited power, sought to defend its Asian interests, real and imagined.

In that decade the European powers and Japan were dividing China, rendered helpless in 1895 after the Sino-Japanese War, into spheres of influence and establishing discriminatory trading privileges in their zones. The McKinley administration in early 1898 watched anxiously as Germany grabbed Jiaozhou (Kiaochow) and Russia gained a lease at Port Arthur on the Liaodong Peninsula. France, already ensconced in Indochina, leased Guangzhou Bay in southern China in April of that year. Japan already had footholds in Formosa and Korea. The British in March 1898 suggested a joint Anglo–American declaration on behalf of equal commercial opportunity in China. In the midst of the Cuban crisis, Washington gave little attention to the request. Britain, which already had Hong Kong, then forced China to give up part of the Shandong Peninsula.

American economic and religious interests in China seemed threatened. The American Asiatic Association and missionary groups appealed to Washington for

American Cigarettes in China. An American soldier in China peddles cigarettes. After the invention of the cigarette machine in 1881, the tobacco tycoon James B. Duke asked to see an atlas. Leafing through the pages, he noticed China's large population of 430 million. "That," he said, "is where we are going to sell cigarettes." Nine years later came the first exports; by 1916 Duke and other American entrepreneurs were selling 12 billion cigarettes in China. (Edward J. Parrish Papers, Duke University Library)

help. Drawing on recommendations from William W. Rockhill, adviser on Asian policy, who in turn consulted his British friend and officer of the Chinese customs service, Alfred Hippisley, Secretary of State John Hay tried words. Even though President McKinley seemed "to want a slice" of China, Hay sent an "Open Door" note on September 6, 1899, to Japan, Germany, Russia, Britain, France, and Italy, asking them to respect equal trade opportunity for all nations in their spheres.[72] It was, of course, a traditional American principle. Noncommittal replies trickled back, but Hay read into them what he wanted and proclaimed definitive acceptance of the Open Door proposal.

Although frail, the Open Door policy carried meaning. Americans knew they had less leverage than the other imperialists in Asia, but they also noted that a delicate balance of power existed there that the United States could unbalance. The European powers and Japan might hesitate to exclude American commerce altogether from China, for fear that the United States would tip that balance by joining one of the powers against the others. They also feared that a world war might erupt from competition in Asia. Americans hoped the Open Door policy would serve their goals in an area where they had little military power. The United States wanted the commercial advantages without having to employ military force, as it

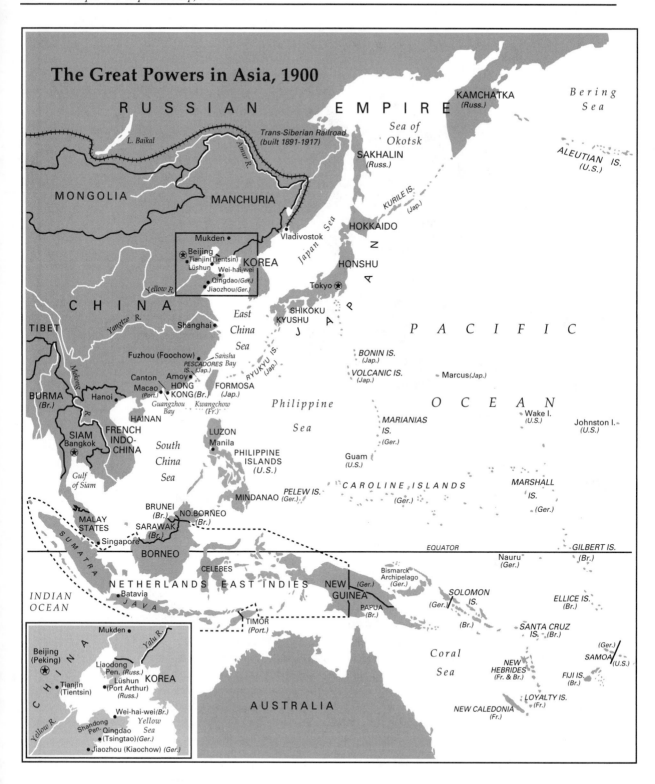

The Great Powers in Asia, 1900

RUSSIAN E M P I R E

KAMCHATKA
(Russ.)

Bering Sea

L. Baikal

*Trans-Siberian Railroad
(built 1891-1917)*

Sea of Okotsk

SAKHALIN
(Russ.)

ALEUTIAN IS.
(U.S.)

Amur R.

MONGOLIA   MANCHURIA

KURILE IS.
(Jap.)

HOKKAIDO

Mukden
Vladivostok

Beijing
Tianjin(Tientsin)   KOREA
Lüshun
Wei-hai-wei
Qingdao(Ger.)
Jiaozhou(Ger.)

Japan Sea

HONSHU

Yellow R.

C H I N A

Tokyo

TIBET

Yangtze R.

Shanghai

East China Sea

SHIKOKU
KYUSHU

J A P A N

P A C I F I C

BONIN IS.
(Jap.)

Mekong R.

Fuzhou (Foochow)

Sansha Bay
PESCADORES IS. (Jap.)

VOLCANIC IS.
(Jap.)

Marcus(Jap.)

Canton   Amoy
Macao   HONG
(Port.)   KONG(Br.)   FORMOSA
(Jap.)

RYUKYU IS. (Jap.)

O C E A N

BURMA
(Br.)

Hanoi

Guangzhou Bay   *Kwangchow (Fr.)*

HAINAN

Philippine Sea

MARIANAS IS.
(Ger.)

Wake I.
(U.S.)

Johnston I.
(U.S.)

SIAM
Bangkok

FRENCH
INDO-
CHINA

South China Sea

LUZON
Manila

Guam
(U.S.)

Gulf of Siam

PHILIPPINE
ISLANDS
(U.S.)

C A R O L I N E   I S L A N D S
(Ger.)

MARSHALL
IS.
(Ger.)

MINDANAO

PELEW IS.
(Ger.)

BRUNEI
(Br.)   NO. BORNEO
(Br.)

SARAWAK
(Br.)

MALAY
STATES

Singapore

SUMATRA

BORNEO

CELEBES

EQUATOR

Nauru
(Ger.)

GILBERT IS.
(Br.)

INDIAN
OCEAN

NETHERLANDS EAST INDIES

Batavia

JAVA

NEW
GUINEA   (Ger.)

Bismarck
Archipelago
(Ger.)

SOLOMON
IS.
(Ger.)

ELLICE IS.
(Br.)

PAPUA
(Br.)

TIMOR
(Port.)

SANTA CRUZ
IS. (Br.)

(Ger.)
SAMOA
(U.S.)

Coral Sea

NEW
HEBRIDES
(Fr. & Br.)

FIJI IS.
(Br.)

LOYALTY IS.
(Fr.)

AUSTRALIA

NEW CALEDONIA
(Fr.)

Inset map:

Mukden

Yalu R.

C H I N A

Beijing
(Peking)

Liaodong
Pen. (Russ.)
Lüshun
(Port Arthur)
(Russ.)

KOREA

Tianjin
(Tientsin)

Yellow R.

Wei-hai-wei(Br.)

Yellow Sea

Shandong
Pen.   Qingdao
(Tsingtao) (Ger.)

Jiaozhou (Kiaochow) (Ger.)

did in Latin America. The policy did not always work, but it fixed itself in the American mind as a guiding principle for Chinese affairs.

The Open Door note notwithstanding, the Manchu dynasty (1644–1912) neared death, unable to cope with the foreign intruders. Resentful nationalistic Chinese, led by a secret society called *Yihequan* ("Righteous and Harmonious Fists," or the "Boxers"), undertook in 1900 to throw out the imperialist aggressors. The Boxers murdered hundreds of Christian missionaries and their Chinese converts, and laid siege to the foreign legations in Beijing (Peking). "If we die we die in peace," one missionary woman wrote just before she was murdered.[73] To head off a complete gouging of China by vengeful Europeans and Japanese, McKinley, without consulting Congress, sent 2,500 American troops to Beijing from the Philippines to join 15,500 soldiers from other nations to lift the siege. And Hay, without consulting the Chinese government, issued another Open Door note on July 3, 1900. He defined U.S. policy as the protection of American life and property, the safeguarding of "equal and impartial trade," and the preservation of China's "territorial and administrative entity."[74] In short, keep the trade door open by keeping China intact.

Certainly these actions did not save China from continued incursion (it had to pay more than $300 million for the Boxers' damages). The United States itself even asked for a territorial concession in late 1900 at Sansha Bay, Fujian Province. The Japanese, catching Hay red-handed, politely reminded him of his notes, and he shelved the request. Thereafter Washington buttressed its support for the Open Door by increasing the Asiatic Squadron to forty-eight warships and earmarking army forces in the Philippines for future emergency deployment in China.

The Elbows of a World Power, 1895–1900

Venezuela, Cuba, Hawai'i, the Philippines, Open Door notes—together they meant an unprecedented set of commitments and responsibilities for the United States. Symbolic of this thrust to world-power status was the ascendancy of the imperialists' imperialist, Theodore Roosevelt, to the presidency in 1901. Peering into the twentieth century, Roosevelt warned Americans to avoid "slothful ease and ignoble peace." Never "shrink from the hard contests"; "let us therefore boldly face the life of strife."[75] Indeed, many diplomats looked back on the triumphs of the 1890s as a testing time when the United States met the international challenge and rightfully asserted its place as a major world power. Europeans watched anxiously. Some, especially Germans, spoke of the "American peril."[76] Russia, however, supported U.S. annexation of Hawai'i because it prevented this "Malta of the Pacific" from becoming Japanese.[77] The United States, European leaders pointed out, had become a factor in the "balance of power." With whom would the nation ally itself?

The odds seemed to favor Great Britain, although the Anglo-American courtship would be prolonged and marriage something for the future. Ever since the eye-opening Venezuelan crisis, the British, in Colonial Secretary Joseph Chamberlain's words, had applauded Washington for "entering the lists and sharing the task which might have proved too heavy for us alone" and pursued what one

John M. Hay (1838–1905). The author of the Open Door notes graduated from Brown University and served as one of President Abraham Lincoln's secretaries. He became a newspaper editor and diplomat and, in 1897, ambassador to Great Britain. The following year McKinley named him secretary of state, a post he held until his death. The historian Christopher Thorne has described the Open Door policy as a "singular blend of evangelicalism, political calculation, benevolent imperialism, and crude self-interest." (National Portrait Gallery, Smithsonian Institution)

Pears Soap advertisement.
This unusual mixture of commercial and diplomatic advertising
salutes Anglo-American rapprochement. (*Life*, 1898)

historian has called the "great rapprochement."[78] Looking for support against an expansionist Germany, John Bull thought Uncle Sam a fit partner. During the Spanish-American-Cuban-Filipino War the British conspicuously tilted toward the
American side and encouraged the subsequent U.S. absorption of Spanish colonies.
American leaders, in turn, sympathized with the British suppression of the Boer Republics in South Africa during 1899–1902, comparing that struggle to their own
war with the Filipinos. Articulate Americans welcomed Britain's implicit acceptance of their imperialism. "Germany, and not England, is the power with whom
we are apt to have trouble over the Monroe Doctrine," wrote Roosevelt in 1898.[79]
Vague Anglo-Saxonism and cultural ties joined British recognition of the power of
the United States to forge more amicable relations. Anglophobes continued to twist
the lion's tail and commercial competition remained intense, but Anglo-American
relations moved from being "cool, grudging, and occasionally hostile" to tolerant
and cordial.[80]

Britain still ranked first in naval power, but in the late 1890s the United States
was growing, standing sixth by 1900. In 1898 alone, spurred by the war with Spain,
the United States added 128 vessels to its navy, at a cost of $18 million. At the 1898
American Historical Association meeting, Professor Edwin A. Grosvenor of
Amherst College caught the new times in his address: "Barriers of national seclu-
sion are everywhere tumbling like the great wall of China. Every nation elbows
other nations to-day."[81] The steel magnate Andrew Carnegie boasted that "the old
nations of the earth creep at a snail's pace," but the United States "thunders past
with the rush of the express."[82] Many commentators reported that the United
States, although still divided North and South on many issues, had united as never
before. Southern racists and northern imperialists now had something in common:
the need to keep inferior peoples in their place. Befitting their new imperial status,
U.S. leaders often used gendered and age-based language that presumed superiority over peoples deemed "emotional, irrational, irresponsible, unbusinesslike, unstable, childlike."[83] If Americans played "the part of China, and [were] content to
rot by inches in ignoble ease within our borders," warned Roosevelt, they will "go
down before other nations which have not lost the manly and adventurous qualities."[84] As one college professor expostulated in 1898: "We must govern as those
who learn; and they must obey as those who are in tutelage. They are children and
we are men in these deep matters of government and justice."[85]

The events of the 1895–1900 period further altered the process of decisionmaking. Both Cleveland and McKinley conducted their own foreign policies, often thwarting or manipulating Congress. "Expansion and disorder abroad equaled
centralization at home," one historian has written.[86] In 1907, looking back on the
days of 1898, Woodrow Wilson, then president of Princeton University, recorded
the historical impact: "The war with Spain again changed the balance of powers.
Foreign questions became leading questions again, as they had been in the first days
of the government, and in them the President was of necessity leader. . . . The nation has risen to the first rank in power and resources. . . . Our President must always, henceforth, be one of the great powers of the world."[87] Wilson exaggerated
America's power, for that strength still largely centered in the Western Hemisphere,
but for the United States, as the *Washington Post* editorialized in 1898, "the policy

of isolation is dead. . . . A new consciousness seems to have come upon us—the consciousness of strength, and with it a new appetite, a yearning to show our strength. . . . Ambition, interest, land-hunger, pride, the mere joy of fighting, whatever it may be, we are animated by a new sensation. . . . The taste of empire is in the mouth of the people, even as the taste of blood in the jungle."[88] After 1900 the task of managing the expansive empire and the global responsibilities that came with it preoccupied U.S. leaders. ·

FURTHER READING FOR THE PERIOD 1895–1900

For the 1890s push for empire and the coming and waging of the Spanish-American-Cuban-Filipino War, see Edward J. Berbusse, *The United States and Puerto Rico, 1898–1900* (1966); Charles H. Brown, *The Correspondents' War* (1967); Richard Challener, *Admirals, Generals,* and *American Foreign Policy, 1898–1914* (1973); Graham A. Cosmas, *An Army for Empire* (1971); Willard B. Gatewood, Jr., *Black Americans and the White Man's Burden, 1898–1903* (1975); Kristin L. Hoganson, *Fighting for American Manhood: How Gender Politics Provoked the Spanish–American and Philippine–American Wars* (1998); John M. Kirk, *José Martí* (1983); Gerald F. Linderman, *The Mirror of War* (1974); Ernest R. May, *Imperial Democracy* (1961); Joyce Milton, *The Yellow Kids* (1989) (journalists); Ian Mugridge, *The View from Xandu* (1995) (Hearst); Ivan Musicant, *Empire by Default* (1998); John L. Offner, *An Unwanted War* (1992); Louis A. Pérez, Jr., *The War of 1898* (1998), *Cuba and the United States* (1997), and *Cuba Between Empires, 1878–1902* (1983); Julius Pratt, *Expansionists of 1898* (1938); Hyman G. Rickover, *How the Battleship* Maine *Was Destroyed* (1976); Emily Rosenberg, *Spreading the American Dream* (1982); Göran Rystad, *Ambiguous Imperialism* (1981); Peggy Samuels and Harold Samuels, *Remembering the Maine* (1995); David F. Trask, *The War with Spain in 1898* (1981); and Paul Wolman, *The Republican Revisionists and U.S. Tariff Policy, 1897–1912* (1992).

For U.S. leaders, see Howard K. Beale, *Theodore Roosevelt and the Rise of America to World Power* (1956); John Braeman, *Albert J. Beveridge* (1971); H.W. Brands, *T.R.* (1997); Charles W. Calhoun, *Gilded Age Cato* (1988) (Gresham); Kenton J. Clymer, *John Hay* (1975); Gerald Eggert, *Richard Olney* (1973); Lewis L. Gould, *The Presidency of William McKinley* (1981); William Harbaugh, *The Life and Times of Theodore Roosevelt* (1975); Margaret Leech, *In the Days of McKinley* (1959); Nathan Miller, *Theodore Roosevelt* (1992); H. Wayne Morgan, *William McKinley and His America* (1963); Edmund Morris, *The Rise of Theodore Roosevelt* (1979); Ronald Spector, *Admiral of the New Empire* (1974) (Dewey); Richard E. Welch, Jr., *The Presidencies of Grover Cleveland* (1988); and William C. Widenor, *Henry Cabot Lodge and the Search for an American Foreign Policy* (1980).

Anti-imperialism is treated in William N. Armstrong, *E. L. Godkin and American Foreign Policy* (1957); Robert L. Beisner, *Twelve Against Empire* (1968); Kendrick A. Clements, *William Jennings Bryan* (1983); Paolo E. Coletta, *William Jennings Bryan* (1964–1969); John C. Farrell, *Beloved Lady* (1967) (Addams); Thomas J. Osborne, *"Empire Can Wait": American Opposition to Hawaiian Annexation, 1893–1898* (1981); E. Berkeley Tompkins, *Anti-Imperialism in the United States* (1970); Hans L. Trefousse, *Carl Schurz* (1982); and Joseph F. Wall, *Andrew Carnegie* (1970).

The Open Door policy and Asia are discussed in Thomas A. Breslin, *China, American Catholicism, and the Missionary* (1980); Charles S. Campbell, *Special Business Interests and the Open Door Policy* (1951); Sherman Cochran, *Big Business in China* (1980) (cigarette industry); Michael Hunt, *Frontier Defense and the Open Door* (1973) and *The Making of a Special Relationship* (1983); Akira Iriye, *Across the Pacific* (1967); Robert McClellan, *The Heathen Chinee* (1971); Thomas McCormick, *China Market* (1967); Valentin H. Rabe, *The Home Base of American China Missions, 1880–1920* (1978); and Marilyn Blatt Young, *The Rhetoric of Empire* (1968). For Hawai'i, see works listed in Chapter 5.

The Philippine rebellion and the American debate receive scrutiny in Teodoro Agoncillo, *Malolos* (1960); A. J. Bacevich, *Diplomat in Khaki* (1989) (General Frank McCoy); Kenton J. Clymer, *Protestant Missionaries in the Philippines, 1898–1916* (1986); John M. Gates, *Schoolbooks and Krags* (1973); Stanley Karnow,

In Our Image (1989); Brian M. Linn, *Guardians of Empire* (1997) and *The U.S. Army and Counterinsurgency in the Philippine War, 1899–1902* (1989); Glenn A. May, *Battle for Batangas* (1991) and *Social Engineering in the Philippines* (1980); Stuart C. Miller, *"Benevolent Assimilation"* (1982); Daniel B. Schirmer, *Republic or Empire* (1972); Peter Stanley, *A Nation in the Making* (1974), and ed., *Reappraising an Empire* (1984); and Richard E. Welch, *Response to Imperialism* (1979).

For the Venezuelan crisis and Anglo–American relations, see Stuart Anderson, *Race and Rapprochement* (1981); Charles S. Campbell, *From Revolution to Rapprochement* (1974); Judith Ewell, *Venezuela and the United States* (1996); Richard B. Mulanax, *The Boer War in American Politics and Diplomacy* (1994); R. G. Neale, *Great Britain and United States Expansion, 1800–1900* (1966); Thomas J. Noer, *Briton, Boer, and Yankee* (1978); Bradford Perkins, *The Great Rapprochement* (1968); Serge Ricard and Hélène Christol, eds., *Anglo-Saxonism in U.S. Foreign Policy* (1991); and Joseph Smith, *Illusions of Conflict: Anglo-American Diplomacy Toward Latin America, 1865–1896* (1979).

See also the General Bibliography, the following notes, and Richard Dean Burns, ed., *Guide to American Foreign Relations Since 1700* (1983).

For comprehensive coverage of foreign-relations topics, see the articles in the four-volume *Encyclopedia of U.S. Foreign Relations* (1997), edited by Bruce W. Jentleson and Thomas G. Paterson.

NOTES TO CHAPTER 1

1. Quoted in Gerald G. Eggert, *Richard Olney* (College Park: Penn State University Press, 1974), p. 208.
2. U.S. Consul Eugene Plumacher quoted in Judith Ewell, *Venezuela and the United States* (Athens: University of Georgia Press, 1996), p. 69.
3. Quoted in Ernest R. May, *Imperial Democracy* (New York: Harper and Row, [1961], 1973), p. 33.
4. Quoted in Charles W. Calhoun, *Gilded Age Cato* (Lexington: University Press of Kentucky, 1988), p. 217.
5. *Foreign Relations, 1895,* Part I (Washington, D.C.: Government Printing Office, 1896), pp. 545–562.
6. Richard E. Welch, Jr., *The Presidencies of Grover Cleveland* (Lawrence: University Press of Kansas, 1988), p. 184.
7. Quoted in Robert L. Beisner, *From the Old Diplomacy to the New, 1865–1900* (Arlington Heights, Ill.: Harlan Davidson, 1986; 2nd ed.), p. 111.
8. Quoted in Howard K. Beale, *Theodore Roosevelt and the Rise of America to World Power* (New York: Collier Books, [1956], 1962), p. 60.
9. Quoted in H. W. Brands, *T.R.* (New York: BasicBooks, 1997), p. 289.
10. Quoted in Eggert, *Olney,* p. 223.
11. Quoted in Stuart Anderson, *Race and Rapprochement* (Rutherford, N.J.: Fairleigh Dickinson University Press, 1981), p. 97.
12. Quoted in Joyce Milton, *The Yellow Kids* (New York: Harper and Row, 1989), p. 27.
13. Quoted in Allan Nevins, *Grover Cleveland* (New York: Dodd, Mead, 1932), p. 644.
14. Quoted in Joseph Smith, *Illusions of Conflict* (Pittsburgh: University of Pittsburgh Press, 1979), p. 207.
15. Quoted in George Young, "Intervention Under the Monroe Doctrine," *Political Science Quarterly, LVII* (June 1942), 277.
16. Henry Cabot Lodge quoted in Fredrick B. Pike, *The United States and Latin America* (Austin: University of Texas Press, 1992), pp. 158–159.
17. Joseph A. Fry, "From Open Door to World Systems," *Pacific Historical Review, LX* (May 1996), 282.
18. Quoted in Richard E. Welch, Jr., *George Frisbie Hoar and the Half-Breed Republicans* (Cambridge: Harvard University Press, 1971), p. 209.
19. Walter Q. Gresham to Carl Schurz, October 6, 1893, Walter Q. Gresham Papers, Library of Congress, Washington, D.C.
20. Quoted in Louis A. Pérez, Jr., *Cuba and the United States* (Athens: University of Georgia Press, 1997; 2nd ed.), p. 80; and John M. Kirk, *José Martí* (Gainesville: University Presses of Florida, 1983), pp. 52, 56, 58, 90, 118.
21. Quoted in Philip S. Foner, *The Spanish-Cuban-American War and the Birth of American Imperialism* (New York: Monthly Review Press, 1972; 2 vols.), I, 21.
22. Quoted in William Manchester, *The Last Lion* (Boston: Little, Brown, 1983), p. 228.
23. Quoted in John L. Offner, *An Unwanted War* (Chapel Hill: University of North Carolina Press, 1992), p. 26.
24. Quoted in Walter LaFeber, *The American Search for Opportunity 1865–1913* (New York: Cambridge University Press, 1993), p. 132.
25. Quoted in Eggert, *Olney,* p. 265.
26. James D. Richardson, ed., *A Compilation of the Messages and Papers of the Presidents, 1789–1897* (Washington, D.C.: Government Printing Office, 1896–1899; 10 vols.), IX, 716–722.
27. Quoted in Edmund Morris, *The Rise of Theodore Roosevelt* (New York: Coward, McCann, & Geoghegan, 1979), p. 610.
28. *Congressional Record, XXXI* (December 6, 1897), 3–5.
29. *Foreign Relations, 1898* (Washington D.C.: Government Printing Office, 1901), pp. 1007–1008.
30. Quoted in Offner, *Unwanted War,* p. 129.
31. *Congressional Record, XXXI* (March 17, 1898), 2916–2919.
32. Quoted in Louis A. Pérez, Jr., *Cuba Between Empires, 1878–1902* (Pittsburgh: University of Pittsburgh Press, 1983), p. 172.
33. Quoted *ibid.,* p. 174.
34. *Foreign Relations, 1898,* p. 746.

35. Quoted in LaFeber, *American Search,* p. 143.

36. *Congressional Record, XXXI* (April 11, 1898), 3699–3702.

37. Pérez, *Cuba Between Empires,* p. 178.

38. Quoted *ibid.,* p. 174.

39. Quoted in H. Wayne Morgan, *America's Road to Empire* (New York: Wiley, 1965), p. 63.

40. Quoted in Winthrop Hudson, "Protestant Clergy Debate the Nation's Vocation, 1898–1899" (unpub. ms., 1974).

41. Rector of Catholic University quoted in Pike, *United States and Latin America,* p. 168.

42. Quoted in John Braeman, *Albert J. Beveridge* (Chicago: University of Chicago Press, 1971), p. 23.

43. Finley Peter Dunne, *Mr. Dooley in Peace and War* (Boston: Small, Maynard, 1899), p. 9.

44. Quoted in Gerald F. Linderman, *The Mirror of War* (Ann Arbor: University of Michigan Press, 1974), p. 125.

45. Quoted in Louis A. Pérez, Jr., "The Meaning of the *Maine,*" *Pacific Historical Review, LVIII* (August 1989), 320.

46. Quoted in Frank Freidel, *The Splendid Little War* (Boston: Little, Brown, 1958), p. 295.

47. Quoted in John A. S. Grenville and George B. Young, *Politics, Strategy, and American Diplomacy* (New Haven: Yale University Press, 1966), p. 278.

48. Quoted in Raymond Carr, *Puerto Rico* (New York: Vintage Books, 1984), p. 25.

49. Quoted in Walter A. McDougall, *Promised Land, Crusader State* (Boston: Houghton Mifflin, 1997), pp. 111–112.

50. Quoted in Robert L. Beisner, "1898 and 1968," *Political Science Quarterly, LXXV* (June 1970), 200.

51. Senator John Daniel quoted in H. W. Brands, *Bound to Empire* (New York: Oxford University Press, 1992), p. 30.

52. Quoted in Hugh Deane, *Good Deeds & Gunboats* (San Francisco: China Books and Periodicals, 1990), p. 65.

53. Quoted in John M. Craig, "Lucia True Ames Mead," in Edward P. Crapol, ed., *Women and American Foreign Policy* (Westport, Conn.: Greenwood, 1992; 2nd ed.), p. 72.

54. Judith Papachristou, "American Women and Foreign Policy, 1898–1905," *Diplomatic History, XIV* (Fall 1990), 493.

55. Quoted in Anders Stephanson, *Manifest Destiny* (New York: Hill & Wang, 1995), p. 98.

56. Quoted *ibid.,* p. 87.

57. Quoted in H. Wayne Morgan, *William McKinley and His America* (Syracuse: Syracuse University Press, 1963), p. 422.

58. Quoted in Kenton J. Clymer, *Protestant Missionaries in the Philippines, 1898–1916* (Urbana: University of Illinois Press, 1986), p. 159.

59. Glenn A. May, *Battle for Batangas* (New Haven: Yale University Press, 1991), pp. 267, 291.

60. *Boston Evening Transcript,* March 1, 1899.

61. Quoted in Stanley Karnow, *In Our Image* (New York: Random House, 1989), p. 191.

62. Quoted in Brian M. Linn, *Guardians of Empire* (Chapel Hill: University of North Carolina Press, 1997), p. 19.

63. Quoted in A. J. Bacevich, *Diplomat in Khaki* (Lawrence: University Press of Kansas, 1989), p. 29.

64. Quoted in John M. Gates, *Schoolbooks and Krags* (Westport, Conn.: Greenwood, 1973), p. vii.

65. Henry F. Graff, ed., *American Imperialism and the Philippine Insurrection* (Boston: Little, Brown, 1969), p. 36.

66. Benjamin Foulois quoted in Linn, *Guardians,* p. 36.

67. Quoted in Donald Smythe, *Guerrilla Warrior* (New York: Charles Scribner's Sons, 1973), p. 198.

68. Quoted in Reynaldo C. Ileto, "Orators and the Crowd," in Peter W. Stanley, ed., *Reappraising an Empire* (Cambridge: Harvard University Press, 1984), p. 103.

69. Quoted in Karnow, *In Our Image,* p. 201.

70. Robert W. Rydell, *World of Fairs* (Chicago: University of Chicago Press, 1993), pp. 75–76.

71. Quoted in Thomas J. McCormick, *China Market* (Chicago: Quadrangle, 1967), p. 119.

72. Quoted in Louis L. Gould, *The Presidency of William McKinley* (Lawrence: University Press of Kansas, 1981), p. 222.

73. Eva Jane Price, *China Journal, 1899–1900* (New York: Charles Scribner's Sons, 1989), p. 232.

74. *Foreign Relations, 1901* (Washington, D.C.: Government Printing Office, 1902), Appendix, p. 12.

75. Quoted in Beale, *Theodore Roosevelt,* p. 84.

76. Quoted in Fareed Zakaria, *From Wealth to Power* (Princeton: Princeton University Press, 1998), p. 133.

77. Mikhail Murav'ev quoted in Normal Saul, *Concord and Conflict* (Lawrence: University Press of Kansas, 1996), p. 438.

78. Quoted in Anderson, *Race and Rapprochement,* p. 127.

79. Quoted in Edward P. Crapol, "From Anglophobia to Fragile Rapprochement," in Hans-Jürgen Schröder, ed., *Confrontation and Cooperation* (Providence, R.I.: Berg, 1993), p. 21.

80. Paul M. Kennedy, *The Rise and Fall of the Great Powers* (New York: Random House, 1987), p. 251.

81. American Historical Association, *Annual Report, 1898* (Washington, D.C.: Government Printing Office, 1899), p. 288.

82. Quoted in Smith, *Illusions of Conflict,* p. 40.

83. Emily S. Rosenberg, "Walking the Borders," in Michael J. Hogan and Thomas G. Paterson, eds., *Explaining the History of American Foreign Relations* (New York: Cambridge University Press, 1991), p. 33.

84. Quoted in Gail Bederman, *Manliness & Civilization* (Chicago: University of Chicago Press, 1995), p. 193.

85. Woodrow Wilson quoted in Tony Smith, *America's Mission* (Princeton: Princeton University Press, 1994), p. 63.

86. LaFeber, *American Search,* p. 117.

87. Quoted in Arthur Link's essay in *Wilson's Diplomacy* (Cambridge: Schenkman, 1973), p. 6.

88. *Washington Post,* June 2, 1898.

Managing, Policing, and Extending the Empire, 1900–1914

"The Thirteenth Labor of Hercules."   *With this official poster by Perham Nahl, the Panama-Pacific Exposition in San Francisco in 1915 celebrated the opening of the Panama Canal. The artist commemorates the ten-year construction project using symbols that reflect the empire-building and male hegemony of the era: A powerful, muscular Hercules (the United States) forcibly parts the land (a yielding Panama) to make space for the canal. (Library of Congress)*

DIPLOMATIC CROSSROAD

Severing Panama from Colombia for the Canal, 1903

"Revolution imminent" warned the cable from the American consul at Colón, a normally quiet Colombian seaport on the Atlantic side of Panama. Acting Secretary of State Francis B. Loomis bridled his curiosity for an hour. Then he fired off an inquiry to the U.S. consul at Panama City, on the Pacific slope: "Uprising on Isthmus reported. Keep Department promptly and fully informed." The response came back in four hours: "No uprising yet. Reported will be in the night. Situation is critical." Loomis's anxiety soon increased when he learned that an "important message" intended for the U.S.S. *Nashville* anchored at Colón had miscarried and troops of the Colombian government had landed in the city.

At the Department of State it was now 8:20 P.M., November 3, 1903. As far as Loomis knew, a revolution had not yet broken out on the isthmus. Nonetheless, he hurriedly drafted instructions for the consuls at Panama and Colón. "Act promptly" to convey to the commanding officer of the *Nashville* this order: "In the interests of peace make every effort to prevent [Colombian] Government troops at Colón from proceeding to Panama [City]." Loomis agonized for another hour. Finally, a new cable arrived in Washington, D.C.: "Uprising occurred to-night . . . no bloodshed. . . . Government will be organized to-night." Loomis had done his part to ensure success in the scheme to acquire a canal controlled by the United States.

If November 3 was busy for Loomis, it was far more hectic for José Augustín Arango and his fellow conspirators in Panama. The tiny band of Panamanians and Americans living on the isthmus had actively plotted revolution since August, when the Colombian congress rejected the treaty that would have permitted the United States to construct an isthmian canal. By late October, they had become convinced that the North American colossus, frustrated in its overtures to Colombia, would lend them moral and physical support. Confident that U.S. naval vessels would be at hand, they selected November 4 as the date of their coup d'état. To their dismay, however, the Colombian steamer *Cartagena* disembarked about 400 troops at Colón early on November 3. Because the "important message" directing him to prevent the "landing of any armed force . . . either Government or insurgent at Colón" had not reached him, Commander John Hubbard of the *Nashville* did not interfere with the landing.

Forced to rely on their own wits, the conspirators made good use of the transisthmian railroad. They deviously separated the Colombian commanding general from his troops, lured him aboard a train, and sped him across the isthmus to Panama City. At 6:00 P.M. on the third, the revolutionaries arrested their guest, formed a provisional government, and paraded before a cheering crowd at the Cathedral Plaza. But the revolution would remain perilously unfinished so long as armed Colombian soldiers occupied Colón. Too weak to expel the soldiers by

Theodore Roosevelt the Pirate. The Colombian minister called the United States a "pirate." When Roosevelt justified to his cabinet the actions he had taken toward Panama in 1903, Secretary of War Elihu Root observed: "You have shown that you have been accused of seduction and you have conclusively proved that you were guilty of rape." Michael C. C. Adams, author of *The Great Adventure: Male Desire and the Coming of World War I* (1990), reads Roosevelt differently, comparing him to Peter Pan, "the boy who would not grow up." (Frank Nankivell, Swann Collection of Caricature and Cartoon)

force, the insurgents gave the colonel in charge $8,000 in gold, whereupon he ordered his troops aboard a departing steamer. The U.S. consul at Panama City cabled: "Quiet prevails." At noon the next day, Secretary of State John Hay recognized the sovereign Republic of Panama.

The frantic pace of isthmian diplomacy continued. The new Panamanian government appointed as its minister plenipotentiary a Frenchman, Philippe Bunau-Varilla, an engineer of an earlier failed Panama canal project. With Gallic flourish, Bunau-Varilla congratulated Secretary Hay for rescuing Panama "from the barbarism of unnecessary and wasteful civil wars to consecrate it to the destiny assigned to it by Providence, the service of humanity, and the progress of civilization."[1] John Hay thoroughly understood Bunau-Varilla's rhetoric and eagerly negotiated the treaty both men wanted. On November 18, 1903, less than two weeks after U.S. recognition of Panama, they signed the Hay–Bunau-Varilla Treaty, by which the United States would build, fortify, and operate a canal linking the Atlantic and Pacific oceans. Washington also guaranteed the "independence of the Republic in Panama," thereby ensuring Panama's national survival against any threat from Colombia.[2]

Hay had at last achieved a goal set by his chief, President Theodore Roosevelt, several years earlier. "I do not see why we should dig the canal if we are not to fortify it," Roosevelt had remarked in 1900. If an unfortified, neutral canal had existed in Central America during the recent war with Spain, Roosevelt argued, the United States would have spent most of the war in "wild panic," fearful that the Spanish fleet would slip through the waterway and rush to the Philippines to attack Commodore Dewey. The obvious lesson: "Better to have no canal at all, than not give us the power to control it in time of war," Roosevelt expostulated.[3]

The Clayton-Bulwer Treaty of 1850, stipulating joint Anglo-American control of any isthmian canal, seemed to block the way. In December 1898, flushed with victory over Spain, President William McKinley had directed Secretary Hay to modify that agreement with the British ambassador, Sir Julian Pauncefote. The Hay-Pauncefote Treaty of February 1900 permitted the United States to build a canal but forbade its fortification, much to the dismay of Roosevelt, then governor of New York. He spearheaded an attack that defeated the treaty in the Senate, forcing renegotiation. On November 18, 1901, with Roosevelt now president, Hay and Pauncefote signed a new pact satisfactory to the Rough Rider.

Then began the complex process of determining the route. In November 1901, after a two-year investigation, the Walker Isthmian Canal Commission reported in favor of Nicaragua. The decisive criterion—cost—seemed exorbitant for Panama because of the obduracy of the New Panama Canal Company, a French-chartered firm that held the Colombian concession for canal rights. The company estimated its assets on the isthmus at $109 million—machinery, property, and excavated soil left by the defunct de Lesseps organization after its failure to cut through Panama in 1888. Purchase of the company's rights and holdings would make a Panama canal prohibitively expensive although technologically easier. For these reasons, the House of Representatives on January 8, 1902, passed the Hepburn Bill authorizing a canal through Nicaragua.

The New Panama Canal Company's American lawyer, William Nelson Cromwell, a partner in the prestigious New York law firm of Sullivan and

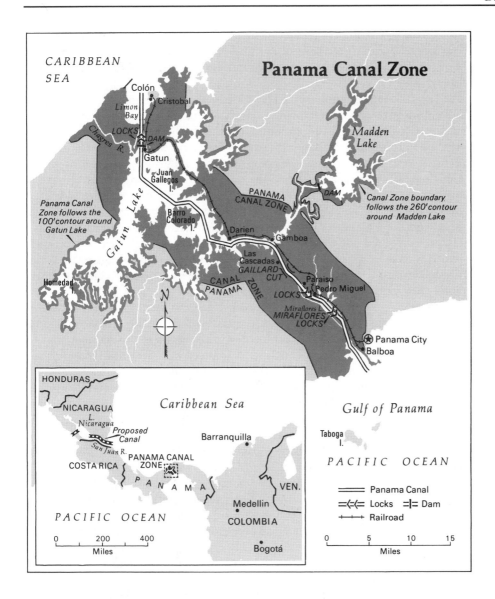

Cromwell, schemed to sell the assets of his French client for the highest possible price. The attorney began to pull strings. Lobbying hard, Bunau-Varilla even exposed the unsuitability of Nicaraguan terrain by deluging Congress with Nicaraguan postage stamps that depicted a belching volcano.

On January 18, 1902, the Walker Commission reversed itself and decided for the technologically preferable Panama passage, citing the company's willingness to sell out for the reduced sum of $40 million. Guided by Roosevelt and Cromwell, Congress five months later chose the Panama route. The State Department soon opened negotiations with Colombia. The annual rent became a stumbling block, which Hay removed only by delivering an ultimatum to the Colombian chargé d'affaires, Tomás Herrán, in January 1903. On January 22 he and Hay signed a treaty granting Colombia an initial payment of $10 million and $250,000 annually. The United States would control the six-mile-wide canal zone for one hundred years, a privilege renewable at the "sole and absolute option" of the North American republic.[4]

The U.S. Senate approved the Hay-Herrán Treaty on March 17, 1903, but the Colombian government attempted to extract a $10 million payment from the New Panama Canal Company for permitting the transfer of its assets to the U.S. government. Cromwell promptly cried foul, whereupon Secretary Hay bluntly announced that any payment by the company to Colombia was "not permissible."[5] The Colombians next tried to raise the initial American cash payment from $10 million to $15 million. Roosevelt exploded against "those contemptible little creatures in Bogotá."[6] The president believed that "you could no more make an agreement with the Colombian rulers than you could nail currant jelly to the wall."[7] TR's intransigence and Hay's extraordinary intercession on behalf of a privately owned foreign corporation increased Colombians' resentment against U.S. infringement on their sovereignty over Panama. The Colombian congress unanimously defeated the treaty on August 12, 1903.

Bogotá's rejection did not catch Roosevelt napping. As early as March 30, U.S. minister Arthur N. Beaupré had warned that "without question public opinion is strongly against its ratification," and Roosevelt had begun to ponder undiplomatic alternatives.[8] On June 13 the ubiquitous Cromwell had met with Roosevelt and then planted a story in the *New York World* reporting that, if Colombia rejected the treaty, Panama would secede and grant to the United States "the equivalent of absolute sovereignty over the Canal Zone," and that "President Roosevelt is said to strongly favor this plan."[9] By now the president was peppering his correspondence with contempt for Colombian "jack rabbits," "foolish and homicidal corruptionists," and "cat-rabbits."[10] Even the usually urbane Hay denounced "the government of folly and graft that now rules at Bogotá."[11]

Roosevelt now considered two options: seizure of Panama by force, or instant recognition and support for any revolutionary regime in Panama. The president inclined sharply toward the latter course after a meeting with Bunau-Varilla on October 10, during which the Frenchman predicted an uprising. When Bunau-Varilla asked what the United States would do, TR replied: "Colombia by her action has forfeited any claim upon the U.S. and I have no use for a government that would do what that government has done."[12] One week later, on October 16, Secretary Hay informed Bunau-Varilla that American naval vessels were heading toward the isthmus. Calculating the steaming time, Bunau-Varilla cabled the revolutionaries waiting on the isthmus that American warships would arrive by November 2. Early that evening the U.S.S. *Nashville* dropped anchor at Colón as predicted. Although the *Nashville* landed troops to keep order *after* the Panamanian junta had gained control, a Colombian diplomat rightfully complained: "The Americans are against us. What can we do against the American Navy?"[13]

In his annual message to Congress after the Panamanian revolution, Roosevelt urged swift ratification of the Hay–Bunau-Varilla Treaty, claiming that Colombia had forced the United States "to take decisive steps to bring to an end a condition of affairs which had become intolerable."[14] When critics complained about his

Panama Canal. The U.S.S. *Ohio* passes through the Culebra Cut (now called the Gaillard Cut) of the Panama Canal about a year after the canal opened to traffic—both warships and commercial vessels. (Library of Congress)

"Bowery-boy" behavior toward Colombia, Roosevelt denounced the "small body of shrill eunuchs who consistently oppose" his "righteous" policies.[15] On February 23, 1904, the Senate approved the treaty by a vote of 66 to 14. The treaty granted the United States "power and authority" within the zone "in perpetuity" as "if it were the sovereign of the territory."[16] Later, in 1911, TR reportedly boasted that "I took the Canal Zone and let Congress debate; and while the debate goes on the Canal does also."[17]

Construction began in mid-1904, and the fifty-mile-long canal opened on August 15, 1914. During the first year of operation alone, 1,058 merchant vessels slid through the locks, while the Atlantic and Pacific fleets of the U.S. Navy freely exchanged ships. In 1922 the United States paid "conscience money" or "canalimony" of $25 million to Colombia but did not formally apologize for having taken the canal zone. Although Roosevelt's handling of the Panama issue constitutes "one of the ineradicable blots on his record," most Americans have applauded his bold meddling in the internal affairs of Colombia.[18] Roosevelt himself ranked it alongside the Louisiana Purchase and the acquisition of Texas.

The Conservative Shapers of Empire

The taking of Panama symbolized the new activism characteristic of American foreign policy after the Spanish-American-Cuban-Filipino War, and construction of the canal ensured the United States virtual hegemony over Latin America. It also

Makers of American Foreign Relations, 1900–1914

Presidents	Secretaries of State
Theodore Roosevelt, 1901–1909	John Hay, 1898–1905
	Elihu Root, 1905–1909
	Robert Bacon, 1909
William Howard Taft, 1909–1913	Philander C. Knox, 1909–1913
Woodrow Wilson, 1913–1921	William Jennings Bryan, 1913–1915

intensified Washington's participation in the global contest for empire among the great powers. "The United States will be attacked as soon as you are about to complete the canal," Germany's Kaiser Wilhelm II predicted to an American diplomat in 1907, identifying Japan as the most likely culprit.[19] Britain, which had the power to challenge U.S. preeminence in the hemisphere, chose to acquiesce in the face of a growing political and naval threat from Germany. In turn, the vigorous German Empire, having expanded its markets and investments in Central and South America to more than 2 billion marks by 1900, seemed "desirous of obtaining a foothold in the Western Hemisphere," as the General Board of the U.S. Navy put it.[20] The kaiser boasted: "We will do whatever is necessary for our navy, even if it displeases the Yankees. Never fear."[21] Revolutionary upheavals in Russia, China, and Mexico produced further shifting in the international balance of power. As European alliances consolidated and lurched toward a world war, it became the task of President Roosevelt and his successors to defend, develop, and enlarge the new U.S. empire in an era of tumultuous transformation.

In the late nineteenth century, Roosevelt had associated closely with the most vocal pressure group agitating for an American canal, the uniformed "professors of war" at the Naval War College.[22] He corresponded regularly with Alfred Thayer Mahan, the navalist who tirelessly explained the strategic advantages of a canal. During the war of 1898, the warship *Oregon* dashed at full speed from San Francisco around South America to Cuba in time to help destroy the Spanish fleet off Santiago. The race of more than 14,000 miles fired American imaginations, but it also consumed sixty-eight days and underscored the need for an interoceanic canal across Central America.

Roosevelt's sense of isthmian strategic necessity reflected a broad worldview he shared with many "progressives" in the early twentieth century. A conservative patrician reformer motivated by noblesse oblige, he "feared that unrest caused by social and economic inequities would impair the nation's strength and efficiency."[23] He saw a similar danger to American interests in unrest abroad, and he sought to exert U.S. influence to create order on a global scale through "proper policing."[24] A quintessential chauvinist, Roosevelt talked about doing the "rough work of the world" and about the need to "speak softly and carry a big stick."[25] Imbibing Darwinist doctrines of "natural selection," Roosevelt proclaimed "our duty toward the people living in barbarism to see that they are freed from their chains, and we can free them only by destroying barbarism itself."[26] For Roosevelt in particular, Anglo-Saxon superiority was best expressed in war. "All the great masterful races have been fighting races," he lectured.[27] Not all Progressive-era reformers joined Roosevelt in advocating a vigorous activism abroad. Wisconsin's Senator Robert M. La Follette, for example, opposed imperialism and contended that the same corporate monopolists they battled at home were dragging the United States into perpetual intervention overseas. Activists in women's organizations bemoaned the "present intoxication with the hashish of conquest" as they urged "women's values" on a male government so as to rein in the "champing steeds" of American militarism and expansion.[28]

Roosevelt vigorously debated his critics and added his unique personal characteristics to American foreign policy. Exuberant and calculating, he centralized foreign-policy decisionmaking, frequently bypassed Congress, and believed "the people" so ignorant about foreign affairs that they should not direct an informed president like himself. At the same time, he kept favorite journalists and other "intelligent observers sufficiently enlightened to prevent their going wrong."[29] Seeking world stability, Roosevelt advocated "minimizing the chances of war among civilized people" and "multiplying the methods and chances of honorably avoiding war in the event of controversy."[30] Indeed, he won the Nobel Peace Prize in 1906 for his mediating effort at the Portsmouth Conference (see pages 52–53). The robust president disliked pomp and ceremony and once broke up a state luncheon by demonstrating jujitsu holds on the Swiss minister. "The biggest matters," this progenitor of the imperial presidency later wrote, "such as the Portsmouth peace, the acquisition of Panama, and sending the fleet around the world, I managed without consultation with anyone; for when a matter is of capital importance, it is well to have it handled by one man only."[31]

Roosevelt and other shapers of American foreign policy before World War I were members of an American quasi aristocracy and sure-footed devotees of "order." Most had graduated from prestigious eastern colleges and distinguished themselves in high political office or in the professions. They moved comfortably in the affluent, cosmopolitan, upper-class society of the Atlantic seaboard. Roosevelt, a graduate of Harvard College and prolific author, had served as assistant secretary of the navy and governor of New York. His successor, Ohioan William Howard Taft, a graduate of Yale, had served as a federal circuit court judge, governor of the Philippines (1901–1904), and secretary of war (1904–1908). Woodrow Wilson earned a Ph.D. from Johns Hopkins, wrote books on government and history, presided over Princeton, and governed New Jersey before entering the White House.

Their secretaries of state, with one exception, belonged to the same elite. John Hay, secretary from 1898 to 1905, was born in Indiana and educated at Brown University. A poet, novelist, biographer, and editor of the *New York Tribune,* the wealthy Hay had served as Lincoln's personal secretary during the Civil War and later as McKinley's ambassador to Great Britain. A chief architect of the Anglo-American rapprochement, Hay regarded "a firm understanding with England" as the "indispensable feature of our foreign policy."[32] His successor, Elihu Root (1905–1909), was born in upstate New York, graduated from Hamilton College, took a law degree at New York University, and became one of America's most successful corporation lawyers. As secretary of war from 1899 to 1904, he created mechanisms, such as the Platt Amendment for Cuba, for managing the American empire. Like TR, he believed that the "main object of diplomacy is to keep the country out of trouble" and maintain order abroad.[33] Philander C. Knox (1909–1913) followed Root. A corporation lawyer born in Pennsylvania, Knox served as attorney general and U.S. senator before entering the State Department. He liked to play golf at Chevy Chase, spend summers with his trotters at his Valley Forge Farms estate, vacation in Florida in the winter, and delegate departmental work to subordinates. He advocated "dollar diplomacy" as a means of creating order in revolution-prone areas—that is, using private financiers and business leaders to promote foreign policy, and using diplomacy to promote American commerce and investment abroad. As his *second* secretary of state President Wilson named New Yorker Robert Lansing (1915–1920), a graduate of Amherst College, son-in-law of a former secretary of state, and practitioner of international law. Reserved and conservative, Lansing also abhorred disorder in the U.S. sphere of Latin America.

William Jennings Bryan, Wilson's *first* appointment (1913–1915), lacked such conservative elite status. The "boy orator" of Nebraska could mesmerize crowds by decrying the "cross of gold" on which eastern capitalists were crucifying western and southern farmers, but he could not win a presidential election (he ran in 1896, 1900, and 1908). The "Great Commoner" languished for years as the most prominent has-been of the Democratic party until Wilson named him secretary of state as a reward for support at the convention of 1912. The president let Bryan appoint "deserving Democrats" to diplomatic posts and indulge his fascination with peace or "cooling off" treaties, but Wilson bypassed him in most important diplomatic decisions, even to the point of composing overseas cables on his own White House typewriter.

These conservative managers of American foreign policy believed that a major component of national power was a prosperous, expanding economy invigorated by a healthy foreign trade. The principle of the "Open Door"—to keep open trade and investment opportunities—became a governing tenet voiced globally, if often tarnished in application. Mahan believed that commerce acted as the "energizer of material civilization," and Roosevelt declared that "America has only just begun to assume that commanding position in the international business world which we believe will more and more be hers."[34] In 1900 the United States exported goods valued at $1.5 billion. By 1914 that figure stood at $2.5 billion. Exports to Latin America increased markedly from $132 million at the turn of the century to $309 million in 1914. Investments there in sugar, transportation, and banking shot up. By 1913 the United Fruit Company, the banana empire, had some 130,000 acres in cultivation in Central America, a fleet of freighters, and political influence as well. By 1914 U.S. entrepreneurs dominated nickel mining in Canada and sugar production in Cuba, and total American investments abroad equaled $3.5 billion.

But those statistics meant more than contributions to pocketbooks. Americans believed that economic expansion also carried abroad the best of "Americanism," the core values of industriousness, honesty, morality, and private initiative. Thus Yale University-in-China and the Young Men's Christian Association (YMCA) joined Standard Oil Company and Singer Sewing in China as advance agents of civilization. And Taft said about the Chinese: "The more civilized they become the more active their industries, the wealthier they become, and the better market they will become for us."[35] President Wilson, who added missionary paternalism to the quest for order, said simply that he would "teach the South American Republics to elect good men."[36] Some foreign observers did not appreciate American beneficence. The typical "Yankee," one German wrote in 1904, was "a boorish fellow . . . who pursued the dollar and sensation, a barbarian in science and art, a bigoted, sanctimonious hypocrite who chewed tobacco and whose chief amusement was found in lynchings."[37] Whatever Americans' intentions or habits, their compulsion to shape the lives of other peoples while denying any desire to dominate brought mixed results.

Cuba's Limited Independence Under the Platt Amendment

In December 1898, President William McKinley promised Cuba "free and independent" status once the American military occupation had achieved "complete tranquility" and a "stable government" on the island.[38] Two months later the Philippine insurrection erupted, and Secretary of War Elihu Root, charged with formulating Cuban occupation policy, feared that in Cuba the United States stood "on the verge daily of the same sort of thing that happened to us in the Philippines."[39]

To accelerate Cuban democracy and stability, Root appointed General Leonard Wood the military governor of the island. A Harvard graduate with a degree in medicine, Wood was a friend of the adventurous Roosevelt. Wood favored outright annexation of Cuba, but he loyally carried out the administration's policy of patrician tutelage. During his tenure as military governor (1899–1902), he worked to eradicate yellow fever, Americanize education, construct highways, and formulate an electoral law guaranteeing order. He even added "before" and "after" photos of public toilets in his reports. The general defined his objectives conservatively: "When money can be borrowed at a reasonable rate of interest and when capital is willing to invest in the Island, a condition of stability will have been reached."[40] Given the war-ravaged Cuban economy, only the North Americans had the resources to generate reconstruction. Those Cuban elites who spoke English and knew American ways could serve as local managers, traders, agents, and advisers. The occupation thus stressed the teaching of English in the public schools because, according to one official, "the Cuban people will never understand the people of the United States until they appreciate our institutions."[41] Many Cubans realized that "to be educated by the people who had conquered them was the extension of conquest, only by another name."[42]

Root began construction of a Cuban-American political relationship designed to weather the storms of independence. Working closely with Senator Orville Platt, Root fashioned the Platt Amendment to the Army Appropriation Bill of 1901. By the amendment's terms, Cuba could not make a treaty with any nation that might impair its independence. Should Cuban independence ever be threatened, or should Cuba fail to protect adequately "life, property, and individual liberty," the

"If General Wood Is Unpopular with Cuba, We Can Guess the Reason." General Leonard Wood (1860–1927), before serving as military governor of Cuba (1899–1902), was a surgeon who entered the army in 1886 and earned a Congressional Medal of Honor for capturing Indian leader Geronimo. He also commanded the Rough Riders at San Juan Hill during the Spanish-American-Cuban-Filipino War. Later he helped govern the Philippines. (*Minneapolis Tribune* in *Literary Digest,* 1901)

United States had the right to intervene. For these purposes, Cuba would cede to the United States "lands necessary for coaling or naval stations."[43]

Cubans howled. On Good Friday 1901, the front page of Havana's *La Discusión* carried a cartoon of "The Cuban Calvary" depicting the Cuban people as Christ and Senator Platt as a Roman soldier. Anti-imperialist critics charged that the amendment extinguished Cuban independence. Root piously denied any "intermeddling or interference with the affairs of a Cuban government," but General Wood privately conceded that "little or no independence [was] left Cuba under the Platt Amendment."[44] A reluctant Cuban convention adopted the measure as an amendment to the new constitution on June 12, 1901, and the two governments signed a treaty embodying the Platt Amendment on May 22, 1903. That same year the U.S. Navy constructed a naval base at Guantánamo Bay; "Gitmo," as the marines christened it, was leased to the United States in perpetuity for a small annual fee. With North American investments pouring into capital-starved Cuba, extending control over sugar, tobacco (the new Tobacco Trust exported 90 percent of Havana cigars by 1902), mining, transportation, utilities, and cattle ranching, the Reciprocity Treaty of 1902 permitted Cuban products to enter the United States at specially reduced tariff rates, thereby further interlocking the economies of the two countries.

The first president of the Republic of Cuba, Tomás Estrada Palma, acted "more plattish than Platt himself."[45] Following his rigged reelection and second inauguration, discontented Cuban nationalists revolted. In September 1906, the U.S. consul general in Havana reported Estrada Palma's inability to quell the rebellion or "protect life and property."[46] President Roosevelt immediately ordered the cruiser *Denver* to Havana, whereupon a battalion of sailors landed at Estrada Palma's request. Roosevelt summarily ordered the men back aboard ship. "I am so angry with that infernal little Cuban republic," exploded the Rough Rider, "that I would like to wipe its people off the face of the earth." All he wanted from the Cubans was that "they should behave themselves."[47]

Into this turmoil stepped the portly secretary of war, William Howard Taft, whom Roosevelt sent to mediate between the warring factions. Estrada Palma resigned, permitting Taft to establish a new government with himself as governor. Taft soon lectured students in Havana that Cubans needed a "mercantile spirit," a "desire to make money, to found great enterprises."[48] He returned home in mid-October, leaving behind a government headed by an American civilian, administered by U.S. Army officers, and supported by more than 5,000 American soldiers. For twenty-eight months Governor Charles E. Magoon attempted to reinstate Leonard Wood's electoral and humanitarian reforms, while Roosevelt publicly scolded the Cubans that if their "insurrectionary habit" persisted, it would be "absolutely out of the question that the Island should continue independent."[49]

Under his successor Taft, and under Taft's successor Woodrow Wilson, U.S. policy toward Cuba reflexively supported existing governments, by force if necessary. Taft and Wilson made no serious effort to reform Cuba in the North American image. Through "dollar diplomacy," the United States sought order in Cuban politics and security for investments and commerce, particularly in sugar. The $50 million invested by Americans in 1896 jumped to $220 million in 1913. By 1920 American-owned mills produced about half of Cuba's sugar. Cuban exports to the United States in 1900 equaled $31 million, by 1914 $131 million, and by 1920 $722 million. U.S. entrepreneurs helped establish missionary schools (such as the Candler school in Havana, named after the founder of Coca-Cola) that, in effect, trained Cubans for employment in North American companies. When revolution threatened these interests, as in May 1912 and February 1917, marines went ashore. After Havana followed Washington's lead and declared war against Germany in April 1917, some 2,500 American troops went to the island, ostensibly to protect the sugar plantations that helped feed the Allied armies.

The Constable of the Caribbean: The Roosevelt Corollary, Venezuela, and the Dominican Republic

President Theodore Roosevelt pondered that most hallowed of American doctrines, the one enunciated by James Monroe in 1823. In his first annual message, on December 3, 1901, Roosevelt called the doctrine "a guarantee of the commercial independence of the Americas." The United States, however, as protector of that independence, would "not guarantee any state against punishment if it misconducts itself, provided that punishment does not take the form of the acquisition of territory by any non-American power."[50] If a Western Hemispheric country misbehaved toward a European nation, Roosevelt would "let the European country spank it."[51]

The president was thinking principally of Germany and Venezuela. Under the rule of Cipriano Castro, an unsavory dictator whom Roosevelt once labeled an "unspeakable villainous monkey," Venezuela perpetually deferred payment on bonds worth more than $12.5 million and held by German investors.[52] Berlin became impatient. Britain also rankled at Venezuelan defaults to British creditors. In December 1902, after clearing the way with Washington, Germany and Britain delivered an ultimatum demanding immediate settlement of their claims, seized several Venezuelan vessels, bombarded two forts, and blockaded all ports. To all of this Roosevelt initially acquiesced, despite the doctrine of Argentina's Foreign Minister Luis M. Drago that "the public debt cannot occasion armed intervention . . . by a European power."[53]

In mid-January 1903, the German navy bombarded two more forts. "Are the people in Berlin crazy?" asked TR.[54] This time the president delivered a quiet warning to desist. He also sent Admiral George Dewey on naval maneuvers in the Caribbean, which were intended, Dewey later boasted, as "an object lesson to the Kaiser."[55] TR privately mused: "The only power which may be a menace to us in anything like the immediate future is Germany."[56] Impressed by the U.S. reaction, Kaiser Wilhelm II replaced his ill-informed ambassador with Hermann Speck von Sternburg, an old friend of Roosevelt. The president urged on him a quick settlement. Thereupon, Britain and Germany in early February lifted the blockade and submitted the dispute to the Permanent Court at The Hague. Prime Minister Arthur Balfour calmed troubled waters by announcing that "the Monroe Doctrine has no enemies in this country."[57] Speck von Sternburg also averred that the kaiser "would no more think of violating that [Monroe] doctrine than he would of colonizing the moon."[58] When the Hague arbiters found in favor of Germany and England in early 1904, a State Department official complained that this decision put "a premium on violence" and made likely similar European interventions in the future.[59]

TR also worried increasingly about the Dominican Republic, revolution-torn since 1899 and seemingly vulnerable to German interests. "I have about the same desire to annex it," Roosevelt said privately, "as a gorged boa constrictor might have to swallow a porcupine wrong-end to."[60] An American firm claimed damages of several million dollars, and European creditors demanded action by their governments. The president prayed that the Dominicans "would behave so that I would not have to act in any way." By spring 1904 he thought he might have to do "what a policeman has to do."[61] If he said "'Hands off' to the powers of Europe, then sooner or later we must keep order ourselves," he told Root.[62]

On December 6, 1904, Roosevelt described to Congress his conception of the United States as hemispheric policeman. "Chronic wrongdoing, or an impotence which results in a general loosening of the ties of civilized society," he proclaimed, "may in America, as elsewhere, ultimately require intervention by some civilized nation, and in the Western Hemisphere the adherence of the United States to the Monroe Doctrine may force the United States, however reluctantly, in flagrant cases of such wrongdoing or impotence, to the exercise of an international police power."[63] With this statement the twenty-sixth president added to the Monroe Doctrine his own corollary, which fundamentally transformed that prohibition on European meddling into a brash promise of U.S. regulation of the Americas.

The Rough Rider soon donned his constable's badge. He assigned a U.S. collector of Dominican customs. "The Constitution," Roosevelt later explained, "did not explicitly give me the power to bring about the necessary agreement with Santo Domingo. But the Constitution did not forbid me."[64] Yet "policing" and "civilizing" the Dominican Republic by presidential order provoked nationalist resentment from Dominicans who, as one naval officer reported in 1906, "are quieting their children with the threat 'There comes an American. Keep quiet or he will kill you.'"[65] Taft's secretary of state, Philander C. Knox, applauded the customs receivership in the Dominican Republic because it denied to rebels the funds they so eagerly "collected" through the capture of customshouses, thus curing "century-old evils."[66] The assassination of the Dominican president in November 1911 suggested that Knox spoke prematurely. And in 1912 revolutionaries operating from contiguous Haiti marauded throughout the Dominican Republic, forcing the closure of several customshouses. To restore order, Taft in September 1912 sent a commission backed by 750 marines. The commissioners redefined the Haitian-Dominican border, forced the corrupt Dominican president to resign, and avoided direct interference in a new election.

His denunciation of "dollar diplomacy" notwithstanding, Woodrow Wilson had written in 1907 that "concessions obtained by financiers must be safeguarded by ministers of state, even if the sovereignty of unwilling nations be outraged in the process."[67] No wonder that President Wilson's search for stability in Latin America retraced familiar steps. When, in September 1913, revolution again threatened the Dominican government, Secretary Bryan promised "every legitimate means to assist in the restoration of order and the prevention of further insurrections."[68] When Wilson ordered naval intervention after further Dominican disorders in May 1916, he said: "If a man will not listen to you quietly in a seat, sit on his neck and make him listen."[69] As the 400 marines of Admiral William Caperton's landing force entered the city of Santo Domingo at dawn on May 15, they found empty streets, bolted doors, shuttered windows, and Dominican flags festooned with black crepe—a "*duelo publico* (public mourning)."[70] A new treaty gave the United States full control over Dominican finances. In November, as U.S. participation in the European war became increasingly probable, Wilson proclaimed the formal military occupation of the Dominican Republic, ostensibly to curtail the activities of revolutionaries suspected of a pro-German bias. Despite an insurgency by peasants in the eastern region of the Dominican Republic, who waged hit-and-run guerrilla warfare, the U.S. Navy formally governed the country until 1922. The main legacy of the occupation, in the historian Bruce Calder's terse judgment, was "a strong anti-U.S. feeling" among the Dominican people.[71]

The Quest for Order in Haiti and Nicaragua

The Dominican Republic shares the island of Hispaniola with Haiti, where revolution became an increasingly popular mode of changing governments. American investments in Haiti were limited to ownership of a small railroad and a one-third share in the Haitian National Bank. Nationals of France and Germany controlled the bank, and disorder thus could give either European nation a pretext for intervention. After the outbreak of World War I, the Wilson administration worried about "the ever present danger of German control" of Haiti and Haiti's deepwater harbor of Môle Saint Nicolas.[72] The Navy Department, content with bases in Cuba and Puerto Rico, nonetheless remembered the German cruiser *Panther*'s sinking a Haitian gunboat in 1902. The State Department sought to buy the Môle "to take it out of the market."[73] To impose order on Haiti, Wilson pressed for an American customs receivership on the Dominican model.

The Haitians resisted successfully until July 1915, when the regime of Guillaume Sam fell in an orgy of grisly political murders. Wilson could stomach no more, and he ordered the navy to invade Haiti. After 2,000 marines imposed martial law and the State Department took over the customshouses, Admiral William B. Caperton reported that "only a government superimposed by the firm hand and supervised under the watchful eye of the United States . . . could ever rescue that unhappy republic from her beastly national sins."[74] Subsequent fighting between occupiers and native guerrillas, which critics perceived as "a racial war of extermination," killed more than 2,250 Haitians compared to 16 marine casualties.[75] An American military regime ruled Haiti until 1934.

The United States also intervened, virtually at will, in Nicaragua. For Theodore Roosevelt, Nicaragua held importance primarily as a potential canal route, a rivalry decided in Panama's favor in 1903. He manifested interest in Nicaragua only briefly thereafter, during 1907, when he and Mexico's president jointly proposed a peace conference to end the incessant warfare among Central American states. As Secretary Root explained, their conduct mattered because the Panama Canal put them "in the front yard of the United States."[76] When President José Santos Zelaya solicited funds to build a second interoceanic canal, especially from Germany (whose capital investments stood three times greater than U.S. properties in Nicaragua), Washington turned against a leader whom some Nicaraguans had compared to Roosevelt himself. For Zelaya's crime of seeking a "better economic position for Nicaragua outside the U.S. economic subsystem," as one historian has written, North Americans labeled him "a tyrannical, self-serving, brutal, greedy disturber of Central American peace, an enemy of U.S. businessmen, and an opponent of all reasonable diplomatic objectives."[77]

After Zelaya "yanked Mr. Taft by the ear" by executing two Americans for aiding rebels, Washington broke diplomatic relations in November 1909, threatened naval intervention, and forced Zelaya into exile.[78] Secretary Knox then negotiated a treaty with the victorious conservatives led by Adolfo Díaz, providing for U.S. control of the customs service and an American loan. Instead of gratitude, "the natural sentiment of an overwhelming majority of Nicaraguans is antagonistic to the United States," the U.S. envoy reported.[79] Rebuffed by the U.S. Senate, Knox and a group of bankers simply went ahead without a treaty. In September 1912, the administration ordered Major Smedley D. Butler and 354 marines into battle on behalf of the Díaz regime, which the State Department deemed representative "of an educated, property-owning and civilized small minority . . . , [and] the ablest people of the country."[80] After tipping the scales against the newest revolutionary army, the leathernecks returned home, leaving one hundred behind as a legation guard in

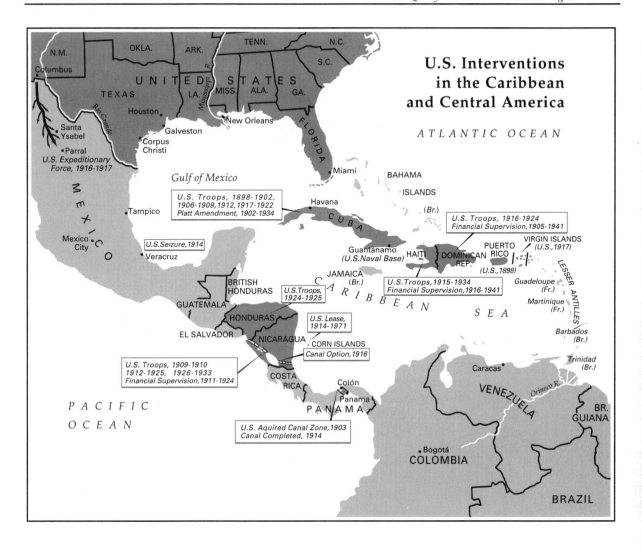

U.S. Interventions in the Caribbean and Central America

ATLANTIC OCEAN

Managua. The marines could prevent a coup d'état, but "*keeping* a surrogate in power in Central America was often as problematical as *putting* him in power."[81]

Bryan in spring 1913 dusted off a shelved draft treaty granting the United States a canal option in Nicaragua in exchange for $3 million. He hoped that this money would "give sufficient encouragement" to American bankers to lend Díaz more.[82] The secretary also added a clause similar to the Platt Amendment before sending the Bryan-Chamorro Treaty to the Senate. When the upper house balked, Bryan had to delete the U.S. right of intervention. Ratification in February 1916 did help Nicaragua's finances. The treaty also effectively excluded European powers from naval bases in the Gulf of Fonseca, and to make that point stick, Wilson ordered U.S. warships to cruise offshore during the 1916 Nicaraguan presidential campaign. Although nominally independent, Nicaragua remained a U.S. protectorate until 1933.

The Mexican Revolution Threatens U.S. Interests

Mexico changed governments with uncharacteristic frequency after the outbreak of revolution in 1910. In 1911 Francisco I. Madero toppled Porfirio Díaz, the aged dictator who had maintained order, personal power, and a healthy environment for North American investments since the late 1870s. U.S. citizens owned more than 40 percent of Mexico's property, and Mexico had become the world's third largest oil producer, thanks to Standard Oil Company, Texas Oil Company (Texaco), and other firms. The revolution thus inevitably took on an anti-Yankee tinge. Despite the threat to American lives and property, Taft determined to "sit tight on the lid and it will take a good deal to pry me off."[83] In February 1913, U.S. ambassador Henry Lane Wilson encouraged one of Madero's trusted generals, Victoriano Huerta, to overthrow the revolutionary nationalist. Indeed, Huerta had Madero shot and then set about to consolidate his own power. The German ambassador called these events "the usual American policy of replacing hostile regimes with pliable ones through revolutions without taking official responsibility for it."[84] But one of the state governors, Venustiano Carranza, organized the "Constitutionalist" revolt on February 26. When American residents became caught in the crossfire, the departing Taft administration refused recognition until Huerta punished the "murderers of American citizens" and ended "discriminations against American interests."[85]

Appalled by Madero's murder, President Wilson vowed not to recognize a "government of butchers."[86] He denounced Huerta as a "diverting brute! . . . seldom sober and always impossible."[87] Seemingly unconcerned about private American properties in Mexico worth some $1.5 billion, Wilson refused to act as "the servant of those who wish to enhance the value of their Mexican investments."[88] When Ambassador Wilson, whom the president suspected of complicity in Madero's ouster, continued to advocate recognition of Huerta to protect those American interests, Washington recalled the U.S. envoy in July 1913 and dismissed him from the diplomatic corps. The president thereafter treated with Mexico through special emissaries, only one of whom spoke fluent Spanish.

In August one such representative, John Lind, arrived in Mexico City. A rabid anti-Catholic and former governor of Minnesota without diplomatic experience, Lind delivered Wilson's proposal for an armistice between Huerta's federalist troops and all revolutionary groups, "an early and free election," and Huerta's promise not to run for president. In exchange, the United States pledged recognition and aid to "the administration chosen and set up . . . in the way and on the conditions suggested." With sublime arrogance, Woodrow Wilson wondered, "can Mexico give the civilized world a satisfactory reason for rejecting our good offices?"[89] Mexican foreign minister Federico Gamboa ridiculed Wilson's "counsels and advice (let us call them thus)," for no Mexican government would ever accept a "veto of any President of the United States."[90] After this snub, Woodrow Wilson announced a restrained policy of "watchful waiting."[91]

Undeterred, Huerta in October dissolved an unruly legislature, arrested its members, and held a special election, which returned an entirely submissive congress ready to extend his presidency indefinitely. Wilson then turned to Carranza in northern Mexico, sending the same proposal Huerta's foreign minister had rejected

William Jennings Bryan (1860–1925), Woodrow Wilson (1856–1924), and Franklin D. Roosevelt (1882–1945), 1913. President Wilson, in white trousers and dark jacket, speaks while Secretary of State Bryan, to the president's right, and Assistant Secretary of the Navy Roosevelt, at the far right of the picture, look on. Wilson spoke proudly of his "missionary diplomacy," for he believed that "every nation needs to be drawn into the tutelage of America." Latin Americans resisted such U.S. paternalism. (Franklin D. Roosevelt Library)

in August. Equally nationalistic, Carranza contemptuously refused Wilsonian mediation and rejected any solution short of his own triumph. Wilson informed the other powers on November 24 of his policy "to isolate General Huerta entirely . . . and so to force him out." If such pressure failed to induce Huerta's retirement, "it will become the duty of the United States to use less peaceful means to put him out."[92]

Most European powers, especially Germany, had recognized Huerta in defiance of Wilson. "Good. Finally unity against the Yankee," the kaiser had noted in July 1913.[93] The British, however, their capital investments in Mexico ranking second only to those of the United States and their navy relying on Mexican oil as a backup to Middle East sources, did not want to antagonize Wilson when tensions were mounting in Europe. The British Foreign Office therefore notified Huerta that it would not support him against the United States, urged him to resign, and recalled Minister Sir Lionel Carden, whose alleged influence over Huerta had provoked American antipathy—all the while viewing Wilson's policies as "most impractical and unreasonable."[94]

With British compliance assured, Wilson lifted the U.S. arms embargo in February 1914 and permitted large quantities of arms to flow to both factions. As Carranza's resupplied forces pushed south, the president sent U.S. naval vessels to the oil-producing town of Tampico on the Gulf of Mexico. On April 9, at Tampico, Huerta's troops arrested several American sailors loading gasoline aboard a whaleboat docked provocatively near the Mexican outpost. The Mexican colonel in charge quickly disavowed the arrests, freed the sailors, and apologized orally. The hotheaded U.S. squadron commander, Rear Admiral Henry T. Mayo, demanded a formal twenty-one-gun salute because Mexico had insulted the flag—"a hostile act, not to be excused."[95] Using Huerta's rejection of the Mayo ultimatum as justification, the president undertook to drive the Mexican leader from power. On April 20, Wilson requested congressional approval to use armed force "to obtain from General Huerta and his adherents the fullest recognition of the rights and dignity of the United States."[96] Rather than protect American-owned oil fields at Tampico, Wilson ordered U.S. warships to the port of Veracruz to stop a German arms shipment intended for Huerta.

On April 21, 1914, 800 American sailors and marines landed. Huerta's troops withdrew from the city, but cadets from the naval academy, joined by prisoners liberated from jails and other irregulars, put up a bloody resistance. Nineteen Americans and several hundred Mexicans died. An anguished Wilson bemoaned that "it was I who ordered those young men to their deaths."[97] Although calculated to undermine Huerta, the historian Ramón E. Ruíz has written, "the capture of Veracruz nearly united Mexicans behind him . . . [because] Mexicans, believing their independence endangered, rushed to enlist in Huerta's army."[98] Rejecting advice from his military advisers, who wanted to march to Mexico City, Wilson accepted mediation when proposed by Argentina, Brazil, and Chile (the ABC powers) on April 25.

A month later, representatives of the United States, Huerta, and the ABC powers met on the Canadian side of Niagara Falls. Intransigence doomed the mediation. Wilson refused to discuss the evacuation of Veracruz or Tampico, a major reason for convening the conference. He sought instead "the entire elimination of General Huerta."[99] But Carranza indignantly boycotted any foreign meeting dealing with Mexico's internal affairs. On July 2 the jilted mediators adjourned, two weeks later Huerta fled to Europe, and on August 20 a triumphant Carranza paraded before enthusiastic throngs in Mexico City.

The Constitutionalist triumph did not last. One of Carranza's northern generals, Francisco (Pancho) Villa, soon broke from the ranks, marched south, and in December occupied Mexico City. Wilson saw Villa as a Robin Hood "robbing the rich in order to give to the poor," a potential client who could be "the sword of the revolution" while Wilson offered "capable and disinterested advice."[100] Because Villa had not criticized Veracruz, the president eased arms exports to him and refused to recognize Carranza. To prevent a military clash with any Mexican faction, all American troops withdrew from Veracruz on November 23, 1914. Once again, Wilson watched and waited.

Relations remained tense during early 1915. Carranza's forces gradually drove Villa north, but in the process Mexico City became a no-man's-land, with bread riots and starvation threatening its inhabitants, including 2,500 Americans and 23,000 other foreign residents. Further complications arose along the Mexico-U.S. borderland, especially in southern Texas, where the massive influx of refugees and revolutionaries exacerbated local tensions between Anglos and *Tejanos*. The Plan of San Diego, an anarchist manifesto in early 1915, demanded return of all lands "robbed in a most perfidious manner," execution of every North American "over sixteen years of age," restoration of Indian lands, and sovereign territory for blacks.[101] The ensuing raids and counterraids turned south Texas into a war zone as vigilantes and

Texas rangers killed at least 150 Mexicans. A new verb—"rangered"—described summary treatment of suspects by Texas authorities.[102] Preoccupied by the *Lusitania* crisis with Germany after May 1915 (see page 68), Wilson reluctantly concluded that "Carranza will somehow have to be digested."[103] With American oil fields under Carranza's protection, Wilson extended de facto recognition to the Constitutionalist regime in June 1915, permitted arms exports (while banning them to opponents), and beefed up the U.S. military presence along the border.

Egged on by German agents who envisaged a Mexican-American war as "a noose . . . to tie the United States to the American continent," Villa denounced *Carranzistas* as "vassals" of the United States.[104] In the predawn hours of March 9, 1916, Villa led a band of *Villistas* across the border into Columbus, New Mexico, initiating a bloody battle that left seventeen Americans and more than a hundred Mexicans dead. Within hours of the attack, Wilson unleashed the Punitive Expedition of 7,000 soldiers, commanded by General John J. Pershing, which penetrated 350 miles into Mexico in a vain search for Pancho Villa. Even though, as Pershing reported, "the natives are not generally arming to oppose us," a clash with *Carranzista* troops occurred at Carrizal in June 1916.[105]

Carranza kept up drumfire demands for U.S. withdrawal, but Wilson hesitated for fear of appearing weak during a presidential election year. Just prior to Germany's resumption of unrestricted submarine warfare, however, Wilson ordered Pershing's troops to disengage; all left Mexico by February 5, 1917. In late February, the secret Zimmermann telegram, proposing an anti–American alliance between Germany and Mexico (and possibly including Japan), came into the hands of the State Department, courtesy of British intelligence. This German ploy accelerated Wilson's movement toward full diplomatic relations with Carranza's government. The United States extended de jure recognition on August 31, 1917, in order to ensure Mexican neutrality during the fight against Germany. After four futile years, Wilson had finally given up trying to tutor the Mexicans. Carranza "may not have fulfilled the social goals of the revolution," as one scholar has written, "but he kept the gringos out of Mexico City."[106]

Francisco (Pancho) Villa (1878–1923). The intelligent, dedicated revolutionary nationalist bedeviled both Mexico and the United States. His daring raid on an American town was calculated to outrage President Wilson, whom he mocked as "an evangelizing professor of philosophy who is destroying the independence of a friendly people." (W. H. Horne postcard. Southwest Collection, El Paso Public Library)

Japan, China, and Dollar Diplomacy in Asia

Managing Asian affairs proved even more difficult. Secretary of State John Hay's Open Door notes did not prevent the further emasculation of China. During the Boxer Rebellion Russia stationed 175,000 troops in Manchuria and demanded exclusive rights from China, including a commercial monopoly. Roosevelt and Hay acquiesced because the Open Door had "always recognized the exceptional position of Russia" in Manchuria and had merely sought the commercial freedom "guaranteed to us by . . . the whole civilized world."[107] Washington retreated because Roosevelt realized that the American people would not fight for nebulous principles of Chinese integrity in Manchuria. He thought it futile "to play the role of an Asian power without military power."[108]

Japan viewed the question quite differently. Russia blocked Japanese economic expansion into Manchuria, posed a potential naval menace, and endangered the

"Spread-eagleism" in China. The missionary teacher Grace Roberts teaches a Bible class in 1903 in Manchuria. Americanism and religious work, flag and missionary, became partners. The mission force was feminized—the majority of missionaries were women. (By permission of the Houghton Library, Harvard University)

Japanese position in Korea. Tokyo covered its flanks with an Anglo-Japanese Alliance in 1902 and prepared for war. On February 8, 1904, the Japanese navy destroyed Russia's Asian fleet in a surprise attack at Port Arthur. At first Roosevelt cheered privately, "for Japan is playing our game," but as the enormity of Japanese victories became apparent he hoped for peace "on terms which will not mean the creation of either a yellow peril or a Slav peril."[109] By spring 1905, Japanese soldiers had triumphed at Mukden, where Russia lost 97,000 men. Revolutionary stirrings had hit St. Petersburg, and Admiral Nakagori Togo had sunk the Russian Baltic fleet. "The Russian bubble has been pretty thoroughly pricked," TR noted.[110] On May 31, Japanese envoy Kogoro Takahira requested Roosevelt "directly and entirely of his own motion and initiative to invite the two belligerents to come together" for direct peace negotiations.[111]

Hoping to balance the belligerents "so that each may have a moderative action on the other" and thus protect American interests in the Pacific and Asia, the president invited Japanese and Russian representatives to meet at Portsmouth, New Hampshire, on August 9, 1905.[112] The Japanese delegates demanded Russia's leasehold on the Liaodong Peninsula and the railroad running from Harbin to Port Arthur, evacuation of Russian troops from Manchuria, and Japan's control of Korea. The Russians quickly conceded these points but rejected additional Japanese requests for an indemnity and cession of the island of Sakhalin. Roosevelt broke the deadlock by proposing division of Sakhalin and agreement "in principle" on an indemnity. Tsar Nicholas II agreed to partition the island but "not a kopeck of compensation."[113] Japan yielded and in late August signed a peace treaty. Roosevelt had earned the Nobel Peace Prize.

The Roosevelt administration's search for equipoise in East Asia neither began nor ended at Portsmouth. As early as March 1904, TR had conceded to Japan a relationship with Korea "just like we have with Cuba."[114] Secretary of War Taft reaffirmed the concession with Prime Minister Taro Katsura on July 27, 1905. In the Taft-Katsura "agreed memorandum of conversation," the prime minister denied Japanese designs on the Philippines, and Taft, in the words of the historian John Wilz, put an American "seal on the death warrant of an independent Korea."[115] A year later the Japanese reopened southern Manchuria to foreign and American trade but discouraged foreign capital investments. Japan formally annexed Korea in 1910.

This studied attempt to balance interests augured well for a continuation of traditional Japanese-American cordiality, until a local dispute in California abruptly undercut Rooseveltian diplomacy. On October 11, 1906, the San Francisco School Board created a special "Oriental Public School" for all Japanese, Chinese, and Korean children. Japan immediately protested, and Theodore Roosevelt denounced the "infernal fools in California" whose exclusion of Japanese from all other public schools was "as foolish as if conceived by the mind of a Hottentot."[116] Given existing federal-state jurisdictions, however, he could do little more than rail against the recalcitrant school board, apply political pressure to the California legislature to prevent statewide discriminatory measures, and propose legislation to naturalize Japanese residing permanently in the United States. Defending segregation, the *San Francisco Examiner* editorialized: "Californians do not want their growing daughters to be intimate in daily school contact with Japanese young men. Is this remarkable?"[117] Always the political realist, Roosevelt accepted what he personally disliked and sought accommodation with Japan. In February 1907, he reached a "Gentlemen's Agreement" with Tokyo, sharply restricting Japanese immigration on a voluntary basis.

Because "the Japanese jingoes are . . . about as bad as ours," the president shrewdly pressed for more battleships and fortification of Hawai'i and the vulnerable Philippines, now America's "heel of Achilles," so that the United States would "be ready for anything that comes."[118] He also dramatized the importance of a strong navy to Congress and to Japan by ordering the battle fleet to the Pacific and around the world. The armada of sixteen battleships steamed out of Hampton Roads, Virginia, on December 16, 1907. Germany's kaiser predicted that U.S. warships in the Pacific "will upset all British and Japanese calculations."[119] Just after the "Great White Fleet" visited Tokyo in October 1908, Ambassador Takahira received instructions to reach an agreement with the United States recognizing the Pacific Ocean as an open avenue of trade, pledging the integrity of Japanese and American insular possessions in the Pacific, and promising equal opportunity in China. The ensuing Root-Takahira declaration of November 30, 1908, seemed to restore Japanese-American harmony.

Elihu Root (1845–1937). Root served as secretary of state (1905–1909). He helped devise methods for managing the American empire. (Library of Congress)

Conflicting Japanese-American goals toward China spoiled the new epoch. Despite John Hay's Open Door notes, American commerce with China stalled during the Roosevelt era, in part because of resurgent nationalism. When Congress barred Chinese immigration in 1904, the Chinese staged a short-lived boycott of American goods and revoked a railroad franchise held by financier J. P. Morgan. As the historian Eileen Scully has noted, moreover, prostitution flourished in China's treaty ports, conducted by "American sex workers and their male compatriots." This illegitimate China trade ("deeply corrupt, overtly predatory, transnational, transracial, conducted without regard to a 'national interest'") undercut the gains of legitimate American commerce in China.[120] Because Roosevelt viewed the Chinese as opulent and effete, "sunk in Oriental stagnation and corruption," he placed strategic interests first and refused to antagonize Japan over China.[121]

Taft thought otherwise. Instead of a decrepit China in decay, Taft envisaged expanded trade with a "young China, rousing from a centuries-old slumber and rubbing the sand of its past from its eyes."[122] During a 1905 trip to East Asia, Taft met the impressive, intensely anti-Japanese American consul general in Mukden, Willard Straight. Two years later Straight proposed the creation of a Manchurian bank, to be financed by the American railroad magnate E. H. Harriman. He condemned the Root-Takahira agreement as "a terrible diplomatic blunder," because it accepted Japan's exploitative position in Manchuria.[123] Under Taft, Straight and the State Department quickly inspired several New York banks to form a combination, headed by J. P. Morgan, to serve as the official agency of American railroad investment in China. As acting chief of the department's new Far Eastern Division, Straight demanded admission of the American bankers into a European banking consortium undertaking construction of the Huguang Railway linking Beijing and Guangzhou (Canton). Straight then resigned from the State Department to become the Morgan group's roving representative.

In November 1909, Washington had proposed to Britain the neutralization of Manchurian railroads through a large international loan to China for the purchase of the lines. Britain, however, joined both Japan and Russia to reject the proposal. Instead of an open door in Manchuria, Secretary of State Knox had "nailed that door closed with himself on the outside."[124] In fall 1910, an agreement expanded the Huguang Railway consortium to include American bankers, but the Chinese Revolution broke out in May 1911 against the Manchu dynasty and foreign interests and delayed railroad construction until 1913. "Dollar diplomacy," Willard Straight ruefully admitted, "made no friends in the Hukuang matter."[125] "We're goin' to give ye [Chinese] a railroad so ye can go swiftly to places that ye don't want to see," observed Finley Peter Dunne's Mr. Dooley.[126]

Hoping to reap tangible benefits by dissociating from the other powers, President Wilson and Secretary Bryan repudiated American participation in the international consortium on March 18, 1913. Failure to cancel the loan, Wilson believed, would have cost the United States "the proud position . . . secured when Secretary Hay stood for the open door in China after the Boxer Uprising." Wilson became the first to extend formal diplomatic recognition to the Chinese Republic on May 6.[127] He had thereby renewed America's commitment to the political integrity of China, a goal pragmatically abandoned by Roosevelt, unsuccessfully resuscitated by Taft, and consistently opposed by Japan.

Events at home soon made Wilson's Asian policy resemble Taft's more than Roosevelt's. In April 1913, Democratic and Progressive politicians placed before the California legislature a bill denying residents "ineligible to citizenship" the right to own land. The measure struck directly at the 50,000 Japanese living in California. Racist passions erupted, with one farmer recoiling from the prospect of racial intermarriage: "What is that baby? It isn't a Japanese. It isn't white. It is a germ of the mightiest problem . . . that will make the black problem of the South look white."[128] Basically sharing the Californians' anti-Japanese prejudices, and philosophically sensitive to states' rights, Wilson sent Bryan to Sacramento to beg for a euphemistic statute. But the California legislature passed the offensive bill on May 3, 1913. When Japan protested the "unfair and intentionally racially discriminatory" measure, Wilson and Bryan lamely argued that one state's legislation did not constitute a "national discriminatory policy."[129]

Wilson's antipathy toward Japan reappeared in fall 1914 when Japan declared war on Germany, seized the German Pacific islands north of the equator, and swept across China's Shandong Peninsula to capture the German leasehold of Jiaozhou. "When there is a fire in a jeweller's shop," a Japanese diplomat theorized, "the neighbours cannot be expected to refrain from helping themselves."[130] Tokyo immediately followed with the Twenty-One Demands of January 18, 1915, creating a virtual protectorate over all of China. Despite stout resistance by Beijing, Japan emerged with extensive political and economic rights in Shandong, southern Manchuria, and Mongolia. Preoccupied with Mexico and the *Lusitania* crisis, the Wilson administration refused to recognize Japan's gains, which amounted to a repudiation of the Open Door policy.

Wilson's nonrecognition policy ran counter to secret treaties in which the European Allies promised to support Japan's conquests at the peace conference after World War I. The United States soon compromised. In an agreement with Viscount Kikujiro Ishii, signed November 2, 1917, Secretary Lansing admitted that "territorial propinquity creates special relationships between countries, and consequently . . . Japan has special interests in China," while Ishii pledged his nation's dedication to the Open Door and integrity of China.[131] The Wilson administration also revived the international banking consortium as the only way to check further unilateral Japanese economic penetration of China proper. The wheel had turned full circle for Wilson. Like Taft before him, Wilson failed to protect China's fragile sovereignty without conciliating or blocking Japan.

Anglo-American Rapprochement and Empire-Building

American policies toward Asia and Latin America often fell short of their proclaimed goals because of the pseudoscientific race thinking of the early twentieth century. Americans viewed Asians as "inscrutable and somnolent," depicted Latin Americans as black children or alluring maidens, imagined Africa as the "dark continent" of "savage beasts and beastly savages," and referred to Filipinos as "our little brown brothers," and these biased stereotypes inevitably impeded statecraft and aroused resentment from Bogotá to Beijing, from Managua to Manila.[132] Yet such Darwinist racial attitudes also facilitated much closer relations between the United States and Great Britain. As the historian Michael H. Hunt has written about the ideology of the time, victory "in the international competition among the races . . . might not go to the refined and peaceful peoples but rather to the amoral, the cunning, the fecund, and the power hungry." Thus "Anglo-Americans might then need to cultivate a sense of solidarity and a capacity for cooperation."[133] Theodore Roosevelt certainly thought so when he claimed that "together . . . the two branches of the Anglo-Saxon race . . . can whip the world."[134] So too did the British, as evidenced by their retreat after the Venezuelan crisis of 1895 and their willingness to accept exclusive American control of a canal in Panama. Also prompted by Britain's search for allies against Germany (evidenced in the Anglo-Japanese Alliance of 1902 and the Entente Cordiale with France in 1904), London's pursuit of what future prime minister Herbert H. Asquith called "the most cordial and constant cooperation" with the United States led to a celebrated "great rapprochement."[135]

The new Anglo-American affinity, however, nearly dissolved in 1903 when the Alaska boundary controversy, which stemmed from Canadian claims to large areas of the Alaskan panhandle, strained relations. As the power responsible for the Dominion's foreign relations (Canada did not establish a foreign office until 1909), Britain found itself backing Ottawa's dubious contention that much of the panhandle's coastline actually belonged to Canada. Roosevelt thought Canada had less right "than the United States did to Cornwall or Kent."[136] The president refused arbitration and sent 800 soldiers to Alaska to awe his opponents. London finally agreed in January 1903 to an American proposal for a mixed boundary commission composed of six "impartial jurists," three from each side.[137] Taking no chances, Roosevelt appointed Senator Henry Cabot Lodge and Secretary Root, hardly disinterested judges, to the commission. He informally warned London he would run the line himself if the commissioners failed to agree. One British commissioner sided with the Americans, and on October 20, 1903, by a vote of 4 to 2, the commission officially decided for the United States. The British "made the inevitable choice to please a power ten times the size of Canada and with more than ten times the wealth."[138]

Canadian-American relations did improve with the Migratory Bird Treaty of 1916. Conservationists and scientists, alarmed by a decline in North American birds caused by reckless sport and commercial hunting, pressed for this agreement under the principle of "common property resources." The death of the last passenger pigeon, in the Cincinnati Zoo in 1914, symbolized the crisis. Because the treaty restricted hunting, especially during the mating season, it sparked some opposition in the United States. Member of Congress John Tillman, a Democrat from Arkansas who defended duck hunting in gendered terms, cried that the accord "should be bedecked with skirts" because it "would feminize our boys."[139] The bird population increased, and such wildlife protection, also evident in the Inland Fisheries

John Bull in Need of Friends. Battered by criticism over its war against the Boers in South Africa and challenged by a rising Germany, Great Britain found a new friend in the United States. Not all Britons embraced Anglo-American affinity. "Only 1/4 of the population of the United States are what you might call natives," wrote a British admiral in 1901, "the rest are Germans, Irish, Italians, and the scum of the earth! all of them hating the English like poison." (*Des Moines Leader* in *Literary Digest,* 1901)

Treaty (1908) and the North Pacific Fur Seal Convention (1911), became landmarks in international environmental history.

Anglo-American entente also characterized the settlement of the North Atlantic fisheries dispute. Since 1782, American fishermen had insisted on retaining their pre-Revolutionary privileges off Canada's Newfoundland. Indeed, "a gilded wooden cod" still hung from the ceiling of the Massachusetts State House.[140] The modus vivendi of 1888, under which they had fished for several years, collapsed in 1905 when Newfoundland placed restrictions on American fishing vessels. Senator

Lodge cried for warships to protect his constituents' livelihood. To avoid a heated quarrel, Roosevelt proposed, and London accepted, arbitration at The Hague Tribunal. In 1910 the tribunal ruled that Britain could oversee fishing off Newfoundland if it established reasonable regulations, that a fisheries commission would hear cases, and that Americans could fish in large bays if they remained three miles from shore. This compromise defused the oldest dispute in American foreign relations and symbolized London's political withdrawal from the Western Hemisphere.

The naval retreat had occurred earlier, when the Admiralty abolished the North Atlantic station based at Jamaica. After 1902 the Royal Navy patrolled the Caribbean only with an annual visit by a token squadron of cruisers. Admiral Sir John Fisher, who oversaw this historic retrenchment, wanted to concentrate his heavy ships in the English Channel and North Sea as monitors of the growing German navy. He regarded the United States as "a kindred state with whom we shall never have a parricidal war."[141]

Even the aggressive hemispheric diplomacy of Taft and Wilson did not undermine Anglo-American rapprochement. Britain criticized dollar diplomacy in Latin America, and Wilson's quixotic efforts to dislodge Huerta from the presidency of Mexico met with little sympathy in England. But Foreign Secretary Sir Edward Grey tersely laid to rest all talk of a challenge: "His Majesty's Government cannot with any prospect of success embark upon an active counterpolicy to that of the United States, or constitute themselves the champions of Mexico or any of these republics against the United States."[142] In reciprocation, Wilson protected British oil interests and made it a "point of honor" to eliminate the one potentially dangerous British grievance inherited from his predecessor.[143] Late in the Taft administration, Congress had exempted American intercoastal shippers from payment of Panama Canal tolls. British opinion condemned this shifting of canal maintenance costs to other users. Because it unfairly discriminated against foreign shipping, Wilson persuaded Congress to revoke the law in June 1914.

In the end, rapprochement meant mutual respect for each other's empires. Roosevelt, for example, encouraged London to frustrate native aspirations for independence in India, while the British accepted the American suppression of the Filipinos and U.S. hegemony in Latin America. American leaders usually spoke favorably of independence for colonial peoples—but independence only after long-term tutelage to make them "civilized" enough to govern. In 1910 in Egypt, where Roosevelt applauded Britain's "great work for civilization," the ex-president even lectured Muslim nationalists about Christian respect for womanhood.[144] In unstable Liberia, where the United States in 1912 instituted a financial receivership in the African nation like that in the Dominican Republic, the British encouraged Washington to use a strong hand in what London called America's "protectorate."[145]

While building an empire, policymakers largely adhered to the tradition of aloofness from continental European political and military affairs. Even Roosevelt overtly tampered only once with Europe's balance of power. In 1904 France acquiesced in British control of Egypt in exchange for primacy in Morocco. A year later, Germany decided to test the solidity of the new Anglo-French entente by challenging France's claims in Morocco. Speaking at Tangier, the kaiser belligerently demanded a German political role in Morocco, which France at once refused. After a brief European war scare, in which Britain stood by its ally, Germany asked Roosevelt to induce France and England to convene a conference to settle Morocco's future. Worried about Kaiser Wilhelm's "violent and often wholly irrational zigzags," Roosevelt accepted the personal invitation only after assuring Paris that he did not act on Berlin's behalf.[146] During the conference, held in early 1906 at Algeciras, Spain, Roosevelt devised a pro-French compromise and persuaded the kaiser to accept it. This political intervention isolated Germany and reinforced the Anglo-French entente, but it generated criticism at home. Roosevelt's successors made sure they did not violate the American policy of nonentanglement with Europe during the more ominous second Moroccan and Balkan crises preceding the First World War.

Nonentanglement also doomed the sweeping arbitration treaties that Secretary Hay negotiated with several world powers. When the Senate attached crippling amendments, Roosevelt withdrew the treaties because they did "not in the smallest degree facilitate settlements by arbitration."[147] After 1905 Secretary Root persuaded Roosevelt to accept watered-down bilateral arbitration treaties, and Secretary Bryan later negotiated a series of supplementary "cooling-off" treaties by which nations pledged to refrain from war during international investigations of serious disputes. None of these arrangements, however, effectively bound signatories, and like the Permanent Court of Arbitration at The Hague, they represented a backwater in international diplomacy. Ambassador Whitelaw Reid compared U.S. participation in the Hague Peace Conference of 1907 to a farmer taking his hog to market: "That hog didn't weigh as much as I expected he would, and I always knew he wouldn't."[148]

The mainstream of American foreign policy between 1900 and 1914 flowed through the Panama Canal, a momentous political, military, and technological achievement. The United States became the unchallenged policeman of the Caribbean region, empowering Washington, in Taft's words, "to prevent revolutions" so that "we'll have no more."[149] Although the German authorities thought that the canal, once completed, would shift American priorities to Asia and "today's Atlantic fleet will become the Pacific fleet," the United States still lacked the power to challenge Japan or Britain.[150] As Roosevelt understood, the Open Door "completely disappears as soon as a powerful nation determines to disregard it."[151] One military officer told Congress in 1910: "We have grown from a little frontier army to one spread all over the world—in America, Porto Rico, Hawai'i, Alaska, the Philippines, and sometimes in Cuba—and we have not got the officers and men to do it."[152]

American insensitivity to the nationalism of other peoples became another imperial legacy. Filipino resistance to American domination, Cuban anger against the Platt Amendment, Colombian outrage over Panama, and Mexican rejection of Wilsonian intervention bore witness to the depth of nationalistic sentiments. Like the European powers who were carving up Asia, Africa, and the Middle East, the United States was developing its empire and subjugating peoples and compromising their sovereignty in Latin America and the Pacific. As a Panamanian diplomat

Naval Arms Race. The international naval competition in the early twentieth century was foreboding. Disarmament talks at The Hague Conferences and arbitration treaties did not curb the arms buildup. Roosevelt's decision to send the "Great White Fleet" around the world in 1907–1908 may have encouraged both Japan and Germany to speed up their naval programs. (*Detroit News* in *Literary Digest*, 1904*)*

later explained: "When you hit a rock with an egg, the egg breaks. Or when you hit an egg with a rock, the egg breaks. The United States is the rock. Panama is the egg. In either case, the egg breaks."[153] With the exception of the Virgin Islands, purchased from Denmark for $25 million in 1917 to forestall any wartime German seizure, the empire grew little from outright territorial gains. It was, instead, an informal empire administered by troops, financial advisers, and reformers who showed contempt for native peoples' culture, politics, and economies through a paternalistic discourse. The U.S. Army marching song—"The Monkeys Have No Tails in Zamboanga"—expressed soldierly disdain for the Filipino populace.

"There is something pathetic and childlike about the people," Roosevelt wrote condescendingly of the Puerto Ricans.[154] Under the Foraker Act (1900), Puerto Rico and its naval base on Culebra became a "new constitutional animal"—an "unincorporated territory" subject to the will of the U.S. Congress and governed by the War Department (until 1934).[155] In a series of decisions called the Insular Cases (1901–1904), the Supreme Court upheld the Foraker Act, providing Washington with a means to govern people it did not wish to organize as a state. In March 1917, Congress granted Puerto Ricans U.S. citizenship just in time for them to be drafted into the U.S. armed forces in the war against Germany. To this day, Puerto Rico remains a colony, or "commonwealth," and Puerto Ricans remain divided in their views about statehood, independence, and commonwealth status.

The adventures of American foreign relations under an imperial ideology and the male ethos in the years 1900–1914 attracted many capable, well-educated young men to diplomatic service. "It was TR's call to youth which lured me to Washington," future under secretary of state William Phillips recalled.[156] Career ambassador Joseph C. Grew first gained presidential favor by shooting a tiger in China. Several of these young foreign-service professionals, virtually all graduates of Ivy League colleges, including Phillips, Grew, Willard Straight, former Rough Rider Henry P. Fletcher, and soldier-diplomat Frank R. McCoy, lived in an exclusive bachelors' townhouse at 1718 H Street during their Washington service. Known among themselves as "the Family," these youthful professionals blended camaraderie with careers and "became the elite or legendary 'inner circle' of the State Department" for the next forty years.[157] The New York attorney Henry L. Stimson, himself a protégé of Elihu Root, served as secretary of war under Taft (1911–1913) and continued this tradition of recruiting some of the brightest public servants in a succession of high-level posts through the end of World War II.

Cultural or public foreign relations also flourished during these years. Just as Buffalo Bill Cody's Wild West Show had "hyped" American cultural myths abroad since the 1890s, Wilbur Wright's airplane tour of Europe in 1908 set records, thrilled crowds, and impressed military strategists.[158] The cruise of the "Great White Fleet" provided as much pageantry as statecraft—"a feast, a frolic, or a fight," as Admiral Robley D. Evans put it.[159] Colonial subjects became popular on college campuses, as anthropologists and ethnographers offered courses on "Savage Childhood" and "Peoples of the Philippines."[160] When academic exchanges with European universities expanded after 1900, Harvard University commemorated its new Germanic Museum by bestowing an honorary doctorate on Prince Henry of Prussia (the kaiser's brother)—"a simple, natural person who got used in a day to our troublesome democratic ways."[161]

Thousands of wealthy Americans traveled abroad clutching their Baedeker guidebooks, spending American dollars, and sometimes acquiring foreign titles through marriage, as in the case of Jennie Jerome and Lord Randolph Churchill, whose son Winston valued Anglo-American partnership. Civic leaders took pride in hosting the Olympic Games in St. Louis in 1904, hailed an American victory in the 1908 Round-the-World Automobile race, became "weekend frontiersmen" after organizing the Boy Scouts of America in 1910, and cheered the gold medals won by Native American Jim Thorpe at the Stockholm Olympics in 1912.[162] Just as they seemed to take up the great game of empire from Great Britain, so too did Americans become proficient in that most diplomatic of athletic competitions, the royal and ancient Scottish sport of golf. For some Americans, true Anglo-American entente did not occur until young Francis Ouimet bested British champions Harry Vardon and Ted Ray in the U.S. Open at Brookline, Massachusetts, in 1913.

Yet beneath the glitter lurked danger. Winston Churchill later wrote of living in two different worlds: "the actual, visual world with its peaceful activities" and "a hypothetical world 'beneath the threshold'"—"a world at one moment utterly fantastic, at the next seeming to leap into reality—a world of monstrous shadows moving in convulsive combination through vistas of fathomless catastrophe."[163] Once the world started spinning around Sarajevo, Bosnia, it became impossible for the growing American empire to escape the maelstrom of world war.

FURTHER READING FOR THE PERIOD 1900–1914

See studies listed in the last two chapters and Michael C. C. Adams, *The Great Adventure: Male Desire and the Coming of World War I* (1990); A. J. Bacevich, *Diplomat in Khaki* (1989) (General Frank McCoy); William H. Becker, *The Dynamics of Business-Government Relations: Industry and Exports, 1893–1921* (1982); Gail Bederman, *Manliness & Civilization* (1995); Lester H. Brune, *The Origins of American Security Policy* (1981); Richard D. Challener, *Admirals, Generals, and American Foreign Policy, 1898–1914* (1973); Kendrick A. Clements, *William Jennings Bryan* (1982); Kurkpatrick Dorsey, *The Dawn of Conservation Diplomacy: U.S.–Canadian Wildlife Protection Treaties in the Progressive Era* (1999); Lloyd C. Gardner, *Safe for Democracy: The Anglo-American Response to Revolution, 1913–1923* (1984); Robert C. Hilderbrand, *Power and the People: Executive Management of Public Opinion in Foreign Affairs, 1897–1921* (1981); E. Berkeley Tompkins, *Anti-Imperialism in the United States* (1970); Richard H. Werking, *The Master Architects* (1977) (foreign service); Rachel West, *The Department of State on the Eve of the First World War* (1978); Rubin F. Westin, *Racism in United States Imperialism* (1972); William C. Widenor, *Henry Cabot Lodge and the Search for an American Foreign Policy* (1980); and Mira Wilkins, *The Emergence of Multinational Enterprise: American Business Abroad from the Colonial Era to 1914* (1970).

Theodore Roosevelt is the subject of Howard K. Beale, *Theodore Roosevelt and the Rise of America to World Power* (1956); John M. Blum, *The Republican Roosevelt* (1954); H. W. Brands, *T.R.* (1997); David H. Burton, *Theodore Roosevelt* (1968); Richard H. Collin, *Theodore Roosevelt: Culture, Diplomacy, and Expansion* (1985); John M. Cooper, Jr., *The Warrior and the Priest: Woodrow Wilson and Theodore Roosevelt* (1983); Thomas G. Dyer, *Theodore Roosevelt and the Idea of Race* (1980); Raymond A. Esthus, *Theodore Roosevelt and the International Rivalries* (1970); Lewis L. Gould, *The Presidency of Theodore Roosevelt* (1991); William H. Harbaugh, *The Life and Times of Theodore Roosevelt* (1975); Frederick W. Marks, *Velvet on Iron* (1979); Natalie A. Naylor et al., eds., *Theodore Roosevelt* (1992); and William N. Tilchin, *Theodore Roosevelt and the British Empire* (1997).

For the Taft administration, see Paolo E. Coletta, *The Presidency of William Howard Taft* (1973); Ralph E. Minger, *William Howard Taft and American Foreign Policy* (1975); and Walter V. Scholes and Marie V. Scholes, *The Foreign Policies of the Taft Administration* (1970).

For Wilson policies, see the next chapter and Frederick S. Calhoun, *Power and Principle: Armed Intervention in Wilsonian Foreign Policy* (1986) and *Uses of Force and Wilsonian Foreign Policy* (1993); Kendrick A. Clements, *The Presidency of Woodrow Wilson* (1990); Edward S. Kaplan, *U.S. Imperialism in Latin America* (1997) (on Bryan's policies); and John M. Mulder, *Woodrow Wilson: The Years of Preparation* (1978).

U.S. relations with Latin America are examined in José A. Cabranes, *Citizenship and the American Empire* (1979) (Puerto Rico); Bruce J. Calder, *The Impact of Intervention* (1984) (Dominican Republic); Raymond A. Carr, *Puerto Rico* (1984); Arturo M. Carrión, *Puerto Rico* (1983); Mark T. Gilderhus, *Pan American Visions* (1986) (Wilson); David Healy, *Drive to Hegemony* (1989) and *Gunboat Diplomacy in the Wilson Era* (1976) (Haiti); Warren G. Kneer, *Great Britain and the Caribbean, 1901–1913* (1975); Walter LaFeber, *Inevitable Revolutions* (1993) (Central America); Lester D. Langley, *Struggle for the American Mediterranean* (1976), *The United States and the Caribbean, 1900–1970* (1980), and *The Banana Wars* (1983); Lester D. Langley and Thomas Schoonover, *The Banana Men* (1995); Dana Munro, *Intervention and Dollar Diplomacy* (1964); Thomas F. O'Brien, *The Revolutionary Mission: American Business in Latin America* (1996); Dexter Perkins, *The Monroe Doctrine, 1867–1907* (1937); Fredrick B. Pike, *The United States and Latin America* (1992); Brenda G. Plummer, *Haiti and the United States* (1992) and *Haiti and the Great Powers, 1902–1915* (1988); Hans Schmidt, *The United States Occupation of Haiti, 1915–1934* (1971); Thomas D. Schoonover, *The United States in Central America, 1860–1911* (1991); and Lars Schoultz, *Beneath the United States* (1998).

For the Panama Canal, see Richard H. Collin, *Theodore Roosevelt's Caribbean* (1990); Michael L. Conniff, *Panama and the United States* (1992); Richard L. Lael, *Arrogant Diplomacy* (1987); Walter LaFeber, *The Panama Canal* (1989); John Major, *Prize Possession* (1993); David McCullough, *The Path Between the Seas* (1977); and Stephen J. Randall, *Colombia and the United States* (1992).

U.S. hegemony in Cuba is discussed in David Healy, *The United States in Cuba, 1898–1902* (1963); José M. Hernández, *Cuba and the United States* (1993); James H. Hitchman, *Leonard Wood and Cuban Independence, 1898–1902* (1971); Allan R. Millett, *The Politics of Intervention* (1968); and Louis A. Pérez, Jr., *Cuba and the United States* (1997) and *Cuba Under the Platt Amendment, 1902–1934* (1986).

Relations with Mexico are treated in Jonathan C. Brown, *Oil and Revolution in Mexico* (1993); Clarence C. Clendenen, *Blood on the Border* (1969); Jules Davids, *American Political and Economic Penetration of Mexico, 1877–1920* (1976); Joseph M. Gilbert, *Revolution from Without* (1982); Mark T. Gilderhus, *Diplomacy and Revolution* (1977); Kenneth J. Grieb, *The United States and Huerta* (1969); John M. Hart, *Revolutionary Mexico* (1988); Larry D. Hill, *Emissaries to a Revolution: Woodrow Wilson's Executive Agents in Mexico* (1973); Friedrich Katz, *The Life and Times of Pancho Villa* (1998) and *The Secret War in Mexico* (1981); Alan Knight, *U.S.–Mexican Relations, 1910–1940* (1987); Daniel Nugent, ed., *Rural Revolt in Mexico and U.S. Intervention* (1988); Robert E. Quirk, *An Affair of Honor* (1962) (Veracruz); Ramón E. Ruíz, *The Great Rebellion* (1980); Karl M. Schmitt, *Mexico and the United States, 1821–1973* (1974); Paul J. Vanderwood and Frank N. Samponaro, *Border Fury* (1988); and Josefina Vázquez and Lorenzo Meyer, *The United States and Mexico* (1985).

For America's interactions with Asia and China, see William R. Braisted, *The United States Navy in the Pacific, 1897–1909* (1958) and *1909–1922* (1971); Jongsuk Chay, *Diplomacy of Asymmetry* (1990) (Korea); Warren I. Cohen, *America's Response to China* (1990); Daniel M. Crane and Thomas A. Breslin, *An Ordinary Relationship: American Opposition to Republican Revolution in China* (1986); Jonathan Goldstein et al., eds., *America Views China* (1991); Robert A. Hart, *The Great White Fleet* (1965); Michael H. Hunt, *The Making of a Special Relationship* (1983); Akira Iriye, *Across the Pacific* (1967); Delber L. McKee, *Chinese Exclusion Versus the Open Door Policy, 1900–1906* (1976); Dennis L. Noble, *The Eagle and the Dragon* (1990); and Noel H. Pugach, *Paul S. Reinsch* (1979).

Japanese-American relations are studied in Burton F. Beers, *Vain Endeavor: Robert Lansing's Attempt to End the American-Japanese Rivalry* (1962); Roger Daniels, *The Politics of Prejudice* (1962) (anti-Japanese sentiment); Raymond A. Esthus, *Double Eagle and Rising Sun* (1988) (Portsmouth) and *Theodore Roosevelt and Japan* (1966); Akira Iriye, *Pacific Estrangement* (1972); Walter LaFeber, *The Clash* (1997); Charles E. Neu, *An Uncertain Friendship* (1967) and *The Troubled Encounter* (1975); and E. P. Trani, *The Treaty of Portsmouth* (1969).

American missionaries, especially in Asia, are covered in Kenton J. Clymer, *Protestant Missionaries in the Philippines, 1898–1916* (1986); Gael Graham, *Gender, Culture, and Christianity* (1995); Patricia R. Hill, *The World Their Household* (1985) (women); Jane Hunter, *The Gospel of Gentility* (1984) (women in China); Xi Lian, *The Conversion of Missionaries* (1997); and James Reed, *The Missionary Mind and American East Asia Policy, 1911–1915* (1983).

U.S. relations with Europe and Great Britain, and rivalry with Germany, are discussed in Stuart Anderson, *Race and Rapprochement* (1981); A. E. Campbell, *Great Britain and the United States, 1895–1903* (1960); Charles S. Campbell, *Anglo-American Understanding, 1898–1903* (1957); David Dimbleby and David Reynolds, *An Ocean Apart* (1989); Holger H. Herwig, *Politics of Frustration: The United States in German Naval Planning, 1889–1941* (1976); Manfred Jonas, *The United States and Germany* (1984); B. J. C. McKercher and Lawrence Aronson, eds., *The North Atlantic Triangle in a Changing World* (1996); Bradford Perkins, *The Great Rapprochement* (1968); Stephen R. Rock, *Why Peace Breaks Out* (1989); Hans-Jürgen Schröder, ed., *Confrontation and Cooperation* (1993) (Germany); and Frederick F. Travis, *George Kennan and the Russian-American Relationship, 1865–1924* (1990).

The peace movement and the role of The Hague are discussed in Peter Brock, *Pacifism in the United States* (1968); Charles Chatfield, *The American Peace Movement* (1992); Merle E. Curti, *Peace or War* (1936); Calvin Davis, *The United States and the First Hague Conference* (1962) and *The United States and the Second Hague Peace Conference* (1975); Charles DeBenedetti, *The Peace Reform in American History* (1980); Sondra R. Herman, *Eleven Against War* (1969); Charles F. Howlett and Glen Zeitzer, *The American Peace Movement* (1985);

C. Roland Marchand, *The American Peace Movement and Social Reform, 1898–1918* (1973); and David S. Patterson, *Toward a Warless World* (1976).

See also the General Bibliography, the following notes, and Richard Dean Burns, ed., *Guide to American Foreign Relations Since 1700* (1983).

For comprehensive coverage of foreign-relations topics, see the articles in the four-volume *Encyclopedia of U.S. Foreign Relations* (1997), edited by Bruce W. Jentleson and Thomas G. Paterson.

NOTES TO CHAPTER 2

1. All quotations from U.S. Congress, *Diplomatic History of the Panama Canal*, Senate Doc. 474 (1914), pp. 345–363.
2. Quoted in John Major, *Prize Possession* (New York: Cambridge University Press, 1993), p. 45.
3. Elting E. Morison, ed., *The Letters of Theodore Roosevelt* (Cambridge: Harvard University Press, 1951–1954; 8 vols.), II, 1185–1187.
4. *Diplomatic History of the Canal*, p. 261.
5. Quoted in Dwight C. Miner, *The Fight for the Panama Route* (New York: Columbia University Press, 1940), p. 275.
6. Quoted in Henry F. Pringle, *Theodore Roosevelt* (New York: Harcourt, Brace, 1931), p. 311.
7. Quoted in Howard K. Beale, *Theodore Roosevelt and the Rise of America to World Power* (Baltimore: Johns Hopkins Press, 1956), p. 33.
8. Quoted in David McCullough, *The Path Between the Seas* (New York: Simon & Schuster, 1977), p. 333.
9. *New York World*, June 14, 1903.
10. Quoted in Pringle, *Roosevelt*, p. 311.
11. Quoted in Tyler Dennett, *John Hay* (New York: Dodd, Mead, 1933), p. 377.
12. Quoted in Thomas Schoonover, "Max Farrand's Memorandum on the U.S. Role in the Panamanian Revolution of 1903," *Diplomatic History*, XII (Fall 1988), 505.
13. Quoted in Stephen J. Randall, *Colombia and the United States* (Athens: University of Georgia Press, 1992), p. 88.
14. Quoted in Lewis L. Gould, *The Presidency of Theodore Roosevelt* (Lawrence: University Press of Kansas, 1991), p. 98.
15. C. F. Adams to Moorfield Story, December 9, 1903, Moorfield Story Papers, Massachusetts Historical Society, Boston; Roosevelt quoted in H. W. Brands, *T.R.* (New York: BasicBooks, 1997), p. 487.
16. Quoted in Walter LaFeber, *The Panama Canal* (New York: Oxford University Press, 1989; updated ed.), pp. 225–226.
17. *New York Times*, March 25, 1911.
18. William H. Harbaugh, *The Life and Times of Theodore Roosevelt* (New York: Oxford University Press, 1975; rev. ed.), p. 197.
19. Quoted in Wayne A. Wiegand, *Patrician in the Progressive Era* (New York: Garland, 1988), p. 120.
20. Quoted in Stephen R. Rock, *Why Peace Breaks Out* (Chapel Hill: University of North Carolina Press, 1989), p. 132.
21. Quoted in Holger H. Herwig, *Politics of Frustration* (Boston: Little, Brown, 1976), p. 67.
22. Ronald H. Spector, *Professors of War* (Newport, R.I.: Naval War College Press, 1977).
23. John Milton Cooper, Jr., "Progressivism and American Foreign Policy," *Mid-America*, LI (October 1969), 261.
24. Quoted in John Morton Blum, *The Republican Roosevelt* (New York: Atheneum [1954], 1973), p. 127.
25. Quoted in Beale, *Theodore Roosevelt*, p. 77; G. Wallace Chessman, *Theodore Roosevelt and the Politics of Power* (Boston: Little, Brown, 1969), p. 70.
26. Quoted in Frank Ninkovich, *Modernity and Power* (Chicago: University of Chicago Press, 1994), p. 6.
27. Quoted in Beale, *Theodore Roosevelt*, p. 140.
28. Quoted in Judith Papachristou, "American Women and Foreign Policy, 1896–1905," *Diplomatic History*, XIV (Fall 1990), 499, 501, 509.
29. Quoted in Frederick F. Travis, *George Kennan and the Russian-American Relationship, 1865–1924* (Athens: Ohio University Press, 1990), p. 266.
30. Quoted in Ninkovich, *Modernity*, p. 13.
31. Quoted in John Milton Cooper, Jr., *The Warrior and the Priest* (Cambridge: Harvard University Press, 1983), p. 75.
32. Quoted in Foster Rhea Dulles, "John Hay," in Norman A. Graebner, ed., *An Uncertain Tradition* (New York: McGraw-Hill, 1961), p. 24.
33. Quoted in Richard W. Leopold, *Elihu Root and the Conservative Tradition* (Boston: Little, Brown, 1954), p. 50.
34. Quoted in David H. Burton, *Theodore Roosevelt* (Philadelphia: University of Pennsylvania Press, 1968), p. 97; *Congressional Record*, XXXV (December 3, 1901), 82–83.
35. Quoted in Ralph E. Minger, *William Howard Taft and United States Foreign Policy* (Urbana: University of Illinois Press, 1975), p. 179.
36. Quoted in Ray S. Baker, *Woodrow Wilson* (Garden City, N.Y.: Doubleday, Doran, 1927–1939; 8 vols.), IV, 289.
37. Quoted in Rock, *Why Peace*, p. 142.
38. *Foreign Relations, 1898* (Washington, D.C.: Government Printing Office, 1901), pp. lxvi–lxvii.
39. Quoted in Philip C. Jessup, *Elihu Root* (New York: Dodd, Mead, 1938; 2 vols.), I, 286–287.
40. Quoted in David F. Healy, *The United States in Cuba, 1898–1902* (Madison: University of Wisconsin Press, 1963), p. 133.
41. U.S. Commissioner Robert P. Porter quoted in Louis A. Pérez, Jr., *Cuba and the United States* (Athens: University of Georgia Press, 1997, 2nd ed.), p. 127.
42. *Ibid.*, p. 128.
43. *Congressional Record*, XXXIV (February 26, 1901), 3036.
44. Quoted in H. Hagedorn, *Leonard Wood* (New York: Harper, 1931; 2 vols.), I, 362; Healy, *United States in Cuba*, p. 178.
45. Quoted in R. H. Fitzgibbon, *Cuba and the United States, 1900–1935* (New York: Russell & Russell, 1964), p. 112.

46. Quoted in Allan R. Millett, *The Politics of Intervention* (Columbus: Ohio State University Press, 1968), p. 72.

47. Quoted in Burton, *Theodore Roosevelt*, p. 106.

48. James D. Richardson, ed., *A Compilation of the Messages and Papers of the Presidents, 1789–1897* (Washington, D. C.: Government Printing Office, 1896–1899; 10 vols.), X, 7436–7437.

49. Quoted in Minger, *William Howard Taft*, p. 136.

50. Fred L. Israel, ed., *The State of the Union Messages* (New York: Chelsea House, 1967; 3 vols.), II, 2038.

51. Morison, *Letters of Roosevelt*, III, 116.

52. *Ibid.*, IV, 1156.

53. Quoted in J. Lloyd Mecham, *A Survey of United States–Latin American Relations* (Boston: Houghton Mifflin, 1965), p. 67.

54. Quoted in William N. Tilchin, *Theodore Roosevelt and the British Empire* (New York: St. Martin's Press, 1997), p. 33.

55. Quoted in John G. Clifford, "Admiral Dewey and the Germans, 1903," *Mid-America, XLIX* (July 1967), 218.

56. Quoted in Manfred Jonas, *The United States and Germany* (Ithaca: Cornell University Press, 1984), pp. 68–69.

57. Quoted in David Dimbleby and David Reynolds, *An Ocean Apart* (New York: Vintage, 1989), p. 38.

58. Quoted in Jonas, *United States and Germany*, p. 73.

59. Quoted *ibid.*, p. 420.

60. Quoted in Brands, *T.R.*, p. 524.

61. Quoted in Dexter Perkins, *The Monroe Doctrine, 1867–1907* (Baltimore: Johns Hopkins Press, 1937), p. 420.

62. Quoted in Warren G. Kneer, *Great Britain and the Caribbean, 1901–1913* (East Lansing: Michigan State University Press, 1975), p. 103.

63. Quoted in Brands, *T.R.*, p. 526.

64. Theodore Roosevelt, *An Autobiography* (New York: Charles Scribner's Sons, 1926), p. 511.

65. Quoted in Richard D. Challener, *Admirals, Generals, and American Foreign Policy, 1898–1914* (Princeton: Princeton University Press, 1973), p. 142.

66. *Foreign Relations, 1912* (Washington, D.C.: Government Printing Office, 1919), p. 1091.

67. Quoted in Lloyd C. Gardner, *Safe for Democracy* (New York: Oxford University Press, 1984), p. 41.

68. *Foreign Relations, 1913* (Washington, D.C.: Government Printing Office, 1920), p. 426.

69. Quoted in Frederick S. Calhoun, *Uses of Force and Wilsonian Foreign Policy* (Kent, Ohio: Kent State University Press, 1993), p. 53.

70. Bruce J. Calder, *The Impact of Intervention* (Austin: University of Texas Press, 1984), p. 12.

71. *Ibid.*, p. 250.

72. Quoted in Dana G. Munro, *Intervention and Dollar Diplomacy in the Caribbean* (Princeton: Princeton University Press, 1964), p. 336.

73. Quoted in Brenda G. Plummer, *Haiti and the Great Powers, 1902–1915* (Baton Rouge: Louisiana State University Press, 1988), p. 188.

74. Quoted in Calhoun, *Uses of Force*, p. 19.

75. Alexander DeConde, *Ethnicity, Race, and American Foreign Policy* (Boston: Northeastern University Press, 1993), pp. 79–80.

76. Quoted in Munro, *Intervention*, p. 155.

77. Thomas D. Schoonover, *The United States in Central America, 1860–1911* (Durham: Duke University Press, 1991), p. 130.

78. Zelaya quoted in Lester D. Langley and Thomas Schoonover, *The Banana Men* (Lexington: University Press of Kentucky, 1995), p. 89.

79. Elliott Northcott quoted in Walter LaFeber, *The American Search for Opportunity, 1865–1913* (New York: Cambridge University Press, 1993), p. 219.

80. Quoted in John E. Findling, *Close Neighbors, Distant Friends* (Westport, Conn.: Greenwood, 1987), p. 61.

81. Langley and Schoonover, *Banana Men*, p. 114.

82. Quoted in Baker, *Wilson*, IV, 436.

83. Quoted in Paolo E. Coletta, *The Presidency of William Howard Taft* (Lawrence: University Press of Kansas, 1973), p. 176.

84. Quoted in Friedrich Katz, *The Secret War in Mexico* (Chicago: University of Chicago Press, 1981), p. 113.

85. *Foreign Relations, 1912*, p. 846.

86. Quoted in Howard F. Cline, *The United States and Mexico* (New York: Atheneum, 1963; rev. ed.), p. 144.

87. Quoted in Arthur S. Link, *Wilson: The New Freedom* (Princeton: Princeton University Press, 1956), p. 360.

88. Quoted in Arthur S. Link, *Wilson: Confusions and Crises, 1915–1916* (Princeton: Princeton University Press, 1964), p. 317.

89. Quoted in Link, *Wilson: New Freedom*, p. 358.

90. Quoted *ibid.*, p. 360.

91. Quoted in Kenneth J. Grieb, *The United States and Huerta* (Lincoln: University of Nebraska Press, 1969), p. 137.

92. Quoted in Link, *Wilson: New Freedom*, pp. 386–387.

93. Quoted in Katz, *Secret War*, p. 216.

94. Quoted in Grieb, *United States and Huerta*, p. 135.

95. Quoted in Robert E. Quirk, *An Affair of Honor* (Lexington: University of Kentucky Press, 1962), p. 26.

96. Quoted in Mark T. Gilderhus, *Diplomacy and Revolution* (Tucson: University of Arizona Press, 1977), p. 11.

97. Quoted in Cary T. Grayson, *Woodrow Wilson* (New York: Holt, Rinehart and Winston, 1960), p. 30.

98. Ramón E. Ruíz, *The Great Rebellion: Mexico, 1905–1924* (New York: Norton, 1980), p. 395.

99. Quoted in Grieb, *United States and Huerta*, p. 160.

100. Quoted in Gardner, *Safe for Democracy*, p. 58.

101. Quoted in Douglas Monroy, "Fence Cutters, *Sedicioso*, and First Class Citizens: Mexican Radicalism in America," in Paul Buhle and Dan Georgakis, eds., *The Immigrant Left in the United States* (Albany: State University of New York Press, 1996), pp. 21–22.

102. Quoted in James A. Sandos, *Rebellion in the Borderlands* (Norman: University of Oklahoma Press, 1992), p. 92.

103. Quoted in Arthur S. Link, *Wilson: The Struggle for Neutrality, 1914–1915* (Princeton: Princeton University Press, 1960), p. 491.

104. Katz, *Secret War*, p. 560; Villa quoted in Friedrich Katz, "Pancho Villa and the Attack on Columbus, New Mexico," *American Historical Review, LXXXIII* (February 1978), 111, 114.

105. Quoted in Ana Maria Alonso, "U.S. Military Intervention," in Daniel Nugent, ed., *Rural Revolt in Mexico and U.S. Intervention* (San Diego: Center for U.S.–Mexican Studies, 1988), p. 217.

106. Lester Langley, *The Banana Wars* (Lexington: University Press of Kentucky, 1983), p. 114.

107. Morison, *Letters of Roosevelt*, III, 497–498.

108. Akira Iriye, *The Cold War in Asia* (Englewood Cliffs, N.J.: Prentice-Hall, 1974), p. 35.

109. Morison, *Letters of Roosevelt*, IV, 724, 761.

110. Quoted in Norman Saul, *Concord & Conflict* (Lawrence: University Press of Kansas, 1996), p. 496.

111. Quoted in Raymond A. Esthus, *Double Eagle and Rising Sun* (Durham: Duke University Press, 1988), p. 39.

112. Quoted in Brands, *T.R.*, p. 534.

113. Quoted in Saul, *Concord*, p. 504.

114. Quoted in Raymond A. Esthus, *Theodore Roosevelt and Japan* (Seattle: University of Washington Press, 1966), p. 101.

115. John Edward Wilz, "Did the United States Betray Korea in 1905?" *Pacific Historical Review, LIV* (August 1985), 252.

116. Quoted in Akira Iriye, *Across the Pacific* (New York: Harcourt, Brace & World, 1967), p. 107.

117. Quoted in Ian Mugridge, *The View from Xanadu: William Randolph Hearst and American Foreign Policy* (Montreal: McGill–Queen's University Press, 1995), p. 51.

118. Quoted in Walter A. McDougall, *Let the Sea Make a Noise* (New York: BasicBooks, 1993), p. 479; Morison, *Letters of Roosevelt, V,* 729–730, 761–762.

119. Quoted in Ute Mehnert, "German *Weltpolitik* and the American Two Front Dilemma," *Journal of American History, LXXXII* (March 1996), 1458.

120. Quoted in Eileen P. Scully, "Taking the Low Road to Sino-American Relations," *ibid., LXXXII* (June 1995), 63–64.

121. Anders Stephanson, *Manifest Destiny* (New York: Hill & Wang, 1995), p. 97.

122. Ninkovich, *Modernity,* p. 25.

123. Quoted in Herbert Croly, *Willard Straight* (New York: Macmillan, 1925), p. 276.

124. A. Whitney Griswold, *The Far Eastern Policy of the United States* (New Haven: Yale University Press, 1938), p. 157.

125. Quoted in Croly, *Straight,* pp. 392–393.

126. Quoted in Walter LaFeber, *The Clash* (New York: Norton, 1997), p. 72.

127. Quoted in Daniel M. Crane and Thomas A. Breslin, *An Ordinary Relationship* (Miami: Florida International University Press, 1986), p. 122.

128. Quoted in Roger Daniels, *The Politics of Prejudice* (New York: Atheneum, [1962], 1968), p. 59.

129. Quoted in Link, *Wilson: New Freedom,* pp. 300–301.

130. Quoted in Kendrick A. Clements, *The Presidency of Woodrow Wilson* (Lawrence: University Press of Kansas, 1990), p. 108.

131. *Foreign Relations, 1922* (Washington, D.C.: Government Printing Office, 1938; 2 vols.), II, 591.

132. Quoted in Michael H. Hunt, *Ideology and U.S. Foreign Policy* (New Haven: Yale University Press, 1987), pp. 69, 71, 79, 81.

133. *Ibid.,* p. 79.

134. Quoted in Beale, *Theodore Roosevelt,* pp. 81, 152.

135. Quoted in Rock, *Why Peace,* p. 51; Bradford Perkins, *The Great Rapprochement* (New York: Atheneum, 1968).

136. Roosevelt quoted in Frederick W. Marks, *Velvet on Iron* (Lincoln: University of Nebraska Press, 1979), p. 168.

137. Quoted in Perkins, *Great Rapprochement,* p. 168.

138. Robert Bothwell, *Canada and the United States* (New York: Twayne, 1992), p. 8.

139. Quoted in Kurk Dorsey, "Scientists, Citizens, and Statesmen," *Diplomatic History, XIX* (Summer 1995), 426.

140. Mark Kurlansky, *Cod* (New York: Walker, 1997), p. 79.

141. Quoted in Arthur Marder, *From the Dreadnought to Scapa Flow* (London: Oxford University Press, 1961–1970; 5 vols.), I, 125.

142. Quoted *ibid.,* p. 201.

143. Quoted in Link, *Wilson: New Freedom,* p. 308.

144. Quoted in Burton, *Theodore Roosevelt,* p. 190.

145. Quoted in Emily S. Rosenberg, "The Invisible Protectorate: The United States, Liberia, and the Evolution of Neocolonialism, 1909–40," *Diplomatic History, IX* (Summer 1985), 194, 198.

146. Quoted in Tilchin, *Theodore Roosevelt,* p. 67.

147. Morison, *Letters of Roosevelt, IV,* 1119.

148. Quoted in Calvin Davis, *The United States and the Second Hague Peace Conference* (Durham: Duke University Press, 1975), p. 296.

149. Quoted in Minger, *William Howard Taft,* p. 106.

150. Quoted in Mehnert, "German *Weltpolitik,*" p. 1461.

151. Quoted in Jerry Israel, *Progressivism and the Open Door* (Pittsburgh: University of Pittsburgh Press, 1971), p. 96.

152. General William Carter quoted in Brian Linn, *Guardians of Empire* (Chapel Hill: University of North Carolina Press, 1997), p. 62.

153. Quoted in Michael L. Conniff, *Panama and the United States* (Athens: University of Georgia Press, 1992), p. 3.

154. Quoted in Arturo Morales Carrión, *Puerto Rico* (New York: Norton, 1983), p. 163.

155. Raymond Carr, *Puerto Rico* (New York: Vintage, 1984), p. 36.

156. William Phillips, *Ventures in Diplomacy* (Boston: Beacon Press, 1952), p. 6.

157. Quoted in A. J. Bacevich, *Diplomat in Khaki* (Lawrence: University Press of Kansas, 1989), p. 48.

158. Emily S. Rosenberg, *Spreading the American Dream* (New York: Hill & Wang, 1982), p. 35.

159. Quoted in Robert A. Hart, *The Great White Fleet* (Boston: Little, Brown, 1965), p. 45.

160. Quoted in Franklin Ng, "Knowledge for Empire," in Robert David Johnson, ed., *On Cultural Ground* (Chicago: Imprint Publications, 1994), p. 135.

161. Charles W. Eliot quoted in Frank Trommler, "Inventing the Enemy," in Hans-Jürgen Schröder, *Confrontation and Cooperation* (Providence, R.I.: Berg Publishers, 1993), p. 101.

162. Arnold Testi, "The Gender of Reform Politics," *Journal of American History, LXXXI* (March 1995), 1522.

163. Winston S. Churchill, *The World Crisis* (New York: Charles Scribner's Sons, 1927; 6 vols.), I, 18.

War, Peace, and Revolution in the Time of Wilson, 1914–1920

Mass Grave of **Lusitania** *Victims.*   *In Queenstown, Ireland, a large burial ground holds more than a hundred victims of the* Lusitania *disaster of 1915, which rudely brought World War I to American consciousness. (U.S. War Department, National Archives)*

DIPLOMATIC CROSSROAD

The Sinking of the *Lusitania,* 1915

"Perfectly safe; safer than the trolley cars in New York City," claimed a Cunard Line official the morning of May 1, 1915.[1] Indeed, the majestic *Lusitania,* with its watertight compartments and swiftness, seemed invulnerable. The British government loaned Cunard the money to build this fast passenger liner, more than twice as long as an American football field. The British Admiralty dictated the coal-burning ship's specifications, so that the 30,396-ton vessel could be armed if necessary during war. "Lucy's" priority was pleasure, not war. Resplendent with tapestries and carpets, the luxurious floating palace dazzled. One impressed American politician found the ship "more beautiful than Solomon's Temple—and big enough to hold all his wives."[2]

A crew of 702 attended the 1,257 travelers who departed from New York's Pier 54 on May 1. Deep in the *Lusitania*'s storage area rested a cargo of foodstuffs and contraband (4.2 million rounds of ammunition for Remington rifles, 1,250 cases of empty shrapnel shells, and eighteen cases of nonexplosive fuses). The Cunarder thus carried, said a U.S. State Department official, both "babies and bullets."[3]

In the morning newspapers of May 1 a rather unusual announcement, placed by the Imperial German Embassy, appeared beside the Cunard Line advertisement. The German "Notice" warned passengers that the waters around the British Isles constituted a war zone wherein British vessels were subject to destruction. Only a handful of passengers canceled their bookings on the *Lusitania.* Few transferred to the *New York,* ready to sail under the American flag that same day. But the unattractive *New York* was slow and for the American "smart set" socially unacceptable. The State Department did not intercede to warn the 197 American passengers away from the *Lusitania.* Most Americans accepted the Cunard Line statement: "She is too fast for any submarine. No German war vessel can get her or near her."[4] During this very time, Secretary of State William Jennings Bryan was trying to persuade President Woodrow Wilson that Americans should be prohibited from traveling on belligerent ships. Bryan made little headway.

Captained by William T. Turner, the *Lusitania* steamed into the Atlantic at half past noon on May 1. Manned by an ill-trained crew (the best now on war duty), "Lucy" enjoyed a smooth crossing in calm water. Despite lifesaving drills, complacency about the submarine danger lulled captain, crew, and passengers alike. Passengers joked about torpedoes, played cards, consumed gallons of liquor, and listened to concerts on deck. On May 6, as the *Lusitania* neared Ireland, Turner received a warning from the Naval Centre at Queenstown: "Submarines active off south coast of Ireland."[5] The captain posted lookouts but took no other precautions, despite follow-up warnings. He had standing orders from the Admiralty to take a zigzag path, to steer a midchannel course, and to steam at full speed—all to make it difficult for lurking German submarines to zero in on their targets. But Turner proceeded straight ahead.

The *Lusitania* and *U-20*.
The majestic passenger liner was sunk by German submarine *U-20* off the coast of Ireland on May 7, 1915. "Suppose they should sink the *Lusitania* with American passengers on board," King George V had mused to Colonel Edward M. House on that fateful morning. (Peabody Museum of Salem; Bundesarchiv)

A beautiful day with unusually good visibility, recorded Lieutenant Walter Schwieger in his log on May 7. The young commander was piloting his *U-20* submarine along the southern Irish coast. That morning it had submerged because British ships capable of ramming the fragile, slender craft were passing by. Schwieger surfaced at 1:45 P.M. and soon spotted a four-funneled ship in the distance. Schwieger quickly submerged and set a track toward the *Lusitania,* eager to take advantage of this chance meeting. At 700 meters the *U-20* released a torpedo. The deadly missile dashed through the water tailed by bubbles. A watchman on the starboard bow of the *Lusitania* cried out. Captain Turner, unaccountably below

Captain William T. Turner (1856–1933). He commanded the *Lusitania* to disaster. (U.S. War Department)

Lieutenant Walter Schwieger (1885–1917). His *U–20* sank the *Lusitania.* (Bundesarchiv)

deck in those dangerous waters, did not hear the megaphone one minute before the torpedo struck. Had he heard the warning, the ship *might* have veered sharply and avoided danger. Turner felt the explosion as it ripped into the *Lusitania*. Schwieger watched through his periscope as the mighty vessel leaned on its starboard side and its bow dipped. Panic swept the passengers as they stumbled about the listing decks or groped in the darkness below. Steam whistled from punctured boilers. Less than half the lifeboats lowered; some capsized or embarked only partially loaded. Within eighteen minutes the "Queen of the Atlantic" sank, killing 1,198—128 of them Americans. A survivor said that when the *Lusitania* went down, "it sounded like a terrible moan."[6]

President Wilson had just ended a cabinet meeting in the White House when he learned of the disaster. His special assistant, Colonel Edward House, then in London, predicted: "We shall be at war with Germany within a month."[7] The pro-British House had actually sailed on the *Lusitania* in February and had witnessed, much to his surprise, the hoisting of an American flag as the ship neared the Irish coast. Fearing war, Secretary Bryan told the president that "ships carrying contraband should be prohibited from carrying passengers. . . . it would be like putting women and children in front of an army."[8] Bellicose ex-president Theodore Roosevelt soon seared the air with his declaration that "this represents . . . piracy on a vaster scale of murder than old-time pirates ever practiced."[9] American after American voiced horror, but few wanted war. Wilson secluded himself to ponder a response to this ghastly event. Just months before, he had said he would hold Berlin strictly accountable for the loss of any American ships or lives because of submarine warfare. Thereafter, Wilson found himself trying to fulfill America's "double

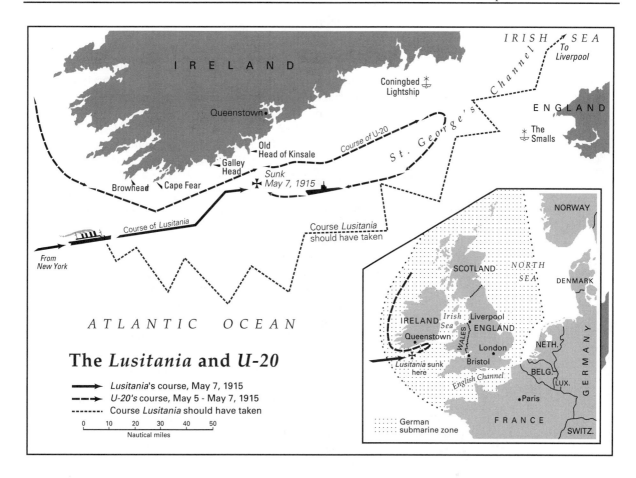

The *Lusitania* and *U-20*

➤ *Lusitania*'s course, May 7, 1915
➤ - ➤ *U-20*'s course, May 5 - May 7, 1915
‧‧‧‧‧‧ Course *Lusitania* should have taken

0 10 20 30 40 50
Nautical miles

wish"—"to maintain a firm front . . . [toward] Germany and yet do nothing that might by any possibility involve us in war."[10]

After reading memoranda from Bryan warning that Americans should not travel on Allied ships carrying contraband, Wilson spoke in Philadelphia on May 10. His words, much misunderstood, suggested he had no backbone: "There is such a thing as a man being too proud to fight. There is such a thing as a nation being so right that it does not need to convince others by force that it is right."[11] When former secretary of state Elihu Root called it "incredible" that Wilson could see "no greater moral question involved," the president regretted his impromptu words.[12] Preoccupied by his intense courtship of his future second wife, Wilson did "not know just what I said in Philadelphia . . . because my heart was in such a whirl."[13] The next morning he told the cabinet that he would send a note to Berlin insisting that Americans had a right to travel on the high seas and demanding a disavowal by the German government of the inhumane acts of its submarine commanders. Bryan sadly approved this first "*Lusitania* note." Long upset about an apparent American double standard in protesting more against German than British violations of American neutral rights, the secretary pleaded for a simultaneous protest to London. But only one note went out on May 13—to Berlin: "The Imperial Government will not expect the United States to omit any word or any act necessary to the performance of its sacred duty of maintaining the rights of the United States and its citizens and of safeguarding their free exercise and enjoyment."[14] In short, end submarine warfare, or else.

The German government took much less pleasure than the German navy did in the destruction of the *Lusitania*. Chancellor Theobold von Bethmann-Hollweg had more than once chastised the navy for inviting war with the United States through submarine attacks on neutral or Allied merchant vessels. On May 28 he sent an evasive reply to Wilson's note. The *Lusitania* case could not be settled, it read, until they clarified certain questions. The German note claimed that the ship was armed, carried munitions, and had orders to ram submarines. Germany asked Washington to investigate. That same day, in a secret meeting with German ambassador Johann von Bernstorff, Wilson proposed that if Germany would settle the *Lusitania* crisis favorably, he would press the British to suspend their blockade and then call a conference of neutrals to mediate an end to the war on the following basis: "1. The status quo in Europe; 2. Freedom of the seas. . . . 3. Adjustments concerning colonial possessions."[15]

Wilson convened the cabinet on June 1. When one member recommended a strong note demanding observance of American rights, another suggested as well a note to England to protest British interference with American commerce. Debate became heated. A majority rejected simultaneous notes. Bryan called the cabinet pro-Ally. Wilson quickly rebuked him for "unfair and unjust" comments.[16] When Germany did not immediately reply to his mediation proposal, Wilson sent a second "*Lusitania* note." This note vigorously demanded an end to warfare by submarine. Wilson rejected Bryan's plea for a warning to passengers and a protest note to England. Sensing that "this will destroy me," Bryan quietly resigned on June 8.[17] Wilson went to the golf links to free himself from the blinding headaches of the past several days. "He is absolutely *sincere*," the president said of Bryan. "That is what makes him dangerous."[18]

More correspondence on the *Lusitania* followed. The United States insisted that Germany admit it had committed an illegal act; but Germany, unwilling to abandon one of its few effective weapons against British mastery of the ocean, refused to admit wrongdoing and asked for arbitration. "Utterly impertinent," sniffed Kaiser Wilhelm II, who preferred victory to Wilson's mediation.[19] Eventually Germany sought compromise. On February 4 it expressed regret over the American deaths and offered to pay an indemnity (eventually paid in the early 1920s). Wilson accepted the German concession.

The horrible deaths from the *Lusitania* remained etched in American memories. The torpedoing of the magnificent Cunarder marked a turning point. The Germans suffered a "naval victory worse than a defeat," as Britons and Americans alike depicted the "Huns" as depraved.[20] The sinking also hardened Wilson's opinion of Germany. After Germany spurned his secret mediation offer, Wilson no longer made diplomatic life easier for the Germans by simultaneously protesting

British infractions. The British were violating property rights, but the Germans violated human rights. He also refused to warn Americans away from belligerent ships. In short, if a U-boat attacked a British ship with Americans aboard, Germany would have to take the consequences. Wilson did not spell out those consequences, but the logical implication was war—just what Bryan feared. His resignation brought pro-Ally Robert Lansing to the secretaryship of state. After the *Lusitania* crisis, Lansing believed "that we would ultimately become an ally of Great Britain."[21] The sinking of the *Lusitania* pointed up, for all to see, the complexities, contradictions, and uncertainties inherent in American neutrality during the European phase of the First World War, 1914–1917.

The Travails of Neutrality

Woodrow Wilson acted virtually as his own secretary of state during those troubled years. "Wilson makes confidant of no one. No one gets his whole mind," an aide wrote.[22] British prime minister Lloyd George put it less kindly: Wilson "believed in mankind but . . . distrusted all men."[23] The president defined the overall character of American foreign policy—what historians call "Wilsonianism." Above all else, Wilson stood for an *open* world unencumbered by imperialism, war, or revolution. Barriers to trade and democracy had to come down, and secret diplomacy had to give way to public negotiations. The right of self-determination would force the collapse of empires. Constitutional procedures would replace revolution. A free-market, humanized capitalism would ensure democracy. Disarmament programs would restrict weapons. The Open Door of equal trade and investment would harness the economic competition that led to war. Wilson, like so many Americans, saw the United States as exceptional—"a sort of pure air blowing in world politics, destroying illusions and cleaning places of morbid miasmic gasses."[24] His reformist, expansionist zeal blended with realism. The president calculated the nation's economic and strategic needs and devised a foreign policy to protect them. Yet many Americans feared that his world-reforming efforts might invite war, dissipate American resources, and undermine reform at home. Wilson led a divided nation.

Few Americans, Wilson included, desired war. Most watched in shock as the European nations savagely slashed at one another in 1914. The progressive faith in human ability to right wrongs, the belief that war belonged to the decadent past, the conviction that civilization had advanced too far for such bloodletting—all were ruthlessly challenged. Before 1914 the new machine guns, howitzers, submarines, and dreadnoughts were simply too awesome for leaders to launch them. The outbreak of World War I smashed illusions and tested innocence. The shock did not become despair, despite the news of poison gas, U-boats, and civilian casualties. The Progressive era exuded optimism, and Americans, particularly the crusading Wilson, sought to retrieve a happier past by assuming the role of civilized instructors: America would help Europe come to its senses by teaching it the rules of humane conduct. The carnage justified the mission. In 1915 alone France suffered 1.3 million

Makers of American Foreign Relations, 1914–1920

President	Secretaries of State
Woodrow Wilson, 1913–1921	William Jennings Bryan, 1913–1915
	Robert Lansing, 1915–1920
	Bainbridge Colby, 1920–1921

casualties, including 330,000 deaths. Germany suffered 848,000 casualties, 170,000 of them deaths. Britain followed with 313,000 casualties, and 73,000 deaths.

Americans had good reason, then, to believe that Europe needed help in cleaning its own house. The outbreak of the war seemed so senseless. By June 1914, the great powers had constructed two blocs, the Triple Alliance (Germany, Austria-Hungary, and Italy) and the Triple Entente (France, Russia, and Great Britain). Some called this division of Europe a balance of power, but an assassin's bullet unbalanced it. Between Austria and Serbia lay Bosnia, a tiny province in the Austro-Hungarian Empire. Slavic nationalists sought to build a greater Serbia—an independent Slavic state—by annexing Bosnia, which the Austro-Hungarian Empire had absorbed just a few years before, in 1909. A Slavic terrorist group, the Black Hand, decided to force the issue. On June 28 the heir to the Hapsburg Crown of Austria-Hungary, Archduke Franz Ferdinand, visited Sarajevo, the capital of Bosnia. As his car moved through the streets of the city, a Black Hand assassin gunned him down.

Austria-Hungary sent impossible demands to Serbia. The Serbs rejected them. Austria-Hungary had already received encouragement from Germany, and Serbia had a pledge of support from Russia, which in turn received backing from France. A chain reaction set in. On July 28 Austria-Hungary declared war on Serbia; on August 1 Germany declared "preventive" war on Russia and two days later on France; on August 4 Germany invaded Belgium, and Great Britain declared war on Germany. In a few weeks Japan joined the Allies (Triple Entente) and Turkey the Central Powers, and Italy entered on the Allied side the next year. As the German leader Otto von Bismarck had once prophesied, "some damned foolish thing in the Balkans" had started a world war.[25]

The Atlantic seemed at first an adequate barrier to insulate the United States. In early August, the U.S. ambassador to England, Walter Hines Page, wrote the president: "Be ready; for you will be called on to compose their huge quarrel. I thank Heaven for many things—first the Atlantic Ocean."[26] Wilson issued a Proclamation of Neutrality on August 4, followed days later by an appeal to Americans to be neutral in thought, speech, and action. Laced with patriotic utterances, the decree sought to cool the passions of immigrant groups who identified with the belligerents. America must demonstrate to a troubled world that it was "fit beyond others to exhibit the fine poise of undisturbed judgment, the dignity of self-control, the efficiency of dispassionate action."[27] A lofty call for restraint, an expression of

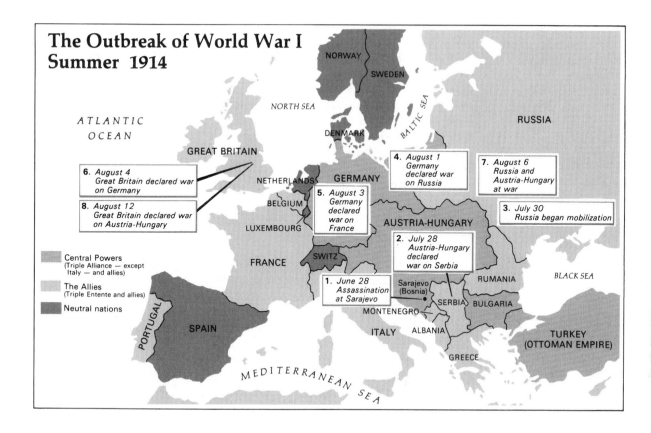

The Outbreak of World War I Summer 1914

6. August 4 Great Britain declared war on Germany

8. August 12 Great Britain declared war on Austria-Hungary

4. August 1 Germany declared war on Russia

7. August 6 Russia and Austria-Hungary at war

5. August 3 Germany declared war on France

3. July 30 Russia began mobilization

2. July 28 Austria-Hungary declared war on Serbia

1. June 28 Assassination at Sarajevo

Central Powers (Triple Alliance — except Italy — and allies)

The Allies (Triple Entente and allies)

Neutral nations

America as the beacon of common sense in a world gone mad, a plea for unity at home—but difficult to achieve.

Few Americans, including officials of the Wilson administration, proved capable of neutral thoughts and deeds. Loyalties to fatherlands and motherlands did not abate. German Americans identified with the Central Powers. Many Irish Americans, nourishing their traditional Anglophobia at a time when Ireland chafed under British rule and readied for rebellion, wished catastrophe on Britain. But Anglo-American traditions and cultural ties, as well as slogans such as "Remember LaFayette," pulled most Americans toward a pro-Allied position. Since the 1890s Anglophobia had weakened in the face of the calming Anglo-American rapprochement. Woodrow Wilson himself harbored pro-British sentiment, telling the British ambassador that "everything I love is at stake" and that a German victory "will be fatal to our form of Government and American ideals."[28] Wilson's advisers, House and Lansing, were ardently pro-British. Ambassador Page became so fiercely pro-British that he wanted Americans "to hang our Irish agitators and shoot our hyphenates and bring up our children with reverence for English history and . . . English literature."[29]

German war actions, exaggerated by British propaganda, also undermined neutrality. To Americans, the Germans, led by arrogant Kaiser Wilhelm II, became symbols of the dreaded militarism and conscription of the Old World. Even Chancellor Bethmann-Hollweg admitted that "we often got on the world's nerves."[30] Germany, too, seemed an upstart nation, an aggressive latecomer to the scramble for imperialist prizes, and a noisy intruder in the Caribbean where the British had already acknowledged U.S. hegemony. Eager to grasp world power and encouraging Austria-Hungary to war, Berlin certainly had little claim on virtue. The European powers had guaranteed Belgium neutrality by treaty, but Bethmann-Hollweg dismissed it as a "scrap of paper."[31] On August 4, 1914, hoping to get at France, the Germans attacked Belgium and, angered that the Belgians resisted, ruthlessly proceeded to raze villages, unleash firing squads against townspeople, and deport young workers to Germany. One magazine called Belgium "a martyr to civilization, sister to all who love liberty, or law; assailed, polluted, trampled in the mire, heel-marked in her breast, tattered, homeless."[32] American hearts and hands went out in the form of a major relief mission headed by a young, wealthy, and courageous mining engineer, Herbert Hoover.

American economic links with the Allies also undercut neutrality. England had always been America's best customer, and wartime conditions simply intensified the relationship. The Allies needed both war matériel and consumer goods. Americans, inspired by huge profits and a chance to pull out of a recession, obliged. In 1914 U.S. exports to England and France equaled $754 million; in 1915 the figure shot up to $1.28 billion; and in 1916 the amount more than doubled to $2.75 billion. Comparable statistics for Germany reveal why Berlin believed the United States was taking sides. In 1914 exports to Germany totaled $345 million; in 1915 they plummeted to $29 million; and in 1916 they fell to $2 million. In 1914–1917 New York's banking house of J. P. Morgan Company served as an agent for England and France and arranged for the shipment of more than $3 billion worth of goods. In April 1915, Britain ordered shells from the American Locomotive Company costing $63.7 million, and that year Bethlehem Steel contracted for some $150 million in ammunition, to cite two examples. By April 1917, British purchasing missions were spending $83 million a week for American copper, steel, wheat, oil, and munitions.

Britain and France sold many of their American securities and liquidated investments to pay for these goods. This netted them several billion dollars. Next, in appeals to prominent American bankers and State Department officials, they also sought loans. In 1914 Bryan discouraged private American loans to the belligerents, because "money is the worst of all contrabands because it commands everything else."[33] Yet in early 1915 the Wilson administration did not object to a Morgan credit to France of $50 million. With Bryan's resignation and Lansing's ascent as secretary of state, the practice became common. As Lansing told Wilson, if Americans did not extend loans to the Allies, it would invite "restriction of output, industrial depression, idle capital, idle labor, numerous failures, financial demoralization, and general unrest and suffering among the laboring classes."[34] The Wilson administration permitted loans to the Allies amounting to $2.3 billion in the years 1914–1917—a sharp contrast to loans of only $27 million to Germany. Once it joined the war as a belligerent, the American economic powerhouse became even more the dispenser of munitions, food, and money to the Allies. Indeed, as the historian Kathleen Burk has written, "the passing of hegemony from Britain to the United States . . . as the leading financial power can be seen occurring, step by step, in the negotiations between the British Treasury mission and the American government during 1917–18."[35]

Berlin protested such "unneutral" economic ties. Yet curbing trade with Britain, which ruled the seas, would have constituted unneutral behavior in favor of the Germans, for under international law a belligerent could buy, at its own risk, contraband and noncontraband goods from a neutral. Neutral or not, the United States had become the arsenal of the Allied war effort. Berlin tried to stop this trade by unleashing *unterseebooten.*

Submarines, Neutral Rights, and Mediation Efforts

To strangle Germany, the British invoked legal doctrines of retaliation and contraband without ever technically declaring a blockade. They mined the North Sea, expanded the contraband list to include foodstuffs and cotton, forced American ships into port for inspection, seized "contraband" from neutral vessels, halted American trade with Germany's neutral neighbors Denmark and Holland, armed British merchant ships, used decoy ships to lure U-boats into traps, flew neutral (often American) flags, and rammed whenever possible any U-boats that complied with international law by surfacing to warn a British merchant vessel of an imminent attack. The British "ruled the waves and waived the rules," so to speak. Defending neutral rights, the Wilson administration issued protests, some mild, some tough, against these illegalities. The Foreign Office usually paid appropriate verbal deference to neutral rights and international law and went right on with its restrictive behavior. Britain sometimes compensated U.S. businesses for damages and purchased large quantities of goods at inflated prices. Americans thus came to tolerate the indignities of British economic warfare. Britain managed brilliantly to sever American economic lines to the Central Powers without rupturing Anglo-American relations.

Germans protested vehemently against American acquiescence in the British "hunger" or "starvation" blockade. To continue the war, Germany had to have imports and had to curb the flourishing Anglo-American trade that fueled the Allied war machine. The German surface fleet, bottled up in ports, seemed inadequate for the task, so German leaders hesitantly turned to a relatively new experimental weapon of limited maneuverability, the submarine. At the start they possessed just 21 U-boats, and at peak strength in October 1917 they had but 127. Only a third of this fleet operated at sea at any one time. On February 4, 1915, Berlin announced that it was retaliating against British strangulation by declaring a war zone around Britain. All *enemy* ships in the area would be destroyed. It warned neutral ships to *stay out* of the zone because of possibly mistaken identity, a real prospect given the British practice of hoisting neutral flags. Passengers from neutral countries were urged, moreover, to *stay off* enemy passenger vessels. Six days later Wilson held Germany to "strict accountability" for the loss of American life and property.[36]

William Jennings Bryan (1860–1925). The great agrarian reformer went to Congress in 1890 as a Democrat from Nebraska. After several unsuccessful runs for the presidency, Bryan endorsed Wilson and became secretary of state in 1913. He favored the arbitration of international disputes, and he perpetuated U.S. interventionist policy in Latin America. Believing that Wilson was tilting toward the British after the *Lusitania* disaster of 1915, Bryan resigned in protest. A colleague called him "too good a Christian to run a naughty world." (National Portrait Gallery, Smithsonian Institution)

The British continued to arm their merchant vessels, which thereby became warships and theoretically ineligible to take on arms or munitions in neutral ports. But Washington invoked a fine distinction between offensive and defensive armaments and permitted such "defensively" armed British craft to carry war supplies from American ports. Crying foul, the Germans also argued that old international law, which Wilson invoked, did not fit the submarine. Rules "adopted during the sailing-ship era" held that an attacking cruiser about to sink or capture enemy merchant vessels had to give adequate warning so as to ensure the safety of passengers and crew.[37] Yet if a submarine surfaced in its sluggish fashion, the merchant ship's crew might sink it with a blast from a deck gun or even a hand grenade, or ram the slow-moving craft. Imagine the problem for Schwieger of *U-20* when he spotted the *Lusitania*. Had he surfaced to warn the ship, the *Lusitania* probably would have attempted to ram *U-20* or flee and would have sent distress signals to British warships in the vicinity. Even if the *Lusitania* had submitted to the warning, it might have taken an hour for passengers to get into lifeboats before Schwieger could torpedo the *Lusitania,* by which time British warships might have closed in. In short, from the German point of view, to comply with an international law that failed to anticipate the submarine was not possible. Wilson retorted that differences over international law could be "adjusted after the war," whereas Germany's "sheer acts of piracy on the high seas . . . might easily lead to actual hostilities."[38]

Secretary Bryan tried diplomacy in early 1915, asking Germany to give up use of unannounced submarine attacks in exchange for a British promise to disarm its merchant carriers and permit food to flow to Germany. The Germans seemed interested, but London refused to abandon its successful blockade. At this point Wilson might have pressed the belligerents to alter their naval strategies or face the prospect of U.S. warships convoying America's neutral ships. Or he might have launched a vigorous diplomatic offensive to delay explosive events on the seas. Yet American armed convoys in the Atlantic could very well draw the country into a war it did not want. A diplomatic offensive, given the intensity of war fever in Europe, seemed a long shot. In March 1915, Wilson did send Colonel House to Europe to sound out possibilities for mediation, but to no avail. Nonetheless, Wilson failed to adjust or shelve ancient international law, which had no provision for the submarine. He accepted British alterations but not German ones, for reasons of both morality and economics.

Between February and May 1915, marauding submarines sank ninety ships in the war zone. One American, on the British passenger ship *Falaba,* died in the sinking of that vessel on March 28. Then came the *Lusitania* in May. Through Wilson's many protest notes, a U.S. posture took shape: uneasy tolerance of British violations of property rights and rejection of German violations of human rights. Despite secret German orders to submarine commanders to avoid a repetition of the *Lusitania* incident, on August 19 the *Arabic,* another British liner, was torpedoed with the loss of two American lives. A worried Ambassador Bernstorff publicly pledged that U-boats would now spare passenger ships.

In early 1916, calling the United States ideally suited as the "mediating nation of the world," Wilson tried to bring the warring parties to the conference table.[39]

Colonel House talked with British officials in London but left with no promises for peace. He journeyed next to Berlin, where German leaders gave no assurances. Both sides would fight on. "Hell will break loose in Europe this spring and summer as never before," House informed Wilson.[40] House then traveled to Paris, where he rashly informed his skeptical French hosts: "If the Allies obtain a small success this spring or summer, the U.S. will intervene to promote a peaceful settlement, but if the Allies have a setback, the United States will intervene militarily and will take part in the war against Germany."[41] House did not report his prediction to the president.

House returned to London to press Sir Edward Grey, British foreign secretary, to heed Wilson's call for a peace conference. The American envoy recorded their agreements in the House-Grey Memorandum of February 22, 1916, a document loaded with "ifs." The first paragraph read: "Colonel House told me that President Wilson was ready, on hearing from France and England that the moment was opportune, to propose that a Conference should be summoned to put an end to the war. Should the Allies accept the proposal, and should Germany refuse it, the United States would probably enter the war against Germany." The record of conversation also reported that House had said that the peace conference would secure terms "not unfavourable to the Allies" and that if the conference failed to achieve peace, "the United States would leave the Conference as a belligerent on the side of the Allies, if Germany was unreasonable."[42] Wilson pronounced the memorandum a diplomatic triumph, but he clouded its meaning all the more by inserting a "probably" before the word "leave" in the sentence quoted above. He took the document much more seriously than did the British or French, who shelved it, snubbed American mediation, and vowed victory over Germany.

As House moved among European capitals, Lansing informed the Allied governments that the United States sought a modus vivendi to defuse naval crises: The Allies would disarm merchant vessels, and the Germans would follow international law by warning enemy merchant ships. This suggestion revealed that the Wilson administration understood the German argument that armed merchant vessels actually operated as offensive craft—that is, warships. The British and Colonel House remonstrated when they received this news. The Germans seemed to endorse the proposal by declaring on February 10 that submarines would henceforth attack only *armed* merchant ships without warning. Suddenly Wilson reversed policy. He abandoned the modus vivendi in order to restore his standing with the British and sustain House's mediation efforts in London. Lansing announced, furthermore, that the United States would not ban its citizens from traveling on "defensively" armed merchant ships.

Edward M. House (1858–1938). This Texas "colonel" served as Wilson's trusted emissary abroad. In the House-Grey Memorandum of 1916 he showed signs of the deviousness that led to his break with the president after the Versailles conference. He misled the British by depicting the mediation overture as a pretext for America's entering the war, and he misled Wilson by reporting that the British were genuinely interested in mediation. (National Portrait Gallery, Smithsonian Institution)

Wilson Leads America into World War

Why let one American passenger and a trigger-happy U-boat captain start a war? asked public critics such as Bryan. Why not, they inquired, keep Americans off belligerent ships and require them instead to sail on American vessels? From August

**Woodrow Wilson
(1856–1924).** Scholar, professor, university president (Princeton), and Democratic governor (New Jersey), Woodrow Wilson was usually cocksure once he made a decision. "I would rather fail in a cause that will ultimately triumph than triumph in a cause that will ultimately fail," he once said. (*Cartoons,* 1912)

1914 to mid-March 1917 only three Americans (on the oil tanker *Gulflight,* May 1, 1915) had lost their lives on an American ship torpedoed by a U-boat. In contrast, about 190 Americans, including the *Lusitania*'s 128, died on belligerent ships. After the *Falaba* was sunk, Bryan, still secretary of state, recognized that Americans had a right to travel on belligerent vessels, but he wanted Wilson to ask them to forgo that right. "I cannot see," Bryan wrote the president, "that he [an American on a belligerent ship] is differently situated from those who by remaining in a belligerent country assume risk of injury."[43] Wilson had, after all, urged Americans to leave war-torn Mexico. Ambassador James W. Gerard in Berlin wondered, "why should we enter a great war because some American wants to cross on a ship where he can have a private bathroom?"[44]

In January 1916, member of Congress Jeff McLemore of Texas, a Democrat, introduced a resolution to prohibit Americans from traveling on armed belligerent vessels. In February, Senator Thomas P. Gore of Oklahoma, another Democrat, submitted a similar resolution in his chamber. Wilson, a firm believer in presidential supremacy in decisionmaking, bristled at this challenge from Congress. He unleashed cabinet members with patronage muscle on timid legislators, suggesting that Gore-McLemore was a pro-German ploy. To halt American passage on belligerent ships, Wilson declared, would be to accept national humiliation and destruction of the "whole fine fabric of international law."[45] In short, he stuck with rigid, archaic concepts, refusing to adjust to the new factor of the submarine or to appreciate the impact on Germany of the obvious British violations of the same law. In early March, the Gore-McLemore resolution lost 68 to 14 in the Senate and 276 to 142 in the House. The resolution asked America to give up very little; despite presidential rhetoric, it did not besmudge national honor. Wilson's message to Berlin rang loud and clear: Do not use your submarines.

In March 1916, another passenger ship, another U-boat, another torpedo, more American injuries: The French ship *Sussex,* moving across the English Channel, took a hit but did not sink. Aboard was a young American scholar, Samuel Flagg Bemis, later a renowned historian of foreign relations but then fresh from archival research on Jay's Treaty. Bemis glimpsed the swirling wake of a torpedo moments before impact. "The entire bow was blown off and with it the people who were in the dining room," he recalled.[46] Although four Americans sustained injuries, a wet Bemis escaped serious harm and managed to save his little bag of note cards.

The *Sussex* attack violated the "*Arabic* pledge," even though the U-boat commander mistook the ship for a minelayer. Lansing wanted to break diplomatic relations with Berlin. Wilson decided instead on an ultimatum. He warned the Germans on April 18 that he would sever relations if they did not halt their submarine warfare against passenger and merchant vessels; he went to Congress the next day and repeated the warning. With the unsuccessful German offensive at Verdun costing more than half a million lives, Berlin did not want war with the United States. In early May Germany promised (the "*Sussex* pledge") that submarines would not attack passenger or merchant ships without prior warning. The Germans also nagged Washington to stop British infractions of international law.

The British, sensing favorable winds, clamped down even harder on trade with the Central Powers. In July, London issued a "blacklist" of more than eighty American companies that had traded with the Central Powers. Even Wilson now fumed that he was "about at the end of my patience with Great Britain and the Allies."[47] He contemplated a ban on loans and exports to them, but he did little. Many Americans also condemned the brutal British smashing of the Irish Easter Rebellion in April 1916.

Shortly after his reelection in 1916, under the slogan "He Kept Us Out of War," the president boldly asked the belligerents to state their war aims. Neither Berlin nor London, still seeking military victory, welcomed Wilson's mediation. Germany coveted Poland, Lithuania, Belgium, and the Belgian Congo; Britain sought German colonies; France wanted Alsace-Lorraine. Wilson pointedly rejected such goals on January 22, 1917, when he called for a "peace without victory" because only through a peace founded on the "equality of nations" could a lasting world order be achieved. He regarded victory as "an intoxicant that fires the national brain and leaves a craving for more."[48] The French novelist Anatole France responded cynically: "Peace without victory is bread without yeast . . . , love without quarrels, a camel without humps, night without moon, roof without smoke, town without brothel."[49]

In early 1917 crises mounted quickly. On January 31 Berlin announced that German submarines would attack without warning and sink all vessels, enemy and neutral, found near British waters. This declaration of unrestricted submarine warfare expressed Germany's calculated risk that it could defeat England and France before the United States could mobilize and send soldiers overseas. The cocky German naval minister remarked: "From a military standpoint, America's entrance is as nothing."[50] German naval officers persuaded the kaiser that the U-boats, now numbering about one hundred, could knock Britain out of the war in six months. Army officers, bogged down in trench warfare, hoped to end their costly immobility through a bold stroke.

On February 3 Washington severed diplomatic relations with Berlin. Wilson still did not want war with Germany, even though he had become incensed by Berlin's most recent decision. According to Lansing, Wilson became "more and more impressed with the idea that 'white civilization' and its domination over the world rested largely on our ability to keep this country intact, as we would have to build up the nations ravaged by the war."[51] Yet Wilson had also committed himself to stand firmly against unrestricted submarine warfare. Allied ships carrying war supplies soon suffered increasing losses, and the few American vessels carrying contraband stayed in port or shifted to trade outside the European war zones. Goods stacked up on wharves. The U.S. economy seemed imperiled.

Next came an apparent challenge to U.S. security. Washington had already endured espionage and sabotage by German agents, most notably the "thunderous" explosions at the Black Tom munitions factories across from the Statue of Liberty in July 1916.[52] In late February the British passed to Ambassador Page an intercepted telegram dated January 16 and sent to Mexico by German foreign minister Arthur Zimmermann. The message proposed a military alliance with the U.S.

Jeannette Rankin (1880–1973). Native of Montana, Rankin, in 1916, became the first woman to be elected to the House of Representatives. A lifelong pacifist, she voted against war in 1917, only to lose her seat the following year. In the interwar period she lobbied for peace and was again elected to Congress in 1940. Once again she refused to send American soldiers into "the foreign slaughterhouse" and cast the only vote against war in 1941. She later marched against the Vietnam War. (Library of Congress)

neighbor. And should war with the United States break out, Germany would help Mexico "reconquer" the territory lost in 1848. Zimmermann also suggested adding Japan to the alliance "at the moment war breaks out between Mexico and the United States."[53] Although the skeptical Mexican government never took up the German offer, Wilson saw the telegram as a direct challenge. "This wd [would] precipitate a war between almost any 2 nations," Page confided to his diary.[54]

Wilson now asked Congress for authority to arm American merchant vessels. On March 1, to create a favorable public opinion for the request, he released the Zimmermann telegram to the press. But antiwar senators Robert La Follette and George Norris led a filibuster—a "little group of willful men," Wilson snarled— that killed the armed ship legislation.[55] Stubbornly ignoring the Senate, Wilson ordered the arming anyway. To no avail: during March 16–18 alone U-boats sunk the American ships *City of Memphis, Illinois,* and *Vigilancia.* Buttressed by the unanimous support of his cabinet, the president decided for war.

After several intense days writing his own speech with help from Colonel House, Wilson played golf with his new wife before addressing a special joint session of Congress on the evening of April 2. He asked for a declaration of war against Germany— a war that Berlin had "thrust" on the United States. The "unmanly business" of using submarines, he asserted, constituted "warfare against mankind." Freedom of the seas, commerce, American lives, human rights—the "outlaw" U-boats challenged all. Economic self-interest, morality, and national honor compelled Americans to fight. He characterized the German government as a menacing monster striking at the "very roots of human life." The "Prussian autocracy" stirred up trouble through spies and the Zimmermann telegram. He also hailed the Russian Revolution of March, which made Russia "a fit partner for a league of honor" in a crusade against autocracy. Then came the memorable words: "The world must be made safe for democracy."[56]

Although the oration simplified issues and promised too much for American intervention, the moment required patriotic fervor. At the end, according to one historian, most listeners "were ready to grasp the Hun by the collar, feeling that surely God was on their side, and if He was not, God this one time must be wrong."[57] By votes of 82 to 6 in the Senate on April 4 (La Follette and Norris among the dissenters) and 373 to 50 in the House on April 6 (Majority Leader Claude Kitchin and nine of Wisconsin's eleven representatives among those voting nay), Congress endorsed Wilson's call for a war for peace. In a rebuke to feminist pacifism, one senator voted for war because it required "a courage both moral and physical, a mind free from trash and slush, flexed muscles and sinews that have not been debilitated, or degenerated by sensuality, security, and luxury."[58]

Submarine warfare precipitated the American decision to enter the war. Had no submarine menaced American lives, property, and the U.S. definition of international law, no American soldiers would have gone to France. Critics have argued, however, that from the German perspective, the submarine became necessary because of the long list of unfriendly American acts: acquiescence in the British blockade, part of a general pro-British bias; huge munitions shipments to the Allies; large loans; an interpretation of neutral rights that insisted that American passengers could sail anywhere, even into a war zone. Take away those acts, which the Germans considered unneutral, and they might not have launched the U-boats. To dissenters it seemed wrong that American ideals and interests could depend so perilously on armed ships carrying contraband, heading for Britain, and steaming through a war zone. Yet Wilson and his advisers had so defined the problem.

Permeating Wilson's policies was the traditional American belief that others must conform to U.S. prescriptions and that America's ideals served as a beacon for the world. "We created this Nation," the president once proclaimed, "not to serve ourselves, but to serve mankind."[59] When the Germans defied America's rules, ideals, and property, and threatened its security through a proposed alliance with Mexico, they had to be punished. Here was an opportunity to protect both humane principles and commercial interests. When Wilson spoke passionately of the right of a neutral to freedom of the seas, he demonstrated the interconnections among American moral, economic, and strategic interests. Wilson sought the role of peacemaker and promised to remake the world in the American image—that is, to create a world order in which barriers to political democracy and the Open Door came down, in which revolution and aggression no longer disturbed world order. As the philosopher John Dewey put it, war came at a "plastic juncture" in history in which Americans could fight to reshape the world according to progressive principles.[60]

The Debate over Preparedness

Berlin's assumption that American soldiers could not reach France fast enough to reverse an expected German victory proved a gross misjudgment. American military muscle and economic power, in fact, decisively tipped the balance against Germany. Given the information available in early 1917, however, the German calculation does not seem so unrealistic. In April the United States had no capacity to send a major expedition to the western front. At that date the Regular Army counted only 130,000 officers and men, backed by 180,000 national guardsmen. Although some American officers had been seasoned by military interventions in Cuba, in the Philippines, and recently in Mexico, many soldiers lacked adequate training. Arsenals had meager supplies of such modern weapons as the machine gun. The "Air Service," then part of the army, did not have a plane of modern design with a machine gun, and some warships had never fired a gun.

An American "preparedness movement" had been under way for months, encouraged by prominent Americans such as the tough-minded Rough Rider and military evangelist General Leonard Wood, who overstated the case when he argued that America's military weakness invited attack, but rang true when he noted that the United States was not recognized as a top-notch military power. After 1914, Wood, Theodore Roosevelt, the National Security League, the Army League, and the Navy League lobbied actively for bigger military appropriations with the argument that "preparedness" offered insurance against war. When the hit pacifist song "I Didn't Raise My Boy to Be a Soldier" became "an icon of popular antiwar sentiment" in 1915, preparedness proponents countered with parodies such as "I Didn't Raise My Boy to Be a Coward."[61] One propaganda film, *The Battle*

Cry of Peace (1916), in showing spike-helmeted soldiers invading America, used gendered images of "a strong manhood ready to protect vulnerable femininity."[62] In another film, *In Again, Out Again* (1917), a virile Douglas Fairbanks ridiculed "puny, pussyfooting pacifists" for "pulling the punch out of preparedness."[63]

Wilson belatedly supported moderate preparedness. He asked Congress in December 1915 for a half-billion-dollar naval expansion program, including ten battleships and one hundred submarines.[64] The president expected the United States to surpass Britain as "incomparably the greatest navy in the world."[65] Land forces would also be enlarged and reorganized.

Perpetuating the antimilitarist tradition of great numbers of Americans, Senator La Follette, Representative Kitchin, and prominent reformers such as William Jennings Bryan, Lillian Wald, and Oswald Garrison Villard spurred a movement against these measures. These peace advocates, the Women's Peace Party, and the League to Limit Armaments argued that war would interrupt reform at home, benefit big business, and curtail civil liberties. Several peace leaders also joined the auto manufacturer Henry Ford in December 1915 as he sailed to Europe on his peace ship, *Oscar II,* to establish a Neutral Conference for Continuous Mediation—a quixotic attempt to end the war and get "the boys out of the trenches by Christmas."[66] The American Union Against Militarism agitated against preparedness with its papier-mâché dinosaur, "Jingo," whose collar read "ALL ARMOR PLATE—NO BRAINS."[67] Because his support of mediation, disarmament, and a postwar association of nations appealed to antiwar liberals and socialists ("progressive internationalists"), Wilson hoped that moderate preparedness would not alienate them.[68] Chicago's famed social reformer Jane Addams remembered "moments of uneasiness," but she and others endorsed Wilson in the 1916 presidential campaign, for it seemed "at last that peace was assured and the future safe in the hands of an executive who had received an unequivocal mandate from the people 'to keep us out of war.'"[69]

In January 1916, Wilson set out on a two-month speaking tour, often criticizing members of his own party for their opposition to a military buildup. U-boat sinkings aided the president's message. In May 1916, Congress passed the National Defense Act, increasing the Regular Army to some 200,000 men and 11,000 officers, and the National Guard to 440,000 men and 17,000 officers. The act also authorized summer training camps, modeled after one held in Plattsburg, New York, in 1915 for the social and economic elite. Despite Jane Addams's query, "Why spend $45,000,000 for warships, when they will only be reduced to scrap heap after this war," the navy bill passed in August 1916.[70] Theodore Roosevelt thought the measures inadequate, but the anarchist Emma Goldman saw no difference between Roosevelt, "the born bully who uses a club," and Wilson, "the history professor who uses the smooth polished mask."[71]

Once in the war, after learning what the Allies "want and need is men, whether trained or not," Wilson relied on the Selective Service Act of May 1917.[72] National military service, proponents believed, would not only prepare the nation for battle but also instill respect for order, democracy, and sacrifice. Thus the Wilson administration transformed the army "into a potent instrument for citizenship inculca-

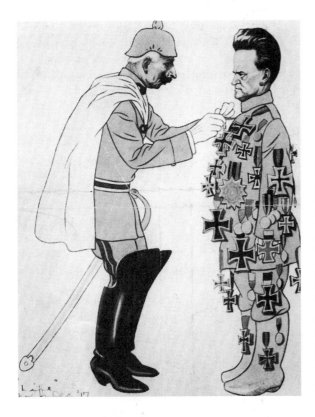

Senator Robert M. La Follette (1855–1925). This *Life* magazine cartoon depicted the antiwar, progressive reformer as a traitor. La Follette wanted a referendum on the war, certain that the American people would vote no. Some Americans thought that he should be expelled from the Senate. Others claimed that he took orders from the German kaiser, here shown pinning medals on the Wisconsin senator. La Follette withstood the intolerance of dissent and continued to speak against organized power and for the powerless, who, he said, were the people destined to do the fighting and dying abroad. (State Historical Society of Wisconsin)

tion," the historian Penn Borden has written, as "the army became sociologist, psychologist, physician, and preacher to the nation."[73] Under the selective service system, 24,340,000 men eventually registered for the draft. Some 3,764,000 men received draft notices, and 2,820,000 were inducted (the others failed preinduction tests, never showed up, or claimed conscientious objector—CO—status). Over all, 4,744,000 soldiers, sailors, and marines served. The typical serviceman was a white, single, poorly educated (most had not attended high school) draftee between twenty-one and twenty-three years of age. Officer training camps turned out "ninety-day wonders," thousands of commissioned officers drawn largely from people of elite background. Although excluded from military combat, women became navy clerks, telephone operators in the Army Signal Corps, and nurses and physical therapists to the wounded and battle-shock cases.

Right after the U.S. declaration of war, the Allies begged for soldiers. General John J. "Black Jack" Pershing, now head of the American Expeditionary Force to Europe, soon sent a "show the flag" contingent to France to boost Allied morale. Neither Wilson nor Pershing, however, would accept the European recommendation that U.S. troops be inserted in Allied units. American units would cooperate in joint maneuvers with other forces, but the U.S. Army would remain separate and independent. National pride dictated this decision, but so did the realization that

Allied commanders had for years wasted the lives of hundreds of thousands in trench warfare. Soldiers jumped out to charge German lines, also a maze of trenches. Machine guns mowed them down; chlorine gas, first used by Germany in 1915, poisoned them. Nor did Wilson wish to endorse exploitative Allied war aims. Thus did the United States call itself an "associated" rather than an "allied" power in the war.

The Doughboys Make the Difference in Europe

On July 4, 1917, General Pershing reviewed the first battalion to arrive in France, as nearly a million Parisians tossed flowers, hugged the "doughboys" (apparently so-called because their buttons resembled dumplings made of dough), and cheered wildly. Enthusiastic but ill-trained recruits, "these men couldn't even slope arms. They were even more dangerous with a loaded rifle," one company commander recalled.[74] But to the war-weary French, these fresh American troops offered inspiration.

To the dismay of American leaders, taverns and brothels quickly surrounded military camps. Alcohol and prostitution, of course, ranked as taboos in the United States during the Progressive era. "Fit to Fight" became the government's slogan, as it moved to close "red-light districts," designated "sin-free zones" around camps, and banned the sale of liquor to men in uniform. Secretary of the Navy Josephus Daniels preached that "men must live straight if they would shoot straight."[75] The YMCA and the Jewish Welfare Board sent song leaders to camps. Movies, athletic programs, and well-stocked stores sought to keep soldiers on the base by making them feel "at home."

Success against venereal disease contrasted with a major flu epidemic, which first struck camps in spring 1918. The extremely contagious flu virus cut across race, gender, and class lines. At Camp Sherman, Ohio, one of the bases hit hardest, 1,101 people died between September 27 and October 13. Whereas about 51,000 soldiers died in battle during the war, some 62,000 soldiers died from diseases. "Dough-boys" infected with the virus carried the flu with them to the European war, where it ignored national boundaries (the Germans called it *Blitzkatarrh*) and turned into a global pandemic that killed more than 21 million people by spring 1919.

Approximately 400,000 African-American troops suffered racism and discrimination during this war "to make the world safe for democracy." Camps were segregated and "white only" signs posted. In 1917 in Houston, Texas, whites provoked blacks into a riot that left seventeen whites and two blacks dead. In the army, three out of every four black soldiers served in labor units, where they wielded a shovel, not a gun, or where they cooked or unloaded supplies. African Americans endured second-class citizenship and the contradiction between America's wartime rhetoric and reality. A statistic revealed the problem: 382 black Americans were lynched in the period 1914–1920. To little effect, Germany's propagandists added a separate unit for "American race problems" to target discontented blacks in the South.[76]

IF YOU FAIL HE DIES

He may be your boy---so help him now.

All proceeds from the sale of this postal card go to the Red Cross. The sender gave his "bit" to save "HIM."

Copyright applied for

Red Cross Postcard. Women served in many roles in the war. They became workers in weapons factories. They sold Liberty Bonds and publicized government mobilization programs as members of the Women's Committee of the Council of National Defense. In France, women nurses and canteen workers became envoys of the U.S. home front, representing the mothers, wives, and sisters left behind. As the historian Susan Zeiger has written, the government's sponsorship of these wartime roles for women cleverly blunted the feminist-pacifist claim that women were "inherently more peaceful than men and would oppose war out of love for their children." (Library of Congress)

The first official American combat death in Europe came only ten days after Congress declared war—that of Edmund Charles Clinton Genet, the great-great-grandson of French Revolutionary diplomat Citizen Genet and member of the famed American volunteer air squadron, the Lafayette Escadrille. Despite Allied impatience, General Pershing hesitated to commit his green soldiers to full-scale battle. As it was, great numbers of troops shipped over in British vessels and had to borrow French weapons. Disease continued to stalk U.S. forces. American reformers hoped soldiers had enough social armor not to be tempted by "sin" overseas, but the venereal-disease rate spiraled up. French premier Georges Clemenceau offered licensed—health-inspected—prostitutes. When Secretary of War Newton Baker received the Gallic proposal, he exclaimed: "For God's sake . . . don't show this to the President or he'll stop the war."[77] Prevention programs and the threat of court-martial eventually reduced the "VD" problem.

By early 1918 the Allies had become mired in a murderous strategy of throwing ground forces directly at enemy ground forces. German troops were mauling

First Division Troops Encounter German Gas Warfare, 1918. Near Soissons, France, U.S. soldiers attacked German lines through air contaminated with poisonous gas. The soldier in the foreground, wounded by fire, tore off his gas mask. (The Bettmann Archive)

Italian forces, and the French army was still suffering from mutinies of the year before. In March, after Germany swallowed large chunks of European Russia through the Brest-Litovsk Treaty, Wilson warned of a German "empire of force" out to "dominate the world itself" and urged Americans to "arm and prepare themselves to contest the mastery of the world."[78] In April he called for "Force, Force to the utmost, Force without stint or limit."[79] U.S. soldiers soon trooped into battle.

In March the German armies, swollen by forty divisions from the Russian front, launched a great offensive. Allied forces retreated, and by late May the kaiser's soldiers encamped near the Marne River less than fifty miles from Paris. Saint-Mihiel, Belleau Wood, Cantigny, Château-Thierry—French sites where U.S. soldiers shed their blood—soon became household words for Americans. In June at Château-Thierry the doughboys dramatically stopped a German advance. From May through September 1918 more than 1 million American troops went to France—2 million by the November armistice. In mid-July the Allies launched a counteroffensive; nine American divisions fought fiercely near Château-Thierry, helping to lift the German threat from Paris. In the Meuse-Argonne offensive (begun in late September), more than 1 million American soldiers joined French and British units to penetrate the crumbling German lines. "The American infantry in the Argonne [Forest] won the war," German marshal Paul von Hindenburg later commented.[80]

On October 4, the German chancellor asked Wilson for an armistice. German troops had mutinied; revolution and riots plagued German cities; Bulgaria had left the war in September. Then Turkey dropped out in late October, and Austria-Hungary surrendered on November 3. Germany had no choice but to seek terms.

The kaiser fled to Holland. On November 11, in a railroad car in the Compiègne Forest, German representatives capitulated.

Wilson Imagines a Better Future: The Fourteen Points and the Peace Conference

During the combat, President Wilson had begun to explain his plans for the peace. He trumpeted his vision most dramatically in his "Fourteen Points" speech before Congress on January 8, 1918. The first five points promised an "open" world after the war, a world distinguished by "open covenants, openly arrived at," freedom of navigation on the seas, equal trade opportunity and the removal of tariffs, reduction of armaments, and an end to colonialism. Points six through thirteen called for self-determination for national minorities in Europe. Point fourteen stood paramount: a "general association of nations" to ensure "political independence and territorial integrity to great and small states alike."[81] His Fourteen Points signaled a generous, nonpunitive postwar settlement. Pacifists felt that they had been "sent up into the very heaven of internationalism."[82] The Fourteen Points served too as effective American propaganda against revenge-fed Allied aims and Russian Bolshevik appeals for European revolution.

Leaders in France, Britain, and Italy feared that Wilson would deny them the spoils of war. In 1915 the Allies had signed secret treaties carving up German territories, including colonies in Africa and Asia. Dreaming of imperial expansion at Germany's expense, the Allies did not appreciate the "modern St. George," as the publicist Herbert Croly depicted Wilson, or his attempts to slay the "dragons of reaction" in Europe.[83] In view of the comparative wartime losses, Europeans believed that Wilson "had bought his seat at the peace table at a discount."[84] When, in September and October 1918, Wilson exchanged notes with Germany and Austria-Hungary about an armistice, the Allied powers expressed strong reservations about the Fourteen Points. General Tasker Bliss, the U.S. representative on the Supreme War Council (established in fall 1917 to coordinate the Allied war effort), despaired that "the war will accomplish more than the abolition of *German* militarism while leaving *European* militarism as rampant as ever."[85] Wilson hinted that the United States might negotiate a separate peace with the Central Powers. The president might even publicize the exploitative Allied war aims. Also facing possible reduced American shipments to Europe, London, Paris, and Rome reluctantly accepted, in the armistice of November, peace negotiations on the basis of the Fourteen Points.

Wilson relished his opportunity. "Never . . . was the world in such plastic state," one Wilsonian adviser explained.[86] The United States could now claim a major role in deciding future international relations. The pictures of dying men dangling from barbed-wire fences and the battle-shock victims who staggered home persuaded many Americans of the need to prevent another conflagration. Wilson's call for a just peace commanded the backing of countless foreigners as well. Italians hoisted banners reading *Dio di Pace* ("God of Peace") and *Redentore dell' Humanità* ("Redeemer of Humanity") to welcome Wilson to Europe.

David Lloyd George (1863–1945). "America," said the British prime minister referring to the League of Nations, "had been offered the leadership of the world, but the Senate had tossed the sceptre into the sea." (Sketch by Anthony Saris, American Heritage Publishing Company)

The president weakened his position even before the peace conference. Congressional leaders wanted him to stay home to handle domestic problems. Lansing feared that Wilson would lose his exalted image in the day-to-day conference bickering. The president would have only one vote, whereas from Washington he could symbolically marshal the votes of humankind. Wilson retorted that distance contributes to confusion and, because "England and France have not the same views with regard to peace that we have," he had to attend personally to defend the Fourteen Points.[87]

Domestic politics soon set Wilson back. In October 1918, Wilson "hurled a brick into a beehive" by asking Americans to return a Democratic Congress loyal to him.[88] Partisan Republicans, resenting Wilson's attempt to identify himself and the Democratic party with the well-being of the nation, proceeded to capture the November election and majorities in both houses of Congress; they would sit in ultimate judgment of Wilson's peacemaking. The president also made the political mistake of not appointing either an important Republican or a senator to the American Peace Commission. Wilson, House, and Lansing sat on it; so did General Bliss and Henry White, a seasoned diplomat and nominal Republican. Some concessions to his political opposition, and to senatorial prerogatives in foreign affairs, might have smoothed the path later for his peace treaty.

On December 4, with great fanfare, Wilson departed from New York aboard the *George Washington*. He settled into a quiet voyage, surrounded by advisers and nearly 2,000 reports produced by "The Inquiry," a group of scholars who had studied issues likely to arise at the peace conference. But the administration had made few plans, and the president continued to speak in vague terms. After reaching France on December 15, Wilson basked in the admiration of enthusiastic Parisian crowds, and later thousands in Italy and England cheered him with near religious fervor. Wilson assumed that this generous outpouring meant that *his* peace plan was universally popular and that *he* had a missionary duty to carry it forward. He would soon discover that such "man-in-the-street" opinion did not impress David Lloyd George, prime minister of Britain, French premier Georges Clemenceau, or Italian prime minister Vittorio Orlando, his antagonists at the peace conference.

Germany and Bolshevik Russia (see page 98) were excluded from the conference of January–May 1919, but thirty-two nations sent delegations, which essentially followed the lead of the "Big Four." Most sessions worked in secrecy, hardly befitting Wilson's first "point." Clemenceau resented Wilson's "sermonettes" and preferred to work with the more compliant Colonel House. "The old tiger [Clemenceau] wants the grizzly bear [Wilson] back in the Rocky Mountains before he starts tearing up the German Hog," commented Lloyd George, who sought to build a strong France and to ensure German purchases of British exports.[89] A fervent Italian nationalist, Orlando concerned himself primarily with enlarging Italian territory. These leaders distrusted American power and sought bigger empires. Lloyd George complained of a chameleon-like Wilson—"the noble visionary, the implacable and unscrupulous partisan, the exalted idealist and the man of rather petty personal rancour."[90] Wilson, in turn, thought the Europeans "too weather-wise to see the weather."[91]

Wilson in Dover, England, 1919.
Wilson received flowers from English schoolchildren. British liberals subsequently voiced their bitter disillusionment. As the economist John Maynard Keynes wrote of Wilson: "He had no plan, no scheme, no constructive ideas whatever for clothing with the flesh of life the commandments which he had thundered from the White House. He could have preached a sermon on any of them or have addressed a stately prayer to the Almighty for their fulfillment, but he could not frame their concrete application when it came [time to act]." (U.S. Signal Corps, National Archives)

Much wrangling occurred over the disposition of colonies and the creation of new countries. Wilson had appealed for self-determination, but the belligerents had already signed secret treaties of conquest. After hard negotiating, the conferees mandated former German and Turkish colonies to the countries that had conquered them, to be loosely supervised under League of Nations auspices. Under the mandate system—a compromise between outright annexation and complete independence—France (with Syria and Lebanon) and Britain (with Iraq, Trans-Jordan, and Palestine) received parts of the Middle East. Japan acquired China's Shandong Province and some of Germany's Pacific islands. After Wilson's reluctant acceptance of the Shandong arrangement, the president lamented that it "was the best that could be had out of a dirty past."[92] Outraged Chinese students in Beijing protested by launching the May Fourth Movement, an increasingly important anti-imperialist voice. France gained the demilitarization of the German Rhineland and a stake in the coal-rich Saar Basin. Italy annexed South Tyrol and Trieste from the collapsed Austro-Hungarian Empire. Some 1,132,000 square miles changed hands. Newly independent countries also emerged from the defunct Austro-Hungarian Empire: Austria, Czechoslovakia, Hungary, Romania, and Yugoslavia. The Allies further exploited nationalism to recognize a ring of hostile states already established around Bolshevik Russia: Finland, Poland, Estonia, Latvia, and Lithuania, all formerly part of the Russian empire (see map on page 93). The mandate system smacked of imperialism, in violation of the Fourteen Points, but the new states in

Europe fulfilled Wilson's self-determination pledge. To assuage French fears of a revived Germany, Britain and the United States signed a security pact with France guaranteeing its border, but Wilson never submitted it for Senate approval.

Reparations proved a knotty issue. The United States wanted a limited indemnity for Germany to avoid a harsh peace that might arouse long-term German resentment or debilitate the German economy and politics. "Our greatest error," Wilson predicted in March 1919, "would be to give her [Germany] powerful reasons for wishing one day to take revenge. Excessive demands would most certainly sow the seeds of war."[93] To cripple Germany, France pushed for a large bill of reparations. The conferees wrote a "war guilt clause," which held Germany responsible for all of the war's damages. Rationalizing that the League would ameliorate any excesses, Wilson gave in on both reparations and war guilt. The Reparations Commission in 1921 presented a hobbled Germany with a huge reparations bill of $33 billion, thereby destablizing international economic relations for more than a decade.

Wilson's primary concern, unlike that of the other participants, was the League of Nations. Drafted largely by Wilson, the League's covenant provided for an influential council of five big powers (permanent) and representatives from smaller nations (by election) and an assembly of all nations for discussion. Wilson saw the heart of the covenant as Article 10, a provision designed to curb aggression and war: "The Members of the League undertake to respect and preserve as against external aggression the territorial integrity and existing political independence of all Members of the League." In case of aggression or threat, "the Council shall advise upon the means by which this obligation shall be fulfilled."[94] Wilson persuaded the conferees to merge the League covenant and the peace terms in a package. The League charter, then, constituted the first 26 articles of a 440-article Treaty of Paris. Wilson deemed the League covenant the noblest part of all—"It is practical, and yet it is intended to purify, to rectify, to elevate."[95]

The Germans signed sullenly on June 28 in the elegant Hall of Mirrors at Versailles. By stripping Germany of 13 percent of its territory, 10 percent of its population, and all of its colonies, and by demanding reparations, the treaty humiliated the Germans without crushing them. In the historian Antony Lentin's words, the treaty contained "a witches' brew" with "too little Wilsonianism to appease, too little of Clemenceau to deter; enough of Wilson to provoke contempt, enough of Clemenceau to inspire hatred."[96] When Wilson died on February 3, 1924, the Weimar Republic in Berlin refrained from issuing an official condolence, and the German Embassy in Washington broke custom by not lowering its flag to half-mast.

Principle, Personality, Health, and Partisanship: The League Fight

Wilson spent almost six months in Europe negotiating the postwar peace. From February 24 to March 14, 1919, he returned to the United States for executive business. On arrival, he vowed not to let "minds that have no sweep beyond the nearest horizon" reject the American purpose of making people free. "I have fight-

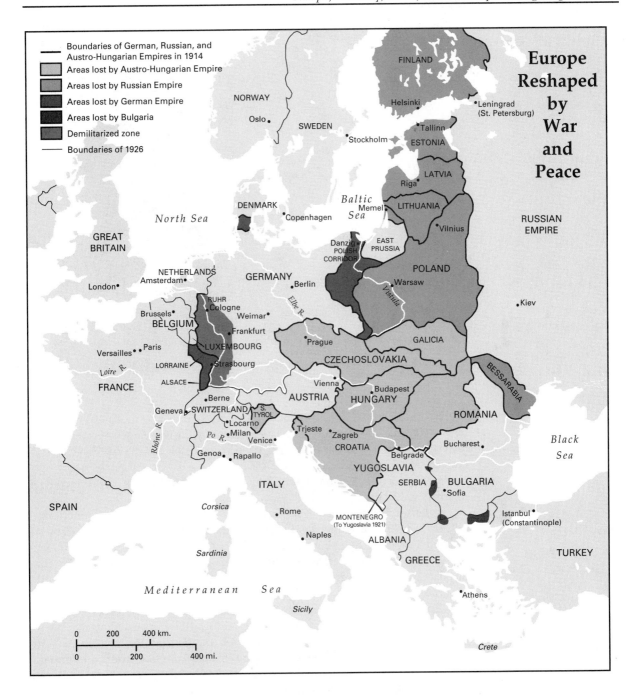

Europe Reshaped by War and Peace

Boundaries of German, Russian, and Austro-Hungarian Empires in 1914
Areas lost by Austro-Hungarian Empire
Areas lost by Russian Empire
Areas lost by German Empire
Areas lost by Bulgaria
Demilitarized zone
Boundaries of 1926

ing blood in me," he asserted.[97] In Washington, Republicans peppered Wilson with questions about the degree to which the covenant limited American sovereignty. When Wilson spoke vaguely, Senator Frank Brandegee of Connecticut felt as if he had been "wandering with Alice in Wonderland and had tea with the Mad

Georges Clemenceau (1841–1929). Auguste Rodin's bronze aptly conveys the formidable stature of "The Tiger" from France, eager for revenge against Germany. (The Rodin Museum, Philadelphia)

Hatter."[98] In early March, Republican senator Henry Cabot Lodge of Massachusetts engineered a "Round Robin," a statement by thirty-nine senators (enough to deny the treaty a two-thirds vote) that questioned the League covenant and requested that the peace treaty and the covenant be acted on separately. Many signers feared that the League would limit U.S. freedom to act independently in international affairs.

A defiant Wilson sailed again for France, determined that "little Americans," full of "watchful jealousies [and] of rabid antagonisms," would not destroy his beloved League.[99] Still, he was politician enough, and stung enough, to seek changes in Paris. He amended the covenant so that League members could refuse mandates, League jurisdiction over purely domestic issues was precluded, and the Monroe Doctrine was safeguarded against League interference. But he would not alter Article 10. When he returned to the United States in July, Wilson submitted the long Treaty of Versailles to the Senate on July 10, with an address that resembled an evangelical sermon: "The stage is set, the destiny disclosed. It has come about by no plan of our conceiving, but by the hand of God, who led us into this way."[100] Asked if he would accept senatorial "reservations" to the treaty, Wilson snapped: "I shall consent to nothing. The Senate must take its medicine."[101]

Wilson, against strong odds, gained a good percentage of his goals as outlined in the Fourteen Points. Self-determination for nationalities advanced as never before in Europe, and the League ranked as a notable achievement. But Wilson did compromise, especially when faced by formidable opposition such as that thrown up by Clemenceau. During the conference, too, both Italy and Japan had threatened to walk out unless they realized some territorial goals. Still, Wilson had so built up a case for an unselfish peace that when the conquerors' hard bargaining and harsh terms dominated the conference, observers could only conclude that the president had failed badly to live up to his millennial rhetoric. "How in our consciences are we to square the results with the promises?" asked the journalist Walter Lippmann.[102] Some critics said that Wilson should have left Paris in protest, refusing to sign, or that he should have threatened the European powers with U.S. economic power by curbing postwar loans and trade. Believing desperately that the League, with Article 10, would rectify all, Wilson instead had accepted embarrassing compromises.

He would not compromise at home, however. And he seldom provided systematic, technical analysis to treaty clauses. He simply expected the Senate dutifully to ratify his masterwork. Yet his earlier bypassing of that body and his own partisan speeches and self-righteousness ensured debate with influential critics. Progressive internationalists protested that "the capitalists wanted the League as a superstate to protect their exploitative concessions in underdeveloped countries."[103] Conservative senator Henry Cabot Lodge asked a key question: "Are you willing to put your soldiers and your sailors at the disposition of other nations?"[104] Senator James Reed of Missouri feared racial peril from a League initially comprising fifteen white nations and seventeen nations of "black, brown, yellow, and red races," which, he claimed, ranked low in "civilization" and high in "barbarism."[105]

Article 10 seemed to rattle everybody. The article did not require members to use force, but it implied they should. Senator William Borah complained that "I may be willing to help my neighbor . . . , but I do not want him . . . [to] decide for me when and how I shall act or to what extent I shall make sacrifice."[106] Because Article 10 seemed to freeze the status quo against colonial rebellion, one Irish-American editor wrote: "Were a League of Nations in existence in the days when George Washington fought and won, . . . we would still be an English colony."[107] The article seemed too open-ended. Yet Wilson argued that without such a commitment to halt warmakers the League would become feeble. "In effect," the historian Roland N. Stromberg has noted, "Wilson and the Democrats wanted to accept an obligation that we might thereafter refuse, while Lodge and the Republicans wanted to refuse an obligation we might thereafter accept."[108]

Henry Cabot Lodge towered as Wilson's chief legislative obstacle. Chair of the Senate Foreign Relations Committee, nationalist-imperialist, author, Republican partisan, like Wilson a scholar in politics, Lodge packed his committee with anti-League senators, dragged out hearings for weeks, kept most Republicans together on treaty votes, and nurtured a personal animosity toward Wilson matched only by Wilson's detestation for Lodge. Whether or not Lodge sought to kill the League in infancy, he attacked obliquely. He proposed "reservations" to the League covenant. Although in retrospect these reservations, intended to guard American sovereignty, do not appear to have been death blows to the League, at the time they stirred impassioned debate. They addressed the central question of American national interest—the degree to which the United States would limit its freedom of action, the degree to which the United States should engage in collective security. In fact, many of the fourteen reservations stated the obvious—that Congress would retain its constitutional role in foreign policy, for example. Others excluded the Monroe

Henry Cabot Lodge (1850–1924). Wilson's partisan rival complained that the president's speeches in Europe "are all in the clouds and fine sentiments that lead nowhere." As for the League covenant, Lodge ridiculed its scholarship. "It might get by at Princeton," Wilson's alma mater, "but certainly not at Harvard," where the senator had earned a Ph.D. in history. (Library of Congress)

Woodrow Wilson After His Stroke. Recent scholarly assessments of medical evidence reveal that Wilson had a long history of cerebrovascular disease. Wilson remained in the White House after his massive stroke in October 1919, while his wife and doctor tried to keep secret the severity of his physical incapacity. Dr. Edwin A. Weinstein, who has studied the relationship among Wilson's health, personality, and decision-making, has noted that the president could not maintain his train of thought and was prone to bursts of temper. (Library of Congress)

Doctrine from League oversight more explicitly than the covenant's version and denied the League jurisdiction over American domestic legislation such as immigration laws. The reservation that qualified Article 10 disclaimed any obligation to preserve the territorial integrity or political independence of another country unless authorized by Congress.

The Senate divided into four groups. Wilson counted on about forty loyal Democrats called the Non-Reservationists. Another group, the Mild-Reservationists, led by Frank B. Kellogg, numbered about thirteen Republicans. The third faction, managed by Lodge, stood together as the Strong-Reservationists—some twenty Republicans and a few Democrats. The fourth group, consisting of sixteen Irreconcilables, ardently opposed the treaty with or without reservations. Most of them were Republicans, including La Follette, George Norris of Nebraska, and Hiram Johnson of California.

Wilson met individually with some twenty-three senators over two weeks, but he suffered a minor stroke on July 19, 1919. He thereafter rigidly refused to accept any reservations. He argued that a treaty ratified with reservations would have to go back to another conference for acceptance and every nation would then rush in with its pet reservations. This argument seemed hollow after the British announced that they would accept American reservations. In September 1919, Wilson set off on a 10,000-mile train trip across the United States. Growing more exhausted with each day, suffering severe headaches and nighttime coughing spells, and showing signs of what the medical historian Bert E. Park has diagnosed as "dementia" from hypertension and cerebrovascular disease, Wilson pounded the podium in forty speeches.[109] He took the offensive, blasting his traducers as "absolute, contemptible quitters."[110] Comparing critics to radical Bolsheviks, he denounced Irish- and German-American opponents—"hyphens are the knives that are being stuck" into the treaty, he asserted.[111] He confused his audiences when he stated that Article 10 meant that the United States had a moral but not legal obligation to use armed force. But he also highlighted often neglected features of the covenant—for example, provisions for the arbitration of disputes and for an international labor conference to abolish child labor and install the eight-hour workday. On September 26, after an impassioned speech in Pueblo, Colorado, he awoke to nausea and uncontrollable facial twitching. "I just feel as if I am going to pieces," he said.[112] When his doctor ordered him to cancel the rest of his trip, Wilson wept.

After Wilson returned to Washington, a massive stroke paralyzed his left side. He lay flat in bed for six weeks and saw virtually no one except his wife and Dr. Cary Grayson. "The government," in the historian Arthur Walworth's terse phrase, "like its president, was paralyzed."[113] For months Mrs. Wilson ran her husband's political affairs, screening messages and banishing House and Lansing, among others, from presidential favor. If the president had resigned, as Dr. Grayson advised him to do, the Senate and Vice President James Marshall almost certainly would have reached some compromise agreement on admission to the League with reservations. As it was, his concentration hampered and his stubbornness accentuated by the stroke, Wilson adamantly refused to change his all-or-nothing position.

In November 1919, the Senate balloted on the complete treaty *with* reservations and rejected it, 39 to 55 (Irreconcilables and Non-Reservationists in the negative). Then it voted on the treaty *without* reservations and also rejected it, 38 to 53

(Irreconcilables and Reservationists in the negative). The president had instructed loyal Democrats not to accept any "reserved" treaty. In March 1920, another tally saw some Democrats vote in favor of reservations. Still not enough, the treaty failed, 49 to 35, short of the two-thirds majority required for approval. "It is dead," Wilson lamented to his cabinet. "Every morning I put flowers on its grave."[114] "We have torn up Wilsonianism by the roots," boasted Senator Lodge.[115] Still a fighter, the president claimed that the election of 1920 would be a "solemn referendum" on the treaty. Other questions actually blurred the League issue in that campaign, and Warren G. Harding, who as a senator had supported reservations, promptly condemned the League after his election as president. In July 1921, Congress officially terminated the war, and in August, by treaty with Germany, the United States claimed as valid for itself the terms of the Treaty of Versailles— exclusive of the League articles.

The memorable League fight had ended. The tragic denouement occurred because of political partisanship, personal animosities, senatorial resentments, the president's failing health, adherence to traditional unilateralism, and disinterest and confusion in the public, which increasingly diverted its attention to readjusting to a peacetime economy. Progressive internationalists, many of them harassed by wartime restrictions on civil liberties and disappointed by Wilson's compromises with the imperial powers, no longer backed a president they thought reactionary. "THIS IS NOT PEACE," shouted a headline in *The New Republic*.[116] Then, of course, there was Wilson himself—stubborn, pontificating, combative, and increasingly ill. But for the "marked and almost grotesque accentuation" of personality traits resulting from Wilson's cerebrovascular disease, he might have conceded that the peace had imperfections.[117] He might have provided more careful analysis of a long, complicated document. He might have remembered when he first learned of the secret treaties. He might, further, have admitted that his opponents held a respectable intellectual position. Instead, he chose often shrill rhetoric and rigid self-righteousness. Most important, he saw the difference between himself and his critics as fundamental: whether it was in America's national interest to participate in collective security or seek safety unilaterally. Traditional American nationalism and nonalignment, or unilateralism, helped decide the debate against Wilson.

Although the League came into being without the United States as a member, none of the great powers wished to bestow significant authority on the new organization. Even if Washington had joined, it most likely would have acted outside the League's auspices, especially regarding its own empire in Latin America. No international association at that time could have outlawed war, dismantled empires, or scuttled navies. Wilson overshot reality in thinking that he could reform world politics through a new international body. Certainly the League represented a commendable restraint against war, but hardly a panacea for world peace.

Red Scare Abroad: Bolshevism and Intervention in Russia

"Paris cannot be understood without Moscow [Russia]," wrote Wilson's press secretary Ray Stannard Baker.[118] Indeed, throughout the Versailles conference, "[V. I.]

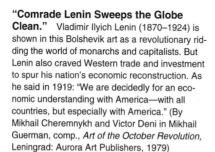

"Comrade Lenin Sweeps the Globe Clean." Vladimir Ilyich Lenin (1870–1924) is shown in this Bolshevik art as a revolutionary ridding the world of monarchs and capitalists. But Lenin also craved Western trade and investment to spur his nation's economic reconstruction. As he said in 1919: "We are decidedly for an economic understanding with America—with all countries, but especially with America." (By Mikhail Cheremnykh and Victor Deni in Mikhail Guerman, comp., *Art of the October Revolution*, Leningrad: Aurora Art Publishers, 1979)

Lenin looms always on the horizon to the East."[119] As he traveled to France aboard the *George Washington,* President Wilson depicted Bolshevism as "the poison of disorder, the poison of revolt, the poison of chaos."[120] Revolutionary and anticapitalist, the Bolsheviks, or Communists, threw fright into the leaders of Europe and America. At home and abroad the peacemakers battled the radical left. In the United States the Wilson administration trampled on civil liberties during an exaggerated "Red Scare," which sent innocent people to jail or deported them. The fluidity of events abroad, however, and the multiplicity of American views led to a range of policy options—from recognizing and taming the Bolsheviks to overthrowing them. Wilson himself seemed to think that "the only way to kill Bolshevism is . . . to open all the doors to commerce."[121] Only belatedly, after authorizing secret aid and espionage against the "Reds," did the president openly "cast in his lot" with the other powers in a futile attempt to destroy the new revolutionary regime.[122]

Most Americans applauded the Russian Revolution of March 1917, which toppled Tsar Nicholas II. Wilson himself viewed it as a thrust against autocracy, war, and imperialism. But when the moderate Provisional government under Alexander Kerensky fell to the radical Bolsheviks in October, Americans responded first with irritation and then anger in March 1918 when the Bolsheviks signed the Brest-Litovsk Treaty with Germany and ceded Ukraine and Finland, among other territories—a total of 1,267,000 square miles, 62,000,000 people, and one-third of Russia's best agricultural land. A necessary peace for a devastated Russia from the Bolshevik perspective, the treaty seemed a stab in the back for the Allies, a decisive victory for Berlin. Because German authorities had allowed Lenin to travel to Russia via Germany in 1917, some irate American officials even considered Bolsheviks pro-German. Others recoiled after Ambassador David Francis's testimony that Bolsheviks had "nationalized women."[123]

Lenin actually treated the United States as a special, favored case, and he consistently sought accommodation with Washington. Described by the Red Cross official Raymond Robins as "heavy set, deliberate, always cool . . . , steadfast, patient, utterly courageous, fanatical and confident," Lenin (and other Soviet officials) held a series of cordial conversations from December 1917 to May 1918 with Robins, a de facto U.S. representative.[124] They reached agreements on food relief, purchase of strategic materials, and exemption of American corporations from Bolshevik nationalization decrees. Prior to Brest-Litovsk, Robins urged prompt recognition of the Bolshevik government to keep Russia in the war, but President Wilson paid more heed to Francis's prediction that the Bolshevik regime would soon collapse.

Although American officials in Russia engaged in propaganda and espionage, and cooperated with Allied and "White" agents in anti-Bolshevik activities after November 1917, Wilson knew only broad outlines of this "secret war" when he sent U.S. troops to Archangel in northern Russia in August 1918. Ordered to avoid military action in the Russian civil war, they inevitably cooperated with British and French forces in attempts to roll back Bolshevik influence. Wilson said publicly that he authorized the expedition only to prevent German seizure of military supplies and a railroad, but he had already authorized $50 million in secret payments to White armies fighting the Bolsheviks. Wilson's motives, according to the historian Robert Foglesong, were "simultaneously anti-German and anti-Bolshevik."[125] Some 5,000 American troops eventually participated. They suffered through a bitter winter of fifty-below-zero temperatures. Their morale sagged; mutiny threatened. In December 1918, Senator Hiram Johnson of California introduced a resolution to withdraw American troops from Russia. It failed by one vote. U.S. soldiers did not leave Russia until June 1919. Two hundred twenty-two American soldiers died on Russian soil.

Wilson always said that he "hoped to avoid intervention, even the appearance of intervening in Russian affairs," preferring to draw the Bolsheviks peacefully into a new world order.[126] But pressure from the deeply anticommunist French and British and expansionist Japanese and his own anti-Bolshevism inclined him to send another expedition, this time to Siberia, where many envisioned the growth of a non-Bolshevik Russian bastion. In July he approved the expedition, later officially explaining to the American people that he was sending the troops (eventually numbering 10,000) to rescue a group of 70,000 Czechs stranded in Russia. Organized earlier as part of the Tsarist Russian army to fight for a Czech homeland in Austria-Hungary, the Czech legion in 1918 was battling Bolsheviks along the Trans-Siberian Railroad in an effort to reach Vladivostok and possible transportation to the western front. Wilson's avowed purpose of evacuating the Czech legion derived also from

A. Mitchell Palmer (1872–1936). When U.S. troops were intervening in Bolshevik Russia, Wilson's attorney general, A. Mitchell Palmer, was chasing suspected radicals at home. An architect of the "Red Scare," Palmer believed that the "blaze of revolution" was "eating its way into the homes of the American workmen, its sharp tongues of revolutionary heat . . . licking the altars of the churches, leaping into the belfry of the school bell, crawling into the sacred corners of American homes, burning up the foundations of society." In January 1920, the "Palmer Raids" put 4,000 people in jail. (Library of Congress)

his "friendly feelings" for Professor Thomas Masaryk and Czechoslovakia's independence, which Wilson soon recognized in October.[127]

Despite his disingenuous official explanation, Wilson believed, as one scholar has put it, that "a limited, indirect intervention to help the Russian people overcome domination by Bolsheviks and Germans would not contradict, but rather facilitate self-determination."[128] Yet intervention in Siberia became openly anti-Bolshevik because the Czechs were fighting Lenin's forces. Once Wilson found it impossible to evacuate the Czechs in time to fight in Europe, he reluctantly bowed to Allied pressure and gave support to the anti-Bolshevik White Russian leader Admiral A. V. Kolchak in the hope that he could form a pro-Western constitutional government. Despite money and supplies from the Allies, Kolchak faltered and his armies were routed before they could reach Moscow in June 1919. American troops in Siberia finally withdrew in early 1920 after thirty-six deaths.

At the Paris peace conference, the victors tried to isolate what they considered revolutionary contagion. The organization of the Third International in Moscow in early 1919 alarmed postwar leaders, as did communist Bela Kun's successful revolution in Hungary in March 1919, which lasted only until August. At Versailles, the conferees granted territory to Russia's neighbors (Poland, Romania, and Czechoslovakia) and recognized the nations of Finland, Estonia, Latvia, and Lithuania as a ring of unfriendly states around Russia. During the conference, besides the military interventions, the Allies imposed a strict economic blockade on Russia, sent aid to the White forces, and extended relief assistance to Austria and Hungary to stem political unrest.

Even though Wilson found the Soviets distasteful for their revolutionary, anticapitalist, anticlerical, authoritarian program, he never settled on a definitive, workable policy to co-opt or smash Bolshevism. Through "a reluctant, chaotic, and capricious process," the president allowed subordinates and circumstances to determine U.S. policy toward Russia.[129] His growing estrangement at Versailles from Colonel House, a conduit for pro-Soviet liberals, meant that the interventionist Allies and the rabidly anti-Bolshevik Secretary Lansing exerted greater influence.

Wilson's one serious effort to end the civil war in Russia through diplomacy came in January 1919 when he invited the warring groups to meet on Prinkipo (Prince's) Island in the Sea of Marmara off the Turkish coast. The Bolsheviks cautiously accepted the invitation, but the anti-Bolsheviks rejected any meeting. Next, in February, House helped arrange a trip by William C. Bullitt, a member of the U.S. delegation at Versailles, and Lincoln Steffens, the radical muckraking journalist, to Russia. Wilson envisioned a fact-finding mission. The ambitious Bullitt, however, negotiated a proposal whereby the Allies would withdraw their troops, suspend military aid to the White forces, and lift the economic blockade. If the Allies accepted these terms, the Soviet government promised to initiate a ceasefire in the civil war and permit its opponents to hold the territories they occupied. Bullitt and Steffens returned to Paris convinced that their agreement would satisfy all parties. Lloyd George squelched it; Wilson ignored it. Bullitt, already disgusted by Wilson's compromises with the Allies at Paris, resigned in protest.

The Allied counterrevolution proved costly. "It intensified the civil war and sent thousands of Russians to their deaths," the British official Bruce Lockhart later wrote. "Its direct effect was to provide the Bolsheviks with a cheap victory, . . .

and to galvanize them into a strong and ruthless organism."[130] Although the Bolshevik emissary Ludwig Martens laid the foundations for future Soviet-American trade during the height of the Red Scare, Kremlin leaders nurtured long memories. "Never have any of our soldiers been on American soil," Premier Nikita S. Khrushchev lectured Americans as late as 1959, "but your soldiers were on Russian soil."[131] Participation by such young men as Allen and John Foster Dulles in Wilson's "secret war" against the Bolsheviks provided "the formative experiences that inclined [them] to rely on propaganda and covert action" when they later directed U.S. policies during the Cold War.[132] Such tactics ultimately backfired, as Wilson recognized before his death. "Bolshevism is a mistake," Wilson said. "If left alone it will destroy itself. It cannot survive because it is wrong."[133]

The Whispering Gallery of Global Disorder

More than 116,000 American soldiers died in World War I, and the conflict cost the U.S. government more than $30 billion. A third of the figure was paid through taxes; the other two-thirds represented borrowed money, which postwar generations would have to pay back. If one counts the long-term expense of veterans' benefits, the cost to the United States probably equaled three times the immediate direct costs. What President Dwight D. Eisenhower would later call the "military-industrial complex" had its origins in a high degree of government-business cooperation during that war; economic decisionmaking for the nation became centralized as never before; and the increased application of efficient methods in manufacturing contributed to American economic power.[134] The era of World War I witnessed other domestic events that impinged on foreign affairs: racial conflict, evidenced by twenty-five race riots in 1919; suppression of civil liberties under the Espionage and Sedition Acts, by which people who dissented from the war were silenced; the stunting of radical commentary (Socialist leader Eugene Debs and the pacifist Alice Paul, among others, went to jail for opposing the war) and hence the imposition of coercive consensus; and the emasculation of the reform impulse. Although Wilson tried to co-opt dissent by appointing labor leaders such as Samuel Gompers to war mobilization agencies, the historian Beth McKillen has argued that the negative response to the League of Nations among immigrants and industrial workers indicated "a revolt against corporatist wartime institutions."[135]

In foreign affairs, the White House assumed more authority in initiating policy and controlling execution. The State Department read diplomatic messages that Wilson had typed on his own machine. Wilson bypassed Congress on a number of occasions, failing to consult that body about the Fourteen Points, the goals at Versailles, and the intervention in Russia. He acted, according to his biographer Arthur S. Link, "like a divine-right monarch in the conduct of foreign relations."[136] The Senate finally rebelled by rejecting the League of Nations, but that negative decision did not reverse the trend of growing presidential power over foreign policy.

World War I took the lives of some 14,663,400 people—8 million soldiers and 6.6 million civilians (flu pandemic victims not included). Russia led with 3.7 million dead; Germany followed with 2.6 million; then came France with 1.4 million, Austria-Hungary with 950,000, and Britain with 939,000. One out of every two

"We Are Making a New World." The British painter Paul Nash rendered this gloomy commentary on the devastation wrought by World War I. (Imperial War Museum, London)

French males between the ages of twenty and thirty-two (in 1914) died during the war. It had been a total war, involving whole societies, not merely their armies. Never before had a war left the belligerents so exhausted, so battered. New destructive weapons made their debut—tanks, airplanes, poison gas, the Big Bertha gun, and submarines—"a preview of the Pandora's box of evils that the linkage of science with industry in the service of war was to mean."[137] The war reinforced American desires to avoid foreign entanglement. Captain Harry S. Truman of Battery D of the 129th Field Artillery Regiment claimed that most soldiers "don't give a whoop (to put it mildly) whether Russia has a Red Government or no government and if the King of the Lollipops wants to slaughter his subjects or his Prime Minister it's all the same to us."[138] Disillusioned intellectuals such as Ernest Hemingway and John Dos Passos mocked the carthaginian peace. E. M. Remarque's *All Quiet on the Western Front* (1929) captured the antiwar mood: "A hospital alone shows what war is."[139]

World War I stacked the cards for the future by bequeathing an unstable international system. Empires broke up—the Turkish, Austro-Hungarian, German, and Russian—creating new and weak nations. The Europe-oriented international order of the turn of the century fragmented and left, in Thomas Masaryk's words, "a laboratory atop a vast cemetery" that included several new states in central and eastern Europe.[140] Nationalists in Asia, such as Mahatma Gandhi in British-dominated India and Ho Chi Minh in French-controlled Indochina, set goals of national liberation based in part on Wilson's ideal of self-determination. "Wilson's proposals, once set forth, could not be recalled," said Sun Zhongshan (Sun Yat-Sen) in 1924 as his China battled imperialist domination.[141] In Latin America, prewar European economic ties withered, inviting the United States to expand its interests there, where nationalists resented the greater North American presence. The rise of Bolshevism in Russia and the hostility it aroused around the world made an already fluid international system even more so. Because of fear of a revived Germany, leaders tried to strip it of power, creating bitter resentments among the German people. Facing reconstruction problems at home, the victors tagged Germany with a huge reparations bill that would disorient the world economy. Nobody seemed happy with the postwar settlement; many would attempt to recapture lost opportunities or to redefine the terms. The high-minded lessons Wilson sought to teach went unlearned. World War I had, surely, created as many problems as it had solved.

During World War I the United States became the world's leading economic power. As Wilson confidently put it: "The financial leadership will be ours. The industrial primacy will be ours. The commercial advantage will be ours."[142] During the war years, to meet the need for raw materials, American companies expanded operations in developing nations. Goodyear went into the Dutch East Indies for rubber, Swift and Armour reached into South America, tin interests tapped Bolivia, copper companies penetrated Chile, and oil firms sank new wells in Latin America and gained new concessions in the Middle East. Washington encouraged this economic expansion by building up the merchant marine, which by 1919 had grown 60 percent larger than its prewar size. By 1920, the United States produced about 40 percent of the world's coal and 50 percent of its pig iron.

Because the U.S. government and American citizens loaned heavily to the Allies during the war, the nation shifted from a debtor to a creditor, with Wall Street replacing London as the world's financial center. Whereas before the war Americans owed foreigners some $3 billion, after the conflict foreigners owed Americans and the U.S. government about $13 billion ($10 billion of this figure represented governments' debts). Americans had devised plans to seize the apparent economic opportunities given them by the war—the Edge Act to permit foreign branch banks, and the Webb-Pomerene Act to allow trade associations to continue to combine for export trading without fear of antitrust action, for example—but a key question remained: How could Europeans pay back their debt to the United States? The answer lay somewhere in a complicated tangle of loans, reparations, tariffs, and world trade. "We are on the eve of a commercial war of the severest sort," predicted Wilson in early 1920.[143]

Economic disorder and political instability thus became the twin legacies of global war. "The world is all now one single whispering gallery," Wilson asserted in September 1919. "All the impulses . . . reach to the ends of the earth; . . . with the tongue of the wireless and the tongue of the telegraph, all the suggestions of disorder are spread." More than most Americans, Woodrow Wilson understood that global interdependence exposed America to the "disorder and discontent and dissolution throughout the world."[144]

FURTHER READING FOR THE PERIOD 1914–1920

Many of the works listed in the last chapter also explore the themes, events, and personalities in the era of World War I. See also John W. Chambers, *The Tyranny of Change* (1992); Paul Fussell, *The Great War and Modern Memory* (1975); Ellis W. Hawley, *The Great War and the Search for a Modern Order* (1992); Clayton D.

James and Anne Sharp Wells, *America and the Great War* (1998); Bernadotte E. Schmitt and Harold C. Vedeler, *The World in the Crucible, 1914–1919* (1984); Tony Smith, *America's Mission* (1994); David Stevenson, *The First World War and International Politics* (1988); and Spencer C. Tucker, *The Great War* (1998).

For Woodrow Wilson and his foreign-policy views, consult Edward H. Buehrig, ed., *Wilson's Foreign Policy in Perspective* (1957); Kendrick A. Clements, *The Presidency of Woodrow Wilson* (1990) and *Woodrow Wilson* (1987); John Milton Cooper, Jr., *The Warrior and the Priest* (1983); Thomas J. Knock, *To End All Wars* (1992); Arthur S. Link, *Wilson* (1960–1965) and *Woodrow Wilson: Revolution, War, and Peace* (1979); Frank Ninkovich, *The Wilsonian Century* (1999); and Jan Willem Schulte Nordholt, *Woodrow Wilson* (1991).

Wilson's health problems and their relationship to decisionmaking are examined in Robert H. Ferrell, *Ill-Advised* (1992), and Edwin A. Weinstein, *Woodrow Wilson: A Medical and Psychological Biography* (1981). See also the essays by Dr. Bert E. Park in volumes of Arthur S. Link et al., eds., *The Papers of Woodrow Wilson*, and Park's *Ailing, Aging, and Addicted* (1993) and *The Impact of Illness on World Leaders* (1986).

Central actors in the period's drama are presented in LeRoy Ashby, *William Jennings Bryan* (1987); Kendrick A. Clements, *William Jennings Bryan* (1982); Paolo Coletta, *William Jennings Bryan* (1956–1969); John Milton Cooper, Jr., *Walter Hines Page* (1977); Ross Gregory, *Walter Hines Page* (1970); George H. Nash, *The Life of Herbert Hoover* (1996); Daniel M. Smith, *Robert Lansing and American Neutrality* (1958); Donald Smythe, *Pershing* (1986); Ronald Steel, *Walter Lippmann and the American Century* (1981); David P. Thelen, *Robert M. La Follette and the Insurgent Spirit* (1976); and William C. Widenor, *Henry Cabot Lodge and the Search for an American Foreign Policy* (1980).

For European questions and the neutrality issue on the U.S. road to World War I, see Thomas A. Bailey and Paul B. Ryan, *The Lusitania Disaster* (1975); Henry Blumenthal, *Illusion and Reality in Franco-American Diplomacy, 1914–1945* (1986); John W. Coogan, *The End of Neutrality* (1981); Patrick Devlin, *Too Proud to Fight* (1975); David M. Esposito, *The Legacy of Woodrow Wilson: American War Aims in World War I* (1996); Robert H. Ferrell, *Woodrow Wilson and World War I* (1985); Ross Gregory, *The Origins of American Intervention in the First World War* (1971); and Ernest R. May, *The World War and American Isolation, 1914–1917* (1959).

The German-American relationship is spotlighted in Reinhard R. Doerries, *Imperial Challenge* (1989); Manfred Jonas, *The United States and Germany* (1984); Hans-Jürgen Schröder, ed., *Confrontation and Cooperation* (1993); and Barbara Tuchman, *The Zimmermann Telegram* (1958).

The Anglo-American relationship is featured in Kathleen Burk, *Britain, America, and the Sinews of War, 1914–1918* (1985); G. R. Conyne, *Woodrow Wilson: British Perspectives, 1912–21* (1992); and Joyce G. Williams, *Colonel House and Sir Edward Grey* (1984).

For the peace movement, see works cited in the previous chapter and Charles DeBenedetti, ed., *Peace Heroes in Twentieth-Century America* (1986); Allen F. Davis, *American Heroine* (1974) (Addams); Barbara S. Kraft, *The Peace Ship* (1978); Erika A. Kuhlman, *Petticoats and White Feathers* (1997); and Ernest A. McKay, *Against Wilson and War* (1996).

America's preparedness and warmaking experiences are discussed in John W. Chambers, *To Raise an Army* (1987); J. Garry Clifford, *The Citizen Soldiers* (1972); Edward M. Coffman, *The War to End All Wars* (1968); Henry A. DeWeerd, *President Wilson Fights His War* (1968); Kenneth J. Hagan, *This People's Navy* (1991); Thomas C. Leonard, *Above the Battle* (1978); Bullitt Lowry, *Armistice, 1918* (1997); David F. Trask, *The AEF and Coalition Warmaking* (1993), *Captains & Cabinets: Anglo-American Naval Relations, 1917–1918* (1980), and *The United States in the Supreme War Council* (1961); and David R. Woodward, *Trial by Friendship: Anglo-American Relations, 1917–1918* (1993).

For the wartime home front, civil-liberties issues, and propaganda, see George T. Blakey, *Historians on the Homefront* (1970); Allan M. Brandt, *No Magic Bullet* (1985) (venereal disease); Alfred W. Crosby, *America's Forgotten Pandemic* (1989); David M. Kennedy, *Over Here* (1980); Seward W. Livermore, *Politics Is Adjourned* (1966); Elizabeth McKillen, *Chicago Labor and the Quest for a Democratic Diplomacy* (1995); Joseph A. McCartin, *Labor's Great War* (1998); Paul L. Murphy, *World War I and the Origin of Civil Liberties* (1979); Horace C. Peterson and Gilbert C. Fite, *Opponents of War, 1917–1918* (1957); Richard Polenberg, *Fighting Faiths* (1987); Ronald Schaffer, *America in the Great War* (1991); John A. Thompson, *Reformers and War* (1986); Stephen Vaughn, *Hold Fast the Inner Lines* (1980) (Committee on Public Information); and Neil Wynn, *From Progressivism to Prosperity* (1986).

The Versailles peacemaking and League debate are discussed in Lloyd E. Ambrosius, *Wilsonian Statecraft* (1991) and *Woodrow Wilson and the American Diplomatic Tradition* (1987); Manfred F. Boemeke et al., eds., *The Treaty of Versailles* (1998); Inga Floto, *Colonel House in Paris* (1973); Lawrence E. Gelfand, *The Inquiry* (1963); Derek Heater, *National Self-Determination* (1994); Warren F. Kuehl, *Seeking World Order* (1969); Warren F. Kuehl and Lynne K. Dunne, *Keeping the Covenant* (1997); Antony Lentin, *Lloyd George, Woodrow Wilson, and the Guilt of Germany* (1985); Herbert F. Margulies, *The Mild Reservationists* (1989); Keith Nelson, *Victors Divided: America and the Allies in Germany, 1918–1923* (1973); Stuart I. Rochester, *American Liberal Disillusionment in the Wake of World War I* (1977); Klaus Schwabe, *Woodrow Wilson, Revolutionary Germany, and Peacemaking* (1985); Alan Sharp, *The Versailles Settlement* (1991); Ralph A. Stone, *The Irreconcilables* (1970); Marc Trachenberg, *Reparations in World Politics* (1986); and Arthur Walworth, *America's Moment, 1918* (1977) and *Wilson and His Peacemakers* (1986).

The U.S. response to Bolshevism, intervention in Russia, and the Red Scare are investigated in Stanley Coben, *A. Mitchell Palmer* (1963); Victor M. Fic, *The Collapse of American Policy in Russia and Siberia, 1918* (1995); David S. Foglesong, *America's Secret War Against Bolshevism* (1995); John Lewis Gaddis, *Russia, the Soviet Union, and the United States* (1990); Lloyd Gardner, *Safe for Democracy* (1984); George F. Kennan, *Russia Leaves the War* (1956) and *The Decision to Intervene* (1958); Linda Killen, *The Russian Bureau* (1983); N. Gordon Levin, Jr., *Woodrow Wilson and World Politics* (1968); Arthur S. Link, ed., *Woodrow Wilson and a Revolutionary World, 1913–1921* (1982); Arno Mayer, *Politics and Diplomacy of Peacemaking* (1967); David W. McFadden, *Alternative Paths: Soviets and Americans, 1917–1920* (1993); Robert K. Murray, *Red Scare* (1955); William Pencak, *For God and Country* (1989) (American Legion); Benjamin D. Rhodes, *The Anglo-American Winter War with Russia, 1918–1919* (1988); Neil V. Salzman, *Reform and Revolution* (1991) (Robins); Ilya Somin, *Stillborn Crusade: The Tragic Failure of Western Intervention in the Russian Civil War* (1996); John Thompson, *Russia, Bolshevism, and the Versailles Peace* (1966); and Betty Miller Unterberger, *America's Siberian Expedition* (1956) and *The United States, Revolutionary Russia, and the Rise of Czechoslovakia* (1989).

U.S. economic expansion abroad during the war is studied in Burton I. Kaufman, *Efficiency and Expansion* (1974); Emily S. Rosenberg, *World War I and the Growth of United States Predominance in Latin America* (1987); and Jeffrey J. Safford, *Wilsonian Maritime Diplomacy, 1913–1921* (1978).

Also see the General Bibliography, the following notes, and Richard Dean Burns, ed., *Guide to American Foreign Relations Since 1700* (1983).

For comprehensive coverage of foreign-relations topics, see the articles in the four-volume *Encyclopedia of U.S. Foreign Relations* (1997), edited by Bruce W. Jentleson and Thomas G. Paterson.

NOTES TO CHAPTER 3

1. Quoted in Thomas Bailey and Paul Ryan, *The* Lusitania *Disaster* (New York: Free Press, 1975), p. 81.
2. Quoted in Edward Ellis, *Echoes of Distant Thunder* (New York: Coward, McCann & Geoghegan, 1975), p. 195.
3. Quoted in Bailey and Ryan, Lusitania *Disaster*, p. 94.
4. Quoted *ibid.*, p. 82.
5. Quoted *ibid.*, p. 133.
6. Quoted in C. L. Droste and W. H. Tantum, eds., *The* Lusitania *Case* (Riverside, Conn.: 7 C's Press, 1972), p. 172.
7. Quoted in Burton J. Hendrick, *Life and Letters of Walter Hines Page* (Garden City, N.Y.: Doubleday, Page, 1922–1925; 3 vols.), *II*, 2.
8. William Jennings Bryan and Mary B. Bryan, *Memoirs* (Chicago: Winston, 1925), pp. 398–399.
9. Quoted in William Harbaugh, *The Life and Times of Theodore Roosevelt* (New York: Oxford University Press, 1975), p. 448.
10. John Milton Cooper, Jr., *The Warrior and the Priest* (Cambridge: Harvard University Press, 1983), p. 288.
11. R. S. Baker and W. E. Dodd, eds., *Public Papers of Woodrow Wilson* (New York: Harper & Brothers, 1926; 2 vols.), *I*, 321.
12. Quoted in Priscilla Roberts, "The Anglo-American Theme," *Diplomatic History*, *XXI* (Summer 1997), 340.
13. Quoted in August Hecksher, *Woodrow Wilson* (New York: Charles Scribner's Sons, 1991), p. 365.
14. *Foreign Relations, 1915, Supplement* (Washington, D.C.: Government Printing Office, 1928), p. 396.
15. Quoted in Richard R. Doerries, *Imperial Challenge* (Chapel Hill: University of North Carolina Press, 1989), p. 105.
16. David F. Houston, *Eight Years with Wilson's Cabinet* (Garden City, N.Y.: Doubleday, Page, 1926), 137.
17. Quoted in LeRoy Ashby, *William Jennings Bryan* (Boston: Twayne, 1987), p. 160.
18. Quoted *ibid.*, p. 161.
19. Quoted in Doerries, *Imperial Challenge*, p. 111.
20. Bailey and Ryan, Lusitania *Disaster*, p. 340.

21. Robert Lansing, *War Memoirs* (Indianapolis: Bobbs-Merrill, 1935), p. 128.
22. Ray S. Baker quoted in Arthur S. Link et al., eds., *The Papers of Woodrow Wilson* (Princeton: Princeton University Press, 1989), *LXI*, 383.
23. Quoted in Rohan Butler, "The Peace Settlement of Versailles, 1918–1933," in C. L. Mowat, ed., *The New Cambridge Modern History*, vol. *XII* (Cambridge, Eng.: Cambridge University Press, 1968), p. 214.
24. Quoted in Frank Ninkovich, *Modernity and Power* (Chicago: University of Chicago Press, 1994), p. 42.
25. Quoted in Barbara Tuchman, *The Guns of August* (New York: Dell, [1962], 1963), p. 91.
26. Quoted in Hendrick, *Life and Letters, I*, 310.
27. Baker and Dodd, *Public Papers, I*, 157–159.
28. Cecil Spring-Rice quoting Wilson in G. R. Conyne, *Woodrow Wilson* (New York: St. Martin's Press, 1992), p. 44.
29. Quoted in Alexander DeConde, *Ethnicity, Race, and American Foreign Policy* (Boston: Northeastern University Press, 1992), p. 86.
30. Quoted in Tuchman, *Guns of August*, p. 349.
31. Quoted *ibid.*, p. 153.
32. *Life* quoted in Mark Sullivan, *Our Times* (New York: Charles Scribner's Sons, 1926–1937; 6 vols.), *V*, 59.
33. Quoted in Ray Stannard Baker, *Woodrow Wilson* (New York: Doubleday, Doran, 1927–1939; 8 vols.), *V*, 175.
34. Quoted in Paul Birdsall, "Neutrality and Economic Pressures, 1914–1917," *Science and Society, III* (Spring 1939), 221.
35. Kathleen Burk, *Britain, America, and the Sinews of War, 1914–1918* (Boston: Allen & Unwin, 1985), p. 5.
36. *Foreign Relations, 1915, Supplement*, p. 99.
37. John W. Coogan, "Submarine Warfare," in Bruce W. Jentleson and Thomas G. Paterson, eds., *Encyclopedia of U.S. Foreign Relations* (New York: Oxford University Press, 1997; 4 vols.), *IV*, 145.
38. Frederick Dixon quoting Wilson in Conyne, *Wilson*, p. 51.
39. Quoted in Frederick S. Calhoun, *Uses of Force and Wilsonian Foreign Policy* (Kent, Ohio: Kent State University Press, 1993), p. 100.
40. Quoted in Arthur S. Link, *Woodrow Wilson and the Progressive Era, 1910–1917* (New York: Harper and Row, 1954), p. 203.
41. French report quoted in Joyce G. Williams, *Colonel House and Sir Edward Grey* (Lanham, Md.: University Press of America, 1984), p. 83.
42. Quoted in Arthur S. Link, *Wilson: Confusions and Crises, 1915–1916* (Princeton: Princeton University Press, 1964), pp. 134–135.
43. Bryan and Bryan, *Memoirs*, p. 397.
44. *Foreign Relations, 1915, Supplement*, p. 461.
45. Link, *Papers of Wilson, XXXVI* (1981), 213–214.
46. Samuel Flagg Bemis, "A Worcester County Student in Wartime London and Paris (via Harvard): 1915–1916," *New England Galaxy, XI* (Spring 1970), 20.
47. Quoted in Patrick Devlin, *Too Proud to Fight* (New York: Oxford University Press, 1975), p. 517.
48. Quoted in Ninkovich, *Modernity and Power*, p. 50.
49. Quoted in Arthur S. Link, *Wilson: Campaigns for Progressivism and Peace, 1916–1917* (Princeton: Princeton University Press, 1965), p. 274.
50. Quoted *ibid.*, p. 289.
51. Lansing, *War Memoirs*, p. 212.
52. Jules Witcover, *Sabotage at Black Tom* (Chapel Hill, N.C.: Algonquin Books, 1989), p. 12.
53. *Foreign Relations, 1917, Supplement 1* (Washington, D.C.: Government Printing Office, 1931), p. 147.
54. Quoted in John Milton Cooper, Jr., *Walter Hines Page* (Chapel Hill: University of North Carolina Press, 1977), p. 369.
55. Quoted in Thomas W. Ryley, *A Little Group of Willful Men* (Port Washington, N.Y.: Kennikat Press, 1975), p. 2.
56. Link, *Papers of Wilson, XLI* (1983), 519–527.
57. Ross Gregory, *The Origins of American Intervention in the First World War* (New York: Norton, 1971), p. 128.
58. Henry F. Ashurst quoted in Erika A. Kuhlman, *Petticoats and White Feathers* (Westport, Conn.: Greenwood, 1997), p. 90.
59. Quoted in Robert E. Osgood, *Ideals and Self-Interest in American Foreign Relations* (Chicago: University of Chicago Press, 1953), p. 177.
60. Quoted in Michael S. Sherry, *In the Shadow of War* (New Haven: Yale University Press, 1995), p. 8.
61. Susan Zeiger, "She Didn't Raise Her Boy to Be a Slacker," *Feminist Studies, XXII* (Spring 1996), 11–12.
62. Kuhlman, *Petticoats*, p. 51.
63. Quoted in Zeiger, "Slacker," p. 18.
64. Quoted in Paolo E. Coletta, "The American Navy Leaders' Preparations for War," in R. J. Q. Adams, ed., *The Great War, 1914–18* (College Station: Texas A & M University Press, 1990), p. 170.
65. Quoted in Kenneth J. Hagan, *This People's Navy* (New York: Free Press, 1991), p. 252.
66. Quoted in Barbara S. Kraft, *The Peace Ship* (New York: Macmillan, 1978), p. 1.
67. Quoted in Thomas J. Knock, *To End All Wars* (New York: Oxford University Press, 1992), p. 63.
68. *Ibid.*, p. 50.
69. Jane Addams, *Peace and Bread in Time of War* (New York: King's Crown Press, 1945), p. 58.
70. Quoted in Kuhlman, *Petticoats*, p. 56.
71. Quoted in J. Garry Clifford, *The Citizen Soldiers* (Lexington: University Press of Kentucky, 1972), p. 123.
72. General Tasker Bliss quoted in Calhoun, *Uses of Force*, p. 114.
73. Penn Borden, *Civilian Indoctrination of the Military* (Westport, Conn.: Greenwood, 1989), p. 143.
74. Quoted in Edward M. Coffman, *The War to End All Wars* (New York: Oxford University Press, 1968), p. 4.
75. Quoted in Allen F. Davis, "Welfare, Reform, and World War I," *American Quarterly, XIX* (Fall 1967), 530.
76. Quoted in Jorg Nagler, "German Imperial Propaganda," in Hans-Jürgen Schröder, *Confrontation and Cooperation* (Providence, R.I.: Berg Publishers, 1993), p. 172.
77. Quoted in Davis, "Welfare," p. 531.
78. Quoted in Ninkovich, *Modernity and Power*, p. 52.
79. Link, *Papers of Wilson, XLVII* (1984), 270.
80. Quoted in Donald Smythe, *Pershing* (Bloomington: Indiana University Press, 1986), p. 237.
81. Link, *Papers of Wilson, XLV* (1984), 529.
82. Addams, *Peace and Bread*, p. 58.
83. Quoted in Selig Adler, *The Isolationist Impulse* (New York: Collier Books, [1957], 1961), pp. 60–61.
84. H. G. Nicholas essay in *Wilson's Diplomacy* (Cambridge: Schenkman, 1973), p. 81.
85. Quoted in David F. Trask, *The United States in the Supreme War Council* (Middletown, Conn.: Wesleyan University Press, 1961), p. 155.
86. Ray S. Baker quoted in John A. Thompson, *Reformers and War* (New York: Cambridge University Press, 1988), p. 234.
87. Quoted in James D. Startt, "American Propaganda in Britain During World War I," *Prologue, XXVIII* (Spring 1996), 20.

88. Knock, *To End All Wars*, p. 180.

89. Quoted in David W. McFadden, *Alternative Paths* (New York: Oxford University Press, 1993), p. 209.

90. Quoted in Herbert Hoover, *The Ordeal of Woodrow Wilson* (New York: McGraw-Hill, 1958), p. 254.

91. Quoted in Walter A. McDougall, *Promised Land, Crusader State* (Boston: Houghton Mifflin, 1997), p. 139.

92. Quoted in Ross Gregory, "To Do Good in the World," in Frank Merli and Theodore Wilson, eds., *Makers of American Diplomacy* (New York: Charles Scribner's Sons, 1974), p. 380.

93. Quoted in Lawrence E. Gelfand, "Where Ideals Confront Self-Interest," *Diplomatic History, XVIII* (Winter 1994), 133.

94. U.S. Congress, Senate, *Treaties*, Senate Doc. 348 (Washington, D.C.: Government Printing Office, 1923), pp. 3336–3345.

95. Link, *Papers of Wilson, LV* (1985), 177.

96. Antony Lentin, *Lloyd George, Woodrow Wilson, and the Guilt of Germany* (Baton Rouge: Louisiana State University Press, 1984), p. 132.

97. Link, *Papers of Wilson, LV* (1985), 238–245.

98. Quoted in D. F. Fleming, *The United States and the League of Nations, 1918–1920* (New York: Russell & Russell, 1968), p. 134.

99. Quoted in Beth McKillen, "The Corporatist Model, World War I, and the Debate over the League of Nations," *Diplomatic History, XV* (Spring 1991), 174.

100. Link, *Papers of Wilson, LXI* (1989), 436.

101. Quoted in Arthur S. Link, *Wilson the Diplomatist* (Chicago: Quadrangle, [1957], 1963), p. 131.

102. Quoted in Thompson, *Reformers and War*, p. 239.

103. Robert David Johnson, *The Peace Progressives and American Foreign Relations* (Cambridge: Harvard University Press, 1995), p. 102.

104. Quoted in William C. Widenor, "The United States and the Versailles Peace Settlement," in John M. Carroll and George C. Herring, Jr., eds., *Modern American Diplomacy* (Wilmington, Del.: Scholarly Resources, 1986), p. 49.

105. Quoted in Lloyd E. Ambrosius, *Woodrow Wilson and the American Diplomatic Tradition* (New York: Cambridge University Press, 1987), p. 139.

106. Quoted in Osgood, *Ideals and Self-Interest*, p. 286.

107. Quoted in McKillen, "Corporatist Model," 292.

108. Roland N. Stromberg, *Collective Security and American Foreign Policy* (New York: Praeger, 1963) p. 37.

109. Bert E. Park, "Wilson's Neurological Illness," in Link, *Papers of Wilson, LXII* (1990), 629.

110. Link, *Papers of Wilson, LXIII* (1990), 35.

111. Quoted in DeConde, *Ethnicity*, p. 97.

112. Quoted in Knock, *To End All Wars*, p. 263.

113. Arthur Walworth, *Wilson and His Peacemakers* (New York: Norton, 1986), p. 533.

114. Quoted in E. David Cronon, ed., *The Cabinet Diaries of Josephus Daniels* (Lincoln: University of Nebraska Press, 1963), p. 520.

115. Quoted in Warren F. Kuehl and Lynne K. Dunne, *Keeping the Covenant* (Kent, Ohio: Kent State University Press, 1997), p. 18.

116. Quoted in Knock, *To End All Wars*, p. 254.

117. Bert E. Park, "The Aftermath of Wilson's Stroke," in Link, *Papers of Wilson, LXIV* (1986), 525.

118. Quoted in John M. Thompson, *Russia, Bolshevism, and the Versailles Peace* (Princeton: Princeton University Press, 1966), pp. 3–4.

119. Ray S. Baker quoted in McFadden, *Alternative Paths*, p. 240.

120. Quoted in David S. Foglesong, *America's Secret War Against Bolshevism* (Chapel Hill: University of North Carolina Press, 1995), p. 25.

121. Quoted in McFadden, *Alternative Paths*, p. 247.

122. Winston Churchill quoting Wilson in Lloyd C. Gardner, *Safe for Democracy* (New York: Oxford University Press, 1984), p. 239.

123. Quoted in Foglesong, *Secret War*, p. 43.

124. Quoted in McFadden, *Alternative Paths*, p. 104.

125. Foglesong, *Secret War*, p. 77.

126. Quoted in Betty Miller Unterberger, *The United States, Revolutionary Russia, and the Rise of Czechoslovakia* (Chapel Hill: University of North Carolina Press, 1989), p. 264.

127. Betty Miller Unterberger, "Woodrow Wilson and the Russian Revolution," in Arthur S. Link, ed., *Woodrow Wilson and a Revolutionary World, 1913–1921* (Chapel Hill: University of North Carolina Press, 1982), p. 70.

128. Foglesong, *Secret War*, p. 190.

129. Victor M. Fic, *The Collapse of American Policy in Russia and Siberia, 1918* (New York: Columbia University Press, 1995), p. 141.

130. Quoted in McFadden, *Alternative Paths*, p. 154.

131. Quoted in Benjamin D. Rhodes, *The Anglo-American War with Russia, 1918–1919* (Westport, Conn.: Greenwood, 1988), p. 123.

132. Foglesong, *Secret War*, p. 296.

133. Quoted *ibid.*, p. 291.

134. Dwight D. Eisenhower, *Waging Peace, 1956–1961* (Garden City, N.Y.: Doubleday, 1965), p. 616.

135. McKillen, "Corporatist Model," 173.

136. Arthur S. Link, *The Higher Realism of Woodrow Wilson* (Nashville: Vanderbilt University Press, 1971), p. 83.

137. Quoted in Gordon A. Craig, "The Revolution in War and Diplomacy," in Jack J. Roth, ed., *World War I* (New York: Knopf, 1967), p. 12.

138. Quoted in Robert H. Ferrell, *Woodrow Wilson and World War I* (New York: Harper and Row, 1985), p. 180.

139. E. M. Remarque, *All Quiet on the Western Front* (London: Putnam, 1929), p. 224.

140. Quoted in Tony Smith, *America's Mission* (Princeton: Princeton University Press, 1994), p. 102.

141. Quoted in Hans Schmidt, "Democracy in China," *Diplomatic History, XXII* (Winter 1998), 28.

142. Link, *Papers of Wilson, LXII* (1990), 47.

143. Quoted in John A. DeNovo, "The Movement for an Aggressive American Oil Policy Abroad, 1918–1920," *American Historical Review, LXI* (July 1956), 858.

144. Quoted in Foglesong, *Secret War*, p. 1.

4

Descending into Europe's Maelstrom, 1920–1939

Trojan Horse?

Trojan Horse?   *Many observers thought that President Franklin D. Roosevelt concealed too much in his foreign policymaking—that he not only misled but also lied. Fred O. Seibel of the* Richmond Times Dispatch *(February 4, 1939) portrayed such thinking shortly after a "Boston" bomber with a French pilot aboard crashed in Los Angeles. The British diplomat Lord Halifax saw as much confusion as deviousness in the Roosevelt administration, which he likened to "a disorderly line of beaters out shooting; they do put the rabbits out of the bracken, but they don't come out where you expect." (Courtesy of* Richmond Times Dispatch/*Franklin D. Roosevelt Library)*

DIPLOMATIC CROSSROAD

Roosevelt's Attempt to Extend America's Frontier to the Rhine, 1939

Daubed with red, white, and blue U.S. Army Air Corps paint, the new A-20 ("Boston") twin-engine light bomber performed high-speed acrobatics over Los Angeles's municipal airport on January 23, 1939. The sleek craft climbed to 3,000 feet at more than 300 miles per hour. Test pilot John Cable then apparently cut one motor to attempt a climb on half power. Suddenly the plane went into a spin and hurtled toward the ground. Cable bailed out at 400 feet but he pulled his parachute ripcord too late. He died on impact.

Three employees from the adjacent North American Aviation plant extricated a civilian-clad survivor from the crashed bomber before it burst into flames. Reporters soon learned that the man with the wrenched back and broken leg was thirty-three-year-old Captain Paul Chemidlin, incognito member of a secret French purchasing mission headed by Jean Monnet to buy American-made warplanes for the French air force. The French were getting ready for World War II, which finally began in September.

Controversy soon engulfed Washington. General Henry "Hap" Arnold of the U.S. Army Air Corps happened to be testifying before the Senate Military Affairs Committee on budgetary issues. Senator Bennett C. Clark of Missouri asked how a French officer could be aboard the "secret" bomber that had just crashed. Arnold disingenuously replied that the Frenchman had gone "out there under the direction of the Treasury Department with a view of looking into possible purchase of airplanes by the French Mission."[1] Formal authorization, he added, had come from the War Department, and all secret equipment was removed from the plane before the French saw it.

Clark and fellow noninterventionist Gerald P. Nye of North Dakota then summoned Treasury Secretary Henry Morgenthau, Jr., and Secretary of War Harry Woodring for further grilling. Morgenthau acidly pointed out that the army had not yet placed orders for the plane, which remained the sole property of the Douglas Company and could hardly be termed "secret" if flown from a municipal airport where anyone could see it. Woodring, however, admitted that the air corps had originally opposed the French mission but that "everyone [was] . . . in accord before the French went to the West Coast."[2] President Franklin D. Roosevelt muddied matters further by denying to the press that "this Government [had] taken any steps to assist or facilitate France in buying planes in this country." But French plane purchases "would be an excellent idea" to help "in building up" U.S. foreign trade, he noted blandly.[3]

A devotee of poker, the president "wasn't ready publicly to show his hand."[4] In seeking to deter a major war through nonmilitary methods, he had talked publicly in recent years about quarantines against aggression, held secret naval talks with the British, and toyed with calling a conference in Washington of major world leaders. His invitation to the king and queen of England to visit America in June 1939 seemed "a safe but effective way of dramatizing Anglo-American amity for the benefit of the dictators and the American public."[5] Roosevelt had mentioned "methods short of war" to Congress in early January, but he gave no details of what would amount to a major shift in American foreign policy in the months prior to World War II.[6]

Ever since the disastrous Munich Conference of September 1938, when England and France had agreed to German territorial demands against Czechoslovakia, FDR had seized on air power as a possible deterrent against another European war. "Had we . . . 5,000 planes and the immediate capacity to produce 10,000 per year," he had mused, "Hitler would not have dared to take the stand he did."[7] When the French financier-diplomat Jean Monnet visited in October 1938, the president confided that "the Germans can produce 40,000 planes per year, Britain and Canada 25,000 and France 15,000. 20–30,000 more will be needed to achieve decisive superiority over Germany and Italy; and they'll have to be found here, in the United States."[8] He urged England and France to place orders, thereby stimulating the lagging U.S. aviation industry and jump-starting military rearmament. When War Department officials balked at showing top-secret prototypes to foreign buyers, Roosevelt argued that "the only check to a world war, which would be understood by Germany, would be the creation of a great [French] air force and a powerful force in this country."[9] Only after a direct presidential order on January 16, 1939, did General Arnold permit the French to inspect the Douglas bomber.

FDR also wanted to revise America's neutrality laws to permit the sale of arms and munitions to belligerents on a cash-and-carry basis. France and Britain could buy weapons legally in peacetime, but the current law forbade such sales in wartime. The president had secretly promised British prime minister Neville Chamberlain "the industrial resources of the American nation . . . in the event of war with the dictatorships."[10] The crash of the plane with the French officer aboard put Roosevelt's plans in jeopardy and threatened to expose rifts in his administration. The designation of his close friend Morgenthau to oversee all foreign purchases had aroused criticism. The bespectacled Treasury secretary served as an "intellectual rough-neck" who "bulled things through" with little regard for bureaucratic sensitivity. In this instance, the chief obstruction proved to be Secretary of War Woodring, a "fourth-rate" former governor of Kansas, "who not only couldn't see that our frontier was the Rhine, but couldn't see across the Hudson River."[11]

Roosevelt invited the Senate Military Affairs Committee to the White House on January 31, 1939. He asked for confidentiality so as not "to frighten the American people." During the meeting, FDR asserted that the growing menace from Germany, Italy, and Japan necessitated fundamental changes in U.S. policies. He denied that "we can draw a line of defense around this country and live completely and solely to ourselves." He cited Thomas Jefferson's embargo—"the damned thing didn't work" and "the country began to strangle" and "we got into the War of 1812." Americans could react to the new threat by hoping that "somebody would assassinate Hitler or that Germany will blow up from within." Or they could "try to prevent the domination of the world—prevent it by peaceful means."

Franklin D. Roosevelt (1882–1945). Although stricken by polio in the 1920s, Roosevelt remained energetic and optimistic. A talented politician who won four presidential elections, he moved haltingly to shore up Britain and France as they faced an aggressive Germany. Here FDR relaxes with stamp collecting, his favorite hobby. During World War II the president once showed British prime minister Winston Churchill a favorite stamp "from one of your colonies." Churchill asked: "Which one?" Roosevelt replied: "One of your last. . . . You won't have them much longer, you know." (Franklin D. Roosevelt Library)

Strengthening America's "first line of defense" offered the best approach. In the Pacific, that defense consisted of "a series of islands, with a hope that through the Army and Navy and the airplanes we can keep the Japanese" from dominating the Pacific and denying "us access to the west coast of South America." In Europe and the Atlantic, the line of defense rested on "the continued independence" of countries from Finland to Turkey. If England and France fell, however, the others would "drop into the [German] basket." Colonial Africa would "automatically" capitulate. The president claimed that the Germans could dominate South and Central America through subversion and economic penetration. He warned: "The Germans have 1,500 bombing planes that can go from Germany to Colombia inside of forty-eight hours. We have, I think, about eighty that can go down there."

Roosevelt emphatically defended the sale of aircraft, saying that "it is to our interest, quite frankly, to do what we can, absolutely as a matter of peace . . . to help the British and French maintain their independence." The American aviation industry also needed foreign orders to expedite mass production and "turn out nine or ten thousand planes per year" without at the same time delaying the buildup of U.S. air forces. As for secrets, he affirmed that the Norden bombsight "has not been disclosed to the French and won't." He vowed to "maintain the independence of these other nations by sending them all they can pay for on the barrelhead. . . . Now, that is the foreign policy of the United States."

A bravura performance, to be sure. Yet when asked if he meant that the United States had the "duty" to "maintain the independence of these nations . . . by whatever efforts may be necessary," Roosevelt shot back: "No. No! Listen: I probably saw more of the war [World War I] in Europe than any other living person." Describing his three-month tour of the battle zones as assistant secretary of the navy in

1918, he "covered the whole coast of France. . . . I spent days on the Belgian front, on the British front, on the French front, and on the American front. . . . Therefore, you may be quite sure that about the last thing this country should do is ever to send an army to Europe again."[12] Senator Nye, listening intently, went back to his office and immediately wrote a nine-page memorandum. "Get the uniforms ready for the boys," he noted. "I saw troops moving even though the Pres[ident] had declared he had no intent to go to war."[13]

The next day word leaked to the press that FDR had proclaimed that "the frontiers of the United States are on the Rhine."[14] The president angrily hit back, calling the leak "a deliberate lie" that "some boob got off." He accused isolationists of trying to "make political capital" out of words he never spoke. He specifically singled out Senator Nye as "an unscrupulous person."[15] As reverberations echoed in the press, the French ambassador lamented "manifestations of isolation in this country," and Neville Chamberlain noted that "Roosevelt is saying Heaven knows what but anyhow something disagreeable to the dictators."[16]

Did FDR lie? According to a stenographic transcript of his meeting with the senators, he never said exactly that America's frontier extended to the Rhine, but his argument that the nation's first line of defense depended on the continued independence of England and France carried the same meaning. Several times, Morgenthau later recalled, the president did say privately: "Our frontier is on the Rhine."[17] Yet in all likelihood Roosevelt sincerely believed he spoke the truth. A deft "juggler" who always kept options open, the smiling squire of Hyde Park wanted above all else to deter a European war while at the same time to prepare for possible U.S. participation.[18] He sought "methods short of war" because "sending a large army abroad was undesirable and politically out of the question."[19] As the historian Michael Sherry has written, "repudiation of armed intervention did not exclude intervention by display of arms. Methods short of war could still embrace the capacity for deterrence that rearmament implied."[20] Roosevelt persisted in selling aircraft to the French and British, even threatening to exile General Arnold to Guam if he did not "play ball."[21] Although the 555 combat planes eventually delivered to France did not deter war, the French orders quadrupled airplane production and laid the foundation "for the gigantic later expansion of the U.S. aircraft industry."[22]

The "cockeyed" affair also caused FDR to abandon any sustained personal effort to educate Congress and public opinion about revising American neutrality laws before the outbreak of war in Europe.[23] Only after the German invasion of Poland in September 1939 did the administration succeed in repealing the arms embargo, and even then the president remained conspicuously in the background. His encounter with the senators over the French air mission remained so disturbing that he hesitated to lead boldly: "Recall the colorful and untrue reports of over a year ago about our frontier being on the Rhine; . . . about the death of a French officer caused by the crash of an airplane in California," he told a prominent publisher in June 1940. "The government . . . cannot change its 'editorial' policy overnight. . . . Governments, such as ours, cannot swing so far or so quickly."[24] Of course, the French officer had not died, but Roosevelt sometimes exaggerated for effect.

Some six years and two months after FDR made his alleged remarks about America's frontier on the Rhine, U.S. soldiers seized the bridge at Remagen and crossed the Rhine into Germany. Another European war, which American diplomacy and arms sales to France had failed to prevent, then definitively extended the frontiers of the United States.

The Independent Internationalists

The French airplane incident of 1939 illustrates salient themes of interwar foreign relations. It demonstrates that even on the eve of World War II in Europe, the United States still sought methods short of war to deter potential aggressors in areas vital to the national interest. Because foreign airplane orders also meant "prosperity in this country and we can't elect a Democratic Party unless we get prosperity," as Roosevelt put it, the episode reveals the impact of the Great Depression on foreign trade, domestic politics, and international security.[25] Even in failure, it shows how an activist president can use subterfuge and surrogates to circumvent bureaucratic rivalries and congressional opposition. The episode underlines the lessons learned from American intervention in World War I and the determination to avoid the mistakes attributed to Woodrow Wilson. In view of FDR's claim that America's national security had become tied to the independence of France and England, it also proves that important U.S. leaders recognized global interdependence and rejected an ostrichlike, isolationist course during the interwar years.

The United States had emerged from World War I a recognized world power. Under the Treaty of Versailles, U.S. military forces even occupied the left bank of the Rhine near Coblenz until early 1923. Postwar American diplomats, closer to a global perspective than ever before, knew that even if they wanted to, Americans could not be bystanders in world affairs. True, between World Wars I and II Americans hoped to avoid foreign entanglements and concentrate on domestic matters. But, within the limits of U.S. power, American leaders pursued an active foreign policy befitting their nation's high international status. They worked to create a community of peaceful nations characterized by legal and orderly processes, the Open Door, and economic and political stability. Washington emphasized nonmilitary means—treaties, conferences, disarmament, economic and financial agreements, banking reform—in its pursuit of world order. Secretary of State Henry L. Stimson remarked that the United States championed a "commercial and non-military stabilization of the world."[26] America between the wars wanted to isolate itself from war, to scale down foreign military interventions, and to preserve the freedom to make independent decisions in international affairs. "Independent internationalism," rather than "isolationism," best characterizes American practice—active on an international scale, but independent in action.[27]

Where the United States lacked viable power, such as in Asia, it moved haltingly. Where it possessed power, as in Latin America, it moved vigorously. As for Europe, "economic imperatives, humanitarian instincts, and ideological impulses compelled American officials to take an active interest."[28] Until 1933 the Republican administrations seriously worked to contain but rehabilitate Germany, relieve

Charles Evans Hughes (1862–1948) and Warren G. Harding (1865–1923). The secretary of state (left) and president were quite different in background and intellect, but as conservatives both sought a stable, nonrevolutionary world order. (Ohio Historical Society)

French strategic anxieties, tame Soviet radicalism while seeking to integrate Russia into the community of nations, advance disarmament proposals, resolve controversies over war debts and reparations, stabilize European currencies, foster American exports, and systematize the flow of private American capital abroad. In seeking a world order of peace and prosperity, the U.S. government encouraged private experts in business, finance, labor, and agriculture to cooperate with public officials in what some historians have called a system of "corporatism." By the mid-1930s, with international stability shattered by the Great Depression and Europe torn by conflict, Americans tried to protect themselves from war through neutrality legislation. Not until 1939 did policymakers again risk war to achieve world order.

In the 1920s especially, weak presidential leadership, congressional-executive competition, and increased professionalism in the Foreign Service characterized U.S. policymaking. Presidents Warren G. Harding and Calvin Coolidge gave minimal attention to foreign affairs, leaving that field to their secretaries of state. Harding's world was his hometown of Marion, Ohio. Wilson's League of Nations fiasco persuaded Harding to eschew a conspicuous role in foreign policy. On one occasion, when a European correspondent for the *New York Times* talked with Harding, the president cut him short: "I don't know anything about this European stuff."[29]

Calvin Coolidge managed in his autobiography to avoid mentioning foreign policy, although as a politician he often waxed noisy on the issue of Bolshevism. The taciturn president once shocked the British ambassador by saying he would "never visit Europe because he could learn everything he needed to know by remaining in America."[30] Coolidge's relaxed approach to problems, exemplified by long afternoon naps in the White House and by his fawning worship of American business, created a deceptively passive image. The simple man from Vermont, preaching the

Makers of American Foreign Relations, 1920–1939

Presidents	Secretaries of State
Woodrow Wilson, 1913–1921	Bainbridge Colby,1920–1921
Warren G. Harding, 1921–1923	Charles E. Hughes, 1921–1925
Calvin Coolidge, 1923–1929	Frank B. Kellogg, 1925–1929
Herbert C. Hoover, 1929–1933	Henry L. Stimson, 1929–1933
Franklin D. Roosevelt, 1933–1945	Cordell Hull, 1933–1944

virtues of self-reliance, grew impatient with Europeans—who, he believed, always looked to the United States to bail them out. "We couldn't help people very much until they showed a disposition to help themselves," he noted in 1926.[31]

Herbert Hoover held much the same philosophy, but he had considerable knowledge about foreign affairs and adopted an active presidential role. His distinguished career included experience in international business (mining), food relief (Belgium and Russia), and diplomacy (reparations adviser at Versailles). As secretary of commerce under Harding and Coolidge, he used his office energetically to expand American economic interests abroad. Known as the "Great Engineer," Hoover had a telephone installed at his elbow in the White House, further enhancing his reputation as a specialist in administrative efficiency. A plodding speaker with a shy personality, Hoover entered the presidency as the Great Depression struck, wrecking his political career. True to his Quaker background, he sought nonmilitary, noncoercive solutions to international crises and emphasized cooperative economic relations.

The secretaries of state in the 1920s often compensated for presidential shortcomings. Magisterial Charles Evans Hughes was a distinguished jurist (Supreme Court), an experienced politician (governor of New York and unsuccessful Republican candidate for president in 1916), and a confirmed nationalist and expansionist. Under Harding and Coolidge the patient, pragmatic Hughes enjoyed considerable freedom in diplomacy, receiving little presidential instruction. International law and the sanctity of treaties served as his primary guides to world order. Frank B. Kellogg succeeded Hughes. Ingloriously called "Nervous Nellie" because of his appearance (one blind eye and a trembling hand), the former senator and ambassador to Britain moved cautiously, often consulting a major critic of interventionism, William Borah, chair of the Senate Foreign Relations Committee. Because of jurisdictional disputes with the Commerce Department, one of Kellogg's subordinates commented: "diplomatic functions today are mainly economic; this places the Department of Commerce in control of the substance of diplomacy, and leaves the State Department with social relationships."[32]

President Hoover named as secretary of state mustachioed Henry L. Stimson, one of America's most distinguished public servants. The strong-willed, confident, reserved, punctual, sexist, mannered, wealthy Stimson lived on his Long Island estate like an English squire. His social pedigree included Phillips Andover Academy, Yale University, Harvard Law School, and tutelage under the eminent Elihu Root.

Herbert Hoover (1874–1964). The thirty-first president graduated from Stanford University. Cautious and stubborn, Hoover advocated healthy trade relations, military retrenchment, and foreign loans for "reproductive purposes" as routes to peace. (Library of Congress)

Before becoming secretary, he headed the War Department under Taft. In 1927 he went as a diplomatic troubleshooter to Nicaragua, and during 1927–1929 he served as governor-general of the Philippines. He had been Colonel Stimson in World War I—and let few forget it. Hoover did not like Stimson's combative personality and his eagerness to use force in foreign affairs.

Franklin D. Roosevelt came to office with some foreign-affairs experience, having served in the Navy Department under Woodrow Wilson. He admired both the big-sticking of his cousin Theodore and the liberal internationalism of Wilson. As a vice-presidential candidate in 1920, Roosevelt had defended the League and the Versailles treaty, but in the 1932 campaign he abandoned the League ("an emasculated constituency") to garner the endorsement of the influential newspaper magnate William Randolph Hearst.[33] The sly Roosevelt actually acted as both a Wilsonian and an isolationist: a Wilsonian because he believed that collective security through an international organization directed by the large powers would help stabilize world politics; an isolationist because he shared, although in differing degrees, the basic components of isolationist thought—(1) abhorrence of war; (2) limited *military* intervention abroad; (3) freedom of action in international relations. At least until 1937, one scholar argues, "Roosevelt offered no signs that American military power would be used abroad in a major war, for he had no intentions that it should be."[34]

Roosevelt relished personal diplomacy, often taking command of negotiations and more than once failing to tell the Department of State what he was doing. He centralized decisionmaking in the White House; but dangers lurked in his methods because too often he possessed only a superficial understanding of other national cultures and histories. Sometimes he misled diplomats with his easy smile; sometimes his agreements lacked precision, depending for their authority on the honor of gentlemen's words; sometimes the formal diplomatic document did not properly capture the "spirit" of a meeting; sometimes U.S. diplomacy moved forward with the dizziness of a confused bureaucracy. A consummate politician, Roosevelt compromised frequently and resorted to deception if it served his goals. One historian has called Roosevelt "an intellectual jumping-jack . . . hopping helter-skelter in several directions at once"; another scholar has likened him to a college professor who prefers to teach without a syllabus.[35]

Roosevelt chose Tennessean Cordell Hull as his secretary of state. A powerful senator devoted to free trade, the chronically ill sexagenarian (he secretly suffered from diabetes, claustrophobia, and tuberculosis) reluctantly accepted. FDR picked Hull not for his views on foreign affairs but because the appointment would please old Democratic party members, southern conservatives, and unreconstructed Wilsonians. Roosevelt often undercut him, although Hull and the State Department remained dominant in formulating Asian and Latin American policy. Rexford Tugwell, a presidential aide, noted as early as 1933 that "Hull doesn't know half of what goes on."[36] Indeed, Roosevelt sent Hull to the World Economic Conference in London that June without consulting him on the makeup of the delegation, and then embarrassed him by rejecting a currency stabilization plan and effectively ending the conference. Once dubbed "Miss Cordelia Dull" for his "congenital procrastination," the secretary had contemplated resigning earlier that spring when the president delayed sending to Congress Hull's pet project, the reciprocal trade bill.[37]

Hull's deliberate methods wearied the president, who preferred quickness and repartee. The secretary resented the president's practice of dispatching personal envoys overseas, of conspicuously excluding Hull from conferences, and of relying on friends such as Sumner Welles (after 1937 under secretary of state), Morgenthau, and Ambassador William C. Bullitt, instead of Hull himself. "They all come at me with knives and hatchets," Hull once complained.[38] But he stayed on until 1944, the longest tenure of any secretary of state, forever disliking the pomp of official dinners, always charming his listeners with his hill-country drawl and lisp, and impressing all with his personal dignity, hard work, and deep commitment to the premise that wars grew out of international economic competition.

The Foreign Service over which Hull presided improved during the interwar period. It certainly needed reform. Frequenting the dark corridors and Victorian furnishings of the old State, War, and Navy Building on Pennsylvania Avenue were U.S. diplomats noted for their elite backgrounds (urban, wealthy, eastern, and Ivy League–educated). Some derided them as "cookie pushers" and "striped pants," as purveyors of "pink peppermint and protocol." Foreign Service Officers nonetheless believed that "they belonged to a pretty good club. That feeling has fostered a healthy *esprit de corps*."[39] Many diplomatic appointees could not speak the language of the country to which they were assigned. Under the spoils system, faithful politicians received top diplomatic posts.

The heavy work load imposed on Foreign Service personnel during World War I had exposed the shortcomings. The immigration laws of 1921 and 1924, establishing quotas, demanded a more efficient consular staff; the revolution in China required observers who could intelligently interpret that convulsion; and economic expansion depended on sound reporting about market conditions abroad. The Rogers Act of 1924 merged the previously unequal consular and diplomatic corps into the Foreign Service of the United States and provided for examinations, increased salaries, promotion by merit, and overseas living allowances. At about the same time, the State Department began training specialists in Soviet affairs, with George F. Kennan and Charles E. Bohlen (both later ambassadors to the Soviet Union) as initiates who mastered the language and culture of Russia. These trainees came to share hard-line attitudes toward the Soviet Union. Despite persistent cliques, political favoritism, snobbery, sexism, anti-Semitism, and lower salaries and staff cutbacks during the depression, the Foreign Service became more efficient and professional.

Cordell Hull (1871–1955). The long-tenured secretary of state (1933–1944) firmly believed that "we cannot have a peaceful world . . . until we rebuild the international economic structure." Although Roosevelt often ignored him, Hull played a central role in Latin American issues, negotiations with Japan, and trade questions. (National Portrait Gallery, Smithsonian Institution)

Economic and Cultural Expansion in a Rickety World

The Foreign Service helped facilitate conspicuous American economic expansion abroad after World War I. Measured by statistics, the United States had become the most powerful nation in the world, accounting for 70 percent of the world's petroleum and 40 percent of its coal production. Most impressive, the United States produced 46 percent of total world industrial goods (1925–1929 figures). It also ranked first as an exporter, shipping more than 15 percent of total world exports in 1929, and it replaced Great Britain as the largest foreign investor and financier of world trade. Throughout the decade the United States enjoyed a favorable balance of trade, exporting more than it imported. In the period 1914–1929, the value of exports more than doubled, to $5.4 billion, and American private investments abroad grew from $3.5 billion in 1914 to $17.2 billion by 1930. "American money power," warned British prime minister Stanley Baldwin, "is trying to get hold of the natural resources of the empire."[40]

"The growth of U.S. stakes abroad during the 1920s represented not simply an increase in scale," the historian Mira Wilkins has noted. "Rather, U.S. companies were (1) going to *more countries*, (2) building *more plants* in a particular foreign country, (3) manufacturing or mining *more end products* in a particular foreign land, (4) investing in a single alien nation in a *greater degree* of integration, and (5) diversifying on a *worldwide* basis."[41] U.S. Rubber bought its first Malayan plantation; Anaconda moved into Chilean copper mining; General Electric joined international cartels and invested heavily in Germany; oil companies began to penetrate the Middle East; Americans controlled 83 percent of the automobile industry in Canada; General Motors purchased Opel, by 1929 the best-selling automobile in Germany; Henry Ford helped build an automobile plant in Soviet Russia; and American firms handled about one-third of oil sales in France.

American culture—including household appliances, foods, language, music, film, and appreciation for machines—also spread worldwide. "Today we go to America as the Japanese once came to Germany," an industrialist from Weimar Germany wrote after visiting Detroit to observe American mass-production techniques.[42] U.S. government support for the expansion of the communications industry helped International Telephone and Telegraph (ITT), Radio Corporation of America (RCA), Associated Press (AP), and United Press (UP) become international giants by 1930. American movies so dominated the global market that the "sun . . . never sets on the British Empire and the American motion picture." Indeed, "trade follows the film," and together they so advertised U.S. culture abroad that some foreigners feared that "Americanization" would engulf them.[43] As "the most pervasive and persuasive of American contributions to European culture," according to one scholar, Hollywood movies "epitomized American culture in its mass orientation, tempo, monumentalism, sensationalism and profit urge."[44] Thus did street urchins in London adopt American slang: "O.K., kid" and "What are you doing tonight, babe?"[45] In 1929 alone, some 251,000 American tourists visited Europe, where they spent $323 million. F. W. Woolworth had opened 350 stores in England, with nothing priced above a sixpence. For German women "Americanization" produced, among other things, an advertisement from Siemens describing "How the Buschmüllers Got a Vacuum."[46] From mass-production methods to soda fountains and gym shoes, American ways claimed an international clientele.

When the Rockefeller Foundation sponsored programs in preventive medicine, hygiene, public health, and nursing in Eastern and Central Europe in the 1920s, this philanthropic institution also introduced America to foreigners. Under Rockefeller auspices, for example, "Kentucky closets" (outdoor toilets) became ubiquitous in Croatian villages.[47] The foundation also battled yellow fever in Latin America and supported colleges to train doctors in Lebanon and China—all under the philosophy that culture adoption, economic expansion, and social and political stability went hand in hand.

The Weight of the United States in the World Economy

Relative Value of Industrial Production, 1925–1929

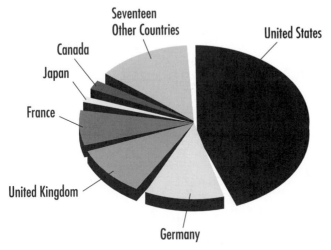

Source: U.S. Department of Commerce, *The United States in the World Economy* (Washington, D.C.: Government Printing Office, 1943), p. 28

This economic-cultural activity faced obstacles. Mexican nationalism, confiscation of property in Soviet Russia, European resentments, a wrecked German economy, wartime destruction in Europe, growing tariff walls, and the dislocation of international finance caused by World War I debts and reparations—all hindered enterprising Americans. U.S. government decisions offered welcome but limited help. The Webb-Pomerene Act (1918) permitted American companies to combine for purposes of foreign trade without prosecution under the antitrust laws; the Edge Act of 1919 legalized branch banks abroad; and the Merchant Marine Act of 1920 authorized the federal government to sell vessels to private companies and to make loans for the construction of new ships. New tax laws also permitted foreign tax credits for American investors abroad. Secretary Hoover put the Department of Commerce behind trade expansion by providing businesses with research data and advice. To help financiers avoid unproductive foreign lending and risky foreign bonds, official Washington tried to oversee loans and bond sales, but the practice never became consistent or thorough. For example, the government discouraged the sale in the United States of the bonds of a Czech brewery because it would violate the "spirit" of prohibition laws, but tolerated an unproductive loan for a sports palace in Germany.

Believing trade essential to domestic prosperity, the United States continued to proclaim the Open Door policy but applied it selectively and imperfectly. U.S. officials usually invoked the policy where the United States faced vigorous competition, as in Asia and the Middle East. In Latin America and the Philippines, however, where American capital and trade dominated, something approximating a "closed

The Contracting Spiral of World Trade

January 1929 to March 1933
Total Imports of 75 Countries in Millions of Dollars

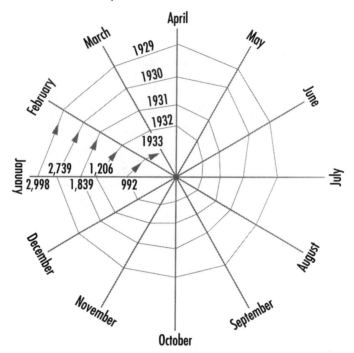

Source: Charles P. Kindleberger, *The World in Depression, 1929–1939* (Berkeley and Los Angeles: University of California Press, 1973), p. 172. Copyright © 1973 by The Regents of the University of California; reprinted by permission of the University of California Press.

door" developed. Europeans complained bitterly that the United States followed a double standard. They also resented American tariff policy, which made it difficult to sell to the United States—as they had to do in order to obtain the dollars necessary to buy American goods. The tariff acts of 1922 (Fordney-McCumber) and 1930 (Hawley-Smoot) raised duties to protect domestic producers and invited retaliation against American products. Economists lamented the irrationality of Washington's seeking, "on the one hand, to promote exports . . . , while on the other hand, by increasing tariffs it makes exportation ever more difficult." They predicted "a tariff war" that would disturb world peace.[48] Some twenty-five nations by 1932 had retaliated against American imports. Hoover held that high tariffs and overseas economic expansion could proceed hand in hand, and until the Great Depression struck in 1929 the seeming contradiction appeared to work.

The depression raised havoc with the international economy. Only two countries might have led the world out of depression, but the "British couldn't and the Americans wouldn't."[49] Economic nationalism guided most countries as they tried to protect themselves from the cataclysm with higher tariffs and import quotas.

World trade declined 40 percent in value and 25 percent in volume from 1929 to mid-1933. In 1933 the United States exported goods worth $2.1 billion, down from the 1929 figure of $5.4 billion. American capital stayed at home, and foreign holders of American loans defaulted. American private investments abroad slumped to $13.5 billion, down from the $17.2 billion figure of 1930. President Hoover flatly—and wrongly—called it a "patently European crisis."[50] His successor, Franklin D. Roosevelt, confronting 13 million unemployed Americans when he took office in 1933, also succumbed to economic nationalism as he created his New Deal recovery program. He abruptly sabotaged the London Economic Conference, indicating that the United States would henceforth "pursue domestic recovery by means of a policy of unilateralism."[51] But Hull gradually persuaded him that lowered tariffs would spur U.S. foreign trade and spark an economic upturn at home. Hull also preached that healthy world trade would contribute to stable politics and peace at a time when Japan, Germany, and Italy were turning to political extremes and threatening aggression. It would also deter Bolshevism from exploiting Europe's economic and social turmoil. "International commerce," Hull avowed, "is not only calculated to aid materially in the restoration of prosperity everywhere, but it is the greatest civilizer and peacemaker in the experience of the human race."[52]

In 1934 Hull piloted through Congress the Reciprocal Trade Agreements Act, which empowered the president to reduce tariffs by as much as 50 percent after agreements with other nations under the doctrine of the most-favored nation. This principle, which had traditionally guided American trade, meant that the United States was entitled to the lowest tariffs imposed by a country (in short, the best favor that country granted any other nation) with which the United States had a reciprocal agreement, and vice versa. The reciprocal trade program did retard the deterioration of world trade, but, as President Roosevelt confessed, "those trade treaties are just too goddamned slow. The world is moving too fast."[53] Hull also created in 1934 the Export-Import Bank, a governmental agency designed to provide loans to expand foreign trade. Washington could give or withhold credits to facilitate foreign-policy goals as well. Yet in 1937 FDR waxed skeptical in thinking that "an economic approach to peace is a weak reed."[54]

The reciprocal trade program and the bank came too late to help solve one of the major troubling legacies of World War I and Versailles—the debts-reparations tangle. Whereas before the war U.S. citizens owed some $3 billion to Europeans, after the war European citizens owed private Americans $3 billion and their governments owed another $10 billion, largely because of wartime loans. America had gone dramatically from a debtor to a creditor nation. But how would Europeans earn dollars to pay such a huge sum? American investments, sale of goods to the United States, U.S. tourist spending, and income from German reparations payments ranked as the most promising sources. But the Germans proved incapable of meeting the indemnity of $33 billion, so in the early 1920s the British began asking for a cancellation of the debts, arguing that Americans should write them off as a contribution to the Allied victory. Europeans, then, looked on the war loans as essentially political in character, rather than as business transactions. Anyway, they pointed out, they had given lives and had endured destruction of property, but the

United States had not suffered military devastation and had enjoyed unprecedented profits from sales to the Allies. America indignantly rejected this argument, prompting Britons to think "Americans are dirty swine."[55]   The humorist Will Rogers captured the American mood: "There is only one way we could be worse with the Europeans, and that is to have helped them out in two wars instead of one."[56] Congress created the War Debt Commission in 1922 to negotiate full payment. The commission ultimately forgave or canceled about half of the Allied debts. From 1918 to 1931 the United States actually received only $2.6 billion in Allied debts payments.

By stabilizing European finances, restoring trade, and encouraging the private flow of capital to Germany, U.S. diplomats sought to "harness Germany's resources to the cause of European recovery without restoring its prewar hegemony or reinvigorating the economic nationalism and autarky" that could lead to world war.[57] The debts-reparations embroglio eventually undercut this strategy. Wild inflation, a crippled economy, inadequate exports, and anti-Versailles hostility prompted the Germans to default on reparations payments in 1922–1923. France and Belgium thereupon aggravated Germany's plight by seizing the rich Ruhr Valley. In 1924 the State Deparment encouraged the businessman Charles G. Dawes to negotiate the Dawes Plan, whereby American investors such as the J. P. Morgan Company loaned millions to Germany and Berlin accepted a systematic reparations payment schedule. But the European economy simply could not bear the heavy debts (Europeans also owed money to other Europeans) and the reparations. Nor could American capital continue to keep Europe afloat. Under the Young Plan of 1929, another salvaging effort reduced German reparations to $9 billion. That year, too, President Hoover informed the British that he would cancel their debt if they transferred Bermuda, British Honduras (Belize), and Trinidad to the United States. London refused. In 1931 Hoover declared a one-year moratorium on debts payments. Thereafter only Finland met its debt obligations, forever winning a place in American hearts.

Debtors defaulted, Germany stopped paying reparations, and the world settled into the devastating depression of the 1930s. "It was hardly surprising," the historian Bruce Kent has written, "that this rickety financial structure, the maintenance of which depended on a vigorous expansion of world trade and a buoyant international credit system, should have been shaken to its foundations by the economic contractions" of the depression.[58]

Peace Seekers for a World Without War

If Europeans and Americans failed to resolve the mammoth problems plaguing the international economy, they also failed to curb a growing arms race, although the Washington treaties of 1922 held promise (see Chapter 5), and peace sentiment ran high in the United States. In 1923, when the publisher Edward Bok sponsored a contest for the best peace plan, he received more than 22,000 entries. Eleanor Roosevelt, Franklin's wife, helped organize the bipartisan peace prize. The winner of $100,000 was a member of the New York Peace Society who recommended joining the World Court and working with the League of Nations. Some peace advocates, such as the Carnegie Endowment for International Peace, placed their hopes in such global institutions. Pacifists in the Fellowship of Reconciliation, the War Resisters League, and the Women's Peace Union, in contrast, renounced individual participation in war. Religious groups pointed to the un-Christian character of war. Salmon Levinson, a Chicago lawyer who organized the American Committee for the Outlawry of War, argued that "war is an institution in the same sense as the church, the school or the home. It will never cease to be an institution until it becomes illegal."[59] Some business leaders, such as Thomas J. Watson of International Business Machines (IBM), endorsed the theme of "world peace through world trade."[60] Women gravitated to their own organizations, such as Carrie Chapman Catt's moderate Committee on the Cause and Cure of War and Jane Addams's and Emily Greene Balch's radical U.S. Section of the Women's International League for Peace and Freedom (WILPF), because they lacked influence in male-dominated groups and because of the popular assumption that women—as life givers and nurturing mothers—had a unique aversion to violence and war. Disarmament and anticolonialism became the missions of many peace-oriented people. Radical pacifists and antiwar advocates agitated for fundamental social and economic change in order to remove social injustice, which they saw as the capitalist wellsprings of imperialism and war. The National Council for the Prevention of War, founded in 1921, served as an organizational umbrella for the divergent peace groups.

Most peace activists or peace-conscious citizens believed that the United States, because of its basically democratic and pacific inclinations, could regenerate habitually war-prone Europe. In the 1920s, such reformist ideas did not seem farfetched: arms seemed controllable (technology had not yet produced global bombers or atomic weapons); domestic economies still did not rely heavily for their prosperity on defense production; the revulsion against World War I remained intense; and few warmongers had yet seized governments. Yet when Dorothy Detzer of WILPF threatened the loss of a million female votes if President Hoover did not name Mt. Holyoke College president Mary Wooley as a delegate to the Geneva Disarmament Conference, Secretary Stimson grumbled that Wooley "knows nothing about the subject. I presume, however, that she can read."[61] Notwithstanding Wooley's active participation, and a WILPF-sponsored Transcontinental Peace Caravan that forwarded several hundred thousand signatures to Geneva, the disarmament talks ran afoul of the Manchurian crisis (see Chapter 5) and accomplished little.

One of the peace movement's few achievements was the Kellogg-Briand Pact of 1928. France, prodded by James T. Shotwell, a Columbia University professor and trustee of the Carnegie Endowment for International Peace, asked the United States to sign a bilateral treaty renouncing war between the two nations. The security-conscious French, ever worried about a revived Germany, seemed to want an "American Locarno," in which Washington would support the European guarantee of France's eastern boundary as stipulated in the Locarno Treaty of 1925.[62] Washington coolly received the request. But a publicity campaign for a multilateral treaty launched by Shotwell, Salmon Levinson, and Senator William Borah, as well as pressure from women's delegations, prodded Secretary Kellogg into action. In February 1928 he sent a draft treaty to France and other powers. Foreign Minister

"Come on in. I'll treat you right. I used to know your daddy." C. D. Batchelor's cartoon won a Pulitzer Prize in 1937. As the historian Michael Sherry has noted, the depiction of war as "a diseased whore luring men to their death" revealed the "strikingly—sometimes maliciously—gendered ways in which war was often portrayed in modern American culture." (Library of Congress)

Aristide Briand fumed; Kellogg and the peace advocates had transformed his Franco-American security treaty into a universal declaration against war. That August in Paris, the signatories, eventually numbering sixty-two, agreed to "condemn recourse to war for the solution of international controversies, and renounce it as an instrument of national policy."[63]

The Kellogg-Briand Pact required no real sacrifices and established no precise responsibilities. On January 15, 1929, the Senate approved it 85 to 1, the lone dissenter being John J. Blaine of Wisconsin, a confirmed Anglophobe. Hardly lulled into a sense of security by the treaty, the Senate that same day approved funds for fifteen new cruisers. Peace advocates did not naively believe that Kellogg-Briand guaranteed a peaceful world. Because "many people . . . are unwilling to support the Secretary of State's proposals for outlawing big wars while he continues to wage little wars" in places such as Nicaragua (see Chapter 5), Dorothy Detzer regarded it as a first step in a long process and championed the pact as a way of alerting the American people to think once again of the costs of war.[64] Thus it held educational value. And the pact gave the Allies the legal grounds after World War II to punish Axis leaders for plotting aggressive war.

The League of Nations, itself designed to check wars, opened in Geneva without the United States. Washington at first ignored League communications. But by 1925 U.S. diplomats were discreetly participating in League functions. By 1930, unofficial American "observers" had attended more than forty League conferences on such questions as health, prostitution, obscene materials, codification of international law, and opium. In October 1931, U.S. envoy Prentiss B. Gilbert formally participated in League Council meetings on the Manchurian crisis, but Washington would only push the League to cite the Kellogg-Briand Pact and condemn Japan for aggression (see Chapter 5). The United States nearly did join the League-sponsored Permanent Court of International Justice (World Court), which sought to arbitrate international disputes when requested to do so. In 1926 the Senate approved U.S. membership but so qualified it that the court could not accept the American proposal. In 1935 a treaty of membership nearly gained the two-thirds vote, aided by FDR's claim that "the sovereignty of the United States [would] in no way be diminished or jeopardized."[65] That eminent jurists such as Charles Evans Hughes did sit as judges in the World Court offered internationalists some solace.

American participation in disarmament conferences in 1922 (Washington), 1927 (Geneva), 1930 (London), 1932–1933 (Geneva), and 1935–1936 (London) also demonstrated America's international but independent diplomatic course. At those conferences, the United States sought arms limitations, especially on navies, in part because it hoped to shackle others at a time when a parsimonious Congress restrained military U.S. growth. Except for some naval restrictions negotiated at the Washington and London conferences, little was accomplished. Without building to treaty limits, the United States sought to check the quantitative growth of other navies; France would not endorse disarmament until it received security guarantees; the British had a huge empire to protect and police by sea; Italy and Germany plotted military buildups; Japan eyed naval expansion in the Pacific. German rearmament under Adolf Hitler after 1933 and Japanese renunciation of Washington treaty provisions in 1934 signalled the failure of the peace seekers as the world stumbled toward global war.

Cold as Steel: Soviet-American Encounters

Soviet Russia signed the Kellogg-Briand Pact and joined the League of Nations in 1934. Yet most European nations and the United States treated Bolshevik Russia as an outsider, a revolutionary disease to be isolated. It was like "having a wicked and disgraceful neighbor," Herbert Hoover wrote. "We did not attack him, but we did not give him a certificate of character by inviting him into our homes."[66] Only when Europe tottered on the brink of war in 1939 did Germany on the one hand and France and Britain on the other seriously woo Soviet Russia. Only grudgingly did the United States establish commercial and diplomatic contacts with the Soviet Union during the interwar years.

Even though V. I. Lenin had said in 1918 that "with the United States we have friction, encounters, struggle, but there can also be agreement," Republican administrations in the 1920s adhered to the nonrecognition policy set by Woodrow Wilson.[67] The Bolsheviks had confiscated American-owned property valued at $336 million, and Russia owed another $192 million to the U.S. government and still another $107 million to American nationals (Tsarist and Provisional government debts). Until Moscow paid, recognition would be denied. Antiradical sentiment in the United States, moreover, saw the Bolsheviks as godless, uncivilized, anticapitalist, violent revolutionaries who chained their workers like slaves to an authoritarian system. The *New York Times,* American Legion, and American Federation of Labor, among others, bitterly castigated the Soviet experiment. Secretary Stimson, ever wary of the American Communist party, promised in 1930 to deny recognition until Russia "ceased to agitate for the overthrow of American institutions by revolution."[68] Only a few Americans, such as Senator Borah and the International Ladies Garment Workers Union, urged tolerance and recognition while they criticized the Soviet system.

If most Americans shunned the Bolsheviks, others edged closer. In 1921 Russia suffered a devastating famine. Secretary of Commerce Herbert Hoover organized shipments of food and medicine to needy areas. Moved by humanitarianism, Hoover also believed that this aid would help implant American influence in Russia and serve as a counterrevolutionary force. From 1921 to 1924 the American Relief Administration collected $50 million from the federal government and private citizens for assistance to 10 million Russians.

American businesses seemed willing to "sell the misguided fanatics all they are willing to pay for."[69] The State Department separated its distaste for Bolshevism from its desire for economic expansion and permitted important commercial relations to develop. International Harvester, General Electric, and Du Pont signed trade and technical assistance contracts with the Soviet government, often through its purchasing agency in New York, the Soviet-owned Amtorg Trading Corporation. By 1924 Soviet purchases of American products had jumped seven times over the 1923 figure. The entrepreneur and future ambassador W. Averell Harriman obtained monopolistic rights to rich manganese deposits in Soviet Georgia valued at $1 billion, from which Harriman eventually secured a "reasonable profit."[70] In 1928, Americans accounted for 24 percent of all foreign investment in Soviet Russia. Communist plans for industrialization and collectivization could not have advanced without American machinery, technology, and engineers (1,000 by 1931), although German trade and investments also figured heavily in Soviet economic growth.

For people who believed that capitalism and communism could never meld, Henry Ford's contract with the Soviet Union in 1929 seemed remarkable. Yet the business magnate agreed to supply technical information needed for the large Nizhni-Novgorod automobile factory, which would buy Ford parts and produce a car like the Model A and a truck like the Model AA. Ford eventually lost $578,000 on this multimillion-dollar venture, which terminated in 1934. Expecting a "market for Ford products which . . . may someday surpass in volume all the rest of Europe and Asia combined," the auto entrepreneur did sell the Soviets on mass-production techniques (*Fordizatsia*).[71] By 1927, 85 percent of the Soviets' tractors were "Fordsons." Once Moscow acquired Western skills and technology, the Soviet leader Leon Trotsky predicted, "Americanized Bolshevism will defeat and crush imperialist Americanism."[72] Not so.

American-Russian economic ties began to loosen in the early 1930s. With the Great Depression causing widespread unemployment, government and business officials resented Soviet announcements in the United States that jobs were available in Russia. Russia also began selling goods ("dumping") in the world market below American prices. The United States banned imports of Soviet paper pulp because convict labor allegedly produced it. In retaliation the Soviets reduced drastically their buying of American products. In another abortive venture, the famed Russian director Sergei Eisenstein came to Hollywood in 1930 to film Theodore Dreiser's *An American Tragedy,* only to have Paramount terminate his contract and U.S. authorities deport him to Mexico. Eisenstein thereafter always expressed contempt for capitalist "Californica."[73] By 1932 American exports to Russia had declined 90 percent from the 1931 trade. Business executives eager for markets began to argue that official diplomatic recognition might restart stalled commercial relations. The Reconstruction Finance Corporation, a U.S. government agency, helped by extending Russia a $4 million credit for the purchase of American cotton.

The Roosevelt administration, because it wanted to improve trade and deter further Japanese encroachment on China, and simply because nonrecognition served no useful purpose, formally recognized the Soviet Union in November 1933. Roosevelt himself conducted the negotiations. "We would recognize the Devil with a false face if he would contract for some pitchforks," Will Rogers quipped.[74] But the exchange of embassies did not smooth relations or halt Japan. American trade with Russia improved little, despite the signing of a trade treaty in 1935 and the establishment of the Export-Import Bank. The loan or credit that Roosevelt and Commissar for Foreign Affairs Maxim Litvinov had discussed at the time of recognition never materialized because of disagreement over compensation for debts. When American communists spoke critically of the United States at Moscow's Seventh International Communist (Comintern) Congress in 1935, Sec-

"So You're the Big Bad Bear!"
Roosevelt and Soviet commissar for foreign affairs Maxim Litvinov met in Washington in 1933. The atmosphere was friendly. (*Washington Evening Star*, Library of Congress)

retary Hull charged a violation of Russia's no-propaganda pledge. The Kremlin expected governments to "fall like ripe fruit from their capitalist treetops," noted another U.S. diplomat.[75]

Other issues disrupted Soviet-American relations. Named the first ambassador to Moscow, William Bullitt left America in 1933 as a friend of Russia. Two years later he resigned, convinced that the Soviet government "is a conspiracy to commit murder and nothing else."[76] He had changed his mind because of difficult living conditions in Moscow, spies among his servants, indignities inflicted by rude Soviet bureaucrats, his own volatile prejudices (he called one Soviet commissar "a wretched little kike"), and the ubiquitous Soviet tyranny.[77] Bullitt soon "deviled the Russians. I did all I could to make things unpleasant."[78] He mocked the Comintern's call for a popular front against Germany as similar to the tiger's "historic ride with the young lady of Niger. The Communists feel sure they will come back from the ride with the Socialists and Democrats inside."[79]

The ghastly purges that began in 1935 also moved Bullitt and others toward the hard line. "The last mass trials were a great success. There are going to be fewer but better Russians," quipped an unsmiling Greta Garbo in the movie *Ninotchka* (1939).[80] Bullitt's successor as ambassador, the wealthy Joseph E. Davies, thought Soviet Premier Joseph Stalin "cold as steel" and the trials "a nightmare."[81] George F. Kennan, a member of the embassy staff, endured a "liberal education in the horrors of Stalinism."[82] Kennan, who had much enjoyed the "fraternity-like atmosphere" and "homosocial bonding" of 1933–1934 (the "the high point of [my] life . . . in comradeship, in gaiety, in intensity of experience"), attended the purge trials in person. So intense was the "eroticized discourse" of Kennan, Bullitt, and other diplomats, the historian Frank Costigliola has suggested, that their passionate outrage at official Soviet cruelties resembled that of spurned suitors thwarted in their wooing of the Russian people. Nondiplomats reacted in much the same way.[83] The journalist Eugene Lyons, a United Press correspondent in Russia from 1928 to 1934, became sickened by the callousness of Stalin's regime: "The great tragic themes of peasant liquidation, persecution of intellectuals, tightening food shortage were bodied forth in hundreds of individual tragedies," he sadly wrote.[84]

If the purges stunned many Americans, the Nazi-Soviet Pact of August 1939 outraged them. Stalin believed that the Western European powers and the United States had let Hitler expand uninhibited to encourage the German's design to conquer Russia. And Stalin had so depleted the officer ranks of his army through the purges that he was in no position to stave off an expected German attack. In the United States, the nonaggression pact, which secretly divided Poland, reinforced charges that Stalin had become Hitler's friend. When World War II erupted in September 1939, many Americans blamed the Soviet Union.

Hitler's Germany, Appeasement, and the Outbreak of War

By exploiting the depression-afflicted economy and the vehement attitudes against the Versailles treaty in Germany, the Nazi leader Adolf Hitler came to power in January 1933. Racist toward Jews, emphatically anti-Bolshevik, and fanatical in his quest for personal power, Hitler set out to recapture past glory through the concept of Pan Germanism. In October 1933, Hitler withdrew Germany from the faltering League of Nations and denounced disarmament talks. He told an associate that the European powers would "never act! They'll just protest. And they will always be too late."[85] Indeed, France and Britain settled on a timid policy of "appeasement," hoping to satisfy what they thought were Hitler's limited goals and to avert another European war. By 1935 Britain, France, Italy, and the League of Nations had censured Germany for building a huge army and air force. Yet at the same time, Britain agreed that Germany could rebuild its navy to 35 percent of the size of the British navy, another costly concession to German militarism.

Hardly adjusted to the rise of Nazi Germany, the world watched as Italy invaded the African state of Ethiopia in October 1935. The fascist Benito Mussolini had governed Italy since 1922, and he had long dreamed of creating an Italian empire. Already holding Somaliland and Eritrea as African colonies, Mussolini gradually pressed Ethiopian leader Haile Selassie until military skirmishes broke out. Then Mussolini invaded and annexed Ethiopia. The League imposed an embargo on the shipment of war-related goods (except oil) to Italy. But the French, with their own empire in Africa, and the British, fearful that Italy might disrupt their imperial lifeline in the Mediterranean, seemed willing to sacrifice Ethiopia, a mere

Benito Mussolini (1883–1945). "Il Duce" excited a revival of Italian imperial grandeur by attacking Ethiopia in 1935. Will Rogers described Mussolini as a "cross between Roosevelt, Red Grange, Babe Ruth . . . , the elder La Follette, a touch of Borah, Bryan of '96, Samuel Gompers, and Tunney." (National Archives)

Adolf Hitler (1889–1945). When Hitler took power in 1933, some Americans likened his mustachioed face to that of the actor Charlie Chaplin. In this propagandistic German painting, the anticommunist, anti-Semitic Nazi leader is surrounded by swastikas and saluting followers. Hitler called the United States a "mongrel society" that was "hopelessly weak," but he learned otherwise. (U.S. Army)

"corridor for camels."[86] They also feared that further hostilities would "play into Germany's hands" and "might mean a general war in Europe."[87]

Apparently encouraged by Anglo-French docility over Ethiopia, Hitler in March 1936 ordered his goose-stepping troops into the Rhineland, the area bordering Belgium and France that the Versailles treaty had declared permanently demilitarized. After World War I, the French had erected the Maginot Line, a series of large guns and defensive bunkers along the German-French border. By seizing the Rhineland, Germany could outflank the line. The French, fearful of igniting another war, did not resist the German advance. Meanwhile, in June, the League of Nations lifted the economic sanctions against Italy. Victories by German athletes at the Berlin Olympiad in summer 1936, moreover, proved "as conducive to [Hitler's] self-esteem as a 98% plebiscite—and perhaps more convincing," observed U.S. ambassador William E. Dodd.[88] In October 1936, Germany and Italy arranged a tenuous alignment, the Rome-Berlin Axis; and a month later Germany and Japan joined in the Anti-Comintern Pact aimed at the Soviet Union.

Spain became contested ground, too. "Nationalist" soldiers under General Francisco Franco started the Spanish civil war in July 1936 by attacking the "Loyalist" Republican government. Eager for a Franco government hostile to France, Hitler and Mussolini poured military equipment and troops into the Nationalist effort. The tepid Anglo-French response produced an International Non-Intervention Committee of twenty-seven nations, remarkably including Germany and Italy. Although the signatories pledged to stay out of the Spanish conflict, Hitler and Mussolini continued covert aid, and France and Britain lived with the fiction that they had isolated the Spanish civil war. The Soviet Union and Mexico sent help to the Republicans, and some 3,000 Americans fought alongside them in the famous Abraham Lincoln Brigade. "We were naive," one volunteer recalled, "but it's the kind of naiveté that the world needs and will always find somewhere, among the youth especially."[89] Franco and his brand of fascism nonetheless prevailed in early 1939.

The mid–1937 election of Neville Chamberlain as British prime minister enshrined the appeasement policy. He believed that Germany had good reason to want to reject the humiliating Versailles treaty and to claim status as a major power. Tolerant of Hitler's demand for mastery over people of German descent living in Austria, Czechoslovakia, and Poland, Chamberlain also judged that "Germany lacked the economic strength and political cohesion seriously to contemplate war and that she could be weaned from aggression by his blend of conciliation and firmness, carrot and stick."[90] Further, an appeased Germany could serve as a useful restraint on Soviet Russia.

In March 1938, German troops crossed into Austria and annexed it to the German Reich. Months of terrorism against Jews and opponents of Nazism in Austria followed. Hitler next demanded the Sudeten region of Czechoslovakia, where 3 million ethnic Germans lived. Hitler assured Chamberlain that this marked Germany's last territorial demand. Britain and France (which had a defense treaty with Prague) granted the Nazi this additional prize. The Czechs had to capitulate. The end of Czechoslovakia's independence came at the Munich Conference of September 29–30, 1938, where Italy, Germany, France, and Britain agreed never to make war against one another and to sever the Sudetenland from Czechoslovakia. The conferees did not consult the Czechs themselves, who were not invited to Munich, Germany. Chamberlain proclaimed "peace with honour" and "peace for our time," but as a precaution Britain launched a rearmament program.[91] Hitler soon accelerated his persecution of German Jews and in March 1939 swallowed the rest of Czechoslovakia. The following month Italy absorbed Albania.

Poland came next. Refusing Hitler's demands for the city of Danzig, the Poles soon faced German pressure. But London and Paris announced in March 1939 that they would stand behind an independent Poland. A grim Chamberlain judged it "impossible to deal with Hitler after he had thrown all his own assurances to the wind."[92] The Soviet Union then emerged as a central actor in the European tu-

Joachim von Ribbentrop (1893–1946) and Joseph Stalin (1879–1953). The German foreign minister (left) and Soviet premier smile their approval of the Nazi-Soviet nonaggression pact signed in August 1939. The news angered but did not surprise American officials, who monitored the secret negotiations through reports from a cooperative German diplomat in Moscow. (World War II Collection of Seized Enemy Records, National Archives)

mult. Germany, Britain, and France opened negotiations with Moscow in attempts to gain Soviet allegiance. Stalin chose Germany. "Britain and France wanted us to be their hired hand . . . and without pay," he remarked.[93] On August 23, Nazi Germany and Soviet Russia signed the nonaggression pact. Poland, the immediate victim, found itself divided between the two powers. As he watched Hitler cavort with the Bolshevik devil, one U.S. senator wrote privately: "If Germany can organize Russia and they make England give up her fleet, look out—we'll have a Nazi, or nasty, world."[94] On September 1, German soldiers invaded Poland. Two days later Britain and France declared war against Germany. On September 17, Soviet troops struck Poland, taking half the nation.

Throughout these years of descent into World War II, Hitler both admired and underrated the United States. Impressed by anti-Semite Henry Ford and his production techniques, he sent German car designers to Detroit before launching the *Volkswagen.* Nonetheless, he scorned the United States's influence in world affairs. Although his advisers told him that American isolationism might not last, he deemed the United States "incapable of conducting war"—a "Jewish rubbish heap," incapacitated by economic and racial crises, crime, and inept political leadership. "The inferiority and decadence of this allegedly new world is evident in its military inefficiency," he claimed.[95] For Hitler, too, the image of the emancipated American woman did not accord with "the Nazi ideal of a devoted Gretchen bearing future soldiers for the Third Reich's wars of conquest."[96] Because America seemed to be a "melting pot" of ethnic diversity, "half Judaized, half negrified," and because it relied on sea power, Hitler underestimated it, although some historians have argued that Hitler's long-range plans included aggressive war against the United States.[97] As the United States after 1938 increasingly tied its fortunes to Britain and France, Hitler's subjective views began to collide with the reality of American power.

American Isolationism and the Neutrality Acts

"This nation will remain a neutral nation," President Roosevelt announced on September 3, 1939, "but I cannot ask that every American remain neutral in thought as well."[98] Second thoughts about neutrality came only late in the decade. During the early 1930s the United States attempted to shield itself from conflict in Europe and remain rigidly neutral. Although most Americans responded hostilely to the rise of Nazism, and strongly disapproved of Hitler's machinations at home and abroad, they tried to isolate themselves from a continent they thought prone to self-destruction. If Britain and France could not handle German aggression in their own backyards, America could not do the job for them.

Americans also drew lessons from World War I. Disillusioned writers and "revisionist" historians argued that Germany had not solely precipitated war in 1914, that business leaders and propagandists had influenced a pro-British Wilson, and that the costs and results of war did not justify American participation. In 1934 the best-selling book *Merchants of Death* (by Helmuth Englebrecht and Frank Hanighen) argued that profiteering arms manufacturers had exploited the American economic and political system to compromise U.S. neutrality. Encouraged by President Roosevelt, Senator Gerald P. Nye held hearings during 1934–1936 to determine if mu-

Senator Hiram W. Johnson (1866–1945). The California progressive reformer, anti-imperialist, and firm isolationist served in the U.S. Senate for twenty-eight years. He opposed U.S. membership in the League of Nations and the World Court and called for strict U.S. neutrality toward Europe. The United States, Johnson insisted, "cannot strut as a knight-errant to reform the world." In 1941, however, he voted for U.S. entrance into World War II after the Japanese attack on Pearl Harbor. (Library of Congress)

nitions makers and bankers had lobbied Wilson into war. The committee never proved the allegation but did uncover substantial evidence that these entrepreneurs had exerted influence on behalf of the Allies. As one historian has concluded, the Nye Committee "exhibited documents which shocked Americans into the realization that there was a difference between selling instruments of human destruction and selling sewing machines or automobiles."[99] Popular sentiment held that World War I had been a tragic blunder and that Americans "must think of the next war as they would of suicide."[100]

Although they might disagree on particulars, peace groups, the scientist Albert Einstein, Herbert Hoover, the anti-Semite Father Charles E. Coughlin, the historian Charles Beard, and Senators William Borah, Hiram Johnson, and George Norris shared the traditional belief in political and military nonentanglement—"a north star, constant and steady, which will hold us true to our course."[101] The antiwar movement grew strong on college campuses and among women. Princeton University students organized the Veterans of Future Wars in 1936 and demanded $1,000 each as a bonus *before* going into battle, because few, they predicted, would live through the next war. The journalist William Allen White predicted that "the next war will see . . . the same bowwow of the big dogs to get the little dogs to go out and follow the blood scent and get their entrails tangled in the barbed wire."[102] In 1938, member of Congress Louis Ludlow introduced a constitutional amendment calling for a national referendum on decisions for war. Warned Ludlow: "It is impossible to imagine the next large-scale war being anything less than a vast carnival of death."[103] Roosevelt claimed that the amendment "would cripple any President in his conduct of our foreign relations," and even the isolationist Senator Arthur Vandenberg protested that it "would be as sensible to require a town meeting before permitting the fire department to put out the blaze."[104] A motion to discharge Ludlow's resolution from the Rules Committee failed by only 209 to 188.

Many so-called progressive isolationists believed that American entry into a European war would undercut the New Deal's attempts to recover from the depression. They remembered how the Wilson administration had savaged critics in World War I, how Wilson had cooperated with big business to win the war. Convinced that business expansionists helped create the conditions that spawned war, progressive isolationists sought to curb business adventures abroad that entangled the United States. The statistics were not as readily available to them as they are now to historians. By 1937, for example, twenty of the top one hundred American corporations had negotiated important agreements with Nazi Germany, some with the core of the German military machine, the I. G. Farben Company. Du Pont, Union Carbide, and Standard Oil signed contracts, with Standard Oil helping Germany develop synthetic rubber and aviation fuel. "American businessmen publicly opposed war as much as anyone else," one scholar has concluded, "but it would seem that the one price they would not pay for peace was private profit."[105]

Although sharply critical of fascism abroad, Dorothy Detzer, the dynamic executive secretary of the WILPF, also feared a "peculiar type of American Fascism" in which "women would be thrown back into the kitchen, as . . . in Germany."[106] Detzer and other peace progressives worked behind the scenes on behalf of the Nye Committee and neutrality legislation. Roosevelt wanted a neutrality law that would permit him to ban sales of arms to aggressors. Congress instead passed the Neutrality Act of 1935, requiring an American arms embargo against all belligerents after the president had officially proclaimed the existence of war. In short, FDR could neither designate nor punish the aggressor. Subsequent legislation banned loans to belligerents (Act of 1936) and required belligerents wishing to trade with the United States to carry away U.S. goods in their own ships ("cash and carry"), after payment on delivery (Act of 1937). The latter also forbade U.S. citizens to travel on belligerent vessels. An amendment of 1937 made the United States neutral in the Spanish civil war.

The Neutrality Acts erred in providing for no discrimination among the belligerents, no punishment of the aggressor. They denied the United States any forceful word in the cascading events in Europe. They amounted to an abdication of power. Yet, at the same time, much of what the isolationists said about the fruits of war rang true. Their criticisms of imperialism and business expansion were honest and telling. They scorned the British Empire and U.S. intervention in Latin America. They compared Italy's subjugation of Ethiopia to Britain's supremacy in India. Many of them warned about increasing the power of the president in foreign affairs beyond congressional reach. Their noble commitment to peace and their rejection of war as a solution to human problems were compelling. "Isolationism was," the historian Manfred Jonas has written, "the considered response to foreign and domestic developments of a large, responsible, and respectable segment of the American people."[107] In condemning all imperialism—American, British, or German—the isolationists often refused to make the choice of the lesser of two or three evils. However praiseworthy their thought, their formulas for the 1930s proved as misguided as Britain's appeasement policy.

Roosevelt Shifts and Congress Balks on the Eve of War

President Roosevelt, sensitive to American sentiment against U.S. entanglement in Europe and sharing much of the pacifist loathing of war, responded haltingly to the events of the 1930s. His foreign policy fed appeasement. When Italy attacked Ethiopia, Roosevelt stated that the United States sought above all to avoid war. America would set a peaceful example for other nations to follow. He and Hull invoked the Neutrality Act, warned Americans not to travel on belligerent ships, and suggested a moral embargo against trade with the warring parties. Actually, American businesses ignored the moral embargo and increased commerce with Italy, especially in oil. Aggression in Africa sparked "the first great manifestation of Afro-American interest in foreign affairs."[108] In addition to anti-Italian boycotts and petitions by black churches to the pope, the African-American poet Langston Hughes composed a "Ballad of Ethiopia" in support of black solidarity.[109] In August 1936, the president gave a stirring speech at Chautauqua, New York, recalling World War I: "I have seen war. . . . I have seen blood running from the wounded. I have seen men coughing out their gassed lungs. . . . I hate war."[110]

In January 1937, Roosevelt asked Congress for an arms embargo against Spain. Congress obliged, but the decision sparked considerable debate. It produced "malevolent neutrality" that worked against the "Loyalist" Republican government and in favor of Franco, who received arms from Germany and Italy.[111] In this case, many isolationists protested neutrality—the sacrifice of Spanish democracy. They agonized: How can one be commited to both peace and liberty? Roosevelt and Hull chose strict neutrality, in essence backing feeble British-French efforts to contain the civil war and aligning themselves with the pro-Franco views of the Catholic hierarchy at home. Yet Roosevelt privately pondered ways to curb the aggressors.

In July, when Japan plunged into undeclared war against China, Roosevelt favored China by not invoking the Neutrality Act, thereby permitting the Chinese government to buy and import American war goods (see Chapter 5). Then in October he delivered his famous "quarantine" speech, calling for the isolation of international lawbreakers. Hoping that "people realize that war will be a greater danger . . . if we close all the doors and windows than if we go in the street and use our influence to curb the riot," FDR approached the British ambassador about a joint cruiser blockade against Japan and sent a naval officer to London for secret staff talks.[112] Under Secretary of State Sumner Welles also proposed a world conference on disarmament and international law in Washington, at which Roosevelt might quietly stiffen British diplomacy. Chamberlain, however, blocked the meeting in early 1938; he feared it would interfere with his efforts to negotiate with the aggressors. Convinced that he could "count on nothing from the Americans but words," Chamberlain continued to pursue appeasement.[113]

During the Czech crisis of 1938 the United States kept at a safe distance. The president appealed for negotiations to head off war, while telling Hitler that the United States had "no political involvements in Europe and will assume no obligations in the conduct of the present negotiations."[114] "Good man," Roosevelt cabled Chamberlain when he heard that the prime minister would go to Munich.[115] Yet the dismemberment of Czechoslovakia, combined with the Japanese terror in China, soon prompted the president to confess privately that he was ashamed of Munich. Worried about the insidious effects of "too much Eton and Oxford," FDR thought the British needed "a good stiff grog, inducing not only the desire to save civilization but the continued belief that they can do it."[116]

In October 1938, Roosevelt asked Congress for $300 million for national defense. He encouraged the State Department and Senator Key Pittman, the hard-drinking, gun-packing, incompetent chair of the Foreign Relations Committee, to lobby for the repeal of the arms embargo law. In November, in protest against Hitler's vicious persecution of the Jews, he recalled Ambassador Hugh Wilson from Berlin and never let him return. That same month, FDR initiated a program to build more than 10,000 warplanes per year, in order "to have something to back up my words."[117] He also secretly arranged for the French government to place orders for planes. In December the administration rallied behind a declaration of joint defense against aggression in the Western Hemisphere and loaned $25 million to China.

In January 1939, Roosevelt again urged revision of the Neutrality Act so that it would not "actually give aid to an aggressor and deny it to the victim."[118] The

"Uncomfortable Grandstand."   The British cartoonist David Low obviously did not think that a neutral United States could remain safe after the outbreak of war in Europe. President Roosevelt turns a quizzical face to Secretary of State Hull as the bombs fly and burst. (*London Evening Standard/* Solo)

crash of the A-20 bomber in Los Angeles and FDR's garbled statement about America's frontier on the Rhine stalled this initiative. The president thus delayed until March the introduction of a bill specifically repealing the arms embargo, and throughout the spring he allowed the erratic Pittman to direct legislative strategy. Reluctant to risk battle against sizable political odds, FDR failed to lead at a critical time. In April he asked Hitler and Mussolini to refrain from attacking countries named on a list, but his request met open derision, Il Duce saying that Italy would not respond to "Messiah-like messages."[119] The Senate Foreign Relations Committee, by a 12 to 11 vote, refused in July to report out a bill repealing the arms embargo. "I've fired my last shot," the president groaned.[120] Not until November 1939—after Germany's conquest of Poland—did Congress finally revise the Neutrality Act so that England and France, as belligerents, could purchase American arms on a cash-and-carry basis.

Even in fall 1939, however, most Americans joined their president in wanting to avoid participation in World War II. "We cannot expect . . . the United States to evolve quicker than we did," the British ambassador reported.[121] By sending Sumner Welles to Berlin, London, Paris, and Rome in the winter of 1940, FDR evidently thought he might mediate the conflict. Hitler's *blitzkrieg* in the west that spring killed any such possibility. The Democratic party platform of 1940, on which Roosevelt ran for a third term, reflected the American desire to avoid war but also to prepare for it: "We will not participate in foreign wars, and we will not send our army, naval or air forces to fight in foreign lands outside of the Americas except in case of attack." Still, it also promised "an invincible air force, a navy strong enough to protect all our seacoasts and our national interests, and a fully equipped and mechanized army."[122] As in World War I, because of their international interests, because U.S. power became intertwined in the war, and because they gradually abandoned neutrality to aid the Allies, Americans once again found themselves risking major war. The interwar quest for world order and peace had failed; the several Neutrality Acts had failed; independent internationalism had failed.

FURTHER READING FOR THE PERIOD 1920–1939

Overviews include Selig Adler, *The Isolationist Impulse* (1957); Warren I. Cohen, *Empire Without Tears* (1987); Robert A. Divine, *The Reluctant Belligerent* (1979); Justus D. Doenecke and John E. Wilz, *From Isolation to War* (1991); Robert Ferrell, *American Diplomacy in the Great Depression* (1957) and *Peace in Their Time* (1952); Sally Marks, *The Illusion of Peace* (1976); Arnold Offner, *The Origins of the Second World War* (1975); Brenda Gayle Plummer, *Rising Wind* (1996) (African Americans); Robert Schulzinger, *The Making of the Diplomatic Mind* (1975); Geoffrey S. Smith, *To Save a Nation* (1992); and Raymond Sontag, *A Broken World, 1919–1939* (1971).

The presidents and their presidencies are treated in David Burner, *Herbert Hoover* (1978); Martin Fausold, *The Presidency of Herbert C. Hoover* (1985); Robert Ferrell, *The Presidency of Calvin Coolidge* (1998); Ellis W. Hawley, ed., *Herbert Hoover: Secretary of Commerce* (1981); Donald R. McCoy, *Calvin Coolidge* (1967); Robert K. Murray, *The Harding Era* (1969); and Joan Hoff Wilson, *Herbert Hoover* (1975).

For Franklin D. Roosevelt, see James M. Burns, *The Lion and the Fox* (1956); Wayne S. Cole, *Roosevelt and the Isolationists* (1983); Robert Dallek, *Franklin D. Roosevelt and American Foreign Policy, 1933–1945* (1979); Kenneth R. Davis, *FDR* (1972–1993); Robert A. Divine, *Roosevelt and World War II* (1969); Frank Freidel, *Franklin D. Roosevelt* (1952–1973) and *Franklin D. Roosevelt* (1990); William E. Leuchtenburg, *Franklin D. Roosevelt and the New Deal* (1963); Frederick W. Marks III, *Wind over Sand* (1988); Willard Range, *Franklin D. Roosevelt's World Order* (1959); Arthur M. Schlesinger, Jr., *The Age of Roosevelt* (1957–1960); and Cornelius A. van Minnen and John F. Sears, eds., *FDR and His Contemporaries* (1992).

For the secretaries of state, see McGeorge Bundy, *On Active Service in Peace and War* (1948) (Stimson); Michael Butler, *Cautious Visionary* (1998) (Hull); L. Ethan Ellis, *Frank B. Kellogg and American and Foreign Relations* (1961); Robert Ferrell, *Frank B. Kellogg* (1963) and *Henry L. Stimson* (1963); Betty Glad, *Charles Evans Hughes and the Illusions of Innocence* (1967); Godfrey Hodgson, *The Colonel* (1990) (Stimson); Elting E. Morison, *Turmoil and Tradition* (1960) (Stimson); Dexter Perkins, *Charles Evans Hughes and American Democratic Statesmanship* (1956); and Julius Pratt, *Cordell Hull* (1964).

Other diplomats and politicians are studied in Leroy Ashby, *The Spearless Leader* (1972) (Borah); Fred A. Bailey, *William Edward Dodd* (1997); Will Brownell and Richard N. Billings, *So Close to Greatness* (1988) (Bullitt); Wayne S. Cole, *Senator Gerald P. Nye and American Foreign Relations* (1962); Ralph de Bedts, *Ambassador Joseph Kennedy* (1985); Irwin Gellman, *Secret Affairs* (1995) (Hull and Welles); Betty Glad, *Key Pittman* (1986); Frank W. Graff, *Strategy of Involvement* (1988) (Welles); Waldo Heinrichs, *American Ambassador* (1966) (Grew); Kenneth P. Jones, *Diplomats in Europe, 1919–1941* (1981); Richard C. Lower, *A Bloc of One* (1993) (Hiram Johnson); Richard Lowitt, *George W. Norris* (1963–1978); Elizabeth K. MacLean, *Joseph E. Davies* (1992); Jesse H. Stiller, *George S. Messersmith* (1987); Michael Weatherson and Hal W. Bochin, *Hiram Johnson* (1995); and Benjamin Welles, *Sumner Welles* (1997).

Economic foreign relations receive attention in Frederick Adams, *Economic Diplomacy* (1976); Derek H. Aldcroft, *From Versailles to Wall Street, 1919–1929* (1977); Joseph Brandes, *Herbert Hoover and Economic Diplomacy* (1962); Patricia Clavin, *The Failure of Economic Diplomacy* (1996); Herbert Feis, *The Diplomacy of the Dollar* (1950); Lloyd C. Gardner, *Economic Aspects of New Deal Diplomacy* (1964); Michael J. Hogan, *Informal Entente* (1977); Burton I. Kaufman, *Efficiency and Expansion* (1974); Charles P. Kindleberger, *The World in Depression, 1929–1939* (1986); Carl Parrini, *Heir to Empire* (1969); Stephen J. Randall, *United States Foreign Oil Policy, 1919–1948* (1986); William Stivers, *Supremacy and Oil* (1982); Mira Wilkins, *The Maturing of Multinational Enterprise* (1974); Joan Hoff Wilson, *American Business and Foreign Policy, 1920–1933* (1971); and Gilbert Ziebura, *World Economy and World Politics, 1924–1931* (1990).

The German reparations issue is explored in Bruce Kent, *The Spoils of War* (1989); Stephen Schuker, *American "Reparations" to Germany* (1988); and Marc Trachtenberg, *Reparation in World Politics* (1980).

Cultural issues and industries are highlighted in Frank Costigliola, *Awkward Dominion* (1984) (Europe); David H. Culbert, *News for Everyman: Radio and Foreign Affairs in Thirties America* (1976); George Q. Flynn, *Roosevelt and Romanism: Catholics and American Diplomacy, 1937–1945* (1976); Emily S. Rosenberg, *Spreading the American Dream* (1982); Thomas J. Saunders, *Hollywood in Berlin* (1994); Lawrence Spinelli, *Dry Diplomacy* (1989) (Prohibition); Richard W. Steele, *Propaganda in an Open Society* (1985); Arnold H. Taylor, *American Diplomacy and the Narcotics Traffic, 1900–1931* (1969); and Robert C. Williams, *Russian Art and American Money* (1980).

Defense preparedness and arms-control questions are discussed in James L. Abrahamson, *America Arms for a New Century* (1981); Thomas Buckley, *The United States and the Washington Conference* (1970); Roger Dingman, *Power in the Pacific: The Origins of Naval Arms Limitation, 1914–1922* (1976); Richard W. Fanning, *Peace and Disarmament* (1995); Emily O. Goldman, *Sunken Treaties* (1994) (naval arms control); Robert Kaufman, *Arms Control During the Pre-Nuclear Age* (1990); Ernest R. May, *Knowing One's Enemy* (1984) (intelligence assessment); Stephen Pelz, *Race to Pearl Harbor* (1974) (Second London Naval Conference); and Michael S. Sherry, *The Rise of American Air Power* (1987).

For peace advocates and the League of Nations, see Harriet H. Alonso, *The Women's Peace Union and the Outlawry of War* (1989); Jason Berger, *A New Deal for the World* (1981) (Eleanor Roosevelt); Charles Chatfield, *For Peace and Justice* (1971); Blanche Wiesen Cook, *Eleanor Roosevelt* (1992); Merle Curti, *Peace or War* (1936); Charles DeBenedetti, *Origins of the Modern American Peace Movement, 1915–1929* (1978) and *The Peace Reform in American History* (1980); Michael Dunne, *The United States and the World Court* (1988); D. F. Fleming, *The United States and World Organization, 1920–1933* (1938); Carrie Foster, *The Women and the Warriors* (1995); Catherine Foster, *Women for All Seasons* (1989); Robert D. Johnson, *The Peace Progressives and American Foreign Relations* (1995); Harold Josephson, *James T. Shotwell and the Rise of Internationalism in America* (1976); Warren F. Kuehl and Lynne K. Dunn, *Keeping the Covenant* (1997) (League); Gary B. Ostrower, *Collective Insecurity* (1979) (League); Lois Scharf, *Eleanor Roosevelt* (1987); Linda K. Schott, *Reconstructing Women's Thoughts* (1997) (WILPF); Joan Hoff Wilson and Marjorie Lightman, eds., *Without Precedent* (1984) (Eleanor Roosevelt); and Lawrence S. Wittner, *Rebels Against War* (1984).

For American isolationism, see overviews cited in the first paragraph and Warren I. Cohen, *The American Revisionists* (1967); Thomas Guinsburg, *The Pursuit of Isolationism* (1981); Manfred Jonas, *Isolationism in America* (1966); Thomas C. Kennedy, *Charles A. Beard and American Foreign Policy* (1975); and John Wiltz, *In Search of Peace* (1963) (Nye Committee).

Relations with Europe and Germany and the coming of World War II are studied in many of the works cited above and in James J. and Patience P. Barnes, *Hitler's* Mein Kampf *in Britain and America* (1980); Edward W. Bennett, *German Rearmament and the West, 1932–1933* (1979); Peter H. Buckingham, *International Normalcy: The Open Door Peace with the Former Central Powers, 1921–29* (1983); Bernard Burke, *Ambassador Frederic Sackett and the Collapse of the Weimar Republic* (1995); James V. Compton, *The Swastika and the Eagle* (1967); Jean-Baptiste Duroselle, *France and the United States* (1978); Barbara R. Farnham, *Roosevelt and the Munich Crisis* (1997); John Haight, Jr., *American Aid to France, 1938–1940* (1970); Melvyn Leffler, *The Elusive Quest* (1979) (France); Charles S. Maier, *Recasting Bourgeois Europe* (1975); Brian McKercher, ed., *Anglo-American Relations in the 1920s* (1991); William C. McNeil, *American Money and the Weimer Republic* (1986); Wolfgang

Mommsen and Lothar Kettenacker, eds., *The Fascist Challenge and the Policy of Appeasement* (1983); John E. Moser, *Twisting the Lion's Tail: American Anglophobia between the World Wars* (1999); Mary Nolan, *Visions of Modernity* (1994) (American business in Germany); Arnold Offner, *American Appeasement* (1969); R. A. C. Parker, *Chamberlain and Appeasement* (1993); Neal Pease, *Poland, the United States, and the Stabilization of Europe, 1919–1933* (1986); David Reynolds, *The Creation of the Anglo-American Alliance, 1937–41* (1982); David Reynolds and David Dimbleby, *An Ocean Apart* (1989); William R. Rock, *Chamberlain and Roosevelt* (1988); David F. Schmitz, *The United States and Fascist Italy* (1988); David F. Schmitz and Richard D. Challener, eds., *Appeasement in Europe* (1990); Dan P. Silverman, *Reconstructing Europe After the Great War* (1982); D. C. Watt, *How War Came* (1989); and Gerhard Weinberg, *The Foreign Policy of Hitler's Germany* (1970, 1980).

Soviet-American relations and recognition are discussed in Edward Bennett, *Recognition of Russia* (1970) and *Franklin D. Roosevelt and the Search for Security* (1985); Peter G. Boyle, *American-Soviet Relations* (1995); Dennis Dunn, *Caught Between Roosevelt and Stalin* (1998); Keith D. Eagles, *Ambassador Joseph E. Davies and American-Soviet Relations, 1937–1941* (1985); Beatrice Farnsworth, *William C. Bullitt and the Soviet Union* (1967); Peter Filene, *Americans and the Soviet Experiment* (1967); John Lewis Gaddis, *Russia, the Soviet Union, and the United States* (1990); Jonathan Haslam, *The Soviet Union and the Struggle for Collective Security in Europe* (1984); George F. Kennan, *Russia and the West Under Lenin and Stalin* (1960); Melvyn Leffler, *The Specter* (1994); James K. Libbey, *Alexander Gumberg and Soviet-American Relations* (1977); Thomas R. Maddux, *Years of Estrangement* (1980); David Mayers, *The Ambassadors and America's Soviet Policy* (1995); Katherine Siegel, *Loans and Legitimacy* (1996); Anthony Sutton, *Western Technology and Soviet Economic Development* (1968); Christine A. White, *British and American Commercial Relations with Soviet Russia* (1993); and Joan Hoff Wilson, *Ideology and Economics* (1974).

For the Spanish civil war, see Michael Alpert, *A New International History of the Spanish Civil War* (1998); Peter N. Carroll, *The Odyssey of the Abraham Lincoln Brigade* (1994); Mark Falcoff and Fredrick B. Pike, *The Spanish Civil War, 1936–1939* (1982); Allen Guttman, *The Wound in the Heart* (1962); Douglas Little, *Malevolent Neutrality* (1985); R. Dan Richardson, *Comintern Army* (1982); and Richard Traina, *American Diplomacy and the Spanish Civil War* (1968).

See also "Further Reading" in Chapters 5 and 6, the General Bibliography, and the following notes.

For comprehensive coverage of foreign-relations topics, see the articles in the four-volume *Encylocpedia of U.S. Foreign Relations* (1997), edited by Bruce W. Jentleson and Thomas G. Paterson.

NOTES TO CHAPTER 4

1. Quoted in Kenneth S. Davis, *FDR: Into the Storm* (New York: Random House, 1993), p. 401.
2. Quoted *ibid.,* p. 402.
3. Quoted *ibid.,* p. 401.
4. Henry Morgenthau, Jr., quoted in conference transcript, March 21, 1946, Box 391, Henry Morgenthau, Jr., Papers, Franklin D. Roosevelt Library, Hyde Park, N.Y.
5. David Reynolds, *The Creation of the Anglo-American Alliance, 1937–1941* (Chapel Hill: University of North Carolina Press, 1982), p. 43.
6. Quoted in Wayne S. Cole, *Roosevelt and the Isolationists* (Lincoln: University of Nebraska Press, 1983), p. 297.
7. Quoted in Michael S. Sherry, *The Rise of American Air Power* (New Haven: Yale University Press, 1987), pp. 79–80.
8. Quoted in Jean Monnet, *Memoirs* (London: Collins, 1978), p. 119.
9. Quoted in Sherry, *Air Power,* p. 80.
10. Quoted in Cole, *Roosevelt and Isolationists,* p. 301.
11. Quoted in conference transcript, "The French Airplane Mission," April 25, 1946, Box 391, Morgenthau Papers.

12. Transcript of "Conference with Senate Military Affairs Committee, Executive Offices of the White House, January 31, 1939, 12:45 P.M.," Personal Files, PPF 1-P, Franklin D. Roosevelt Papers, Roosevelt Library.
13. Quoted in J. Garry Clifford, "A Note on the Break Between Senator Nye and President Roosevelt in 1939," *North Dakota History,* XLIX (Summer 1982), 17.
14. *New York Times,* February 1, 1939.
15. Quoted in Clifford, "A Note," p. 14.
16. Entry of February 7, 1939, diary of J. Pierrepont Moffat, Houghton Library, Harvard University, Cambridge; and quoted in Reynolds, *Creation,* p. 37.
17. Transcript, "French Airplane Mission."
18. Warren F. Kimball, *The Juggler* (Princeton: Princeton University Press, 1991), p. 7.
19. Quoted in Sherry, *Air Power,* p. 79.
20. *Ibid.,* p. 82.
21. Henry Arnold quoted in John M. Haight, Jr., *American Aid to France, 1938–1940* (New York: Atheneum, 1970), p. 204.

22. Francois Duchêne, *Jean Monnet* (New York: Norton, 1994), p. 69.

23. Raymond Clapper to Alfred M. Landon, February 7, 1939, Landon Papers, Kansas State Historical Society, Topeka.

24. Franklin D. Roosevelt to Helen Rogers Reid, June 6, 1940, Reid Papers, Library of Congress, Washington, D.C.

25. Quoted in John M. Blum, *From the Morgenthau Diaries* (Boston: Houghton Mifflin, 1959–1967; 3 vols.), I, 118.

26. Quoted in Melvyn P. Leffler, "Political Isolationism: Economic Expansionism or Diplomatic Realism?" *Perspectives in American History, VIII* (1974), 419.

27. Joan Hoff Wilson, *American Business and Foreign Policy, 1920–1933* (Boston: Beacon Press, 1973 [c. 1971]), p. x.

28. Melvyn P. Leffler, *The Elusive Quest* (Chapel Hill: University of North Carolina Press, 1979), p. 362.

29. Quoted in L. Ethan Ellis, *Republican Foreign Policy, 1921–1933* (New Brunswick, N.J.: Rutgers University Press, 1968), p. 40.

30. Robert H. Ferrell, *The Presidency of Calvin Coolidge* (Lawrence: University Press of Kansas, 1988), p. 145.

31. Howard H. Quint and Robert H. Ferrell, eds., *The Talkative President* (Amherst: University of Massachusetts Press, 1964), p. 298.

32. Quoted in Frank Ninkovich, *Modernity and Power* (Chicago: University of Chicago Press, 1994), p. 80.

33. Warren F. Kuehl and Lynne K. Dunne, *Keeping the Covenant* (Kent, Ohio: Kent State University Press, 1997), p. 196.

34. Michael A. Sherry, *In The Shadow of War* (New Haven: Yale University Press, 1995), p. 28.

35. Willard Range, *Franklin D. Roosevelt's World Order* (Athens: University of Georgia Press, 1959), p. xii.

36. Quoted in Frank Freidel, *Franklin D. Roosevelt: Launching the New Deal* (Boston: Little, Brown, 1973), p. 459.

37. Benjamin Welles, *Sumner Welles* (New York: St. Martin's Press, 1997), p. 199.

38. Quoted in Jordan A. Schwarz, *Liberal* (New York: The Free Press, 1987), p. 191.

39. Wilbur Carr quoted in Martin Weil, *A Pretty Good Club* (New York: Norton, 1978), p. 47.

40. Quoted in Gregory Johnson and David A. Lenarcic, "The Decade of Transition," in B. J. C. McKercher and Lawrence Aronson, eds., *The North Atlantic Triangle in a Changing World* (Toronto: University of Toronto Press, 1996), p. 99.

41. Mira Wilkins, *The Maturing of Multinational Enterprise* (Cambridge: Harvard University Press, 1974), p. 138.

42. Quoted in Mary Nolan, *Visions of Modernity* (New York: Oxford University Press, 1994), p. 24.

43. Edward G. Lowry, "Trade Follows the Film," *Saturday Evening Post, CXCVIII* (November 7, 1925), 12.

44. Thomas Saunders, *Hollywood in Berlin* (Berkeley: University of California Press, 1994), p. 11.

45. Quoted in David Reynolds and David Dimbleby, *An Ocean Apart* (New York: Vintage, 1989), p. 116.

46. Quoted in Nolan, *Visions*, p. 216.

47. Quoted in Paul Weindling, "Public Health and Political Stabilization: The Rockefeller Foundation in Central and Eastern Europe Between the Two World Wars," *Minerva, XXXI* (Autumn 1993), 261.

48. *New York Times*, May 5, 1930.

49. Charles Kindleberger, *The World in Depression, 1929–1939* (Berkeley: University of California Press, 1973), p. 222.

50. Quoted in Patricia Clavin, *The Failure of Economic Diplomacy* (New York: St. Martin's Press, 1996), p. 16.

51. Quoted in Robert A. Hathaway, "1933–1945: Economic Diplomacy in a Time of Crisis," in William H. Becker and Samuel F. Wells, Jr., eds., *Economics and World Power* (New York: Columbia University Press, 1984), p. 285.

52. Quoted in Julius W. Pratt, *Cordell Hull* (New York: Cooper Square, 1964; 2 vols.) I, 112.

53. Quoted in Blum, *Morgenthau Diaries, I*, 151.

54. Quoted in Richard A. Harrison, "The United States and Great Britain," in David F. Schmitz and Richard D. Challener, eds., *Appeasement in Europe* (Westport, Conn.: Greenwood, 1990), p. 116.

55. Foreign Office diplomat quoted in Brian McKercher, "Wealth, Power, and the New International Order," *Diplomatic History, XII* (Fall 1988), 421.

56. Will Rogers, *Letters of a Self-Made Diplomat to His President* (New York: A. & C. Boni, 1926), p. xii.

57. Michael J. Hogan, "Revival and Reform," *Diplomatic History, VIII* (Fall 1984), 289.

58. Bruce Kent, *The Spoils of War* (New York: Oxford University Press, 1989), p. 10.

59. Quoted in Harold Josephson, *James T. Shotwell and the Rise of Internationalism in America* (Rutherford, N.J.: Fairleigh Dickinson University Press, 1975), p. 140.

60. Quoted in Charles DeBenedetti, "Peace Was His Profession," in Frank Merli and Theodore A. Wilson, eds., *Makers of American Diplomacy* (New York: Charles Scribner's Sons, 1974), p. 390.

61. Quoted in Rhodri Jefferys-Jones, *Changing Differences* (New Brunswick, N.J.: Rutgers University Press, 1995), p. 53.

62. James Shotwell quoted in Charles DeBenedetti, *Origins of the Modern American Peace Movement, 1915–1929* (Milwood, N.Y.: KTO Press, 1978), p. 187.

63. *The General Pact for the Renunciation of War* (Washington, D.C.: Government Printing Office, 1928).

64. Quoted in Richard W. Fanning, *Peace and Disarmament* (Lexington: University Press of Kentucky, 1995), p. 85.

65. Quoted in Michael Dunne, *The United States and the World Court* (New York: St. Martin's Press, 1988), p. 264.

66. Quoted in Melvyn P. Leffler, *The Specter of Communism* (New York: Hill & Wang, 1994), p. 19.

67. Quoted in David McFadden, *Alternative Paths* (New York: Oxford University Press, 1993), p. 26.

68. Quoted in David J. Danelski and Joseph S. Tulchin, eds., *The Autobiographical Notes of Charles Evans Hughes* (Cambridge: Harvard University Press, 1973), p. 262.

69. Loy Henderson quoted in Peter G. Boyle, *American-Soviet Relations* (London: Routledge, 1995), p. 23.

70. Katherine A. S. Siegel, *Loans and Legitimacy* (Lexington: University Press of Kentucky, 1996), p. 126.

71. Quoted in Christine A. White, *British and American Commercial Relations with Soviet Russia, 1918–1924* (Chapel Hill: University of North Carolina Press, 1992), p. 223.

72. Quoted in Reynolds and Dimbleby, *Ocean Apart*, p. 118.

73. Quoted in David Bordwell, *The Cinema of Eisenstein* (Cambridge: Harvard University Press, 1993), p. 19.

74. Will Rogers, *How We Elect Our Presidents* (Boston: Little, Brown, 1952), p. 148.

75. John Wiley quoted in Thomas R. Maddux, *Years of Estrangement* (Tallahassee: University Presses of Florida, 1980), p. 21.

76. Quoted in Irwin Gellman, *Secret Affairs* (Baltimore: Johns Hopkins University Press, 1995), p. 141.

77. Quoted in David Mayers, *The Ambassadors and America's Soviet Policy* (New York: Oxford University Press, 1995), p. 113.

78. Quoted in Beatrice Farnsworth, *William C. Bullitt and the Soviet Union* (Bloomington: Indiana University Press, 1967), p. 153.

79. Quoted in Mayers, *Ambassadors*, p. 115.

80. Quoted in Melvin Small, "Buffoons and Brave Hearts: Hollywood Portrays the Russians, 1939–1944," *California Historical Quarterly, LII* (Winter 1973), 327.

81. Quoted in Elizabeth Kimball MacLean, *Joseph E. Davies* (Westport, Conn.: Praeger, 1992), pp. 50, 55.

82. George F. Kennan, *Memoirs, 1925–1950* (Boston: Little, Brown, 1967), p. 67.

83. Frank Costigliola, "'Unceasing Pressure for Penetration,'" *Journal of American History, LXXXIII* (March 1997), 1316, 1321, 1329.

84. Eugene Lyons, "To Tell or Not to Tell," *Harper's, CLXXI* (June 1935), 102.

85. Quoted in Arnold A. Offner, *American Appeasement* (New York: Norton, 1976 [c. 1969]), p. 50.

86. Quoted in Raymond J. Sontag, *A Broken World, 1919–1939* (New York: Harper and Row, 1971), p. 290.

87. Ambassador Robert Bingham quoted in David F. Schmitz, *The United States and Fascist Italy, 1922–1940* (Chapel Hill: University of North Carolina Press, 1988), pp. 161–162.

88. Quoted in George Eisen, "The Voices of Sanity: American Diplomatic Reports from the 1936 Berlin Olympiad," *Journal of Sports History, XI* (Winter 1984), 75.

89. Don MacLeod quoted in Peter N. Carroll, *The Odyssey of the Abraham Lincoln Brigade* (Stanford: Stanford University Press, 1994), p. 4.

90. Reynolds, *Creation*, p. 9.

91. Quoted in A. J. P. Taylor, *The Origins of the Second World War* (New York: Fawcett, 1966 [c. 1961]) p. 181.

92. Quoted in Roy Douglas, "Chamberlain and Appeasement," in Wolfgang J. Mommsen and Lothar Kettenacker, eds., *The Fascist Challenge and the Policy of Appeasement* (London: Allen & Unwin, 1983), p. 87.

93. Quoted in Leffler, *Specter*, p. 26.

94. Harry S. Truman quoted in Robert H. Ferrell, ed., *Dear Bess* (New York: Norton, 1983), p. 419.

95. Quoted in James V. Compton, *The Swastika and the Eagle* (Boston: Houghton Mifflin, 1967), pp. 17, 25.

96. V. R. Berghahn, "Germany's America," *American Heritage, XLVI* (May/June 1995), 68.

97. Quoted in Compton, *Swastika*, p. 33.

98. Samuel I. Rosenman, ed., *Public Papers . . . of Franklin D. Roosevelt, 1939* (New York: Macmillan, 1938–1950; 13 vols.), *VIII*, 463.

99. John E. Wiltz, "The Nye Committee Revisited," *The Historian, XXIII* (February 1961), 232.

100. Eleanor Roosevelt quoted in Blanche Wiesen Cook, "Eleanor Roosevelt and Human Rights," in Edward P. Crapol, ed., *Women and American Foreign Policy* (Wilmington, Del.: Scholarly Resources, 1992; 2nd ed.), p. 97.

101. Ernest Lundeen quoted in Thomas N. Guinsburg, "The Triumph of Isolationism," in Gordon Martel, ed., *American Foreign Relations Reconsidered, 1890–1993* (London: Routledge, 1994), p. 99.

102. Quoted in Sherry, *Shadow of War*, p. 26.

103. Quoted in Thomas G. Paterson, *Meeting the Communist Threat* (New York: Oxford University Press, 1988), p. 216.

104. Quoted in Robert A. Divine, *The Reluctant Belligerent* (New York: Wiley, 1979; 2nd ed.), p. 52; and in Justus D. Doenecke and John E. Wilz, *From Isolation to War* (Arlington Heights, Ill.: Harlan Davidson, 1991; 2nd ed.), p. 15.

105. Offner, *American Appeasement*, p. 103.

106. Quoted in Carrie Foster, *The Women and the Warriors* (Syracuse: Syracuse University Press, 1995), p. 190.

107. Manfred Jonas, *Isolationism in America, 1935–1941* (Ithaca: Cornell University Press, 1966), p. viii.

108. Brenda Gayle Plummer, *Rising Wind* (Chapel Hill: University of North Carolina Press, 1996), p. 37.

109. Quoted in Alexander DeConde, *Ethnicity, Race, and American Foreign Policy* (Boston, Northeastern University Press, 1992), p. 107.

110. Rosenman, *Public Papers, 1936, V*, 289.

111. Douglas Little, *Malevolent Neutrality* (Ithaca: Cornell University Press, 1985), p. 265.

112. Roosevelt to Edward M. House, October 19, 1937, Edward M. House Papers, Sterling Library, Yale University, New Haven, Conn.

113. Quoted in Christopher Thorne, *Allies of a Kind* (New York: Oxford University Press, 1978), p. 38.

114. *Foreign Relations, 1938, I* (Washington, D.C.: Government Printing Office, 1955), 685.

115. *Ibid.*, p. 688.

116. Quoted in Reynolds, *Creation*, p. 43.

117. Quoted in Blum, *Morgenthau Diaries, II*, 49.

118. Rosenman, *Public Papers, 1939, VIII*, 4.

119. Quoted in William L. Langer and S. Everett Gleason, *The Challenge to Isolation* (New York: Harper & Brothers, 1952), p. 87.

120. Quoted in Robert Dallek, *Franklin D. Roosevelt and American Foreign Policy, 1932–1945* (New York: Oxford University Press, 1979), p. 192.

121. Lord Lothian to Lord Halifax, September 27, 1939, vol. 24, Halifax Papers, Public Record Office, Kew, Eng.

122. Kirk H. Porter and Donald B. Johnson, eds., *National Party Platforms, 1840–1972* (Urbana: University of Illinois Press, 1973), p. 382.

Asia, Latin America, and the Vagaries of Power, 1920–1939

William E. Borah (1865–1940) and Henry L. Stimson (1867–1950). *The Idaho senator (left) chaired the Foreign Relations Committee (1925–1933). An isolationist, he opposed U.S. membership in the League of Nations and promoted neutrality; an anti-imperialist, he condemned U.S. interventions in Latin America; a peace advocate, he saluted the Kellogg-Briand Pact. A noted orator, Borah said much on most issues. "Borah this and Borah that, Borah here and there, Borah does and Borah doesn't, until you wish that Borah wasn't," wrote a journalist. In a February 1932 letter to Borah, Secretary of State Stimson explained U.S. defense of the Open Door policy during the Manchurian crisis. (Library of Congress)*

DIPLOMATIC CROSSROAD

The Manchurian Crisis, 1931–1932

It apparently started with thirty-one inches of steel. At 10:20 P.M., a few miles outside the Manchurian capital of Mukden on September 18, 1931, an explosion apparently blasted a short section from the South Manchurian Railway. Japanese soldiers apparently shot and killed some Chinese attempting to escape from the area. Apparently? Yes, because Japanese army officers had a most difficult time explaining the events of that dark night. The Mukden Express somehow crossed over that very section of track *after* the alleged explosion. It appears that independent-minded young officers of the Guandong (Manchurian) army fabricated the "Mukden Incident" of September 18. They had plotted for months to seize Manchuria from China. Feverish in their quest for Japanese grandeur and Asian power, they or their followers had already, in 1930, assassinated the Japanese premier. So when the news from Mukden reached Tokyo, one civilian official remarked, "They've done it at last."[1]

For the Japanese—civilian or military—Manchuria ranked as a vital interest. Comprising an area as large as France and Germany with a population of 30 million (28 million of them Chinese), Manchuria served as a defensive buffer against the Russians and their communism. More important, the territory teemed with the raw materials (coal, iron, timber, soybeans) so desperately needed by the import-hungry Japanese islands. Manchuria held more than half of Japan's foreign investments. The Japanese-run South Manchurian Railway interlaced these large economic holdings. Ever since their 1905 victory in the Russo-Japanese War, the Japanese had been driving in their imperial stakes. By treaty they had acquired the right to station troops along the railroad. The United States had recognized Japan's primacy in Manchuria through the Root-Takahira and Lansing-Ishii agreements (see Chapter 2).

Chinese nationalists throughout the 1920s had resisted Japanese intrusions. Nationalist leader Jiang Jieshi (Chiang Kai-shek) encouraged Chinese to move to Manchuria and sought to build a railroad to compete with the South Manchurian. The Chinese boycotted Japanese products, a particularly alarming practice during the Great Depression, when Japan's foreign trade slumped. Chinese and Japanese blood spilled in isolated incidents. Such cumulative provocations amounted to "a case where a thousand pinpricks equalled a slash of the saber."[2]

The Mukden news of September 18, 1931, reached an irritable Secretary of State Henry L. Stimson, worn low by Washington's hot, humid temperatures before the age of the air conditioner. The weather accentuated what President Herbert Hoover called Stimson's "combat psychology."[3] The forthright secretary shared prevalent American attitudes toward "inferior" races and the "Oriental mind."[4] He also embraced the Open Door policy and the sanctity of law. Japanese aggression in Manchuria violated treaties signed at the Washington Conference

"The Open Door."   The Japanese thrust into Manchuria in 1931 called into question the peace and disarmament agreements of the previous decade. A. U.S. diplomat described Japan in 1934 as "the combination of national centralization with feudal loyalty, of mysticism with technical efficiency, of medievalism with tanks and airplanes. . . . They dwell in a no-man's zone of time, their springs of action in the Middle Ages, their instruments of action out of the twentieth century." (*The Outlook*, 1931)

(1922), which endorsed the Open Door, and the Kellogg-Briand Pact (1928), which outlawed war. Stimson saw the Manchurian crisis as "an issue between the two great theories of civilization and economic methods."[5]

Stimson hoped at first that the "Mukden Incident" would remain a localized mutiny of the Japanese army. No American wanted the United States to become ensnarled "all by itself" in this imbroglio "full of hidden explosives, dense underbrush, [and] quicksand," noted State Department official Stanley K. Hornbeck.[6] The United States possessed little power in Asia. The British, interested in preserving their own Asian empire and hobbled by economic crisis at home, preferred to appease Japan. The French foundered in their frequent domestic political confusion. Soviet Russia, still not recognized by the United States, could hardly be called on for help. And the feeble League of Nations, the humorist Will Rogers astutely observed, could "make the little fellows behave" but had "no more power than a Senate investigating committee" to discipline "the big fellows."[7]

Stimson decided on a meek policy of letting "the Japanese know we are watching them."[8] On September 24, 1931, he urged the Chinese and Japanese to cease hostilities. A few days later the League began to discuss the Manchurian crisis, and an American representative sat at the League table, but only as an "observer." Stimson and Hoover feared that the international organization would "dump" the

"Manchurian baby" in Washington's lap, but the League passed mild peace resolutions and set up the Lytton Commission to investigate.[9] After Japanese forces occupied all of Manchuria by early December, Stimson thought Japan "in the hands of virtually mad dogs," with its army "running amok."[10]

The secretary of state had few options. He could not intervene militarily. Economic sanctions seemed a possibility. Stimson knew that the island empire depended on imports of American oil, that it was the third largest buyer of American exports, and that the United States took about 40 percent of Japan's exports. Maybe economic pressure would force Tokyo to disgorge Manchuria. Hoover, however, refused to stick "pins in tigers."[11]

Thus, nonrecognition. On January 7, 1932, Stimson issued what became known as the Stimson Doctrine. He threw tradition and law against Japan: The United States would not recognize any arrangements in China that might impair American treaty rights, violate the Open Door policy, or subvert the Kellogg-Briand Pact. Defiantly, on January 28, the Japanese marched into Shanghai, far to the south of Manchuria. A belligerent Stimson persuaded Hoover to reinforce the American military garrison in that city. Reminded of the German attack on Belgium in 1914, the secretary drew a historical lesson and set his jaw against this new aggression.

Stimson tried to bluff. He wanted to frighten Japan without revealing that it had no reason to be afraid. On February 23, 1932, Stimson sent a public letter to Senator William Borah, chair of the Senate Foreign Relations Committee, which the secretary hoped would "encourage China, enlighten the American public, exhort the League, stir up the British, and warn Japan."[12] Citing the Open Door policy as an instrument, Stimson chastised Japan for violating the administrative and territorial integrity of China and the Kellogg-Briand agreement. He threatened to fortify Guam and build up the U.S. Navy in the Pacific if Japan did not halt its aggression. This protest made little impact, although Japan soon signed an armistice in Shanghai and the League endorsed nonrecognition. In February, Japan actually reconstituted Manchuria as the puppet state of Manchukuo. In October the Lytton Commission chided the Japanese for misconduct in Manchuria. Japan thereupon resigned from the League in early 1933. "In Japan," Stimson wrote, "the cause of Mr. Hyde against Mr. Jekyll has in large measure been victorious, and my efforts on behalf of the latter without much seeming result."[13]

A Question of Power

Stimson's diplomatic efforts raise questions about the choices, opportunities, and limitations facing U.S. leaders in the 1920–1939 period. Was it wise for Stimson to rail against Japanese machinations in Manchuria? Did it perhaps help the Japanese military gain support from other nationalists who also considered Manchuria vital? Did the nonrecognition policy reveal just how weak the United States was in Asia? Did it not also expose China's abandonment by other nations? Yet, should and could Stimson have ignored the violations of the treaties? Or should he have let the Asians settle their own differences? Did the Manchurian crisis threaten America's national interest?

Makers of American Foreign Relations, 1920–1939

Presidents	Secretaries of State
Woodrow Wilson, 1913–1921	Bainbridge Colby, 1920–1921
Warren G. Harding, 1921–1923	Charles E. Hughes, 1921–1925
Calvin Coolidge, 1923–1929	Frank B. Kellogg, 1925–1929
Herbert C. Hoover, 1929–1933	Henry L. Stimson, 1929–1933
Franklin D. Roosevelt, 1933–1945	Cordell Hull, 1933–1944

Years after 1931, Stimson admitted that nonrecognition had not worked. Moral exhortation and lecturing may only have soothed the American conscience and stirred up the aggressor, to nobody's benefit. The diplomat Hugh Wilson reflected on Stimson's tactics: "If the nations of the world feel strongly enough to condemn, they should feel strongly enough to use force." He went on: "Condemnation creates a community of the damned who are forced outside the pale, who have nothing to lose by the violation of all laws of order and international good faith."[14] Still, despite minimal American economic interests in Manchuria, the principle of the Open Door, both as diplomatic tool and as ideology, stood at risk. If Tokyo could violate the Open Door in Manchuria, it could do so elsewhere, Stimson argued.

America's timid response to the Manchurian crisis demonstrated that the United States could not manage affairs in Asia. U.S. gunboats still chugged on Chinese rivers, American troops garrisoned on Chinese soil, American business interests formed the Shanghai Power Company in 1928 and thus "Americanized" the city, and the Philippines remained a colony, but in Asia the Japanese had hegemony.[15] America could lecture but not enforce.

By contrast, the United States held considerable power—economic, naval, military, political—in Latin America. Central America and the Caribbean were to the United States what China, especially Manchuria, was to Japan. The Japanese, in fact, often commented that their actions in China simply resembled U.S. actions in Latin America. In Latin America the United States practiced the "closed door"; in Asia it appealed for the "Open Door." In both areas, the viability of American foreign policy depended on power.

The Manchurian crisis also revealed the ineffectiveness of the treaties of the 1920s and the reluctance of the European powers to check aggression in the 1930s, when appeasement became the policy of the day (see Chapter 4). What frightened Stimson and Hoover, in one scholar's words, was "not so much China's fate as the specter of the great powers seizing new empires to rescue themselves from economic depression."[16] Japan's violation of the Nine Power Treaty eroded "the Washington Conference system," threatening international stability.[17] Given the timidity of the Europeans and the League of Nations, Americans recognized the limits of their own power and nurtured their independent internationalism. The United States worked to create with nonmilitary means a world characterized by legal, orderly processes, the Open Door, and economic and political stability. The Hoover-Stimson response to the Manchurian episode typified these goals and methods. America hoped to muzzle the dogs of war in order to stimulate domestic prosperity, expand foreign trade, and ensure national security. As in Europe, so in Asia would U.S. efforts come up short.

Facing Japan: The Washington Naval Disarmament Conference and China

The American pursuit of independent internationalism and a nonmilitary foreign policy began conspicuously at the Washington naval conference of November 12, 1921, through February 6, 1922. After World War I a naval arms race loomed among the United States, Britain, and Japan. All parties recoiled from the spiraling financial costs. Japan was pumping as much as one-third of its national budget into naval construction. The United States, possessing the second largest navy in the world, alarmed third-ranked Japan by stationing most of its heaviest battleships in the Pacific Fleet, by developing the base at Pearl Harbor, and by speculating about fortifying the Philippines and Guam. First-ranked Britain already had Singapore, but lacked funds to engage in a naval arms race. The U.S. Congress might not appropriate funds either. Thus all three powers welcomed arms control to check one another. With prodding from Senator Borah, the Harding administration invited eight nations (Britain, France, Italy, Japan, China, Belgium, the Netherlands, and Portugal) to Washington to discuss naval arms limitations and competition in Asia.

The Washington conference opened with dramatic words from bewhiskered Secretary of State Charles Evans Hughes. He announced that the United States would scrap thirty ships. Then he turned to the British delegation and sank twenty-three of its ships. British admiral Lord David Beatty, noted a reporter, leaned forward like a "bulldog, sleeping on a sunny doorstep, who has been poked in the stomach by the impudent foot of an itinerant soap canvasser."[18] The secretary next scuttled twenty-five Japanese vessels. One commentator wrote that "Hughes sank in thirty-five minutes more ships than all the admirals of the world have sunk in a cycle of centuries."[19]

Despite grumblings of doom from navy officers, the diplomats hammered out a naval limitations pact—the Five Power Treaty. It set a ten-year moratorium on the construction of capital vessels (defined as warships of more than 10,000 tons displacement or carrying guns larger than eight inches in bore diameter) and limited the tonnage for aircraft carriers. The treaty also established a tonnage ratio for capital ships of 5 : 5 : 3 : 1.75 : 1.75 (United States : Britain : Japan : France : Italy; 1 equaling approximately 100,000 tons displacement). The top three naval powers agreed to dismantle sixty-six capital ships, many of them battleships. They also pledged not to build new fortifications in their Pacific possessions, such as the Philippines and Hong Kong, thus reassuring the Japanese, who had sarcastically accepted naval inferiority by translating 5 : 5 : 3 as Rolls Royce : Rolls Royce : Ford.

Another treaty—the Four Power—abolished the Anglo-Japanese Alliance and simply obligated signatories to respect each other's Pacific territories. All delegations also signed the Nine Power Treaty, an endorsement of the Open Door for the preservation of China's administrative integrity and equal trade opportunity there. In other agreements, Japan consented to evacuate troops from the Shandong Peninsula; the United States obtained cable rights to the Pacific island of Yap; and Japan withdrew its troops from Russian Siberia and the northern half of Sakhalin Island. Hughes's diplomatic success owed much to the State Department's "Black Chamber" code-breakers, who deciphered some 1,600 secret Japanese cables during the conference, proving that "stud poker is not a very difficult game after you've seen your opponent's hole card."[20]

The treaties signed in Washington essentially recognized the status quo in Asia. Japan had regional superiority, and the other powers could not challenge it without undertaking massive naval construction and prohibitively expensive fortifications. Geography clearly worked in Japan's favor in Asia, as it did for the United States in Latin America. The United States gave up only the *potential* of naval superiority—ships that Congress had no intention of funding ("phantom vessels sailing on seas of fancy," as one diplomat remarked).[21] The United States secured temporary protection of the vulnerable Philippines and abolition of the Anglo-Japanese Alliance.

Shortcomings emerged. The Five Power Treaty did not limit submarines, destroyers, or cruisers, thus sparking in those categories an arms race that agreements at the London conference of 1930 only partly curbed. Nor did the naval treaty provide means for verification other than good faith. Russia, with major stakes in Asia, did not attend the Washington conference, since the major powers were still attempting to isolate the Bolsheviks. None of the pacts contained enforcement provisions. In time, the Washington treaties fell victim to what one historian has called the "Icarus Factor"—that is, the "waxwork of political webs" that sustained disarmament at the beginning and later "melted" before the "Rising Sun" of Japanese expansion.[22]

China lost the most. Not representing Sun Zhongshan's (Sun Yat-sen's) Guomindang government at Guangzhou (Canton), Chinese delegates spoke instead for the weak Beijing regime (the British cynically described it as "a group of persons who call themselves a government but who have long ceased to function as such").[23] Chinese pleas for tariff autonomy, withdrawal of foreign troops, and an end to extraterritoriality fell on stony ground. Washington helped by negotiating the Japanese out of Shandong, but the imperial powers rejected full sovereignty for China and continued to do so even as the Guomindang triumphed over its rivals later in the decade. The Washington conference took a worthy step toward disarmament, but the absence of enforcement provisions left China vulnerable to foreign aggression.

U.S. relations with the anti-imperialist, nationalist Chinese proved nettlesome. In 1898 Americans had perceived the Philippines as stepping-stones to China; three decades later, in a historical flipflop, a strong, friendly China seemed necessary to protect the islands. China thus took on strategic importance for Americans in the 1920s and 1930s. Also, many Americans remained mesmerized by the mirage of the China market and the inviolability of the Open Door principle. Sentimental considerations partly accounted for the American attachment to China, especially in the

American Gunboat on the Yangtze River, China. The shallow-draft gunboat U.S.S. *Monocacy* served in the Yangtze Patrol, evacuating besieged Americans and protecting missionaries and commerce. After entanglement with Chinese civil disturbances and Japanese military thrusts, the *Monocacy* in 1939 was decommissioned, towed to sea, and sunk. (U.S. Navy)

1930s. Pearl Buck's best-selling *The Good Earth* (1931), made into a powerful movie six years later, captured for Americans the romance of the hard-working, persevering Chinese peasants. John Paton Davies, a young Foreign Service Officer in China during the depression decade, recalled America's "righteous infatuation" with China, stemming from years of religious missionary activity and a misguided and self-congratulatory belief that the United States had become China's special friend by virtue of the Open Door notes. In Asia, wrote Davies, "Washington preached to everyone, including the Chinese."[24]

Washington sermonized most fervently to the Japanese, Soviets, and Chinese Nationalists, all of whom strove to limit the influence of the United States and the other Western imperialists in Asia. For the United States, peaceful change, the Open Door, protection of American property and citizens, and the treaty rights of trade and judicial extraterritoriality (criminal trials for its nationals in American rather than Chinese courts) seemed threatened. Sun Zhongshan, leader of the Chinese Revolution from its outbreak in 1911 until his death in 1925, bristled when U.S. gunboats visited Guangzhou in 1923 to halt a potential Chinese takeover of foreign-dominated customshouses. After declaring that the Chinese Revolution took its inspiration from America, the Christian, English-speaking Sun "might well have expected that an American Lafayette would fight on our side in this good cause. In the twelfth year of our struggle towards liberty there comes not a Lafayette but an American Admiral with more ships of war than any other nation in our waters."[25]

The United States did little to assist the two potential roadblocks to Japanese expansion—Soviet Russia and the Chinese Nationalists. Americans applauded the Chinese nationalistic spirit but insisted on U.S. treaty privileges. The Chinese turned to another possible means of support, Soviet Russia. Seeking to restrain Japan, spank imperialist capitalists, and implant communism, Moscow sent Michael Borodin to help the Nationalists centralize the structure of the Guomindang party. Americans understood neither the depth of Chinese nationalism nor Sun's use of

Soviet agents for Chinese purposes; some Americans attributed China's intense antiforeign sentiment to Bolshevik agitation.

In 1925, Sun died and the Nationalist outpouring in the May 30th Movement of that year led to attacks on foreign nationals and missionaries. Lieutenant Colonel George C. Marshall summed up his experience with the Fifteenth Infantry in China over the next two years: "We are either just out of near trouble with the Chinese or trouble is just hovering near us."[26] Anti-imperialist opinion at home and Chinese pressure prompted Washington to reconsider treaty privileges. The outbreak of civil war within the Nationalist ranks also dictated a reevaluation. The ambitious Guomindang leader Jiang Jieshi turned fiercely on his communist allies in 1926–1927, booting Borodin back to Moscow and killing Chinese communists by the thousands. The communist leader Mao Zedong fled south to Kiangsi Province, where he set up a rebel government. Jiang told U.S. officials that only American assistance could buttress China in "holding off" Japan and Soviet Russia and averting "a great war in the Pacific."[27] Washington responded to Jiang's assertion of power by signing in 1928 a new treaty restoring tariff autonomy to China and providing for most-favored-nation treatment. By 1930 more than 500 American companies were operating in China, with investments amounting to $155 million, yet they represented only 1 percent of total American foreign investments. From 1923 to 1931 the United States sent only 3 percent of its total exports to China. American trade with Japan totaled twice as much.

Although at least one U.S. sailor left China having "seen enough of this yeller race to suit me awhile," Washington waxed hopeful because American-trained Chinese "cosmopolitans" such as H. H. Kung, Hu Shi, and T. V. Soong were gaining influence in the Guomindang.[28] The Rockefeller Foundation was training an English-speaking elite through institutions such as the Peking Union Medical College, where American "modernizers" introduced "scientific medicine" for a country short on physicians.[29] Jiang had joined the crusade against communism. In 1930, furthermore, he converted to Christianity and married Meiling Soong, daughter of the American-educated, prominent Chinese businessman Charles Soong. "Part dreamy lotus flower, part sullen tiger lily, and part American rose," the Wellesley College honors graduate spoke impeccable English and soon established ties with prominent Americans, later called the China Lobby.[30] The beautiful, intelligent, and "Westernized" Madame Jiang became the perfect "damsel in distress" as she— and the new God-fearing China—appealed to American notions of "mission, chivalry, and machismo."[31]

Japan's March for a New Pacific Order

Zealous expansionists, the Japanese feared the future. As their population grew, land became scarce (in 1931, 65 million people lived in an area smaller than Texas), and they became dependent on outside sources for vital raw materials. The Japanese also complained that Western nations had for years intruded into their sphere of influence and controlled products central to their economy, such as oil. Japan sought self-sufficiency because "a tree must have its roots," citing U.S. "roots" in Latin

America as an example.[32] Claiming "equality" with the Western powers, the Japanese often explained their expansion in the broadest terms: All major powers were doing it. One diplomat claimed that the Western powers taught Japan the game of poker but then, after acquiring most of the chips, pronounced the game immoral and took up contract bridge. In August 1936 Tokyo secretly adopted the "Fundamental Principles of National Strategy," which called for both southern expansion "by peaceful means" toward the British, Dutch, and French empires of Southeast Asia (favored by the navy) and a northern advance into China and Mongolia (favored by the army).[33] Three years later Japan announced its imperial ambitions by defining the "Greater East Asia Co-Prosperity Sphere."

Japan ranked the United States first on its list of potential enemies. A Japanese navy study of 1936 stated that "in case the enemy's [America's] main fleet is berthed at Pearl Harbor the idea should be to open hostilities by surprise attacks from the air."[34] American naval leaders used Japan as the enemy on the war-game board at the Naval War College. Naval competition intensified in 1935–1936 when the London conference broke up without agreement and Japan announced its abrogation of earlier treaties. The American Immigration Act of 1924, blatantly discriminatory in excluding Japanese citizens from entering the United States, rankled Tokyo. Secretary Hughes lamented that the legislation had "undone the work of the Washington conference and implanted the seeds of an antagonism sure to bear fruit in the future."[35] Trade disputes also intensified. Inexpensive Japanese goods, especially textiles, entered the American market, undercutting some domestic producers. "Buy America" campaigns and public boycotts of Japanese goods followed. Japan began to close the trade and investment door in China.

Japan and the United States did have two common interests: Their mutual trade continued at high levels, and both counted Communist Russia as a threat (Japan joined the Anti-Comintern Pact with Germany in 1936).

When Franklin D. Roosevelt became president in early 1933, he continued Stimson's nonrecognition policy. This policy reflected American weakness in Asia. But at least until 1937, the long lull in fighting between China and Japan did not seem to require U.S. action. Roosevelt did move to bring the navy up to the strength permitted by the Washington and London conference treaties. Under New Deal programs in 1933, the president allocated funds for thirty-two new vessels, including two aircraft carriers, and by 1937 naval appropriations had doubled. Two years earlier the United States staged large-scale naval maneuvers near Midway Island in the Pacific to impress the Japanese. Instead of deterring Tokyo, these naval activities reinforced Japan's secret decision in May 1937 to outbuild the Americans and construct warships "above and beyond the quantitative and qualitative limits of the naval treaties"—including the huge 80,000-ton battleships *Yamato* and *Musashi*.[36] Roosevelt's diplomatic recognition of Soviet Russia in 1933 was intended in part to frighten Japan with the suspicion that Moscow and Washington had linked arms in Asia. Four years later, Captain Claire Chennault, retired from the U.S. Army Air Corps, joined the Chinese air force as chief adviser. By 1940 American volunteer pilots manned his "Flying Tigers" unit.

On July 7, 1937, Japanese and Chinese troops clashed at the Marco Polo Bridge near Beijing. This skirmish grew quickly into the "China Incident" (not a "war" because the Kellogg-Briand Pact outlawed wars). Fighting spread throughout China.

Shanghai, China, 1937. This photograph of a baby amid the ruins of North Station after Japanese bombing galvanized American opinion. Senator George Norris, who gradually abandoned his isolationism because of scenes like this, denounced the Japanese as "disgraceful, ignoble, barbarous, and cruel, even beyond the power of language to describe." (United Press International)

Shanghai fell to Japan in November after a costly battle and the cruel bombing of civilians. The "rape" of Nanjing followed in December. "Dead Chinese, dead Chinese, dead Chinese" were all that one journalist could see, as Japanese soldiers raped 80,000 women and massacred 260,000 residents of China's then capital city.[37] A U.S. military observer recoiled at bloated corpses—"grotesque inflated rubber figures which children sometimes play with . . . at seaside resorts. The stench was almost unbearable."[38]

To make matters worse, the civil war between Jiang's Guomindang forces and Mao Zedong's communists further sapped China. The communists had declared war on Japan in 1932, charging Jiang with appeasing Tokyo. Until 1937 Jiang fought the communists more than he fought the Japanese. From 1935 to 1937, the communists took the dramatic "Long March" from their southern haven to Yan'an (Yenan) in the north—an expedition of 6,000 miles. In late 1936 dissident Chinese army forces in Manchuria kidnapped Jiang, hoping to end the civil war by creating a coalition government. Joseph Stalin and the Chinese communists soon secured his release and persuaded him to institute a tenuous united front against Japan in early 1937. Indeed, a Sino-Soviet nonaggression pact in August led to what one scholar has called a "multifaceted alliance" wherein Moscow increased arms sales and technical assistance to Jiang and Soviet troops actually routed the Japanese in border clashes along the Manchurian and Mongolian frontiers in 1938 and 1939.[39]

Having refused to invoke American neutrality after the Marco Polo Bridge incident, thereby permitting valuable trade to continue with China, Roosevelt addressed a Chicago audience on October 5, 1937. He called vaguely for a "quarantine" on aggressors to check the "epidemic of world lawlessness."[40] After the speech, FDR admitted that he evoked an attitude more than a "policy." He privately toyed with economic warfare—a naval blockade or embargo—but American isolationists responded to the speech by warning against trying "to police a

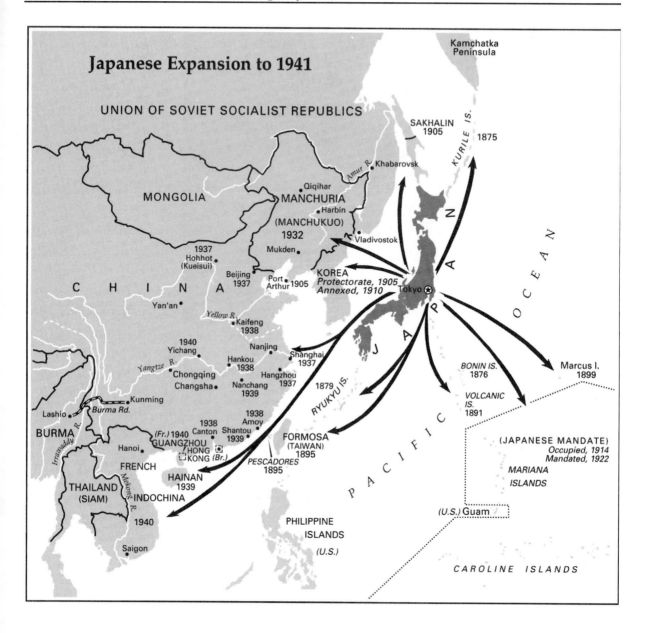

Japanese Expansion to 1941

world that chooses to follow insane leaders" and recalling "our plunge into the European war in 1917."[41] In November Roosevelt sent U.S. representatives to a conference in Brussels, but it disbanded without taking a stand—only the Soviet Union pushed for reprisals against Japan. In December the American gunboat *Panay*, escorting on the Yangtze River three Standard Oil Company tankers flying American flags, took destructive fire from zealous Japanese pilots. Three Americans died. Under pressure from Ambassador Joseph Grew, Tokyo quickly apologized and paid an indemnity of $2,214,007.36.

As Japan plunged deeper into China in 1938 and U.S. military observers reported that "the Japanese fly has at last got himself well entangled in the Chinese flypaper," the Roosevelt administration cautiously initiated new measures.[42] First, in purchasing Chinese silver, the United States gave China dollars with which to buy American military equipment. Second, Secretary Hull imposed a "moral embargo" on the sale of aircraft to Japan. Third, the United States extended technical assistance to improve the Chinese transportation system. Fourth, a naval bill authorized two new carriers and the doubling of naval airplanes. Fifth, the United States occupied several Pacific islands (Enderbury, for example) as potential naval bases. Sixth, Roosevelt sent a secret naval emissary to London to discuss contingency plans in case of war in the Pacific. These actions did not deter the Japanese, who by the end of 1938 controlled virtually all major Chinese seaports, had established exploitative development companies, and had begun to install a puppet Chinese regime. An American trade commissioner in Shanghai accurately noted that the "Open Door" was being "banged, barred, and bolted."[43]

With war clouds billowing in Europe in summer 1939 (see Chapter 4), Hull and Roosevelt abrogated the Japanese-American commercial treaty of 1911. They hoped the threat of economic pressure might cause the Japanese to temper their onslaught in China. In 1938 the United States had supplied Japan with 44 percent of its imports, mostly automobiles, machinery, copper, oil, iron, and steel. The abrogation, effective January 1940, by no means ended trade, for Washington remained reluctant to impose a rigid economic embargo. Grew's talks with the Japanese foreign minister in the fall of 1939 failed to secure American trading rights in China but did elicit a Japanese pledge to curtail brutalities against foreigners. In November 1939 another American naval bill authorized two more battleships. By then World War II had begun to bloody Europe, and Japanese-American relations had stalemated. Unwilling to fight over China, Washington had to decide what to do if Japan expanded beyond China.

Making and Managing Good Neighbors in Latin America

In contrast with Asia, U.S. power in the Western Hemisphere remained unmatched and U.S. methods bold. Indeed, shortly after World War I, U.S. armed forces used the Caribbean for maneuvers—as preparation for a possible war with Japan in the Pacific. And when Germany and Japan marched aggressively in the 1930s, the United States brought most of the Latin American states into a virtual alliance to resist foreign intrusions in the U.S. sphere of influence. The U.S. imperial net in Latin America had been stitched before and during World War I, especially in Central America and the Caribbean, through military occupations, naval demonstrations, the Panama Canal, the management of national finances, the threat of intervention, nonrecognition, and economic ties. A U.S. diplomat in Guatemala reported in 1921 that "the bacillus of revolution is in the blood of these people, and will never be eradicated until some strong hand is placed over them and the serum of hard work is injected into them by force."[44] The Roosevelt Corollary to the Monroe Doctrine provided the overriding justification for U.S. hegemony (see Chapter 2).

Charles A. Lindbergh (1902–1974) Returns from Latin America, 1928. Lindbergh made aviation history on May 20, 1927, when he flew nonstop from New York to Paris in the *Spirit of St. Louis.* To promote U.S. goodwill toward Latin America, the aviator began a tour in December 1927 that first took him to Mexico. There he met Anne Morrow, the daughter of Ambassador Dwight Morrow; later Lindbergh would marry her. After visiting Guatemala, Panama, Venezuela, and other countries, Lindbergh returned from Cuba in February 1928. In the late 1930s Lindbergh became an isolationist, and in his last years he earned yet another reputation as a conservationist. (Lindbergh Picture Collection, Yale University Library)

Swaggering American marines in the streets of Havana, Managua, or Port-au-Prince represented only the most conspicuous evidence of North American imperial management.

The use of marines as instruments of policy, however, became unpopular and counterproductive, and nationalist sentiment, especially in Mexico and Argentina, placed limits on U.S. power. Anti-imperialists such as Senators George Norris and William Borah demanded self-determination for Latin Americans. Congress resented the costs of military interventions, as well as the president's usurpation of Congress's power to declare war when he unilaterally dispatched troops to the Caribbean. Business leaders came to believe that military expeditions, because they aroused anti-U.S. sentiment and violence, endangered rather than protected their properties. Referring to Japan's seizure of Manchuria, and alert to a double standard, Secretary Stimson commented in 1932: "If we landed a single soldier among those South Americans now . . . it would put me absolutely in the wrong in China, where Japan has done all this monstrous work under the guise of protecting her nationals with a landing force."[45]

Between the world wars, therefore, the United States increasingly sought nonmilitary methods to maintain its hegemony in Latin America. Washington forswore armed interference and employed economic penetration, political subversion, nonrecognition, support for dictators who kept order, arbitration treaties, Pan Americanism, financial supervision, Export-Import Bank loans, and the training of national guards. At times U.S. officials pressed for negotiated settlements, as when, in 1929, Secretary Kellogg helped settle the Tacna-Arica dispute between Chile and

Peru. These tactics translated into a catchy phrase popularized (but not invented) by Franklin D. Roosevelt—the Good Neighbor policy. The president hailed in early 1933 "the policy of the good neighbor—the neighbor who resolutely respects himself and, because he does so, respects the rights of others—the neighbor who respects his obligations and respects the sanctity of his agreements in and with a world of neighbors."[46] Although Latin Americans welcomed the new spirit, the goal of U.S. hegemony in the hemisphere had not changed, only the means for maintaining it. Roosevelt defined the "new approach" toward Latin America: "Give them a share. They think they are just as good as we are, and many of them are."[47] As the Axis specter loomed larger in the late 1930s, the Good Neighbor policy came to mean cooperation against the European aggressors.

Economic decisions by U.S. leaders, private and governmental, held immense importance for Latin American nations. In the Dominican Republic, Cuba, and Haiti, for example, officials had to obtain U.S. consent before borrowing foreign capital. With its ambassador in Washington working to influence U.S. decisions on copper purchases and Chilean bonds, both vital to his nation's livelihood, Chile in the 1930s had never "felt so totally controlled by the unpredictable attitudes of a foreign power."[48] In Cuba, where North American interests accounted for about two-thirds of sugar production, U.S. investments helped lock the country into a risky one-crop economy subject to fluctuating world sugar prices. In Honduras, U.S. companies provided cannon and machine guns to one political group that conducted a successful coup in 1924. In 1929 U.S. firms produced more than half of Venezuela's oil. Their bribery of Venezuelan government officials, including the president, was not uncommon. In Guatemala, the arrogance of American shipping and rail magnates caused a State Department official in 1938 to question "the propriety of an American corporation, possessing a monopoly of essential transportation facilities in a foreign country, and operating in virtually complete independence of . . . either the American or Guatemalan governments."[49]

In a process sometimes called "colonialism by contract," professional economists such as Edward Kemmerer of Princeton University served as financial advisers (or "money doctors") to Colombia, Chile, Ecuador, and Peru during the 1920s, usually recommending gold-exchange currency reforms managed by a central bank, new taxes, revised tariffs, and private American loans for public-works projects tied to U.S. firms.[50] These icons of "progress who emblemized manly professionalism" devised systems to instill "duty, regularity, self-restraint, and responsibility," thus embodying the "spirit of (white) manhood and its destiny to supervise lesser beings."[51] Popular at first, such programs aroused nationalist backlashes in the 1930s when declining exports, excessive indebtedness, and contracting capital markets caused massive defaults throughout Latin America, where "money doctors" were again seen as Wall Street, Yankee imperialists.

The Argentine writer Manuel Ugarte bluntly identified a "new Rome" in the mid-1920s. The United States, he explained, annexed wealth rather than territory, thus enjoying the "essentials of domination" without the "dead-weight of areas to administrate and multitudes to govern." He deplored the consequences of U.S. economic penetration: "Its subtle intrusion into the private affairs of each people has always in consecrated phrase invoked peace, progress, civilization, and culture;

Marine Recruiting Poster. Marines saw many parts of Latin America, especially the Caribbean. But battle and occupation conditions were hardly as pleasant as depicted in James Montgomery Flagg's drawing. And, asked critics, once you are on the jaguar's back, how do you get off? (Library of Congress)

but its motives, procedure, and results have frequently been a complete negation of these premises."[52] Nonetheless, President Roosevelt's smiling personification of the Good Neighbor seemed to make the Yankee presence more palatable. "Here was a gringo in the Latin mold, a man they could understand and empathize with as a projection of their own political style," the scholar Fredrick B. Pike has written. "The man was so simpatico: and that papered over a multitude of sins."[53]

Although Latin American intellectuals often regarded North American "intruders as crass émigrés from a materialist culture," a U.S. consul in Brazil appreciated one of the ways the United States cultivated ruling elites.[54] He praised Rotary International, whose "meetings are attended by members of the Federal Cabinet, mayors of cities, and other officials who . . . welcome our support and cooperation."[55] Still, too many North Americans resembled the boorish member of Congress who insulted a Latin American diplomat's wife: "Señora, I regret that I know only two words of your beautiful language: mañana, which means tomorrow, and pyjama, which means tonight."[56] When a young Nelson Rockefeller visited Venezuela in the early 1930s to look after his oil investments, he noticed that U.S. citizens there seldom learned Spanish. "Why should I?" asked one American. "Who would I talk to in Spanish?"[57] Rockefeller thereupon hired twelve Berlitz instructors to begin Spanish classes for company employees. A decade earlier the Rockefeller Foundation had begun to spend millions to destroy the mosquito in Latin America to combat yellow fever and succeeded in "unhooking the hookworm" in Colombia.[58]

U.S. investments in and trade with Latin America reached a "boom" stage after World War I. The direct investments of U.S. citizens (excluding bonds and securi-

Nelson A. Rockefeller (1908–1979) and Anastasio Somoza García (1896–1956). The grandson of Standard Oil millionaire John D. Rockefeller, Sr., Nelson served as director of the family oil business in Venezuela during the 1930s. An advocate of improved U.S. cultural, scientific, and educational relations within the hemisphere, Rockefeller served as coordinator of the Office of Inter-American Affairs for the State Department during World War II. Elected governor of New York in 1958, Rockefeller became vice president in 1974 under President Gerald Ford following President Richard Nixon's resignation during the Watergate scandal. Rockefeller is dining here with Nicaraguan strongman Somoza, who ruled from 1937 to 1956, aligned himself with the United States, and created a corrupt family dynasty in his country. (National Archives)

ties) jumped from $1.26 billion in 1914 to $3.52 billion in 1929, mostly in electric power, railroads, bananas, sugar, oil, and minerals. By 1936, because of the devastating impact of the global depression, the amount dropped to $2.77 billion. These figures represented about one-third of total U.S. investments abroad. One of the nation's largest corporations, Standard Oil of New Jersey, operated in eight countries, and United Fruit Company held a large stake in the "banana republics" of Central America. International Telephone and Telegraph controlled communications in Cuba, where, between 1919 and 1933, overall U.S. investments increased 536 percent. Worried about diminishing domestic oil reserves after World War I, Washington urged "companies to acquire oil territory in South America and elsewhere before the European companies preempted all of it." Commerce Secretary Hoover described the result: "a conference of the leading oil producers was called and such action taken that most of the available oil lands in South America were acquired by Americans."[59] In the period 1925–1929 in Latin America, the average annual income outflow from U.S. investments totaled $100 million more than the U.S. capital inflow.

Confirming the axiom that "trade follows investments," U.S. exports to Latin America tripled in value from 1914 to 1929, reaching the billion-dollar figure, approximately 20 percent of total U.S. exports. Although this impressive trade slumped during the Great Depression, for many Latin American countries commercial relationships with the United States remained critical. Nicaragua, for example, shipped 96 percent of its exports to the United States by 1941. In 1920 the United States supplied Cuba with 73 percent of its imports; that trade shrank to 59 percent in 1929 because of the depressed Cuban sugar economy. Cuba's exports to the United States also dropped off, although they still comprised 68 percent of all the island's exports. American investments in and trade with Venezuela moved the British out and helped that country to become the world's leading exporter of oil. Trade with Chile in nitrates and copper jumped after U.S. investments there doubled from $200 million in 1920 to $400 million in 1928. Worried by declining world trade during the 1930s, Secretary Hull sought wider markets in Latin America when he launched the Export-Import Bank (directing loans to inter-American commerce) and the Reciprocal Trade Agreements Program. His efforts helped increase exports to Latin America from $244 million in 1933 to $642 million in 1938.

Building Dictators and Guards: The Dominican Republic, Nicaragua, and Haiti

After Spain left the Dominican Republic in 1865 and until the U.S. military occupation in 1916, that impoverished Caribbean country knew little peace. Corrupt politics and mismanagement of national revenues produced economic stagnation, political factionalism, foreign indebtedness, and U.S. intervention (see Chapter 2). In May 1916, when a contest between the Dominican congress and president threatened to postpone U.S. demands for expanded authority, American marines went ashore. Although U.S. forces occupied the major cities and established martial law, the peasants and caudillos in the mountainous east waged bloody guerrilla war from 1917 to 1922. The marines retaliated in kind against rebels who "are almost all touched with the tarbrush," as Military Governor Harry Knapp crudely put it.[60] Marine atrocities against Dominican people of color usually went unpunished. Sumner Welles, the American commissioner to the Dominican Republic (1922–1924), later criticized the U.S. officers who ran the occupation—"none of whom had any knowledge or experience of Dominican affairs or problems, and the great majority of whom could not even speak the language of the country."[61]

The military intervention in the Dominican Republic, became a hot political issue at home and abroad. Warren G. Harding accused Wilson of the "rape of Haiti" in the 1920 campaign but continued the Dominican and Haitian occupations as president.[62] *The Nation* (1920) demolished the argument that improved hospitals and schools justified imperialism by noting that the "Germans improved sanitation during their occupation of some of the villages of northern France, but no officer of the Marine Corps ever suggested that these reforms justified the German presence in France."[63] When Washington ended the occupation in 1924, after forcing on the Dominican government a stabilization loan to liquidate past debt, and when the new national guard consumed a quarter of the Dominican budget, Hughes ingeniously claimed that the departure proved that the United States was "anti-imperialistic."[64] Franklin D. Roosevelt agreed in a 1928 article in *Foreign Affairs:* "We accomplished an excellent piece of constructive work, and the world ought to thank us."[65] With Americans running the country's fiscal affairs until 1941, FDR blithely ignored Welles's observation of "the lasting hostility towards the American people which the occupation created in the hearts of . . . the Dominican people."[66]

The U.S. occupation also begot Rafael Leonidas Trujillo. In early 1919 he received a commission as a second lieutenant in the U.S.-created national guard. The onetime thief, forger, and pimp earned high marks from American military officers and became chief of staff of the National Army in 1928. Through the fraudulent election of 1930, Trujillo won the presidency. Washington worried that his authoritarian methods would spawn new insurrections but gradually warmed to him when his strong-arm tactics created internal order and precluded U. S. military intervention. Thanks to beneficent U.S. control of the customs, Trujillo could divert funds to his army for the suppression of internal dissent. Political corruption, military muscle, torture, murder, nepotism, commercial monopolies, and raids on the national treasury enabled Trujillo to quiet opponents and amass a fortune of $800 million.

From 1930 until his assassination in 1961, sometimes as president, sometimes through puppets, Trujillo ruled. U.S. military arms filled Domincan arsenals. U.S. business leaders, who dominated sugar production, endorsed him. Most imports came from the United States. The National City Bank became the official depository for Dominican revenues. By World War II the Dominican Republic stood as a success story for the new Good Neighbor policy. But good neighbors with whom? Roosevelt reportedly gave an answer in reference to Trujillo: "He may be an S.O.B., but he is our S.O.B."[67]

Rafael Trujillo (1891–1961). The strongman of the Dominican Republic graduated from an American military training school and went on to rule his nation from 1930 to 1961, when he was assassinated. The historian Eric Paul Roorda explains that a "group of pro-Trujillo businessmen, legislators, and paid advocates constituted a kind of 'Dominican Lobby' in the United States with Joseph E. Davies at the center." In 1933 Davies became Trujillo's counsel—negotiating, lobbying, and propagandizing for the regime in the United States. Four years later President Roosevelt appointed his friend Davies U.S. ambassador to the Soviet Union. (*The Reporter*, 1961. Copyright 1961 by The Reporter Magazine Co.)

Nicaragua, like the Dominican Republic, developed in the twentieth century under the weight of U.S. military occupation and the Good Neighbor policy. From 1912 to 1925 the United States ruled Nicaragua and kept in power the pliant Conservative party. Nicaragua by 1925 appeared to be solvent, secure, and stable. The marines departed, but in late 1926 they returned because, in President Coolidge's words, Nicaragua "went to hell in a hack."[68] The Coolidge administration explained—in an overstated report titled "Bolshevik Aims and Policies in Mexico and Latin America"—that communists were fomenting trouble in Nicaragua. The U.S. embassy in Mexico had greatly exaggerated the activities of American leftists in Mexico (including the Marxist writer Bertram Wolfe), and Washington found the anti-Bolshevik rationale irresistible. In fact, Nicaraguan Liberals had used Mexico as a sanctuary to challenge the Conservatives. "We are not making war on Nicaragua," Coolidge opined, with tones of the Roosevelt Corollary, "any more than a policeman on the street is making war on passersby."[69] Nicaraguans in the Coco River basin saw it differently: "The Machos are coming," they said of the marines. "They will burn our houses."[70]

The Nicaraguan intervention generated rancorous debate in the United States. The assertion of a communist plot persuaded few. Congress again resented presidential initiatives that ignored the legislature's power to declare war. Senator Burton K. Wheeler suggested that if U.S. soldiers intended to "stamp out banditry, let's send them to Chicago to stamp it out there. . . . I wouldn't sacrifice . . . one American boy for all the damn Nicaraguans."[71] Bloodshed and destruction in Nicaragua raised further outcries after Secretary of the Navy Curtis D. Wilbur matter-of-factly reported in 1928: "Several houses were destroyed in the village of Quilali in order to prepare a landing field for airplanes so that 19 wounded Marines could be evacuated to a hospital."[72] From 1927 to 1933 the Liberal insurgent César Augusto Sandino, who protested "the corrupting vice of the dollar in Nicaragua," earned an international reputation as he waged guerrilla war against U.S. troops, which numbered 50,000 in early 1929.[73] To dampen Latin American attraction to the Sandino

César Augusto Sandino (1895–1934). President Hoover called him a "cold-blooded bandit," but Nicaraguans have hailed Sandino as a hero. Determined that Nicaragua control its natural resources and help the poor, Sandino blasted the Monroe Doctrine as meaning "America for the Yankees." Accused of administering "machete justice" to members of the Guardia Nacional, Sandino explained that "liberty is not conquered with flowers." The revolutionaries who overthrew the Somoza dictatorship in 1979 called themselves "Sandinistas." (Library of Congress)

insurgency, Washington pressed El Salvador, Honduras, and Costa Rica to suppress anti-imperialist leaders and newspapers in those Central American nations.

Sensitive to criticism of the U.S. presence in Nicaragua, special emissary Henry L. Stimson brought Liberals and Conservatives together in the "Peace of Tipitapa" (1927) and provided for U.S. supervision of the election of 1928. Most important, he and General Frank R. McCoy created an American-trained national guard to perpetuate the domestic order that the marines had imposed. Shortly after U.S. troops withdrew in 1933, Sandino signed a truce with the Nicaraguan government. But General Anastasio Somoza, who had studied at a business school in Philadelphia and knew colloquial English, gained command of the American-trained Guardia Nacional. Somoza then captured and executed Sandino, notwithstanding his "word of honor" that no harm would come to him.[74] In 1936 Somoza seized power and established a self-enriching family dictatorship that lasted until 1979. An American collector-general remained to handle customs collections until 1944, and the United States retained canal rights and a naval base. The Roosevelt administration in 1939 constructed an interoceanic highway (the Rama Road) for several million dollars to spur economic development.

Few benefits accrued to the United States from its years of interference in Nicaragua. Trade never reached important levels, although the United States dominated the Central American nation's economy. From 1914 to 1930 U.S. investments grew from $4.5 million to $13 million. Although the stormy occupation of Nicaragua may have indirectly fostered the Good Neighbor policy, for Nicaraguans that policy meant continued foreign financial management and replacement of the U.S. Marine Corps by a home-grown dictator and a national guard traveling the Rama Road to suppress critics of the regime.

Haiti, too, drew Washington's hegemonic attention. A marine officer depicted the Haitians as "real nigger and no mistake—there are some very fine looking, well educated polished men here but they are real nigs beneath the surface."[75] When U.S. soldiers went abroad, of course, they carried American prejudices as well as canteens. For nineteen years, from 1915 to 1934, marines governed the tiny black French-speaking nation of Haiti in the Caribbean. The venture only deepened Haiti's distress. The Wilson administration ordered the marines into Haiti on July 28, 1915, because it feared German intrigue during World War I, sought to protect American financial interests, and insisted on order in the Caribbean.

The occupation built highways, technical schools, lighthouses, hospitals, and railroads. Americans improved public health and sanitation, but never eradicated Haiti's profound human squalor. By the mid-1960s Haiti had the lowest life expectancy (thirty-five years) and the lowest literacy rate (10 percent) in Latin America. Many of the roads had been built in 1916–1918 by forced labor—the *corvée* system under which Admiral William Caperton ordered workers into labor gangs. NAACP official James Weldon Johnson, who toured Haiti, protested: "They were maltreated, beaten and terrorized . . . [like] the convicts in the Negro chain gangs that are used to build roads in many of our southern states."[76] Haitians rebelled against the *corvée;* in 1919 alone the marines killed 2,000 to quell the insurrection.

American racism reached into Haiti. U.S. personnel introduced to Haitians the words "nigger," "gook," and "coon" and enforced segregation between blacks and

Comic Strips in Nicaragua. In this 1927 photograph of the tranquil side of intervention, marines read newspaper comic strips to Nicaraguan children. Said Clifford Hamm, collector-general of customs in Nicaragua: "Three cheers for the American marine who is teaching baseball and sportsmanship! It is the best step towards order, peace, and stability." (Marine Corps, National Archives)

whites. When an aide objected to inviting Haitian diplomats to tea, Secretary Hull responded in both race and class terms: "When they [blacks] speak French, that's different."[77] Americans bestowed higher status on the mulattos (the "elites") than on the *authentiques* (blacks) but neither wooed nor fraternized with the Haitian bourgeoisie. They did not do so because of intense hostility to mixed bloods based on the belief, in the historian Brenda Plummer's words, "that such persons, as links between the races, endangered the established order in what should be a rigidly color-defined world."[78] Anthropological research in the 1930s by Franz Boaz and others that showed complex linkages among African, European, and indigenous cultures could not displace the prevailing Hollywood film stereotype of Haiti as the land of voodoo and zombies.

Transportation improvements expanded commercial contacts between cities and rural farmers. Pan American Airways began flights between Miami and Port-au-Prince. Irrigation systems and a telephone network contributed to economic growth. Sugar and cotton exports increased, although the heavy dependence on one crop, coffee, left Haiti susceptible to fluctuations in world prices. The United States became Haiti's largest trading partner. American capital investments grew from $11.5 million in 1914 to $28.5 million in 1930. The National City Bank of New York owned the Banque Nacional. Under U.S. financial supervision, Haiti actually paid its foreign debts (largely French) ahead of schedule.

U.S. military authorities trained a national guard, the Garde d'Haiti. A majority of the officers of this gendarmerie actually consisted of Americans; no Haitian had reached captain's rank by 1930. The first commandant, Major Smedley D. Butler of the marines, had experience in putting down "natives" in China, Honduras,

"The Rights of Small Nations: Haiti." A harshly critical view of the marine occupation of Haiti, 1915–1934. (*Good Morning,* 1921)

Nicaragua, Panama, and Mexico. The brash Butler vowed to use "my little chocolate soldiers . . . to make a real and happy nation out of this blood crazy Garden of Eden."[79] The national guard served as judges, tax collectors, and paymasters for teachers, enforced martial law, and wielded deciding political force.

The United States failed to establish respect for honest government by law and neglected to train efficient civil servants. Washington officials drafted the 1918 constitution and forced it on Haitians; the press was censored and elections were rigged. U.S. authorities suspended the legislature for thirteen years. When President Philippe Sudre Dartiguenave's term ended in 1922, Americans jilted him in favor of Louis Borno, an acquiescent lawyer who collaborated with the American high commissioner, General John H. Russell of Georgia, to rule Haiti from 1922 to 1930. Borno "has never taken a step without first consulting me," Russell boasted.[80] The American general wrote Haitian legislation, directed public projects, and when Borno seemed obstinate, ordered the American financial adviser to withhold the president's salary.

Haitians resented their colonial status. The peaking of discontent in 1929 came after a slump in coffee prices and exports and exposure of Borno's political machinations. Protests and strikes spread across the country. President Hoover appointed an investigating commission chaired by W. Cameron Forbes, former governor-general of the Philippines. His report of 1930 noted "the failure of the Occupation to understand the social problems of Haiti."[81] The commission promoted "Haitianization" to ease Haitians into positions of responsibility. Hoover started the withdrawal; Roosevelt completed it in 1934.

After the marines departed, strong-arm presidents ruled with the help of Export-Import Bank loans and ties with Washington. During World War II the United States used Haitian bases, and until 1947 U.S. officials supervised Haitian national finances. A revolution in 1946 placed the government in the hands of the Garde, and the revolution of 1956–1957 produced the callous dictatorship of Dr. François ("Papa Doc") Duvalier. He ruled with the ruthless help of his secret police force, the Touton Macoutes, until his death in 1971, when his son "Baby Doc" assumed power. Driven out in 1986, he left behind abject poverty and rampant civil strife. In 1994 U.S. armed forces once again invaded Haiti to stabilize politics (see Chapter 12).

Subverting Nationalism in Cuba and Puerto Rico

Cubans bristled under the Platt Amendment and U.S. military interventions (see Chapter 2). Through the 1920s and into the 1930s the United States helped conduct elections, enlarged the national army, managed the national budget, and maintained economic control over the island. North American investment, particularly in sugar, soared to $1.5 billion in 1929. Approximately half a million fun-seeking Americans a year visited the capital city of Havana, where, declared one tourist, "it is hot, it is 'wet,' it is . . . Wide Open."[82]

Gerardo Machado ruled from 1924 to 1933; he suppressed free speech, jailed or murdered leftists, journalists, labor leaders, and students, and used the army as a political weapon. Obtaining loans from U.S. bankers, he prohibited strikes and looked after North American business interests "as if they were my own."[83] Cuban resentment against Machado intensified in the late 1920s when sugar prices began to drop. Dependent on sugar and exports to the United States, Cuba sank further into economic crisis when the United States instituted the restrictive Smoot-Hawley Tariff of 1931. Unemployment rates shot up. Machado's army beat back protesters. Because armed intervention would violate the newly stated Good Neighbor policy, Roosevelt and his advisers chose to ease out the unpopular Machado.

Suave Sumner Welles, a Groton School friend of Roosevelt already experienced in the Dominican Republic, went as ambassador to Havana in 1933. While U.S. warships patrolled Cuban waters and a general strike rocked the country, Welles persuaded Machado to flee. But Welles lost control; "his" handpicked government, led by Carlos Manuel de Céspedes, lasted less than a month. Military dissidents, commanded by Sergeant Fulgencio Batista, staged the "Sergeants' Revolution" of September 1933, deposed the lackluster Céspedes, and installed Professor Ramón Grau San Martín as president.

An exile under Machado, critic of the Platt Amendment, and friend of the left, Grau stood as "the hope and the symbol of the forces of nationalism, patriotism, and reform."[84] Yet the U.S. ambassador refused recognition because "we owe it to the Cuban people not to assist in saddling upon them for an indefinite period a government which every responsible element in the country violently opposed."[85] Grau soon promulgated economic and social reforms, suspended payment on Chase National Bank loans, and seized some North American–owned sugar mills. Welles decried the "confiscatory" decrees of this "social revolution" and conspired with Batista, who feared that Grau's economic nationalism would spawn U.S. intervention.[86] Welles left Cuba in December 1933, and in January Batista toppled Grau, who fled to Mexico. A Batista-backed president took over, and the United States quickly granted recognition.

Batista ruled Cuba, sometimes as president, sometimes from the shadows, from 1934 to 1959. At the start of the Batista era, the United States abrogated the unpopular Platt Amendment (1934), lowered the sugar tariff, granted a favorable quota to Cuban sugar imports (1934), and issued Export-Import Bank loans ($8 million in 1934). In 1940, Cuba granted American armed forces the use of ports and airfields (besides Guantánamo) in exchange for military aid. One Cuban nationalist, Julio César Fernández, reflected on the lost opportunity of 1933: "American diplomacy has many resources; when the steel of her warships is not convenient, she uses the docile backbone of her native lackeys."[87]

Elsewhere in the Caribbean, Puerto Rico stagnated under American paternalism. Throughout the interwar years, mediocre and often crude U.S. governors who could not speak Spanish castigated Puerto Ricans as "unsteady, unprincipled children" unable to govern themselves.[88] Although the Jones Act of 1917 had granted Puerto Ricans U.S. citizenship, Washington stiff-armed requests for the colony's independence or statehood. Puerto Ricans did not gain the right to elect their own governor until 1947. Absentee American landowners and sugar barons ran the island's economy. Despite improved roads and new schools, Governor Theodore Roosevelt, Jr. (1929–1932), observed "farm after farm where lean underfed women

Fulgencio Batista (1901–1973). Born of farm folk in the United Fruit Company town of Banes, Batista joined the Cuban army at age twenty. A smiling, ruthless dictator, he became a staunch U.S. ally, bought real estate in Daytona Beach, Florida, and turned Havana into a playground of casinos and brothels for American tourists. Fidel Castro's 26th of July Movement overthrew the corrupt regime in 1959. Batista died in exile in Portugal. (National Archives)

Ponce, Puerto Rico, 1938.
The U.S. Farm Security Administration photographer Edwin Rosskam captured class divisions in Puerto Rico, where U.S. neglect helped perpetuate the island's poverty. At the top of the hill sits the villa of the owner of a sugar plantation and refinery. The shacks of workers cling to the hillside. (Library of Congress)

and sickly men repeated again and again the same story—little food and no opportunity to get more."[89] Eighty percent of peasants remained landless and many crowded into urban slums.

Encouraged by New Deal reformers to act "as a cultural bridge between the Americas," faculty and alumni at the University of Puerto Rico actually became critical of U.S. hegemony.[90] The Harvard-educated lawyer Pedro Albizu Campos headed the Nationalist party, which advocated the violent overthrow of U.S. rule. On Palm Sunday, 1937, police fired on unarmed Nationalist marchers, killing nineteen in the "Ponce Massacre." Abizu went to federal prison until 1947. Other Puerto Ricans rallied behind the socialist Luis Muñoz Marín, whose Popular Democratic party ultimately advocated "commonwealth" status (attained in 1952). Muñoz Marín worked with New Dealers in the 1930s to obtain relief and public-works projects amounting to $1 million a month, but when Governor Rexford Tugwell arrived in 1941, he found Puerto Rico "still sunk in hopeless poverty."[91]

Compromising with Mexico: Oil and Nationalism

The ongoing Mexican Revolution, which began in 1910, presented the United States with a test of the nonmilitary emphasis of the Good Neighbor policy. Before the 1920s it had appeared that Mexico would be treated like other U.S. neighbors—invaded, occupied, and owned by Americans, who by 1910 controlled 43 percent of Mexican property and produced more than half of Mexico's oil. Hollywood films perpetuated stereotypes by portraying the Mexican as a bandit or villainous "greaser."[92] Scholars and artists promoted cultural interaction to counter such negative images. Professor Herbert E. Bolton of the University of California, Berkeley, emphasized a shared borderlands history, drawing large numbers of students to his course on "Greater America." In the 1930s at U.S. universities, the Mexican artist José Clemente Orozco painted colorful murals of revolutionary struggle. A decade earlier Mexico City had become a "Yankee Bohemia" where expatriot writers and artists sympathetically interpreted Mexican politics and culture.[93] These contacts did not diminish the nationalism of either nation, but they probably did encourage an environment of tolerance and understanding based on mutual experience that undercut war hawks bent on military confrontation.

The Mexican Constitution of 1917 alarmed capitalist Americans, because its Article 27 held that all "land and waters" and all subsoil raw materials belonged to the Mexican nation. Three hundred million dollars in American investments in oil and mines seemed jeopardized. Mexico also began to tax American oil producers heavily. Unwilling to see its resources "rapidly sucked away by international firms," as the historian Linda B. Hall has written, Mexico proved that "it was not a Caribbean nation that the United States could push around at will."[94]

Washington continued to claim economic rights for its nationals in Mexico and refused to recognize the Mexican government of Alváro Obregón. In 1923, however, Mexico and the United States signed the Bucareli Agreements. In exchange for U.S. recognition, Mexico agreed that Americans who held subsoil rights before the 1917 Constitution could continue those concessions and that Americans whose agricultural lands were expropriated would receive Mexican bonds in compensation. At the time Americans owned about 60 percent of Mexico's oil industry. But a new law passed by the Mexican congress in 1925 stated that oil lands secured before 1917 could be held for a maximum of only fifty years. In part because American oil companies had begun to exploit the rich oil fields of Venezuela, Washington rejected appeals to intervene and resorted to nonmilitary methods instead.

In early 1927, President Coolidge selected Dwight W. Morrow, an old college chum and a partner in the Wall Street firm of J. P. Morgan and Company, as the new ambassador to Mexico City. An oil lobbyist advised that Morrow, the "trainer," faced a "vicious animal" in Mexico: "If the trainer showed fear, the animal would attack him, but if he showed courage and force, the animal would submit."[95] Learning a little Spanish, having "Lone Eagle" Charles Lindbergh fly nonstop from Washington, D.C., and even bringing the humorist Will Rogers to the Mexican capital, Morrow ingratiated himself. He then negotiated an agreement that confirmed *pre-1917* ownership of petroleum lands. Thus in 1927–1928 the oil controversy seemed defused through compromise. The United States protected its citizens' oil investments and tacitly conceded that Mexico legally controlled its own raw materials. This arrangement lasted until 1938, when President Lázaro Cárdenas defiantly expropriated the property of all foreign oil companies, then attempting to thwart an oil workers' strike for higher wages. "An entire nation, accustomed for centuries to the perpetual humiliation of the underdog, reared its head proudly for

Lázaro Cárdenas (1895–1970) and Josephus Daniels (1862–1949). A former newspaper publisher and secretary of the navy during the Wilson administration, Daniels donned Mexican national costumes, adopted a warm, folksy style, and became a popular ambassador to Mexico (1933–1941) under his friend President Franklin D. Roosevelt. As president of Mexico (1934–1940), Cárdenas attempted to regain control of his nation's oil resources from multinational corporations. In contrast to the frightened pro-business attitudes of professional diplomats in Mexico, and to FBI director J. Edgar Hoover's warning that Cárdenas was "anti-foreign due to his Indian antecedents," Daniels assured FDR that Cárdenas was simply another "New Dealer" trying to improve his country's living conditions. According to the historian Friedrich E. Schuler, Daniels, through his defense of Cárdenas's expropriation of U.S. oil companies in 1938, "represented the proverbial good neighbor in Mexico more than any other U.S. ambassador to Latin America during all of Roosevelt's administrations." (Library of Congress)

the first time," wrote one Mexican journalist. "No more humble pie, no more kowtowing to arrogant foreign officials."[96]

Ambassador Josephus Daniels, who as secretary of the navy in 1914 had ordered the marines to Veracruz, dispelled early suspicions and persuaded Mexican leaders that he and Washington had changed. Daniels would not accept Hull's "get tough" policies, softening an intemperate State Department blast when he delivered it to the Mexican foreign minister. Refusing to see the Good Neighbor policy "drown in Mexican oil," Daniels opposed Washington's economic coercion through the reduction of U.S. purchases of Mexican silver.[97] For their part the American oil companies refused to sell petroleum equipment to Mexico, and they persuaded shipping firms not to carry Mexican oil. Standard Oil of New Jersey financed false propaganda in the United States with the message that Cárdenas plotted to turn Mexico communist. In 1938 Daniels cabled Hull that "some of the oil men are predicting revolution" so that they can "return to conditions here as existed under Díaz or Huerta."[98]

Viewing Cárdenas as "one of the few Latin leaders who was actually preaching and trying to practice democracy," FDR ruled out intervention and sought compensation.[99] Increased purchases of Mexican oil by Germany, Italy, and Japan underscored the urgent need for a diplomatic settlement. Indeed, once war broke out in Europe in September 1939, the "nervous Nelly of American intelligence," FBI director J. Edgar Hoover, reported false rumors about 250 Nazi pilots in Mexico, eight German submarines operating out of Veracruz, and Hitler's promise of British Honduras if Mexico agreed to supply Germany with petroleum.[100] Protracted Mexican-American talks finally produced an agreement in 1941. The United States conceded the principle that Mexico owned its own raw materials, and Mexico promised to pay for expropriated properties. The Export-Import Bank extended a

$30 million loan. Washington's compromise with Mexican nationalism illustrated the Good Neighbor policy's abandonment of military intervention. The change paid strategic dividends as the United States readied itself for World War II.

Pan Americanism and the Approach of the Second World War

In 1889, Secretary of State James G. Blaine spurred formation of the International Bureau of American Republics, renamed in 1910 the Pan American Union. The U.S. secretary of state became its permanent chair. "Pan Americanism" at first focused on improvement of trade in the Western Hemisphere and symbolized a mythical inter-American "cooperative ideal."[101] The union's elegant quarters, financed by steel baron Andrew Carnegie, stood, significantly, near the Department of State building. One Argentine diplomat sneered that "there is no Pan Americanism in South America; it exists only in Washington."[102] The declarations of neutrality during World War I by seven Latin American governments suggested the hollowness of Pan American solidarity.

In 1923 the Fifth International Conference of American States met in Santiago, Chile. The United States controlled the agenda, and the delegates endorsed a Treaty to Avoid or Prevent Conflicts Between the American States (Gondra Treaty). The Havana conference of 1928 proved quite different, because it convened shortly after U.S. troops had landed in Nicaragua. Washington anticipated trouble and thus appointed former secretary of state Hughes to head its delegation. Even President Coolidge traveled to Cuba to address the conference with soothing banalities. The cooperative Machado dictatorship censored critical newspaper comments about the United States. At the conference, the delegate from El Salvador boldly moved that "no state has the right to intervene in the internal affairs of another."[103] Mexico and Argentina backed this challenge to the United States. Hughes defended the right of "interposition of a temporary character," and he manipulated the conference to table the resolution.[104]

The seventh Pan American conference, in Montevideo, Uruguay (1933), met under the aura of the Good Neighbor policy. The nonintervention resolution was once again introduced. Secretary Hull cast an affirmative vote but retained a U.S. right to intervene "by the law of nations as generally recognized and accepted."[105] Further confusion about the meaning of the nonintervention pledge became evident at the 1936 Buenos Aires conference, where the United States seemingly endorsed an unequivocal statement. The U.S. definition, however, intended to outlaw *military* intervention, whereas many Latin American countries argued that Washington could not interfere through economic or political pressure when countries nationalized American-owned property.

Pan Americanism took a decided turn toward hemispheric security in the late 1930s, as Germany, Italy, and Japan attempted to improve their economic and political standing in Latin America. As Germany's trade with Latin America climbed, Hull thought the danger "not limited to the possibility of a military invasion. It was more acute in its indirect form of propaganda, penetration, organizing political parties, buying some adherents, and blackmailing others."[106] Adolf Hitler dreamed of creating "a new Germany" in Brazil and instigated subversive activities there and in Uruguay, Argentina, and Mexico, but the United States overreacted.[107] With such fears, Washington decided to form what Assistant Secretary of State Adolf Berle called "a north–south axis" at the Lima Pan American conference of 1938, where Argentina, Uruguay, and Chile fought Hull's proposal to knit the Latin American countries together in a quasi alliance.[108] The anti-German sentiment of most delegates, aroused by the recent Munich crisis, helped Hull achieve solidarity. The conferees endorsed the Declaration of Lima, a pledge to resist foreign intervention in the Americas. A secret U.S. Army Air Corps study in early 1939 warned that secret "airdromes in the north-west part of Brazil . . . would place Nazi-Fascist bombers less than 1,000 miles from the Panama Canal, well within their operating radius of action with [a] heavy load of bombs."[109] That autumn the Declaration of Panama established a security belt around the Western Hemisphere to rebuff possible Axis intrusions. At the same time, the United States persuaded Latin American nations to reduce or cease trade with the Axis powers and to ship strategic raw materials to the United States. To advance hemispheric unity even more, Roosevelt in 1940 appointed the energetic Nelson Rockefeller to the new post of coordinator of inter-American affairs. His office encouraged Hollywood to produce films, such as *The Road to Rio* (1941) and *Simon Bolivar* (1941), which "strengthened popular support for U.S. foreign policy."[110]

The post–World War I search for international order had broken down by 1939. In both Asia and Latin America, fervent nationalists challenged the United States. In both areas the viability of American diplomacy derived from the power the United States possessed and exercised. In Asia, after the Manchurian crisis of 1931–1932, the United States sought, without success, to build a counterforce to Japan. Even the Philippines became a virtual hostage that the U.S. military said it could not defend. By spring 1939 the possibility of simultaneous war with Germany, Italy, and Japan prompted the U.S. Joint Army-Navy Board to modify war plan ORANGE (which emphasized a naval offensive in the Pacific) in favor of RAINBOW plans for hemispheric defense based on the primacy of the Atlantic and Caribbean approaches.

The Great Depression prostrated international relations. World trade and investment collapsed; tariffs went up. The island-bound and trade-conscious Japanese accelerated efforts to build a "co-prosperity" sphere in Asia. In Latin America, where many countries depended on the exportation of one commodity, revolutions and coups erupted, feeding on incipient nationalism. Social unrest and political instability rocked the area from which the United States was withdrawing its marines. Political upheavals in the Dominican Republic, Argentina, Brazil, and Chile in 1930, Peru in 1931, Cuba in 1933—all threatened U.S. hegemony. Devastated by the depression, Latin Americans gained a new awareness of the extent to which foreigners made their national choices and the degree to which foreign companies drained profits from them. By World War II, Latin Americans held a more favorable image of the United States, which seemed to have abandoned military intervention under the Good Neighbor policy. But they harbored fresh suspicions that invigorated inter-

American economic relations would continue U.S. hegemony. Yankeephobia simmered even as Latin Americans joined the United States in the fight against the Axis.

FURTHER READING FOR THE PERIOD 1920–1939

For general studies and biographies for this period, see works cited in Chapter 4.

For Asia, see Irvine H. Anderson, *The Standard-Vacuum Oil Company and United States East Asia Policy* (1974); Richard D. Burns and Edward M. Bennett, eds., *Diplomats in Crisis* (1974); Roger Dingman, *Power in the Pacific* (1976); Herbert Feis, *The Road to Pearl Harbor* (1950); Akira Iriye, *Across the Pacific* (1967), *After Imperialism* (1969), and *The Origins of the Second World War in Asia and the Pacific* (1987); Brian M. Linn, *Guardians of Empire: The U.S. Army and the Pacific, 1902–1940* (1997); Jonathan Marshall, *To Have and Have Not: Southeast Asian Raw Materials and the Origins of the Pacific War* (1995); William R. Nestor, *Power Across the Pacific* (1996); and Gerald Wheeler, *Prelude to Pearl Harbor: The United States Navy and the Far East, 1921–1931* (1963).

For relations with Japan, consult Michael Barnhart, *Japan Prepares for Total War* (1987); Dorothy Borg and Shumpei Okamoto, eds., *Pearl Harbor as History* (1973); Justus D. Doenecke, *When the Wicked Rise* (1984) (Manchurian crisis); Peter Duus et al., eds., *The Japanese Wartime Empire, 1931–1945* (1996); Carol Gluck and Stephen Graubard, eds., *Showa: The Japan of Hirohito* (1992); Saburō Ienaga, *The Pacific War* (1978); Manny T. Koginos, *The Panay Incident* (1967); Walter LaFeber, *The Clash* (1997); Frank P. Mintz, *Revisionism and the Origins of Pearl Harbor* (1985); James W. Morley, ed., *Deterrent Diplomacy: Japan, Germany and the U.S.S.R., 1934–1940* (1977); Charles E. Neu, *The Troubled Encounter* (1975); William L. Neumann, *America Encounters Japan* (1963); Christopher Thorne, *The Limits of Foreign Policy* (1972); and Jonathan G. Utley, *Going to War with Japan, 1937–1941* (1985).

China and the United States are explored in Russell D. Buhite, *Nelson T. Johnson and American Policy Toward China* (1968); Mary B. Bullock, *An American Transplant* (1980) (Rockefeller Foundation); Warren I. Cohen, *America's Response to China* (1990) and *The Chinese Connection* (1978); Bernard Cole, *Gunboats and Marines* (1983); John W. Garver, *Chinese-Soviet Relations, 1937–1945* (1988); David H. Grover, *American Merchant Ships on the Yangtze* (1992); Shizhang Hu, *Stanley K. Hornbeck and the Open Door Policy* (1995); T. Christopher Jespersen, *American Images of China* (1996); Kathleen Lodwink, *Educating the Women of Hainan* (1995); Patricia Neils, *China Images in the Life and Times of Henry Luce* (1990); Youli Sun, *China and the Origins of the Pacific War* (1993); Barbara Tuchman, *Stilwell and the American Experience in China* (1971); and Stephen J. Valone, *"A Policy Calculated to Benefit China"* (1991).

Inter-American relations and the Good Neighbor policy are treated in Cole Blasier, *The Hovering Giant* (1976); John A. Britton, *Carleton Beals* (1987); Marcos Cueto, ed., *Missionaries of Science* (1994) (Rockefeller Foundation); Alexander DeConde, *Herbert Hoover's Latin American Policy* (1951); Alton Frye, *Nazi Germany and the American Hemisphere, 1933–1941* (1967); Irwin F. Gellman, *Good Neighbor Diplomacy* (1979); Mark T. Gilderhus, *The Second Century* (2000); David Green, *The Containment of Latin America* (1971); Kenneth J. Grieb, *The Latin American Policy of Warren G. Harding* (1976); David G. Haglund, *Latin America and the Transformation of U.S. Strategic Thought, 1936–1940* (1984); Thomas L. Karnes, *Tropical Enterprise: The Standard Fruit and Steamship Company in Latin America* (1978); Michael L. Krenn, *U.S. Policy Toward Economic Nationalism in Latin America* (1990); Lester D. Langley, *America and the Americas* (1989); Abraham F. Lowenthal, ed., *Exporting Democracy* (1991); John Major, *Prize Possession* (1993) (Panama Canal); Carlos Marichal, *A Century of Debt Crises in Latin America* (1989); Thomas O'Brien, *The Revolutionary Mission: American Enterprise in Latin America* (1996); Fredrick B. Pike, *FDR's Good Neighbor Policy* (1995); Emily S. Rosenberg, *Financial Missionaries to the World* (1999); Lars Schoultz, *Beneath the United States* (1998); David F. Schmitz, *Thank God They're on Our Side* (1999) (dictatorships); James Schwoch, *The American Radio Industry and Its Latin American Activities* (1990); Sarah E. Sharbach, *Stereotypes of Latin America* (1993); Peter H. Smith, *Talons of the Eagle* (1996); Joseph Tulchin, *The Aftermath of War: World War I and U.S. Policy Toward Latin America* (1971); and Bryce Wood, *The Making of the Good Neighbor Policy* (1961).

For the Caribbean and Central America, see G. Pope Atkins and Larman C. Wilson, *The United States and the Trujillo Regime* (1972) and *The Dominican Republic and the United States* (1998); Bruce Calder, *The Impact of Intervention* (1984) (Dominican Republic); Raymond Carr, *Puerto Rico* (1984); Arturo Morales Carrión, *Puerto Rico* (1983); Truman P. Clark, *Puerto Rico and the United States, 1917–23* (1975); Paul J. Dosal, *Doing Business with the Dictators* (1993) (United Fruit, Guatemala); Ronald Fernandez, *The Disenchanted Island* (1992) (Puerto Rico); Walter LaFeber, *Inevitable Revolutions* (1993); Lester D. Langley, *The United States and the Caribbean* (1980); Rayford W. Logan, *Haiti and the Dominican Republic* (1968); A. W. Maldonado, *Teodoro Moscoso and Puerto Rico's Operation Bootstrap* (1997); Dana Munro, *The United States and the Caribbean Republics, 1921–1933* (1974); Brenda G. Plummer, *Haiti and the United States* (1992); Eric Paul Roorda, *The Dictator Next Door* (1998) (Trujillo); Robert I. Rotberg, *Haiti* (1971); Richard V. Salisbury, *Anti-Imperialism and International Competition in Central America* (1989); and Hans Schmidt, *The United States Occupation of Haiti* (1971) and *Maverick Marine* (1987) (Butler).

For Nicaragua and the U.S. intervention, see Paul C. Clark, Jr., *The United States and Somoza* (1992); Thomas J. Dodd, *Managing Democracy in Central America* (1992); William Kamman, *A Search for Stability* (1968); Neil Macaulay, *The Sandino Affair* (1967); Richard Millett, *Guardians of the Dynasty* (1977); and Knut Walter, *The Regime of Anastasio Somoza* (1993).

For South America, see Elizabeth A. Cobbs, *The Rich Neighbor Policy: Rockefeller and Kaiser in Brazil* (1992); Paul W. Drake, *The Money Doctor in the Andes* (1988); Stanley Hilton, *Brazil and the Great Powers* (1975); Michael Grow, *The Good Neighbor Policy and Authoritarianism in Paraguay* (1981); Frank McCann, *The Brazilian-American Alliance* (1973); Michael Montéon, *Chile in the Nitrate Era* (1982); Stephen G. Rabe, *The Road to OPEC* (1982) (Venezuela); and Stephen J. Randall, *The Diplomacy of Modernization* (1977) (Colombia).

Studies of U.S.-Mexican relations include Leslie Bethell, ed., *Mexico Since Independence* (1991); John A. Britton, *Revolution and Ideology: Images of the Mexican Revolution in the United States* (1995); E. David Cronon, *Josephus Daniels in Mexico* (1960); Helen Delpar, *The Enormous Vogue of Things Mexican* (1992) (culture); Linda B. Hall, *Oil, Banks, and Politics* (1995); Dan LaBotz, *Edward L. Doheny* (1991) (oil); Lorenzo Meyer, *Mexico and the United States in the Oil Controversy* (1977); Stephen R. Niblo, *War, Diplomacy, and Development* (1995); W. Dirk Raat, *Mexico and the United States* (1996); Ramón Ruíz, *The Great Rebellion* (1980); Friedrich E. Schuler, *Mexico Between Hitler and Roosevelt* (1998); and Robert F. Smith, *The United States and Revolutionary Nationalism in Mexico* (1972).

For Cuba, see Jules R. Benjamin, *The United States and Cuba* (1978); Irwin F. Gellman, *Roosevelt and Batista* (1973); Louis A. Pérez, Jr., *Cuba and the United States* (1997) and *Cuba Under the Platt Amendment* (1968); and Ramón Ruíz, *Cuba* (1968).

See also the General Bibliography and the following notes.

For comprehensive coverage of foreign-relations topics, see the articles in the four-volume *Encyclopedia of U.S. Foreign Relations* (1997), edited by Bruce W. Jentleson and Thomas G. Paterson.

NOTES TO CHAPTER 5

1. Quoted in Elting E. Morison, *Turmoil and Tradition* (New York: Atheneum, 1964), p. 312.
2. Robert H. Ferrell, "The Mukden Incident," *Journal of Modern History*, XXVII (March 1955), 67.
3. Quoted in Morison, *Turmoil and Tradition*, p. 308.
4. Quoted in Richard N. Current, "Henry L. Stimson," in Norman A. Graebner, ed., *An Uncertain Tradition* (New York: McGraw-Hill, 1961), pp. 171, 169.
5. Quoted in Frank Freidel, *Franklin D. Roosevelt: Launching the New Deal* (Boston: Little, Brown, 1973), p. 120.
6. Quoted in Richard Dean Burns, "Stanley K. Hornbeck," in Richard Dean Burns and Edward M. Bennett, eds., *Diplomats in Crisis* (Santa Barbara: ABC-CLIO Press, 1974), p. 103.
7. Quoted in Justus D. Doenecke, *When the Wicked Rise* (Lewisburg, Pa.: Bucknell University Press, 1984), p. 37.
8. Quoted in Christopher Thorne, *The Limits of Foreign Policy* (New York: Capricorn, 1973), p. 158.
9. Quoted in Morison, *Turmoil and Tradition*, p. 310.
10. Quoted in Walter LaFeber, *The Clash* (New York: Norton, 1997), p. 70.

11. Quoted in Morison, *Turmoil and Tradition,* p. 315.

12. Quoted in Norman A. Graebner, "Hoover, Roosevelt, and the Japanese," in Dorothy Borg and Shumpei Okamoto, eds., *Pearl Harbor as History* (New York: Columbia University Press, 1973), p. 30.

13. Quoted in LaFeber, *Clash,* p. 173.

14. Hugh R. Wilson, *Diplomat Between the Wars* (New York: Longmans, Green, 1941), p. 280.

15. Edgar Snow quoted in James L. Huskey, "The Cosmopolitan Connection," *Diplomatic History, XI* (Summer 1987), 241.

16. Michael Schaller, *The U.S. Crusade in China, 1938–1945* (New York: Columbia University Press, 1979), p. 5.

17. Akira Iriye, *The Origins of the Second World War in Asia and the Pacific* (London: Longman, 1987), p. 16.

18. Quoted in Thomas H. Buckley, *The United States and the Washington Conference, 1921–1922* (Knoxville: University of Tennessee Press, 1970), p. 72.

19. *Ibid.,* p. 73.

20. Cryptographer Herbert Yardley quoted in LaFeber, *Clash,* p. 140.

21. Robert Vansittart quoted in Richard W. Fanning, *Peace and Disarmament* (Lexington: University Press of Kentucky, 1995), p. 153.

22. Thomas H. Buckley, "The Icarus Factor," *Diplomacy & Statecraft, IV* (November 1993), 125.

23. Quoted in David Armstrong, "China's Place in the New Pacific Order," *Diplomacy & Statecraft, IV* (November 1993), 263.

24. John Paton Davies, *Dragon by the Tail* (New York: Norton, 1972), p. 95.

25. Quoted in Akira Iriye, *Across the Pacific* (New York: Harcourt Brace & World, 1967), p. 148.

26. Quoted in Dennis L. Noble, *The Eagle and the Dragon* (Westport, Conn.: Greenwood, 1990), p. 192.

27. Quoted in Bernard D. Cole, *Gunboats and Marines* (Newark: University of Delaware Press, 1983), p. 145.

28. Ernie Place quoted in Noble, *Eagle,* p. 150; Huskey, "Cosmopolitan Connection," p. 228.

29. Mary B. Bullock, *An American Transplant* (Berkeley: University of California Press, 1980), pp. 44, 47.

30. Clare Boothe Luce quoted in T. Christopher Jesperson, *American Images of China, 1931–1949* (Stanford: Stanford University Press, 1996), p. 54.

31. *Ibid.,* p. 91.

32. Quoted in Justus D. Doenecke and John E. Wilz, *From Isolation to War, 1931–1941* (Arlington Heights, Ill.: Davidson, 1991; 2nd ed.), p. 23.

33. Quoted in William R. Nestor, *Power Across the Pacific* (New York: New York University Press, 1996), p. 117.

34. Quoted in Asada Sadao, "The Japanese Navy and the United States," in Borg and Okamoto, *Pearl Harbor,* p. 238.

35. Quoted in William L. Neumann, *America Encounters Japan* (Baltimore: Johns Hopkins University Press, 1963), p. 176.

36. Robert G. Kaufman, *Arms Control During the Pre-Nuclear Era* (New York: Columbia University Press, 1990), p. 181.

37. Quoted in Iris Chang, *The Rape of Nanking* (New York: Basic Books, 1998), p. 22.

38. Roger B. Jeans, ed., *Good-Bye to Old Peking* (Athens: Ohio University Press, 1998), p. 11.

39. John W. Garver, *Chinese-Soviet Relations 1937–1945* (New York: Oxford University Press, 1988), p. 15.

40. Samuel I. Rosenman, ed., *Public Papers and Addresses of Franklin D. Roosevelt* (New York: Macmillan, 1938–1943; 13 vols.), *VI,* 406–411.

41. Senator Gerald P. Nye quoted in Wayne S. Cole, "Congress and Political Parties," in Borg and Okamoto, *Pearl Harbor,* p. 314.

42. Major David Barrett quoted in Youli Sun, *China and the Origins of the Pacific War* (New York: St. Martin's Press, 1993), p. 134.

43. Quoted in Frederick C. Adams, *Economic Diplomacy* (Columbia: University of Missouri Press, 1976), p. 233.

44. Quoted in Stephen M. Streeter, "Waging the Counterrevolution: The United States and Guatemala, 1954–1961" (Ph.D. diss., University of Connecticut, 1994), p. 4.

45. Quoted in Arthur P. Whitaker, "From Dollar Diplomacy to the Good Neighbor Policy," *Inter-American Economic Affairs, IV* (Spring 1951), 18.

46. Rosenman, *Public Papers, II,* 14.

47. Quoted in Mark T. Gilderhus, *The Second Century* (Wilmington, Del.: Scholarly Resources, 2000), p. 89.

48. Fredrick B. Pike, *Chile and the United States* (South Bend, Ind.: University of Notre Dame Press, 1963), p. 236.

49. Sumner Welles quoted in Paul J. Dosal, *Doing Business with Dictators* (Wilmington, Del.: Scholarly Resources, 1993), p. 8.

50. Emily S. Rosenberg and Norman L. Rosenberg, "From Colonialism to Professionalism," *Journal of American History, LXXIV* (June 1987), 79; Paul W. Drake, *The Money Doctor in the Andes* (Durham: Duke University Press, 1989).

51. Emily S. Rosenberg, "Revisiting Dollar Diplomacy," *Diplomatic History, XXII* (Spring 1998), 173–174.

52. C. Neale Ronning, ed., *Intervention in Latin America* (New York: Knopf, 1970), pp. 42–49.

53. Fredrick B. Pike, *FDR's Good Neighbor Policy* (Austin: University of Texas Press, 1995), p. 137.

54. Lester D. Langley, *America and the Americas* (Athens: University of Georgia Press, 1989), p. 125.

55. Quoted in Emily Rosenberg, *Spreading the American Dream* (New York: Hill & Wang, 1982), p. 112.

56. Quoted in Benjamin Welles, *Sumner Welles* (New York: St. Martin's Press, 1997), p. 93.

57. Quoted in Elizabeth A. Cobbs, *The Rich Neighbor Policy* (New Haven: Yale University Press, 1992), p. 28.

58. Christopher Abel, "External Philanthropy and Domestic Change in Colombian Health Care," *Hispanic-American Historical Review, LXXV* (August 1995), 350.

59. Herbert Hoover, *Memoirs: The Cabinet and the Presidency, 1920–1933* (New York: Macmillan, 1952), p. 69.

60. Quoted in Bruce J. Calder, *The Impact of Intervention* (Austin: University of Texas Press, 1984), p. 124.

61. Sumner Welles, *Naboth's Vineyard* (New York: Payson and Clark, 1928; 2 vols.), *II,* 797–798.

62. Quoted in Magdaline W. Shannon, *Jean Price-Mars, the Haitian Elite, and the American Occupation, 1915–1935* (New York: St. Martin's Press, 1996), p. 166.

63. Quoted in Joseph R. Juárez, "United States Withdrawal from Santo Domingo," *Hispanic American Historical Review, XLII* (May 1962), 180.

64. Quoted *ibid.*

65. Franklin D. Roosevelt, "Our Foreign Policy," *Foreign Affairs, VI* (July 1928), 583.

66. Quoted in Calder, *Impact of Intervention,* p. 252.

67. Quoted in Robert F. Smith, *The United States and Cuba* (New York: Bookman, 1960), p. 184.

68. Quoted in Benjamin T. Harrison, *Dollar Diplomat* (Pullman: Washington State University Press, 1988), p. 91.

69. Quoted in Albert K. Weinberg, *Manifest Destiny* (Chicago: Quadrangle, 1963 [c. 1935]), p. 441.

70. Quoted in Carleton Beals, "This Is War, Gentlemen!" *The Nation*, CXXVI (April 11, 1928), 406.

71. Quoted in Ivan Musicant, *The Banana Wars* (New York: Macmillan, 1990), p. 328.

72. U.S. Navy, *Operation of Naval Service in Nicaragua* (Senate Doc. 86, 70 Cong., 1 Sess., 1928), pp. 5–6.

73. Sergio Ramírez, ed., *Sandino* (Princeton: Princeton University Press, 1990), p. 239.

74. Quoted in Walter LaFeber, *Inevitable Revolutions* (New York: Norton, 1993; 2nd ed.), p. 70.

75. Colonel Littleton Waller quoted in Robert I. Rotberg, *Haiti* (Boston: Houghton Mifflin, 1971), pp. 137–138.

76. James Weldon Johnson, "The Truth About Haiti," *The Crisis*, XX (September 1920), 223.

77. Quoted in Branda Gayle Plummer, *Rising Wind* (Chapel Hill: University of North Carolina Press, 1996), p. 100.

78. Brenda G. Plummer, *Haiti and the United States* (Athens: University of Georgia Press, 1992), p. 129.

79. Quoted in Hans Schmidt, *Maverick Marine* (Lexington: University of Kentucky Press, 1987), p. 84.

80. Quoted in Donald B. Cooper, "The Withdrawal of the United States from Haiti, 1928–1934," *Journal of Inter-American Studies, V* (January 1963), 83.

81. Quoted in Dana G. Munro, *The United States and the Caribbean Republics, 1921–1933* (Princeton: Princeton University Press, 1974), pp. 314–315.

82. Quoted in Louis A. Pérez, Jr., *Cuba and the United States* (Athens: University of Georgia Press, 1990), p. 142.

83. Quoted in Thomas F. O'Brien, *The Revolutionary Mission* (New York: Cambridge University Press, 1996), p. 228.

84. Quoted in Luis E. Aguilar, *Cuba 1933* (New York: Norton, 1974), p. 167.

85. Sumner Welles quoted in Irwin F. Gellman, *Secret Affairs* (Baltimore: Johns Hopkins University Press, 1995), p. 80.

86. Quoted in Louis A. Pérez, Jr., *Cuba Under the Platt Amendment, 1902–1934* (Pittsburgh: University of Pittsburgh Press, 1986), pp. 323–324.

87. Quoted in Aguilar, *Cuba 1933*, pp. 228–229.

88. Arturo Morales Carrión, *Puerto Rico* (New York: W. W. Norton, 1983), p. 206.

89. Quoted in Raymond Carr, *Puerto Rico* (New York: Vintage, 1984), p. 54.

90. Ernest Gruening quoted in Robert David Johnson, "Anti-Imperialism and the Good Neighbour Policy," *Journal of Latin American Studies, XXIX* (February 1997), 109.

91. Quoted in Carr, *Puerto Rico*, p. 61.

92. Quoted in Helen Delpar, *The Enormous Vogue of Things Mexican* (Tuscaloosa: University of Alabama Press, 1992), p. 5.

93. John A. Britton, *Revolution and Ideology* (Lexington: University Press of Kentucky, 1995), p. 52.

94. Linda B. Hall, *Oil, Banks, and Politics* (Austin: University of Texas Press, 1995), p. 179.

95. Delbert Haff quoted in Michael L. Krenn, *U.S. Policy Toward Economic Nationalism in Latin America, 1917–1929* (Wilmington, Del.: Scholarly Resources, 1990), p. 62.

96. Verna Carlton Millan quoted in Britton, *Revolution*, p. 130.

97. Quoted in W. Dirk Raat, *Mexico and the United States* (Athens: University of Georgia Press, 1996), p. 145.

98. Quoted in Stephen R. Niblo, *War, Diplomacy, and Development* (Wilmington, Del.: Scholarly Resources, 1995), p. 45.

99. Quoted in Pike, *FDR's Good Neighbor*, p. 192.

100. David A. Haglund, *Latin America and the Transformation of U.S. Strategic Thought, 1936–1940* (Albuquerque: University of New Mexico Press, 1984), p. 154.

101. David Sheinin, "Pan Americanism," in Bruce W. Jentleson and Thomas G. Paterson, eds., *Encyclopedia of U.S. Foreign Relations* (New York: Oxford University Press, 1997), III, 356.

102. Quoted in J. Lloyd Mecham, *A Survey of United States–Latin American Relations* (Boston: Houghton Mifflin, 1965), p. 100.

103. Quoted in Samuel Guy Inman, *Inter-American Conferences* (Washington, D.C.: University Press, 1965), p. 117.

104. Quoted in Richard V. Salisbury, *Anti-Imperialism and International Competition in Central America, 1920–1929* (Wilmington, Del.: Scholarly Resources, 1989), p. 121.

105. Quoted in Bryce Wood, *The Making of the Good Neighbor Policy* (New York: Columbia University Press, 1961), p. 119.

106. Cordell Hull, *Memoirs* (New York: Macmillan, 1948; 2 vols.), I, 602.

107. Quoted in Holger H. Herwig, *Politics of Frustration* (Boston: Little, Brown, 1976), p. 187.

108. Quoted in Jordan A. Schwarz, *Liberal* (New York: Free Press, 1987), p. 123.

109. Quoted in John Major, *Prize Possession* (New York: Cambridge University Press, 1993), p. 295.

110. Peter H. Smith, *Talons of the Eagle* (New York: Oxford University Press, 1996), p. 85.

Survival and Spheres: The Allies and the Second World War, 1939–1945

Church Service on the* Prince of Wales. *On August 10, 1941, President Franklin D. Roosevelt and Prime Minister Winston S. Churchill, with their staffs, attended a stirring service aboard the British warship during the Atlantic Charter Conference. (Franklin D. Roosevelt Library)*

DIPLOMATIC CROSSROAD

The Atlantic Charter Conference, 1941

In the longest walk he had attempted since contracting polio twenty years earlier, President Franklin D. Roosevelt slowly limped the entire length of the battleship H.M.S. *Prince of Wales* to take his place of honor on the quarterdeck. More than 1,500 men, including British prime minister Winston S. Churchill, stood at rigid attention as the president took his tortured steps. "He was determined to walk along that deck even if it killed him," observed a Britisher.[1] Roosevelt finally reached his seat near the bow, side by side with Churchill. British and American chiefs of staff stood behind them, near impressive ranks of sailors and marines. Roosevelt and Churchill were attending church services in the quiet waters of Placentia Bay near the harbor of Argentia, Newfoundland, on August 10, 1941.

The Sunday services aboard the *Prince of Wales* marked the "keynote" of the four-day summit meeting between the two leaders (August 9–13, 1941), some four months before Pearl Harbor catapulted the United States into World War II as a formal belligerent.[2] The text of the sermon, from Joshua 1:1–9, seemed directed at the president: "As I was with Moses, so I will be with thee: I will not fail thee, nor forsake thee." And suggesting the need for the U.S. to aid in the war against Hitler was the hortatory hymn, "Onward Christian Soldiers," with its call for volunteers "marching as to war." For Roosevelt, who had already supplied destroyers, Lend-Lease, and other aid short of war, the moment evoked a rush of emotion. "If nothing else had happened," he later told his son, "that would have cemented us. 'Onward Christian Soldiers.' We *are,* and we *will,* go on, with God's help."[3] Churchill found symbolic unity that morning—"the Union Jack and the Stars and Stripes draped side by side on the pulpit; . . . the highest naval, military, and air officers of Britain and the United States grouped together behind the President and me; the close-packed ranks of British and American sailors, completely intermingled . . . and joining fervently in the prayers and hymns familiar to both."[4] Nobody aboard the *Prince of Wales* could know, of course, that Japanese bombs would destroy the majestic battleship off the coast of Malaya on December 10, 1941.

The four-day meeting in Placentia Bay was the first of many conferences between Roosevelt and Churchill during World War II; altogether, the two leaders would spend some 120 days in each other's company. Notwithstanding the fears that the meeting might spark a clash of "prima donnas," the personalities blended well.[5] Churchill's willingness to pay deference to a man he regarded "almost with religious awe" and his own pride in being half-American (his mother) made him an ardent advocate of Anglo-American solidarity.[6] Roosevelt, although he sometimes saw the prime minister as the last of the Victorians, reciprocated Churchill's friendship. Under their leadership the two countries became "mixed up together . . . for mutual and general advantage" to a degree unmatched in modern times.[7] Indeed, the cultural "invasion" of the British Isles over the next four years by nearly 3 million rowdy, "jitterbugging and gum-chewing" American military personnel accelerated a trend that "began during the Jazz Age" and "continued on via the gyrations of Elvis Presley" to the present day.[8] "Trust me to the bitter end," FDR told his British partner in early 1942.[9]

Aside from the personal equation and cultural symbolism, Argentia produced few decisive results. The British asked for men, ships, planes, and tanks. Churchill urged that the American navy extend its convoying of British vessels farther into the German submarine-infested North Atlantic. The British military chiefs, remembering the frightful casualties of World War I, argued that bombing, blockades, and propaganda might so weaken the Germans that they would surrender without a full-scale invasion. The Americans favored a more direct strategy, insisting on large ground armies. Army chief of staff General George C. Marshall declared that a U.S. military buildup had to take priority over British requests for weapons and equipment; "the hungry table," as Churchill described the demands on U.S. defense production, simply did not have enough for all who wanted to eat.[10] In the one tangible military commitment at Argentia, FDR promised to order his navy to convoy British merchant ships as far as Iceland, but he delayed any public declaration until September, when a German submarine fired torpedoes at the U.S. destroyer *Greer* near Iceland. Neglecting to mention that the *Greer* had shadowed the U-boat for three hours prior to the attack, Roosevelt announced over worldwide radio on September 11 that henceforth American naval vessels would shoot at German submarines. Undeclared naval action (or "war in masquerade") was as far as Roosevelt would go in the months before Pearl Harbor.[11]

At Argentia, discussions about Japan exposed British and American differences. Foreign Office diplomats argued that Japan, which had recently occupied the southern half of French Indochina, should receive an explicit U.S. warning against further encroachments, and that the United States should commit itself to war if the Japanese attacked British or Dutch territory in Southeast Asia. U.S. officials avoided any definite commitment. Roosevelt did promise a "mighty swat" at Japan. But when the president returned to Washington, Secretary of State Cordell Hull watered down the proposed statement. Instead of announcing that continued Japanese aggression would cause the United States to take measures that "might result in war," the actual postconference warning to the Japanese ambassador merely read that Washington would take steps necessary "toward insuring the safety and security of the United States."[12] Roosevelt preferred to delay a confrontation in the Pacific until he strengthened his army and navy and cultivated a more favorable public opinion. He also intended to beat Hitler first.

The most famous product of the summit came in the eight-point statement of war aims—the Atlantic Charter. Reminiscent of Woodrow Wilson's Fourteen Points, the Atlantic Charter reaffirmed the principles of collective security, national self-determination, freedom of the seas, and liberal trading practices (see Chapter 3). The signatories also disclaimed any territorial aggrandizement and pledged economic collaboration leading to "social security." Behind the vision of a postwar world, however, lay Anglo-American differences. The Americans, particularly Under Secretary of State Sumner Welles, pressed for a statement explicitly endorsing freer trade. The British wanted to protect their discriminatory system of imperial preferences. The compromise called for "access, on equal terms, to the trade and to the raw materials of the world," leaving the British an escape clause that promised

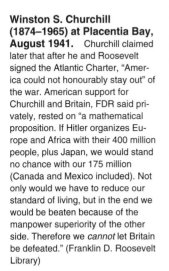

Winston S. Churchill (1874–1965) at Placentia Bay, August 1941. Churchill claimed later that after he and Roosevelt signed the Atlantic Charter, "America could not honourably stay out" of the war. American support for Churchill and Britain, FDR said privately, rested on "a mathematical proposition. If Hitler organizes Europe and Africa with their 400 million people, plus Japan, we would stand no chance with our 175 million (Canada and Mexico included). Not only would we have to reduce our standard of living, but in the end we would be beaten because of the manpower superiority of the other side. Therefore we *cannot* let Britain be defeated." (Franklin D. Roosevelt Library)

"due respect for their existing obligations." When he read this vague language later, Hull felt "keenly disappointed."[13] Churchill failed to gain Roosevelt's backing for a new League of Nations. Roosevelt would endorse only "the establishment of a wider and permanent system of general security."[14] As "both realist and idealist, both fixer and preacher, both a prince and a soldier," the president wanted to be as cautious as he was eloquent about postwar goals.[15]

The Atlantic Charter became a propaganda tool for the war against the Axis. Within months Voice of America radio broadcasts hailed the charter's call to "fight on all the world's battlefields for these essential liberties: liberty of expression, of religion, and the right to live protected from need and from fear."[16] In September 1941, at an Inter-Allied meeting in London, representatives of the nations battling Hitler formally adhered to the "common principles" set forth in the Atlantic Charter.[17] The Soviet Union gave qualified approval. Twenty-six nations, on January 1, 1942, signed the Declaration of the United Nations, which pledged cooperation in achieving the aims of the Atlantic Charter. Churchill and Roosevelt, however, provided no procedures for enforcement or implementation. Indeed, the prime minister insisted that the charter applied only to "nations of Europe now under the Nazi yoke," not to "the regions and peoples which owe allegiance to the British Crown."[18] Roosevelt came to view the principles as a "beautiful idea" rather than as set rules.[19] However much the president believed in the Argentia ideals, he seemed willing to postpone their application or compromise them to accommodate pressing military and diplomatic priorities. "I dream dreams but am, at the same time, an intensely practical person," he once said.[20]

By meeting secretly with Churchill on board a British battleship, Roosevelt demonstrated America's commitment to the defense of Britain by all means short of war. Whatever his hopes that the theatrics of Argentia would galvanize American opinion for a firmer policy, Roosevelt maintained a "policy of influence without belligerence," as one historian has put it.[21] Not "a single American officer has shown the slightest keenness to be in the war on our side," one British participant noted.[22] Yet the Atlantic Charter, the Churchill-Roosevelt friendship, the Anglo-American strategic conversations, even the divergent views on international organization and postwar economic policy—all struck chords that would echo through the next four years of war. That the Soviet Union, which Germany had invaded some six weeks earlier, had no representatives at Argentia did not mean that the conferees did not discuss Soviet cooperation against the Axis. Presidential aide Harry Hopkins had visited Moscow two weeks before the Argentia conference, and his assurances that the USSR would withstand the Nazi onslaught buoyed the two leaders. In a joint communication to Stalin from Argentia, Churchill and Roosevelt hailed "the splendid defense that you are making against the Nazi attack" and promised the "very maximum" of supplies.[23] This Anglo-American commitment to the Soviet Union against Hitler also carried large implications for the future.

Juggling Between War and Peace, 1939–1941

The conversations at Placentia Bay exemplified Roosevelt's distinctly personal approach to diplomacy during World War II. A deft juggler who "could keep all his balls in the air without losing his own," as Vice President Henry Wallace quipped, FDR delighted in face-to-face confrontations, always confident in his ability to charm foreign leaders.[24] It mattered little to Roosevelt that Secretary Hull learned of the conference when he read about it in the newspapers. The president did not mind that his military and naval advisers often had short notice to prepare for meetings. Roosevelt kept close aides such as Harry Hopkins and Sumner Welles nearby and watched the spotlight focus on himself. If not the evil Machiavelli of the isolationists' fantasy, the president, with his formidable style and strong personality, could be unsettling. British foreign secretary Anthony Eden once compared Roosevelt to "a conjurer, skillfully juggling with balls of dynamite, whose nature he failed to understand."[25]

The juggling act had begun two years earlier, when Germany started World War II by attacking Poland. FDR had avowed on September 3, 1939, just two days after the German invasion, that "this nation will remain a neutral nation." Still, "I cannot ask that every American remain neutral in thought as well."[26] Thus, in words pointedly different from Wilson's in 1914, did Roosevelt project the next twenty-six months of U.S. policy toward the war in Europe. Roosevelt proceeded from neutrality to nonbelligerency to undeclared war in the Atlantic and finally, after Pearl Harbor, to full-scale war against the Axis powers. Hoping to avoid war while at the same time giving as much aid as possible to Hitler's opponents, the

Makers of American Foreign Relations, 1939–1945

Presidents	Secretaries of State
Franklin D. Roosevelt, 1933–1945	Cordell Hull, 1933–1944
	Edward R. Stettinius, Jr., 1944–1945
Harry S. Truman, 1945–1953	James F. Byrnes, 1945–1947

president did not always speak candidly to the public about the possible and ultimate contradiction between these two goals.

On September 21, 1939, Roosevelt asked Congress to repeal the arms embargo
in the Neutrality Act as the best way to keep the United States out of the war. He
stressed this deceptive argument, knowing that the real purpose of repeal was to
permit England and France, with their superior sea power, to purchase arms and
munitions on a cash-and-carry basis. He persuaded William Allen White, the Republican sage from Emporia, Kansas, to form a Non-Partisan Committee for Peace
Through Revision of the Neutrality Act. Although isolationists such as Republican
senator Charles Tobey of New Hampshire opposed "our changing the rules after
the war has broken out," the president's tactics worked.[27] By a vote of 63 to 30 in
the Senate and 243 to 181 in the House, the revised Neutrality Act became law on
November 4, thus permitting Britain and France to buy arms on a cash-and-carry
arrangement.

The Pan American Conference at Panama City (September 23–October 3,
1939) also signaled the pro-Allied emphasis of U.S. policy. The conferees proclaimed neutrality, established a committee for economic coordination, and created
a neutral zone 300 miles wide along the entire coast of the Western Hemisphere
(except Canada), in which belligerent naval operations were prohibited. Roosevelt
had told his cabinet in April 1939 that the Atlantic fleet would patrol such areas and
"if we fire and sink an Italian or German [submarine] . . . we will say it the way
the Japs do, 'so sorry.' 'Never happen again.' Tomorrow we sink two."[28] These
"neutrality patrols" actually became the first step toward Anglo-American naval cooperation. By late summer 1940, conversations between staff officers began in London, soon followed by exchanges of personnel and cryptographic intelligence,
actual coordination against German naval operations (such as the sighting and sinking of the battleship *Bismarck* in May 1941), and, in autumn 1941, the convoying
of merchant ships across the Atlantic. Justified in terms of contingency planning and
aid short of war, such naval measures nonetheless led the chief of naval operations,
Admiral Harold R. Stark, to conclude in early 1941: "We cannot avoid having it
[war] thrust upon us or our deliberately going in. . . . It may be a matter of weeks
or days."[29]

Germany's *blitzkrieg* humbled Poland in two weeks, and then in winter
1939–1940 came a "phony war," or *sitzkrieg*. Most battle news from November to
March flowed from northern Europe, where the Soviet Union defeated Finland in

the "Winter War." Roosevelt sent his sympathies but little else to Finland. The fall of France in June 1940 stung FDR into bold measures. In a speech on June 10, Roosevelt condemned Italy for holding the dagger that "struck . . . the back of its neighbor," and he pledged to England "the material resources of this nation."[30] A week later he named the prominent Republicans Henry L. Stimson and Frank Knox, both vocal advocates of aid to Britain, as secretary of war and secretary of the navy, respectively. Then, after careful preparations and intricate negotiations, the president announced on September 3, 1940, that he was transferring to England some fifty old destroyers in exchange for leases to eight British bases stretching from Newfoundland to British Guiana. Two weeks later, he signed into law the Selective Service Act of 1940, the first peacetime military draft in American history.

That Roosevelt could accomplish so much at a time when isolationist sentiment still prevailed and he was seeking a controversial third presidential term testifies to his political astuteness. As for both selective service and the destroyers-for-bases agreement, FDR learned that his Republican presidential opponent, Wendell L. Willkie, would not make them campaign issues. In both cases Roosevelt also encouraged influential private citizens (the Century Group for the destroyers deal and the Military Training Camps Association for selective service) to lobby for his objectives. The larger Committee to Defend America by Aiding the Allies, headed by William Allen White, soon rallied behind the president to counter the isolationist America First Committee set up in September 1940. FDR avoided congressional scrutiny of the destroyers deal by presenting it as an executive agreement rather than as a treaty, and he deflected political opposition to conscription by having men of integrity, such as Secretary Stimson and General Marshall, attest to the military's need for a draft. Furthermore, Roosevelt continued to promise that his policies would keep America out of war. Although Germany could regard the destroyers deal as an act of war, FDR called it instead "the most important action in the reinforcement of our national defense . . . since the Louisiana Purchase."[31] When Willkie made last-minute charges during the fall campaign that Roosevelt secretly sought war, the White House struck back: "Your boys are not going to be sent into any foreign wars." Willkie exploded: "That hypocritical son of a bitch! This is going to beat me!"[32] It did.

As Roosevelt took a postelection cruise in the Caribbean, Churchill cabled: "The moment approaches when we shall no longer be able to pay cash for shipping and other supplies."[33] Roosevelt soon held one of his breezy, jaunty press conferences, saying that he favored lending or leasing supplies to Britain. He likened it to lending a garden hose to a neighbor whose house was burning. Once the fire is out, "he gives it back to me and thanks me very much for the use of it."[34] In a fireside chat on December 29, FDR admitted that sending armaments to Britain risked war, but the "sole purpose is to keep war away from our country and our people." Then, in a ringing phrase, Roosevelt called on the United States to "become the great arsenal of democracy."[35]

Over the next two months, Americans debated the Lend-Lease bill "in every newspaper, on every wave length—over every cracker barrel in all the land."[36] Although the vote of 60 to 31 in the Senate and 317 to 71 in the House seemed substantial, the White House did not win without a struggle. Senator Burton K.

The German Onslaught 1939–1942

Wheeler, an isolationist Democrat from Montana, warned that aid short of war was a dangerous delusion—"You can't put your shirt tail into a clothes wringer and pull it out suddenly when the wringer keeps turning."[37] Right-wing mothers' groups picketed the White House for "scheming to embroil . . . their sons" in a "Jewish" war.[38] A bit of benevolent deception occurred in the numbering of the bill in the House. The administration's floor manager, Representative John W. McCormack, worried because his Irish constituents in South Boston would surely protest any "McCormack Bill" designed to aid the British Empire, induced the House parliamentarian to tag the Lend-Lease bill H.R. 1776. When one irate constituent still berated him, the future Speaker of the House thought quickly: "Madam, do you

Lend-Lease to the USSR. A U.S. Lend-Lease official checks American food destined for the Soviet Union's hard-pressed people. The Soviets eventually lost nearly 27 million people in the war. (U.S. Information Agency, National Archives)

realize that the Vatican is surrounded on all sides by totalitarianism? Madam, this is not a bill to save the English, this is a bill to save Catholicism."[39]

The Lend-Lease Act became law on March 11, 1941. Under its terms the president could "sell, transfer title to, exchange, lease, lend, or otherwise dispose of" defense articles to "any country whose defense the President deems vital to the defense of the United States."[40] Although the initial appropriation totaled $7 billion, by war's end the United States had expended more than $50 billion on Lend-Lease. England eventually received $31.6 billion in Lend-Lease assistance during the war.

With German U-boats sinking more than 500,000 tons of shipping a month, it seemed logical that the United States would use its navy to ensure that Lend-Lease supplies reached England safely. But FDR hesitated, partly because of public opinion, but also because the Atlantic fleet lacked operational readiness. Instead, he extended naval "patrols" halfway across the Atlantic, announcing in April that American vessels would monitor German warships. "We have got a tadpole that someday may be a frog," Secretary Hull told an aide.[41] U.S. troops also occupied Greenland the same month. Although interventionists urged U.S. Navy convoys for British ships, FDR declared a national emergency in late May but took no new action. He told the cabinet that "he expected a clash sooner or later but said the Germans would have to fire the first shots."[42]

When Hitler occupied the Balkans and invaded the Soviet Union in June 1941, the president announced the next month that 4,000 American marines would occupy Iceland for hemispheric defense. Roosevelt also began military Lend-Lease aid to the USSR in November, notwithstanding opinions from State Department and military advisers that the Soviet Union would quickly fall. (By the end of the war the USSR had received $11 billion in Lend-Lease.) "Now comes this Russian diversion," FDR wrote four days after the German assault. "If it is more than just that it will mean the liberation of Europe from Nazi domination."[43] When bureaucratic tangles inhibited the flow of goods to the USSR, Roosevelt snapped that "the only answer I want to hear is that it is under way."[44] Then the president held his dramatic meeting with Churchill at Placentia Bay, and in early September, after German torpedoes just missed the *Greer,* he publicly ordered naval convoys as far as Iceland and issued a "shoot-on-sight" command to the navy.

By autumn 1941, Roosevelt probably anticipated an "incident" to induce U.S. entry into the war against Hitler. After the Placentia Bay conference, the president told Churchill that "he would wage war, but not declare it, and that he would become more and more provocative. If the Germans did not like it, they could attack American forces."[45] When a U-boat torpedoed the destroyer *Kearny* off Iceland on October 17, killing eleven men, the president seized the moment: "The shooting has started. And history has recorded who fired the first shot."[46] Roosevelt then flourished a map that purportedly showed Nazis plans to reorganize Central and South America as vassal states. Through these histrionics the president hoped to persuade Congress to repeal the sections of the 1939 Neutrality Act that prohibited the arming of merchant ships and banned such vessels from war zones. After a U-boat sank the destroyer *Reuben James* on October 31, killing more than one hundred men, the isolationist America First Committee charged that the White House was "asking Congress to issue an engraved drowning license to American seamen."[47] Following bitter debate, repeal passed in November by narrow margins, 50 to 37 in the Senate and 212 to 194 in the House. For the first time since the outbreak of war in 1939, U.S. merchant vessels could carry munitions to England.

Roosevelt charted an oblique course toward war because he believed he had no other choice. "Haranguing the country doesn't help," he said. "It will take a 'shock' like 1932" to change isolationist attitudes.[48] In October 1941 he bluntly told the British ambassador that "if he asked for a declaration of war, he wouldn't get it, and opinion would swing against him."[49] FDR thus chose indirection over candor and relied on events and his own manipulative ability to inch ahead. Without decisive presidential leadership, the internationalist-isolationist debate thus hardened into stalemate by autumn 1941. Some 80 percent of the American people still opposed entering the war, while a higher percentage wanted an Axis defeat. In the Chicago area, for example, "at no time did more than a minority of the proponents of aid view the policy as a springboard to full U.S. entry into the war. Until Pearl Harbor, most Americans desired peace. But they wanted even more to see Hitler beaten."[50] So long as FDR touted aid to the Allies as the best way to avoid war, Americans could apparently fulfill both goals. The narrow vote over repeal of the Neutrality Act in November reinforced the president's reluctance to ask for outright intervention. "The day of the white rabbits has passed," Senator Josiah Bailey of North Carolina wrote, "and the great magician who could pull them out of any silk hat . . . cannot find the rabbit."[51]

Asian Collision Course: Japanese-American Relations, 1939–1941

Events in Asia, not Europe, plunged the United States into World War II. Ambassador Joseph C. Grew expressed surprise at increased anti-Japanese sentiment during a trip home in the summer of 1939, as his old Groton and Harvard friend Franklin Roosevelt talked truculently of intercepting the Japanese fleet if it moved against the Dutch East Indies. With the announcement in July that the 1911 commercial treaty with Japan would terminate in six months, Grew feared that economic sanctions and war might follow. "[It] is going to be up to me," he noted, "to let this American temper discreetly penetrate into Japanese consciousness. Sparks will fly before long."[52]

Grew had failed to grasp the Europe-first emphasis of Roosevelt's foreign policy. After 1937, when Japan marched deeper into China, Washington angrily reacted with protests but lacked the power to challenge Japanese predominance in East Asia. Even Roosevelt's much-heralded refusal to apply the Neutrality Act to the "incident" in China, thus making it legal to sell arms to Jiang Jieshi's government, could not obscure the preponderance of U.S. trade with Japan. As late as 1940, $78 million in American exports went to China, whereas $227 million were shipped to Japan. Abrogation of the 1911 commercial treaty permitted economic sanctions against Japan, but oil, the most vital ingredient in Japan's war machine, flowed until July 1941. In keeping with Roosevelt's policy of all-out aid to England short of war, the navy revised its strategic thinking in November 1940. "Plan Dog" called for a defensive posture in the Pacific, depicted Germany as the country's number one enemy, and made preservation of England its principal goal. Roosevelt still hoped to avoid a confrontation, because "I simply have not got enough Navy to go around—and every little episode in the Pacific means fewer ships in the Atlantic."[53]

Japanese movement into Southeast Asia placed Washington and Tokyo on a collision course. With the Asian colonies of France and the Netherlands lying unprotected, Japanese expansionists demanded a thrust southward, thus completing the strangulation of China and transforming the whole region into the Greater East Asia Co-Prosperity Sphere. Japan pressed England and France to close down supply routes to the Guomindang through Burma and Indochina. Tokyo also demanded economic concessions from the petroleum-rich Dutch East Indies. Then, only four days after Vichy French representatives allowed Japanese troops to occupy northern Indochina, Japan signed the Tripartite Pact with Germany and Italy on September 27. The signatories pledged to aid one another if attacked by a nation not currently involved in the war. Because the pact explicitly exempted the Soviet Union, Washington had no doubt about being its target.

A new, more militant Japanese government, with Prince Fumimaro Konoe as prime minister and General Hideki Tojo as war minister, took the fateful steps. Foreign Minister Yosuke Matsuoka, who had lived in America and thought he understood Americans, articulated the advantages of boldness—"one cannot obtain a tiger's cub unless he braves the tiger's den."[54] Matsuoka intended the Tripartite Pact to deter the United States from intervening in the Atlantic or the Pacific, and to facilitate a rapprochement between Japan and the Soviet Union, which remained aligned with Germany in the Nazi-Soviet Pact. Tokyo might then induce Jiang Jieshi to join the Co-Prosperity Sphere, after which Japanese troops would gradually withdraw from China and civilian authorities could reassert control over the army.

Washington flashed warning signals. In July 1940, Roosevelt withheld aviation fuel and top-grade scrap iron sought by Japan. In September, at the time of the Tripartite Pact, he extended the embargo to all scrap metals. Even Grew urged firmness, labeling Japan "one of the predatory powers," lacking "all moral and ethical sense."[55] Administration "hawks" pressed the president to shut off oil exports as well. Backed by Hull and the Joint Chiefs, however, Roosevelt kept the oil flowing to Japan. Recognizing the interconnectness of Asian and European events, FDR expedited aid to China to keep Japan's army "busy and more or less tied up" so it could not "move southward in full force."[56] The president hoped to aid England while avoiding a showdown in the Pacific, which an oil embargo would likely precipitate.

In February 1941, Admiral Kichisaburo Nomura became ambassador to Washington. A personal friend of President Roosevelt, Nomura accepted the appointment only when assured by Konoe and Matsuoka that peace with the United States took precedence over Japan's commitment to the Axis. A group of private citizens known as the "John Doe Associates" and led by two Catholic missionaries, Father James M. Drought and Bishop James E. Walsh, also tried to effect conciliation. They held interviews with Prince Konoe, Hull, and Roosevelt. Drought enthusiastically forwarded his own "Draft Understanding" to Hull in early April. It called for a Konoe-Roosevelt meeting and U.S. pressure on China to recognize Japanese domination of Manchuria in exchange for Japanese disavowal of the Tripartite Pact. Hull thought the "Understanding" a Japanese proposal and accepted it as a basis of discussion, noting, however, that any agreement had to satisfy four basic principles: respect for the territorial integrity and sovereignty of all nations; noninterference in the internal affairs of other nations; respect for the equality of commercial opportunity, or the Open Door; and support for peaceful change in the Pacific. Nomura failed to attach appropriate importance to Hull's four points when he reported to Tokyo. Not until September did Tokyo learn that Hull's four principles could block any settlement of the China war. The John Doe efforts also muddled a possible Roosevelt-Konoe summit, as Tokyo asked in August for a meeting they thought the Americans had proposed in April, but Washington then rejected any high-level meeting without assurances on outstanding problems. Both sides suspected the other of retreating from earlier positions.

Japan's determination to hold China and to expand farther doomed these diplomatic efforts. "The Japs are having a real drag-down," Roosevelt observed in early July 1941, "trying to decide which way they are going to jump—attack Russia, attack the South Seas . . . or whether they will sit on the fence and be more friendly with us."[57] When word reached Washington on July 24 that Japanese troop transports were steaming toward southern Indochina, FDR signed an executive order freezing all Japanese funds in the United States. Hard-line bureaucrats interpreted the order to mean stopping all trade with Japan—including oil. Thereafter, Washington and Tokyo steered "a collision course that even statesmen of great flexibility would find it difficult to avoid."[58]

Unless the sale of American oil resumed, Japan determined to seize Dutch and British petroleum fields. But the United States would not turn on the oil spigot un-

The PURPLE Machine. In September 1940, U.S. cryptanalysts of the Signal Intelligence Service cracked Japan's most secret diplomatic code. The American code-breakers, under Operation MAGIC, not only deciphered thousands of intercepted messages sent by Japanese officials around the world, but also duplicated the machine, called PURPLE, that generated the codes. Important intercepts went to a select group of U.S. officials, including the president. Although these dispatches revealed through 1941 that Japan expected all-out war with the United States, they did not reveal military plans or the planned attack on Pearl Harbor. (National Archives)

til Tokyo agreed to Hull's four principles, especially the pledge to respect China's sovereignty and territorial integrity. Key American officials also knew from cracking the Japanese diplomatic code (Operation MAGIC) that Japan's forces were massing to strike southward after mid-November, although most officials did not think Japan would attack the United States. Hard-liners such as Henry L. Stimson viewed the Japanese as "notorious bluffers" who backed down when confronted firmly.[59] As late as November 27, when MAGIC intercepts revealed the imminence of a Japanese strike somewhere, State Department Asian expert Stanley K. Hornbeck challenged his colleagues: "Tell me of one case in history when a nation went to war out of desperation."[60] Amid this atmosphere, the urging of army and navy leaders to string out negotiations until the Philippines could be reinforced went unheeded. An eleventh-hour modus vivendi envisioned a trickle of oil to Japan and negotiations between Chongqing and Tokyo, while maintaining American aid to China; Japan would have to abrogate the Tripartite Pact and accept basic principles of international conduct. Exhausted from months of negotiations, Hull advised Roosevelt to shelve the proposal. The secretary of state told Stimson: "It is now in the hands of . . . the Army and Navy."[61]

After months of discussion among civilian and military leaders, the Japanese Imperial Conference of September decided to fight the United States if Washington did not lift the embargo on strategic materials by October 15—a date later extended to November 25 and then to November 29. Tokyo's final decision to attack the United States did not stem from irrationality or suicidal tendencies. Japan required 12,000 tons of oil each day, and desperate moderates and militants alike read U.S. pressure as provocative and life-strangling. In a choice between fighting the United States or pulling out of China, no Japanese leader recommended the latter. They knew America's power and industrial potential well enough, but, as Tojo (who replaced Konoe as prime minister) put it: "You have to plunge into war if there is some chance, however slight, of winning victory."[62] The Japanese did not expect America to surrender (an invasion of the United States was out of the question), but they hoped that a stalemated war of endurance might persuade tired Americans to negotiate a compromise peace. In any case, Japan refused to give up its empire, to "lie prostrate at the feet of the United States."[63]

On November 25, 1941, a huge task force that included six carriers bearing some 350 airplanes headed across 3,000 miles of the Pacific Ocean. The target: Pearl Harbor, Hawai'i. After receiving the message "Climb Mt. Niitake" on December 2, every ship maintained radio silence to avoid detection and ensure complete surprise.[64] In the early morning of Sunday, December 7, the carriers launched their planes. After a flight of 220 miles, the aircraft swept down on the unsuspecting American naval base, dropping torpedoes and bombs, strafing buildings. Within a few hours eight U.S. battleships had been sunk or damaged and 2,403 Americans had died. The stunning news shot around the world. In London, Winston Churchill thought: "So we had won after all!" Indeed, "greater good fortune has rarely happened to the British Empire."[65] In Chongqing, Jiang Jieshi "sang an old opera air, and played the Ave Maria all that day," also rejoicing in his new ally.[66]

Critics have charged that Roosevelt and his top advisers deliberately sacrificed the Pacific fleet to get into the war with Hitler via the "back door."[67] Most scholars reject the conspiracy theory and explain Pearl Harbor as the consequence of mistakes, missed clues, overconfidence, and plain bad luck. Better intelligence in Washington might have alerted Hawai'i, but American errors weighed less than the enormous care and skill with which the Japanese planned the attack. MAGIC intercepts on November 30, for example, read "that there is extreme danger that war may suddenly break out between the Anglo-Saxon nations and Japan . . . ; this war may come quicker than anyone dreams."[68] Yet the intercepts never revealed military plans, and Washington thought Japan would strike Southeast Asia, where troop ships were spotted heading for Malaya; no one thought Tokyo could undertake two major operations at once. As to hints of major Japanese interest in Pearl Harbor, including Grew's warning in February 1941 of a possible sudden attack, one scholar has written: "After the event a signal is always crystal clear. . . . But before the event it is obscure and pregnant with conflicting meanings. . . . In short, we failed to anticipate Pearl Harbor not for want of the relevant materials, but because of a plethora of irrelevant ones."[69] Many "ifs" cloud the question. If the radar operator had been able to convince his superiors on Oahu that the blips really were planes, if General Marshall had sent his last-minute warning by navy cable instead of Western Union telegraph, if MAGIC could have read Japan's naval communications as well as its diplomatic cables, if . . .

For Japan, Pearl Harbor proved a tactical victory but a strategic disaster. When President Roosevelt, referring to the "date which will live in infamy," asked for a declaration of war, Congress responded on December 8 with a unanimous vote in the Senate and only one dissent in the House—that of Jeannette Rankin, who had also voted "no" in 1917.[70] For Senator Vandenberg, the Japanese attack on Hawai'i "ended isolationism for any realist."[71] The deadly event acted "like a reverse earthquake, that in one terrible jerk shook everything disjointed, distorted, askew back into place. Japanese bombs had finally brought national unity to the U.S."[72]

Pearl Harbor. A Japanese pilot's perspective on Ford Island, Pearl Harbor, Hawai'i. The three Pacific U.S. aircraft carriers were not in port and escaped the attack. Of the eight battleships hit at Pearl Harbor, six were repaired and eventually participated in the war. By coincidence, the eighteenth issue of *National Comics,* featureing the super-hero Captain America, appeared on newsstands in early November 1941, depicting a Japanese attack on Pearl Harbor a month before one actually happened. (Navy Department, National Archives)

Hitler's declaration of war against the United States on December 11, and Congress's immediate answer in a resolution affirming a state of war with Germany, confronted Americans with a daunting two-theater war.

The Big Three: Strategies and Fissures, 1941–1943

The Atlantic Charter Conference and the events of 1939–1941 foreshadowed well the themes of wartime diplomacy. Giving material aid to Hitler's opponents through the "arsenal of democracy" became the main U.S. contribution to victory in Europe. Washington's commitment to a "Europe First" strategy derived from Anglo-American staff discussions prior to Pearl Harbor, as did the different American and British conceptions of that strategy. Americans favored a "massive thrust at the enemy's heart," and the British preferred "successive stabs around the periphery . . . like jackals worrying a lion before springing at his throat."[73] During the war Americans also revived Wilsonianism but combined it with a pragmatic determination to avoid Wilson's mistakes. This time the United States would join an international organization to maintain peace, even if it meant adding blatant balance-of-power features to the institution under Roosevelt's concept of the "Four Policemen" (United States, USSR, Britain, and China), each of which would maintain peace in a sphere of influence. This time there would be no debts-reparations tangle because Lend-Lease would eliminate the dollar sign. This time the enemy must surrender unconditionally. This time tariff walls must fall and trade doors must open. This time there would be postwar cooperation with the Soviets. With

"Jap . . . You're Next!"
James Montgomery Flagg, already famous for his "I Want You" poster of World War I, offered this version of Uncle Sam in 1942. After Pearl Harbor, posters such as Flagg's helped focus public resentment on Japan, rather than on Hitler. "I can see why we are fighting the Japanese," observed one Gallup Poll respondent, "but I can't see why we are fighting the Germans." Yet Roosevelt did not want to adopt a "Pacific First" strategy and kept his "Europe First" strategy alive by supporting British proposals to invade North Africa in November 1942. (National Archives)

FDR's encouragement, Hollywood turned out pro-Soviet films such as *The North Star* (1943) and *Mission to Moscow* (1943), and *Life* magazine described Russians as "one hell of a people" who "look like Americans, dress like Americans, and think like Americans."[74]

Global war brought new power and confidence to U.S. diplomacy. The Atlantic Charter reflected a commitment to shaping the postwar world in an American image. As Henry Luce's best-selling *American Century* phrased it in 1941, the United States must "exert upon the world the full impact of our influence, for such purposes as we see fit and by such means as we see fit."[75] By rearming, acquiring new bases, raising an army of more than 2 million, welding hemispheric unity, and revving up its industries, the United States built the sinews of global power even before Pearl Harbor. Churchill told Roosevelt in 1944: "You have the greatest navy in the world . . . the greatest air force . . . the greatest trade. You have all the gold." But Churchill hoped that the Americans "will not give themselves over to vainglorious ambitions, and that justice and fair-play will be the lights that guide them."[76] FDR's anticolonial ambitions, stirred by a wartime visit to the poverty-stricken British West African colony of Gambia ("the most horrible thing I have ever seen in my life"), often irritated his European allies, for the president said he intended to break up colonial empires after the war and set long-abused people free.[77] Churchill retorted: "I have not become the King's First Minister in order to preside over the liquidation of the British Empire."[78]

American-British-Soviet diplomacy in the "Grand Alliance" centered on two issues: boundaries in Eastern Europe and the timing of an Anglo-American "second front" in Western Europe. Shortly after Pearl Harbor, Premier Stalin said he had no objections to the Atlantic Charter, which he regarded as "algebra," but he preferred "practical arithmetic"—that is, an agreement guaranteeing Soviet boundaries with Eastern Europe as they stood prior to Hitler's attack in 1941.[79] The British seemed inclined to grant what Stalin wanted, but Roosevelt told the Soviet ambassador that "under no conditions would he subscribe to any secret treaty. Nor could he subscribe to any open public treaty with regard to definite frontiers until the war had been won."[80]

FDR viewed the second front with great urgency. The Soviets, fighting some 200 German divisions and dying by the hundreds of thousands, pleaded for a cross-channel attack as quickly as possible. Assuring V. M. Molotov in May 1942 that Roosevelt ardently supported a second front, Harry Hopkins urged the diplomat to paint a deliberately "gloomy picture of the Soviet position to make the American generals understand the gravity of the situation."[81] Although Molotov's visit generated a joint communiqué promising a second front in 1942, the Anglo-American invasion of France did not take place until June 6, 1944, and during the interim, as FDR acknowledged, "the Russian armies are killing more Axis personnel and destroying more Axis material than all other twenty-five United Nations put together."[82] The delay produced serious fissures in the Grand Alliance.

American military leaders urged a cross-channel attack by spring 1943 at the latest, but the British, with Roosevelt's reluctant compliance, decided otherwise. A new plan, Operation TORCH, called for the invasion of French North Africa in November 1942, a decision that led logically to operations against Sicily and Italy in the summer of 1943 and effectively postponed a cross-channel attack (later dubbed Operation OVERLORD) until 1944. When General Dwight D. Eisenhower learned that the second front had been postponed, he pronounced it the "blackest day in history" if the Soviet Union did not stay in the war.[83] At numerous military conferences in 1942–1943, the Americans always suspected that British fixation on the Mediterranean demonstrated a desire to shore up imperial lifelines and not, as the British claimed, a coherent strategy to bloody Germany on the periphery before launching a full-scale invasion of France. Churchill said he no longer needed to woo the United States; "now that she is in the harem, we talk to her quite differently."[84] British strategy predominated in the two years after Pearl Harbor because England had fully mobilized, whereas America had not, and any combined operation had to depend largely on British troops, shipping, and casualties. U.S. matériel and forces, moreover, were being diverted to the Pacific theater at the insistence of General Douglas MacArthur and Admiral Ernest King. Once American production and manpower began to predominate in 1943, combined strategy gradually shifted toward Operation OVERLORD. A symbolic clash between the two competing strategies occurred in early 1944. Churchill insisted on an invasion of Rhodes, off the Turkish coast. "No American soldier is going to die on that goddam beach," barked General Marshall.[85] None did.

Roosevelt and Churchill knew how intensely Stalin wanted a full-scale second front in France, not in North Africa or Italy. The Red Army had stopped the Germans short of Moscow in 1941, but in summer 1942 German *panzers* drove into the Caucasus oil fields and laid siege to Stalingrad (present-day Volgograd). Churchill told Stalin in August 1942 that a cross-channel attack was planned for spring 1943. Not until June 1943 did the Soviets learn officially that a cross-channel assault would not happen at all that year. "Need I speak of the dishearteningly negative expression that this fresh postponement of the second front . . . will produce in the Soviet Union?" Stalin wrote Roosevelt.[86]

Tensions increased that summer, when the Soviet Union broke off diplomatic relations with the Polish exile government in London after the Poles asked the International Red Cross to investigate charges that the Russians had murdered more than 10,000 Polish prisoners (many of them senior army officers) in the Katyn Forest in 1941. (Soviet archives opened after the Cold War revealed that Stalin had ordered the Polish executions.) The Soviets also protested when the Allies suspended convoys carrying vital Lend-Lease supplies to Murmansk because of shipping needs in the Mediterranean and Pacific. In August 1943, Stalin complained to Roosevelt about separate peace talks with Italy. (The Italians formally surrendered in early September, then declared war against Germany, only to have German forces occupy most of the peninsula before Anglo-American troops could land in force.) Britain and the United States, said Stalin, only "informed" the USSR, and "this situation cannot be tolerated any longer."[87]

Stalin had to be "courted, wooed, constantly chatted up," so Churchill urged the Poles not to protest the Katyn massacre because "nothing you can do will bring them [the dead officers] back."[88] FDR expedited Lend-Lease supplies to Russia without the usual quid pro quo arrangements. At the Casablanca Conference in January 1943, he announced that "the elimination of German, Japanese, and Italian war power means the unconditional surrender by Germany, Italy, and Japan."[89] Coming shortly after the Anglo-Americans made an agreement with the Vichy French collaborator Admiral Jean-François Darlan to gain French cooperation in North Africa, Roosevelt's "unconditional surrender" announcement signaled to a suspicious Stalin that Britain and the United States would not make a separate German peace with one of Hitler's subordinates. The doctrine brought a modicum of Allied unity by concentrating on a total military victory over Hitler, deferring troublesome peace terms until afterward. "Roosevelt is more friendly to us than any other prominent American," the Soviet ambassador reported in 1943, "and it is quite obvious that he wishes to cooperate with us."[90]

The foreign ministers' meeting in Moscow (October 19–30) established an Advisory Council for Italy to coordinate Allied policy and a European Advisory Commission to make recommendations for a final peace settlement. The Soviets told Hull that the 200,000 American battle casualties did not amount to much—"we lose that many each day before lunch. You haven't got your teeth in the war yet."[91] Hull replied: "When I was young I knew a bully in Tennessee. He used to get a few things his way by being a bully and bluffing other fellows. But he ended up by not having a friend in the world."[92] Suffering from tuberculosis, the seventy-two-year-old Hull got what he wanted: a Declaration of Four Nations on General Security (China included), the first definite commitment to a postwar replacement for the defunct League of Nations.

The Moscow Conference seemed a mere appetizer for "the turning point" at Teheran, Iran, November 28–December 1, 1943.[93] Meeting the mustachioed Soviet leader for the first time, FDR thought Stalin "very confident, very sure of himself."[94] From the start, an American general recalled, "Uncle Joe had talked straight from the shoulder," telling Churchill and Roosevelt that he favored a firm commitment to OVERLORD as opposed to any Anglo-American operations in the Balkans.[95] When Churchill backed an Adriatic landing, Stalin asked: "Do the British really believe in OVERLORD or are they only saying so to reassure the Russians?" Churchill lamely replied that "it was the duty of the British Government to hurl every scrap of strength across the channel."[96] At a dinner party two nights later Stalin playfully advocated the summary execution of 50,000 German officers, whereupon the prime minister protested that the British would "never tolerate mass execution."[97] When Roosevelt joked that only 49,000 should be shot, Churchill walked out in a huff. The prime minister complained that the "great Russian bear" and the "great American buffalo" were squeezing the "poor little English donkey."[98]

At Teheran, FDR called for a new international organization dominated by the "Four Policemen," who would deal immediately with any threat to peace. Stalin agreed but doubted that the new peacekeeping body alone could block future German and Japanese aggression. He suggested the creation of "strong physical points"—bases—near the two nations to deter them.[99] The president said that the United States would supply only air and naval support in the event of a crisis in postwar Europe; troops would have to come from Britain and the USSR.

The conferees also discussed the postwar status of Eastern Europe and Germany. Churchill had proposed moving Poland's boundaries a considerable distance to the west, incorporating German lands. Polish territory in the east would pass to

Major Wartime Conferences, 1941–1945

Conference	Date	Participants	Results
Argentia, Newfoundland	August 9–12, 1941	Roosevelt, Churchill	Atlantic Charter
Washington, D.C.	December 22, 1941–January 14, 1942	Roosevelt, Churchill	Combined Chiefs of Staff; priority in war effort against Germany; United Nations Declaration
Washington, D.C.	June 19–25, 1942	Roosevelt, Churchill	North African campaign strategy
Moscow, USSR	August 12–15, 1942	Churchill, Stalin, Harriman	Postponement of second front
Casablanca, Morocco	January 14–24, 1943	Roosevelt, Churchill	Unconditional surrender announcement; campaign against Sicily and Italy
Washington, D.C.	May 12–25, 1943	Roosevelt, Churchill	Scheduling of cross-channel landing for May 1, 1944
Quebec, Canada	August 14–24, 1943	Roosevelt, Churchill	Confirmation of cross-channel landing (OVERLORD)
Moscow, USSR	October 19–30, 1943	Hull, Eden, Molotov	Postwar international organization to be formed; Russian promise to enter the war against Japan after Germany's defeat; establishment of European Advisory Commission
UNRRA, Washington, D.C.	November 9, 1943	44 nations	Creation of UNRRA
Cairo, Egypt	November 22–26, 1943	Roosevelt, Churchill, Jiang	Postwar Asia: China to recover lost lands; Korea to be independent; Japan to be stripped of Pacific islands
Teheran, Iran	November 27–December 1, 1943	Roosevelt, Churchill, Stalin	Agreement on cross-channel landing and international organization; Soviet reaffirmation of intent to enter the war against Japan
Bretton Woods, New Hampshire	July 1–22, 1944	44 nations	Creation of World Bank and International Monetary Fund
Dumbarton Oaks, Washington, D.C.	August 21–October 7, 1944	U.S., Britain, USSR, China	United Nations Organization
Quebec, Canada	September 11–16, 1944	Roosevelt, Churchill	"Morgenthau Plan" for Germany
Moscow, USSR	October 9–18, 1944	Churchill, Stalin	Spheres of influence in Balkans (percentage scheme)
Yalta, USSR	February 4–11, 1945	Roosevelt, Churchill, Stalin	Polish governmental structure, elections, and boundaries; United Nations; German reparations; USSR pledge to declare war against Japan and to recognize Jiang's government; some Japanese territories to USSR
San Francisco, California	April 25–June 26, 1945	50 nations	United Nations Organization Charter
Potsdam (Berlin), Germany	July 17–August 2, 1945	Truman, Churchill/Attlee, Stalin	German reconstruction and reparations; Potsdam Declaration to Japan; Council of Foreign Ministers established

the Soviets to secure their western frontier. Roosevelt acquiesced in these plans for Poland but said he could not "publicly take part in any such arrangement at the present time." The election of 1944 loomed, and "as a practical man," he would not risk the votes of millions of Polish-Americans. Roosevelt also mentioned self-determination for the Baltic states. Stalin bristled. Those states, he insisted, belonged to the Soviet Union. Roosevelt replied that the American people "neither knew nor understood." Stalin shot back that "some propaganda work should be done."[100] But FDR never did explain publicly the differences between the Atlantic Charter and Soviet demands for security in Eastern Europe. On Germany, the conferees debated ways to divide the nation, but they left specific plans for "retribution" against Germany to the future.[101]

Although inconclusive on many points, the Teheran discussions pleased the Americans, especially because Stalin had confirmed that, once Hitler was defeated, the USSR would fight against Japan. In response, Roosevelt suggested that the Soviets obtain a Chinese "free port" at Dairen (Dalian) as a reward. Stalin's preference for OVERLORD instead of a Balkans operation also resolved the Anglo-American debate over strategy, thus making Britain a "junior partner" to "its increasingly unsympathetic senior colleague."[102] General sentiment in favor of a peace dictated by the big powers, an international organization, and a weakened postwar Germany signified important Allied cohesion. Stalin also paid tribute to Lend-Lease: "Without these planes from America the war would have been lost."[103] After Teheran the president optimistically told a national radio audience: "We are going to get along very well with him [Stalin] and the Russian people—very well indeed."[104] The Grand Alliance had temporarily closed some fissures.

In Search of a China Policy

Visiting Washington in December 1941, Winston Churchill was astonished that his hosts "rated the Chinese armies as a factor to be mentioned in the same breath as the armies of Russia."[105] America's infatuation with China, the legacy of the Open Door, the false image of Jiang Jieshi as a democratic leader—all reinforced an American determination that China should not "take the wrong path, like the Japs," as a British diplomat put it.[106] Some Americans, President Roosevelt included, even envisioned a strong, united China as a postwar client of the United States and a bridge to Asian peoples freeing themselves from colonialism. China's military importance soon diminished, however, as Japanese victories in early 1942 sent the British and Americans reeling. The fall of Burma in May closed the last remaining land route to Chongqing. The Americans wanted to keep China in the war, yet Roosevelt could not send troops needed elsewhere. He sent General Stilwell instead.

Joseph W. Stilwell arrived in Chongqing with the impressive titles of Chief of Staff to Generalissimo Jiang Jieshi and Commanding General of the United States Forces in India, Burma, and China. As a junior officer he had served two tours of duty in China, had become fluent in Chinese, and had developed great admiration for the Chinese people. But he thought Jiang an untrustworthy scoundrel. In his diary, the always blunt Stilwell called the British "pig fuckers" and Roosevelt "old

Rubberlegs."[107] In Chongqing "Vinegar Joe" sought to train and equip Chinese divisions. With these modernized forces, plus British help from India, Stilwell planned to reopen Burma, increase supplies to China, and thus make the mainland the staging point for the final invasion of Japan.

Stilwell's plans for military reform cut at the heart of the Guomindang system, which one journalist described as combining the "worst features of Tammany Hall and the Spanish Inquisition."[108] The general sputtered in his diary: "Why doesn't the little dummy [Jiang] realize that his only hope is the 30-division plan, and the creation of a separate, efficient, well-equipped, and well-trained force?"[109] Most of Jiang's armies were actually controlled by twelve commanders, several of them virtually autonomous warlords. Before making a decision, the generalissimo always had to ask: "What orders will my generals accept from me?"[110] Jiang wanted Stilwell's equipment but not his advice. Some 500,000 of the Guomindang's best troops had orders to blockade the communists in Yan'an. Jiang wanted to wait out the war and then muster his strength for a final showdown with Mao Zedong. He would not fight in Burma unless the British and Americans gave more support, and the British balked at a Burma campaign. "It is an affectation to pretend that China is a Great Power," said Churchill privately, as he pushed for higher Anglo-American priorities in the Mediterranean.[111] Shortly after the landings in North Africa, Stilwell described his strategic dilemma: "Peanut [Jiang] and I are on a raft, with one sandwich between us, and the rescue ship is heading away from the scene."[112]

President Roosevelt sought conciliation. To Chongqing he sent a stream of personal emissaries to buoy Chinese morale. Jiang received a half-billion dollar loan in 1942, and in January 1943 the State Department negotiated a treaty abolishing the U.S. right of extraterritoriality in China. The following month Roosevelt hosted Madame Jiang at the White House. The Wellesley College alumna addressed Congress and garnered applause for speaking "not only the language of your hearts, but also your tongue. So coming here . . . I am also coming home."[113] At the Cairo Conference in November 1943, Churchill and Roosevelt met with Jiang and formally pledged the return, after the war, of Taiwan, Manchuria, and other areas "stolen by Japan."[114] In December Congress repealed the exclusion laws, which had prohibited Chinese immigration. Roosevelt talked confidently of postwar China as one of his "Four Policemen" that would keep the peace.

FDR also endorsed a plan of General Claire Lee Chennault, whom the Office of Strategic Services (OSS) thought had "fought the Japs more successfully and dealt with the Chinese more successfully than any other American."[115] The famed "Flying Tiger" claimed that with "a very modest American air force equipped with modern airplanes" he could destroy Japanese air power in "six months."[116] When Chennault's bombers began to draw blood in spring 1944, Japanese armies launched a massive counterattack and nearly overran all of the American air bases. Jiang then refused to fight. This time Roosevelt made the extraordinary proposal that Jiang give Stilwell unrestricted command of all forces, Chinese and foreign, in China. The generalissimo stalled for two months; then Roosevelt sent an ultimatum to empower Stilwell that Stilwell delivered in person. "I handed this bundle of paprika to the Peanut and then sank back with a sigh. The harpoon hit the little bugger right in the solar plexus, and went right through him," Stilwell wrote in his diary on

The Cairo Conference. Jiang Jieshi (1887–1975) and Madame Jiang (1897-   ) with Roosevelt and Churchill in November 1943. Although President Roosevelt publicly heaped praise on the Chinese leader, FDR privately told General Stilwell at the Cairo meeting: "If you can't get along with Chiang [Jiang], and can't replace him, get rid of him once and for all. You know what I mean, put someone in you can manage." (Franklin D. Roosevelt Library)

September 19, 1944.[117] Jiang never forgave Stilwell for such a personal humiliation, and rather than antagonize Jiang further, FDR soon replaced Stilwell.

In November, General Patrick J. Hurley became ambassador to China. A blunt-talking sixty-one-year-old Oklahoma Republican, Hurley concentrated on forming a coalition between Jiang's government and the communists. Even though the Soviets, like the Americans, sent military supplies to Jiang's forces and not to Mao Zedong's communists, the communist-led troops had waged successful guerrilla war against the Japanese. The Yan'an communists had an effective intelligence network that extended behind Japanese lines. Claiming to "carry on today the very same work which was carried on earlier in America by Washington, Jefferson, and Lincoln," Mao, Zhou Enlai, and other communist leaders welcomed an American "Observer Mission."[118] The communist revolutionary leadership, according to Foreign Service Officer John S. Service, "has improved the political, economic and social status of the peasant [and] . . . the Communists are certain to play a large, if not dominant, part in China's future."[119] Because most Americans in China shared the belief that the communists might defeat Jiang in a postwar struggle for power, Hurley's initial efforts at coalition building received unified support.

Hurley's first visit to communist Yan'an, in November 1944, provided a grand spectacle. Hurley alighted from his plane "with enough ribbons on his chest to represent every war . . . in which the United States had ever engaged except possibly Shays's Rebellion."[120] Then he completely discombobulated Zhou Enlai by letting out Choctaw war whoops. Later, after the communists rejected Jiang's offer of a virtually worthless seat on the National Military Council in return for merging the Yan'an army under Nationalist control, Hurley accepted Mao's counterproposal for full coalition and communist sharing in Lend-Lease supplies. Mao

Mao Zedong (1893–1976) and Patrick J. Hurley (1883–1963). The Chinese communist leader (second from left) seems less than moved by Ambassador Hurley's dramatic gesture of welcome at Chongqing in 1945. Mao thought Hurley a "clown" who favored Jiang. Hurley once bellowed that Mao was a "motherfucker." The U.S. embassy staff soon called the ambassador "Colonel Blimp" and accused him of "crass stupidity," of being a "stuffed shirt playing at being a great man." The Office of Strategic Services (OSS) in China gave Hurley the code name "Albatross." In November 1945, Hurley suddenly resigned and flung wild charges at Foreign Service Officers who had disagreed with him. (National Archives)

concluded that U.S. policy had changed from "uniting with the CCP [Communists] and pressuring Jiang" to "supporting Jiang, dragging the CCP along [in order to] beat the Japanese."[121]

At this point Hurley began to diverge markedly from the Foreign Service Officers. The ambassador decided on his own that his objective was not to mediate but rather to "sustain" Jiang Jieshi and "to prevent the collapse of the Nationalist government."[122] The communists would undoubtedly have to come to terms. Hurley had formed these views during an earlier visit to Moscow in August 1944, when Molotov had told him that the Chinese communists "had no relation whatever to Communism" and the Soviets would support Jiang Jieshi.[123] Other American officials in China knew that Mao's followers were agrarian-based communists, and they feared that if denied U.S. aid, Mao would obtain assistance from Moscow and thus create a postwar squabble between the United States and the USSR over China. Contrary to Hurley, these "China hands" believed that the rift between the communists and Guomindang ran deep, and that they could obtain Chinese unity only by dealing with Yan'an separately as a way of pressing Jiang. Preliminary talks had already begun in Yan'an, and on January 9, 1945, the head of the American Military Observers Mission cabled that "Mao and Zhou will be immediately available . . . should President Roosevelt express desire to receive them at White House as leaders of a primary Chinese party."[124] The Soviet representative in Yan'an depicted Mao as "clearly offering himself" to the United States to counterbalance the Soviet Union.[125] Mao hoped that if American forces landed in China, Roosevelt would abandon the "militarily impotent Nationalists" and choose "military cooperation" with the communists.[126]

The predictable explosion occurred when Hurley returned to Washington in February 1945 for consultations following the Yalta Conference. In Hurley's absence, the embassy officers at Chongqing sent a telegram to Washington urging the president to inform Jiang "in definite terms that we are required by military necessity to cooperate with and supply the communists and other suitable groups who can aid in this war against the Japanese."[127] These young "China hands" did not know that Stalin had reaffirmed future Soviet entry into the Japanese war at Yalta and, accordingly, that the military rationale for a Guomindang-communist coalition now became less urgent. When Hurley read the telegram, he stormed about Washington, claiming that his subordinates had betrayed him. He called on Roosevelt, then about to take his final journey to Warm Springs, and the weary president gave him what he wanted—unqualified backing for Jiang's regime. The embassy diplomats, including John S. Service and John Paton Davies, found themselves transferred out of China as a timid State Department bowed to the demands of the rambunctious ambassador.

Roosevelt's wartime policy toward China exposed the disparity between his military strategy and postwar political goals. When it became obvious in 1944 that China would not play a major role in the Japanese war and hardly deserved rank as one of the "Four Policemen," Roosevelt faced a choice. He could accelerate American military activities in China, giving the United States more leverage, and press Jiang to undertake the reforms necessary to maintain him in power. Or the president could scale down his political expectations for China and limit military operations there. In fact, Roosevelt "tried to do both and ran the risk of succeeding in neither. He kept talking to and about China as a great power even while he was giving higher and higher military priorities to other military theaters."[128] When the feud between Hurley and the "China hands" ignited, moreover, Roosevelt chose to drift with existing policy rather than take a hard look at Chinese politics. As happened often, when the smiling squire of New York could not easily resolve dilemmas, he left them to the future.

Bystanders to the Holocaust: Americans and the Murder of the Jews

Another problem finessed for the future was that of the refugees, hundreds of thousands of them Jews from Nazi-occupied territories. Many sought asylum in the United States. Although most Americans denounced Hitler's crusade to preserve the purity of the "Aryan race" through the persecution and extermination of European Jews, translating moral revulsion into effective policy proved difficult. U.S. immigration laws, traditional anti-Semitism, the depression, bureaucratic procedures, wartime fear of spies, and domestic politics shaped the timid American response.

The dark story began in 1933 when Hitler initiated his attacks on "non-Aryans." Throughout the 1930s, the Nazis systematically eliminated Jews from the professions and denied them ownership of businesses. In 1935 the Nuremberg Laws stripped Jews of their civil and political rights, in essence making them stateless beings. Hatemongers plastered signs on buildings: "Whoever buys from a Jew is a traitor."[129] In November 1938 a distraught Jewish youth living in Paris entered the German embassy and killed a German official. Germany erupted in anti-Semitic violence. Nazi thugs beat up Jews on the streets, sacked and burned synagogues, and destroyed Jewish shops. After this *Kristallnacht,* or "Night of the Breaking Glass," the German government fined its Jewish subjects $400 million and sent 50,000 Jews to concentration camps at Dachau and Buchenwald, detention centers where tortures and executions became common. President Roosevelt called the U.S. ambassador home in protest, remarking, "I myself could scarcely believe that such things could occur in a twentieth century civilization."[130]

The brutal events occurred again in Austria, Czechoslovakia, Poland, Hungary, and elsewhere as the Third Reich overran Europe. Urgent requests for transit to the United States flooded American embassies and consulates. American immigration law, however, prescribed a quota for each country. The National Origins Act of 1924 openly discriminated against immigrants from eastern and southern Europe, the source, said member of Congress J. M. Tincher of Kansas, of "Bolshevik Wops, Dagoes, Kikes and Hunkies."[131] The annual quota for Great Britain and Ireland was 83,575, for Germany and Austria 27,370, for Poland 6,000, for Italy 5,500, and for Romania 300. American consular officers also inhibited immigration by strictly enforcing procedures. Potential immigrants had to present documents attesting to their birth, health, financial status, and crime-free background. Many of these papers had to be obtained from uncooperative Nazi officials. Americans also rigidly denied entry to people "likely to become a public charge," which meant that persons could gain a place on the quota list only if they proved that they could support themselves once in the United States. Yet under Nazi law Jews could not take their property or savings from Germany. These restrictions, combined with the evaporation of American jobs during the depression, created a revealing statistic for the period 1933–1938: 174,067 people entered the United States and 221,239 departed, or a net *loss* of 47,172. To have opened America's doors to refugees, in short, would not have inundated a nation of 130 million.

The American Federation of Labor and patriotic groups nonetheless lobbied against any revision in the quotas or visa requirements. Foreigners should not compete with U.S. citizens for scarce jobs—a telling argument during the depression. Longstanding anti-Semitism fed such nativist thought. Father Charles E. Coughlin, a fiery Catholic priest from Michigan, equated Judaism and communism in his radio broadcasts, which reached 3.5 million listeners a week. Even the distinguished anti-Nazi diplomat George Messersmith, known as the "Jews' man" in the State Department, opposed the establishment of a University of Exile at the New School for Social Research in New York because he feared that Jews teaching there would undermine the basic Anglo-Saxon Protestant nature of American society.[132] Opinion polls revealed that more than 80 percent of Americans opposed revision of the quotas to admit European refugees. Congress stood firmly behind the quota system. Already blistered by charges that his domestic reform program was a "Jew Deal," a label attached because he appointed such Jews as Henry Morgenthau, Jr., and Felix Frankfurter to prominent positions, the president played it safe. Thwarted in his ill-fated "court-packing" attempt in 1937 and his futile effort to purge conservatives from the Democratic party in 1938, Roosevelt would not risk another political setback.

Roosevelt mostly left the refugee problem to the Department of State, which "clung to a policy that was timid, rigidly legal, and without innovation."[133] In 1934 the department lobbied successfully against a Senate resolution condemning Germany's treatment of the Jews, fearful that the resolution would spark German comment about the segregation of black Americans. Despite his own wife's Jewish heritage, Secretary Hull opposed boycotts organized by American Jews against German products because such behavior interrupted normal trade channels. FDR "did quietly manipulate at the margins" with executive orders that combined German and Austrian quotas in 1938–1939 and temporarily relaxed enforcement of the "likely to become a public charge" clause, but many Jews still could not obtain the necessary documents.[134] The result: The German-Austrian quota went unfilled in 1933–1938 and 1940–1945; only in 1939 did it fill. Emanuel Celler, member of Congress from New York, thought the State Department a "heartbeat muffled in protocol."[135]

In 1938 Roosevelt did call for an international conference on refugees, which met in Evian, France, to establish an Intergovernmental Committee on Refugees (IGC). Plans for refugee havens in Latin America and central Africa faltered. Hitler sneered that "the entire democratic world dissolves in tears of pity, but then, in spite of its obvious duty to help, closes its heart to the poor, tortured people."[136] In early 1939 Senator Robert Wagner of New York introduced a bill to allow 20,000 German refugee children to enter above the quota. With revision of the Neutrality Act then pending, the president scratched "File No action FDR," and the bill died in committee.[137]

In mid-1939 the ship *St. Louis* steamed toward Cuba from Hamburg carrying 930 Jewish refugees. Havana officials, however, would not permit them to land without proper visas. The ship then headed for Miami, tailed by Coast Guard cutters. American immigration officials would not let the passengers disembark, so the *St. Louis* had to return to Europe. Its passengers ultimately scattered to Britain, the Netherlands, Belgium, and France after refugee societies pressed their governments.

The plight of Jewish refugees deepened after the outbreak of war. The State Department actually tightened visa requirements because it feared refugees might include saboteurs and spies. In the State Department, refugee questions fell under the authority of Breckinridge Long, a southern aristocrat, old Wilsonian, former ambassador to Italy, and large financial contributor to the Democratic party. Believing that refugees might become a fifth column in the United States, he and other officials blocked numerous private efforts to save them and later suppressed information about Hitler's plan to exterminate European Jewry. U.S. consuls increasingly rejected applications for visas, and ships headed to American shores half empty. Washington tried futilely to persuade Latin American countries to take refugees. When the State Department asked the British to approach Portugal about opening its African colony of Angola, Lord Halifax snapped: "Let the Americans do it."[138] Resettlement proposals for British Guiana, French Madagascar, and the Philippines also fell through; Britain restricted the movement of Jews to Palestine.

In August 1942 reliable evidence reached the State Department that Germany had begun to exterminate the entire Jewish population of Europe. When Jan Karski, a Polish courier who had witnessed mass executions at Belzec and Treblinka, briefed FDR and Hull, they had trouble grasping the full reality of the Holocaust. Even a Zionist such as Justice Felix Frankfurter told Karski that "he

Buchenwald Concentration Camp, Germany. This large Nazi concentration camp held Jews and others who served as slave labor for local factories during World War II. Although Buchenwald did not have death-dealing gas chambers, many prisoners died there from disease, malnutrition, beatings, medical experiments, and executions. The journalist Andy Rooney, who reported on the liberation of Buchenwald for *Stars and Stripes,* later recalled: "I stared. I stared in embarrassed silence. . . . For the first time, I knew for certain that any peace is not better than any war." (Library of Congress)

didn't believe what he was being told."[139] Yet the evidence mounted. The Jewish ghetto in Warsaw became a target of German barbarity; by fall 1942 only 70,000 of its 380,000 residents remained, and they desperately rebelled in the spring of the next year. Using Zyklon B gas and large crematoria, German officials murdered a million victims in the most notorious extermination camp at Auschwitz, Poland. Scholars have debated the feasibility of bombing Auschwitz and surrounding rail lines. The U.S. air force probably could have destroyed these installations by August 1944, "but only by diverting substantial resources" and killing "thousands of camp inmates." Such an operation would have required authorization from FDR, who "was never seriously asked for such approval" because the War Department opposed any "diversions" that would delay victory, seen as the best hope for the Jews.[140] Perhaps only the assassination of Hitler in 1943 or 1944 could have saved "hundreds of thousands of Jews—if not more," but the Allies never tried, and attempts by German dissidents failed.[141] Of 10 million Jews in Nazi-occupied Europe in 1940, at least 5.5 million had died by 1945.

In early 1943 representatives of Britain and the United States met in Bermuda to discuss the refugee problem; in essence they reported that they had done all they could to help. After the conference, Hull informed the president: "The unknown cost of moving an undetermined number of persons from an undisclosed place to an unknown destination, a scheme advocated by certain pressure groups, is, of course, out of the question."[142] Hull never sought to solve the unknowns. Secretary of the Treasury Henry Morgenthau, Jr., did. At his request, Treasury general counsel Randolph Paul submitted the *Report to the Secretary on the Acquiescence of This Government in the Murder of the Jews,* a frank critique of the State Department. "It takes months and months to grant the visa and then it usually applies to a corpse," Paul wrote. Morgenthau then told Roosevelt that the rescue of Jews "is a trust too great to remain in the hands of men indifferent, callous and perhaps hostile."[143] In January 1944 the president created the War Refugee Board, outside the auspices of the State Department. Using private and public funds, board operatives established refugee camps in Italy, Morocco, Hungary, Sweden, Palestine, and Switzerland. The board thus saved some 200,000 Jews and 20,000 non-Jews by war's end. "What we did was little enough. . . . Late and little," its director concluded.[144] Given the "yawning gap" between the "benevolent rhetoric" of the Roosevelt administration and its actual achievements, Jewish refugees themselves took command of their survival after the war by leading the "exodus" to Palestine and creating the new nation of Israel in 1948.[145] Nearly a half-century later, the director Steven Spielberg, in the movie *Schindler's List* (1993), drove home what a few heroically dedicated individuals might have done to save thousands of lives.

Planning the Postwar Peace, 1943–1945

The great European military battles of 1944, wherein the Anglo-American D-Day invasion of France in June coincided with a massive Soviet offensive that reached the Vistula River by August, gave postwar planning higher priority. Taking advantage of a "second chance" to overcome isolationism, economic depression, and war, U.S. officials helped launch several international organizations to secure peace and prosperity. Indeed, when FDR saw the Hollywood film *Wilson* (1944), with vivid scenes of his predecessor losing his health and the League, he exclaimed, "By God, that's not going to happen to me."[146] He thus made the Atlantic Charter a more flexible guide than the Fourteen Points. During 1943–1945 the United Nations Relief and Rehabilitation Administration (UNRRA), World Bank, International Monetary Fund, and United Nations Organization took form. Unlike World War I, this time the establishment of postwar institutions would not await the grand deliberations of one conference. Nor would plans to reform Germany.

On November 9, 1943, at the White House, forty-four nations signed the UNRRA agreement for the "relief of victims of war . . . through the provision of food, fuel, clothing, shelter and other basic necessities, medical and other essential services."[147] Some leaders feared that hungry, displaced people might, in desperation, turn to political extremes like communism; food and medicine would help stem postwar political chaos. The Department of State insisted that an American head UNRRA. Operating until mid-1947, UNRRA had a budget of $4 billion, $2.7 billion of which the United States donated. UNRRA dispensed 9 million tons of food; built hundreds of hospitals; prevented epidemics of diphtheria, typhoid, cholera, and venereal disease; revived transportation systems; and cared for at least a million displaced persons. China, Italy, Greece, and Austria absorbed about half of UNRRA's assistance. The other half went to Poland, other Eastern European nations, and the Soviet Union. American critics protested that an international organization was spending taxpayers' dollars to shore up communist governments. In fact, UNRRA tried to avoid politics, refusing to apply political tests to the needy. But Americans expected food aid to bring political returns. When it did not, Washington killed UNRRA in 1947 by cutting off funds.

Two other organizations proved more permanent. From July 1 to 22, 1944, the delegates of forty-four nations negotiated at Bretton Woods in New Hampshire. Working from an Anglo-American proposal, the conferees created the International Bank for Reconstruction and Development (World Bank) and the International Monetary Fund (IMF). The World Bank could extend loans to "assist in the reconstruction and development" of members, to "promote private investment," and to "promote the long-range balanced growth of international trade."[148] The IMF was intended to facilitate world trade by stabilizing the international system of payments through currency loans. After much debate, with critics charging "the worst swindle . . . in the history of the nation," Congress passed the Bretton Woods Agreement Act by margins of 345 to 18 and 61 to 16 in July 1945.[149]

From the start, U.S. economic power dominated the two organizations. Located in Washington, D.C., the World Bank has always had an American as president. The United States also possessed one-third of the votes in the bank by committing $3.175 billion of the total of $9.100 billion initial subscriptions. The United States also held one-third of the votes in the fund. As payer of the "piper," the United States would "call the tune."[150] Britain begrudged U.S. control but joined. The USSR did not join the bank or fund because the Soviets practiced state-controlled trade and finance, feared having to divulge economic data, and could not accept the emphasis on "private" enterprise or the U.S. domination. Moscow's absence augured poorly for postwar Allied cooperation.

From August to October 1944, representatives of the United States, Britain, the Soviet Union, and China met in the Dumbarton Oaks mansion in Washington, D.C., to shape the United Nations Organization (UN). Public opinion polls indicated that Americans strongly endorsed a new collective-security organization, and Congress had passed favorable resolutions. The conferees hammered out the UN's charter, providing for a powerful Security Council dominated by the great powers and a weak General Assembly. The Security Council, empowered to use force to settle crises, had five permanent members. When the United States pushed China as a permanent member, Churchill proposed France, calling China a "faggot vote on the side of the United States."[151] After some grumbling, the Soviet Union accepted both China and France, feeling secure in the veto power that each permanent member of the Security Council possessed.

Two other issues also proved contentious: voting procedures in the Security Council and membership in the Assembly. The Soviet Union advocated an absolute veto for permanent members, whereas the United States argued that parties to a conflict should not veto discussion or action. Not until the Yalta Conference in early 1945 did the Allies agree that the veto would apply only to substantive questions such as economic or military sanctions, not to procedural questions. As for membership in the Assembly, Moscow brazenly requested seats for all sixteen

United Nations Symbol. A sign of peace for the new international organization. (United Nations)

"The Two Thousand Yard Stare." Combat artist Tom Lea captures the zombie-like demeanor of a young marine who has endured too much. Lea painted this portrait during the battle for Peleliu in the Palau Islands (September–November 1944), in which 2,000 Americans were killed and more than 8,500 were wounded. Some 11,000 Japanese also died. "In the last war, they sent a guy to France," another G.I., alert to the global role of the United States, wrote in 1944. "Then he went home. . . . Real simple. . . . But what do they do this time? . . . They send you to Tunisia, and then they send you to Sicily, and they send you to Italy. . . . Maybe we'll be in France next year. . . . Then we'll work our way east. Yugoslavia. Greece. Turkey. No, not Turkey. All I know is, in 1958, we're going to fight the battle of Tibet." (U.S. Army, Center of Military History)

Soviet republics. That outlandish request derived from Soviet fears of being badly outnumbered in the Assembly by the British Commonwealth "bloc" and the U.S.–Latin America "bloc." As the historian Robert Hilderbrand has written, "the Big Three saw the defense of their own security, the protection of their own interests, and the enjoyment of the fruits of their victory in the world war as more important than the creation of an international organization to maintain world peace."[152] At Yalta the Soviets accepted a compromise of three votes in the Assembly (see page 207).

Although Republican support for Dumbarton Oaks seemed as likely as "the Sermon on the Mount . . . being endorsed by the Gestapo," Secretary Hull successfully appealed to GOP presidential candidate Thomas E. Dewey to keep the issue of international organization out of the political campaign.[153] The resulting nonpartisanship and the inclusion of senators in the Dumbarton Oaks delegation helped the Roosevelt administration build its case for the UN. On January 10, 1945, the influential Senator Arthur H. Vandenberg of Michigan, an arch prewar isolationist expected to insist on reservations much as Lodge had a generation earlier (see pages 95–96), delivered a stunning speech urging U.S. participation in collective security as a curb on aggression. He further advised the major Allies to sign a security treaty to keep the Axis nations permanently demilitarized; he hoped thereby to allay Soviet fears of a revived Germany and hence render Soviet expansion unnecessary. Vandenberg could accept American membership in the United Nations because "this is anything but a wild-eyed internationalist dream of a world State."[154]

Roosevelt rewarded Vandenberg for his support by naming him a delegate to the San Francisco Conference of April 25–June 26, 1945, convened to launch the United Nations. The new secretary of state after Hull's retirement in November 1944, Edward R. Stettinius, Jr., managed the conference. The 282 delegates did not make decisions without prior approval of the representatives of the big powers, who met each evening in Stettinius's penthouse at the Fairmont Hotel. The United States refused to admit Poland, because its government had not reorganized as required by Yalta (see p. 206). But then the American delegation shocked all by requesting participation for Argentina, which had only declared war against Germany in March. The United States, believing that the Latin American republics would not vote for three Soviet seats in the Assembly unless Argentina were included, would not relent. By the lopsided vote of 32 to 4, with 10 abstentions, Argentina won its seat. When African-American leader W. E. B. Du Bois complained that Dumbarton Oaks had disenfranchised 750 million "colored peoples" who could seek equality only "through the philanthropy of masters," Stettinius replied that his "job in San Francisco was to create a charter," not to solve "the negro's question."[155]

Henry Morgenthau, Jr. (1891–1967). A long-time friend of Franklin D. Roosevelt, Morgenthau served as FDR's secretary of the treasury (1933–1945) but often participated in the making of foreign policy. A deft bureaucratic infighter, Morgenthau pressed during World War II for an active U.S. stance against the genocide in Europe and for harsh peace terms against the Nazis after the war. Although successful in creating the War Refugee Board, he failed to impose the Morgenthau Plan on defeated Germany. (Franklin D. Roosevelt Library)

Journalists detected an American "steamroller" at San Francisco.[156] So did the Soviet Union, which objected in blunt language. And so did smaller states, which protested their exclusion from key decisions and their impotence in the new United Nations Organization. Fifteen nations abstained in the vote on the veto formula. The UN Charter, as finally adopted, included the Economic and Social Council and the Trusteeship Council. The latter looked to the eventual independence of colonial areas but left the British and French empires intact and permitted the United States to absorb former Japanese-dominated islands in the Pacific (Marianas, Carolines, and Marshalls). *Time* magazine aptly termed the United Nations "a charter for a world of power."[157] Indeed, that characterization applied also to Article 51, which permitted regional alliances such as that the United States and Latin America outlined in the Act of Chapultepec in March. The United States, as one official observed, would "have our cake and eat it too"—freedom of action in the Western Hemisphere and an international organization to curb aggression in Europe.[158] Amid memories of 1919, the Senate approved the UN Charter on July 28, 1945, by a vote of 89 to 2.

While these plans for the victors unfolded, the debate over the fate of a defeated Germany centered on a "constructive" policy (rehabilitation, economic unity, and integration into the European economy) or a "corrective" policy (strict reduction in industry, large reparations, and a decentralized economy).[159] At the center of the controversy stood Treasury Secretary Henry Morgenthau, Jr., who proposed a "corrective" plan designed to despoil Germany of industries having potential military value. In early September 1944 he had advised Roosevelt that the coal- and iron-rich Ruhr area should be stripped of industry. At the Quebec Conference of September 12–16, 1944, the president gained Churchill's reluctant signature to a memorandum "eliminating the war-making industries in the Ruhr and in the Saar" and "converting Germany into a country primarily agricultural and pastoral in its character."[160] Churchill apparently had approved the Morgenthau scheme in exchange for the promise of a postwar American loan.

"Uncle Sam Pulls the Lever at the UN."   Many foreign commentators believed that the United States dominated the new United Nations Organization. *(Ta Kung Pao* of Shanghai–Hong Kong in *United Nations World,* 1951)

Back in Washington, critics lambasted the Morgenthau Plan. Secretaries Hull and Stimson opposed a harsh economic peace. "Prosperity in one part of the world helps to create prosperity in other parts of the world," Stimson advised. "Poverty in one part of the world induces poverty in other parts."[161] Germany had to revive to spur postwar prosperity in Western Europe. Using his special access to the president, Morgenthau persuaded Roosevelt in September to approve an interim Joint Chiefs of Staff directive (JSC/1067), which ordered denazification and demilitarization, the dismantling of iron, steel, and chemical industries, a controlled economy, and limited rehabilitation. The new president, Harry S. Truman, however, thought "Morgenthau didn't know sh— from apple butter" and began a gradual retreat from the Morgenthau Plan and JCS/1067, especially after he eased Morgenthau out of office in July 1945.[162] By the end of the war, then, U.S. plans for postwar Germany remained unsettled.

Compromises at the Yalta Conference

Near the end of the European war Churchill, Roosevelt, and Stalin met once again, at the Livadia Palace near Yalta in the Crimea. Meeting from February 4 to 11, 1945, the Big Three, after considerable compromise, made important decisions for the war against the Axis and for the postwar configuration of international affairs, the Yalta "system." After the conclave, Yalta aroused heated controversy akin to the Munich Conference. To some critics, Yalta symbolized a "sell-out" to the Soviets, an example of Roosevelt's coddling of the communist menace. Worn low by the illness that would take his life two months later, critics have claimed, Roosevelt gave in to a guileful Stalin and failed to use superior U.S. economic power to force concessions. The president's detractors also pointed an accusing finger at Alger Hiss, a U.S. official at Yalta who later went to jail on a perjury charge for testifying that he had not served Moscow as a spy. Although one among hundreds of decrypted Soviet cables from World War II now available suggests that Hiss was "probably" an agent named "Ales," no corroborating evidence has yet turned up in former Soviet (now Russian) archives.[163]

The Big Three entered the conference with different goals. Britain sought a zone in Germany for France, a curb on Soviet expansion into Poland, and protection of the British Empire. The Soviet Union wanted reparations to rebuild its devastated economy, possessions in Asia, influence over Poland, and a Germany so weakened that it could never again march eastward. The United States wanted a U.S.-managed United Nations, a Soviet declaration of war against Japan, a reduction of communist political power in Poland, and elevation of China to big-power status. Although each participant suspected the others' motives, "a high incidence of consensus was reached at the Conference."[164]

The "consensus" at Yalta reflected the military and diplomatic realities of the moment. Britain and the United States had delayed the opening of the second front until June 6, 1944, and then, from mid-December to mid-January 1945—just before Yalta—Anglo-American troops bogged down in the Battle of the Bulge in Belgium. Asked to take pressure off the western front by stepping up the Soviet winter offensive in the east, Stalin obliged on January 12. "I am most grateful to you for your thrilling message," a relieved Churchill replied.[165] Throughout 1944 the Red Army had cut deeply into German lines on the eastern front. Indeed, by the time of the Yalta Conference, Russian soldiers were sweeping westward along a wide front through Poland, Czechoslovakia, and Hungary, with Romania already freed from German clutches. The Red Army, not Roosevelt, gave the Soviet Union influence in Eastern Europe.

Asian military realities also shaped diplomatic decisions. Japan was fiercely battling American forces in Luzon and the Marianas, and still had 1 million soldiers in China, 2 million in the home islands, and another 1 million in Manchuria and Korea. With some 54 percent of American battle deaths in the Pacific occurring in the last year of the war, both sides fought with increasing savagery. Japanese authorities depicted Americans as "albino apes" and "carnivorous beasts," and according to the war correspondent Ernie Pyle, marines in the Pacific called the enemy "Japes," a combination of "Jap" and "ape."[166] "We shot prisoners in cold blood, wiped out hospitals, strafed lifeboats," one U.S. war correspondent admitted, and "boiled the flesh off enemy skulls to make table ornaments for sweethearts, or carved their bones into letter openers."[167] One U.S. general saw "dead Germans and I thought about their wives and children," but "with these [Japanese] bastards, that doesn't even occur."[168] Japan's suicidal *Kamikaze* resistance on Okinawa still lay in the future. In short, Roosevelt and Churchill still needed Soviet help to defeat Japan.

The Soviets strained to make their guests comfortable at Yalta, offering servants and lavish meals. The meetings proceeded amicably, although Stalin once became ruffled when he took Roosevelt's name for him—"Uncle Joe"—as ridicule rather than as a term of endearment, and Molotov wore his customary stone face. At the

The Yalta Conference. In this meeting with Churchill, a haggard Roosevelt betrayed symptoms of the cardiovascular disease that would kill him in April 1945. Robert H. Ferrell's *The Dying President* (1998), utilizing the records and diaries of FDR's heart doctor, concludes that the president was "arguably as incapacitated as President Wilson had been, a shell of his former self, unable to keep abreast of the great decisions he had left to the end of the war, too ill or too arrogant to inform his successor about them." (Franklin D. Roosevelt Library)

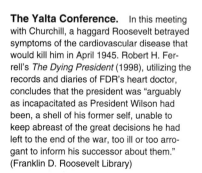

final dinner, Churchill informed Stalin that with general elections scheduled soon "I shall have to speak very harshly about the Communists. . . . You know we have two parties in England." "One party is much better," Stalin deadpanned.[169]

For Churchill, Poland counted as "the most urgent reason for the Yalta Conference."[170] Two Polish governments claimed legitimacy. The British and Americans recognized the conservative exiled government in London, led by Stanislas Mikolajczyk. Moscow recognized the communist-led provisional government in Lublin. Repeatedly reminding everyone that Germany had attacked the Soviet Union through the Polish corridor twice in the century, Stalin insisted not only on Allied support for the Lublin government but also on boundaries that gave Poland part of Germany (Oder-Neisse line in the west) and Russia part of Poland (Curzon line in the east). Churchill and Roosevelt opposed a communist Poland but had little bargaining power because Soviet troops occupied much of the country. Roosevelt said he had several million Polish voters back home who demanded a more representative Polish government. Stalin remained adamant.

Compromises emerged. The Curzon line was temporarily set as the eastern boundary. The Yalta agreement stipulated also that a "more broadly based" government would be created in Poland, that the "Provisional Government . . . should be therefore reorganized on a broader democratic basis with the inclusion of democratic leaders from Poland itself and from Poles abroad," with "free and unfettered elections" held as soon as possible.[171] Roosevelt wanted the first election in Poland "to be like Caesar's wife. I did not know her but they said she was pure." "They said that about her," Stalin corrected, "but in fact she had her sins."[172] Until such an election the communist Lublin group would comprise the nucleus of the Polish government. When later asked about the Polish agreement by Assistant Secretary of State A. A. Berle, FDR replied: "I didn't say it was good, Adolf, I said it was the best I could do."[173] Churchill swallowed the bitter pill, in part because Stalin assured him that the Soviet Union would not intrude in British-dominated Greece, then in the throes of civil war. Compromises on other issues also made the Polish settlement tolerable.

Britain reluctantly accepted Germany's "dismemberment" so long as its ally France received a zone of occupation. Noting that Roosevelt had said that American troops would not long remain in Europe, Churchill cited France as a bulwark against Germany. Stalin grudgingly accepted a French zone. On reparations, which the Soviets vigorously demanded, Britain and America agreed on German reparations "in kind" and the creation of a Reparations Commission, but they refused to set a figure until they determined Germany's ability to pay.

The conferees reached compromises on Asia and the Pacific, where Japan enjoyed the strategic advantage of a one-front war, unlike Germany, which was pinched hopelessly between Allied armies to the east and west. By February 1945, the Japanese were reeling northward as General MacArthur's amphibious forces pressed them from the southwest Pacific and Admiral Chester Nimitz's carrier-backed amphibians forced them to retreat across the central Pacific. The home islands were under sustained attack by U.S. heavy bombers, but the Americans still feared the dismaying prospect of very high casualties in the planned invasion of Japan. Soviet intervention and a Red Army thrust across Manchuria would draw off defenders and materially reduce American casualties during the landings in Kyushu and Honshu. FDR therefore desperately sought Stalin's pledge to enter the Pacific war. Stalin promised to declare war against Japan two or three months after Hitler's defeat, enough time to transfer his troops to Asia. Stalin also agreed to sign a pact of friendship and alliance with Jiang Jieshi's regime, not with Mao Zedong's rival communists. In return, the Soviet Union regained what Russia had lost in 1905: the southern part of Sakhalin, Dairen (Dalian) as a free port, Port Arthur as a naval base, and joint operation of Manchurian railroads. The Soviet Union also obtained the Kurile Islands. On these agreements the Big Three never consulted China, a clear loser at Yalta.

The Allies reached agreement on the United Nations Organization. Dumbarton Oaks had added France and China as "permanent" members of the Security Council, possessing the veto. Although Churchill thought China would vote with the United States, FDR and Stalin expected France to support British positions. Thus outnumbered in the council, Stalin asked at Yalta for membership of all sixteen Soviet republics in the General Assembly. He also insisted on an absolute veto in the council on all issues, procedural and substantive. Roosevelt agreed to three Soviet seats in the General Assembly, and Stalin shelved the veto for procedural questions (such as whether the council should take up an issue to which the permanent member is a party). The conference also reaffirmed national self-determination in the "Declaration of Liberated Europe," which Stalin signed because "we can fulfill it in our own way. What matters is the correlation of forces."[174]

Yalta marked the "dawn of the new day," said Harry Hopkins. "We were absolutely certain that we had won the first great victory of the peace."[175] "Poor Neville Chamberlain believed he could trust Hitler," Churchill commented after Yalta. "He was wrong. But I don't think I'm wrong about Stalin."[176] Roosevelt, Churchill, and Stalin had deftly played the great-power game of building spheres of influence. Each went home with some major objectives satisfied. Although they had postponed some tough questions and written some vague language, they had faced military and political realities. None of the leaders, of course, had consulted weaker nations on whom the Yalta decisions weighed heavily.

Later, when the Yalta agreements collapsed, critics ignored U.S. gains from the conference—broadening of the Polish government, a UN voting formula, delay of the reparations question, the significant Soviet pledge to enter the Pacific war—and charged that FDR had conceded too much. But he had little to give away. The United States might have used its economic power in the form of reconstruction aid as a diplomatic weapon, but such tactics would have spoiled the spirit of compromise at Yalta, which served American interests. Churchill recognized the necessity of conciliation: "What would have happened if we had quarrelled with Russia while the Germans still had three or four hundred divisions on the fighting front?"[177] Indeed, "had the Grand Alliance fallen apart at Yalta or immediately after because Roosevelt refused to recognize Russia's security needs," the historian Lloyd C. Gardner has written, postwar Europe might have descended into "a series of civil wars or possibly an even darker Orwellian condition of localized wars along an uncertain border."[178] The spheres-of-influence agreement, the Yalta leaders believed, would serve as a transition to peace.

To Each Its Own: Allied Divergence and Spheres of Influence

Throughout World War II, the Allies attempted to protect and, if possible, extend their spheres of influence. Churchill's defense of the British Empire, from Argentia through Yalta, reflected this characteristic of wartime diplomacy. "If the Americans want to take Japanese islands," he remarked, "let them do so with our blessing. . . . But 'Hands Off the British Empire' is our maxim."[179] With vital interests in the Mediterranean and Persian Gulf, as well as in Asia, Britain resisted postwar United Nations–mandated trusteeships. Some Americans suspected that Churchill's constant postponement of the second front and his strategies for North Africa and Italy aimed at preserving British interests. His advice to American military leaders, near war's end, that they drive quickly to Berlin, and if possible even farther into Eastern Europe, to beat the Soviets there, also aroused this suspicion.

The Churchill-Stalin percentage agreement of October 1944 was emblematic. In early 1944 Churchill concluded that "we are approaching a showdown with the Russians" in the Balkans, and he called for a frank settlement. Roosevelt agreed to a trial division of authority. Instability plagued Romania, where Soviet troops dominated; Yugoslavia, where independent communist Josip Tito and his Partisans were emerging; Bulgaria, where an indigenous communist movement grew with Soviet influence; and Greece, a British-dominated area plagued by civil war. At an October conference with Stalin in Moscow, Churchill scribbled some percentages on a piece of paper. In Romania, Russia would get 90 percent of the power and Britain 10 percent; in Greece, Britain would enjoy 90 percent and Russia 10 percent; in Yugoslavia and Hungary, a 50-50 split; and in Bulgaria, 75 percent would go to Russia and 25 percent to "others." Churchill "pushed this across to Stalin," who "took his blue pencil and made a large tick upon it."[180] Stalin liked this arrangement that granted the Soviets predominant influence in Eastern Europe:

The Allies Push Japan Back, 1942–1945

Japanese-held areas

Limit of Japanese conquest

Norman Adams

"The United Kingdom had India and the Indian Ocean in her sphere of influence; the United States, China and Japan; the USSR had nothing."[181] Roosevelt did not protest.

Soviet support for the Lublin government, demands for Polish and Romanian territory, efforts to exclude the United States and Britain from the joint control commissions in Eastern Europe, and seizure of German-operated property underscored the growing power of the Soviet Union among its neighbors. Soviet handling of the Warsaw uprising of July 31, 1944, alarmed Western observers. With Soviet armies some twelve miles from Warsaw, the Polish underground gambled and attacked German forces, hoping that Soviet troops would dash to their aid. But the Red Army stopped. Over the next two months the Germans leveled half the city and killed 166,000 Poles, most of whom owed allegiance to the exiled government in London. "Confident that the alliance will not break up over Poland," Stalin dropped supplies to the besieged city in September but refused at first to let Allied planes land at Soviet airfields after carrying supplies to Warsaw.[182] He called the uprising a "reckless and fearful gamble" by "power-seeking criminals."[183] Whatever the military realities—Stalin claimed that his soldiers were meeting heavy German resistance—many charged that Stalin abetted the slaughter of the Warsaw Poles. Ambassador to the Soviet Union W. Averell Harriman called the Soviets a "world bully" who "misinterpreted our generous attitude toward them."[184] The liberation of Poland by Soviet forces in 1944 ultimately fixed a communist regime in Warsaw—one that Roosevelt's compromises at Yalta essentially recognized.

The United States itself was expanding and building spheres of influence during the war. Having drawn most of the Latin American states into a defense community at the Lima Conference (1938) and in the Declaration of Panama (1939), the United States moved to drive German investments and influence from the Western Hemisphere. The Export-Import Bank loaned $130 million to twelve Latin American nations in 1939–1941 to help them oust German businesses, cut trade with the Axis, stabilize their economies, and bring them into alignment with U.S. foreign policy. During the war, the United States increased its stake in Bolivian tin, helped build Brazilian warships, expanded holdings in Venezuelan oil, acquired bases in Panama and Guatemala, and nourished the Dominican dictatorship of Rafael Trujillo. The American military also began to coordinate armaments and military training with Latin American forces. During the war Latin America shipped 50 percent of its exports, largely much needed raw materials, to the United States. At the Rio de Janeiro Conference (January 15–28, 1942), all but Chile and Argentina voted to break diplomatic relations with the Axis nations. In March 1945, in the Act of Chapultepec, the United States and Latin America took another step toward a regional defense alliance. In early 1945 Secretary Stettinius unwittingly reminded many of Yankee dominance: "The United States looks upon Mexico as a good neighbor, a strong upholder of democratic traditions in this hemisphere, and a country we are proud to call our own."[185] Even Canadian prime minister W. L. Mackenzie King worried that Washington intended to take Canada "out of the orbit of the British Commonwealth and into their own orbit."[186]

U.S. leaders also sought to direct events in postwar Italy and Asia. They essentially excluded the Soviets from the Italian surrender agreement in 1943 and denied

Pacific Fleet Carriers. After Japan's attack on Pearl Harbor ended the U.S. Navy's addiction to the irresistible masculine sensuality of battleships, a major reason for U.S. victories in the Pacific and for a substantial American role in postwar Asia was the air superiority provided by aircraft carriers. The light aircraft carrier *Langley* and the heavy carrier *Ticonderoga* lead this Pacific fleet task group. From 1940 to June 1945, the U.S. Navy grew from 1,099 to 50,759 vessels, including 8 new battleships, 92 new aircraft carriers, and 43,255 new landing craft. (Navy Department, National Archives)

them a role in the control commission. Some American officials recognized that Italy, where predominant power rested in their hands, set a precedent for later Soviet predominance in Romania and Hungary. U.S. officials also insisted on holding the conquered Japanese islands in the Pacific and in unilaterally governing postwar Japan. Hoping to "steer this great unwieldy barge . . . into the right harbor," the British Ministry of Information, in its propaganda efforts in the United States, emphasized the common theme of "white men in tough places" to encourage Americans to "see themselves as a global caretaker of many subject races."[187] With U.S. forces spearheading the counteroffensive in the southwest Pacific, Australian prime minister John Curtin acknowledged allegiance "to America, free of any pangs to our traditional links with the United Kingdom."[188] Thus did Washington envisage closer postwar ties with India, Australia, New Zealand, and Jiang's China.

In the Middle East the United States also expanded. In 1939 the Arabian-American Oil Company (Aramco) began to tap its 440,000-square-mile concession in Saudi Arabia's rich oil fields. By 1944 American corporations controlled 42 percent of the proved oil reserves of the Middle East, a nineteenfold increase since 1936. In 1944, American companies, with Washington's encouragement, applied for an oil concession in Iran, then occupied by British and Soviet troops and used as a corridor for Lend-Lease shipments to the Soviet Union. This request touched off a three-cornered competition for influence in the heretofore British-dominated country. When Roosevelt promised in 1944 not to deprive the British of their traditional stakes in the Middle East, Churchill tartly thanked him "for your assurances about no sheeps' eyes at our oil fields in Iran and Iraq. Let me reciprocate by giving you fullest assurance that we have no thought of trying to horn in upon your interests or property in Saudi Arabia."[189]

Harry Hopkins (1890–1946).
A progressive reformer, the Iowa-born Hopkins became one of Franklin D. Roosevelt's most trusted New Deal administrators and advisers. During World War II, Roosevelt sent Hopkins on special missions and utilized his counsel at international conferences, including Yalta. When he traveled to Moscow for Truman in May 1945, Hopkins was suffering from the cancer that would cause his death within months. (Courtesy of FDR Library)

On a global scale, then, the Big Three jockeyed for power. "Spheres of influence do in fact exist," concluded Roosevelt's State Department in early 1945. "In view of the actual Eastern European sphere and the Western Hemispheric bloc (Act of Chapultepec), we are hardly in a position to frown upon . . . measures designed to strengthen the security of nations in other areas of the world."[190]

With Germany's surrender on May 8, 1945, the Third Reich collapsed in the rubble of bombed-out Berlin. President Harry S. Truman quickly ended Lend-Lease aid to the Soviet Union (he soon partially restarted it), thereby stirring up a hornet's nest in Moscow. With this issue and the Polish question troubling Soviet-American relations, the president sent Harry Hopkins to see Stalin in May, to "use diplomatic language or a baseball bat."[191] An irate Stalin warned Hopkins that the Americans had made "a fundamental mistake" in halting Lend-Lease "as pressure on the Russians in order to soften them up."[192] Hopkins expressed growing U.S. dismay about Stalin's apparent obstruction of the Yalta agreement on elections in Poland—a symbol of Soviet-American trust. Stalin would not permit the anti-Soviet London Poles (the most likely winners of an election) to govern postwar Poland, because Poland had twice "served as a corridor for German attacks. . . . It is therefore in Russia's vital interest that Poland should be both strong and friendly."[193] Ambassador Harriman also reported to Truman that Stalin wondered "why we should want to interfere with Soviet policy in a country like Poland, which he considers so important to the USSR's security, unless we have some ulterior motive."[194] Stalin did agree that a few ministries should go to non-Lublin Poles. He also assured Hopkins, as promised at Yalta, that the Soviet Union would enter the war against Japan and respect Jiang's government. Truman then noted in his diary: "I'm not afraid of Russia. . . . They've always been our friends and I can't see any reason why they shouldn't always be."[195]

The Potsdam Conference and the Legacy of the Second World War

As the war in Asia wound down and the occupation of Germany commenced, the Big Three gathered near Berlin for the Potsdam Conference (July 16–August 2, 1945). While Churchill "gave me a lot of hooey," Truman's first impression of his Soviet counterpart was favorable: "I can deal with Stalin. He is honest—but smart as hell."[196] That impression soon changed. Truman wrote his family that "you never saw such pigheaded people as are the Russians."[197] Harriman called the Russians "those barbarians."[198] Churchill took a liking to the new president, whom he described as a "man of exceptional character and ability with . . . simple and direct methods of speech, and a great deal of self-confidence and resolution."[199] Reports of the successful explosion of an atomic device in New Mexico had "tremendously pepped up" the president.[200]

By Potsdam, American intentions toward postwar Germany had moved a good distance from the Morgenthau Plan and JCS/1067. Reconstruction now became the watchword. U.S. officials saw Germany as a vital link in the economic recovery of Western Europe. When Germany came up for discussion, Truman thus resisted dismemberment and large reparations. The final Potsdam accord stated that Germany would be managed by military governors in four zones, treated as "a single economic unit," and permitted a standard of living higher than its low level of 1945.[201] Transportation, coal, agriculture, housing, and utilities industries were to be rehabilitated. As for reparations, desired by the Soviet Union for both revenge and the recovery of its hobbled economy, Stalin had to settle for an agreement that each occupying power would take reparations from its own zone and that the USSR would get some industrial equipment from the Western zones. In return, the Soviet Union would send food to the other three zones. The diplomat George F. Kennan described the reparations deal as "catch as catch can."[202]

When Churchill complained about the absence of free elections in Poland, Stalin mentioned the British domination of Greece. They did agree, however, to set the Oder-Neisse line as Poland's temporary western boundary, thereby granting Poland large chunks of German territory. The Soviet Union agreed to accept Italy as a member of the United Nations. The big powers also established the Council of Foreign Ministers to continue discussion on issues not resolved at Potsdam: peace treaties for the former German satellites; withdrawal of Allied troops from Iran; postwar control of the Dardanelles; internationalization of inland waterways; and disposition of Italian colonies. Stalin promised again to enter the war against Japan, but U.S. officials also learned that they possessed a new atomic weapon that might force Japan's surrender. Britain and the United States issued the "Potsdam Declaration," demanding Japan's unconditional surrender and threatening it with destruction.

The seemingly minor issue of waterways became for Truman a test of Soviet intentions. At Potsdam he pushed for an international authority to govern the 800-mile-long Danube River, which wound its way through several countries, including the Soviet Union, to the Black Sea. Essentially combining two traditional American principles—free navigation and the Open Door—the proposal antagonized Moscow, which countered with a commission limited to those states through which the river flowed. When Churchill backed Truman on the question, Molotov pressed: "If it was such a good rule why not apply it to the Suez?"[203] Churchill evaded the comparison, and the president simplistically concluded: Stalin's attitude on waterways showed "what he was after. . . . The Russians were planning world conquest."[204] For his part, Stalin interpreted London and Washington as wanting to "force us" to accept "their plans on questions affecting Europe and the world. Well, that's not going to happen."[205]

Potsdam, aptly code-named TERMINAL, left the world much as it had found it—divided and devastated. World War II ended on August 14, 1945, with Japan's surrender after Soviet intervention and two atomic bombs decimated Hiroshima and Nagasaki (see pages 222–228). But peace remained elusive because of the war's vast social, economic, and political dislocations in Europe and Asia. World War II claimed the lives of at least 55 million people—27 million of them in the USSR. Poland and Germany lost 6 million each; Yugoslavia suffered at least 1.6 million dead; Britain lost 400,000. The toll mounted in Asia, too: 15 million Chinese, 4 million Indonesians, 3 million Japanese, 1 million Vietnamese, 120,000 Filipinos, and more. A total of 405,395 Americans died fighting in the war. A generation of

Bombed-out French Town, 1944. Europe lay in ruins at the end of the war, and American help became essential to the reconstruction effort. (U.S. Office of War Information, National Archives)

young European people in their twenties and thirties virtually disappeared. Millions of displaced persons became separated from their homelands. Transportation systems, communications networks, and factories shut down. Cities entered the postwar era as rubble heaps, including the German city of Dresden, which Allied planes had punished in February 1945 in a merciless attack of questionable necessity. The firebombing of Tokyo killed 100,000. When General Dwight D. Eisenhower flew into the Soviet Union after V-E Day, he "did not see a house standing between the western borders of the country and the area around Moscow."[206] An unprecedented reconstruction task lay ahead.

With the imperial powers in disarray, their Asian colonies, encouraged by Japan during the waning days of the war, became rebellious. Without the necessary resources and manpower to curb the nationalist revolutions, the European empires began to crumble. The Dutch battled their Indonesian subjects; France fought the Vietnamese in Indochina; Britain reluctantly began its exit from Burma, India, and Ceylon (Sri Lanka).

The rise of the Soviet Union as a major international player counts as another legacy of World War II. The "greatest crime of Hitler," said Ambassador Harriman, was that his defeat opened parts of Europe to Soviet influence.[207] The Soviets resented any intimation that they should not have an influential voice in postwar questions. Reeling from heavy wartime losses, they asked for much and grabbed what they could before the war ended. "Whoever occupies a territory imposes on it his own social system," said Stalin. "It cannot be otherwise."[208]

The USSR rose, Britain declined, China floundered, and the United States galloped. The American economy, untouched by enemy bombers or marauding armies, moved in high gear at war's end. The U.S. gross national product jumped from $90.5 billion in 1939 to $211.9 billion in 1945. Observers spoke of an American "production miracle."[209] By the end of the war, in one historian's words, the United States had become "the global workshop and banker, umpire and policeman, preacher and teacher."[210]

Alone in a position to provide the capital and goods for recovery abroad, Washington felt flushed with power. "Instead of being looked upon as . . . an ordinary, common, American official," a Foreign Service Officer recalled, "people just practically fawned in front of us."[211] Imbibing lessons from the 1930s about the need to avoid Munichs, Americans looked forward to creating the stable world order that had eluded them between the two world wars. State Department official Dean Acheson observed that the "great difference in our second attempt . . . is the wide recognition that peace is possible only if countries work together and prosper together. That is why the economic aspects are no less important than the political aspects of the peace."[212] Through the war years the United States had constructed institutions—UNRRA, World Bank, International Monetary Fund, United Nations—to ensure that peace.

The war also wrought changes in the decisionmaking process in the United States. Agencies in the government handling national security matters ballooned in size. The defense establishment became more active in making diplomatic choices. In comparison, the State Department, so frequently bypassed by Roosevelt, slipped in power. The war spawned a large espionage establishment, beginning with the Office of Strategic Services (OSS) in 1942 and culminating in the Central Intelligence Agency (CIA) five years later. The president centralized decisionmaking in the White House, while Congress neglected its foreign-affairs prerogatives in the constitutional system and applauded bipartisanship. Another consequence of the war was an enlarged "military-industrial complex," a partnership between business executives eager for lucrative defense contracts and military brass eager for increased budgets. The recruitment of universities bequeathed a long-term legacy. Science professors had developed the atomic bomb at the Universities of Chicago and California, Berkeley. Princeton received grants for ballistics research. Postwar federal subsidies flowed to colleges for arms development, research on Soviet studies, and intelligence gathering.

"The world was fluid and about to be remade" in 1945, the journalist Theodore White remembered.[213] After the setbacks of depression and war, the historian Allan Nevins wrote, "the old self-confident America is coming into its stride again."[214] But it did so now as the world's strongest power.

FURTHER READING FOR THE PERIOD 1939–1945

Biographical studies include Rudy Abrahamson, *Spanning the Century* (1992) (Harriman); James M. Burns, *Roosevelt: The Soldier of Freedom* (1970); Kenneth R. Davis, *FDR* (1972–1993); Martin Gilbert, *Winston S. Churchill* (1983); Waldo H. Heinrichs, *American Ambassador* (1966) (Grew); Warren F. Kimball, *The Juggler*

(1991) (FDR); Joseph P. Lash, *Roosevelt and Churchill, 1939–1941* (1976); George McJimsey, *Harry Hopkins* (1987); Forrest C. Pogue, *George C. Marshall* (1963–1987); Mark A. Stoler, *George Marshall* (1989); and works cited in Chapters 4 and 5.

FDR's health is the subject of Kenneth R. Crispell and Carlos F. Gomez, *Hidden Illness in the White House* (1988); Robert H. Ferrell, *The Dying President* (1998) and *Ill-Advised* (1992); and Bert E. Park, *The Impact of Illness on World Leaders* (1986).

For the United States and Europe, 1939–1941, and debates at home, see Patrick Abbazia, *Mr. Roosevelt's Navy* (1975); Mark Chadwin, *The Hawks of World War II* (1968); J. Garry Clifford and Samuel R. Spencer, Jr., *The First Peacetime Draft* (1986); Wayne S. Cole, *America First* (1953) and *Roosevelt and the Isolationists* (1983); James V. Compton, *The Swastika and the Eagle* (1967); Robert A. Divine, *The Reluctant Belligerent* (1979); Justus Doenecke, *The Battle Against Intervention* (1997); Silvo Hietanen, ed., *The Road to War* (1993); Travis B. Jacobs, *America and the Winter War, 1939–1940* (1981); Manfred Jonas, *The United States and Germany* (1984); Warren F. Kimball, *The Most Unsordid Act* (1969) (Lend-Lease); James R. Leutze, *Bargaining for Supremacy: Anglo-American Naval Collaboration* (1977); Mark A. Lowenthal, *Leadership and Indecision: American War Planning and Policy Process, 1937–1942* (1988); Arnold A. Offner, *The Origins of the Second World War* (1975); David L. Porter, *The Seventy-Sixth Congress and World War II, 1939–1940* (1979); Anthony Read and David Fisher, *The Deadly Embrace* (1989) (Nazi-Soviet Pact); David Reynolds, *The Creation of the Anglo-American Alliance, 1937–1941* (1982); James C. Schneider, *Should America Go to War?* (1989); Kevin Smith, *Conflict over Convoys* (1996) (U.S.-Britain); D. C. Watt, *How War Came* (1989); and Theodore A. Wilson, *The First Summit* (1991).

For the advent of war with Japan, see the books by Borg and Okamoto, Burns and Bennett, Feis, and Neu cited in Chapter 5; Michael A. Barnhart, *Japan Prepares for Total War* (1987); Robert J. C. Butow, *Tojo and the Coming of the War* (1961) and *The John Doe Associates* (1974); Hilary Conroy and Harry Wray, eds., *Pearl Harbor Reexamined* (1990); Ladislas Farago, *The Broken Seal* (1967) (MAGIC); Akira Iriye, *The Origins of the Second World War in Asia and the Pacific* (1987); Walter LaFeber, *The Clash* (1997); Robert W. Love, Jr., ed., *Pearl Harbor Revisited* (1994); Peter Lowe, *Great Britain and the Origins of the Pacific War* (1977); Martin V. Melosi, *The Shadow of Pearl Harbor* (1977); Samuel Eliot Morison, *The Rising Sun in the Pacific* (1973); James Morley, ed., *The Fateful Choice: Japan's Advance into Southeast Asia, 1939–1941* (1980), ed., *The Final Confrontation* (1994), and, ed., *Japan's Road to the Pacific War: Japan's Negotiations with the United States, 1941* (1994); Gordon W. Prange, *At Dawn We Slept* (1981) and *Pearl Harbor* (1986); Paul W. Schroeder, *The Axis Alliance and Japanese-American Relations, 1941* (1958); Youli Sun, *China and the Origins of the Pacific War* (1993); Jonathan Utley, *Going to War with Japan* (1984); and Roberta Wohlstetter, *Pearl Harbor* (1962).

Allied relations and postwar planning are explored in Michael C. C. Adams, *The Best War Ever* (1993); Alan H. Bath, *Tracking the Axis Enemy* (1998); Robert Beitzell, *The Uneasy Alliance* (1972); Edward M. Bennett, *Franklin D. Roosevelt and the Search for Victory* (1990); Douglas Brinkley and David Facey-Crowther, eds., *The Atlantic Charter* (1994); Susan A. Brewer, *To Win the Peace* (1997); A. Russell Buchanan, *The United States and World War II* (1964); Mark J. Conversino, *Fighting with the Soviets* (1997); R. D. Cuff and J. L. Granatstein, *Canadian-American Relations in Wartime* (1975); Robert Dallek, *Franklin D. Roosevelt and American Foreign Policy* (1979); Robert A. Divine, *Second Chance* (1967) and *Roosevelt and World War II* (1969); Alan P. Dobson, *U.S. Wartime Aid to Britain* (1986); Robin Edmonds, *The Big Three* (1991); Lloyd C. Gardner, *Spheres of Influence* (1993); George C. Herring, Jr., *Aid to Russia, 1941–1946* (1973); Gary R. Hess, *The United States at War, 1941–1945* (1986); Gregory Hooks, *Forging the Military-Industrial Complex* (1990); Barry M. Katz, *Foreign Intelligence* (1989); Helen Keyssar and Vladimir Posner, eds., *Remembering War* (1990) (USSR); Warren F. Kimball, ed., *America Unbound* (1992); Gabriel Kolko, *The Politics of War* (1968); Eric Larrabee, *Commander in Chief* (1987); Ralph Levering, *American Opinion and the Russian Alliance* (1976); David MacIsaacs, *Strategic Bombing in World War Two* (1976); Vojtech Mastny, *Russia's Road to the Cold War* (1979); Steven M. Miner, *Between Churchill and Stalin* (1988); Samuel Eliot Morison, *Strategy and Compromise* (1958); J. Robert Moskin, *Mr. Truman's War* (1996) (end of World War II); William O'Neill, *A Democracy at War* (1993); R. C. Raack, *Stalin's Drive to the West, 1938–1945* (1995); David Reynolds et al., eds., *Allies at War* (1994) and *Rich Relations: The American Occupation of Britain* (1995); Ronald Schaffer, *Wings of Judgment* (1985) (U.S. bombing);

Michael S. Sherry, *Preparing for the Next War* (1977); Bradley F. Smith, *Sharing Secrets with Stalin: How the Allies Traded Intelligence* (1996); Gaddis Smith, *American Diplomacy During the Second World War* (1985); Mark A. Stoler, *The Politics of the Second Front* (1977); Dwight W. Tuttle, *Harry L. Hopkins and Anglo-American-Soviet Relations, 1941–1945* (1983); Piotr S. Wandycz, *The United States and Poland* (1980); Gerhard L. Weinberg, *A World at Arms* (1994); Steve Weiss, *Allies in Conflict* (1996); Randall B. Woods, *A Changing of the Guard* (1990) (U.S.-Britain); and Llewellyn Woodward, *British Foreign Policy in the Second World War* (1970–1971).

For the Churchill-Roosevelt relationship and assessments of Churchill, see John Charmley, *Churchill's Grand Alliance* (1995); Martin Gilbert, *Winston S. Churchill* (1983–1986); Warren F. Kimball, *Forged in War* (1997); and Keith Sainsbury, *Churchill and Roosevelt at War* (1994).

Big Three summit meetings are treated in Russell O. Buhite, *Decisions at Yalta* (1986); Diane Shaver Clemens, *Yalta* (1970); Keith Eubank, *Summit at Teheran* (1985); Herbert Feis, *Between War and Peace* (1960) (Potsdam); Keith Sainsbury, *The Turning Point* (1985) (Cairo and Teheran); and John L. Snell, ed., *The Meaning of Yalta* (1956).

For the creation of new international organizations, see Thomas Campbell, *Masquerade Peace* (1973) (UN); Robert C. Hilderbrand, *Dumbarton Oaks* (1990); Townsend Hoopes and Douglas Brinkley, *FDR and the Creation of the U.N.* (1997); and Greg Schild, *Bretton Woods and Dumbarton Oaks* (1995).

Propaganda and the mobilizing of public opinion in the era of World War II are studied in Nicholas Cull, *Selling War* (1995) (British propaganda in the United States); Clayton Koppes and Gregory Black, *Hollywood Goes to War* (1987); Clayton Laurie, *The Propaganda Warriors* (1996); George H. Roeder, Jr., *The Censored War* (1993); Holly C. Shulman, *The Voice of America* (1991); and Richard Steele, *Propaganda in an Open Society* (1985).

For the Pacific theater, China, and decolonization, see Wesley M. Bagby, *The Eagle-Dragon Alliance* (1992); David D. Barrett, *Dixie Mission* (1970); Günter Bischof and Robert Dupont, eds., *The Pacific War Revisited* (1997); Russell D. Buhite, *Patrick J. Hurley and American Foreign Policy* (1973); Warren I. Cohen, *America's Response to China* (1990); John W. Dower, *War Without Mercy* (1986); Suburō Ienaga, *The Pacific War* (1978); Akira Iriye, *Power and Culture* (1981); E. J. Kahn, Jr., *The China Hands* (1975); Xiaoyuan Liu, *A Partnership for Disorder* (1996) (China); William R. Louis, *Imperialism at Bay* (1978) (decolonization); Michael Schaller, *The U.S. Crusade in China, 1938–1945* (1978); John J. Sbrega, *Anglo-American Relations and Colonialism in East Asia* (1983); Michael M. Sheng, *Battling Western Imperialism* (1997); Leon V. Sigal, *Fighting to the Finish: The Politics of War Termination in the United States and Japan, 1945* (1988); Ronald H. Spector, *Eagle Against the Sun* (1984); Christopher Thorne, *Allies of a Kind* (1977) and *The Issue of War* (1985); Barbara Tuchman, *Stilwell and the American Experience in China, 1911–1945* (1971); and Odd Arne Westad, *Cold War and Revolution* (1993) (China).

For wartime relations with Latin America, see works cited in Chapter 5; Michael J. Francis, *The Limits of Hegemony* (1977) (Argentina and Chile); Michael Grow, *The Good Neighbor Policy and Authoritarianism in Paraguay* (1981); Stanley Hilton, *Hilter's Secret War in South America, 1939–1945* (1981); Frank D. McCann, Jr., *The Brazilian-American Alliance, 1937–1945* (1973); Stephen R. Niblo, *War, Diplomacy, and Development* (1995) (Mexico); María Emilia Paz, *Strategy, Security, and Spies* (1997) (Mexico); David Rock, ed., *Latin America in the 1940s* (1994); and Randall B. Woods, *The Roosevelt Foreign Policy Establishment and the "Good Neighbor"* (1980) (Argentina).

For U.S. interest in the Middle East and oil, consult Irvine H. Anderson, *Aramco, the United States, and Saudi Arabia* (1981); Philip J. Baram, *The Department of State in the Middle East, 1919–1945* (1978); Aaron D. Miller, *Search for Security* (1980) (Saudi Arabia); and Michael B. Stoff, *Oil, War, and American Security* (1980).

The Holocaust and refugee problem are recounted in Robert H. Abzug, *Inside the Vicious Heart* (1985); Yehuda Bauer, *Jews for Sale?* (1994); Richard Breitman and Alan M. Kraut, *American Refugee Policy and European Jewry* (1987); Richard Breitman, *Official Secrets* (1998); Christopher Browning, *The Path to Genocide* (1992); Leonard Dinnerstein, *America and the Survivors of the Holocaust* (1982); Henry L. Feingold, *Bearing Witness* (1995) and *Politics of Rescue* (1970); Martin Gilbert, *Auschwitz and the Allies* (1981); Walter Laqueur, *The Terrible Secret* (1980); Deborah E. Lipstadt, *Beyond Belief* (1993); Arthur D. Morse, *While Six Million Died* (1968); William E. Nawyn, *American Protestantism's Response to Germany's Jews and Refugees* (1982); Verne

Newton, ed., *FDR and the Holocaust* (1995); Arnold Offner, *American Appeasement* (1964); Monty N. Penkower, *The Jews Were Expendable* (1983); and David Wyman, *The Abandonment of the Jews* (1984), *Paper Walls* (1968), and ed., *The World Reacts to the Holocaust* (1996).

See also the General Bibliography and the following notes.

For comprehensive coverage of foreign-relations topics, see the articles in the four-volume *Encyclopedia of U.S. Foreign Relations* (1997), edited by Bruce W. Jentleson and Thomas G. Paterson.

NOTES TO CHAPTER 6

1. Quoted in Theodore A. Wilson, *The First Summit* (Lawrence: University Press of Kansas, 1991), p. 98.
2. FDR quoted in Warren F. Kimball, *Forged in War* (New York: Morrow, 1997), p. 98.
3. Elliott Roosevelt, *As He Saw It* (New York: Duell, Sloan, and Pearce, 1946), p. 33.
4. Winston S. Churchill, *The Grand Alliance* (Boston: Houghton Mifflin, 1950), p. 431.
5. Quoted in Robert E. Sherwood, *Roosevelt and Hopkins* (New York: Harper & Brothers, 1948), p. 236.
6. Harold Nicolson, *Diaries and Letters* (New York: Atheneum, 1966–1968; 3 vols.), II, 385.
7. Churchill quoted in David Reynolds, "Churchill, Roosevelt, and the Wartime Anglo-American Alliance, 1939–1945," in William Roger Louis and Hedley Bull, eds., *The "Special Relationship"* (New York: Oxford University Press, 1986), p. 40.
8. David Reynolds, *Rich Relations* (New York: Random House, 1995), p. 438.
9. Quoted in David Reynolds and David Dimbleby, *An Ocean Apart* (New York: Vintage, 1989), p. 151.
10. Quoted in Forrest C. Pogue, *George C. Marshall* (New York: Viking, 1963–1987; 4 vols.), II, 46.
11. David Reynolds, *The Creation of the Anglo-American Alliance, 1937–1941* (Chapel Hill: University of North Carolina Press, 1981), p. 195.
12. Quoted in Raymond Esthus, "President Roosevelt's Commitment to Britain to Intervene in a Pacific War," *Mississippi Valley Historical Review, L* (June 1963), 31.
13. Cordell Hull, *Memoirs* (New York: Macmillan, 1948; 2 vols.), II, 975–976.
14. *Foreign Relations, 1941* (Washington, D.C.: Government Printing Office, 1958), I, 368–369.
15. James MacGregor Burns, *Roosevelt: The Soldier of Freedom* (New York: Harcourt Brace Jovanovich, 1970), p. 550.
16. Quoted in Holly C. Shulman, *The Voice of America* (Madison: University of Wisconsin Press, 1990), p. 72.
17. *Foreign Relations, 1941*, I, 378.
18. Quoted in William H. McNeill, *America, Britain, & Russia* (London: Oxford University Press, 1953), p. 41.
19. Quoted in Lloyd C. Gardner, *Spheres of Influence* (Chicago: Ivan R. Dee, 1993), p. 241.
20. Quoted in Burns, *Soldier*, p. 609.
21. Mark A. Lowenthal, *Leadership and Indecision* (New York: Garland, 1988), p. 633.
22. Ian Jacob quoted in Martin Gilbert, *Winston S. Churchill* (Boston: Houghton Mifflin, 1983), p. 1161.
23. Quoted in Wilson, *First Summit*, p. 182.
24. Quoted in J. Garry Clifford, "Juggling Balls of Dynamite," *Diplomatic History, XVII* (Fall 1993), 636.
25. Anthony Eden, *The Reckoning* (Boston: Houghton Mifflin, 1965), p. 433.
26. Samuel I. Rosenman, ed., *Public Papers . . . of Franklin D. Roosevelt, 1939* (New York: Macmillan, 1938–1950; 13 vols.), VIII, 463.
27. Charles Tobey to James Richardson, September 28, 1939, Tobey Papers, Dartmouth College Library, Hanover, N.H.
28. Quoted in John M. Blum, *From the Morgenthau Diaries: Years of Urgency* (Boston: Houghton Mifflin, 1965), p. 91.
29. Quoted in B. Mitchell Simpson, *Admiral Harold R. Stark* (Columbia: University of South Carolina Press, 1989), p. 99.
30. Rosenman, *Public Papers, 1940, IX,* 263.
31. *Ibid.*, 391.
32. FDR quoted in Robert A. Divine, *Foreign Policy and U.S. Presidential Elections, 1940–1948* (New York: New Viewpoints, 1974), pp. 82–83.
33. Warren F. Kimball, ed., *Churchill & Roosevelt* (Princeton: Princeton University Press, 1984; 3 vols.), I, 108.
34. Rosenman, *Public Papers, 1940, IX,* 607.
35. *Ibid.*, pp. 640–643.
36. Quoted in George C. Herring, Jr., *Aid to Russia, 1941–1946* (New York: Columbia University Press, 1973), p. 4.
37. Quoted in Nicholas Cull, *Selling War* (New York: Oxford University Press, 1995), p. 75.
38. Glen Jeansome, *Women of the Far Right* (Chicago: University of Chicago Press, 1996), pp. 7–9.
39. Quoted in Warren F. Kimball, *The Most Unsordid Act* (Baltimore: Johns Hopkins University Press, 1969), p. 153.
40. *Congressional Record, LXXVII* (March 8, 1941), 2097.
41. Breckinridge Long Diary, May 12, 1941, Long Papers, Library of Congress, Washington, D.C.
42. Claude Wickard Diary, May 2, 1941, Wickard Papers, Franklin D. Roosevelt Library, Hyde Park, N.Y.
43. Quoted in Calvin L. Christman, "Franklin D. Roosevelt and the Craft of Strategic Assessment," in Williamson Murray and Allen R. Millett, eds., *Calculations* (New York: Free Press, 1992), p. 256.
44. Quoted in Blum, *Morgenthau Diaries*, p. 264.
45. August 19, 1941, CAB 65/19, War Cabinet Records 84, Public Record Office, London.
46. Rosenman, *Public Papers, 1941, X,* 438, 439.
47. Quoted in Wayne S. Cole, *America First* (Madison: University of Wisconsin Press, 1953), p. 163.
48. FDR quoted in Joseph Lash Diary, February 5, 1940, Joseph Lash Papers, Roosevelt Library.

49. Quoted in Reynolds, *Rich Relations*, p. 11.

50. James C. Schneider, *Should America Go to War?* (Chapel Hill: University of North Carolina Press, 1989), p. 219.

51. Josiah Bailey to I. M. Meekins, September 6, 1941, Bailey Papers, Duke University Library, Durham, N.C.

52. Quoted in Edward M. Bennett, "Joseph C. Grew," in Richard Dean Burns and Edward M. Bennett, eds., *Diplomats in Crisis* (Santa Barbara: ABC-CLIO, 1974), p. 78.

53. Harold L. Ickes, *The Secret Diary of Harold L. Ickes* (New York: Simon & Schuster, 1953; 3 vols.), III, 567.

54. Quoted in Charles E. Neu, *The Troubled Encounter* (New York: Wiley, 1975), p. 168.

55. *Foreign Relations, 1940* (Washington, D.C.: Government Printing Office, 1955), IV, 602.

56. Quoted in Christopher Thorne, *The Issue of War* (New York: Oxford University Press, 1985), p. 22; Jonathan Marshall, *To Have and Have Not* (Berkeley: University of California Press, 1995), p. 251.

57. Quoted in Herbert Feis, *The Road to Pearl Harbor* (New York: Atheneum, 1967), p. 206.

58. Jonathan Utley, *Going to War with Japan, 1937–1941* (Knoxville: University of Tennessee Press, 1984), p. 156.

59. Ickes, *Secret Diary, III*, 346.

60. Quoted in James C. Thomson, Jr., "The Role of the Department of State," in Dorothy Borg and Shumpei Okamoto, eds., *Pearl Harbor as History* (New York: Columbia University Press, 1973), p. 101.

61. Quoted in Kimball, *Forged in War*, p. 118.

62. Quoted in Walter LaFeber, *The Clash* (New York: Norton, 1997), p. 208.

63. Japanese Liaison Conference quoted in Scott D. Sagan, "The Origins of the Pacific War," *Journal of Interdisciplinary History, XVIII* (Spring 1988), 912.

64. Quoted in James W. Morley, ed., *The Final Confrontation* (New York: Columbia University Press, 1994), p. 332.

65. Quoted in Thorne, *Issue of War*, p. 10.

66. Youli Sun, *China and the Origins of the Pacific War* (New York: St. Martin's Press, 1993), p. 155.

67. Charles Tansill, *Back Door to War* (Chicago: Regnery, 1952).

68. Quoted in Carl Boyd, *Hitler's Japanese Confidant* (Lawrence: University Press of Kansas, 1993), p. 36.

69. Roberta Wohlstetter, *Pearl Harbor* (Stanford: Stanford University Press, 1962), p. 387.

70. Rosenman, *Public Papers, 1941, X*, 514.

71. Arthur H. Vandenberg, Jr., ed., *The Private Papers of Senator Vandenberg* (Boston: Houghton Mifflin, 1952), p. 1.

72. *Time* quoted in George H. Roeder, Jr., *The Censored War* (New Haven: Yale University Press, 1993), p. 153.

73. Samuel E. Morison, *Strategy and Compromise* (Boston: Little, Brown, 1958), p. 25.

74. Quoted in Roeder, *Censored War*, p. 129.

75. Quoted in Geoffrey Perrett, *Days of Sadness, Years of Triumph* (Baltimore: Penguin, 1973), p. 197.

76. Quoted in Warren F. Kimball, "Churchill and Roosevelt," *Prologue, VI* (Fall 1971), 181.

77. Quoted in Brenda Gayle Plummer, *Rising Wind* (Chapel Hill: University of North Carolina Press, 1996), p. 114.

78. Quoted in Warren F. Kimball, *The Juggler* (Princeton: Princeton University Press, 1991), p. 136.

79. Eden, *Reckoning*, pp. 336–337.

80. Quoted in Steven M. Miner, *Between Churchill and Stalin* (Chapel Hill: University of North Carolina Press, 1988), p. 217.

81. Quoted in Oleg Rzheshevsky, ed., *War and Diplomacy: Documents from Stalin's Archives* (Amsterdam, Neth.: Harwood, 1996), p. 120.

82. Quoted in Herbert Feis, *Churchill, Roosevelt, Stalin* (Princeton: Princeton University Press, 1957), p. 42.

83. Quoted in Harry C. Butcher, *My Three Years with Eisenhower* (New York: Simon & Schuster, 1946), p. 29.

84. Quoted in Kimball, *Forged in War*, p. 130.

85. Quoted in Mark A. Stoler, *George Marshall* (Boston: Twayne, 1989), p. 106.

86. *Correspondence Between the Chairman . . . U.S.S.R. and the Presidents of the U.S.A. and the Prime Ministers of Great Britain* (Moscow: Foreign Languages Publishing House, 1957; 2 vols.), II, 70–71.

87. Quoted in Robert Beitzell, *The Uneasy Alliance* (New York: Knopf, 1972), p. 159.

88. D. C. Watt, *Succeeding John Bull* (Cambridge, Eng.: Cambridge University Press, 1984), p. 101; Winston S. Churchill, *The Hinge of Fate* (Boston: Houghton Mifflin, 1950), p. 759.

89. Quoted in Raymond G. O'Connor, *Diplomacy for Victory* (New York: Norton, 1971), p. 52.

90. Maxim Litvinov quoted in John Lewis Gaddis, *We Now Know* (New York: Oxford University Press, 1997), p. 15.

91. Memorandum of Conversation with Cordell Hull, November 30, 1943, "Black Notebooks," Box 1, Arthur Krock Papers, Princeton University Library, Princeton, N.J.

92. Hull, *Memoirs, II*, 1297.

93. Keith Sainsbury, *The Turning Point* (New York: Oxford University Press, 1985), p. 307.

94. Quoted in Keith Eubank, *Summit at Teheran* (New York: Morrow, 1985), p. 248.

95. Henry H. Arnold, *Global Mission* (New York: Harper & Brothers, 1949), p. 465.

96. Quoted in Mark A. Stoler, *The Politics of the Second Front* (Westport, Conn.: Greenwood Press, 1977), p. 149.

97. Churchill, *Hinge of Fate*, p. 374.

98. Quoted in David Reynolds, "The Erosion of British Influence," in Charles Brower, ed., *World War II in Europe: The Final Year* (New York: St. Martin's Press, 1998), p. 40.

99. Quoted in Robert Dallek, *Franklin D. Roosevelt and American Foreign Policy* (New York: Oxford University Press, 1979), p. 435.

100. *Foreign Relations, Cairo and Teheran* (Washington, D.C.: Government Printing Office, 1961) pp. 594–595.

101. Churchill quoted in Sainsbury, *Turning Point*, p. 300.

102. Kevin Smith, *Conflict over Convoys* (Cambridge, Eng.: Cambridge University Press, 1996), p. 239.

103. Quoted in Burns, *Soldier*, p. 411.

104. Rosenman, *Public Papers, 1943, XII*, 558.

105. Churchill, *Hinge of Fate*, p. 133.

106. Nevile Butler quoted in LaFeber, *The Clash*, p. 231.

107. Quoted in Jonathan Spence, *To Change China* (Boston: Little, Brown, 1969), p. 236; Christopher Thorne, "Indochina and Anglo-American Relations, 1942–1945," *Pacific Historical Review, XLIV* (February 1976), 76.

108. Theodore White quoted in LaFeber, *The Clash*, p. 232.

109. Theodore H. White, ed., *The Stilwell Papers* (New York: William Sloane Associates, 1948), p. 157.

110. Quoted in Robert P. Newman, *Owen Lattimore and the "Loss" of China* (Berkeley: University of California Press, 1992), p. 70.

111. Quoted in Sainsbury, *Turning Point*, p. 156.

112. Quoted in Herbert Feis, *The China Tangle* (Princeton: Princeton University Press, 1953), p. 51.

113. Quoted in T. Christopher Jesperson, *American Images of China, 1931–1949* (Stanford: Stanford University Press, 1996), p. 94.

114. Quoted in Akira Iriye, "Japan Against the ABCD Powers," in Akira Iriye and Warren Cohen, eds., *American, Chinese, and Japanese Perspectives on Wartime Asia, 1931–1949* (Wilmington, Del.: Scholarly Resources, 1989), p. 233.

115. Quoted in Maochun Yu, *OSS in China* (New Haven: Yale University Press, 1996), p. 66.

116. Quoted in Martha Byrd, *Chennault* (Tuscaloosa: University of Alabama Press, 1987), p. 174.

117. White, *Stilwell Papers*, p. 333.

118. Mao quoted in Michael H. Hunt, *The Genesis of Chinese Communist Foreign Policy* (New York: Columbia University Press, 1996), p. 154.

119. *Foreign Relations, 1944* (Washington, D.C.: Government Printing Office, 1967), *VI*, 631–632.

120. David D. Barrett, *Dixie Mission* (Berkeley: University of California, 1970), p. 56.

121. Quoted in Michael M. Sheng, *Battling Western Imperialism* (Princeton: Princeton University Press, 1997), p. 94.

122. Quoted in Feis, *China Tangle*, p. 213.

123. Quoted in Russell D. Buhite, *Patrick J. Hurley and American Foreign Policy* (Ithaca: Cornell University Press, 1973), p. 152.

124. Quoted in Carolle J. Carter, *Mission to Yenan* (Lexington: University Press of Kentucky), p. 147.

125. Pyotr Vladimirov quoted in Wesley M. Bagby, *The Eagle-Dragon Alliance* (Newark: University of Delaware Press, 1992), p. 122.

126. Hunt, *Genesis*, p. 156.

127. Quoted in Feis, *China Tangle*, p. 269.

128. Burns, *Soldier*, p. 545.

129. Quoted in Moshe Gottlieb, "The Berlin Riots and Their Repercussions in America," *American Jewish Historical Quarterly, LIX* (March 1970), 306.

130. Quoted in Cyrus Adler and Aaron M. Margalith, *With Firmness in the Right* (New York: American Jewish Committee, 1946), p. 381.

131. Quoted in Saul S. Friedman, *No Haven for the Oppressed* (Detroit: Wayne State University Press, 1973), p. 21.

132. Quoted in Jesse H. Stiller, *George S. Messersmith* (Chapel Hill: University of North Carolina Press, 1987), p. 123.

133. Arnold A. Offner, *American Appeasement* (New York: Norton, 1976 [c. 1969]), p. 92.

134. Richard Breitman quoted in Verne Newton, ed., *FDR and the Holocaust* (New York: St. Martin's Press, 1996), p. 14.

135. Quoted in Henry L. Feingold, *Politics of Rescue* (New Brunswick, N.J.: Rutgers University Press, 1970), p. 19.

136. Quoted in Friedman, *No Haven*, p. 83.

137. Quoted in David Wyman, *Paper Walls* (Amherst: University of Massachusetts Press, 1968), p. 97.

138. Quoted in A. J. Sherman, *Island Refuge* (Berkeley: University of California Press, 1973), p. 207.

139. Quoted in Henry L. Feingold, "Courage First and Intelligence Second: The American Secular Jewish Elite, Roosevelt, and the Failure to Rescue," in Michael Marrus, ed., *The Nazi Holocaust: Bystanders to the Holocaust* (Westport, Conn.: Meckler, 1989; 9 vols.) *II*, 781.

140. Richard H. Levy, "The Bombing of Auschwitz Revisited," in Newton, *FDR and the Holocaust*, p. 262.

141. Yehuda Bauer, *Jews for Sale?* (New Haven: Yale University Press, 1994), p. 254.

142. Quoted in Arthur D. Morse, *While Six Million Died* (New York: Random House, 1968), p. 63.

143. Quoted *ibid.*, pp. 93, 95.

144. Quoted in David Wyman, "The United States," in Wyman, ed., *The World Reacts to the Holocaust* (Baltimore: Johns Hopkins University Press, 1996), p. 707.

145. Henry L. Feingold, *Bearing Witness* (Syracuse: Syracuse University Press, 1995), p. 8.

146. Henry Bruenn quoted in Keith W. Olson, "Franklin D. Roosevelt, the Ghost of Woodrow Wilson, and World War II," in Silvo Hietanen, ed., *The Road to War* (Tampere, Finland: University of Tampere, 1993), p. 62.

147. Quoted in George Woodbridge et al., *The History of the United Nations Relief and Rehabilitation Administration* (New York: Columbia University Press, 1950), *I*, 4.

148. *Treaties and Other International Acts* (Washington, D.C.: Government Printing Office, 1946), series 1501–1502.

149. Congresswoman Jesse Sumner quoted in Randall B. Woods, *A Changing of the Guard* (Chapel Hill: University of North Carolina Press, 1990), pp. 236–237.

150. *Manchester Guardian* quoted in Richard N. Gardner, *Sterling-Dollar Diplomacy* (New York: McGraw-Hill, 1969; rev. ed.), p. 267.

151. Quoted in Diane Shaver Clemens, *Yalta* (New York: Oxford University Press, 1970), p. 48.

152. Robert C. Hilderbrand, *Dumbarton Oaks* (Chapel Hill: University of North Carolina Press, 1990), p. 246.

153. *New Republic* quoted in Townsend Hoopes and Douglas Brinkley, *FDR and the Creation of the U.N.* (New Haven: Yale University Press, 1997), p. 161.

154. Quoted in Gabriel Kolko, *The Politics of War* (New York: Random House, 1968), pp. 270–271.

155. Quoted in Carol Anderson, "From Hope to Disillusion," *Diplomatic History, XX* (Fall 1996), 535, 536.

156. Walter Lippmann quoted in Robert A. Divine, *Second Chance* (New York: Atheneum, 1967), p. 291.

157. Quoted *ibid.*, p. 297.

158. John J. McCloy quoted in Kolko, *Politics of War*, p. 470.

159. Arnold Wolfers, *United States Policy Toward Germany* (New Haven: Yale Institute of International Studies, 1947), p. 3.

160. *Foreign Relations, Conference at Quebec, 1944* (Washington, D.C.: Government Printing Office, 1972), p. 467.

161. Henry L. Stimson to the president, September 15, 1944, Box 100, James Forrestal Papers, Princeton University Library.

162. Notebooks, Interview with Harry S. Truman, November 12, 1949, Box 85, Jonathan Daniels Papers, University of North Carolina Library, Chapel Hill.

163. Quoted in Robert L. Benson and Michael Warner, eds., *Venona* (Laguna Hills Calif.: Aegean Park Press, 1996), p. 423.

164. Clemens, *Yalta*, p. 287.

165. *Correspondence Between the Chairman, I,* 295.

166. Quoted in Alexander DeConde, *Ethnicity, Race, and American Foreign Policy* (Boston: Northeastern University Press, 1992), p. 123; Pyle quoted in Gerald Linderman, *The World Within War* (New York: Free Press, 1997), p. 169.

167. Edgar Jones quoted in John W. Dower, *War Without Mercy* (New York: Pantheon, 1986), p. 64.

168. General Holland Smith quoted in Ronald H. Spector, "Fourth Dimension of Strategy," in Günter Bischof and Robert L. Dupont, eds., *The Pacific War Revisited* (Baton Rouge: Louisiana State University Press, 1997), pp. 46–47.

169. Quoted in Martin Gilbert, *Winston S. Churchill: Road to Victory, 1941–1945* (Boston: Houghton Mifflin, 1986), p. 1208.

170. Churchill, *Triumph and Tragedy*, p. 366.

171. *Foreign Relations, Yalta* (Washington, D.C.: Government Printing Office, 1955), p. 973.

172. Quoted in Gardner, *Spheres,* p. 236.

173. Quoted in William L. O'Neill, *A Democracy at War* (New York: Free Press, 1993), p. 196.

174. Stalin quoted in Vojtech Mastny, *The Cold War and Soviet Insecurity* (New York: Oxford University Press, 1996), p. 22.

175. Quoted in Sherwood, *Roosevelt and Hopkins,* p. 870.

176. Quoted in Reynolds, "Erosion," p. 51.

177. Churchill, *Triumph and Tragedy,* p. 402.

178. Gardner, *Spheres,* p. xiii.

179. Quoted in Kolko, *Politics of War,* p. 465.

180. Churchill, *Triumph and Tragedy,* pp. 227–228.

181. Quoted in Robin Edmonds, *The Big Three* (New York: Norton, 1991), p. 419.

182. Stalin quoted in Mastny, *Soviet Insecurity,* p. 20.

183. Quoted in Mark J. Conversino, *Fighting with the Soviets* (Lawrence: University Press of Kansas, 1997), pp. 136–137.

184. Quoted in Rudy Abrahamson, *Spanning the Century* (New York: Morrow, 1992), p. 383.

185. Quoted in Richard L. Walker, *E. R. Stettinius, Jr.* (New York: Cooper Square Publishers, 1965), p. 333.

186. Quoted in John A. English, "Not an Equal Triangle," in B. J. C. McKercher and Lawrence Aronson, eds., *The North Atlantic Triangle in a Changing World* (Toronto: University of Toronto Press, 1996), p. 174.

187. Quoted in Mark A. Stoler, "Strategy, Grand and Otherwise," in Brower, *World War II,* pp. 58–59; Susan A. Brewer, *To Win the Peace* (Ithaca: Cornell University Press, 1997), pp. 170, 198.

188. Quoted in Kimball, *Forged in War,* p. 134.

189. *Foreign Relations, 1944* (Washington, D.C.: Government Printing Office, 1965), III, 103.

190. Quoted in Kolko, *Politics of War,* p. 482.

191. Harry S. Truman, *Memoirs* (Garden City, N.Y.: Doubleday, 1955–1956; 2 vols.), I, 258.

192. *Foreign Relations, Berlin* (Washington, D.C.: Government Printing Office, 1960; 2 vols.), I, 33.

193. *Ibid., I,* 39.

194. *Ibid., I,* 61.

195. Quoted in James L. Gormly, *From Potsdam to the Cold War* (Wilmington, Del.: Scholarly Resources, 1990), p. 21.

196. Quoted in Robert H. Ferrell, ed., *Off the Record* (New York: Harper and Row, 1980), p. 53.

197. Truman, *Memoirs, I,* 402.

198. Journal, August 1, 1945, Box 19, and Memorandum of Conversation with Harriman, July 17, 1945, Box 18, Joseph Davies Papers, Library of Congress.

199. "Note of the Prime Minister's Conversation with President Truman at Luncheon, July 18, 1945," Prem. 3, Prime Minister's Office Records, Public Record Office.

200. Quoted in Robert L. Messer, "World War II and the Coming of the Cold War," in John M. Carroll and George C. Herring, eds., *Modern American Diplomacy* (Wilmington, Del.: Scholarly Resources, 1986), p. 121.

201. *The Tehran, Yalta & Potsdam Conferences: Documents* (Moscow: Progress Publishers, 1969), p. 323.

202. George F. Kennan, *Memoirs, 1925–1950* (Boston: Little, Brown, 1967), p. 260.

203. *Foreign Relations, Berlin,* II, 365.

204. Truman, *Memoirs, I,* 412.

205. Stalin quoted in Andrei Gromyko, *Memoirs* (New York: Doubleday, 1989), p. 110.

206. Quoted in Donald W. White, *The American Century* (New Haven: Yale University Press, 1996), p. 43.

207. Quoted in Walter Millis, ed., *The Forrestal Diaries* (New York: Viking, 1951), p. 79.

208. Quoted in Peter G. Boyle, *American-Soviet Relations* (New York: Routledge, 1993), p. 45.

209. Peter F. Drucker, *The Concept of the Corporation* (New York: New American Library, 1964; 2nd ed.), p. xi.

210. Thomas J. McCormick, *America's Half-Century* (Baltimore: Johns Hopkins University Press, 1989), p. 33.

211. Constance Ray Harvey quoted in Ann Miller Morin, *Her Excellency* (New York: Twayne, 1994), p. 27.

212. *Department of State Bulletin, XXII* (April 22, 1945), 738.

213. Theodore H. White, *In Search of History* (New York: Warner, 1979), p. 224.

214. Allan Nevins, "How We Felt About the War," in Jack Goodman, ed., *While You Were Gone* (New York: Simon & Schuster, 1946), p. 23.

7

All-Embracing Struggle: The Cold War Begins, 1945–1950

Atomic Blast. *The second atomic bomb fell on Nagasaki August 9, 1945, killing at least 60,000. When the renowned scientist Albert Einstein heard that Japan had been blasted with an atomic bomb, he said: "Ach! The world is not ready for it." (U.S. Air Force)*

DIPLOMATIC CROSSROAD

The Atomic Bomb at Hiroshima, 1945

The crew of the B-29 group scrawled rude anti-Japanese graffiti on the "Little Boy." A major, thinking about his son and a quick end to the war, scratched "No white cross for Stevie" on the 10,000-pound orange and black bomb.[1] The 509th Bombardment Group had been training on the Mariana Island of Tinian since May. At last, the United States's secret atomic development program (Manhattan Project) neared fruition. In the evening of August 5, 1945, Colonel Paul Tibbets informed his crew for the first time that their rare cargo was "atomic." He did not explain the scientific process in which two pieces of uranium (U-235), placed at opposite ends of a cylinder, smashed into one another to create tremendous energy. Yet they knew what the equivalent of 20,000 tons of TNT meant.

At 1:37 A.M. on August 6 three weather planes took off for the urban targets of Hiroshima, Kokura, and Niigata. At 2:45, Tibbets's heavily laden B-29, the *Enola Gay,* named after his mother, lifted ponderously off the Tinian runway. The six-hour flight was uneventful except for the nerve-wracking final assembly of the bomb's inner components. Followed by two observation planes stocked with cameras and scientists, the *Enola Gay* spotted the Japanese coast at 7:30 A.M. The weather plane assigned to Hiroshima, the primary target, reported that "everything was peachy keen."[2] Tibbets headed for that city.

"This is history," he intoned over the intercom, "so watch your language."[3] But in those anxious moments someone forgot to switch on the tape recorder. At 31,600 feet and 328 miles per hour the *Enola Gay* began its run on Hiroshima. Crew members fastened on goggles. Bombardier Thomas Ferebee prepared to cross the hairs in his bombsight. At 8:15 A.M. he shouted "bombs away." The *Enola Gay* swerved quickly to escape. "Little Boy" fell for fifty seconds and then exploded about 2,000 feet above ground, a near perfect hit at hypocenter. A brilliant flash temporarily blinded the fliers. The aircraft trembled. "It looked like a pot of black, boiling tar," thought navigator Theodore Van Kirk, as he watched the huge cloud of smoke, dust, and debris rise 40,000 feet into the atmosphere.[4] "What we saw made us feel that we were Buck Rogers twenty-fifth century warriors," co-pilot Robert Lewis remembered.[5]

Hiroshima ranked as Japan's eighth largest city, with 250,000 people. Manhattan Project director Lieutenant General Leslie Groves, with the president's approval, had put it first on the target list because it housed regional military headquarters, even though largely a residential and commercial city. On the cloudless, warm morning of August 6, 1945, Hiroshima's inhabitants heard the bombing alert siren. An "all clear" sounded when only a weather plane passed over. Everything seemed routine, for Hiroshima had largely escaped American bombs during the war. Forty-five minutes later, at 8:15 A.M., few heard the *Enola Gay* overhead. Suddenly a streak of light raced through the sky. A blast of lacerating heat traveling

Enola Gay.   On August 6, 1945, just before takeoff, Colonel Paul Tibbets waved from the cockpit of his aircraft *Enola Gay.* Tibbets hailed from Miami and had served in the European theater. For commanding the atomic mission, Tibbets received the Distinguished Service Cross. (U.S. Air Force)

"Little Boy."   The nuclear weapon detonated over Hiroshima was 120 inches long and 28 inches in diameter and weighed about 10,000 pounds. (Los Alamos Scientific Laboratory, courtesy of the Harry S. Truman Library)

near the speed of light rocked the city. The temperature soared to suffocating levels. Trees were stripped of their leaves. Buildings blew apart like firecrackers. Debris shot through the air like bullets. Permanent shadows etched themselves into concrete. The sky grew dark, lighted only by the choking fires that erupted everywhere. Winds swirled violently. In an example of "psychic numbing," one survivor recalled that the agony around him "no longer moved me in the slightest. At that time human beings on the point of death were no longer human: they became mere substance."[6]

As the giant mushroom cloud churned above, dazed survivors stumbled about like scarecrows, their arms raised to avoid the painful rubbing of burned flesh. The victims remembered skin peeling off like ribbons, gaping wounds, vomiting and diarrhea, intense thirst. A badly wounded Dr. Michihiko Machiya said that "no one talked, and the ominous silence was relieved only by a subdued rustle among so many people, restless, in pain, anxious, and afraid, waiting for something else to happen."[7] The nightmare registered in statistics: about 130,000 dead, as many wounded, and 81 percent of the city's buildings destroyed. Some twenty-three

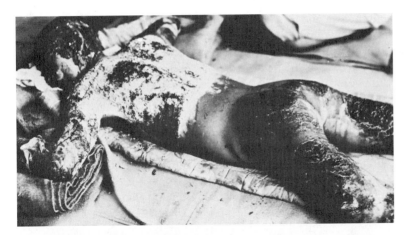

Victims at Hiroshima. Flash-burned victims shortly after the destruction of Hiroshima. The total of immediate and longer-term deaths caused by the two bombings may be as high as 300,000. Official Japanese registries in the 1980s recognized 368,259 *hibakusha* (survivors). Of these, the vast majority—71 percent in Hiroshima and 69 percent in Nagasaki—suffered acute radiation sickness immediately after the explosions. In the conventional bombing of Tokyo and other Japanese cities in 1945, as many as 600,000 Japanese were killed and more than 1 million wounded. The battle for Okinawa, which ended in June 1945, saw 12,000 American deaths and 60,000 wounded; 70,000 Japanese soldiers died, along with 150,000 Okinawan noncombatants killed. (Photographs courtesy of Dr. A. A. Liebow, Army Institute of Pathology)

American prisoners of war also perished there. Nine days later in Fukuoka, Japan, seventeen captured American airmen were beheaded by Japanese soldiers, allegedly in retaliation for the "indiscriminate bombing" of civilians.[8]

American aircraft continued their destructive conventional bombing of other Japanese cities. On August 9, a second atomic bomb smashed Nagasaki, killing at least 60,000. The next day, shaken after "killing all those kids," President Harry S. Truman decided not to unleash a third atomic bomb.[9] The Japanese surrendered four days later. "We cried with relief and joy," a twenty-one-year-old lieutenant recalled. "We were going to grow up to adulthood after all."[10] Presidential aide Admiral William D. Leahy later regretted that "in being the first to use it, we had adopted the ethical standard common to the barbarians of the Dark Ages."[11] No military or naval adviser, however, told Truman before Hiroshima that "the use of the A-bomb was unnecessary, or that the weapon should not be used, or both."[12]

The decision to use the atomic bomb against an urban center did meet criticism within the small circle of government officials and scientists privy to the Manhattan Project. Although Truman claimed that his atomic bomb decision became necessary to end the war and thus save American lives, some advisers and scientists disagreed. They presented what they considered viable alternatives to dropping the bomb on a civilian population: (1) follow up Japanese peace feelers; (2) blockade and bomb Japan conventionally; (3) have the USSR declare war on Japan; (4) warn Tokyo about the bomb and threaten its use; (5) demonstrate the bomb on an unpopulated island or area with international observers, including Japanese; (6) conduct a military landing on the outlying Japanese island of Kyushu. Many scientists believed that use of the bomb would constitute a moral blot on the American record, that it would jeopardize chances of postwar international control of the awesome weapon, and that it was unnecessary because Japan tottered on the verge of surrender.

Those who chose to drop the atomic bomb on populated targets stressed that they wanted to end the war as quickly as possible to save American lives. "Think of the kids who won't be killed!" Truman wrote from the Potsdam Conference.[13] That simple reason helps to explain the decision, but decisions seldom derive from single factors and this one is no exception. Three primary and intertwined motives induced policymakers to inflict atomic horror on the citizens of Japan. Together, the three suggest the central point: Truman found no compelling reasons against dropping atom bombs on Hiroshima and Nagasaki and important advantages in doing so.

The first motive—emotion—dated from December 7, 1941, when the Japanese bombed Pearl Harbor without warning. Vengeful Americans never forgot or forgave that disaster. Nor did they forget the Bataan Death March and other Japanese atrocities. Revenge became the order of the day. Racialized American images of the Japanese as treacherous agents of a "Yellow Peril" strengthened this popular wartime attitude. Comics and movies crudely disparaged this people of color as "yellowbellies" and "yellow monkeys." One weapons manufacturer acclaimed its machine gun for "blasting red holes in little yellow men."[14] *Kamikaze* air attacks in 1945 persuaded many that the Japanese, suicidal and bloodthirsty, deserved the worst of punishments. Americans hated the Japanese—the "slant-eyes"—more than they hated the Germans, and 13 percent in a Gallup Poll of December 1944 recommended the extermination of all Japanese. Others advised sterilization. A post-Hiroshima cartoon in the *Atlanta Constitution,* titled "Land of the Rising Sons," depicted apelike figures being propelled skyward by the atomic blast. This angry emotion carried influence. Truman himself said on August 11, 1945: "When you have to deal with a beast you have to treat him as a beast."[15]

The second motive—military momentum—merged with the first and dated from the establishment of the Manhattan Project in August 1942. This program began after European scientists, through a letter from Albert Einstein to President Franklin D. Roosevelt, warned that Germany might develop a nuclear device for military purposes. Officials in charge of the $2 billion project always assumed that once they developed a bomb they would use it to end the war. Truman inherited this assumption from the Roosevelt administration. Put another way, Truman really did not *decide* to drop the bomb. Rather, as General Leslie Groves remarked, the president practiced "noninterference—basically a decision not to upset the existing plans."[16] By 1945, too, the large-scale bombing of civilians, as in Dresden and

Hiroshima. The ruins of Japan's eighth largest city bespoke the birth of the atomic age. Regarding the reasons for Japan's surrender, the historian Herbert Bix writes: "The twin psychological shocks of the first atomic bomb and the Soviet entry into the war, coupled with . . . concern over the growing popular criticism of the throne and its occupant, and the possibility that, sooner or later, the people would react violently against their leaders if they allowed the war to go on much longer—these factors finally caused Hirohito to accept, in principle, the terms of the Potsdam Declaration." (U.S. Air Force)

Tokyo, had become accepted conduct. By August 1945, however, compelling momentum had taken on an irrational quality, for the Germans had surrendered and Japan faced certain defeat.

The third factor that helped unleash the atomic bomb was the diplomatic advantage that might accrue to the United States. The diplomatic bonus materialized when American leaders, while at Potsdam, learned about the successful test explosion at Alamogordo, New Mexico, on July 16, 1945. "Japs will fold up before Russia comes in," Truman wrote on learning the details. "I am sure they will when Manhattan appears over their homeland."[17] Throughout the war, Churchill and Roosevelt tried to keep the secret of the bomb from the Soviet Union, in part to use it for diplomatic leverage in the postwar period. Some scientists and advisers protested that excluding the Soviet Union, an ally, from any knowledge, would jeopardize postwar negotiations. At Potsdam, Truman did cryptically inform Stalin that the United States had "a new weapon of unusual destructive force."[18] In fact, despite Soviet penetration of the Manhattan Project through espionage, Stalin "had no conception of the impact" of atomic weapons until after Hiroshima and Nagasaki.[19] Suddenly aware that the bomb had "shaken the whole world," Stalin in mid-August authorized an accelerated program to catch up.[20] A nuclear arms race ensued.

Churchill learned about the test in New Mexico directly from the American delegation at Potsdam. "When he [Truman] got to the meeting after having read

James F. Byrnes (1879–1972) and Harry S. Truman (1884–1972). Both the secretary of state and the president, here on their way back from the Potsdam Conference, welcomed the atomic bomb as a diplomatic bargaining weapon in the postwar period. Although Truman publicly insisted for the rest of his life that he never had qualms about his atomic bomb decision, he reportedly told a former U.S. diplomat in 1962 that he suffered "recurring nightmares about the dropping of the bombs and that he considered that it was the greatest mistake of his life." (U.S. Navy, courtesy of the Harry S. Truman Library)

this report [from New Mexico] he was a changed man," the prime minister noted. "He told the Russians just where they got on and off and generally bossed the whole meeting."[21] Two diplomatic advantages suggested themselves. First, the bomb might strengthen the United States's negotiating position vis-à-vis the Soviets. An intimidated Russia might offer concessions on Eastern Europe if the bomb revealed its destructive power on a Japanese city. Second, the bomb might end the war in the Pacific before the Soviets could declare war against Japan. Even though Washington had sought Soviet intervention against Japan prior to Alamogordo, quick use of the bomb might forestall Soviet military entry into Manchuria and deny the USSR any part of the postwar control of Japan. As it turned out, Moscow's declaration of war against Japan on August 8 caused greater alarm in Tokyo than did news of Hiroshima. "Now the jig is up," said Prime Minister Kantaro Suzuki as he and Emperor Hirohito maneuvered the deadlocked Supreme War Council into accepting surrender.[22]

All three factors—emotion, military momentum, and diplomatic advantage—explain the tragedies at Hiroshima and Nagasaki. The diplomatic aspect emerged as a late bonus; Truman would have dropped the bomb whether such a consideration existed or not. To have decided against dropping the atomic bomb, Truman would have had to deny the passion and momentum that had built up by mid-summer 1945. He could avenge Pearl Harbor, end the war quickly, save American lives, and shore up the U.S. diplomatic position—the advantages far outweighed the disadvantages in his mind. Still, the costs were not inconsequential. Some of the alternatives, or a combination of them, might have terminated the war without the heavy death toll and the grotesque suffering of the survivors. The failure to discuss atomic development and control with the Soviets during the war bequeathed to the postwar generation both division and fear. "Seldom, if ever," the CBS radio commentator Edward R. Murrow stated, "has a war ended leaving the victors with such . . . a realization that the future is obscure and survival is not assured."[23]

The Big Two and the International System: Sources of the Long War

Because World War II left the international system in disarray, the transition to peace proved rough and contentious. Broken societies and economies needed repair, and competing models for a new future produced wrenching political turmoil. Some 35 million people died in Europe during the war, and hungry, homeless survivors struggled to live in the rubble. The contrast with prosperous Americans, untouched by enemy bombers or soldiers, became stark. "Like mice in the cage of the elephant," noted the British magazine *The Economist* in comparing the rest of the world to the United States, "they follow with apprehension the movements of the mammoth."[24] The war so weakened the imperial French, British, and Dutch, moreover, that they began to retreat from empire. Britain granted independence to India in 1947 and Burma in 1948, and the Dutch left Indonesia a year later. The French clung precariously to Indochina in the face of nationalist rebellions (see Chapter 9). The decolonization process accelerated in what became known as the Third World.

As Washington moved to fill the power vacuums left by the defeated Axis and retreating colonial powers, it encountered an obstreperous competitor in Joseph Stalin's Soviet Union. Soon a bipolar international structure emerged from the Soviet-American rivalry—the Cold War. The Soviets' pushy behavior, suspiciousness, and blunt language rankled Americans. Truman complained that they negotiated "with a boorishness worthy of stable boys."[25] At the end of the war, the Soviet Union had troops in several Eastern European countries and part of Germany. It lacked an effective navy or air force and had no atomic bomb, but it possessed strong regional power by virtue of its military exploits. Motivated by traditional Russian nationalism and communist ideology, craving security against a revived Germany and facing a huge task of reconstruction, the Kremlin determined to make the most of its limited power. Often rude and abusive, yet cautious and realistic, Stalin determined never again to see his country invaded through Eastern Europe. Still, compared with the United States, as chargé d'affaires George F. Kennan reported from Moscow, the Soviet Union stood as the "weaker force."[26]

The United States emerged from World War II a full-fledged global power for the first time in its history. An asymmetry—not a balance—of power existed. Washington possessed what political scientists call "compellent" power and flexed its multidimensional muscle to build even more power. Because of domestic public pressure, Washington may have demobilized its troops faster than Truman wished, but the Soviet Union also demobilized millions of soldiers. With troops in Asia and Europe, the world's largest navy and air force, a monopoly of the atomic

Joseph Stalin (1879–1953). General secretary of the Soviet Communist party since 1922, he ran an authoritarian state and conducted a foreign policy of suspiciousness. Because Stalin often played "good cop" to Molotov's "bad cop," President Truman once called the Soviet dictator a "prisoner of the Politburo," and Ambassador Averell Harriman wrote that if "it were possible to see [Stalin] more frequently . . . many of our difficulties would be overcome." (*The Reporter*, 1952. Copyright 1952 by Fortnightly Publishing Co., Inc.)

Makers of American Foreign Relations, 1945–1950

President	Secretaries of State
Harry S. Truman, 1945–1953	Edward R. Stettinius, Jr., 1944–1945
	James F. Byrnes, 1945–1947
	George C. Marshall, 1947–1949
	Dean G. Acheson, 1949–1953

bomb, and a high-gear economy, the United States claimed first rank in world affairs. The United States wielded the "prime weapon of *de*struction—the atomic bomb—and the prime weapon of *recon*struction—such wealth as no nation hitherto had possessed."[27] In contrast, a Moscow study estimated that total Soviet war damages surpassed "the national wealth of England or Germany" and constituted "one-third of the overall national wealth of the United States."[28]

American ideology held that world peace and order depended on the existence of prosperity and political democracy. Poverty and economic depression bred totalitarianism, revolution, communism, the disruption of world trade, and war. Prosperity became the handmaiden of stability, political freedom, unrestricted trade, and peaceful international relations. Americans had long believed that they were prosperous because they were democratic and democratic because they were prosperous.

American leaders determined that *this time,* unlike after World War I, the United States would seize the opportunity to fulfill its ideological premises. As the historian Gaddis Smith has described the diplomat Dean Acheson's historical understanding, "only the United States had the power to grab hold of history and make it conform."[29] The lessons of the 1920s and 1930s admonished the leaders of the 1940s to throw off the mistakes of the past, to make the most of the "second chance," and to install America's concept of "peace and prosperity" as the world's way.

The vital needs of the U.S. economy also influenced postwar expansionism. Truman and other leaders frankly stated that the United States *had* to export American goods and *had* to import strategic raw materials. By 1947 U.S. exports accounted for one-third of total world exports and were valued at $14 billion a year. Pivotal industries, such as automobiles, trucks, machine tools, steel, and farm machinery, relied heavily on foreign trade for their well-being. Farmers exported about half of their wheat. Many Americans, remembering the Great Depression, predicted economic catastrophe unless U.S. foreign trade continued and expanded. Although less than 10 percent of the GNP, exports exceeded in volume such elements of the GNP as consumers' expenditures on durable goods, total expenditures by state and local governments, and private construction. Further, imports of manganese, tungsten, and chromite, to name a few, had become essential to America's industrial system. Foreign trade, however, was threatened by the sickness of America's best customer, Europe, which lacked the resources to purchase American

"What Next?"   Jack Lambert's 1946 cartoon of Harry S. Truman captured the feeling of many Americans that the president, new at his job, was overwhelmed by postwar problems. FDR had kept Truman in the dark on foreign affairs. Recalling their first contentious meeting in April 1945, Molotov thought Truman "half-witted" and "far behind Roosevelt in intellect." Stalin called the president a "gentleman shopkeeper." (Jack Lambert, *Chicago Sun Times*)

products, and also by nationalists in former colonial areas, who controlled raw materials sources for both Europe and America. To protect its interests and to fulfill its ideology the United States undertook foreign-aid programs that eventually became global in scale.

President Truman felt the flush of American power, shared the ideology, and knew well the economic needs of the country. A Democratic party regular from the Pendergast machine in Kansas City, Missouri, Truman had long experienced rough-and-tumble politics. "The buck stops here" read a sign on his desk. He prided himself on blunt language and quick decisions. The British ambassador once dismissed Truman as "an honest and intelligent mediocrity"—"a bungling if well-meaning amateur."[30] With intense eyes peering through thick lenses, Truman relished the verbal brawl. His hurried simplification of issues, superficial application of lessons from the past, and quick-tempered style spawned jokes that often fit the truth. Somebody rewrote a proverb: "To err is Truman." Although intelligent and energetic, Truman was a provincial nationalist of narrow vision who believed he could win the Cold War through the projection of U.S. power, and he expected the world to go America's way. When it did not, he sometimes lost his temper and spoke carelessly. His assistant Clark Clifford later commented that the president "*never* got involved in the complexities of the period"; he saw the world in black and white terms.[31]

In April 1945, Soviet foreign minister V. M. Molotov visited the White House. President Truman gave him a vigorous tongue-lashing, charging that Moscow had not honored the Yalta accords. After the encounter, the first meeting between the new president and a high-ranking Soviet official, Truman gloated to a friend: "I gave it to him straight 'one-two to the jaw.' I let him have it straight."[32] Truman's assertive, "get tough" style drew strength from actual American power. Truman told Ambassador W. Averell Harriman that he did not fear the Soviets, because they "needed us more than we needed them." He did not expect to win 100 percent of the American case, but "we should be able to get 85 percent."[33] Indeed, although U.S. resources did not always reach as far as American goals because the unstable international system, political leftists, and nationalists put up obstacles, Washington possessed unusual power.

The confrontation between the United States and the Soviet Union derived from the different postwar needs, ideology, style, and power of the two rivals and drew on a historical legacy of frosty relations. Each saw the other, in mirror image, as the world's bully. Each charged the other with assuming Hitler's aggressive mantle. Americans compared Nazism and communism, Hitler and Stalin, and coined the phrase "Red Fascism." Moscow and Washington became trapped in a "security dilemma": Every step taken by one side to ensure its security appeared to the other to be provocative. Still, one historian has argued, "in view of the overwhelming power of the United States and in view of the relative restraint exhibited by the Kremlin *outside its immediate periphery,* U.S. officials might have displayed more tolerance for risk."[34]

The advent of the air and nuclear ages made all nations vulnerable to surprise attack. "We are for all time de-isolated," wrote one observer.[35] And the Soviet and American quests for spheres of influence kindled a global contest for advantage— an "all embracing struggle" with an expensive arms race, military alliances, trade restrictions, and repeated interventions and client-state wars.[36] The Cold War era lasted more than forty years, claimed the lives of millions of victims, and nearly bankrupted the main protagonists because they eventually suffered decline from "imperial overstretch."[37]

Challenging the Soviet Sphere in Eastern Europe

The Soviet presence in Eastern Europe before 1947–1948 was neither uniform nor consistent. Although Stalin had stated bluntly at Potsdam that "a freely elected government in any of these countries would be anti-Soviet, and that we cannot allow," Moscow had no imperial blueprint for its neighbors.[38] Poland, with its communist Lublin government in control, fell firmly within the Soviet grasp. Romania, an anti-Soviet German satellite during the war, suffered under a Soviet-imposed government. The Soviet Union gained territory at the expense of Poland, Finland, and Romania after postwar boundary settlements. Bulgaria had a large indigenous communist movement, which gained control through elections without much help from Moscow.

Changes in Europe After World War II

▨ Territorial Changes After World War II

Notes: -The United States, British, and French Zones of Germany merged in 1949 as the Federal Republic of Germany.

-The Russian Zone of Germany became the German Democratic Republic in 1949.

-The four zones of Austria merged in 1955 to become the Federal Republic of Austria.

NORWAY

SWEDEN

FINLAND
To Russia

Leased to Russia until 1955

L. Ladoga

Leningrad

Gulf of Finland

NORTH SEA

DENMARK

ESTONIA
to Russia

L. Pskov

BALTIC SEA

To Russia
LATVIA

LITHUANIA
To Russia
Niemen R.

To Russia

EAST PRUSSIA
To Poland

Danzig

To Poland

Vistula R.

U.S. ZONE

NETH.

BRITISH ZONE

Berlin

GERMANY
W.

E.

RUSSIAN ZONE

POLAND

Oder R.

Neisse R.

To Russia

BEL.

Rhine R.

LUX.

FRENCH ZONE

UNITED STATES ZONE

CZECHOSLOVAKIA

Don R.

FRANCE

SWITZ.

FRENCH

RUSSIAN

Vienna

U.S.

AUSTRIA

BRITISH

BRATISLAVA BRIDGEHEAD
To Czech.

SUBCARPATHIAN RUTHENIA

NORTHERN BUKOVINA

Dniester R.

BESSARABIA
To Russia

Prut R.

VENEZIA-GIULIA
To Yugoslavia

To France

Po R.

Trieste

HUNGARY

Drava R.

ROMANIA

CORSICA

ITALY

Rome

ADRIATIC SEA

YUGOSLAVIA

Danube R.

BLACK SEA

DOBRUJA
To Bulgaria

SARDINIA

BULGARIA

ALBANIA

GREECE

TURKEY

AEGEAN SEA

SICILY

MALTA (Br.)

DODECANESE IS.
(To Greece from Italy)

CRETE

MEDITERRANEAN SEA

SOVIET RUSSIA

"Red Fascism." This popular notion among Americans suggested that German Nazism and Soviet communism were really one and the same and that the 1940s would suffer totalitarian aggression like that of the 1930s. Such thinking aroused fears of another "Munich" or "appeasement" and thereby hindered negotiations. (*The Reporter,* 1950. Copyright 1950 by Fortnightly Publishing Co., Inc.)

Hungary and other nations developed differently. The conservative Hungarian Smallholders' party of Ferenc Nagy won national elections in November 1945 by routing the communists, who gained only 17 percent of the vote. Although the communists ousted Nagy in spring 1947, a year later the U.S. minister still believed that "the Soviets and their Hungarian Communist allies are far too clever at this stage . . . to bring Hungary under complete domination."[39] In Finland, to demonstrate further the political complexity in Eastern Europe, noncommunist leaders recognized their precarious position with respect to the neighboring Soviet Union and adopted a neutral position vis-à-vis the Soviet-American confrontation. Finland thus retained its independence and in 1948 even ousted from its cabinet the lone communist member. Yugoslavia, although a communist state, established its independence from Moscow under the leadership of Josip Broz Tito. When Belgrade and Moscow bitterly split in 1948, Washington at first considered the schism "a rathole to be watched, not an opportunity for decisive exploitation."[40] Once Yugoslavia demonstrated "a loyal and cooperative attitude in its international relationships," as the State Department put it, the United States pursued closer ties as part of a "wedge" strategy to weaken Soviet dominance in Eastern Europe.[41] In Czechoslovakia, an independent socialist country with a democratic political process and ties to the West, officials recognized the advisability of a middle course in the developing Cold War. A coalition government under noncommunist president Eduard Beneš and Foreign Minister Jan Masaryk assumed office after free elections in May 1946. Communists held membership in the government, with 9 of 26 top-level positions and 114 of 300 National Assembly seats, but the Soviet Union for a time refrained from meddling directly in Czech affairs. In February 1948, after the Cold War had intensified, communists seized control of Czechoslovakia during a domestic crisis.

The Soviet presence in Eastern Europe before 1948, then, became conspicuous and often repressive, but not absolute. Stalin told French communists in 1947 that "cooperation between different systems . . . is completely possible."[42] In early 1945, he emphasized security: "Throughout history Poland has been the corridor for attack. . . . Russia wants a strong, independent, and democratic Poland. . . . It is not only a question of honor for Russia, but one of life and death."[43] Still bitter over the *cordon sanitaire* the Western powers constructed around Soviet Russia after World War I and staggering from the loss of 27 million dead during the recent war, Soviet leaders demanded security. "Give them twelve to fifteen years and they'll be on their feet again," Stalin said of the Germans.[44] They also believed that the Yalta accords acknowledged their primary position in Eastern Europe. Thus the Soviets began building their own *cordon sanitaire*.

Washington sought "free elections" and the "Open Door" for trade, both traditional principles calculated in part to reduce Soviet influence. The Soviets signed bilateral trade treaties with many Eastern European states, which established favors anathema to America's multilateral approach to trade. Despite minimal commercial ties with Eastern Europe, U.S. diplomats preached the Open Door as a way of driving a wedge into the area. "Free elections" proved difficult in Eastern Europe. First, except for Czechoslovakia, the region lacked democratic traditions. Second, free elections in most of those nations would have produced strongly anti-Soviet governments threatening Soviet security. The question of elections in Hungary demonstrates the complexity of the question. During late 1946 it was the *noncommunist* Nagy who delayed elections, because he knew that the communists would lose badly, alarming Moscow and perhaps triggering Soviet intervention.

The Soviets charged the United States with a double standard. When American leaders consciously excluded the USSR from participation in the postwar reconstruction of Italy and Japan, the Soviets cited them as precedents for their machinations in Eastern Europe. Secretary of War Henry L. Stimson remarked: "Some Americans are anxious to hang on to exaggerated views of the Monroe Doctrine and at the same time butt into every question that comes up in Central Europe."[45] Molotov contended that an Open Door in Eastern Europe would mean ultimate American economic domination of war-weakened nations.

At the Yalta and Potsdam conferences, at the foreign ministers' conferences in London (September–October 1945) and Moscow (December 1945), at the Paris Peace Conference (April–October 1946), and in numerous diplomatic notes, the United States sought influence in Eastern Europe to counter the Soviets. Washington tried nonrecognition of the pro-Soviet governments but abandoned that tactic after slight Soviet concessions, such as adding a few noncommunists to the Polish government. Some American leaders thought the atomic bomb would act as a compellent. Stimson recorded in his diary that Byrnes "looks to having the presence of the bomb in his pocket" at the London Conference.[46] At that conference, Molotov actually asked Byrnes if he had "an atomic bomb in his side pocket." "You don't know Southerners," Byrnes parried. "We carry our artillery in our pocket. If you don't cut out all this stalling and let us get down to work, I am going to pull an atomic bomb out of my hip pocket and let you have it."[47] Still, the implied threat of the bomb did not budge the Soviets from Eastern Europe, and the United States never practiced a blatant "atomic diplomacy" of direct threat.

Stimson opposed the use of the bomb as a diplomatic weapon when he told Truman in September 1945 that the United States should share the secret of the bomb to spur postwar cooperation. "For if we fail to approach them now and merely continue to negotiate with them, having this weapon rather ostentatiously on our hip, their suspicions and their distrust of our purposes and motives will increase." Stimson, then seventy-eight, offered the president some sage advice: "The only way you can make a man trustworthy is to trust him; and the surest way you can make a man untrustworthy is to distrust him and show your distrust."[48] Stimson gained the support of Secretary of Commerce Henry Wallace, but Secretary of the Navy James V. Forrestal rejected any effort to "buy [Soviet] understanding and sympathy. We tried that once with Hitler."[49] Truman sided with Forrestal.

The United States also used foreign aid as a diplomatic weapon in Eastern Europe. Byrnes stated the policy in 1946: "We must help our friends in every way and refrain from assisting those who either through helplessness or for other reasons are opposing the principles for which we stand."[50] In short, no loans or aid for Eastern Europe. This policy backfired, for it left those countries dependent on Soviet aid and drove them deeper into the Soviet orbit. In Czechoslovakia, for example, the United States abruptly severed an Export-Import Bank loan. Noncommunist foreign trade minister Hubert Ripka complained bitterly in late 1947: "These idiots

"I Can't Give You All Up for One Angel of Peace."   The burly Soviet savors the attention of the Eastern Europeans in this critical Turkish cartoon. The brutish caricature suggests a certain truth. According to the historian Norman Naimark, "women in the Eastern zone" of Germany "shared an experience for the most part unknown in the West, the ubiquitous threat and reality of rape, over a prolonged period of time." The raping by Soviet troops of an estimated 2 million German women prompted the U.S. military governor Lucius Clay to write: "We began to look like angels, not because we were angels, but we looked [like] that in comparison to what was going on in Eastern Europe." (*ULUS,* Ankara, in *United Nations World,* 1947)

started the usual blackmail: 'Okay, you can have 200,000 or 300,000 or even 500,000 tons of wheat, but on one condition only—that you throw the Communists out of the Czechoslovak Government.'" The result: "And now these idiots in Washington have driven us straight into the Stalinist camp."[51]

Washington exaggerated the extent of Soviet control in Eastern Europe, and pressure tactics helped intensify the Cold War—that is, Moscow leaders read American policies as threats to their security and so tightened their grip. George F. Kennan has suggested that the Czech coup of 1948 represented the Soviet response to the Marshall Plan, a major American aid program that the Soviets considered a challenge to their tenuous position in Eastern Europe (see pages 245–248).

Stiffening Up: Early Cold War Crises

The question of Eastern Europe broke up the London Conference of Foreign Ministers (September–October 1945). Byrnes demanded representative governments in Bulgaria and Romania before he would sign any peace treaties with the former German satellites. Molotov countered with questions about British-dominated Greece and American-dominated Japan. The conferees left London unable to agree even on a public communiqué. At the Moscow Conference in December 1945, the secretary of state tempered his tough stand, and Stalin permitted a token broadening of the Romanian and Bulgarian regimes. The Soviets also accepted Byrnes's

Winston S. Churchill (1874–1965) in Fulton.
Churchill (far left) received applause from President Harry S. Truman (far right) during the former British prime minister's visit to Westminster College in Fulton, Missouri. There Churchill delivered his provocative oration against the "iron curtain." (Truman Library and Westminster College)

ideas for a general peace conference to be held in Paris and a United Nations Atomic Energy Commission to prepare plans for international control.

Truman grew impatient. In early 1946 he said "stop babying the Russians," and instructed Byrnes to "stiffen up," to make no compromises with the Soviets.[52] News of a Canadian spy ring that had sent atomic secrets to Moscow broke in February, about the time that Stalin gave a preelection speech that persuaded some Americans that the Soviets had become intractable. From Moscow, on February 22, chargé d'affaires George F. Kennan wrote an alarmist and influential cable that declared that "we have here a political force committed fanatically to the belief that with [the] US there can be no permanent modus vivendi." Widely read in Washington, this "long telegram" depicted, in gendered terms, a rapacious, aggressive, hypermasculine Soviet Union, guided by an implacable communist ideology and a "neurotic view of world affairs."[53] Kennan, as one scholar has noted, repeated the word "penetration" five times in "reference to the Soviets' insistent, unwanted intrusion" into central Europe. To reassure the "tired and frightened" Europeans, Kennan urged the United States to "tighten" up, assert greater "cohesion, firmness and vigor," and rely on the manly virtues of "courage, detachment, objectivity, and . . . determination not to be provoked" in dealing with Moscow.[54]

On March 5, Winston Churchill, no longer prime minister, spoke in Fulton, Missouri. President Truman sat prominently on the platform and, with pleasure, heard the eloquent orator lash out at the Soviets: "From Stettin in the Baltic to Trieste in the Adriatic, an iron curtain has descended across the Continent."[55] Most Americans liked his stern anti-Soviet tone, but they warmed much less to his call for an Anglo-American alliance outside the fledgling United Nations Organization. The reporter David Brinkley recalled that Churchill "threw his whole body" into the speech but "managed to do so without excessive gestures or histrionics," his speaking style "the highly distilled product of a thousand years of upper-class English language and rhetoric." Churchill was "not talking to those of us in the hall. He was talking to the world."[56]

W. Averell Harriman (1891–1986). Graduate of Yale, heir to the Harriman railroad empire, investment banker of Brown Brothers, and diplomat, Harriman was one of America's great public servants in the twentieth century. He served as ambassador to Russia (1943–1946), ambassador to Great Britain (1946), secretary of commerce (1946–1948), and U.S. representative in Europe for the Marshall Plan. Later he advised Presidents John F. Kennedy and Lyndon B. Johnson. Maxim Litvinov once asked: "How can a man with a hundred million dollars look so sad?" (*The Reporter*, 1950. Copyright 1950 by Fortnightly Publishing Co., Inc.)

The Iranian crisis disturbed Soviet-American relations at the same time. The crisis began quietly in 1944 when British and American oil companies applied for Iranian concessions. In a classic example of competition for spheres of influence, the Soviet Union soon applied for an oil concession too. By 1944 U.S. corporations controlled 42 percent of the "proved" oil reserves of the Middle East, a nineteen-fold increase since 1936. Both the British and the Soviets grew alarmed by U.S. oil expansion, but the declining British saw the United States as a counterweight to the Soviets in the region.

A 1942 treaty with Iran allowed the British and Soviets to occupy the country and required them to leave six months after the end of the war. U.S. soldiers and supply units also went to Iran, primarily to facilitate Lend-Lease shipments to the Soviet Union. In mid-1945 the Soviets backed an indigenous rebellion in northern Iran (Azerbaijan) against the central government in Teheran. In January 1946, working with U.S. officials, Iran took the question to the new United Nations Organization. Teheran and Moscow entered direct negotiations but did not reach an accord by March 2, when all foreign troops, by treaty, had to depart. U.S. soldiers had withdrawn in January but left military advisers behind; British troops departed in early March. The Soviets thus stood alone in defiance of the treaty and, in Truman's exaggerated view, threatened a "giant pincers movement" toward the Mediterranean and the Near East.[57] In April, however, Moscow and Teheran concluded an agreement and Soviet forces withdrew. In exchange, Iran agreed to establish a joint Iranian-Soviet oil company, subject to approval by its parliament. Stalin abandoned his Azerbaijani clients. In late 1946, Iranian armed forces, advised by Major General Robert W. Grow of the U.S. Army, crushed the insurrection in northern Iran. Not until October 1947 did Iran's legislature consider the joint oil company, rejecting it by a vote of 102 to 2.

The Soviets exploded in anger. They had departed Iran while Britain and the United States had driven in stakes. Arthur C. Millspaugh, former U.S. financial adviser to the Iranian government, pinpointed the security issue: "Iran's geographic relation to the Soviet Union is roughly comparable to the relation of Mexico or Canada to the United States."[58] The Soviets wanted what the British and Americans already had—oil and influence—and feared the foreign penetration of a neighboring state. Years later, Truman embellished the Iranian story by claiming that he had sent the Soviets an ultimatum to get out of Iran or face U.S. troops, but the State Department has denied the existence of such a message. Yet this myth suggests the simple lesson Americans drew from the conflict: "Get tough" and the Soviets will give way. Secretary Wallace, however, told a Madison Square Garden audience in September 1946: "'Getting tough' never brought anything real and lasting—whether for schoolyard bullies or businessmen or world powers. The tougher we get, the tougher the Russians will get."[59] Truman fired him from the cabinet, lumping Wallace with "parlor pinks and soprano-voiced men" as a "national danger" and "a sabotage front for Uncle Joe Stalin."[60]

Other issues heightened friction in 1946 and illustrated Truman's "get tough" policy. During the war, Moscow asked Washington for a major postwar reconstruction loan. Seeing U.S. aid as one of America's "cards" in the Cold War game, Truman decided to comply assistance for the USSR's massive reconstruction task as a weapon rather than as a tool.[61] But as Ambassador Harriman admitted, U.S. rejection of the Soviet loan request in early 1946 actually "may have contributed to their avaricious policies" in Eastern Europe.[62] In contrast, Washington granted Britain a $3.75 billion loan in mid-1946 in return for British promises to open trade in their Sterling Bloc.

The Baruch Plan of July 1946 also divided Washington and Moscow. The plan emerged from months of intra-administration talks, but its final touches belonged to Bernard Baruch, the uncompromising American negotiator. He outlined the proposal for control of atomic weapons: (1) the creation of an international authority; (2) the international control of fissionable raw materials by this authority; (3) inspections to prevent violations; (4) no Security Council vetoes of control or inspections; (5) global distribution of atomic plants for peaceful purposes; (6) cessation of the manufacture of atomic bombs; (7) destruction of existing bombs; (8) these procedures to occur in stages, with abandonment of the U.S. atomic bomb monopoly coming last.

Not until after the Soviets had given up atomic bomb development and fissionable materials within their country, and submitted to inspections, would the United States relinquish its "winning weapon."[63] The United States would also control a majority of the members of an international authority, with most plants in areas friendly to the United States. "We are telling the Russians that if they are 'good boys' we may eventually turn over our knowledge of atomic energy to them," Wallace wrote to the president.[64] About the same time, the Soviet ambassador in Washington, Nikolai Novikov, warned his superiors that the United States was "striving for world supremacy."[65] Moscow not surprisingly rejected the Baruch Plan, and the stalemate persisted until 1949, when the Soviets successfully exploded their first atomic device.

The issue of Germany—zones, reparations, central administration, demilitarization, and the dismantling of war-oriented factories—deepened the schism. *"Deutschland unter Allies"* consisted of British, French, American, and Soviet zones, wherein each occupying power did what it liked.[66] The vengeful French proved the most obstructionist, refusing to permit any centralized German agencies and pushing for permanent dismemberment. The Soviets tried with mixed success to grab reparations, thereby weakening the entire German economy. The British tried to bestow socialism on their district but generally wanted a strong Germany to which they could sell goods and from which they could receive coal. The United States sought, according to the Potsdam accords, to treat Germany as one economic unit to speed reconstruction. Never again, vowed Truman, would America "pay reparations, feed the world, and get nothing for it but a nose thumbing."[67] With the Morgenthau Plan shelved, new plans evolved to reconstruct steel- and coal-rich Germany as the vital center of a revived European economy. Washington also implemented Project Paperclip to bring German scientists and technicians to the United States to assist in the "development of new types of weapons."[68]

The dismantling of industrial plants slowed, and in May 1946 U.S. military governor Lucius Clay halted all reparations shipments from the American zone. No more reparations, he told the Soviets, until they contributed to German economic unity. As former president Herbert Hoover concluded after a fact-finding mission: "We can keep Germany in these economic chains but it will also keep Europe in rags."[69] In December 1946, the British and Americans combined their zones into

Berlin Airlift. In May 1949, at the close of the crisis over the Berlin blockade, American military personnel celebrate victory for "Operation Vittles." According to the historian Richard Pells, "American soldiers [in Germany]—tossing chewing gum and chocolate to the natives, trading stockings and cigarettes for women's favors, threatening to flatten pedestrians as they roared through town in their Jeeps and luxuriously upholstered cars, noisily invading the neighborhood pubs, bulging with dollars to spend on the black market—aroused a mixture of feelings, from fascination to exasperation to envy." (U.S. Air Force)

"Bizonia." "We really do not intend to accept German unification in any terms that the Russians might agree to," one U.S. diplomat wrote privately.[70] The Federal Republic of Germany (West Germany), a consolidation of "Bizonia" with the French zone, was formed in May 1949. The Soviets, after looting their zone, established their own client, the German Democratic Republic (East Germany), in October 1949. The Russians "bolshevised" their zone, in one historian's words, "not because there was a plan to do so, but because that was the only way they knew how to organize society."[71]

"Perhaps we can kick them out," Stalin told a German communist as he initiated the Berlin blockade (June 1948–May 1949) to impede unification of the western zones.[72] Fearful of a Germany linked to the West, the Soviets sealed off land, rail, and water access to Berlin (inside the Soviet zone). Truman answered with an airlift. U.S. planes soon swept into the western part of the city with food, fuel, and other supplies. He also ordered B-29 bombers to England, concealing the fact that they went without any of the fifty atomic bombs then in the U.S. arsenal. Although Truman thought it "no time to be juggling an atom bomb," the Soviet ambassador reported a "war psychosis" rampant in Washington.[73] Gambling that "the American administration was not run by frivolous people who would start a nuclear war over such a situation," Stalin nonetheless never interfered with the airlift and even permitted a half-million tons of supplies to reach Berlin from the Soviet zone.[74] Moscow lifted the blockade, but only after suffering worldwide reproach and the creation of the West Germany it had so wanted to prevent. Americans drew another Cold War lesson: To win, never flinch in the face of communist aggression.

The Truman Doctrine, Israel, and Containment

On March 12, 1947, President Harry S. Truman spoke dramatically to a special joint session of Congress. Greece and Turkey, he said, faced grave threats. Unless the United States offered help, "we may endanger the peace of the world—and we shall surely endanger the welfare of this Nation." His most famous words became known as the Truman Doctrine: "It must be the policy of the United States to support free peoples who are resisting attempted subjugation by armed minorities or by outside pressures."[75] Truman asked for $400 million to ensure this policy's success. The president's address was short on analysis of the civil war in Greece and the Soviet-Turkish controversy over the strategic Dardanelles, but long on clichés and alarmist language. He played on the words *free* and *democratic,* implying that they fit the Greek and Turkish governments. Presidential aide Clark Clifford called it "the opening gun in a campaign to bring the people up to [the] realization that the war isn't over by any means."[76]

A lingering squabble over the Dardanelles and a British request for help in Greece served as immediate catalysts for the Truman Doctrine. When the Germans withdrew from Greece in 1944, much of the countryside had come under the control of communist and other leftist Greek nationalist resistance fighters—the ELAS (National Popular Liberation Army) and their political arm, the EAM (National Liberation Front). Intent on preserving their influence in the eastern Mediterranean, the British soon reinstated the Greek government-in-exile. Violence erupted in December 1944. British troops, transported to Greece on U.S. ships, joined by rightist sympathizers, and spurred by Churchill's pledge of "no peace without victory," engaged the leftists in vicious warfare.[77] The rebels, hoping to gain political power through elections, signed a peace treaty in February 1945.

From then until March 1946, when the civil war flared again, the corrupt British-sponsored Athens regime set about to eliminate its political foes. The United States sent warships to Greek ports and offered aid through the Export-Import Bank. In September, Navy Secretary Forrestal announced the positioning of a permanent U.S. fleet in the Mediterranean. Although wary about a Greek government that one American official described as "completely reactionary, . . . incredibly weak, stupid, and venal," Washington still considered a friendly regime better than a leftist or communist one.[78] Greece limped along, staggered by war-wrought devastation and civil turmoil. Britain, suffering its imperial death throes, could no longer pay the Greek bill. On February 21, 1947, the British informed Washington that they were pulling out. Truman's special message to Congress answered the British appeal with uncommon alacrity.

Critics charged that Truman backed a ruthless Greek regime. Others worried about the cost of the program, preferred economic over military aid, recommended United Nations action, and feared that the Soviets would interpret the Truman Doctrine as threatening a world crusade. Critics also challenged the contention that Soviet aggression threatened Greece and Turkey. The EAM, although communist-led, had minimal ties with the Soviet Union. Despite Stalin's apparent desire for a "soft" Greece with "pro-Soviet elements powerful enough to veto any anti-Soviet initiatives," Churchill always credited Stalin for keeping the bargain he made at their 1944 Moscow conference to stay out of the Greek imbroglio.[79] In fact, Stalin disliked the nationalist Greek communists because the independent-minded Yugoslav leader Tito gave them aid. Yet Truman claimed that all communists took their orders from Moscow.

The Truman administration enlisted the support of Senator Arthur M. Vandenberg in a prime example of bipartisan foreign policy. The Michigan Republican predicted a "Communist chain reaction from the Dardanelles to the China Sea and westward to the rim of the Atlantic."[80] Most leaders accepted what would later be called the "domino theory." On April 22 the Senate passed the act for aid to Greece and Turkey, 67 to 23; the House followed on May 15 with a positive voice vote.

The Dardanelles question also had more complexity than Truman acknowledged. The United States urged international control over the straits. But the Soviets saw the issue quite differently, for the Turks during World War II had permitted German warships to pass through the straits into the Black Sea. Stalin insisted at Yalta that the Soviet Union could no longer "accept a situation in which Turkey had a hand on Russia's throat."[81] And, if internationalization of the waterway was such a good idea, why not internationalize the U.S. Panama Canal? When Turkey refused joint control with the Soviets, Moscow threatened to take action. The presence of Soviet troops near the Turkish border in August 1946 prompted the State-War-Navy Coordinating Committee to assert that "the only thing which will deter the Russians will be the conviction that the United States is prepared . . . to meet aggression with the force of arms."[82] Truman's ostentatious dispatch of a U.S. carrier task force to Constantinople may have caused the Soviets to moderate their demands. "We of course overdid it a bit," Molotov later recalled, but "backed down in time."[83] Ignoring legitimate Soviet concerns about the Dardanelles, Truman drew the simplistic conclusion that Stalin sought to subjugate Turkey. U.S. aid to Turkey under the Truman Doctrine pulled that Mediterranean nation and Soviet neighbor into the U.S. orbit.

American aid and advisers flowed to Greece after 1947, with U.S. officials taking charge of the Greek government. More than 350 American officers accompanied the Greek army in its campaign against the EAM. Dependent on American assistance, Greece too entered the U.S. sphere of influence. Truman claimed another Cold War victory, but the Greek insurgents lost in October 1949 not only because of American intervention but because the Soviet Union refused to help them and Tito sealed off the Yugoslav border to deny Greek leftists a sanctuary.

U.S. interest in the Mediterranean region also entangled the United States in the Palestine question, "an open sore, the infection from which tends to spread rather than to become localized."[84] Zionists had long sought a Jewish homeland, and at the end of World War II they pressed London and Washington to open

Founders of the New Israel, 1948. Formerly the High Commissioner for Refugees under the League of Nations, America's first ambassador to Israel James G. MacDonald (1886–1964; on left) enjoys tea after presenting his credentials to Israel's President Chaim Weizmann (1874–1952) and Prime Minister David Ben-Gurion (1886–1973; on right). The historian Michelle Mart has observed that "Jews in the postwar period first symbolized a complete lack of masculinity for their role as victims and then masculine resurgence in their survival and construction of a new state," an image that commanded respect from Americans. (National Archives)

British-mandated Palestine to Holocaust survivors. As Britain stalled, blocking immigration and turning back ships such as the *Exodus* loaded with Jewish refugees, extremist Zionists vowed to take up arms. At first, U.S. Mideast policy sought to satisfy the Arabs, who opposed increased Jewish immigration and a new Jewish state, because Washington valued Mideast oil and Arab anticommunism. At the same time, many Americans, including President Truman, welcomed the humanitarian opportunity to assist displaced persons once terrorized by Nazism. The astute politician in Truman also spoke: "I have to answer to hundreds of thousands who are anxious for the success of Zionism," he told U.S. diplomats posted in the Middle East. "I do not have hundreds of thousands of Arabs among my constituents."[85]

The beleaguered British decided to abandon the Palestine question to the United Nations, whose special commission recommended partition into Jewish and Arab states, with 56 percent of the mandate area assigned to the Zionists. America's UN ambassador embarrassingly exhorted Arabs and Jews to "settle this problem in a true Christian spirit."[86] Truman groped for a policy while he exploded against Zionists who castigated him for not demanding an independent Jewish nation: "Jesus Christ couldn't please them when he was here on earth, so how could anyone expect that I would have any luck?"[87] Although such statements smacked of anti-Semitism, the president hoped to win the large Jewish vote in the forthcoming presidential election, and he resented unyielding State Department officials who kept predicting that partition would alienate Arabs. In fall 1947 Truman chose partition. Fighting between Arabs and Jews escalated, and millions of private dollars

George F. Kennan (b. 1904).
Graduate of Princeton, Pulitzer Prize–winning historian, career diplomat, and recognized expert on Soviet affairs, Kennan was Mr. "X" in 1947 when he articulated the containment doctrine. This brilliant man served Ambassador Harriman in Moscow and then headed the State Department's Policy Planning Staff (1947–1949). Later he became ambassador to Russia (1952) and Yugoslavia (1961–1963). In the 1970s and 1980s he emerged as a leading critic of the nuclear arms race, imploring leaders to "cease this madness." (The Institute for Advanced Study, Princeton, New Jersey)

from Jewish Americans flowed to co-religionists in Palestine to buy weapons. (By war's end in early 1949, some 780,000 of 1,300,000 Arab residents had been displaced; many of these Palestinians became refugees in Lebanon and Jordan. Having jettisoned the partition plan, Jews came to occupy 77 percent of Palestine.)

Truman tilted further toward the Zionists after his old business partner Eddie Jacobson arranged a visit from Chaim Weizmann in March 1948. This Zionist leader (soon to be the first president of Israel) had once thought Truman "will never jeopardize his oil concessions for the sake of the Jews, although he may need them when the time of election arrives."[88] For reasons of politics and Cold War strategy, Truman formally extended diplomatic recognition to the new Jewish state on May 14, 1948, just nine minutes after Zionists declared the existence of Israel. Two presidential aides and Zionist sympathizers, David Niles and Max Lowenthal, had persuaded Truman that Israel would "line up on the side of the United States a far abler force" than the Arabs, thereby bolstering the American position vis-à-vis the Soviet Union in the Middle East.[89] And Clark Clifford, another pro-Zionist assistant, advised that "shilly-shallying appeasement" of the Arabs would cause "contempt" for the United States around the world, thus serving Soviet ambitions.[90] Despite Secretary of State George Marshall's blunt comment that he "would vote against the president" in the election if Truman recognized Israel for political expediency, subsequent Israeli military victories over the armies of five Arab states prompted even the State Department to reassess Israel's importance as a potential ally in the containment of the Soviet Union.[91] Moscow itself recognized Israel, reducing the risk that U.S. recognition would drive angry Arabs into the Soviet camp.

Containment became the byword of the time, and George F. Kennan, director of the State Department's Policy Planning Staff, wrote the definitive statement. The July 1947 issue of the prestigious journal *Foreign Affairs* carried "The Sources of Soviet Conduct," written by a mysterious Mr. "X," soon revealed as Kennan. The United States must adopt a "policy of firm containment," he wrote, "designed to confront the Russians with unalterable counterforce, at every point where they show signs of encroaching upon the interests of a peaceful and stable world." Such pressure might force the "mellowing" of Soviet policy. Kennan sketched a picture of an aggressive, uncompromising Soviet Union driven by ideology. Mechanistic Soviet power, he wrote, "moves inexorably along a prescribed path, like a persistent toy automobile wound up and headed in a given direction, stopping only when it meets some unanswerable force."[92] Even though Kennan, as the historian Wilson Miscamble has noted, actually preferred "political, rather than military, means" to implement containment, his muscular language suggested otherwise.[93]

One of the most vocal critics of containment, the journalist Walter Lippmann, predicted trouble. Lippmann called containment a "strategic monstrosity" because it did not distinguish vital from peripheral areas. Containment would test American resources and patience without limit. What if Congress should decide not to fund some presidential ventures in "counter-force"? Lippmann also prophetically observed that the "policy can be implemented only by recruiting, subsidizing and supporting a heterogeneous array of satellites, clients, dependents and puppets." Instead, he proposed the removal of all foreign troops from Europe to ease tension. He denied that Soviet forces stood poised to attack Western Europe, a point on which he and Kennan agreed. Finally, Lippmann sadly concluded that Truman and Mr. "X" in their major statements had abandoned their essential responsibility—diplomacy. "For a diplomat to think that rival and unfriendly powers cannot be brought to a settlement is to forget what diplomacy is about."[94]

The Marshall Plan, NATO, and the Division of Europe

In 1947–1948, under the banner of containment, U.S. goals for Western Europe crystallized: economic reconstruction and hunger relief, linkage of Germany's western zones with a Western European economic system, reinvigorated trade with the United States, prevention of leftist political gains, ouster of communists from governments (especially in Italy and France), settlement of colonial disputes (as in Indochina and Indonesia) that were draining funds, blockage of neutralist tendencies, and building military allies. By 1947 the United States had already spent $9 billion in the region. Despite assistance through the United Nations Relief and Rehabilitation Administration (UNRRA), the World Bank, and the International Monetary Fund, plus the loan to Britain and expenditures for the military occupation of Germany, Washington had failed to secure peace and prosperity. Europe remained economically hobbled, and Americans predicted that communists would exploit the economic chaos. Europe's multibillion-dollar deficit also meant that Europeans could not buy American products unless they received dollars from the United States.

V. M. Molotov (1890–1986). Popularly known as "stone ass," the Soviet foreign minister (1939–1949; 1952–1956), a tough-minded negotiator, cleared most decisions with Stalin. When he became angry, a bump appeared on his forehead, alerting adversaries of trouble. In his memoirs Molotov stressed *realpolitik*: "What we did . . . we did superbly, we strengthened the Soviet state. That was my chief task. My task as minister of foreign affairs was to see to it that we weren't cheated." (*The Reporter*, 1956. Copyright 1956 by The Reporter Magazine Co.)

On June 5, 1947, at Harvard University, Secretary of State George C. Marshall called for a comprehensive, coordinated program to put Europe back on its feet. A halting, quiet orator, Marshall delivered a monumental message in only 1,500 words. A distraught Europe needed help to face "economic, social and political deterioration of a very grave character."[95] He vaguely called on the European nations to initiate a collective plan. Recognizing that "if we want to act singlehandedly, we lose everything," British foreign secretary Ernest Bevin and French foreign minister Georges Bidault conferred and soon accepted Marshall's proposal, ultimately shaping it according to American specifications.[96] They reluctantly invited Soviet foreign minister V. M. Molotov to join them for a meeting in Paris in June.

Kremlin leaders sniffed a capitalist trap. Opposed to any program dominated by the United States, Molotov suggested loosely structured arrangements designed to protect national sovereignties. Bevin and Bidault, knowing that Washington insisted on an integrated effort, rejected national shopping lists. Molotov abruptly left Paris, and he recalled in his unrepentant memoirs that "if *they* think we made a mistake in rejecting the Marshall Plan, that means we acted correctly."[97] The United States had never wanted Soviet participation in the European Recovery Program (ERP), as the Marshall Plan became known. "At best," the historian Michael J. Hogan has written, "American officials saw Marshall's plan as a way to break Soviet influence in Eastern Europe; at worst, they were counting on Soviet opposition to galvanize support for the plan in Congress."[98] Moscow rejected the Marshall Plan because Eastern Europe was expected to ship raw materials to industrial Western Europe, ensuring dependency on the West; because a large influx of dollars into the

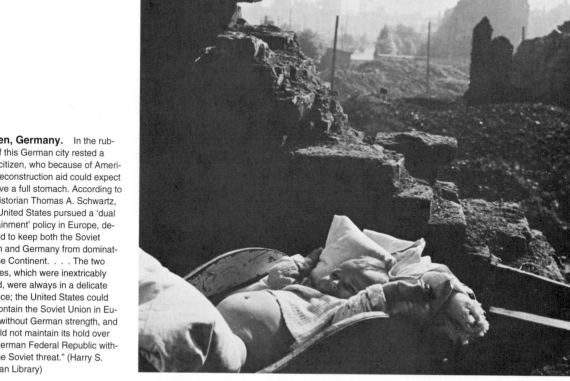

Essen, Germany. In the rubble of this German city rested a new citizen, who because of American reconstruction aid could expect to have a full stomach. According to the historian Thomas A. Schwartz, "the United States pursued a 'dual containment' policy in Europe, designed to keep both the Soviet Union and Germany from dominating the Continent. . . . The two policies, which were inextricably linked, were always in a delicate balance; the United States could not contain the Soviet Union in Europe without German strength, and it could not maintain its hold over the German Federal Republic without the Soviet threat." (Harry S. Truman Library)

Soviet sphere of influence would directly challenge Soviet interests; and because the plan sought to revive West Germany. In any case, Congress would probably have shunned funding a recovery program that included the Soviet Union and its neighbors. Finally demanding "total conformity and obedience" from his allies, Stalin announced the division of the world into "two camps" and instituted a feeble Molotov Plan for Eastern Europe to compete with the Marshall Plan.[99]

Congress in March 1948 passed the Economic Cooperation Act. The coup in Czechoslovakia, elections in Italy (would they go communist?), and the growing crisis over Germany, together with a March 17 Truman war-scare speech to a joint session of Congress, garnered the Marshall Plan a vote of 69 to 17 in the Senate and 329 to 74 in the House. Congress approved $4 billion for the program's first year. Before ending in December 1951, the Economic Cooperation Administration had sent $12.4 billion into the needy European economy.

The Marshall Plan proved a mixed success. In Europe it caused inflation, failed to solve a serious balance-of-payments problem, and took only tentative steps toward economic integration. But it sparked impressive Western European industrial production and investment and started the region toward self-sustaining economic growth. The ERP, remarked Bevin, acted "like a lifeline to sinking men."[100] The Marshall Plan stimulated the U.S. economy by requiring recipients to spend some aid in the United States on American goods; in this way, the profitable flow of American exports to traditional European markets continued. The program "aided and accelerated . . . the anti-Communist shift of the European trade union movement," and it won votes for political parties that backed the generous U.S. project.[101]

The Marshall Plan had shortcomings, too. Europe became dependent on American aid, less able to make its own choices. The French complained about "Coca-colonization."[102] The publisher of *Le Monde* hyperbolically remarked to Walter Lippmann that "France under the Marshall Plan and the Truman Doctrine was becoming a sort of Philippines."[103] Some American money funded European resistance to colonial wars. The program bypassed the United Nations and the Economic Commission for Europe, where it might have operated with less divisiveness. The ERP encouraged restrictions on East-West trade and helped revive West Germany, thereby arousing Moscow's fears of its nemesis. In 1951 the Economic Cooperation Administration merged into the Mutual Security Administration, with 80 percent of American aid to Western Europe becoming military in nature.

Dollar and Atomic Diplomacy. In this Soviet view of U.S. foreign policy, Truman wields the atomic bomb and the money bag. Note Winston S. Churchill on the right. (*Krokodil*, USSR)

Believing the Soviets capable of overrunning Western Europe in six months, bombing Alaska and Puget Sound, and even causing "serious internal disorders by subversion," the Pentagon sought greater rearmament without knowing that "the Soviet army in Germany was configured for defensive operations, rather than the quick march to the English Channel that formed the basis of U.S. military planning."[104] In July 1947, Congress passed the National Security Act, which streamlined the military establishment. The act created the Department of Defense, the National Security Council (NSC) to advise the president, and the Central Intelligence Agency (CIA) to gather and collate information through spying and other unspecified functions, which later came to mean covert activities against foreign governments or citizens. In Europe in March 1948, Britain, France, and the three Benelux nations, with U.S. encouragement, signed the Brussels Treaty for collective defense. In June the Senate passed (64 to 4) Vandenberg's resolution applauding that effort and suggesting American participation.

The United States also implemented the Fulbright Program in 1948, "the most significant movement of scholars across the earth since the fall of Constantinople in 1453," as an Oxford don remarked.[105] The brainchild two years earlier of Senator J. William Fulbright, Democrat of Arkansas and a former Rhodes scholar and university president, this example of "public diplomacy" sought to breach cultural barriers and inculcate a favorable image of the United States among foreign peoples. The Fulbright Program sponsored educational exchanges; faculty and students went abroad to teach and study, and their counterparts from other countries came to the United States. By 1953 elites in twenty-eight nations participated in the program in Europe, Asia, and the Middle East. In some countries, former Fulbrighters achieved political prominence and helped keep their governments friendly to Washington. To combat anti-American propaganda in what President Truman described as a "struggle, above all else, for the minds of men," some American and European intellectuals organized the Congress of Cultural Freedom in 1950; the CIA secretly subsidized this effort to promote America in Europe.[106]

The United States also endorsed in 1948 the World Health Organization (WHO), a specialized United Nations agency (and successor to UNRRA) that fulfilled a "two-pronged strategy of education and disease-fighting." Targeting borderless epidemic diseases such as malaria, tuberculosis, and syphilis, with a "sense of

Dean Acheson (1893–1971).
A graduate of Yale and Harvard and a wealthy lawyer, Acheson became secretary of state in 1949. He described himself as "always a conservative." Polished and arrogant, he served as secretary of state until 1953. "There's no way to argue with a river," Acheson once said about the Soviets. "You can channel it; you can dam it up. But you can't argue with it." (Portrait by Gardner Cox, National Portrait Gallery, Smithsonian Institution, Gift of Covington and Burling)

international fellowship," WHO physicians blanketed the earth to promote prevention and administer vaccines.[107] Washington has traditionally supplied the largest share of WHO's budget.

Truman summarized American foreign policy in his inaugural address of January 20, 1949. Articulating simple juxtapositions of "communism" and "democracy," the president listed four central points. First, he endorsed the United Nations. Second, he applauded the European Recovery Program. Third, he announced that the United States was planning a North Atlantic defense pact. And fourth, "we must embark on a bold new program" of technical assistance for "underdeveloped areas," a reference to the Point Four Program, launched in 1950.[108]

On April 4, 1949, the North Atlantic Treaty was signed in Washington by the five Brussels Treaty countries of Britain, France, Belgium, the Netherlands, and Luxembourg, as well as by Denmark, Iceland, Italy, Norway, Portugal, Canada, and the United States. (Greece and Turkey joined in 1952 and West Germany in 1954.) Article 5 provided "that an armed attack against one or more . . . shall be considered an attack against them all."[109] This article, said critics, would draw America into a war even if it did not want to go. "Mr. Republican," Senator Robert Taft of Ohio, saw NATO as a threat to the Soviet Union that would eventually force the United States to send military aid to Europe and spur an arms race. Taft also noted that the president could commit American troops almost at will without constitutional restraint. Some dissenters questioned the precise nature of the Soviet threat: Was it military, political, or ideological? After all, no Soviet military attack seemed imminent. Other critics from both left and right thought that the United States was overextending itself. George F. Kennan, increasingly disaffected from the American militarization and nuclearization of the Cold War, argued that, because few U.S. leaders anticipated a Soviet military thrust, NATO served no military need.

The United States welcomed NATO as much for political as for military purposes. A popular saying explained that NATO kept the Soviets out, the Americans in, and the Germans down. In other words, NATO gave the United States influence in Europe—an extension of the Monroe Doctrine, one senator claimed. Through NATO Washington could blunt neutralist tendencies or revival of an "appeasement psychology."[110] The alliance also permitted the United States to rearm West Germany while reassuring Europeans that Germany would be controlled by a multinational organization. U.S. officials also believed that Western Europe needed a "general stiffening of morale" through the creation of NATO, to stimulate capital investment and encourage an energetic reconstruction effort.[111] Depicting new allies as insecure members of the same family who "sublimated fear" of their "own inadequacy," Kennan recommended that "we must exhibit more confidence in them than we may actually feel—string them along a little."[112] "Europe under American water cans handled by British gardeners blossoms into a happy Garden of Eden," as one diplomat phrased it.[113]

On July 21, 1949, the Senate approved the NATO Treaty by a handsome 82 to 13 margin. Truman ratified the treaty two days later. That day he also sent the Mutual Defense Assistance Bill to Congress requesting more than a billion dollars for European military aid. Containment had taken a distinct turn to military means, and the stakes became bigger. After the Soviets exploded an atomic device in August 1949, Truman ordered crash development of a thermonuclear or hydrogen "superbomb," saying that "since we can't obtain international control we must be strongest in atomic weapons."[114] By mid-1950 the U.S. arsenal already included some 300 atomic bombs and more than 260 aircraft that could drop them on Soviet targets. The Soviets responded to NATO with the Warsaw Pact in 1955, the same year that they detonated their first hydrogen bomb, three years after the U.S. H-bomb.

In late January 1950, Truman ordered a comprehensive review of U.S. military and foreign policy. Eventually tagged National Security Council Paper Number 68 (NSC-68), the April report predicted prolonged global tension, Soviet military expansion, and relentless communist aggression (some officials regarded Mao's recent triumph in China as an example of an international conspiracy). According to one student of national security policy, "conventional rearmament and strategic superiority were now deemed indispensable for the risk-taking necessary to co-opt the industrial core of Eurasia, integrate it with the Third World periphery, and maintain America's preponderant position in the international system."[115] Washington had to persuade the public to support larger defense budgets and higher taxes. Paul Nitze, who replaced Kennan as head of the Policy Planning Staff, wrote most of NSC-68, and he glossed over complexities and ambiguities. The document treated communism as a monolith, ignoring differences within the communist community. It spoke of the "free world," overlooking the many nations allied with the United States that had undemocratic governments. It postulated that communism orchestrated the world's troubles, neglecting the indigenous character of nationalist movements that challenged the imperial powers. It made sweeping assumptions about Soviet motives and capabilities without evidence. The report, in short, exaggerated the "threat." Lippmann's counsel against indiscriminate globalism went unheeded; the United States prepared to become the world's policeman. But how to convince Americans to support the report's prescriptions? "We were sweating over it, and then—with regard to NSC-68—thank God Korea came along," recalled an Acheson aide.[116] In September 1950, a few months after the outbreak of the Korean War, Truman ordered NSC-68's implementation.

Stalin initially responded to NATO and American rearmament with disdain. "America, though it screams war, is actually afraid of war," he told Mao Zedong in December 1949.[117] Yet as the two sides consolidated their respective spheres, Moscow appealed in spring 1950 for a Soviet-American dialogue to reduce tensions. Secretary of State Dean Acheson ridiculed the Soviet "Trojan dove," vowing to contest the Soviets by building U.S. "situations of strength" throughout the world.[118] As Walter Lippmann had predicted, diplomacy became a victim of the Cold War.

Asian Allies: Restoring Japan and Backing Jiang in China

Asia experienced a major reconfiguration at the end of World War II. In Indochina, Burma, and Indonesia the old imperial system crumbled. The colonial powers looked to the United States to help them salvage what they could. Japan suffered defeat and occupation. Korea, formerly dominated by Japan, was divided along the thirty-eighth parallel by the Soviet Union and the United States. Civil war loomed in China.

The Pacific Ocean was becoming an American sphere of influence. If the Soviets ran some of the Eastern European countries, the Supreme Commander for the Allied Powers, General Douglas MacArthur, ran Japan. Unlike Germany, Japan had no zones. Despite a Far Eastern Advisory Commission with Soviet membership, the United States rejected Soviet requests for shared power, and MacArthur treated Stalin's representative like "a mere piece of furniture."[119] The United States also assumed control over Micronesia (the Marianas, Marshalls, and Carolines), Okinawa, Iwo Jima, and more than a hundred other Pacific outposts. As if to demonstrate the point, on July 7, 1946, the United States tested an atomic bomb on the Marshall Island of Bikini. To avoid the charge of imperial land grabbing, Washington had the United Nations place Micronesia under U.S. trusteeship. In 1949 MacArthur declared that "the Pacific had become an Anglo-Saxon lake," and State Department official Dean Rusk wanted "to control every wave in the Pacific."[120]

The first two years of occupation brought major reforms to Japan: a new constitution, war crimes trials, women's rights, dismantling of feudal landownership, even American censorship of Japanese films so as to depict Emperor Hirohito not as a god but as a constitutional monarch and "symbol of the people's unity."[121] Japan seemed to bury its militarism as a more pacifist culture emerged. Then U.S. officials reversed course as the Cold War progressed and it appeared that communist Mao Zedong would win in China. Americans now needed a "stable Japan, integrated into the Pacific, friendly to the U.S., and, in case of need, a ready and dependable ally."[122] During 1947–1950, labor unions were restricted, the reparations program was curtailed, production controls in war-related industries were relaxed, the antitrust program was suspended, communists were barred from government and university positions, and former Japanese leaders were reinstated. As a result, as the historian John W. Dower has noted, "the ideals of peace and democracy took root in Japan—not as a borrowed ideology or imposed vision, but as a lived experience and a seized opportunity."[123]

The restoration of Japan carried international ramifications. The Chinese communists feared a devilish scheme to rebuild Japan as a base for aggression against China. Japanese recovery, U.S. officials argued in early 1950, also required the development of markets for Japanese products in Southeast Asia, Indonesia, the Philippines, southern Korea, and India, and hence, application of the containment doctrine to undercut communists. The Soviet Union suspiciously eyed U.S. expansion in Asia and protested America's peace treaty negotiations with Japan. In September 1951, the United States and fifty other nations signed a peace treaty that restored Japanese sovereignty, gave the United States a base on Okinawa, and permitted the retention of foreign troops in Japan. Moscow refused to sign. A separate Japanese-American security pact also permitted American troops and planes on Japanese soil. From Pearl Harbor, a merciless war, and the atomic blasts to a peaceful occupation and Japanese-American cooperation—how to explain the dramatic shift? Continued demonic images and punishment no longer served the interests of either party. Americans sought a Cold War ally, and the Japanese sought a helping hand. Luckily, "the same stereotypes that fed superpatriotism and outright race hate were adaptable to cooperation." For example, Americans considered the Japanese, in MacArthur's words, "like a boy of twelve" and able to become "good pupils" under U.S. tutelage. And the Japanese philosophy of "proper place" meant that the Japanese could become "good losers" who, as Prime Minister Shigeru Yoshida put it, end up "winning by diplomacy after losing in war."[124]

Americans wanted a peaceful China within their sphere of influence too. For decades they had preached the Open Door, dreamed of vast Chinese markets and Christian havens, and considered China a special friend, if not client. A recovering Japan also needed Asian markets. "Whether China is red or green," said Yoshida, "China is a natural market."[125] The Chinese communists had other ideas, challenging the American-backed regime of Jiang Jieshi. During 1945–1949, the United States became a counterrevolutionary force in a revolutionary country.

American postwar goals sought a united noncommunist country under Jiang, trade with the United States, China as a keeper of the balance of power in Asia, and a U.S. ally. At the end of the war, American troops took positions in northern China, including Beijing and Tianjin. They transported Jiang's soldiers to Manchuria in a race to beat Mao Zedong's communists there. As he promised at Yalta, Stalin signed a treaty of friendship with Jiang's regime in August 1945, telling Nationalist diplomats that "Japan will restore her might in 20, 30 years . . . our relations with China is [*sic*] based on this."[126] When pressed by Stalin not to renew civil war and to cooperate with Jiang, Mao grumbled that "the Soviet Union cannot help us."[127] Perhaps hoping that a "cooperative Nationalist China" might act as "a buffer" against a revived Japan, Stalin preferred a China that would pose no threat along the 4,150 miles of the Sino-Soviet border.[128] Mao seemed too independent-minded, too "Titoist" for the Soviet taste. Stalin called the Chinese "margarine" communists.[129] U.S. Foreign Service Officers such as John Paton Davies and John S. Service reported from China that relations between Moscow and Mao remained fractious and that the communists would probably defeat Jiang without much help from Moscow, despite the presence of Soviet troops in Manchuria.

Swashbuckling Ambassador Patrick J. Hurley managed to bring Mao and Jiang together for talks in fall 1945, but Jiang refused to make concessions, confident that "the evolution of the international situation" would bring him American backing.[130] The talks failed. In November, Hurley, with his typical blast-furnace approach, resigned and charged that "a considerable section of our State Department is endeavoring to support communism in . . . China," in favor of "Mouse Dung" and "Joe N. Lie" (as he called Mao and Zhou Enlai).[131] Hurley's attack on the professional diplomats fed the conspiracy-minded who needed scapegoats for the American frustration over China. The "China experts" had not preferred Mao; they had simply reported that Jiang was corrupt, reactionary, and unlikely to gain the allegiance of the Chinese people, and that the communists would thus gain support. Paying for their accuracy, the China hands were criticized for having "warm hearts, but thick heads" and eventually were forced from the State Department under pressure from red-baiting Senator Joseph McCarthy.[132]

After the Hurley debacle, in December 1945, Truman sent the "Marshall Mission" to China. Headed by the highly respected General George C. Marshall, it sought to unite the factions under a noncommunist government. The communists,

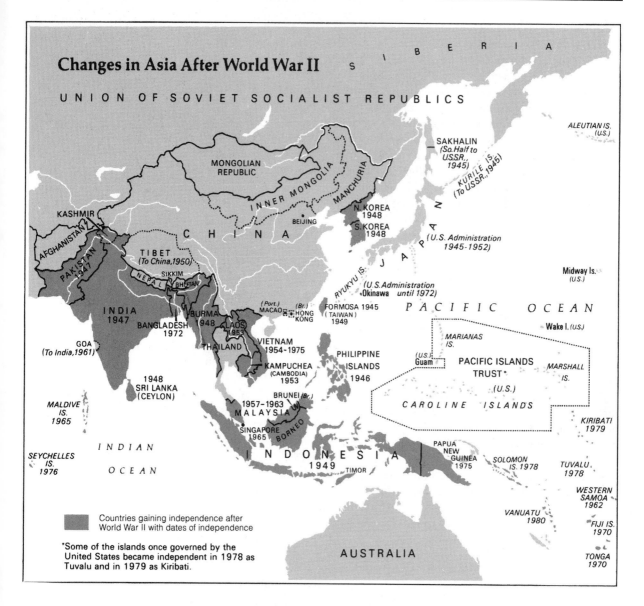

Changes in Asia After World War II

Countries gaining independence after World War II with dates of independence

*Some of the islands once governed by the United States became independent in 1978 as Tuvalu and in 1979 as Kiribati.

not wanting a bloody civil war and seeing coalition government as a nonviolent route to power, accepted Marshall's cease-fire in January 1946. About the same time, the Soviets pulled out of Manchuria, after having seized equipment as war booty, leaving the area to superior communist forces. By May 1946, 90 percent of Manchuria rested in communist hands. Jiang's decision to storm into Manchuria to challenge Mao doomed the cease-fire. Marshall and the 1,000 U.S. military and naval personnel who advised Jiang's forces could not restrain the overconfident generalissimo. "We were taken in," said Mao of U.S. mediation efforts; "we won't be cheated again."[133] For the next two years the communists adopted a "talking but not doing" approach—namely, castigating the United States but avoiding direct conflict.[134] A chagrined Marshall returned to the United States in January 1947 to become secretary of state.

Still hopeful of preventing a communist victory, Truman dispatched the "Wedemeyer Mission" to China in July 1947. General Albert C. Wedemeyer criticized the disarray of the Nationalists but concluded that China, like Greece, needed an aid program to curb the communist menace. He also suggested that a UN commission govern Manchuria. Secretary Marshall vetoed both proposals as impractical. But Marshall did release undelivered Lend-Lease goods to Jiang. In autumn 1947 Marshall offered the Nationalists arms and ammunition and authorized the Army Advisory Group to train Chinese combat troops on Formosa. In part to answer critics who asked why Greece but not China should be saved from communism, the White House asked Congress in early 1948 for $570 million in China aid. Under the China Aid Act of April, China obtained $400 million.

Despite $3 billion in aid to Jiang since V-J Day, Washington failed to stop Mao's ascent. Jiang let inflation run rampant, neglected tax and land reforms, launched risky military expeditions, tolerated corruption, and rejected negotiations. Dispirited soldiers defected from his army. U.S. military equipment fell into communist hands; ironically, in this roundabout way, Mao's troops got more aid from America than from the Soviet Union. "We picked a bad horse," the president lamented.[135] *Life* magazine called Mao's triumph "a victory for the Soviet Union and a moral disaster for the U.S."[136]

"The Open Door." The communists, led by Mao Zedong, defeated the crumbling forces of Jiang Jieshi in 1949, opening a door that the United States had tried to keep closed. The American imperialists, Mao claimed, would "make trouble, fail, make trouble again, fail again . . . till their doom." (*The Reporter,* 1950. Copyright 1950 by Fortnightly Publishing Co., Inc.)

The People's Republic of China and U.S. Nonrecognition

In June 1949, Mao Zedong stated that he was leaning to the side of socialism (the Soviet Union) against that "one great imperialist power" (the United States).[137] For many Americans, Mao's strident address simply confirmed Moscow's creation of another puppet state. Even though Stalin had given the Chinese communists only "limited" military aid ("not even a fart," as Mao overstated it), Americans preferred the words of Secretary Acheson, in the *China White Paper* of August 1949, that "the Communist regime serves not [Chinese] interests but those of Soviet Russia."[138] The *White Paper* documents showed little the United States could have done because Jiang himself would do so little. In January 1949 he sent China's gold supplies to the island of Formosa (Taiwan); in December, his Nationalist government followed. Mao's People's Republic, established on October 1, assumed power.

Critics such as the publisher Henry R. Luce of *Time* magazine, Republican members of Congress, and missionaries trumpeted that "China had been sold down the Yangtze" by the Democrats.[139] Senator Styles Bridges and Representative Walter Judd headed an informal and influential "China Lobby," which for years had advocated a major U.S. intervention in the Chinese civil war. They asked: If American foreign policy sought the containment of communism without geographical limit, as stated in the Truman Doctrine and the "X" article, why did not the United States intervene in China? Truman administration officials answered that China was too large, that a land war in Asia was unthinkable, that Jiang was unmanageable, and that the monetary costs were prohibitive. "The Chinese just seem unable to do anything positive themselves," a U.S. diplomat reported. "They always want the United States to do it first and for them."[140] Jiang's mishandling of U.S. funds confirmed Truman's private view of the Guomindong as "grafters and crooks."[141]

After Mao's victory over Jiang, the United States refused to recognize the People's Republic of China. Behind the nonrecognition policy lay mounting Sino-American animosities. In June 1949 communist leaders asked American ambassador J. Leighton Stuart to meet with them. The Truman administration vetoed contact. Not only did Truman fear howling protest from the "China Lobby," but he also resented Chinese communist behavior. In bombastic speeches, they reminded Americans of their imperialist past, including military participation in the Boxer Rebellion, support for Japan's seizure of Shandong in 1919, and naval gunboat patrols on Chinese rivers in the 1920s and 1930s (see Chapter 5). They confiscated American property and, apparently following Soviet advice, used calculated harassment to "squeeze out" Western diplomatic personnel in Manchuria.[142] They kept the U.S. consul general at Mukden under house arrest for two years before expelling him as a spy in October 1949.

From December 1949 through February 1950, in Moscow, Mao negotiated a treaty of friendship and alliance. Fearful of a revived Japan and of the expanded U.S. presence in Asia, Mao needed an ally. Wary of a Chinese Tito, Stalin avoided substantive talks until Mao blurted: "I only have had three tasks here: the first was to eat, the second was to sleep, and the third was to shit."[143] Mao eventually obtained what he wanted, an alliance obligating both parties to come to each other's assistance if attacked by a third party—"a big political asset to deal with the imperialist countries of the world."[144] American observers played down both the meager foreign aid that Moscow promised and Sino-Soviet differences over Mongolia and Manchuria. Despite Acheson's belief that "the very basic objectives of Moscow are very hostile to the basic objectives of China," Truman publicly stressed Sino-Soviet ideological affinity and denounced the treaty as the Soviet conquest of China.[145] The "Chi Commies," as official U.S. cables tagged the new Chinese leaders, would not receive U.S. diplomatic recognition. Born in failure, misinterpretation, and exaggeration, the nonrecognition policy set the United States firmly against the largest (650 million people) and potentially most influential nation in Asia. Hoping eventually to drive a wedge between the two communist powers, Assistant Secretary of State Dean Rusk in early 1951 taunted the Chinese: "The Peiping regime may be a colonial Russian government—a Slavic Manchukuo on a larger scale. It is not the Government of China. It does not pass the first test. It is not Chinese."[146]

The Cold War Mentality Takes Root

"We thought we could do anything," noted a U.S. writer who recalled the end of World War II. "We were heirs to a smiling and victorious confidence."[147] Although Western Europeans sometimes complained about the "ham-fisted" style, they usually welcomed the American presence.[148] In addition to soldiers and dollars, Washington exported jazz and baseball, "blue jeans and T-shirts, Coca-Cola and chewing gum, U.S. comics and movie stars."[149] As early as August 1945, an occupation official in Austria cabled Washington: "They're killing me with inquiries about Walt Disney films. . . . The American occupation cannot be complete without Mickey Mouse and Donald Duck."[150] Because Western Europeans had "invited" the United States to create an empire and include them within it, some scholars have argued, Washington pursued its economic, ideological, and strategic goals all the more zealously.[151] When an ally behaved erratically, as the French seemed to do on occasion, Americans used gendered discourse to rationalize their dominance, evoking images of "the whimsical airhead, the flirt, the hysteric, the seductress, the female who was willful and wrongheaded."[152] Shorn of their ignoble "isolationism," determined to throw off the failures of the depression decade, and committed to a world of peace and prosperity on their terms, Americans grew outraged when the Soviet Union challenged the U.S. mission and opportunity.

"After World War II," Senator J. William Fulbright remembered, "we were sold on the idea that Stalin was out to dominate the world . . . Henry Wallace sensed it [differently], he had a feeling about it, but he was ridiculed for being a visionary, an appeaser, unrealistic."[153] As Fulbright suggested, a popular idea captivated many Americans in the early Cold War: The Soviet Union had launched a crusade to communize the world. Appearances fed such a notion. Austere, intransigent, and ruthless, Stalin became in American eyes an obstructionist. Soviet diplomatic machinations and strong-arm rule in Eastern Europe alarmed Washington, and simple-minded communist propaganda offended. With threats and restricted contacts more common than compromises, the rude Soviet diplomatic style caused Western diplomats to repond in the same "crabbed and rancorous" manner.[154]

In the turmoil of the immediate postwar years, Americans exaggerated the Soviet/communist threat, imagining an omnipresent force. Americans made the communist adversary into something it was not, claiming for it a strength it did not possess, blaming it for trouble it did not start, identifying a monolith it did not resemble, and attributing to it accomplishments it did not achieve. True, the tough-talking Soviets eventually turned Eastern Europe into client states and probed in Berlin, but right after World War II the Soviets acted cautiously because they lacked a long-range air force, air defenses, the atomic bomb, and a surface fleet. Moscow actually snubbed independent communists such as Tito and Mao and could not control communists in Western Europe. "The most important thing," Stalin told an Albanian communist in January 1948, "is not to provoke our former allies."[155]

Americans nonetheless came to believe that Moscow ignited, fueled, and exploited unrest around the world, including revolutions. Most upheaval actually sprang from indigenous sources—colonial, tribal, ethnic, religious, cultural, economic. Yet Americans posited a mechanistic "domino theory." Erecting a global wall against communism, the United States supported imperialist allies such as France, which attempted to restore its colonial power in Vietnam against a popular nationalist movement (see pages 321–323). Believing that the Soviet Union masterminded revolutions directed specifically against U.S. interests, Washington sniffed international conspiracy and refused to recognize the People's Republic of

"Uncle Sam's World Wide Umbrella."   As the donor of large amounts of foreign aid, as the chief partner in military alliances, and as the professor of the containment doctrine, the United States undertook new global responsibilities after World War II. The depiction of smaller countries as children and Uncle Sam as the adult protector suggests a favorite American image/metaphor of family in which difficult allies were seen as naive children in need of tutelage and nurturing from the altruistic United States. (*The Reporter*, 1950. Copyright 1950 by Fortnightly Publishing Co., Inc.)

China, hardly a Soviet puppet. Only with respect to Finland ("the only [U.S.] penetration yet achieved in any part of the [Iron] Curtain") did the United States refrain "from acts . . . which might reasonably be regarded by the Soviet Union as a challenge to its essential interests."[156] Dependent on imports of uranium and other strategic minerals from South Africa to sustain a Cold War nuclear strategy and economy, the Truman administration backed white, anticommunist regimes that suppressed black nationalism, acting, in the historian Thomas Borstelmann's phrase, "as a reluctant uncle—or godparent—at the baptism of apartheid."[157]

Even in Latin America, indirect U.S. intervention to oust communists from the Costa Rican government in 1948 "mirrored the hardening of Washington's policies toward worldwide communism."[158] In 1945–1946 Washington had given tacit support for democratic interventions by exile groups against Caribbean dictatorships, but by the end of the decade it "placed a premium on stability out of concern that Communists might exploit situations of unrest."[159] Thus did Panama receive Point Four assistance in 1950 to combat "Communist-influenced subversive elements," and military aid flowed to the Péron regime in Argentina after 1947 because of Cold War fears.[160]

The Cold War mentality framed discourse in a "system of symbolic representation that defined America's national identity by reference to the un-American 'other,' usually the Soviet Union."[161] The malevolent Soviets acted; the heroic Americans reacted. The Soviets aggressed; Americans defended. Hollywood still featured films about World War II, but "the real unseen enemy was Communism," and postwar movies such as *Sands of Iwo Jima* (1949) and *Twelve O'Clock High* (1949) stressed the "psychological conditioning necessary for a new kind of 'war.'"[162] The expansive term "national security" took on an almost sacred aura, justifying huge military budgets that starved the infrastructure, the suspension of diplomacy in favor of confrontation, interventions far distant from the United States, a secrecy that undermined constitutional procedures, and actions Americans condemned others for—manipulating foreign governments, assassinating political foes abroad, and disseminating false information ("disinformation"). Because the Soviets acted similarly, they share responsibility for the extremes of the long Cold War.

To meet the communist threat and to protect and extend traditional overseas interests through preponderant power, American diplomats in the early Cold War pursued a self-conscious, expansionist, often unilateral foreign policy. In a world ravaged by war, American business and government officials cooperated to expand U.S. foreign trade. By 1947 the United States accounted for one-third of the world's exports. Americans exploited Middle Eastern oil and tapped the raw materials of the Third World, importing manganese ore from Brazil and India, for example. Open Door pronouncements helped spur this trade and facilitate the investment of $12 billion abroad by 1950. Stalin thought the "Open Door policy as dangerous to a nation as foreign military invasion."[163] Further, the expenditure of $1.314 billion in arms aid to NATO in 1949 marked "the beginning of an enormously costly program that," as one official feared, "will go first to Europe and then perhaps to Asia and then to South America and where does it stop?"[164]

The containment doctrine became the commanding dogma. When Americans had doubts, the containment doctrine told them what to do. "Like medieval theologians," Fulbright noted, "we had a philosophy that explained everything to us in advance, and everything that did not fit could be readily identified as a fraud or a lie or an illusion. . . . The perniciousness of the anti-Communist ideology . . . arises . . . from its universalization and its elevation to the status of a revealed truth."[165] Americans henceforth applied the historical lessons of the 1940s, failing to define precisely the "threat," placing few geographical limits on containment, and increasingly adopting military methods. Whereas Washington explained its mission as containment, Moscow charged encirclement.

Another legacy of the early Cold War reshaped the American political process. The Truman administration, sometimes using scare tactics, influenced the thinking of the "foreign-policy public." Most foreign-policy debates centered on how much to spend, not whether to spend. Congress sometimes proved obstinate, but on the whole Truman got what he wanted. Bipartisanship also helped the president dominate the making of foreign policy. Leaders said that Americans had to speak with unity. As bipartisan leader Vandenberg proudly concluded, "our Government did not splinter. It did not default. It was strong in the presence of its adversaries."[166] But bipartisanship too often meant that legislation received superficial analysis, that debate became pro forma, and that Congress permitted the president considerable freedom in foreign policy.

Democratic values inevitably suffered. As the historian Thomas A. Bailey rationalized, "the masses are notoriously short-sighted and generally cannot see the danger until it is at their throats." Therefore, concluded Bailey, in an unabashed endorsement of executive infallibility in 1948: "deception of the people may in fact become increasingly necessary."[167] Acheson bluntly remarked: "Bipartisan foreign policy is the ideal for the executive because you cannot run this damned country any other way except by fixing the whole organization so it doesn't work the way it is supposed to work. Now the way to do that is to say politics stops at the seaboard—and anyone who denies that postulate is a son-of-a-bitch and a crook and not a true patriot. Now if people will swallow that, then you're off to the races."[168]

People swallowed it. Debate—testing assumptions and holding government leaders accountable—became shallow. Tolerance of dissenting views and the fearless inquiry so essential to democracy deteriorated during the early Cold War. Unprincipled demagogues exploited public anxiety about national security, charging that communist conspiracies wormed through official Washington. During the 1948 campaign, the president himself practiced the "red-baiting" so common to Cold War politics when he deliberately linked Progressive party candidate Henry A. Wallace, dissenter from the "get-tough" policy, to the communists. Three years before demagogic Senator Joseph McCarthy charged government officials with treason, the Truman administration itself instituted a federal employee loyalty program to identify and ferret out suspected subversives. With no precise definition of disloyalty, zealous witch-hunters confused criticism with subversion. In this milieu of suspicion, an ever-increasing public cynicism infected politics.

As the Cold War grew more perilous, so too did the ominous presence of the atomic bomb. As much as Truman said he "disliked relying on nuclear weapons, he disliked deficits and taxes [from the costs of conventional forces] even more."[169]

With growing arsenals and increasingly horrific strategies of "overkill" on both sides, people recognized that the Cold War "might not end in *one* Rome but with *two* Carthages," that nuclear war invited apocalypse.[170] Government officials, magazine editors, strategic analysts, scientists, and fiction writers alike, again and again, issued doomsday forecasts, sketching pictures of a radioactive global wasteland if nuclear weapons were not controlled. In a best-selling book, *No Place to Hide* (1948), David Bradley, a physician who witnessed the Bikini atomic test, chillingly depicted "the shadow of the colossus which looms behind tomorrow."[171] In 1949, in the apocalyptic Cold War film *White Heat,* James Cagney played a gangster who makes it to the "top of the world" perched on a globe-shaped chemical tank that explodes in a mushrooming fireball.[172] Late that year, after the Soviet atomic success, the *Bulletin of the Atomic Scientists* moved the hands of its "doomsday clock" to three minutes before midnight. A few months after the United States exploded the first hydrogen bomb in 1953, the hands moved to two minutes before midnight. America, the poet Robert Frost wrote, had "invented a new Holocaust."[173]

FURTHER READING FOR THE PERIOD 1945–1950

Some works cited in Chapter 6 cover particular leaders and the transition from war to peace.

For general studies of the Cold War era relevant to this chapter and others that follow, see Stephen Ambrose and Douglas Brinkley, *Rise to Globalism* (1997); S. J. Ball, *The Cold War* (1998); Richard Barnet, *Roots of War* (1972); H. W. Brands, *The Devil We Knew* (1993); Warren Cohen, *America in the Age of Soviet Power* (1993); Gordon A. Craig and Francis L. Lowenheim, eds., *The Diplomats, 1939–1979* (1994); Philip J. Funigiello, *American-Soviet Trade in the Cold War* (1988); John Lewis Gaddis, *The Long Peace* (1987), *Russia, the Soviet Union, and the United States* (1990), and *We Now Know* (1997); Alexander L. George et al., eds., *U.S.-Soviet Security Cooperation* (1988); Alexander L. George and Richard Smoke, *Deterrence in American Foreign Policy* (1974); Allen Hunter, ed., *Rethinking the Cold War* (1998); Robert H. Johnson, *Improbable Dangers: Conceptions of Threat in the Cold War and After* (1994); Charles W. Kegley, ed., *The Long Postwar Peace* (1991); Gabriel and Joyce Kolko, *The Limits of Power* (1972); Walter LaFeber, *America, Russia, and the Cold War* (1993); Deborah W. Larson, *Anatomy of Mistrust* (1997); Stuart W. Leslie, *The Cold War and American Science* (1994); Ralph Levering, *The Cold War* (1994); Geir Lundestad, *The American "Empire"* (1990); Michael Mandelbaum, *The Fate of Nations* (1988); Thomas J. McCormick, *America's Half Century* (1994); Frank A. Ninkovich, *Modernity and Power* (1994); David S. Painter, *The Cold War* (1999); Thomas G. Paterson, *Meeting the Communist Threat* (1988) and *On Every Front* (1992); James T. Patterson, *Grand Expectations* (1996); Edward Pessen, *Losing Our Souls* (1993); Michael S. Sherry, *In the Shadow of War* (1995); Hugh Thomas, *Armed Truce* (1987); and Adam Ulam, *Expansion and Coexistence* (1974).

U.S. leaders in the early Cold War period are studied in Rudy Abrahamson, *Spanning the Century* (1992) (Harriman); Allida Black, *Casting Her Own Shadow* (1995) (Eleanor Roosevelt); H. W. Brands, *Inside the Cold War* (1991) (Henderson); Douglas Brinkley, ed., *Dean Acheson and the Making of U.S. Foreign Policy* (1993); David Callahan, *Dangerous Capabilities* (1990) (Nitze); James Chace, *Acheson* (1998); Robert H. Ferrell, *George C. Marshall* (1966) and *Harry S. Truman* (1994); Alonzo Hamby, *Man of the People* (1995) (Truman); James G. Hershberg, *James B. Conant and the Birth of the Nuclear Age* (1993); Townsend Hoopes and Douglas Brinkley, *Driven Patriot* (1992) (Forrestal); Walter Isaacson and Evan Thomas, *The Wise Men* (1986); David McCullough, *Truman* (1992); David McLellan, *Dean Acheson* (1976); William E. Pemberton, *Harry S. Truman* (1989); Forrest C. Pogue, *George C. Marshall* (1963–1987); Alan R. Raucher, *Paul G. Hoffman* (1986); David Robertson, *Sly and Able* (1994) (Byrnes); T. Michael Ruddy, *The Cautious Diplomat* (1986) (Bohlen); Jordan A. Schwarz, *The Speculator* (1981) (Baruch); Gaddis Smith, *Dean Acheson* (1972); Ronald Steel, *Walter Lippmann and the American Century* (1980); Mark A. Stoler, *George C. Marshall* (1989); J. Samuel Walker, *Henry A. Wallace and American Foreign Policy* (1976); and Graham White and John Maze, *Henry A. Wallace* (1995).

Many books, all with the main title *Stalin,* include and critique the Soviet leader's foreign policy: Robert Conquest (1991); Isaac Deutscher (1967); Walter Laqueur (1990); Robert H. McNeal (1988); Edward Radzinsky (1996); and Dmitri Volkogonov (1991).

The ideas and career of George F. Kennan are explored in Barton Gellman, *Contending with Kennan* (1984); Walter Hixson, *George F. Kennan* (1990); David Mayers, *George Kennan and the Dilemmas of U.S. Foreign Policy* (1988); Wilson D. Miscamble, *George F. Kennan and the Making of American Foreign Policy* (1992); and Anders Stephanson, *George Kennan and the Art of Foreign Policy* (1989).

For the origins of the Cold War, see works cited in the paragraphs above and Barton J. Bernstein, ed., *Politics and Policies of the Truman Administration* (1970); Kendrick A. Clements, ed., *James F. Byrnes and the Origins of the Cold War* (1982); Robert J. Donovan, *Conflict and Crisis* (1977); John Lewis Gaddis, *The United States and the Origins of the Cold War* (1972); Lloyd Gardner, *Architects of Illusion* (1970); Francesca Gori and Silvio Pons, *The Soviet Union and Europe in the Cold War* (1996); James L. Gormly, *The Collapse of the Grand Alliance* (1987); George Herring, *Aid to Russia, 1941–1946* (1973); Lynn B. Hinds and Theodore O. Windt, Jr., *The Cold War as Rhetoric* (1991); Michael J. Hogan, *A Cross of Iron: Harry S. Truman and the Origins of the National Security State* (1998); Frank Kofsky, *Harry S. Truman and the War Scare of 1948* (1993); Gabriel Kolko, *The Politics of War* (1968); Deborah W. Larson, *Origins of Containment* (1985); Melvyn P. Leffler, *A Preponderance of Power* (1992) and *The Specter of Communism* (1994); Donald R. McCoy, *The Presidency of Harry S. Truman* (1984); Vojtech Mastny, *The Cold War and Soviet Insecurity* (1996); Robert Messer, *The End of an Alliance* (1982); Chester J. Pach, *Arming the Free World* (1991); Thomas G. Paterson, ed., *Cold War Critics* (1971); David Reynolds, ed., *The Origins of the Cold War in Europe* (1994); William Taubman, *Stalin's American Policy* (1982); Daniel Yergin, *Shattered Peace* (1977); and Vladislav Zubok and Constantine Pleshakov, *Inside the Kremlin's Cold War* (1996).

For the early years of the United Nations Organization, see James Barros, *Trygvie Lie and the Cold War* (1989); Thomas Campbell, *Masquerade Peace* (1973); Robert A. Divine, *Second Chance* (1967); Robert C. Hilderbrand, *Dumbarton Oaks* (1990); Townsend Hoopes and Douglas Brinkley, *FDR and the Creation of the U.N.* (1997); Evan Luard and Derek Herter, *The United Nations* (1993); and George Mazuzan, *Warren R. Austin at the U.N., 1946–1953* (1977).

The atomic bomb, nuclear questions, and their cultural impact are discussed in Gar Alperovitz, *Atomic Diplomacy* (1985) and *The Decision to Use the Atomic Bomb* (1995); Barton J. Bernstein, ed., *The Atomic Bomb* (1975); Kai Bird and Lawrence Lifschultz, eds., *Hiroshima Shadows* (1998); Paul Boyer, *By the Bomb's Early Light* (1986) and *Fallout* (1998); McGeorge Bundy, *Danger and Survival* (1990); Robert J. C. Butow, *Japan's Decision to Surrender* (1954); Herbert Feis, *The Atomic Bomb and the End of World War II* (1966); Jonathan E. Helmreich, *Gathering Rare Ores: The Diplomacy of Uranium Acquisition* (1986); Margot A. Henriksen, *Dr. Strangelove's America* (1997); Gregg Herken, *The Winning Weapon* (1981); Richard Hewlett and Oscar Anderson, *The New World* (1962); Michael J. Hogan, ed., *Hiroshima in History and Memory* (1996); David Holloway, *The Soviet Union and the Arms Race* (1984) and *Stalin and the Bomb* (1994); Robert Jay Lifton and Greg Mitchell, *Hiroshima in America* (1995); M. Susan Lindee, *Suffering Made Real: American Science and the Survivors at Hiroshima* (1994); Robert J. Maddox, *Weapons for Victory* (1995); Robert P. Neuman, *Truman and the Hiroshima Cult* (1995); John Newhouse, *War and Peace in the Nuclear Age* (1989); Martin Sherwin, *A World Destroyed* (1975); Ronald Takaki, *Hiroshima* (1995); J. Samuel Walker, *Prompt and Utter Destruction* (1997); Samuel R. Williamson and Steven L. Rearden, *The Origins of U.S. Nuclear Strategy* (1993); Allan M. Winkler, *Life Under a Cloud* (1993); Lawrence S. Wittner, *The Struggle Against the Bomb* (1993) (disarmament movement); and Peter Wyden, *Day One* (1984). The H-bomb is treated in Richard Rhodes, *Dark Sun* (1987), and Herbert F. York, *The Advisors* (1975).

Studies that focus on Eastern Europe and Finland include Phyllis Auty, *Tito* (1970); Michael M. Boll, *Cold War in the Balkans* (1984); Charles Gati, *Hungary and the Soviet Bloc* (1983); Jussi M. Hanhimäki, *Containing Coexistence* (1997) (Finland); Lorraine M. Lees, *Keeping Tito Afloat* (1997); Richard Lukacs, *Bitter Legacy* (1982) (Poland); Geir Lundestad, *The American Non-Policy Towards Eastern Europe* (1975) and *America, Scandinavia, and the Cold War* (1980); Stanley Max, *The United States, Great Britain, and the Sovietization of Hungary* (1985); Eric Roman, *Hungary and the Victor Powers* (1996); Walter Ullman, *The United States in Prague* (1978); Piotr Wandycz, *The United States and Poland* (1980); and Patricia Ward, *The Threat of Peace* (1979).

Anglo-American relations are discussed in Terry H. Anderson, *The United States, Great Britain, and the Cold War* (1981); Elisabeth Barker, *The British Between the Superpowers* (1983); Richard A. Best, Jr., *"Cooperation with Like-Minded Peoples"* (1986); Alan Bullock, *Ernest Bevin* (1984); Robin Edmonds, *Setting the Mould* (1987); Fraser J. Harbutt, *The Iron Curtain* (1986); Robert M. Hathaway, *Ambiguous Partnership* (1981); John Kent, *British Imperial Strategy and the Origins of the Cold War* (1993); W. Roger Louis and Hedley Bull, eds., *The Special Relationship* (1986); Ritchie Overdale, *The English Speaking Alliance* (1985); Kenneth W. Thompson, *Winston Churchill's World View* (1983); and Randall B. Woods, *A Changing of the Guard* (1990).

The United States in the world economy and economic expansion are treated in Irvine H. Anderson, *Aramco, the United States, and Saudi Arabia* (1981); Fred L. Block, *The Origins of International Economic Disorder* (1977); Alfred E. Eckes, Jr., *A Search for Solvency* (1975) (Bretton Woods) and *The United States and the Global Struggle for Minerals* (1979); Diane Kunz, *Butter and Guns* (1997); Aaron D. Miller, *Search for Security* (1980) (Saudi Arabia's oil); David S. Painter, *Oil and the American Century* (1986); Stephen J. Randall, *United States Foreign Oil Policy, 1919–1984* (1985); and Michael B. Stoff, *Oil, War, and American Security* (1980).

Cultural relations are specifically explored in Tom Engelhardt, *The End of Victory Culture* (1995); Kyoko Hirano, *Mr. Smith Goes to Tokyo* (1992) (cinema in Japan); Lary May, ed., *Recasting America* (1989); Frank A. Ninkovich, *The Diplomacy of Ideas* (1981); Richard Pells, *Not like Us: How Europeans Have Loved, Hated, and Transformed American Culture* (1997); and Reinhold Wagnleitner, *Coca-Colonization and the Cold War* (1994) (Austria).

For Western European issues, including economic reconstruction, Austria, and the Marshall Plan, see Josef Becker and Franz Knipping, *Power in Europe?* (1986); Anthony Carew, *Labour Under the Marshall Plan* (1987); Frank Costigliola, *France and the United States* (1992); Audrey K. Cronin, *Great Power Politics and the Struggle over Austria* (1986); David W. Ellwood, *Rebuilding Europe* (1992); Chiarello Esposito, *America's Feeble Weapon* (1994) (Marshall Plan); Richard Gardner, *Sterling-Dollar Diplomacy* (1969); Haim Genizi, *America's Fair Share* (1993) (displaced persons); John L. Harper, *America and the Reconstruction of Italy* (1986) and *American Visions of Europe* (1994); Michael J. Hogan, *The Marshall Plan* (1987); Boris N. Liedtke, *Embracing a Dictatorship* (1998) (Spain); Richard Mayne, *Recovery of Europe* (1973); James E. Miller, *The United States and Italy* (1986); Alan S. Milward, *The Reconstruction of Western Europe, 1945–51* (1984); Thomas G. Paterson, *Soviet-American Confrontation* (1973); Sallie Pisani, *The CIA and the Marshall Plan* (1991); Robert A. Pollard, *Economic Security and the Origins of the Cold War* (1985); Federico Romero, *The United States and the European Trade Union Movement* (1992); Mark Trachtenberg, *A Constructed Peace* (1999); Irwin M. Wall, *The United States and the Making of Postwar France* (1991); Donald R. Whiting and Edgar Erickson, *The American Occupation of Austria* (1985); Imanuel Wexler, *The Marshall Plan Revisited* (1983); and John W. Young, *Britain, France, and the Unity of Europe* (1984).

For Germany, see John H. Backer, *Winds of History* (1984); Tom Bower, *The Paperclip Conspiracy* (1988); Anne Deighton, *The Impossible Peace* (1990); Jeffrey M. Diefendorf et al., eds., *American Policy and the Reconstruction of West Germany* (1993); Carolyn Eisenberg, *Drawing the Line* (1996); John Gimbel, *The American Occupation of Germany* (1968), *The Origins of the Marshall Plan* (1976), and *Science, Technology, and Reparations* (1990); Bruce Kuklick, *American Policy and the Division of Germany* (1972); Clarence G. Lasby, *Project Paperclip* (1971); Norman Naimark, *The Russians in Germany* (1995); Edward N. Peterson, *The American Occupation of Germany* (1978); Daniel Rogers, *Politics After Hitler* (1995); Thomas A. Schwartz, *America's Germany* (1991); Avi Shlaim, *The United States and the Berlin Blockade, 1948–1949* (1983); Christopher Simpson, *Blowback* (1988) (recruitment of Nazis); and Jean Smith, *The Defense of Berlin* (1963).

For the Truman Doctrine and containment, consult G. M. Alexander, *The Prelude to the Truman Doctrine* (1984); David J. Alvarez, *Bureaucracy and Cold War Ideology* (1980) (Turkey); Richard Barnet, *Intervention and Revolution* (1972); Robert Frazier, *Anglo-American Relations with Greece* (1991); Richard Freeland, *The Truman Doctrine and the Origins of McCarthyism* (1971); John Lewis Gaddis, *Strategies of Containment* (1981); Charles Gati, ed., *Caging the Bear* (1977); John O. Iatrides, *Revolt in Athens* (1972), ed., *Greece in the 1940s* (1981), and ed., *Greece at the Crossroads* (1995); Howard Jones, *"A New Kind of War"* (1989); Jon V. Kofas, *Intervention and Underdevelopment* (1989) (Greece); Bruce R. Kuniholm, *The Origins of the Cold War in the Near East* (1980); and Lawrence S. Wittner, *American Intervention in Greece, 1943–1949* (1982).

NATO and military questions are studied in John Baylis, *The Diplomacy of Pragmatism* (1993) (Britain); Timothy P. Ireland, *Creating the Entangling Alliance* (1981); Lawrence S. Kaplan, *The United States and NATO* (1984), *NATO and the United States* (1988), and *The Long Entanglement: NATO's First Fifty Years* (1999); Steven L. Rearden, *History of the Office of the Secretary of Defense* (1984); Olav Riste, ed., *Western Security* (1985); Edward J. Sheehy, *The U.S. Navy, the Mediterranean, and the Cold War* (1992); Michael S. Sherry, *The Rise of American Air Power* (1987); Nicholas Sherwen, ed., *NATO's Anxious Birth* (1985); E. Timothy Smith, *The United States, Italy, and NATO* (1991); and Joseph Smith, ed., *The Origins of NATO* (1990). See also Samuel F. Wells, Jr., "Sounding the Tocsin: NSC-68 and the Soviet Threat," *International Security* (1979).

U.S. relations with Asia, including decolonization, are discussed in Robert Blum, *Drawing the Line* (1982); Russell Buhite, *Soviet-American Relations in Asia, 1945–1954* (1982); Kenton J. Clymer, *Quest for Freedom* (1995) (India); Nick Cullather, *Illusions of Influence* (1994) (Philippines); Edward Friedman and Mark Selden, eds., *America's Asia* (1971); Marc S. Gallicchio, *The Cold War Begins in Asia* (1988); Gary Hess, *America Encounters India, 1941–1947* (1971) and *The United States' Emergence as a Southeast Asian Power, 1940–1950* (1987); Akira Iriye and Warren Cohen, eds., *American, Chinese, and Japanese Perspectives on Wartime Asia, 1931–1949* (1990); James I. Matray, *The Reluctant Crusade* (1985) (Korea); Robert J. McMahon, *Colonialism and Cold War* (1981) (Indonesia), *The Cold War on the Periphery* (1994) (India and Pakistan), and *The Limits of Empire* (1999) (Southeast Asia); Yōnosuke Nagai and Akira Iriye, eds., *The Origins of the Cold War in Asia* (1977); Anita I. Singh, *The Limits of British Influence* (1994) (South Asia); and William Stueck, *The Road to Confrontation* (1981). For works on Vietnam and Indochina, see Chapter 9.

For Japan and the American occupation, see William S. Borden, *The Pacific Alliance* (1984); Roger Buckley, *Occupation Diplomacy* (1982); John W. Dower, *Empire and Aftermath* (1979), *War Without Mercy* (1986), and *Embracing Defeat* (1999); Herbert Feis, *Contest over Japan* (1967); Richard B. Finn, *Winners in Peace* (1992); D. Clayton James, *The Years of MacArthur* (1985); Walter LaFeber, *The Clash* (1997); Philip R. Piccigallo, *The Japanese on Trial* (1979); Michael Schaller, *The American Occupation of Japan* (1985), *Douglas MacArthur* (1989), and *Altered States* (1997); and Gary H. Tsuchimochi, *Education Reform in Postwar Japan* (1993).

For China and the recognition question, see Dorothy Borg and Waldo Heinrichs, eds., *Uncertain Years* (1980); Russell Buhite, *Patrick J. Hurley and American Foreign Policy* (1973); Carolle J. Carter, *Mission to Yenan* (1997); Gordon Chang, *Friends and Enemies* (1990); Thomas J. Christensen, *Useful Adversaries* (1996); Warren Cohen, *America's Response to China* (1990); Sergei Goncharov, John Lewis, and Xue Litai, *Uncertain Partners* (1993); Harry Harding and Yuan Ming, eds., *Sino-American Relations, 1945–55* (1989); Michael H. Hunt, *The Genesis of Chinese Communist Foreign Policy* (1996); T. Christoper Jesperson, *American Images of China* (1996); E. J. Kahn, Jr., *The China Hands* (1975); Ronald C. Keith, *The Diplomacy of Zhou Enlai* (1989); Ross Koen, *The China Lobby in American Politics* (1974); Paul G. Lauren, ed., *The China Hands' Legacy* (1987); Gary May, *China Scapegoat* (1979); David A. Mayers, *Cracking the Monolith* (1986); Robert P. Newman, *Owen Lattimore and the "Loss" of China* (1992); James Reardon-Anderson, *Yenan and the Great Powers* (1979); Michael M. Sheng, *Battling Western Imperialism* (1998); William Stueck, *The Wedemeyer Mission* (1984); Nancy B. Tucker, *Patterns in the Dust* (1983) and *Taiwan, Hong Kong, and the United States* (1994); Odd Arne Westad, *Cold War and Revolution* (1993); Shaw Yu-Ming, *John Leighton Stuart and Twentieth-Century Chinese-American Relations* (1992); and Shu Guang Zhang, *Deterrence and Strategic Culture* (1992).

For the Middle East, Iran, and the new state of Israel, see books on oil cited above and Michael J. Cohen, *Palestine and the Great Powers* (1983) and *Truman and Israel* (1990); Leonard Dinnerstein, *America and the Survivors of the Holocaust* (1982); Bruce J. Evensen, *Truman, Palestine, and the Press* (1992); Louise L. Fawcett, *Iran and the Cold War* (1992) (1946 crisis); Zvi Ganin, *Truman, American Jewry, and Israel, 1945–1948* (1979); James F. Goode, *The United States and Iran, 1946–51* (1989); Peter L. Hahn, *The United States, Great Britain, and Egypt* (1991); Burton I. Kaufman, *The Arab Middle East and the United States* (1996); George Lenczowski, *American Presidents and the Middle East* (1989); William Roger Louis, *The British Empire in the Middle East, 1945–1951* (1984); William Roger Louis and Robert W. Stookey, eds., *The End of the Palestine Mandate* (1986); Mark H. Lytle, *The Origins of Iranian-American Alliance, 1941–1953* (1987); John Quigley, *Palestine and Israel* (1990); Barry Rubin, *The Great Powers in the Middle East, 1941–1947* (1980); David

Schoenbaum, *The United States and the State of Israel* (1993); John Snetsinger, *Truman, the Jewish Vote, and the Creation of Israel* (1974); and Robert W. Stookey, *America and the Arab States* (1975). See also works on the Middle East cited in following chapters.

Relations with other Third World nations, including Latin America, are explored in Charles D. Ameringer, *The Caribbean Legion* (1996); Scott L. Bills, *Empire and Cold War* (1990) and *The Libyan Arena* (1995); Thomas Borstelmann, *Apartheid's Reluctant Uncle* (1993) (South Africa); Zachary Karabell, *Architects of Intervention* (1999); Michael L. Krenn, *The Chains of Interdependence* (1996) (Central America); Walter LaFeber, *Inevitable Revolutions* (1993); Thomas M. Leonard, *The United States and Central America, 1944–1949* (1984); Kyle Longley, *The Sparrow and the Hawk* (1997) (Costa Rica); Fredrick B. Pike, *The United States and Latin America* (1992); and Gaddis Smith, *The Last Years of the Monroe Doctrine* (1994).

For Canada-U.S. relations, see Robert Bothwell, *Canada and the United States* (1992); Joseph Jockel, *No Boundaries Upstairs* (1989); B. J. C. McKercher and Lawrence Aronsen, eds., *The North Atlantic Triangle in a Changing World* (1996); Denis Smith, *Diplomacy of Fear* (1988); and John H. Thompson and Stephen J. Randall, *Canada and the United States* (1998).

For espionage and the origins of the Central Intelligence Agency, see Obert Benson and Michael Warner, eds., *Venona: Soviet Espionage and the American Response* (1996); Arthur B. Darling, *The Central Intelligence Agency* (1990); Evan Thomas, *The Very Best Men* (1995); and Thomas F. Troy, *Wild Bill and Intrepid* (1996).

For domestic politics, anticommunism, interest groups, and public opinion in the early Cold War period, see Robert Divine, *Foreign Policy and U.S. Presidential Elections, 1940–1960* (1974); Justus Doenecke, *Not to the Swift: The Old Isolationists in the Cold War Era* (1979); Bruce E. Field, *Harvest of Dissent: The National Farmers Union and the Early Cold War* (1998); Richard M. Fried, *Nightmare in Red* (1990) and *The Russians Are Coming! The Russians Are Coming!* (1998); Robert Griffith and Athan Theoharis, eds., *The Specter* (1974); John E. Haynes, *Red Scare or Red Menace?* (1996); William Keller, *The Liberals and J. Edgar Hoover* (1989); Harvey Klehr and Ronald Radosh, *The Amerasia Spy Case* (1996); William L. O'Neill, *A Better World: Stalinism and the American Intellectuals* (1983); Brenda Plummer, *Rising Wind* (1996) (African Americans); Ronald Radosh, *American Labor and U.S. Foreign Policy* (1969); Colin Shindler, *Hollywood Goes to War* (1979); Peter L. Steinberg, *The Great "Red" Menace* (1984); Athan Theoharis, *The Yalta Myths* (1970), *Seeds of Repression* (1971), and ed., *Beyond the Hiss Case: The FBI, Congress, and the Cold War* (1982); Penny von Eschen, *Race Against Empire* (1997) (African Americans); Stephen J. Whitfield, *The Culture of the Cold War* (1991); and Lawrence Wittner, *Rebels Against War: The American Peace Movement, 1941–1960* (1984). For works on McCarthyism, see Chapter 8.

See also the General Bibliography and the following notes.

For comprehensive coverage of foreign-relations topics, see the articles in the four-volume *Encyclopedia of U.S. Foreign Relations* (1997), edited by Bruce W. Jentleson and Thomas G. Paterson.

NOTES TO CHAPTER 7

1. Quoted in Hanson W. Baldwin, "Hiroshima Decision," in *Hiroshima Plus 20* (New York: Delacorte, 1965), p. 41.
2. Harold M. Agnew quoted in *Time, CXXVI* (July 29, 1985), 46.
3. Quoted in John Toland, *The Rising Sun* (New York: Random House, 1970), p. 780.
4. Quoted in *New York Times*, August 6, 1995.
5. Quoted in William L. Laurence, *Dawn over Zero* (New York: Knopf, 1946), pp. 219, 221.
6. Wakashi Shigetosi quoted in M. Susan Lindee, *American Science and the Survivors at Hiroshima* (Chicago: University of Chicago Press, 1994), p. 4.
7. Michihiko Hachiya, *Hiroshima Diary* (Chapel Hill: University of North Carolina Press, 1955), p. 6.
8. Quoted in Timothy L. Francis, "The Japanese Execution of American Aircrew at Fukuoka, Japan, During 1945," *Pacific Historical Review, LXVI* (November 1997), 481.
9. Quoted in John M. Blum, ed., *The Price of Vision* (Boston: Houghton Mifflin, 1973), p. 474.
10. Paul Fussell, "Hiroshima," in Michael B. Stoff, ed., *The Manhattan Project* (New York: McGraw-Hill, 1991), p. 276.
11. William D. Leahy, *I Was There* (New York: Whittlesey, 1950), p. 441.

12. Barton J. Bernstein, "Understanding the Atomic Bomb," *Diplomatic History, XIX* (Spring 1995), 267.

13. Quoted in Robert Messer, "American Perspectives on the Origins of the Cold War in Asia, 1945–1949," in Akira Iriye and Warren Cohen, eds., *American, Chinese, and Japanese Perspectives on Wartime Asia, 1931–1949* (Wilmington, Del.: Scholarly Resources, 1990), p. 251.

14. Quoted in John W. Dower, *War Without Mercy* (New York: Pantheon, 1986), p. 162.

15. Quoted in Barton J. Bernstein, "Roosevelt, Truman and the Atomic Bomb, 1941–1945," *Political Science Quarterly, XC* (Spring 1975), 61.

16. Quoted in Michael S. Sherry, *The Rise of American Air Power* (New Haven: Yale University Press, 1987), p. 341.

17. Quoted in Marc S. Gallicchio, *The Cold War Begins in Asia* (New York: Columbia University Press, 1988), p. 44.

18. Harry S. Truman, *Memoirs* (Garden City N.Y.: Doubleday 1955–56; 2 vols.), I, 416.

19. David Holloway, *Stalin and the Bomb* (Stanford: Stanford University Press, 1994), p. 115.

20. Quoted *ibid.*, p. 132.

21. Quoted in Martin J. Sherwin, *A World Destroyed* (New York: Knopf, 1975), p. 224.

22. Quoted in Alvin D. Coox, "The *Enola Gay* and Japan's Struggle to Surrender," *Journal of American-East Asian Relations, IV* (Summer 1995), 165.

23. Quoted in Lawrence S. Wittner, *One World or None* (Stanford: Stanford University Press, 1993), p. 58.

24. Quoted in Donald W. White, *The American Century* (New Haven: Yale University Press, 1996), pp. 81–82.

25. Harry S. Truman to Eleanor Roosevelt, December 12, 1948, Box 4560, Eleanor Roosevelt Papers, Franklin D. Roosevelt Library, Hyde Park, N.Y.

26. *Foreign Relations, 1946* (Washington, D.C.: Government Printing Office, 1969), VI, 707.

27. Jeanette P. Nichols, "Dollar Strength as a Liability in United States Diplomacy," *Proceedings of the American Philosophical Society, III* (February 17, 1967), 47.

28. Quoted in Vladislav Zubok and Constantine Pleshakov, *Inside the Kremlin's Cold War* (Cambridge: Harvard University Press, 1996), p. 31.

29. Gaddis Smith, *Dean Acheson* (New York: Cooper Square, 1972), p. 416.

30. Lord Inverchapel quoted in Peter Boyle, "America's Hesitant Road to NATO, 1945–1949," in Joseph Smith, ed., *The Origins of NATO* (Exeter, Eng.: University of Exeter Press, 1990), p. 76.

31. Quoted in Frank Ninkovich, *Modernity and Power* (Chicago: University of Chicago Press, 1994), p. 138.

32. Quoted in John Lewis Gaddis, *The United States and the Origins of the Cold War* (New York: Columbia University Press, 1972), p. 205.

33. Quoted in John Lewis Gaddis, "Harry S. Truman and the Origins of Containment," in Frank Merli and Theodore Wilson, eds., *Makers of American Diplomacy* (New York: Charles Scribner's Sons, 1974), p. 500.

34. Quoted in Melvyn P. Leffler, *A Preponderance of Power* (Stanford: Stanford University Press, 1992), p. 99.

35. Lester Markel, "Opinion—A Neglected Instrument," in Lester Markel et al., *Public Opinion and Foreign Policy* (New York: Harper, 1949), p. 4.

36. *Public Papers, Truman, 1952–53* (Washington, D.C.: Government Printing Office, 1966), p. 1199.

37. Paul Kennedy, *The Rise and Fall of the Great Powers* (New York: Random House, 1987), p. 515.

38. Quoted in Edward Pessen, *Losing Our Souls* (Chicago: Ivan R. Dee, 1993), p. 62.

39. U.S. Minister Selden Sapin quoted in Eric Roman, *Hungary and the Victor Powers, 1945–1950* (New York: St. Martin's Press, 1996), p. 189.

40. CIA estimate quoted in Jussi Hanhimäki, *Containing Coexistence* (Kent, Ohio: Kent State University Press, 1997), p. 52.

41. Quoted in Lorraine M. Lees, *Keeping Tito Afloat* (University Park: Penn State University Press, 1997), p. 53.

42. Quoted in Melvyn P. Leffler, *The Specter of Communism* (New York: Hill & Wang, 1994), p. 43.

43. *Foreign Relations, Yalta* (Washington, D.C.: Government Printing Office, 1955), p. 669.

44. Quoted in Vladislav Zubok and Constantine Pleshakov, "The Soviet Union," in David Reynolds, ed., *The Origins of the Cold War in Europe* (New Haven: Yale University Press, 1994), p. 62.

45. Quoted in Lloyd C. Gardner, *Economic Aspects of New Deal Diplomacy* (Madison: University of Wisconsin Press, 1964), p. 308.

46. Quoted in Barton J. Bernstein, "American Foreign Policy and the Origins of the Cold War," in Barton J. Bernstein, ed., *Politics and Policies of the Truman Administration* (Chicago: Quadrangle, 1970), p. 36.

47. Quoted in Gregg Herken, *The Winning Weapon* (New York: Knopf, 1980), p. 48.

48. Henry L. Stimson and McGeorge Bundy, *On Active Service in Peace and War* (New York: Harper & Brothers, 1948), p. 644.

49. Walter Millis, ed., *The Forrestal Diaries* (New York: Viking, 1951), p. 96.

50. *Foreign Relations 1946, VII* (Washington, D.C.: Government Printing Office, 1969), 223.

51. Quoted in Alexander Werth, *Russia: The Post-War Years* (New York: Taplinger, 1971), pp. 328, 329.

52. Quoted in James L. Gormly, *The Collapse of the Grand Alliance, 1945–1948* (Baton Rouge: Louisiana State University Press, 1987), p. 147.

53. Quoted in Thomas G. Paterson, *Meeting the Communist Threat* (New York: Oxford University Press, 1988), pp. 114, 115.

54. Frank Costigliola, "'Unceasing Pressure for Penetration,'" *Journal of American History, LXXXIV* (March 1997), 1333.

55. Quoted in Fraser J. Harbutt, *The Iron Curtain* (New York: Oxford Univerity Press, 1986), p. 186.

56. David Brinkley, *David Brinkley* (New York: Knopf, 1995), p. 74.

57. Quoted in Louise L. Fawcett, *Iran and the Cold War* (Cambridge, Eng.: Cambridge University Press, 1992), p. 125.

58. Arthur C. Millspaugh, "Memorandum on . . . Iran," September 8, 1948, Box 20, John W. Snyder Papers, Harry S. Truman Library, Independence, Mo.

59. *Vital Speeches, XII* (October 1, 1946), 738–741.

60. Quoted in Arnold A. Offner, "Another Such Victory?" *Diplomatic History, XXIII* (Spring 1999), 138.

61. Quoted in U.S. Congress, Senate, Judiciary Committee, *Morgenthau Diary (Germany),* (Washington, D.C.: Government Printing Office, 1967; 2 vols.), II, 1555.

62. W. Averell Harriman, "Certain Factors Underlying Our Relations with the Soviet Union," November 14, 1945, Harriman Papers, Library of Congress, Washington, D.C.

63. Baruch quoted in Shane J. Maddock, "The Nth Country Conundrum" (Ph.D. diss., University of Connecticut, 1997), p. 123.

64. Henry A. Wallace, "The Path to Peace with Russia," *The New Republic, CXV* (September 30, 1946), 401–406.

65. "The Novikov Telegram, Washington, September 27, 1946," *Diplomatic History, XV* (Fall 1991), 527.

66. Bob Hope, *So This Is Peace* (New York: Simon & Schuster, 1946), p. 167.

67. Quoted in Arnold A. Offner, "Harry S. Truman as Parochial Nationalist," in Thomas G. Paterson and Robert J. McMahon, eds., *The Origins of the Cold War* (Lexington, Mass.: Heath, 1991; 3rd ed.), p. 56.

68. Quoted in John Gimbel, "Project Paperclip," *Diplomatic History, XIV* (Summer 1990), 351.

69. Quoted in Thomas A. Schwartz, *America's Germany* (Cambridge: Harvard University Press, 1991), p. 31.

70. Walter Bedell Smith quoted in Carolyn Eisenberg, *Drawing the Line* (New York: Cambridge University Press, 1996), p. 488.

71. Norman Naimark, *The Russians in Germany* (Cambridge: Harvard University Press, 1995), p. 467.

72. Quoted in Zubok and Pleshakov, *Kremlin's Cold War*, p. 52.

73. Quoted in John Newhouse, *War and Peace in the Nuclear Age* (New York: Knopf, 1989), p. 67; Alexander Paniushkin quoted in Vojtech Mastny, *The Cold War and Soviet Insecurity* (New York: Oxford University Press, 1966), p. 59.

74. Andrei Gromyko quoted in Holloway, *Stalin and the Bomb*, p. 260.

75. *Public Papers, Truman, 1947* (Washington, D.C.: Government Printing Office, 1963), pp. 176–180.

76. Quoted in David W. Ellwood, *Rebuilding Europe* (London: Longman, 1992), p. 69.

77. Quoted in John O. Iatrides, *Revolt in Athens* (Princeton: Princeton University Press, 1972), p. 208.

78. Paul Porter quoted in Howard Jones, *"A New Kind of War"* (New York: Oxford University Press, 1989), p. 30.

79. Peter J. Stavrakis, "Soviet Policy on Greece," in John O. Iatrides and Linda Wrigley, eds., *Greece at the Crossroads* (University Park: Penn State University Press, 1995), p. 228.

80. *Congressional Record, XCIII* (April 22, 1947), 3772–3773.

81. *Foreign Relations, Yalta*, p. 903.

82. Quoted in Eduard Mark, "The War Scare of 1946," *Diplomatic History, XXI* (Summer 1997), 383.

83. Quoted *ibid.*, p. 414.

84. Loy Henderson quoted in H. W. Brands, *Inside the Cold War* (New York: Oxford University Press, 1991), p. 177.

85. Quoted in George Lenczowski, *American Presidents and the Middle East* (Durham: Duke University Press, 1990), p. 30.

86. Warren Austin quoted in Mark A. Stoler, *George C. Marshall* (Boston: Twayne, 1989), p. 172.

87. Quoted in Michael J. Cohen, *Truman and Israel* (Berkeley: University of California Press, 1990), p. 136.

88. Quoted *ibid.*, p. 122.

89. Quoted *ibid.*, p. 193.

90. Quoted in Bruce J. Evensen, *Truman, Palestine, and the Press* (New York: Greenwood, 1992), p. 180.

91. Quoted in David Schoenbaum, *The United States and the State of Israel* (New York: Oxford University Press, 1993), p. 34.

92. "X," "The Sources of Soviet Conduct," *Foreign Affairs, XXV* (July 1947), 566–582.

93. Kennan quoted in Wilson D. Miscamble, *George F. Kennan and the Making of American Foreign Policy, 1947–1950* (Princeton: Princeton University Press, 1992), p. 67.

94. Walter Lippmann, *The Cold War* (New York: Harper & Brothers, 1947), pp. 18, 21, 60.

95. *Department of State Bulletin, XVI* (July 15, 1947), 1159–1160.

96. Bidault quoted in René Girault, "The French Decision-Makers and Their Perception of French Power in 1948," in Josef Becker and Franz Knipping, eds., *Power in Europe?* (Berlin: Walter de Gruyer, 1986), p. 61.

97. Quoted in Woodford McClellan, "Molotov Remembers," *Cold War International History Project Bulletin*, no. 1 (Spring 1992), 18.

98. Quoted in Michael J. Hogan, *The Marshall Plan* (New York: Cambridge University Press, 1987), p. 52.

99. Quoted in Vladislav Zubok, "Stalin's Plans and Russian Archives," *Diplomatic History, XXI* (Spring 1997), 299.

100. Quoted in Richard McKinzie and Theodore Wilson, "The Marshall Plan in Historical Perspective" (unpub. paper, American Historical Association, 1972), p. 8.

101. Frederico Romero, *The United States and the European Trade Union Movement, 1944–1951* (Chapel Hill: University of North Carolina Press, 1992), p. 216.

102. Quoted in Irwin M. Wall, *The United States and the Making of Postwar France, 1945–1954* (Cambridge, Eng.: Cambridge University Press, 1991), p. 122.

103. Diary, November 23, 1948, Walter Lippmann Papers, Yale University Library, New Haven, Conn.

104. Joint Chiefs quoted in Mastny, *Soviet Insecurity*, p. 58; Matthew Evangelista, "The 'Soviet Threat,'" *Diplomatic History, XXII* (Summer 1998), 444.

105. Quoted in Randall B. Woods, *Fulbright* (New York: Cambridge University Press, 1994), p. 136.

106. Quoted in Richard Pells, *Not like Us* (New York: St. Martin's Press, 1993), p. 109.

107. Amy L. S. Staples, "Constructing International Identity" (Ph.D. diss., Ohio State University, 1998), pp. 361, 373.

108. *Public Papers, Truman, 1949* (Washington, D.C.: Government Printing Office, 1964), p. 114.

109. *Department of State Bulletin, XX* (March 20, 1949), 340.

110. Quoted in Thomas G. Paterson, *On Every Front* (New York: Norton, 1992; rev. ed.), p. 87.

111. John Hickerson in *Foreign Relations, 1948* (Washington, D.C.: Government Printing Office, 1974), *III*, 183.

112. Quoted in Frank Costigliola, "The Nuclear Family," *Diplomatic History, XXI* (Spring 1997), 165, 166.

113. Pierson Dixon quoted in Anne Deighton, *The Impossible Peace* (New York: Oxford University Press, 1990), p. 190.

114. Quoted in Samuel R. Williamson and Steven L. Reardon, *The Origins of U.S. Nuclear Strategy, 1945–1953* (New York: St. Martin's Press, 1993), p. 109.

115. Leffler, *Preponderance of Power*, p. 314.

116. Edward W. Barrett in "Princeton Seminar," October 10–11, 1953, Box 65, Dean Acheson Papers, Truman Library.

117. Conversation between Stalin and Mao, December 16, 1949, in *Cold War International History Project Bulletin*, nos. 6–7 (Winter 1995/1996), 5.

118. Dean Acheson, *Present at the Creation* (New York: Norton, 1969), p. 379; *Department of State Bulletin, XXII* (March 20, 1950), 1037.

119. Stalin quoted in D. Clayton James, *The Years of MacArthur: Triumph and Disaster, 1945–1964* (Boston: Houghton Mifflin, 1985), pp. 26–27.

120. Quoted in John W. Dower, "Occupied Japan and the American Lake, 1945–1950," in Edward Friedman and Mark Selden, eds., *America's Asia* (New York: Vintage, 1971), p. 170; Dean Rusk, *As I Saw It* (New York: Norton, 1990), p. 123.

121. Quoted in Kyoko Hirano, *Mr. Smith Goes to Tokyo* (Washington, D.C.: Smithsonian Institution Press, 1992), p. 113.

122. John Paton Davies quoted in Michael Schaller, "Securing the Great Crescent," *Journal of American History,* LXXIX (September 1982), 395.

123. John W. Dower, *Embracing Defeat* (New York: Norton, 1999), p. 23.

124. Dower, *War Without Mercy,* pp. 302, 305; MacArthur and Yoshida quoted in Michael A. Schaller, *Altered States* (New York: Oxford University Press, 1997), pp. 7, 9.

125. Quoted in Walter LaFeber, *The Clash* (New York: Norton, 1997), p. 280.

126. Quoted in Sergei Goncharov, John Lewis, and Xue Litai, *Uncertain Partners* (Stanford: Stanford University Press, 1993), p. 10.

127. Quoted in Michael M. Sheng, *Battling Western Imperialism* (Princeton: Princeton University Press, 1997), p. 104.

128. John Lewis Gaddis, *We Now Know* (New York: Oxford University Press, 1997), p. 60.

129. Quoted in Herbert Feis, *The China Tangle* (New York: Atheneum, 1965), p. 140.

130. Jiang quoted in Edmund S. Wehrle, "Marshall, the Moscow Conference, and Harriman," in Larry I. Bland, ed., *George C. Marshall's Mediation Mission to China* (Lexington, Va.: George C. Marshall Foundation, 1998), p. 89.

131. Quoted in John Maxwell Hamilton, *Edgar Snow* (Bloomington: Indiana University Press, 1988), p. 171; Robert A. Hart, *The Eccentric Tradition* (New York: Charles Scribner's Sons, 1976), p. 156.

132. Clare Booth Luce quoted in T. Christopher Jesperson, *American Images of China* (Stanford: Stanford University Press, 1996), p. 181.

133. Quoted in He Di, "The Evoluton of the Chinese Communist Party's Policy Toward the United States," in Harry Harding and Yuan Ming, eds., *Sino-American Relations, 1945–1955* (Wilmington, Del.: Scholarly Resources, 1989), p. 40.

134. Quoted in Zhang Baijia, "The Shaping of New China's Diplomacy," *Chinese Historians,* VII (Spring and Fall 1994), 58.

135. Quoted in Thomas G. Paterson, "If Europe, Why Not China?" *Prologue,* XIII (Spring 1981), 37.

136. Quoted in Michael H. Hunt, "East Asia in Henry Luce's 'American Century,'" *Diplomatic History,* XXIII (Spring 1999), 328.

137. Quoted in William Stueck, *The Road to Confrontation* (Chapel Hill: University of North Carolina Press, 1981), p. 124.

138. Odd Arne Westad, "Losses, Chances, and Myths," *Diplomatic History,* XXI (Winter 1997), 108; Mao quoted in Li Zhisui, *The Private Life of Chairman Mao* (New York: Random House, 1994), p. 117; *United States Relations with China* (Washington, D.C.: Department of State, 1949), p. xvii.

139. Geraldine Fitch quoted in Jesperson, *American Images,* p. 179.

140. Lewis Clark quoted in Nancy Bernkopf Tucker, *Taiwan, Hong Kong, and the United States, 1945–1992* (New York: Twayne, 1994), p. 21.

141. Quoted in Gordon H. Chang, *Friends and Enemies* (Stanford: Stanford University Press, 1990), p. 13.

142. Quoted in Michael Sheng, "The United States, the Chinese Communists, and the Soviet Union, 1948–1950," *Pacific Historical Review,* LXIII (November 1994), 529.

143. Memorandum of Mao conversation, July 22, 1958, in *Cold War International History Project Bulletin,* nos. 6–7 (Winter 1995/1996), 156.

144. Quoted in Shu Guang Zhan, "In the Shadow of Mao," in Gordon A. Craig and Francis L. Loewenheim, eds., *The Diplomats* (Princeton: Princeton University Press, 1994), p. 349.

145. Quoted in Gaddis, *We Now Know,* p. 62.

146. *Department of State Bulletin,* XXIV (May 28, 1951), 847.

147. L. E. Sissman, "Missing the Forties," *Atlantic Monthly,* CCXXXII (October 1973), 35.

148. M. E. Dening quoted in William Roger Louis, *Imperialism at Bay* (New York: Oxford University Press, 1978), p. 550.

149. Reinhold Wagnleitner, "The Irony of American Culture Abroad," in Lary May, ed., *Recasting America* (Chicago: University of Chicago Press, 1989), p. 295.

150. Eugen Sharin quoted *ibid.,* p. 285.

151. Geir Lundestad, "'Empire by Invitation' in the American Century," *Diplomatic History,* XXIII (Spring 1999), 189–217.

152. Costigliola, "Nuclear Family," p. 170.

153. Quoted in Daniel Yergin, "Fulbright's Last Frustration," *New York Times Magazine,* November 24, 1974, p. 87.

154. British Ambassador Clark Kerr quoted in Frank Costigliola, "'Mixed Up' and 'Contact': Culture and Emotion in the Second World War," *International History Review,* XX (December 1998), 803.

155. Quoted in Mastny, *Soviet Insecurity,* p. 38.

156. H. Freeman Matthews quoted in Hanhimäki, *Containing Coexistence,* p. 17.

157. Thomas Borstelmann, *Apartheid's Reluctant Uncle* (New York: Oxford University Press, 1993), p. 197.

158. Kyle Longley, *The Sparrow and the Hawk* (Wilmington, Del.: Scholarly Resources, 1997), p. 159.

159. Charles D. Ameringer, *The Caribbean Legion* (University Park: Penn State University Press, 1996), p. 10.

160. Ambassador Monnet Davis quoted in John Major, *Prized Possession* (New York: Cambridge University Press, 1993), p. 273.

161. Michael J. Hogan, *A Cross of Iron* (New York: Cambridge University Press, 1998), p. 17.

162. Garry Wills, *John Wayne's America* (New York: Simon & Schuster, 1997), p. 154.

163. Quoted in W. Averell Harriman and Elie Abel, *Special Envoy to Churchill and Stalin* (New York: Random House, 1975), p. 528.

164. Paul Hoffman quoted in Chester J. Pach, *Arming the Free World* (Chapel Hill: University of North Carolina Press, 1991), p. 231.

165. J. William Fulbright, "Reflections: In Thrall to Fear," *The New Yorker,* XLVII (January 8, 1972), 43.

166. Arthur H. Vandenberg, Jr., ed., *The Private Papers of Senator Vandenberg* (Boston: Houghton Mifflin, 1952), pp. 550–551.

167. Thomas A. Bailey, *The Man in the Street* (New York: Macmillan, 1948), p. 13.

168. Quoted in Theodore Wilson and Richard McKinzie, "White House Versus Congress" (unpub. paper, Organization of American Historians, 1973), p. 2.

169. Williamson and Reardon, *U.S. Nuclear Strategy,* p. 191.

170. Harold D. Lasswell, *Power and Personality* (New York: Norton, 1948), p. 180.

171. Quoted in Paul Boyer, *By the Bomb's Early Light* (New York: Pantheon, 1985), p. 92.

172. Quoted in Margot A. Henriksen, *Dr. Strangelove's America* (Berkeley: University of California Press, 1997), p. 23.

173. Quoted in Allan M. Winkler, *Life Under a Cloud* (New York: Oxford University Press, 1993), p. 50.

Global Watch: The Korean War and Eisenhower Foreign Relations, 1950–1961

Blair House Meeting. *Attorney General J. Howard McGrath, President Harry S. Truman, and Secretary of Defense Louis Johnson break for lunch on June 27, 1950, after discussing the Korean crisis. Truman believed that "punishment always followed transgression," and he intended to punish the "pagan wolves" of North Korea. (Harry S. Truman Library)*

DIPLOMATIC CROSSROAD

The Decision to Intervene in the Korean War, 1950

American ambassador to South Korea John J. Muccio picked up the phone at 8:00 A.M. "Brace yourself for a shock," his chief deputy said, "the Communists are hitting all along the front!"[1] Muccio rushed out to check the alarming reports. United Press correspondent Jack James, also in Seoul, alertly did the same and earned himself a rare scoop. At 9:50 A.M. he cabled UP in the United States that North Korean troops had crossed into South Korea. Muccio also cabled Washington about "an all-out offensive."[2]

At 4:00 A.M. that rainy Sunday morning of June 25, 1950, some 75,000 troops of the Democratic People's Republic of Korea (North Korea) bolted across the thirty-eighth parallel, the boundary drawn after World War II by the United States and the Soviet Union, cutting Korea into North and South. North Korean units attacked along a 150-mile front with armor and heavy artillary. As Soviet-made tanks rumbled forward, South Korean forces collapsed in a rout. General Douglas MacArthur remembered that the North Korean army "struck like a cobra."[3]

James's cable beat Muccio's to the United States, more than 7,000 miles away, by a few minutes. It was a hot, humid Saturday evening (June 24) in Washington, D.C., thirteen hours behind Seoul time. UP called the Department of State to verify James's report. Dumbfounded officers had no information. They phoned Assistant Secretary of State Dean Rusk, then dining out. Rusk left dinner about the time that Muccio's cable reached the State Department. About 10:00 P.M. the bad news reached Secretary of State Dean Acheson, resting at his Maryland farm just outside the capital. When General MacArthur received word at his Tokyo post, he told visiting envoy John Foster Dulles: "This is probably only a reconnaissance in force. . . . I can handle it with one hand tied behind my back."[4] Dulles expected worse: "To sit by while Korea is overrun," he cabled, "would start a disastrous chain of events leading most probably to world war."[5]

Acheson decided to convene an emergency session of the United Nations Security Council. The United States dominated that body, and the principle of collective security in the face of aggression seemed at issue. At 11:20 P.M. Acheson rang up President Harry S. Truman, at home in Independence, Missouri, with his family, saying that the president could do little at that point, so he should remain in Missouri, get a good night's sleep, and come to Washington the next day, Sunday, June 25. State Department personnel worked through the night drafting a Security Council resolution that charged North Korea with a "breach of the peace."[6] Meetings in the Pentagon and the State Department debated courses of action. Orders went out to evacuate Americans from Seoul. World War III, thought some officials, had started.

President Truman boarded his plane early Sunday afternoon. According to one biographer, the president possessed "an appetite, too much of one, really, for unhesitating decision."[7] Truman stood low in the public opinion polls at the time, in

Dean Acheson (1893–1971).
He, like the president, assumed
that Moscow had initiated the Korean War and urged resolute
American reaction. The new crisis,
coming after Acheson's National
Press Club speech of January 12,
1950, and other foreign-policy
woes such as the communist victory in China, emboldened some
of his critics to ask once again for
his resignation. (*The Reporter*,
1952. Copyright 1952 by Fortnightly Publishing Co., Inc.)

large part because Senator Joseph McCarthy of Wisconsin was charging him with
softness toward communism. Former State Department official Alger Hiss, to right-
wing critics the ultimate "sell-out" spy, had been convicted of perjury in January,
and China had "fallen" a few months before. Bold action now would disarm the
president's critics. Truman pondered history. He frequently drew facile lessons
from the past. Korea was the American Rhineland, he thought. The 1930s all over
again: "Communism was acting in Korea just as Hitler, Mussolini, and the Japanese had acted ten, fifteen, and twenty years earlier."[8] No appeasement this time!
Mean-while, the Security Council passed the U.S. resolution condemning North
Korea. Except for Yugoslavia's abstention, all members present voted "yes." The
Soviet delegation, which could have vetoed the measure, remained surprisingly absent, boycotting the United Nations over its refusal to seat the new communist government in China.

A stern, short-tempered Truman deplaned in Washington and headed for a
meeting with top officials. Nobody present doubted that the Soviet Union had engineered the attack, using its North Korean allies to probe for a soft spot in the
American containment shield. The relationship between the Soviet Union and
North Korea, one official remarked, was like "Walt Disney and Donald Duck."[9]
Worse still, the thrust into South Korea might be only one component of a worldwide communist assault. "If we let Korea down," Truman predicted, "the Soviet
[*sic*] will keep right on going and swallow up one piece of Asia after another. . . .
[Then] the Near East would collapse and no telling what would happen in Europe."[10] Truman ordered General MacArthur in Japan to send arms and equipment
to the South Koreans and to use U.S. war planes to attack the North Korean spear-
head. Further, he sent the Seventh Fleet into the waters between the Chinese mainland and Formosa to forestall conflict between the two Chinas.

Despite widespread bipartisan support for Truman's decisions, some conservative Republicans seized the moment to indulge in McCarthyite recriminations.
Senator William E. Jenner of Indiana waxed splenetic: "The Russian bear is
sprawled across the Eurasian continent, biding its time, digesting its prey, and dig-
ging itself in for a long and cruel international winter. The Korean debacle also reminds us that the same sell-out-to-Stalin statesmen, who turned Russia loose, are
still in the saddle, riding herd on the American people."[11]

By Monday evening, North Korean forces neared Seoul. Truman learned
about a downed North Korean plane, which he hoped "was not the last."[12] Diplomats and military leaders believed that the reputation of the United States stood at
risk. If America did not defend its principle of containment, its image would tarnish
and its power erode. Korea became a supreme Cold War test, a symbol, a link in a
Cold War chain of events. To falter would forfeit world leadership, Truman officials claimed.

Truman ordered U.S. aircraft and warships into full-scale action below the
thirty-eighth parallel; he declared Formosa (Taiwan) off limits to the mainland
Chinese; and he dispatched military aid to Indochina and the Philippines. The
president did not ask Congress for a declaration of war. Senator Tom Connally of
Texas, chair of the Foreign Relations Committee, advised:"You might run into a
long debate in Congress which would tie your hands completely. You have the

right to do it as Commander-in-Chief and under the UN Charter."[13] Truman simply informed key legislators about his decisions. On Tuesday, June 27, Americans applauded Truman's response. "Never . . . have I felt such a sense of relief and unity pass through the city," wrote one veteran reporter.[14] The United Nations passed another U.S.-sponsored resolution urging members to aid South Korea, in essence endorsing actions the United States had already taken. Seoul nonetheless fell.

The continued North Korean push into the South sparked talk on June 28 and 29 of sending U.S. troops. Presidential supporters cited historical precedent: Jefferson had ordered action against the Barbary pirates and McKinley had sent troops into China during the Boxer Rebellion without prior congressional sanction. On the twenty-ninth, Truman ordered U.S. pilots to attack above the thirty-eighth parallel. On Friday, June 30, after visiting the war front, MacArthur asked Truman to send U.S. soldiers to Korea. The president soon gave the order, amid reports that the North Korean surge was pushing the South Koreans into a small area at the bottom of the peninsula, the Pusan perimeter. The nation mobilized for an undeclared but initially popular war against communism. Truman tagged it a "police action."[15]

The Korean War Intensifies the Cold War

At first the war went badly for the United States, South Korea, and the small number of troops offered by allies, all nominally under United Nations auspices. America's initial combat units took heavy losses, buying time to equip and transport a substantial force for offensive operations in Korea. Discusssions began on whether American troops should cross the thirty-eighth parallel and attempt to liberate the North from the communist camp. In August the president decided in favor of this drastic change in U.S. war aims.

Meanwhile, MacArthur persuaded a reluctant Joint Chiefs of Staff to approve a daring, difficult amphibious assault at Inchon, hundreds of miles behind North Korean lines. On September 15, 1950, U.S. marines landed at Inchon, pushed the North Koreans back, and quickly cut to Seoul. North Korean troops retreated north. "We want you to feel unhampered tactically and strategically to proceed north of the 38th Parallel," Secretary of Defense George C. Marshall cabled MacArthur.[16]

The Chinese warily watched these events. When Truman sent the Seventh Fleet to neutralize Formosa on June 27, Beijing called the decision "armed aggression against Chinese territory," revealing the "true imperialist face" of the United States.[17] Shortly after the Inchon landing, Mao Zedong, vowing not to wait "year after year unsure of when the enemy will attack us," began preparations to send "volunteers" into Korea.[18] Worried about Chinese security, Mao and Zhou Enlai also warned the United States to keep its troops away from the Yalu River boundary. MacArthur was certain the Chinese were bluffing. Even British intelligence dismissed reports of Chinese intervention as "based upon a single unconfirmed statement made by a single enemy prisoner of war who does not know what he is talking about."[19]

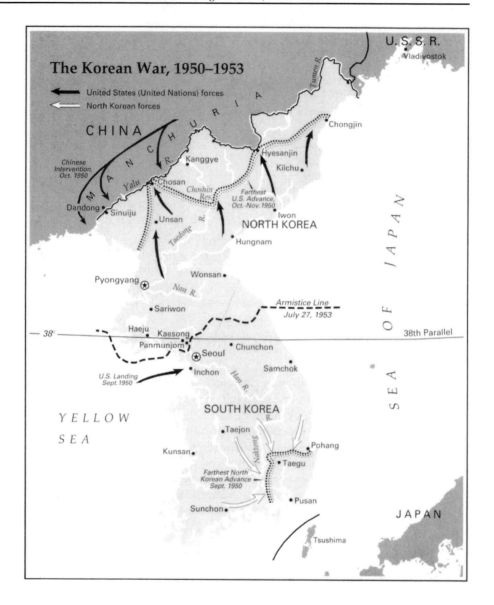

The Korean War, 1950–1953

Stalin cabled Mao on October 1, urging the Chinese to "move at least five or six divisions toward the 38th parallel at once."[20] Mao cabled back the next day, ruling out intervention because it would provoke "open conflict" with the United States. "The wounds inflicted on the people by the [Chinese Civil] war have not healed, we need peace." After further appeals from Stalin and offers of Soviet air support, and after intense debate in Beijing, Mao reversed course because the "Americans would run more rampant" unless stopped.[21]

On October 8, United Nations forces under U.S. command trooped across the thirty-eighth parallel and marched deep into North Korea. Even after Stalin reneged on his promise of Soviet air support, 250,000 Chinese troops quietly crossed the Yalu on October 19. On October 26, Chinese forces attacked. After fierce fighting, however, they retreated—"purposely showing ourselves to be weak," as their commander put it, "increasing the arrogance of the enemy, letting him run amuck, and luring them deep into our area."[22] U.S. officials abandoned caution. On November 8, for the first time, B-29 bombers struck bridges across the Yalu— bridges that linked North Korea and China. Then, on November 24, MacArthur launched a major offensive. Victory appeared near. Two days later, what one U.S. general called "a glut of Chinamen" swept down on MacArthur's unsuspecting armies.[23] Within weeks Chinese engulfed the North. MacArthur asked Washington, without success, to approve air strikes against China. The United Nations soon branded China an "aggressor," and Truman hinted publicly that using nuclear weapons was under "active consideration."[24] "You can use the atomic bomb," Mao reportedly boasted. "I will respond with my hand grenade. I will catch the weak point on your part and defeat you."[25] British prime minister Clement Attlee hastened to Washington to protest that the United States should seek negotiations, not a dangerously expanded war. To Truman's assertion that the Chinese communists were "complete satellites" of Moscow, the British ambassador argued that war with China would tighten a Sino-Soviet alliance based "on a coincidence of Chinese and Russian views, not Chinese subservience to Russian views."[26] In fact, Truman and his advisers rejected a wider war because they deemed the nuclear arsenal too small and feared Soviet retaliation in Europe.

Douglas MacArthur (1880–1964). The West Point graduate commanded U.S. troops in Asia during World War II, directed the postwar occupation of Japan, and headed forces in Korea until relieved of duty by the president in April 1951. MacArthur later said he could have ended the Korean War in ten days: "I would have dropped between 30 and 50 atomic bombs" on China. (Library of Congress)

By March 1951 MacArthur had managed to shove communist forces back across the thirty-eighth parallel. With fighting stabilized at roughly the prewar boundary, Truman contemplated negotiations, but MacArthur grew restless, hellbent on reversing earlier defeats and slashing China on behalf of the crusade against international communism. MacArthur "seems to want a war with China. We do not," the British protested.[27] The general with the Napoleonic ego began to make public statements suggesting that his commander in chief practiced appeasement. To Representative Joseph Martin, he wrote, in a letter made public in April: "There is no substitute for victory."[28] On April 11 Truman, backed strongly by the Joint Chiefs of Staff, fired the seventy-one-year-old MacArthur for insubordination.

The vain general, who had so badly miscalculated Chinese reactions, returned home to ticker-tape parades. In a televised address he told Congress on April 19 that the war must be expanded. He closed with now-famous words: "Old soldiers never die; they just fade away."[29] Congressional hearings soon revealed that many Americans shared MacArthur's frustrations over military restraint. Americans were used to winning wars; Truman was now conducting something alien—a "limited war," localized and without atomic weapons. Senator McCarthy spewed his venom, too, calling Truman "a rather sinister monster of many heads and many tentacles, a monster conceived in the Kremlin, and then given birth to by Acheson . . . , and then nurtured into Frankenstein proportions by the Hiss crowd, who still run the State Department."[30] The debate focused on different strategies for rolling back communism. "There was MacArthur's, which resembled a locomotive with no brakes. And there was Acheson's, a controlled rollback limited to Korea."[31]

Truman and Acheson pointed to the risk of world war. The chair of the Joint Chiefs of Staff, General Omar Bradley, argued that escalating the war would by no means guarantee victory, that it might bring the Soviets in, and that the United

States would lose angry allies. A showdown with Soviet communism in Korea, he said, would be "the wrong war, at the wrong place, at the wrong time, and with the wrong enemy."[32] As one scholar points out, Bradley implied that the *right war* should be against the Soviet Union, "and the *right place* to fight it was not at the periphery, but at the heart of Soviet power," and the *right time* was only after the buildup of American power under NSC-68.[33]

Peace talks began at Panmunjom in July 1951. They made little headway and the fighting continued. Americans "want to subjugate the world," mocked Stalin in 1952, "yet they cannot subdue little Korea."[34] During the 1952 presidential campaign, Republican candidate Dwight D. Eisenhower pledged, if elected, to go to Korea to find a way to end the conflict. Elected in good part because of American frustration with limited war, Ike did go to Korea but found no easy solution. The most serious obstacle centered on the disposition of prisoners of war (POWs). Thousands of Chinese and North Korean soldiers, encouraged by a "re-education" program in the South, refused repatriation. A few hundred captives in the North, having undergone communist "brainwashing," elected to remain above the thirty-eighth parallel. Despite the usual diplomatic practice of returning all prisoners, "the allure of many Chinese voting with their feet for Chiang [Jiang] rather than Mao validated" an American policy toward Nationalist China that was "unpopular internationally."[35]

By 1953 the military buildup under NSC-68 had erased doubts about U.S. capabilities that had precluded escalation earlier in the war. Announcing that the United States considered "the atomic bomb as simply another weapon in our arsenal," Eisenhower tried to intimidate the Chinese.[36] And Washington unleashed Jiang Jieshi to attack the mainland: Nationalist bombing raids soon followed. The March death of Stalin, combined with these actions, probably helped bring the peace talks to a conclusion. A more flexible Moscow urged Beijing to settle the prisoner question. When South Korean president Syngman Rhee tried to sabotage the talks by releasing thousands of North Korean POWs, the Chinese launched a final offensive against South Korean positions.

On July 27, 1953, the adversaries signed an armistice. They agreed to turn over the POW issue to a committee of neutral nations (ultimately the POWs stayed where they chose—including twenty-one Americans in North Korea). The conferees drew a new boundary line close to the thirty-eighth parallel, which gained South Korea 1,500 square miles of territory. The agreement also provided for a demilitarized zone between the two Koreas.

The Korean War ranks as one of the costliest in twentieth-century history. More then 4 millon died: 2 million North Korean civilians and 500,000 North Korean soldiers; 1 million South Korean civilians and some 47,000 South Korean soldiers; and offical Chinese statistics list 148,000 dead. The United States lost 54,246 dead and 105,000 wounded and spent some $20 billion. The United States supplied 80 percent of the naval power and 90 percent of the air support, as well as 90 percent of foreign combat troops, in this "United Nations" effort.

The Korean War has left many questions, some of which the partial opening of Chinese and Russian archives are helping to answer. Did Moscow start the Korean War? Truman officials claimed that the Soviet Union induced its North Korean client to attack. Perhaps Moscow sensed an opportunity, because Acheson had indicated in a speech before the National Press Club on January 12, 1950, that South Korea lay outside the American defense perimeter. Acheson's speech "produced a certain influence" on the young North Korean leader Kim Il Sung, who visited Moscow in April and promised a surprise attack that would win the war in three days.[37] A cautious Stalin told Kim to check with Mao, who cited possible American intervention but endorsed Kim's plans apparently without realizing that the timetable would precede China's projected invasion of Taiwan. Stalin then backed Kim's scheme, probably gambling that North Korea could score a quick victory.

The "gamble thesis" raises difficult questions. Why did the Soviet delegate absent himself from the United Nations at such a crucial time, especially if Stalin had approved the attack? Why did Stalin give such inadequate aid to the North Koreans and Chinese during the war? Why did Moscow launch a European movement for peaceful coexistence and then torpedo that effort by provoking war in Asia? "We are thus left to reconcile the ubiquitous American assumption that Stalin started the war," one scholar notes, "with the unambiguous evidence that he distanced Soviet interests, prestige, and armed might from the conflict, allowing the United States ultimately to pulverize North Korea."[38]

Soviet relations with China influenced Stalin's decisions on Korea. If he refused to support Kim's goal of unifying Korea, Stalin might invite the charge that he hindered revolution in Asia, thereby boosting Mao's China as a potential rival. Stalin may further have calculated that even if the United States did not defend South Korea, Washington would never permit the additional loss of Taiwan. The Americans would then move to protect Jiang Jieshi's government on the island, thus preventing any rapprochement between the United States and the People's Republic of China and forcing Mao to "continue to turn to the Soviet Union for economic and military aid."[39] Whatever Stalin's precise motives, he hesitated, because a war in Korea risked Soviet economic and strategic interests in Northeast Asia. As for Mao, who expected U.S. aggression against China in the future, he leaned toward intervention in Korea *after* Truman sent the Seventh Fleet into the Taiwan Strait, which "tore up all international argeements" and "exposed its [America's] imperialist face."[40] The initiative, and probably the timing, for the war came from Pyongyang, not from Moscow or Beijing.

This interpretation seems plausible because since 1945 a two-part civil war had wracked Korea: the conflict in the South and the conflict between South and North. In the South, "people's committees" resisted the rightist state backed by the United States. Peasant uprisings, leftist-initiated labor strife, and guerrilla warfare claimed tens of thousands of lives. The North encouraged the rebellions in the South, and skirmishes between northern and southern soldiers intensified in 1949 along the dividing parallel. Both Kim Il Sung's North Korean communist government and Syngman Rhee's Republic of Korea in the South craved national unification. Both tapped foreign sources for material aid. Rhee, who had lived in the United States for almost four decades, used his American political connections well. In February 1950, Congress authorized $60 million in economic aid for South Korea; in March it voted almost $11 million in military assistance; and on June 5 it added another $100 million in military aid. Although U.S. occupation troops had departed in mid-1949, a U.S. Military Advisory Group remained to train Rhee's forces. In May elections, Rhee lost control of the South Korean National Assembly. All the while, Rhee "seemed like a tethered hound, constantly pulling at the [U.S.] leash."[41]

With a 150,000-soldier army well supplied with Soviet arms, including 150 T-34 tanks, Kim's authoritarian regime probably decided to strike before Rhee could utilize U.S. aid and stabilize his precarious political position. In any case, scholars interpret the major war that exploded in June 1950 as an extension of the ongoing civil war waged by North and South Korea, not simply as a conflagration ignited by the two Cold War superpowers.

Despite uncertainty over the war's origins, we *can* measure its consequences. In the United States, it meant the repudiation of the Democrats in 1952 and the election of a Republican administration, both made possible by popular exasperation with the stalemate in Korea. The Korean War wounded bipartisanship and fueled McCarthyism. It helped set off a "great debate" in the early 1950s over whether Europe or Asia ranked higher in the campaign against communism and whether the United States had overcommitted itself around the globe. Truman's handling of the Korean War also confirmed presidential supremacy in foreign policy; he neither consulted Congress nor asked for a declaration of war. Acheson did not wish to invite hearings that might produce that "one more question in cross-examination which destroys you, as a lawyer." He did not wish to answer "ponderous questions" that might have "muddled up" Truman's policy.[42]

The Korean War poisoned Sino-American relations while it strengthened Japanese-American relations. The United States continued to intervene in the Chinese civil war by aiding Jiang on Formosa. Washington more than ever adamantly refused to recognize Mao's government, now that it had shed American blood. At the same time, the war enabled the Chinese communists to consolidate their revolution at home and gain international prestige from battling the United States to a draw. The Korean War also bolstered Japan and its alliance with the United States. Some $3 billion in U.S. procurement orders during the war revived Japanese industry. The "seedbed" for the Japanese economic "miracle" of the 1960s and 1970s was "planted."[43]

The Korean War further divided the world into two competing camps and drew Third World nations into its destructive wake as the domino theory took on new vigor. "We are fighting in Korea," Truman proclaimed in fall 1952, "so we won't have to fight in Wichita, or in Chicago, or in New Orleans, or on San Francisco Bay."[44] South Korea became a staunch ally, receiving, in 1953–1972, $5.5 billion in foreign aid from the United States. Viewing nationalist movements as potential Soviet allies, and determined to back allies in the aggravated Cold War, Washington increased aid to the French in their battle against Vietnamese nationalists (see Chapter 9).

The Truman administration utilized the Korean War to fulfill other goals. As Acheson noted, the dispatch of troops to Korea "removed the recommendations of NSC-68 from the realm of theory and made them immediate budget issues."[45] The Defense Department budget for fiscal year 1953 reached $52.6 billion, up from $17.7 billion in 1950. U.S. military expansion included a much enlarged army; de-

Makers of American Foreign Relations, 1950–1961

Presidents	Secretaries of State
Harry S. Truman, 1945–1953	Dean G. Acheson, 1949–1953
Dwight D. Eisenhower, 1953–1961	John Foster Dulles, 1953–1959
	Christian A. Herter, 1959–1961

velopment of tactical nuclear weapons; four more army divisions for Europe, making a total of six there; the 1952 maiden flight of a new jet bomber, the B-52; the explosion of a thermonuclear device in November 1952; and expansion of the Strategic Air Command (SAC) to 1,600 aircraft (nearly all atomic capable). The United States also acquired bases in Saudi Arabia and Morocco, began successful talks with fascist Spain for an air base, and initiated plans for the rearmament of West Germany. In 1951 the United States, Australia, and New Zealand formed the ANZUS Pact. The United States created a military alliance with Pakistan in 1954. Strategies for psychological warfare and propaganda culminated in the creation of the United States Information Agency (USIA) in 1953. The Korean War's most lasting legacy was the quickened militarization of the Cold War.

Ambivalent Cold Warrior: Dwight D. Eisenhower

The stalemated Korean War and the "loss" of China provided Republicans with political ammunition in the 1952 presidential campaign. Although their candidate, General Dwight D. Eisenhower, conducted a smiling, moderate campaign, his party's right wing attacked vehemently. The Truman administration, which had launched containment, gotten "tough" with the Soviets, and established an internal security system, had somehow grown soft on communism. Vice-presidential candidate Richard M. Nixon ridiculed Democratic candidate Adlai E. Stevenson as a graduate of "Acheson's Cowardly College of Communist Containment."[46] The Republican party platform, written by John Foster Dulles, hurled invective at the Truman administration for ineptly squandering U.S. power.

Republicans called containment defensive and immoral. Dulles proposed "liberation" as a replacement.[47] By that he meant lifting the communist yoke from Eastern Europe. He never explained precisely how to do so.

"Liberation" did not decide the election of 1952, but the rhyme "I like Ike" may have. Eisenhower came across as a sincere, modest, wholesome, and honest person, whose simple rhetoric and homespun illustrations made him attractive. Because the Cold War seemed more than ever a military matter, this professional soldier seemed better qualified than did Stevenson. Eisenhower's "I shall go to Korea" statement of October 24 certainly helped him win election with 55 percent of the popular vote.[48]

The first Republican president since Hoover, Eisenhower appeared, but was not, simple-minded. He lacked a surefootedness for grammar. His utterances often

Richard M. Nixon (1913–1994). Before being elected vice president in 1952, Nixon graduated from Whittier College, earned a law degree from Duke University, served in Congress (1946–1951), and represented California as senator (1951–1953). An anticommunist alarmist who often used excessive language to score debating points, Nixon was, said Adlai Stevenson, "the kind of politician who would cut down a redwood tree, and then mount the stump and make a speech for conservation." (*The Reporter,* 1960. Copyright 1960 by The Reporter Magazine Co.)

displayed mangled syntax and colloquialisms that produced dizziness in his listeners. "His ad-libbed sentences bounced around like dodgem cars at a carnival . . . with nobody quite sure what he said," remembered the journalist David Brinkley.[49] This idiosyncratic style masked a skillful politician whose "hidden hand" leadership dominated the policy process.[50] But the president's meandering remarks, platitudes, and apparent moments of confusion left the impression of a "good-natured bumbler who preferred to sneak off to the golf course," out of touch with details, and vulnerable to the wiles of demagogic right-wingers in his party.[51]

Raised in Abilene, Kansas, Eisenhower graduated from West Point and led an obscure military life until appointed the supreme allied commander in Europe during World War II. After the war he served as army chief of staff, president of Columbia University, and NATO commander. Eisenhower admired business leaders and appointed many to high office in agencies shaping foreign policy. Representatives of business, finance, and law held 76 percent of such posts under Eisenhower, whereas the figure for Truman had been 43 percent. Conservative advocates of "private enterprise" in a world increasingly turning toward revolution and socialism, these "national security managers" sought to impose order on international relations.[52]

Believing in a "mutually cooperative, voluntarist society," Eisenhower and his advisers saw capitalist development as a deterrent to communism.[53] Healthy world trade, they argued, helped stimulate cooperative capitalism. Eisenhower appointed a Commission on Foreign Economic Policy in 1953, and it urged a more liberal trade policy through tariff reduction. The president extended the reciprocal trade agreements program, expanded the lending authority of the Export-Import Bank, and relaxed controls on trade with Eastern European nations. Total American exports expanded from $15 billion in 1952 to $30 billion in 1960. At first Eisenhower favored trade over aid. But he came to see foreign aid "as the cheapest insurance in the world" and soon shifted to a mix of trade and extensive military aid to balance the budget and help developing nations.[54] During the 1950s, the United States spent more than $3 billion a year in foreign military assistance under the Mutual Security program. Eisenhower also added a new program in 1954, later called "Food for Peace," wherein the United States disposed of its agricultural surplus overseas. In ten years this program accounted for $12.2 billion in farm exports. And in 1959, after years of ignoring ardent Latin American requests, the United States established the Inter-American Development Bank to spur hemispheric economic projects.

Eisenhower also emphasized propaganda through the Voice of America, Radio Free Europe, and Radio Liberty, all of which beamed incendiary anti-Soviet messages beyond the Iron Curtain. The Soviets jammed these broadcasts, but many got through. Some historians argue that propaganda and cultural contacts "parted the curtain" and cultivated anticommunist values that eventually undermined pro-Soviet regimes.[55] Others regard such efforts as having been counterproductive because they raised hopes—ultimately false—that Washington would back its calls for "liberation" with military power.

The Eisenhower administration elevated the CIA as a major instrument of foreign policy. Under its director Allen W. Dulles, brother of Secretary of State John

Foster Dulles, the CIA hired many Ivy League–educated lawyers and academicians to gather data on foreign countries and to prepare "estimates" about their policies, motives, and capabilities. But the agency also provided the president with the "quiet option," including "termination with extreme prejudice" or "health alteration"—that is, assassination.[56] Working under the assumption that the Cold War had "no rules" and that "longstanding American concepts of 'fair play' must be reconsidered," the CIA became empowered "to subvert, sabotage, and destroy our enemies."[57] Among those included on the CIA's assassination hit list were the Congo's Patrice Lumumba and Cuba's Fidel Castro. Encouraged by Eisenhower to conduct widespread psychological warfare, the agency hired mercenaries, conducted sabotage, co-opted labor unions, planted stories in newspapers, covertly bribed foreign leaders such as King Hussein of Jordan, and staged coups. The CIA helped overthrow governments in Iran (1953) and Guatemala (1954) but failed to overthrow the Indonesian government in 1958. In the Philippines, the CIA in 1959 spent a million pesos to influence elections, but, as the historian Nick Cullather has concluded, CIA operations there "were long on ambition and short on results," especially in countering a growing "Filipino First" movement.[58]

At home, the CIA put American journalists and professors on its payroll, recruited business executives as "fronts," financed the National Student Association, funded research projects at universities, and used philanthropic foundations to pass money to organizations for anticommunist activities. By the mid-1960s, the CIA had clandestinely subsidized publication of some 1,000 books. In the name of Cold War research and without the knowledge of the victims, the agency used Americans as guinea pigs. Under a program called MKULTRA, researchers subjected unwitting Americans to the mind-altering drug LSD. Other governmental projects sought to measure the effects of radioactivity by injecting unsuspecting Americans at schools and hospitals with radioactive materials. Eisenhower once remarked that he "knew so many things that I am almost afraid to speak to my wife."[59] Although sometimes characterized as a "rogue elephant" acting on its own, the agency's "mahout, the driver who sits on top and steers it," as two scholars have put it, "is always the president."[60]

Unlike Truman and Acheson, Eisenhower at least seemed willing to negotiate with the Soviets. Stalin's death in March 1953 removed one of the original Cold War architects, and in April Eisenhower seized the opportunity to deliver a stirring address titled "The Chance for Peace." The president invited more friendly relations and revealed his discomfort with militarism. "Every gun that is made, every warship launched, every rocket fired signifies, in the final sense, a theft from those who hunger and are not fed."[61] A tougher speech by Secretary Dulles two days later, however, caused Soviet intelligence to report that the Eisenhower administration contained "resolute enemies of any attempts at peaceful accommodations."[62]

Fearing nuclear war, Eisenhower often recommended arms-control measures, but "denunciations of overkill or sheer explosions of temper" could not halt the technological momentum that pushed nuclear weapons to dangerous levels.[63] Eisenhower's "Atoms for Peace" speech in December 1953 called for contributions of fissionable materials to an International Atomic Energy Agency that would then

Dwight D. Eisenhower (1890–1969).
Well experienced in world affairs before becoming president, Eisenhower nurtured a "deeply rooted anti-Communism" and "an obsession with falling dominoes." He also "realized that unlimited war in the nuclear age was unimaginable, and limited war unwinnable," writes the biographer Stephen E. Ambrose. Eisenhower suffered a coronary thrombosis in September 1955 but went on to win reelection in 1956 against Democratic candidate Adlai Stevenson. (Dwight D. Eisenhower Library)

develop nonmilitary uses for atomic energy. Hardly slowing the arms race, the proposal did lead to the United States's signing agreements with thirty-nine nations to develop nuclear energy for peaceful purposes. In 1954 the president rejected advice that the United States use nuclear weapons or send troops to Indochina to forestall a Vietnamese victory over the French. In his "Farewell Address" of early 1961, Eisenhower warned against a "military-industrial complex" (a potent lobby of "an immense military establishment and a large arms industry") and a government-university scientific complex that threatened the "democratic process" and "possible domination of the nation's scholars by federal employment, project allocations, and the power of money."[64]

Ike's peace initiatives fizzled, and his antimilitarist sentiments seldom translated into effective policies. He unilaterally halted nuclear tests in 1958, but America's stockpile of nuclear weapons during his presidency rose from 1,200 to 22,229. He sent troops to Lebanon, and by 1959 a million Americans served overseas in forty-two countries. By 1960 the Defense Department controlled 35 million acres of land at home and abroad. Defense budgets averaged more than $40 billion a year, although Eisenhower, fearful of "busting ourselves" by overspending, angered generals who disputed his cuts in army personnel.[65]

John Foster Dulles, McCarthyism, and the New Look

Although Secretary of State John Foster Dulles (1953–1959) seemed, from his stern public image, a less flexible Cold Warrior than Eisenhower, he and the president "held strikingly parallel views," and "the documents confirm that it was the president who made the decisions."[66] Tutelage from his Presbyterian minister father, education at Princeton and George Washington Law School, service as a negotiator on reparations at the Paris Peace Conference at Versailles, membership in the prestigious Wall Street firm of Sullivan and Cromwell, and worldwide activity on behalf of the Federal Council of Churches gave Dulles a varied, cosmopolitan experience before World War II. After the war he helped promote bipartisanship. In 1952 he assailed the very policies of the Truman administration he had helped to shape, but he later admitted that his desire to elect Eisenhower had fueled this political gambit.

Forceful, ambitious, sharp, and self-righteous, Dulles combined moral idealism with hard-nosed realism. He pursued ideals through the exercise of power. He once told a journalist that the United States "is almost the only country strong enough and powerful enough to be moral."[67] A dull, flat speaker with a lecturing tone, he preferred face-to-face negotiations with foreign diplomats. He disliked compromise. If every "detail was not buttoned up," he once warned, "the Soviets would take advantage of any loopholes."[68] Dulles's calculated public reputation for being a "simplistic, hard-line, rigid thinker," one colleague remarked, "was absolutely just at odds with what one saw . . . around the table within the department arguing about what should be done."[69] Still, foreigners thought his incantations too hectoring and his anticommunist public stances too overstated and too unbending.

Stalin's death and growing Soviet nuclear capabilities prompted an early reassessment of defense strategy, code-named Solarium, which predicted as many as 12 million U.S. casualties if Moscow launched a surprise attack by 1955. The resulting Eisenhower-Dulles "New Look" sought conventional military forces "adequate to deter or initially counter aggression" but emphasized "massive atomic capability" in order to keep defense costs down.[70] What Dulles called "massive retaliation," the president tersely described as "blow hell out of them in a hurry if they start anything."[71] It was cheaper to rely on nuclear deterrence because "if we let defense spending run wild," the president reasoned, "you get inflation . . . then controls . . . then a garrison state . . . and *then* we've lost the very values we were trying to defend."[72] Later in the decade, Eisenhower and Dulles moved toward the idea of a "firebreak"—a delay between the beginning of a crisis and the launching of strategic nuclear weapons.[73]

With its huge nuclear arsenal and strong armed forces, the United States practiced "brinkmanship": not backing down in a crisis, even if it meant going to the brink of

John Foster Dulles (1888–1959). Watching Dulles "grapple with a problem," an aide recalled, "was like watching a bird dog sniffing for its prey. He got a little excited as he worked over a solution, breathed a little faster, and obviously enjoyed the thinking process." More biting, Soviet foreign minister V. M. Molotov described Dulles and his brother Allen, the CIA director, as "the sort who would pick your pockets and cut off your head in one stroke." (*The Reporter*, 1956. Copyright 1956 by the Reporter Magazine Co.)

**Joseph McCarthy
(1909–1957).** The Republican senator from Wisconsin used the "big lie." Graduate of Marquette University, judge, and marine, the demagogue was once known as the "Pepsi-Cola Kid" for protecting the interests of that company. The Senate "condemned" him in December 1954. The scholar Ellen Schrecker, noting that anticommunist excesses were widespread, argues that McCarthy was the "creature" not the "creator" of the 1950s Red scare. (*The Reporter*, 1951. Copyright 1951 by Fortnightly Publishing Co., Inc.)

war. "Victory goes to him who can keep his nerve to the last fifteen minutes," Dulles wrote.[74] Keep enemies guessing, Dulles advised. But what if they guessed wrong?

As for the Third World, Eisenhower in 1954 commented: "You have a row of dominoes set up, you knock over the first one, and . . . the last one . . . will go over very quickly."[75] Thus if one country in Asia fell to the communists, others supposedly would fall in rapid succession. The 1957 "Eisenhower Doctrine" stipulated that the United States would intervene in the Middle East if any government threatened by a communist takeover requested aid. Sold as dynamic departures from the Truman administration, such slogans offered only tactical changes in a continuing containment strategy.

Eisenhower once said that "sometimes Foster is just too worried about being accused of sounding like Truman and Acheson."[76] Dulles had witnessed the harassment of Acheson by Republican right-wingers. To avoid a similar fate, Dulles showed his anticommunist colors early. He appointed an ex-FBI man and henchman of Senator Joseph McCarthy, Scott McLeod, as the chief security officer of the State Department. After seven months of tapping phones, McLeod's investigators fired 193 "security risks," only one of them a suspected subversive. The people "don't care whether they were drunks, perverts or communists," McLeod explained. "They just want us to get rid of them."[77] In early 1953, Dulles ordered books authored by "Communists, fellow travellers, et cetera" to be removed from the libraries of American overseas information centers.[78] Who was an "et cetera"? Bureaucrats gave the broadest interpretation and tossed out the books of such people as the historian Foster Rhea Dulles, the secretary of state's own cousin.

One prominent and tragic case centered on Foreign Service Officer John Carter Vincent, an independent-minded "China hand" who during World War II reported that Jiang Jieshi would probably lose. McCarthyites took this professional analysis to mean that Vincent plotted to defeat Jiang. A State Department Loyalty Board cleared Vincent, but the Civil Service Loyalty Review Board, by a vote of 3 to 2, doubted his loyalty to the United States. Dulles forced Vincent out by questioning his standards as an officer. Dulles once asked Vincent if he had read Stalin's *Problems of Leninism*. Vincent said he had not, and Dulles replied that Vincent would not have advocated the China policy he did if he had read it. One student of China affairs has commented that "since Stalin failed in China no less than Truman, one may wonder whether Stalin read his own book."[79] Another China specialist, John Paton Davies, also lost his job even though nine security reviews had cleared him. McCarthyism left deep wounds. "It's like a car that's been in an accident," one ambassador recalled. "You repair it, but somehow it's never quite the same."[80] "The wrong done," the journalist Theodore H. White has written, "was to poke out the eyes and ears of the State Department on Asian affairs, to blind American foreign policy."[81]

The Glacier Grinds On: Khrushchev, Eisenhower, and the Cold War

Like a huge glacier, the Cold War continued to move across the international landscape. After Stalin's death, Eisenhower asked, "what is the Soviet Union ready to

"I Hear There's Something Wrong with Your Morale." Secretary Dulles launched a damaging purge of Foreign Service Officers. President Eisenhower, refusing to get into "a pissing contest with that skunk" McCarthy, whom he privately viewed as "a pimple on [the] path of progress," did nothing to halt the political onslaught against the State Department. (*Herblock's Here and Now*, Simon & Schuster, 1955)

do?"[82] The early signs for improved Soviet-American relations seemed auspicious. Moscow helped end the deadlock over Korea, opened diplomatic relations with Yugoslavia and Greece, abandoned territorial claims against Turkey, toned down its anti-American rhetoric, and launched a "peace offensive." Although the Soviet crushing of an East Berlin riot in June 1953 reminded Americans of the past, the freeing of Stalinist victims from forced labor camps conversely suggested that Stalin's heirs would not mimic their long-time autocrat.

Soviet leaders scrambled for position in the succession crisis. Nikita S. Khrushchev, for years the Communist party boss of the Ukraine, eventually climbed to the top of the Kremlin hierarchy. By September 1953, Khrushchev had

Nikita S. Khrushchev (1894–1971). "I made speeches to bolster the morale of my people," Premier Khrushchev recalled. "I wanted to give our enemy pause. . . . I exaggerated a little. I said that we had the capability of shooting a fly out of space with our missiles." He fell from power in 1964 and until his death aired his views through his memoirs. (*The Reporter*, 1956. Copyright 1956 by The Reporter Magazine Co.)

become first secretary of the Central Committee of the party; five years later he became premier. Portly and amiable, Khrushchev impressed people as an impulsive, competitive person of coarse speech. Eisenhower found him "shrewd, tough, and coldly deliberate even when he was pretending to be consumed by anger."[83]

Eisenhower and Khrushchev continued their nations' military buildups. Although Soviet ground forces outnumbered their American counterparts by a 2 to 1 margin, the United States possessed a far wider margin in strategic bombers and stood ready to vaporize hundreds of Soviet targets with nuclear bombs. In an attempt to bolster Western defenses through greater integration, including West German units, Dulles sponsored the European Defense Community (EDC). When the French balked, he warned them that the United States would undertake an "agonizing reappraisal"of U.S. security commitments.[84] Paris called his bluff and rejected EDC. The secretary did gain West German membership in NATO in May 1955. That same year SEATO went into effect (see page 292), the American defense treaty with nationalist China became active, the Baghdad Pact formed, and West Germany joined NATO. In response, the Soviets formed their own military organization, the Warsaw Pact of Eastern European states.

On one issue, Austria, the two great powers cooperated in a rare example of productive Cold War diplomacy. They agreed by treaty in May 1955 to end their ten-year occupation and to create an independent, neutral Austria. The agreement emerged not only because the Austrians adeptly pressed for it but because both the Soviets and the Americans found elements of "victory": Each side effectively denied Austria to the other's sphere; Moscow demonstrated a commitment to peaceful coexistence; Washington welcomed a possible model for Eastern European nations eager to roll back Soviet power. As Dulles remarked, he expected the Red Army's withdrawal from Austria to become "contagious."[85]

Also in May 1955, the Soviet Union and the United States, under United Nations–sponsored negotiations, seemed close to an agreement to prohibit the use and manufacture of nuclear weapons, reduce conventional forces, and create an inspection system to monitor compliance—all terms that the United States had insisted on for years. "The whole thing looks too good to be true," remarked the French representative on the UN Disarmament Subcommittee.[86] So it was. Within months, the United States backed away from the disarmament proposal. Why? Steeped in the Cold War mentality, U.S. officials, especially the Joint Chiefs of Staff, still did not trust the Soviets and expected them to cheat. But more important, Dulles and Eisenhower sought to win the Cold War, not negotiate its end.

Throughout 1954–1955 came calls for a summit meeting of the great powers. Winston Churchill made an eloquent plea, and Democrats in Congress urged negotiations. Dulles countered: A summit conference would permit the Soviets to use propaganda on a grand scale; it would let them appear equal to Americans; it might encourage neutralism, for other countries would fear less and align less; and the Soviets would not bargain seriously because totalitarianism depended on an outside enemy. Better to wait until West Germany had rearmed. Eisenhower, however, decided to test Soviet intentions. Overruled, Dulles nonetheless feared that the overly "generous" Eisenhower "might accept a [Soviet] promise or proposition at face value and upset the apple cart."[87]

The Soviet Union, the United States, Britain, and France met in Geneva, Switzerland, July 18–23, 1955. Eisenhower and Dulles assured members of Congress that "Geneva was not going to be another Yalta."[88] The reference was timely, for early in 1955 Dulles had engineered the publication of once-secret documents in the *Yalta Papers* in an abortive attempt to embarrass the Democrats. Geneva did not repeat Yalta, because the Big Four struck no concrete agreements. Everybody tried to score points for prestige. East and West wanted to unite Germany, but each on its own terms. Americans sought a unified Germany in NATO. Both sides favored arms control but parted over methods. Eisenhower dramatically presented his "Open Skies" proposal, which called for the Soviet Union and the United States to exchange maps and submit their military installations to aerial inspection to ensure compliance with agreements.[89] On this American propaganda ploy designed to counter pre-Geneva Soviet appeals for disarmament, Eisenhower later remarked: "We knew the Soviets wouldn't accept it. We were sure of that, but we took a look and thought it was a good move."[90] "A bald espionage plot," sniffed Khrushchev.[91] Indeed, secrecy comprised one of the Soviets' deterrents, keeping Americans guessing on whether the inferior Soviets were catching up in airborne striking power. That secrecy ended in 1956 when the United States began covert reconnaisance flights by high-altitude U-2 planes over the Soviet Union.

When Eisenhower returned home, he applauded a "new spirit of conciliation and cooperation" and assured Americans that he had not penned any secret agreements.[92] Soviets and Americans at Geneva drank "coexistence cocktails"—vodka and Coke.[93] After the largely ceremonial conference, Moscow recognized West Germany and Khrushchev endorsed "détente." Yet, he went on: "If anybody thinks that for this reason we shall forget about Marx, Engels, and Lenin, he is mistaken. This will happen when shrimps learn to whistle."[94]

The Geneva summit did initiate cultural exchanges, most notably Vice President Nixon's 1959 trip to the Soviet Union, where at a display of American products in a Moscow exhibition, he engaged Khrushchev in the "kitchen debate" on capitalism, communism, and the "commodity gap."[95] Even more impressive in spreading the American message were goodwill jazz tours by American "jambassadors" such as Dizzy Gillespie, who reported to Eisenhower in 1956: "Our interracial group was powerfully effective against Red propaganda. Jazz . . . communicates with all people regardless of language or social barriers."[96] In summer 1957, 30,000 young people danced to U.S. musicians at a Moscow festival, picking up slang ("see ya later, alligator") and calling themselves *bitniki* (beatniks).[97] As the "Cool War" gained converts, the Voice of America program "Music USA" attracted far more listeners than did its political broadcasts.[98] In one historian's words, Washington's containment strategists never imagined "rollback as rock 'n' roll back."[99]

The Soviet-American confrontation in Europe nonetheless accelerated. Neither Moscow nor Washington had the power to force significant changes in European alignments, and neither side wanted to risk war to alter the status quo. The Soviets said they could wait for serious negotiations—"our asses aren't freezing in the wind," Khrushchev told West German Chancellor Konrad Adenauer.[100] Moscow still wanted Germany removed from NATO and NATO expunged from

Preparation for the "Kitchen Debate."   Khrushchev and Vice President Richard M. Nixon sip Pepsi-Cola at the American National Exhibition in Moscow in July 1959, just before their "kitchen debate" in which the Soviet leader admitted American superiority in consumer goods but boasted "when we catch you up, in passing you by, we will wave to you." (PepsiCo, Inc.)

Europe. The United States still wanted the Soviets excluded from Eastern Europe and the indefinite perpetuation of U.S. nuclear superiority.

In February 1956, Khrushchev, once the loyal supporter of Stalin's bloody purges of the 1930s, delivered a secret speech to the Twentieth Party Congress. He denounced Stalin for domestic crimes, initiated a "de-Stalinization" program, endorsed peaceful coexistence, and seemed to endorse different brands of communism. After the CIA obtained a copy of the speech and published it, Khrushchev's apparent acceptance of Titoism emboldened nationalists and victims of Stalinism to challenge Stalinist leaders in Eastern Europe. The abolition of the Cominform in April seemed to demonstrate Moscow's new tolerance for diversity. Young people and intellectuals especially embraced self-determination. In Poland, for example, a labor dispute in mid-1956 evolved into national resistance to Soviet tutelage. After using force to put down riots, Moscow compromised with Polish nationalism by reluctantly accepting Wladyslaw Gomulka as the Polish Communist party chairman, heretofore denied influence because Stalin thought him too "Titoist." The United States, which had been giving aid to Tito himself for years, soon offered Poland economic assistance.

Revolt erupted next in Hungary. Young revolutionaries marched and fought in the streets of Budapest. A new government, backed by local revolutionary councils throughout the country, took a drastic step when it announced that Hungary was pulling out of the Warsaw Pact and becoming neutral in the Cold War. The Anglo-French invasion of Egypt on October 31 (see page 301) gave the previously

"I'll Be Glad to Restore Peace to the Middle East, Too." The ugly Soviet suppression of the Hungarian rebellion of 1956 prompted this telling cartoon by Herblock. (*Herblock's Special for Today,* Simon & Schuster, 1958)

reluctant Khrushchev a "favorable moment" for the Red Army to crush the revolt; to do nothing "will give a great boost to the Americans, English, and French," he warned.[101] The courageous hand-to-tank combat of underarmed students and workers in the streets of Budapest in early November stirred global sympathy. Approximately 20,000 Hungarians and 3,000 Soviet troops died.

The Polish and Hungarian rebellions seemed to satisfy Dulles's dream of "liberation." In 1953, Congress had passed the first annual Captive Peoples' Resolution to spur self-determination in Eastern Europe. The Eisenhower administration had been encouraging discontent in Eastern Europe through the Voice of America and CIA-financed Radio Free Europe, which beamed anti-Soviet propaganda broadcasts into the Soviet sphere. "Sure, we never said rise up and revolt," one CIA agent recalled, "but there was a lot of propaganda that led the Hungarians to believe that we would help."[102] A covert CIA program called RED SOX/RED CAP trained East European émigrés for paramilitary missions. Still, Budapest was "as inaccessible to us as Tibet."[103] Hungary exposed "liberation" as a sham slogan that was aimed largely at winning votes in elections from Americans of East European background. The Eisenhower administration lowered immigration barriers to permit more than 20,000 Hungarian refugees to enter the United States and introduced a resolution condemning Soviet force in the General Assembly of the United Nations. Lacking power in the Soviet sphere, Washington could do nothing more.

Propaganda Balloons for Eastern Europe.   Although the United States did not send troops or military supplies to Hungary during the 1956 uprising, in the 1950s the Free Europe Committee floated message-filled balloons across the Iron Curtain from West Germany to stir up unrest. The CIA-front organization launched its first polyethylene balloons in 1951; its leaflets read: "Freedom will rise again." (Franklin D. Roosevelt Library)

Missile Race, Berlin, and the U-2 Mess

In 1956–1957, the United States seemed on the defensive and the Soviets on the offensive. Washington hastened to patch up its crumbling European alliance, rocked by U.S. disapproval of British-French military actions in the Middle East. Washington reinvigorated NATO and deployed intermediate-range ballistic missiles in Britain and tactical nuclear weapons in Western Europe. Still, the French became bogged down in a colonial war in Algeria and shifted many of their NATO contingents to Africa. Many Western Europeans remained suspicious of the U.S. push for German rearmament, worried about a resurgence of McCarthyism, and resented U.S. strictures on trade with communist countries. People in NATO nations also expressed doubt about America's credibility as an ally. Might not Americans fail to defend Western Europe against a Soviet attack lest U.S. countermeasures in Europe invite a Soviet nuclear onslaught against the United States itself? An American economic recession in 1957 further sapped Western vitality. John Foster Dulles's cancer surgery in November 1956 meant that President Eisenhower had to steer the United States through Eastern European and Mideast crises without his trusted adviser, who died in May 1959.

On October 4, 1957, the Soviets launched into outer space the world's first artificial satellite, *Sputnik.* Two months earlier the Soviets had fired the first intercontinental ballistic missile (ICBM). A Turkish official commented, "Sputniks are the bows and arrows of tomorrow. You Americans will find something to top them."[104] But many critics lambasted Eisenhower for apparently letting American power and prestige slip. Even though the USSR had test-fired only six ICBMs, Khrushchev bragged about turning out rockets "like sausages."[105] In fact, Khrushchev ran a "bluff"; he actually deployed only four unwieldy ICBMs by 1960, giving "the impression of Soviet strength . . . while actually playing from a position of inferiority."[106] A presidential commission study, the "Gaither Report," fed popular fears that the Soviets were outstripping the United States both militarily and economically. This bellicose report of November 1957 urged a large, expensive military buildup to improve U.S. "deterrent power."[107]

Eisenhower recoiled from the prospects of expanding the budget deficit but did agree to develop more ICBMs and disperse Strategic Air Command bombers. He nonetheless knew that *Sputnik* had not undermined U.S. security, because since 1956 American U-2 spy planes, flying at high altitude with sensitive instruments, had been gathering information on Soviet military capabilities. Privately fuming about "neurotic demagogues" who "leaked security information" that "misled the public," the president tried to reassure Americans without releasing the intelligence data.[108] He failed.

In January 1958, rocket scientists successfully launched an American satellite named Explorer I. In July, Congress created the National Aeronautics and Space Administration (NASA), soon to be, with the Pentagon, the chief federal funding source for high-tech research in universities such as Stanford and Massachusetts Institute of Technology, where academic agendas came to follow "the requirements of the national security state."[109] *Sputnik* also boosted secondary education so that "Johnny" could keep up with "Ivan." The National Defense Education Act (NDEA), passed in September 1958, provided federal aid to finance new educational programs in the sciences, mathematics, and foreign languages.

The continued militarization of the Cold War and the new emphasis on missile development alarmed George F. Kennan, an earlier architect of the containment doctrine. In 1957 Kennan delivered the "Reith Lectures" in London, calling for the "disengagement" of foreign troops from Eastern Europe and Germany, restrictions on nuclear weapons in that area, and a unified, nonaligned Germany. Earlier in the year, Polish foreign minister Adam Rapacki had advocated a "denuclearized zone" in Central and Eastern Europe.[110] The U.S. ambassador in Warsaw thought the Rapacki Plan would cause "trouble between the Poles and the U.S.S.R.," but Dulles and Eisenhower rejected the proposal as "highly dangerous," despite their own appeals for disarmament.[111] Kennan tried to keep the idea alive through his eloquent lectures, widely broadcast over BBC radio. Also, in order to reduce Moscow's security fears, he sought to remove Germany from the Cold War and thereby permit a withdrawal of Soviet troops from Eastern Europe. Finally, Kennan urged the administration to "put our military fixations aside," to exercise diplomacy rather than to strengthen NATO.[112]

Kennan's suggestions sparked furious debate. Former secretary of state Dean Acheson joined the fray. Should Kennan's plan become reality, Acheson scolded, the Soviet Union might reintroduce troops into Eastern Europe, threaten Western Europe, and actually sign an anti-American military pact with the new united Germany. A rearmed West Germany must remain in the U.S. camp. The United States, Kennan answered, would never know Moscow's intentions unless it negotiated. Walter Lippmann, who had criticized Kennan's containment in 1947, stood with him in 1957. Acheson and other hard-liners, Lippmann complained, resembled "old soldiers trying to relive the battles in which they won their fame and glory. . . . Their preoccupation with their own past history is preventing them from dealing with the new phase of the Cold War."[113]

A new crisis over Berlin demonstrated the importance of Kennan's suggestions for defusing European issues. West Berlin, 110 miles inside communist East Germany, stuck like a bone in the Soviet throat, as Khrushchev put it. Some 3 million East German defectors, many of them skilled workers, had used West Berlin as an escape route since 1949. For Americans and their allies, the city operated as an espionage and propaganda center. West Berlin's prosperity, induced by billions of dollars in U.S. aid, glittered next to drab East Berlin. Washington heated Soviet tempers by crowing about West Berlin's economic success and applauding the East German exodus. The United States also insisted that the two Germanies unite under free elections and refused to recognize the East German government. Finally, the continued rearmament of West Germany, including U.S. planes capable of dropping nuclear bombs, alarmed Moscow, which had endorsed the Rapacki Plan.

In November 1958 the Soviet Union boldly issued an ultimatum to solve the German "problem." Within six months, warned Khrushchev, unless East-West talks on Germany had begun, Moscow would sign a peace treaty with East Germany, thereby ending the occupation agreements still in effect from World War II and turning East Berlin over to the East German regime. He recommended that Berlin become a "free city" without foreign troops. Washington knew that to deal with East Germany would confirm the Soviet claim of two Germanies. Such a confirmation would surrender the post–World War II occupation rights and hence the U.S. presence within West Berlin itself. Eisenhower feared that "if we let the Germans down they might shift their own position and even go neutralistic."[114] Urged to test Soviet intentions by sending U.S. military units through the corridors to West Berlin, the president rejected such inflammatory advice and stalled. He said privately that "in this gamble, we are not going to be betting white chips, building up the pot gradually and fearfully. Khrushchev should know that when we decide to act, our whole stack will be in the pot."[115] Khrushchev wanted to talk, not fight. "Do not hurry. . . . The conditions are not ripe as yet for a new scheme of things," he told the militant East German leaders.[116] He dropped his ultimatum and agreed to a foreign ministers conference for May 1959, which proved inconclusive, a trip in September 1959 to the United States to speak directly with Eisenhower, and ultimately a Paris summit meeting in May 1960.

"Braggers." In this Japanese cartoon, Khrushchev and Eisenhower brag about their missiles. Despite his menacing public boasts, Khrushchev, like Eisenhower, dreaded the consequences of nuclear war. "We could never possibly use these weapons," he told an Egyptian journalist, "but all the same we must be prepared." (Nasu, courtesy of the State Historial Society of Missouri)

Warmly welcomed by Eisenhower, Khrushchev began his visit to the United States in September 1959 with a dramatic speech at the United Nations, where he proposed "general and complete disarmament in three years."[117] More in the forefront of diplomacy following Dulles's death from cancer in May, the president hoped that firsthand exposure to America's vastness and variety would make a favorable "chip in the granite."[118] The portly premier, seeming altogether human, inspected an IBM plant, marveled at the fecundity of Midwest grain fields, and visited a Hollywood movie set where he took offense at the bare legs exposed in a can-can dance—a sign to him of the decadence of Western capitalism. Khrushchev plugged "peaceful coexistence" and said that no one should take his "we will bury capitalism" statement in a literal or military sense: "You may live under capitalism and we will live under socialism and build communism. The one whose system proves better will win."[119] The Soviet leader reminded Americans that they had sent troops into the Russian civil war during the World War I period, and they reminded him of American relief aid in the early 1920s. After ten days on the road, the Soviet premier went to Camp David, that quiet, secluded presidential retreat near the Catoctin Mountains in Maryland. For two days the two leaders exchanged war stories and discussed Berlin. Eisenhower would not agree to a new summit meeting until Khrushchev abandoned his Berlin ultimatum. The premier agreed to do so, thus evoking the "Spirit of Camp David"—a willingness on both sides to talk their way to détente. Eisenhower "sincerely wanted to liquidate the 'cold war' and improve relations," Khrushchev later told the Politburo, adding that the moderates who advised Eisenhower had gained the upper hand over the "madmen."[120]

In 1959–1960 Eisenhower himself took goodwill foreign trips in a deliberate effort to ease tensions. Just before Khrushchev's visit to the United States, the president had flown to London, Paris, and Bonn for talks with European leaders. In December he traveled 22,000 miles to eleven nations in Europe, Asia, and North

"So Russia Launched a Satellite, But Has It Made Cars with Fins Yet?"   Ross Lewis's cartoon suggested that Americans had become too fascinated by 1950s consumer products while the Soviets were advancing missile technology. It did not take long for the United States to establish superiority in the nuclear arms race through new intercontinental ballistic missiles. (Milwaukee Public Library)

Africa. In February 1960, he toured Latin America for two weeks and encountered a mixed reception. And then he departed for the Paris summit meeting in May.

Two weeks before that summit meeting, on May 1, 1960, an American airplane carrying high-powered cameras and other reconnaissance instruments was shot down over Sverdlovsk in the Ural Mountains of northern Russia, 1,200 miles inside the Soviet Union. On a CIA mission, the U–2 intelligence plane was flying from a base in Pakistan to one in Norway. Although such flights had gone on for four years and the Soviets knew about them, this was the first time that Soviet firepower had reached the high-altitude craft. Pilot Francis Gary Powers's U–2 evidently had engine trouble and dropped several thousand feet before being shot down. He parachuted and was captured immediately, unable or unwilling to kill himself by taking his CIA-issued poison. NASA, used as "cover," announced routinely on May 3 that a "research airplane" studying weather patterns over Turkey had apparently crashed. When Khrushchev declared that an American airplane had been shot down after it had violated Soviet air space, the State Department fabricated a statement that a weather plane piloted by a civilian had probably strayed over Soviet territory by mistake. On May 6 Khrushchev demolished that story by displaying photographs of the uninjured pilot, his spy equipment, and the crashed U–2. Eisenhower then took responsibility for the U–2 reconnaissance flights as necessary to prevent another Pearl Harbor.

Berlin and controls on nuclear-weapons testing stood high on the agenda of the Paris summit meeting. Apparently preferring to wait until a new president took of-

Titan II Missile. Ten stories high and packing in one nuclear warhead the explosive power of 9 million tons of TNT (equivalent to 700 Hiroshima bombs), this intercontinental ballistic missile (ICBM) stands ready for launching from its underground silo. The decision to develop the Titan I came in 1955; the Titan booster was successfully tested four years later; and in 1962 the bigger and longer Titan II was developed. In 1963, this missile became part of the Strategic Air Command, deployed at bases in Arizona, Kansas, and Arkansas. (U.S. Air Force)

fice, perhaps seizing an opportunity to show domestic hard-liners and Chinese critics of peaceful coexistence that he could be tough, and certainly angry about U.S. violations of Soviet air space, Khrushchev denounced American aggression, demanded an apology for the U-2 flights, and stalked out. Thinking that a real opportunity to wind down the Cold War had been lost, Eisenhower bemoaned "the stupid U-2 mess" and looked forward to retirement on his Gettysburg farm.[121]

To the Brink with China; To the Market with Japan

The Chinese communists did not mourn this deterioration in Soviet-American relations. From the mid-1950s onward, Beijing castigated any sign of Soviet-American rapprochement. China repeatedly criticized Khrushchev for "yielding to evil" and "coddling wrong."[122]

As the Sino-Soviet schism widened, it became less tenable for U.S. officials to speak of a communist monolith, although many still did. But even John Foster Dulles admitted the split, and, seizing the opportunity, he worked to drive a wedge between Moscow and Beijing by "exerting maximum strain" on the Chinese communists to force them to ask the Soviets for help, "thereby placing additional stress on Russian-Chinese relations."[123] Many reasons other than U.S. pressure explain the Sino-Soviet split, including Moscow's refusal to help China develop nuclear capability. Scholars debate whether the hard-line U.S. posture produced better results

U-2. The United States began work on this high-altitude reconnaissance aircraft in 1954. In 1956, the Lockheed-built 49-foot-long spy plane began overflights of the Soviet Union to gather intelligence on Soviet missile development, despite Khrushchev's warning that "we will shoot down all uninvited guests." With a range of 2,200 miles and a cruising speed of 460 miles per hour, the U-2 also conducted surveillance during the Suez crisis. On May 1, 1960, a U-2 piloted by Francis Gary Powers crashed well inside the Soviet Union. President Eisenhower's announcement that flights over Soviet territory would continue so angered Premier Khrushchev that he walked out of the Paris summit meeting. (National Air and Space Museum, Smithsonian Institution, Photo No. 85-7309)

than a softer policy of trade and engagement might have achieved. In any case, under Eisenhower-Dulles policies, the Sino–American chasm gaped ever wider.

In early 1953, to press the People's Republic of China to accept an armistice in the Korean War, President Eisenhower announced that the Seventh Fleet would no longer block Jiang Jieshi's attempts to attack the mainland. Jiang actually lacked the resources for a major fight, but the decision alarmed Beijing, especially after Nationalist bombing raids began to hit the coast. Throughout the 1950s Jiang pledged a return to China. In that decade, he received an annual average of more than $250 million in U.S. economic and military aid. The Seventh Fleet remained in the Taiwan Strait, for U.S. policy valued Jiang's Formosa as a military partner in Asia. In December 1954, Taiwan and the United States signed a mutual defense treaty. The following month, Congress, by a vote of 83 to 3 in the Senate and 410 to 3 in the House, gave the president authority in the Formosa Resolution to employ American troops if necessary to defend Taiwan and adjoining islands.

In fall 1954 the United States created SEATO, an alliance with France, Britain, Australia, New Zealand, Thailand, Pakistan, and the Philippines. The Southeast Asia Treaty Organization targeted "Red China" and Beijing's support of revolution in Indochina. Washington also resisted cultural or economic contacts with China. U.S. officials forbade American journalists to accept China's 1956 invitation to visit the mainland. The State Department even banned the shipment of a panda to the United States because of its Chinese origins. At the 1954 Geneva Conference on Indochina (see next chapter), Chinese and American diplomats barely mixed. At one point Foreign Minister Zhou Enlai approached Secretary Dulles intending to shake hands, but Dulles, afraid that photographers would record this contaminating event, brusquely shunned Zhou's outstretched hand by turning his back. Washington also imposed a trade embargo on China.

In a crisis that "illustrates the danger of mutual isolation," China and the United States lurched toward the brink in 1954–1955.[124] Jinmen (Quemoy) and Mazu (Matsu) lay just a few miles off the southeastern China coast in the Taiwan Strait, two of some thirty small offshore islands that the Nationalists had managed to hold when they fled to Taiwan in 1949. Jiang had fortified the two islands with thousands of troops and used the outposts to raid the mainland. As the United States negotiated the defense treaty with Jiang in summer 1954, Beijing unfurled a "Liberate Taiwan" global propaganda campaign to counter the anticipated alliance. In response to the "plot of making a mutual security treaty" and to divert attention from preparations to invade another offshore island group called the Dachens, Chinese shore batteries began to bombard Jinmen early in September.[125] The Chinese did not intend to invade Jinmen, and they certainly did not anticipate the U.S. response.

Deeming the offshore islands militarily valuable to Taiwan (some 100 miles away), Washington had cautioned Jiang against escalating coastal warfare. "Quemoy is not our ship," Eisenhower said at first. People would ask, "What do we care what happens to those yellow people out there?"[126] The president changed his view, however, interpreting the shelling as a stab at American credibility, as a Cold War probe. Jinmen and Mazu, Vice President Nixon asserted, had become "stakes" in the "poker game of world politics."[127]

"Vastly overestimating the military capability of the Chinese to mount an assault" on Taiwan, yet seeking flexibility and hoping to deter further Chinese military action, Eisenhower decided to keep Mao puzzled about U.S. intentions.[128] Despite British warnings that Jiang was a "palooka" who might ignite war "through impulsiveness," the United States signed the defense treaty with Taiwan, and Congress gave the president a blank check in the Formosa Resolution. Mao also practiced brinkmanship.[129] In mid-January 1955, he sent his army to overrun the Dachens. Heeding U.S. advice, Jiang pulled his troops out; then Washington took up Mao's challenge. Eisenhower brandished nuclear weapons, stating publicly that he would use them "just exactly as you would use a bullet or anything else."[130] The Joint Chiefs of Staff readied plans to drop several Hiroshima-size bombs on coastal cities with expected casualties in the millions.

Dismissing the atomic threat, but lacking guaranteed support from the Soviet Union and reacting to alarms voiced by Asian nations attending the Bandung Conference (see page 299), China offered in April to discuss tensions with the United States. The crisis quickly quieted. In Geneva, and after 1958 in Warsaw, Chinese and American officials talked at the ambassadorial level about Taiwan, trade, and other topics. These limited discussions constituted the only sensible, civil element in Sino-American relations.

After the deployment of U.S. tactical nuclear weapons on Taiwan, and after Jiang had augmented his forces to more than 100,000 on the offshore islands, Mao answered in August 1958 by once again shelling Jinmen and Mazu. During the new crisis, Eisenhower resisted military advice to counterattack with "low yield" nuclear strikes "deep into Communist China" causing "millions of non-combatant casualties."[131] Instead he ordered U.S. airlifts and Seventh Fleet escorts for Nationalist supply ships. America's European allies urged caution. Beijing vowed "to deal resolute blows and take necessary military action" against Jiang's "clique," but care-

Mao Zedong (1893–1976). Chief of the Communist party in "Red China," father of the successful Communist Revolution, and radical philosopher-poet, Mao said of the Taiwan Strait crisis: "I did not expect that the whole world would be so deeply shocked." (National Archives)

Neighborhood Street and Coca-Cola in Tokyo, Japan.   Although Japan developed a booming export economy in the 1950s, it also imported famous U.S. products. Wherever U.S. troops were stationed during the Cold War, Coca-Cola followed, as the Georgia-based company greatly expanded its global marketing. Despite complaints about "Coca-colonization," the beverage quickly became a popular soft drink abroad. "One could swallow it," one scholar notes, "without giving up one's cultural loyalties or sense of national identity." (Library of Congress)

fully refrained from firing at U.S. warships.[132] Mao told Soviet foreign minister Andrei Gromyko that "it's getting so hot, and we want Eisenhower to take a shower."[133] Gromyko urged a peaceful settlement instead.

Eisenhower stepped back from the brink, as did the People's Republic. After Dulles and Jiang agreed in October that Jiang would not use force against the mainland, the Nationalist leader withdrew some troops from Jinmen and Mazu and Eisenhower suspended escorts of Nationalist vessels. Beijing relaxed its bombardment of the islands. "The islands," Mao told his doctor, "are two batons that keep Khrushchev and Eisenhower dancing, scurrying this way and that."[134] After the Taiwan Strait crises, Beijing became more determined to acquire its own nuclear deterrent, setting off alarm bells in both Moscow and Washington.

As it went to the brink with the People's Republic, the United States continued to rebuild Japan, cultivating it as a dependent, anticommunist partner, all the while worrying China, the Soviet Union, the Koreas, and other past victims of Japanese aggression. Two September 8, 1951, agreements guided Japanese-American relations for the decade. The first, a peace treaty signed by the United States and forty-seven other nations, provided for the ending of American occupation on April 28, 1952. The second, the Mutual Security Treaty signed by Washington and Tokyo, provided for U.S. defense of Japan and the stationing of American arms and forces on Japanese soil. Japan agreed to create a 110,000-strong military (Self-Defense Forces), which could not be used outside the nation. The military pact provoked considerable friction. Many Japanese resented the U.S. bases and the U.S. pressure to rearm, and throughout the 1950s, with popular opinion favoring "rice before guns," mass street demonstrations strained relations.[135] Meanwhile, American leaders who insisted that Japan pay for more of its own defense sharply criticized the Tokyo government for obstructing rearmament.

The plight of the *Fukuryu Maru* (*Lucky Dragon*), a Japanese fishing boat, heightened the debate. On March 1, 1954, the United States tested its new hydrogen bomb in the Bikini Atoll (Marshall Islands). The *Lucky Dragon* was fishing for tuna near the area. After the huge fireball erupted, shifting winds sprinkled radioactive fallout on the crew. The contaminated ash caused severe nausea, fever, and blisters, eventually killing one crew member. When Washington waited many months before compensating the victims, Japanese citizens protested American insensitivity. Two years later, in *Godzilla* (1956), movie audiences experienced an "eerie and realistic recalling . . . of the *Lucky Dragon*" as a prehistoric monster, revived by atomic bomb tests, rampaged through Tokyo.[136]

After negotiators signed a renewed Japanese-American defense pact in January 1960, hundreds of thousands marched and rioted against the retention of U.S. bases. Although the Japanese government pushed the new treaty through the Diet (parliament), the prime minister was forced to resign, and President Eisenhower had to cancel his goodwill trip to Japan.

Even though huge U.S. military purchases in Japan during the Korean War—for Toyota trucks, for example—spurred economic recovery, Secretary Dulles still complained in 1954 that Japan "has been listless and drifting and apparently expecting merely to be taken care of by [the] U.S."[137] Eager to lower the costs of subsidizing Japanese reconstruction and to blunt possible communist exploitation of economic instability, U.S. officials encouraged Japan to develop a prosperous export-oriented economy. A bullish consumerism was inspired in part by the Japanese desire to adopt aspects of the American lifestyle after seeing Hollywood movies. By the mid-1950s, Japan began to enjoy double-digit economic growth by using large sums of U.S. foreign aid, buying and copying American technology (Motorola helped start the electronics industry), inviting an industrious and loyal work force to cooperate closely with management for efficiency and quality control, practicing trade protectionism, and spending money on research and development rather than on military weaponry. With its populace aspiring to purchase the "three sacred treasures" (television, washing machine, and refrigerator), and with 2,500 Japanese intellectuals visiting the United States through academic exchange programs in the 1950s ("spreading favorable images of America as a model and . . . inspiration"), Japan became not only America's military ally but also eventually its economic competitor.[138]

The Third World Rises: Revolutionary Nationalism and Nonalignment

In the years 1946–1960, thirty-seven new nations emerged from colonial status in Asia, Africa, and the Middle East. Eighteen countries became independent in 1960 alone. In 1958, twenty-eight prolonged guerrilla insurgencies raged. Revolutions

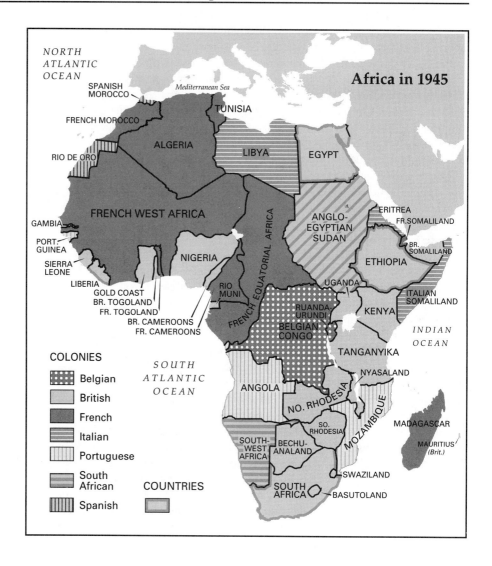

and the collapse of empires thus claimed a central place in international affairs. These great changes occurred in the "Third World"—a term for nations that belonged neither to the capitalist "West" nor to the communist "East." At first called "backward" and then "developing" countries, Third World nations generally consisted of non-white, agricultural peoples in the southern half of the globe. U.S. officials feared that Soviet offers of trade and aid to Third World countries such as India and Egypt "will create an even more serious threat to the Free World than did Stalin's aggressive postwar policies."[139] These countries abounded in raw materials and had served the needs of the industrial nations. In 1959 more than one-third of American direct private investments abroad were in the Third World. These nations also bought manufactured goods and provided sites for air and naval bases and intelligence facilities.

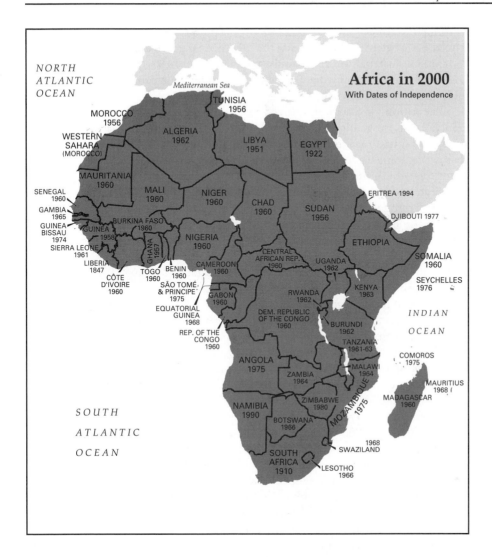

Volatile conditions in these "emerging" nations did not permit easy management by outsiders. Nationalism flourished. Many of their leaders were anticolonial revolutionaries who established leftist, undemocratic regimes. Long exploited, these poor countries eagerly sought economic improvement without foreign ownership. Many new nations declared themselves uncommitted, nonaligned, or neutral in the Cold War. In longer-established Third World nations, particularly in Latin America, in an effort to beat back rebel challenges, the United States continued to support governments controlled by military, political, or economic elites.

The Eisenhower administration fumbled this new "hot potato."[140] American leaders disparaged "neutralism," claiming that it only helped the communist cause. They assumed that Moscow inspired much of the trouble in the Third World. "Yet to blame the danger of these [explosions] on the presence of Communists," one scholar has written, "is like blaming the inherent danger in a huge mass of exposed combustible materials on the possible presence of arsonists."[141] The Eisenhower-Dulles team tried to apply the venerable containment doctrine to these regions in a futile effort to curb the new challenge.

The nation's great wealth proved a mixed blessing. Known as the "People of Plenty," to borrow the title of a 1954 book by the historian David M. Potter, Americans found that foreigners both envied and resented America's unmatched abundance; some wanted to acquire American material culture—from blue jeans to sports cars—but carped about the difficulty of doing so. The image of the "Ugly American" exacerbated foreign resentment. In 1958 William J. Lederer and Eugene Burdick wrote a novel with that title to warn that "fat," "ostentatious," "loud," and "stupid" Americans flaunted their wealth and that U.S. diplomats often isolated themselves by living lavishly in a "Golden Ghetto."[142] The authors appealed for Foreign Service Officers who spoke the language of the host country. Unless U.S. officials moved more among "the people," they argued, Washington would lose the struggle against communism.

American racism, symbolized by Jim Crow practices, handicapped the United States. In December 1952, when the attorney general asked the Supreme Court to strike down segregation in public schools, his brief read that "it is in the context of the present world struggle between freedom and tyranny that the problem of racial discrimination must be viewed."[143] So it was. In 1955 an airport restaurant in Texas refused service to the Indian ambassador because of his dark skin. In 1957, on Route 40 leading into Washington, the finance minister of Ghana was denied food at a Howard Johnson restaurant. President Eisenhower tried to assuage the insult by inviting him to breakfast at the White House. In the same year, when Eisenhower sent federal troops to Little Rock, Arkansas, to escort black children to school in the midst of ugly white protest, Dulles bemoaned the effect of the action on Asia and Africa, suggesting that it would be worse for Americans than Hungary was for the Soviets. With the candid admission that "17 million Negroes have yet to win all of the equal rights promised them by American democratic society," the State Department constructed a controversial exhibit for the Brussels World Fair of 1958 that featured a life-size photograph of multiracial children playing ring-around-the-rosy.[144] Despite favorable reactions from Europeans, Eisenhower quietly withdrew the display after protests from segregationists in Congress.

Gender stereotypes combined with racism and other cultural biases in shaping U.S. policies toward the Third World. On the Indian subcontinent, for example, U.S. officials preferred the "tough," "martial" Pakistanis ("energetic Western types . . . good people, good fighters") over the "mystics, dreamers, hypocrites" of "effeminate" India, not the least because Pakistan joined both SEATO and the Baghdad Pact while India stayed neutral.[145] One of Dulles's associates complained of the "almost feminine hypersensitiveness" that most Indians displayed about their country's prestige, whereas Prime Minister Jawaharlal Nehru once described a "loathsome Uncle Sam seeking to seduce the lovely virgin India."[146] Similarly, Washington's policies toward the Middle East were conditioned by changing ideas

Eisenhower and Prime Minister Jawaharlal Nehru (1889–1964). The Indian prime minister is shown visiting Eisenhower's Gettysburg, Pennsylvania, farm in 1956. Despite his irritation at Washington's military alliance with Pakistan in 1954 and Nehru's own leadership of the nonaligned Third World countries, the British-educated Brahmin enjoyed more cordial relations with President Eisenhower than he did with either President Truman or John F. Kennedy. The Truman administration resented India's friendly ties with the People's Republic of China during the Korean War. (Dwight D. Eisenhower Library, White House Album)

about Jewish masculinity. Israel, having shed the stereotype of passive victim of the Holocaust for that of "tough Jew" or "virile, throbbing civilization" surrounded by "hostile enemies," took on the role of America's "democratic *bulwark*." By contrast, Americans portrayed the Arab states, despite their valuable oil, as cowardly "marauders," "devious" and undisciplined soldiers who fought mostly with "windy communiques."[147]

When early-twentieth-century revolutions such as those in Mexico, China, and Russia rocked international equilibrium, the United States increasingly found itself a target rather than a model of revolution. One government report put the problem frankly in 1945: "The United States leans toward propertied classes who place a premium on order and trade."[148] So it was during the Eisenhower years. In late 1960, when forty-three Afro-Asian states, led by India, sponsored a United Nations resolution championing liberation from colonialism, the United States abstained from voting, lest it offend such Cold War friends as Portugal.

The Soviets had their troubles in the Third World, too. On the ideological level, both Marxism and the USSR's professed anticolonialism enjoyed wide appeal. In the mid-1950s Khrushchev toured India, Burma, and Afghanistan. The Soviet Union, however inexpertly, launched a foreign-aid offensive. It funded a steel plant in India and the Aswan Dam in Egypt. Between 1954 and 1959 Indonesia received the equivalent of a quarter-billion dollars in Soviet aid. At the Bandung Conference of April 1955, where twenty-nine "nonaligned" states representing about one-quarter of the world's population met to applaud "neutralism" and the

Soviet call for "peaceful coexistence," it became evident that the "free world" held less popularity than the "Communist world" in the Third World.

Yet the Soviet Union bumped up against nationalism, too, and gained few allies. Egypt's Gamal Abdul Nasser and India's Jawaharlal Nehru would not become the "plaything" or "pawn" of either side.[149] During a 1955 trip in India, Khrushchev vehemently denounced the West; the neutralist Indians resented this blatant effort to bring the Cold War into their country. Then, too, Arab nationalism, not Soviet communism, dominated the Middle East. And in Latin America, between 1945 and 1955, sixteen nations outlawed the Communist party. The Soviets, like the Americans, could not tolerate or exploit independent nationalism. Nor did they have the economic resources to make good on many of their foreign-aid promises. Finally, they could not explain away the contradiction between their rhetoric on self-determination and their suppression of Eastern European countries.

American officials remained fearful, however, that communism would exploit nationalistic sentiment and poverty in the Third World. Foreign aid became a primary U.S. tool. Whereas during the 1949–1952 period some three-quarters of total U.S. economic assistance went to Europe, in the years 1953–1957 three-quarters flowed to developing countries. By 1961 more than 90 percent of U.S. aid targeted the Third World. But to Washington's distress, many recipients refused to choose sides in the Cold War, thus drawing fire from Americans who demanded political returns from foreign aid. To Dulles, neutralism seemed but a deceitful stage on the road to communism. He declared it an "immoral and shortsighted conception."[150]

Stormy Weather: Nationalism in the Middle East and Latin America

Crises in the Middle East and Latin America illustrated troubled U.S. relations with the Third World and elevated the CIA as a major instrument of foreign policy. The Middle East became a particularly tumultuous region (see map, page 375). In 1952 Gamal Abdul Nasser led young Egyptian army officers against King Farouk, who fled to Europe with his harem and his wealth. Nasser initiated land reform and pledged to eliminate British control of the Suez Canal. A 1954 agreement, reluctantly signed by London, provided for a phased withdrawal. To maintain Western influence in the Middle East, thwart Soviet expansion, and fill what U.S. officials called a defense "vacuum," Washington in 1955 promoted the Baghdad Pact, a military alliance of Britain, Turkey, Iran, Iraq, and Pakistan.[151] Iran had been won over in 1953 when the United States, through the intervention of the CIA and a cut-off of foreign aid, helped overthrow the nationalist regime of Mohammed Mossadegh, who had attempted to nationalize foreign oil interests. U.S. companies produced about 50 percent of the Middle East's petroleum. Of Europe's crude oil imports in 1955, 89 percent came from that region.

Israel drew closer to the United States through foreign aid totaling $374 million from 1952 to 1961. Yet bitter Arab-Israeli conflict thwarted U.S. hopes for order in the Middle East. After the Israelis raided the Gaza Strip in 1955 and exposed Egypt's military weakness, Cairo signed an arms agreement with Czechoslovakia.

Heretofore Western nations had monopolized arms sales in the Middle East. Meanwhile, Palestinian refugees languished in squalid camps, growing more militant each year. As Israel rejected Washington's advice to compensate the homeless Palestinians, U.S. officials became annoyed. "Drop the attitude of a conqueror and the conviction that force . . . is the only policy that your neighbors will understand," Assistant Secretary of State Henry Byroade lectured the Israelis. He also implored Arabs to accept Israel's existence "as an accomplished fact."[152]

Despite his dislike for Nasser's Pan Arabism and neutralism, Dulles tried to entice him toward the West with foreign aid. In December 1955 the secretary offered to fund Nasser's dream of the Aswan Dam on the Nile, a potential source of electricity and irrigation. During the next year the World Bank crafted a $1.3 billion project utilizing British, American, and World Bank monies. About the same time, Egypt joined an anti-Israeli military alliance with Saudi Arabia, Syria, and Yemen. Jewish Americans protested in Washington, while southern members of Congress balked at a project that would permit Egypt to produce competitive cotton. Eisenhower and Dulles worried that a Czech/Egyptian arms deal signified alignment with the Soviets. Cairo had also recognized the People's Republic of China. Dulles asked: "Do nations which play both sides get better treatment than nations which . . . work with us?"[153] Nassar always replied that nationalism provided the best defense against communism, and that Zionism and Western imperialism, not communism, ranked as Egypt's greatest enemies.

To no avail. On July 19, 1956, Dulles informed the Egyptian ambassador that the United States would not fund the Aswan Dam. The State Department publicly insulted the Egyptians by explaining that their credit was no good—this despite the World Bank's decision that the dam represented a sound investment. "May you choke to death on your fury," Nasser jeered.[154] As a warning to Egypt and other neutrals to align with the United States, this hard-knuckled economic diplomacy failed miserably. Nasser quickly seized the Suez Canal, intent on using its $25 million annual profit to help build the Aswan Dam.

Without consulting Washington, and defiant of U.S. advice to avoid violence, the British and French huddled with Israel to plan a military operation. In late October and early November 1956, British, French, and Israeli forces invaded Egypt and nearly captured the canal. "Nothing justifies double-crossing us," an irate Eisenhower told his aides. "We're going to apply sanctions, we're going to the United Nations, we're going to do everything we can to stop this thing."[155] With Dulles in the hospital for treatment of his cancer, Eisenhower publicly upbraided the British and French for taking military action that might draw the Soviets into the Middle East and that took the spotlight off the simultaneous Soviet invasion of Hungary (see page 285). The Soviets, preoccupied with Eastern Europe, actually did little during the Suez crisis except wail against the invaders.

U.S. officials introduced a UN resolution demanding withdrawal and refused Britain oil shipments to make up for losses due to the closing of the Suez Canal and the destruction of oil pipelines. Washington also refused to aid Britain financially when its currency (the pound) faltered and Bank of England reserves dwindled because of a dollar drain. Bowing to U.S. pressure, French and British troops pulled out by late December. Only after Washington threatened sanctions (economic aid

Gamal Abdul Nasser (1918–1970). The bold Egyptian leader once told John Foster Dulles that the Russians "have never occupied our territory . . . but the British have been here for seventy years." Nasser went on: "How can I go to my people and tell them I am disregarding a killer with a pistol sixty miles from me at the Suez Canal to worry about somebody who is holding a knife a thousand miles away?" (*The Reporter,* 1956. Copyright 1956 by The Reporter Magazine Co.)

had already been suspended) did Israel disengage its forces from the Sinai in March 1957. A UN peacekeeping force then took positions and returned the canal, now clogged with sunken ships, to Egypt.

After the Suez crisis, although the United States retained its oil interests, Washington failed to dissuade Muslims from seeing the United States as anything more than another Western usurper. After all, the United States still stood at odds with the most popular Arab leader, Nasser, whom Eisenhower labeled an "evil influence" but whom Arabs hailed as a hero for his daring confrontation with Western imperialism.[156] By withdrawing the High Dam offer and letting Moscow build the imposing structure, Eisenhower signalled his choice to assume the role of Middle East policeman—because "the Bear is still the central enemy."[157] Anti-imperialist and anti-Israeli Arabs bristled against the U.S. presumption that they needed a protective sheriff. Relations with Britain and France had fractured, but Eisenhower's ire soon subsided in favor of strengthening the NATO alliance. Suez nonetheless accelerated Britain's decline. As for Israel, Eisenhower coveted it as an anticommunist ally, and in August 1958 Washington made its first arms sale to the Jewish state.

Claiming that communists schemed to exploit the Mideast "vacuum" and that "it is 'curtains' for Israel" if the United States did not thwart Soviet-backed Arab radicals, the president and a recuperating Dulles revitalized containment in the Eisenhower Doctrine.[158] In a speech before Congress on January 5, 1957, Eisenhower requested authority to use U.S. armed forces in the Middle East to help nations there resist "overt armed aggression from any nation controlled by International Communism" and authority to send military and economic assistance to the region.[159] On January 30, both houses approved the request in a resolution (72 to 19 in the Senate and 350 to 60 in the House). Although Iran and Lebanon endorsed the doctrine, Syria, Egypt, and Jordan soundly rejected it, and Iraq and Saudi Arabia seemed lukewarm.

Tests soon came. In April 1957, when pro-Nasser Jordanians threatened to overthrow King Hussein, Eisenhower ordered the Sixth Fleet to patrol off the coast of Lebanon and suggested that he would send U.S. marines too. Although the king had appealed for implementation of the Eisenhower Doctrine, this first application of the doctrine actually targeted Nasserite Arabs, not communists. In any case, the revolt failed. The second test came in Syria, where pro-Nasser radical military officers gained power and negotiated aid from the Soviet Union. Syrian officials exposed a CIA plot to oust them, and Dulles declared Syria a virtual Soviet satellite. In fact, the anticommunist Syrians looked mostly to Cairo, not Moscow. In February 1958, Syria and Egypt merged as the United Arab Republic; Nasser quickly banished the Communist party from Syria.

Lebanon and Iraq claimed attention next. In May 1958, a civil war erupted between Christians and pro-Nasser Muslims in multireligious Lebanon. A few months later, when Nasserites overthrew the regime in Iraq, Washington, fearing the spread of Arab radicalism, took firm action to save the Christian-led, pro-American government in Lebanon. On July 15, 14,000 U.S. marines waded ashore in Lebanon. U.S. officials intimidated Lebanese rebels by pointing out that one "aircraft, armed with nuclear weapons, could obliterate Beirut . . . from the face of the earth."[160] The marines departed in October after American diplomats negotiated an end to the civil war. Although acclaimed for decisively defending the Eisenhower Doctrine, the president actually set "dangerous precedents" by emphasizing U.S. "credibility as a guarantor, by misrepresenting the Third World nationalism as Soviet inspired, and by waging what amounted to a limited but undeclared presidential war."[161]

Nationalism also challenged in Latin America. Through the Rio Pact (a defensive military alliance formed in 1947), the Organization of American States (launched the following year but formally established in 1951 to help settle inter-American disputes), investments of $8.2 billion by 1959, economic assistance totaling $835 million for the period 1952–1961, and support for military dictators such as Fulgencio Batista in Cuba, the United States perpetuated its hegemony over neighbors to the south. But many Latin Americans grew restless, and their nationalism became strident. Latin American poverty remained stark; illiteracy rates stood high; health care proved inadequate; a population explosion threatened scarce resources; productivity showed minuscule growth; profits from raw materials such as sugar and oil flowed through American companies to the United States. "To arrest the drift in the area toward radical and nationalistic regimes," Dulles said, the United States would intervene, the Good Neighbor policy notwithstanding.[162]

Guatemala became a test case in which U.S. anticommunism, economic stakes, and hegemonic presumption prompted intervention. Jacobo Arbenz Guzmán won election as president by a wide margin, and after his inauguration in spring 1951, he set land reform as his central goal. Only 2 percent of the population owned 70 percent of the land. Under the agrarian reform law of mid-1952, the government eventually expropriated about one-quarter of the nation's arable land and distributed it to some 500,000 peasants. Food production increased. Soon after expropriation, however, Arbenz clashed with the United Fruit Company (UFCO), the U.S.-owned banana exporter and Guatemala's largest landowner. UFCO had to give up more than 400,000 acres of uncultivated land. When Arbenz offered compensation in government bonds, using the value of the land the company itself, for tax purposes, set at $1.2 million, UFCO claimed the expropriated properties represented $19 million. The State Department sided strongly with UFCO, which hired lobbyists and propagandists to spread a story in the United States: Communism had secured a beachhead in Central America.

The Soviet Union, prudently honoring the law of "geographical fatalism" in the face of superior U.S. regional power, actually showed little interest in Latin America in the 1950s.[163] Moscow looked skeptically at Arbenz and other anti-Yankee leftists who seemed more reformist than radical or communist. Still, indigenous communists backed Arbenz. He welcomed their help against entrenched interests, and he appointed some of them to administer land reform projects. Arbenz insisted that he would become neither a communist nor an anticommunist, but he defended the communists as servants of Guatemalan nationalism who respected the electoral process. Given their Cold War mentality, however, U.S. diplomats thought the worst. As Ambassador John Peurifoy remarked, Arbenz "talked like a Communist, he thought like a Communist, he acted like a Communist, and if he is not one . . . , he will do until one comes along."[164]

The desire to save UFCO properties also motivated U.S. actions, but what worried Washington most was "the strong appeal" among Central American neighbors of Guatemala's "broad social program of aiding workers and peasants."[165] Simply put, Arbenz challenged U.S. hegemony in the region. "They would have overthrown us even if we had grown no bananas," Arbenz's friend José Manuel Fortuny recalled.[166]

Eisenhower approved a CIA plan to overthrow the Arbenz government. Using a base in Florida and $5–7 million, the CIA recruited Guatemalan exiles. Training camps in Nicaragua and Honduras prepared them for an invasion. Colonel Carlos Castillo Armas, a graduate of the army staff school at Fort Leavenworth, Kansas, won favor as the president-to-be. In early 1954 Washington prodded the Organization of American States to declare, by a 17 to 1 vote, that the domination of any American state by the international communist movement would constitute a threat to the hemisphere. Washington also cut off technical assistance to Guatemala. After learning that the United States plotted his ouster, Arbenz turned to Czechoslovakia. A Czech arms shipment triggered the last stage of the CIA operation called PBSUCCESS.

On June 18, after the CIA bribed Guatemalans, planted fictitious news stories about Arbenz's submission to the Soviets, and dropped supplies at United Fruit facilities, Castillo Armas's small force attacked from Honduras. U.S.-supplied rebel planes bombed Guatemala City. Abandoned by his military and fearful that Washington would order U.S. marines to Guatemala if Castillo Armas's invasion failed, an anguished Arbenz fled to Mexico, where he died in 1971.

Castillo Armas soon returned UFCO lands, jailed his detractors, and set Guatemala on a course of government-sponsored terror that by 1990 had left 100,000 Guatemalans dead. In 1957 he fell to assassination, but the new regime remained a staunch U.S. ally. When a cabinet member, following the Guatemala coup, urged that "we . . . stop talking so much about democracy" and say "we . . . support dictatorships of the right if their policies are pro-American," Eisenhower interjected: "you mean they're OK if their *our* s.o.b.s?"[167]

Vice President Richard Nixon felt Latin American resentment firsthand in April–May 1958 when he traveled south on a goodwill tour. In Montevideo, Uruguay, anti-Yankee pickets mingled with the cheering crowds when Nixon motored through the city. Determined to counter what he considered communist agitation, Nixon stopped at the University of the Republic and engaged students in debate on U.S. foreign policy. Nixon claimed a "victory" and went on to Peru, where anti-Yankee sentiment welled up at San Marcos University. Nixon went there anyway, vowing to contest a "bunch of Communist thugs."[168] Stoned and spat on, he then headed for Caracas.

In Venezuela all hell broke loose. Earlier in 1958 a military junta had overthrown the dictatorship of Marcos Pérez Jiménez ("P.J."). A special friend of the United States during his seven-year rule, Jiménez "adopted the kind of policies which we think that other countries of South America should adopt," said Dulles. "Namely, they have adopted policies which provide in Venezuela a climate which is attractive to foreign capital to come in."[169] When Jiménez fled Caracas and the Eisenhower administration gave him asylum, Venezuelan bitterness toward the United States deepened.

Into this volatile environment stepped Nixon, emboldened by his earlier tangles with protesting students. Crowds blocked Nixon's motorcade en route to a wreath-laying ceremony at the tomb of Simón Bolívar; demonstrators stoned his car, shattering windows. They smashed fenders, rocked the automobile, and threatened the vice president's life. Nixon's car somehow sped away. In Operation Poor Richard, Eisenhower dispatched two airborne infantry companies to the Caribbean, in case Nixon had to be rescued. He did not. His toughness in the face of danger gained him public admiration in the United States. "A national defeat," noted one journalist, "has been parlayed into a personal political triumph."[170]

After Nixon's trip, Washington began to send more economic and military aid to the hemisphere. In 1959 the United States subscribed $500 million to the new Inter-American Development Bank. To combat communist propaganda and dissuade opinion makers in Latin America from criticizing the United States, Nixon recommended that Washington distance itself somewhat from unpopular rulers: "a formal handshake for dictators; an *embraso* [*abrazo*] for leaders in freedom."[171] That advice proved inadequate. In 1959, students and other nationalists in Panama rioted against U.S. control of the Canal Zone and tried to plant Panamanian flags there. Zone police and U.S. infantry beat them back. Recognizing that "one good missile with an atomic bomb could knock out one whole end of the Canal structure," Eisenhower eventually permitted the Panamanian flag to fly over the zone for the first time since the early twentieth century.[172] In Cuba, too, the United States met challenge. Nationalistic insurgents led by Fidel Castro overthrew Batista and launched a revolution to expel U.S. economic and military interests from the island (see pages 333–335). "Batten down the hatches," Assistant Secretary Thomas Mann told Latin American specialists in the State Department. "There's going to be some real stormy weather."[173]

Cultural Expansion and the Globalized Cold War

By decade's end, one of the most conspicuous signs of U.S. influence abroad came in the proliferation of American mass consumer culture and the foreign adoption of American ways. As economic recovery occurred in Western Europe and Japan, people spent proportionally more of their incomes on luxuries such as electrical appliances, hi-fi phonographs, televisions, leisurewear, even glossy, befinned American cars. Although some foreign elites sneered at "fast-food emporiums, sugar-saturated soft drinks, . . . *Der Spiegel*-like imitations of *Time* and *Newsweek*," youth culture made clear choices—"worn-out jeans vs. neat trousers, 'Elvis-quiff' and ponytail vs. orderly . . . hairstyles, uninhibited rock'n'roll vs. civilized ballroom dancing, comic strips vs. Goethe."[174] At trade fairs, the USIA adopted the theme of "People's Capitalism" to tout middle-class consumerism.[175] At the Moscow exhibition of 1959, site of the Nixon-Khrushchev debate, the Miracle Kitchen of Today served up "17,500 dishes ranging from ready-to-bake biscuits and oven-ready vegetable pies to instant coffee and Jello."[176] The continued appeal of Hollywood films demonstrated what one Austrian scholar has called the "Marilyn Monroe Doctrine."[177] "Is the World 'Going American'?" *U.S. News & World Report* asked, as it described Hula-Hoops in France, canned beer in British pubs, traffic jams in Rome, Bonn, and Sydney.[178] Such "cultural infiltration" may have helped to undermine communist authority in the Soviet empire, as people abroad came to identify Americans not only with nuclear superiority but with wealth and freedom.[179] In this sense, Americanization became a component of national security policy,

Mobile Motion Picture Unit.   In the 1950s, these specially outfitted Jeeps equipped with projectors, screens, and films, according to the State Department, were sent to "isolated areas of the world to distribute the U.S. information program." Believing that social modernization and economic progress would undercut leftist ideas, U.S. propaganda officials dispatched these vehicles, for example, into rural Mexico, seeking to reach "illiterates" through films on U.S. sports, music, health, and agriculture. These films, writes the historian Seth Fein, "privileged U.S. property relations and cultural values" by depicting, for example, "privately owned family farms as models for rural development." This anticommunist propaganda program in Mexico constituted an "attempt at cultural conquest" to "influence political behavior" to favor the United States in the Cold War. (National Archives)

equating consumerism with freedom. Yet cultural expansion generated both adoption *and* rejection, setting off cultural wars, as demonstrated by the "Ugly American" image in the Third World and French hostility to things American, including American English.

The Eisenhower administration promoted the expansion of American culture and Americanization abroad as one of several means to contest and undermine the appeal of Arab nationalism, Latin American revolution, Third World neutralism, communism, the Soviet Union, and China. Despite the catchy phrases of the Eisenhower-Dulles years, however, no dramatic new departures occurred in foreign policy. "Liberation" and "rollback" had always been the ultimate goal of "containment." The "Eisenhower Doctrine" extended the "Truman Doctrine." Dulles's strictures against neutralism sounded very much like Truman's declaration that all nations must choose between two ways of life. The "domino theory" in Asia differed little from Truman's alarmist predictions that if Greece fell, the Middle East would fall and then Europe collapse. Eisenhower and Dulles reinforced the Truman-Acheson hostility to "Red China." Both administrations intervened, with different methods, in the Middle East. Both sped the growth of the nation's nuclear arsenal. Both nourished overseas economic interests as essential to U.S. and world stability. Both sought to draw West Germany into Western Europe. America's Cold War institutions, its high defense budgets, its large foreign-affairs bureaucracy, its assumptions from the past, its export of culture—all ground on.

But the world had changed. In 1945 the United States sat atop the international system. Few restraints obstructed its exercise of power. Americans confidently placed restraints on others. But as the Soviet Union and the United States built their economies and military forces toward a stalemate, particularly in Europe, the bonds of stability loosened elsewhere. Throughout the 1950s new nations claimed independence, threw off the shackles of colonialism, and refused to join sides in the Cold War. Troubles for the two major powers also erupted in their own spheres of influence, as client states and allies challenged great-power hegemony. Latin America became less responsive to U.S. tutelage, and political turmoil and anti-Yankeeism grew apace. The 1959 victory of nationalists in the Cuban Revolution symbolized the new challenge (see next chapter). Anti-American Japanese rioters forced Eisenhower to cancel his trip to Japan, and Europeans such as Charles de Gaulle of France resisted U.S. influence. The Soviets faced the Hungarian Revolution, growing discontent in Eastern Europe, and the Sino-Soviet split. In short, Dulles and Eisenhower "overestimated the reach of communism" and "underestimated the power of nationalism."[180] Nuclear proliferation scared both sides. "Soon even little countries will have a stockpile of these bombs," Eisenhower noted in 1954, "and then we *will* be in a mess."[181] Britain (1952), France (1960), and China (1964) independently developed atomic bombs.

The bipolar world gradually became multipolar. Neither the Soviet Union nor the United States, tied to rigid policies and military programs, adjusted well to the more fluid international system. Although each professed an understanding of Third World needs and aspirations, both sought curbs on nationalism. After all, notwithstanding their propaganda, they wanted friends or allies, not fulfillment of the principle of self-determination. The two antagonists, in their drive to win friends through foreign aid and subversion, saw Third World nations manipulate the Cold War competition to gain economic assistance and military hardware from both sides. The U.S. antipathy toward revolutionary nationalism, socialism, expropriation of land and industry, and neutralism created a backlash in the Third World. Nor did alliances such as SEATO and the Baghdad Pact, CIA activities in Iran and Guatemala, training of counterrevolutionaries in South Vietnam (see next chapter), and sending of troops to Lebanon reveal an American grasp of the new challenge.

Unimaginative in dealing with the Third World, the Eisenhower administration also lacked innovation in its relations with the Soviet Union or China. The arms race continued, evolving into a space race and missile race. Washington seemed only minimally interested in reducing tension in Central Europe and Germany, quickly rejecting the Rapacki Plan and "disengagement" proposals. The Soviet Union seemed serious about cooling the arms race, but Moscow, too, so distrusted the other side that negotiations produced little. Nonrecognition of China simply isolated the United States from one of the world's important nations. Standing firmly with Jiang on Formosa revealed obstinacy, not wisdom, when many other Western nations recognized Beijing and traded with the People's Republic.

McCarthyism inhibited movement toward détente, but it had waned by 1954. The president also deflected another challenge, a proposed amendment to the Constitution. The Bricker Amendment, first offered in 1951 by Republican senator John Bricker of Ohio, sought primarily to limit the effects in the United States of UN-sponsored agreements on human rights. But it also included restrictions on executive agreements to ensure that presidents did not skirt the treaty-making power of the Senate. Hoping to force the president to consult more with Congress on foreign-policy issues and to forestall another Yalta, the amendment's backers insisted that executive agreements be voted on like treaties. Seeing an assault on presidential authority, Eisenhower, with help from liberal Democrats and moderate Republicans, beat back the amendment in a close Senate vote in February 1954. Eisenhower thereafter consulted regularly with legislators on major foreign policies, with the conspicuous exception of covert operations. Congress usually granted his requests. The Cold War consensus shaped in the 1940s continued strong. The Eisenhower administration failed to devise new policies for new realities, then, not because of Joe McCarthy and the China Lobby but because of its own uncompromising assumptions.

In the election of 1960, the Democrats claimed that the Cold War could be won. They differed from Eisenhower over methods to continue the old fight and to reverse the declining position of the United States in the Third World. The Democratic party and its presidential candidate, Senator John F. Kennedy, embraced the anticommunist absolutes of the era as heartily as John Foster Dulles ever had. Eisenhower's political critics charged that he and his secretary of state had caused the United States to fall behind in the missile race and that they had squandered American power.

Historical assessments of the Eisenhower administration used to stress its rigid conservatism, passive style, limited achievements, and hesitancy to adjust to new circumstances. They highlighted the president's apparent failure to keep abreast of events and his timidity in coming down hard on Joe McCarthy. Eisenhower's loyalty program damaged the Foreign Service. His expansion of the CIA and covert operations proved dangerous and short-sighted. Subsequent revelations of CIA assassination plots tarnished Ike's reputation. Whatever his doubts about the insanity of the nuclear arms race, he advanced it and left a legacy of nuclear fear. The 1950s generation would long remember going through the duck-and-cover drills of civil defense and watching Hollywood films of nuclear holocaust such as *On the Beach* (1959). Eisenhower distrusted Jiang's Nationalists and seemed to prefer a "two Chinas" policy, but a hard-line posture toward the People's Republic of China tempted nuclear war more than once. After researching the now-declassified documents of the 1950s, many scholars now emphasize Eisenhower's influential style, command of the policymaking process, political savvy, sensibly moderate approach to most problems, commitment to nuclear arms control, and curbing of the military. He was, in short, not an aging bystander in the 1950s. Such "Eisenhower revisionism" has stimulated a healthy reconsideration of the period. But we should not praise him too much for not going over the brink, for Eisenhower remained a zealous anticommunist of little flexibility and little innovation whose diplomatic record is at best mixed.

FURTHER READING FOR THE PERIOD 1950–1961

Some works cited in Chapter 7 also cover this period.

The Korean War is explored in Frank Baldwin, ed., *Without Parallel* (1975); Ronald Caridi, *The Korean War and American Politics* (1969); Bruce Cumings, *The Origins of the Korean War* (1981 and 1990), *Korea's Place in the Sun* (1997), and ed., *Child of Conflict* (1983); Rosemary Foot, *The Wrong War* (1985) and *A Substitute for Victory* (1990); Sergei N. Goncharov, John W. Lewis, and Xue Litai, *Uncertain Partners: Stalin, Mao, and the Korean War* (1994); John Halliday and Bruce Cumings, *Korea* (1988); D. Clayton James, *The Years of MacArthur* (1985) and *Refighting the Last War* (1992); Jian Chen, *China's Road to the Korean War* (1994); Burton I. Kaufman, *The Korean War* (1986); Peter Lowe, *The Origins of the Korean War* (1997); Callum A. MacDonald, *Korea* (1987); John Merrill, *Korea* (1989); Glenn D. Paige, *The Korean Decision* (1975); Stanley Sandler, *The Korean War* (1999); Michael Schaller, *Douglas MacArthur* (1989); William Stueck, *The Korean War* (1995); John Toland, *In Mortal Combat* (1991); Richard Whelan, *Drawing the Line* (1990); and Shu Guang Zhang, *Mao's Military Romanticism* (1996).

For the 1950s and President Dwight D. Eisenhower, see Craig Allen, *Eisenhower and the Mass Media* (1993); Stephen E. Ambrose, *Eisenhower* (1983–1984) and *Nixon* (1987); Michael R. Beschloss, *MAYDAY* (1986) (U-2); Günter Bischof and Stephen E. Ambrose, eds., *Eisenhower* (1995); H. W. Brands, Jr., *Cold Warriors* (1988); Jeff Broadwater, *Eisenhower and the Anti-Communist Crusade* (1992); Blanche W. Cook, *The Declassified Eisenhower* (1981); Robert A. Divine, *Eisenhower and the Cold War* (1981); Saki Dockrill, *Eisenhower's New-Look National Security Policy* (1996); Fred I. Greenstein, *The Hidden-Hand Presidency* (1982); Robert H. Johnson, *Improbable Dangers: U.S. Conceptions of Threat in the Cold War and After* (1994); Burton I. Kaufman, *Trade and Aid* (1982); Michael T. Klare, *American Arms Supermarket* (1985); Michael L. Krenn, *Black Diplomacy: African Americans and the State Department, 1945–1969* (1998); Elaine Tyler May, *Homeward Bound* (1988); Chester J. Pach, Jr., and Elmo Richardson, *The Presidency of Dwight D. Eisenhower* (1991); Herbert S. Parmet, *Eisenhower and the American Crusades* (1972); James T. Patterson, *Grand Expectations* (1996); William B. Pickett, *Dwight David Eisenhower and American Power* (1995); Brenda Gayle Plummer, *Rising Wind* (1996) (African Americans); Caroline Pruden, *Conditional Partners* (1998) (United Nations); Michael S. Sherry, *In the Shadow of War* (1995); and Duane Tananbaum, *The Bricker Amendment Controversy* (1988).

John Foster Dulles is studied in Louis Gerson, *John Foster Dulles* (1968); Richard Goold-Adams, *The Time of Power* (1962); Michael Guhin, *John Foster Dulles* (1972); Townsend Hoopes, *The Devil and John Foster Dulles* (1973); Richard H. Immerman, ed., *John Foster Dulles and the Diplomacy of the Cold War* (1990) and *John Foster Dulles* (1999); Frederick W. Marks, *Power and Peace* (1993); and Ronald W. Pruessen, *John Foster Dulles* (1982).

Other biographical studies include Jeff Broadwater, *Adlai Stevenson* (1994); Gayle Montgomery and James Johnson, *One Step from the White House* (1998) (Senator William Knowland); G. Bernard Noble, *Christian A. Herter* (1970); and James T. Patterson, *Mr. Republican* (1972) (Senator Robert Taft).

For the Soviet Union and Europe, consult Günter Bischof and Saki Dockrill, eds., *Cold War Respite: The Geneva Summit of July 1955* (1999); George W. Breslauer, *Khrushchev and Brezhnev as Leaders* (1982); Frank Costigliola, *France and the United States* (1992); Audrey K. Cronin, *Great Power Politics and the Struggle over Austria* (1986); Ennio Di Nolfo, ed., *Power in Europe? II* (1992); Michael P. Gehlen, *The Politics of Coexistence* (1967); Alexander L. George et al., eds., *U.S.-Soviet Security Cooperation* (1988); Alfred Grosser, *The Western Alliance* (1975); Wolfram F. Hanrieder, *Germany, America, Europe* (1989); William Roger Louis and Hedley Bull, eds., *The Special Relationship* (1986) (Britain); Thomas Risse-Kappan, *Cooperation Among Democracies: The European Influence on U.S. Foreign Policy* (1995); Jack M. Schick, *The Berlin Crisis* (1971); and Michel Tatu, *Power in the Kremlin* (1969).

The nuclear arms race, missile development, and antinuclear views are treated in Edmund Beard, *Developing the ICBM* (1976); Howard Ball, *Justice Downwind* (1986); Timothy Botti, *Ace in the Hole* (1996) (why nuclear weapons were not used); McGeorge Bundy, *Danger and Survival* (1988); Craig Campbell, *Destroying the Village: Eisenhower and Thermonuclear War* (1998); Ian Clark, *Nuclear Diplomacy and the Special Relationship* (1994) (U.S.-Britain); Barbara B. Clowse, *Brainpower for the Cold War: The Sputnik Crisis and the National Defense Education Act of 1958* (1981); Robert A. Divine, *Blowing on the Wind* (1978) and *The Sputnik Challenge* (1993); Gregg F. Herken, *Counsels of War* (1985); Richard G. Hewlett and Jack M. Holl, *Atoms for Peace* (1989); Jerome H. Kahan, *Security in the Nuclear Age* (1975); Fred Kaplan, *The Wizards of Armageddon* (1983); Milton S. Katz, *Ban the Bomb* (1986); Michael Mandelbaum, *The Nuclear Question* (1979); Walter A. McDougall, *The Heavens and the Earth* (1985); Peter Roman, *Eisenhower and the Missile Gap* (1995); David L.

Snead, *The Gaither Committee, Eisenhower, and the Cold War* (1999); Marc Trachtenberg, *History and Strategy* (1991); Andreas Wenger, *Eisenhower, Kennedy, and Nuclear Weapons* (1997); Lawrence S. Wittner, *The Struggle Against the Bomb* (1998); and Ernest J. Yanarella, *The Missile Defense Controversy* (1977).

For culture and cultural expansion, see works cited in Chapter 7 and Manuela Aguilar, *Cultural Diplomacy and Foreign Policy* (1996) (U.S.-Germany); Robert H. Haddow, *Pavilions of Plenty* (1997); Margot A. Henriksen, *Dr. Strangelove's America* (1997); and Walter L. Hixson, *Parting the Curtain: Propaganda, Culture, and the Cold War* (1997).

Asian questions, including China, the offshore islands crises, and Japan, are studied in Robert Accinelli, *Crisis and Commitment* (1996) (Taiwan); Stanley D. Bachrack, *The Committee of One Million* (1976) (China Lobby); William D. Borden, *The Pacific Alliance* (1984) (Japan); Roger Buckley, *U.S.-Japan Alliance Diplomacy, 1945–1990* (1992); Gordon H. Chang, *Friends and Enemies: The United States, China, and the Soviet Union, 1948–1972* (1990); Thomas J. Christensen, *Useful Adversaries* (1996); Warren I. Cohen, *America's Response to China* (1990); Nick Cullather, *Illusions of Influence* (1994) (Philippines); Harry Harding and Yuan Ming, eds., *Sino-American Relations, 1945–1955* (1989); Audrey R. Kahin and George McT. Kahin, *Subversion as Foreign Policy* (1995) (Indonesia); Peter Lowe, *Containing the Cold War in East Asia* (1997); David A. Mayers, *Cracking the Monolith: U.S. Policy Against the Sino-Soviet Alliance* (1986); Nancy B. Tucker, *Taiwan, Hong Kong, and the United States* (1994); Odd Arne Wested, ed., *Brothers in Arms: The Rise and Fall of the Sino-Soviet Alliance, 1945–1963* (1999); Kenneth T. Young, *Negotiating with the Chinese Communists* (1968); Qiang Zhai, *The Dragon, the Lion, & the Eagle* (1994); and Shu Guang Zhang, *Deterrence and Strategic Culture* (1992) (China). Studies of Indochina/Vietnam appear in Chapter 9.

For the Third World, see Richard J. Barnet, *Intervention and Revolution* (1972); H. W. Brands, *The Specter of Neutralism* (1989); Melvin Gurtov, *The United States Against the Third World* (1974); Gabriel Kolko, *Confronting the Third World* (1988); Robert J. McMahon, *The Cold War on the Periphery* (1994) (India and Pakistan); Thomas J. Noer, *Cold War and Black Liberation* (1985) (Africa); Peter J. Schraeder, *United States Foreign Policy Toward Africa* (1994); L. S. Stavrianos, *Global Rift* (1981); and Stanley Wolpert, *Nehru* (1997). See also works cited in Chapters 7, 9–12.

For U.S. relations with the Middle East, especially with Egypt and Israel, see Isaac Alteras, *Eisenhower and Israel* (1993); Nigel J. Ashton, *Eisenhower, Macmillan, and the Problem of Nasser* (1996); George W. Ball and Douglas B. Ball, *The Passionate Attachment* (1992) (Israel); Abraham Ben-Zvi, *Decade of Transition* (1998) (Israel); William J. Burns, *Economic Aid and American Policy Toward Egypt* (1985); Irene Gendzier, *Notes from the Minefield* (1997) (Lebanon); Peter L. Hahn, *The United States, Great Britain, and Egypt* (1991); Mary Ann Heiss, *Empire and Nationhood* (1997) (Iranian oil); George Lenczowski, *The Middle East in World Affairs* (1980); Zach Levy, *Israel and the Western Powers* (1998); S. Neil MacFarlane, *Superpower Rivalry and Third World Radicalism* (1985); Gail E. Meyer, *Egypt and the United States* (1980); Michael Oren, *The Origins of the Second Arab-Israeli War* (1993); William R. Polk, *The Arab World Today* (1991); Cheryl Rubenberg, *Israel and the American National Interest* (1986); Barry Rubin, *The Arab States and the Palestine Conflict* (1981); Bonnie Saunders, *The United States and Arab Nationalism* (1996) (Syria); David Schoenbaum, *The United States and the State of Israel* (1993); Steven L. Spiegel, *The Other Arab-Israeli Conflict* (1985); and Robert W. Stookey, *America and the Arab States* (1975).

The Suez crisis is included in many of the works above, but especially see Chester L. Cooper, *The Lion's Last Roar* (1978); Steven Freiberger, *Dawn over Suez* (1992); Diane B. Kunz, *The Economic Diplomacy of the Suez Crisis* (1991); Donald Neff, *Warriors at Suez* (1981); William Roger Louis and Roger Owen, eds., *Suez 1956* (1989); and Selwyn Troen, ed., *The Sinai-Suez Crisis, 1956* (1990).

Latin American–U.S. relations and the intervention in Guatemala are treated in Cole Blasier, *The Hovering Giant* (1976); Elizabeth A. Cobbs, *The Rich Neighbor Policy* (1992); Nick Cullather, *Secret History* (1999) (CIA in Guatemala); Michael D. Gambone, *Eisenhower, Somoza, and the Cold War in Nicaragua* (1997); Piero Gleijeses, *Shattered Hope* (1991) (Guatemala); Richard Immerman, *The CIA in Guatemala* (1982); Stephen Kinzer and Stephen Schlesinger, *Bitter Fruit* (1982) (Guatemala); Walter LaFeber, *The Panama Canal* (1989) and *Inevitable Revolutions* (1993) (Central America); Abraham F. Lowenthal, ed., *Exporting Democracy* (1991); A. W. Maldonado, *Teodoro Moscoso and Puerto Rico's Operation Bootstrap* (1997); Nicola Miller, *Soviet Relations with Latin America, 1959–1987* (1989); Thomas G. Paterson, *Contesting Castro* (1994); Stephen G. Rabe,

Eisenhower and Latin America (1988); Ramón Ruíz, *Cuba* (1968); David F. Schmitz, *Thank God They're on Our Side* (1999) (right-wing dictatorships); Lars Schoultz, *Beneath the United States* (1998); Gaddis Smith, *The Last Years of the Monroe Doctrine* (1994); Peter H. Smith, *Talons of the Eagle* (1996); and Bryce Wood, *The Dismantling of the Good Neighbor Policy* (1985).

For the Central Intelligence Agency and its covert activities, see Stephen E. Ambrose, *Ike's Spies* (1981); Sigmund Diamond, *Compromised Campus: The Collaboration of Universities with the Intelligence Community* (1992); Peter Grose, *Gentleman Spy* (1994) (Allen Dulles); Loch K. Johnson, *America's Secret Power* (1989); Ludwell L. Montagne, *General Walter Bedell Smith as Director of Central Intelligence* (1992); John Ranelagh, *The Agency* (1986); Evan Thomas, *The Very Best Men* (1995); and Robin W. Winks, *Cloak & Gown* (1987).

For the impact of McCarthyism, consult works cited in Chapter 7 and Michael R. Belknap, *Cold War Political Justice* (1977); Robert Griffith, *The Politics of Fear* (1987); M. J. Heale, *McCarthy's Americans* (1998); William W. Keller, *The Liberals and J. Edgar Hoover* (1989); Stanley I. Kutler, *The American Inquisition* (1982); Mary S. McAuliffe, *Crisis on the Left* (1978); Thomas C. Reeves, *The Life and Times of Joe McCarthy* (1982); Ellen W. Schrecker, *No Ivory Tower: McCarthyism and the Universities* (1986) and *Many Are the Crimes* (1998); Athan Theoharis and John S. Cox, *The Boss* (1988) (J. Edgar Hoover); Stephen Vaughn, *Ronald Reagan in Hollywood* (1994); and Stephen J. Whitfield, *The Culture of the Cold War* (1991).

See also the following notes and the General Bibliography.

For comprehensive coverage of foreign-related topics, see the articles in the four-volume *Encyclopedia of U.S. Foreign Relations* (1997), edited by Bruce W. Jentleson and Thomas G. Paterson.

NOTES TO CHAPTER 8

1. Quoted in Glenn D. Paige, *The Korean Decision* (New York: Free Press, 1968), p. 82.
2. Glenn D. Paige, ed., *1950: Truman's Decision* (New York: Chelsea House, 1970), p. 49.
3. Quoted in David Rees, *Korea* (London: Macmillan, 1964), p. 36.
4. Quoted in John Toland, *In Mortal Combat* (New York: Morrow, 1991), p. 34.
5. Quoted in Ronald W. Pruessen, *John Foster Dulles* (New York: Free Press, 1982), p. 454.
6. Paige, *1950*, p. 63.
7. Robert J. Donovan, *Tumultuous Years* (New York: Norton, 1982), p. 202.
8. Harry S. Truman, *Memoirs* (Garden City, N.Y.: Doubleday, 1955–1956; 2 vols.), *II*, 333.
9. Quoted in *New York Times*, June 26, 1950.
10. Quoted in Melvyn P. Leffler, *A Preponderance of Power* (Stanford: Stanford University Press, 1992), p. 366.
11. *Congressional Record*, *XCVI* (June 26, 1950), 9188.
12. *Foreign Relations, 1950, VII* (Washington, D.C.: Government Printing Office, 1976), 179.
13. Quoted in Toland, *In Mortal Combat*, p. 41.
14. Joseph C. Harsch quoted in Bruce Cumings, *The Origins of the Korean War* (Princeton: Princeton University Press, 1981, 1990; 2 vols.), *II*, 628.
15. Quoted in Bruce Cumings, *Korea's Place in the Sun* (New York: Norton, 1997), p. 265.
16. Quoted in D. Clayton James, *Refighting the Last War* (New York: Free Press, 1993), p. 16.
17. Mao Zedong quoted in Hao Yufan and Zhai Zhihai, "China's Decision to Enter the Korean War," *China Quarterly*, no. 121 (May 1990), 101.
18. Quoted in Rosemary Foot, "Leadership, Perception, and Interest," *Diplomatic History*, *XX* (Summer 1996), 479.
19. Air Marshal Cecil Boucher quoted in Peter Lowe, *Containing the Cold War in East Asia* (New York: Manchester University Press, 1997), p. 206.
20. Quoted in Shen Zhihua, "The Discrepancy on Chinese Entry into the Korean War," *Cold War International History Project Bulletin*, nos. 8–9 (Winter 1996/1997), 237.
21. Quoted in Thomas G. Paterson, "The Korean War," in Bruce W. Jentleson and Thomas G. Paterson, eds., *Encyclopedia of U.S. Foreign Relations* (New York: Oxford University Press, 1997), *III*, 31.
22. Quoted in Melvyn P. Leffler, *The Specter of Communism* (New York: Hill & Wang, 1994), p. 107.
23. Edward Almond quoted in Cumings, *Origins*, *II*, 742.
24. Quoted in Callum A. MacDonald, *Korea* (New York: Free Press, 1987), p. 71.
25. Quoted in Philip West, "Confronting the West," *Journal of American–East Asian Relations*, *II* (Spring 1993), 6–7.
26. Truman quoted in Arnold A. Offner, "Another Such Victory," *Diplomatic History*, *XXIII* (Spring 1999), 151; Oliver Franks quoted in Thomas J. Christensen, *Useful Adversaries* (Princeton: Princeton University Press, 1996), p. 184.
27. Quoted in Laura Belmonte, "Anglo-American Relations and the Dismissal of General MacArthur," *Diplomatic History*, *XIX* (Fall 1995), 663.
28. Quoted in Michael Schaller, *Douglas MacArthur* (New York: Oxford University Press, 1989), p. 335.
29. *Congressional Record*, *XCVII* (April 19, 1951), 4125.
30. *Ibid.*, April 24, 1951, p. 4261.
31. Cumings, *Origins*, *II*, 713.
32. Quoted in Michael D. Pearlman, *Warmaking and American Democracy* (Lawrence: University Press of Kansas, 1999), p. 293.
33. Marc Trachtenberg, "A 'Wasting Asset': American Strategy and the Shifting Nuclear Balance," *International Security*, *XIII* (Winter 1988/1989), 27.

34. Stalin–Zhou Enlai conversation, August 20, 1952, *Cold War International History Project Bulletin*, nos. 6–7 (Winter 1995/1996), 12–13.

35. Rosemary Foot, *A Substitute for Victory* (Ithaca: Cornell University Press, 1990), p. 220.

36. Quoted in Thomas Risse-Kappen, *Cooperation Among Democracies* (Princeton: Princeton University Press, 1995), p. 62.

37. General Chung Sang-chin of North Korea quoted in Kathryn Weathersby, "Soviet Aims in Korea and the Origins of the Korean War, 1945–1950," Working Paper no. 8, *Cold War International History Project* (Washington, D.C., November 1993), p. 26.

38. Cumings, *Origins, II*, 643.

39. Weathersby, "Soviet Aims," p. 31.

40. Mao quoted in Christensen, *Useful Adversaries*, p. 162.

41. John Halliday and Bruce Cumings, *Korea* (New York: Pantheon, 1988), p. 34.

42. "Princeton Seminar," February 13–14, 1954, Box 66, Dean Acheson Papers, Harry S. Truman Library, Independence, Mo.

43. Quoted in Walter LaFeber, *The Clash* (New York: Norton, 1997), p. 294.

44. *Public Papers, Truman, 1952–1953* (Washington, D.C.: Government Printing Office, 1966), p. 708.

45. Dean Acheson, *Present at the Creation* (New York: Norton, 1969), p. 420.

46. Quoted in Stephen E. Ambrose, *Nixon* (New York: Simon & Schuster, 1987), p. 297.

47. Quoted in John Lewis Gaddis, *Russia, the Soviet Union, and the United States* (New York: McGraw Hill, 1990; 2nd ed.), p. 216.

48. Quoted in Stephen E. Ambrose, *Eisenhower, 1890–1952* (New York: Simon & Schuster, 1983), p. 569.

49. David Brinkley, *David Brinkley* (New York: Ballantine, 1995), p. 125.

50. Fred I. Greenstein, *The Hidden-Hand Presidency* (New York: Basic Books, 1982).

51. Nancy B. Tucker, *Taiwan, Hong Kong, and the United States* (New York: Twayne, 1994), p. 36.

52. Richard J. Barnet, *Intervention and Revolution* (New York: New American Library, 1972; rev. ed.), p. 36.

53. Quoted in Robert Griffith, "Dwight D. Eisenhower and the Corporate Commonwealth," *American Historial Review, LXXXVII* (February 1982), 91.

54. Quoted in Robert J. McMahon, "The Illusion of Vulnerability," *International History Review, XVIII* (August 1996), 617.

55. Walter L. Hixson, *Parting the Curtain* (New York: St. Martin's Press, 1997).

56. Quoted in Loch K. Johnson, *America's Secret Power* (New York: Oxford University Press, 1989), pp. 17, 27.

57. Hoover Commission quoted *ibid.*, p. 10.

58. Nick Cullather, *Illusions of Influence* (Stanford: Stanford University Press, 1994), p. 176.

59. Quoted in Stephen E. Ambrose, *Eisenhower, the President* (New York: Simon & Schuster, 1984), p. 226.

60. Audrey R. Kahin and George McT. Kahin, *Subversion as Foreign Policy* (New York: New Press, 1995), p. 8.

61. *Public Papers, Eisenhower, 1953* (Washington, D.C.: Government Printing Office, 1960), pp. 182–183.

62. Quoted in Vladislav Zubok, "Soviet Intelligence and the Cold War," *Diplomatic History, XIX* (Summer 1995), 461.

63. Michael S. Sherry, *In the Shadow of War* (New Haven:Yale University Press, 1995), p. 203.

64. *Public Papers, Eisenhower, 1960–61* (Washington, D.C.: Government Printing Office, 1961), pp. 1035–1040.

65. "Discussion at the 309th Meeting of the National Security Council, Friday, January 11, 1957," Box 7, NSC Summaries, NSC Series, Ann Whitman File, Dwight D. Eisenhower Papers, Dwight D. Eisenhower Library, Abilene, Kan.

66. Richard H. Immerman, "Conclusion," in Immerman, ed., *John Foster Dulles and the Diplomacy of the Cold War* (Princeton: Princeton University Press, 1990), p. 266.

67. Quoted in Herbert S. Parmet, "Power and Reality," in Frank Merli and Theodore Wilson, eds., *Makers of American Diplomacy* (New York: Charles Scribner's Sons, 1974), p. 593.

68. Quoted in Deborah Welch Larson, *Anatomy of Mistrust* (Ithaca: Cornell University Press, 1997), p. 65.

69. Robert Bowie quoted in *John Foster Dulles* (Princeton: Woodrow Wilson School of Public and International Affairs, Princeton University, 1988), p. 10.

70. Quoted in William B. Pickett, *Dwight David Eisenhower and American Power* (Arlington Heights, Ill.: Harlan Davidson, 1995), p. 104.

71. Quoted in Ronald E. Powaski, *The Cold War* (New York: Oxford University Press, 1998), p. 102.

72. Quoted in Shane J. Maddock, "The Fourth Country Problem," *Presidential Studies Quarterly, XXVIII* (Summer 1998), 554.

73. Wolfram F. Hanrieder, *Germany, America, Europe* (New Haven: Yale University Press, 1989), p. 70.

74. Quoted in Gordon H. Chang, *Friends and Enemies* (Stanford: Stanford University Press, 1990), p. 116.

75. *Public Papers, Eisenhower, 1954* (Washington, D.C.: Government Printing Office, 1960), p. 383.

76. Quoted in Emmett John Hughes, *The Ordeal of Power* (New York: Dell, 1964 [c. 1962]), p. 98.

77. Quoted in J. Garry Clifford, "McCarthyism," in Jentleson and Paterson, *Encyclopedia, III,* 120.

78. Quoted in Earl Latham, *The Communist Controversy in Washington* (New York: Atheneum, 1969), p. 338.

79. Ross Terrill, "When America 'Lost' China," *Atlantic Monthly, CCXXIV* (November 1969), 79.

80. Margaret Joy Tibbetts quoted in Ann Miller Morin, *Her Excellency* (New York: Twayne, 1994), p. 57.

81. Theodore H. White, *In Search of History* (New York: Warner, 1978), p. 395.

82. *Public Papers, Eisenhower, 1953*, p. 187.

83. Quoted in Steven I. Levine, "Soviet Asian Policy in the 1950s," in Warren I. Cohen and Akira Iriye, eds., *The Great Powers in East Asia, 1953–1960* (New York: Columbia University Press, 1990), p. 298.

84. Quoted in John Lewis Gaddis, *Strategies of Containment* (New York: Oxford University Press, 1982), p. 153.

85. Quoted in Kurt Steiner, "Negotiations for an Austrian State Treaty," in Alexander L. George et al., eds., *U.S.-Soviet Security Cooperation* (New York: Oxford University Press, 1988), p. 75.

86. Quoted in Matthew Evangelista, "Cooperation Theory and Disarmament Negotiations in the 1950s," *World Politics, XLII* (July 1990), 503.

87. Quoted in *Foreign Relations of the United States, 1955–1957* (Washington, D.C.: Government Printing Office, 1988), *V*, 301.

88. Sherman Adams, *Firsthand Report* (New York: Popular Library, 1962 [1961]), p. 177.

89. Quoted in Richard G. Hewlett and Jack M. Holl, *Atoms for Peace and War* (Berkeley: University of California Press, 1989), p. 299.

90. Quoted in Herbert S. Parmet, *Eisenhower and the American Crusades* (New York: Macmillan, 1972), p. 406.

91. Quoted in Michael R. Beschloss, *MAYDAY* (New York: Harper and Row, 1986), p. 103.

92. *Public Papers, Eisenhower, 1955*, p. 730.

93. Quoted in James T. Patterson, *Grand Expectations* (New York: Oxford University Press, 1996), p. 302.

94. Quoted in Denis Healey, "'When Shrimps Learn to Whistle,'" *International Affairs, XXXII* (January 1956), 2.

95. Elaine Tyler May, *Homeward Bound* (New York: Basic Books, 1988), p. 164.

96. Quoted in Penny V. von Eschen, *Race Against Empire* (Ithaca: Cornell University Press, 1997), pp. 177–178.

97. Hixson, *Parting*, p. 159.

98. Reinhold Wagnleitner, "The Irony of American Culture Abroad," in Lary May, ed., *Recasting America* (Chicago: University of Chicago Press, 1989), p. 295.

99. Reinhold Wagnleitner, *Cocacolonization and the Cold War* (Chapel Hill: University of North Carolina Press, 1994), p. 4.

100. Quoted in Vladislav Zubok and Constantine Pleshakov, *Inside the Kremlin's Cold War* (Cambridge: Harvard University Press, 1996), p. 180.

101. Quoted in Mark Kramer, "New Evidence on Soviet Decision-Making and the 1956 Polish and Hungarian Crises," *Cold War International History Project Bulletin*, nos. 8–9 (Winter 1996/1997), 370.

102. Thomas Polgar quoted in Evan Thomas, *The Very Best Men* (New York: Simon & Schuster, 1995), p. 147.

103. Quoted in Chester J. Pach, Jr., and Elmo Richardson, *The Presidency of Dwight D. Eisenhower* (Lawrence: University Press of Kansas, 1991), p. 132.

104. Quoted in Philip Nash, *The Other Missiles of October* (Chapel Hill: University of North Carolina Press, 1997), p. 5.

105. Quoted in Gregg Herken, *Counsels of War* (New York: Oxford University Press, 1987), p. 130.

106. Zubok and Pleshakov, *Kremlin's Cold War*, p. 172.

107. Quoted in Michael Mandelbaum, *The Nuclear Question* (New York: Cambridge University Press, 1979), p. 66.

108. Quoted in Peter Roman, *Eisenhower and the Missile Gap* (Ithaca: Cornell University Press, 1995), p. 139.

109. Stuart Leslie, *The Cold War and American Science* (New York: Columbia University Press, 1993), pp. 2, 43.

110. Noble Frankland, ed., *Documents on International Affairs, 1957* (London: Oxford University Press, 1960), p. 157.

111. Jacob Beam and Dulles quoted in Piotr Wandycz, "Adam Rapacki," in Gordon A. Craig and Francis L. Loewenheim, eds., *The Diplomats, 1939–1979* (Princeton: Princeton University Press, 1994), pp. 299–300.

112. George F. Kennan, *Russia, the Atom, and the West* (New York: Harper & Brothers, 1958), p. 92.

113. Quoted in Thomas G. Paterson, ed., *Containment and the Cold War* (Reading, Mass.: Addison-Wesley, 1973), p. 116.

114. Quoted in William Burr, "New Sources on the Berlin Crisis, 1958–1962," *Cold War International History Bulletin*, no. 2 (Fall 1992), 22.

115. Quoted in Townsend Hoopes, *The Devil and John Foster Dulles* (Boston: Little, Brown, 1973), p. 470.

116. Quoted in Hope M. Harrison, "Ulbricht and the Concrete 'Rose,'" Working Paper no. 5, *Cold War International History Project* (Washington, D.C., May 1993), p. 21.

117. Quoted in Zubok and Pleshakov, *Kremlin's Cold War*, p. 200.

118. Dwight D. Eisenhower, *The White House Years: Waging Peace, 1956–1961* (Garden City, N.Y.: Doubleday, 1965), p. 432.

119. *Khrushchev in America* (New York: Crosscurrents, 1960), p. 120.

120. Quoted in Larson, *Anatomy*, p. 96.

121. Quoted in Ambrose, *Eisenhower, President*, p. 580.

122. Quoted in Edward Crankshaw, *The New Cold War* (Baltimore: Penguin, 1965 [c. 1963]), p. 81.

123. Quoted in John Lewis Gaddis, *The United States and the End of the Cold War* (New York: Oxford University Press, 1992), p. 75.

124. Gordon H. Chang and He Di, "The Absence of War in the U.S.-China Confrontation over Quemoy and Matsu in 1954–1955," *American Historical Review, XCVIII* (December 1993), 1523.

125. Military orders quoted in Xiaobing Li and Honshan Li, eds., *China and the United States* (Lanham, Md.: University Press of America, 1998), p. 55.

126. Quoted in Waldo Heinrichs, "Eisenhower and the Sino-American Confrontation," in Cohen and Iriye, *Great Powers*, p. 99.

127. Richard M. Nixon, *Six Crises* (Garden City, N.Y.: Doubleday, 1962), p. 273.

128. Robert Accinelli, *Crisis and Commitment* (Chapel Hill: University of North Carolina Press, 1996), p. 223.

129. Quoted in Qiang Zhai, *The Dragon, the Lion, & the Eagle* (Kent, Ohio: Kent State University Press, 1994), p. 161.

130. Quoted in Shu Guang Zhang, *Deterrence and Strategic Culture* (Ithaca: Cornell University Press, 1992), p. 214.

131. Gerard Smith memorandum for Secretary Herter, August 13, 1958, National Security Archive, Washington, D.C.

132. Quoted in Melvin Gurtov, "The Taiwan Strait Crisis Revisited," *Modern China, II* (January 1976), 79.

133. Quoted in Zhang, *Deterrence*, p. 255.

134. Quoted in Li Zhisui, *The Private Life of Chairman Mao* (New York: Random House, 1994), p. 270.

135. Quoted in Roger Buckley, *U.S.-Japan Alliance Diplomacy, 1945–1990* (Cambridge, Eng.: Cambridge University Press, 1992), p. 57.

136. Margot A. Henrikson, *Dr. Strangelove's America* (Berkeley: University of California Press, 1997), p. 58.

137. Quoted in Stuart Auerbach, "How the U.S. Built Japan, Inc.," *Washington Post National Weekly Edition,* July 26–August 1, 1993.

138. Quoted in *Washington Post National Weekly Edition,* August 21–27, 1995; in Akira Iriye, "Japan Returns to the World," in Craig and Loewenheim, *Diplomats,* p. 334.

139. Quoted in McMahon, "Illusion of Vulnerability," p. 600.

140. Henry Cabot Lodge quoted in Caroline Pruden, *Conditional Partners* (Baton Rouge: Louisiana State University Press, 1998), p. 176.

141. Robert L. Heilbroner, "Making a Rational Foreign Policy Now," *Harper's, CCXXXVII* (September 1968), 65.

142. Quoted in Hixson, *Parting,* p. 126; William J. Lederer and Eugene Burdick, *The Ugly American* (New York: Fawcett, 1958), p. 234.

143. Quoted in C. Vann Woodward, *The Strange Career of Jim Crow* (New York: Oxford University Press, 1974; 3rd ed.), p. 132.

144. Quoted in Michael L. Krenn, "Unfinished Business," *Diplomatic History, XX* (Fall 1996), 598.

145. Elbert Matthews quoted in Andrew Rotter, "Gender Relations, Foreign Relations," *Journal of American History, LXXXI* (September 1994), 538.

146. Eustace Seligman and Nehru quoted *ibid.,* pp. 525, 539.

147. Quoted in Michelle Mart, "Tough Guys and American Cold War Policy," *Diplomatic History, XX* (Summer 1996), 366, 371, 376, 379.

148. SWNCC, "Political and Military Problems in the Far East," November 29, 1945, James F. Byrnes Papers, Clemson University Library, Clemson, S.C.

149. Quoted in Robert J. McMahon, *The Cold War on the Periphery* (New York: Columbia University Press, 1994), p. 38.

150. *Department of State Bulletin, XXXIV* (June 18, 1956), 1000.

151. Quoted in Thomas G. Paterson, *Meeting the Communist Threat* (New York: Oxford University Press, 1988), p. 161.

152. Quoted in William R. Polk, *The Arab World Today* (Cambridge: Harvard University Press, 1991), p. 388.

153. Quoted in Hoopes, *Devil,* p. 337.

154. Quoted in Gail E. Meyer, *Egypt and the United States* (Rutherford, N.J.: Fairleigh Dickinson University Press, 1980), p. 146.

155. Quoted in Peter L. Hahn, *The United States, Great Britain, and Egypt, 1945–1956* (Chapel Hill: University of North Carolina Press, 1991), p. 230.

156. Cablegram, December 12, 1956, Box 20, DDE Diary Series, Whitman File, Eisenhower Papers.

157. Quoted in David Schoenbaum, *The United States and the State of Israel* (New York: Oxford University Press, 1993), p. 117.

158. John Foster Dulles quoted in Douglas Little, "The Making of a Special Relationship: The United States and Israel, 1957–68," *International Journal of Middle East Studies, XXV* (1993), 564.

159. Quoted in Ambrose, *Eisenhower, President,* p. 382.

160. Robert Murphy quoted in Irene L. Gendzier, *Notes from the Minefield* (New York: Columbia University Press, 1997), p. 316.

161. Douglas Little, "His Finest Hour?" *Diplomatic History, XX* (Winter 1996), 28.

162. Quoted in Thomas G. Paterson, *Contesting Castro* (New York: Oxford University Press, 1994), p. 10.

163. Quoted in Nicola Miller, *Soviet Relations with Latin America, 1959–1987* (Cambridge, Eng.: Cambridge University Press, 1989), pp. 5–6, 10.

164. Quoted in Richard H. Immerman, *The CIA in Guatemala* (Austin: University of Texas Press, 1982), p. 181.

165. U.S. official Burrows quoted in Piero Gleijeses, *Shattered Hope* (Princeton: Princeton University Press, 1991), p. 365.

166. Quoted *ibid.,* p. 4.

167. George Humphrey and Eisenhower quoted in Stephen M. Streeter, "Managing the Counterrevolution: The United States and Guatemala, 1954–1961" (Ph.D. diss., University of Connecticut, 1994), p. 78.

168. Nixon, *Six Crises,* pp. 198–199.

169. U.S. Senate, Committee on Finance, *Trade Agreements Extension* (Hearings), 84 Cong., 1 Sess. (1955), Part 4, p. 2049.

170. James Reston quoted in J. Fred Rippy, "The Hazards of Dale Carnegie Diplomacy," *Inter-American Economic Affairs, XII* (Summer 1958), 35.

171. Quoted in Stephen G. Rabe, *Eisenhower and Latin America* (Chapel Hill: University of North Carolina Press, 1988), p. 104.

172. Quoted in John Major, *Prized Possession* (New York: Cambridge University Press, 1993), p. 334.

173. Quoted in Robert A. Stevenson Oral History, Foreign Affairs Oral History Program, Lauinger Library, Georgetown University, Washington, D.C., p. 29.

174. Richard Pells, "American Culture Abroad," in R. Kroes et al., *Cultural Transmissions and Receptions* (Amsterdam, Neth.: Vu University Press, 1993), p. 78; Kaspar Maase, "American Mass Culture in the Federal Republic of Germany," *ibid.,* p. 167.

175. Quoted in Hixson, *Parting,* p. 133.

176. Robert J. Haddow, *Pavilions of Plenty* (Washington, D.C.: Smithsonian Institution Press, 1997), pp. 212–213.

177. Wagnleitner, *Cocacolonization,* p. 4.

178. Quoted in Donald W. White, *The American Century* (New Haven: Yale University Press, 1996), p. 241.

179. Hixson, *Parting,* p. ix.

180. Richard Immerman, *John Foster Dulles* (Wilmington, Del.: Scholarly Resources, 1999), p. 196.

181. Quoted in Shane J. Maddock, "The Nth Country Conundrum" (Ph.D. diss., University of Connecticut, 1997), p. 189.

Passing the Torch: The Vietnam Years, 1961–1969

*"**Wise Men.**" So named, this group of experienced statesmen met periodically to advise President Lyndon Johnson on Vietnam from 1965 to 1968. George Ball (far left), Dean Acheson (with mustache), and Dean Rusk (looking at the president, seated to right) are pictured here with Johnson and aides on March 16, 1968. After the Tet offensive, when the "Wise Men" told LBJ that they no longer supported the war, the president grudgingly accepted their advice. (Lyndon Baines Johnson Library)*

DIPLOMATIC CROSSROAD

The Tet Offensive in Vietnam, 1968

"They're coming in! They're coming in! VC in the compound," the young MP shouted into his radio.[1] Seconds later Vietcong (VC) commandos gunned him down. Moments before, about 3:00 A.M. that January 30, 1968, the compound of the U.S. Embassy in Saigon, South Vietnam, was quiet, the only noise coming from the whirring air conditioners and the fireworks exploding in celebration of Tet, the Lunar New Year. Completed in 1967 at a cost of $2.6 million, the six-story embassy building was protected by shatterproof Plexiglas windows, a concrete sun shield covering the entire structure, and a thick, eight-foot-high outer wall. Topped by a helicopter pad, the fortified building had become "the symbol of America's power" in Vietnam.[2]

At 2:45 A.M., a taxi cab and truck moved into the darkness from a repair shop near the embassy. About fifteen Vietcong leaped from their vehicles. Soon a huge explosion blew a three-foot hole in the wall. The VC scrambled through, firing automatic rifles at two embassy MPs (military police), who managed to radio for help before they died. The invaders then unleashed their antitank guns and rockets, transported into Saigon weeks before under shipments of tomatoes and firewood. The thick teakwood embassy doors took a direct hit, sending the U.S. seal crashing to the ground. Inside, a skeleton crew of Central Intelligence Agency and Foreign Service officials felt as if they were "in a telephone booth in the *Titanic*."[3] A few blocks away, aides roused Ambassador Ellsworth Bunker and whisked him away to a secret hiding place.

The news of the attack quickly reached the United States. Few American leaders could believe that the enemy had breached "Bunker's bunker." After all, on January 17, in his State of the Union message, President Lyndon B. Johnson himself had called most of South Vietnam secure, and the embassy seemed the most secure of any site.

In Saigon's dim morning light, American soldiers counterattacked. Paratroopers landed by helicopter on the roof. By 9:15 A.M., with the compound secure, General William C. Westmoreland counted nineteen dead Vietnamese (four were friendly embassy employees), five dead Americans, and two Vietcong prisoners. He then declared an American victory. One reporter described the compound as a "butcher shop in Eden."[4]

The bold sally against the embassy comprised but one part of the massive, well-coordinated Tet offensive conceived in communist North Vietnam by General Vo Nguyen Giap, famous for his defeat of the French at Dienbienphu in 1954. The forays struck thirty-six of the forty-four provincial capitals, some one hundred other villages, the gigantic Tan Son Nhut air base, and numerous sites in Saigon (see map, page 350). The communist forces attacked after half of the South Vietnamese Army (ARVN) had gone on leave for the Tet holiday. The VC, or National Liberation

"What the Hell's Ho Chi Minh Doing Answering Our Saigon Embassy Phone . . . ?" Paul Conrad's cartoon of President Lyndon B. Johnson expressed well the startled American response to the attack on the U.S. Embassy in South Vietnam in January 1968. Johnson had earlier reported that most of South Vietnam had been secured against the Vietcong and North Vietnamese. But General Earl Wheeler explained that "in a city like Saigon people can inflitrate easily. . . . This is about as tough to stop as it is to protect against individual muggings in Washington, D.C." (© 1968, *Los Angeles Times*. Reprinted with permission Los Angeles Times Syndicate)

Front (NLF), and North Vietnamese hoped to seize the cities, foment a general sympathetic uprising, force ARVN and U.S. troops to move to the cities—leaving a vacuum in the countryside—and disrupt the governmental bureaucracy. In the end, Washington would presumably negotiate American withdrawal.

Yet the ARVN and U.S. armies struck back: "Forced to fight in the cities, they bombed, shelled, and strafed the most populous districts as if they saw no distinction between them and the jungle."[5] Americans at home watched the counterattacks on color television, and many recoiled from the carnage. To fight enemy troops in Hue, South Vietnam's old imperial capital, American and ARVN forces used everything from nausea gas to rockets. After three weeks of vicious warfare, the communists fled, 100,000 people had become refugees, thousands lay dead, and American bombings had reduced a once-beautiful city to rubble. The Vietcong executed hundreds, perhaps thousands, of civilians, most of them connected with the South Vietnamese government or Americans. The Vietcong commander at Hue later wrote: "There is never an easy 'political' victory . . . without first having to shed blood and scatter bones on the battlefield."[6]

In the northwest corner of South Vietnam, U.S. soldiers bravely resisted a siege of their two-square-mile hillside at Khe Sanh, which, according to Westmoreland, "served to lure North Vietnamese to their deaths."[7] Hundreds of Americans died during the first months of 1968, as enemy rockets zeroed in on the strategic but vulnerable base. American B-52s countered by dropping tons of bombs on the surrounding area. By April, remembered a colonel, "the jungle had become literally a desert—vast stretches of scarred, bare earth . . . , a landscape of splinters and bomb craters."[8] Although the communists never launched a major assault, the sight of pinned-down GIs at Khe Sanh signaled a new defensive posture for the United States in Vietnam.

The provincial capital of Ben Tre symbolized the costs of the Tet offensive. To ferret out the VC, American and ARVN forces leveled Ben Tre, killing a thousand civilians. In unforgettable words, a U.S. officer declared that "it became necessary to destroy the town to save it."[9] That statement joined a visual image to sear American memory. The NBC Huntley-Brinkley news program of February 2 showed a brief film clip of the national police chief of South Vietnam pointing a pistol at the head of a suspected VC. General Nguyen Ngoc pulled the trigger and blasted the young man. The fifty-two seconds of footage, said an NBC producer, broadcast the "rawest, roughest film anyone had ever seen."[10]

The Johnson administration, having claimed before Tet that South Vietnam had gained the upper hand in the war and having said that U.S. officials had expected a communist offensive, suffered an ever-growing "credibility gap" with the American people. January proved a bad month for Lyndon B. Johnson. On the twenty-third the North Koreans captured the American spy ship *Pueblo* and its entire crew off the Korean coast. The international balance of payments for the United States, Johnson learned, was running at an annual deficit of $7 billion. A B-52 with four H-bombs aboard crashed in Greenland. And Senator Eugene McCarthy, a "dove" on Vietnam, challenged Johnson's renomination to the presidency.

Critics probed the administration's assertion that Tet counted as a triumph. Senator Robert F. Kennedy, soon to become a candidate for the Democratic presidential nomination, said: "It is as if James Madison [had claimed] victory in 1812 because the British only burned Washington instead of annexing it to the British Empire."[11] After Secretary McNamara recited enemy casualties, a reporter queried: "Isn't there something Orwellian about it, that the more we kill, the stronger they get?"[12] When the popular television newscaster Walter Cronkite of CBS judged the war a stalemate, LBJ moaned: "If I've lost Cronkite, I've lost middle America."[13]

Some 45,000 Vietcong, 2,000 ARVN, and 1,000 American soldiers died. Vietnamese civilians suffered a heavy toll, too. More than 14,000 died and 24,000 were wounded. One-eighth of the South Vietnamese people became homeless refugees in their own land. "We didn't . . . spur uprisings throughout the south," a North Vietnamese general later admitted, and "making an impact in the U.S. . . . had not been our intention—but it turned out to be a fortunate result."[14] Nonetheless, Tet had freed thousands of prisoners, disrupted the South Vietnamese governmental structure, crippled the U.S. pacification program in the countryside, and heaped monstrous refugee and reconstruction problems on the Saigon regime.

Johnson authorized 10,500 more troops for Vietnam, gave hawkish speeches against quitting under fire, and flamboyantly toured U.S. military bases. "Give me the lesser of evils," said LBJ as he asked the new secretary of defense, Clark Clif-

Lyndon B. Johnson (1908–1973). A tired president confers with Generals Creighton Abrams and Earl Wheeler at the National Security Council meeting of March 27, 1968. A few days later, Johnson removed himself as a candidate in the presidential race. Johnson's wife Lady Bird later described the Vietnam War as "just a hell of a thorn stuck in [LBJ's] throat. It wouldn't come up; it wouldn't go down. . . . It was just pure hell." (Courtesy of The Lyndon B. Johnson Library)

ford, a former Truman adviser, to undertake a major review of Vietnam policy.[15] In late February General Westmoreland had recommended that an additional 206,000 American troops join the more than 500,000 already there. The generals planned a major new ARVN-U.S. offensive. Within the Pentagon, formerly timid dissenters pleaded for deescalation. Americans could not save Vietnam by destroying it, Under Secretary of the Air Force Townsend Hoopes and Deputy Secretary of Defense Paul Nitze counseled. "Let's go in and win or else get out," a group of U.S. governors recommended.[16] In early March, too, Secretary of State Dean Rusk suggested curtailing the bombing of North Vietnam to induce peace talks. In the New Hampshire Democratic primary on March 12, McCarthy made a strong showing by polling 42 percent of the vote to Johnson's 49 percent. Speaking for the "Wise Men" (an advisory group comprised largely of Truman-era diplomats and generals), former secretary of state Dean Acheson put it bluntly: "We can no longer do the job we ought to do in the time we have left and we must begin to take steps to disengage."[17]

Clifford came to the same conclusion. He grew appalled that the generals could not say for how long or how many more troops might be needed. "Nothing had prepared me for the weakness of the military's case," he recalled.[18] His Ad Hoc Task Force on Vietnam recommended in early March sending 20,000 additional American troops. But Clifford's group found "no reason to believe" that 206,000 more troops—"or double or triple that quantity"—could achieve victory. The strategy of attrition had created "a sinkhole," said the report. "We put in more— they match it. We put in more—they match it."[19] Johnson's advisers also expressed alarm that the Vietnam War had initiated a gold and dollar crisis that threatened the economic well-being of the United States. Nervous foreigners—especially Europeans—rushed to exchange their dollars for gold. On March 14 alone, foreigners redeemed $372 million for gold. A post-Tet military buildup would cost billions more, further bloat the deficit-burdened budget, and panic foreign owners of dollars even more. Clifford's friends in the business community found America "in a hopeless bog."[20] The "sheer accumulation" of negative views from advisers, opinion polls, the news media, and Congress turned Johnson toward deescalation. In a dream he also saw himself as Woodrow Wilson paralyzed from the neck down.

On March 31 LBJ spoke on prime-time television. "We are prepared to move immediately toward peace through negotiations," he announced. Although another 13,500 soldiers would go to South Vietnam, he reported that U.S. airplanes would halt their bombing of a major portion of North Vietnam. "Even this limited bombing of the North could come to an early end—if our restraint is matched in Hanoi [the North Vietnamese capital]."[21] To the amazement of viewers, Johnson also declared that he would not seek reelection. On April 3 the North Vietnamese agreed to go to the conference table. Discussions began on May 14. The fighting and talking—and dying—would go on for several years more. Many GIs no longer thought the war worth fighting, as they said in their familiar slogan: "It don't mean nothin'."[22]

Vietnamese Wars Before 1961

Why Vietnam? Why did this Southeast Asian land of peasant farmers become the site of America's longest war? The origins are found in the centuries-long story of Vietnamese resistance to foreigners—Chinese, French, Japanese, and American. In 1867 France colonized Vietnam and soon began to exploit the country's raw materials, as well as those of Laos and Cambodia, which became protectorates in 1883 and part of French Indochina in the 1890s. Rice, rubber, tin, and tungsten from the area flowed to European markets. France constructed a repressive imperial government and monopolized land holdings, while some 80 percent of the Vietnamese people subsisted as poor, rural peasants. From 1867 onward the embittered Vietnamese battled their French overlords.

Vietnam's most famous nationalist leader was Ho Chi Minh, born in 1890 to a low-level government employee. Later described by a U.S. intelligence officer as a "wisp of a man . . . intelligent, well-versed in the problems of his country, rational, and dedicated," Ho traveled to Europe and at the time of World War I lobbied for independence.[23] In Paris, Ho sent a memorandum to the Big Four leaders at Versailles, but his reference to Woodrow Wilson's principle of self-determination did not move the conferees. Because the Communist party seemed the only political force vigorously denouncing colonialism, Ho and other nationalists joined it. Throughout the twenties and thirties he lived and agitated in China and Russia. In 1930–1931 the French brutally suppressed a Vietnamese peasant rebellion, killing 10,000 and deporting another 50,000.

During 1940–1941 the Japanese took over Vietnam but left collaborating French officials in charge. Vietnamese nationalists, including Ho's communists, went underground, used China as a base, and in 1941 organized the Vietminh, a coalition of nationalist groups led by the Communist party. In the final days of World War II, Vietminh guerrillas tangled with Japanese troops, liberated some northern provinces, and cooperated with the U.S. Office of Strategic Services (OSS). "Deer Team" grew fond of Ho, designated him OSS Agent 19, gave his troops weapons-training, and hoped to work with him after the war. Ho sent formal messages to Washington, asked for recognition, and often spoke in understandable English about America—its history, its political ideals, its endorsement of self-determination, its support for "free, popular governments all over the world."[24] In late August 1945, Ho's Vietminh organized the Democratic Republic of Vietnam (DRV) in Hanoi. On September 2, he proclaimed Vietnam's independence, borrowing phrases from America's document of July 4, 1776. Still, jilted in the past, Ho remained privately suspicious of Americans as "only interested in replacing the French. . . . They want to reorganize our country to control it. They are capitalists to the core."[25]

During World War II, President Franklin D. Roosevelt often remarked that France should relinquish Indochina. He toyed with the idea of a trusteeship. The Department of State valued the Southeast Asian countries as "potentially important markets for American exports. They . . . have important bearing on our security and the security of the Philippines."[26] Some American officials also worried that denying France its empire would alienate a potential European ally needed to stabilize the postwar world. Prime Minister Winston Churchill, moreover, informed Roosevelt in no uncertain terms that Britain opposed the breakup of empires. Just before he died, Roosevelt retreated. He "did not want to get mixed up in any Indochina decision" with an agitated Churchill at Yalta, he said.[27] Roosevelt's anticolonial instincts never became policy.

The French, with British military help and American acquiescence, returned to Vietnam. Ignored by the United States, receiving no support from Moscow, and now facing French forces, the Vietminh accepted a compromise with France in March 1946: DRV status as a "free state" in the French Union and French military occupation of northern Vietnam. Vietminh and French soldiers clashed in December. One French bombardment of Haiphong killed several thousand civilians. The Vietminh responded with guerrilla terror. For the next eight years Vietnam endured bloody combat, with the French holding the cities and the Vietminh the countryside.

To win Paris's favor for its postwar policies in Europe, Washington tolerated the return of French colonialism to Vietnam. Conditioned by traditional notions of American cultural and racial superiority, U.S. diplomats dismissed the Vietnamese as not "particularly industrious"—lacking such traits as "honesty, loyalty, or veracity."[28] As the Cold War intensified in 1946–1947, Ho's Moscow "training" became a topic of American discussion. The Department of State designated him an agent of international communism, although some diplomats pointed out that Vietnamese leaders were nationalists, not servants of Moscow, and that Ho stood as an Asian Tito. Ho himself had earlier described himself to an OSS officer as a "progressive-socialist-nationalist"—that is, the leader of both a colonial rebellion against France and a social revolution for Vietnam.[29]

In 1948 the French installed Emperor Bao Dai, who had served the Japanese in World War II, as their Vietnamese leader. U.S. officials accepted this French puppet as an alternative to "Commie domination of Indochina."[30] In February 1950, in what now appears as a momentous decision based on mistaken Cold War notions that the Soviet Union instigated nationalist rebellions and that Mao's China might engulf the region, Washington recognized the Bao Dai government. In May, moreover, the Truman administration extended aid to the French for their war in Vietnam.

The Korean War accentuated Washington's interest in the outcome of the Vietnamese rebellion. In 1950 Truman sent $150 million and a contingent of military advisers to Vietnam. For 1945–1954 the United States gave $2 billion of the $5 billion that Paris spent to keep Vietnam within the French empire. In 1954 U.S. aid covered 78 percent of the cost of the war, and some 300 Americans went to Vietnam as part of the Military Assistance Advisory Group—all to no avail.

In spring 1954, at Dienbienphu, a fortress where the besieged French had chosen to stand or fall, Vietminh forces moved toward a major, symbolic victory. To save the fortress, the French sought U.S. intervention. President Eisenhower received conflicting advice. The chair of the Joint Chiefs of Staff, Admiral Arthur Radford, urged massive night attacks on Vietminh positions by 300 U.S. carrier aircraft, possibly including tactical nuclear weapons. Army chief of staff Matthew Ridgeway, however, judged intervention "altogether disproportionate to the liability it would incur."[31] A Defense Department analyst agreed that "one cannot go over Niagara Falls in a barrel only slightly."[32]

The president cited the "falling domino" analogy to explain U.S. interests in Southeast Asia and then sounded out Congress, France, and Britain about internationalizing the war through "United Action." But members of Congress warned against an air strike that might lead next to ground troops and another Korea. The British also balked. Without U.S. intervention, French forces at Dienbienphu surrendered on May 7.

A few days earlier, on April 26, 1954, representatives from France, the Soviet Union, Britain, China, the United States, Bao Dai's Vietnam, the DRV, Laos, and Cambodia met in Geneva to discuss Asian issues. The Eisenhower administration, fearing a French retreat, reluctantly agreed to discuss Vietnam at the conference. In fact, a new French government, headed by Pierre Mendès-France, came to power on June 12 and pledged to end the war. President Eisenhower expected to "gag" on any Geneva agreement but vowed to "salvage something" by organizing Southeast Asian states into a military pact and defending the southern half of Vietnam.[33] China's Zhou Enlai pressed Ho's Vietminh (now controlling two-thirds of Vietnam) to make peace so as to "isolate the USA."[34]

On July 20 the DRV and France signed the Geneva agreements. The terms: temporary partition of Vietnam at the seventeenth parallel; French withdrawal to below that latitude; neither North nor South Vietnam to sign military alliances or permit foreign bases on Vietnamese soil; national elections to be held in 1956; unification of the country after elections; and elections also in neighboring strife-torn Laos and Cambodia, the other territories in French Indochina. Refusing to endorse the accords, the United States did state that it would "refrain from the threat or the use of force."[35] The National Security Council found the Geneva settlement a "disaster" that represented a "major forward stride of Communism which may lead to the loss of Southeast Asia."[36] Quite an exaggeration, but the United States believed that Communist China, which had sent some aid to the Vietminh, would use Vietnam as a base for expansion.

Because "we can't go on losing areas of the free world forever," Eisenhower established the Southeast Asia Treaty Organization in September 1954 to protect Cambodia, Laos, and South Vietnam from communist subversion and aggression.[37] SEATO violated the spirit of the Geneva Accords by specifying the defense of the southern half of Vietnam—now treated as a separate state. Although Great Britain, France, Pakistan, the Philippines, Thailand, Australia, and New Zealand joined the United States in the pact, only the last three later sent troops to fight in Vietnam. (SEATO disbanded in 1977.)

In the South, the United States backed the new government of Prime Minister Ngo Dinh Diem, a Vietnamese nationalist and Catholic who impressed U.S. diplomats as "a Messiah without a message."[38] A four-year residence in the United States gained him prominent friends such as Cardinal Francis Spellman, Supreme Court Justice William O. Douglas, and Senators Mike Mansfield and John F. Kennedy, who together constituted what might be called the Vietnam Lobby. An enlarged contingent of American advisers, in violation of Geneva, began to train a South Vietnamese army, and millions of dollars in U.S. military and economic aid flowed to Diem. He and U.S. officials cooperated to displace Bao Dai and the remnants of French influence. In mid-1955 the North proposed preliminary talks to plan the national election scheduled by Geneva for 1956. Diem refused, and the Eisenhower administration, certain that Ho would win an election, endorsed cancellation of the electoral provisions of the Geneva Accords, thereby thwarting unification. In October 1955 Diem held his own referendum in the South. That blatant fraud gave him 98.2 percent of the vote.

The two Vietnams went their separate ways, with Ho's North receiving aid from both the Soviet Union and China, cautiously avoiding dependence on either. Ho launched land reform, ending a landlord system that had largely excluded peasants. Diem's Republic of Vietnam received U.S. aid of about $300 million a year (80 percent of it for the military). Working under CIA contract, Michigan State University police experts began to train a "Civil Guard" to capture suspected Vietminh. Air Force colonel Edward Lansdale, on loan to the CIA, inaugurated a propaganda campaign. Slogans such as "Christ has gone to the South" along with disinformation about impending communist bloodbaths served to scare Catholics in the North into moving to the South. Some 900,000 people, most of them Catholics, made the trek.[39] Adopting the motto "To defeat the brigands, you must become brigands," Lansdale directed sabotage operations in the North and helped Diem defeat local rivals through bribes and threats, thus persuading skeptical U.S. officials that "proud, doughty little Ngo Dinh Diem" could bring "peace and stability" to his country.[40] In 1956 Diem jailed 20,000 to 30,000 suspected communists in "reeducation" camps. Torture became routine. In 1957 and 1958

Eisenhower, Ngo Dinh Diem (1901–1963), and Dulles. The South Vietnamese nationalist Diem, from a mandarin and Catholic family, spent time in exile in the United States before returning to his country as premier (1954–1963). His police-state rule did not seem to upset President Eisenhower or Secretary Dulles in May 1957 when they met with Diem in Washington. (Dwight D. Eisenhower Library)

southern rebels retaliated by killing village teachers, police, officers, and government officials.

Capitalizing on general anti-Diem dissent, the Vietminh organized the National Liberation Front (NLF) in December 1960 as an umbrella organization. Hanoi encouraged this communist-dominated group. In the rural areas they controlled, NLF cadres won favor from peasants by distributing land and reducing rents. In contrast, Diem resisted land reform and placed family members in profitable positions, grafting corruption onto an already unpopular regime. "Our choice," said member of Congress Walter Judd, "was between a 'bad' government that was friendly, and a worse government that was *hostile* to us."[41] Ambassador Elbridge Durbrow criticized Diem for not initiating reforms, but U.S. military advisers defended the premier, who once startled Americans by regretting that "it would not be possible to use atomic weapons" if North Vietnamese forces infiltrated through Laos.[42]

U.S. officials charged that North Vietnamese aggression initiated this new war in the South, but most scholars conclude that the NLF sprang from the peculiar, repressive environment of Diem's South. Vietnam's history had thus evolved from a colonial rebellion to expel the French from Vietnam into several interacting wars and revolutions: post-Geneva social revolution in the North; civil war within Diem's South; civil war between North and South; and, finally, an anti-imperialist war to force the Americans out. Imbued with the Cold War mentality that crammed events into an East-West frame, however, Americans failed to understand the singularly *Vietnamese* character of the Vietnamese wars. Senator John F. Kennedy in 1956 called Diem's Vietnam the "cornerstone of the free world in Southeast Asia, the keystone of the arch, the finger in the dike."[43] In 1961 Kennedy became president.

John F. Kennedy and His "Action Intellectuals"

Vietnam actually figured little in the 1960 presidential contest between Richard M. Nixon and John F. Kennedy, both Cold Warriors who differed more in style than on policy. Kennedy, who won by a narrow margin, aroused support through the slogan "I think it's time America started moving again."[44] Both Nixon and Kennedy belonged to the "containment generation" that imbibed the popular lessons of World War II and the Cold War. Both had won seats in Congress in 1946 and endorsed the Truman Doctrine the following year. In 1960, Kennedy charged that the Eisenhower-Nixon administration had neglected the Third World, losing it to communism. With the U-2 affair, the collapse of the Paris summit meeting, an adverse balance of payments, cancellation of a presidential visit to Japan, and crises in Cuba, the Congo, and Indochina as the immediate backdrop, Kennedy claimed that the United States was losing the Cold War. "History will make a judgment," JFK stated during the 1960 campaign, "that these were the days when the tide began to run out"—"when the communist tide began to pour in."[45] Warning that the country had "gone soft—physically, mentally, spiritually soft," he ridiculed Nixon for saying in the "kitchen" debate with Khrushchev that, although behind in space, "we were ahead in color television." Asserted Kennedy: "I would rather take my television black and white and have the largest rockets in the world."[46]

Kennedy did not mind being called Truman with a Harvard accent. Born in 1917 to wealthy, Catholic, politically active parents, John Fitzgerald Kennedy graduated from Harvard College and served with honor in World War II. At the time his father served as ambassador to Great Britain, his senior thesis appeared as a book titled *Why England Slept* (1940), with the theme that England should have resisted Nazi aggression with force. For Kennedy's generation, the Munich agreement became the "Munich syndrome." As he said in 1962: "The 1930s taught us a clear lesson: aggressive conduct, if allowed to go unchecked and unchallenged, ultimately leads to war."[47]

The new president exuded charisma. "All at once you had something exciting," recalled a student campaigner in comparing Eisenhower and Kennedy. "You had a young guy who had kids, and who liked to play football on his front lawn."[48] Call it psychology, charm, image, or mystique, Kennedy had it. Photogenic and quick-witted, he became a television star. Handsome, articulate, ingratiating, dynamic, energetic, competitive, athletic, cultured, bright, self-confident, cool, analytical, mathematical, zealous—these were the traits universally ascribed to the president. People often listened not to what he said but to how he said it, and he usually said it with verve. Dean Rusk remembered him as an "incandescent man.

John F. Kennedy (1917–1963). Before becoming president, JFK represented Massachusetts in the House (1947–1953) and the Senate (1953–1961). His ghostwritten book *Profiles in Courage* (1957) won a Pulitzer Prize. One of the president's underpublicized achievements was the Trade Expansion Act of 1962 and the subsequent "Kennedy Round" of trade negotiations, which reduced tariffs. (*The Reporter*, 1962. Copyright 1962 by The Reporter Magazine Co.)

Kennedy and Kwame Nkrumah (1909–1972). Shown here greeting the president of Ghana in 1961, Kennedy won praise from African leaders because of his previous support of Algerian independence and for speeches advocating "a world safe for democracy." A student in the United States (1935–1945) before becoming his country's first president in 1957, Nkrumah welcomed American Peace Corps volunteers to train Ghana's educators and U.S. aid to build hydroelectric dams. While calling Kennedy "a real friend," Nkrumah also condemned Western imperialism and invited young Soviet "volunteers" to compete with the Peace Corps. On a visit to China in 1966 as a self-appointed mediator of the Vietnam War, Nkrumah was deposed by his own army. (John F. Kennedy Library)

He was on fire, and he set people around him on fire."[49] For the historian and presidential assistant Arthur M. Schlesinger, Jr., JFK had "enormous confidence in his own luck," and "everyone around him thought he had the Midas touch and could not lose."[50]

Style and personality influence diplomacy. Many of his friends have commented that a desire for power drove John F. Kennedy, because power ensured victory. His father, Joseph P. Kennedy, "pressed his children hard to compete, never to be satisfied with anything but first place. The point was not just to try; the point was to win."[51] Although Kennedy suffered from near-fatal Addison's disease and received regular injections of potent drugs, all of which he concealed through public disclaimers, JFK nonetheless projected the image of a healthy, vigorous man who played to win. His appearances with Hollywood actresses such as Marilyn Monroe and his frequent extramarital sexual liaisons reflected his macho self-image. John F. Kennedy also saw foreign affairs as an arena for proving his toughness. "Who gives a shit about the minimum wage?" he once asked.[52] Kennedy soon gave Americans box scores on the missile race, the arms race, and the space race. He introduced new slogans: "The Grand Design" for Europe; the "New Africa" policy; "Flexible Response" for the military; and the "Alliance for Progress" for Latin America. Cocky, thinking themselves the "right" people, Kennedy and his advisers were, as one official complained, "sort of looking for a chance to prove their muscle."[53] Schlesinger captured the mood: "Euphoria reigned; we thought for a moment that the world was plastic and the future unlimited."[54] Kennedy's alarmist inaugural address pledged that "the torch has been passed to a new generation." He paid homage to historical memories when he noted that his generation had been "tem-

Makers of American Foreign Relations, 1961–1969

Presidents	Secretary of State
John F. Kennedy, 1961–1963	Dean Rusk, 1961–1969
Lyndon B. Johnson, 1963–1969	

pered by war" and "disciplined by a hard and bitter peace." Then came those moving, but in hindsight dangerously expansive, words: "We shall pay any price, bear any burden, meet any hardship, support any friend, oppose any foe to assure the survival and the success of liberty."[55]

The Kennedy people considered themselves "can-do" types who with careful calculation could manage crises and revive an ailing nation and world. Theodore H. White tagged them "the Action Intellectuals."[56] They had an inordinate faith in data. When a White House assistant attempted to persuade Secretary of Defense Robert McNamara, the "whiz kid" from Ford Motor Company, that the Vietnam venture would fail, McNamara shot back: "Where is your data? Give me something I can put in the computer. Don't give me your poetry."[57] Danger lurked in a heavy reliance on quantified information. "Ah, *les statistiques,*" said a Vietnamese general to a U.S. official. "If you want them to go up, they will go up. If you want them to go down, they will go down."[58]

Kennedy's secretary of state, Dean Rusk, worked uncomfortably with the crusading "action intellectuals" but remained a loyal member of the team. Rusk had served as a military intelligence officer in Asia during World War II, as an assistant secretary of state under Truman, and as president of the Rockefeller Foundation in the 1950s. "The gentle, gracious Rusk," the presidential assistant Theodore C. Sorensen later noted, "deferred almost too amiably to White House initiatives and interference."[59] A native of Georgia and the son of a Presbyterian minister, Rusk agonized over Vietnam, opposing Americanization of the war but refusing to advise withdrawal until a noncommunist government stood secure. So he ended up backing military escalation. Lyndon Johnson appreciated his loyalty: "He has the compassion of a preacher and the courage of a Georgia cracker."[60]

Next to Attorney General Robert F. Kennedy, the president's brother who served as troubleshooter and confidant, McGeorge Bundy became Kennedy's chief foreign-relations counselor. The brilliant forty-one-year-old former Harvard dean had helped Henry L. Stimson write his memoirs and had worked for the Marshall Plan. As national security affairs adviser, Bundy centralized decisionmaking in the White House and controlled the flow of information to the president. Colleagues stood in awe of Bundy's "mathematical mind. . . . very clipped. Almost surgical," while others thought him "cold as ice and snippy about everything."[61] A self-professed member of the well-born elite dedicated to public service, Bundy arrogantly asserted that "the United States is the engine of mankind, and the rest of the world is the caboose."[62]

Robert Strange McNamara (b. 1916). The mathematically minded secretary of defense graduated from the University of California, Berkeley. A former Ford Motor Company executive, McNamara applied efficiency methods to his department and served as war minister for Vietnam. In 1968 he became president of the World Bank. In the 1980s he criticized the nuclear arms race that he had accelerated in the 1960s. Senator Barry Goldwater called McNamara "an IBM machine with legs," and LBJ referred to "that man with the Stay-Comb in his hair." McNamara finally published a memoir, *In Retrospect* (1995), wherein he confessed that America's war in Vietnam had been "wrong, terribly wrong." (*The Reporter*, 1967. Copyright 1967 by The Reporter Magazine Co.)

Arms Buildup, Berlin Crisis, and Nation Building

The Kennedy administration emphasized military expansion. Kennedy had charged that the Eisenhower administration was losing the Cold War by tolerating a "missile gap" favorable to the Soviets. Eisenhower knew the politically motivated and unsubstantiated charge was nonsense. U-2 intelligence flights revealed a modest Soviet missile program. The United States had immense superiority. Kennedy and McNamara learned this, too, but, worried by Soviet boasting and Third World insurgencies, they began a mighty expansion of the military arsenal.

The administration called its defense strategy "flexible response," providing a method for every conceivable kind of war.[63] The Special Forces, or Green Berets, would conduct counterinsurgency against wars of national liberation; conventional forces would handle limited wars; more and better missiles would deter war or serve as primary weapons in nuclear war; at home, fallout shelters would protect Americans under a civil defense plan. In 1961 Kennedy increased the defense budget by 15 percent. By 1963 the United States had 275 major bases in 31 nations, 65 countries hosted U.S. forces, and the American military trained soldiers in 72 countries. Also, one and a quarter million military-related American personnel were stationed overseas. In 1961 the United States had 63 ICBMs; by 1963, 424. During 1961–1963, NATO's nuclear firing power increased 60 percent. Kennedy also created the U.S. Arms Control and Disarmament Agency, but his military buildup took priority.

The more missiles Americans acquired, the more vulnerable Americans seemed to become, because the Soviets tried to catch up by also building more. With Khrushchev about to test a fifty-megaton bomb "to hang over the heads of the capitalists," Kennedy sought to reassure Americans about nuclear supremacy as well as to warn Moscow not to miscalculate.[64] On October 21, 1961, Secretary McNamara's deputy, Roswell Gilpatric, announced that the United States had such a powerful nuclear retaliatory force that it could withstand a Soviet nuclear strike and still have enough missiles remaining to annihilate the Soviet Union. Moscow reacted to the speech by speeding up its ICBM program.

Kennedy met with Khrushchev at Vienna in June 1961 to discuss a test ban treaty, Berlin, and Laos. Aides warned that Khrushchev's style ranged from "cherubic to choleric."[65] Kennedy went to Vienna to show the Soviets that they "must not crowd him too much."[66] With 30,000 refugees each month escaping from East Germany to West Berlin, Khrushchev speculated that "soon there will be nobody left in the GDR [East Germany] except for [Communist boss Walter] Ulbricht and his mistress."[67] Khrushchev told Kennedy that Berlin must become a "free city," thereby ending Western occupation. If the United States did not negotiate, Moscow would sign a separate treaty with East Germany, thus terminating the Soviet commitment to postwar occupation rights in Berlin. "Berlin is the testicles of the West," Khrushchev privately quipped. "Every time I want to make the West scream, I squeeze on Berlin."[68] Kennedy exploded: "That son of a bitch won't pay any attention to words. He has to see you move."[69] Although the Kremlin leader may have left Vienna thinking that he had outdueled the young president, records of their meetings reveal that a tenacious Kennedy gave as good as he got. Still,

U.S.S. *Sam Rayburn*.   Launched in 1962, this nuclear-powered submarine with sixteen Polaris ballistic missiles, each with a range of 2,875 miles, became part of a large Kennedy-inspired military buildup. The first Polaris submarine was commissioned in 1959. The deployment of Polaris submarines enabled the United States to withdraw from Italy and Turkey the land-based Jupiter missiles that so complicated the Cuban missile crisis in 1962. (U.S. Navy, Naval Photographic Center)

because news accounts depicted Kennedy as "shaken and angry," the public perception developed that the Soviet leader had pushed Kennedy around.[70]

After Vienna the administration decided to force the Berlin question. On July 25, calling Berlin "the great testing place of Western courage and will," the president asked Congress for a $3.2 billion addition to the regular defense budget and authority to call up military reservists. He also requested $207 million to begin a civil defense, fallout shelter program—"in the event of an attack."[71] In a meeting with East German comrades, Khrushchev snorted that if Kennedy "starts a war then he would probably become the last president of the United States of America."[72]

On August 13 the East Germans, backed by Moscow, suddenly put up a barbed wire barricade, followed by an ugly concrete block barrier, between the two Berlins. Worried that his East German ally Walter Ulbricht might try to capture West Berlin, Khrushchev welcomed the wall solution to defuse the crisis. The wall did shut off the exodus of refugees. Judging that "a wall is a hell of a lot better than

The Berlin Wall. This photograph, taken a decade after the concrete wall went up, shows a trench filled with oil and barbed-wire fencing, all designed to deter East Germans from scaling the Wall. From 1961 to 1989, East German guards killed eighty people trying to escape across the Wall. Mayor Willy Brandt, later West Germany's chancellor, grew disillusioned with the United States because it "merely frowned" when the Wall went up. "What was called my Ostpolitik was formed against this background. . . . Traditional formulas of Western policies had been shown to be ineffective and unrealistic." (National Archives)

a war," Kennedy acquiesced.[73] But he speculated that "we shall probably come very close to the edge" of nuclear war.[74] Unbeknownst to the president, his special representative in Berlin, General Lucius Clay, took it on himself to arm U.S. tanks with bulldozer attachments to knock down the wall. Soviet intelligence learned of these preparations. Ten American M-48 tanks suddenly found themselves facing ten Russian tanks on opposite sides of Checkpoint Charlie on October 27, nearly precipitating "a nuclear-age equivalent of the Wild West Showdown at the OK Corral."[75] With the NSC staff simulating war games in which European fatalities reached tens of millions, Kennedy used a secret channel to negotiate with Khrushchev. After sixteen tense hours, both Soviet and U.S. tanks withdrew and the crisis passed. West Germans scowled at Kennedy's unwillingness to destroy the Wall. To assuage bruised feelings, Washington filled the airwaves with rhetorical commitments to the reunification of Germany. Kennedy himself visited West Berlin in June 1963 to underscore the American will to stay.

Kennedy also attended to the Third World, the region he thought most vulnerable to revolution and communism and at the same time most susceptible to U.S. influence. "Nation building" became his watchword. Recognizing the force of nationalism in the Third World, the "action intellectuals" sought to use or channel it. They hoped that through modernization, or what the Kennedy team called middle-class revolution, Third World nations would grow from economic infancy to economic and political maturity, and that evolutionary economic development would ensure noncommunist political stability. "Modern societies must be built," one of the chief theoreticians, Walt W. Rostow, declared, "and we are prepared to

"Could You Point Out the Ground You've Taken? We're Here to Secure and Develop It Economically."
A "nation-building" team cooperates with a counterinsurgency team in this parody of the "modernization" efforts of Americans overseas. (Editorial cartoon by Pat Oliphant, © 1976, *Los Angeles Times*. Reprinted with permission of Universal Press Syndicate)

help build them."[76] Kennedy, for example, counted populous India as a particularly good candidate because it followed a noncommunist model of economic development, bordered the People's Republic of China, and led the nonaligned movement. India might be won for the West through U.S. economic and military aid. Although dollar assistance to India angered Pakistan, a U.S. ally, Washington nonetheless tilted toward New Delhi, especially during the Sino-Indian border war of fall 1962. In the early 1960s, India became the world's largest recipient of U.S. economic aid, for, if "we lose" the neutrals, "the balance of power could swing against us."[77]

Khrushchev's pledge of January 1961 to support wars of national liberation—such as that in Vietnam—seemed to raise the stakes in the Third World. To meet this test, U.S. counterinsurgency took several forms: the training of native police forces and bureaucrats, flood control, transportation and communications improvements, and community action projects. U.S. Special Forces units—Green Berets—received special attention. Kennedy personally elevated their status in the military and supervised their choice of equipment. Washington assumed it could apply America's finest technology in Vietnam to succeed where the French had failed.

Kennedy also created the Peace Corps. Established by executive order in 1961, this volunteer group of mostly young Americans numbered 6,646 by mid-1963 and 15,000 by mid-1966. Seeking "to live out the ideals of their culture," as one volunteer put it, they went into developing nations as teachers, agricultural advisers, and technicians.[78] Heeding Vice President Lyndon Johnson's admonition to reject any volunteers who matched the "three C's—the Communists, the consumptives, and the cocksuckers," Peace Corps officials won plaudits for their efforts to improve Third World living conditions.[79] Peace Corps monuments—irrigation systems, water pumps, larger crops—arose throughout Latin America and Africa, but the corps's humanitarian efforts fell far short of eradicating the Third World's profound squalor. In some cases, as in Ethiopia, Peace Corps volunteers went abroad with too little understanding of foreign languages and cultures.

The Kennedy administration also embarked on the Alliance for Progress in Latin America to head off Cuban-style revolution and communist subversion. Launched at the Punta del Este meeting of the Organization of American States in August 1961, the alliance envisioned spending $20 billion in funds from the United States and international organizations. In return, Latin Americans promised land and tax reform, housing, and health improvements. Initiated with great fanfare, the

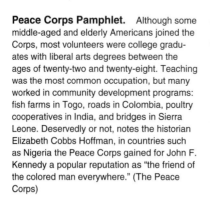

Peace Corps Pamphlet. Although some middle-aged and elderly Americans joined the Corps, most volunteers were college graduates with liberal arts degrees between the ages of twenty-two and twenty-eight. Teaching was the most common occupation, but many worked in community development programs: fish farms in Togo, roads in Colombia, poultry cooperatives in India, and bridges in Sierra Leone. Deservedly or not, notes the historian Elizabeth Cobbs Hoffman, in countries such as Nigeria the Peace Corps gained for John F. Kennedy a popular reputation as "the friend of the colored man everywhere." (The Peace Corps)

alliance soon sputtered. American businesses did not invest as expected; the State Department dragged its feet; Latin American nationalists disliked U.S. control; elites resisted reforms and pocketed U.S. dollars; middle-class Latin Americans, whom Washington counted on, proved selfish. In the end, adult literacy and infant mortality rates improved, but Latin American economies registered unimpressive growth rates, class divisions widened, unemployment climbed, and agricultural production per person declined. The *Alianza para el Progreso* became another tool to maintain U.S. hegemony in the hemisphere and to wage the Cold War. By the mid-1960s, under the leadership of the staunchly conservative diplomat Thomas Mann, the Alliance had turned its resources to military purposes, such as internal security forces. Washington abandoned its requirement that political democracy accompany economic change. Cuba's Fidel Castro acknowledged the Alliance as "a politically wise concept put forth to hold back the tide of revolution." But it did not work, he noted, "because those in charge of seeing that the agrarian reform was implemented in Latin America were the very owners of the lands."[80]

The difficulties of nation building appeared dramatically in the Congo, which obtained hurried independence from Belgium in mid-1960. Civil war quickly erupted. Backed by U.S. and European cobalt and copper interests, Moise Tshombe tried to detach Katanga Province from the new central government headed by Patrice Lumumba. The United States, fearing Soviet influence in "another Cuba," helped a UN mission quell the Katanga insurrection.[81] Although Lumumba was killed in 1961, by early 1963 the central Congolese government had defeated Tshombe. About a year later, however, a major leftist revolt supported by the Soviet Union, China, and Ghana broke out. With UN forces gone, the CIA

Where Are We? The Alliance for Progress moved slowly and eventually abandoned its initial objective of reforming military dictatorships in Latin America. The diplomat Willard L. Beaulac concluded: "We told people whom we did not know how to solve problems that we did not understand." One architect of the alliance, Richard Goodwin, later admitted: "I had never set foot south of the border (aside from one orgiastic night just beyond the Texas border during the [1960] campaign which had little to do with high policy, but which an exceptionally imaginative psychiatrist might conclude had planted the seed of my love affair with Latin America)." (Edmund Valtman, *The Hartford Times*)

soon bolstered former enemy Tshombe as the new leader of the central government, and with direct U.S. aid, including military advisers, he recruited white mercenaries. The rebels responded by terrorizing white foreigners. In November 1964 a small force of Belgian paratroopers dropped from U.S. aircraft into the Congo to rescue Belgian and U.S. citizens. Although a serious communist threat never emerged in the Congo, the Kennedy administration, caught up in the Cold War mentality, had thrust itself into the shaky politics of Africa. U.S. ambassador to Guinea William Attwood noted that leading African nationalists felt humiliated by foreign intervention in the Congo, because "the white man with a gun, the old plunderer who had enslaved his ancestors, was back again, doing what he pleased. . . . And there wasn't a damn thing Africa could do about it, except yell rape."[82] Attwood identified the chief source of resistance to American nation building—nationalism itself.

The Most Dangerous Area in the World: The Cuban Revolution and Latin America

In Latin America, events surrounding the Cuban Revolution claimed center stage. Because Cuba might export revolution to its neighbors, Kennedy considered Latin America "the most dangerous area in the world."[83] On July 26, 1953, a young lawyer and Cuban nationalist, Fidel Castro, attempted to overthrow the American-backed regime of Fulgencio Batista. Imprisoned and later released, Castro fled to Mexico. In late 1956, under the banner of the 26th of July Movement, he returned to Cuba. Almost captured, he escaped into the mountains, where for two years he augmented his guerrilla forces, gained popular support, and fought Batista's U.S.-supplied army. In January 1959, despite CIA plots to deny him power, the bearded rebel marched into Havana and initiated social and economic programs designed to reduce extensive U.S. interests that had developed since 1898 and had come to dominate Cuba's sugar, mining, and utilities industries.

Determined to dilute the North American cultural influence that they believed had undermined Cuba's national identity, the Castroites crippled the gangster-run gambling casinos and ousted from government the *batistianos* who had profited from close contact with U.S. investors. Castro avowed that "we no longer live in times when one had to worry when the American Ambassador visited the [Cuban] Prime Minister."[84] Indeed, "what happened in Guatemala will not happen here."[85] When Castro visited Washington in April 1959, Eisenhower ostentatiously went south to play golf.

Fearing that a successful Cuban revolution would cause the United States to "get kicked around in the hemisphere," but finding no evidence that Castro was a communist, Washington soon applied a series of tests: Cuba must respect North American–owned property, continue alignment with the United States on international questions, and adhere to a democratic politics that permitted pro-U.S. "moderates" to sustain ties with Washington.[86] Cuba failed the U.S. tests. Land reform struck at U.S. interests, the execution of Batista supporters reduced U.S. influence, and the moderates faltered in their competition with Castroite radicals. Castro postponed elections and evicted the U.S. military missions that had supported Batista. In vehement anti-Yankee orations, Castro also called for revolutions throughout Latin America. Washington warned against his "Nasser-like ambition."[87] In late 1959 the CIA began to work with Castro's rivals to "replace" the revolutionary regime.[88] In January 1960, a furious Eisenhower labeled Castro a "mad man . . . who is going wild and harming the whole American structure."[89]

In March 1960, the president ordered the CIA to train Cuban exiles for an invasion of their homeland—this shortly after Cuba signed a trade treaty with the Soviet Union. In mid-1960, as the revolutionary government nationalized foreign properties, the United States suspended imports of Cuban sugar and then forbade U.S. exports to the island. These strong measures only pushed Cuba toward a new economic lifeline—the Soviet Union. As Khrushchev later told President Kennedy, Castro was no communist but "you are well on your way to making him a good one."[90] Embracing the thesis that Castro had moved from neutralism to communism, Washington broke diplomatic relations with Cuba in early January 1961.

"The Castro regime is a thorn in the flesh," Senator J. William Fulbright argued, "but it is not a dagger in the heart."[91] Still, ignoring the U.S. contribution to Castro's anti-Americanism, President Kennedy defined Cuba as a test of will and gave the green light for a "covert" assault, dubbed "Operation Castration" by White House aide Arthur Schlesinger.[92] The CIA assured him that it could deliver another Guatemala, as in 1954. The Agency predicted that the Cuban people would rise up against Castro and a CIA-hired assassin's bullet would kill him. The CIA pinpointed Bahía de Cochinos (Bay of Pigs) as the invasion site and organized a Cuban Revolutionary Council to take office. Uneasy with the plan, Kennedy nonetheless approved it, although he prohibited direct U.S. military participation. The CIA did not protest this prohibition because "we felt that when the chips were down," Allen Dulles later wrote, "any action required for success would have been authorized [by the president] rather than permit the enterprise to fail."[93] Kennedy worried that the trained exiles would embarrass him politically if he scotched the expedition—the "disposal" problem.[94] The new administration neither talked with the Castro government nor consulted Congress before launching its war against Cuba.

In mid-April 1961, 1,453 CIA-trained commandos departed from Nicaragua for Cuba (see map, page 417). They met early resistance from Castro's militia, no sympathetic insurrection occurred, and within two days the invasion had become a fiasco. One hundred fourteen commandos died, and more than 1,100 were captured. Some 150 Cuban defenders were killed. Four American pilots also died in the operation. Attorney General Robert Kennedy found defeat difficult to accept: "We just could not sit and take it." Walt Rostow, who pandered to Kennedy machismo, reassured him that "we would have ample opportunity to prove we were not paper tigers in Berlin, Southeast Asia, and elsewhere."[95] After the disaster, President Kennedy, who had vetoed a desperate CIA request for U.S. air attacks during the last hours of the failing invasion, blamed the CIA and Joint Chiefs of Staff for faulty intelligence and sloppy execution. Cuban exiles cried betrayal, saying it was "like John Wayne backing down from a gunfight with an evil dwarf."[96] But even if the president had ordered more air strikes, then what? The brigade's meager forces would have had to face Castro's army of 25,000 and the nation's 200,000-strong militia.

Little sobered by the Bay of Pigs setback, Kennedy issued secret orders making Cuba the "top priority . . . all else is secondary—no time, money, effort, or manpower is to be spared."[97] During the next year, the United States imposed a tighter economic blockade, evicted Cuba from the Organization of American States, directed U.S. Information Agency propaganda at the Havana regime, and continued assassination plots on Castro's life. Under Operation Mongoose, CIA agents cooperated with anti-Castro exiles to stage hit-and-run sabotage raids against oil facilities and other island targets. This multitrack campaign did not knock Castro from his perch. What next? "If I had been in Moscow or Havana at that time," Secretary of Defense McNamara later remarked, "I would have believed the Americans were preparing for an invasion."[98]

Spinning out of Control: The Cuban Missile Crisis

Critical to understanding the missile crisis of fall 1962 is the relationship and timing between U.S. activities and Soviet/Cuban decisions to place on the island nuclear weapons that could strike areas of the United States where 92 million people lived. In May 1962, Soviets and Cubans first discussed the idea of such weapons; in July, during a trip by Raúl Castro to Moscow, representatives initialed a draft agreement; in late August/early September, during a trip by the Cuban leader Che Guevara to

NOW IT'S OFFICIAL!

The Sun-Telegram, San Bernardino, Ca.

"Now It's Official."   Jeff Yohn's anti-Castro, anti-Soviet cartoon appeared in the *San Bernadino Sun-Telegram* (California) newspaper in 1961. In July 1960, when the Soviet Union agreed to purchase Cuban sugar after the Eisenhower administration ended sugar imports from the island, Soviet premier Nikita Khrushchev declared the Monroe Doctrine dead and pledged military aid to Cuba—"if it became necessary." During the April 1961 Bay of Pigs crisis, Khrushchev told President Kennedy that the Soviets would give "to the Cuban government all the necessary assistance to repel aggression." In 1962 such aid included nuclear-tipped SS-4 missiles, setting off yet another crisis. (Library of Congress)

Moscow, an accord became final. These steps were taken while the United States was pressing Cuba on all fronts.

Not only did Castro learn about the assassination plots and witness the sabotage attacks, but his spies heard about possible U.S. military action against Cuba. The director of Operation Mongoose, Brigadier General Edward Lansdale, planned to ignite a revolt against Castro in October 1962 and recommended the use of U.S. forces to ensure success. American military maneuvers heightened Cuban fears. One well-publicized U.S. exercise, staged during April, included 40,000 troops and an amphibious landing on a small island near Puerto Rico. Some noisy American politicians, throughout 1962, called for the real thing: an invasion of Cuba. "Were we right or wrong to fear direct invasion?" Castro later asked.[99]

By midsummer, Cuban-Soviet plans for nuclear defense crystallized. After the Bay of Pigs invasion, Moscow had begun military shipments that included small arms, howitzers, armored personnel carriers, patrol boats, MIG jet fighters, and tanks. Under the Moscow-Havana agreement, the Soviets intended to send surface-to-air missiles (SAMs), 48 medium-range (SS-4) missiles, 32 intermediate-range (SS-5) missiles, 48 light IL-28 bombers, tactical nuclear weapons, and nuclear warheads. U.S. photointerpreters had to rely on the "fledgling science of cratology" to guess what crates on Soviet merchant ships actually contained.[100] By mid-October only the intermediate-range missiles had not reached Cuba.

Had there been no Bay of Pigs invasion, no destructive covert activities, no assassination plots, no military maneuvers and plans, and no economic and diplomatic steps to harass, isolate, and destroy the Castro government, there might have been no Cuban missile crisis. The origins of the October 1962 crisis derived largely from the concerted U.S. campaign to quash the Cuban Revolution and from the Soviet-Cuban effort to deter the United States through missile deployment. Scholars have attributed other motives to the Soviets, such as their wanting to force negotiations on Berlin, to compel a trade for U.S. missiles stationed in Turkey and pointed at the Soviet Union, or to undermine Chinese criticism that Moscow had become too tolerant of the West. Perhaps because Pentagon officials had publicly announced decisive American nuclear superiority, Moscow also may have hoped to catch up in the nuclear arms race. But to stress only the global, Cold War dimension slights the local or regional sources of the conflict and misses the central point: Khrushchev would never have had the opportunity to install dangerous nuclear weapons in the Caribbean if the United States had not been attempting to overthrow the Cuban government. The United States helped precipitate what Dean Rusk called "an utterly crashing crisis."[101]

On October 14, a U-2 reconnaissance plane photographed medium-range (1,100-mile) missile sites under construction in Cuba. After gathering more data, American officials informed the president on October 16 that the Soviet Union had indeed placed missiles in Cuba. Kennedy created an Executive Committee of the National Security Council (Ex Comm), consisting of his "action intellectuals" and experienced diplomats from the Truman years. Joining McNamara, brother Robert, McGeorge Bundy, and Theodore Sorensen were Dean Acheson, Paul Nitze, and Robert Lovett, among others.

Kennedy's immediate preference became clear: "We're certainly going . . . to take out these . . . missiles."[102] Ex Comm considered four options: "talk them out," "squeeze them out," "shoot them out," and "buy them out."[103] Ex Comm advisers initially gave only slight attention to negotiations and concentrated on military action. Acheson, among others, favored an air strike. Under Secretary of State George Ball countered that even a successful air strike would mean "carrying the mark of Cain on your brow for the rest of your life."[104] Air force officials reported they could not guarantee 100 percent success; some missiles might remain in place for firing against the United States. The Joint Chiefs of Staff recommended a full-scale military invasion. Although alluring, such a scheme could mean a prolonged war with Cuba, heavy U.S. casualties, and a Soviet retaliatory attack on Berlin. Ex Comm ruled out a private overture to Castro. Ambassador to the United Nations Adlai Stevenson's proposal that the United States publicly offer to trade the missiles in Turkey for those in Cuba met open derision. Ex Comm members, tired and irritable, finally settled on a naval blockade or quarantine of future arms shipments to Cuba. The quarantine, pushed ardently by McNamara as "a communications exercise, not a military operation," left open options for further escalation.[105]

Kennedy went on national television on October 22, announcing a blockade and insisting that Khrushchev "halt and eliminate this clandestine, reckless and provocative threat to world peace."[106] More than 180 warships patrolled the Caribbean, and marines reinforced the U.S. naval base at Guantánamo, on Cuba. A B-52 bomber force loaded with nuclear bombs took to the skies. On October 24, Soviet vessels approached the blockade, but the ships stopped. Assembly of the missiles already in Cuba continued. Secretary General of the United Nations U Thant

Soviet Missile Site at San Cristóbal, Cuba. This revealing U-2 photograph was taken in October 1962, when Soviet technicians were busily trying to assemble the various components of medium-range missiles. (U.S. Air Force)

urged talks; Khrushchev called for a summit meeting. Kennedy demanded removal of the missiles first. On October 26, in a confusing episode, ABC News correspondent John Scali heard a Soviet agent suggest one possible solution whereby Moscow would disengage its missiles if Washington publicly pledged not to invade Cuba. Scali reported the conversation to U.S. officials as a genuine Soviet proposal from "very high sources," but the KGB agent had not been authorized to make the offer.[107] A long letter from Khrushchev soon arrived, however, proposing much the same settlement but still insisting that the missiles were defensive, not offensive.

The next day, October 27, the crisis intensified. A Soviet surface-to-air missile shot down a U-2 plane over Cuba. The Americans prepared to retaliate, not knowing that Soviet commanders had tactical nuclear weapons ready to use against an invasion. Later in the day, a U.S. spy aircraft strayed into Soviet air space, nearly setting off a dogfight with Soviet MIGs. By this time U.S. officials were analyzing another Khrushchev letter. The premier raised the stakes: He would withdraw the missiles from Cuba if the United States removed its missiles from Turkey. "We can't very well invade Cuba," JFK mused, "when we could have gotten them [Soviet ballistic missiles] out by making a deal on . . . Turkey."[108] Sidestepping this proposal, the president endorsed Khrushchev's first proposal: removal of the missiles in Cuba in exchange for a public U.S. pledge not to invade Cuba. Robert Kennedy assured the Soviets in private ("You have my word on this," he told Ambassador Anatoly Dobrynin) that the Jupiter missiles would be withdrawn from Turkey, but he warned that if Moscow divulged this secret deal, Washington would disavow it.[109] A "very upset" Bobby said that "time is of the essence," that "many unreasonable heads" are "itching for a fight," that "a chain reaction will start that will be very hard to stop," and "millions of Americans and Russians will die."[110] If Khrushchev had balked, Rusk had secretly arranged for the United Nations to propose removing missiles from both Turkey and Cuba; "Kennedy would not let the Jupiters in Turkey become an obstacle," Rusk has insisted.[111] Despite Chinese charges of "wish-washiness" and Munich-style appeasement, Khrushchev agreed to withdraw his missiles.[112] The military forces at his command could not prevent or repel a U.S. invasion, a bellicose Castro seemed to urge a preemptive Soviet nuclear strike, and the imminence of doomsday so unnerved the Kremlin leader that a colleague claimed he "shitted his pants."[113] Having at least secured Cuba from invasion, Khrushchev said he was no "czarist officer who has to kill myself if I fart at a masked ball. It is better to back down than go to war."[114] He appreciated Kennedy's restraint: "He had us by the balls and didn't squeeze."[115]

Adlai Stevenson (1900–1965). Governor of Illinois and twice a Democratic presidential candidate, Stevenson became ambassador to the United Nations under Kennedy. During the missile crisis, Stevenson urged removal of Soviet missiles from Cuba *and* U.S. missiles from Turkey—advice that prompted President Kennedy to tell journalists that "Adlai wanted a Munich." Because Kennedy, in the final settlement, *secretly* promised the Soviets that the Jupiter missiles would be withdrawn from Turkey, the historian Mark White ranks Stevenson as "the unsung hero of the missile crisis." (National Portrait Gallery, Smithsonian Institution)

"We were in luck," John Kenneth Galbraith later commented, "but success in a lottery is no argument for lotteries."[116] As McGeorge Bundy remembered, the crisis came "so near to spinning out of control."[117] Close calls (the U-2 incidents), flawed intelligence (Soviet troops in Cuba numbered 42,000, not the estimated 10,000), an inability to control local events (U.S. warships forced Soviet submarines to the surface without Kennedy's knowledge), inaccurate perceptions (the Soviet ambassador at first misreported Kennedy as a "hot-tempered gambler" already committed to invading Cuba), near nervous breakdowns (reportedly both Rusk and Stevenson suffered incapacitating stress)—all reveal something quite short of the artful crisis management often attributed to the president.[118] NATO allies pointedly complained that they "can live with Soviet MRBMS, why can't [Americans]?"[119] Why not reduce tensions by publicly trading missiles in Turkey that U.S. officials privately considered "a pile of junk" and "worse than useless"?[120] Even the aftermath proved messy. Washington demanded that the IL-28 bombers that the Soviets had given to Cuba must be removed along with the missiles. Not until November 13 did Khrushchev agree to pull the IL-28s out. The three protagonists, moreover, never signed a formal agreement, leaving enough ambiguity to cause later crises in Cuban-Soviet-American relations (see pages 381, 426). A quarter-century later, McNamara offered a somber reassessment: "You *can't* manage" crises because of all the "misinformation, miscalculation, misjudgment, and human fallibility."[121]

The Cuban missile crisis both slowed and accelerated the Cold War. Having found communication difficult during the event, the antagonists installed a "hot line" or Teletype link between the White House and Kremlin. Both sides seemed frightened enough by nuclear danger to move toward a more accommodating relationship, producing the Limited Test Ban Treaty of July 1963, which prohibited atmospheric and underwater nuclear testing. In a speech at American University in June ("the best . . . by any president since Roosevelt," according to Khrushchev) Kennedy revealed uneasiness with large weapons spending, appealed for arms control, and asked Americans to reexamine Cold War attitudes.[122] Later Kennedy speeches, however, sounded hawkish once again.

The missile crisis carried long-term detrimental effects. The Soviet Union, revealed as a nuclear inferior, pledged to catch up in the arms race. That part of the Cold War contest was ratcheted up with new and more dangerous weapons systems. As for Cuba, despite a Castro initiative for rapprochement, U.S. officials

The Green Berets.   President Kennedy helped select equipment for the U.S. Army Special Forces units like this one at Fort Bragg, North Carolina. The Green Berets were trained in counterguerrilla methods and sent into the mountains and jungles of Vietnam and Laos. (U.S. Army)

vowed to intensify "our present nasty course."[123] The CIA quickly launched new dirty tricks and revitalized its assassination option by making contact with a traitorous Cuban official, Rolando Cubela Secades. Bearing the code name AM/LASH, he plotted with the CIA to kill Fidel Castro. On the very day that President Kennedy fell to assassination, AM/LASH rendezvoused with CIA agents in Paris, where he received a ballpoint pen rigged with a poisonous hypodermic needle. Like all other assassination plots against Castro, this one failed. The new Johnson administration put exploratory Cuban-American contacts at the United Nations on ice. From that time onward, U.S.-Cuba relations remained frozen.

Success in the missile crisis had emboldened Kennedy's civilian advisers, especially Secretary McNamara, in their belief that "carefully controlled and sharply limited military actions were reversible . . . at minimum risk and cost."[124] Proud of keeping their generals "on a short leash," they could confidently avoid nuclear holocaust, confine actual combat to Third World insurgencies, and win the Cold War through a calculated "display of superior American nerve and resolve."[125] Or so they thought until Vietnam changed many of their minds.

Laos, Vietnam, and the Kennedy Legacy

Continued unrest in Laos and Vietnam placed them high on President Kennedy's agenda. Rostow saw an opportunity to use "our unexploited counterguerrilla assets"—helicopters and Special Forces units. "We are not saving them for the Junior Prom," he told Kennedy.[126] Landlocked Laos, wracked by civil war, became a testing ground. Granted independence at Geneva in 1954, Laos chose nonalignment in the Cold War when the nationalist leader Souvanna Phouma organized a coalition government of neutralists and the procommunist Pathet Lao in 1957. The Eisenhower administration opposed the government and built up the right-wing Laotian army. In 1958 CIA-backed rightists displaced Souvanna Phouma and shaped a pro-American government without Pathet Lao participation. Washington soon dispatched military advisers to the new but shaky regime. Souvanna Phouma returned to power after a coup in 1960, but the United States again undermined him by equipping rightist forces. Seeking a counterweight, Souvanna took assistance from Moscow and North Vietnam. But in December he fled his country. For Eisenhower, "the fall of Laos to Communism" would initiate "a chain of events [that] would open the way to Communist seizure of all Southeast Asia."[127] Laos constituted the "cork in the bottle," claimed Ike.[128]

The incoming Kennedy administration did not perceive the Laotian problem much differently. As conspicuous Soviet aid flowed to the Pathet Lao, Kennedy ordered the Seventh Fleet into the South China Sea and moved marines with helicopters into Thailand. Then the Bay of Pigs disaster struck. Fearing to appear weak with one arm tied down in Cuba, Kennedy swung the other in Laos. The president instructed the several hundred American military advisers in Laos, heretofore restricted to only covert operations, to discard their civilian clothes and dress in more ostentatious military uniforms as a symbol of U.S. resolve. The Soviets wanted no fight in Laos. In April 1961 they endorsed Kennedy's appeal for a cease-fire. But the Pathet Lao battled on alone. Kennedy asked the Joint Chiefs of Staff if an American military expedition could succeed. The military experts said they could proceed so long as they had "120,000–140,000 men, with authority to use nuclear weapons if necessary."[129]

The solution came in Geneva, where a conference on Laos began in May 1961. Although it took deft diplomatic pressure from W. Averell Harriman, continued bloodshed in Laos, and hard bargaining lasting until June 1962, the major powers did sign what Harriman called "a good, bad deal."[130] Laos would become neutral; it could not enter military alliances or permit foreign military bases on its soil. Souvanna Phouma headed the new government. Still, peace did not come. In late 1962, in clear violation of the agreement it had just signed, Washington secretly shipped arms to Souvanna's government, which increasingly turned to the right. North Vietnamese soldiers in the north served as the pretext. Without informing the American people, the United States began secret bombing raids against Pathet Lao forces in 1964, after a right-wing coup had diminished Souvanna's authority. By then the problem of Laos derived from the country's proximity to Vietnam.

After the Bay of Pigs fiasco, the erection of the Berlin Wall, and the neutralization of Laos, Vietnam seemed to assume greater urgency. Rejecting Charles de Gaulle's warning that in Vietnam "we failed and you will fail," Kennedy advisers considered the corrupt Ngo Dinh Diem a liability, but as Vice President Lyndon B. Johnson put it, "Sh—, man, he's the only boy we got out there."[131] Kennedy said he did not want to launch a white man's war in Asia; Asians had to fight their own battles. But because he accepted the domino theory, thought that China fomented Vietnamese turmoil, and believed that nation building promised success, he expanded the U.S. presence. In January 1961, Kennedy authorized $28.4 million to enlarge the South Vietnamese army and another $12.7 million to improve the civil

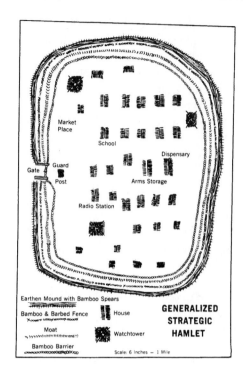

Earthen Mound with Bamboo Spears

Bamboo & Barbed Fence

Moat

Bamboo Barrier

House

Watchtower

GENERALIZED STRATEGIC HAMLET

Scale: 6 Inches — 1 Mile

Strategic Hamlet, South Vietnam. Introduced by the Diem regime in 1962, inspired by British counterinsurgency expert Sir Robert Thompson (based on his experience in Malaya and the Philippines), and funded by the United States, the strategic hamlet program sought to separate the Vietcong from their supporters among the people. Peasants had to move from ancestral lands and live in quarters surrounded by barbed wire and bamboo spears. Many of the 6,000 hamlets were poorly managed and defended, alienating the very people the Saigon government tried to win over. (Courtesy of M. W. Dow, from M. W. Dow, *Nation Building in Southeast Asia.* Boulder, Colo.: Pruett Press, 1966; rev. ed.)

guard. In May he ordered 400 Special Forces soldiers and another 100 military "advisers" to South Vietnam. Meanwhile, the Vietcong captured more territory and accelerated the violence through assassinations of village chiefs. In October a U.S. intelligence study indicated that 80 to 90 percent of the 17,000 Vietcong in South Vietnam came from the South, not from North Vietnam, and that most of their supplies originated in the South. Although it contradicted official claims that the Vietnamese crisis started because of aggression by North Vietnam, the report apparently did not influence Kennedy.

The president in October dispatched two hawks, General Maxwell Taylor and Walt Rostow, to South Vietnam to study the war firsthand. Diem asked for more American military aid. The duo recommended sending 8,000 U.S. combat troops to avoid the "sickly pallor" of appeasement.[132] Rusk questioned such advice, arguing that Diem must first reform his conservative government. Conscious that his decision violated the Geneva Accords but unwilling to say so publicly, Kennedy in November authorized an increase in U.S. forces or "advisers" in South Vietnam. By the end of 1961 they numbered 3,205. During the next year the figure jumped to 9,000, and at the time of Kennedy's death in November 1963 these forces had reached 16,700. American troops, helicopter units, minesweepers, and air reconnaissance aircraft went into action. In 1962, 109 Americans died and in 1963, 489. The strategic hamlet program fortified villages but proved disruptive and unpopular with villagers and permitted the Vietcong to appear as Robin Hoods. In Febru-

A Suicide in Protest, Saigon. Quang Duc, a Buddhist monk aged seventy-three, set his gasoline-drenched yellow robes afire in June 1963 to protest Diem's restrictions on Buddhists. (Wide World Photos)

ary 1963, Rusk nonetheless announced that the "momentum of the Communist drive has been stopped."[133]

In May 1963 the difficulties of nation building became exposed when South Vietnamese troops opened fire on protesting and unarmed Buddhists in the city of Hue, massacring nine. The incident erupted after a Catholic provincial chief had enforced an old decree prohibiting the flying of Buddhist flags. A Catholic oligarchy governed the predominantly Buddhist population. The Buddhist demonstrations also expressed longstanding nationalist sentiment, an appeal for peace talks with the NLF, and resentment against U.S. interference in Vietnamese politics. In early June a Buddhist monk sat in a Saigon street, poured fuel over his body, and immolated himself. Appalled, Kennedy reportedly told a confidant that the Vietnamese "hate us. . . . they'll kick our asses out of there."[134] Madame Nhu chortled about Buddhist "barbecues."[135] During summer and fall the protest spread; so did Diem's suppression, including an attack on Hue's pagodas. Also, authorities arrested thousands of students. Kennedy publicly chastised Diem and reduced aid. Senior South Vietnamese generals, now aware that Diem no longer had American favor, asked U.S. officials how they would respond to a coup d'état. The new ambassador, Henry Cabot Lodge, unsuccessful Republican vice presidential candidate in 1960, wanted to dump Diem, but officials in Washington hesitated. When a new mission headed by a marine general and a State Department official gave conflicting advice, a puzzled Kennedy asked: "You two did visit the same country, didn't you?"[136]

Washington continued cool relations with Diem, who proved more and more resistant to U.S. advice. In early October 1963 the Vietnamese generals prepared a coup. Judging Diem's removal imperative to bring "this medieval country into the 20th century," Lodge did not discourage them, a signal the generals grasped.[137] On November 1 the generals took Diem prisoner and murdered him. A few weeks later, on November 22, Kennedy himself was assassinated in Dallas. Some Kennedy advisers have suggested that after the presidential election of 1964 he would have withdrawn from Vietnam. Despite Kennedy's exploratory planning to bring home 1,000 military advisers in 1964, the removal of Diem only accentuated the political instability that undercut U.S. efforts to defeat the NLF and thus necessitated continued intervention. Given his Cold War mentality, his unwillingess to change U.S. nonrecognition policy toward China, his personal aversion to defeat, his political alertness to charges of being soft on communism, and the persistently poor prospects of victory in Vietnam, Kennedy probably would have pushed on in Vietnam, much as did his successor, Lyndon B. Johnson.

Nose to Nose: Lyndon B. Johnson and the World

Johnson kept on many of Kennedy's advisers. McNamara stayed until early 1968; Rusk until the end; replacing Bundy in 1966 was the zealous Walt Rostow, soon dubbed "the American Rasputin" by the veteran diplomat W. Averell Harriman.[138] Johnson had his own brand of international reform, derived from a sensitivity to the travails of poverty. Influenced by his New Deal reform years, he declared: "I want to leave the footprints of America there [Vietnam]. I want them to say, 'This is what the Americans left—schools and hospitals and dams. . . .' We can turn the Mekong [River area] into a Tennessee Valley."[139] He asserted: "Old Ho can't turn me down."[140] Intensely committed to his domestic agenda, Johnson believed that "foreign policy was something you had, like the measles, and got over . . . as quickly as possible."[141]

An experienced political operator, Johnson came from the poor hill territory of Texas between Fort Worth and San Antonio. He gulped his meals and talked incessantly. LBJ would thrust "his face close to the face of the person he was talking to, practically touching the other's nose," the Soviet ambassador wrote, "often pulling him closer by the lapel . . . in a heroic effort at persuasion."[142] It was "like being licked by a Great Dane," recalled one journalist.[143] Dean Acheson once called Johnson "a real centaur—part man, part horse's ass."[144] LBJ reminded Clark Clifford of "a powerful old-fashioned locomotive roaring unstoppably down the track."[145] In his first year as president, LBJ helped prevent a Turkish-Greek war over Cyprus by telling the Greek ambassador: "America is an elephant. Cyprus is a flea. Greece is a flea. If these two fellows continue itching the elephant, they may just get whacked by the elephant's tail, whacked good."[146] A "credibility gap" dogged the administration, not so much because Johnson told barefaced lies, but because he consciously downplayed his commitment to "that bitch of a war" lest it divert attention from the "woman I really loved—the Great Society" domestic reform program.[147] "Don't give a damn about those little pinkos on the campuses," he admonished. "They're just waving their diapers and bellyaching. . . . The great black beast for us is the right wing."[148]

Johnson left relations with the Soviet Union and China much as he had found them—calmer after the Cuban missile crisis but still strained and based on intense military competition. He met Soviet premier Aleksei Kosygin in Glassboro, New Jersey, in 1967, but the heralded "spirit of Glassboro" did not last. That year the Johnson administration asked Congress for an anti-ballistic missile system (ABM) to maintain the posture of massive retaliation or deterrence. The Soviets already had a limited ABM system. The heated debate over further enlargement of the arms race via the ABM still raged after Johnson left office (see Chapter 10). The United States, the Soviet Union, and more than fifty other nations signed a nuclear nonproliferation treaty in 1968 (ratified in 1969), a pledge not to spread nuclear weapons to other nations. But France and China, both members of the nuclear club, refused to sign. Nonsigner India joined the elite nuclear club in 1974, demonstrating again the diffusion of power in the international system.

In Latin America, smoldering nationalism, frequent military coups, and Castro's defiant survival defined Johnson's policies. Johnson put Assistant Secretary of State Thomas C. Mann in charge of the Alliance for Progress, and it soon withered away from neglect. Mann declared that the United States preferred to support anticommunist governments rather than to oppose military regimes. In 1964 Washington officials "did not try to hide their elation" over a military takeover in Brazil, and when Panamanians rioted against U.S. control of the Canal Zone, Johnson lectured the president of Panama that the United States would not tolerate insults to the American flag.[149] Despite his vow not to get into "any Bay of Pigs deal," Johnson sent 24,000 American soldiers into the Dominican Republic in 1965.[150] The trouble had started when, in late 1962, after the assassination of the dictator Rafael Trujillo the year before, radical reformer Juan Bosch won election as president of the economically depressed Caribbean country. Ten months later a military coup ousted him. But in April 1965, pro-Bosch rebels launched a new civil war against the military regime. Johnson and his advisers, with quick trigger fingers and fragmentary evidence, assumed that "the choice is: Castro in the Dominican Republic or U.S. intervention."[151] After sending in the troops, the president ordered the FBI to "find me some Communists in the Dominican Republic."[152] Thus was "a democratic revolution smashed by the leading democracy of the world," Bosch lamented.[153] The Dominican generals took over once again.

The president announced that the United States would henceforth prevent a communist government from taking office in the hemisphere. This frank statement of hegemony attempted to maintain the U.S. sphere in Latin America. (In 1968, after the Soviets had ruthlessly invaded rebellious Czechoslovakia, the Kremlin's explanations sounded much like those of Johnson in 1965.) Knowing that with LBJ "anything less than 100% support was rank desertion," Senator Fulbright nonetheless denounced the Dominican intervention for its "vain attempt to preserve the status quo."[154]

Abe Fortas Gets the Johnson Treatment. President Lyndon B. Johnson (1908–1973) used his formidable presence to cajole and persuade. Here the recipient of the famed treatment is Abe Fortas (1910–1982), Washington, D.C. lawyer, Supreme Court justice (1965–1969), and occasional presidential adviser on Vietnam. (Lyndon Baines Johnson Library)

"The Biggest Damned Mess": Johnson's Vietnam War

During Johnson's five years in office, Vietnam consumed his energies, his ambitions, his reputation. After Diem's death, the time seemed propitious for a political settlement. The National Liberation Front, Secretary General U Thant of the United Nations, the French government, and many Americans who recoiled from an Asian land war called for a coalition government in Saigon and the neutralization of Vietnam. Johnson would have none of it. In December 1963, he insisted on "victory" to prevent "a communist takeover."[155] For Johnson and his advisers, Vietnam occupied only one front in the Cold War; to falter in Southeast Asia, they believed, would send a false signal that the United States would retreat elsewhere, too.

By early 1964, however, the war was going badly. "We ought [not] to take this government seriously," said Ambassador Lodge (who treated the South Vietnamese like an "emperor dealing with barbarian tribes"). "We have to do what we think we ought to do regardless of what the Saigon government does."[156] The Army of the Republic of Vietnam (ARVN) proved ineffective in the field, and desertions ran high. The strategic hamlet program collapsed, and governmental administration in rural areas weakened. A coup by General Nguyen Khanh brought little progress, as Secretary McNamara reported that the Vietcong controlled 40 percent of the South Vietnamese countryside by March 1964. "We're getting into another Korea," a prophetic LBJ grumbled in May. "I don't think it's worth fighting for and I don't think we can get out. It's just the biggest damned mess."[157]

Deterioration in Vietnam gave Johnson's political foes an issue in the 1964 presidential campaign. Conservative Republican candidate Barry Goldwater urged military action against Ho Chi Minh's North. The president publicly chided Goldwater as a dangerous warmonger. But in private his administration was already implementing plans and developing new contingencies to increase the U.S. presence in South Vietnam and U.S. pressure against North Vietnam. In early 1964, Washington dispatched additional military advisers (reaching 23,000 by the end of the year). Air strikes hit Laos, through which supplies flowed south. In February a covert operation, tagged OPLAN 34-A, began to air-drop commandos into the North to conduct sabotage. To stiffen the Khanh government and to give Johnson flexibility to reverse the negative trend in Vietnam, aides urged the president in June to ask Congress for a resolution "conveying our firmness of purpose in Southeast Asia."[158]

On August 2, 1964, North Vietnamese torpedo patrol boats opened fire on the American destroyer *Maddox* some ten miles offshore. American aircraft from the U.S.S. *Ticonderoga* entered the fray. U.S. forces drove off the attackers, sinking one boat and damaging others, with no American casualties. The *Maddox* was on an espionage mission, called a "DeSoto patrol," collecting intelligence on radar and coastal defenses. As the president admitted privately, "we were playing around up there" in support of an OPLAN 34-A operation against two islands, "and they came out, gave us a warning, and we knocked hell out of 'em."[159] After the incident, almost as if to bait North Vietnam, the *Maddox* and *C. Turner Joy* steered to within

Vietcong Tunnels. One writer described "a formless war against a formless enemy who evaporated into the morning jungle mists only to materialize in some unexpected place." When a Vietnamese communist was told that his side had never beaten U.S. troops in a major battle, he replied: "That is correct. It is also irrelevant." Guerrillas win as long as they do not lose. Well-hidden tunnels helped the Vietcong defy superior U.S. military power. The most famous tunnels, in the Cu Chi region near Saigon, served as a staging area for the Tet offensive. (U.S. Army)

four miles of the islands. Rusk remarked: "If they [North Vietnamese] do it again, they'll get another sting."[160]

After dark on August 4, the captain of the *Maddox* interpreted his sonar data to mean that North Vietnamese gunboats had attacked the two ships. The *Maddox* and *C. Turner Joy* fired away wildly and American warplanes flew in to help. No evidence has ever confirmed a North Vietnamese attack. The ship's sonar may have picked up the sound of turbulent water, a thunderstorm, or the destroyer's own propellers. James B. Stockdale, who flew a Crusader jet from the *Ticonderoga* that night, saw "no boats, no wakes, no richochets off boats, no boat impacts, no torpedo wakes—nothing but black sea and American firepower."[161] "Those dumb, stupid sailors were just shooting at flying fish!" the president later said.[162]

Despite the CIA's report that the North Vietnamese were simply defending their territory against commando raids, Johnson exploited the moment to punish North Vietnam and to seek passage of a congressional resolution. On August 4, the president announced air strikes against the North. Saying nothing about destroyer operations against the North, he charged the enemy with deliberate aggression in international waters. Johnson consciously misled the American people and the Congress. The "Tonkin Gulf Resolution" passed on August 7 without much debate and by huge margins, 416 to 0 in the House and 88 to 2 in the Senate. Many voted "aye" unenthusiastically. Only Senators Ernest Gruening of Alaska and Wayne Morse of Oregon dissented. The resolution authorized the president to "take all necessary measures to repel armed attack against the forces of the United States and to prevent further aggression."[163] The resolution, said Johnson, was "like grandma's nightshirt—it covered everything."[164] In 1970, regretting this open-ended concession to the president, the Senate repealed it.

On February 7, 1965, the Vietcong attacked an American airfield at Pleiku and killed eight Americans. Johnson immediately ordered retaliatory strikes against the North. "I'm going up Ho Chi Minh's leg an inch at a time," he said.[165] By March the United States had undertaken a sustained bombing program—Operation Rolling Thunder. When the Joint Chiefs of Staff in April urged calling up the reserves to "show the American people we were serious," the president said: "You leave the American people to me. I know more about . . . [them] than anybody in this room."[166] With 80,000 U.S. troops operating in the South by July, the military asked for 100,000 more. On July 21 the president convened his high-level advisers. Only Under Secretary of State George W. Ball argued that the United States could not win a protracted war in an Asian jungle. "Take our losses, let their government fall apart, negotiate, discuss, knowing full well there will be a probable take-over by the Communists," he advised. Sending more troops would be "like giving cobalt treatment to a terminal cancer case." In the long run, then, the war "will disclose our weakness, not our strength." Johnson jumped in: "But, George, wouldn't all these countries say that Uncle Sam was a paper tiger," with America losing its credibility? "No sir," Ball answered. "The worse blow would be that the mightiest power on earth is unable to defeat a handful of guerrillas."[167]

Friction between Johnson and his military advisers accompanied the decision to escalate. "Bomb, bomb, bomb. That's all you know," LBJ bellowed at one point. "You're not giving me . . . any solutions for this damn little pissant country."[168] Unwilling to let "some military idiots talk him into World War III," the president once told the Joint Chiefs to "get the hell out of my office."[169] Cowed by such tirades, the military professionals ("five silent men") never confronted Johnson with "the total forces they believed would ultimately be required in Vietnam."[170] The result was a McNamara-dominated strategy of graduated pressure, in which the Joint Chiefs "signed on" to ensure consensus, and ground forces went to Vietnam in increments.

By the end of the year nearly 200,000 American troops were fighting in Vietnam; a year later the number reached 385,000. Not wanting to jeopardize Great Society reforms, Johnson built up forces without mobilizing the reserves or raising taxes. As Rusk later said: "In a nuclear world it is just too dangerous for an entire people to get too angry and we deliberately tried to do in cold blood what perhaps can only be done in hot blood."[171]

In 1966 American bombers hit oil depots in the North, and by midyear 70 percent of the North's storage capacity had been destroyed. With North Vietnamese and Vietcong forces increasing from 116,000 to 282,000 during the 1965–1967 period, the heavy bombing apparently had little impact on the enemy's ability to resist. During 1965–1968 the United States tried, in air force general Curtis LeMay's infamous phrase, "to bomb them back into the stone age" by dropping 400 tons of ordnance per day.[172] But the United States lost 918 aircraft valued at $6 billion. By war's end more than 7 million tons of U.S. bombs had battered Vietnam, the equivalent of 400 Hiroshima atomic blasts. General William Westmoreland kept asking for more troops, even though Secretary McNamara reported in October 1966 that

Caught in Battle. A Vietnamese peasant mother and her children emerge after battle between ARVN forces and Vietcong guerillas near the village of Phung Hiep on July 23, 1965. Such a photograph is an exception to the caricatured images of the Vietnamese at war—"the shadowy foe darting through the underbrush or lying crumpled on the ground, the prostitute or crowd of children outside an American base camp, the venal official hobbling the Saigon government's war effort, the child in frightful flight from napalm," as the historian Michael H. Hunt has observed. (National Archives)

"pacification has, if anything, gone backward."[173] The president nonetheless kept sending troops—peaking at 543,400 in early 1969.

At a "Wise Men's" meeting in November 1967, George Ball made "his usual plea for extrication to the usual deaf ears." Then he lost his temper: "You're like a flock of buzzards sitting on a fence, sending the young men off to be killed."[174] President Johnson took comfort in simplistic historical analogies: "Just like FDR and Hitler, just like Wilson and the Kaiser," Americans had to stop "aggression."[175]

In this period of escalation, 1965–1968, the bloodshed and dislocation staggered the Vietnamese people. Under General Westmoreland's ("Waste-more-men") questionable strategy of "attrition," American and South Vietnamese forces bombed and destroyed villages that harbored suspected Vietcong, the "Charlie."[176] Hundreds of thousands of civilians died, many from fiery napalm attacks in areas called "free fire zones." "After . . . a while you forget that there are people down there," an American pilot explained.[177] Counting enemy bodies became "a macabre statistical competition" for Captain Colin Powell, who later recalled the nightly ritual: "'How many did your platoon get?' 'I don't know. We saw two for sure.' 'Well, if you saw two there were probably eight. So lets's say ten.'"[178] To deny the enemy food and to expose hideouts, American defoliation teams sprayed chemicals such as Agent Orange on crops and forests, denuding the landscape and inadvertently exposing GIs to the dioxin-tainted herbicide. (After the war, some 39,000 veterans with cancer and nerve diseases filed claims with the U.S. government.) Beginning in 1967 the CIA supervised the Phoenix program, in which

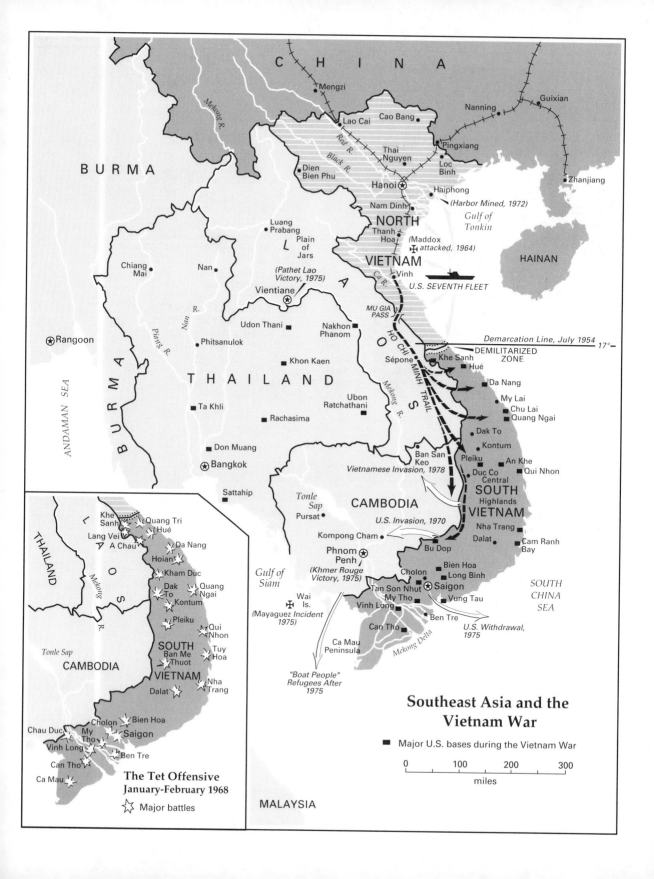

CHINA

Mengzi

Nanning • Guixian

Lao Cai • Cao Bang

Pingxiang

Thai
Nguyen

Loc
Binh

Zhanjiang

BURMA

Dien
Bien Phu

Red R.

Black R.

Hanoi ✦

Haiphong

(Harbor Mined, 1972)

Nam Dinh

Luang
• Prabang

Plain
of
Jars

L

Thanh
Hoa

NORTH

VIETNAM

*Gulf of
Tonkin*

HAINAN

Chiang
Mai

Nan

A

Ca R.

Vinh

*(Maddox
attacked, 1964)*

Vientiane ✦

O

U.S. SEVENTH FLEET

Nan R.

Rangoon ✦

Piang R.

Udon Thani

Nakhon
Phanom

S

MU GIA
PASS

Demarcation Line, July 1954

17°—

Phitsanulok

Sépone

HO CHI MINH TRAIL

Khe Sanh

DEMILITARIZED
ZONE

Hué

THAILAND

Khon Kaen

Da Nang

My Lai
Chu Lai
Quang Ngai

Ta Khli

Ubon
Ratchathani

Mekong R.

Dak To

Kontum

Rachasima

Ban San
Keo

Pleiku

An Khe

Qui Nhon

Don Muang

Vietnamese Invasion, 1978

Duc Co
Central

Bangkok ✦

*Tonle
Sap*

CAMBODIA

SOUTH

Highlands

VIETNAM

Sattahip

Pursat •

U.S. Invasion, 1970

Nha Trang

Dalat

Cam Ranh
Bay

*Gulf of
Siam*

Kompong Cham

Bu Dop

Bien Hoa
Long Binh

Phnom
Penh ✦

*(Khmer Rouge
Victory, 1975)*

Cholon

*SOUTH
CHINA
SEA*

Wai
Is.
*(Mayaguez Incident
1975)*

Tan Son Nhut

My Tho

Vinh Long

Saigon ✦

Vung Tau

Ben Tre

*U.S. Withdrawal,
1975*

Can Tho

Ca Mau
Peninsula

Mekong Delta

*"Boat People"
Refugees After
1975*

Southeast Asia and the
Vietnam War

■ Major U.S. bases during the Vietnam War

0   100   200   300

miles

Inset map (lower left):

Khe
Sanh

Quang Tri

L

Hué

Lang Vei

A Chau

Da Nang

THAILAND

Hoian

Kham Duc

Mekong R.

Dak
To

Quang
Ngai

Kontum

Pleiku

Qui
Nhon

O

SOUTH

Tuy
Hoa

S

Ban Me
Thuot

VIETNAM

Nha
Trang

Tonle Sap

Dalat

CAMBODIA

Chau Duc

Cholon

Bien Hoa

My
Tho

Saigon

Vinh Long

Ben Tre

Can Tho

Ca Mau

The Tet Offensive
January–February 1968

✦ Major battles

MALAYSIA

*Pathet Lao
Victory, 1975*

ANDAMAN SEA

South Vietnamese operatives infiltrated rural areas and "neutralized" thousands of suspected Vietcong. "Infiltration of a couple of guys into our ranks created tremendous difficulties," a Vietcong leader later admitted.[179] To many Americans, the My Lai massacre of March 16, 1968, where a U.S. Army platoon commanded by Lieutenant William Calley shot to death scores of helpless women and children, or "gooks," represented a depravity unbecoming to a civilized nation. Because of official cover-ups, the My Lai story did not become public until twenty months later. Despite documented incidents of the deliberate shooting, raping, and torturing of civilians and prisoners, however, most U.S. soldiers were not committing atrocities. They were trying instead to save their young lives—the average age of the Vietnam GI was only nineteen—from snipers, booby traps, ambushes, mortar attacks, and firefights. Etched in their memories, too, was the inhospitable environment, "as if the sun and land were in league with the Vietcong," recalled the marine officer Philip Caputo in *A Rumor of War* (1977), "wearing us down, driving us mad, killing us."[180]

As the Doves Dissent, the Peace Efforts Fail

"Can the tortoise of progress in Vietnam stay ahead of the hare of dissent at home?" one official asked.[181] It could not. Students and faculties at universities began to hold "teach-ins" in 1965, first at the University of Michigan in March. Hundreds refused military draft calls and went to jail or fled to Canada. Others obtained deferments. The protest songs of Bob Dylan, Pete Seeger, and Joan Baez inspired rallies. The National Student Association, secretly funded by the CIA, found itself upstaged by the radical Students for a Democratic Society (SDS). Sit-ins greeted representatives of major corporations such as Dow Chemical, a maker of napalm, when they attempted to recruit on campus. In early 1967, 300,000 demonstrators marched in New York City; in November, 100,000 surrounded the Pentagon. With LBJ's encouragement, the CIA and FBI spread rumors that antiwar activists had come under the control of communists.

Prominent intellectuals, such as the linguist Noam Chomsky, the political scientist Hans Morgenthau, Jr., and the disaffected Arthur M. Schlesinger, Jr., called for withdrawal from Vietnam. Business executives, lawyers, and members of the clergy, too, joined antiwar groups. The pediatrician Benjamin Spock and Dr. Martin Luther King, Jr., the civil rights crusader, added their voices to the protest. Among scores of alternative press outlets, *Ramparts* magazine became famous for its coverage of Vietnam brutalities and university-Pentagon links. The U.S. ambassador to India captured Third World peoples' hostility to U.S. military intervention when he commented that they saw a "powerful white Western nation attempting to clobber a small underdog brown-skinned Asian nation."[182] Radical pacifists, liberal reformers, conservative constitutionalists, strategic realists, religious moralists, hippies, trade unionists, and many others melded into a national, largely unstructured antiwar movement. Often stereotyped as the haven for long-haired, bearded college-age youth, the movement actually encompassed a wide spectrum of people. The strongest opposition to the war came from four groups: older, black, female,

Harvard Strike, 1969. A clenched fist and V-shaped fingers became symbols of the antiwar movement. The scholar Tom Wells, in *The War Within* (1994), describes the antiwar movement as "a bountiful mix of political notions and visions that brought together teenagers and senior citizens, Democratic Party lobbyists and Maoist revolutionaries, pacifists and streetfighters, letter writers and draft resisters, healers and bomb makers." (Homer Babbidge Library, University of Connecticut)

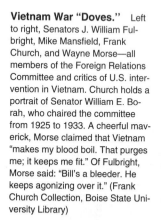

Vietnam War "Doves." Left to right, Senators J. William Fulbright, Mike Mansfield, Frank Church, and Wayne Morse—all members of the Foreign Relations Committee and critics of U.S. intervention in Vietnam. Church holds a portrait of Senator William E. Borah, who chaired the committee from 1925 to 1933. A cheerful maverick, Morse claimed that Vietnam "makes my blood boil. That purges me; it keeps me fit." Of Fulbright, Morse said: "Bill's a bleeder. He keeps agonizing over it." (Frank Church Collection, Boise State University Library)

and lower-class Americans. Younger, white, male, and middle-class citizens tended to support escalation of the war and follow the president's lead—at least until 1968. In February of that year, after Tet, a majority of polled Americans for the first time said that the United States had made a "mistake" in sending troops to Vietnam.

The critics offered multifaceted arguments: The war cost too much and weakened needed reform at home; America's youth was dying—30,000 by 1968; inflation and a worsening balance of payments undermined the economy; the ghastly bloodshed and U.S. conduct of the war were immoral; the war damaged relations with allies and foes alike; Washington and Saigon could not win the war; the president was undermining the constitutional system of checks and balances; U.S. behavior in Vietnam debased the American principles of fair play and right to self-determination; and dissension was ripping domestic America apart. Above all else, the United States had succumbed to a debilitating globalism of anticommunism, overcommitment, and overextension. In short, some critics complained about how the war was being conducted, whereas others, more searching, criticized globalism and the containment doctrine itself.

The growing public disaffection encouraged dissent in Congress. Lingering doubts about the Tonkin Gulf Resolution prompted Senator Fulbright to hold publicly televised hearings before his committee. LBJ ridiculed him as Senator "Half Bright"—"a crybaby" because "I can't . . . kiss him every morning."[183] But dissenting senators kept asking the administration to explain exactly what in Vietnam the United States was trying to contain. The Soviet Union? China? North Vietnam? The Vietcong? Rusk settled on China as the main culprit, especially after the Chinese leader Lin Biao declared in 1965 that China would encourage wars of national liberation in the Third World. "It is on this spot," as Rostow once asserted, "that we have to break the liberation war—Chinese type." Otherwise, "we shall have to face it again in Thailand, Venezuela, elsewhere."[184] Chinese supplies to North Vietnam predominated until 1966, whereupon Moscow increased efforts to woo Hanoi to its side in the Sino-Soviet split. Many administration officials overlooked the fundamental fact that the conflict in South Vietnam grew from indigenous roots—it was a civil war. The surprise testimony at the Fulbright hearings came from George F. Kennan. He insisted that the containment doctrine, designed for a stable European nation-state context in the 1940s, did not fit Asia. He urged a gradual withdrawal from Vietnam. So did Senator Eugene McCarthy, who declared in late 1967 that he would challenge President Johnson for the 1968 Democratic nomination. To stay "clean for Gene," student activists temporarily abandoned their unisex hairdos, "tie-dyed T-shirts, torn jeans, and sandals," all of which offended middle America.[185] In March 1968, Senator Robert F. Kennedy, the slain president's brother, also entered the Democratic race as an antiwar candidate.

The Johnson administration lashed back, citing polls showing that most Americans, before 1968, favored escalation, not withdrawal. Rostow tried to reassure Johnson with statistical charts showing the enemy's large losses, yet the most heavily industrialized, the most militarily powerful, the richest nation on earth could not subdue what LBJ once called that "raggedy-ass little fourth-rate country."[186] Doubters grew more numerous within administration ranks. In 1967 Johnson's advisers generally favored the "stick it out" option, but by Tet the president heard words such as "disengagement," "deescalation," "withdrawal," and "sinkhole."[187] McNamara's increasing disenchantment and 1967 resignation angered the president. McGeorge Bundy, George Ball, and close political adviser Bill Moyers had already departed. With victory an increasingly elusive goal by 1967–1968, Johnson seemed determined at least not to lose.

Throughout the 1965–1968 escalation period, international groups, including the United Nations and the Vatican, suggested avenues for peace. Even the Soviet Union urged peace talks because it sought closer ties with Washington as a bulwark against the "adventurous schemes" of Mao's China—whom the North Vietnamese soon called "La Grand Impuissance" (Great Non-Power).[188] In 1965, through Italy, North Vietnam offered a plan resembling the 1954 Geneva agreements. LBJ sent prominent emissaries to foreign capitals to explore peace. In January 1966, he halted the bombing of North Vietnam. But during this bombing pause, he also increased U.S. troop strength in Vietnam, raising doubts about his intentions. Washington would not talk until North Vietnam ceased its "aggression" and would not recognize the National Liberation Front as a political force in the South. Hanoi, increasingly speaking for the Vietcong, would not negotiate until U.S. bombing stopped and Saigon granted the NLF political rights. Assistant Secretary of Defense John McNaughton, another "hawk" becoming a "dove," concluded that Washington wanted "capitulation by a Communist force that is far from beaten."[189] A

Antiwar Buttons. Opponents of the Vietnam War demonstrated their protest in a panoply of buttons urging withdrawal and peace. (Division of Political History, Smithsonian Institution)

promising diplomatic contact (codenamed MARIGOLD) arranged through a Polish representative, in December 1966, aborted when American bombers stepped up air strikes around Hanoi. Another bombing pause came in February 1967, in part induced by McNamara's argument that the bombing did not seriously impede the flow of arms and soldiers into the South over narrow, jungle paths (the "Ho Chi Minh Trail"; see map, on page 350). After each pause, the bombing intensified.

And then the Tet offensive of early 1968 wrought its havoc; military escalation and Johnson's political career derailed; the bombing scaled down; and the peace talks finally began in Paris. In November, Richard M. Nixon defeated Vice President Hubert Humphrey for the presidency. In 1961 John F. Kennedy had asked Americans to "pay any price" and "bear any burden." By 1969, many refused. The new Nixon administration faced the task of maintaining U.S. interests abroad while at the same time mollifying the evident discontent with globalism and the Vietnam War.

FURTHER READING FOR THE PERIOD 1961–1969

Several works cited in Chapters 7 and 8 on the Cold War and the Third World also survey this period, and not all are repeated here.

For John F. Kennedy and his foreign relations, see James D. Barber, *The Presidential Character* (1992); Irving Bernstein, *Promises Kept* (1991); Michael Beschloss, *The Crisis Years* (1991); Douglas Brinkley and Richard T. Griffiths, eds., *John F. Kennedy and Europe* (1999); Kenneth R. Crispell and Carlos F. Gomez, *Hidden Illness in the White House* (1989); Robert H. Ferrell, *Ill-Advised* (1992); James N. Giglio, *The Presidency of John F. Kennedy* (1991); Doris Kearns Goodwin, *The Fitzgeralds and the Kennedys* (1987); David Halberstam, *The Best and the Brightest* (1972); Seymour Hersh, *The Other Side of Camelot* (1997); Montague Kern et al., *The Kennedy Crises* (1983); William E. Leuchtenburg, *In the Shadow of FDR* (1989); Timothy P. Maga, *John F. Kennedy and New Frontier Diplomacy* (1994); Bert Park, *Ill-Fated History* (1993); Herbert S. Parmet, *JFK* (1983); Thomas G. Paterson, ed., *Kennedy's Quest for Victory* (1989); Richard Reeves, *President Kennedy* (1993); Thomas C. Reeves, *A Question of Character* (1991); J. Richard Snyder, ed., *John F. Kennedy* (1988); Mark J. White, *Kennedy* (1998); and Garry Wills, *The Kennedy Imprisonment* (1982). For Kennedy and specific countries and crises, see below.

For Lyndon B. Johnson and his administration (see Vietnam below), see Irving Bernstein, *Guns or Butter* (1996); Vaughn D. Bornet, *The Presidency of Lyndon B. Johnson* (1983); H. W. Brands, *The Wages of Globalism* (1995) and ed., *The Foreign Policies of Lyndon Johnson* (1999); David Burner, *Questioning History* (1996); Warren I. Cohen and Nancy B. Tucker, eds., *Lyndon Johnson Confronts the World* (1995); Paul K. Conkin, *Big Daddy from the Pedernales* (1986); Robert Dallek, *Flawed Giant* (1998); Robert A. Divine, *Exploring the Johnson Years* (1981) and ed., *The Johnson Years* (1987–1994); Peter Geyelin, *Lyndon B. Johnson and the World* (1966); Paul Y. Hammond, *LBJ and the Presidential Management of Foreign Relations* (1993); Doris Kearns, *Lyndon Johnson and the American Dream* (1976); and Diane Kunz, ed., *The Diplomacy of the Crucial Decade* (1994).

For other prominent Americans, see Leroy Ashby and Rod Gramer, *Fighting the Odds* (1994) (Frank Church); William C. Berman, *William Fulbright and the Vietnam War* (1988); James A. Bill, *George Ball* (1997); Kai Bird, *The Color of Truth* (1998) (Bundy); Douglas Brinkley, *Dean Acheson* (1992); Jeff Broadwater, *Adlai Stevenson* (1994); Warren I. Cohen, *Dean Rusk* (1980); David L. DiLeo, *George Ball, Vietnam, and the Rethinking of Containment* (1991); Gilbert C. Fite, *Richard B. Russell, Jr.* (1991); Dorothy Fosdick, ed., *Staying the Course* (1987) (Henry Jackson); Robert A. Goldberg, *Barry Goldwater* (1995); Walter Isaacson and Evan Thomas, *The Wise Men* (1986); Robert David Johnson, *Ernest Gruening and the American Dissenting Tradition* (1998); John B. Martin, *Adlai Stevenson and the World* (1977); Barry Riccio, *Walter Lippmann* (1989); Howard B. Schaffer, *Chester Bowles* (1993); Thomas J. Schoenbaum, *Waging Peace and War* (1988) (Rusk); Deborah Shapley, *Promise and Power* (1993) (McNamara); Carol Solberg, *Hubert Humphrey* (1984); Ronald Steel, *Walter Lippmann and the American Century* (1980); Randall B. Woods, *Fulbright* (1995); and Thomas W. Zeiler, *Dean Rusk* (1999).

Economic issues and trade policy are scrutinized in David P. Calleo, *The Imperious Economy* (1982); John W. Evans, *The Kennedy Round* (1971); and Thomas Zeiler, *American Trade and Power in the 1960s* (1992).

Europe, the Berlin crisis, and the nuclear arms race are the subjects of Desmond Ball, *Politics and Force Levels* (1980); McGeorge Bundy, *Danger and Survival* (1988); Curtis Cate, *The Ides of August* (1978) (Berlin); Honoré Catudal, *Kennedy and the Berlin Wall Crisis* (1980); Frank Costigliola, *France and the United States* (1992); Bernard Firestone, *The Quest for Nuclear Stability* (1982); Alfred Grosser, *The Western Alliance* (1980); Michael Harrison, *The Reluctant Ally* (1981) (France); Michael Mandelbaum, *The Nuclear Question* (1979); Frank A. Mayer, *Adenauer and Kennedy* (1996); David Nunnerly, *President Kennedy and Britain* (1972); Kendrick Oliver, *Kennedy, Macmillan, and the Nuclear Test Ban Treaty* (1998); Thomas Risse-Kappen, *Cooperation Among Democracies* (1995); Jack Schick, *The Berlin Crisis* (1971); Glenn T. Seaborg and Benjamin S. Loeb, *Kennedy, Khrushchev, and the Test Ban* (1981) and *Stemming the Tide* (1987) (arms control); Robert Slusser, *The Berlin Crisis of 1961* (1973); Andreas Wenger, *Living with Peril: Eisenhower, Kennedy, and Nuclear Weapons* (1997); Peter Wyden, *The Wall* (1989); and Ernest J. Yanarella, *The Missile Defense Controversy* (1977).

Aspects of relations with the Third World in the 1960s include Abraham Ben-Zvi, *Decade of Transition* (1998) (Israel); Melvin Gurtov, *The United States and the Third World* (1974); Gabriel Kolko, *Confronting the Third World* (1988); Timothy P. Maga, *John F. Kennedy and the New Pacific Community* (1990); Robert J. McMahon, *Cold War on the Periphery* (1994) (India and Pakistan) and *The Limits of Empire* (1999); Robert A. Packenham, *Liberal America and the Third World* (1973); David L. Schalk, *War and the Ivory Tower* (1991) (Algeria); and Penny M. von Eschen, *Race Against Empire: Black Americans and Anticolonialism* (1998).

For the Cuban Revolution, Fidel Castro, Bay of Pigs, and missile crisis, see Graham Allison, *Essence of Decision* (1971); Jules Benjamin, *The United States and the Origins of the Cuban Revolution* (1990); James G. Blight, *The Shattered Crystal Ball* (1990); James G. Blight and Peter Kornbluh, eds., *Politics of Illusion* (1998) (Bay of Pigs); James G. Blight and David A. Welch, *On the Brink* (1989); James G. Blight et al., *Cuba on the Brink* (1993); Herbert Dinerstein, *The Making of a Missile Crisis* (1976); Jorge Domínguez, *Cuba* (1978) and *To Make a World Safe for Revolution* (1989); Alexander Fursenko and Timothy Naftali, *"One Hell of a Gamble"* (1997); Raymond L. Garthoff, *Reflections on the Cuban Missile Crisis* (1989); Alexander L. George, ed., *Avoiding War* (1991); Trumbull Higgins, *The Perfect Failure* (1987) (Bay of Pigs); Donna R. Kaplowitz, *Anatomy of a Failed Embargo: U.S. Sanctions Against Cuba* (1998); Richard Lebow and Janice G. Stein, *We All Lost the Cold War* (1994); Felix Masud-Piloto, *From Welcomed Exiles to Illegal Immigrants* (1995) (Cuban migration); Ernest R. May and Philip D. Zelikow, eds., *The Kennedy Tapes* (1997); Morris Morley, *Imperial State and Revolution* (1987); Philip Nash, *The Other Missiles of October* (1997) (Jupiters); James A. Nathan, ed., *The Cuban Missile Crisis Revisited* (1992); Louis A. Pérez, Jr., *Cuba and the United States* (1997); Scott D. Sagan, *The Limits of Safety* (1993); Tad Szulc, *Fidel* (1986); Lucien S. Vandenbroucke, *Perilous Options* (1993) (Bay of Pigs); and Mark J. White, *The Cuban Missile Crisis* (1996) and *Missiles in Cuba* (1997).

U.S.–Latin America relations, including the Alliance for Progress, are explored in Samuel Baily, *The United States and . . . South America* (1976); Jan K. Black, *United States Penetration of Brazil* (1977); Cole Blasier, *The Hovering Giant* (1976); Theodore Draper, *The Dominican Revolt* (1968); Piero Gleijeses, *The Dominican Crisis* (1978); Walter LaFeber, *Inevitable Revolutions* (1993); Lester D. Langley, *The United States and the Caribbean in the Twentieth Century* (1982) and *America and the Americas* (1989); Ruth Leacock, *Requiem for Revolution* (1990) (Brazil); Jerome Levinson and Juan de Onís, *The Alliance That Lost Its Way* (1970); Abraham F. Lowenthal, *Exporting Democracy* (1991); John D. Martz, ed., *United States Policy in Latin America* (1988); Phyllis Parker, *Brazil and the Quiet Intervention* (1979); Stephen G. Rabe, *The Most Dangerous Area in the World* (1999) (JFK); L. Ronald Scheman, ed., *The Alliance for Progress* (1988); Lars Schoultz, *Beneath the United States* (1998); and W. Michael Weis, *Cold Warriors & Coups D'État* (1993) (Brazil).

Studies of U.S. relations with Africa include David N. Gibbs, *The Political Economy of Third World Intervention* (1991) (Congo); Madeline G. Kalb, *The Congo Cables* (1982); Richard D. Mahoney, *JFK* (1983); Thomas J. Noer, *Cold War and Black Liberation* (1985); Joseph E. Thompson, *American Policy and African Famine* (1990) (Nigeria); and Stephen Weissman, *American Foreign Policy in the Congo* (1974).

For the Peace Corps, see Julius A. Amin, *The Peace Corps in Cameroon* (1992); Fritz Fischer, *Making Them Like Us* (1998); Elizabeth Cobbs Hoffman, *All You Need Is Love* (1998); and Gerald T. Rice, *The Bold Experiment* (1985).

For Vietnam, especially the experience of the 1960s, see David L. Anderson, ed., *Shadow on the White House* (1993) and *Facing My Lai* (1998); Loren Baritz, *Backfire* (1985); David M. Barrett, *Uncertain Warriors* (1993); Larry Berman, *Planning a Tragedy* (1982) and *Lyndon Johnson's War* (1989); Anne Blair, *Lodge in Vietnam* (1995); Robert K. Brigham, *Guerrilla Diplomacy: The NLF's Foreign Relations and the Viet Nam War* (1999); Robert Buzzanco, *Vietnam and the Transformation of American Life* (1999); Larry Cable, *Unholy Grail* (1991); William J. Duiker, *U.S. Containment Policy and the Conflict in Indochina* (1994); John Ernst, *Forging a Fateful Alliance* (1998) (Michigan State University contracts and Vietnam); Frances FitzGerald, *Fire in the Lake* (1972); Ilya V. Gaiduk, *The Soviet Union and the Vietnam War* (1996); Lloyd C. Gardner, *Pay Any Price* (1995); William C. Gibbons, *The U.S. Government and the Vietnam War* (1986–1994); Fred Greenstein et al., eds., *How Presidents Test Reality* (1989); Ellen J. Hammer, *A Death in November* (1987) (Diem); Patrick L. Hatcher, *The Suicide of an Elite: American Internationalists and Vietnam* (1990); George C. Herring, *LBJ and Vietnam* (1994) and *America's Longest War* (1996); Paul Hendrickson, *The Living and the Dead* (1996); Gary R. Hess, *Vietnam and the United States* (1998); Michael H. Hunt, *Lyndon Johnson's War* (1996); Susan Jeffords, *The Remasculinization of America: Gender and the Vietnam War* (1989); George McT. Kahin, *Intervention* (1986); Stanley Karnow, *Vietnam* (1991); Yuen Foong Khong, *Analogies of War* (1992); Gabriel Kolko, *Anatomy of a War* (1985); David W. Levy, *The Debate over Vietnam* (1991); Fredrik Logevall, *Choosing War* (1999); H. R. McMaster, *Dereliction of Duty* (1997); Edwin F. Moïse, *Tonkin Gulf and the Escalation of the Vietnam War* (1996); Joseph G. Morgan, *The Vietnam Lobby* (1997); John M. Newman, *JFK and Vietnam* (1992); Caroline Page, *U.S. Official Propaganda During the Vietnam War* (1996); Douglas Pike, *Vietnam and the Soviet Union* (1987); William J. Rust, *Kennedy in Vietnam* (1985); Robert D. Schulzinger, *A Time for War* (1997); Orrin Schwab, *Defending the Free World* (1998); Neil Sheehan, *A Bright Shining Lie* (1988); Anthony Short, *The Origins of the Vietnam War* (1989); Ronald H. Spector, *After Tet* (1993); William S. Turley, *The Second Indochina War* (1986); Brian VanDeMark, *Into the Quagmire* (1991) (Johnson); Frank E. Vandiver, *Shadows of Vietnam* (1997); Jayne S. Werner and Luu Doan Huynh, eds., *The Vietnam War* (1992); Marilyn Young, *The Vietnam Wars* (1991); and James J. Wirtz, *The Tet Offensive* (1992).

Laos and Cambodia are discussed in many of the studies above and in Timothy N. Castle, *At War in the Shadow of Vietnam* (1993) (Laos); David P. Chandler, *The Tragedy of Cambodian History* (1991); Michael Haas, *Cambodia, Pol Pot, and the United States* (1991); Jane Hamilton-Merritt, *Tragic Mountain* (1993) (Laos); Marie A. Martin, *Cambodia* (1994); William Shawcross, *Sideshow* (1979) (Cambodia); and Charles Stevenson, *The End of Nowhere* (1972) (Laos).

The colonial history of Vietnam, its wars against foreigners, and the development of its politics are examined in Joseph Buttinger, *Vietnam* (1970); William Duiker, *The Communist Road to Power in Vietnam* (1981); Bernard Fall, *The Two Viet-Nams* (1967); James P. Harrison, *The Endless War* (1982); Ronald E. Irving, *The First Indochina War* (1975); David Marr, *Vietnamese Anti-Colonialism, 1885–1925* (1971) and *Vietnamese Tradition on Trial, 1920–1945* (1981); John T. McAlister, Jr., *Vietnam* (1971); and Douglas Pike, *History of Vietnamese Communism* (1978) and *Viet Cong* (1972).

Specific studies of the Truman and Eisenhower administrations and Vietnam are David L. Anderson, *Trapped by Success* (1991) (Eisenhower); Melanie Billings-Yun, *Decision Against War* (1988) (Dienbienphu); Lloyd C. Gardner, *Approaching Vietnam* (1988); Lloyd C. Gardner and Ted Gittinger, eds., *Vietnam: The Early Decisions* (1998); Ellen J. Hammer, *The Struggle for Vietnam, 1945–1955* (1966); Lawrence S. Kaplan et al., eds., *Dien Bien Phu and the Crisis of Franco-American Relations* (1990); David G. Marr, *Vietnam 1945* (1995); Andrew J. Rotter, *The Path to Vietnam* (1987); Martin Shipway, *The Road to War* (1996) (French policy); and Stein Tönnesson, *The Vietnamese Revolution of 1945* (1991).

For the My Lai massacre, see David L. Anderson, *Facing My Lai* (1998); Seymour M. Hersh, *Cover-Up* (1972); James S. Olson and Randy Roberts, *My Lai* (1998); and Kevin Sim and Michael Bilton, *Four Hours in My Lai* (1992).

For province- and village-level studies that probe American interactions with a peasant society, see William Andrews, *The Village War* (1973); Eric M. Bergerud, *The Dynamics of Defeat* (1991); Jeffrey Race, *War Comes to Long An* (1972); and James W. Trullinger, Jr., *Village at War* (1980).

Military decisions and operations and the soldier's experience in Vietnam are studied in Christian G. Appy, *Working-Class War* (1993); Robert Buzzanco, *Masters of War: Military Dissent and Politics in the Vietnam*

Era (1996); Jeffrey J. Clarke, *United States Army in Vietnam* (1988); Mark Clodfelter, *The Limits of Power* (1989) (bombing); Robert L. Gallucci, *Neither Peace nor Honor* (1975); Douglas Kinnard, *The War Managers* (1977) and *The Certain Trumpet* (1991) (Taylor); Andrew F. Krepinevich, Jr., *The Army and Vietnam* (1986); Otto J. Lehrack, *No Shining Armor* (1992) (marines); Guenter Lewy, *America in Vietnam* (1978); Donald J. Mrozek, *Air Power & the Ground War in Vietnam* (1989); Edgar O'Ballance, *The Wars in Vietnam* (1975); Douglas Pike, *PAVN: People's Army of Vietnam* (1986); John Prados and Ray Stubbe, *Valley of Decision* (1991) (Khe Sanh); Ronald H. Spector, *United States in Vietnam* (1983); Shelby Stanton, *The Rise and Fall of an American Army* (1985); Harry G. Summers, *On Strategy* (1981); and James C. Thompson, *Rolling Thunder* (1980).

American public opinion, media, and the antiwar movement are discussed in many of the works above and specifically in Peter Braestrup, *Big Story* (1977); Charles DeBenedetti and Charles Chatfield, *An American Ordeal* (1990) (antiwar movement); Terry Dietz, *Republicans and Vietnam* (1986); G. David Garrow, *Bearing the Cross* (1986) (Martin Luther King, Jr.); Daniel C. Hallin, *The "Uncensored War"* (1986); Kenneth J. Heineman, *Campus Wars* (1993); Allen J. Matusow, *Unraveling of America* (1984); Melvin Small, *Johnson, Nixon, and the Doves* (1988) and *Covering Dissent* (1994); Melvin Small and William D. Hoover, eds., *Give Peace a Chance* (1992); William Prochnau, *Once upon a Distant War* (1995) (journalists); Amy Swerdlow, *Women Strike for Peace* (1993); Robert R. Tomes, *Apocalypse Then: American Intellectuals and the Vietnam War, 1954–1975* (1998); Kathleen J. Turner, *Lyndon Johnson's Dual War* (1985); Tom Wells, *The War Within* (1994); Lawrence S. Wittner, *Rebels Against War* (1984); Clarence R. Wyatt, *Paper Soldiers* (1993); and Nancy Zaroulis and Gerald Sullivan, *Who Spoke Up?* (1984).

See also the General Bibliography and the following notes.

For comprehensive coverage of foreign-related topics, see the articles in the four-volume *Encyclopedia of U.S. Foreign Relations* (1997), edited by Bruce W. Jentleson and Thomas G. Paterson.

NOTES TO CHAPTER 9

1. Quoted in J. L. Dees, "The Viet Cong Attack That Failed," *Department of State News Letter*, no. 85 (May 1968), 22.
2. Tran-van Dinh, "Six Hours That Changed the Vietnam Situation," *Christian Century*, LXXXV (March 6, 1968), 289.
3. Don Oberdorfer, *Tet!* (Garden City, N.Y.: Doubleday, 1971), p. 25.
4. Quoted *ibid.*, p. 33.
5. Frances FitzGerald, *Fire in the Lake* (New York: Vintage, 1972), p. 524.
6. Tran Van Tra, "Tet," in Jayne Werner and Luu Doan Huynh, eds., *The Vietnam War* (Armonk, N.Y.: Sharpe, 1992), p. 58.
7. William C. Westmoreland, *A Soldier Reports* (Garden City, N.Y.: Doubleday, 1976), p. 348.
8. Quoted in Townsend Hoopes, *The Limits of Intervention* (New York: McKay, 1969), p. 213.
9. Quoted in George Kahin and John Lewis, *The United States in Vietnam* (New York: Dell, 1969), p. 373.
10. Quoted in George A. Bailey and Lawrence W. Lichty, "Rough Justice on a Saigon Street," *Journalism Quarterly*, XLIX (Summer 1972), 222.
11. Quoted in *Newsweek*, LXXI (February 19, 1968), 24.
12. *Department of State Bulletin*, LVIII (February 26, 1968), 261.
13. Quoted in Philip B. Davidson, *Vietnam at War* (Novato, Calif.: Presidio Press, 1988), p. 486.
14. Tran Do quoted in Timothy J. Lomperis, *From People's War to People's Rule* (Chapel Hill: University of North Carolina Press, 1996), p. 338.
15. Quoted in George C. Herring, *LBJ and Vietnam* (Austin: University of Texas Press, 1994), p. 158.
16. Quoted in Robert Dallek, *Flawed Giant* (New York: Oxford University Press, 1998), p. 506.
17. McGeorge Bundy's notes of Wise Men's meeting, March 26, 1968, in David M. Barrett, ed., *Lyndon B. Johnson's Vietnam Papers* (Austin: University of Texas Press, 1998), p. 713.
18. Clark Clifford, *Counsel to the President* (New York: Random House, 1991), p. 494.
19. Quoted in Robert Buzzanco, *Masters of War* (New York: Cambridge University Press, 1996), p. 333; in Herring, *LBJ and Vietnam*, p. 160.
20. David M. Barrett, *Uncertain Warriors* (Lawrence: University Press of Kansas, 1993), p. 111.
21. *Public Papers, Johnson, 1968* (Washington, D.C.: Government Printing Office, 1970), p. 470.
22. Quoted in Christian G. Appy, *Working-Class War* (Chapel Hill: University of North Carolina Press, 1993), p. 208.
23. Archimedes Patti quoted in Stein Tönnesson, *The Vietnamese Revolution of 1945* (Newbury Park, Calif.: Sage, 1991), p. 311.
24. Quoted in David Marr, *Vietnam, 1945* (Berkeley: University of California Press, 1995), p. 289.
25. Quoted in Lloyd C. Gardner, *Approaching Vietnam* (New York: Norton, 1988), p. 65.
26. Quoted in Christopher Thorne, "Indochina and Anglo-American Relations, 1942–1945," *Pacific Historical Review*, XLIV (February 1976), 93.
27. Quoted in Richard H. Immerman, "Why and Why Not Vietnam," *New England Journal of History*, LII (April 1998), 25.

28. Quoted in George C. Herring, *America's Longest War* (New York: Knopf, 1996; 3rd ed.), p. 12.

29. Quoted in Archimedes L. A. Patti, *Why Vietnam?* (Berkeley: University of California Press, 1980), p. 203.

30. Dean Acheson in *Foreign Relations, 1950* (Washington, D.C.: Government Printing Office, 1976), *VI*, 692.

31. Quoted in Melanie Billings-Yun, *Decision Against War* (New York: Columbia University Press, 1988), p. 91.

32. Quoted in Herring, *America's Longest War*, p. 34.

33. Quoted *ibid.*, p. 41.

34. Quoted in John Lewis Gaddis, *We Now Know* (New York: Oxford University Press, 1997), p. 163.

35. Quoted in Marilyn Young, *The Vietnam Wars* (New York: Harper-Collins, 1991), p. 42.

36. Quoted in *New York Times, The Pentagon Papers* (New York: Bantam, 1971), p. 14.

37. Quoted in Robert J. McMahon, *The Limits of Empire* (New York: Columbia University Press, 1999), p. 67.

38. Chargé Robert McClintock in David Anderson, *Trapped by Success* (Columbia: University of Missouri Press, 1991), pp. 60–61.

39. Quoted in Robert D. Schulzinger, *A Time for War* (New York: Oxford University Press, 1997), p. 81.

40. Lansdale quoted in Anderson, *Trapped by Success*, p. 76; *Time* quoted in Michael H. Hunt, "East Asia and The American Century," *Diplomatic History*, *XXIII* (Spring 1999), 329.

41. Quoted *ibid.*, p. 207.

42. Quoted in Schulzinger, *Time for War*, p. 91.

43. Quoted in George W. Ball, *The Past Has Another Pattern* (New York: Norton, 1982), p. 364.

44. Quoted in Theodore C. Sorensen, *Kennedy* (New York: Harper and Row, 1965), p. 199.

45. *New York Times*, August 25, 1960.

46. Quoted in Robert D. Dean, "Masculinity as Ideology," *Diplomatic History*, *XXII* (Winter 1998), 29, 45, 46.

47. *Public Papers, Kennedy, 1962* (Washington, D.C.: Government Printing Office, 1963), p. 807.

48. Don Ferguson in Peter Joseph, *Good Times* (New York: Morrow, 1974), p. 4.

49. Quoted in Thomas G. Paterson, "Introduction," in Thomas G. Paterson, ed., *Kennedy's Quest for Victory* (New York: Oxford University Press, 1989), p. 14.

50. Arthur M. Schlesinger, Jr., *A Thousand Days* (Boston: Houghton Mifflin, 1965), p. 259.

51. James Barber, *The Presidential Character* (Englewood Cliffs, N.J.: Prentice-Hall, 1992; 4th ed.), p. 345.

52. Quoted in Michael Beschloss, *The Crisis Years* (New York: Harper-Collins, 1991), p. 48.

53. Oral History Interview by Chester Bowles, pp. 49, 90, John F. Kennedy Library, Boston.

54. Schlesinger, *Thousand Days*, p. 217.

55. *Public Papers, Kennedy, 1961* (Washington, D.C.: Government Printing Office, 1962), pp. 1–3.

56. Theodore H. White, "The Action Intellectuals," *Life, LXII* (June 1967), 43.

57. Quoted in David Halberstam, "The Programming of Robert McNamara," *Harper's, CCXLII* (February 1971), 62.

58. Quoted in Roger Hilsman, *To Move a Nation* (Garden City, N.Y.: Doubleday, 1967), p. 523.

59. Sorensen, *Kennedy*, p. 270.

60. "Memorandum of Conversation with President Johnson," by Max Frankel, July 8, 1965, Box 1, Arthur Krock Papers, Princeton University Library, Princeton, N.J.

61. Harvard Professor and Chester Cooper quoted in Kai Bird, *The Color of Truth* (New York: Simon and Schuster, 1998), pp. 190–191.

62. Quoted in Michael H. Hunt, *Lyndon Johnson's War* (New York: Hill & Wang, 1996), p. 48.

63. Quoted in Michael Mandelbaum, *The Nuclear Question* (New York: Cambridge University Press, 1979), p. 90.

64. Khrushchev quoted in Viktor Adamsky and Yuri Smirnov, "Moscow's Biggest Bomb," *Cold War International History Project Bulletin*, no. 4 (Fall 1994), 120.

65. Briefing Book, June 1961, Box 126, President's Office File, John F. Kennedy Papers, Kennedy Library.

66. Schlesinger, *Thousand Days*, p. 348.

67. Quoted in Vladislav M. Zubok, "Khrushchev and the Berlin Crisis," *Cold War International History Project, Working Paper no. 6* (May 1993), 20.

68. Quoted in Dean Rusk, *As I Saw It* (New York: Penguin, 1991), p. 227.

69. Quoted in Schlesinger, *Thousand Days*, p. 391.

70. James Reston quoted in James N. Giglio, *The Presidency of John F. Kennedy* (Lawrence: University Press of Kansas, 1991), p. 78.

71. *Public Papers, Kennedy, 1961*, pp. 534, 536.

72. "Khrushchev's Secret Speech on the Berlin Crisis," *Cold War International History Project Bulletin*, no. 2 (Fall 1993), 59.

73. Quoted in Beschloss, *Crisis Years*, p. 278.

74. Quoted in Frank Costigliola, "The Pursuit of Atlantic Community," in Paterson, *Kennedy's Quest*, p. 40.

75. Raymond L. Garthoff, "Berlin 1961," *Foreign Policy*, no. 84 (Fall 1991), 142.

76. Marcus G. Raskin and Bernard B. Fall, eds., *The Viet-Nam Reader* (New York: Vintage, 1967; rev. ed.), p. 113.

77. John F. Kennedy quoted in Robert J. McMahon, *The Cold War on the Periphery* (New York: Columbia University Press, 1994), p. 273.

78. Lawrence Fuchs quoted in Elizabeth A. Cobbs, "The Foreign Policy of the Peace Corps," *Diplomatic History, XX* (Winter 1996), 104.

79. Johnson quoted in Elizabeth Cobbs Hoffman, *All You Need Is Love* (Cambridge: Harvard University Press, 1998), p. 70.

80. Quoted in Frank Mankiewicz and Kirby Jones, *With Fidel* (New York: Ballantine, 1975), p. 175.

81. Quoted in Thomas Noer, "New Frontiers and Old Priorities in Africa," in Paterson, *Kennedy's Quest*, p. 262.

82. William Attwood, *The Reds and the Blacks* (New York: Harper and Row, 1967), p. 219.

83. Quoted in Stephen G. Rabe, *The Most Dangerous Area in the World* (Chapel Hill: University of North Carolina Press, 1999), p. 19.

84. Quoted in Jules Benjamin, *The United States and the Origins of the Cuban Revolution* (Princeton: Princeton University Press, 1990), p. 182.

85. Quoted in Thomas G. Paterson, *Contesting Castro* (New York: Oxford University Press, 1994), p. 242.

86. Roy R. Rubottom, Jr., in *Foreign Relations, 1958–1960, VI*, 656.

87. Quoted in Paterson, *Contesting*, p. 257.

88. Quoted in Piero Gleijeses, "Ships in the Night," *Journal of Latin American Studies, XXVII* (February 1995), 3.

89. Quoted in Stephen G. Rabe, *Eisenhower and Latin America* (Chapel Hill: University of North Carolina Press, 1988), p. 128.

90. Quoted in Anatoli I. Gribkov and William Y. Smith, *Operation Anadyr* (Chicago: Edition Q, 1994), p. 12.

91. Quoted in Schlesinger, *Thousand Days*, p. 251.

92. Quoted in Dean, "Masculinity," 48.

93. Quoted in Lucien S. Vandenbroucke, "The 'Confessions' of Allen Dulles," *Diplomatic History, VIII* (Fall 1984), 369.

94. Allen Dulles quoted in Lucien S. Vandenbroucke, *Perilous Options* (New York: Oxford University Press, 1993), p. 22.

95. Walt W. Rostow, *The Diffusion of Power* (New York: Macmillan, 1972), pp. 210–211.

96. Quoted in James G. Blight and Peter Kornbluh, eds., *Politics of Illusion* (Boulder, Colo.: Lynne Rienner, 1998), p. 150.

97. Richard Helms memorandum, January 30, 1962, *ibid.*, p. 247.

98. Quoted in *New York Times*, February 5, 1989.

99. Quoted in Mankiewicz and Jones, *With Fidel*, p. 130.

100. John Hughes, "The San Christobel Trapezoid," *Studies in Intelligence, XXXVI* (1992), 61.

101. Quoted in Ernest R. May and Philip D. Zelikow, eds., *The Kennedy Tapes* (Cambridge: Harvard University Press, 1997), p. 258.

102. Transcript, "Off-the-Record Meeting on Cuba," 11:50 A.M.–12:57 P.M., October 16, 1962, Presidential Recordings, Kennedy Library.

103. Maxwell Taylor quoted in J. Anthony Lukacs, "Class Reunion," *New York Times Magazine*, August 30, 1987, p. 58; Abram Chayes quoted in James A. Nathan, "The Heyday of the New Strategy," in Nathan, ed., *The Cuban Missile Crisis Revisited* (New York: St. Martin's Press, 1992), p. 24.

104. Quoted in May and Zelikow, *Kennedy Tapes*, p. 149.

105. Quoted in H. R. McMaster, *Dereliction of Duty* (New York: HarperCollins, 1997), p. 30.

106. *Public Papers, Kennedy, 1962*, p. 808.

107. Quoted in James T. Graham, "Kennedy, Cuba, and the Press," *Journalism History, XXIV* (Summer 1998), 64.

108. Transcript, "Cuban Missile Crisis Meetings," October 27, 1962, Presidential Recordings, Kennedy Library.

109. Quoted in Philip Nash, *The Other Missiles of October* (Chapel Hill: University of North Carolina Press, 1997), p. 151.

110. Anatoly Dobrynin cable to Soviet Foreign Ministry, October 27, 1962, *Cold War International History Project Bulletin*, no. 5 (Spring 1995), 79.

111. Quoted in Barton J. Bernstein, "Reconsidering the Missile Crisis," in Nathan, *Cuban Missile Crisis*, p. 100.

112. Chen Yi quoted in M. Y. Prozumenschikov, "The Sino-Indian Conflict, the Cuban Missile Crisis, and the Sino-Soviet Split," *Cold War International History Project Bulletin*, nos. 8–9 (Winter 1996/1997), 255.

113. Vassily Kuznetsov quoted in Vladislav Zubok and Constantine Pleshakov, *Inside the Kremlin's Cold War* (Cambridge: Harvard University Press, 1996), p. 266.

114. Quoted in Richard Ned Lebow and Janice Gross Stein, *We All Lost the Cold War* (Princeton: Princeton University Press, 1994), p. 110.

115. Aleksei Adzhubei quoting Khrushchev, *ibid.*, p. 145.

116. John Kenneth Galbraith, "The Plain Lessons of a Bad Decade," *Foreign Policy*, no. 1 (Winter 1970–1971), 32.

117. Quoted in McGeorge Bundy, *Danger and Survival* (New York: Random House, 1988), p. 426.

118. Dobrynin quoted in James G. Hershberg, "New Evidence on the Cuban Missile Crisis," *Cold War International History Project Bulletin*, nos. 8–9 (Winter 1996/1997), 273.

119. McGeorge Bundy quoted in Thomas Risse-Kappen, *Cooperation Among Democracies* (Princeton: Princeton University Press, 1995), p. 148.

120. McNamara and Bundy quoted in Nash, *Other Missiles*, p. 3.

121. Quoted in James Blight and David Welch, *On the Brink* (New York: Hill & Wang, 1989), p. 100; Marc Trachtenberg, "Commentary," *Diplomatic History, XIV* (Spring 1990), 242.

122. Quoted in Seymour Hersh, *The Other Side of Camelot* (Boston: Little, Brown, 1997), p. 383.

123. McGeorge Bundy quoted in Stephen G. Rabe, "The Caribbean Triangle," *Diplomatic History, XX* (Winter 1996), 77.

124. McMaster, *Dereliction*, p. 326.

125. Michael S. Sherry, *In the Shadow of War* (New Haven: Yale University Press, 1995), p. 243.

126. Walt W. Rostow, Memorandum, March 29, 1961, Box 193, National Security File, Kennedy Papers.

127. Eisenhower, *Waging Peace*, p. 607.

128. Quoted in Edmund F. Wehrle, "'A Good, Bad Deal,'" *Pacific Historical Review, LXVII* (April 1998), 353.

129. JCS quoted in Timothy N. Castle, *At War in the Shadow of Vietnam* (New York: Columbia University Press, 1993), p. 41.

130. Quoted in Wehrle, "'Good, Bad Deal,'" p. 349.

131. Quoted in Frank Costigliola, *France and the United States* (Boston: Twayne, 1992), p. 140; in David Halberstam, *The Best and the Brightest* (Greenwich, Conn.: Fawcett, 1973), p. 77.

132. Walt Rostow quoted in Hunt, *Johnson's War*, p. 58.

133. U.S. Senate, Foreign Relations Committee, *Foreign Assistance Act of 1968*, Part 1: *Vietnam* (Washington, D.C.: Government Printing Office, 1968), p. 218.

134. Charles Bartlett quoting Kennedy in Hersh, *Dark Side*, p. 418.

135. Quoted in Beschloss, *Crisis Years*, p. 651.

136. Quoted in Herring, *America's Longest War*, p. 111.

137. Quoted in McMahon, *Limits of Empire*, p. 111.

138. Quoted in Anatoly Dobrynin, *In Confidence* (New York: Random House, 1995), p. 174.

139. Quoted in Lloyd C. Gardner, *Pay Any Price* (Chicago: Ivan R. Dee, 1995), p. 197.

140. Quoted in Brian VanDeMark, *Into the Quagmire* (New York: Oxford University Press, 1991), p. 123.

141. Eric Goldman quoted in Nancy Bernkopf Tucker, "Lyndon Johnson," in Warren I. Cohen and Nancy Bernkopf Tucker, eds., *Lyndon Johnson Confronts the World* (New York: Cambridge University Press, 1994), p. 212.

142. Dobrynin, *In Confidence*, p. 120.

143. Ben Bradlee, *A Good Life* (New York: Simon & Schuster, 1995), p. 263.

144. Quoted in Douglas Little, "Crackpot Realists and Other Heroes," *Diplomatic History, XIII* (Winter 1989), 103.

145. Clifford, *Counsel*, p. 385.

146. Quoted in H. W. Brands, *The Wages of Globalism* (New York: Oxford University Press, 1995), p. 80.

147. Quoted in Hunt, *Johnson's War*, p. 72.

148. Quoted in Walter LaFeber, "Johnson, Vietnam, and Tocqueville," in Cohen and Tucker, *Johnson Confronts*, p. 50.

149. W. Michael Weis, *Cold Warriors & Coups D'État* (Albuquerque: University of New Mexico Press, 1993), p. 163.

150. Johnson telephone conversation, December 2, 1963, in Michael Beschloss, ed., *Taking Charge* (New York: Simon & Schuster, 1997), p. 87.

151. Jack Valenti quoted in Walter LaFeber, "Latin American Policy," in Robert A. Divine, ed., *The Johnson Years* (Lawrence: University Press of Kansas, 1987–1994; 3 vols.), I, 76.

152. Quoted in Randall Bennett Woods, *Fulbright* (New York: Cambridge University Press, 1995), p. 382.

153. Quoted in *Newsweek, LXV* (May 17, 1965), 52.

154. McGeorge Bundy quoted in Woods, *Fulbright*, p. 385; J. William Fulbright, *The Arrogance of Power* (New York: Vintage, 1966), pp. 91, 92.

155. Quoted in Kahin and Lewis, *U.S. and Vietnam*, p. 152.

156. Senator Richard Russell quoted in Michael D. Pearlman, *Warfighting and American Democracy* (Lawrence: University Press of

Kansas, 1999), p. 357; Lodge quoted in Gardner, *Pay Any Price*, p. 232.

157. Johnson telephone conversation, May 27, 1965, in Beschloss, *Taking Charge*, p. 370.

158. McGeorge Bundy in Summary Record of Meeting, June 10, 1964, in Barrett, *LBJ's Vietnam Papers*, p. 54.

159. Johnson telephone conversation, August 3, 1964, in Beschloss, *Taking Charge*, p. 493.

160. Quoted in Herring, *America's Longest War*, p. 134.

161. Quoted in George Kahin, *Intervention* (New York: Knopf, 1986), p. 223.

162. Quoted in Dallek, *Flawed Giant*, p. 155.

163. *Congressional Record*, CX (August 7, 1964), 18471.

164. Quoted in Stanley Karnow, *Vietnam* (New York: Viking, 1991; rev. ed.), p. 374.

165. Quoted in LeRoy Ashby and Rod Gramer, *Fighting the Odds: The Life of Frank Church* (Pullman: Washington State University Press, 1994), p. 199.

166. Quoted in Lewis Sorley, *Honorable Warrior: General Harold K. Johnson* (Lawrence: University Press of Kansas, 1998), p. 202.

167. Quoted in Jack Valenti, *A Very Human President* (New York: Norton, 1975), pp. 329, 334, 335.

168. Quoted in Herring, *LBJ and Vietnam*, p. 31.

169. Quoted in Dallek, *Flawed Giant*, p. 342.

170. McMaster, *Dereliction*, pp. 328, 330.

171. Quoted in George C. Herring, "The Reluctant Warrior," in David L. Anderson, ed., *Shadow on the White House* (Lawrence: University Press of Kansas, 1993), p. 93.

172. Quoted in James P. Harrison, "History's Heaviest Bombing," in Werner and Huynh, *Vietnam War*, p. 135.

173. Quoted in Eric M. Bergerud, *The Dynamics of Defeat* (Boulder, Colo.: Westview Press, 1991), p. 163.

174. Quoted in David L. DiLeo, *George Ball, Vietnam, and the Rethinking of Containment* (Chapel Hill: University of North Carolina Press, 1991), p. 170.

175. Quoted in Doris Kearns, *Lyndon Johnson and the American Dream* (New York: Harper and Row, 1976), p. 329.

176. Quoted in Buzzanco, *Masters*, p. 350.

177. Quoted in Jonathan Mirsky, "The Root of Resistance," *The Nation*, CCVII (August 5, 1968), 90.

178. Colin L. Powell, *My American Journey* (New York: Random House, 1995), p. 146.

179. Quoted in Karnow, *Vietnam*, p. 617.

180. Philip Caputo, *A Rumor of War* (New York: Ballantine, 1977), p. 100.

181. Nicholas Katzenbach quoted in Larry Berman, *Lyndon Johnson's War* (New York: Oxford University Press, 1989), pp. 106–107.

182. Quoted in Richard Dauer, "Great Expectations Unrealized: Chester Bowles and U.S. Cold War Policy, 1951–1969" (Ph.D. diss., University of Connecticut, 1998), p. 343.

183. Johnson telephone conversation, March 27, 1964, in Beschloss, *Taking Charge*, p. 298; quoted in LaFeber, "Johnson," in Cohen and Tucker, *Johnson Confronts*, p. 49.

184. Quoted in Stephen Ambrose, *Rise to Globalism* (Baltimore: Penguin, 1993; 7th ed.), pp. 201–202.

185. Melvin Small, *Covering Dissent* (New Brunswick, N.J.: Rutgers University Press, 1994), p. 163.

186. Quoted in Herring, *LBJ and Vietnam*, p. 37.

187. Barrett, *Uncertain Warriors*, p. 158.

188. Soviet Foreign Office quoted in Dobrynin, *In Confidence*, p. 157; quoted in Ivan V. Gaiduk, *The Soviet Union and the Vietnam War* (Chicago: Ivan R. Dee, 1996), p. 150.

189. Quoted in Donald F. Lach and Edmund S. Wehrle, *International Politics in East Asia* (New York: Praeger, 1975), p. 338.

CHAPTER

❖ 10 ❖

Détente and Disequilibrium, 1969–1977

Richard M. Nixon (1913–1994) and Zhou Enlai (1898–1976), 1972. *During his historic trip to China in February 1972, President Nixon met with the Chinese premier. Zhou asked at one point: "Can [the] U.S. control the 'wild horse' of Japan?" Nixon replied: "The United States can get out of Japanese waters, but others will still fish there"—a veiled reference to the Soviet Union. (Nixon Presidential Materials Project/National Archives)*

DIPLOMATIC CROSSROAD

Richard M. Nixon's Trip to China, 1972

The president's chief security officer aboard the aircraft radioed to the Beijing airport: "What about the crowd?" The answer came back: "There is no crowd." The disbelieving officer asked: "Did you say, 'No crowd'?"[1] Indeed, when President Richard M. Nixon's jet, the *Spirit of '76*, touched down that wintry morning of February 21, 1972, the reception was decidedly restrained. Apparently the Chinese wanted observers to think that the United States desired this dramatic meeting more eagerly than did the People's Republic of China (PRC). Cheering schoolchildren usually greeted visiting dignitaries, but "a vast silence" welcomed Nixon.[2]

At the foot of the stairs stood trim seventy-three-year-old Premier Zhou Enlai, a veteran communist who had served Chairman Mao Zedong as key administrator since the success of the Chinese Revolution in 1949. Nixon and Zhou formally shook hands—the very gesture that Secretary John Foster Dulles had spurned at Geneva in 1954. The television cameras whirred, sending back to the United States, via satellite, picture postcards of the historic encounter. Zhou and Nixon sped toward Beijing. Portraits of Mao and political signs hung everywhere. The Chinese had painted over one poster that read: "We Must Defeat the U.S. Aggressors and All Their Running Dogs."[3]

Nixon's "journey for peace" contrasted sharply with the previous quarter-century of no formal diplomatic relations between the two countries.[4] For years they had harangued each other as warmongers and had fought one another in Korea. The United States maintained close ties with the PRC's archenemy Jiang Jieshi in Taiwan, while China aided America's foe in Vietnam. Nixon and Zhou had not forgotten this history of hostility, but each now recognized that cooperation best served his own country's interests.

In 1969, newly inaugurated President Nixon had asked his assistant for national security affairs, Henry A. Kissinger, to review relations with China. When border fighting between the Soviet Union and China broke out that year, Nixon told his cabinet: "The worst thing that could happen to us would be for the Soviet Union to gobble up Red China."[5] He soon sent signals to Beijing by scaling back U.S. Seventh Fleet operations in the Taiwan Strait and relaxing trade restrictions with China. The Chinese picked up the signals. Early in 1970 PRC diplomats once again began meeting with U.S. officials in Warsaw—talks that China had suspended two years earlier as a protest against American warfare in Vietnam. In December, Mao told the visiting American journalist Edgar Snow that he would welcome Nixon to China, "either as a tourist or as President."[6] Nixon responded by lifting restrictions against Americans wanting to travel to the People's Republic. In April 1971 a U.S. table tennis team competing in Japan accepted an invitation to visit China. Quips about "Ping-Pong diplomacy" and "the Ping heard round the world" did not detract from the symbolic significance of the trip.[7]

Marco Polo. The political cartoonist Ray Osrin portrayed two reasons for the Nixon journey to China, 1972. Kissinger's secret 1971 trip to China was code-named "Polo." (Ray Osrin in *The Cleveland Plain Dealer*)

Using U.S. ally Pakistan as an intermediary, Kissinger made plans to go to China himself. In Islamabad (the Pakistani capital) in early July, he secretly boarded a plane for Beijing. Kissinger soon reported that "the process we have now started will send enormous shock waves around the world."[8] On July 15, President Nixon made the startling announcement that he would go to China to "seek the normalization of relations."[9]

Renewed Sino-American relations seemed to promise advantages. Because of the gaping Sino-Soviet split, American recognition of the People's Republic would keep Moscow wondering what Washington intended. "We're using the Chinese thaw to get the Russians shook," Nixon told an aide.[10] With the U.S. economy sagging, moreover, the legendary China market once again loomed large in American imaginations. Nuclear arms race questions also shaped U.S. motives. Having joined the nuclear club in 1964, China had rejected the 1968 Treaty on the Nonproliferation of Nuclear Weapons, and Washington sought Beijing's adherence. Then, too, U.S. recognition of China might influence Beijing to press North Vietnam to accept a political settlement of the Vietnam War.

The China trip also promised Nixon political profits at home. An antiwar Democrat, Senator George McGovern, had launched a campaign against the Nixon administration's continued intervention in Vietnam, and in March, New Hampshire would hold the first presidential primary of 1972. Even though "the libs [liberals] will try to piss on it as an election year gimmick," Kissinger frankly remarked that Nixon's "political ass was on the line."[11] Liberal-left Americans had advocated relations with China for years, and Democrats soon applauded the Nixon journey. At the same time, the right wing of the Republican party could hardly charge that Nixon, a proven anticommunist, had turned soft on communism. Finally, the China journey was central to the general Nixon-Kissinger policy of "détente"—the relaxation of international tensions with communist nations to protect American interests. "We needed China to enhance the flexibility of our diplomacy," said Kissinger.[12]

The Chinese, still reeling from their destructive internal Cultural Revolution, had their own reasons for inviting Nixon. The United States no longer ranked as their number one threat. The Soviet Union did. Military skirmishes in 1969 on the shared 4,150-mile border caused many Chinese, recalling the Soviet invasion of Czechoslovakia in 1968, to fear a Soviet attack on China. The Soviet Union constructed an air base in Mongolia; the Chinese dug bomb shelters and tunnel networks. Resuming Sino-American ties, then, might deter the "polar bear" to the north.[13] In classic Chinese practice, Beijing hoped to play one barbarian against the other. "We can work together to commonly deal with a bastard," Mao told Kissinger.[14] China also feared a revived Japan, and a Sino-American rapprochement might keep Tokyo off guard and cautious. Or it might, as actually happened, lead to the opening of Sino-Japanese relations, thereby strengthening China against the Soviet Union. Finally, China wanted trade and a reduced U.S. commitment to Taiwan.

On the flight to China, Nixon studied notebooks about Chinese politics, culture, and diplomacy. Included were CIA analyses of Mao and Zhou and "talking points" that Nixon committed to memory. Joining the presidential party of thirty-seven—which included Secretary of State William Rogers, upstaged as always by Kissinger—was a press corps of eighty-seven, heavy with television news personalities. Telling CBS reporter Dan Rather that there would be "tough, hard bargaining between people who have very great differences," the president carefully staged his pageant for the prime-time screens back home.[15]

Nixon soon met Chairman Mao. Seated in overstuffed chairs, Nixon, Kissinger, Mao, and Zhou talked warmly for about an hour. Tang Wensheng, a Brooklyn-born Radcliffe graduate who had become a Chinese citizen, served as interpreter. Seventy-eight-year-old Mao, although suffering from congestive heart disease, remained an imposing figure, esteemed by the Chinese as the leader of the Long March and father of the People's Republic. Mao smiled and bantered. "Your book, *Six Crises,* is not a bad book," Mao commented. After the translation of that lukewarm review of his prepresidential memoirs, Nixon looked at Zhou and said: "He reads too much."[16] Born into a well-to-do mandarin family, Zhou spoke English, Russian, French, and Japanese as well as his native Chinese. A skillful negotiator with a sharp memory, Zhou shunned the limelight. U.S. diplomats contrasted his quiet, patient style with the blunt, haggling manner of Soviet diplomats.

That evening, in the Great Hall of the People, Zhou hosted a banquet for 800 guests. Sipping glasses of *mao tai,* a 150-proof rice liquor "roughly equivalent to lawn mower fuel," Americans and Chinese generously toasted one another.[17] Zhou had the Chinese military band play "America the Beautiful"—as "a toast to your next Inaugural," he whispered to Nixon.[18] Then, tearing a page from Chinese communist history, Nixon called for a "long march together." And he even quoted Mao himself: "Seize the day, seize the hour. This is the hour."[19] "I like to deal with rightists," said Mao privately of Nixon. "They say what they really think—not like the leftists, who say one thing and mean another."[20]

On February 22, Nixon and Zhou conferred while journalists filed reports on the Chinese lifestyle—clean streets, gauze masks to prevent infectious diseases, acupuncture techniques for surgery, anti-imperialist banners, expertise in table tennis, regimented schools, puritanical social habits, improved nutrition and health since 1949, Mao's photographs plastered on walls, bicycles, the monotony of blue dress. After watching Chinese bank clerks use an abacus to exchange dollars "in almost unbelievable quick time," a Nixon aide noted: "The total honesty is astonishing."[21] After years of thinking the Chinese a bestial enemy, Americans now found them loving and suffering like the rest of humanity. Whereas in the 1960s Americans used words such as "ignorant, warlike, treacherous, and sly" to describe the "Red Chinese," after the 1972 trip they described them as "hard-working, intelligent, progressive, artistic, and practical."[22]

After late-night social events, an exhausted Kissinger helped fashion language for a joint communiqué. Issued on February 27, the document followed Zhou's formula of "seeking common ground while reserving differences."[23] Affirming existing ties with South Korea and Japan, Nixon assured his hosts that a continued U.S. military presence in Asia was "China's [best] hope for Jap restraint."[24] The Americans then stated their opposition to "outside pressure or intervention" in Asia—meaning Vietnam. The Chinese declared that they would continue to support "the struggles of all oppressed people" against large nations that attempt to "bully" the small. All foreign troops should withdraw from Asia, especially Vietnam. As for Taiwan, which the United States still recognized as the official government of China, the Chinese part of the communiqué admonished the United States to remove its military forces from the island. There was only one China. Having promised the Chinese Nationalists that "I will never sell you down the river," Nixon equivocated, calling for a "peaceful settlement of the Taiwan question by the Chinese themselves."[25] Both parties agreed, however, that "neither should seek hegemony in the Asia-Pacific region and each is opposed to efforts by any other country or group of countries to establish such hegemony"—a slap at the Soviet Union. Finally, both sides appealed for increased cultural and commercial contacts.[26]

Diplomacy done, on the seventh day of his trip, February 28, the president bade farewell at Shanghai and proclaimed that "this was the week that changed the world."[27] Nixon had rushed to judgment.

Nixon, Kissinger, and Their Critics

Nixon and Kissinger, quite different individuals who shared basic assumptions about U.S. foreign relations, orchestrated this surprising turnabout in Sino-American relations. Richard Milhous Nixon, the grocer's son from Whittier, California, relished the big play in politics; his "biggest asset," one scholar notes, was "his appreciation, abstract but keen, of the need and means to change course."[28] Nixon also wanted the Soviets and North Vietnamese to think him irrational and unpredictable. This self-professed "madman theory" would supposedly deter adversaries or cause them to settle on American terms.[29] A secretive, suspicious man,

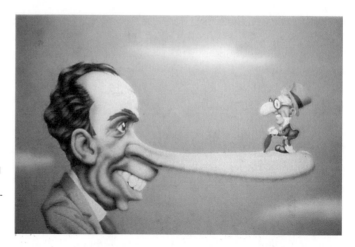

Pinocchio and Jiminy Cricket. "A two-fisted, bare-faced liar"—so Republican Senator Barry Goldwater described Nixon before the Watergate crisis forced him from office. Using characters from the popular story of Pinocchio, the cartoonist Robert Grossman depicts Nixon as the untruthful youngster and Henry A. Kissinger as his faithful adviser. (© Robert Grossman)

Nixon "could forgive and even embrace his enemies abroad," one biographer writes, but he "could not . . . forgive his enemies at home."[30] He became convinced that the news media schemed to "get" him, and he had such scorn for the State Department that he offered ambassadorships to campaign contributors willing to pay "at least $250,000."[31]

His administration guarded itself against its critics through secrecy and executive crimes and corrupt political practices later known collectively as Watergate. Because he wanted documentation for his memoirs and to protect himself against misinformation, Nixon secretly recorded conversations in the White House. When made public by court order, the tapes inspired an impeachment process that Nixon himself, caught in lies, terminated by resigning from the presidency on August 8, 1974, thereby elevating Vice President Gerald Ford to the White House. Exposure of criminality such as the burglary of Democratic party headquarters and the payment of hush money weakened the executive branch in its ongoing struggle with Congress over foreign policy. Watergate also caused bewilderment abroad, as Moscow "did not (or would not) understand how the president of the United States could be prosecuted for what it viewed as a 'small matter.'" Not until the "last moment," recalled the Soviet ambassador, did the Kremlin grasp that "Nixon could be forced to resign."[32]

After Nixon's ignoble departure, Henry A. Kissinger stayed on. Presidential assistant for national security affairs (1969–1976) and secretary of state (1973–1977), Kissinger thought Nixon an "egomaniac" apparently "obsessed by the fear that he was not receiving adequate credit" for foreign-policy triumphs such as the change in China policy.[33] An ambitious political scientist of German-Jewish ancestry, Kissinger had escaped from Nazism in 1938. Reflective, witty, energetic, persistent, and vain, "Henry the Navigator" became one of the most traveled diplomats in history. He reveled in personal diplomacy, in the give-and-take, the manipulation of power and people. His "devilish nimbleness" and evident rapport with people of different cultures brought him negotiating successes.[34] As the nation's principal diplomatic leader in the 1969–1977 period, Kissinger managed an impressive number of roles: theorist, policymaker, negotiator, presidential adviser, bureaucratic in-

Makers of American Foreign Relations, 1969–1977

Presidents	Secretaries of State
Richard M. Nixon, 1969–1974	William P. Rogers, 1969–1973
Gerald Ford, 1974–1977	Henry A. Kissinger, 1973–1977

fighter, and public spokesperson. He and Nixon agreed early that they would make policy in the White House, often sidestepping the foreign-affairs bureaucracy. Kissinger used private, secret "back channels" to communicate with foreign governments. William P. Rogers served as a loyal secretary of state until 1973, but Nixon granted him little authority. Resenting its exclusion from policymaking, Congress reasserted its prerogatives by passing, over Nixon's veto, the War Powers Resolution (1973): The president could commit American troops abroad for no more than sixty days, and after that period he had to obtain congressional approval. Congress also vexed Kissinger by cutting foreign aid to Turkey, Cambodia, South Vietnam, and Angola. Without Watergate and without congressional interference, Kissinger lamented, he could have accomplished so much more. He nonetheless shared with North Vietnamese negotiator Le Duc Tho the Nobel Peace Prize in 1973.

"Some Chicken, Some Egg."   Henry A. Kissinger (b.1923) received his doctorate in 1954 from Harvard, where he taught until Nixon appointed him national security affairs adviser in 1969. An architect of détente, Kissinger also undertook extensive travel to trouble spots such as the Middle East and Africa to conduct personal negotiations. Critics on the left compared him to "Dr. Strangelove," the fictional Germanic presidential adviser, played by Peter Sellers in the movie of that name, who was so deranged that he welcomed a nuclear holocaust. Critics on the right thought Kissinger too conciliatory to the communists. (*The Economist,* London, 1975)

"Inconsiderate of his staff, intolerant, often contemptuous of less brilliant but more practical men," Kissinger nonetheless remained a popular figure.[35] He charmed journalists and leaked secret information to them to generate favorable newspaper stories. A self-proclaimed "swinger" prior to his 1974 marriage, Kissinger once accused Anne Armstrong, the first U.S. woman ambassador to Britain, of crying when he excluded her from negotiations. "I might have bitten him," recalled Armstrong, "but I wasn't going to cry."[36] He once boasted to an interviewer: "I've always acted alone. . . . Americans admire the cowboy leading the caravan alone astride his horse."[37] Soviet foreign minister Andrei Gromyko thought him "slippery as a snake."[38]

Kissinger's critics rarely underestimated him. They questioned the secrecy that surrounded foreign relations. When academicians, business executives, and lawyers, many of whom wrote for the prestigious journal *Foreign Affairs,* became disenchanted, Kissinger exploded: "What the hell is an Establishment for, if it's not to support the President?"[39] Critics argued that Kissinger followed the ruthless maxim that the ends justify the means: He wiretapped aides and journalists; he defended the president in the lowest days of Watergate; he relied recklessly on huge arms sales; he sponsored CIA plots abroad that held America up to ridicule for advocating democracy but undermining it; and he approved the deadly bombing of the peoples of Southeast Asia. Accused of first aiding and then abandoning Kurdish rebels in Iraq (thousands of whom later died at the hands of Iraqi dictator Saddam Hussein), Kissinger coldly replied that "one must not confuse the intelligence business with missionary work."[40] The veteran diplomat George Ball noted that Kissinger's "tactical virtuosity" and "adroit manipulation" violated "a set of standards widely regarded as equitable."[41]

Kissinger and Nixon considered themselves pragmatists, not ideologues. "[Woodrow] Wilson had the greatest vision of America's world role," the president once remarked. "But he wasn't practical enough."[42] Kissinger sought to purge "sentimentality" from U.S. foreign relations.[43] The term that most generally described the thrust of the Nixon-Kissinger diplomacy was "détente": limited cooperation with the Soviet Union and the People's Republic of China within a general environment of rivalry. Détente became a means, a process, a climate in which to reduce international tensions and sustain U.S. leadership in world politics. Détente was supposed to produce a geopolitical balance of power, or "equilibrium," by containing the Soviet Union and China and curbing radical revolution.[44] To Nixon, the world divided into roughly five power centers. Under détente, each great center had the responsibility to keep order among smaller states and clients in its region and to refrain from intervening in another's sphere. "It will be a safer world," Nixon explained, "if we have a stronger, healthy United States, [Western] Europe, Soviet Union, Japan, and China, each balancing the other, not playing one against the other, an even balance."[45]

Nixon and Kissinger saw Soviet-American competition as the primary element in world affairs. They understood that by 1970 the Soviet Union had achieved nuclear parity or equality with the United States, that the Soviets suffered severe internal economic problems and needed outside help, that the Sino-Soviet split had widened, and that world power (capital and weaponry) had become diffused as nations had recovered from World War II and colonies had broken away from empires. Recognizing that Washington could not "conceive *all* the plans, design *all* the programs, execute *all* the decisions," the duo sought to move the United States from containment through confrontation to containment through negotiation.[46]

Détente, SALT, and the Nuclear Arms Race

The Nixon administration emphasized the triangular relationship formed by the Soviet Union, China, and the United States and attempted to play the two communist states off against one another, to keep one worrying about what the United States was doing with the other. For the Soviets there would be both incentives (capital and trade) to encourage restraint, and penalties (large arms sales to Soviet adversaries and closer ties to China) to punish unacceptable behavior.

The new approach to the major communist countries made sense to European allies who abhorred the U.S. "obsession with Southeast Asia."[47] Moscow and Beijing might help the United States extricate itself from war in Vietnam. The Cold War was also costing too much; détente supposedly offered a cheaper way of pursuing containment by reducing the necessity for interventions, spiraling military expenditures, and new nuclear weapons systems. The Nixon administration cut the armed forces from 3.5 million in 1968 to 2.3 million in 1973, ended the draft, and in 1972 negotiated a strategic arms limitation treaty. At a time when U.S. foreign trade needed a boost to eliminate a billion-dollar deficit in the balance of payments, détente conjured up images of expanded markets. Massive grain shipments flowed to the Soviet Union—in 1972, 25 percent of the American wheat crop—and corporations such as Pepsi-Cola and Chase Manhattan Bank started operations in the USSR. U.S. exports to the Soviet Union reached $2.3 billion in 1976. Businesses also revived the great China market dream.

Nixon-Kissinger grand strategy rested on some questionable assumptions. It overestimated the usefulness of China as a check on Moscow. It assumed wrongly that the Soviets could manage their "friends" in North Vietnam or India or the Middle East and that great-power cooperation could calm Third World problems. Still viewing small states as proxies of the great powers, the Nixon administration paid too little attention to the local sources of disputes and the fierce independence of nationalist and neutralist governments. Kissinger spent much of his time trying to keep détente glued together against the backdrop of violent conflicts in Asia, Africa, and the Middle East, and economic challenges from the Organization of Petroleum Exporting Countries (OPEC). Even America's friends caused difficulty: Iran insisted on huge arms shipments but raised oil prices, threatening the U.S. economy; Saudi Arabia demanded sophisticated weaponry but refused to help resolve the Arab-Israeli conflict.

Détente also ran afoul of domestic dissenters. In 1974 conservatives and liberals in Congress cooperated to deny most-favored-nation trade status to the Soviet Union until it permitted Jewish emigration. Americans of Eastern European descent berated détente as sellout—an abandonment of their homelands to Soviet domination. Liberals criticized Kissinger's arrogant presumption of superpower domination and his tolerance of authoritarian regimes that trampled on human

Beijing Ball Park. This American magazine advertisement, titled "Yankees come here," appeared after Nixon's trip. It read: "The way things are going in China, hot dogs will be sold right along with egg rolls." Mao, of course, never donned a baseball uniform or blasted a home run over the Great Wall, but Sino-American détente inspired exaggerations like this. (Lucy Gould, *Parade.* Courtesy of Frankfurt Communications, Inc., New York)

rights. The Nixon and Ford administrations contradicted themselves, for example, by appealing for arms control while they broke records for arms sales abroad ($10 billion in 1976 alone). Hard-line anticommunists labeled Kissinger an appeaser who conceded the communists too much and who squandered U.S. supremacy in the international system. By 1976 the secretary of state bemoaned that "the principal danger we face is our own domestic divisions."[48]

The Nixon administration nonetheless claimed diplomatic triumphs. The opening to China ranked highest. The turnaround helped thwart reconciliation between the two communist giants. It tied down several Soviet military divisions in Asia—away from NATO. It spawned new ties between Japan and China that contributed to Asian stability. And it nurtured a promising trading partnership. In 1973 large companies such as Boeing, Radio Corporation of America, and Monsanto Chemical signed contracts with the Chinese. Sino-American trade began to climb, reaching $700 million in 1973. Also, cultural exchanges and travel between the once-distant nations reduced mutual ignorance. In 1973 Washington and Beijing exchanged "Liaison Offices" or mini-embassies. Formal diplomatic relations had to wait until 1979, after Watergate, Nixon's resignation, the 1976 presidential election, the deaths of Mao and Zhou, and new political alignments within China.

The Sino-American rapprochement did have some tragic side effects. In 1971 the Bengalis of East Pakistan rebelled against the military dictatorship of (West) Pakistan and declared the independent nation of Bangladesh. The Pakistani government attempted to crush the revolution and carried out a slaughter that U.S. officials at the scene called genocide. India, which had just signed a treaty of friendship with the Soviet Union, intervened on behalf of the rebels. The White House, against considerable State Department objection, ordered a "tilt" in favor of Pakistan.[49] As an ally, Pakistan had granted the United States bases for U-2 flights over the Soviet Union and intelligence-gathering posts to monitor Soviet nuclear testing. American weapons soon flowed to Pakistan, foreign aid to India stopped, and a naval task force steamed into the Bay of Bengal without specific orders. "We can't allow a friend of ours and China's [Pakistan] to get screwed in a conflict with a friend of Russia's [India]," Kissinger fumed.[50] Indeed, the White House took a global rather than regional view of the crisis and saw India acting as Moscow's surrogate. But India never attacked West Pakistan, and the Soviet Union never encouraged it to attack. Pakistan, India, China, and the Soviet Union—*before* Kissinger's "frenetic crisis fever, histrionic signals, . . . and the meanderings of the American fleet"—all had indicated support for an agreement that matched the outcome: an end to hostilities and independence for Bangladesh.[51]

Despite blunt exchanges over the hot line during the Indo-Pakistani conflict, détente remained U.S. policy. The president and his national security affairs adviser traveled to the Soviet capital in May 1972 for a productive summit meeting. "My reputation is one of being a very hard-line, cold-war-oriented, anti-communist," Nixon told President Leonid Brezhnev, but Nixon now believed that capitalism and communism could "live together and work together."[52] They struck agreements on cooperation in space exploration (culminating in a joint space venture in 1975) and trade (large grain sales soon followed). The leaders also discussed Vietnam and concluded that small nations should not disrupt détente. Only a few weeks earlier, when Nixon had escalated the bombing of North Vietnam, he feared that an angry Moscow might cancel the summit. The Soviets did not; to them détente came first.

The summit conferees concentrated on the Strategic Arms Limitation Talks (SALT) agreements. When the Nixon administration entered office, it inherited a legacy of doctrines and missiles that defined U.S. nuclear strategy. (See glossary, p. 373.) In the 1960s, the doctrine of "massive retaliation" evolved into the concept of "mutual assured destruction," or MAD. MAD's viability depended on each side's "second-strike capability": the capacity to absorb a first strike and still destroy the attacker with a retaliatory or second strike. By 1969 American strategists sought a superiority of forces through the triad: land-based intercontinental ballistic missiles (ICBMs), long-range B-52 bombers, and submarine-launched ballistic missiles (SLBMs), all armed with nuclear weapons. To help guarantee superiority, the United States had also begun to flight-test the "multiple independently targetable reentry vehicle" (MIRV). Finally, Nixon inherited initial planning for an "antiballistic missile" (ABM) system to defend cities and ICBMs vulnerable to Soviet attack. Because ABMs theoretically protected offensive weapons from attack, critics feared that the ABM would stimulate the Soviets to build more missiles to overwhelm the ABM protection, thus further accelerating the nuclear arms race.

By 1968 Washington had deployed 1,054 ICBMs to the Soviets' 858; the United States also led in SLBMs 656 to 121, and in long-range bombers 545 to 155. The United States ranked first in total nuclear warheads, about 4,200 to 1,100, and in the accuracy of its weapons systems. Yet U.S. officials knew that the Soviets were constructing new missiles, submarines, and bombers at a pace that would soon give the Soviets nuclear parity with the United States. The two great nuclear powers had become "fencers on a tightrope: each facing the other, weapon in hand, balancing precariously; neither willing . . . to thrust decisively because such a thrust would topple them both, attacker and victim, to mutual disaster."[53]

President Nixon soon abandoned the untenable doctrine of superiority and accepted parity of forces with the Soviet Union. Still, he decided to phase in the ABM system. Nixon also ordered the installations of MIRVs. Thus the United States could enter the SALT talks, he said, from a position of strength.

The first SALT talks began in Helsinki in November 1969 and alternated between that city and Vienna until 1972. SALT-I culminated on May 26, 1972, at the Moscow summit with two agreements. The first, a treaty, limited the deployment of ABMs for each nation to two sites. In essence the accord sustained the MAD doctrine, because it left urban centers in both countries vulnerable. The other accord, an interim agreement on strategic offensive arms, froze the existing number of ICBMs already deployed or in construction. At the time, the Soviet Union led 1,607 to 1,054. The interim agreements also froze SLBMs at 740 for the USSR and 656 for the United States. SALT-I did not limit the hydra-headed MIRVs, thus leaving the United States superior in deliverable warheads, 5,700 to 2,500. Nixon and Kissinger underestimated the speed with which the Soviets would deploy their own MIRVs on heavier missiles, and by not seeking a ban on MIRVs, which the Pentagon regarded as America's technological "trump card," they rendered American ICBMs theoretically vulnerable to a first strike.[54] After joking, "What are 3,000 MIRVs among friends," Kissinger later regretted that he had not "thought through the implications of a MIRVed world more thoughtfully."[55] Nor did the agreement restrict long-range bombers, in which the United States held a 450 to 200 advantage. Finally, SALT-I did not prohibit the development of new weapons. The United States, for example, moved ahead on the Trident submarine (to replace the Polaris-Poseidon fleet), the B-1 bomber (to replace the B-52), and the cruise missile. Indeed, as Kissinger remarked: "The way to use this freeze is for us to catch up."[56]

Still, SALT-I did begin frank strategic arms talks and placed limits on specified nuclear weapons. In August 1972, the Senate passed the ABM treaty by an 88 to 2 vote; a joint congressional resolution later endorsed the interim agreement. Détente's reputation soared. Conservative critics charged, however, that despite possessing more nuclear warheads, the United States still lagged behind the Soviet Union in delivery vehicles (ICBMs, SLBMs, and strategic bombers). "What in the name of God is strategic superiority?" Kissinger challenged his detractors. "What do you do with it?"[57]

Negotiations on SALT-II opened in late 1972, but progress came slowly. At Vladivostok, in November 1974, Presidents Ford and Brezhnev initialed a set of

The Nuclear Arms Race: A Glossary

Anti-ballistic missile (ABM):   A defensive missile designed to destroy an incoming enemy ballistic missile before its warhead reaches its target.

Ballistic missile: A rocket-propelled missile that leaves the atmosphere and returns to earth in a free fall.

Cruise missile: A guided missile that flies to its target within the earth's atmosphere, close to the surface. The cruise missile can carry a nuclear warhead and can be launched from the air, land, or sea.

Delivery vehicle: A missile or strategic bomber that delivers a warhead to its target.

Deployment: Installing weapons, making them ready for action.

First strike: An initial nuclear attack by one country intended to destroy an adversary's strategic nuclear forces.

Intercontinental ballistic missile (ICBM):   A land-based missile capable of traveling more than 3,000 nautical miles to deliver one or more warheads.

Intermediate-range nuclear forces (INF):   Sometimes called theater nuclear forces, these weapons have a range of about 3,000 miles.

Missile experimental (MX):   An American ICBM capable of carrying as many as ten MIRVs.

Multiple independently targetable reentry vehicle (MIRV):   A vehicle loaded with a warhead and mounted, along with similar vehicles, on one ballistic missile. Once separated from the missile, each MIRV can be directed against a different target.

Mutual assured destruction (MAD):   The ability of both the United States and the Soviet Union to inflict damage so severe that neither is willing to initiate a nuclear attack.

Neutron bomb: An "enhanced radiation weapon," this nuclear bomb is designed primarily to kill people and to inflict less damage on buildings than other bombs.

Nuclear freeze: The immediate halt to the development, production, transfer, and deployment of nuclear weapons.

Second strike: A retaliatory nuclear attack launched after being hit by an opponent's first strike.

Strategic Defense Initiative (SDI):   Popularly known as "Star Wars," SDI was President Ronald Reagan's 1983 proposal to build a space-based, defensive system that could establish a protective shield over the United States and its allies with the capability to shoot down incoming ballistic missiles.

Strategic weapons or arms: Long-range weapons capable of hitting an adversary's territory. ICBMs, SLBMs, and strategic bombers are so classified.

Submarine-launched ballistic missile (SLBM):   A ballistic missile carried in and launched from a submarine.

Surface-to-air missile (SAM):   A missile launched from the earth's surface for the purpose of knocking down an adversary's airplanes.

Tactical nuclear weapons: Low-yield nuclear weapons for battlefield use.

Triad: The three-part structure of American strategic forces (ICBMs, SLBMs, and strategic bombers).

Warhead: The part of a missile that contains the nuclear explosive intended to inflict damage.

principles to guide the talks. They agreed, first, to place a ceiling of 2,400 on the total number of delivery vehicles permitted each side. They agreed, second, that each side could equip no more than 1,320 missiles with MIRVs. Critics noted that the numerical ceilings actually projected higher levels than either side had reached.

After 1974 the SALT-II talks bogged down over which types of weapons should count in the 2,400 ceiling. The United States insisted that the new Soviet bomber, the Backfire, be included, and the Soviet Union demanded inclusion of the U.S. cruise missile. Neither Moscow nor Washington yielded before 1977, the year the SALT-I agreements expired. By then the United States wielded 8,500 warheads, compared with 5,700 in 1972; comparable Soviet figures equaled 4,000 and 2,500. Total strategic delivery vehicles by 1978 numbered 2,059 for the United States and 2,440 for the Soviet Union. Détente had not checked the nuclear arms race.

In Europe, however, détente worked to ease tensions. Willy Brandt, the West German chancellor, pursued a policy of *Ostpolitik* to remove the two Germanies from great-power competition. A West German–Soviet treaty of August 1970 identified détente as the goal of both countries and recognized the existence of two Germanies. A few months later Brandt signed an agreement with Poland that confirmed the latter's postwar absorption of German territory to the Oder-Neisse line. Then, in June 1972, the four powers occupying Berlin signed an agreement wherein the Soviet Union guaranteed Western access to the city and relaxed restrictions on travel between the two Berlins. Finally, in December 1972, the two Germanies themselves initialed a treaty that provided for the exchange of diplomatic representatives and membership in the United Nations for both (effected in 1973). European East-West trade boomed, with the West German economy the chief beneficiary.

At the Conference on Security and Cooperation in Helsinki, Finland, in summer 1975, thirty-five nations assembled in what some observers called the peace conference that officially ended World War II. The delegates accepted the permanence of existing European boundaries, including adjustments made in Germany and Eastern Europe three decades earlier. The conferees pledged themselves to détente and endorsed human rights for all Europeans. Although many Americans greeted this endorsement with skepticism, dozens of "Helsinki groups" sprang up to press communist governments to honor the pledge about human rights. Such groups included Charter 77, headed by Václav Havel in Czechoslovakia, and Solidarity, led by Lech Walesa in Poland. Instead of the "consolidation of the postwar order that Moscow had so long desired," a Kissinger aide later noted, "the political status quo in Eastern Europe began to unravel."[58] In the short run, however, the Kremlin arrested Soviet intellectuals who demanded freedom of speech. When the dissident writer Aleksandr Solzhenitsyn, whose *Gulag Archipelago* (1974) described and condemned Soviet oppression, asked to visit the White House, President Ford turned down the "goddamned horse's ass" because he did not want to jeopardize progress toward SALT-II.[59]

Arab-Israeli War and the Mideast Arms Race

The Nixon Doctrine, announced in July 1969, declared that henceforth the United States would supply military and economic assistance but not soldiers to help na-

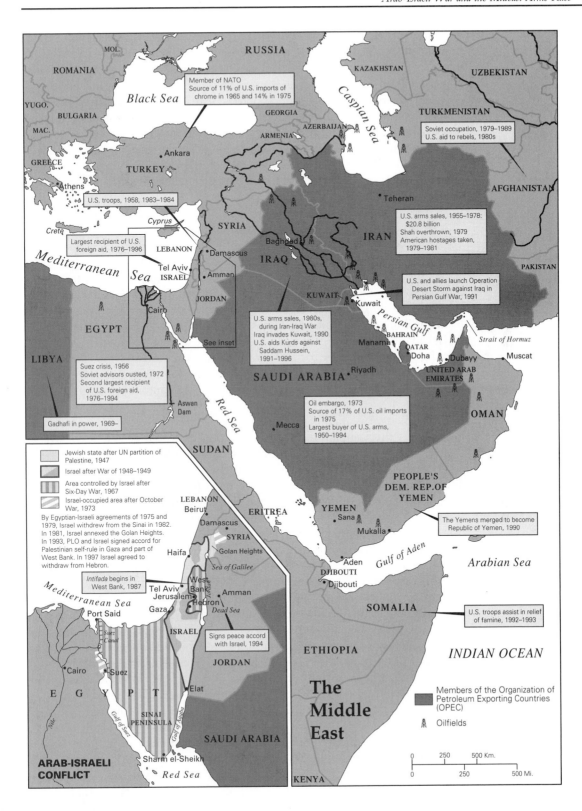

The Middle East
RUSSIA
MOL.
ROMANIA
KAZAKHSTAN
UZBEKISTAN
Member of NATO
Source of 11% of U.S. imports of chrome in 1965 and 14% in 1975
Black Sea
Caspian Sea
YUGO.
BULGARIA
GEORGIA
TURKMENISTAN
MAC.
AZERBAIJAN
ARMENIA
Soviet occupation, 1979–1989
U.S. aid to rebels, 1980s
Ankara
GREECE
TURKEY
Athens
AFGHANISTAN
Teheran
U.S. troops, 1958, 1983–1984
Cyprus
Crete
SYRIA
U.S. arms sales, 1955–1978: $20.8 billion
Shah overthrown, 1979
American hostages taken, 1979–1981
IRAN
Largest recipient of U.S. foreign aid, 1976–1996
Baghdad
LEBANON
Damascus
IRAQ
Mediterranean Sea
Tel Aviv
ISRAEL
Amman
PAKISTAN
U.S. and allies launch Operation Desert Storm against Iraq in Persian Gulf War, 1991
KUWAIT
Kuwait
JORDAN
Cairo
Persian Gulf
EGYPT
U.S. arms sales, 1980s, during Iran-Iraq War
Iraq invades Kuwait, 1990
U.S. aids Kurds against Saddam Hussein, 1991–1996
BAHRAIN
Strait of Hormuz
See inset
Manama
QATAR
Doha
Dubayy
Muscat
LIBYA
Suez crisis, 1956
Soviet advisors ousted, 1972
Second largest recipient of U.S. foreign aid, 1976–1994
Riyadh
UNITED ARAB EMIRATES
SAUDI ARABIA
Aswan Dam
Red Sea
Oil embargo, 1973
Source of 17% of U.S. oil imports in 1975
Largest buyer of U.S. arms, 1950–1994
OMAN
Mecca
Gadhafi in power, 1969–
SUDAN
PEOPLE'S DEM. REP. OF YEMEN
ERITREA
YEMEN
Sana
Mukalla
The Yemens merged to become Republic of Yemen, 1990
Gulf of Aden
Aden
Arabian Sea
DJIBOUTI
Djibouti
SOMALIA
U.S. troops assist in relief of famine, 1992–1993
ETHIOPIA
INDIAN OCEAN
Members of the Organization of Petroleum Exporting Countries (OPEC)
Oilfields
0 250 500 Km.
0 250 500 Mi.
KENYA
ARAB-ISRAELI CONFLICT
Jewish state after UN partition of Palestine, 1947
Israel after War of 1948–1949
Area controlled by Israel after Six-Day War, 1967
Israel-occupied area after October War, 1973
By Egyptian-Israeli agreements of 1975 and 1979, Israel withdrew from the Sinai in 1982. In 1981, Israel annexed the Golan Heights. In 1993, PLO and Israel signed accord for Palestinian self-rule in Gaza and part of West Bank. In 1997 Israel agreed to withdraw from Hebron.
LEBANON
Beirut
Damascus
SYRIA
Haifa
Golan Heights
Sea of Galilee
Intifada begins in West Bank, 1987
West Bank
Jordan
Tel Aviv
Jerusalem
Amman
Hebron
Dead Sea
Mediterranean Sea
Gaza
Port Said
ISRAEL
Signs peace accord with Israel, 1994
Suez Canal
JORDAN
Cairo
Suez
E G Y P T
Elat
SINAI PENINSULA
Gulf of Suez
Gulf of Aqaba
Nile
SAUDI ARABIA
Sharm el-Sheikh
Red Sea

tions defend themselves. "We must avoid that kind of policy that will make countries in Asia so dependent upon us that we are dragged into conflicts such as the one that we have in Vietnam."[60] Washington sought to build up regional surrogate powers, such as Iran and Israel, thus apparently retiring its badge as the world's policeman. Not quite. Third World countries held a place in the Nixon-Kissinger scheme for equilibrium because of their vulnerability to destabilizing radicalism and hence to pernicious Soviet influence. Kissinger cited Moscow's endorsement of national liberation movements to argue, therefore, that the internal politics of developing nations intertwined with the "international struggle."[61] When troubles arose in the Third World, Nixon, Ford, and Kissinger reflexively interpreted them as moves in the game of great-power politics.

Problems in the Middle East sorely tested détente. Basic U.S. goals since World War II had been consistent for the region: ensure oil supplies; contain the Soviet Union; protect Israel; challenge neutralism; and blunt the appeal of Arab nationalism. After the 1956 Suez crisis (see Chapter 8), the Soviet Union and the United States armed Egypt and Israel respectively. In June 1967, after years of threats and counterthreats, Israel attacked Egypt and Syria. In the Six-Day War, the Israelis, using American-supplied weapons, scored a devastating victory by capturing the West Bank, including the ancient city of Jerusalem, from Jordan, the Golan Heights from Syria, and the entire Sinai Peninsula, including the eastern bank of the Suez Canal, from Egypt (see map, page 375). Half of the Arab states broke diplomatic relations with Washington. Soviet vessels obtained access to Arab ports. With pressure from the pro-Israel lobby, the United States sold fifty F-4 Phantom jets to Israel in December 1968.

The Middle East, said Nixon, had become a "powder keg."[62] His administration worried that the persistent Arab-Israeli conflict would open a Soviet avenue into the Middle East. As U.S. Phantom jets began to arrive in Israel, and as the Israelis conducted bombing raids deep into Egypt in January 1970, the Soviets shipped surface-to-air missiles (SAMs) to Egypt to defend against the Phantoms. Thousands of Soviet troops, advisers, and pilots answered Egypt's call for assistance. Washington gave Israel more F-4s and electronic equipment to improve Israeli accuracy. U.S. military credits for Israel totaled $1.2 billion from 1971 to 1973.

Meanwhile, Palestinian Arabs, many of them refugees ousted from their homes in 1948 when Israel won nationhood, grew more frustrated. The Palestine Liberation Organizaion (PLO), formed in 1964 by several guerrilla groups, came under the aggressive leadership of Yasir Arafat four years later. Many Arab leaders backed the organization in its demand for the elimination of the Jewish state and for the creation of a Palestinian homeland. In 1970 a radical wing of the PLO hijacked airliners and temporarily seized passengers, including Americans, as hostages. That same year, PLO troops with Syrian help battled King Hussein's armies in Jordan. Palestinian terrorists murdered Israeli athletes at the 1972 Olympic Games in Munich. The Israelis retaliated, assassinating PLO figures abroad.

Soviet relations with the PLO and Egypt grew frosty in the early 1970s, as Moscow tried to restrain both out of fear that Washington would scuttle détente if Mideast tensions continued. For its part, the Nixon administration, from 1970 to 1973, followed a "standstill diplomacy."[63] Israel possessed military superiority, Moscow displayed restraint, and a new, seemingly more moderate Egyptian gov-

Golda Meir (1898–1978), Nixon, and Kissinger. In early 1973, the prime minister of Israel met with the president, who promised more U.S. airplanes. Nixon once told her "he had gotten only 8% of the Jewish vote and he was supporting Israel not for political reasons for the first time in recent history." (Department of State *Newsletter*)

ernment under the leadership of Anwar el-Sadat came to power after Nasser's death in September 1970. Fearful that détente would condemn Egypt to a "no war, no peace" paralysis, Sadat plotted a new strike against Isreal.[64] He withstood a Soviet-supported coup d'état attempt, and in summer 1972 he abruptly expelled several thousand Soviet technicians and military advisers. The United States continued to arm Israel; in early 1973 Washington promised more airplane deliveries. On October 6, 1973 (Yom Kippur, the holiest day on the Jewish calendar), Egyptian forces struck across the canal into Sinai while Syrian troops attacked Israel's northern border. The attack took Israel and the United States by surprise. At first the Israelis suffered heavy losses, and the Arabs regained land lost in 1967. Nixon promised Tel Aviv more Phantoms. "The best result," a cold-blooded Kissinger predicted, "would be if Israel comes out a little ahead but got bloodied in the process, and if the U.S. stayed clean."[65] Moscow hurried military equipment to Syria.

In the midst of the crisis, the shadow of Watergate lengthened over the Nixon administration. On October 10, Vice President Spiro Agnew resigned after evidence surfaced that he had accepted payoffs as governor of Maryland years before. Ten days later Nixon fired the special Watergate prosecutor for getting too close to damaging evidence. The concatenation of domestic and foreign crises frayed nerves. The White House staff feared that Moscow might think the U.S. government weak or incapacitated.

On October 13, Nixon ordered a massive airlift of military matériel to Israel. Soviet premier Aleksei Kosygin flew to Cairo to persuade Sadat to accept a cease-fire. Kissinger flew to Moscow on October 20, learning en route that the Saudis had embargoed oil to the United States. By October 21 most Arab members of the Organization of Petroleum Exporting Countries had joined the embargo. Kissinger and the Soviets finally arranged a cease-fire on October 22. But the Israelis ignored the truce and surrounded the Egyptian Third Army. When Moscow pressed for Soviet and U.S. troops to enforce the truce jointly, Washington overreacted. An inebriated Nixon called it "the most serious thing since the Cuban Missile Crisis.

**"You're Like a Bunch of . . . of . . . of . . . CAPI-
TALISTS!!"** The oil embargo by the OPEC nations in 1974
produced anger among Americans who found that gasoline
stations ran out of fuel or that what they could buy had drastically risen in price. Venezuela and the Arab nations replied
that they were only doing what the developed nations had
done to them for decades. (Dennis Renault, *Sacramento Bee*)

Words won't do the job. We've got to act."[66] Kissinger thereupon ordered all U.S.
forces on nuclear alert, a calculated ploy to shock Soviet decisionmakers. Amid
charges that Kissinger "lied to us" and that "frightened" Americans sought to "unleash World War III," the Kremlin chose not to intervene unilaterally.[67] Kissinger
pressed the Israelis to honor the truce. A new cease-fire held.

The Arab-Israeli contest threatened the American economy as well as the
economies of U.S. allies. Arab states such as Saudi Arabia, which for three decades
had supplied Western nations with inexpensive petroleum, now used their black
riches as a weapon: They embargoed petroleum shipments to the United States
and quadrupled the price of crude oil for Western Europe and Japan. "We are masters of our own commodity," the Saudi oil minister announced.[68] The United
States, importing between 10 and 15 percent of its oil from the Middle East, suffered an energy crisis. Gasoline prices at the pumps spun upward, and anxious dri-
vers lined up, sometimes for hours, hoping to fuel their automobiles. The embargo
ended in March 1974, but prices remained high and America's vulnerability had
been exposed.

Kissinger launched "shuttle diplomacy" to prevent another Mideast blowup.
With impressive stamina and patience, he bargained in Cairo and Tel Aviv and

other capitals intermittently for two years. "Dr. Henry, you are my favorite magician," said Sadat.[69] Finally, on September 1, 1975, Egypt and Israel initialed a historic agreement that provided for an eventual Israeli pullback from part of the Sinai, created a United Nations–patrolled buffer zone, and placed U.S. technicians in "early warning" stations to detect military activities. Washington also promised substantial foreign aid to both Egypt and Israel.

Thorny problems remained. The Palestinian Arabs still lived in refugee camps and demanded a homeland, while Israelis entrenched themselves in occupied territories, building industries, farms, and houses. Jordan still demanded the return of the West Bank, and Syrian-Israeli hostility persisted with the Golan Heights in Israel's hands. A bloody civil war broke out in Lebanon, which prompted Syria to send in troops in 1976. Washington continued to ship weapons to both Arabs and Israelis after the October war. In 1976, Sadat, who needed American technology and mediation, denounced the Soviet Union, saying that "99 percent of the cards in the game are in America's hands whether the Soviet Union likes it or not."[70] Once Cairo turned emphatically toward the United States, American policy in the Middle East looked more like old-fashioned containment than détente. Kissinger's refusal to include the Soviets and Palestinians (despite secret messages from the PLO "expressing willingness to coexist with Israel") in Mideast diplomacy precluded a full Arab-Israeli settlement.[71] Moscow reacted by backing Libya's President Moammar Gadhafi, a radical anti-American, Pan-Arabist who came to power in 1969 and denounced all peace efforts.

As a counterweight to the Soviets and radical Arabs, the Nixon and Ford administrations fashioned a closer alliance with the Shah of Iran. In 1972 Nixon and Kissinger promised the Shah non-nuclear weapons and U.S. technicians. The Shah's military gorged itself on huge amounts of modern American arms, paid for by galloping oil revenues ("petro-dollars"). American corporate executives rushed to Iran to display their submarines, fighter aircraft, assault helicopters, and missiles. In 1977 his nation ranked as the largest foreign buyer of American-made arms, spending $5.7 billion that year alone. His armed forces became the most powerful in the region. But doubters in the shahdom thought such excessive military spending foolhardy when the Iranian per capita income stood at only $350 and such funds could have helped alleviate the nation's economic woes. Ruthlessly suppressing all dissent, the Shah said that "if there was any rough stuff it was necessary and that was the end of that."[72] To improve his image in the United States, the Shah hired a New York advertising agency and lavishly bestowed gifts on prominent Americans. Official Washington regarded Iran as "an unconditional ally," in the turbulent Middle East, but the huge infusion of weapons further fueled a dangerous regional arms race.[73]

Covert Action Against Radicals in Latin America and Africa

Latin America remained an area of intense interest to the United States. Thousands of Latin American military officers still trained in the United States, some at the Inter-American Defense College in Washington, D.C., where they learned urban counterinsurgency and jungle warfare techniques. U.S. trade with the Western

Frank Church (1924–1984).
Democratic senator from Idaho
(1957–1981), Church became a
major figure on the Foreign Relations Committee, serving as its
chair (1979–1981). A critic of the
Vietnam War and a great orator,
Church chaired Senate investigations that revealed U.S. complicity
in the overthrow of Chile's Salvador Allende and exposed CIA
abuses such as assassination attempts on foreign leaders. One
staff member quipped that
Church's report should be titled
"Bugs, Drugs, and Thugs." (Frank
Church Collection, Boise State
University Library)

Hemisphere continued large. In the early 1970s one-third of Latin American exports went to the U.S. and two-fifths of the region's imports came from the United
States. In 1976, Latin American countries supplied 34 percent of the United States'
petroleum imports, 68 percent of its coffee, 57 percent of its sugar, 47 percent of its
copper, and 98 percent of its bauxite. In that year U.S. direct investments in its
southern neighbors totaled $17 billion. Despite these strong ties, Latin American
governments increasingly challenged Washington. Soon after taking office, Nixon
sent Governor Nelson Rockefeller on a fact-finding mission to Latin America.
Demonstrations erupted, and parts of his trip had to be canceled. The governor reported in August 1969 that the United States caused deep resentment through its
"paternalistic attitude" and attempts to "direct the internal affairs of other nations
to an unseemly degree."[74]

Mexico refused to honor the economic blockade of Cuba, strongly criticized
the 1965 Dominican intervention, and, in its 1972 Charter of Economic Rights and
Duties of Nations, boldly proclaimed the economic independence of small states
and their right to expropriate foreign enterprises. The charter further urged that developed nations share their wealth with poorer countries. In 1974 the United Nations approved the charter by a 120 to 6 vote, with the United States voting no.
The United States also engaged Peru and Ecuador in a "tuna war," after those nations declared a 200-mile territorial limit and began seizing American fishing vessels in coastal waters. After 1968, a new, radical (noncommunist) military
government in Peru deliberately set out to break the country's economic dependence on the United States by nationalizing an Exxon oil subsidiary and other
American-owned properties. Lima also defiantly purchased Soviet MIGs.
Venezuela, too, searched for ways to reduce its economic reliance on the United
States. A founding member of OPEC in 1960, Caracas joined the Arabs in drastically raising petroleum prices in the 1970s, and in 1976 it too nationalized
American-owned oil companies.

Chile attracted Washington's rapt attention as a threat to U.S. hegemony in
September 1970. That month Chileans elected as their president Salvador Allende,
a physician by profession and a founder of Chile's Socialist party. The CIA had sent
hundreds of thousands of dollars in bribe and propaganda money to Chile to thwart
his electoral victory. The CIA also cooperated with the International Telephone
and Telegraph Company's covert effort to back a right-wing candidate. Fearing a
"democratically elected version of Fidel Castro," Nixon personally gave CIA official Richard Helms full authority ("a marshal's baton") to undermine the Allende
government.[75] Following presidential instructions to "make the economy scream"
in Chile in order to block the nationalization of American-owned copper corporations (Kennecott and Anaconda), the CIA worked with U.S. companies to stop the
shipment of spare parts.[76] Washington also cut off economic aid and denied Export-
Import Bank loans to Chile. Military assistance continued as the CIA conspired
with Chilean army officers and spent $6 million to subsidize newspapers and polit-
ical parties opposed to Allende. Allende criticized U.S. pressure—"an always
oblique attack, covert, sinuous, but nonetheless harmful for Chile."[77]

In 1973 a military junta overthrew Allende. In the chaos, military officers murdered him, or he committed suicide. U.S. complicity probably stopped short of di-

rect participation in the coup. "U.S. authorities did not create the factors" that overthrew the government, Allende's foreign minister has written, "but rather increased and intensified the impact of those factors."[78] Vivid images of Allende's ouster recurred in the 1982 film *Missing*, starring Jack Lemmon and Sissy Spacek, a taut thriller in which Chilean authorities kill an American journalist fingered by the U.S. Embassy because he detected U.S. machinations. Although Ambassador Nathaniel Davis refuted the main thesis of the film, it still reinforced the culpability many Americans felt about meddling in the internal politics of a sovereign state and about the many Chileans who lost their lives. The new junta returned companies to private hands, suspended freedom of speech and press, jailed dissenters, and gained notoriety for torturing and killing political opponents.

The Nixon and Ford administrations also sought to keep Cuba isolated. Under Fidel Castro, Cuba had become a communist state and close Soviet ally. In fall 1970, Nixon concluded from sketchy U-2 evidence that the Soviets were building a nuclear submarine base at Cienfuegos, Cuba, in violation of their understanding after the 1962 missile crisis to refrain from placing offensive weapons on the island (see Chapter 9). The president and Kissinger decided "to face the Soviets down."[79] Moscow assured Washington that the Soviets were not building a naval facility. The crisis quickly passed, but the Nixon administration claimed a victory that "reaffirmed," "clarified," and "amplified" the 1962 understanding by prohibiting Soviet nuclear submarine facilities in Cuba.[80] In mid-1971, swine fever swept Cuba, causing health authorities to slaughter half a million pigs to prevent further spread of the disease. Not until 1977 did U.S. investigative journalists reveal that the CIA and an exile group had introduced the deadly virus into Cuba—another CIA dirty trick. Still seeking some accommodation with North America in the early 1970s, Castro deemphasized the export of revolution and aid to insurgencies, and in 1973 he signed an antihijacking treaty with Washington to discourage terrorism in the airways. Two years later the Organization of American States lifted its economic blockade of Cuba. During 1974–1975, U.S. officials met secretly with Cuban diplomats to explore possibilities for détente. In mid-1975 Kissinger rejected baseball commissioner Bowie Kuhn's efforts to arrange games between the United States and Cuba. When Cuban troops in Africa helped Angolan radicals come to power, hopes for a Cuban-American détente faded.

Until the mid-1970s, Africa stood low on the Nixon-Ford-Kissinger list of diplomatic priorities. Administration policy sought to expand U.S. material interests, strengthen ties with white minority regimes in Portuguese Angola, Rhodesia, and South Africa, and yet encourage progress toward racial harmony. The National Security Council explained in a memorandum (NSSM 39) that "the whites are here to stay and the only way that constructive change can come about is through them."[81] Washington calculated that the black majorities feared white military superiority and would therefore refrain from major violent confrontation. In February 1970, Nixon told Kissinger, then preparing a presidential message to Congress on foreign policy, to "make sure there's something in it for the jigs, Henry."[82] This crude, condescending remark about black Africans reflected the cynicism underlying U.S. policy. Washington relaxed the arms embargo to white South Africa; Congress in 1971 passed the Byrd Amendment permitting the United States to buy chromium from Rhodesia despite a United Nations–declared economic boycott of Ian Smith's white minority government. Although the chair of the Congressional Black Caucus resigned from the U.S. delegation to the United Nations because of the "stifling hypocrisy" of Nixon's policy toward Africa, CIA director Richard Helms claimed "they [black Africans] need us."[83] Others cited the more than $2 billion invested in black Africa and U.S. purchases of cobalt, oil, manganese, and platinum.

Events in Angola eventually shattered American complacency. Since the early 1960s, black rebel groups had battled the Portuguese in Angola. Playing a double game in that decade, the CIA channeled funds to a faction of independence fighters while Washington officially backed Portugal and sold it military equipment to quell the nationalist rebellion. The Soviets began to support one of the guerrilla groups, the Popular Movement for the Liberation of Angola (MPLA). In 1975 the CIA spent $32 million on covert operations for propaganda, arms, communications gear, the hiring of white mercenaries, and payments to anti-MPLA political figures. The State Department official in charge of African affairs, Nathaniel Davis, argued that U.S. resources simply could not control the revolution or local events in Africa, but would stimulate increased Soviet activity. Davis urged that the United States appeal to African leaders in Tanzania and Zambia to negotiate a diplomatic solution. For "a test of strength with the Soviets," he advised Kissinger, "we should find a more advantageous place."[84] When President Ford nevertheless decided on covert intervention, Davis resigned.

In November 1975, Portugal granted independence to Angola. The insurgent factions then fought one another in a civil war, with the American clients doing poorly despite support from the United States and China. South Africa and Zaire also dispatched troops to support an American-backed group. "On their own and without consulting us," as one Soviet diplomat put it, the Cubans dispatched 12,000 troops and substantially increased their aid to the MPLA that fall; Moscow hesitated (lest it scuttle détente) but also sent arms and advisers when South African forces intervened.[85] Davis's resignation and leaks about the secret intervention stirred some members of Congress. Another Vietnam? The administration asked for $25 million for arms. "That's when Congress pulled the plug," President Ford later wrote.[86] In December the Senate voted to stop military expenditures for Angola; the House followed suit in January 1976.

Kissinger upbraided Congress for missing a strategic opportunity to confront the Soviets. Opponents replied that the United States should never have viewed an African civil war through a Cold War, ideological prism. The MPLA, after all, did not molest American oil companies and never ranked as a Soviet puppet. Given the MPLA's success, the United States hurt itself by choosing the losing side. Discussions with the MPLA—preventive diplomacy—might have reduced the violence. "You may be right in African terms, but I'm thinking globally," Kissinger retorted.[87] Such complaints about "8,000 Cubans running around" Angola actually encouraged Moscow, heretofore very cautious about backing revolutionary movements "outside its neighboring countries," to defend "African liberation and global anti-imperialism" in far-off Angola, where success fueled further "limited interventions" in Africa and Asia, ultimately leading to the Soviet disaster in Afghanistan in the 1980s (see Chapter 11).[88]

The Ford administration's ban on using the word *détente* after Angola pointedly exposed the differing Soviet and American interpretations of that concept. What Nixon-Kissinger-Ford had intended as arms agreements and codes of conduct that would restrain Soviet expansion, Moscow saw as "the natural result of the correlation of forces in the world arena," a peaceful coexistence between superpowers that "cannot in the slightest abolish or change the laws of the class struggle."[89] Thus, as Washington sustained its regional clients and kept the Soviets out of the Mideast peace process, for example, the Brezhnev regime sought "to perform our international duty to other peoples" by assisting national liberation movements against imperialists and their allies.[90]

Gerald R. Ford (b. 1913). In October 1973 Vice President Spiro Agnew pleaded no contest to charges of income-tax evasion and acceptance of bribes and resigned. Ford then assumed the office of vice president. A long-time conservative member of Congress from Michigan, Ford aroused controversy when, as president, he pardoned Richard M. Nixon. Ford tried to maintain a U.S. presence in Vietnam and Angola, but Congress rejected funding. (The White House)

The Angolan experience prompted reconsideration of U.S. policy toward Africa. So did the outbreak of racial violence in South Africa, where the white government in 1976 crushed a black rebellion in the township of Soweto. America's desire for bountiful Nigerian oil also suggested a change of course. The United States, reasoned Kissinger, faced isolation from the continent, with black radicals, Soviets, and Cubans denying Americans economic links and naval facilities. The United States must do something to "avoid a race war," to contain foreign intervention, and to "prevent the radicalization of Africa," Kissinger concluded.[91] Arms shipments went to Kenya and Zaire. Economic ties were strengthened through investments by companies such as Bethlehem Steel and Kaiser Aluminum, in pursuit of titanium and bauxite, respectively. The secretary of state began to disengage the United States from white minority regimes in Rhodesia and South Africa, urging the latter to abandon its segregationist policy of apartheid. Such changes underscored the fact that Africa had become a Cold War arena.

Economic Competition, Environmental Distress, and the North-South Debate

"History has shown that international political stability requires international economic stability," Kissinger observed.[92] The 1970s marked a disturbing watershed in the history of the world economy. The international economic order created after World War II foundered. The Bretton Woods monetary mechanism (see pages 200–201) faltered; the dollar skidded; famines starved millions at a time when grain stocks fell to record postwar lows; dwindling natural resources spawned political tensions; and the former colonies of the Third World challenged the industrial nations to share power. The worldwide recession of the early 1970s became the worst since the 1930s. Inflation raised the cost of industrial goods for developing countries. Protectionist barriers rose, further impeding world trade. Dramatically climbing OPEC oil prices hit poor and rich nations alike, while the price of some other commodities, such as copper, slumped, causing economic downturns in nations dependent on the export of one product. Economists coined the term "Fourth World"—poor, less developed countries (LDCs) that lacked profitmaking raw materials, relied heavily on imports of food, and built up large debts owed to governments and private banks.

The Soviet Union and the People's Republic of China engaged in world trade as never before, in quest of agricultural products and high technology, and enlarged East-

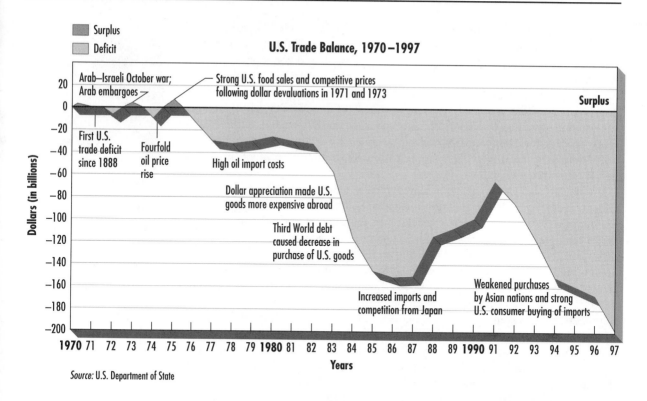

U.S. Trade Balance, 1970–1997

Surplus
Deficit

Source: U.S. Department of State

West trade became a headline issue. So did the questions of how to regulate ocean-bed mineral resources and how to deal with powerful multinational corporations.

In this chaotic economy, the United States produced about one-third of all the world's goods and services and remained the world's largest trading nation. In 1970 U.S. exports stood at $27.5 billion; by 1977 they had climbed to $121.2 billion. Large firms such as Coca-Cola, Gillette, and IBM earned more than half of their profits abroad. Many American jobs depended on healthy foreign trade. In 1976, for example, one out of every nine manufacturing workers produced goods for export. Exports accounted for one out of every four dollars of agricultural sales in 1977.

American industry also relied on imports of raw materials: 75 percent of the tin, 91 percent of the chrome, 99 percent of the manganese, and 64 percent of the zinc consumed by Americans in 1975 came from foreign sources. In 1977 the nation imported more than 40 percent of the petroleum it used. These import needs had become conspicuous in 1971 when, for the first time since the depression decade of the 1930s, the United States suffered a trade deficit, importing more than it exported (see chart). Six years later, the trade imbalance reached $26.5 billion, due in large part to imported energy sources.

U.S. direct investments abroad—about half of the world's total of foreign direct investments—equaled $75.5 billion in 1970 and $149.8 billion in 1977, thus further defining the United States as a fulcrum of the international economy. The greatest part of these investments remained in developed countries (73 percent in 1975). Some investments faced political unrest, terrorist acts, and nationalization.

Despite its commanding status, the United States seemed to be losing its competitive edge. In the 1970s, ninety-eight nations had higher rates of economic growth than the United States. Japan and West Germany, strategic allies but commerical rivals, challenged America in the international marketplace. In fact, Japanese automobiles, televisions, and electronic equipment seized a large share of markets within the United States. Once dominant, American producers of computers, high technology, and aerospace machinery now struggled to retain high rank. Then, too, Americans worried that wealthy Arabs were buying up American banks, companies, and real estate.

The descent of the once mighty dollar further demonstrated the declining U.S. position. A "dollar glut" developed abroad, induced by U.S. foreign-aid programs, military expenditures ($90 billion in 1970 alone), private investments, inflation, and purchases of higher-priced oil. Foreigners held $78 billion in 1969; by 1977 the figure had jumped to $373 billion. Foreign holders of dollars wanted to exchange them for gold, thus putting pressure on America's diminishing gold stock. The dollar declined in value against currencies such as the German mark and Swiss franc. The United States faced a serious balance-of-payments crisis.

The Nixon administration adopted unilateral policies that shocked foreign capitals and upset the Bretton Woods system of cooperation. In August 1971, after the dollar had fallen to its lowest point against the mark since World War II, Nixon devalued the dollar (by increasing the dollar price of an ounce of gold) and suspended its convertibility into gold. The president also cut foreign aid by 10 percent and imposed a 10 percent surtax on all imports, seeking thereby to reduce the influx of Japanese and European goods and to put diplomatic pressure on other nations to revalue their currencies to make them less competitive with the dollar. Treasury Secretary John Connally asserted that "foreigners are out to screw us. Our job is to screw them first."[93] Kissinger approvingly called this "declaration of economic war on the other industrial democracies" an example of "brutal unilateralism."[94]

In December, representatives of ten leading trading nations gathered at the Smithsonian Institution in Washington to try to stabilize the international monetary system. After stormy sessions, America's economic competitors agreed to revalue their currencies to bring them more into line with the dollar. The United States then lifted its import surcharge and once more made the dollar exchangeable for gold. But the Smithsonian agreement did not work for long; in early 1973 the United States again devalued the dollar, this time letting it "float," its value determined no longer by agreement but by supply and demand in the monetary marketplace. Efforts by the International Monetary Fund to restore an orderly system fell short.

International money problems intersected with foreign trade problems. Higher priced American goods could not easily compete with Japanese or European products, and the European Common Market engaged in preferential trade arrangements and export subsidies that hurt American sales abroad. Highly protectionist at home yet aggressively penetrating global markets, Japan was "like the golfer who is shooting in the 80s with the same 25 handicap he used when he was shooting in the 100s."[95] When Nixon in 1971 threatened quotas, the Japanese agreed voluntarily to limit their textile exports to the United States, thus averting a trade war. Multilateral trade negotiations, under the auspices of the long-working General Agreement on Tariffs and Trade (1947), began in Tokyo in 1974. Five years later the "Tokyo Round" of negotiations finally produced accords that shrank tariffs about 30 percent. The signatories, including the United States, also wrote codes to regulate other practices such as subsidies and dumping. Yet they failed to liberalize trade in agriculture. Many protectionist practices continued, prompting the chief American negotiator in 1980 to remark that "the free flow of world trade remains largely an ideal."[96]

Economic relations with Third World nations also grew troubled. In 1972, although the developing world had 74 percent of the world's population, it represented only 17 percent of the world's combined gross national product (GNP). From the perspective of the developing nations (the "South"), it seemed imperative that wealthier industrial nations (the "North") charge less for manufactured goods and technology, offer foreign assistance and loans at low rates, reduce tariff barriers, pay more for imported raw materials through commodity price agreements, and allow Third World nations to restrict foreign-owned corporations. Developing countries also insisted on a greater voice in international institutions such as the World Bank. "The object is to complete the liberation of the Third World countries from external domination" by changing the "structure of power," explained Tanzania's Julius K. Nyerere.[97]

The Group of 77, a coalition of developing nations organized in 1964, articulated the Third World's economic demands. More than one hundred countries by the 1970s, this consortium dominated the United Nations General Assembly, and in 1974 that body endorsed a New International Economic Order encompassing their goals. The United States, Japan, and Western European nations agreed to talk, and struck some compromises, but by the early 1980s a stalemate existed. U.S. officials did not take kindly to charges of American greed when many Third World nations themselves indulged in financial corruption and wasted resources on weaponry. India, fearing Chinese and Pakistani nuclear capabilities, allotted billions to produce a nuclear bomb in 1974 instead of devoting those funds to alleviating severe food shortages.

Global leaders also made little headway against famine. Insufficient fertilizer, inadequate farm acreage, pollution, droughts, and shrinking fish supplies due to overharvesting condemned one-quarter of humankind to hunger. The drought that swept Africa in the early 1970s caused at least 10,000 deaths a day. A high birth rate and falling death rate put severe pressure on available food supplies. In 1975 the world's population passed 4 billion. Nutritionists estimated that between a half-billion and one billion people ate less than the calories required to sustain ordinary physical activity.

At the 1974 World Food Conference in Rome, the United States voted to help finance an International Fund for Agricultural Development to expand food production in developing countries. But the United States continued to market surplus food for profit, most notably in large grain sales to the dollar-paying Soviet Union. And food aid, always political, became more so; in 1973–1974 more than half of U.S. food assistance went to clients South Vietnam, Cambodia, and South Korea. At the same time, because of rising petroleum costs, the United States reduced its exports of petroleum-derived fertilizers, thus contributing to a worldwide decline in grain production of 15 million tons in 1974. As the CIA noted, "in bad

Famine in Chad, Africa.   Drought-stricken Chad was only one of many poor nations that suffered in the world hunger crisis of the 1970s. Millions died. (CARE, New York)

years . . . Washington would acquire virtual life-and-death power over the fate of the multitudes of the needy."[98] The 1970s ranked as bad years.

U.S. foreign-aid strategy in the early 1970s aimed to assist especially the most impoverished people through projects to improve nutrition, family planning, health, education, and food production. But developing nations complained that the United States was cutting back when the need was greatest. Although total foreign aid (economic and military) had increased from $6.6 billion in 1970 to $7.8 billion in 1977, the proportion of GNP devoted to development assistance actually decreased. In 1977 Americans spent about four times as much on tobacco products as their government expended on development aid. Kissinger attempted to meet some of the developing nations' demands; he nonetheless voiced a growing American impatience with their "confrontational" manner and their assumption that growth was "a quick fix requiring only that the world's wealth be properly redistributed through tests of strength instead of a process of self-help over generations."[99]

North-South relations also became contentious over environmental issues. In the United States, books such as Rachel Carson's *Silent Spring* (1962), Paul Erlich's *The Population Bomb* (1968), and Barry Commoner's *The Closing Circle* (1971) raised public consciousness about environmental degradation and the growing imbalance between food supplies and burgeoning populations. Grassroots organizations such as the Worldwatch Institute reiterated the message that "the earth is in danger, that everything is connected to everything else, that too many people live here, that smaller is better."[100] In 1969 Greenpeace organized to protest nuclear-weapons tests, and the following year Americans celebrated the first Earth Day. Nixon bowed to congressional pressure and helped create the Environmental Protection Agency (EPA). Oil spills from oceangoing tankers, unsafe disposal of hazardous wastes, and the contamination of water sources revealed environmental questions as borderless, transnational issues requiring international attention. As environmental groups around the world pressed for action, countervoices challenged the doomsday forecasts and "eco-hysterics" of "econuts."[101]

Swedish scientists and diplomats, alarmed by increasing air pollution and the resultant acid rain, championed an international conference. In June 1972 the United Nations sponsored the Conference on the Human Environment in Stockholm. More than one hundred nations, 19 intergovernmental organizations (IGOs), and 400 nongovernmental organizations (NGOs) attended. North-South differences surfaced. Third World nations feared that measures to protect the environment would slow their economic development. Might not they be told to remain "green areas so that the constructed areas could continue to develop without being disturbed?" asked the Brazilian foreign minister.[102] The South demanded compensation for stricter environmental controls. The South also asked for the North's commitment to additional foreign-assistance funds earmarked for environmental projects. Developed nations in turn worried that Third World industrialization would overwhelm the biosphere.

President Nixon cautiously endorsed the global conference, pledged U.S. monies to the new environmental fund, and supported a ten-year moratorium on commercial whaling. But the administration balked at more financial assistance to Third World countries and resented delegates' complaints that the United States had battered the natural environment in Indochina. Conference resolutions did not bind any states that opposed them. Still, the global conference stimulated national environmental policies, set up Earthwatch to survey environmental conditions, and spotlighted transboundary pollution.

Water covers 70 percent of the earth's surface. In the 1960s a new question became urgent: Who owned the rights to the gas, petroleum, and minerals such as manganese and nickel that rested in the deep seabed? Offshore oil drilling was well advanced, but the exploitation of the ocean's mineral riches was just beginning. American companies such as Kennecott Copper and United States Steel invested large sums in new technology to explore the ocean floor. From the perspective of developing nations, the seabed resources belonged to all nations as a "common heritage of mankind."[103] The United States endorsed this principle in 1970, but at the UN-sponsored Law of the Sea Conference, which opened in 1973 and continued into the early 1980s, U.S. officials rejected the South's call for a powerful international seabed agency with exclusive rights over the mining of ocean resources. Because the new authority would operate on a one-nation, one-vote basis, the United States and other industrial nations would lose their competitive advantage. Washington insisted on private commercial exploitation, with no limits on profits or access to sites. But in 1976–1977 the United States compromised, now recommending a dual system: private development and an international authority, the latter to be assigned exclusive exploitation of certain mining sites. Until such an agreement, Kissinger insisted, the United States would explore and mine on its own.

The South and North also debated multinational corporations, the South seeking tighter controls and a larger proportion of the giant companies' profits earned from operations in developing nations. Ten of the top twelve multinationals in the mid-1970s were U.S.-based, including General Motors, Exxon, and Ford Motor. They intervened in the politics of other nations or bribed foreign leaders to gain contracts. Lockheed Aircraft and Exxon, among others, spent millions to bribe overseas politicians—a practice Congress tried to halt through the 1977 Foreign Corrupt Practices Act. The multinationals' economic decisions—where to locate a plant, for example—held real importance for developing nations that welcomed multinational investments but resented outside control. The South also protested that the multinationals employed too few "locals" in high positions and exploited natural resources without adequate compensation. The multinationals, some charged, had become global mini-empires, beyond the reach of national laws. Defenders replied that multinational enterprises brought benefits to developing nations in higher wages, tax revenues, and technology transfers. Whether beneficial or detrimental, multinational corporations by the early 1970s had become major actors in the international system. Washington balked at restraining them because they brought profits home, but the South vowed to restrict them—one of the many economic issues that challenged the Nixon-Kissinger quest for a stable world order.

Vietnamization, Cambodia, and a Wider War

"What we are doing now with China is so great, so historic, the word 'Vietnam' will be only a footnote when it is written in history," Kissinger boasted in 1971.[104] With superpower relations paramount in Nixon-Kissinger foreign relations, Vietnam became simply a "cruel side show."[105] Cruel but no side show, America's longest war continued to claim rapt attention until 1975. The Nixon administration constantly worried that the persistent war could damage the president at home and spoil détente. "I'm not going to end up like LBJ," Nixon early assured his advisers. "I'm going to stop that war. Fast."[106] But under what terms would the United States withdraw? During the 1968 presidential campaign Nixon hinted at a plan for ending the war. President Eisenhower had brought the Korean War to a close shortly after taking office, and Nixon recalled that Ike had threatened the use of nuclear weapons. But, like Ike in 1952, Nixon had no clear plans in 1968.

At the outset, Nixon weighed his options. He could simply pull out of the war, "lock, stock and barrel," as one senator advised.[107] Nixon vetoed that suggestion. He would not sacrifice an ally. Nixon vowed to end the war but not lose it—his purpose was not to defeat North Vietnam but "to avoid [the] defeat of America."[108] His strategy had several components. Washington capitalized on détente, trying to persuade China and the Soviet Union to force Hanoi to compromise. The United States itself, through military escalation, signaled Ho Chi Minh that Nixon intended to punish the enemy harshly where Johnson had not. North Vietnam had to have a breaking point. Nixon exploited his "madman" image to keep Hanoi wondering if he might order an atomic attack on the North Vietnamese capital. The president would strengthen South Vietnam through huge infusions of foreign aid and the training of a larger South Vietnamese army (ARVN). Underscoring the Nixon Doctrine's emphasis on self-help, Vietnamization meant, said one critic, "only that the color of the bodies is now different."[109] Nixon gradually withdrew

U.S. troops from Vietnam and gave flag-waving speeches to counteract the doves and growing public disapproval of the war. In the cynical belief that most antiwar protesters simply feared "getting their asses shot off," he cut back draft calls, announced a draft lottery in May 1969, removed the controversial General Lewis B. Hershey as Selective Service head, and promised to end the draft soon.[110]

The multifaceted scheme did not work. Ho Chi Minh and the Vietcong leaders did not bow to foreign wishes, whether from Washington, Moscow, or Beijing, and the Soviet Union and China continued to supply their ally. Having outlasted the Japanese and the French, Ho's legions had no intention of surrendering to the Americans. As for dissent at home, every new escalation swelled the ranks of the critics and finally prompted Congress to limit the president's ability to enlarge the war. By summer 1971, according to one survey, only 31 percent of the American people approved Nixon's Vietnam policies. Nor did Vietnamization convert South Vietnam into a secure military state. Although U.S. ships, planes, helicopters, rifles, and millions of dollars poured in, South Vietnam became dependent on U.S. aid to keep its gorged army in the field, thus undermining the ultimate objective of standing on its own feet. Aid sustained the corrupt regime of General Nguyen Van Thieu, a government of self-serving officials—"a network of cliques held together by American subsidies," unpopular and ultimately incapable of conducting a winning effort.[111] Finally, Vietnamization diminished *American* military effectiveness. "Why get killed now?" a U.S. marine recalled. "You didn't have that 'let's go out and find them' attitude anymore."[112]

In early 1969 the Paris peace negotiations stalled over Nixon's demand for North Vietnam to pull its forces out of the South and for the survival of the Thieu government. The communists continued to advance on the ground. Nixon decided to bomb communist sanctuaries in Cambodia—but secretly, so that neither Congress nor the American people knew about it. Code-named MENU, the secret bombing of Cambodia began in March 1969 with punishing B-52 sorties. But leaks soon brought the story into the newspapers. A self-proclaimed "paranoiac . . . with regard to secrecy," Nixon ordered the FBI to wiretap several journalists and government officials in a futile attempt to catch the leakers.[113]

Kissinger, in August 1969, began a series of secret meetings with North Vietnamese representatives that lasted into 1973. In the first encounter in Paris, Kissinger warned North Vietnam to change its rigid stance or face grave consequences. Meanwhile, U.S. soldiers were coming home, so that by the end of 1971 the troop level had dropped to 139,000. Protest against the war continued nonetheless. On October 15, 1969, a quarter-million people peacefully marched in Washington, calling for a moratorium on the war. The president asked the "great silent majority of my fellow Americans" to back him, and he urged Vice President Spiro Agnew to attack the news media.[114]

Events in Cambodia actually prompted the Nixon administration to expand the war. In March 1970, a pro-American general, Lon Nol, overthrew the neutralist government of Prince Norodom Sihanouk. Nixon saw new opportunities: Aid Lon Nol against the Khmer Rouge (Cambodian communists) and the North Vietnamese, who used Cambodian territory as a staging area to attack South Vietnam; step up the attack on the North Vietnamese in Cambodia, already targets of American bombing raids; send unmistakable signals to Hanoi that it had better relent; and

"We Demand: Strike!" The U.S. thrust into Cambodia in 1970 prompted a new wave of protests, including a demand from the radical Boston paper *Old Mole* that students go on strike. Many universities temporarily suspended classes to discuss the costly war. In some cases, radical campus groups trashed buildings and police and troops occupied college grounds. (*Old Mole,* 1970, University of Connecticut Library)

show his critics "who's tough."[115] Despite considerable opposition from the State and Defense departments, the president ordered U.S. troops to invade Cambodia in late April.

A cascade of protest rolled across America. Antiwar demonstrations rocked college campuses, as inexperienced national guard troops shot and killed four students at Kent State University in Ohio. Two students at all-black Jackson State College in Mississippi died when state police fired on a women's dormitory. Within the administration, three Kissinger aides, including Anthony Lake, resigned in protest against the thrust into Cambodia. In June the Senate terminated the Tonkin Gulf Resolution of 1964 and passed the Cooper-Church Amendment cutting off funds for military operations in Cambodia. Although the House failed to pass this measure, a "siege mentality" gripped the White House.[116]

Nixon declared the Cambodian operation a success. Communist arms, equipment, and food had been captured and hundreds of enemy troops killed. Although the invasion probably slowed the communist momentum and bought time for Vietnamization, the bold venture also widened the war, caused the sanctuaries to spread out, and further bloodied Cambodia. North Vietnam substantially increased its aid to the Khmer Rouge insurgents, who gained new recruits radicalized by the U.S. invasion. Lon Nol became another besieged Asian leader dependent on U.S. assistance.

As the peace negotiations in Paris made little headway, the war in Vietnam dragged on. Nixon ordered "protective reaction strikes" against North Vietnam after American reconnaissance planes were shot down. In early 1971, he approved a South Vietnamese invasion of Laos, where in six weeks of heavy fighting ARVN forces "got their tail beat off," thus turning Vietnamization's "first test" into its "biggest failure."[117]

At home the wider war wrought more turmoil. After a court-martial in March 1971 found First Lieutenant William Calley guilty of murdering unresisting children, women, and old men at My Lai in 1968 (see page 351), Nixon ordered him released from jail (Calley won parole in November 1974). Army juries acquitted and army officials dismissed murder and cover-up charges against all other personnel connected with the massacre. The uproar over the Calley case had hardly subsided when, in June 1971, the *New York Times* began to print the *Pentagon Papers,* a long, secret Defense Department history of U.S. intervention in Vietnam. Leaked by a former Pentagon official, Daniel Ellsberg, the papers fortified critics in their argument that American presidents consistently had tried to win a military victory and frequently had withheld facts from the American public. "This will totally destroy American credibility forever," groaned Kissinger.[118] After the Supreme Court refused to halt publication of the *Pentagon Papers,* Nixon set up a "plumbers" group to stop leaks and to find ways to discredit Ellsberg. Watergate soon followed.

The year 1972 saw the presidential trip to China and SALT-I—and even greater escalation in Vietnam. In Paris, Kissinger continued to meet with North Vietnamese representatives, always rejecting the communist demand that the United States abandon Thieu. Following its strategy of "fighting while negotiating," North Vietnam sent its own message to Washington in March of that year by way of a surprise onslaught that struck deep into South Vietnam and threw the Saigon government into disarray.[119] Soon American B-52 bombers pummeled fuel depots around Hanoi and Haiphong, where four Soviet merchant ships were sunk. Kissinger warned the Soviets that détente was threatened unless the communist offensive ceased. "Why are you turning against *us* when it is Hanoi that has challenged you?" asked Ambassador Anatoly Dobrynin.[120] In May the president announced the mining of Haiphong harbor, a naval blockade of the North, and more massive bombing raids code-named LINEBACKER-I. "The bastards have never been bombed like they're going to be bombed this time," he growled.[121] During the seven months of LINEBACKER-I, American aircraft flew 41,653 sorties and dropped 155,000 tons of bombs on North Vietnamese storage facilities, air bases, power plants, bridges, tunnels, and by mistake, hospitals. Supplies to the South slowed but did not stop.

The Peace Agreement, Withdrawal, and Defeat

In early October 1972, Kissinger and the North Vietnamese negotiator Le Duc Tho finally reached an agreement that provided for U.S. withdrawal sixty days af-

"Une Grande, une Immense Majorité Silencieuse." President Nixon claimed support for his policies from the majority of Americans who remained silent during the vocal protests of the 1960s and 1970s. In this harsh sketch, Vazquez de Sola portrays Nixon's "silent majority" as war dead who cannot protest. (Swann Collection of Caricature and Cartoon)

ter a cease-fire, the return of American prisoners of war, and a political arrangement in the South that ultimately included elections. In short, both sides made concessions—North Vietnam gave up its demand that Thieu resign, and the United States dropped its insistence that North Vietnamese troops pull out of the South. When Kissinger traveled to Saigon, however, Thieu balked. Resentful at not having been consulted and opposed to North Vietnamese troops in the South, the South Vietnamese president refused to sign. When Kissinger bemoaned "the greatest failure of my diplomatic career," Thieu asked: "Are you rushing to get the Nobel Prize?"[122] Fearing that Thieu might cry betrayal just a few days before the U.S. presidential election, Nixon sent Kissinger back to the negotiating table. The communists, suspecting trickery, published the agreement that they had crafted with Kissinger. Still, on October 31, Kissinger told the press "peace is at hand."[123] Not so.

Back in Paris, on November 20, Kissinger and Le Duc Tho resumed their meetings. In early December they reached terms very much like those Thieu and Nixon had torpedoed in October. But a final agreement faltered over the status of the Demilitarized Zone (DMZ). Kissinger suspected the communists of stalling, perhaps counting on military victory. So he broke off the talks.

The carrot for Saigon (more arms), the stick for Hanoi. Nixon ordered the bombing of North Vietnam above the twentieth parallel. From December 18 to 28, LINEBACKER-II planes pounded North Vietnam hour upon hour in saturation bombing that Kissinger called "brutal unpredictability."[124] Everything from factories to water supplies took hits in the "Christmas bombing." Fifty-foot bomb craters gaped in Hanoi and Haiphong. North Vietnam's largest hospital was destroyed in error—"by bombs escaping the normal bomb train."[125] At least 2,000 civilians perished. Swedish prime minister Olof Palme cited such atrocities as "Guernica, Oradour, Katyn, Lidice, Sharpville, Treblinka. Now there is another name to add to the list—Hanoi, Christmas 1972."[126]

On December 22 Washington informed Hanoi that the bombing would stop if the North Vietnamese would reopen negotiations. The talks resumed, and on January 27, 1973, Kissinger and Le Duc Tho signed an accord. The United States promised to withdraw its remaining troops within sixty days; both sides would exchange prisoners; an international commission would oversee the cease-fire; and a coalition would conduct elections in the South. New language settled the DMZ issue. Although the Vietcong accepted the terms, Thieu as before stood aloof. If Thieu "bucks more," advised Senator Barry Goldwater, "to hell with him."[127] Nixon gave his secret promise that "we will respond with full force" if Hanoi violated the agreement. This promise, combined with the bombing of the North, persuaded Thieu to capitulate, albeit bitterly.[128] "Ah, these great powers who divide the world among themselves!" he remarked.[129] In the four years of the Nixon-Kissinger war, 20,553 Americans and half a million Vietnamese had died when "we could have gotten essentially the same deal anytime after the 1968 bombing halt," as one diplomat put it.[130]

Nixon claimed that the bombings had forced the enemy to accept U.S. terms. A Kissinger aide stated more accurately: "We bombed the North Vietnamese into accepting our concessions."[131] In the twelve days of bombing, the United States lost twenty-six planes over North Vietnam, fifteen of them expensive B-52s. In private, Nixon "kept coming back to the B-52 loss problem, saying we can't back off, but will we get three losses every time [we raid]?"[132] The final agreement, moreover, resembled the one reached in October, before the bombing. Finally, the popular outcry in the United States against Nixon's "war by tantrum" grew so loud that the president could not ignore it.[133] With Congress about to reconvene, many legislators wanted to eliminate funds for the bombing. Perhaps through North Vietnam's willingness to resume negotiations, "Nixon got himself off the hook," as one scholar has written.[134]

The cease-fire broke down quickly as each side moved to strengthen itself militarily. The United States maintained military and CIA "advisers" in Vietnam and transferred millions of dollars' worth of equipment and bases to the Saigon regime. One peace provision called for the United States to provide Hanoi with substantial reconstruction funds. But when the cease-fire collapsed, that agreement died. U.S. warships still cruised off the coast, and the bombing of Cambodia continued. Congress acted again, this time against a president weakened by Watergate revelations, voting in June 1973 to require the president to cease military actions in all parts of Indochina. Nixon vetoed the measure but accepted a compromise deadline of August 15. In November came the War Powers Resolution. In 1974 Congress rejected Kissinger's appeal for $1.5 billion in military aid for Thieu's collapsing government, voting $700 million instead.

Pressed by North Vietnamese and Vietcong advances, Thieu and his coterie seemed paralyzed by early 1975. Then the communists launched an offensive whose swift success surprised even themselves. The Army of the Republic of Vietnam disintegrated as a fighting force. Many ARVN troops deserted, were captured, or were killed. Refugees clogged highways; the turmoil in the countryside and cities left some civilians near starvation. ARVN forces abandoned vast amounts of American-made military hardware to the enemy.

On April 30, 1975, the victorious Vietcong and North Vietnamese streamed into Saigon. For days, frantic Vietnamese had surged toward the Tan Son Nhut air base near Saigon, where American planes loaded evacuees. But there were not enough airplanes, people blocked the runways, and enemy rockets smashed into frightened crowds. Thousands of scrambling, crying Vietnamese engulfed the U.S. Embassy, whose roof served as a landing pad for helicopters from offshore ships. Thieu, the generals, other high-ranking officials, and those who had the money to bribe their passage, had managed to escape earlier, but they abandoned thousands of Vietnamese compromised by their years of cooperation with the United States. Some were later sent to communist "reeducation camps." Others escaped as "boat people" and sailed away in unseaworthy craft with inadequate water and food. Human tragedy also struck Cambodia and Laos, where, in 1975, the communist insurgents also triumphed. In Cambodia the Khmer Rouge imposed a genocidal regime that killed millions.

The Americans exited from their longest war without victory. At least 58,000 Americans died in Vietnam. At least 3 million Vietnamese died. Hundreds of thousands of people were maimed, and millions became refugees. Civilian deaths in Cambodia and Laos, before and after 1975, also numbered in the millions. The United States spent at least $170 billion in Southeast Asia. Perhaps another $200 billion would be paid to American veterans of the war in the future. The prolonged Vietnam War alienated U.S. allies, undercut détente, and spoiled relations with the Third World. At home the war fueled inflation and political instability. Nixon's Watergate abuses stemmed in large part from the strains the war placed on the White House and from frustrations over leaks. The war wrecked two presidencies—Johnson's and Nixon's—and weakened the institution of the presidency. Believing that their highest officials had too often lied and deceived, Americans' trust in their government plummeted. Blaming others rather than his own flawed policies for failure in Vietnam, the historian Jeffrey Kimball has noted, Nixon "contributed to the bitterness that haunted American politics and the confusion of purpose and meaning that plagued American foreign policy in the years ahead."[135]

The Many Lessons and Questions of Vietnam

Americans only reluctantly searched for lessons after the Vietnam debacle, and most discussion took place among the intellectual and governmental elite. Most citizens seemed more relieved that it had ended than inquisitive about consequences. They switched it off like a TV set. The 1976 presidential campaign passed with barely a word uttered about Vietnam.

Hawkish leaders feared that defeat in Vietnam had weakened U.S. credibility, inviting the nation's adversaries to exploit Washington's setback. They decried a "Vietnam syndrome" that allegedly prevented America from sustaining its role as world leader. "Sir, do we get to win this time?" asked the fictional John Rambo as he returned to Vietnam in the popular film *Rambo II* (1985).[136] Generals Maxwell Taylor and William Westmoreland lamented that they could have gained victory if only the American people had not suffered a failure of will during the Tet offensive: Just let the military do its job next time, unencumbered by fickle public opinion, inquisitive journalists, and public congressional watchdogs. "We didn't know our ally [South Vietnam]," Taylor later admitted, but "we knew even less about the enemy. And, the last, most inexcusable of our mistakes, was not knowing our own people."[137] Other hawks considered Vietnam the wrong terrain on which to battle communism: Next time the United States should choose a more strategically advantageous site and use aerial and naval power rather than troops, or change strategy to emphasize limited or theater nuclear warfare.

Some political scientists, such as Graham Allison in *Essence of Decision* (1971), emphasized a bureaucratic politics model to interpret events. They suggested that it is difficult to hold individuals accountable for decisions and "outcomes," because of the way the impersonal, oversized bureaucracy resists change, follows standard operating procedures, and becomes rutted in traditional channels.[138] This bureaucracy had to be reformed to encourage more intragovernment dissent and debate, eschew fixed doctrines and kneejerk anticommunism, and "think in time"—that is, become alert to the historical record to avoid making the same mistakes again and again.[139] Critics of this analysis, however, blamed Vietnam on strong presidents such as Johnson, who actually controlled the bureaucracy through appointments, an overpowering personality, and a pervasive ideology. This viewpoint implied that a future change in presidents would bring about diplomatic reformation. A more assertive Congress, some argued, could rein in the "imperial presidency," as exposed by Senator Frank Church's 1975 intelligence committee revelations about CIA "abuses and aberrations," including attempted assassinations of Fidel Castro and other foreign leaders.[140]

Other opinions differed radically: Vietnam was a prime example of American global expansionism and arrogance, encouraged by a zealous belief that the United States, through superior power and ideals, could and should manage events almost everywhere. Richard J. Barnet of the Institute for Policy Studies in Washington, D.C., in his *Roots of War* (1972), wrote that the nation had to examine "those drives . . . that impel us toward destruction," among them a capitalist economy and business creed that required intervention abroad.[141]

The *Mayaguez* incident of May 1975 seemed to suggest as much. Just as opinion polls in Europe indicated "major declines in U.S. standing" after the fall of Saigon, Cambodian patrol boats seized the American merchant ship *Mayaguez*.[142] "Let's look ferocious," said Kissinger, so as to refute charges that the United States had become a helpless giant after Vietnam.[143] U.S. marines assaulted Koh Tang Island off the Cambodian coast, and U.S. warships and planes attacked Cambodian boats and bases, nearly killing the *Mayaguez* crew in the process. Cambodians released the *Mayaguez* and its crew, but forty-one Americans died. Senator Barry Goldwater crowed "we've still got balls."[144]

The Vietnam War, said other critics, revealed the shortcomings of the containment doctrine, which had failed to make distinctions between peripheral and vital areas and which applied military force to political problems. The analyst Ed-

Vietnam Refrain. Presidents Eisenhower through Ford kept predicting victory in Vietnam but kept losing the war. In 1975, Ford made a last-ditch effort to gain a small victory in the tragic *Mayaguez* affair. (Mike Peters, *Dayton Daily News,* 1975)

mund Stillman wrote: "Freedom *is* divisible. Some places are worthy of defense. Some are not. Some are capable of being defended. Some are not."[145] Ronald Steel, an eloquent critic of *Pax Americana,* likewise concluded: "Never confuse knights and bishops with pawns."[146]

The historian Henry Steele Commager wondered why "we find it so hard to accept this elementary lesson of history, that some wars are so deeply immoral that they must be lost, that the war in Vietnam was one of these wars, and that those who resist it are the truest patriots."[147] To some, then, defeat became a victory for humane values. In contrast to those who blamed the antiwar activists for encouraging the enemy and weakening congressional resolve, historians of the peace movement have offered a more modest judgment. Antiwar opponents "produced an awareness of an alternative America that stripped away through dissent and resistance the rational, moral, and political legitimacy of Washington's war in Indochina."[148] Thus: "The dissidents did not stop the war. But they made it stoppable."[149] Some commentators urged "neo-isolationism" after Vietnam. "Compared to people who thought they could run the universe," remarked the famed journalist Walter Lippmann, "I *am* a neo-isolationist and proud of it."[150] Never again should the United States practice unrestrained global interventionism.

By the late 1970s public discussion of the Vietnam experience and its consequences increased. Films such as *Coming Home* (1978), *The Deer Hunter* (1978), and *Apocalypse Now* (1979) heightened public attention. Depicting the soldiers' Vietnam were memoirs such as C. D. B. Bryan's *Friendly Fire* (1976), Ron Kovic's *Born on the Fourth of July* (1976), Philip Caputo's *A Rumor of War* (1977), and Michael Herr's *Dispatches* (1977); oral histories such as Al Santoli's *Everything We Had* (1981) and Mark Baker's *Nam* (1981); and novels such as James Webb's *Fields of Fire* (1978).

The dedication of the Vietnam Veterans Memorial in Washington in November 1982 gave the 2.8 million survivors of service in the war "a wailing wall. We came to find the names of those we lost in the war, as if by tracing the letters cut

Vietnam Memorials. These statues, part of the memorial site in Washington, D.C., honor the men and women who served in the Vietnam War. On the left is the Vietnam Veterans Memorial by Frederick Hart, and on the right is the Vietnam Women's Memorial by Glenna Goodacre. Both stand near the long wall on which the names of Americans who died in Vietnam are etched. (National Park Service)

into the granite we could find what was left of ourselves."[151] Hundreds of thousands of veterans suffered from post-traumatic stress disorder. An ex-marine remembered crawling "around on the floor with my .357 Magnum in my house looking for North Vietnamese soldiers with my wife and kids terrorized."[152] For thirteen years a former army nurse woke up each night to wash her hands. "Like Lady Macbeth. I couldn't get the blood of Vietnam off my hands," she recalled.[153] By the early 1990s, thousands of veterans of the Vietnam War had committed suicide.

Post-Vietnam writings, television documentaries, and college courses on the war have emphasized the *American* experience in Vietnam, even as hundreds of thousands of Vietnamese, Cambodian, and Laotian refugees came to the United States and gained citizenship over the next two decades. When one professor asked his students to consider the Vietnamese and their response to the war, he found that most "cannot grasp that the war had something to do with other people." Instead of a real country on the far side of the Pacific with its own history and culture, Vietnam had become, as one writer put it, "another word for mistakes or dishonesty or whatever."[154] The only "Vietnamese words we learned were the cusswords," recalled one veteran.[155]

Debate on the war came to center on whether the United States could have won. Many conservatives articulated a "stab-in-the-back" theory, namely, that the United States could have won had protesters not impeded the war effort and had civilian officials not restrained the military.[156] President Ronald Reagan declared that American troops "were denied permission to win."[157] "It takes the full strength of a tiger to kill a rabbit," argued General William C. Westmoreland.[158]

Doubters have raised imposing questions about such thinking. Because the bombing of North Vietnam did not significantly impede the flow of matériel and soldiers to the South, perhaps only a U.S. invasion of the North would have sufficed to defeat the enemy. This strategy would have entailed heavy American casualties and a long occupation of a hostile population that had demonstrated its tenacity against foreigners through decades of warfare. Would Americans accept the killing of tens of thousands of people by bombing the irrigation dikes of the North? Would Americans volunteer for a cause with such an uncertain end? Would they tolerate huge draft calls? An invasion of the North, moreover, would have risked war with both the Soviet Union and China. Détente might have restrained the Soviets from rescuing the North, but China sent 320,000 troops to North Vietnam between 1965 and 1969, credibly threatening intervention if the United States moved north with "dire consequences for the world."[159] To say that the United States lacked the "will" to win misses the real limits on American power. "What distinguishes me from [Lyndon] Johnson," Nixon once said, "is that I have the *will* in spades."[160] Yet Nixon wisely rejected tactical nuclear weapons or an invasion of the North, because he recoiled from the domestic and international consequences.

To have won, suggested some, the United States would also have had to destroy what it was trying to save—that is, using more military power would have produced more deaths and more refugees. What would remain after "victory"? Perhaps at best an internally divided, economically feeble nation needing huge infusions of American aid but still vulnerable to collapse. Even with the military unleashed—and dropping on Indochina three times the tonnage of bombs used in all theaters during World War II hardly suggests restraint—it would still have faced intractable problems: an inhospitable terrain and climate; jungle, leeches, malaria, and enemy booby traps; an elusive adversary deeply committed to its cause, battle-tested, and able to live off the land (*its* land); and a South Vietnamese people who often sheltered communist soldiers. Doubters of the "win" thesis also note that the United States received very little help from its allies. In fact most European partners urged Washington to stop wasting its resources on a fruitless venture. Of America's forty allies by treaty, only Australia, New Zealand, South Korea, and Thailand sent combat troops.

The United States could not have won, others have argued, because it lacked a political base on which to build. Coups and attempted coups too often rocked the unpopular Saigon governments. The South Vietnamese desertion rate ran high. ARVN troops were "armed farces," said one U.S. adviser, "very poor fighters" with "absolutely no discipline" whose "timidity endangered American lives."[161] ARVN forces suffered the same problems that afflicted their government: poor morale, corruption, and nepotism. The "war of attrition" alienated many South Vietnamese, as did the unsettling strategic hamlet program, disruptive "search and destroy" missions, leveling of villages, requiring of identity cards, bombings of innocents, and spraying of Agent Orange. Cultural differences also separated Americans from Vietnamese. Bars and prostitution flourished in a rural Buddhist society made rapidly urban by fleeing refugees. High-tech computers hummed and giant war machines rumbled in a land of water buffalo, rice paddies, and traditional peasant folk.

Problems in the U.S. military itself reduced the chances for victory. Because officers wanted to reassure superiors that they were turning back the enemy, some suppressed intelligence information and submitted false reports on the numbers killed. "If he's dead and Vietnamese, he's VC [Vietcong]" became the prevailing assumption in the field.[162] Decisionmakers in Washington did not fully know how badly the war was going. The military also suffered from corruption and mismanagement—even a black market for equipment developed. By early 1971 some 40,000 GIs had become heroin addicts. Racial tension between "bloods" (blacks) and "honkies" (whites) and "fragging"—the murder of officers by enlisted soldiers by means of a hand grenade or other weapon—further reduced combat effectiveness. Educational deferments under the draft system meant that "high school dropouts were three times more likely to experience heavy combat than were college graduates."[163] The rotation system for officers—one year in Vietnam to "punch your ticket"—undermined military cohesion and the benefits of experience. "About the time they [officers] gain the experience and not get your butt killed," one enlisted man remembered, "they get sucked back in the rear with the gear, and you get a brand-new butter bar and . . . go through the whole process again."[164] Disgusted with the "groupthink pressure"and "pretense," General Colin Powell later wrote that many of "my generation . . . vowed that when our turn came to call the shots, we would not quietly acquiesce in half-hearted warfare for half-baked reasons that the American people could not understand or support."[165]

The United States also faced tenacious adversaries who suffered remarkable losses but kept coming. "I know Americans," Ho had said. "They are an impatient people. They will leave."[166] Defending their nation against outsiders, the Vietnamese enemy seemed indomitable. "Everything we knew commanded us to fight," a Vietcong veteran remembered. "Our ancestors called us to war. Our myths and legends called us to war."[167] General Bruce Palmer, Jr., remembered that "their will to resist was inextinguishable."[168] The Vietnamese had always fought those who brought "elephants home to trample the graveyards of their ancestors."[169] Such elephants "could make the earth tremble" but "couldn't conquer the ants that lived on it."[170]

Whatever the answer to the Vietnam tragedy, succeeding administrations would have to operate in a domestic political setting of uncertainty about the direction of American foreign relations. Conservative defenders of the war stood ready to criticize any policy that smacked of retrenchment or "another Munich." Liberals and radicals stood alert to dispute any policy that seemed to offer "another Vietnam." And in this highly charged environment, the unfulfilled Nixon-Kissinger grand design disintegrated further.

FURTHER READING FOR THE PERIOD 1969–1977

See works on the Cold War, the Third World, and other topics cited in earlier chapters.

For foreign relations during the Nixon and Ford presidencies, and for Richard M. Nixon the person, see Stephen E. Ambrose, *Nixon* (1989, 1991); James Cannon, *Time and Chance* (1994) (Ford); Terry L. Deibel, *Presidents, Public Opinion, and Power* (1987); Leon Friedman and William F. Levantrosser, eds., *Cold*

War Patriot and Statesman (1993) (Nixon); Michael Genovese, *The Nixon Presidency* (1990); John R. Greene, *The Limits of Power* (1992) and *The Presidency of Gerald R. Ford* (1994); Seymour Hersh, *The Price of Power* (1983); Joan Hoff, *Nixon Reconsidered* (1994); Stanley Hoffmann, *Primacy or World Order* (1978); Ole Holsti and James R. Roseneau, *American Leadership in World Affairs: Vietnam and the Breakdown of Consensus* (1984); Robert C. Johansen, *The National Interest and the Human Interest* (1980); Richard A. Melanson, *American Foreign Policy Since the Vietnam War* (1996); Roger Morris, *Richard Milhous Nixon* (1989); Franz Schurmann, *The Foreign Politics of Richard Nixon* (1987); Lewis Sorley, *Arms Transfers Under Nixon* (1983) and *A Better War* (1999); and Garry Wills, *Nixon Agonistes* (1970).

For Henry A. Kissinger, see Dan Caldwell, ed., *Henry Kissinger* (1983); Gregory D. Cleva, *Henry Kissinger and the American Approach to Foreign Policy* (1989); Gordon A. Craig and Francis L. Lowenheim, eds., *The Diplomats* (1994); Stephen Graubard, *Kissinger* (1973); Walter Isaacson, *Kissinger* (1992); Bernard and Marvin Kalb, *Kissinger* (1974); Roger Morris, *Uncertain Greatness* (1977); Robert D. Schulzinger, *Henry Kissinger* (1989); Harvey Starr, *Henry Kissinger* (1984); and John Stoessinger, *Henry Kissinger* (1976).

For Congress, including the Church committee's investigations, see Thomas Franck and Edward Weisband, *Foreign Policy by Congress* (1979); Loch K. Johnson, *A Season of Inquiry* (1985); and Kathryn S. Olmsted, *Challenging the Secret Government* (1997).

For Soviet-American relations, détente, and SALT, see Richard J. Barnet, *The Giants* (1977); Robert F. Byrnes, *Soviet-American Academic Exchanges, 1958–1975* (1976); Robin Edmonds, *Soviet Foreign Policy* (1983); Michael B. Froman, *The Development of the Idea of Détente* (1992); Raymond L. Garthoff, *Détente and Confrontation* (1995); Alexander L. George et al., eds., *Managing U.S.-Soviet Rivalry* (1982); Marshall I. Goldman, *Détente and Dollars* (1975); Jonathan Haslam, *The Soviet Union and the Politics of Nuclear Weapons in Europe* (1990); David Holloway, *The Soviet Union and the Arms Race* (1983); Robert S. Litwak, *Détente and the Nixon Doctrine* (1984); Michael Mandelbaum, *The Nuclear Question* (1979); Keith L. Nelson, *The Making of Détente* (1995); John Newhouse, *Cold Dawn* (1973); Morton Schwartz, *Soviet Perceptions of the United States* (1978); Gordon B. Smith, ed., *The Politics of East-West Trade* (1984); Paula Stern, *Water's Edge* (1979) (Jackson Amendment); Richard W. Stevenson, *The Rise and Fall of Détente* (1985); Terry Terriff, *The Nixon Administration and the Making of U.S. Nuclear Strategy* (1995); and Adam B. Ulam, *Dangerous Relations* (1983).

For China and Japan, see Warren I. Cohen, *America's Response to China* (1990); Rosemary Foot, *The Practice of Power* (1995); Gene T. Hsiao, ed., *Sino-American Détente and Its Policy Implications* (1974); Arnold Xiangze Jiang, *The United States and China* (1988); Ronald C. Keith, *The Diplomacy of Zhou Enlai* (1989); Walter LaFeber, *The Clash* (1997) (Japan); James Mann, *About Face* (1999) (China); Robert S. Ross, *Negotiating Cooperation* (1995); Michael Schaller, *The United States and China* (1990) and *Altered States* (1997) (Japan); David Shambaugh, *Beautiful Imperialist* (1991); Robert G. Sutter, *The China Quandary* (1983); Ross Terrill, *Mao* (1993); and Nancy B. Tucker, *Taiwan, Hong Kong, and the United States* (1994).

The end and lessons of the Vietnam War are explored in Anthony S. Campagna, *The Economic Consequences of the Vietnam War* (1991); Walter H. Capps, *The Unfinished War* (1982); John H. Ely, *War and Responsibility* (1993); Leslie H. Gelb and Richard K. Betts, *The Irony of Vietnam* (1979); Allan E. Goodman, *The Lost Peace* (1978); John Hellmann, *American Myth and the Legacy of Vietnam* (1986); Rhodri Jeffreys-Jones, *Peace Now! American Society and the Ending of the Vietnam War* (1999); Jeffrey Kimball, *Nixon's Vietnam War* (1998); Anthony Lake, ed., *The Vietnam Legacy* (1976); Timothy J. Lomperis, *The War Everyone Lost—and Won* (1984); Myra MacPherson, *Long Time Passing* (1984); Richard A. Melanson, *Writing History and Making Policy* (1983) and *Reconstructing Consensus* (1990); Gareth Porter, *A Peace Denied* (1975); Earl C. Ravenal, *Never Again* (1978); William Shawcross, *Sideshow* (1979) (Cambodia); and W. Scott Thompson and Donaldson D. Frizzill, eds., *The Lessons of Vietnam* (1977). See also works listed in Chapter 9.

International economic questions, including the North-South debate, are covered in Richard J. Barnet, *The Lean Years* (1980); Richard J. Barnet and Ronald Müller, *Global Reach* (1974); David P. Calleo, *The Imperious Economy* (1982); Albert L. Danielson, *The Evolution of OPEC* (1982); I. M. Destler, *Making Foreign Economic Policy* (1980); I. M. Destler, Haruhiro Fukui, and Hideo Sato, *The Textile Wrangle* (1979); Jeffrey A. Hart, *The New International Economic Order* (1983); Stephen Krasner, *Defending the National Interest* (1978); Diane B. Kunz, *Butter and Guns* (1997); Allen J. Matusow, *Nixon's Economy* (1998); David Morawetz, *Twenty-five Years of Economic Development* (1977); Robert K. Olson, *U.S. Foreign Policy and the New International*

Economic Order (1981); Robert A. Pastor, *Congress and the Politics of U.S. Foreign Economic Policy* (1980); Joan E. Spero, *The Politics of International Economic Relations* (1985); and Brian Tew, *The Evolution of the International Monetary System* (1982).

Environmental issues, population, food, and their intersection with the international economy and world politics are examined in Robert Boardman, *International Organization and the Conservation of Nature* (1981); Lynton K. Caldwell, *International Environmental Policy* (1984); Alfred E. Eckes, Jr., *The United States and the Global Struggle for Minerals* (1977); Ann L. Hollick, *U.S. Foreign Policy and the Law of the Sea* (1981); Raymond F. Hopkins and Donald J. Puchala, *Global Food Interdependence* (1980); John McCormick, *Reclaiming Paradise: The Global Environmental Movement* (1989); William Murdoch, *The Poverty of Nations* (1980); William and Paul Paddock, *Time of Famines* (1976); Clyde Sanger, *Ordering the Oceans* (1987); Ross B. Talbott, *The Four World Food Agencies in Rome* (1990); Mitchel B. Wallerstein, *Food for War–Food for Peace* (1980).

For Africa and some Third World issues, see Fernando A. Guimarães, *The Origins of the Angolan Civil War* (1998); Charles A. Jones, *The North-South Dialogue* (1983); Anthony Lake, *The "Tar Baby" Option* (1976) (Southern Rhodesia); Robert J. McMahon, *The Limits of Empire* (1999); and P. David Searles, *The Peace Corps Experience: Challenge and Change, 1969–1976* (1997).

For the Middle East, oil, and the Arab-Israeli conflict, see George W. Ball and Douglas B. Ball, *The Passionate Attachment* (1992) (Israel); James A. Bill, *The Eagle and the Lion* (1988) (Iran); George W. Breslauer, *Soviet Strategy in the Middle East* (1990); Trevor N. Dupuy, *Elusive Victory* (1978); James F. Goode, *The United States and Iran* (1997); Robert D. Kaplan, *The Arabists* (1993); George Lenczowski, *The Middle East in World Affairs* (1980); Donald Neff, *Warriors Against Israel* (1988); William R. Polk, *The Arab World Today* (1991); William B. Quandt, *Decade of Decisions* (1977); Bernard Reich, *Quest for Peace* (1977); Cheryl A. Rubenberg, *Israel and the American National Interest* (1986); Barry Rubin, *Paved with Good Intentions* (1977) (Iran); Yezid Sayigh, *Armed Struggle and the Search for State* (1998) (Palestinians); David Schoenbaum, *The United States and the State of Israel* (1993); Mohammed K. Shadid, *The United States and the Palestinians* (1981); Edward R. F. Sheehan, *The Arabs, Israelis, and Kissinger* (1976); Benjamin Shwadran, *Middle East Oil* (1977); Steven L. Spiegel, *The Other Arab-Israeli Conflict* (1985); and Daniel Yergin, *The Prize* (1991) (oil).

Latin America–U.S. relations, including Chile, are treated in Robert J. Alexander, *The Tragedy of Chile* (1978); Richard R. Fagen, ed., *Capitalism and the State in U.S.–Latin American Relations* (1979); T. H. Moran, *Multinational Corporations and the Politics of Dependence: Copper in Chile* (1974); Morris H. Morley, *Washington, Somoza, and the Sandinistas* (1994); James Petras and Morris Morley, *The United States and Chile* (1975); Stephen G. Rabe, *The Road to OPEC* (1982) (Venezuela); Lars Schoultz, *Beneath the United States* (1998); Paul E. Sigmund, *The United States and Democracy in Chile* (1993); Peter H. Smith, *Talons of the Eagle* (1996); and Arthur P. Whitaker, *The United States and the Southern Cone* (1976).

See also the General Bibliography and the following notes.

For comprehensive coverage of foreign-relations topics, see the articles in the four-volume *Encyclopedia of U.S. Foreign Relations* (1997), edited by Bruce W. Jentleson and Thomas G. Paterson.

NOTES TO CHAPTER 10

1. Quoted in Bernard Kalb and Marvin Kalb, *Kissinger* (Boston: Little, Brown, 1974), p. 266.
2. Hugh Sidey in *Life, LXXII* (March 3, 1972), 12.
3. *Newsweek, LXXIX* (February 28, 1972), 13.
4. *Department of State Bulletin, LXVI* (March 6, 1972), 290.
5. Quoted in John Lewis Gaddis, *Strategies of Containment* (New York: Oxford University Press, 1982), p. 296.
6. Quoted in John Maxwell Hamilton, *Edgar Snow* (Bloomington: Indiana University Press, 1988), p. 269.
7. Quoted in Robert D. Schulzinger, *Henry Kissinger* (New York: Columbia University Press, 1989), p. 85.

8. Henry Kissinger, *White House Years* (Boston: Little, Brown, 1979), p. 754.
9. *Public Papers, Nixon, 1971* (Washington, D.C.: Government Printing Office, 1972), p. 819.
10. Entry of April 20, 1971, in H. R. Haldeman, *The Haldeman Diaries* (New York: Putnam, 1994), p. 275.
11. Quoted in Joan Hoff, "A Revisionist View of Nixon's Foreign Policy," *Presidential Studies Quarterly, XXVI* (Winter 1996), 117.
12. Kissinger, *White House Years*, p. 1049.
13. Mao quoted in Li Zhisui, *The Private Life of Chairman Mao* (New York: Random House, 1994), p. 565.

14. Quoted in Rosemary Foot, *The Practice of Power* (New York: Oxford University Press, 1995), p. 137.

15. Quoted in Robert S. Ross, *Negotiating Cooperation* (Stanford: Stanford University Press, 1995), p. 45.

16. Richard Nixon, *RN* (New York: Grosset & Dunlap, 1978), p. 564.

17. Walter Isaacson, *Kissinger* (New York: Simon & Schuster, 1992), p. 402.

18. Entry of February 22, 1972, *Haldeman Diaries*, p. 416.

19. Kissinger memorandum of conversation, February 21, 1972 in William Burr, ed., *The Kissinger Transcripts* (New York: New Press, 1998), p. 64.

20. Quoted in Li, *Chairman Mao*, p. 514.

21. Entry of February 22, 1972, *Haldeman Diaries*, p. 417.

22. George Gallup in *Hartford Courant*, March 12, 1972.

23. Quoted in Ronald C. Keith, *The Diplomacy of Zhou Enlai* (New York: St. Martin's Press, 1989), p. 199.

24. Quoted in Michael A. Schaller, *Altered States* (New York: Oxford University Press, 1997), p. 227.

25. Nixon quoted in Nancy Bernkopf Tucker, *Taiwan, Hong Kong, and the United States* (New York: Twayne, 1994), p. 104.

26. *Department of State Bulletin*, LXVI (March 20, 1972), 435–438.

27. Nixon, *RN*, p. 580.

28. Michael S. Sherry, *In the Shadow of War* (New Haven: Yale University Press, 1995), p. 310.

29. H. R. Haldeman, *The Ends of Power* (New York: Times Books, 1978), p. 98.

30. Stephen E. Ambrose, *Nixon: Ruin and Recovery, 1973–1990* (New York: Simon & Schuster, 1991), p. 58.

31. Tape recording, June 23, 1971, in Stanley I. Kutler, ed., *Abuse of Power* (New York: Free Press, 1997), p. 4.

32. Anatoly Dobrynin, *In Confidence* (New York: Random House, 1995), p. 310.

33. Quoted in Richard Valeriani, *Travels with Henry* (New York: Berkley, 1980), p. 123; Kissinger, *White House Years*, p. 1094.

34. Stanley Hoffmann, *Primacy or World Order* (New York: McGraw-Hill, 1978), p. 33.

35. James Reston, *Deadline* (New York: Random House, 1991), pp. 419–420.

36. Quoted in Ann Miller Morin, *Her Excellency* (New York: Twayne, 1994), p. 110.

37. "An Interview with Oriana Fallaci: Kissinger," *New Republic*, CLXVII (December 16, 1972), 21–22.

38. Quoted in *Time*, CXXV (February 11, 1985), 65.

39. Quoted in J. Garry Clifford, "Change and Continuity," in James Patterson, ed., *Paths to the Present* (Minneapolis: Burgess, 1975), p. 137.

40. Quoted in Thomas G. Paterson, "Oversight or Afterview?" in Michael Barnhart, ed., *Congress and United States Foreign Policy* (Albany: State University of New York Press, 1987), p. 155.

41. Quoted in James A. Bill, *George Ball* (New Haven: Yale University Press, 1997), p. 217.

42. Quoted in Garry Wills, *Nixon Agonistes* (Boston: Houghton Mifflin, 1970), p. 20.

43. Kissinger, *White House Years*, p. 191.

44. *Ibid.*, p. 55.

45. Quoted in John Lewis Gaddis, "The Statecraft of Henry Kissinger," in Gordon A. Craig and Francis L. Loewenheim, eds., *The Diplomats, 1939–1979* (Princeton: Princeton University Press, 1994), p. 574.

46. Kissinger quoted in Robert J. McMahon, *The Limits of Empire* (New York: Columbia University Press, 1999), p. 157.

47. Memorandum of White House meeting, December 7, 1970, Box 68, Dean Acheson Papers, Yale University, New Haven, Conn.

48. Elaine P. Adam and Richard P. Stebbins, eds., *American Foreign Relations, 1976* (New York: New York University Press, 1978), p. 13.

49. Quoted in Robert J. McMahon, *The Cold War on the Periphery* (New York: Columbia University Press, 1994), p. 346.

50. Quoted in Nixon, *RN*, p. 527.

51. Raymond G. Garthoff, *Détente and Confrontation* (Washington, D.C.: Brookings Institution, 1995; rev. ed.), p. 311.

52. Nixon, *RN*, p. 527.

53. Michael Mandelbaum, *The Nuclear Question* (Cambridge, Eng.: Cambridge University Press, 1979), p. 218.

54. Gerard C. Smith, *Disarming Diplomat* (New York: Madison Books, 1996), p. 167.

55. Kissinger memorandum of conversation, March 27, 1974, in Burr, *Kissinger Transcripts*, p. 258; quoted in Gregg Herken, *Counsels of War* (New York: Oxford University Press, 1987), p. 255.

56. Kissinger, *White House Years*, p. 1245n.

57. Quoted in Donald R. Baucom, *The Origins of SDI* (Lawrence: University Press of Kansas, 1992), p. 75.

58. William Hyland quoted in Isaacson, *Kissinger*, p. 663.

59. Ford quoted in John Robert Greene, *The Presidency of Gerald R. Ford* (Lawrence: University Press of Kansas, 1995), p. 151.

60. *Public Papers, Nixon, 1969*, p. 548.

61. Kissinger, *White House Years*, p. 117.

62. Quoted in David Schoenbaum, *The United States and the State of Israel* (New York: Oxford University Press, 1993), p. 171.

63. William B. Quandt, *Decade of Decisions* (Berkeley: University of California Press, 1977), p. 127.

64. Sadat quoted in Yazid Sayigh, *Armed Struggle and the Search for State* (New York: Oxford University Press, 1997), p. 152.

65. Quoted in Richard Ned Lebow and Janice Gross Stein, *We All Lost the Cold War* (Princeton: Princeton University Press, 1994), p. 189.

66. Alexander Haig quoting Nixon in Garthoff, *Détente and Confrontation*, p. 426.

67. Aleksei Kosygin and Yuri Andropov quoted in Victor Israeyan, *Inside the Kremlin During the Yom Kippur War* (University Park: Penn State University Press, 1995), p. 180.

68. Ahmed Zakhi Yamani quoted in Daniel Yergin, *The Prize* (New York: Simon & Schuster, 1991), p. 606.

69. Quoted in Edward R. F. Sheehan, "How Kissinger Did It," *Foreign Policy*, no. 22 (Spring 1976), 48.

70. Quoted in *New York Times*, March 15, 1976.

71. Sayigh, *Armed Struggle*, p. 333.

72. Richard Helms quoting the Shah in James F. Goode, *The United States and Iran* (New York: St. Martin's Press, 1997), p. 186.

73. Kissinger quoted in James A. Bill, *The Eagle and the Lion* (New Haven: Yale University Press, 1988), p. 203.

74. Quoted in Samuel Baily, *The United States and the Development of South America* (New York: New Viewpoints, 1976), p. 118.

75. Walter LaFeber, "The Tension between Democracy and Capitalism," *Diplomatic History, XXIII* (Spring 1999), 178; Helms quoted in William Bundy, *A Tangled Web* (New York: Hill & Wang, 1998), p. 201.

76. Quoted in U.S. Senate, Select Committee . . . Intelligence Activities, *Covert Action in Chile* (Washington, D.C.: Government Printing Office, 1975), p. 33.

77. Quoted in William F. Sater, *Chile and the United States* (Athens: University of Georgia Press, 1990), p. 184.

78. Clodomiro Almeyda quoted *ibid.*, p. 187.

79. Kissinger, *White House Years*, p. 645.

80. Quoted in Garthoff, *Détente and Confrontation*, p. 92.

81. Quoted in Stephen Weissman, "CIA Covert Action in Zaire and Angola," *Political Science Quarterly*, XCIV (Summer 1979), 281.

82. Quoted in Roger Morris, *Uncertain Greatness* (New York: Harper and Row, 1977), p. 131.

83. Quoted in Steven Metz, "Congress, the Antiapartheid Movement, and Nixon," *Diplomatic History, XII* (Spring 1988), 177.

84. Nathaniel Davis, "The Angola Decision of 1975," *Foreign Affairs*, LVII (Fall 1978), 114.

85. Anatoly Dobrynin quoted in Piero Gleijeses, "Havana's Policy in Africa," *Cold War International History Project Bulletin*, nos. 8–9 (Winter 1996/1997), 13.

86. Gerald R. Ford, *A Time to Heal* (New York: Harper and Row, 1979), p. 345.

87. Quoted in Thomas W. McCormick, *America's Half Century* (Baltimore: Johns Hopkins University Press, 1996; rev. ed.), p. 189.

88. Kissinger memorandum of conversation, January 21, 1977, in Burr, *Kissinger Transcripts*, p. 445; Soviet Foreign Office quoted in Arne Odd Westad, "Moscow and the Angolan Crisis," *Cold War International History Project Bulletin*, nos. 8–9 (Winter 1996/1997), 27, 29.

89. Leonid Brezhnev quoted in Garthoff, *Détente and Confrontation*, p. 41.

90. Dobrynin, *In Confidence*, p. 472.

91. *Department of State Bulletin*, LXXV (July 12, 1976), 46.

92. *Ibid.*, LXXII (June 2, 1975), 713.

93. Quoted in Diane B. Kunz, *Butter and Guns* (New York: Free Press, 1997), p. 218.

94. Kissinger, *White House Years*, pp. 955, 962.

95. U.S. business executive quoted in Walter LaFeber, *The Clash* (New York: Norton, 1997), p. 353.

96. Reuben Askew quoted in Charles W. Kegley, Jr., and Eugene R. Wittkopf, *World Politics* (New York: St. Martin's Press, 1981), p. 181.

97. Quoted in Thomas G. Paterson, *On Every Front* (New York: Norton, 1992; 2nd ed.), p. 217.

98. Quoted in Robert C. Johansen, *The National Interest and the Human Interest* (Princeton: Princeton University Press, 1980), p. 13.

99. Quoted in Adam and Stebbins, *American Foreign Relations, 1976*, p. 478.

100. Quoted in Mark H. Lytle, "An Environmental Approach to American Diplomatic History," *Diplomatic History, XX* (Spring 1996), 287.

101. Petr Beckmann quoted in John McCormick, *Reclaiming Paradise* (Bloomington: Indiana University Press, 1989), p. 85.

102. Mario Gibson Barbaroza quoted in Charles McGraw, "Removed from Planet Earth" (Unpub. paper, University of Connecticut, 1994), p. 7.

103. United Nations, General Assembly, *Official Records*, 22nd Session, August 18, 1967, Document A/6695, p. 1.

104. Quoted in Michael Roskin, "An American Metternich," in Frank J. Merli and Theodore A. Wilson, eds., *Makers of American Diplomacy* (New York: Charles Scribner's Sons, 1974), p. 698.

105. White House official quoted in Tad Szulc, "How Kissinger Did It," *Foreign Policy*, no. 15 (Summer 1974), 35.

106. Quoted in McMahon, *Limits of Empire*, p. 255.

107. Mike Mansfield quoted in Stanley Millet, ed., *South Vietnam* (New York: Facts on File, 1973–1974; 7 vols.), *IV*, 358.

108. H. R. Haldeman notes quoted in Michael A. Genovese, *The Nixon Presidency* (Westport, Conn.: Greenwood, 1990), p. 134.

109. Quoted in Clarence R. Wyatt, *Paper Soldiers* (New York: Norton, 1993), p. 193.

110. Quoted in Melvin Small, "Containing Domestic Enemies," in David L. Anderson, ed., *Shadow on the White House* (Lawrence: University Press of Kansas, 1993), p. 137.

111. Frances FitzGerald, *Fire in the Lake* (New York: Vintage, 1972), p. 544.

112. Ken George quoted in Otto J. Lehrack, *No Shining Armor* (Lawrence: University Press of Kansas, 1992), pp. 337–338.

113. Quoted in *Time*, CXXIII (April 16, 1984), 24.

114. *Public Papers, Nixon, 1969*, p. 909.

115. Morris, *Uncertain Greatness*, p. 175.

116. Charles Colson quoted in George C. Herring, *America's Longest War* (New York: Knopf, 1986), p. 239.

117. Ambassador William Sullivan and Foreign Minister Nguyen Co Thach quoted in McMahon, *Limits of Empire*, p. 264.

118. Quoted in Isaacson, *Kissinger*, p. 329.

119. Ho quoted in Ilya V. Gaiduk, *The Soviet Union and the Vietnam War* (Chicago: Ivan R. Dee, 1996), p. 231.

120. Quoted in Nixon, *RN*, p. 605.

121. Quoted in Herring, *America's Longest War*, p. 247.

122. Quoted in Nguyen Tien Hung and Jerrold L. Schecter, *The Palace File* (New York: Harper and Row, 1986), p. 105.

123. Kissinger, *White House Years*, p. 1399.

124. Entry of December 28, 1972, *Haldeman Diaries*, p. 557.

125. Guenter Lewy, *America in Vietnam* (New York: Oxford University Press, 1978), p. 414.

126. Quoted in Fredrik Logevall, "The Swedish-American Conflict over Vietnam," *Diplomatic History, XVII* (Summer 1993), 441.

127. Quoted in Robert Alan Goldberg, *Barry Goldwater* (New Haven: Yale University Press, 1995), p. 269.

128. Quoted in Bundy, *Tangled Web*, p. 362.

129. Quoted in Oriana Fallaci, *Interview with History* (Boston: Houghton Mifflin, 1976), p. 56.

130. Richard Holbrooke quoted in Isaacson, *Kissinger*, p. 483.

131. John Negroponte quoted in Marilyn B. Young, *The Vietnam Wars* (New York: HarperCollins, 1991), p. 279.

132. Entry of December 20, 1972, *Haldeman Diaries*, p. 558.

133. Reston, *Deadline*, p. 408.

134. Herring, *America's Longest War*, p. 281.

135. Jeffrey Kimball, *Nixon's Vietnam War* (Lawrence: University Press of Kansas, 1998), p. 371.

136. Quoted in George C. Herring, "Vietnam: The War That Never Seems to Go Away," *New England Journal of History*, LIV (Spring 1998), 8.

137. Quoted in Thomas G. Paterson, "Historical Memory and Illusive Victories," *Diplomatic History, XII* (Winter 1988), 14.

138. Quoted in J. Garry Clifford, "Bureaucratic Politics," in Michael J. Hogan and Thomas G. Paterson, eds., *Explaining the History of American Foreign Relations* (New York: Cambridge University Press, 1991), p. 141.

139. Richard E. Neustadt and Ernest R. May, *Thinking in Time* (New York: Free Press, 1986).

140. Church quoted in Kathryn S. Olmstead, *Challenging the Secret Government* (Chapel Hill: University of North Carolina Press, 1996), p. 81.

141. Richard J. Barnet, *Roots of War* (Baltimore: Penguin, 1972), p. 9.

142. USIA memorandum quoted in Caroline Page, *U.S. Official Propaganda During the Vietnam War* (New York: Leicester University Press, 1996), p. 296.

143. Quoted in Greene, *Ford*, p. 150.

144. Quoted in Young, *Vietnam Wars*, p. 301.

145. Edmund Stillman, in "America Now: A Failure of Nerve?" *Commentary*, LX (July 1975), 83.

146. Ronald Steel, *ibid.*, p. 79.

147. Henry Steele Commager, "The Defeat of America," *New York Review of Books*, October 5, 1972, p. 13.

148. Charles DeBenedetti, *The Peace Reform in American History* (Bloomington: Indiana University Press, 1980), p. 174.

149. Charles DeBenedetti, "On the Significance of Peace Activism," *Peace and Change*, IX (Summer 1983), 14.

150. Quoted in Ronald Steel, *Walter Lippmann and the American Century* (Boston: Little, Brown, 1980), p. 586.

151. Bruce Weigl quoted in Young, *Vietnam Wars*, p. 328.

152. Jim Yost quoted in Lehrback, *No Shining Armor*, p. 356.

153. Joan Furey quoted in Laura Palmer, "How to Bandage a War," *New York Times Magazine*, November 7, 1993, p. 40.

154. William Duiker and Kevin Farrell quoted in Arnold R. Isaacs, *Vietnam Shadows* (Baltimore: Johns Hopkins University Press, 1997), p. 147.

155. C. W. Bowman quoted in Eric Bergerud, *Red Thunder, Tropic Lightning* (New York: Penguin, 1994), p. 224.

156. Jeffrey P. Kimball, "The Stab-in-the-Back Legend and the Vietnam War," *Armed Forces and Society*, XIV (Spring 1988), 433–458.

157. Quoted in George C. Herring, "The 'Vietnam Syndrome,'" *Virginia Quarterly Review*, LVII (Fall 1981), 595.

158. Quoted in Thomas G. Paterson, *Meeting the Communist Threat* (New York: Oxford University Press, 1988), p. 259.

159. Qiang Zhai, "Reassessing China's Role in the Vietnam War," in Xiaobing Li and Hongshan Li, eds., *China and the United States* (Lanham, Md.: University Press of America, 1998), p. 111.

160. Quoted in Gaddis, *Strategies*, p. 300.

161. John Pancrazio quoted in Bergerud, *Red Thunder*, p. 246.

162. Quoted in Philip Caputo, *A Rumor of War* (New York: Ballantine, 1977), p. 69.

163. Christian G. Appy, *Working Class War* (Chapel Hill: University of North Carolina Press, 1993), p. 26.

164. John Kniffen quoted in Richard Stacewicz, *Winter Soldiers* (New York: Twayne, 1997), p. 107.

165. Colin L. Powell, *My American Journey* (New York: Random House, 1995), p. 149.

166. Quoted in McMahon, *Limits of Empire*, p. 132.

167. Le Ly Hayslip, *When Heaven and Earth Changed Places* (Garden City, N.Y.: Doubleday, 1989), p. xiv.

168. Bruce Palmer, Jr., *The 25-Year War* (Lexington: University Press of Kentucky, 1984), p. 176.

169. Quoted in Ngo Vinh Long, "Vietnamese Perspectives," in Stanley I. Kutler, ed., *Encyclopedia of the Vietnam War* (New York: Scribner, 1996), p. 608.

170. Alistair Cooke quoted in Donald W. White, *The American Century* (New Haven: Yale University Press, p. 378.

❖ 11 ❖

To Begin the World Over Again: Carter, Reagan, and Revivalism, 1977–1989

American Hostage in Iran. *On November 8, 1979, this blindfolded, hand-tied American captive was paraded on the grounds of the U.S. Embassy in Teheran. A jeering crowd taunted the frightened American early in the Iranian hostage crisis. (AP/Wide World Photos)*

DIPLOMATIC CROSSROAD

The Iranian Hostage Crisis, 1979–1981

"Death to the Shah! Death to Carter! Death to America!" chanted the radical Islamic student demonstrators outside the U.S. Embassy in Teheran, Iran, on November 4, 1979.[1] Suddenly, they stormed the embassy that their religious leader Ayatollah Ruhollah Khomeini had branded a "nest of spies."[2] Hundreds of shouting students spread over the twenty-seven-acre compound. In the chancery, CIA officers operating undercover as Foreign Service personnel shredded classified documents. "Man, we're gonna have an Alamo," said one U.S. marine as the armed militants broke into rooms and seized frightened Americans, including Ann Swift, a political officer who maintained contact with Washington until she put down the telephone and surrendered.[3] "We're paying you back for Vietnam," snarled one attacker.[4]

All told, sixty-six Americans were captured. Three were visiting the Iranian Foreign Ministry at the time; they remained there throughout the crisis. A few U.S. officials escaped, and Canadian diplomats later spirited them out of Iran. According to the jubilant students, the kidnapped Americans would go free only after Shah Mohammad Reza Pahlavi returned to Iran for trial.

The admission of the exiled Shah to a New York hospital two weeks earlier had provided the immediate catalyst for seizing the embassy. But Iranian hostility had been smoldering since the 1950s. The Shah had risen to power in 1941, replacing his father, who had claimed the Peacock Throne by force in the 1920s. The young Shah increasingly relied on U.S. advice and assistance—a dependence demonstrated most emphatically in 1953 after he left Iran, when nationalists, led by Prime Minister Mohammad Mossadegh, gained control of the government and nationalized the Anglo-Iranian Oil Company. In Operation AJAX, the CIA plotted with royalist Iranians and British officials, restored the Shah to the throne, and drove Mossadegh from the country. The Shah soon became a staunch anticommunist ally of the United States. In 1957, with CIA assistance, he organized SAVAK, a secret police organization that suppressed dissent and terrorized the population. "We will teach the CIA not to do these things in our country," said a militant student to one hostage.[5]

In the 1970s popular discontent with the Shah swelled. Muslim clergy resented Western influences, including Hollywood movies and rights for women. Intellectuals and students protested the suppression of civil liberties. Social democrats who had fled with Mossadegh in the 1950s demanded a constitutional government. For different reasons, merchants, young workers, and feudal landholders felt aggrieved by the Shah's modernization of the Iranian economy. Inflation, unemployment, inadequate housing, and preferential jobs for skilled foreigners also created unrest. Ethnic separatists in Kurdistan fought for autonomy. SAVAK, symbol of the Shah's police state, committed untold brutalities that helped to unite disparate groups against the monarch and his sponsor, the United States.

Some Iranians also objected to massive purchases of arms from the United States. In the period 1973–1978, the Shah spent $19 billion of the nation's oil wealth on American weapons. He bought helicopters, fighter aircraft, destroyers, and missiles, because, he argued, Iran had to fend off numerous enemies—the Soviet Union, Iraq, radical Arabs, domestic radicals—and had to police the Persian Gulf. Iran possessed the mightiest military in the Middle East, but many Iranians thought that the Shah squandered the nation's resources as a stooge of the United States.

President Jimmy Carter, visiting Teheran in late 1977, toasted the Shah for making Iran "an island of stability" and for earning the "admiration and love which your people give to you."[6] U.S. diplomats were "dumbfounded" by Carter's remarks, for the president had identified the pursuit of human rights (hardly the Shah's strongest point) as a major U.S. foreign-policy goal.[7] The president, of course, was paying polite deference to an ally, and after Vietnam, American leaders looked to regional powers such as Iran to assist the United States in preserving its global interests. Reports of unrest in Iran elicited a standard Washington response: "It's not our country; the Shah is in control; we don't know enough about what could happen if he lost control—the communists might take over."[8] Carter did not know that the Shah was dying of cancer—a condition perhaps making the monarch fatalistic and lethargic.

In 1978, demonstrations, riots, and strikes shook Iran. The Shah declared martial law, and the United States equipped his forces with riot-control equipment. "Hang firm and . . . count on our backing," Carter told him.[9] National Security Affairs Adviser Zbigniew Brzezinski urged that the Iranian army smash the opposition and stage a coup. Secretary of State Cyrus Vance rebutted that the "iron fist" belied the central thrust of Carter's foreign policy and would not work because the largely conscript Iranian army would disintegrate.[10] From Teheran, U.S. ambassador William Sullivan sided with Vance. Officials in Washington had rejected Sullivan's advice to open direct communication with Khomeini, the evident leader of the revolution, then in exile in Paris. Even though "we did not know beans . . . about the people around Khomeini," Washington officials agreed to welcome the Shah if he ever gave up his throne.[11]

The Shah appointed a civilian government acceptable to his generals and flew to Egypt on January 16, 1979. Making it clear that Islamic clerics intended to govern Iran, the Ayatollah rejected the new regime and soon installed his own. When he fueled rampant anti-Americanism in angry speeches to cheering Iranians, American citizens began to depart the convulsed nation. On February 14 a revolutionary group seized the U.S. Embassy, but the Iranian government forced the intruders to abandon the compound.

After leaving Teheran, the Shah moved from Egypt to Morocco to the Bahamas to Mexico. Few nations wanted to give sanctuary to a repudiated despot. Even Carter rescinded the offer of welcome to the Shah. Former secretary of state Henry A. Kissinger and David Rockefeller, whose Chase Manhattan Bank had substantial financial ties to Iran, petitioned the White House to cease treating the Shah like "a flying Dutchman" in search of a safe place to land.[12] In October the president learned that the Shah would die of a malignant lymphoma unless a New York hospital admitted him. Despite warnings that such a move could ignite protest against Americans in Iran, Carter invited him to the United States. The Shah arrived in New York on October 22; on November 4 militant students seized the embassy.

As stunned Americans watched "America Held Hostage" each night on television, it became clear that the hostage-takers wanted more than the Shah.[13] First, the hostage-grabbing was Iran's way of preventing the Shah from launching a counter-revolution from the United States; many Iranians painfully remembered 1953. Second, the hostage-taking helped Iran break diplomatic relations with the United States, which Khomeini called a "global Shah" never to be trusted.[14] Finally, the hostage drama permitted the eighty-one-year-old Khomeini—whose dark, piercing eyes glared from posters hung throughout the country—to use anti-Americanism to overwhelm civilian moderates who competed with his clerics for control of the revolution.

Spending sleepless nights, President Carter felt "the same kind of impotence that a powerful person feels when his child is kidnapped."[15] Within the administration, Vance and Brzezinski differed bitterly. The latter advocated retaliatory action to preserve U.S. honor, even at the cost of lives. Vance countered that the crisis called "not for rhetoric, but for quiet, careful and firm diplomacy."[16] On November 14 the president froze Iranian assets in the United States valued at about $8 billion. U.S. officials secretly asked Palestine Liberation Organization leader Yasir Arafat to help. He did, persuading the revolutionary government to release thirteen hostages (most of those released were women and African Americans). All other efforts through intermediaries came to naught.

As the diplomats struggled to negotiate with an Iranian government that often seemed incapable of functioning, the hostages languished in captivity. Although never mutilated or sexually abused, the hostages suffered through an ordeal lasting 444 days. At first blindfolded with their hands and feet tied, they thought that they would be either released quickly or killed. For a long time they could not speak or read newspapers. The hostages lost weight, and became sick. They received books and games later, but they constantly fought boredom, melancholy, and fear. The worst terror they endured was a mock execution, preceded by abusive interrogation. Asked later if he would ever return to Iran, one freed hostage shot back: "Yeah, in a B-52."[17]

On April 7, 1980, after Teheran jettisoned another secret diplomatic overture, the United States broke relations with Iran. When the CIA reported that "pulling a Mussadiq [overthrowing the regime] is beyond our reach," Carter ordered the Joint Chiefs of Staff to launch a rescue mission.[18] "Stunned and angry that such a momentous decision had been made in my absence," Vance asked for reconsideration when he returned from a trip.[19] Carter called a meeting of the National Security Council to hear Vance's objections. First, the secretary said, the United States had just pressed its allies to impose economic sanctions on Iran; a military maneuver, without prior warning, would make them feel deceived. Second, the Iranian parliament, about to meet, might provide a solution to the crisis. Third, the hostages faced no immediate physical danger. Even if the raid succeeded, numerous hostages would die. Fourth, the Iranians might retaliate by seizing U.S. journalists and other Americans in Teheran, creating another hostage crisis. Fifth, the

Jimmy Carter's World. The Iranian crisis joined domestic economic turmoil to trouble President Carter. A White House aide remembered that "before conferring with a foreign leader, Carter would often sit by his globe . . . trying to imagine the political, economic, and military pressures experienced by the leader." (Cartoon by Tony Auth. Reprinted with permission from *Foreign Policy,* no. 31, Summer 1978. Copyright 1978 by the Carnegie Endowment for International Peace)

whole Middle East might become inflamed. And last, such a military venture might push the Iranians into the arms of the Soviets. No one at the meeting agreed with Vance. "I will stick with the decisions I made," stated a grim-faced Carter.[20] The time had now come to "lance the boil" of American frustration, Brzezinski concluded.[21] "America needs a win . . . real, real bad," remarked "Chargin' Charlie" Beckwith, the rescue mission's ground commander.[22] Later he admitted that "the probability of success was about 50 percent."[23]

On April 24, eight helicopters lifted off the supercarrier *Nimitz* in the Arabian Sea. At the same time, six C–130 Hercules transports took to the skies from Egypt. All the aircraft headed for a rendezvous in the Iranian desert; from there rescue teams of Green Berets and Rangers planned to infiltrate Teheran and assault the U.S. Embassy to free the hostages. But the helicopters had to fly through unexpected dust clouds, two malfunctioned before reaching Iran, and another lost a hydraulic line at the rendezvous point. The president accepted Colonel Beckwith's recommendation to abort the mission. In the hasty and dusty exit, a helicopter and a C–130 collided, killing eight crew members. The saddened president asked for a copy of the speech that John F. Kennedy had made after the disastrous 1961 Bay of Pigs invasion; then he told the nation the news. Vance, who said that he would resign whether or not the rescue attempt succeeded, quietly left the administration. Critics pounded Carter for undertaking a project sure to cause the deaths of many hostages. "Thank God for the sandstorm," later remarked one hostage.[24] While some speculated that Carter may have ordered the risky operation to bolster his sagging political fortunes, others asked if "the Three Stooges now directed foreign policy."[25]

After the rescue attempt, Americans seemed resigned to a prolonged crisis. Many citizens displayed yellow ribbons to symbolize their prayers, while others pasted stickers on their car bumpers: "NUKE THE AYATOLLAH" and "Ayatollah Assa Hola." "People who ran around in robes and looked funny could do all this to us and we couldn't do anything about it," lamented Carter's press secretary.[26]

Four events finally facilitated a resolution. First, the Shah died in Egypt in July 1980. Second, Khomeini's Islamic clerics won control of the parliament and thus no longer needed the hostages for their political purposes. Third, in September, Iraq and Iran went to war, and Iran found that it had few friends or funds. Iran's oil exports had slowed because of equipment breakdowns and war-related destruction of petroleum facilities and pipelines. And fourth, Ronald Reagan, who promised a tougher posture, was elected president.

As these events unfolded, American and Iranian diplomats met with Algerian mediators. On the day before Reagan took office, an agreement was struck: release of the hostages in exchange for unfreezing Iranian assets in the United States. On January 20, 1981—shortly after Reagan's inauguration—the hostages gained their freedom. After 444 days they returned home to a relieved nation that celebrated briefly and then tried to forget.

"*No one* spoke to any of the Persian-speaking political officers among the hostages to find out what happened" until months later, because U.S. officials "just didn't care," one hostage recalled.[27] Some second-guessing did occur. Should Carter have played up the hostage issue so much, thereby signaling to the Iranians that they had in fact stung and would continue to sting Americans? But with the

The Hostages Return. After 444 days in captivity, the fifty-two Americans held prisoner in Iran came home to celebrations. At the start, sixty-six had been seized. Fourteen had been released from bondage earlier. This placard awarded victory to the United States. (U.S. Department of State. Photograph by Rover Kaiser)

Iranians jeering Washington day after day, with television cameras daily chronicling this gross violation of diplomatic immunity, with Carter's vaunted compassion for other human beings—could the president have removed the issue from the spotlight?

The United States had lost an ally with a large army, huge quantities of oil, intelligence posts that yielded critical data on Soviet missile tests, and billions of dollars to spend on American-made weapons. The long crisis had wounded American pride, raising questions in the post-Vietnam era about the ability of the United States to lead. The hostage ordeal helped bring down the Carter presidency. President Reagan drew a simple lesson: America had to build up its military to deter enemies. Other Americans urged separation from right-wing regimes and clients so that the United States could avoid becoming the target of revolutionary ire. Perhaps the hostage travail reinforced a lesson of Vietnam: American aid and weaponry, such as had flowed to the Shah, cannot guarantee the survival of an unpopular regime. As the Iranian revolution descended into tyranny, executions of Khomeini foes, and disputes with other Muslims in the Middle East, some Americans prided themselves on once having supported the Shah. Others found comfort in the fact that Washington's loss did not automatically become Moscow's gain: The Iranians remained ardently anti-Soviet.

The outpouring of emotional patriotism that greeted the returning hostages suggested another conclusion: The nation hungered for heroes who could rekindle American pride. "If television coverage of Vietnam had converted the American people into temporary pacifists," wrote one analyst, "the video images from Iran turned them into a pack of snarling wolves."[28] An Oklahoma man who judged Carter too timid looked to the imperial past for inspiration: "I agree with Teddy Roosevelt. Walk softly and carry a big stick," the Oklahoman said. "And club the hell out of them if you need to."[29]

Zbigs and Zags: Carter's Divided Administration

Teddy Roosevelt's "big stick" was exactly what Jimmy Carter had found wrong with American foreign policy when he came to office in 1977—too much bluster, too much military, and too much insensitivity toward Third World peoples. During the 1976 campaign, Carter joined critics of the Nixon-Ford-Kissinger years in demanding "no more Vietnams" and "no more Chiles." He promised to reduce military budgets, bring some of America's overseas forces home, trim arms sales abroad, and slow nuclear proliferation. He berated the Republicans for supporting dictatorial regimes. Yet at times Carter sounded like an inveterate Cold Warrior. He claimed that the Republicans had permitted a decline of U.S. power. He mocked détente: "We've been outtraded in almost every instance."[30] He criticized the White House for accepting Soviet domination of Eastern Europe and authorizing huge grain sales to the Soviet Union. President Gerald Ford thought that Carter was cynically attracting the hawks by bemoaning the descent of American power and wooing the doves by advocating cuts in defense spending. "He wavers, he wanders, he wiggles, and he waffles," Ford complained.[31]

After the downbeat years of Watergate, Vietnam, CIA abuses, and soaring OPEC oil prices, the election of the wealthy peanut farmer with a toothy smile inspired hope. After graduating from the Naval Academy and serving on a nuclear submarine, Carter entered politics as a Georgia state senator in the 1960s and, in 1970, became governor. After a four-year gubernatorial term, this relatively obscure Democrat set out to win the presidency and astounded the professionals by doing so. Carter cherished hard work, family responsibility, and religion. A devout Baptist, he became a "born again" Christian, awakened to a religious revival by his evangelical sister Ruth, a faith-healer. Energetic, ambitious, and self-confident, Carter seemed to some people sanctimonious and arrogant. A quick learner, he paid meticulous attention to details. Carter ran the presidency like a "family farmer: Plow the field, plant the seeds, fertilize the crop, . . . overseeing every last detail."[32] Unwilling to prioritize, he tried to be "desk officer for everything."[33]

An "outsider" to Washington politics, Carter had little experience in foreign affairs. He did hold membership in the Trilateral Commission, organized by the Columbia University political scientist Zbigniew Brzezinski and the banker David Rockefeller to bring together business, political, and academic notables for discussions of global problems bedeviling industrial nations. And Carter had followed the fractious debate over Vietnam and knew that a new national foreign-policy consensus had not yet taken form. "Deeply troubled by the lies our people had been told," he sensed a need for national redemption.[34]

Carter selected Cyrus Vance as his secretary of state. A wealthy, West Virginia–born, Yale-educated lawyer, Vance held top posts in the Department of De-

Cyrus R. Vance (b. 1917). "Cy" Vance brought extensive diplomatic experience to his post as secretary of state. Vance won plaudits for negotiating the Panama Canal treaties and SALT-II. His resignation in 1980 was the first such act made in protest by a secretary of state since that of William Jennings Bryan in 1915. (National Archives)

Makers of American Foreign Relations, 1977–1989

Presidents	Secretaries of State
Jimmy Carter, 1977–1981	Cyrus R. Vance, 1977–1980
	Edmund Muskie, 1980–1981
Ronald Reagan, 1981–1989	Alexander M. Haig, Jr., 1981–1982
	George P. Shultz, 1982–1989

fense in the 1960s. He doubted the efficacy of military intervention, having learned from Vietnam that the United States could not "prop up a series of regimes that lacked popular support."[35] He did not believe that the Soviets fomented most local conflicts, and he advised quiet diplomacy to find avenues toward Soviet-American cooperation. When Vance resigned in April 1980, he did so not only to protest the hostage rescue mission, but also to register his disenchantment with Carter for embracing the "visceral anti-Sovietism" of Zbigniew Brzezinski, the national security affairs adviser.[36]

Outspoken and tenacious, arrogant and aggressive, Brzezinski blamed most of the world's troubles on the Soviets. He sought military superiority and worked to play China off against the Soviet Union. To counter Vance's argument that a military coup in Iran would produce bloodshed, Brzezinski coldly lectured President

Carter (b. 1924) and Zbigniew Brzezinski (b. 1928). A Warsaw-born son of a Polish diplomat, Brzezinski emigrated to the United States in 1953. A long-time professor of political science at Columbia University, he became noted for his Cold War views before serving as Carter's adviser. According to one White House staffer, Brzezinski relished his role as "the first Pole in 300 years in a position to really stick it to the Russians." Brzezinski told an interviewer: "I'm pretty good at winning. I win a great deal. I seldom lose, very seldom." (Carter Presidential Materials Project, Atlanta)

Andrew Young (b. 1932).
A graduate of Howard
University and the Hartford
Theological Seminary, the
Reverend Young had been
Dr. Martin Luther King's right-
hand man in the civil rights
movement of the 1950s–
1960s and a member of
Congress from Georgia be-
fore Carter named him am-
bassador to the United
Nations. Young was forced to
resign in 1979 when he admitted meeting with representatives of the Palestine
Liberation Organization,
whose participation in negotiations he deemed essential
to Middle East peace. (United
Nations. Photograph by Y.
Nagata)

Carter that "world politics was not a kindergarten."[37] State Department officers often bristled over Brzezinski's strong-arm bureaucratic methods, his attempts to become a public spokesperson for policy, and his back-channel contacts with foreign
leaders. "While Mr. Vance played by the Marquis of Queensberry rules," remarked
one official, "Mr. Brzezinski was more of a street fighter."[38]

The president believed that Vance and Brzezinski would balance one another
in both style and substance, and that he could manage any conflict: "Zbig would be
the thinker, Cy would be the doer, and Jimmy Carter would be the decider."[39] But
acrimonious infighting soon made the administration's foreign policy appear inconsistent, marked by zigs and zags between caution and hyperbole.

The Carter administration pursued basically traditional goals. "U.S. foreign
policy is like an aircraft carrier," remarked Brzezinski. "You simply don't send it
into a 180-degree turn; at most you move a few degrees to port or starboard."[40] At
the start Carter officials rejected the extreme options of "Fortress America" (isolationism) and "Atlas America" (global policeman) in favor of "Participant America."[41] That meant emphasizing worldwide preventive diplomacy: advancing the
peace process in the Middle East; reducing nuclear arms; normalizing relations with
China; mediating conflict in the Third World; stimulating improvements in human
rights; and creating economic stability through talks on the law of the sea, energy,
and clean air and water. The president wanted to avoid a reactive foreign policy en-
meshed in short-term, day-to-day crises. With reformist zeal, Carter set out to apply "morality, reason, and power" to American diplomacy.[42]

Carter especially sought to restore U.S. power and influence in the Third
World. He preferred to emphasize North-South rather than East-West issues and
to make concessions to nationalism, even to leftist regimes. Third World problems,
he argued, sprang not from communist plots but from deep-seated, indigenous economic, social, racial, and political problems. The appointment of Andrew Young
as ambassador to the United Nations symbolized Carter's sympathetic approach. An
African American once active in the civil rights movement, Young gradually improved the U.S. dialogue with suspicious Third World diplomats. But in 1979
Carter had to fire Young after the ambassador made unauthorized contact with representatives of the Palestine Liberation Organization, a group that the United States
refused to recognize. It later became known that the U.S. ambassador to Lebanon
also held thirty-five secret yet officially sanctioned meetings with PLO representatives during the same period.

The soul of American foreign policy, Carter insisted, should be the defense and
expansion of human rights for foreign peoples. By internationalizing the Bill of
Rights, America could recover its prestige and pride and add moral force to the nation's arsenal. Drawing on his own religious commitment, Carter vowed to win for
all peoples the freedom to work, vote, worship, travel, speak, assemble, and receive
a fair trial. Slavery, genocide, torture, forced labor, arbitrary arrest, rigged elections,
and suspensions of civil liberties all became anathema. Dictators must respect human rights or face cutbacks in American foreign aid.

Although Carter emphasized that Americans should put their "inordinate fear
of communism" behind them, he actually reinvigorated the containment doctrine
by initiating new weapons systems and streamlining conventional forces, by en-

couraging nationalism in Eastern Europe, and by cultivating Third World governments.[43] Improved Sino-American ties (the "China card"), continued strategic arms limitations talks, and public denunciations of Soviet violations of human rights also might check Moscow. By 1979 Carter, having moved closer to Brzezinski's views, sounded the familiar Cold War calls for "a more muscular foreign policy."[44] The following year he proclaimed the Carter Doctrine, or containment in the Middle East. Confrontation more than cooperation came to mark Soviet-American relations under Carter.

The Panama Canal and Nationalism in High Voltage: Latin America

Although the Iranian hostage crisis and the rivalry with the Soviet Union came to dominate the president's foreign policy, at the outset Carter launched an active diplomacy toward Latin America, the Middle East, and Africa. In Latin America, still beset by poverty, rapid population growth, and natural disasters, Carter championed human rights and democratization and worked to accommodate the United States to nationalism. More than ever before, the Latin American governments claimed an independent role in world politics and shunned U.S. advice. They petitioned Washington for lower tariffs, higher commodity prices, less diplomatic backing of North American corporations locked in disputes with their governments, and the transfer of technology on convenient terms. The Carter administration saw high stakes: $59 billion in trade (1979); investments of $24.4 billion (1979); vital imports of petroleum, copper, and tin; and Latin America's thirty votes in the United Nations. Foreign aid ($726 million in 1977–1978) continued as one means of exerting influence, but Carter also sought negotiations.

Panama became the first testing ground. Panamanians had long resented the 1903 treaty granting the United States the Canal Zone, a ten-mile-wide, 500-square-mile slice of territory that cut their nation in half—"a foreign flag piercing its own heart," according to Panamanian General Omar Torrijos.[45] After bloody anti-American riots in 1964, President Lyndon B. Johnson had started talks, but they barely crawled forward.

Carter brought the negotiations to fruition. Two treaties were signed in 1977 and ratified the following year. One treaty, abrogating the 1903 document, provided for the integration of the Canal Zone into Panama and increased Panama's percentage of the canal's revenues to boost the small nation's ailing economy. The other treaty stated that the United States had the right to defend the "neutrality" of the canal forever. In a national vote, Panamanians approved the treaties by a 2 to 1 margin, but nationalistic sentiment against a continued U.S. role in Panamanian affairs ran high. When Torrijos identified "lots of electric currents" in his country, the U.S. negotiator Ellsworth Bunker thanked him for "keeping the voltage down."[46]

Conservative critics in the United States soon denounced the treaties as diabolical instruments of appeasement and retreat. After Vietnam, Americans had to draw the line somewhere: "Panama is the place and now is the time."[47] Many Americans thought that the United States owned the canal. Ronald Reagan mangled the historical record: "We bought it, we paid for it, it's ours, and we're going to keep it."[48] Giving up a key waterway would supposedly weaken U.S. defense and leave Panama vulnerable to Soviet or Cuban subversion. Veterans' groups lined up against the treaties, and the Conservative Caucus flooded senatorial offices with claims that the treaty would turn the Caribbean into a "Red Lake."[49]

The Carter administration countered with a full-court press. The Committee of Americans for the Canal Treaties enlisted veteran diplomat W. Averell Harriman, labor leader George Meany, and army general Maxwell Taylor, among others. Gerald Ford and Henry Kissinger also worked for approval. Executives of the National Association of Manufacturers and multinational corporations holding large investments in Latin America endorsed the agreements. Treaty advocates stressed the goodwill that Washington would gain after terminating the imperialistic document of 1903. If the United States insisted on staying in Panama, it might invite a protracted guerrilla war. "A single Panamanian" with a bazooka "could put the great locks out of commisson for months."[50] The canal's value had dimininshed because modern aircraft carriers had too much beam to pass through the waterway. Moreover, less than 10 percent of U.S. foreign trade went through it, and the new, large cargo ships and supertankers could not squeeze through the locks. The actor John Wayne, a personal friend of General Torrijos, publicly rebuked Governor Reagan "point by God damn point in the Treaty where you are misinforming people."[51]

As the debate peaked in early 1978, the administration used arguments that alarmed Panamanians. A "memorandum of understanding," signed by Torrijos and Carter and later added to the treaty by the Senate, provided for U.S. intervention after the year 2000 to thwart "any aggression or threat directed against the Canal or against the peaceful transit of vessels through the Canal."[52] When asked what the United States would do after 2000 if the Panamanians closed the canal for repairs, Brzezinski answered: "Close down the Panamanian government for repairs."[53] A "condition," which an annoyed Torrijos accepted only after Carter's personal plea, stated that if canal operations ever stopped, the United States had the right to intervene, "including the use of military force in the Republic of Panama."[54] On March 16, 1978, the Senate approved the neutrality treaty 68 to 32; the other treaty passed on April 18 by a similar count—in both cases with only one vote more than the two-thirds tally mandated by the Constitution. Carter later acknowledged that "some fine members of Congress had to pay with their political careers for their votes."[55]

The Carter administration also contended with nationalist stirrings in Nicaragua. Since 1936 the Somoza family had ruled that Central American state (see pages 156–160). Dictatorial, brutal, and corrupt, the Somoza dynasty nevertheless had gained grudging U.S. support as a reliable anticommunist ally and had received military aid, which it often used to suppress critics. Nicaragua had served as a staging area for CIA operations against Guatemala (1954) and Cuba (1961). All the while, Nicaraguans suffered high rates of poverty, malnutrition, and illiteracy, and the Somozas amassed great wealth, coming to own much of the country's land and industry. After a devastating 1972 earthquake, the Somoza family callously drained off international relief aid. A long-smoldering popular rebellion exploded

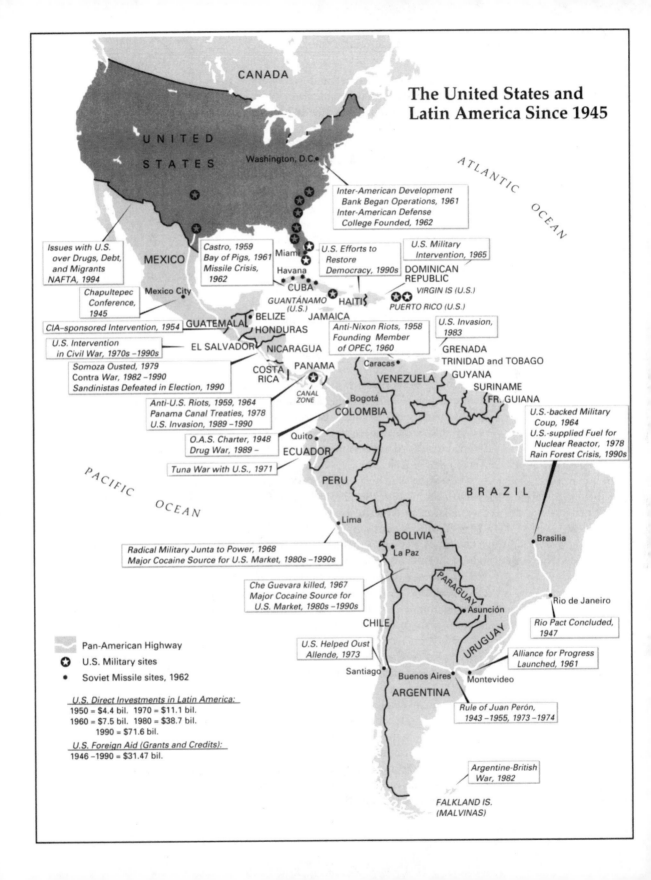

The United States and Latin America Since 1945

CANADA

UNITED STATES

Washington, D.C.

**Inter-American Development Bank Began Operations, 1961
Inter-American Defense College Founded, 1962**

ATLANTIC OCEAN

Issues with U.S. over Drugs, Debt, and Migrants NAFTA, 1994

MEXICO

**Castro, 1959
Bay of Pigs, 1961
Missile Crisis, 1962**

Miami

Havana

U.S. Efforts to Restore Democracy, 1990s

U.S. Military Intervention, 1965

DOMINICAN REPUBLIC

VIRGIN IS (U.S.)

Chapultepec Conference, 1945

Mexico City

CUBA

GUANTÁNAMO (U.S.)

HAITI

JAMAICA

PUERTO RICO (U.S.)

CIA–sponsored Intervention, 1954

GUATEMALA

BELIZE

HONDURAS

**Anti-Nixon Riots, 1958
Founding Member of OPEC, 1960**

U.S. Invasion, 1983

U.S. Intervention in Civil War, 1970s –1990s

EL SALVADOR

NICARAGUA

GRENADA

TRINIDAD and TOBAGO

**Somoza Ousted, 1979
Contra War, 1982 –1990
Sandinistas Defeated in Election, 1990**

COSTA RICA

PANAMA

CANAL ZONE

Caracas

VENEZUELA

GUYANA

SURINAME

FR. GUIANA

**Anti-U.S. Riots, 1959, 1964
Panama Canal Treaties, 1978
U.S. Invasion, 1989 –1990**

Bogotá

COLOMBIA

**U.S.-backed Military Coup, 1964
U.S.-supplied Fuel for Nuclear Reactor, 1978
Rain Forest Crisis, 1990s**

**O.A.S. Charter, 1948
Drug War, 1989 –**

Quito

ECUADOR

Tuna War with U.S., 1971

PERU

B R A Z I L

PACIFIC OCEAN

Lima

BOLIVIA

La Paz

Brasilia

**Radical Military Junta to Power, 1968
Major Cocaine Source for U.S. Market, 1980s –1990s**

**Che Guevara killed, 1967
Major Cocaine Source for U.S. Market, 1980s –1990s**

PARAGUAY

Asunción

Rio de Janeiro

Rio Pact Concluded, 1947

Pan-American Highway

⭐ U.S. Military sites

• Soviet Missile sites, 1962

CHILE

U.S. Helped Oust Allende, 1973

URUGUAY

Alliance for Progress Launched, 1961

Santiago

Buenos Aires

Montevideo

ARGENTINA

U.S. Direct Investments in Latin America:
1950 = $4.4 bil. 1970 = $11.1 bil.
1960 = $7.5 bil. 1980 = $38.7 bil.
1990 = $71.6 bil.

U.S. Foreign Aid (Grants and Credits):
1946 –1990 = $31.47 bil.

Rule of Juan Perón, 1943 –1955, 1973 –1974

Argentine-British War, 1982

FALKLAND IS. (MALVINAS)

in 1978, led by the leftist Sandinista National Liberation Front (FSLN). Founded in 1962, the FSLN took its name from the insurgent César Augusto Sandino, who had fought U.S. occupation in the 1920s and 1930s (see pages 159–160). Business executives, Catholic clergy, and intellectuals joined the crusade to unseat the Somozas and reduce U.S. influence. General Anastasio Somoza Debayle, a graduate of West Point (1946), answered with torture, executions, and bombings of civilians.

Carter tried to shape a new government that would ensure Somoza's departure and restrict the radical Sandinistas. Somoza balked and the effort failed. After the FSLN opened its final offensive in mid-1979, Washington encouraged the national guard—Somoza's hated personal army—to preserve order. When this tactic also misfired, diplomats pressed the new, broadly based provisional government to share power with more nonradicals or else forfeit reconstruction assistance. On July 17, 1979, Somoza and his entourage fled the battle-scarred country; he was later assassinated in Paraguay. Carter had abandoned a client government supported by seven previous U.S. administrations.

The new Nicaraguan government promised a mixed economy and pluralistic politics. But only after Mexico, Venezuela, and others offered loans did Carter ask Congress to appropriate $75 million in economic assistance for Nicaragua. Not until July 1980 did Congress allocate funds, with conservatives calling the Sandinistas communists because they welcomed Cuban advisers and issued caustic anti-Yankee propaganda. Many Nicaraguans resented Washington's long-time ties with Somoza, which Nicaraguans saw as "a needle in the spine."[56] Tension soon ran high, especially when Carter suspended economic aid in early 1981 after the Sandinistas aided rebels who were challenging the U.S.-backed government of El Salvador (see pages 441–443).

Mexico's announcement in 1981 that it was "tightening the links of friendship that bind us with the revolutions of Cuba and Nicaragua" suggested diplomatic troubles even closer to home.[57] Commercial and other questions troubled Mexican-American relations. By 1980 Mexico ranked as the United States's third most important trading partner, after Japan and Canada, yet the two neighbors squabbled over oil and natural gas prices. Crossing the shared 2,000-mile border in the 1970s, at least 2 million Mexicans, most of them young males, entered the United States without immigration papers. U.S. border patrols probably turned back as many. "It is not a crime to look for work," remarked President José López Portillo, especially when U.S. employers offered jobs.[58] U.S. critics contended that these illegal laborers displaced American workers, drove down wages, and burdened taxpayers by ending up on the welfare rolls. U.S. law seemed contradictory: It was illegal for undocumented migrants to take jobs but legal for employers to hire them. Carter tackled the *indocumentado* controversy early. In August 1977, he asked for new legislation, but not until 1986 did Congress pass the Immigration Reform and Control Act, which provided amnesty and legal residence for illegal migrants already in the United States, fines for employers who hired undocumented workers, and stricter border controls.

Elsewhere in Latin America, Cuba remained high on the hemisphere's agenda. Carter initially sought to reduce tensions with Fidel Castro. In March 1977, U.S. and Cuban negotiators began to discuss normalization of relations. In September,

Cuba and the United States established "interests sections" in each other's country (essentially embassies without full diplomatic recognition). Carter also lifted the ban on travel to Cuba. Castro in 1978 made gestures toward improved relations by releasing 3,600 political prisoners. Several irritants diminished these positive steps. The Soviet Union was pouring about $3 million a day into Cuba to sustain the island's fragile economy, weakened by the longstanding U.S. trade embargo and Castro's mismanagement. Washington argued that Cuba had become a Soviet puppet and charged that Cuban troops in Angola and Ethiopia acted as Soviet surrogates. Castro retorted that he was pursuing Cuba's commitment to revolutions in the Third World. The Cubans had entered Angola as early as the 1960s, independently of the Soviets. Secret, high-level U.S.-Cuba talks in 1978–1980 failed to normalize relations or relax the trade embargo. And the question of a Soviet brigade in Cuba poisoned chances for rapprochement with Havana (see page 426).

In spring 1980, Castro suddenly announced that Cubans wishing to leave the country could use Peruvian visas if they could get them. Thousands jammed into the Peruvian Embassy grounds in Havana. Carter thereupon announced that the United States would accept Cubans who wanted to join their families already in the United States. Castro soon declared that any Cuban who wanted to emigrate could do so by boat from the port of Mariel. All makes and shapes of watercraft began to shuttle between Cuba and Florida in a "freedom flotilla"; about 100,000 Cubans entered U.S. processing centers. Castro emptied his jails of "undesirables" and cynically put them on boats to the United States. "Fidel has flushed his toilet on us," the mayor of Miami bitterly charged.[59] Many new arrivals languished in detention centers in the United States; others rioted. Americans felt tricked, especially as evidence mounted that many *Marielitos* had criminal records.

Elsewhere in Latin America, right-wing governments resisted Carter's efforts to improve human rights, although Haiti, Argentina, and the Dominican Republic did release hundreds of political prisoners. In 1977 Carter suspended military aid to Guatemala when its regime sanctioned the murder and torture of political opponents; two years later he froze U.S. aid to Bolivia after that nation's military seized power. Military assistance to Latin America dropped from $210 million in 1977 to only $54 million in 1979, as Carter kept dictators at arms' length. Henry Forde, prime minister of Barbados, remarked that Carter had done much "to correct the image of the United States as an unfeeling giant."[60]

Carter's Activism in the Middle East and Africa

The Iranian revolution and hostage crisis, civil war in Lebanon, Arab-Israeli conflict, Iran-Iraq War, Soviet thrust into Afghanistan (see page 427), and Western reliance on Persian Gulf oil put the Middle East in the headlines. The United States had significant economic, military, and diplomatic interests there. Saudi Arabia served as America's largest supplier of imported oil. In 1980 Israel and Egypt together received about one-third of all U.S. foreign aid. During the period 1971–1981, the United States sold $47.7 billion worth of armaments to Middle Eastern countries. American weapons became the instruments of war in the region:

Israel used U.S. warplanes to attack Palestinian communities in Lebanon and revolutionary Iran used American arms to battle Iraq. Syrians and Iraqis, however, brandished Soviet armaments.

Building on Kissinger's earlier efforts, the Carter administration concentrated on bringing Egypt and Israel to the peace table. Israeli leaders encouraged the president, because "if you take one wheel off a car, it won't drive. If Egypt is out of the conflict, there will be no more war."[61] President Anwar el-Sadat of Egypt personally advanced the peace process. In November 1977 he astonished the world by journeying to Jerusalem to offer peace and security to Israel in exchange for an Israeli withdrawal from lands occupied since 1967. When the Sadat initiative faltered, Carter interceded, inviting Sadat and Israeli prime minister Menachem Begin to Camp David. Brzezinski wanted to bug the Egytian and Israeli cabins so "we all knew what they were saying," but Carter and Vance overruled him.[62] From September 5 to 17, 1978, the three leaders and their aides engaged in often heated discussion. Carter pressed Begin to withdraw to Israel's 1967 borders in the hope that the restored territories might become a homeland for Palestinians. Israel could not have both peace and captured territories, Carter reasoned. Like his predecessors, Carter favored an agreement based on the 1967 United Nations Resolution 242, by which Arabs would recognize Israel's right to live in peace and security in exchange for Israeli withdrawal from territories seized in the war. Playing "the role of draftsman, strategist, therapist, friend, adversary, and mediator," Carter wooed and cajoled.[63] Worried about the Jewish vote in the United States and confronted with Begin's intransigence, Carter persuaded Sadat to accept compromises since the Egyptian leader seemed to want an agreement more than did Begin. He promised both sides huge amounts of foreign aid if they would settle some of their differences.

Egypt and Israel signed two Camp David Accords. The first agreement stated goals: negotiations leading to self-government for the West Bank and Gaza and subsequent participation of Jordanians and Palestinians in the peace process. The second agreement, a "framework" for peace, provided for Israeli withdrawal from the Sinai in exchange for Egyptian diplomatic recognition. Once resumed, the Egyptian-Israeli negotiations stumbled again. Carter pressed for compromise. In March 1979, he flew to the Middle East to meet separately with Begin and Sadat.

The presidential presence worked again. Signed on March 26, 1979, the Egyptian-Israeli Peace Treaty provided for the phased withdrawal of Israel from the Sinai, to be completed in 1982; the stationing of United Nations forces along the Egyptian-Israeli boundary to monitor the agreement; full economic and diplomatic relations between Cairo and Tel Aviv; and the opening of negotiations on Palestinian rights in the occupied West Bank and Gaza (see map, page 375). After thirty years of war, peace formally came to part of the Middle East. Other Arabs, especially the PLO, denounced the treaty for not recognizing the right of Palestinians to a homeland. Even Jordan's King Hussein, long considered an Arab moderate, blasted the peace as a "dead horse" because it ignored the homeland question.[64] By the end of Carter's administration, the troops of Israel and the PLO, the latter with Syrian help, were shooting at one another in Lebanon (see page 446).

Although sub-Saharan African issues lacked the urgency of Middle Eastern problems, the Carter administration strove to identify the United States with black African nationalism and to end the "last vestiges of colonialism" in Zim-

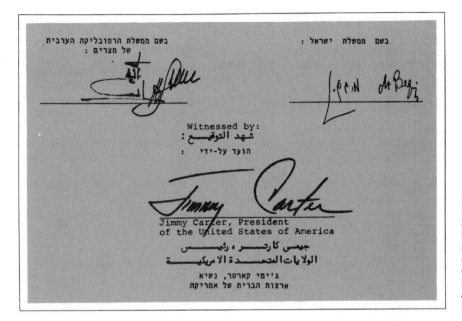

בשם ממשלת הרפובליקה הערבית
של מצרים :

בשם ממשלת ישראל :

בשם ממשלת ישראל

Witnessed by:
شهد التوقيع :

הועד על-ידי :

Jimmy Carter, President
of the United States of America

جيمي كارتــــر ، رئيــــس
الولايات المتحــــدة الأمريكيـــة

ג'ימי קארטר, נשיא
ארצות הברית של אמריקה

Signatures on the Egyptian-Israeli Peace Treaty of March 26, 1979. The historic document, hammered out under the patient guidance of the American president, was signed by Egypt's president Anwar el-Sadat, Israeli prime minister Menachem Begin, and President Jimmy Carter. (U.S. Department of State)

babwe/Rhodesia and Namibia.[65] Ambassador Andrew Young became the president's chief adviser, with "African solutions for African problems" as his motto.[66] He believed that U.S. support for a strong and stable black Africa, through foreign aid and trade, would reduce Soviet influence on the continent. African nationalism, not U.S. intervention, would contain the Soviet Union and protect U.S. interests.

Much seemed at stake in Africa. The continent had political clout—a third of the membership in the United Nations. Africa possessed a bulging storehouse of raw materials. For example, Zaire ranked as the United States's largest supplier of cobalt; Nigeria ranked as the second largest source of imported oil; Gabon supplied manganese; Namibia had the world's largest uranium mine; and South Africa shipped manganese, platinum, chromium, and antimony to the United States. Africa held great trade and investment potential, because the fifty nations hungered for development capital and modern technology. By 1979 Americans had invested some $4 billion in black Africa and about $2 billion in South Africa. Total annual trade with Africa passed the $30 billion figure. Africa's strategic location also aroused interest. Its ports and airfields lay along major sea lanes through the Persian Gulf, Indian Ocean, and Atlantic Ocean. The region's political instability made it an arena for great-power competition. Because American blacks had descended from Africans, they kept national leaders alert to African issues and politically accountable for their decisions.

The Carter administration worked especially hard to cultivate Nigerian friendship. Africa's most populous nation, Nigeria ranked seventh in world oil production and carried weight in African politics. Nigeria became independent in 1960 and in 1967 suffered a civil war in which victory over Biafran separatists cost more than half a million lives. World opinion, including that of the United States, grew hostile toward the military regime that had perpetrated this tragedy. But in the 1970s, when America endured its energy crisis and Nigeria expanded its oil production, relations improved. Both Carter and Young visited Nigeria, acknowledging the nation's importance to Africa's future.

South Africa's riches, traditional ties to the United States, occupation of Namibia, blatant racism, and white minority government ensured its continuing prominence on the U.S. diplomatic agenda. Carter chided white South African rulers for apartheid—an official system of segregating nonwhites and whites that included removals of blacks to designated homelands, discriminatory wages based on race, and denial of voting rights and civil liberties for blacks. Visiting South Africa, Vice President Walter Mondale angered whites by calling for a one-person, one-vote policy (85 percent of South Africa was nonwhite), because "perpetuating an unjust system is the surest incentive to increase Soviet influence and even racial war."[67] Carter rejected economic sanctions as a means to foster change, because trade stood at $4 billion in 1979 and the largest concentration of American investment in the continent rested in South Africa. In the mid-1970s, twenty-nine of America's top fifty corporations operated there, with General Motors, Mobil, Exxon, Ford, General Electric, and Firestone heading the list. Although critics argued for disinvestment, the most some American companies would do was to accept the Sullivan Principles. Devised by the black Philadelphia minister Leon H. Sullivan, also a member of the General Motors board of directors, the guidelines amounted to a voluntary pledge to follow nondiscriminatory employment practices in South Africa. By 1979 only 116 of the 300 American firms active there had endorsed the principles.

Many black African leaders favored a U.S. economic boycott and protested the sale of American aircraft to the regime. They criticized Carter's approval of Export-Import Bank loans (subsequently stopped by Congress). One Nigerian official condemned America's "outright collaboration with South Africa" and pressed Washington to honor its rhetoric of human rights.[68] The Carter administration defended its policies: The United States needed strategic minerals from South Africa; disinvestment would hurt native blacks by causing unemployment; if American investors pulled out, competitors would simply move in, denying the United States both profits and leverage on the regime; and economic warfare would have limited impact, given South Africa's unusual self-sufficiency. Carter officials believed that steady pressure, short of economic sanctions, would move South Africa to reform. The white regime's changes, however, amounted to little more than the "desegregation of the deck chairs on the *Titanic*."[69]

In Zimbabwe/Rhodesia, the civil war between whites and insurgent blacks finally ended. Ian Smith's white government, formed in 1965, had made token gestures to black majority rule, but Carter insisted on real change. The president persuaded Congress in 1977 to repeal the Byrd Amendment (1971), which had permitted the United States to trade with Zimbabwe/Rhodesia in chromium, despite the UN-declared economic boycott of Smith's regime. Carter in 1979 refused to accept white-manipulated elections. Finally, in a rare example of a civil war resolved by diplomacy, British-led negotiations culminated in an all-races, nationwide election held in April 1980, which produced a new government led by the former black rebel Robert Mugabe.

By the end of Carter's term, U.S. influence in Africa stood higher than ever, and trade with black Africa was improving. The United States gained access to military facilities in Somalia after that nation expelled the Soviets in 1977. Soviet and Cuban influence in Africa confined itself mainly to Ethiopia and Angola. Nigeria's President Obasanjo reflected widespread opinion when he warned Moscow and Havana that Africa would not welcome a "new imperial power."[70] Zambia's President Kenneth Kaunda hailed President Carter for bringing "a breath of fresh air to our troubled world."[71]

The Red Thread: SALT-II, Afghanistan, and the Carter Record

Carter's efforts in the Third World ultimately became overshadowed by the old question of containing the Soviet Union. From the outset, conflicting interpretations of Soviet behavior beset the Carter administration. Some officials believed that global problems did not always stem from Soviet intrigue and that the Soviet Union suffered domestic troubles, an unimaginative and aged leadership, and nationalist stirrings in Eastern Europe. "Are the Soviets five feet tall or ten feet tall?" asked Marshall Shulman, an aide to Vance.[72] Shulman and others in the State Department saw the Soviets as adversaries with whom the United States could negotiate, but Brzezinski and his NSC staff countered that Soviet expansionism in the Middle East and Africa had to be faced down, not negotiated away.

Buffeted by these competing views, Carter once asked Vance and Brzezinski to submit separate memoranda for a major 1978 speech on Soviet-American relations. Predictably, two contrasting statements reached the Oval Office. In essence stapling the different papers together, the president gave an address marked by a glaring contradiction between toughness and conciliation, between the "mailed fist and the dove's coo."[73] Still, the president eventually leaned toward Brzezinski's counsel of confrontation.

Barely a month in office, the administration exhorted Moscow to permit Dr. Andrei Sakharov, a leading dissident, to speak freely against the Soviet government. The Kremlin testily warned Americans to stop meddling in Soviet domestic affairs. "For the sake of arms control," Soviet ambassador Anatoly Dobrynin recalled, "we were prepared to consider some concessions," but "President Carter continued to attack us in public, in public, in public. Always in public."[74] The Soviets defied Carter's sermons by harassing Jews who applied to emigrate from the Soviet Union to Israel and dissident intellectuals who criticized the communist regime. From the American perspective, too, the Soviets seemed bent on a military buildup: Cuban troops and Soviet advisers stayed in Angola; the Soviet navy and Warsaw Pact forces modernized; and greater numbers of missiles pointed at NATO countries. U.S. arms expansion and activism abroad, Moscow retorted, explained the Soviet steps. In any case, détente never meant to them that they must abandon their support for leftist Third World nations. In this environment laced with suspicion and hostility, Secretary Vance journeyed to Moscow in March 1977 to reenergize SALT (Strategic Arms Limitation Talks) with a sudden, publicized proposal for deep cuts in ICBMs—precisely the category in which the Soviets were strongest. The Soviets

U.S. Dependence on Imports of Raw Materials, 1980

RAW MATERIALS	PERCENT OF DOMESTIC CONSUMPTION DERIVED FROM IMPORTS	MAJOR FOREIGN SOURCES AND USES
Columbium	100%	Brazil, Canada, Thailand – Boiler steel, refinery equipment, jet engines, gas turbines
Mica (sheet)	100%	India, Brazil, Madagascar – Electrical and electronic equipment
Strontium	100%	Mexico – Color television picture tubes, pyrotechnics
Graphite	100%	Mexico, South Korea, Madagascar, U.S.S.R. – Steel, refractories, lubricants
Industrial diamonds	100%	Ireland, South Africa, Belg.-Lux., U.K. – Abrasives, drills, phonograph needles, glass cutters
Magnese	97%	South Africa, Gabon, Brazil, France – Steel, dry cell batteries, chemicals, paints
Tantalum	97%	Thailand, Canada, Malaysia, Brazil – Electronic components, machinery
Bauxite & alumina	94%	Jamaica, Guinea, Australia, Suriname – Pots and pans, window frames, house siding, abrasives
Cobalt	93%	Zaire, Belg.-Lux., Zambia, Finland – Gas turbine engines, magnetic materials, mining tools
Chromium	91%	South Africa, U.S.S.R., Philippines, Turkey – Metals, chemicals, refractories, jet engines
Platinum – Group metals	87%	South Africa, U.S.S.R., U.K. – Jewelry, chemicals, fuel cells, electrodes, dental fillings
Fluorspar	84%	Mexico, South Africa, Spain – Chemicals, water fluoridation
Tin	84%	Malaysia, Bolivia, Thailand, Indonesia – Cans, containers, ceramics, pigments
Asbestos	76%	Canada, South Africa – Asbestos-cement pipe, flooring, insulation, gaskets
Nickel	73%	Canada, Norway, New Caledonia, Dom. Rep. – Steel, electroplating, nuclear reactors
Potassium	62%	Canada, Isreal – Fertilizers, chemicals, soap
Cadmium	62%	Canada, Australia, Mexico, Belg.-Lux. – Hardware, batteries, pigments, plastics
Zinc	58%	Canada, Spain, Mexico, West Germany – Galvanizing iron and steel, die castings, bleaches, paints
Tungsten	54%	Canada, Bolivia, Thailand, South Korea – Incandescent lamps, jet engines, high pressure equipment
Antimony	53%	South Africa, Mexico, Bolivia, China – Ammunition, flame retardants, batteries, glass
Mercury	49%	Spain, Algeria, Italy, Canada, Yugoslavia – Catalyst for plastics and resins, gauges, thermostats
Titanium (ilmenite)	47%	Australia, Canada, South Africa – Jet engines, missile parts, pigments, bottle helmets
Selenium	40%	Canada, Japan, Yugoslavia – Electronic components, photocopiers, glass, chemicals
Barium	38%	Peru, Ireland, Mexico, Morocco – Well-drilling, television picture tube, optical glass
Gypsum	38%	Canada, Mexico, Jamaica – Plasters, cements
Petroleum	31%	Saudi Arabia, Nigeria, Libya, Mexico – Fuels, asphalt, plastics, synthetic rubber
Gold	28%	Canada, U.S.S.R., Switzerland – Jewelry, electronics, dental fillings, investment bars
Iron ore	22%	Canada, Venezuela, Brazil, Liberia – Steel, ships, machine tools, razor blades, nuts and bolts
Vanadium	15%	South Africa, Chile – Construction equipment, pipelines, welding rods
Copper	14%	Canada, Chile, Zambia, Peru – Electrical wire, bearings, coins, steel cases

Source: 1976–1979 data from U.S. Department of the Interior, U.S. Department of Energy, and the U.S. Department of the Navy.

**We have 10,000 tanks.
He has 45,000.**

**Honeywell technology helps
even the odds.** Being outnumbered is nothing new.
Being outsmarted is unacceptable.
Honeywell's technology base and systems
experience are committed to finding

14   NATIONAL DEFENSE

Honeywell Corporation Exploits the Cold War Rivalry. Defense firms such as Honeywell, as this magazine advertisement of 1978 illustrates, frankly played on Cold War tensions and the arms race. In this case, Honeywell pictures a manacing Soviet officer and claims that the United States lagged far behind the Soviet Union in tanks. Although President Eisenhower had warned against a "military-industrial complex," Honeywell and other companies championed themselves as necessary elements of national defense in order for the United States to compete with the Soviet Union. In the 1980s, the Pentagon spent vast sums and defense contractors earned impressive incomes by building armaments, but American business lost its global reputation for Yankee know-how in automobiles and machine tools. (Honeywell)

thought Carter was saying: "Either you accept our position or we start an arms race and the Cold War again." Washington "was weaseling out of the SALT process," a Brezhnev aide remarked.[75] Vance made no headway: "We got a wet rug in the face and were told to go home."[76]

In March 1978 Carter denounced the Kremlin for conducting a proxy war in Ethiopia by using Cubans to battle Somalia, a newfound American friend that had futilely invaded Ethiopia to seize disputed land. The president's blunt speech, boasted Brzezinski, meant "we weren't soft."[77] In May, Brzezinski traveled to China with the intention of signaling the Soviets that they should worry about Sino-American "parallel interests."[78] After the NSC adviser challenged his hosts to a footrace at the Great Wall, saying the "last one to the top fights the Russians in Ethiopia," the Chinese dubbed him "the polar bear tamer."[79] Hints of American arms sales to the People's Republic prompted one Soviet official to complain that the United States was "smuggling" weapons aimed against the USSR through the "back door" in Asia.[80] As Soviet-American trade increased, Moscow understandably expressed puzzlement over "constant zigzags" in U.S. behavior.[81]

The two superpowers gradually moved toward a new strategic arms limitation agreement. In the SALT-II talks of 1977–1979, the Soviets tried but failed to block American development of the new MX (missile experimental), an improved ICBM designed to carry ten MIRVs; the Trident-II submarine-launched ballistic missile, capable of carrying fourteen warheads; and the cruise missile (see Glossary, page 373). The Americans sought but failed to restrict the new Soviet supersonic "Backfire" bomber. Its range of 5,500 miles threatened Western Europe and China, and in a desperate one-way mission it could also strike the United States. Prolonged negotiations nonetheless culminated in the SALT-II treaty, signed at the Vienna summit in June 1979.

The agreement for the first time established numerical equality between the United States and the Soviet Union in total strategic nuclear delivery vehicles, each limited to 2,400 (reduced to 2,250 in 1982). The treaty capped MIRVed launchers at 1,200 and limited the number of warheads per delivery vehicle. Whereas the treaty required the Soviets to dismantle more than 250 existing delivery vehicles, the Americans could expand from their current 2,060 to the ceiling of 2,250. Each nation could conduct technical verification of the other's compliance without interference.

SALT-II soon fell victim to the deteriorating Soviet-American relationship. The influential Paul Nitze, who had composed NSC-68 in 1950, opposed the accord because "it is time for the United States to stand up and not be a patsy."[82] In the Senate, opponents argued that progress on nuclear-arms control should be linked to Soviet behavior on other issues, such as human rights and Africa. Democratic senator Henry Jackson of Washington and other hawks also claimed that the Soviets, by the mid-1980s, could destroy America's land-based missiles in a first strike. SALT-II therefore endangered American security. Conservatives asserted, too, that accurate verification could not be guaranteed. Dovish critics, however, found SALT-II limitations too meager, permitting continued nuclear-weapons growth.

Admitting that SALT-II was but a small step toward deep-cut agreements, the Carter administration concentrated on rebutting conservative critics. Without SALT-II, the State Department explained, the Soviets would enlarge their nuclear forces at a brisker pace. Compelled to keep up, the United States would fuel an expensive, spiraling arms race. As for the alleged vulnerability of American ICBMs, Carter officials explained that the Soviets would have to deposit two warheads squarely on every ICBM silo to ensure destruction—an unlikely scenario: The timing would have to be near-perfect so that one incoming warhead would not explode and destroy other warheads before they reached their targets ("fratricide"). The Soviets would have to assume that the president would stand by—even with twenty to thirty minutes' warning—and let American ICBMs be destroyed in their silos. Even if a Soviet first strike somehow destroyed the land-based ICBMs (only 30 percent of U.S. nuclear forces), the rest of the triad—SLBMs and strategic bombers—would remain to annihilate tens of millions of Soviet people. "They [Soviets] are not supermen; they are not fools either," remarked one official.[83]

Carter jeopardized ratification by mishandling a "pseudo-crisis" in fall 1979.[84] He accused the Soviets of sneaking a combat brigade of 2,600 troops into Cuba to threaten other Caribbean islands. When the surprised yet conciliatory Soviets replied that the unit had been stationed there for many years, Carter retreated from the storm he had stirred up. Asked later why the episode had ever occurred, Under Secretary of State David D. Newsom fingered politics: "The White House is naturally conscious of the Presidential image."[85] The episode further poisoned the atmosphere for SALT-II by suggesting that the Soviets were once again up to no good and that Carter was inept. Senator Frank Church of Idaho, chair of the Foreign Relations Committee, temporarily postponed hearings on SALT-II and exploited the brigade issue in order to improve his own chances in a tough reelection campaign.

With senatorial approval of the treaty in doubt, Carter tried to win votes from hawks by announcing an expensive five-year military expansion program and a plan to deploy 572 Pershing-II ballistic missiles and ground-launched cruise missiles in Western Europe to counter the Soviet medium-range SS-20 missiles aimed at America's allies.

The Soviet invasion of Afghanistan in late December 1979 killed the SALT-II treaty and elevated to orthodoxy Brzezinski's hard-line views about a malevolent Soviet Union. Some 50,000 Red Army troops marched into neighboring Afghanistan to sustain a Soviet client challenged by Islamic rebels. The Soviets also intervened because they wanted to maintain Afghanistan as a "buffer" against the spread of Islamic fundamentalism in central Asia.[86] Moscow feared that covert CIA assistance to the insurgents since July might cause the Afghans to "do a Sadat on us" by aligning with the United States.[87] Carter used the "hot-line" to vent his rage at Soviet premier Leonid Brezhnev. About one-third of America's oil imports came from the Persian Gulf region; Japan and allies in Western Europe imported three-quarters and two-thirds, respectively. Did Afghanistan signal a Soviet master plan to deny America and its allies vital fuel? Would the Soviets move against Iran too? With an eye on domestic opinion, the Carter administration acted as if it feared the worst. "Putting 'a Red thread' through the complexities of the Gulf area seemed to us to be a desirable and justified simplification" to arouse the American people, Brzezinski later admitted.[88]

In early 1980 Carter tried to punish the Soviet Union. He withdrew the SALT-II treaty from the Senate. He stopped high-technology sales and grain shipments to the USSR. He pulled the United States out of the Summer Olympic Games scheduled for Moscow and urged other nations to boycott the event. Carter also outlined military measures: arms assistance for Pakistan, a state bordering the Soviet Union; creation of U.S. naval facilities in Oman, Kenya, Somalia, and Egypt; formation of a rapid deployment force for use in the Middle East; positioning of two aircraft carrier groups in the region; and a much increased defense budget. Further, the president asked an obliging Congress to require young men to register for the draft so as to mobilize forces quickly in the event of war. And last, CIA assistance helped the Afghan resistance to thwart Moscow's prediction that "it would be over in a few weeks time."[89]

In his State of the Union address of January 24, 1980, the president proclaimed the Carter Doctrine: "An attempt by any outside force to gain control of the Persian Gulf region will be regarded as an assault on the vital interests of the United States of America, and such an assault will be repelled by use of any means necessary, including military force."[90] As a statement of containment, it sounded familiar themes. But serious problems impeded implementation. When Washington offered $400 million to Pakistan, its prime minister said "peanuts" and demanded more.[91] The Saudis refused to let the U.S. military use their facilities. When Carter admitted the Soviets would not evacuate Afghanistan, West German chancellor Helmut Schmidt concluded that "what he [Carter] was after was domestic prestige" and thus refused to stop German trade with the USSR and Eastern Europe.[92] Most nations rejected the Olympics boycott.

MX Launch Test. The "missile experimental" carried ten warheads and was first deployed in 1986. President Reagan decided to place MX missiles in fixed ICBM silos, reversing President Carter's decision to deploy the missiles in a network of tracks and underground shelters, shuttling the MXs so that the Soviets could not target them. (U.S. Air Force)

The Carter Doctrine also sparked debate at home. George F. Kennan denied that the Soviet attack on Afghanistan signaled further aggression. Carter also had played all of his cards at the outset, and the Soviets remained in Afghanistan. Other critics thought that Carter had capitulated fully to Cold Warriors such as Brzezinski in another diplomatic lurch, going too far too fast, and that he had exaggerated the issue to boost his low political standing. A State Department official later revealed that the Carter Doctrine "grew out of last-minute pressures for a presidential speech" rather than from a cool calculation of policy.[93]

As Soviet-American relations deteriorated, Sino-American relations improved. After formal recognition of the People's Republic of China in early 1979, Washington and Beijing sought to use each other to contain the Soviet Union. While Washington played its "China card" in the anti-Soviet game, Beijing played its "America card." A U.S.-China trade agreement took effect in early 1980, and the Export-Import Bank extended credit to China. American companies signed contracts to tap China's oil. Chinese markets beckoned American farmers. In 1977–1980 China ranked fourth in the world as a buyer of U.S. agricultural exports, taking about half of the nation's cotton exports in 1979 alone. Mineral-short America eyed China's large deposits of tin, chrome, and tungsten. In 1980 American exports to China totaled $4 billion, up from $807 million in 1974. China replaced the Soviet Union as the United States's largest communist trading partner; in 1980 U.S. exports to the Soviet Union stood at a comparatively low $1.5 billion.

Taiwan's status, however, remained contentious. The United States severed formal diplomatic relations with the Republic of China on Taiwan, unilaterally terminated the 1954 mutual defense treaty, and withdrew all U.S. forces and military installations from the island. But private Americans maintained strong economic links, and the U.S. government continued low-level official ties through an "Institute." Washington also kept up the flow of military aid. The People's Republic insisted on ultimately repossessing Taiwan, but threats of force subsided. U.S. cultural interactions with Taiwan remained strong, especially so when Taiwanese teams won a "series of world championships" in Little League baseball during the 1970s.[94]

During the Carter presidency, many Americans sensed that the nation's power had slipped, that its role as the world's sheriff, banker, business manager, and teacher had eroded. High OPEC prices, huge deficits in the balance of payments, haunting memories of Vietnam, revolution in Nicaragua, return of the Canal Zone to Panama, Castro's defiance, Soviet nuclear equivalence and the jilted SALT-II, the Iranian hostage crisis, and Afghanistan—all seemed to project an image of American weakness. (See graph on p. 424 for growing dependence on imports.) Carter had failed to persuade Americans that a decline in U.S. power was inevitable in an interdependent, multipolar world of some 150 nations. He talked bluntly of the 1970s and 1980s as decades of limits and scarcity. Yet when he urged energy conservation as "the moral equivalent of war," wags spelled out the acronym MEOW.[95] When Carter called America a "good" country rather than a "great" one, most Americans rejected both the sobering message and the messenger.[96] The American people, concluded one historian, suffered "a serious case of empire shock for the first time in their cultural history."[97]

Carter left a mixed record. Too often, administration policy appeared erratic because of the constant feuding between the State Department and Brzezinski's National Security Council. Carter also seldom gave a rousing speech or pounded the bully pulpit—too "de-pomped," wrote one specialist on presidential power.[98] Carter lacked FDR's charm, Eisenhower's popularity, JFK's television presence, LBJ's ability to handle Congress, and Nixon's talent for exploiting the spectacular. Carter also violated some of his stated goals. Despite his pledge to reduce the American military presence abroad, more military personnel served overseas in 1980 (489,000) than in 1976 (460,000). He promised to withdraw U.S. forces from South Korea but then reversed himself. Strongly advocating nuclear nonproliferation, he nonetheless agreed in 1980 to ship 38 metric tons of enriched uranium fuel to India, even though New Delhi had snubbed the nonproliferation treaty. He promised to reduce defense spending but actually increased the Pentagon's budget, recommending for fiscal year 1982 a 14.5 percent rise over 1981. Although the president vowed to trim arms sales abroad, they climbed from $12.8 billion in 1977 to $17.1 billion in 1980.

Carter's human-rights policy also appeared inconsistent. While condemning Soviet mistreatment of dissidents and securing the emigration of more than 100,000 Soviet Jews, he muted criticism of abuses by U.S. friends. Amnesty International, the London-based independent organization founded in 1961 to monitor the worldwide status of human rights, cited the governments of Argentina, Brazil, Guatemala, Indonesia, Iran, Morocco, the Philippines, South Korea, Taiwan, and Thailand for condoning or practicing torture, political terrorism, or arbitrary arrest. In 1976–1980 the United States delivered $2.3 billion in military aid to those ten nations and sold them weapons worth $13.7 billion. Thousands of foreign officers and police also trained at U.S. military schools. Conservative critics, in contrast, complained that Carter was behaving like an evangelical preacher in a world of sinners, that he invited revolutions such as the one in Iran by weakening leaders whom America needed as strategic partners. Carter's human-rights efforts led to the freeing of hundreds of political prisoners abroad, but the president's detractors faulted his effort as either too little or too meddlesome.

The president's defenders attributed his uneven record to domestic politics. Carter may have played politics with the Cuban brigade issue, the rescue attempt in Iran, and the Afghan crisis, they admitted, but vigorous right-wing pressure made him do so. They blamed noisy Cold Warriors in the Committee on the Present Danger. Founded in 1976, this pressure group included hawks such as former secretary of state Dean Rusk and the veteran policymaker Paul Nitze. The organization advocated scrapping SALT-II and enlarging the military. Carter's bow to the conservatives epitomized the dictum that "smart politics produce bad policies."[99]

Carter officials believed that the administration pursued noble goals and achieved diplomatic successes and infused morality into American foreign policy to prove that U.S. power lay not simply in military capabilities but also in the nation's values. The administration candidly explained the limits of U.S. influence in a world of diffused power and stressed the need to deal with long-range issues, not just immediate crises. Pointing to the Egyptian-Israeli peace, Panama Canal treaties, normalization of relations with China, progress on the law of the sea, North-South dialogue, end to civil war in Zimbabwe, nuclear modernization of NATO, and an improved American status in Africa, Professor Brzezinski proudly filled out the administration's report card: A−/B+.

Coke in China. In 1981 the Coca-Cola Company opened a plant in China, where the famous soft drink is known as "tasty happiness." The humorist Art Buchwald commented: "I don't mind 800 million Chinese drinking a bottle a day, but I don't want them to bring back the empties." (Courtesy The Coca-Cola Company, 1979)

The 1980 Republican presidential candidate, Ronald Reagan, disputed that high grade. The former Hollywood actor and California governor slammed Carter for leading America into decline. In a display of raw anticommunism, Reagan declared that an expansionist Soviet Union "underlies all the unrest that is going on. If they weren't engaged in this game of dominoes, there wouldn't be any hot spots in the world."[100] Confounded by domestic economic troubles, the unresolved Iranian hostage crisis, and Carter's unsteady leadership, and rallying to Reagan's promise to "make America great again," the electorate turned Carter out by giving him only 41 percent of the popular vote.[101] The Republicans also gained control of the Senate; liberal, dovish senators Birch Bayh of Indiana, Frank Church of Idaho, John Culver of Iowa, and George McGovern of South Dakota joined Carter in defeat.

Ronald Reagan's Mission to Revive Hegemony

Ronald Reagan had no experience in national government or foreign affairs before he became president. He preferred movies and television to reading books, riding horses to roundtable discussions. Time and time again, he revealed an ignorance of fundamental information. After returning from his first trip to South America, he announced: "Well, I learned a lot. You'd be surprised. They're all individual countries."[102] When Reagan told French president François Mitterrand, a Socialist, that he thought communism and socialism were the same thing, Mitterrand wondered: "What planet is that man living on?"[103] Reagan also became noted for reckless and exaggerated statements, factual inaccuracies, and right-wing sloganeering. He acted more on his instincts than on patient reasoning. His staff, fearing ill-thought utterances, carefully managed his public performances. Surrounded by pollsters and communications specialists who tapped his natural talent, Reagan proved an effective communicator. His aw-shucks style deflected criticism and camouflaged his shallow grasp of many issues. "Being a good actor pays off," he told students at China's Fudan University.[104]

Reagan became a very popular president, winning a landslide reelection in 1984 against former vice president Walter Mondale. Americans liked Reagan even when he suffered setbacks. They applauded his poised, amiable, down-to-earth, speak-from-the-heart manner, his self-deprecating humor (especially about his age), and his dogged consistency in voicing his convictions. This "warmly ruthless man," one aide wrote, made decisions like "a Turkish pasha, passively letting his subjects serve him, selecting only those morsels of public policy that were especially tasty."[105]

Several beliefs rooted in the American past guided the Reagan administration. First, Reagan and his conservative allies believed in a devil theory: A malevolent Soviet Union instigated international insecurity—the bully on the block who ignited civil wars, promoted terrorism, and built an "evil empire."[106] Soviet leaders, the president avowed, stood poised "to commit any crime, to lie, to cheat" to achieve a communist world.[107] Such rhetoric poisoned the diplomatic environment. Reagan's dark view of the Soviets overlooked the many successful Soviet-

American agreements of the recent past. He also left the United States open to charges of a double standard, because Washington itself sponsored "disinformation" programs and engaged in covert skullduggery. Reagan officials thought in terms of an earlier age of bipolarism, global containment, and confrontation—with one exception: They lifted the grain embargo so that U.S. farmers could sell billions of dollars of wheat and corn to the Soviet Union.

Second, because the Soviets had allegedly "engaged in the biggest military buildup in the history of man" and had achieved "a definite margin of superiority," Reagan vowed to surpass them.[108] "Defense is not a budget item," he told the Pentagon. "Spend what you need."[109] They did—and more. Running up huge federal deficits, he launched the largest peacetime arms buildup in American history, spending $2 trillion. Reagan pushed plans for the B-1 bomber (Carter had refused to fund this plane); ordered the stockpiling of the neutron bomb (Carter had vetoed this weapon); and resumed production of poison gas for chemical warfare. The administration, moreover, expanded the navy, beefed up special forces units for counterinsurgency warfare, and continued the Trident-II submarine, MX, cruise missile, Stealth bomber, and mobile Midgetman missile programs. "Now they're going to be faced with . . . an arms race and they can't keep up," said Reagan of the Soviets.[110] Once the buildup was underway, he told Helmut Schmidt, "we will negotiate and negotiate and negotiate."[111] Military appropriations increased by 50 percent, growing from $143.9 billion in 1980 to $294.7 billion in 1985. In 1985 the Pentagon was spending $28 million an hour, twenty-four hours a day, seven days a week. Reagan also embraced a nuclear abolitionist's faith that American technology could devise an invulnerable space shield that would protect civilian populations from nuclear annihilation. The former actor likened the arms race to "two Westerners standing in a saloon aiming their guns at each other's heads—permanently. There had to be a better way."[112]

Third, Reagan believed it important to change America's mood to gain public support for a more militarized, interventionist foreign policy. He implored the American people to abandon their post-Vietnam "self-doubt" in favor of a "national reawakening."[113] Using his exceptional communicating skills to whip up emotional patriotism, Reagan reassured Americans that "we've closed the door on a long, dark period of failure."[114]

The fourth driving force became known as the Reagan Doctrine. Dubbed "the Will Rogers of intelligence—he never met a covert operation he didn't like," the president in 1985 pledged support for anticommunist "freedom fighters" who battled the Soviets or Soviet-backed governments.[115] The CIA, with congressional approval, funneled aid to insurgents in Afghanistan, Nicaragua, Angola, Cambodia, and Ethiopia. Reagan made overt what had been covert: the attempted overthrow of governments deemed inimical to U.S. interests. The Reagan Doctrine emphasized a commitment to low-intensity conflict: military action through allies, proxies, and paramilitary assets so that fewer American soldiers would fight and die in foreign lands as elite forces organized others to do the dirty work of shadow wars.

Fifth, Reagan and his advisers believed that nations must embrace private capitalism and privatize managed economies. American leaders frequently lectured Third World nations on the "magic of the marketplace."[116] The United States even

Ronald Reagan (b. 1911). Born in Illinois, a graduate of Eureka College, a long-time professional actor, and governor of California, (1967–1975), Reagan displayed a sunny disposition that helped return optimism, even chauvinism, to the national mood. As the vaunted "Great Communicator," Reagan proved adept at "using every communications medium save Morse Code and smoke signals," according to one journalist. Although one White House adviser claimed that Reagan never spent "one nano-second" on planning or analysis, his wife Nancy remarked: "He is more complex then people think." (Peter Souza Photo, The White House)

cast the only "no" vote against a UN resolution to restrict the sale of baby formula in developing nations. Medical authorities had reported that companies marketed their infant products so aggressively that many mothers were forgoing healthy breastfeeding in favor of the artificial liquid, which they then mixed with polluted water. The Reagan administration also refused to sign the long-awaited Law of the Sea Treaty, protesting that the agreement did not adequately protect American deep-sea mining companies.

Sixth, drawing lessons from the failure of the Carter administration to support friendly dictators in Iran and Nicaragua, the Reaganites accepted Ambassador to the United Nations Jeane Kirkpatrick's distinction between "authoritarian" and "totalitarian" regimes.[117] Authoritarian regimes in countries such as the Philippines, Chile, South Korea, and South Africa sustained capitalist economies and would supposedly respond to U.S. suggestions for reform. Communist totalitarian regimes imposed managed economies and resisted change. Given such thinking, Reagan officials downgraded human-rights tests for friendly authoritarian governments.

Finally, another central belief of the Reagan team was that the United States must serve as a model for other nations and reform a reprobate world. "The United States is the economic miracle," bragged the president. "The world's hopes rest with America's future."[118] This reformist zealotry found expression through institutions such as the National Endowment for Democracy, created in 1983 as a propaganda agency using federal and private funds to promote free enterprise and democratic politics. The endowment gave millions of dollars to foreign political parties, labor unions, and publishers, many with an antileft bias. Reagan even quoted Tom Paine of the American Revolution: "We have it in our power to begin the world over again."[119]

Reagan named General Alexander M. Haig, Jr., secretary of state. A steely-eyed military professional who became famous for his mixed metaphors and his ambition, Haig feuded with just about everybody. "Sometimes our right hand doesn't know what our far-right hand is doing," Reagan once joked.[120] The volatile secretary abruptly resigned in June 1982. Haig found the White House "as mysterious as a ghost ship; you heard the creak of the rigging and the groan of the timbers and even glimpsed the crew on deck. But which one of the crew was at the helm?"[121]

"Give War a Chance."   During his confirmation hearings in January 1981, Secretary of State–designate Alexander M. Haig, Jr., said: "There are more important things than peace—there are things which we Americans must be willing to fight for." Some people thought him too eager to apply military solutions to political problems and too inclined toward confrontation with the Soviet Union and leftist Third World nations. As for El Salvador, where Haig and Reagan thrust the United States into a civil war, the secretary declared: "We are going to succeed and not flounder as we did in Vietnam." (Bob Englehart, *Hartford Courant*)

George P. Shultz followed Haig. A founding member of the Committee on the Present Danger, Shultz was an economist and business executive. He often clashed with Secretary of Defense Caspar W. ("Cap") Weinberger, especially after Weinberger announced in 1984 that the United States should use military force only under certain conditions: with long-term public and congressional support; for "clearly defined political and military objectives"; and with "the clear intention of winning."[122] Shultz chastised Weinberger as a big spender who refused to use newly augmented U.S. forces. "A somewhat stolid, serious, and utterly dependable conversational partner," according to one diplomat, Shultz also battled hawkish CIA director William J. Casey (whom Shultz saw "as independent as a hog on ice" and "as confident [as he was] wrong"). [123]

Richard V. Allen, a business consultant noted for his anticommunist zeal, became Reagan's assistant for national security affairs. After Allen departed in 1982 under suspicion of scandal, the office of national security adviser suffered instability, further undistinguished leadership, and more scandal. Under William Clark, Reagan's political crony from California, NSC staffwork became so cumbersome that Shultz thought it "worse than a university."[124] Then came Robert C. McFarlane, a former marine who never argued against misguided policies because "if I'd done that, Bill Casey, Jeane Kirkpatrick, and Cap Weinberger would have said I was some kind of commie."[125] John M. Poindexter, an active-duty admiral with a Ph.D. in nuclear physics, succeeded McFarlane, but he had to resign in late 1986 when the Iran-Contra affair erupted.

Despite strong opposition from Weinberger and Shultz, President Reagan ordered the National Security Council to carry out a covert project to trade arms to Iran in return for the release of U.S. hostages held in Lebanon. Because he also empowered the NSC secretly to aid the Nicaraguan *contras* (see page 444), the two operations eventually commingled. To ensure secrecy, McFarlane and Poindexter ran both schemes in total disregard of Congress and almost completely outside the purview of the Defense and State Departments. Relying on CIA connections, the action officer in charge of both operations, marine lieutenant colonel Oliver North, flaunted his contempt for Congress, professional diplomats, and traditional bureaucrats. "Colonel North was given a very broad charter," Poindexter later testified, "and I did not micromanage him."[126] When North diverted profits from the Iranian arms sales to the *contras,* Poindexter approved but said he did not tell Reagan because he wanted the president "to have some deniability so that he would be protected."[127] Shultz later portrayed Reagan as an innocent dupe misled by his inner circle. Yet the record shows that at top-level meetings on Iran-Contra, President Reagan spoke more than his advisers and made the basic decisions, without monitoring every operational detail. "The old man loves my ass," North boasted, but White House logs show that Reagan met North only four times and never saw him alone.[128]

Reagan's appointment of Frank C. Carlucci, a seasoned diplomat and administrator, and then General Colin Powell, as his next NSC advisers did not quiet a national crisis that badly besmirched the Reagan presidency. In 1989 North was found guilty of three felonies (obstructing congress, destroying documents, and receiving illegal gratuities), and in early 1990 Poindexter was convicted of five felony

July 4, 1986. Here, with Nancy Reagan, the president stands before a ship's gun on Independence Day. Mrs. Reagan encouraged her husband to negotiate with the Soviets. After a private White House dinner, she whispered the word "peace" when saying good-bye to Soviet foreign minister Andrei Gromyko. "Tell that to your husband tonight in your bedroom," Gromyko replied. (Terry Arthur Photo, The White House)

Reagan in Doubt. When the crisis over the arms sale to Iran and aid to the *contras* erupted in 1986–1987, Reagan could not remember the details of his decisions. Diagnosis of Alzheimer's disease in 1994 raised the question of whether Reagan had suffered any mental impairment during his presidency. His official biographer, Edmund Morris, writes that after Reagan's near assassination in March 1981 "he lost his quickness. And for the rest of his presidency it was a very, very slow and steady mental and physical decline." Because doctors had apparently not tested him for Alzheimer's disease while president, it seemed impossible to judge whether Reagan's mental lapses were the result of dementia or simply the normal failings of an elderly president who remembered only the details that interested him. (Bill Schorr © 1987, The Los Angeles Times Syndicate)

" WHAT DO I KNOW ... AND WHEN WILL I KNOW IT ? "

charges, including lying to Congress. A federal appeals court later overturned both convictions because Congress had granted immunity to the two men for testimony given to congressional committees. President George Bush later pardoned CIA officers guilty of a cover-up, and when Secretary of Defense Caspar Weinberger was indicted, Bush also pardoned him before a trial could take place. All told, some 190 Reagan officials were indicted or convicted of illegal activities.

Soviet-American Crises and Antinuclearism

Reagan assumed that the Soviet Union outspent the United States on armaments and outdistanced it in nuclear weapons. He had campaigned on an anti–SALT-II platform and displayed undisguised distaste for nuclear-arms control talks. The United States had to close the "window of vulnerability"—the theoretical vulnerability of American land-based ICBMs to a Soviet first strike—by enlarging the American nuclear arsenal.[129] The Soviets outranked the United States in ICBMs and SLBMs but lagged behind in strategic bombers and nuclear warheads. And at least two-thirds of Soviet nuclear arms consisted of vulnerable ICBMs in fixed silos. The president failed to count on the American side the defense spending of NATO allies. As for the "window of vulnerability," in 1983 the president's own Commission on Strategic Forces reported that the window did not exist and that America's triad of air-, sea-, and land-based nuclear weapons provided sufficient deterrence.

Statements by Reagan officials about winning a nuclear war stimulated a transatlantic debate. The evangelist Billy Graham, World Council of Churches, and Union of Concerned Scientists urged restraint in the nuclear arms race. The American Medical Association declared that "there is no adequate medical response to a nuclear holocaust," and one doctor called nuclear war the "final epidemic."[130] George F. Kennan added his voice to the antinuclear movement. "Cease this madness," he implored.[131] Calling Reagan's views on the USSR "an intellectual primitivism," Kennan recommended an immediate 50 percent cut in nuclear arsenals on both sides, the denuclearization of much of Europe, a complete ban on nuclear testing, and a freeze on new weapons.[132] The House of Representatives in 1983 also passed a freeze resolution. Proponents argued that America's infrared satellites and other intelligence techniques could verify a freeze on the testing and deployment of ballistic missiles.

In May 1983 the Roman Catholic Bishops of the United States issued a pastoral letter that labeled nuclear weapons immoral: "We are the first generation since Genesis with the power to virtually destroy God's creation," read the 150-page document.[133] Feminists ridiculed the sexual nature of the discourse on nuclear strategy wherein "white men in ties" talked about "missile size, . . . vertical erector launchers, thrust-to-weight ratios, soft lay downs, deep penetrations," and what one Reagan adviser called "releasing 70 to 80 percent of our megatonnnage in one orgasmic whump."[134] In November 1983 an ABC television dramatization titled *The Day After* left President Reagan and the American people "greatly depressed" by its vivid depiction of the human costs of a nuclear war.[135] Scientists postulated that even people who survived a nuclear exchange would face a devastating "nuclear winter": Clouds of debris, dust, and smoke from mass fires would block the sun's rays, cooling the earth's temperatures and killing plant and animal life.

Europeans also vigorously spoke out. In 1981, huge crowds in Bonn, London, Rome, and Amsterdam called for a ban on the installation of Pershing and cruise missiles. "The most important mass-based challenge to NATO in its entire history" demanded that both Washington and Moscow sit down to talk and that the NATO countries forswear the new weapons.[136] Statements by U.S. officials evoked alarm. Reagan mentioned the possibility of a limited nuclear war in Europe, thus sparing the two great powers. On other occasions he revealed his "stunning ignorance about the capabilities of the weapons over which he had authority."[137] He once stated that cruise missiles were defensive weapons—in fact, they were designed to penetrate Soviet defenses and to strike targets deep in the USSR. He even said that SLBMs could be recalled after firing.

To satisfy Western European leaders who welcomed U.S. missiles but wanted less domestic protest, and to quiet the American antinuclear movement, Reagan reluctantly agreed to begin talks in Geneva on intermediate-range nuclear forces (INF) in Europe. For these negotiations, which opened in November 1981, the United States proposed to stop planned deployment of the new Pershings and cruise missiles in NATO nations if the Soviet Union would dismantle its growing arsenal

George Shultz (b. 1920). A graduate of Princeton University (he had a tiger tattoo on his buttocks) and the Massachusetts Institute of Technology (Ph.D., 1949), Shultz served as secretary of labor, director of the Office of Management and Budget, and secretary of the treasury in the Nixon administration. In 1982 he joined the Reagan cabinet as secretary of state. One pundit said Shultz had "the charisma of a drowsy clam." (Department of State)

Antinuclear March.
In October 1983, the civil rights leader Jesse Jackson (front, left) led a march in Cambridge, Massachusetts, against nuclear weapons, especially the Pershing-II missiles scheduled for deployment in Europe. This protest was part of an international weekend campaign. According to the Pentagon official Thomas K. Jones, Americans could easily survive nuclear war: "Dig a hole, cover it up with a couple of doors and then throw three feet of dirt on top. . . . If there are enough shovels to go around, everybody's going to make it." (AP/Wide World Photos)

of SS-20, SS-4, and SS-5 missiles pointed at Western Europe. The Soviets initially rejected this "zero option," because it excluded British and French nuclear forces and U.S. weapons on submarines and aircraft. Also, argued Moscow, the new NATO missiles could reach the USSR, but the SS-20s could not hit the United States. The Soviets deployed more triple-warhead SS-20s, and the United States began in 1983 to put Pershing-IIs into NATO countries, first Great Britain and then West Germany. In November 1983, to express their displeasure over these new missiles, the Soviets suspended the INF talks. Meetings did not resume until early 1985, only to falter again. Pentagon hard-liners did not mind. Without an agreement, the U.S. arms buildup continued.

Negotiations on strategic nuclear weapons did not fare much better. Reagan replaced SALT with START—Strategic Arms Reduction Talks. ("How about 'Faster Arms Reduction Talks'?" one White House aide quipped.)[138] Negotiations began in Geneva in 1982, but the U.S. proposal for deep cuts stalled. The reason became obvious: The American plan sought drastic reductions in those very weapons that constituted the bulk of Soviet deterrent power.

Chances for a START agreement also became complicated because of President Reagan's announcement of the Strategic Defense Initiative in March 1983.

"Star Wars" in 1984.
President Reagan made a passionate case for the Strategic Defense Initiative to prevent a "madman" with missiles from blackmailing "all of us." Some scientists assured him that they could create his "dream"—an effective ballistic missile defense system. In this artist's sketch, a space-based electromagnetic ray gun destroys a nuclear-armed reentry vehicle presumably launched from the Soviet Union. SDI development still limped along in the late 1990s. (U.S. Army/Department of Defense, Still Media Records Center)

Soon dubbed "Star Wars," SDI envisioned an anti-ballistic missile defense system in space—a laser or particle beam shield over the United States that could intercept Soviet ballistic missiles and destroy them in space. Jerome B. Wiesner, former scientific adviser to the White House, skeptically cited "10,000 or more nuclear weapons on each side. A defense system that would knock out 90 or 95 percent would be a miracle—and the remaining 5 or 10 percent would be enough to totally destroy civilization."[139] Others argued that if SDI ever did work, it would undermine deterrence itself by eliminating the danger of Soviet attack, thus freeing the United States to use nuclear weapons without fear of retaliation. Although some saw SDI as a multibillion-dollar "turkey," it acted as a "secret weapon . . . to undercut the freeze crusade."[140] The president optimistically viewed it as the perfect defense, a way to "get rid of those atomic weapons. Every one," he said privately.[141] As SDI research advanced, with some test results actually faked to keep congressional funds flowing, START sputtered.

Other events spoiled the negotiating environment. As the Reagan administration closed out its first year, the Solidarity labor movement in Poland, having earned concessions from the communist government through strikes and protests, called for a national referendum on the future of that government and for a reexamination of Poland's military alliance with the Soviet Union. For months Moscow had warned the Poles against weakening the communist regime. In December the Polish military cracked down, imposing martial law and arresting Solidarity leaders. Washington reacted quickly. It suspended economic agreements with Poland and blamed Moscow for unleashing the "forces of tyranny" against its neighbor.[142] Reagan cut back Soviet-American trade and banned Soviet airline flights to the United States but elected to do no more. NATO countries reacted cautiously, in part because they possessed little leverage in Polish affairs and because they wanted to continue their lucrative trade with the Soviets and Soviet clients.

On September 1, 1983, Korean Air Lines Flight 007, en route from Anchorage, Alaska, to Seoul, South Korea, strayed some 300 miles off course and for a time cruised in Soviet airspace near a strategic nuclear base. Soviet planes scrambled. When the Korean pilot did not acknowledge warning signals and shots, a Soviet jet blasted the Boeing 747 with one missile, killing all 269 passengers aboard. Reagan branded the shootdown "an act of barbarism."[143] Even though jet pilot Gennadi Osipovich identified KAL 007 as "a civilian plane," Soviet officials claimed it was on a spy mission for the United States.[144] Moscow later revealed that the shootdown had occurred in international airspace and that Soviet authorities had crudely covered up their error. Yet the "simplistic overreaction" to the shootdown in the United States so exacerbated tensions that NATO military exercises in November caused the frightened Kremlin leadership to fear a nuclear first strike.[145] Informed about this nuclear "near-miss," Reagan recited to aides the biblical story of Armageddon and made his first public plea to banish nuclear weapons "from the face of the earth."[146] Until tempers cooled, we "can't cook porridge together," Ambassador Dobrynin told U.S. officials.[147]

Another obstacle to an arms-control agreement was the instability and incapacity of Soviet leadership—until the arrival of Mikhail S. Gorbachev in 1985. Leonid Brezhnev died in 1982; his first successor, Yuri Andropov, died in 1984; and his second successor, Konstantin Chernenko, died the following year after a prolonged illness. Gorbachev became the new general secretary of the Communist party, at age fifty-four one of the Soviet Union's youngest leaders, with a personality quite "different from the wooden ventriloquism of the average Soviet apparatchik," as British prime minister Margaret Thatcher put it.[148] Determined to reform the sluggish Soviet economy through restructuring (*perestroika*) and to open the suffocating authoritarian political system through liberalization (*glasnost*), Gorbachev initiated stunning changes in his own nation and across the globe (see Chapter 12).

"Deeply affected" by the disastrous accident at the Chernobyl nuclear power station in 1986, the new secretary general altered the Soviet position on nuclear weapons.[149] He unilaterally stopped further deployment of intermediate-range missiles. He halted nuclear-weapons tests. In November 1985 Gorbachev and Reagan met in Geneva. Although they could not agree on SDI or an extension of SALT-II, they established warm personal relations during their talks. "I bet the hard-liners in both our countries are bleeding," whispered Reagan as he shook Gorbachev's hand.[150] Then in early 1986 Gorbachev called for an end to all nuclear weapons by the year 2000. Another summit meeting in Reykjavík, Iceland, in October 1986, seemed close to producing a substantial treaty. The conferees made tremendous progress by agreeing to reduce warheads, missiles, and bombers and to remove all American and Soviet intermediate missiles from Europe. Reagan found the results "breathtaking." But when Gorbachev said that "this all depends, of course, on your

Mikhail Gorbachev (b. 1932) and Reagan. In May 1988, at the Moscow summit meeting, the two leaders continued the warm personal relationship that helped end the Cold War. (Photo by Bill Fitz-Patrick, The White House, Courtesy Ronald Reagan Library)

giving up SDI," Reagan "reacted as if he had been asked to toss his favorite child into an erupting volcano."[151] The meeting quickly ended. Yet the atmosphere had clearly changed for the better.

The Washington summit meeting in December 1987 finally saw the signing of the Intermediate-Range Nuclear Forces (INF) Treaty, which provided for the elimination of all U.S. and Soviet INF missiles anywhere and verification of their destruction through on-site inspections. What had changed? Gorbachev had taken the initiative by accepting the "zero option" and giving Washington "120 percent of what it wanted" in negotiaions.[152] The warmth between Reagan and Gorbachev facilitated negotiations. "When I told him [Gorbachev] we should put our cards on the table, he took out his Visa and Mastercard," Reagan later joked.[153] Schultz similarly found Soviet foreign minister Eduard Shevardnadze a welcome change from the dour Andrei Gromyko. "I, too, have problems with my bureaucracy," Shultz told the Soviets, before the resignations of Weinberger and other hard-liners.[154] The antinuclear movement had produced strong antinuclear public opinion in Europe and America. Most obvious, the two superpowers saw the treaty as beneficial to their quite different national interests. Both faced economic troubles spawned by the long Cold War. "Our economy," one Soviet official told his colleagues, "has been literally eviscerated by military spending."[155] In May the Senate approved the treaty by a 93 to 5 vote. On June 1, 1988, the INF Treaty went into force and missiles began to be destroyed.

Destruction of a Cruise Missile under the INF Treaty. Under the terms of the Intermediate-Range Nuclear Forces Treaty, signed in late 1987 and effective in mid-1988, both the United States and the Soviet Union (and its successor states) eliminated INF missiles in Europe, including Soviet SS-20s and U.S. Pershing-II and cruise missiles. To destroy this cruise missile, a demolition crew cut it in half. (U.S. Arms Control and Disarmament Agency)

Gorbachev also boldly advanced other issues. In April 1988 he signed a UN-mediated accord providing for the withdrawal of all Soviet forces from Afghanistan. They departed early the next year, acknowledging a conspicuous defeat for the Soviet military, caused in part by the "Stinger" antiaircraft weapons that the United States had shipped to the Afghan *mujahedeen* ("holy warriors"). In December 1988 the Soviet leader announced a unilateral Soviet cut of 500,000 ground troops. Moscow also reduced its support for the Sandinistas in Nicaragua and negotiated for the removal of Cuban troops from Angola. The Soviets also stopped jamming Voice of America broadcasts.

The "Backyard": Central America and the Caribbean

The Reagan administration read events in the Third World as related chapters in an East-West, Cold War book written by the two superpowers, not as independent short stories composed by distinct, indigenous sources. In the Third World, argued Reagan officials, U.S. influence had to be restored to repel "beachheads of tyranny, subversion, and terror."[156] Hegemony was at stake. Reagan quoted the Truman

Doctrine, resuscitated the domino theory, and stressed military and covert means over negotiations. Central America, long in the United States's grip but restless under the burden of profound economic, political, and social divisions, figured prominently in Reagan's counterrevolutionary crusade.

The State Department claimed that Moscow used Cuba to propagandize revolution, train insurgents, and promote "Cuba-model states" that would "provide platforms for subversion, compromise vital sea lanes, and pose a direct military threat at or near our borders."[157] At times President Reagan imagined radicals crossing the border from Mexico into Texas, but increasingly he made a strategic case: As a major trade route, the Caribbean provided "our lifeline to the outside world," and "Soviet military theorists want to destroy our capacity to resupply Western Europe in case of an emergency. They want to tie down our attention and forces on our own southern border and so limit our capacity to act in more distant places such as Europe, the Persian Gulf, the Indian Ocean, the Sea of Japan."[158] Fearing "another Cuba," Reagan officials determined to defeat leftist insurgents in El Salvador, to topple the Sandinista government in Nicaragua, and to draw Guatemala and Honduras into a tighter U.S. military network. Through billions of dollars in aid (including the Caribbean Basin Initiative announced in 1982), CIA operations, weapons and advisers, splashy military maneuvers, and support for the anti-Sandinista army known as the *contras,* Washington plunged more deeply into Central America—"the most important place in the world," Ambassador Kirkpatrick solemnly avowed (see map, page 417).[159]

Critics charged that Reagan exaggerated the Soviet-Cuban threat, underplayed the local causes of disorder, bypassed opportunities for negotiations, and shored up the right wing and military, thus spurring further political polarization. Such policies helped invite what Washington wanted most to prevent: Soviet influence in the area. Senator Christopher Dodd, a Democrat from Connecticut and former Peace Corps volunteer in Latin America, decried the "ignorance" of the Reagan diplomats who "seem to know as little about Central America in 1983 as we knew about Indochina in 1963." Downplaying a Soviet threat and emphasizing Central America's economic underdevelopment, inadequate medical care, illiteracy, and class structure, Dodd declared that "if Central America were not racked with poverty, there would be no revolution."[160]

In El Salvador, the Reagan administration nevertheless found "a textbook case of indirect armed aggression by Communist powers."[161] El Salvador seemed a place where the United States could "win one for a change."[162] A presidential assistant explained that "El Salvador itself doesn't matter—we have to establish credibility."[163] Reagan said it simply: "We are the last domino."[164] El Salvador was a poor country plagued by a high infant mortality rate, illiteracy, and violence. The army and a small landed elite had long ruled the nation. Two percent of the people owned half the land. In October 1979, however, reform-minded colonels seized power and organized a new government under José Napoleón Duarte, a Christian Democratic party leader. The elite responded by organizing "death squads" to assassinate moderates and radicals alike. Leftists formed the Farabundo Martí Front for National Liberation (FMLN). In 1980 national guard troops raped and killed four American churchwomen, but the Salvadoran government refused to prosecute the officers who ordered the murders. Ambassador Kirkpatrick

"Communism."   Critics of Reagan's interventionism in Central America believed that the president misread the sources of instability in the region. (Dennis Renault, *Sacramento Bee*)

seemed to excuse the slayings by saying "the nuns were not just nuns" but "political activists" for the FMLN.[165]

Determined to find a non-Marxist solution to the Salvadoran civil war through land reform, the Carter administration had extended economic aid to the Duarte government. But it had also dispatched military advisers and military aid. The Reagan administration dramatically increased the military assistance program and expanded economic aid. Reagan explained that "we have training squads in more than thirty countries, so this isn't an unusual thing that we are doing."[166] "They thought it was like rolling a drunk," former ambassador to El Salvador Robert E. White remarked.[167]

While reluctantly funding Reagan's Salvadoran programs, Congress insisted that the administration certify human-rights progress in the country. Every six months officials dutifully issued optimistic but disingenuous statements. "Everybody *knew,* Congress *knew,* what they [Salvadoran military forces] were doing," a U.S. Embassy official recalled. "What's improvement, any way? You kill eight hundred and it goes down to two hundred, that's improvement. The whole thing was an exercise in the absurd."[168] The UN Truth Commission reported in 1993 that 85 percent of the 75,000 people killed in the Salvadoran civil war died at the hands of government forces and gun-for-hire death squads. U.S. military advisers trained some of the units responsible for murdering civilians. Although they wanted to curb death-squad killings, U.S. diplomats did not exert "high-level pressure for change on Salvadoran military leaders."[169]

The election of 1982, boycotted by the FMLN, installed a right-wing government. The Reagan administration improved the Salvadoran military's ability to stage air assaults and bombing raids, but the growing civilian death count from the air war actually may have facilitated the FMLN's recruitment of followers. Although Reagan spent $4.5 billion in El Salvador during the 1980s, victory in the bloody civil war still eluded him when he left office. Only after four more years of killing on both sides, including the murder of six Jesuit priests by government forces, did the combatants finally negotiate a United Nations–sponsored peace in January 1992.

The Reagan administration blamed much of the Salvadoran trouble on Cuba and Nicaragua, which sent small supplies of arms to the insurgents. Secretary Haig announced that the Soviets had a "hit list" of Central American states, with Nicaragua first, El Salvador second.[170] The Sandinistas invited thousands of Cuban medical specialists and teachers into their poor country, used Cuban advisers and Soviet weapons to build a strong military, and limited free speech as they moved to a one-party government. "Our function [once] was to grow sugar, cocoa, and coffee for the United States; we served the dessert at the imperialist dinner table," remarked Minister of Agrarian Reform Jaime Wheelock. "We have to be against the United States in order to reaffirm ourselves as a nation."[171]

As the United States had treated Cuba in the 1950s and 1960s, so it treated Nicaragua in the 1980s: putting pressure on a small, proud, doggedly radical government to the point where it faced a choice between capitulation or seeking outside help for defense. Reagan first cut off all foreign aid. In November 1981, he ordered the CIA to train and arm the anti-Sandinista *contras* in a prime example of the low-intensity-conflict strategy. If the United States did not stop radicals "in our own backyard, it was far less likely that we could do so . . . in more distant locations," a top U.S. official later explained.[172] "Let's make the bastards sweat," CIA director William Casey told his covert operators.[173] A mercenary army of 15,000, including former supporters of Somoza, the *contras* were "a mixed bag," according to General Colin Powell. "We worked with what we had."[174] From bases in Honduras and Costa Rica the *contras* raided Nicaragua, sabotaging bridges, oil facilities, and crops, and using CIA "coercive techniques" (including "direct physical brutality") against civilians.[175]

Although in 1982 Congress had prohibited the use of funds to overthrow the Nicaraguan government, Reagan officials winked at the restriction. In early 1984 Congress discovered that the CIA had worked with *contra* commandos to mine three Nicaraguan ports. "I am pissed off," roared Senator Barry Goldwater at the CIA's Casey. "It is an act of war. . . . I don't see how we're going to explain it."[176] When Nicaragua went to the World Court to charge a breach of international law, Washington refused to recognize the court's jurisdiction. (In June 1986, the court decided that the United States had violated international law by funding

The Vietnam Syndrome Cured by the Reagan Doctrine. President Reagan's interventionism in the Third World supposedly ended the Vietnam syndrome, but many critics, including a majority of the American people, feared another Vietnam. (Dan Wasserman for *The Boston Globe* © 1985, Los Angeles Times Syndicate. Reprinted with permission)

the *contras* and ordered Washington to pay an indemnity to Nicaragua; Reagan ignored the ruling.) In mid-1984, Congress banned aid to the *contras*. Meanwhile, Nicaraguan-American talks in Mexico produced no agreement.

The congressional prohibition did not stop aid to the *contras*. Following Reagan's explicit instructions "to do whatever you have to do to help these people keep body and soul together," CIA, Pentagon, and NSC officials rerouted money from Defense appropriations and solicited funds from foreign countries and private donors to supply the *contras*.[177] In 1985–1986 Colonel North of Reagan's NSC shifted to the *contras* profits from secret arms sales to Iran by using Israeli intermediaries and a Swiss bank account. North also coordinated a network of planes and ships (without "USG fingerprints") and funded the building of a large airstrip in Costa Rica—all without informing Congress.[178] As an independent federal prosecutor later concluded, President Reagan "created the conditions which made possible the crimes committed by others" and "knowingly participated" in the illegal aid effort.[179] Reagan said that if the "story gets out, we'll all be hanging by our thumbs in front of the White House."[180] Defeating "Communism in Central America" took precedence over "obeying the law," one scholar has written, so Reagan officials "lied about what they were doing—publicly, privately, repeatedly, egregiously."[181]

In early 1985 Reagan admitted publicly what he had long denied: Washington sought to topple the Sandinista government—he wanted it to say "uncle."[182] In

May he imposed an economic embargo. The United States also blocked loans to Nicaragua from the World Bank and the Inter-American Development Bank. Congress grew more obliging; it appropriated $27 million for "humanitarian" aid to the *contras*. Still, the *contra* war did not go well. The insurgents constantly feuded among themselves, generated little popular support in Nicaragua, and could not seize and hold towns. But they forced the Sandinistas to shift funds from social programs to defense and to tighten controls on civil liberties, thus slowing the revolution and arousing internal dissent. An opponent of *contra* aid, Republican Mark O. Hatfield of Oregon, remembered Vietnam: "Here we are again, old men creating a monster for young men to destroy."[183]

"Don't be a pilgrim," Casey once told George Shultz. "What's that?" "An early settler," said Casey.[184] Hence Reagan officials treated negotiations as "nothing more than a necessary smokescreen to quiet opposition to the paramilitary program."[185] Washington snubbed the Contadora group (Mexico, Venezuela, Panama, and Colombia), which in 1983 had persuaded the five Central American states to limit foreign advisers, reduce arms, and promote democracy. Reagan officials stiff-armed the 1987 peace plan by Costa Rican president Oscar Arias Sánchez but had to negotiate when Congress again banned military aid (which it had reinstated in 1986) and the *contras* agreed to a cease-fire in March 1988. Hobbled by the Iran-Contra scandal, Reagan resisted appeals for more aid to the *contras*. When Reagan left office, the Sandinistas still governed. Under arrangements brokered by the Central American presidents, the Washington-backed candidate Violetta Barrios de Chamorro soundly defeated Sandinista President Daniel Ortega Saavedra in elections finally held in 1990. After nearly a decade of civil war, 30,000 Nicaraguans had died and the ravaged economy had sunk to the second poorest in the hemisphere.

Washington had "proof" that Cuba was "exporting revolution and bloodshed" to El Salvador and Nicaragua, Secretary Haig lectured Cuba's foreign minister during secret talks in 1981.[186] He promised to "close Castro down" by going to the "source."[187] "I'll make that island a fucking parking lot," Haig thundered.[188] Reagan rejected such extremes but banned tourist and business visits to Cuba, denied Cuban officials visas for travel in the United States, and restricted importation of Cuban newspapers and magazines. As for Central America, Cuba endorsed the Contadora process and urged the Salvadoran rebels and Nicaraguans to negotiate in order to obviate U.S. intervention. In December 1984 Havana and Washington did sign an immigration agreement: The United States would return to Cuba about 2,700 criminals who had come by boat in the 1980 Mariel exodus, and Cuba would let Cubans reunite with families in the United States. But when the United States, in mid-1985, started up Radio Martí to act as "an electronic Bay of Pigs" beaming propaganda into Cuba, Castro angrily abrogated the accord and "defiantly prepared to be the last adversary of the United States."[189] America's allies, such as Canada and Britain, undermined the U.S. economic embargo by expanding their trade with Cuba.

When U.S. troops invaded the tiny Caribbean island of Grenada on October 25, 1983, Washington wanted to "send shivers up Castro's spine about whether or not they [the Cubans] might be next."[190] In what one reporter called a "lovely little war," more than 6,000 Americans went ashore to oust a Marxist regime that

Reagan termed "a Soviet-Cuban colony, being readied as a major military bastion to export terror."[191] More than 100 people died, including about 25 Cubans helping to build an airstrip. Reagan claimed that the airfield would serve the Cuban and Soviet militaries, but British engineers explained that its purpose was to boost Grenada's tourist trade. The administration also justified the invasion as the rescue of 1,000 Americans, many of them medical students. But critics argued that the Americans faced no immediate danger. By mid-December, having deported surviving Cubans from the island and closed the Soviet Embassy, U.S. forces evacuated Grenada. The mission had cost $75.5 million. World opinion disapproved this modern example of a "Gilbert-and-Sullivan war."[192] When the UN Security Council deplored the invasion, the United States vetoed the resolution. North Americans celebrated victory, only days after a bomb killed 241 American soldiers in Lebanon (see page 447).

Endangered Interests in the Middle East, Africa, and Asia

The Reagan administration failed to sustain Carter's initiatives in the Middle East. A "Hollywood poolside Zionist" who had resigned from a country club in 1948 to protest the exclusion of Jews, Reagan sought to gain some sort of homeland for the Palestinians and to guarantee Israel's security through a new Arab-Israeli accord.[193] But the peace process stalled. Lebanon descended into savage civil war and suffered a punishing Israeli invasion and Syrian occupation; the Iran-Iraq War disrupted oil shipments; Libya and the United States skirmished; Israel and the United States bickered bitterly; and terrorists victimized the innocent, including many Americans. Saudi Arabia and Jordan refused to relax tensions with Israel yet kept placing large orders for arms. (For example, Reagan in 1981 approved the sale of high-tech military equipment valued at $8.5 billion to the Saudis.) Reaganites assumed that the Soviet Union coveted the region. But Israel considered the PLO and Arab nationalism the greater threats; and the Arabs designated Israel, not Moscow, as enemy number one.

In late 1981, in open defiance of Reagan's position, Israel suddenly announced its annexation of the Golan Heights. Secretary Weinberger complained: "How long do we have to go on bribing Israel," getting little cooperation in return?[194] When Reagan suspended an Israeli-American military agreement, Prime Minister Menachem Begin exploded, "Are we a banana republic?" To American protests against Israeli bombing raids of PLO camps in Lebanon, Begin cited U.S. bombing in Vietnam—"You don't have a right, from a moral perspective, to preach to us."[195] Then came the Egyptian radicals' assassination of President Sadat and Israel's invasion of Lebanon.

Lebanon had long suffered factionalism, especially between Muslims and Christians. For decades, displaced Palestinians had moved into the country, and in 1970–1971 PLO fighters driven from Jordan joined them. When civil war erupted in the mid-1970s, Lebanon invited Syria to restore order; Syrian troops arrived and stayed. From bases in Lebanon the PLO harassed and murdered Israelis. Israel invaded Lebanon in June 1982 in the hope of "cleansing" the nation of Palestinians.[196] Israeli forces drove all the way to Beirut, helping to destroy much of the capital city. Reagan finally telephoned Begin. "Menachem, this is a holocaust," he said. "Mr. President," Began replied, "I think I know what a holocaust is."[197] Nonetheless the Israeli bombing of Beirut stopped.

U.S. officials arranged the withdrawal of both the PLO and Israel from Beirut and created a peacekeeping force that included U.S. marines. Soon Muslims targeted Americans. In April 1983 bombs hit the U.S. Embassy in Beirut, killing 63 people; mortar and sniper fire took the lives of marines over the next several months. Then, in October, a terrorist drove a truck loaded with explosives into a building full of sleeping American troops, killing 241 of them. Weinberger's aide, General Colin Powell, wanted to use military force when it made sense, "but Beirut wasn't sensible. . . . It was goofy from the beginning."[198] Powell criticized the fuzzy idea of providing a "presence," a word "used to give the appearance of clarity to mud."[199] In February 1984, with public criticism rising, Reagan withdrew the marines.

After 533 days and scores of deaths, the marines could not quell Lebanon's multifaceted war. Critics chastised the administration for compliantly following Israel's lead into disaster and for not penalizing Israel for its use of American weapons in violation of contractual restrictions. When the veteran diplomat George Ball claimed that Israel's "roving Air Force" and "rampaging Army" had "devastated a nation [Lebanon]," Cold War hawks accused him of anti-Semitism.[200] The Reagan administration soon patched up relations with Israel, which in 1985 received the largest U.S. foreign-aid package of any nation—$3 billion, or more than $700 per person.

Israeli-American relations soured again after the Palestinian uprising (in Arabic, the *intifada*) began in December 1987 in the West Bank and Gaza. The Israelis had been ruling the 1.5 million inhabitants since 1967. Like other Palestinians in the Middle East (some 5 million), the PLO-backed participants in the *intifada* wanted a homeland. As youthful demonstrators were shot down by Israeli troops, and as shopkeepers organized anti-Israeli boycotts, Shultz urged convocation of an international conference to work out a "land for peace" solution. Both Israel and the PLO adamantly rejected the idea. Jordan decided to relinquish the West Bank to the PLO, which then declared an independent Palestinian state and endorsed UN Resolution 242 (see page 420). PLO leader Yasir Arafat launched a peace initiative of his own, but when he asked to speak before the General Assembly, Shultz denied him a visa. UN members thereupon voted to hear Arafat in Geneva, Switzerland, where the PLO leader recognized Israel's right "to exist in peace and security" and "absolutely" renounced "all forms of terrorism."[201] Shultz accepted Arafat's pledge, and U.S. diplomats on December 16, 1988, opened official talks in Tunisia with the PLO for the first time ever. The Israeli government denounced the negotiations.

Terrorism spread beyond the Middle East (the Baader-Meinhof gang operated in West Germany, and death squads killed in El Salvador). In 1985 alone, more than 800 terrorist incidents in the world claimed some 900 lives, 23 of them Americans. But Mideast terrorists drew the greatest attention. Passengers on American commercial jets became hijack and murder victims, and U.S. citizens were taken

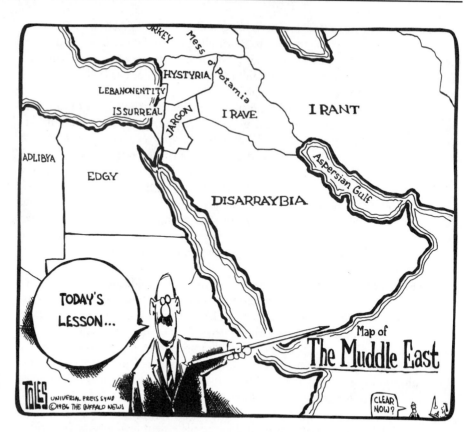

The Muddle East. To many Americans, including the cartoonist Toles, the turbulent Middle East seemed a strange, even irrational region. (TOLES © 1986 The Buffalo News. Reprinted with permission of UNIVERSAL PRESS)

hostage. In one case in 1985, U.S. warplanes forced to the ground an Egyptian airliner known to be carrying four Palestinians who had earlier seized the Italian cruise ship *Achille Lauro* and murdered a wheelchair-bound American. "You can run but you can't hide," warned Reagan.[202]

The Reagan administration especially blamed Libyan radical Islamic ruler Moammar Gadhafi for much of the terrorism. Diplomatic relations between Libya and the United States were severed in early 1981; the following year Washington imposed an embargo on oil imports from Libya; and in early 1986 Reagan banned all trade. After a series of terrorist attacks at busy European airports, Reagan officials fingered Libyan responsibility, sent U.S. warships into the Gulf of Sidra, and attacked patrol boats, shore batteries, and radar sites. A few months later, in April 1986, the bombing of a West Berlin discotheque killed one American soldier and wounded others. Reagan declared Gadhafi the "mad dog of the Middle East."[203] Within days U.S. planes again bombed Libya, coming close to killing Gadhafi himself. The raid did slay his adopted infant daughter.

The Iran-Iraq War also engaged the U.S. military. Deaths ran in the hundreds of thousands as each side savagely attacked the other. Iraq had initiated the war in 1980 to gain Iranian oil lands, control the Shatt al Arab waterway, and topple the Khomeini regime, which had incited Shiite Muslims in Iraq to rebel. Iraq began to

Hunger in Africa. These refugees in a camp in Ethiopia in 1984 await food or death. During the 1980s, several African countries experienced severe drought and famine. Concerned people around the world raised money and sent food and supplies, but millions of Africans still starved to death. (Courtesy CARE)

sink oil tankers in the Persian Gulf. As Iran retaliated in the "tanker war," the United States vowed to keep the Gulf open to international commerce. In May 1987 two sea-skimming missiles fired by an Iraqi aircraft hit the U.S. frigate *Stark,* killing 37 crewmen. Iraq apologized. Reagan soon beefed up the U.S. naval presence in the Gulf and "reflagged" Kuwaiti oil tankers as American vessels. In October, after Iranian missiles struck a reflagged Kuwaiti tanker, American aircraft attacked two Iranian oil platforms. The next year, in July, the U.S.S. *Vincennes,* thinking itself under attack despite sophisticated equipment that should have told its captain otherwise, shot down a civilian Iranian airliner, killing all 290 aboard. Washington admitted error while covering up the fact that the *Vincennes,* violating international law, was inside Iranian territorial waters at the time of the shootdown. At last, in August 1988, Iran and Iraq agreed to end their costly war.

In Africa, too, Reagan had to deal with knotty, long-term issues. Death-dealing famine, as in Sudan in the mid-1980s; civil wars in Angola and Ethiopia, where Soviet and Cuban troops assisted ruling regimes and covert CIA aid helped insurgents; the unresolved status of South Africa–dominated Namibia; and the dehumanizing policy of apartheid in South Africa—all demanded attention. Reagan again espied Soviet adventurism. Toward white-ruled South Africa he at first launched "constructive engagement."[204] Because the United States could not coerce South Africa to abandon its oppression of the black majority, Assistant Secretary of State Chester Crocker argued, Americans should disapprove apartheid but refrain from economic sanctions, and instead encourage gradual reform. This policy amounted to a "kid-glove, all carrot-and-no-stick approach," some analysts dissented.[205]

Reagan abandoned constructive engagement for several reasons. The South African government would not entertain serious reform, and black South Africans marched, protested, and died, demanding that people around the world take sides. As violence spread across South Africa, Reagan worried that the opportunistic Soviets might exploit the turmoil. Protest in the United States, led by the Free South Africa Movement, a broad-based coalition, forced the issue onto the American political agenda. Claiming that "sanctions may hurt, but apartheid kills," members of Congress joined with church, labor, and intellectual leaders to picket the South African embassy in Washington, D.C.[206] South African bishop Desmond M. Tutu, the 1984 Nobel Peace Prize recipient, toured the United States appealing for economic pressure against his government. Cities (Boston, Philadelphia, and others) and states (Connecticut, Maryland, and Nebraska among them) passed divestiture laws requiring the sale of stock they owned in U.S. companies operating in South Africa. Anti-apartheid groups also pressed U.S. corporations to begin divestment— the sale of their businesses in South Africa. Some companies pulled out; by 1986, U.S. investments had dropped to $1.3 billion from $2 billion in 1981.

To head off congressional action, Reagan, in September 1985, added a few sanctions to the earlier (1962) embargo on arms sales to South Africa. This time he restricted nuclear and computer sales and prohibited American bank loans to the South African government. But in October 1986, with an unusual bipartisan consensus and over Reagan's veto, Congress passed stiffer economic sanctions, including a ban on new American investments in and oil exports to South Africa and on imports of certain South African products.

Good news did come from Namibia. South Africa had governed this former German colony since World War I, even defying the United Nations when it revoked Pretoria's mandate in 1966 and demanded independence. Since the early 1970s the radical South West African People's Organization (SWAPO), with Cuban and Soviet support, had battled South African armies from bases in Angola and Zambia. After twelve years of sporadic negotiations, however, Angola, Cuba, and South Africa signed a U.S.-mediated agreement in December 1988 for a Cuban troop withdrawal from Angola and black majority rule in Namibia. Formal independence came in March 1990.

In Asia, Ferdinand Marcos's Philippines became a troublesome ally. Elected president in 1965, Marcos had created a dictatorship marked by corruption, martial law, and personal enrichment. By the early 1980s his country groaned under a huge foreign debt of more than $20 billion, high unemployment, and economic stagnation. He jailed critics, whom security forces tortured and murdered. Business, Roman Catholic Church, civil libertarian, and professional leaders demanded reform. Two insurgencies fed on Filipino discontent: the New People's Army led by communists and the Moro National Liberation Front of Muslims in the south. The accelerating discontent with Marcos came suddenly to a head in August 1983, after assassins gunned down the anti-Marcos leader Benigno S. Aquino. The evidence pointed to a successful military conspiracy.

American investments of $2 billion, trade sales of similar value, and outstanding debts owed to American banks seemed in jeopardy. So, too, did two major American bases: Subic Bay Naval Station and Clark Air Base. The Reagan administration distanced itself from Marcos and pressed for reforms. When Marcos stole an election from Benigno Aquino's widow, Corazon Aquino, turmoil tore across the Philippines. Besieged by his own people and abandoned by the United States, Marcos, on February 25, 1986, went into exile in Hawai'i. U.S. aid soon flowed to the Aquino government.

An altogether different kind of issue stood at the center of Japanese-American relations: a huge trade deficit. Although Japan remained a solid strategic partner, providing bases for the U.S. military and foreign aid to U.S. allies such as South Korea, Turkey, and Pakistan, it also grew dramatically as an economic competitor. "We send Japan low-value soybeans, wheat, coal and cotton," one business leader remarked. "They send us high-value autos, motorcycles, TV sets, and oil-well casings. It's 1776 and we're a colony again."[207] In 1985 the total U.S. trade deficit (more imports than exports) mounted to an all-time high of $148.5 billion—$50 billion of it with Japan. The overall deficit derived in large part from the strong dollar abroad (making American goods expensive in other countries and imports less expensive in the United States) and the indebtedness of Third World nations, which forced them to buy fewer U.S. products. Japan's tariff barriers, cartels, and government subsidies also made it difficult for American goods such as plywood, paper, and cosmetics to penetrate Japanese markets. Protectionists demanded retaliatory, higher tariffs on Japanese goods so that ailing American industry could better meet import competition and American workers could hold their jobs. In 1985 Japan voluntarily set quotas on automobile and carbon-steel shipments to the United States and promised trade liberalization at home, but Washington wanted more. In 1987 Reagan imposed restrictions on some Japanese imports. The 1988 Omnibus Trade and Competitiveness Act "had Japan in its sights" when it authorized U.S. retaliation against nations that refused to negotiate reductions in trade barriers.[208] As the Reagan era ended, Japan's foreign minister characterized the Japanese-American trade relationship as "at its worst since the war."[209]

Triumphs and Time Bombs: The Reagan Legacy

Reagan claimed foreign-policy successes, especially in the twilight of his presidency: Namibia, the INF Treaty, the departure of dictators in Haiti (Jean-Claude Duvalier) and the Philippines (Ferdinand Marcos), termination of the Iran-Iraq War, talks with the PLO, and Cuban withdrawal from Angola. At the end, Reagan seemed less ideological, more adaptable. Improved relations with the Soviet Union suggested that the Cold War was winding down (see Chapter 12). The Soviets pulled out of Afghanistan and loosened their grip on Eastern Europe. Some analysts argued that the huge Reagan military spending forced the economically hobbled Soviets to make concessions. Others noted that much of the money was misspent and wasted (especially on SDI), and that the remarkable changes initiated by Gorbachev sprang not from U.S. pressure but from a new generation of Soviet leaders and courageous Eastern European dissidents. The large U.S. defense buildup may actually have delayed the end of the Cold War by undermining Soviet moderates in their struggle against Kremlin hawks. Reagan very well may have undercut

American power and prestige in the long run by spending the United States into tremendous debt and neglecting to repair the American economy or to improve American education to make the United States more competitive in the international marketplace. The conservative columnist George F. Will wrote that Reagan "has been a great reassurer, a steadying captain who calmed the passengers and, to some extent, the sea." But, Will added, Reagan's "cheerfulness" was "a narcotic, numbing the nation's senses about hazards just over the horizon."[210]

President Reagan bequeathed to his successor, Republican Vice President George Bush, several failures and unresolved international issues. Reagan (and Bush) had paid little attention to global environmental questions. Soil erosion reduced food production at a time when the world's population was growing rapidly. Toxic wastes, acid rain, shortages of clean water, the overcutting of forests, and the overgrazing of fields hurried environmental decline, which in turn burdened governments. "Encroaching deserts now pose a greater threat to national security, and indeed national survival, than do invading armies," warned one development specialist.[211] A warming of the earth's climate owing to the "greenhouse effect" of carbon dioxide and other gases building up in the atmosphere, scientists reported, might raise ocean levels, flooding farmlands and dislocating millions of people. Unless corrected, these environmental and economic problems would spawn political unrest. Some positive signs appeared: population-control programs in many Third World nations; public-health programs providing an effective vaccine against malaria; massive immunization programs against measles and polio; India's attainment of self-sufficiency in food production; and the conservation of dwindling supplies of minerals. But the Reagan administration barely noticed.

Environmental questions also figured in Canadian-American relations. Canadians grew alarmed that polluted American air in the form of acid rain was destroying their forests and contaminating their water. Tension between Ottawa and Washington reached an awkward high. Canadian prime minister Pierre Trudeau once mused, "Living next to you is in some ways like sleeping with an elephant. No matter how friendly and even-tempered is the beast, if I may call it that, one is affected by every twitch and grunt."[212] Although Reagan showed scant interest in acid rain, he did launch negotiations leading to the United States–Canada Free Trade Agreement of 1988. This accord created the world's largest free trade area. The two nations exchanged more goods and services each year, worth about $166 billion in 1989, than any other two countries.

Any accounting of the Reagan legacy includes the president's failure to energize the peace process in the Middle East. The Iran-Contra scandal and intervention in Lebanon rank as major foreign-policy blunders. In Central America, Reagan registered a large death count, continued civil wars, economic disarray, and a bankrupt attachment to the *contras*. On South Africa, Congress had to push Reagan to express serious disapproval of apartheid. The trade and budget deficits grew to huge proportions in the Reagan years (the national debt tripled to $2.8 trillion), and the United States became a debtor nation. Trade conflict with Japan intensified as the United States struggled to compete with the trans-Pacific power. The Third World "debt bomb" also jeopardized a stable economic future.

In the 1980s, after Vietnam and the Iranian hostage crisis, Americans worked to reassert their international supremacy. They built up massive military and nuclear forces; they financed insurgencies; they defended their global interests; they continued to assume that they had answers to others' problems; they reaffirmed their self-appointed mission to purify an imperfect world; they restated their belief in American exceptionalism. In his upbeat farewell address, Ronald Reagan declared that "America is respected again in the world, and looked to for leadership."[213] Other voices suggested that he "may have left time bombs ticking away for the future."[214]

FURTHER READING FOR THE PERIOD 1977–1989

For overviews and various topics, see William C. Berman, *America's Right Turn* (1994); John Ehrman, *The Rise of Neoconservatism: Intellectuals and Foreign Affairs, 1945–1994* (1995); Tom J. Farer, *The Lost Consensus* (1987); Raymond L. Garthoff, *Détente and Confrontation* (1985) and *The Great Transition* (1994); Robert C. Gray and Stanley J. Michalak, Jr., eds., *American Foreign Policy Since Détente* (1984); Ole R. Holsti and James N. Rosenau, *American Leadership in World Affairs* (1984); Robert C. Johansen, *The National Interest and the Human Interest* (1980); Paul Kennedy, *The Rise and Fall of the Great Powers* (1987); Don Oberdorfer, *From the Cold War to a New Era* (1998); and Odd Arne Westad, ed., *The Fall of Détente* (1995). See also books listed in Chapters 7, 10, and 12.

For Jimmy Carter and his foreign relations (specific policies and regions are listed later), see Douglas Brinkley, *The Unfinished Presidency: Jimmy Carter's Journey Beyond the White House* (1998); John Drumbell, *The Carter Presidency* (1993); Gary M. Fink and Hugh Davis Graham, eds., *The Carter Presidency* (1998); Betty Glad, *Jimmy Carter* (1980); Erwin C. Hargrove, *Jimmy Carter as President* (1988); Burton I. Kaufman, *The Presidency of James Earl Carter, Jr.* (1993); David S. McLellan, *Cyrus Vance* (1985); Kenneth E. Morris, *Jimmy Carter, American Moralist* (1996); A. Glenn Mower, *The United States, the United Nations, and Human Rights* (1979) and *Human Rights and American Foreign Policy* (1987); Nancy P. Newell and Richard S. Newell, *The Struggle for Afghanistan* (1981); Kenneth A. Oye et al., eds., *Eagle Entangled* (1979); Jerel A. Rosati, *The Carter Administration's Quest for Global Community* (1987); Herbert O. Rosenbaum and Alexej Ugrinsky, eds., *Jimmy Carter* (1993); David Skidmore, *Reversing Course* (1996); Gaddis Smith, *Morality, Reason, & Power* (1986); and Sandy Vogelsang, *American Dream, Global Nightmare* (1980) (human rights).

Reagan policies are studied in Coral Bell, *The Reagan Paradox* (1989); Larry Berman, ed., *Looking Back on the Reagan Presidency* (1990); Sidney Blumenthal and Thomas B. Edsall, eds., *The Reagan Legacy* (1988); Paul Boyer, ed., *Reagan as President* (1990); Lou Cannon, *President Reagan* (1991); Robert Dallek, *Ronald Reagan* (1984); Theodore Draper, *A Very Thin Line* (1991) (Iran-Contra); Beth A. Fischer, *The Reagan Reversal* (1997); Allan Gerson, *The Kirkpatrick Mission* (1991) (UN); J. David Hoeveler, Jr., *Watch on the Right* (1991); Haynes Johnson, *Sleepwalking Through History* (1991); Peter Kornbluh and Malcolm Byrne, eds., *The Iran-Contra Scandal* (1993); David E. Kyvig, ed., *Reagan and the World* (1990); Mark P. Lagon, *The Reagan Doctrine* (1994); Alexandre Laurien, *The Voice of America* (1988); Thomas E. Mann, *A Question of Balance* (1990) (Congress); Jeff McMahan, *Reagan and the World* (1986); Morris Morley, *Crisis and Confrontation* (1988); Edmund Morris, *Dutch* (1999); Roger Morris, *Haig* (1982); Kenneth A. Oye et al., eds., *Eagle Defiant* (1983) and *Eagle Resurgent?* (1987); William E. Pemberton, *Exit with Honor* (1997); Michael Rogin, *Ronald Reagan* (1987); Michael Schaller, *Reckoning with Reagan* (1992); James M. Scott, *Deciding to Intervene* (1996) (Reagan Doctrine); and Garry Wills, *Reagan's America* (1987). Specific topics and regions are listed below.

Economic and environmental issues can be explored in C. Fred Bergsten and William R. Cline, *The United States–Japan Economic Problem* (1987); Margaret P. Doxey, *Economic Sanctions and International Enforcement* (1980); Robert Gilpin, *The Political Economy of International Relations* (1987); Edward Goldsmith and

Nicolas Hildyard, eds., *The Earth Report* (1988); Edward M. Graham and Paul R. Klugman, *Foreign Direct Investment in the United States* (1995); Gary C. Hufbauer et al., *Economic Sanctions Reconsidered* (1985); Anne G. Keatley, ed., *Technological Frontiers and Foreign Relations* (1985); John H. Makin, *The Global Debt Crisis* (1984); John McCormick, *Reclaiming Paradise* (1989); Jürgen Schmandt et al., eds., *Acid Rain and Friendly Neighbors* (1988); Jeffrey J. Schott, *The Uruguay Round* (1994); Gilbert R. Winham, *International Trade and the Tokyo Round Negotiations* (1986); and Donald Worster, ed., *The Ends of the Earth* (1988).

For relations with the Soviet Union (except for the nuclear arms race, listed below), see Garthoff above; Dana H. Allin, *Cold War Illusions: America, Europe, and Soviet Power* (1995); Seweryn Bialer, *The Soviet Paradox* (1986); Seweryn Bialer and Michael Mandelbaum, eds., *Gorbachev's Russia and American Foreign Policy* (1988); Archie Brown, *The Gorbachev Factor* (1996); Alexander Dallin, *Black Box* (1985) (KAL 007); Seymour M. Hersh, *"The Target Is Destroyed"* (1986); Jerry Hough, *Russia and the West* (1988); Bruce Jentleson, *Pipeline Politics* (1986) (East-West energy trade); Robert G. Kaiser, *How Gorbachev Happened* (1991); Michael MccGwire, *Perestroika and Soviet National Security* (1991); Michael Mandelbaum and Strobe Talbott, *Reagan and Gorbachev* (1987); Jerry Sanders, *Peddlers of Crisis* (1983); and Strobe Talbott, *The Russians and Reagan* (1984).

For the nuclear arms race, SALT-II, SDI, and the antinuclear movement, see Ruth Adams and Susan Cullen, eds., *The Final Epidemic* (1981); William Arkin and Richard Fieldhouse, *Nuclear Battlefields* (1985); Donald C. Baucom, *The Origins of SDI* (1992); Dan Caldwell, *The Dynamics of Domestic Politics and Arms Control* (1991) (SALT-II); David Callahan, *Dangerous Capabilities* (1990) (Nitze); Sidney D. Drell et al., *The Reagan Strategic Defense Initiative* (1985); Lynn Eden and Steven E. Miller, eds., *Nuclear Arguments* (1989); Matthew Evangelista, *Innovation and the Arms Race* (1988); Jonathan Haslam, *The Soviet Union and the Politics of Nuclear Weapons in Europe* (1990); Robert Jervis, *The Meaning of the Nuclear Revolution* (1989); William W. Kaufmann, *A Reasonable Defense* (1986); Michael T. Klare, *American Arms Supermarket* (1984); Edward T. Linenthal, *Symbolic Defense* (1989) (SDI); David S. Meyer, *A Winter of Discontent* (1990) (freeze); John Mueller, *Retreat from Doomsday* (1989); John Newhouse, *War and Peace in the Nuclear Age* (1989); Janne E. Nolan, *Guardians of the Arsenal* (1989); Andrew J. Pierre, *The Global Politics of Arms Sales* (1982); Jerome Price, *The Antinuclear Movement* (1989); Thomas R. Rochon, *Mobilizing for Peace* (1988); Scott D. Sagan, *Moving Targets* (1989); David N. Schwartz, *NATO's Nuclear Dilemmas* (1983); Leon V. Sigal, *Nuclear Forces in Europe* (1984); Steven K. Smith and Douglas A. Wertman, *U.S.–Western European Relations During the Reagan Years* (1992); Strobe Talbott, *Endgame* (1979) (SALT-II), *Deadly Gambits* (1984), and *The Master of the Game* (1988) (Nitze); Douglas C. Waller, *Congress and the Nuclear Freeze* (1987); Daniel Wirls, *Buildup* (1992); and Thomas W. Wolfe, *The SALT Experience* (1979).

The CIA, U.S. covert operations, counterinsurgency, and counterrevolution are explored in Daniel P. Bolger, *Americans at War, 1975–1986* (1988); Anne H. Cahn, *Killing Détente: The Right Attacks the CIA* (1998); Loch Johnson, *America's Secret Power* (1989); Michael T. Klare and Cynthia Arnson, *Supplying Repression* (1981); Michael T. Klare and Peter Kornbluh, eds., *Low-Intensity Warfare* (1988); David C. Martin and John Wolcott, *Best Laid Plans* (1988); Michael McClintock, *Instruments of Statecraft* (1992); Kathryn S. Olmsted, *Challenging the Secret Government* (1996) (investigations of CIA); Joseph E. Persico, *Casey* (1990); John Prados, *Presidents' Secret Wars* (1986); John Ranelagh, *The Agency* (1986); D. Michael Shafer, *Deadly Paradigms* (1988); and Gregory F. Treverton, *Covert Action* (1987).

For U.S. relations with the Third World, see Richard E. Feinberg, *The Intemperate Zone* (1983); John L. Girling, *America and the Third World* (1980); Melvin Gurtov and Ray Maghroori, *Roots of Failure* (1984); Gabriel Kolko, *Confronting the Third World* (1988); Stephen D. Krasner, *Structural Conflict* (1985); Barry Rubin, *Modern Dictators* (1987); Peter J. Schraeder, *Intervention in the 1980s* (1989); and Marshall D. Shulman, ed., *East-West Tensions in the Third World* (1986).

Middle East topics, Arab-Israeli conflict, and the peace process are examined in Fouad Ajami, *The Arab Predicament* (1981); George W. Ball, *Error and Betrayal in Lebanon* (1984); Mahmoud G. ElWarfally, *Imagery and Ideology in U.S. Policy Toward Libya* (1988); George Lenczowski, *American Presidents and the Middle East* (1989) and *The Middle East in World Affairs* (1980); Zachary Lochman and Joel Beinin, eds., *Intifada* (1989); A. F. K. Organski, *The $36 Billion Bargain* (1990) (aid to Israel); Don Peretz, *Intifada* (1990); William R. Polk, *The Arab World Today* (1991); William B. Quandt, *Camp David* (1986), *The United States and Egypt* (1990), and *The Peace Process* (1993); Cheryl Rubenberg, *Israel and the American National Interest* (1986); Yezid Sayad, *Armed Struggle and the Search for State* (1997); David Schoenbaum, *The United States and the State of Israel* (1993); Steven L. Spiegel, *The Other Arab-Israeli Conflict* (1985); and Daniel Yergin, *The Prize* (1991) (oil).

For U.S.-Iranian relations and the hostage crisis, see James A. Bill, *The Eagle and the Lion* (1988); Richard Cottam, *Iran and the United States* (1988); Charles-Phillippe David et al., *Foreign Policy in the White House* (1993); Mark J. Gasiorowski, *U.S. Foreign Policy and the Shah* (1991); James E. Goode, *The United States and Iran* (1997); Nikki R. Keddie, *Iran, the United States, and the Soviet Union* (1990); Russell L. Moses, *Freeing the Hostages* (1996); R. K. Ramazani, *Revolutionary Iran* (1987); Barry Rubin, *Paved with Good Intentions* (1980); Paul Ryan, *The Iranian Rescue Mission* (1985); Amin Saikal, *The Rise and Fall of the Shah* (1980); William Shawcross, *The Shah's Last Ride* (1988); Gary Sick, *All Fall Down* (1985) and *October Surprise* (1991) (hostages and Reagan election); and Marvin Zonis, *Majestic Failure* (1991).

For Asia, see David Bain, *Sitting in Darkness* (1984) (Philippines); C. Fred Bergsten and William R. Cline, *The United States–Japan Economic Problem* (1987); Raymond Bonner, *Waltzing with a Dictator* (1987) (Marcos); H. W. Brands, *Bound to Empire* (1992) (Philippines); Roger Buckley, *U.S.-Japan Alliance Diplomacy* (1992); Sandra Burton, *Impossible Dream* (1989); Warren I. Cohen, *America's Response to China* (1990); Lynn D. Feintech, *China's Four Modernizations and the United States* (1982); Yufan Hao and Guocang Huan, eds., *The Chinese View of the World* (1989); Harry Harding, *A Fragile Relationship* (1992) (China); Stanley Karnow, *In Our Image* (1989) (Philippines); Richard J. Kessler, *Rebellion and Repression in the Philippines* (1989); Walter LaFeber, *The Clash* (1997); Michael Schaller, *The United States and China in the Twentieth Century* (1989) and *Altered States* (1997); and Stephen R. Shalom, *The United States and the Philippines* (1981).

For Latin America and the Panama Canal treaties, see Paul Drake and Iván Jaksić, eds., *The Struggle for Democracy in Chile* (1991); David W. Engstrom, *Presidential Decision Making Adrift* (1997) (Mariel boatlift); William L. Furlong and Margaret E. Scranton, *The Dynamics of Foreign Policymaking* (1984) (Panama); J. Michael Hogan, *The Panama Canal in American Politics* (1986); Eldon Kenworthy, *America/Américas* (1995); Walter LaFeber, *The Panama Canal* (1989); Gordon K. Lewis, *Grenada* (1987); Abraham F. Lowenthal, ed., *Partners in Conflict* (1987) and *Exporting Democracy* (1991); John Major, *Prize Possession* (1993) (Panama); Christopher Mitchell, ed., *Western Hemisphere Immigration and United States Foreign Policy* (1992); Louis A. Pérez, Jr., *Cuba and the United States* (1997); and Lars Schoultz, *Human Rights and United States Policy Toward Latin America* (1981), *National Security and United States Policy Toward Latin America* (1987), and *Beneath the United States* (1998).

Mexican-American relations are the subject of Wayne Cornelius, *Building the Cactus Curtain* (1980); Paul R. Erlich et al., *The Golden Door* (1981); George W. Grayson, *The Politics of Mexican Oil* (1980) and *Oil and Mexican Foreign Policy* (1988); Robert H. McBride, ed., *Mexico and the United States* (1981); Robert A. Pastor and Jorge G. Castañeda, *Limits of Friendship* (1988); Susan K. Purcell, ed., *Mexico–United States Relations* (1981); W. Dirk Raat, *Mexico and the United States* (1996); Peter H. Smith, *Mexico* (1980); and Stanley Weintraub, *Marriage of Convenience* (1989).

For Central America, especially Nicaragua and El Salvador, see Ariel C. Armony, *Argentina, the United States, and the Anti-Communist Crusade in Central America* (1997); Cynthia J. Arnson, *Crossroads* (1994); Bruce M. Bagley, ed., *Contadora and the Diplomacy of Peace in Central America* (1987); Leslie Bethell, ed., *Central America Since Independence* (1991); Morris J. Blachman et al., eds., *Confronting Revolution* (1986); Kenneth M. Coleman and George C. Herring, eds., *Understanding the Central American Crisis* (1991); Roy Gutman, *Banana Diplomacy* (1987) (Nicaragua); Martha Honey, *Hostile Acts* (1994) (Costa Rica); Stephen Kinzer, *Blood of Brothers* (1991) (Nicaragua); Peter Kornbluh, *Nicaragua* (1988); Clifford Krauss, *Inside Central America* (1991); Walter LaFeber, *Inevitable Revolutions* (1993); Anthony Lake, *Somoza Falling* (1989); William M. LeoGrande, *Our Own Backyard* (1998); Morris H. Morley, *Washington, Somoza, and the Sandinistas* (1994); Robert Pastor, *Condemned to Repetition* (1987) (Nicaragua); Holly Sklar, *Washington's War on Nicaragua* (1988); Christian Smith, *Resisting Reagan: The U.S. Central America Peace Movement* (1996); Gaddis Smith, *The Last Years of the Monroe Doctrine, 1945–1993* (1994); and Thomas W. Walker, *Reagan vs. the Sandinistas* (1987), and ed., *Revolution and Counterrevolution in Nicaragua* (1991).

South Africa and African questions are treated in Pauline H. Baker, *The United States and South Africa* (1989); James Barber and John Barratt, *South Africa's Foreign Policy* (1990); Gerald J. Bender et al., eds., *African*

Crisis Areas and U.S. Foreign Policy (1985); Christopher Coker, *The United States and South Africa* (1986); Alexander deWaal, *Famine That Kills: Darfur, Sudan, 1984–1985* (1989); Peter Duignan and Lewis H. Gann, *The United States and Africa* (1987); Arthur Gaushon, *Crisis in Africa* (1981); Richard W. Hull, *American Enterprise in South Africa* (1990); Janice Love, *The U.S. Anti-Apartheid Movement* (1985); Robert K. Massie, *Loosing the Bonds* (1997) (South Africa); Martin Meredith, *In the Name of Apartheid* (1988); William Minter, *King Solomon's Mines Revisited* (1986); Robert I. Rotberg, *Suffer the Future* (1980); and Jennifer S. Whitaker, *Conflict in Southern Africa* (1978) and *How Can Africa Survive?* (1987).

See also the General Bibliography and the following notes.

For comprehensive coverage of foreign-relations topics, see the articles in the four-volume *Encyclopedia of U.S. Foreign Relations* (1997), edited by Bruce W. Jentleson and Thomas G. Paterson.

NOTES TO CHAPTER 11

1. Quoted in Robert D. McFadden et al., *No Hiding Place* (New York: Times Books, 1981), p. 3.
2. Quoted in William B. Quandt, "The Middle East Crisis," *Foreign Affairs: America and the World, 1979, LVIII* (1980), 544.
3. Moorhead Kennedy quoting a marine in discussion of "Iran Hostage Mission" in Herbert B. Rosenbaum and Alexej Ugrinsky, eds., *Jimmy Carter* (Westport, Conn.: Greenwood, 1994), p. 232.
4. Quoted in Doyle McManus, *Free at Last!* (New York: New American, 1981), p. 16.
5. Quoted in Tim Wells, *444 Days* (San Diego: Harcourt Brace Jovanovich, 1985), p. 70.
6. *Public Papers, Carter, 1977* (Washington, D.C.: Government Printing Office, 1977–1978; 2 vols.), II, 2221.
7. Pierre Salinger, *America Held Hostage* (Garden City, N.Y.: Doubleday, 1981), p. 5.
8. Quoted in James F. Goode, *The United States & Iran* (New York: St. Martin's Press, 1997), p. 186.
9. Jimmy Carter, *Keeping Faith* (New York: Bantam, 1982), p. 439.
10. Cyrus Vance, *Hard Choices* (New York: Simon & Schuster, 1983), p. 331.
11. Carter official quoted in Russell L. Moses, *Freeing the Hostages* (Pittsburgh: University of Pittsburgh Press, 1996), p. 89.
12. Quoted in *New York Times*, November 18, 1979.
13. Quoted in Daniel Yergin, *The Prize* (New York: Simon & Schuster, 1991), p. 701.
14. Quoted in Harold H. Saunders, "Diplomacy and Pressure," in Warren Christopher et al., *American Hostages in Iran* (New Haven: Yale University Press, 1982), p. 102.
15. Quoted in McFadden, *No Hiding Place*, p. 214.
16. Quoted in Burton I. Kaufman, *The Presidency of James Earl Carter, Jr.* (Lawrence: University Press of Kansas, 1993), p. 160.
17. Quoted in Wells, *444 Days*, p. 439.
18. Stansfield Turner quoted in Moses, *Freeing*, p. 186.
19. Vance, *Hard Choices*, p. 409.
20. Zbigniew Brzezinski, *Power and Principle* (New York: Farrar, Straus & Giroux, 1985; rev. ed.), p. 494.
21. Zbigniew Brzezinski, "The Failed Mission," *New York Times Magazine*, April 18, 1982, p. 64.
22. Quoted in Phillip Keisling, "Desert One," *Washington Monthly*, XV (December 1983), 56.
23. Quoted in Lucien S. Vandenbroucke, *Perilous Options* (New York: Oxford University Press, 1993), p. 140.
24. Quoted in Paul B. Ryan, *The Iranian Rescue Mission* (Annapolis, Md.: Naval Institute Press, 1985), p. 127.
25. Michael Schaller, *Reckoning with Reagan* (New York: Oxford University Press, 1992), p. 21.
26. Hodding Carter quoted in John Dumbrell, *The Carter Presidency* (New York: Manchester University Press, 1993), p. 169.
27. John Limbert quoted in James A. Bill, *The Eagle and the Lion* (New Haven: Yale University Press, 1988), p. 303.
28. Sanford J. Ungar, "The Roots of Estrangement," in Ungar, ed., *Estrangement* (New York: Oxford University Press, 1985), p. 7.
29. Quoted in Steven V. Roberts, "The Year of the Hostage," *New York Times Magazine*, November 2, 1980, p. 63.
30. Quoted in Jules Witcover, *Marathon* (New York: Viking, 1977), p. 596.
31. Quoted in Betty Glad, *Jimmy Carter* (New York: W. W. Norton, 1980), p. 391.
32. Douglas Brinkley, "The Rising Stock of Jimmy Carter," *Diplomatic History, XX* (Fall, 1996), 515.
33. William Quandt in discussion of "Negotiations at Home and Abroad" in Rosenbaum and Ugrinsky, *Carter*, p. 62.
34. Carter, *Keeping Faith*, p. 143.
35. Quoted in *Washington Post*, January 12, 1977; *New York Times*, May 2, 1979.
36. Vance, *Hard Choices*, p. 394.
37. Brzezinski, *Power and Principle*, p. 380.
38. Leslie H. Gelb in *New York Times*, April 29, 1980.
39. Hamilton Jordan, *Crisis* (New York: G.P. Putnam's Sons, 1982), p. 47.
40. Quoted in *Newsweek, LXXXVIII* (December 27, 1976), 19.
41. Marina Whitman, "Leadership without Hegemony," *Foreign Policy*, no. 20 (Fall 1975), 138.
42. Gaddis Smith, *Morality, Reason, & Power* (New York: Hill & Wang, 1986).
43. Quoted in John Lewis Gaddis, *Strategies of Containment* (New York: Oxford University Press, 1982), p. 345.
44. Smith, *Morality, Reason, & Power*, p. 9.
45. Quoted in Richard Hudson, "Storm Over the Canal," *New York Times Magazine*, May 16, 1976, p. 24.

46. Quoted in William J. Jorden, *Panama Odyssey* (Austin: University of Texas Press, 1984), p. 436.

47. Quoted in William L. Furlong and Margaret E. Scranton, *The Dynamics of Foreign Policymaking* (Boulder, Colo.: Westview Press, 1984), p. 55.

48. Quoted in Lou Cannon, *President Reagan* (New York: Simon & Schuster, 1991), p. 342.

49. Quoted in Leroy Ashby and Rod Gramer, *Fighting the Odds* (Pullman: Washington State University Press, 1994), p. 543.

50. Sol Linowitz quoted in John Major, *Prize Possession* (New York: Cambridge University Press, 1993), p. 351.

51. Quoted in Ashby and Gramer, *Fighting*, p. 544.

52. *Department of State Bulletin, LXXVIII* (May 1978), 52.

53. Brzezinski, *Power and Principle*, p. 136.

54. *Department of State Bulletin, LXXVIII* (May 1978), 53.

55. Quoted in Charles O. Jones, *The Trusteeship Presidency* (Baton Rouge: Louisiana State University Press, 1988), p. 160.

56. Minister of Planning Henry Ruíz quoted in Morris H. Morley, *Washington, Somoza, and the Sandinistas* (New York: Cambridge University Press, 1994), p. 306.

57. López Portillo quoted in W. Dirk Raat, *Mexico and the United States* (Athens: University of Georgia Press, 1992), p. 161.

58. Quoted in Michael S. Teitelbaum, "Right Versus Right," *Foreign Affairs, LIX* (Fall 1980), 46.

59. Quoted in Saul Landau, "The Bay of Pigs," *Los Angeles Times*, April 19, 1981.

60. Quoted in *Hartford Courant*, November 20, 1980.

61. Moshe Dayan quoted in William B. Quandt, *Peace Process* (Washington, D.C.: Brookings, 1993), p. 268.

62. William Quandt in discussion of "The Camp David Accords," in Rosenbaum and Ugrinsky, *Carter*, p. 186.

63. William B. Quandt, *Camp David* (Washington, D.C.: Brookings, 1986), p. 258.

64. Quoted in *Hartford Courant*, December 22, 1980.

65. Andrew Young in Elaine P. Adam and Richard P. Stebbins, eds., *American Foreign Relations, 1977* (New York: New York University Press, 1979), p. 301.

66. Quoted in Walter LaFeber, *America, Russia, and the Cold War, 1945–1992* (New York: McGraw-Hill, 1993; 7th ed.), p. 292.

67. In Adam and Stebbins, *American Foreign Relations, 1977*, p. 309.

68. General Obasanjo quoted in Donald Rothchild, "U.S. Policy Styles in Africa," in Kenneth A. Oye et al., eds., *Eagle Entangled* (New York: Longman, 1979), p. 327.

69. Clyde Ferguson and William R. Cotter, "South Africa," *Foreign Affairs, LVI* (January 1978), 262.

70. Quoted in Foreign Policy Association, *Great Decisions, '79* (New York: Foreign Policy Association, 1979), p. 60.

71. Quoted in Kaufman, *Carter*, p. 91.

72. Quoted in *New York Times*, December 7, 1978.

73. Hodding Carter III, "Life Inside the Carter State Department," *Playboy, XXVIII* (February 1981), 215.

74. Quoted in Odd Arne Westad, "The Fall of Détente and the Turning Tides of History," in Westad, ed., *The Fall of Détente* (Boston: Scandinavian University Press, 1995), p. 17.

75. Georgy Kornienko quoted in Vladislav Zubok, "An Offered Hand Rejected?" in Rosenbaum and Ugrinsky, *Carter*, p. 365.

76. Quoted in Westad, "Fall of Détente," p. 16.

77. Quoted in Lawrence Caldwell and Alexander Dallin, "U.S. Policy Toward the Soviet Union," in Oye, *Eagle Entangled*, p. 220.

78. Quoted in *New York Times*, May 29, 1978.

79. Quoted in Thomas J. McCormick, *America's Half-Century* (Baltimore: Johns Hopkins University Press, 1996, rev. ed.), p. 206.

80. Georgi Arbatov quoted in Joseph Kraft, "Letter from Moscow," *The New Yorker, LIV* (October 16, 1978), 122–124.

81. Quoted in George McGovern, "How to Avert a New 'Cold War,'" *Atlantic Monthly, CCXLV* (June 1980), 52.

82. Quoted in David Callahan, *Dangerous Capabilities* (New York: HarperCollins, 1990), p. 409.

83. Leslie H. Gelb, "The Facts of SALT II," April 1979, Department of State Current Policy No. 65.

84. Senator Robert Byrd quoted in *New York Times*, October 4, 1979.

85. Quoted in Robert Shaplen, "Eye of the Storm—III," *The New Yorker, LVI* (June 16, 1980), 76.

86. Garthoff, *Détente and Confrontation*, p. 928.

87. Leonid Shebarshin quoted in Odd Arne Westad, "New Russian Evidence on the Soviet Intervention in Afghanistan," *Cold War International History Project Bulletin*, nos. 8–9 (Winter 1996/1997), 130.

88. George Urban, "A Long Conversation with Dr. Zbigniew Brzezinski," *Encounter, LVI* (May 1981), 18.

89. Leonid Brezhnev quoted in Odd Arne Westad, "The Road to Kabul," in Westad, *Fall of Détente*, p. 141.

90. *Department of State Bulletin, LXXX* (February 1980), Special B.

91. Quoted in Smith, *Morality, Reason, & Power*, p. 232.

92. Helmut Schmidt, *Men and Powers* (New York: Random House, 1989), p. 207.

93. David D. Newsom, "America Engulfed," *Foreign Policy*, no. 43 (Summer 1981), 17.

94. Nancy Bernkopf Tucker, *Taiwan, Hong Kong, and the United States* (New York: Twayne, 1994), p. 156.

95. Quoted in Michael S. Sherry, *In the Shadow of War* (New Haven: Yale University Press, 1995), p. 350.

96. Quoted in Timothy Maga, *Hands Across the Sea* (Athens: Ohio University Press, 1997), p. 110.

97. William A. Williams letter, *The Nation, CCXXXII* (February 14, 1981), 162.

98. Richard E. Neustadt, *Presidential Power and the Modern Presidents* (New York: Free Press, 1990), p. 261.

99. Cyrus Vance quoted in *New York Times*, June 6, 1980.

100. Quoted in Hedrick Smith, "Reagan," *New York Times Magazine*, November 16, 1980, p. 172.

101. Quoted in Cecil V. Crabb, Jr., "The Reagan Victory," in Ellis Sandoz and Cecil V. Crabb, Jr., eds., *A Tide of Discontent* (Washington, D.C.: Congressional Quarterly Press, 1981), p. 158.

102. Quoted in Robert G. Kaiser, "Your Host of Hosts," *New York Review of Books*, June 28, 1984, p. 38.

103. Quoted in Pierre E. Trudeau, *Memoirs* (Toronto: McClellan and Stewart, 1993), p. 332.

104. Quoted in Kaiser, "Your Host," p. 39.

105. Martin Anderson, *Revolution* (Stanford: Stanford University Press, 1990), pp. 288, 290.

106. Quoted in Strobe Talbott, *The Russians and Reagan* (New York: Vintage, 1984), p. 32.

107. *Public Papers, Reagan, 1981* (Washington, D.C.: Government Printing Office, 1982), p. 57.

108. Reagan quoted in David Wirls, *Buildup* (Ithaca: Cornell University Press, 1992), pp. 32–33.

109. Quoted in Schaller, *Reckoning*, p. 47.

110. Quoted in Raymond L. Garthoff, *The Great Transition* (Washington, D.C.: Brookings, 1994), p. 11.

111. Quoted in Schmidt, *Men and Powers*, p. 243.

112. Ronald Reagan, *An American Life* (New York: Simon & Schuster, 1990), p. 547.

113. *Public Papers, Reagan, 1981*, p. 464; *ibid., 1983* (Washington D.C.: Government Printing Office, 1984–1985, 2 vols.), I, 265.

114. *Public Papers, Reagan, 1983*, II, 1189.

115. CIA official quoted in Robert Alan Goldberg, *Barry Goldwater* (New Haven: Yale University Press, 1995), p. 319.

116. *Department of State Bulletin, LXXXIV* (May 1984), 4.

117. Quoted in Walter LaFeber, *Inevitable Revolutions* (New York: Norton, 1993; 2nd ed.), p. 276.

118. *Weekly Compilation of Presidential Documents, XXII* (February 10, 1986), 136, 140.

119. *Department of State Bulletin, LXXXIV* (November 1984), 7.

120. Quoted in Cannon, *President Reagan*, p. 160.

121. Alexander M. Haig, Jr., *Caveat* (New York: Macmillan, 1984), p. 85.

122. Quoted in Michael McClintock, *Instruments of Statecraft* (New York: Pantheon, 1992), p. 378.

123. Hans-Dietrich Gentscher, *Rebuilding a House Divided* (New York: Broadway Books, 1998), p. 205; George P. Shultz, *Turmoil and Triumph* (New York: Charles Scribner's Sons, 1993), p. 84.

124. Shultz, *ibid.*, p. 275.

125. Quoted in Robert A. Pastor, "The Centrality of Central America," in Larry Berman, ed., *Looking Back on the Reagan Presidency* (Baltimore: Johns Hopkins University Press, 1990), p. 40.

126. Quoted in Theodore S. Draper, *A Very Thin Line* (New York: Simon & Schuster, 1991), p. 565.

127. Quoted *ibid.*, p. 560.

128. North quoted in William E. Pemberton, *Exit with Honor* (Armonk, N.Y.: Sharpe, 1998), p. 173.

129. Quoted in Robert E. Osgood, "The Revitalization of Containment," *Foreign Affairs: America and the World, 1981, LX* (1982), 475.

130. Quoted in *New York Times*, December 10, 1981.

131. George F. Kennan, "Cease This Madness," *Atlantic Monthly, CCXLVII* (January 1981), 25–28.

132. George F. Kennan, "On Nuclear War," *New York Review of Books*, January 21, 1982, pp. 10, 12.

133. Quoted in *New York Times*, May 4, 1983.

134. General William Odum quoted in Carol Cohn, "Sex and Death in the Rational World of Defense Intellectuals," *Signs, XII* (Autumn 1987), 692–693.

135. Reagan quoted in Beth A. Fischer, *The Reagan Reversal* (Columbia: Unviersity of Missouri Press, 1997), p. 120.

136. Steven K. Smith and Douglas A. Wertman, *US–West European Relations During the Reagan Years* (New York: St. Martin's Press, 1992), p. 58.

137. Strobe Talbott, *The Master of the Game* (New York: Viking, 1989), p. 5.

138. James Baker quoted in Strobe Talbott, *Deadly Gambits* (New York: Viking, 1984), p. 223.

139. Quoted in *New York Times*, March 27, 1983.

140. Gregory Fossedal of the Heritage Foundation quoted in Wirls, *Buildup*, p. 149.

141. Suzanne Massie quoting Reagan in Deborah H. Strober and Gerald S. Strober, eds., *Reagan* (Boston: Houghton Mifflin, 1998), p. 128.

142. Reagan quoted in *Washington Post*, December 24, 1981.

143. Ronald Reagan, "Korean Airline Massacre," September 5, 1983, Department of State Current Policy no. 507.

144. Quoted in *New York Times*, December 9, 1996.

145. Geoffrey Howe, *Conflict of Loyalty* (London: Macmillan, 1994), p. 350.

146. Reagan quoted in Fischer, *Reagan Reversal*, p. 135.

147. Anatoly Dobrynin, *In Confidence* (New York: Random House, 1995), p. 538.

148. Margaret Thatcher, *The Downing Street Years* (New York: Harper-Collins, 1993), p. 461.

149. George Shultz quoted in Archie Brown, *The Gorbachev Factor* (New York: Oxford University Press, 1996), p. 231.

150. Quoted in Robert G. Kaiser, *How Gorbachev Happened* (New York: Simon & Schuster, 1991), p. 119.

151. Reagan, *American Life*, p. 675; Jack F. Matlock, *Autopsy on an Empire* (New York: Random House, 1995), p. 97.

152. Ambassador Jack Matlock quoted in Carolyn M. Ekedal and Melvin A. Goodman, *The Wars of Eduard Shevardnadze* (University Park: Penn State University Press, 1997), p. xix.

153. Quoted in LaFeber, *America, Russia*, p. 325.

154. Quoted in Ekedahl and Goodman, *Shevardnadze*, p. 147.

155. Georgi Arbatov, *The System* (New York: Times Books, 1992), p. 350.

156. Reagan quoted in Knud Krakau, "Policy as Myth and Myth as Policy," *Revue Française d'Études Americaines, XVII* (August 1994), 263.

157. Quoted in Harold Molineu, *U.S. Policy toward Latin America* (Boulder, Colo.: Westview Press, 1986), p. 176; NSC paper of April 1982 quoted in *New York Times*, April 7, 1983.

158. *Public Papers, Reagan, 1983, I*, 373, 601.

159. Quoted in William M. LeoGrande, *Our Own Backyard* (Chapel Hill: University of North Carolina Press, 1998), p. 581.

160. Quoted in *New York Times*, April 28, 1983.

161. *Department of State Bulletin, LXXXI* (March 1981), 7.

162. U.S. Senator quoted in *New York Times*, April 26, 1981.

163. Quoted in William M. LeoGrande, "A Splendid Little War," *International Security, VI* (Summer 1981), 27.

164. Quoted *ibid.*, p. 45.

165. Quoted in LaFeber, *Inevitable Revolutions*, p. 277.

166. *Department of State Bulletin, LXXXI* (April 1981), 12.

167. Quoted in Marvin Gettleman et al., eds., *El Salvador* (New York: Grove, 1981), p. 355.

168. Howard Lane quoted in Mark Danner, "The Truth of El Mozote," *The New Yorker, LXIX* (December 6, 1993), 118.

169. Thomas Carothers, "Reagan Years," in Abraham F. Lowenthal, ed., *Exporting Democracy* (Baltimore: Johns Hopkins University Press, 1991), p. 93.

170. Quoted in *New York Times*, March 19, 1981.

171. Quoted in Stephen Kinzer, "Nicaragua," *New York Times Magazine*, August 28, 1983, p. 24.

172. Quoted in Peter Kornbluh, "The U.S. Role in the Counterrevolution," in Thomas W. Walker, ed., *Revolution & Counterrevolution in Nicaragua* (Boulder, Colo.: Westview, 1991), p. 325.

173. Quoted in Bob Woodward, *Veil* (New York: Simon & Schuster, 1987), p. 281.

174. Colin L. Powell, *My American Journey* (New York: Random House, 1995), p. 339.

175. CIA manual quoted in *New York Times*, January 29, 1997.

176. Quoted in Thomas G. Paterson, "Oversight or Afterview?" in Michael Barnhart, ed., *Congress and United States Foreign Policy* (Albany: State University of New York Press, 1987), p. 154.

177. Quoted in Pemberton, *Exit*, p. 173.

178. Oliver North to John Poindexter, September 25, 1986, in Tom Blanton, ed., *White House E-Mail* (New York: New Press, 1995), p. 99.

179. Lawrence Walsh quoted in Theodore Draper, "Walsh's Last Stand," *New York Review of Books*, March 3, 1994, p. 27.

180. Quoted in Joel Brinkley, "The Cover-Up That Worked," *New York Times*, January 23, 1994.

181. LeoGrande, *Backyard,* p. 587.

182. Quoted in *New York Times,* February 23, 1985.

183. Quoted *ibid.,* August 13, 1986.

184. Shultz, *Turmoil and Triumph,* p. 305.

185. Robert M. Gates, *From the Shadows* (New York: Simon & Schuster, 1996), p. 273.

186. Quoted in Peter Kornbluh, "The Haig-Rodríguez Secret Talks," *Cold War International History Project Bulletin,* nos. 8–9 (Winter 1996/1997), 219.

187. Quoted in Robert McFarlane, *Special Trust* (New York: Cadell & Davies, 1991), p. 177.

188. Michael Deaver quoting Haig in Schaller, *Reckoning,* p. 123.

189. Laurien Alexandre, *The Voice of America* (Norwood, N.J.: Ablex, 1988), p. 139; Kenneth N. Skoug, Jr., *The United States and Cuba Under Reagan and Shultz* (Westport, Conn.: Praeger, 1996), p. 207.

190. Robert McFarlane quoted in Strober and Strober, *Reagan,* p. 290.

191. Quoted in Michael D. Pearlman, *Warfighting and American Democracy* (Lawrence: University Press of Kansas, 1999), p. 397; quoted in Lars Schoutz, *Beneath the United States,* (Cambridge: Harvard University Press, 1998), p. 365.

192. Sherry, *Shadow,* p. 339.

193. Quoted in David Schoenbaum, *The United States and the State of Israel* (New York: Oxford University Press, 1993), p. 273.

194. Quoted in Haig, *Caveat,* p. 328.

195. Quoted in *New York Times,* December 21, 1981.

196. Ariel Sharon quoted in Quandt, *Peace Process,* p. 346.

197. Quoted in Schoenbaum, *U.S. and Israel,* p. 285.

198. Quoted in Caspar W. Weinberger, *Fighting for Peace* (New York: Warner, 1990), p. 160.

199. Powell, *American Journey,* p. 291.

200. Quoted in James A. Bill, *George Ball* (New Haven: Yale University Press, 1997), pp. 194–195.

201. Quoted in Yezid Sayid, *Armed Struggle and the Search for State* (New York: Oxford University Press, 1997), p. 624.

202. Quoted in *New York Times,* October 15, 1985.

203. Quoted *ibid.,* April 20, 1986.

204. Chester A. Crocker, "South Africa: Strategy for Change," *Foreign Affairs, LIX* (Winter 1980/1981), 346.

205. Donald Rothchild and John Ravenhill, "From Carter to Reagan," in Kenneth Oye et al., eds., *Eagle Defiant* (Boston: Little, Brown, 1983), p. 349.

206. Member of Congress William Gray quoted in Stephen R. Weissman, *A Culture of Deference* (New York: BasicBooks, 1995), p. 171.

207. Lee Iacocca quoted in Donald W. White, *The American Century* (New Haven: Yale University Press, 1996), p. 395.

208. George Shultz quoted in Walter LaFeber, *The Clash* (New York: Norton, 1997), p. 380.

209. Abe Shintaro quoted *ibid.*

210. George F. Will, "How Reagan Changed America," *Newsweek, CXIII* (January 9, 1989), 13, 17.

211. Lester R. Brown quoted in *World Development Forum, IV* (August 31, 1986), 1.

212. Quoted in Ivo D. Duchacek, *Nations and Men* (Hinsdale, Ill.: Dryden Press, 1975; 3rd ed.), p. 146.

213. Quoted in Foreign Policy Association, *Great Decisions 1990* (New York: Foreign Policy Association, 1990), p. 16.

214. Terry Deibel, "Reagan's Mixed Legacy," *Foreign Policy,* no. 75 (Summer 1989), 49.

CHAPTER

❖ 12 ❖

Sheriff of the Posse: Americans and the World Since 1989

The Berlin Wall Comes Down, 1989.   *Berliners celebrate atop the partially dismantled Berlin Wall on November 12, 1989. East Germans (back to camera) crowd through the opening into West Berlin at Potsdamer Platz. The opening of the Wall three days earlier led to the reunification of East and West Germany. Watching the scene on television, Secretary of State James Baker found it "hard to hold back tears of joy as the trickle of people seeking freedom in the West turned into a torrent." (Wide World Photos)*

Diplomatic Crossroad

The Berlin Wall Comes Down, 1989

The partying began at midnight. Earlier on that afternoon of November 9, 1989, the East Berlin Communist party boss had announced that starting at midnight, citizens of the German Democratic Republic (GDR) could leave the country at any spot, including the crossing points along the infamous 28-mile-long Berlin Wall. The news sped through both parts of the divided city, to the 1.3 million inhabitants of East Berlin and the 2 million in the West. At Checkpoint Charlie in the American sector of West Berlin, a raucous crowd gathered, carrying bottles of beer and sparkling wine to celebrate.

At midnight, thousands of East Berliners filed through. Soon West Berlin exploded with trumpet blasts, fireworks, and dancing. Strangers embraced amid a cacophony of honking horns. Atop the ten-foot Wall in front of the Brandenburg Gate, Berliners linked arms, pranced, and sang the popular folk song, "Such a Beautiful Day Should Last Forever."[1] New signs soon covered the graffiti along the Wall: "Stalin Is Dead, Europe Lives" and "Only Today Is the War Really Over."[2] During the ensuing three-day weekend, more than 2 million Easterners crossed into West Berlin to walk along the Kurfurstendamm boulevard, an upscale shopping district suddenly converted into "one vast mall, its six lanes and median strip given over to strollers," where the migrants eagerly spent the hundred Deutschemarks ($60) given to them by West German authorities as "welcome money."[3] Everywhere people grabbed their new freedom. Thousands of East Germans in their two-cylinder Trabant cars wheezed onto the autobahns to visit friends and relatives inside West Germany.

The British scholar Timothy Garton Ash also participated in "the greatest street party in the history of the world." As he strolled through the Potsdamer Platz on Sunday morning, November 12, he could see workers dismantling the famous platform where distinguished visitors, including John F. Kennedy and Ronald Reagan, had hurled defiant speeches across the Berlin Wall. Soon the platform disappeared "like an unneeded stage prop." To Garton Ash, the weekend had a certain "magic, Pentecostal quality . . . when you feel that somewhere an angel has opened his wings."[4] The German wife of a U.S. diplomat kept saying: "I don't believe it. I just don't believe it."[5] West German chancellor Helmut Kohl told President George Bush by phone: "Without the United States this day would not have been possible."[6]

The foundations of the Wall had begun to crumble the previous May, when Hungary opened its border with Austria. In August tens of thousands of East Germans went on holiday to Hungary, then traveled across the Austro-Hungarian border and eventually to West Germany, where they could obtain automatic rights of citizenship. East Germany soon banned travel to Hungary, but this restriction only temporarily stemmed the flood, as more East Germans voted with their feet, some escaping through Czechoslovakia. By late October the number of refugees from the GDR had swelled to 200,000.

Exodus of East Germans. On October 4, 1989, some 10,000 refugees from East Germany milled outside the West German Embassy in Prague, Czechoslovakia, waiting for special buses to take them to West Germany, where they could obtain automatic citizenship. Five weeks later, the Berlin Wall opened. (AP/Wide World Photos)

That same month, popular demonstrations in Leipzig and East Berlin led to the resignation of Erich Honecker's government. His successor, Egon Krenz, tried to stop the hemorrhaging by opening the Wall on November 9 and promising free elections for 1990, a signal that East Germany would soon join Hungary and Poland in abandoning orthodox communism for some combination of democratic socialism and market capitalism. The day after the Wall came down, moreover, a bloodless coup in Sofia, Bulgaria, ousted Todor Zhivkov, the hard-line Communist party boss for the past thirty-five years. By the end of November, mass demonstrations were peacefully terminating communist rule in Czechoslovakia, and during Christmas week a bloody popular uprising toppled the tyrannical regime of Nicolae Ceausescu in Romania.

The breaching of the Wall also raised the prospect of German reunification. "The wheel of history is turning faster now," chancellor Kohl proclaimed. "We are and remain one nation. Long live a free German fatherland!"[7] The precise blueprints and timetables for reunification remained vague, but "it was one of those rare times," according to *Time* magazine, "when the tectonic plates of history shift beneath men's feet, and nothing after is quite the same."[8]

Mikhail Gorbachev and the Revolutions of 1989

The seismic events of the *annus mirabilis* (year of miracles) 1989 would not have occurred without major impetus from Soviet president Mikhail S. Gorbachev. Since his accession to leadership in the Kremlin in March 1985, Gorbachev's bold effort

Meeting at Camp David, 1990.
Secretary of State James Baker
(b. 1930), Barbara Bush (b. 1925),
President George Bush (b. 1924),
Raisa M. Gorbachev (b. 1936),
President Mikhail S. Gorbachev
(b. 1932), and Foreign Minister
Eduard Shevardnadze, Assistant
for National Security Affairs Brent
Scowcroft (b. 1925), and Marshal
Sergei Akhromeyev (1923–1991; left
to right) at an informal meeting on
June 2, 1990, at the Maryland presidential retreat. Raisa Gorbachev impressed people during the
Gorbachevs' tour of the United
States. The first wife of a Soviet
leader to appear prominently in public with her husband, she held a
graduate degree in the philosophy of
science and could lecture on Marxism or missiles. (Courtesy of the
Bush Presidential Materials Project)

at reforming the Soviet Union through political liberalization (*glasnost*) and economic restructuring (*perestroika*) had acquired a momentum of its own. To revive
the sick Soviet economy, plagued by declining productivity and a demoralized
work force, the Soviet leader warned at the outset that "everyone must change,
from the worker to the minister to the secretary of the central committee."[9] Freeing up emigration, permitting religious freedom, eliminating censorship, guaranteeing opposition parties and free elections, and overhauling the economy required
changes in external policies. What started out as a fairly limited foreign-policy
agenda—ending the war in Afghanistan, improving relations with China, and negotiating arms-control agreements with the United States—quickly mushroomed.

Gorbachev identified the huge drain on Soviet resources caused by the superpower competition as one area of potential savings. He decided on military cuts *despite* the Reagan military buildup. "These were unnecessary and wasteful
expenditures that we were not going to match," he later insisted.[10] Improving East-
West trade and achieving serious arms reductions meant that Gorbachev could not
simultaneously reform Soviet society and carry on the Cold War as usual. Thus, on
December 7, 1988, Gorbachev astounded the world by announcing that over the
next two years his country would unilaterally cut its military forces by 500,000 men
and 10,000 tanks, approximately 10 percent of the total Soviet manpower and 25
percent of the Red Army's tanks in Eastern Europe. In visits to Western Europe in
spring and summer 1989, the charismatic Soviet leader elaborated on his proposals
for a "common European home" that would eliminate "the probability of an armed
clash and the very possibility of the use of force."[11] Gorbachev quietly passed the
word to East European officials that Soviet troops would not intervene to put down
uprisings—the Brezhnev Doctrine was dead.

The veteran communist oligarchs of Eastern Europe heard the message and lost
their nerve. At year's end in Prague, a large sign tallied up the revolutionary results:

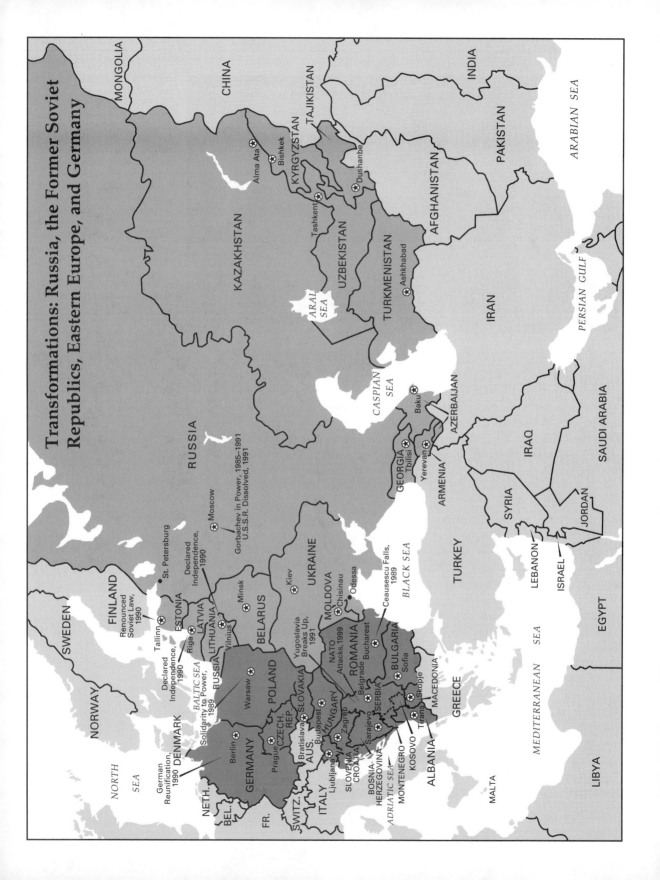

Transformations: Russia, the Former Soviet Republics, Eastern Europe, and Germany

"Poland—10 Years / Hungary—10 Months / East Germany—10 Weeks / Czechoslovakia—10 Days / Romania—10 Hours."[12]

Whether or not Gorbachev expected Eastern Europe "to crumble like a dry Saltine cracker in just a few months," he encouraged the process.[13] "Life punishes harshly anyone who is left behind in politics," Gorbachev told cheering crowds in Berlin on October 7, the fortieth anniversary of the founding of the GDR.[14] Gorbachev advised East Germans to open the Wall—it would "let off steam" and "avoid an explosion."[15]

Just as *glasnost* and *perestroika* accelerated the liberation of Eastern Europe, so too did the toppling of communist regimes have repercussions inside the Soviet Union. During late August 1989, more than a million citizens of Estonia, Latvia, and Lithuania linked arms to form a human chain some four hundred miles long in protest against the fiftieth anniversary of the Nazi-Soviet Pact that had led to Stalin's annexation of the Baltic states. In December Lithuanian Communists broke with the party leadership in Moscow. In March 1990 the Lithuanian Parliament declared formal independence from the Soviet Union, and Estonia's governing body renounced Soviet law. In May Latvia declared independence, and in July Ukraine proclaimed itself sovereign. Gorbachev tried to slow, if not reverse, the surging separatist tide, but he promised not to use force.

Facing down the Soviet "political and military nomenklatura" (officialdom) who accused him of "sell-outs to an alleged enemy," Gorbachev went from confident master of events to bewildered victim of forces he had unleashed.[16] He won the Nobel Peace Prize but lost his country. By the end of 1991 the economically hobbled Soviet Union had disintegrated into sixteen squabbling independent nations. The Communist party disbanded, the weakened central government recognized the independence of the three Baltic states, and most of the republics signed a new union treaty that left the Soviet government virtually impotent. Russia declared its independence and with many of the republics formed the Commonwealth of Independent States in December. Boris Yeltsin's Russian government soon took over the Kremlin, the KGB, and the Soviet Foreign Ministry. A president without a country or even an office, Gorbachev stepped down. On Christmas Day 1991, at 7:32 P.M. (Moscow time), the red hammer-and-sickle flag atop the Kremlin fluttered downward for the last time, soon replaced by the red, white, and blue Russian flag.

Václav Havel (b. 1936) of Czechoslovakia. When this former Prague brewery worker, playwright, and political prisoner was sworn in as president of Czechoslovakia by communist officials who had jailed him twice, one observer said, "it was as though Kafka's Joseph K. had been re-tried and acquitted." Havel eloquently proclaimed that "all of us are responsible, each to a different degree, for keeping the totalitarian machine running. None of us is merely a victim, because all of us helped to create it together." When Czechoslovakia splintered in 1993, Havel became president of the Czech Republic. (Courtesy of the Bush Presidential Materials Project, photo by Carol T. Powers)

Not Just Another Country: Bush, Clinton, and Post–Cold War Priorities

Studied nonchalance appeared to be the official U.S. reaction to the opening of the Berlin Wall. No special "Berlin task force" monitored events. President George Bush remained subdued and noncommittal. In one scholar's words, the president left "the impression that he didn't know quite what to do but was determined to do it prudently."[17]

Appearances were partly deceiving. Although the process of reassessment took several months, by the time the Berlin Wall came down the Bush administration

McDonald's in Moscow. A worldwide symbol of capitalist bounty came to Moscow in early 1990 when McDonald's opened a fast-food restaurant in Pushkin Square. McDonald's Canadian subsidiary had spent fourteen years negotiating a contract with Soviet authorities. (McDonald's Corporation)

had made up its collective mind that Gorbachev was "for real," that his reforms in the Soviet Union and Eastern Europe served America's national interest, and that Washington would cooperate with Moscow in smoothing the transition to a post–Cold War world.[18] The quiescent response to events in Berlin was deliberate—a signal to the Soviet Union that the United States did not seek to exploit the upheavals in Eastern Europe.

Prudence became the watchword. George Bush and his foreign-policy team were cautious about almost everything. "People say I'm indecisive," Bush once joked. "Well, I don't know about that."[19] Reactive, ad hoc, adaptable rather than ideologically zealous, conservative, fearful of doing the wrong thing, Bush "always seemed a step behind," observed one U.S. diplomat. Wary of the future, "he concentrated on managing the present and avoiding the mistakes of the past."[20] A manager and a doer rather than an intellectual, Bush refused "to hypothecate [*sic*]" beyond the immediate, as he once put it.[21] A former Yale University baseball captain, Bush could quote the famed Yankee catcher Yogi Berra: "I'll make plenty of mistakes, but I don't want to make the wrong mistakes."[22] Although many applauded the absence of Reaganite hyperbole and misstatement, others thought that Bush should shape fast-moving events. Brent Scowcroft, Bush's assistant for national security affairs, put it succinctly: "We prefer what is, as opposed to the alternative."[23]

Bush's conservatism had deep roots. "George Bush was born on third base and thinks he hit a triple," quipped a fellow Texan.[24] Born in Massachusetts in 1924 to a wealthy, old Yankee family, Bush became a decorated navy pilot in World War II, attended Yale (B.A., 1948), and then moved to Texas, where he amassed greater wealth in the booming oil industry of the 1950s. After serving in Congress (1967–1971) and as ambassador to the United Nations (1971-1973), chair of the Republican National Committee (1973-1974), U.S. representative to China

Nobel Peace Prize Winners, 1981–1998

1981	Office of the United Nations High Commissioner for Refugees.
1982	Alva Myrdal of Sweden and Alfonso García Robles of Mexico, disarmament advocates.
1983	Lech Walesa of Poland, leader of the Solidarity trade union movement.
1984	Bishop Desmond M. Tutu of South Africa, a leader of the antiapartheid movement.
1985	International Physicians for the Prevention of Nuclear War, an organization jointly headed by a Soviet and an American doctor.
1986	Elie Wiesel, American writer on the Holocaust and a Nazi death camp survivor.
1987	President Oscar Arias Sánchez of Costa Rica, author of a peace plan for Central America.
1988	United Nations peacekeeping forces.
1989	Dalai Lama, exiled leader of Tibet.
1990	Mikhail S. Gorbachev, Soviet leader who launched *glasnost* and *perestroika*.
1991	Daw Aung San Suu Kyi, Burmese woman who organized political opposition to the repressive military government in her country.
1992	Rigoberta Menchú, Guatemalan woman who struggled for the rights of indigenous peoples.
1993	Frederick W. de Klerk, president of South Africa, and Nelson Mandela, head of the African National Congress, who cooperated to end apartheid and initiate majority rule in South Africa.
1994	Yasir Arafat, Chair of the Palestine Liberation Organization, and Prime Minister Yitzhak Rabin and Foreign Minister Shimon Peres of Israel, who negotiated a peace accord.
1995	Joseph Rotblat and the Pugwash Conferences on Science and World Affairs which Rotblat helped found in Great Britain, for their campaign against nuclear weapons.
1996	Carlos Filipe Ximenes Belo and José Ramos-Horta of East Timor, who worked for peace in East Timor.
1997	The International Campaign to Ban Landmines and its coordinator Jody Williams of the United States.
1998	John Hume, head of the Catholic Social Democrat and Labor Party, and David Trimble, leader of the Ulster Unionist Party, both of Northern Ireland, for their key role in securing the Good Friday Accord to reduce conflict in Northern Ireland.

(1974-1975), and CIA director (1976–1977), he unsuccessfully challenged Ronald Reagan for the Republican presidential nomination in 1980 and then accepted second spot on the ticket. Always a loyalist, Bush supported Reagan's policies and traveled widely to broaden an international experience that few men have brought to the White House.

Bush selected a compatible secretary of state in James A. Baker III, a close friend from Texas who had skillfully managed his political campaigns. Like Bush, born (1930) to the elite, Baker had become a Texas corporate lawyer after graduation from Princeton University. The secretary's "pragmatic" problem-solving abilities lay in the art of "fixing," British prime minister Margaret Thatcher observed.[25] Baker had won high marks as Reagan's White House chief of staff and secretary of the treasury. "This is a man I can accomplish things with," Soviet foreign minister Eduard Shevardnadze reported after their first meeting.[26] Reactive and conservative like Bush, Baker preferred to deal with the task at hand rather than with the

Makers of American Foreign Relations Since 1989

Presidents	Secretaries of State
George Bush, 1989–1993	James A. Baker III, 1989–1992
	Lawrence Eagleburger, 1992–1993
Willliam J. Clinton, 1993–	Warren M. Christopher, 1993–1997
	Madeleine K. Albright, 1997–

opportunity ahead. Scowcroft worked well with Baker and with Baker's successor, Lawrence Eagleburger, thus avoiding the feuding that had marred previous administrations. A former army general from Utah, with a doctorate in international relations from Columbia University, Scowcroft defined his role as facilitator, broker, and coordinator, not as architect of policy.

The election of former five-term Arkansas governor Willam J. Clinton in 1992 seemed to bring a different generational perspective to the White House. A graduate of Georgetown University and Yale Law School, Rhodes scholar, intern to Senator J. William Fulbright, Vietnam War protester and draft avoider, and at age forty-six the second youngest elected president, Clinton pledged during the campaign to maintain America's global leadership. Yet he came to Washington hoping to "keep foreign policy submerged" until he dealt with domestic priorities such as taxes, deficits, economic growth, health care, and welfare reform.[27] One student of the presidency compared Clinton's extemporaneous, "perfectly grammatical 100-odd-word sentences" with Bush's "fractured prose," and noted Clinton's "energy, enthusiasm, intelligence, and devotion to policy," as well as an "absence of self-discipline" and "hubristic confidence in his own views and abilities."[28] Notwithstanding Clinton's election to a second term in 1996, Republican majorities in Congress after 1994 brought to the fore "a very strong element that is anti-internationalist, unilateralist, even isolationist—very xenophobic, extremely touchy," as one diplomat put it.[29] Cuts in foreign aid and delays in ambassadorial appointments challenged the president's foreign-policy leadership. In 1998 impeachment by the House of Representatives with respect to Clinton's apparent perjury over a sex scandal also bedeviled the president. Like Jay Gatsby in F. Scott Fitzgerald's novel, Clinton was "popular but not respected."[30]

Sixty-seven-year-old Warren M. Christopher became Clinton's first secretary of state. An alumnus of the University of Southern California and Stanford Law School, this "lawyer's lawyer" had served as deputy secretary of state during the Carter years and had negotiated the release of American hostages from Iran in 1980–1981.[31] Disciplined and dignified, dour and aloof, Christopher "practiced diplomacy as though it were a contract that needed a bit more work before it was ready for signature."[32] Replacing Christopher for the second term was UN ambassador Madeleine Albright, a former assistant to Zbigniew Brzezinski and Georgetown University professor who resurrected Cold War certitudes. "My mindset is Munich," she proclaimed. "Most of my generation's is Vietnam."[33] An insider through friendship with fellow Wellesley College alumna Hillary Rodham Clin-

Madeleine Korbel Albright (b. 1937). Born in Prague, the daughter of a Czech diplomat who defected to the United States In 1948, Albright was raised as a Roman Catholic and apparently did not learn until she became secretary that her parents had been born Jewish and three of her grandparents had died in the Holocaust. The family experience of "being driven twice from our home in Czechoslovakia—first by Hitler and then by Stalin" greatly shaped her worldview. After attending Wellesley College (B.A. 1959) and earning a Ph.D. at Columbia University (1976), Albright served on the National Security Council staff during the Carter administration and later taught political science at Georgetown University. As President Clinton's ambassador to the United Nations (1993-1996), she at first supported the UN's expanded role in international peacekeeping. Dubbed "Lady of Steel" by Russian diplomats, Secretary Albright advocated "threat-based diplomacy," proved adept at cultivating the media, and even charmed the cantankerous Jesse Helms, chair of the Senate Foreign Relations Committee. (Bureau of Public Affairs, U.S. Department of State)

ton, the blunt-speaking Albright quickly earned a hawkish reputation. "Madeleine is willing to fire a missile at anybody," remarked one admirer.[34]

Christopher maintained collegial relations with Clinton's national security affairs adviser, Anthony Lake. Educated at Harvard and Cambridge, with a Ph.D. from Princeton, Lake had entered the Foreign Service in 1962 but resigned from Henry Kissinger's National Security Council staff in protest against the U.S. invasion of Cambodia in 1970. He served in the Carter State Department and later taught political science at Mount Holyoke College. Described by associates as "a stalwart Puritan," "immensely kind," "the opposite of a self-promotor," Lake exhibited little of the egotism and manipulative qualities often found in White House advisers.[35] Asked to define a new grand strategy for the post–Cold War era, Lake in 1993 proposed the "enlargement" of free markets and democracies as a substitute for containment. Using the word *market* forty-one times, his speech fell flat— "low-grade, low-wattage Wilsonian rhetoric concerned with prodding the world toward universal democracy."[36] Lake's equally self-effacing deputy and successor, Samuel R. "Sandy" Berger, a specialist in global monetary transactions, outlined more concrete goals for Clinton's second term—integrating Eastern and Western Europe without provoking Russia; more liberal trade expansion; cooperation against "transnational threats" such as terrorism and drugs; and working toward a "strong, stable Asia Pacific Community."[37]

Clinton faced an increasingly disinterested public who thought the American "eagle had completed a great adventure and was returning to its nest, and that's where they wanted it."[38] As the U.S. economy improved in the 1990s, the president quickly recognized that the "new virility symbols are exports and productivity and growth rates" rather than nuclear missiles.[39] He vowed to "expand and strengthen the world's community of market-based economies," and he demanded that Japan open its market to more U.S. exports.[40] He skillfully lobbied through Congress the North American Free Trade Agreement (NAFTA) (see page 482). In 1994, Washington signed the "Uruguay Round" of GATT accords liberalizing world trade. The agreement also created a new World Trade Organization, which Clinton hailed as promoting "a vision of economic renewal" for the United States and the world.[41] In pushing as well for U.S. participation in both a future Free Trade Area of the Americas and the Asia Pacific Economic Cooperation forum, the president preached the new "gospel of geoeconomics."[42] He seemed "more interested in helping Toys 'R' Us and Nike to flourish in Central Europe and Asia than in dispatching Marines to quell unrest in economically inconsequential nations."[43] Worrisome, however, was the 1998 U.S. trade deficit of $233.4 billion—a record.

Nowhere was the primacy of geoeconomics more evident than in American initiatives, in conjunction with the International Monetary Fund (IMF), to rescue faltering economies and act as the "drivewheel" of the international political economy.[44] When the Mexican peso collapsed in 1994, Washington fashioned an international financial bailout that included a $50 billion credit, with the United States ($20 billion) and the IMF ($18 billion) the chief backers. With the United States contributing 18 percent of the IMF's resources, the announcement of a $10.2 billion credit line to Russia during Boris Yeltsin's reelection campaign in 1996 clearly reflected Washington's policy preferences. The United States contributed $5 billion to an overall $41.5 billion loan to Brazil in November 1998, provided that Brazil implement IMF-approved measures to balance its huge budget deficit.

During the Asian financial crisis of 1997–1998, U.S. Treasury officials, working through the IMF, orchestrated a financial package of $115 billion, in return for which Asian countries pledged to adopt banking and budget reforms. With financial markets gyrating wildly in January 1998, Deputy Treasury Secretary Lawrence Summers jetted to China, Hong Kong, Thailand, Malaysia, Singapore, and South Korea to contain the "Asian economic flu."[45] Despite conservative criticism of IMF bailouts for encouraging irresponsible policies by governments and investors, and leftist complaints that IMF requirements undercut social welfare reforms and increased unemployment, Summers contrasted Clinton's successful rescue operation with the Coolidge-Hoover failure to assist the war-stricken European economies in the 1920s and 1930s. "At this point in the world the United States has a very special role," he asserted. "We are not just another country."[46]

Europe Transformed: Soviet Disintegration, German Reunification, NATO Expansion, Balkan Hell

Bush's initial response to Gorbachev was to institute "the pause."[47] Hard-line "squeezers" who sought to harass the Kremlin into choosing between collapse and the abandonment of communism still competed with "dealers" who thought the time ripe to negotiate with the Soviets on a whole spectrum of issues.[48] A national security review eventually endorsed the banal goal of "status quo plus."[49] Skeptical statements emanating from Washington prompted a message from Gorbachev: "Tell the president . . . to please be a little more considerate."[50]

The turning point seems to have been Secretary Baker's visit to Moscow in early May 1989, when Gorbachev offered specific reductions for the Conventional Forces in Europe negotiations (CFE) under way in Vienna; the numbers were so close to NATO's proposals that Washington officials became persuaded that Gorbachev seriously sought further arms agreements. A cordial meeting in September between Baker and Foreign Minister Shevardnadze in Jackson Hole, Wyoming, broke the impasse over Strategic Arms Reduction Talks (START) when the Soviets dropped their demand that the United States abandon its SDI research. Baker soon affirmed that *perestroika* "will bring about a less aggressive Soviet Union."[51] At year's end, Bush promised that the United States would remove discriminatory trade barriers as soon as Moscow passed formal legislation permitting free emigration. At the Washington summit of June 1990, Bush and Gorbachev signed agreements to improve trade, to reduce chemical weapons, to expand university undergraduate exchanges, and to negotiate deeper cuts in strategic arms.

As the Soviet Union gradually disintegrated over the next two years, Bush continued to solicit a special relationship with Gorbachev. During Germany's rapid reunification Bush and Baker helped to ensure Soviet acquiescence by emphasizing that only Germany's membership in NATO could keep the new Germany from ever moving hostilely eastward. When Iraq invaded Kuwait in early August 1990, Washington and Moscow jointly called for an "international cutoff of all arms supplies" to Iraq.[52] As the United States contemplated military action against Iraq, Shevardnadze told Baker: "If you're going to use force, you have to know that you will succeed."[53] Bush kept in telephone touch with Gorbachev throughout the Gulf crisis (see pages 488–491).

The Bush-Gorbachev relationship also paid off in the START-I accord signed in Moscow in July 1991. Bypassing hard-liners in their respective military bureaucracies, the two presidents ironed out the final compromises in personal correspondence. They inked the treaty and accompanying protocols using pens made of metal salvaged from missiles banned under the earlier INF Treaty. The treaty limited each nuclear superpower to 1,600 delivery vehicles and 6,000 strategic nuclear devices. Only 4,900 such devices could be carried by intercontinental ballistic missiles (ICBMs) or sea-launched missiles (SLBMs) deployed on submarines. The remaining 1,100 devices permitted under the treaty included warheads and bombs carried by cruise missiles and strategic bombers. In effect, the Americans and Soviets undertook an "arms race downhill" in reverse by pledging to reduce their nuclear arsenals by half.[54]

Then came the abortive coup against Gorbachev of August 18–21. The conspirators proved inept. Russian president Boris Yeltsin and his top aides holed up in the Russian parliament building and called for a general strike. Bush failed to condemn the coup but tried several times to telephone Gorbachev. Not until the third day did he call Boris Yeltsin, who had rallied mass demonstrations. By the fourth day the revolt had fizzled. Bush and his advisers understood that legitimate authority had shifted to Yeltsin and the Russian republic. Bush preferred Gorbachev to the volatile Yeltsin ("you dance with who is on the dance floor") and the U.S. president feared the centrifugal forces surging through the Soviet Union.[55] He saw a strong central government as essential for keeping control over the Soviet nuclear arsenal and fending off renegade military units. In the end, his caution did not prevent Washington from working harmoniously with a Yeltsin-led Russia, as evidenced by a $24 billion Western aid package to Russia and further negotiations on nuclear arms reductions. Just before Bush left office in January 1993, he and Yeltsin signed a START-II agreement in Moscow that provided for the cutting of nuclear warheads and bombs to 3,500 (U.S.) and 2,997 (Russia) and for eliminating all multiple warhead (MIRV) intercontinental missiles by the year 2003.

The Clinton administration also pursued a "Russia first" policy.[56] Former president Richard Nixon told Clinton that "peripheral issues . . . don't amount to a hill of beans compared to Russia: Russia is the big one."[57] The administration's principal expert on Russian affairs, Strobe Talbott, had been a roommate and fellow Rhodes scholar with Clinton at Oxford and a reporter and editor at *Time* magazine. Talbott advised Clinton to back Yeltsin's free-market reforms with financial assistance even though they resulted in hardship for the Russian people, including high unemployment and the removal of social-security safety nets. Clinton regularly wrote Yeltsin detailed letters and gave Yeltsin unconditional support when he dissolved the Russian Duma (parliament) in October 1993 and then turned army guns on recalcitrant legislators holed up in the building. The favorable showing of ultranationalists in elections to the new Duma prompted Clinton's decision not to offer more than a loose partnership status in NATO to former Warsaw Pact members. Russia itself accepted partnership status.

Clinton's critics claimed that by putting all his chips on Yeltsin he was repeating Bush's mistake with Gorbachev. Such criticism seemed valid, as Russia's gross national product fell by 20 percent during the first four years of reforms, as inflation ate up personal savings, as thousands of Russian troops failed to suppress a revolt in the breakaway republic of Chechnya in 1994–1996, as a Russian Mafia ("Comrade criminals") exploited a growing black market in Russia's cities, as the economy became "dominated by seven banking houses in unholy collusion with remnants of the old state apparatus."[58] Notwithstanding seven summit meetings with "my friend Bill" in five years and his own reelection in 1996, Yeltsin's failing health and inability to cope with Russia's economic crisis made him an unreliable partner.[59] Clinton and Yeltsin did reach agreement in 1997 on a START-III Treaty that would cut strategic nuclear weapons by one-third of the limits in START-II, but the Russian Duma, angry over the expansion of NATO eastward (see page 475), dragged its feet, not ratifying either START-II or START-III. Nor could more than $60 billion in Western loans since 1992 forestall the collapse of Russia's "virtual economy" in August 1998.[60] With an ill and politically embattled Yeltsin struggling to hang on to power as the Duma considered his impeachment, with Communists and neo-fascists in the Duma blaming "yids" and "Jewish bankers" for Russia's economic plight, and with disaffected military officers complaining about national humiliation, Washington could only hope that the new Russia would not suffer Weimar Germany's fate and turn to extremism.[61]

A United Germany in NATO.   Mikhail Gorbachev, remembering with many other Soviet citizens the German onslaught of World War II, at first resisted the U.S. push for a united Germany in the North Atlantic Treaty Organization (NATO). But Gorbachev recognized that he could not stop the realignment of European power. (By permission of Mike Luckovich and Creators Syndicate)

As for the new Germany, just after the Berlin Wall opened in 1989, Chancellor Kohl put forward a plan for confederation between East and West Germany, thus making reunification "a matter for Germans to decide."[62] Although Bush tried to influence the process by keeping an "arm around the shoulder" of the West Germans, the pell-mell rush of events upset predictions.[63] East Germany's citizens continued to migrate to the West at a rate of 2,000 to 3,000 a day. Local government, public services, the economy, and civic morale in the GDR steadily eroded. In early 1990, West German politicians and parties began to funnel campaign money to new political groups in order to build alliances in the East for an anticipated postelection unification. German reunification became "a kind of runaway freight train that nobody—East or West—seems able to contain."[64] The Kohl-supported center-conservative coalition won a landslide victory in the March GDR elections. Kohl initiated currency union and economic merger in July 1990. Then, in September, the four powers agreed to end their postwar occupation. In October the two Germanies formally reunited.

Washington backed Kohl's quest for rapid reunification because of the chancellor's continued commitment to NATO and European integration. "The more you resist," said one U.S. official, "the more likely you are to create the kind of Germany you don't want—resentful, angry."[65] Bush's advisers believed that "an unattached Germany on the loose in Central Europe" looked more threatening to Moscow "than one embedded in NATO."[66] In July 1990 Gorbachev dropped objections to a reunited Germany in NATO in exchange for a promise of Western economic aid and a smaller German army. Bush had "provided a skillful accompaniment" to European events, one scholar has noted, "but the main musicians were not in Washington; they were in Bonn and in Moscow."[67]

"Now That You're a Capitalist."
The Poles and other Eastern Europeans may have abandoned communism, but, the cartoonist Jeff Danziger reminds us, they exchanged one set of problems for a new set all too familiar to capitalist countries. The rough transition to a postcommunist world grafted harsh reality onto the initial euphoria many felt when the failed communist regimes collapsed. (Jeff Danziger/*Christian Science Monitor.* © 1989 Los Angeles Times Syndicate

What Margaret Thatcher nervously called "the German juggernaut" stood in the center of Europe—nearly 80 million people between the Rhine and the Oder with a potential combined military force of 1.8 million and a strong export-driven economy.[68] Kohl moved quickly to dispel fears of "hob-nailed boots and spike helmets" by limiting future troop strength and pledging never to build nuclear, chemical, or biological weapons.[69] Germany became the dominant voice in the European Community (EC), pressed for aid to Eastern Europe and the former Soviet republics, pledged billions of dollars (but not troops) to the Gulf War (see pages 488–491), and extended quick diplomatic recognition to Croatia and Slovenia as they broke from Yugoslavia in 1991. Because Germany's new constitution also explicitly welcomed refugees, thus implying "some sort of national atonement for past aggressions."[70] Germany absorbed some 400,000 war refugees from Croatia and Bosnia by 1996. Steadfast in their commitment to European integration and NATO, Germans chose the "European road" rather than "go their own special, isolated way," as Foreign Minister Hans-Dietrich Gentscher put it.[71] Bonn contributed to peacekeeping missions in the Persian Gulf, Somalia, and Yugoslavia. Clinton established his friendliest European relationship with Chancellor Kohl, even kidding him about their "sumo wrestler" girths after one diplomatic banquet.[72] Further economic integration with Europe and greater competition with the United States in global markets meant that future German leaders would likely be "not so much against but rather not so much for their American partner in world affairs."[73]

The conversion of the Economic Community into the European Union (EU) through ratification of the Maastricht Treaty in fall 1993 advanced integration in the west but ignored disintegration in the east. "We fiddled in Maastricht while Sarajevo burned," observed one scholar, as European reluctance to intervene in Bosnia underscored the continent's continued disunity.[74] In the Eastern European nations, Poland, Hungary, and Czechoslovakia (divided into Czech and Slovak republics in 1993) progressed most quickly in organizing market economies and democratic governments and looked to membership in the European Union. Bulgaria, Romania, Albania, Slovenia, Croatia, Estonia, Latvia, Lithuania, and other former Soviet republics faced tremendous obstacles, not the least of which were smoldering ethnic and national rivalries long frozen by the Cold War. The European Union nonetheless established budgetary and financial criteria for entry that East European countries could not possibly meet. The EU Council decided in 1995 to establish a European Central Bank, issue a common currency (the "Euro"), and complete European Monetary Union by July 2002.

Partly to compensate for Eastern Europe's exclusion from the EU, President Clinton announced in 1994 that the question of NATO expansion eastward was no longer "whether" but "when and how."[75] A bruising bureaucratic battle preceded this "most important political-military decision for the United States since the collapse of the Soviet Union."[76] Despite Pentagon fears that expansion would "dilute" the alliance and "we should do nothing to offend Russia," National Security Affairs Adviser Lake and Assistant Secretary of State for European Affairs Richard Holbrooke "bludgeoned" the decision through.[77] The prospect of winning ethnic votes in the 1996 election also appealed to Clinton, who publicly designated Poland, Hungary, and the Czech Republic as the first beneficiaries of NATO membership. European leaders proceeded to rubber-stamp Clinton's proposals, notwithstanding reports that "Russians at all levels are opposed to NATO enlargement" and George F. Kennan's prediction that this "most fateful error" would "impel Russian foreign policy in directions decidedly not to our liking."[78] In a vote of 80 to 19 to approve the new NATO members in mid-1998, U.S. senators seemed more concerned about the costs of enlargement (perhaps as much as $35 billion) than about the strategic implications of angering Russia. The three new members officially joined NATO in March 1999.

NATO had already demonstrated its ineffectiveness in dealing with the Balkan crisis. In October 1990 the CIA had predicted that, with the collapse of communism, Yugoslavia would disintegrate into bloody ethnic violence and Serbia would use force to seize as much of the country as possible. The Bush administration nonetheless deferred to European allies when they recognized the independence of Croatia and Slovenia in summer 1991. Talks with Balkan leaders convinced Secretary Baker that the region was "sleep-walking into a car wreck."[79] Yet the United States "had no dog in that fight," he later remarked.[80] Serbia proclaimed a new Federal Republic of Yugoslavia (including Montenegro) and incited Serbs living in the other republics—especially in Bosnia—to take up arms. Croats and Muslims living in Bosnia declared an independent state. After Bosnia-Herzegovina became independent in April 1992, Serbs began to shell Sarajevo, the city where a 1914 assassination had triggered World War I. Bosnian Serbs grabbed territory and displaced Bosnian Muslims through the horrors of "ethnic cleansing," which included the mass rape of Muslim women by Serbian soldiers.[81]

The European Community, having failed in mediation efforts, imposed trade sanctions on Serbia-Montenegro and handed the issue over to the United Nations. As UN mediators tried futilely to negotiate a peace settlement, Serbian militia seized approximately 70 percent of the Bosnian hinterland while systematically bombarding and starving the people of Sarajevo. France and Britain dispatched

President William Jefferson Clinton (b. 1946) and Richard C. Holbrooke (b. 1941). Photographed in 1997, President Clinton (right) was using crutches because of a knee injury. Clinton's presidency subsequently suffered a serious blow when a sex scandal caused him to become only the second president to be impeached. A former aide to Henry Kissinger, Holbrooke served in Jimmy Carter's State Department and later as ambassador to Germany, assistant secretary of state for Europe, and chief diplomatic troubleshooter in the Balkans for the Clinton administration. After successfully negotiating the 1995 Dayton agreement, which ended the war in Bosnia, Holbrooke in 1998 helped to broker a temporary cease-fire in the southern Yugoslavian province of Kosovo, where Muslim ethnic Albanians battled against their Serbian overlords. A persistent negotiator, Holbrooke characterized diplomacy not as chess but "more like jazz—a constant improvisation on a theme." (White House Photo)

"Blue Helmets" (UN troops) to safeguard relief supplies but recoiled from military intervention. By 1993 perhaps as many as 150,000 people had perished.

Clinton inherited this "problem from hell."[82] Though moved by the suffering in Bosnia, Americans feared getting bogged down in age-old ethnic rivalries impervious to outside influence. When Clinton asked for military options, moreover, the Pentagon took note of the rugged terrain in the region and reportedly told him: "We do deserts, we don't do mountains."[83] The pressure to act mounted during the spring of 1993. Ambassador Madeleine Albright asked: "What's the point of having this superb military . . . if we can't use it?" General Colin Powell promised to "carry out any mission [he] was handed," but the "tough political goals had to be set first."[84] Although Clinton issued warnings to the Serbs and proclaimed America's humane concern, he lacked foreign support and a domestic consensus. Accused of "Hamlet-like deliberations," he backed away.[85] When Clinton proposed the lift and strike option (lifting the arms embargo against Bosnia and launching air strikes against the Bosnian Serbs), NATO allies balked because of their own peacekeeping forces on the ground. Critics called it "rift and drift."[86]

Starting in February 1994, NATO did carry out air strikes against Serbian planes in "no-fly" zones and against Serb artillery that was shelling Sarajevo and other safe havens. Bosnian Serbs nonetheless succeeded in displacing Muslims from much of Bosnia, despite formation of a Croat-Muslim federation and Washington's announcement that it would no longer enforce the arms embargo against Muslims.

A cease-fire negotiated by former president Carter in November 1994 did not prevent renewed violence the following spring. When Bosnian Serbs in July seized the safe havens of Srebenica and Zepa and massacred thousands of Muslims within sight of UN peacekeepers, Washington flashed a green light, whereupon the Croatian army overran Serb-held territory in northwest Bosnia and NATO intensified its air attacks. As new refugees fled into Serbia, Yugoslav president Slobodan Milosevic asserted his authority over the Bosnian Serbs and agreed to a cease-fire in October 1995.

A peace conference convened at Wright-Patterson Air Force Base in Ohio. Assistant Secretary Holbrooke "cajoled, harassed, and pressured" the presidents of Serbia, Bosnia, and Croatia into an agreement.[87] The Dayton Accords of December 14, 1995, retained a Croat-Muslim Federation and a Serb Republic within a single Bosnian state, with Sarajevo to remain as a multiethnic capital. The United States agreed to contribute 20,000 personnel as part of a 60,000-member NATO implementation force that would separate the parties and assist in reconstruction. Some 8,000 U.S. troops still remained in Bosnia four years later, having sustained a fragile peace at a cost of more than $7 billion.

In 1999, Kosovo became the next Balkan crisis to spark international consequences. In this largely ethnic Albanian, Muslim province of Yugoslavia, President Milosevic ordered and his Serb forces implemented a brutal ethnic cleansing. After he rejected NATO demands to halt the persecution and preserve Kosovo's autonomy, NATO began in March to bomb military and communications sites throughout Yugoslavia. The bombing unleashed even more cruelties in Kosovo as the Serbs systematically moved against ethnic Albanians, massacring and raping them, burning their homes, and forcing 800,000 of them to flee as refugees to neighboring Albania and Macedonia. Pounded by air attacks, encircled by hostile nations, and suffering a NATO-imposed oil embargo at sea, Milosevic relented in early June under an agreement to withdraw his forces from Kosovo, permit the return of refugees, accept a NATO security presence, and grant greater autonomy to Kosovo. The International War Crimes Tribunal at the Hague indicted Milosevic and his top aides for atrocities against the people of Kosovo.

Hope and Tragedy in Africa

As communism collapsed in Eastern Europe, apartheid began its descent in South Africa. As with the dynamics of change in Europe, the main impetus for reversing decades of social, political, and economic discrimination came from within—in this case, from within a nation of 35 million blacks, people of mixed race, and Asians ruled by 6.7 million whites. The United States played a modest role in nurturing the process.

One of the last diplomatic achievements of the Reagan administration, the mediation of the Namibia-Angola agreement in 1988 prepared the way. These accords established independence for Namibia and called for the staged withdrawal of Cuban and South African troops from Angola. South Africa's antiapartheid organi-

Nelson Mandela (b. 1918).
A founder of the African National Congress (ANC), this attorney and member of the Xhosa tribe was a young man when the white South African government jailed him in November 1962. Following his release from prison in February 1990, Mandela gave the black-nationalist salute.
(Reuters/Bettmann)

zations now found it increasingly difficult to obtain outside assistance and weapons to mount guerrilla campaigns inside South Africa. Harsh measures by Pretoria's security police during four years of the state of emergency since 1986 also neutralized most armed black nationalist activity. Thus when South Africa's white leaders, P. W. Botha and his successor, F. W. de Klerk, recommended negotiating an end to apartheid, beleaguered black activists responded positively.

The Bush administration pressed Pretoria to negotiate by maintaining economic sanctions against South Africa. From 1986 to 1989, sanctions cost South Africa $32 billion to $40 billion, including $11 billion in capital outflows and $4 billion in lost export earnings. When de Klerk became president in September 1989, reforms quickly followed. He lifted prohibitions against dissent, stopped executions, freed selected political prisoners, legalized banned organizations such as the African National Congress (ANC), and desegregated beaches and some housing areas. He offered to talk with black leaders to devise a new constitution in which blacks would share governing power. De Klerk also released the political prisoner and ANC leader Nelson Mandela on February 11, 1990. When the gray-haired, seventy-one-year-old Mandela, the symbol of resistance to apartheid, walked through a police cordon outside a prison near Cape Town, he raised his right arm in the black nationalist salute—the first time he could freely do so in nearly twenty-eight years.

Serious talks for a democratic South Africa did not begin until December 1991. They stalled the following year as bloody skirmishes and massacres erupted from rivalry between the ANC and the Zulu-based Inkatha Freedom party, backed by government and police officials. Despite continued violence—among black groups (especially Zulus versus Xhosas), between blacks and the government, and by white extremists such as the Afrikaner Resistance Movement—twenty-six parties resumed constitutional talks in early 1993. Four straight years of zero economic growth helped to spur compromises. Agreement on a constitutional democracy finally came in September 1993, and South Africa's first all-race elections were held in April 1994. The ANC handily won the elections, and Mandela became South Africa's first black president. The new parliament drew up a new constitution. The U.S. Congress repealed sanctions. Mandela and de Klerk shared the Nobel Peace Prize in 1993.

Mandela's regime welcomed U.S. aid and investment. Firms that had previously disinvested, such as Ford, Honeywell, General Electric, Sara Lee, and Citibank, quickly returned, and Coca-Cola and Pepsi "zoomed" into South Africa to compete "in their global cola war."[88] By 1996 more than 500 U.S. companies were operating in South Africa, with a total asset value of $3.5 billion. A Truth and Reconciliation Commission attempted to heal the past. The U.S. ambassador hailed "the symbiotic relationship between two countries that are multi-racial, multi-ethnic, and working to make such diverse societies work in spite of histories of prejudice and discrimination."[89]

Less successful was the U.S. intervention in Somalia. In December 1992, after he had lost the election, President Bush ordered 28,150 U.S. troops to the Horn of Africa on a humanitarian mission to feed the people of civil-war-torn Somalia (see map, page 299). Ghastly television pictures of emaciated children and adults starv-

U.S. Marines in Somalia.
Armed with M-16A2 5.56mm rifles
equipped with grenade launchers,
these marines escorted relief workers
in December 1991 as they delivered
sacks of grain to a Somalian village
during Operation Restore Hope. "We
had a good plan for going in. But we
didn't have such a good plan for getting out," one marine observed.
(Courtesy of U.S. Navy/Department of
Defense, Still Media Records Center)

ing while armed thugs stole food from their bowls stirred Americans. Somalia
ranked as "a tragedy of major proportions," Acting Secretary of State Eagleburger
emphasized, "and, underline this, *one that we had to do something about.*"[90] Deploy-
ing troops despite Pentagon misgivings, Bush hoped that U.S. forces could restore
order, move relief supplies to desperate Somalis, and then turn peacekeeping duties
over to the United Nations.

Somalia ranked as one of Washington's Cold War orphans. When the Soviet
Union in 1977 began wooing the Marxist regime in Ethiopia, the Carter administration backed Somalian dictator Siad Barre, a former Soviet client, and thus gained
access to the former Soviet air base at Berbera on the Gulf of Aden. Somalia became a pivotal pro-West ally. Over the next decade, despite harsh repression of internal dissent, Siad Barre received nearly $1 billion in U.S. assistance. As the Cold
War waned, Somalia's strategic importance diminished. Clan rivalries led to a ferocious civil war that destroyed half the capital city of Mogadishu and forced Siad
Barre to flee in January 1991. The United States withdrew its diplomatic mission—
in effect "turned out the light, closed the door and forgot about the place."[91] The
civil war intensified. By 1993 some 300,000 Somalis had died.

Bush's Operation Restore Hope succeeded at first. U.S. marines landed with
reporters and camera crews waiting on the beach. U. S. officials initiated cooperative relations with the most powerful Somali warlord, General Mohamed Farah
Aidid, who controlled Mogadishu. Relief operations fed the hungry, and media-

tion efforts progressed, with clan leaders agreeing to negotiate national reconcilia-tion. President Clinton began to pull U.S. forces out. "We can go abroad and accomplish some distinct objectives," the president announced, "then come home again when the mission is accomplished."[92] Not quite.

With starvation stopped, the United Nations tried to restore political stability to the country. Without consulting Congress, the Clinton administration left 8,000 U.S. logistical troops in Somalia, along with a 1,000-person quick-reaction force. Such attempts at nation building, even under UN auspices, aroused nationalist resentment. In June 1993 Aidid's forces attacked Pakistani peacekeeping troops, killing twenty-four. The Security Council protested, and U.S. forces under UN command tried unsuccessfully to kill Aidid in a "decapitation mission" in early July.[93]

In early October, the warlord's forces killed nineteen U.S. Army Rangers in a bloody firefight deep within "Indian country," as the U.S. commander put it.[94] A shocked Clinton watched television pictures of dead U.S. soldiers being dragged through the streets of Mogadishu by seemingly jubilant Somalis. "It turned my stomach," he told aides.[95] Clinton quickly backtracked, claiming that "it is not our job to rebuild Somalia's society."[96] He withdrew all U.S. forces by April 1994, leaving the mission to the UN. Clinton's Presidential Decision Directive 25 thereafter established a rigid framework for U.S. participation in peacekeeping operations. Somalia remained tumultuous.

Just a month after U.S. personnel departed Somalia, mass killing erupted in the central African republic of Rwanda. A suspicious April 1994 plane crash that killed the presidents of Rwanda and Burundi, both members of the dominant Hutu majority, touched off massacres of the Tutsi minority that left more than 800,000 dead in eighty-nine days, "nearly three times the rate of Jewish dead during the Holocaust."[97] With macabre television images reinforcing American stereotypes about "backward" and "savage" Africans, the Clinton administration resisted proposals for vigorous intervention, concentrated on evacuating U.S. citizens and reducing UN peacekeeping forces, and even instructed officials to avoid the term *genocide*.[98] Not until the massacres had ended did Clinton order U.S. troops in July to secure the airport in Kigala so that relief supplies could flow directly to Rwanda and stem the flood of refugees into neighboring Burundi, Tanzania, and Zaire.

The Rwanda massacres embarrassed Washington. On visiting Africa in 1998, President Clinton apologized for not "calling these crimes by their rightful name: genocide."[99] Susan E. Rice, the new assistant secretary of state for Africa, vowed to "do everything in my power . . . to make sure [never] to see that again."[100] She helped create the African Crisis Response Initiative, designed to assist African countries to organize joint forces for rapid intervention in the future. Despite such plans, further fighting flared between Hutus and Tutsis in Burundi in 1996, and the next year a revolt, backed by Rwanda, Uganda, and Eritrea, toppled long-time U.S. client Mobutu Sese Seko in Zaire (renamed the Democratic Republic of Congo). "Caught with our pants down," Washington recognized the new government of Laurent Kabila, whose troops promptly slaughtered thousands of Hutu *genocidaires* exiled in the eastern provinces.[101] The Democratic Republic of Congo became convulsed by civil war.

U.S. relations also fared badly with Sudan, whose Islamic regime sponsored terrorist groups. After closing its embassy in Khartoum for security reasons in 1996, Washington fired cruise missiles at a Sudanese pharmaceutical plant in August 1998 in retaliation for deadly terrorist attacks on U.S. embassies in Kenya and Tanzania attributed to Osama bin Laden, a Saudi extremist with close ties to Sudan. (U.S. forces also bombed sites associated with bin Laden in Afghanistan.) Despite official claims of "convincing evidence" that the factory produced nerve gas, skeptics wondered if Clinton, facing impeachment, was following a *"Wag the Dog"* strategy—so named for a contemporary movie in which a president deflects attention from a sex scandal by fomenting a phony war.[102]

Elsewhere in Africa the U.S. record was mixed. Washington maintained close ties with General Sani Abachi's repressive military regime in Nigeria, which exported $6.3 billion in oil, gas, and other commodities to the United States in 1997, making it the fifth largest supplier of foreign oil. Abachi's death in 1998 raised hopes for a transition to civilian rule. Although civil wars destabilized former Cold War clients such as Liberia, Sudan, Somalia, and Zaire, recent targets of U.S. assistance (South Africa, Ghana, Ethiopia, Mozambique, Uganda, and Mali) made significant political and economic progress in the 1990s. In 1996 the Botswanan ambassador hosted a dinner in Washington to give thanks for $203 million in U.S. aid, sent over three decades, which enabled his country to "graduate" from the foreign-assistance rolls.[103] That same year American trade with the eleven countries of southern Africa totaled $9 billion, the equivalent of U.S. trade with Russia and former Soviet republics. During a six-nation visit in March 1998, President Clinton hailed the "beginning of a new African Renaissance," but Congress killed his proposed Africa Trade and Investment Act.[104] Modest bilateral programs continued.

Markets and Invasions in Latin America

The Bush administration only slowly reversed past policies toward Latin America. The president himself held traditional proprietary North American ideas about the region, and he had helped devise and administer Reagan's interventionism. The Western Hemisphere seemed to be advancing from military regimes to popularly elected governments (as in Argentina, Chile, and Brazil), yet at the time of Bush's inauguration many of the 1980s interventionist U.S. policies had failed: Narcotics continued to flow into the profitable U.S. marketplace despite expensive antidrug operations; the Latin American debt, rampant inflation, and sluggish growth rates imperiled economies; a graying Fidel Castro still bedeviled Washington; an escalating crisis with Panama threatened further instability in the Caribbean. But after the Sandinistas lost elections in 1990 to U.S.-backed Violeta Barrios de Chamorro and her National Opposition Union, the civil war in Nicaragua finally ended. The civil war in El Salvador was stopped under a UN-brokered agreement in 1992, leaving Central America with staggering costs of reconstruction and reconciliation and tens of thousands dead. Latin America's economic linkage with the United States nonetheless remained strong: In 1990 40 percent of the region's exports flowed to the United States.

Bush's and Clinton's sponsorship of NAFTA, as well as the agreement to implement a Free Trade Area of the Americas (FTAA) by 2005, held the promise of a more prosperous Latin America. "A rising tide lifts all boats," Clinton said at the Summit of the Americas in 1994, whereupon the prime minister of Barbados reminded him that "a rising tide can . . . overturn small boats."[105]

Debt continued to burden Latin America. By 1990 Latin American nations owed more than $400 billion (total Third World debt stood at more than $1.3 trillion). Brazil, Mexico, and Argentina owed the most, and much of it to U.S. banks. One economist blamed "Stupid bankers [who] made stupid loans to stupid countries."[106] Others pointed to global trends: the worldwide economic recession of the early 1980s, rising interest rates, higher oil prices, and falling export earnings. The debt crisis hurt the United States. As debtors struggled to meet debt-service payments, they trimmed their imports; U.S. exports then slumped by billions of dollars, and North American jobs were lost. Latin migrants trying to escape grinding poverty pressed against U.S. immigration gates. The narcotics trade expanded as poor farmers and laborers turned to lucrative drug crops for income. Because health services and educational outlays had to be reduced and economic-development projects scuttled throughout Latin America, political unrest spread.

Secretary of the Treasury Nicholas F. Brady instituted a program in 1989 that provided for some debt relief and lower interest rates, but the U.S. government increasingly urged banks "to paddle their own leaky canoes."[107] Several agreements between commercial banks and Latin American governments, and backed by the International Monetary Fund, cut debt burdens by about one-third. In return, Latin American debtors accepted market-opening requirements—controlling inflation, attracting foreign investment, and reducing trade restrictions. As Latin American governments in the early 1990s instituted reforms to improve "investor confidence" and advanced regional economic integration based on a "free trade" philosophy, "swelling flows of foreign direct investment" helped ease the debt crisis and raised hopes that the hemisphere's groaning poverty and environmental deprivation could find relief.[108] Still, as former Argentine president Raúl Alfonsín remarked, market forces were not enough to provide welfare. Nonetheless, spurred by NAFTA and planning for the Free Trade Area of the Americas, Latin American exports grew from an average 4.5 percent during the 1980s to 9.9 percent in the 1990s, while foreign investments leaped from $6.7 billion in 1990 to $22.4 billion in 1996. Measured as a percentage of overall exports, Latin America's debt fell from 384 percent in 1987 to 227 percent in 1997.

When President Carlos Salinas of Mexico proposed a free trade agreement with Washington in 1990, he reversed more than a century of "building walls to keep out U.S. goods, investment, and influence."[109] Embraced by the Bush administration, signed by Canada, Mexico, and the United States in 1992, approved by Congress in 1993, the resulting North American Free Trade Agreement created the world's largest free trade bloc, comprising 370 million people with a combined gross domestic product of $6.5 trillion. President Clinton subsequently negotiated side agreements with Mexico to protect workers' rights and environmental standards, and he mobilized an effective lobbying effort that included former presidents and secretaries of state. Billionaire Ross Perot's prediction that a "great sucking sound" would accompany the flight of jobs, factories, and capital southward proved incorrect.[110] Notwithstanding a Mexican financial crisis in 1994, bilateral trade rose by $17 billion annually between 1993 and 1996, with a $7 billion net surplus for U.S. exports. Statistics revealed 100,000 U.S. jobs lost due to NAFTA by 1997, but unemployment rates reached historic lows as the revived U.S. economy created 2.5 million new jobs per year in the mid-1990s. U.S. direct investments in Mexico averaged $3.1 billion annually after 1994. Mexico even paid back, with interest, $13.5 billion loaned by the U.S. Treasury in 1995 as part of the $50 billion financial package to rescue the Mexican peso. Despite continuing bilateral problems with drugs and illegal immigration, NAFTA promised to expand an already burgeoning "Mexamerica," the 2,000-mile border society where two cultures blended "like reluctant lovers in the night, embracing for fear that letting go could only be worse."[111]

Many Americans believed that the flourishing drug trade endangered international stability and hence U.S. security. President Clinton called narcotrafficking "an unusual and extraordinary threat to . . . national security."[112] Between 1985 and 1995 the world production of opium and coca leaves roughly tripled, as drug prices dropped and U.S. prisons filled to capacity with people convicted of drug-related crimes. "This is more serious than the Vietnam War," claimed the governor of Maryland.[113] As the Cold War receded, the "Drug War" accelerated.

The United States spent upwards of $3 billion a year in a supply-side war against foreign sources and middlemen. In 1986, for example, American troops and army Blackhawk helicopters helped the Bolivian military swoop down on jungle cocaine laboratories. Under Bush and Clinton, U.S. counternarcotics aid flowed to the Andean nations of Peru, Bolivia, and Colombia, but Washington also increasingly stressed the importance of staunching demand inside the United States itself. This apparent change stemmed in part from pressure from Latin Americans who feared new U.S. interventionism; they had grown bitter over the drug issue, because they contended that North Americans unfairly blamed them for the problem. "No one is forcing the gringos to snort coke, so let Washington deal with it," they seemed to say.[114] For example, an estimated 72 million Americans (34 percent of the population) had used illegal drugs, while only 3.9 percent of Mexico's population had done the same. How can "small, poor countries," asked the prime minister of St. Kitts, "defeat the wealthy drug lords if the rich countries . . . are unsuccessful in limiting the demand?"[115]

Mexico had become a major source of marijuana (a hemp plant, *Cannabis sativa*) and heroin (a white powder processed from opium poppies) and a major highway for South American cocaine shipments destined for the United States. From Bolivia, Peru, and Colombia came coca, which was processed into cocaine and crack. (Tons of opium/heroin also entered the United States from the "Golden Triangle" of Burma, Thailand, and Laos and the "Golden Crescent" of Iran, Afghanistan, and Pakistan.) Any nation that came into contact with the drug trade became exposed to corruption, drug addiction, violence, and death. Illegal drug money bribed politicians in some Latin American states. In Colombia the sharpshooters of the militarized drug cartels assassinated judges, journalists, police officers, and government officials. "Narcoterrorism" destabilized Peru: Leftist guerrillas called the *Sendero Luminoso* (Shining Path) used the drug trade to help finance their

McDONALD
DIARIO EL HERALDO
San Pedro Sula
HONDURAS

THE AMERICAN
ADDICTION

The American Addiction.
This political cartoon from a Honduran newspaper reflected the Latin American perspective that the drug crisis in the United States stemmed not from the production of cocaine in Latin America but from the consumption of dangerous drugs in North America. Could the cartoonist also be suggesting that the drug trade was destroying Latin America? (McDonald/Diario El Heraldo, San Pedro Sula, Honduras)

rebellion.[116] Drug profits, not reinvested in long-term development, distorted regional economies; the "laundering" of "narcodollars" befouled banking systems. Colombia took courageous steps to defeat the drug lords of the Medellín and Cali cartels, only to produce the "hydra effect" of more dispersed operations and new drug fiefdoms in Mexico, Venezuela, and Brazil.[117] By 1998, 75% of the cocaine entering the United States arrived through Mexico. Of the five to seven tons of illegal drugs crossing the southwest border every day, authorities confiscated only an estimated 15 percent. "We find [drugs] in drive shafts, in car bumpers, in beer coolers . . . in butane tanks, gas tanks, in air conditioner vents, in the pistons of cars being towed," said a border agent.[118] The arrest, trial, and requested extradition of three Mexican druglords, (the so-called "Kings of Methamphetamines") in 1998 became a litmus test of U.S.-Mexican cooperation against "rivers of gold . . . and their enormous capacity for corruption."[119] Narcotics had become "a shared tragedy for both halves of the hemisphere."[120]

The drug issue became central to Panamanian–United States relations. After the United States signed the 1978 canal treaties with Panama's military government (see pages 415–416), the Carter administration tried to nudge the country toward civilian rule. But the military solidified its hold. In 1983 General Manuel Antonio Noriega took power. As the intelligence chief of the Panama Defense Forces, he had come to know Panama's thriving world of drug trafficking. As Panamanian banks laundered drug money, Noriega became a millionaire by cutting deals with Colombia's cocaine barons. By the late 1980s his dictatorial rule and drug-running had stirred anger in North Americans eager to blame the swaggering Panamanian for U.S. drug problems.

Little did the American people know that official Washington and General Noriega had long been allies. As a young officer in the 1960s, Noriega received regular payments from the Central Intelligence Agency. During the 1980s he helped the United States aid and train the *contras*. Grateful for this cooperation, Washington turned a blind eye to reports of his links with drug traffickers. In mid-1987 a former Noriega aide exposed in detail the general's corrupt practices. Anti-Noriega protests rocked Panama. Sensing the popular Panamanian resentment against the general, U.S. officials halted foreign aid to Panama. In February 1988, two Florida grand juries indicted the dictator for shipping Colombian drugs to the United States. Washington froze Panamanian assets in the United States and offered Noriega safe haven in another country (such as Spain). Yet Noriega would agree to nothing until the indictments were dropped. Washington broke off the talks in May 1988.

President Bush suffered frustration because economic pressure failed to topple Noriega. A "wet-noodle approach to Panama," complained one Washington journalist.[121] In late fall 1989, Noriega's rhetoric heated up in angry anti-*yanqui* public rallies. Violent and harassing incidents against U.S. military personnel in Panama soon grabbed front-page headlines. "This president is going to do something," snapped Bush, who ordered an invasion.[122] The chair of the Republican National Committee called the Panama invasion a "political jackpot" for a president many were calling a "wimp."[123]

In the early hours of December 20, 1989, Operation Just Cause commenced. The invasion of Panama by 22,500 troops proved a violent success. A billion dol-

General Colin Powell's Briefing on Panama.   Born in New York City in 1937, Powell earned a B.S. degree from the City University of New York before he began his military career. In 1987–1989 the army general served as assistant to the president for national security affairs, and in 1989 he was named chair, Joint Chiefs of Staff. Here he gives a briefing, on December 20, 1989, shortly after U.S. troops attacked Panama. The popular Powell retired from the army in 1993, and political observers then mentioned him as a possible presidential candidate. (Department of Defense)

lars' worth of property in Panama City was damaged and more than 300 Panamanians died. Only 23 American soldiers perished. The resistance had been greater than anticipated. Reflecting North American prejudice about the character of Latin Americans, one U.S. official remarked that "we thought if there was a lot of noise outside of the front door, they would go out the back."[124] When U.S. troops finally located Noriega in the Vatican Embassy in Panama City, the psychological operations team resorted to rock-and-roll music boomed over loudspeakers to induce surrender. Among the musical messages played were "Born to Run," "Crying in the Chapel," "I Fought the Law and the Law Won," and "We Gotta Get Outta This Place."[125] On January 4, 1990, Manuel Antonio Noriega became a federal prisoner in Miami awaiting trial on drug charges. Foiled in his efforts to reveal CIA secrets and embarrass President Bush, Noriega was convicted of cocaine smuggling in April 1992 and went to prison.

President Bush Directs the Invasion of Panama.   President Bush liked to use the telephone. Here, on December 20, 1989, he communicates with U.S. officials in Panama after he ordered the invasion. Critics bemoaned another example of "gunboat diplomacy," but Bush's popularity at home rose. Pummeled by massive U.S. firepower, Panama sank into deep economic crisis. Hundreds of Panamanian lives were lost. As many as 60 percent of American casualties were caused by "friendly fire"— Americans killed or wounded by mistake by other Americans. (Carol T. Powers, The White House)

Bush's popularity shot up after the military invasion of Panama. Democrats and Republicans alike cheered even though Bush had not consulted Congress. For General Powell, Panama vindicated the lessons of Vietnam: "Have a clear political objective and stick to it. Use all the force necessary, and do not apologize for going in big if that's what it takes."[126] Critics, however, lambasted the administration for violating the UN Charter and the OAS Charter, which contain nonintervention provisions. The Organization of American States censured the United States, and only a U.S. veto prevented passage of a UN Security Council resolution condemning the invasion. Most Latin American governments applauded the Noriega ouster but did not think a U.S. military attack the best way to oust him. President Alan García Pérez of Peru branded the invasion a "criminal act."[127]

The U.S. military also intervened in poverty-stricken Haiti to restore a deposed president. Elected in 1990, the Reverend Jean-Bertrand Aristide fled nine months later when Haitian military leaders resisted his plans for demilitarization and social reform. With Aristide exiled to the United States, a junta headed by General Raul Cedras terrorized and tortured political opponents. As thousands of Haitians tried to escape on makeshift boats, both Bush and Clinton, fearing an immigration crisis, denounced the junta but ordered the U.S. Coast Guard to turn back refugees seeking asylum. Backed by a UN-sponsored embargo, U.S. officials negotiated an agreement in July 1993 that would have reinstated Aristide in return for amnesty for Cedras and his cohorts. Yet when U.S. and Canadian peacekeepers arrived in October aboard the U.S.S. *Harlan County* to supervise the transition to civilian rule, armed rioters forced the vessel to turn back. Amid charges that "America turns tail," the Clinton administraiton seemed paralyzed, with the Pentagon reluctant to intervene so soon after the Somalia debacle, with the CIA leaking reports that Aristide was a "certifiable psychopath," and with members of the Congressional Black Caucus charging racism because Washington granted asylum to Cubans fleeing Castro but not to Haitians.[128]

Despite strong public opposition to intervention, Clinton decided to deploy force in late summer 1994. With jet fighters taking off for Port-au-Prince and a 20,000-strong invasion force set to land within thirty-six hours, a negotiating team headed by Jimmy Carter and General Colin Powell persuaded the junta to step down to avert bloodshed. Operation Uphold Democracy, the second U.S. military occupation of Haiti in this century (see pages 45–46), disarmed the Haitian military, returned Aristide to power, did what it could to create "a secure and stable environment" for 5 million Haitians, then left on schedule in April 1995, whereupon UN peacekeeping forces took over and supervised new elections.[129] Meager foreign aid did little to lift Haiti's living standards, the poorest in the hemisphere. "We're still gonna have a shitload of people in boats wanting to go to America," one U.S. soldier predicted.[130]

Boat people also troubled Cuban-American relations in the 1990s. The end of the Cold War caused Castro's Cuba to retrench but not repent, as it repatriated its military forces from abroad and began to adapt to world markets. While hosting an international symposium on the history of the missile crisis in 1992, Castro announced that Cuba would no longer give military support to revolutionary movements. Cuba was "desovietized forever," as one scholar put it.[131] The end of Soviet

Cuban Refrain. The cartoonist Mike Peters captures the words of nine U.S. presidents who thought they could overthrow Cuba's defiant leader. Forty years after hs accession to power in 1959, an unrepentant Fidel Castro still vowed "Socialism or death" and accused Wall Street capitalists of playing "Russian roulette" with the world economy. The price of free markets, he claimed, is paid in human misery, child labor, prostitution, and drug traffic. (© 1984 Mike Peters/Dayton Daily News)

subsidies, however, produced tremendous economic hardship in Cuba, thereby increasing the number of Cubans fleeing in makeshift rafts across the Florida Straits. After thirty-seven refugees drowned when Cuban authorities sank their hijacked boat in August 1994, rioting in Havana prompted Castro to denounce the United States for encouraging hijackers; henceforth Cuban police would not stop people from leaving so long as they did not hijack boats or planes. More than 35,000 departed in the next month.

President Clinton responded on both the domestic and the international levels. Recalling the Mariel boatlift of 1980, he consulted with the conservative anti-Castro Cuban American National Foundation (CANF) and Florida governor Lawton Chiles, who persuaded Clinton to "demagnetize" the United States by barring entry to the *balseros* (rafters).[132] Clinton then reached an agreement with Havana that increased to 20,000 the legal immigrants permitted into the United States annually, required Cuba to halt illegal immigration, and placed refugees under detention at the Guantánamo naval base and in Panama. A subsequent agreement in May 1995 allowed the detainees to enter the United States. To discourage a new exodus, Washington promised to return all future boat people to Cuba. To gain Castro's concurrence, Clinton promised to oppose further anti-Cuban sanctions sponsored by Republicans Senator Jesse Helms of North Carolina and Representative Dan Burton of Indiana.

Cooperation between Cuban and U.S. authorities in resolving the refugee problem ended abruptly. Three civilian aircraft piloted by a Cuban-American group called Brothers to the Rescue flew toward Cuba in Feburary 1996 in search of boat people. Because the Brothers organization had been warned about previous violations of Cuban air space, Cuban MiGs gave chase and shot down two of the planes, killing four crew members. "This is not *cojones* [testicles]," Madeleine Albright lectured Havana, "this is cowardice."[133]

Congress quickly passed the Helms-Burton bill by large majorities, and Clinton signed it into law on the eve of the Florida primary. The legislation not only allowed U.S. citizens (including naturalized Cuban-Americans) to sue foreign companies that did business using properties confiscated by the Castro regime; it also barred any relaxation of sanctions until a democratic government ruled in Cuba. "Adiós, Fidel," bragged Senator Helms.[134] Although such blatant Yankee economic interference did discourage foreign investment, Mexico, Canada, and the EU protested the measure for interrupting their lucrative trade with and investment in Cuba. The Helms-Burton Act actually made it easier for Castro to suppress dissent. "If you want to let light into the island," Cuba's leading human-rights activist advised, "then don't keep trying to keep all its windows shut."[135] On visiting Cuba in 1998, Pope John Paul II offered a prayer: "May Cuba . . . open itself up to the world, and may the world open itself up to Cuba."[136] When the EU claimed that Helms-Burton violated the rules of the new World Trade Organization, Clinton temporarily suspended suits against foreign firms while maintaining the punishing embargo. Castro continued to rail about North America's "canned culture" invasion that "transmits poisonous messages . . . to all families, to all homes, to all children."[137] In terms of Cuban-American relations, the Cold War had grown "colder."[138]

A modest thawing came in January 1999. Clinton, worried about a possibly violent transition to a post-Castro Cuba and about long-term Cuban resentment against the United States because of the hurtful economic embargo, authorized American citizens to send at least $1,200 a year to Cuban families, increased charter passenger flights to and from Cuba, established direct mail service, and permitted the sale of food to nongovernmental enterprises on the island. Pressed to jettison the embargo altogether by many foreign-policy analysts, Catholic archbishops, peace groups, the U.S. Chamber of Commerce, and many American companies eager to enter the Cuban marketplace, Clinton and his expected successor, Vice President Al Gore, alert to the voting power of vehemently anti-Castro Cuban-Americans in Florida and New Jersey, took the politically safe route of modest changes.

Mideast Tests: Persian Gulf War and Arab-Israeli Peace Process

The invasion of Kuwait by Iraq on August 2, 1990, led to a most significant exercise of U.S. power. Instead of paying back billions of dollars in loans received from Kuwait during the eight-year war between Iran and Iraq, Iraq's dictator, Saddam Hussein used old territorial claims and invasion to annex Kuwait in the name of all "zealous Arabs who believe in one Arab nation."[139] Washington feared that Saddam might next invade Saudi Arabia and thus control 40 percent of the world's oil. Bush also saw the Iraq-Kuwait crisis as the first post–Cold War "test of our mettle" at a time when "declinists" questioned the U.S. capacity to lead.[140] Exhorted by Prime Minister Margaret Thatcher not "to go wobbly," Bush pledged: "This will not stand."[141] He organized an international coalition of thirty countries to liber-

World Orders, Old and New.
In 1991, as the United States fought the Persian Gulf War, the cartoonist Jim Borgman linked past (Theodore Roosevelt) and present (George Bush) to suggest that the United States still saw itself as—and acted like—an international policeman. Not much had changed, it seemed to many Americans, since the early twentieth-century days of the Roosevelt Corollary and the Big Stick. (Jim Borgman, Cincinnati Enquirer © 1991. Reprinted with special permission of King Features Syndicate)

ate Kuwait. By November the UN had imposed economic sanctions and demanded Iraqi withdrawal. Bush initially sent some 200,000 American troops as part of a multinational peacekeeping force to defend Saudi Arabia (Operation Desert Shield). In early November he increased the expeditionary force to more than 500,000; contingents from other allied countries brought the troop level to 700,000. The Security Council commanded Iraq to evacuate Kuwait by January 15, 1991, or else face military attack.

Saddam Hussein had provoked unprecedented international unity among the United States and most NATO members; Iraq's former military patron, the Soviet Union; and several Arab states, including Egypt and Syria. The Iraqi despot no doubt found Washington's outraged reaction puzzling in view of recent efforts by the Reagan and Bush administrations to befriend Iraq. Off-the-books arms transfers to Iraq were kept secret from Congress from 1982 to 1987, in violation of the law. Washington had supplied intelligence data to Baghdad during the Iran-Iraq War, and Bush had blocked congressional attempts to deny agricultural credits to Iraq, charged with human-rights abuses. The Bush administration had also winked at secret and illegal bank loans that Iraq had used to purchase some $5 billion in Western technology for its burgeoning nuclear and chemical weapons programs. Only a week before the invasion, Ambassador April Glaspie informed Saddam Hussein that Washington had no "opinion on inter-Arab disputes such as your border dispute with Kuwait."[142]

"Maybe I'll turn out to be a Teddy Roosevelt," mused Bush in the first weeks of the crisis.[143] "It must be done as massively and decisively as possible," the Vietnam-conscious JCS chair Powell advised. "Choose your target, decide on your objective, and try to crush it."[144] Bush did not announce the offensive buildup until after the November mid-term elections. All the while he expanded U.S. goals from defending Saudi Arabia to liberating Kuwait, to crippling Iraq's war economy, to stopping Saddam Hussein from acquiring nuclear weapons. UN sanctions cut off 90 percent of Iraq's imports and 97 percent of its exports. Iraq replied that it would consider withdrawal from Kuwait only if the United States forced Israel to relinquish its occupied territories.

When Bush asked for authorization to send U.S. troops into combat under a UN resolution, Congress debated for four days. Senator Joseph Biden of Delaware declared that "none [of Iraq's] actions justify the deaths of our sons and daughters."[145] Senator George Mitchell of Maine cited the risks: "an unknown number of casualties and deaths, billions of dollars spent, a greatly disrupted oil supply and oil price increases, a war possibly widened to Israel, Turkey or other allies, the possible long-term American occupation of Iraq, increased instability in the Persian Gulf region, long-lasting Arab enmity against the United States, a possible return to isolationism at home."[146] Senator Robert Dole of Kansas rebutted that "Saddam . . . may think he's going to be rescued, maybe by Congress."[147] Despite jokes about "a war to make the world safe for gas-guzzlers," a majority in both houses narrowly approved Bush's request to use force.[148]

Operation Desert Storm began with a spectacular aerial bombardment of Iraq and Kuwait on January 16. For five weeks satellite television coverage via Cable News Network (CNN) enabled Americans to watch Tomahawk cruise missiles hit Iraqi targets and U.S. Patriot missiles intercept Iraqi Scud missiles. Bush and Baker masterfully kept the coalition intact, persuading Israel not to retaliate after Iraqi Scud attacks and keeping Gorbachev "steadfast" as allied bombs devastated Russia's erstwhile client. Finally, on February 23, hundreds of thousands of allied ground forces invaded Kuwait and eastern Iraq. Iraq's largely conscript army put up little resistance. Iraqi troops scrambled to leave Kuwait, blowing up as many as 800 oil wells as they retreated. Allied aircraft flew hundreds of sorties along the "Highway of Death" from Kuwait City to Basra. After only one hundred hours of fighting on the ground, Iraq accepted a UN-imposed cease-fire. An exultant Bush proclaimed: "By God, we've kicked the Vietnam syndrome once and for all."[149]

Burning Oil Fields in Kuwait.
Months after Operation Desert Storm freed Kuwait from Iraqi rule, oil fields blazed, creating an environmental disaster. Some oil facilities were hit in the fighting. Retreating Iraqi forces also torched Kuwait's oil industry. Soot and unburned crude oil billowed into the air and then polluted soils, vegetation, and Persian Gulf waters. (U.S. Navy/Department of Defense, Still Media Records Center)

Estimates vary and remain disputed, but Iraq's casualties numbered some 40,000 military dead; U.S. forces suffered only 148 deaths and 458 wounded (out of a coalition total of 240 and 776). A public-health crisis soon beset the Iraqi people, who had seen their infrastructure disabled by air attacks; cholera and typhoid spread. A UN inspection team reported that Iraq had been "relegated to a preindustrial age, but with all the disabilities of postindustrial dependency on an intensive use of energy and technology."[150]

Bush did not send U.S. forces to Baghdad to capture Saddam Hussein. General Powell reminded him that "our practical intention was to leave Baghdad enough power to survive as a threat to an Iran that remained bitterly hostile to the United States," even though the result was, as Marine Corps Lieutenant General Bernard E. Trainor later criticized Powell, that the United States snatched "a modest victory from the jaws of triumph."[151] Bush hoped that the Iraqi military or disgruntled associates in the Ba'ath party would oust Saddam in a coup. Yet when Kurds in northern Iraq and Shi'ites in the south rebelled, Bush did little to help. Wary of a Mideast quagmire, Bush said: "We are not going to permit this to drag on in terms of [a] significant U.S. presence à la Korea."[152] Saddam Hussein used his remaining tanks and helicopters to crush both rebellions. Public pressure persuaded Bush to send thousands of U.S. troops to northern Iraq, where the United Nations designated a "no-fly" zone prohibiting Iraqi aircraft from attacking Kurdish refugees. Saddam Hussein's remarkable survival left a sour taste. As Margaret Thatcher commented in 1996: "There is the aggressor, Saddam Hussein, still in power. There is the president of the United States, no longer in power. I wonder who won?"[153]

Under Security Council Resolution 687, Iraq had to accept the inviolability of the boundary with Kuwait; tolerate the presence of UN peacekeepers on its borders; and fully disclose all chemical, biological, and nuclear weapons, including missiles, and cooperate in their destruction. Bush had boasted during the air war that "our pinpoint attacks have put Saddam out of the nuclear bomb-building business for a long time to come."[154] Not so. What allied bombs had missed, UN inspectors tried to locate. Saddam Hussein's scientists and engineers had built more than twenty nuclear facilities that were within months of producing nuclear weapons when the Gulf War began. Air attacks had only inconvenienced Iraqi efforts to build a bomb. Inspectors found and destroyed more than 100 Scud missiles, 70 tons of nerve gas, and 400 tons of mustard gas.

Saddam Hussein nonetheless continued to bedevil Washington. In retaliation for an apparent Iraqi assassination plot against former president Bush, Clinton ordered missile attacks on Baghdad in 1993. He sent 36,000 troops to Kuwait the following year to deter Iraqi military movements southward, then bombed Iraq again in 1996 when Saddam Hussein crushed a Kurdish revolt in northern Iraq. Despite continued economic sanctions until all weapons of mass destruction were accounted for, Baghdad played a six-year shell game by interfering with UN inspectors as they searched for chemical weapons and small, easily hidden biological stores of anthrax, botulinum, and aflatoxin. "When we go to a site," the American UN inspector Scott Ritter declared to his colleagues, "they're gonna know we've been there, we're gonna raise our tails and we're gonna spray urine all over their walls."[155] The Iraqi government protested UN inspection teams' zealotry and their sharing of intelligence data with U.S. officials—information later used to target sites for U.S. air strikes. In February and November 1998 the United States rushed forces to the Persian Gulf (both deployments cost a billion dollars), each time deferring attack when Iraq promised complete access for inspectors. Despite CIA funding of $100 million to Kurds and other anti-Saddam groups since 1991, Clinton publicly promised "overt covert operations" to "work for" a different regime in Baghdad.[156]

When Saddam Hussein again stiff-armed UN inspectors on the eve of Clinton's impeachment in December 1998, the president launched Operation Desert Fox, a joint Anglo-American bombing campaign aimed at "degrading" Iraq's military capabilities.[157] Several hundred Tomahawk missiles (more than in the Gulf War) fired over a period of four days set back Iraq's weapons program by "a year or more," but also provoked criticism from China, Russia, and France.[158] And that "very, very bad bastard," as British prime minister Tony Blair called Saddam Hussein, remained in power, an Islamic "hero who faced down U.S. imperialism."[159] Intermittent air attacks continued into 1999.

To the surprise and welcome of many, the Gulf War spurred the Arab-Israeli peace process. When Bush took office in early 1989 the peace process had stalled. *Intifada* deaths continued to mount as Israelis used uncompromising military force to quell the Palestinian insurrection. The conservative Likud party took power in Israel in mid-1990, vowing never to give up the occupied territories. Radical Palestinian factions at the same time refused to abandon their "Holy war" *(jihad)* against the Jewish state. Secretary Baker pressed both sides but particularly implored Israel to negotiate: "Forswear annexation. Stop settlement activity. . . . Reach out to the Palestinians as neighbors who deserve political rights."[160]

The end of the Cold War, the Gulf War, and growing dissatisfaction with Israel's hard-line stance among American Jews improved the diplomatic climate. The Soviet Union's collapse robbed the PLO of outside support. Yasir Arafat's ill-fated backing of Iraq during the Gulf War caused the oil-rich governments of Saudi Arabia and the Gulf states, in retaliation, to curtail their financial assistance to the PLO. Hard-line Islamic fundamentalists in the Hamas movement challenged Arafat's leadership within the PLO. Thus when Israel showed restraint in the face of Iraqi missile attacks and the United States promised moderate Arabs an expanded peace process after the Gulf War, Arafat opted to negotiate despite his fear of becoming "a male bee that fertilizes once and then dies."[161] Secretary Baker traveled to the Mideast eight times in 1991 to arrange for multilateral negotiations in Madrid in 1992. President Bush withheld $10 billion in loan guarantees so long as the hard-line Likud government expanded Israeli settlements in the occupied territories; this pressure helped to elect a more flexible Labor government, headed by Yitzhak Rabin and Shimon Peres, in July 1992.

The breakthrough came little more than a year later, after secret meetings between Israeli and PLO representatives in Norway. In Washington on September 13, 1993, Arafat and Rabin signed a declaration of principles for eventual Palestinian self-rule in the Gaza Strip and in the Jericho area of the West Bank. Terrorist attacks by both sides delayed implementation. Resumed talks finally produced agreement in May 1994, when Israeli forces withdrew from the Gaza Strip and Jericho and Palestinian autonomy began in those two areas. Israel and Jordan signed

PLO-Israeli Agreement.
On September 13, 1993, President Clinton acted as stage manager on the South Lawn of the White House when Israeli prime minister Yitzhak Rabin (left), and Palestine Liberation Organization chair Yasir Arafat (right), signed a historic accord for Palestinian self-rule in the Gaza Strip and Jericho—first steps, perhaps, toward a Palestinian homeland. After Rabin and Arafat affixed their signatures, Clinton shook hands with both men and then stepped back and gestured with his arms. Arafat reached his hand out, and after several long seconds, Rabin responded. (The White House)

a peace accord in July after the United States agreed to forgive Jordan's foreign debt, but Syria refused to make peace despite a personal visit by President Clinton to Damascus.

The assassination of Rabin by a Jewish extremist in November 1995, Palestinian bombings that killed more than sixty Israelis the following spring, and the election of hard-line Prime Minister Benjamin Netanyahu in 1996 threatened to unravel the Palestinian-Israeli accord. Clinton, who had admired Rabin greatly, came away from his first meeting with Netanyahu feeling that "he had been dissed by the leader of a country smaller than Vermont that gets three billion dollars in aid every year."[162] Except for relinquishing Hebron in 1997, Netanyahu balked at any more Israeli withdrawals. Finally brought together by Clinton at a nine-day summit in Maryland during October 1998, Arafat and Netanyahu agreed to further Israeli pullbacks from jointly held territory and a phased release of Palestinian prisoners in return for Arafat's fulfilling previous promises of changes in the PLO charter calling for Israel's destruction. Repudiated by hard-liners in his own Likud party, Netanyahu called for and lost a national election in Spring 1999. His successor, Ehud Barak, promised to attempt good-faith negotiations with the Palestinians.

Feuding and Trading with China, Vietnam, and Japan

Human rights and trade issues continued to dominate U.S. relations with Asia under Bush and Clinton. During the night of June 3–4, 1989, Chinese soldiers and tanks stormed into Beijing's Tiananmen Square. The epicenter of Chinese life "became a killing field" in which hundreds—perhaps thousands—of demonstrators lay dead.[163] For weeks unarmed students had been holding peaceful prodemocracy rallies and appealing for talks with government leaders. The movement had attracted wide support, including the backing of some Chinese party officials. China's octogenarian rulers, however, in contrast to their counterparts in much of Eastern Europe, chose repression over constructive change—"to haul China back twenty years to terror and Orwellian groupthink."[164] The most powerful leader in the Chinese government, Deng Xiaoping, saw the students' call for political liberalization to match economic reforms as an attempt "to create chaos under the heavens."[165] Deng not only crushed the prodemocracy movement; he also purged the government of reformers and ordered the arrest and execution of protesters. World opinion became outraged, because "Tiananmen was a record-breaking world event on television."[166]

Bush sent signals to China "that we want the relationship to stay intact, but it's hard when they are executing people, and we have to respond," he noted in his diary.[167] Washington suspended weapons sales to China (and then soon lifted the ban) and deferred consideration of new World Bank loans to China. Yet Bush continued Beijing's most-favored-nation trade status. He calculated that China's aging leaders would once again travel the reform path, and he argued that America's global security required stable and friendly Sino-American ties. China, Bush implored, should not be isolated in the international community. Brent Scowcroft flew secretly to Beijing on June 30 with the message that "we can do a lot more for them when they aren't killing their own people."[168]

Critics charged that the United States was shortsightedly allying itself with China's elderly clique while alienating the nation's younger, progressive, future leaders. Bush cheered such leaders in Bucharest, Prague, and Warsaw but snubbed them in Beijing. The debate centered on a classic question: When calls for human rights and calculations of global power politics collide, must either give way?

Prodemocracy Courage, Tiananmen Square, Beijing, China. In early 1989 university students and sympathizers camped in Beijing's great square. They made hopeful speeches about democracy and even built a towering replica of the Statue of Liberty. Drawing inspiration from Poland's Solidarity movement, the young prodemocracy activists pleaded with their nation's aged leaders to liberalize China's politics. In June the military swept into the square. After the massacre, one person—probably a student—braved tanks in a sobering example of the classic contest between the courageous individual and the powerful state. (AP/Wide World Photos)

Despite China's negative record on human rights, its economy boomed during the 1990s. U.S. trade with China reached $33.1 billion in 1992, with an $18.3 billion surplus in China's favor; by 1997 the figures climbed to $63 billion and $39.5 billion. Some analysts suggested that the "Asia card" of market growth might ensure "success in the revitalization of the U.S. economy."[169] The Clinton administration renewed China's most-favored-nation trading privileges in June 1993 after the Beijing government released several prominent dissidents. Beijing's establishment of diplomatic ties with South Korea in 1992, its growing trade with Seoul, and its quiet pressure on North Korea to permit international nuclear inspection also pleased Washington. When Clinton again granted China most-favored-nation status in 1994, he frankly declared that human rights and trade issues were henceforth delinked.

Tensions nonetheless increased when Washington permitted a visit by Taiwan's president to his Cornell University alma mater in May 1995. Accusing Washington of abetting Taiwanese independence as part of a plot to "divide, weaken, and contain China," Beijing precipitated a crisis in March 1996 by firing three ballistic missiles close to Taiwan and conducting military exercises in the Taiwan Strait.[170] Chinese officials discounted any U.S. response: "We've watched you in Somalia, Haiti, and Bosnia, and you don't have the will."[171] Secretary of Defense William Perry thereupon warned a visiting Chinese diplomat of "grave consequences" if any missiles struck Taiwan, and two U.S. carrier task forces steamed ostentatiously toward the region.[172] Both sides soon backed off, as the United States officially reaffirmed its support of "one China," and the Chinese agreed not to sell nuclear technology to Iran and other states that supported terrorism. Despite Republican charges ("donorgate") that Chinese agents had attempted to "buy" the 1996 U.S. elections by funneling money to Democratic candidates, a week-long state visit to the United States by Chinese president Jiang Zemin in October 1997 produced a "constructive strategic partnership."[173] The United States and China cooperated to help defuse a crisis between India and Pakistan over nuclear testing the following year.[174] The announcement during Clinton's own visit to China in 1998 that Washington and Beijing "will do whatever we can to restore confidence in Japan's economy" led the Japanese to suspect that the United States wanted to play "both a China card and a Japanese card."[175] Whether as "military adventurists or as venture capitalists," China's growing power and influence—and its poor human-rights record—kept it high on Washington's agenda.[176]

U.S. relations with Vietnam also improved. In fall 1992, President Bush announced that "we can begin writing the last chapter of the Vietnam War."[176] Bush referred to the protracted negotiations with Hanoi to reach a full accounting for the 2,265 American military personnel still listed as missing in action (MIAs) from the Vietnam War. In February 1994, after the Clinton administration satisfied itself that Vietnamese officials had made a sincere effort to identify and return remains, Washington lifted the nineteen-year-old trade embargo. Within hours PepsiCo erected a giant, inflated can of soda in the middle of Ho Chi Minh City and gave away 40,000 cans of the international soft drink. Caterpillar, Otis, and other companies hoped to win contracts worth billions of dollars to repair Vietnam's infrastructure. Mobil expected to begin pumping oil in the South China Sea. General

Electric set up offices two blocks from the infamous "Hanoi Hilton" prison.[177] Despite a devastating war and two decades of isolation, many of the 71 million Vietnamese apparently retained a certain attraction to things American. "English is the language of money, the language of our future," said a Vietnamese diplomat.[178] Having opened its economy to foreign investment and trade, Hanoi undoubtedly saw a strong U.S. economic presence as a possible counter to its giant neighbor China.

President Clinton established full diplomatic relations in July 1995, and his appointment as ambassador of Pete Peterson, a former prisoner of war in North Vietnam for seven years, proved "a political masterstroke" in defusing much of the resentment against normalization.[179] Billboards championing American products soon greeted tourists on the highway connecting Hanoi airport with the city, as low-wage Vietnamese workers manufactured Nike athletic shoes and other products for global markets. Joint historical symposia on the Vietnam War, with Robert McNamara and General Nguyen Giap among the participants, also helped to reconcile the past.

Trade issues also dominated the Japanese-American relationship. Anti-Americanism in Japan and "Japan bashing" *(Nihon tataki)* in the United States bedeviled the world's two major economies.[180] In 1990 the world's ten largest banks had headquarters in Japan, and several of the world's premier public companies were Japanese. Japan's biggest company, NTT, was more than twice the size of America's leading corporation, IBM. The best-selling car in America in 1989 was the Honda Accord. In response to Japanese comments about "lazy" and "illiterate" U.S. workers, South Carolina senator Ernest Hollings suggested drawing "a mushroom cloud and put underneath it: 'Made in America by lazy and illiterate Americans and tested in Japan.'"[181]

"The Japanese Have Bought Pearl Harbor." Huge Japanese investments in the United States prompted the cartoonist Don C. Wright to remember December 7, 1941, when Japan attacked Pearl Harbor. By the 1980s Japan had become an economic behemoth. Americans grumbled that the Japanese were buying up the United States. But, remarked Chrysler Corporation chair Lee Iacocca, Americans had nobody but themselves to blame. "You can't get mad at them [Japanese] for saying. 'We'll take as much as you give us.'" (© 1988 Don Wright, *The Miami News)*

Many Americans especially worried that the dollar-rich Japanese were buying up too many businesses in the United States. By 1990 Japanese interests controlled 25 percent of California's banking assets and owned almost half of downtown Los Angeles. When Japanese firms acquired the MCA and Columbia movie studios in the early 1990s, it seemed that Godzilla was mounting a cultural invasion. "Why should the Japanese bomb Pearl Harbor when they can buy it?" people asked.[182]

Predictions of Japan's global economic hegemony dwindled. The Japanese variant of capitalism, characterized by government management of the economy and close ties among corporate "families" of manufacturers, suppliers, exporters, and banks, proved ill adapted to globalization and to emerging industries such as biotechnology, computer software, and digital imaging. Japan's highly structured society encouraged high production and savings from its citizens but discouraged bold Japanese entrepreneurs equivalent to America's Ted Turner or Bill Gates. "There are whole sectors, like the Internet, that don't develop" in Japan, noted one U.S. economist. "If you are wild and crazy, you have to go somewhere else."[183] Japanese investments in Hollywood soured because industrial know-how had little relevance to a field such as entertainment. As the New York stock exchange soared in the mid-1990s, Tokyo's Nikkei average slumped to half the levels of the late 1980s. U.S. exports to Japan jumped from $27 billion in 1986 to $47.8 billion in 1992 to $66 billion in 1997, even though the trade deficit (in Japan's favor) still hovered around $50 billion in the mid-1990s. McDonald's ranked as Japan's largest restaurant chain by 1995 and Apple Computer became the second largest vendor of personal computers. The vulnerability of Japan's banking system during the Asian financial crisis in 1997–1998 led some Japanese to bemoan "the second defeat in the Pacific War," as the $8 trillion U.S. economy stood roughly twice as large as Japan's by 1999.[184] Nonetheless, Tokyo still maintained large trade surpluses, with every dollar earned adding to Japan's huge foreign investments. "Japan is still the main source of long-term capital for the world today," noted a long-time Asia watcher, "and the United States is still the largest debtor nation."[185]

Washington much valued Japan's close military alliance with the United States (more than 50,000 American military personnel served there) and its shouldering of more of the mutual defense costs. American officials praised Tokyo for applying Japanese funds to relieve the international debt problem and for providing economic assistance to developing nations such as the Philippines. A North Korean threat to build nuclear weapons and China's potential menace to Taiwan reinforced Tokyo's desire for continuing military ties even in the absence of a Soviet enemy. The rape of a twelve-year-old girl on Okinawa by three U.S. servicemen in 1995 temporarily strained relations but did not alter the commitment of Japan's ruling parties to its $40 billion per year self-defense forces (plus paying 70 percent of burden-sharing for U.S. troops). By century's end, many Americans still held ambivalent attitudes about their erstwhile enemy and long-time ally—as "miracle and menace, docile and aggressive, fragile blossom and Tokyo Rose."[186] Nonetheless, given the mutual popularity of samurai movies, "teenage mutant ninja turtles," and American baseball, Ambassador Walter Mondale jokingly predicted that neither he nor his Japanese counterpart could have "nearly the influence on bilateral relations as Hideo Nomo will," referring to the star Japanese pitcher who, at the time, played for the Los Angeles Dodgers.[187]

Global Bewilderments

"Gosh, I miss the Cold War," President Clinton half-joked after American soldiers were killed in Somalia.[188] Indeed, the post–Cold War era seemed less manageable than the bipolar system that had preceded it—so full of "outlaws," so rife with religious, tribal, and ethnic tensions, so overarmed, so wracked by economic catastrophes, so divided on the basis of gender, so plagued by illicit drugs, crime, and AIDS, so threatened by the proliferation of nuclear weapons and the deterioration of the natural environment, so burdened by overpopulation and famines, so disunited just when it appeared that the United Nations had emerged as a major builder of coalitions.[189]

Arms sales accelerated across the post–Cold War world. Surface-to-surface missiles were showing up in the world arms market. So were U.S. Stinger missiles that the Reagan administration had given in the 1980s to radical Islamic rebels for their war against the Soviet-backed government in Afghanistan. After the Soviet withdrawal, Reagan's Afghan "freedom fighters" used the weapons against their rivals, became traffickers in heroin, trained *jihad* terrorists and assassins, and suppressed the rights of indigenous Afghan women. The United States continued as the world's leading arms merchant, exporting $15 billion in weapons each year as Third World governments lined up to buy Patriot missiles with money better spent on health and education.

Other weapons posed deadly threats. The release of a killer gas into the Tokyo subway by a Japanese religious cult in 1995 suggested that terrorists could disperse a vial of anthrax over Washington, D.C., and kill more than a million people. With biological weapons banned since 1972, the 1993 Chemical Convention (ratified by Washington in 1997) required signatories to destroy all chemical weapons by the year 2005 and to submit to rigorous inspection. More than one hundred nations in 1997 signed a treaty banning antipersonnel land mines. The American activist Jody Williams shared the Nobel Peace Prize for her work in behalf of the treaty, but President Clinton refused to sign it because U.S. troops in Korea relied on mines to protect against a North Korean attack.

Nuclear proliferation remained a threat to all nations. Although Argentina and Brazil signed a pact never to build nuclear weapons and South Africa publicly announced in 1993 that it had dismantled its nuclear-weapons program, Israel, Pakistan, and India had joined the elite nuclear club—and each refused to sign the nonproliferation treaty. U.S. intelligence learned in May 1990 that Pakistan had deployed as many as ten nuclear weapons on American-made F-16 fighter planes and seemed poised to strike India. Only an eleventh-hour U.S. plea defused a crisis that one CIA official called "far more frightening than the Cuban missile crisis."[190] As for the former Soviet republics, Congress provided nearly $1.5 billion to help Russia, Belarus, Ukraine, and Kazakhstan dismantle much of the former Soviet nuclear arsenal and safeguard the remaining nuclear materials inside Russia. In a "Megatons to Megawatts" arrangement, President Clinton promised to buy from Russia 500 metric tons of highly enriched uranium over a 20-year period for $12 billion, and in 1994 U.S. nuclear technicians in Project SAPPHIRE spirited out of Kazakhstan some 600 kilograms of uranium to prevent its theft or sale.[191] Calling nonproliferation "one of our nation's highest priorities," the Clinton administration did what

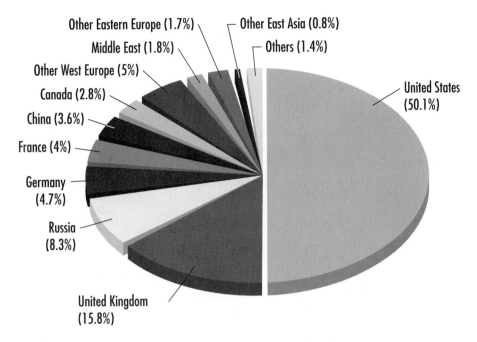

Other Eastern Europe (1.7%)
Other East Asia (0.8%)
Middle East (1.8%)
Others (1.4%)
Other West Europe (5%)
Canada (2.8%)
China (3.6%)
France (4%)
Germany (4.7%)
Russia (8.3%)
United States (50.1%)
United Kingdom (15.8%)

U.S. Government

it could to prevent "nuclear yardsales" and to maintain nuclear security inside Russia.[192] Clinton's success in renewing the Treaty on the Nonproliferation of Nuclear Weapons (NPT) in 1995 and negotiating a comprehensive test ban treaty in 1996 only partly dissipated nuclear nightmares.

The discovery that Kim Il Sung's North Korean regime had built facilities that could produce small nuclear weapons spawned a short-lived crisis in the early 1990s. Pyongyang refused to cooperate with the International Atomic Energy Agency, which sought to inspect suspected plants, and threatened to withdraw from the NPT, which North Korea had signed in 1985. It seemed puzzling that the octogenarian Kim Il Sung would seek one or two nuclear weapons, the use of which "would mean the end of their country as they know it," as President Clinton so bluntly put it.[193] "North Korea could explode or implode," predicted the commander of U.S. forces in South Korea.[194] A "private" visit by former president Jimmy Carter to North Korea led to negotiations betwen Washington and Pyongyang. In October 1994, North Korea agreed to dismantle its nuclear-weapons program and submit to international inspection, and in return the United States promised $4 billion in energy aid. The agreement eliminated, at least temporarily, the threat of a "backlash state" with nuclear weapons.[195]

"Until now the cold war provided an alibi" to avoid tackling many global issues, wrote a leading analyst. "No longer."[196] The deterioration of the international environment and deteriorating public health not only endangered economic prosperity; it also threatened to undermine international stability. A sample of recent data revealed problems:

- The world's population in 1998 reached 6 billion and was rising at a rate of 90 million every year.
- The World Health Organization in 1997, calling smoking "a fire in the global village," predicted that 3.5 million deaths would increase to 10 million yearly with the growing popularity in Asia of Western-style cigarettes from multinational firms.[197]
- Without effective curtailment of greenhouse gases, average global temperatures will increase between 2 and 6.5 degrees Fahrenheit by the end of the twenty-first century.
- Americans use about one-third of all chlorofluorocarbons (CFCs) in the world—the chemical most responsible for depletion of the ozone layer that shields the earth from the sun's deadly ultraviolet rays.
- By 1998, 33 million people had become infected with AIDS, more than two-thirds of them living in sub-Saharan Africa.
- Industrial countries produce more than 90 percent of the 400 million tons of hazardous waste entering the biosphere each year.
- "World food production will have to increase by more than 75% over the next thirty years to keep pace with population growth," a UN official has estimated.[198]
- Diarrhea kills nearly 3 million children under age five every year.
- "Tropical forests cover only 7 percent of Earth's land surface," according to the World Resources Institute, "but they contain more than half of all living species. Yet these forests are being cut and cleared at a very rapid rate—an area of about 40 million acres (about the size of the state of Washington) every year."[199]

As evidenced by "collapsing fisheries, falling water tables, shrinking forests, dying lakes, crop-withering heat waves, and disappearing species," the world faced a host of borderless issues.[200] The catapulting growth in population meant a greater use of scarce resources, more pollution, more disease, and more famines such as those that wracked Africa in the 1980s and 1990s. Overgrazing and tree-cutting in many parts of the Third World, as in Bangladesh, produced quick runoffs of rainfalls and flooding, washing away precious topsoil and killing hundreds. In turn, these ecological/economic problems generated political instability and social disintegration. Food riots and migrations of refugees challenged governments, many of which seemed immobilized. Yet the Bush administration vetoed monies for the UN Population Fund in 1989 because the agency supported birth-control programs that allowed abortions. Because Washington did not want the 1982 Convention on the Law of the Sea to restrict private American business, not until fall 1997 did President Clinton transmit the treaty to the Senate, where it remains pending.

If "all of your people want to get rich in exactly the same way we got rich," President Clinton admitted to China's president in 1996, "we won't be breathing

Deforestation of the Amazon.   The burning of tropical forests in order to open land to farming, grazing, and settlement has eliminated hundreds of plant and animal species. The clearing has also accelerated soil erosion and filled the atmosphere with carbon dioxide, one of the greenhouse gases causing global warming. In the years 1981–1990, more than 40 million acres of tropical forests were lost each year. The photograph on the left was taken by Skylab 2 in 1973 on a partly cloudy day in the Amazon basin. The photograph on the right, taken by the crew of the space shuttle *Discovery* in 1988, reveals the effects of burning as thick smoke covers the same area. (Courtesy of NASA)

very well" and will face "irreparable damage to the global environment."[201] Yet less developed countries resented lectures from industrial nations that had perpetrated environmental wrongs for decades. And, "you can't have an environmentally healthy planet in a world that is socially unjust," noted the president of Brazil at the 1992 Earth Summit in Rio de Janeiro.[202] At that summit, attended by 178 nations, Bush spoke against strong environmental protection rules, charging that they would cost jobs. He refused to sign the Biodiversity Treaty designed to slow the loss of endangered species. Clinton, however, signed the treaty in 1993 (it remains pending in the Senate) and also agreed to reduce emissions of greenhouse gases (this Global Warming Convention also remains pending in the Senate, as of this writing). The Clinton administration's increased attention to environmental issues was due in no small measure to Vice President Al Gore, whose book *Earth in the Balance: Healing the Global Environment* (1992) had established his credentials.

"We do not have generations," noted the Worldwatch Institute's Lester R. Brown. "We only have years in which to turn things around."[203] Pressure from environmentalists forced the U.S. tuna industry to stop using fish-netting techniques that killed 100,000 dolphins annually. Entertainers regularly supported environmental causes through events such as the 1989 "Don't Bungle the Jungle" concert staged by Madonna and the Grateful Dead. At the same time, the United States helped establish an international ban on ivory in order to save the vanishing elephant. The Clean Air Act of 1990 took steps to reduce acid rain and toxic wastes in the air. Washington also began "debt-for-nature swaps" wherein Third World nations willing to undertake major programs to protect the environment enjoyed some debt reduction.[204]

The UN Environmental Program kept "global commons" issues alive. Eighty-six nations agreed at Helsinki in mid-1989 to phase out the manufacture and use of ozone-destroying chemicals by the year 2000; by 1994 their efforts had reduced by half the *increase* in the concentration of CFCs in the atmosphere. Through the efforts of the World Health Organization (WHO), infectious diseases such as small-pox and malaria have nearly been eliminated. Combating the global spread of AIDS is the organization's next daunting task. Genetic-engineering programs funded by the World Bank hope to launch a "gene revolution" to improve farm productivity.[205] Some 100 countries signed the Convention on Desertification in 1994 and pledged to channel $10 billion to $20 billion through a UN program over the next twenty years to support land preservation and reclamation. Finally, a conference in Kyoto in 1997 attended by 166 countries agreed to a Global Warming Convention under which developed nations must reduce carbon dioxide, methane, and other greenhouse gas emissions by 6 to 8 percent below their 1990 levels. Because of expected increases from Third World nations, scientists predicted that Kyoto will produce only "a small decrease in the rate of increase" in greenhouse gas emissions.[206] President Clinton voiced approval of the treaty.

In early 1994 the State Department focused for the first time on the treatment of women in its annual human-rights report. Its grim findings included forced sterilizations and abortions in China; coerced prostitution in Thailand and Burma; females spending one-third as much time in school as males in Zaire; "dowry deaths" in India (husbands killing their wives because of insufficient dowries); laws making adultery illegal for women but not for men in Morocco and the Republic of the Congo. Of 1.3 billion people living in poverty, the UN Development Program reported in 1995, "70 percent are women."[207] Worldwide, women held only 14 percent of top managerial jobs, 10 percent of seats in national legislatures, and 6 percent of cabinet-level posts. The following year, U.S. courts granted asylum to a nineteen-year-old woman who had fled her native Togo to avoid having "my woman's parts . . . scraped off"; the United States thus joined Canada in making genital mutilation (2 million victims per year) and other gender-based abuses grounds for asylum.[208] Hillary Rodham Clinton headed a U.S. delegation that attended a World Conference on Women in Beijing in 1995, and Secretary Albright promised higher priority for women's issues because it "is the right" and "smart thing to do."[209] Still, as of 1999, the United States had not approved the convention banning discrimination against women and the Convention on the Rights of the Child.

Because "information, ideas, and money now pulse across the planet at light speed," international communications issues assumed new importance.[210] Since the 1970s, developing nations had been calling for a "New Information Order" in which the powerful developed nations would have to democratize access to information and to report news accurately and fairly. Third World critics charged that the control of information by developed nations—especially the United States—created dependency and retarded economic growth. Because of its remote-sensing satellites, the United States allegedly could marshal greater information (data on weather and market conditions, mineral deposits, and agricultural output) than

American Decline, American Ignorance. Peter C. Vey's cartoon speaks to a major point that "declinists" made to explain why U.S. power slipped: The American educational system needed reform. American students were ignorant of the wider world. A 1989 Gallup poll discovered that 14 percent of the American respondents could not pick out the United States on a world map and that 50 percent did not know that the Sandinistas and U.S.-backed *contras* were battling in Nicaragua. A 1990 Gallup survey found that one-third of the interviewees did not know whether the United States had fought on the side of the South Vietnamese or North Vietnamese in America's longest war. (P. C. Vey, reprinted from the *New York Times*)

weaker states in negotiations on tariffs and other issues. Through the International Telecommunications Satellite Consortium (INTELSAT), founded in 1964 to coordinate the use of satellites, the United States has also preserved control of the majority of the electromagnetic spectrum for itself and its allies. By 1999, Time Warner, the world's largest TV producer and distributor, was selling thousands of hours of programs to 175 countries. Such dominance helped, for example, to increase sales of sneakers to China through video images of Michael Jordan slam-dunking ("*kou qui*") a basketball.[211] An international agreement in 1997 opened the $600 billion global telephone market to greater competition, with U.S. companies poised to increase their one-third share. Despite sites on the World Wide Web in many languages, morever, most of the software, search engines, and information were in English, as was an estimated 90 percent of all Internet traffic.

Another aspect of communications technology revealed that powerful governments could be rendered powerless to silence critics who had easy access to inexpensive equipment for disseminating their messages. In the 1980s, videocassettes of American and Japanese newscasts of the assassination of Benigno Aquino were smuggled into the Philippines, where they were copied and distributed to home viewers, thus helping to topple the dictatorship of Ferdinand Marcos, an American ally. In 1989 protesting Chinese students listened to Voice of America radio broadcasts to follow events throughout China and used fax machines to communicate with the outside world. International revulsion against the Chinese crackdown was so extensive largely because the ghastly events appeared on worldwide television. In an "anomaly of history" in 1989, East Europeans "watched the revolution on CNN relayed by a Russian satellite and mustered the courage to rebel against their own sovereigns."[212] Nor could Islamic censorship in Iran suppress the "tide of god-lessness" represented by bootleg videocassettes of "Baywatch" and *Titanic*.[213] Even the Pentagon, which relied by the late 1990s on 2 million computers to coordinate its missions, had to guard against "electronic Pearl Harbors" because of their vulnerability to hackers and viruses.[214]

Globalization made foreign relations less foreign. "From the floor of the stock exchange in Singapore to the roof of the world over Patagonia where there is a hole in the ozone layer, what happens there matters here—and vice versa," noted one diplomat.[215] The impact of NAFTA on both St. Joseph, Missouri, and Racine, Wisconsin, for example, was the loss of manufacturing jobs when textiles and refrigeration plants relocated to Mexico, and the addition of employees by high-tech firms eager to take advantage of the booming export market. Even college sports became globalized, as the popularity of National Basketball Association basketball, enhanced by the televised triumphs of America's "Dream Team" in the 1992 Olympics, attracted nearly 300 student athletes from 59 countries to accept basketball scholarships at American universities by 1998. Conversely, the growth of international sports stimulated globalized gambling via the Internet, most notably through the World Sports Exchange on the Caribbean island of Antigua, thus making it easier for criminals to launder money through a $100 billion gambling industry. "It's the wild, wild West out there on the Internet," a State Department official acknowledged.[216]

As the millennium approached, the United States not only faced a global agenda of unusual complexity; it also had to deal with profound domestic problems. Americans ballyhooed victory in the Cold War and the triumph of capitalism. "So then why doesn't it feel better?" asked one journalist.[217] The Paris-based Organization for Economic Cooperation and Development reported in late 1998 that the United States trailed twenty-two other leading industrialized nations in high-school graduation rates. Even with a revived economy and balanced budget by 1999, America's increasing divisions between rich and poor, skilled and unskilled, suggested that "a nation prey to drugs, guns, and violence . . . , torn by racial tension, and riven by insecurity," might eventually prove to be "a weak player on the world stage."[218] Whereas Bush had not, President Clinton acknowledged the point: "The currency of national strength in this new era will be denominated not only in ships and tanks and planes, but in diplomas and patents and paychecks."[219]

Despite the end of the Cold War, new arguments came from Clinton officials and others for old hegemonic policies, a major global if not interventionist role for the United States, and continued high-profile military readiness. First, it was argued, the disintegration of the Soviet Union had not reduced the level of international threat. The National Security Agency, which eavesdrops on potential enemies, laid off Russian speakers to hire specialists in Swahili and Farsi. Second, the end of Soviet-American bipolarity led to greater complexity and instability. Rather than "the lone global policeman," suggested one sympathetic analyst, "the United States can frequently serve as sheriff of the posse, leading shifting coalitions of friends and allies to address shared security concerns."[220] Third, only the United States had the power to fashion global solutions. Fourth, the United States held a unique moral responsibility to uphold humanitarian ideals and serve human rights.

Fifth, the United States could not pass up the opportunity to promote free-market capitalism in the wake of communism's demise. Sixth, because the U.S. economy intermeshed with the world economy, "we'll need to control the seas regardless of what happens in Moscow," as Secretary of Defense Richard Cheney once put it.[221]

Others made a seventh point about domestic economic imperatives. In 1992, for example, Representative Sam Gedjenson of Connecticut, one of the most liberal Democrats in Congress, fought to rescue the multibillion-dollar Seawolf submarine project after the Bush administration had cut it from the Pentagon budget. Why? Because the nuclear submarines were constructed at the Electric Boat shipyards in Groton, part of Gedjenson's home district, where cutbacks in defense spending meant high unemployment rates. Some forty-four states benefited from subcontracts under Seawolf. In short, even without a Soviet enemy, the U.S. defense budget remained on "Cold War autopilot" ($270 billion in 1999).[222]

Indeed, after the Gulf War the U.S. military devised new weapons and strategies for use against "rogue" states and terrorists.[223] The air force abandoned strategic nuclear bombing in favor of "stealth" aircraft that could deliver "smart" bombs and missiles without alerting enemy radar. The navy reluctantly planned new generations of cruise-missile ships to replace the aging supercarriers whose aviators were vulnerable to capture and torture by foes who knew how to manipulate the global media. The army forced itself to stress hand-to-hand combat by small units of "Rangers" at some cost to the historically preferred large-scale battles of maneuver by divisions and corps. Most important, the marine corps rose to a new level of parity with the other services as the arm that could most readily attack from the sea with ship-based helicopters, close air-support jets, tanks, and troops. Dubbed "Tomahawk Diplomacy" after the American cruise missile of choice, the new strategy smacked of nineteenth-century British and U.S. "gunboat diplomacy"—the arbitrary application of military and naval force against less "civilized" peoples to teach them proper behavior.[224] Given the uncertain results of this new strategy (evidenced by Saddam Hussein's continuing defiance), the perils of peacekeeping in Bosnia and elsewhere, and expansive post–Cold War commitments to NATO, Japan, and South Korea, the Pentagon tried to prepare for what George F. Kennan called the "bewilderments" of the new millennium.[225]

"Great tests" existed everywhere, Czech Republic president Václav Havel reminded Americans, because "everything is interrelated." Americans should know, he wrote, that "the future of the United States or the European Union is being decided in suffering Sarajevo or Mostar, in the plundered Brazilian rain forests, in the wretched poverty of Bangladesh or Somalia." When he implored Americans to exercise "global responsibility," they debated his meaning and his advice—much as they had done with other prescriptions throughout their history.[226]

FURTHER READING FOR THE PERIOD SINCE 1989

Some works listed in Chapter 11 also cover topics in this period.

Studies that emphasize the Bush-Clinton years and characteristics of the post–Cold War world include William C. Berman, *America's Right Turn* (1994); Michael Beschloss and Strobe Talbott, *At the Highest Levels* (1993); Colin Campbell and Bert A. Rockman, *The Bush Presidency* (1991); James Chace, *The Consequences of the Peace* (1992); Michael Cox, *U.S. Foreign Policy After the Cold War* (1995); James E. Cronin, *The World the Cold War Made* (1996); Michael Dobbs, *Madeleine Albright* (1999); H. Richard Frimen, *NarcoDiplomacy* (1996); Raymond Garthoff, *The Great Transition* (1994); William Greider, *Fortress America* (1998); William G. Hyland, *Clinton's World* (1999); Ronald H. Hinckley, *People, Polls, and Policymakers* (1992); Stanley Hoffmann, *World Disorders* (1999); Robert L. Hutchings, ed., *At the End of the American Century* (1998); Robert J. Lieber, ed., *Eagle Adrift* (1997); Michael Mandelbaum, *The Dawn of Peace in Europe* (1997); Richard A. Melanson, *Reconstructing Consensus* (1991); C. Richard Nelson and Kenneth Weisbrode, eds., *Reversing Relations with Former Adversaries* (1998); Kenneth A. Oye et al., eds., *Eagle in a New World* (1992); Herbert S. Parmet, *George Bush* (1998); Randall B. Ripley and James M. Lindsay, eds., *U.S. Foreign Policy After the Cold War* (1997); John G. Ruggie, *Winning the Peace* (1996); James M. Scott, *After the End* (1999); Paul B. Stares, *Global Habit* (1996) (drugs); Ronald Steel, *Temptations of a Superpower* (1995); Jessica Stern, *The Ultimate Terrorists* (1999); Robert W. Tucker and David C. Henrickson, *The Imperial Temptation* (1992); and Stephen R. Weissman, *A Culture of Deference* (1995) (Congress).

For the dramatic changes in the Soviet Union and Eastern Europe, for why the Cold War ended, and for the consequences of these changes for U.S. foreign relations, see Timothy Garton Ash, *The Uses of Adversity* (1989) and *The Magic Lantern* (1990); David Armstrong and Erik Goldstein, eds., *The End of the Cold War* (1990); Anders Åslund, *Gorbachev's Struggle for Economic Reform* (1989); Archie Brown, *The Gorbachev Factor* (1996); J. F. Brown, *Surge to Freedom* (1991); Dusko Doder and Louise Branson, *Gorbachev* (1990); John Lewis Gaddis, *The United States and the End of the Cold War* (1992); Matthew Evangelista, *Unarmed Forces* (1999); Michael Hogan, ed., *The End of the Cold War* (1992); Geoffrey Hosking, *The Awakening of the Soviet Union* (1990); Jerry F. Hough, *Democratization and Revolution in the U.S.S.R., 1985–1991* (1997); Robert G. Kaiser, *Why Gorbachev Happened* (1991); William W. Kaufmann, *Glasnost, Perestroika, and U.S. Defense Spending* (1990); Charles W. Kegley, Jr., ed., *The Long Postwar Peace* (1991); Richard Lebow and Janice Gross Stein, *We All Lost the Cold War* (1993); Allen Lynch, *The Cold War Is Over—Again* (1992); Michael Mandelbaum, ed., *Central Asia and the World* (1994) (former Soviet republics); Michael MccGwire, *Perestroika and Soviet National Security* (1991); Thomas G. Paterson, *On Every Front* (1992); David Remnick, *Lenin's Tomb: The Last Days of the Soviet Empire* (1993); and Nicholas X. Rizopoulos, ed., *Sea-Changes* (1990).

For Germany and reunification, see Timothy Garton Ash, *In Europe's Name* (1993); Dan Diner, *German Anti-Americanism* (1995); Michael A. Freney and Rebecca S. Hartley, *United Germany and the United States* (1991); Charles S. Maier, *Dissolution* (1997) (East Germany); Stephen F. Szabo, *The Diplomacy of German Unification* (1992); Gregory F. Treverton, *America, Germany, and the Future of Europe* (1992); and Peter Wyden, *The Wall* (1989).

For the wars in the former Yugoslavia and the international response, see Michael E. Brown, ed., *The International Dimensions of Internal Conflict* (1996); Donald C. F. Daniel et al., *Coercive Inducement and the Containment of International Crises* (1999); James Gow, *The Triumph of the Lack of Will* (1997); James Mayall, ed., *The New Interventionism* (1996); and Susan L. Woodward, *Balkan Tragedy* (1995).

For the thesis that the United States has suffered decline, see Michael A. Bernstein and David E. Adler, eds., *Understanding American Economic Decline* (1994); David P. Calleo, *Beyond American Hegemony* (1987); Jim Hanson, *The Decline of the American Empire* (1993); Paul Kennedy, *The Rise and Fall of the Great Powers* (1987); Thomas J. McCormick, *America's Half-Century* (1995); Walter Russel Mead, *Mortal Splendor* (1987); and Michael E. Porter, *The Competitive Advantage of Nations* (1990). Critics of the declinist thesis are Henry Nau, *The Myth of America's Decline* (1990); Joseph S. Nye, Jr., *Bound to Lead* (1990); and Richard Rosecrance, *America's Economic Resurgence* (1990).

The spread of nuclear weapons and efforts at nonproliferation are explored in Ronald J. Bee, *Nuclear Proliferation* (1995); William E. Burrows and Robert Windrem, *Critical Mass* (1994); Stephen I. Schwartz, ed., *Atomic Audit* (1998); Leon V. Sigal, *Disarming Strangers* (1998) (North Korea); and Raju Thomas, *The Nuclear Nonproliferation Regime* (1997).

International economic issues are discussed in Richard J. Barnet and John Cavanagh, *Global Dreams: Imperial Corporations and the New World Order* (1994) ("imperial corporations"); C. Fred Bergsten, *Dilemmas of the Dollar* (1996); Barry Eichengreen and Peter H. Lindert, eds., *The International Debt Crisis in Historical Perspective* (1990); Edward M. Graham and Paul Klugman, *Foreign Direct Investment in the United States* (1989);

Otis L. Graham, *Losing Time: The Industrial Policy Debate* (1992); George W. Grayson, *The North American Free Trade Agreement* (1995); Ricardo S. Grinspun and Maxwell A. Cameron, eds., *The Political Economy of North American Free Trade* (1993); Gary G. Hufbauer and Jeffrey J. Schott, *NAFTA* (1993); Patrick Low, *Trading Free* (1993); William A. Orme, Jr., *Understanding NAFTA* (1996); Louis W. Pauly, *Who Elected the Bankers?* (1997); Stephen J. Randall and Herman W. Konrad, eds., *NAFTA in Transition* (1995); Robert Solomon, *Money on the Move: The Revolution in International Finance Since 1980* (1999); Wayne Sandholtz et al., *The Highest Stakes* (1993); and James L. Watson, ed., *Golden Arches East: McDonald's in East Asia* (1998).

Environmental issues are explored in Richard E. Benedick, *Ozone Diplomacy* (1998); David E. Fisher, *Fire and Ice* (1990); Laurie Garrett, *Microbes Versus Mankind: The Coming Plague* (1997); Thomas F. Homer-Dixon, *Environmental Scarcity and Global Security* (1993); Alexander King and Bertrand Schneider, *The First Global Revolution* (1991); Paul Klugman, *The Age of Diminished Expectations* (1990); Jim MacNeill et al., *Beyond Interdependence* (1991); Jessica T. Mathews, *Preserving the Global Environment* (1990); George D. Moffett, *Global Population Growth* (1994); World Resources Institute, *Environmental Almanac* (1991); and Donald Worster, ed., *The Ends of the Earth* (1989).

For refugees and relief and immigration policy, see Frank B. Bean et al., *At the Crossroads* (1998) (Mexico); John F. Hutchinson, *Champions of Charity* (1996) (Red Cross); Gil Loescher, *Beyond Charity* (1993); Michael S. Teitelbaum and Myron Weiner, eds., *Threatened Peoples, Threatened Borders* (1995); and Reed Ueda, *Postwar Immigrant America* (1994).

For cultural relations, communications, and globalization see Thomas L. Friedman, *The Lexus and the Olive Tree* (1999); Richard F. Kuisel, *Seducing the French: The Dilemma of Americanization* (1993); Frank Ninkovich, *U.S. Information Policy and Cultural Diplomacy* (1996); and Donald Wilhelm, *Global Communications and Political Power* (1990).

For Japan, China, and Asia, see Chu-yuan Cheng, *Behind the Tiananmen Massacre* (1990); Stephen D. Cohen, *Cowboys and Samurai* (1991); Bruce Cumings, *Divided Korea* (1995); Craig C. Garby and Mary Brown Bullock, eds., *Japan* (1994); John Gittings, *China Changes Face* (1990); Harry Harding, *A Fragile Relationship* (1992) (China); Sheila K. Johnson, *The Japanese Through American Eyes* (1990); Paul Klugman, ed., *Trade with Japan* (1992); Walter LaFeber, *The Clash* (1997) (Japan); Edward J. Lincoln, *Japan's Unequal Trade* (1990); Robert S. McMahon, *The Limits of Empire* (1999) (Southeast Asia); Kenneth Pyle, *The Japanese Question* (1992); Michael Schaller, *Altered States* (1997) (Japan); Patrick Smith, *Japan* (1997); Jonathan Spence, *The Search for Modern China* (1990); and Lester Thurow, *Head to Head* (1992).

For Africa, including intervention in Somalia, see the Brown, Daniel, and Mayall books cited above, and Michael Clough, *Free at Last?* (1992); John L. Hirsch and Robert B. Oakley, *Somalia and Operation Restore Hope* (1995); Heidi Holland, *The Struggle* (1990) (ANC in South Africa); Jeffrey A. Lefebvre, *Arms for the Horn* (1991) (Ethiopia and Somalia); Fatima Meer, *Higher Than Hope* (1990) (Mandela); Robert K. Massie, *Loosing the Bonds* (1998) (South Africa); Larry Minear and Thomas G. Weiss, *Humanitarian Politics* (1995); Peter J. Schraeder, *United States Foreign Policy Toward Africa* (1994); and Jonathan Stevenson, *Losing Mogadishu* (1995).

The Palestinian question, Israel, and the Middle East are discussed in Deborah J. Gerner, *One Land, Two Peoples* (1990); F. Robert Hunter, *The Palestinian Uprising* (1991); Burton I. Kaufman, *The Arab Middle East and the United States* (1996); Louis Kriesberg, *International Conflict Resolution* (1992); David McDowall, *Palestine and Israel* (1990); William B. Quandt, *Peace Process* (1993) and *The United States and Egypt* (1990); Yezid Sayigh, *Armed Struggle and the Search for State* (1997); David Schoenbaum, *The United States and the State of Israel* (1993); and Daniel Yergin, *The Prize* (1991).

Iraqi-U.S. relations and the Persian Gulf War and its impact are the subject of Deborah Amos, *Lines in the Sand* (1992); Rick Atkinson, *Crusade* (1993); Lawrence Freedman and Efraim Karsh, *The Gulf Conflict* (1993); Stephen R. Graubard, *Mr. Bush's War* (1992); Avigdor Haselkorn, *The Continuing Storm: Iraq, Poisonous Weapons, and Deterrence* (1999); Efraim Karsh and Inari Rautsi, *Saddam Hussein* (1991); John R. MacArthur, *Second Front* (1992) (censorship); Ken Matthews, *The Gulf Conflict and International Relations* (1993); Judith Miller and Laurie Mylroie, *Saddam Hussein* (1990); John Mueller, *Policy and Opinion in the Gulf War* (1994); Joseph S. Nye, Jr., and Roger K. Smith, eds., *After the Storm* (1992); Michael A. Palmer, *Guardians of the Gulf* (1992); Jean Edward Smith, *George Bush's War* (1992); Philip M. Taylor, *War and the Media* (1992); and Kenneth R. Timmerman, *The Death Lobby: How the West Armed Iraq* (1991).

For U.S. relations with Latin America, see Jan S. Adams, *A Foreign Policy in Transition* (1992) (Central America); Sergio Aguayo, *Myths and (Mis)Perceptions* (1998) (Mexico); John Booth and Thomas Walker, *Understanding Latin America* (1993); Timothy J. Dunn, *The Militarization of the U.S.-Mexico Border* (1996); Guy Gugliotta and Jeff Leen, *Kings of Cocaine* (1989); Susanne Jonas, *The Battle for Guatemala* (1991); Walter LaFeber, *Inevitable Revolutions* (1993); Abraham F. Lowenthal, *Partners in Conflict* (1990); Abraham F. Lowenthal and Katrina Burgess, eds., *The California-Mexico Connection* (1993); Donald J. Mabry, ed., *The Latin American Narcotics Trade and U.S. National Security* (1989); Christopher Mitchell, ed., *Western Hemisphere Immigration and United States Foreign Policy* (1992); Robert A. Pastor, *Whirlpool* (1992) and *Integration with Mexico* (1993); Brenda Gayle Plummer, *Haiti and the United States* (1992); Susan K. Purcell and Robert M. Immerman, ed., *Japan and Latin America in the New Global Order* (1992); W. Dirk Raat, *Mexico and the United States* (1996); Lars Schoultz, *Beneath the United States* (1998); Peter D. Scott and Jonathan Marshall, *Cocaine Politics: Drugs, Arms, and the CIA in Central America* (1991); Peter H. Smith, *Talons of the Eagle* (1996); Howard J. Wiarda, *American Foreign Policy Toward Latin America in the 80s and 90s* (1992); and Sidney Weintraub et al., eds., *U.S.-Mexican Industrial Integration* (1991).

For Panama and the war against Noriega, consult Kevin Buckley, *Panama* (1991); John Dinges, *Our Man in Panama* (1990); Frederick Kempe, *Divorcing the Dictator* (1990); R. M. Koster and Guillermo Sanchez, *In The Time of the Tyrants* (1990); Walter LaFeber, *The Panana Canal* (1989); and Margaret E. Scranton, *The Noriega Years* (1991).

See also the General Bibliography and the following notes.

For a comprehensive survey of foreign-relations topics, see the articles in the four-volume *Encyclopedia of U.S. Foreign Relations* (1997), edited by Bruce W. Jentleson and Thomas G. Paterson.

NOTES TO CHAPTER 12

1. *Newsweek, CXIV* (November 20, 1989), 28.
2. Timothy Garton Ash, "The German Revolution," *New York Review of Books,* December 21, 1989, p. 14.
3. G. Jonathan Greenwald, *Berlin Witness* (University Park: Penn State University Press, 1993), p. 270.
4. Ash, "German Revolution," p. 14.
5. Gaby Greenwald quoted in Greenwald, *Berlin,* p. 264.
6. Quoted in George Bush and Brent Scowcroft, *A World Transformed* (New York: Knopf, 1998), p. 151.
7. Quoted in *Time, CXXXIV* (November 20, 1989), 29.
8. *Ibid.,* p. 25.
9. Quoted in *Washington Post National Weekly Edition,* January 1–7, 1990.
10. Quoted in Richard Ned Lebow and Janice Gross Stein, "Reagan and the Russians," *The Atlantic Monthly, CCLXXIII* (February 1994), 36.
11. Quoted in Jim Hoagland, "Europe's Destiny," *Foreign Affairs: America and the World,* 1989/90, *LXIX* (1990), 38.
12. Quoted in *Time, CXXXV* (January 1, 1990), 53.
13. Robert G. Kaiser, "The End of the Soviet Empire," *Washington Post National Weekly Edition,* January 1–7, 1990.
14. Quoted in Mikhail Gorbachev, *Memoirs* (New York: Doubleday, 1996), p. 525.
15. Quoted in Michael Beschloss and Strobe Talbott, *At the Highest Levels* (Boston: Little, Brown, 1993), p. 134.
16. Vyacheslav Dashichev quoted in Archie Brown, *The Gorbachev Factor* (New York: Oxford University Press, 1996), p. 245.
17. Richard J. Barnet, "Reflections: After the Cold War," *The New Yorker, LXV* (January 1, 1990), 66.
18. Quoted in Elizabeth Drew, "Letter from Washington," *ibid., LXV* (November 22, 1989), 122.
19. Quoted in *New York Times,* April 3, 1989.
20. Jack F. Matlock, Jr., *Autopsy of an Empire* (New York: Random House, 1995), p. 91.
21. Quoted in Editors of The New Republic, *Bushisms* (New York: Workman, 1992), p. 58.
22. Quoted in Beschloss and Talbott, *Highest,* p. 205.
23. Quoted in *Washington Post National Weekly Edition,* October 23–29, 1989.
24. Quoted in *Time, CXXXII* (August 1, 1988), 21.
25. Margaret Thatcher, *The Downing Street Years* (New York: Harper-Collins, 1993), p. 783.
26. Quoted in Beschloss and Talbott, *Highest,* p. 41.
27. Senior official quoted in Elizabeth Drew, *On the Edge* (New York: Simon & Schuster, 1994), p. 138.
28. Fred I. Greenstein, "The Presidential Leadership Style of Bill Clinton," *Political Science Quarterly, CVIII* (Winter 1993–1994), 593–594.
29. Brian Urquhart in "The Talk of the Town," *The New Yorker, LXXII* (December 2, 1996), 45.
30. Quoted in *Washington Post National Weekly Edition,* July 14, 1997.
31. Quoted in *New York Times,* December 23, 1992.
32. Quoted in *Washington Post National Weekly Edition,* January 18–24, 1993.
33. Mark Danner, "Marooned in the Cold War," *World Policy Journal, XIV* (Fall 1997), 11.
34. Four-star general quoted in Seymour Hersh, "The Missiles of August," *The New Yorker, LXXIV* (October 12, 1998), 37.

35. Quoted in *Time, CXL* (November 30, 1992), 36.

36. David Calleo, "A New Era of Overstretch?" *World Policy Journal, XV* (Spring 1998), 13.

37. Quoted in *Washington Post National Weekly Edition,* July 4, 1997.

38. Robert A. Pastor, "The Clinton Administration and the Americas," *Journal of Interamerican Studies & World Affairs, XXXVIII* (Winter 1996), 99.

39. Martin Walker, "The Clinton Doctrine," *The New Yorker, LXXII* (October 7, 1996), 7.

40. Quoted in *New York Times,* September 28, 1993.

41. Quoted in *Hartford Courant,* December 16, 1993.

42. Douglas Brinkley, "Democratic Enlargement: The Clinton Doctrine," *Foreign Policy,* no. 106 (Spring 1997), 125.

43. *Ibid.*

44. Robert Kagan, "The Benevolent Empire," *Foreign Policy,* no. 111 (Summer 1998), 25.

45. Quoted in John T. Rourke, *International Politics on the World Stage* (New York: Dushkin/McGraw-Hill, 1999; 7th ed.), p. 476.

46. Quoted in John Cassidy, "The Triumphalist," *The New Yorker, LXXIV* (July 6, 1998), 57.

47. Fred I. Greenstein, "Ronald Reagan, Mikhail Gorbachev, and the End of the Cold War," in William C. Wohlforth, ed., *Witnesses to the End of the Cold War* (Baltimore: Johns Hopkins University Press, 1996), p. 216.

48. Arnold L. Horelick, "U.S.–Soviet Relations," *Foreign Affairs: America and the World, 1989/90, LXIX,* (1990), 54–55.

49. Quoted in *New York Times,* April 9, 1989.

50. Quoted in Matlock, *Autopsy,* p. 198.

51. James A. Baker III, "Points of Mutual Advantage," speech, October 16, 1989, U.S. Department of State.

52. Quoted in *New York Times,* August 5, 1990.

53. Quoted in James A. Baker III, *The Politics of Diplomacy* (New York: G. P. Putnam's Sons, 1995), p. 310.

54. Gorbachev quoted in Raymond Garthoff, *The Great Transition* (Washington, D.C.: Brookings, 1994), p. 491.

55. Diary entry of March 17, 1991, in Bush and Scowcroft, *World Transformed,* p. 500.

56. Quoted in Charles William Maynes, "A Workable Clinton Doctrine," *Foreign Policy,* no. 93 (Winter 1993/1994), 3; Paul D. Wolfowitz, "Clinton's First Year," *Foreign Affairs, LXXIII* (January/February 1994), 41.

57. Quoted in Monica Crowley, *Nixon in Winter* (New York: Random House, 1998), p. 146.

58. Stephen Handelman, *Comrade Criminal* (New Haven: Yale University Press, 1994); Jonathan Haslam, "Russia's Seat at the Table," *International Affairs, LXXIV* (January 1998), 125.

59. Quoted in Raymond Garthoff, "The United States and the New Russia," *Current History, XCVI* (October 1997), 307.

60. Clifford Gaddy quoted in *Time, CLII* (September 7, 1998), 33.

61. Quoted in *Newsweek, CXXXII* (December 7, 1998), 40.

62. Jim Hoagland, "Europe's Destiny," *America and the World, 1989/90,* p. 41.

63. Bush aide quoted in Frank Costigliola, "An 'Arm Around the Shoulder': The United States, NATO, and German Unification, 1989–1990," *Contemporary European History, III* (March 1994), 88.

64. Richard Helms in *Hartford Courant,* March 4, 1990.

65. Quoted in Elizabeth Drew, "Letter from Washington," *The New Yorker, LXV* (March 19, 1990), 104.

66. Brent Scowcroft quoted in James Chace, "New World Disorder," *New York Review of Books,* December 17, 1998, p. 60.

67. Stanley Hoffmann, "Bush Abroad," *New York Review of Books,* November 5, 1992, p. 54.

68. Thatcher, *Downing Street,* p. 797.

69. John S. Duffield, *World Power Forsaken: German Security After Unification* (Stanford: Stanford University Press, 1998), p. viii.

70. Stephen R. Graubard, "A Common Discontent," *Foreign Affairs, LXXII* (Summer 1993), 5.

71. Hans-Dietrich Gentscher, *Rebuilding a House Divided* (New York: Broadway, 1998), p. 361.

72. Quoted in Rourke, *International Politics,* p. 282.

73. Lewis J. Edinger and Brigitte L. Nacos, "From Bonn to the Berlin Republic," *Political Science Quarterly, CXIII* (Summer 1998), 189.

74. Timothy Garton Ash, "Europe's Endangered Liberal Order," *Foreign Affairs, LXXVII* (March/April 1998), 61.

75. Quoted in James Goldgeier, "NATO Expansion: Anatomy of a Decision," *The Washington Quarterly, XXI* (Winter 1998), 94.

76. *Ibid.,* p. 85.

77. U.S. diplomat quoted in Haslam, "Russia's Seat," p. 124.

78. William Perry quoted in Victor Israelyan, "Don't Tease a Wounded Bear," *The Washington Quarterly, XXI* (Winter 1998), 53; Kennan quoted in *New York Times,* February 5, 1997.

79. Baker, *Politics of Diplomacy,* p. 483.

80. Brent Scowcroft quoting Baker in Michael Kelly, "Surrender and Blame," *The New Yorker, LXX* (December 19, 1994), 45.

81. Andrew Bell Fialkoff, "A Brief History of Ethnic Cleansing," *Foreign Affairs, LXXII* (Summer 1993), 120.

82. Warren Christopher quoted in Richard J. Barnet, "Groping for a Security Blanket," *The Progressive, LVIII* (January 1994), 21.

83. Quoted in John Newhouse, "No Exit, No Entrance," *The New Yorker, LXIX* (June 28, 1993), 46.

84. Colin L. Powell, *My American Journey* (New York: Random House, 1995), pp. 576–577.

85. Richard Nixon quoted in Monica Crowley, "Nixon Unplugged," *The New Yorker, LXXII* (July 29, 1996), 50.

86. Quoted in Drew, *On the Edge,* p. 159.

87. Richard Holbrooke, "Why We Are in Bosnia, "*The New Yorker, LXXIV* (May 18, 1998), 43.

88. Robert K. Massie, *Loosing the Bonds* (New York: Doubleday, 1998), p. 689.

89. Princeton Lyman, "South Africa's Promise," *Foreign Policy,* no. 102 (Spring 1996), 4.

90. Quoted in *Washington Post National Weekly Edition,* December 14–20, 1992.

91. T. Frank Crigler quoted *ibid.,* October 26–November 1, 1993.

92. Quoted in *New York Times,* May 6, 1993.

93. Quoted in *Washington Post National Weekly Edition,* October 18–24, 1993.

94. General Thomas Montgomery quoted in Danial P. Bolger, *Savage Peace* (Novato, Calif.: Presidio Press, 1995), p. 314.

95. Quoted in *Time, CXLII,* (October 18, 1993), 38.

96. Quoted in *New York Times,* October 8, 1993.

97. Philip Gourevitch, "After the Genocide," *The New Yorker, LXXI* (December 18, 1995), 78.

98. Quoted in David F. Gordon and Howard Wolpe, "The Other Africa," *World Policy Journal, XV* (Spring 1998), 52.

99. Quoted in *Hartford Courant,* March 26, 1998.

100. Quoted in Frank Smyth, "A New Game: The Clinton Administration on Africa," *World Policy Journal, XV* (Summer 1998), 85.

101. State Department official quoted *ibid.,* 90.

102. Intelligence official quoted in Hersh, "Missiles," 37; *Washington Post National Weekly Edition,* August 24, 1998.

103. Quoted in Gordon and Wolpe, "Other Africa," 58.

104. Quoted in *Washington Post National Weekly Edition,* December 21–28, 1998.

105. Quoted in *New York Times*, December 12, 1994.

106. Cheryl Payer quoted in *Great Decisions 1989* (New York: Foreign Policy Association, 1989), p. 30.

107. Harlan Cleveland, *Birth of a New World* (San Francisco: Jossey-Bass, 1993), p. 172.

108. Inter-American Dialogue, *Convergence and Community* (Washington, D.C.: Aspen Institute, 1992), p. 9.

109. Pastor, "Clinton Administration," p. 101.

110. Quoted in M. D. Baer, "Misreading Mexico," *Foreign Policy*, no. 108 (Fall 1997), 144.

111. Tom Miller, *On the Border* (1981), quoted in W. Dirk Raat, *Mexico and the United States* (Athens: University of Georgia Press, 1992), p. 173.

112. Quoted in Sewall H. Menzel, *Cocaine Quagmire* (New York: University Press of America, 1997), p. 153.

113. Quoted in "The Talk of the Town," *The New Yorker*, LXV (January 1, 1990), 21.

114. Patrick Lloyd Hatcher, "The Unwinnable War on the Drug Trade," *Orbis*, XLI (Fall 1997), 659.

115. Denzil Douglas quoted in George Getta and Ellen James Martin, "From Communism to Cocaine," *Foreign Service Journal*, LXXVII (October 1998), 20.

116. Quoted in William O. Walker III, "Drug Control and National Security," *Diplomatic History*, XII (Spring 1988), 188.

117. Eva Bertram and Kenneth Sharpe, "The Unwinnable Drug War," *World Policy Journal*, XIII (Winter 1996/1997), 45.

118. Quoted in *Washington Post National Weekly Edition*, January 5, 1998.

119. Mexican attorney general Jorge Madrazo quoted *ibid.*, November 2, 1998.

120. Sol M. Linowitz, "Latin America," *Foreign Affairs*, LXVII (Winter 1988/1989), 56.

121. David S. Broder in *Washington Post National Weekly Edition*, September 18–24, 1989.

122. *Bushisms*, p. 65.

123. Quoted in Lars Schoultz, *Beneath the United States* (Cambridge: Harvard University Press, 1998), p. 371.

124. Quoted in *Washington Post National Weekly Edition*, January 8–14 1990.

125. Public Affairs After Action Report, December 20, 1989–January 31, 1990, National Security Archive, Washington, D.C.

126. Powell, *American Journey*, p. 434.

127. Quoted in *Time*, CXXXV (January 29, 1990), 28.

128. Quoted in Morris Morley and Chris McGillion, "The Clinton Administration and Haiti," *Political Science Quarterly*, CXII (Fall 1997), 370, 371.

129. Quoted in Tracy Kidder, "The Siege of Mirebalais," *The New Yorker*, LXXI (April 17, 1995), 84.

130. Quoted *ibid.*, p. 85.

131. Jorge Domínguez, "U.S.- Cuban Relations: From the Cold War to the Colder War," *Journal of Interamerican Studies and World Affairs*, XXXIX (Fall 1997), 54.

132. Quoted in William M. LeoGrande, "From Havana to Miami," *ibid.*, XL (Spring 1998), 77.

133. Quoted in Ann Blackman, *Seasons of Her Life* (New York: Charles Scribner's Sons, 1998), p. 246.

134. Quoted in Wayne S. Smith, "Our Dysfunctional Cuban Embargo," *Orbis*, XLII (Fall 1998), 537.

135. Elizardo Sanchez quoted *ibid.*, p. 542.

136. Quoted in Rourke, *International Politics*, p. 172.

137. Quoted in *Washington Post National Weekly Edition*, November 30, 1998.

138. Domínguez, "Colder War," p. 49.

139. Quoted in Deborah Amos, *Lines in the Sand* (New York: Simon & Schuster, 1992), p. 82.

140. Quoted in Thomas G. Paterson, *On Every Front* (New York: Norton, 1992; rev. ed.), p. 226.

141. Quoted in Michael Howard, "The Prudence Thing," *Foreign Affairs*, LXXVII (November/December 1998), 131.

142. Quoted in Lawrence Freedman and Efraim Karsh, *The Gulf Conflict* (Princeton: Princeton University Press, 1993), p. 53.

143. Quoted in John T. Rourke, *Presidential Wars and American Democracy* (Washington, D.C.: Paragon, 1993), p. 14.

144. Quoted in Pierre Salinger and Eric Laurent, *Secret Dossier* (New York: Penguin, 1991), p. 110.

145. Quoted in *Hartford Courant*, January 13, 1991.

146. Quoted in Freedman and Karsh, *Gulf*, p. 293.

147. Quoted in Rourke, *Presidential Wars*, p. 59.

148. H. W. Brands, *What America Does for the World* (New York: Cambridge University Press, 1998), p. 306.

149. *Weekly Compilation of Presidential Documents*, XXVII (March 1, 1991), 233.

150. Quoted in Robert W. Tucker and David C. Hendrickson, *The Imperial Temptation* (New York: Council on Foreign Relations Press, 1992), p. 76.

151. Powell, *American Journey*, p. 531; Trainor quoted in Kenneth J. Hagan "On (the Gulf) War," *Naval History*, XIII (April 1999), 20.

152. Quoted in Rick Atkinson, *Crusade*, (Boston: Houghton Mifflin, 1993), p. 491.

153. Quoted in Michael Sterner, "Closing the Gate: The Persian Gulf War Revisited," *Current History*, XCVI (January 1997), 13.

154. Quoted in Atkinson, *Crusade*, p. 496.

155. Quoted in Peter J. Boyle, "Scott Ritter's Private War," *The New Yorker*, LXXIV (November 9, 1998), 66.

156. Quoted in *Washington Post National Weekly Edition*, November 28, 1998.

157. Quoted in *New York Times*, December 17, 1998.

158. William Cohen quoted in *Newsweek*, CXXXII (December 28, 1998), 48.

159. Blair quoted *ibid.*, p. 48; Hamad Bayati quoted in *Time*, CLII (December 28, 1998), 73.

160. James Baker, "Principles and Pragmatism," May 22, 1989, Department of State Current Policy no. 1176.

161. Quoted in Yezid Sayigh, *Armed Struggle and the Search for State* (New York: Oxford University Press, 1997), p. 654.

162. David Remnick, "The Outsider," *The New Yorker*, LXXIV (May 25, 1998), 95.

163. Baker, *Politics of Diplomacy*, p. 103.

164. Winston Lord, "China and America," *Foreign Affairs*, LXVIII (Fall 1989), 3.

165. Quoted in Roderick MacFarquhar, "The End of the Chinese Revolution," *New York Review of Books*, July 20, 1989, p. 8.

166. John K. Fairbank, "Why China's Rulers Fear Democracy," *New York Review of Books*, September 28, 1989, p. 33.

167. Entry of June 20, 1989, Bush and Scowcroft, *World Transformed*, p. 102.

168. Lawrence Eagleburger quoted in Baker, *Politics of Diplomacy*, p. 110.

169. Yoichi Funabashi, "The Asianization of Asia," *Foreign Affairs*, LXXII (November/December 1993), 85.

170. Quoted in Jonathan D. Pollock, "The United States and Asia in 1996," *Asian Survey*, XXXVII (January 1997), 97.

171. U.S. official quoting Chinese diplomats in *Washington Post National Weekly Edition*, June 29, 1998.

172. William Perry quoted *ibid.*

173. Quoted in Lucien W. Pye, "The United States and Asia in 1997," *Asian Survey, XXXVII* (January 1998), 99; quoted in Yoichi Funabashi, "Tokyo's Depression Diplomacy," *Foreign Affairs, LXXVII* (November/December 1998), 32.

174. Quoted in Ted Galen Carpenter, "Roiling Asia," *Foreign Affairs, LXXVII* (November/December 1998), 4.

175. Richard Haass, "Fatal Distraction: Bill Clinton's Foreign Policy," *Foreign Policy,* no. 108 (Fall 1997), 120.

176. Quoted in Robert B. Oxnam, "Asia/Pacific Challenges," *Foreign Affairs: America and the World 1992/93, LXXII* (January 1993), 71.

177. *Washington Post National Weekly Edition,* August 8–14, 1994.

178. Quoted in *New York Times,* February 6, 1994.

179. Robert J. McMahon, *The Limits of Empire* (New York: Columbia University Press, 1999), p. 224.

180. Quoted in James Fallows, "Getting Along with Japan," *The Atlantic Monthly, CCLXIV* (December 1989), 55.

181. Quoted in Michael A. Schaller, *Altered States* (New York: Oxford University Press, 1997), p. 258.

182. Joseph Joffe quoted in John Ikenberry, ed., *American Foreign Policy* (New York: Longman, 1999), p. 600.

183. Richard Samuels quoted in *Washington Post National Weekly Edition,* April 7, 1997.

184. Quoted in Funabashi, "Depression Diplomacy," 32.

185. Chalmers Johnson quoted in *Washington Post National Weekly Edition,* August 24, 1998.

186. Bruce Cumings quoted in Benjamin Schwartz, "Why America Thinks It Has to Run the World," *The Atlantic Monthly, CCLXXVII* (June 1996), 94.

187. Quoted in Nicholas D. Kristof, "Japan's Full Story," *Foreign Affairs, LXXVI* (November/December 1997), 145.

188. Quoted in *Washington Post National Weekly Edition,* October 25–31, 1993.

189. Anthony Lake, "Confronting Backlash States," *Foreign Affairs, LXXIII* (March/April 1994), 55.

190. Richard Kerr quoted in Seymour Hersh, "On the Nuclear Edge," *The New Yorker, LXIX* (March 29, 1993), 55.

191. Quoted in Arjun Makhijani et al., "Dismantling the Bomb," in Stephen I. Schwartz, ed., *Atomic Audit* (Washington, D.C.: Brookings, 1998), p. 346.

192. Quoted in Michael Klare, *Rogue States and Nuclear Outlaws* (New York: Hill & Wang, 1995), p. 125.

193. Quoted in *Newsweek, CXXIII* (February 21, 1994), 29.

194. General Robert RisCassi quoted in Bruce Cumings, "Time to End the Korean War," *The Atlantic Monthly, CCLXXIX* (February 1997), 73.

195. Lake, "Confronting," p. 45.

196. Strobe Talbott in *Time, CXXXV* (January 1, 1990), 72.

197. Hirosha Nakajima quoted in *Hartford Courant,* August 26, 1997.

198. Jacques Diouf quoted in *Great Decisions, 1997* (New York: Foreign Policy Association, 1997), p. 59.

199. World Resources Institute, *Environmental Almanac* (Boston: Houghton Mifflin, 1992), p. 13.

200. Lester R. Brown, "The Acceleration of History," in Worldwatch Institute, *State of the World 1996* (New York: Norton, 1996), p. 4.

201. Quoted in *New York Times,* April 17, 1996.

202. Quoted in Rourke, *International Politics,* p. 47.

203. Quoted in *Time, CXXXIII* (January 2, 1989), 30.

204. James Baker, "Diplomacy for the Environment," February 26, 1990, Department of State Current Policy no. 1254.

205. Quoted in Cleveland, *Birth,* p. 46.

206. Quoted in *New York Times,* November 3, 1997.

207. Quoted in *Hartford Courant,* August 25, 1995.

208. Fauziya Kassindja quoted in Rourke, *International Politics,* p. 512.

209. Quoted in *Washington Post National Weekly Edition,* March 31, 1997.

210. Anthony Lake quoted in Brinkley, "Democratic," p. 117.

211. Quoted in Rourke, *International Politics,* p. 181.

212. Walter B. Wriston, "Bits, Bytes, and Diplomacy," *Foreign Affairs, LXXVI* (September/October 1997), 175.

213. Quoted in *Washington Post National Weekly Edition,* December 14, 1998.

214. Writson, "Bits," p. 180.

215. Strobe Talbott, "Globalization and Diplomacy," *Foreign Policy,* no. 108 (Fall 1997), 79.

216. Jonathan Winer quoted in *Sports Illustrated, LXXXVIII* (January 26, 1998), 86.

217. Maureen Dowd in *New York Times,* March 4, 1990.

218. Ronald Steel, "The Domestic Core of Foreign Policy," *The Atlantic Monthly, CCLXXV* (June 1995), 86.

219. Quoted in Jonathan Clarke, "The Conceptual Poverty of U.S. Foreign Policy," *The Atlantic Monthly, CCLXXII* (September 1993), 62.

220. Joseph S. Nye, Jr., "Future Wars," *Current* (March/April 1996), 38.

221. Quoted in *Hartford Courant,* April 5, 1990.

222. Robert Worth, "Clinton's Warriors," *World Policy Journal, XV* (Spring 1998), 47.

223. Klare, *Rogue States,* p. 1.

224. *Time, CLII* (October 19, 1998), 60.

225. George F. Kennan, "Correspondence," *World Policy Journal, XV* (Spring 1998), 107.

226. Václav Havel, "A Call for Sacrifice," *Foreign Affairs, LXIII* (March/April 1994), 7.

APPENDIX

Makers of American Foreign Relations

Presidents	Secretaries of State	Chairs of the Senate Foreign Relations Committee
George Washington (1789–1797)	Thomas Jefferson (1790–1793) Edmund Randolph (1794–1795) Timothy Pickering (1795–1797)	
John Adams (1797–1801)	Timothy Pickering (1797–1800) John Marshall (1800–1801)	
Thomas Jefferson (1801–1809)	James Madison (1801–1809)	
James Madison (1809–1817)	Robert Smith (1809–1811) James Monroe (1811–1817)	James Barbour (1816–1817)
James Monroe (1817–1825)	John Quincy Adams (1817–1825)	James Barbour (1817–1818) Nathaniel Macon (1818–1819) James Brown (1819–1820) James Barbour (1820–1821) Rufus King (1821–1822) James Barbour (1822–1825)
John Quincy Adams (1825–1829)	Henry Clay (1825–1829)	Nathaniel Macon (1825–1826) Nathan Sanford (1826–1827) Nathaniel Macon (1827–1828) Littleton W. Tazewell (1828–1829)
Andrew Jackson (1829–1837)	Martin Van Buren (1829–1831) Edward Livingston (1831–1833) Louis McLane (1833–1834) John Forsyth (1834–1837)	Littleton W. Tazewell (1829–1832) John Forsyth (1832–1833) William Wilkins (1833–1834) Henry Clay (1834–1836) James Buchanan (1836–1837)
Martin Van Buren (1837–1841)	John Forsyth (1837–1841)	James Buchanan (1837–1841)
William H. Harrison (1841)	Daniel Webster (1841)	William C. Rives (1841)
John Tyler (1841–1845)	Daniel Webster (1841–1843)	William C. Rives (1841–1842)

Makers of American Foreign Relations *(continued)*

Presidents	Secretaries of State	Chairs of the Senate Foreign Relations Committee
	Abel P. Upshur (1843–1844)	William S. Archer (1842–1845)
	John C. Calhoun (1844–1845)	
James K. Polk (1845–1849)	James Buchanan (1845–1849)	William Allen (1845–1846)
		Ambrose H. Sevier (1846–1848)
		Edward A. Hannegan (1848–1849)
		Thomas H. Benton (1849)
Zachary Taylor (1849–1850)	John M. Clayton (1849–1850)	William R. King (1849–1850)
Millard Fillmore (1850–1853)	Daniel Webster (1850–1852)	Henry S. Foote (1850–1851)
	Edward Everett (1852–1853)	James M. Mason (1851–1853)
Franklin Pierce (1853–1857)	William L. Marcy (1853–1857)	James M. Mason (1853–1857)
James Buchanan (1857–1861)	Lewis Cass (1857–1860)	James M. Mason (1857–1861)
	Jeremiah S. Black (1860–1861)	
Abraham Lincoln (1861–1865)	William H. Seward (1861–1865)	Charles Sumner (1861–1865)
Andrew Johnson (1865–1869)	William H. Seward (1865–1869)	Charles Sumner (1865–1869)
Ulysses S. Grant (1869–1877)	Elihu B. Washburne (1869)	Charles Sumner (1869–1871)
	Hamilton Fish (1869–1877)	Simon Cameron (1871–1877)
Rutherford B. Hayes (1877–1881)	William M. Evarts (1877–1881)	Hannibal Hamlin (1877–1879)
		William W. Eaton (1879–1881)
James A. Garfield (1881)	James G. Blaine (1881)	Ambrose E. Burnside (1881)
		George F. Edmunds (1881)
Chester A. Arthur (1881–1885)	Frederick T. Frelinghuysen (1881–1885)	William Windon (1881–1883)
		John F. Miller (1883–1885)
Grover Cleveland (1885–1889)	Thomas F. Bayard (1885–1889)	John F. Miller (1885–1887)
		John Sherman (1887–1889)
Benjamin Harrison (1889–1893)	James G. Blaine (1889–1892)	John Sherman (1889–1893)
	John W. Foster (1892–1893)	
Grover Cleveland (1893–1897)	Walter Q. Gresham (1893–1895)	John T. Morgan (1893–1895)
	Richard Olney (1895–1897)	John Sherman (1895–1897)
William McKinley (1897–1901)	John Sherman (1897–1898)	William P. Frye (1897)
	William R. Day (1898)	Cushman K. Davis (1897–1901)
	John Hay (1898–1901)	
Theodore Roosevelt (1901–1909)	John Hay (1901–1905)	William P. Frye (1901)
	Elihu Root (1905–1909)	Shelby M. Cullom (1901–1909)
	Robert Bacon (1909)	
William Howard Taft (1909–1913)	Philander C. Knox (1909–1913)	Shelby M. Cullom (1909–1913)

Makers of American Foreign Relations *(continued)*

Presidents	Secretaries of State	Chairs of the Senate Foreign Relations Committee
Woodrow Wilson (1913–1921)	William Jennings Bryan (1913–1915) Robert Lansing (1915–1920) Bainbridge Colby (1920–1921)	Augustus O. Bacon (1913–1915) William J. Stone (1915–1919) Henry Cabot Lodge (1919–1921)
Warren G. Harding (1921–1923)	Charles E. Hughes (1921–1923)	Henry Cabot Lodge (1921–1923)
Calvin Coolidge (1923–1929)	Charles E. Hughes (1923–1925) Frank. B. Kellogg (1925–1929)	Henry Cabot Lodge (1923–1924) William E. Borah (1925–1929)
Herbert C. Hoover (1929–1933)	Henry L. Stimson (1929–1933)	William E. Borah (1929–1933)
Franklin D. Roosevelt (1933–1945)	Cordell Hull (1933–1944) Edward R. Stettinius, Jr. (1944–1945)	Key Pittman (1933–1940) Walter F. George (1940–1941) Tom Connally (1941–1945)

Presidents	Secretaries of State	Chairs of the Senate Foreign Relations Committee	Secretaries of Defense	Assistants to the President for National Security Affairs
Harry S. Truman (1945–1953)	Edward R. Stettinius, Jr. (1945) James F. Byrnes (1945–1947) George C. Marshall (1947–1949) Dean G. Acheson (1949–1953)	Tom Connally (1945–1947) Arthur H. Vandenberg (1947–1949) Tom Connally (1949–1953)	James V. Forrestal (1947–1949) Louis A. Johnson (1949–1950) George C. Marshall (1950–1951) Robert A. Lovett (1951–1953)	
Dwight D. Eisenhower (1953–1961)	John F. Dulles (1953–1959) Christian A. Herter (1959–1961)	Alexander Wiley (1953–1955) Walter F. George (1955–1957) Theodore F. Green (1957–1959) J. William Fulbright (1959–1961)	Charles E. Wilson (1953–1957) Neil H. McElroy (1957–1959) Thomas S. Gates, Jr. (1959–1961)	Robert Cutler (1953–1955 & 1957–1958) Dillon Anderson (1955–1956) William H. Jackson (1956) Gordon Gray (1958–1961)
John F. Kennedy (1961–1963)	Dean Rusk (1961–1963)	J. William Fulbright (1961–1963)	Robert S. McNamara (1961–1963)	McGeorge Bundy (1961–1963)
Lyndon B. Johnson (1963–1969)	Dean Rusk (1963–1969)	J. William Fulbright (1963–1969)	Robert S. McNamara (1963–1968) Clark M. Clifford (1968–1969)	McGeorge Bundy (1963–1966) Walt W. Rostow (1966–1969)

Makers of American Foreign Relations *(continued)*

Presidents	Secretaries of State	Chairs of the Senate Foreign Relations Committee	Secretaries of Defense	Assistants to the President for National Security Affairs
Richard M. Nixon (1969–1974)	William P. Rogers (1969–1973) Henry A. Kissinger (1973–1974)	J. William Fulbright (1969–1974)	Melvin R. Laird (1969–1973) Elliot L. Richardson (1973) James R. Schlesinger (1973–1974)	Henry A. Kissinger (1969–1974)
Gerald R. Ford (1974–1977)	Henry A. Kissinger (1974–1977)	J. William Fulbright (1974–1975) John Sparkman (1975–1977)	James R. Schlesinger (1974–1976) Donald Rumsfeld (1976–1977)	Henry A. Kissinger (1974–1975) Brent Scowcroft (1975–1977)
James E. Carter (1977–1981)	Cyrus R. Vance (1977–1980) Edmund Muskie (1980–1981)	John Sparkman (1977–1979) Frank Church (1979–1981)	Harold Brown (1977–1981)	Zbigniew Brzezinski (1977–1981)
Ronald W. Reagan (1981–1989)	Alexander M. Haig, Jr. (1981–1982) George P. Shultz (1982–1989)	Charles Percy (1981–1985) Richard G. Lugar (1985–1987) Claiborne Pell (1987–1989)	Caspar Weinberger (1981–1987) Frank C. Carlucci (1987–1989)	Richard Allen (1981) William P. Clark, Jr. (1981–1983) Robert C. McFarlane (1983–1985) John M. Poindexter (1985–1986) Frank C. Carlucci (1986–1987) Colin L. Powell (1987–1989)
George H. W. Bush (1989–1993)	James A. Baker III (1989–1992) Lawrence Eagleburger (1992–1993)	Claiborne Pell (1989–1993)	Richard B. Cheney (1989–1993)	Brent Scowcroft (1989–1993)
William J. Clinton (1993–)	Warren M. Christopher (1993–1997) Madeleine K. Albright (1997–)	Claiborne Pell (1993–1995) Jesse Helms (1995–)	Les Aspin (1993–1994) William J. Perry (1994–1997) William S. Cohen (1997–)	Anthony Lake (1993–1996) Samuel R. Berger (1996–)

GENERAL BIBLIOGRAPHY

General Reference Works

See also "Overviews of Relations with Countries, Regions, and Other Places of the World" and "Overviews of Subjects," both below, and your library's computer-based sources. Comprehensive bibliographies also appear in the four volumes of Bruce W. Jentleson and Thomas G. Paterson, eds., *Encyclopedia of U.S. Foreign Relations* (1997).

Annual Surveys: *Facts on File* (1941–); *Human Development Report* (1990–); *Keesing's Record of World Events* (also titled *Keesing's Contemporay Archives*) (1931–); London Institute of World Affairs, *The Yearbook of World Affairs* (1947–); Alan F. Pater and Jason R. Pater, eds., *What They Said In . . . : The Yearbook of World Opinion* (1971–); *Political Handbook of the World* (1928–); *The Statesmen's Year-Book World Gazetteer* (1864–); United Nations, *Demographic Yearbook* (1948–); *The World Bank Atlas* (1967–); *World Development Report* (1978–). See also "Statistics."

Atlases and Gazetteers: Ewan W. Anderson and Don Shewan, *An Atlas of World Political Flashpoints* (1993); Andrew Boyd, *An Atlas of World Affairs* (1998); Anna Bramwall, *The Atlas of Twentieth Century History* (1989); Gerard Chaliand and Jean-Pierre Rageau, *Strategic Atlas* (1990); Rodger Doyle, *Atlas of Contemporary America* 1994); Robert Ferrell and Richard Natkiel, *Atlas of American History* (1987); *Hammond Atlas of the World* (1992); Eric Homberger, *The Penguin Historical Atlas of North America* (1995); Michael Kidron and Ronald Segal, *The State of the World Atlas* (1995); Catherine Mattson and Mark T. Mattson, *Contemporary Atlas of the United States* (1998); David Munro, ed., *Chambers World Gazetteer* (1988); *National Geographic Atlas of the World* (1992); Richard Natkiel et al., eds., *Atlas of the Twentieth Century* (1982); *The New York Times Atlas of the World* (1992); *Oxford Atlas of the World* (1992); Rand McNally, *Today's World* (1996); Dan Smith, *The State of War and Peace Atlas* (1997); *The Times Atlas of World History* (1993).

Bibliographies: Samuel Flagg Bemis and Grace Gardner Griffin, *Guide to the Diplomatic History of the United States, 1775–1921* (1935); Richard Dean Burns, ed. *A Guide to American Foreign Relations Since*

1700 (1982); Congressional Information Service, *American Foreign Policy Index* (1994–); Council on Foreign Relations, *Foreign Affairs Bibliography* (1933–1972); Byron Dexter, ed., *The Foreign Affairs 50-Year Bibliography* (1972); Frank Freidel, ed., *Harvard Guide to American History* (1974); Mary Beth Norton, ed., *Guide to Historical Literature* (1995); Francis P. Prucha, *Handbook for Research in American History* (1987). The journal *Diplomatic History* regularly publishes articles that review the historiography of major topics and periods and provide extensive bibliographical guidance. The *Journal of American History* regularly lists recent publications. Journals such as *Foreign Affairs* and *Political Science Quarterly* regularly publish reviews of recent books.

Biographical Aids: John S. Bowman, *The Cambridge Dictionary of American Biography* (1995); Asa Briggs, *A Dictionary of Twentieth Century World Biography* (1990); Mari Jo Buhle et al., eds., *The American Radical* (1994); David Crystal, ed., *The Cambridge Biographical Encyclopedia* (1994); *Current Biography* (1940–); *Dictionary of American Biography* (1928–); *Encyclopedia of World Biography* (1998); John A. Garraty and Mark C. Carnes, eds., *American National Biography* (1999); John Garraty and Jerome L. Stersbstin, eds., *The Encyclopedia of American Biography* (1996); *International Who's Who* (1935–); Bernard K. Johnpoll and Harvey Klehr, eds., *Biographical Dictionary of the American Left* (1986); Warren F. Kuehl, ed., *Biographical Dictionary of Internationalists* (1983); *National Cyclopedia of American Biography* (1898–); Alan Palmer, *Who's Who in Modern History* (1980); Philip Rees, *Biographical Dictionary of the Extreme Right Since 1890* (1991); Frank W. Thackery and John E. Findling, eds., *Statesmen Who Changed the World* (1993); U.S. Department of State, *Biographic Register* (1860–1974) and *Foreign Service List* (1929–); *Who Was Who in America* (1963–); *Who's Who in America* (1899–); *Who's Who in the World* (1971–).

Chronologies: Lester H. Brune, *Chronological History of U.S. Foreign Relations* (1985, 1991); Gorton Carruth, *The Encyclopedia of American Facts and Dates* (1993) and *The Encyclopedia of World Facts and Dates* (1993); Council on Foreign Relations, *Foreign Affairs Chronology, 1978–1989* (1990) and *The United States in World Affairs* (1932–

1972); Robert H. Ferrell and John S. Bowman, eds., *The Twentieth Century* (1984); Bernard Grun, *The Timetables of History* (1991); John E. Jessup, *A Chronology of Conflict and Resolution, 1945–1985* (1989); Thomas Parker and Douglas Nelson, *Day by Day: The Sixties* (1983); Royal Institute of International Affairs, *Survey of International Affairs, 1920–1963* (1972–1977); Laurence Urdang, ed., *The Timetables of American History* (1996). See also "Annual Surveys."

Documentary Collections and Series: Martin P. Claussen, ed., *The National State Papers of the United States: Texts of Documents (1789–1817)* (1980–   ); Council on Foreign Relations, *Documents on American Foreign Relations, 1938/1939–1970* (1939–1973); Royal Institute of International Affairs, *Documents on International Affairs, 1928–1963* (1929–1973); Arthur M. Schlesinger, Jr., ed., *The Dynamics of World Power: A Documentary History of U.S. Foreign Policy, 1945–1973* (1973); U.S. Congress, *American State Papers* (1852–1859); U.S. Department of State, *A Decade of American Foreign Policy: Basic Documents, 1941–1949* (1985), *American Foreign Policy: Basic Documents, 1950–1955* (1957), *American Foreign Policy: Basic Documents, 1977–1980* (1983–1986), *American Foreign Policy: Current Documents, 1956–1967* (1956–1967), *American Foreign Policy: Current Documents, 1981–*   (1984–   ), *Bulletin* (1938–   ), *Dispatch* (1990–   ), *Foreign Relations of United States, 1861–*   (1862–   ), and *Press Conferences of the Secretaries of State, 1922–1974* (n.d.); *Vital Speeches of the Day* (1934–   ).

Encyclopedias and Dictionaries: Alexander DeConde, *Encyclopedia of American Foreign Policy* (1978); Margaret Denning and J. K. Sweeney, *Handboook of American Diplomacy* (1992); John Drexel, ed., *The Facts on File Encyclopedia of the 20th Century* (1991); Graham Evans and Jeffrey Newnham, eds., *The Dictionary of World Politics* (1990); John M. Farragher, ed., *The American Heritage Encyclopedia of American History* (1998); John E. Findling, *Dictionary of American Diplomatic History* (1989); Stephen A. Flanders and Carl N. Flanders, *Dictionary of American Foreign Affairs* (1991); Charles W. Freeman, Jr., *The Diplomat's Dictionary* (1997); Jack P. Greene, ed., *Encyclopedia of American Political History* (1984); Kenneth L. Hill, *Encyclopedia of Conflicts Since World War II* (1998); Stanley Hochman, *The Penguin Dictionary of Contemporary American History* (1997); Bruce W. Jentleson and Thomas G. Paterson, eds., *Encyclopedia of U.S. Foreign Relations* (1997); Joel Krieger et al., eds., *The Oxford Companion to the Politics of the World* (1993); Stanley I. Kutler, ed., *Encyclopedia of the United States in the Twentieth Century* (1995); Richard B. Morris et al., *Encyclopedia of American History* (1996); Jack C. Plano and Ray Olton, *The International Relations Dictionary* (1988); Jack E. Vincent, *A Handbook of International Relations* (1968); *Worldmark Encyclopedia of the Nations* (1995).

Statistics: Erik W. Austin and Jerome C. Clubb, *Political Facts of the United States Since 1789* (1986); International Monetary Fund, *International Financial Statistics* (1948–   ); George T. Kurian, ed., *The Illustrated Book of World Rankings* (1996); Victor Showers, *World Facts and Figures* (1989); Ruth L. Sivard, *World Military and Social Expenditures* (1974–   ); Charles L. Taylor and David A. Jodice, *World Handbook of Political and Social Indicators* (1983); United Nations, *Demographic Yearbook* (1948–   ), *Report on the World Social Situation* (1952–   ), and *Statistical Yearbook* (1948–   ); U.S. Agency for International Development, *United States Overseas Loans and Grants and Assistance from International Organizations, July 1, 1945–Sept. 30, 1980* (1981); U.S. Bureau of the Census, *Historical Statistics of the United States* (1975) and *Statistical Abstract of the United States* (1878–   ); U.S. Central Intelligence Agency, *Handbook of International Economic Statistics* (1971–   ) and *The World Factbook* (1981–   ); World Bank, *World Tables* (1974–   ); World Resources Institute, *World Resources* (1990–   ). See also "Annual Surveys."

Overviews of Relations with Countries, Regions, and Other Places of the World, Including Atlases and Gazetteers (A), Annual Surveys and Chronologies (AS), Bibliographies (B), Biographical Aids (BA), Chronologies (C), Encyclopedias and Dictionaries (E), and Statistics (S)

Afghanistan: Anthony Arnold, *Afghanistan* (1985); Henry S. Bradsher, *Afghanistan and the Soviet Union* (1985); B. S. Gupta, *Afghanistan* (1986); M. Hassar Kakar, *Afghanistan: The Soviet Invasion and the Afghan Response* (1995); Nancy P. Newell and Richard S. Newell, *The Struggle for Afghanistan* (1981); Leon B. Poullada, *The Kingdom of Afghanistan and the United States, 1828-1973* (1995); Stanley Wolpert, *Roots of Confrontation in South Asia* (1982).

Africa: Chris Cook and David Killinway, *African Political Facts Since 1945* (1991) (E); Peter Duignan and Lewis H. Gann, *The United States and Africa* (1987); Dennis Hickey and Kenneth White, *An Enchanting Darkness* (1993); Lawrence C. Howard, *American Involvement in Africa South of the Sahara, 1800–1860* (1988); Henry F. Jackson, *From the Congo to Soweto* (1982); Zaki Laidi, *The Superpowers and Africa* (1990); Colin Legum, ed., *Africa Contemporary Record* (1968–   ) (AS); Michael McCarthy, *Dark Continent* (1983); Lysle E. Meyer, *The Farther Frontier* (1992); Thomas Noer, *Cold War and Black Liberation* (1985); Anthony G. Pazzanita and Tony Hodges, *Historical Dictionary of Western Sahara* (1994) (E); Peter J. Schraeder, *United States Foreign Policy Toward Africa* (1994); Elliot P. Skinner, *African-Americans and*

U.S. Policy Toward Africa, 1850–1924 (1992); U.S. Library of Congress, *The United States and Sub-Saharan Africa* (1984) (B). See also countries.

Alaska: Paul S. Holbo, *Tarnished Expansion* (1983); Ronald J. Jensen, *The Alaska Purchase* (1975); Walter A. McDougall, *Let the Sea Make a Noise* (1993). See also Kushner and Saul in "Russia and the Soviet Union."

Albania: William B. Bland, *Albania* (1988) (B).

Algeria: Charles-Robert Ageron, *Modern Algeria* (1992); Helen C. Metz, ed., *Algeria* (1994); Martin Stone, *The Agony of Algeria* (1997). See also "North Africa."

Angola: Richard Black, *Angola* (1992) (B); Susan H. Broadhead, *Historical Dictionary of Angola* (1992) (E); Thomas Collelo, ed., *Angola* (1990); Fernando A. Guimarães, *The Origins of the Angolan Civil War* (1998); Lawrence W. Henderson, *Angola* (1979); John A. Marcum, *The Angolan Revolution* (1969, 1978); Kenneth Mokoena and Nicole Gaymon, eds., *The Angola Crises* (1991); Inge Tvedten, *Angola* (1997). See also "Africa."

Antarctica: Peter J. Beck, *The International Politics of Antarctica* (1986); Robert Headland, *Chronological List of Antarctic Expeditions* (1989) (E and C); Christopher C. Joyner and Ethel R. Theis, *Eagle over the Ice* (1997); Frank G. Klotz, *America on the Ice* (1990); Jeffrey D. Myhre, *The Antarctic Treaty System* (1986); John Stewart, *Antarctica* (1990) (E); Gilligan D. Triggs, ed., *The Antarctic Treaty Regime* (1987).

Arab World: See "Israel, Palestine, and Arab-Israeli Conflict" and "Middle East."

Arctic: Elizabeth B. Elliot-Meisel, *Arctic Diplomacy: Canada and the United States in the Northwest Passage* (1998); Clive Holland, *Arctic Exploration and Development* (1993) (E). See also "Canada."

Argentina: Alan Biggs, *Argentina* (1991) (B); Harold F. Peterson, *Argentina and the United States* (1964); David Rock, *Argentina* (1985); David Sheinin, *Searching for Authority* (1998); Joseph Tulchin, *Argentina and the United States* (1990); Arthur P. Whitaker, *The United States and the Southern Cone* (1976). See also "Latin America."

Armenia: Vrej Nerses Neressian, *Armenia* (1993) (B).

Asia and Pacific Islands: Alexander Besher, *The Pacific Rim Almanac* (1991) (E); Jessica S. Brown et al., eds., *The United States in East Asia* (1985) (B); Frederica M. Bunge and Melinda W. Cooke, eds., *Oceania* (1985); I. C. Campbell, *A History of the Pacific Islands* (1989); Sucheng Chan, *Asian-Americans* (1991); Warren I. Cohen, ed., *Pacific Passage* (1996); Donald Denoon and Stewart Firth, eds., *The Cambridge History of the Pacific Islanders* (1997); John C. Dorance, *The United States and the Pacific Islands* (1992); Norman Douglas and Ngaire Douglas, eds., *Pacific Islands Yearbook* (1932–) (AS); Arthur P. Dudden, *The American Pacific* (1992); Ainslie T. Embree, *Encyclopedia of Asian History* (1988) (E); Gerald Fry, *Pacific Basin and Oceania* (1987) (B); Roger W. Gale, *The Americanization of Micronesia* (1979); Arrell M. Gibson, *Yankees in Paradise* (1993); Akira Iriye, *Across the Pacific* (1967); Donald D. Johnson, *The United States in the Pacific* (1995); John C. Perry, *Facing West* (1994); Deryck Scarr, *The History of the Pacific Islands* (1990); Gerald Segal, *Rethinking the Pacific* (1990); David Shavit, *The United States in Asia* (1990) (E); Roger C. Thompson, *The Pacific Rim Since 1945* (1994); James C. Thomson, Jr., et al., *Sentimental Imperialists* (1981). See also countries and "Vietnam and Southeast Asia."

Australia: Glen St. John Barclay, *Friends in High Places* (1985); Philip Bell, *Implicated* (1993); Norman Harper, *A Great and Powerful Friend* (1987); Joseph Siracusa and Yeong-Han Cheong, *America's Australia, Australia's America* (1997). See also "Asia and Pacific Islands."

Austria: William Bader, *Austria Between East and West* (1966); Audrey K. Cronin, *Great Power Politics and the Struggle over Austria, 1945–1955* (1986); Barbara Jelavich, *Modern Austria* (1988); Mellany A. Sully, *A Contemporary History of Austria* (1990); Reinhold Wagnleitner, *Coca-Colonization and the Cold War* (1994). See also "Europe."

Azerbaijan: Ian Bremmer and Ray Taras, eds., *Nations and Politics in the Soviet Successor States* (1993). See also "Russia and the Soviet Union."

The Bahamas: Paul G. Boultbee, *The Bahamas* (1989) (B).

Bahrain: F. Gregory Gauss, *Oil Monarchies* (1994). See also "Middle East" and "Persian Gulf."

Baltic States: Walter C. Clemens, Jr., *Baltic Independence and Russian Empire* (1991); David Flint, *The Baltic States* (1992); Kristian Gerner, *The Baltic States and the End of the Soviet Empire* (1993); Walter R. Iwaskiw, ed., *Estonia, Latvia, and Lithuania* (1996); Anatol

Lieven, *The Baltic Revolution* (1993); Inese A. Smith and Marita V. Grunts, *The Baltic States* (1993). See also "Estonia."

Bangladesh: See Brown in "India."

Belarus: Helen Fedor, *Belarus and Moldova* (1995).

Belgium: Jonathan E. Helmreich, *United States Relations with Belgium and the Congo* (1998); Frank E. Hugget, *Modern Belgium* (1969). See also "Europe."

Belize: O. Nigel Bolland, *Belize* (1996). Also see Merrill in "Guyana."

Berlin: See "Germany and Berlin."

Bhutan: See "Nepal."

Bolivia: Rex A. Hudson and Dennis M. Haggerty, eds., *Bolivia* (1991); Waltraud Q. Morales, *Bolivia* (1992); Lawrence Whitehead, *The United States and Bolivia* (1969); J. W. Wilkie, *The Bolivian Revolution and U.S. Aid Since 1952* (1969). See also "Latin America" and Pike in "Peru."

Bosnia-Herzegovina: Noel Malcolm, *Bosnia* (1994). See also "Yugoslavia."

Brazil: Jan Black, *United States Penetration of Brazil* (1977); Elizabeth A. Cobbs, *The Rich Neighbor Policy: Rockefeller and Kaiser in Brazil* (1992); John Dickenson, ed., *Brazil* (1997) (B); Gerald K. Haines, *The Americanization of Brazil* (1989); Stanley Hilton, *Brazil and the Great Powers* (1975); Rex A. Hudson, ed., *Brazil* (1998); Frank McCann, *The Brazilian-American Alliance, 1937–1945* (1973); Joseph Smith, *Unequal Giants* (1991); Steven C. Topik, *Trade and Gunboats* (1996); W. Michael Weis, *Cold Warriors and Coups d'État* (1993). See also "Latin America."

Bulgaria: Glenn A. Curtis, ed., *Bulgaria* (1993). See also "Europe."

Burma: See "Myanmar."

Burundi: Morna Daniels, *Burundi* (1992) (B). See also "Africa."

Cambodia: MacAlister Brown and Joseph J. Zasloff, *Cambodia Confronts the Peacemakers, 1979–1998* (1998); David P. Chandler, *The Tragedy of Cambodian History* (1991); Michael Haas, *Cambodia, Pol Pot, and the United States* (1991); Henry Kamm, *Cambodia* (1998); Ben Kiernan, *How Pol Pot Came to Power* (1985) and *The Pol Pot Regime* (1996); Russell R. Ross, ed., *Cambodia* (1990); William Shawcross, *The Quality of Mercy* (1984) and *Sideshow* (1979). See also "Southeast Asia."

Cameroon: Julius A. Amin, *The Peace Corps in Cameroon* (1992); Mark DeLancey, *Cameroon* (1986) (B); Mark DeLancey and H. Mbella Mokeba, *Historical Dictionary of Cameroon* (1990) (E). See also "Africa."

Canada: David J. Bercuson and J. L. Granatstein, *The Collins Dictionary of Canadian History* (1988) (E); Robert Bothwell, *Canada and the United States* (1992); Charles Doran, *Forgotten Partnership* (1984); Charles Doran and John H. Sigler, *Canada and the United States* (1985); William T. Fox, *A Continent Apart* (1985); J. L. Granatstein and Robert Bothwell, *Pirouette* (1990); J. L. Granatstein and Norman Hillmer, *For Better or For Worse* (1992); Archie Hobson, *The Cambridge Gazetteer of the United States and Canada* (1996) (A); Lansing Lamont and Duncan Edmonds, eds., *Friends So Different* (1989); Seymour Martin Lipset, *Continental Divide* (1990); Lawrence Martin, *The Presidents and the Prime Ministers* (1982); J. F. Rooney, Jr., et al., eds., *This Remarkable Continent* (1982) (A); Denis Smith, *Diplomacy of Fear* (1988); Reginald C. Stuart, *United States Expansionism and British North America 1775–1871* (1988); John H. Thompson and Stephen J. Randall, *Canada and the United States* (1998). See also "Great Britain."

Caribbean: Charles D. Ameringer, *The Caribbean Legion* (1974); David Healy, *Drive to Hegemony* (1988); Roger Hughes, *The Caribbean* (1987) (B); Lester D. Langley, *The United States and the Caribbean, 1900–1970* (1980) and *The United States and the Caribbean in the Twentieth Century* (1989); Sandra W. Meditz and Dennis M. Hanratty, eds., *Islands of the Commonwealth Caribbean* (1989); Robert F. Smith, *The Caribbean World and the United States* (1994). See also "Central America," "Latin America," and countries.

Central African Republic: Pierre Kalck, *Historical Dictionary of the Central African Republic* (1992) (E). See also "Africa."

Central America: Tom Barry, *Central America Inside Out* (1991) (C and E); Leslie Bethel, ed., *Central America Since Independence* (1991); Morris J. Blachman et al., eds., *Confronting Revolution* (1986); John Booth and Thomas Walker, *Understanding Central America* (1993); John Coatsworth, *Central America and the United States* (1994); Kenneth M. Coleman and George C. Herring, eds., *Understanding the Central American Crisis* (1991); John E. Findling, *Close Neighbors, Distant Friends* (1987); Kenneth J. Grieb, *Central America in the Nineteenth and Twentieth Centuries* (1988) (B); Walter LaFeber, *Inevitable Revolutions* (1993); Thomas M. Leonard, *Central America and the United*

States (1991) and *Central America and U.S. Policies, 1820s–1980s* (1985) (B); Thomas D. Schoonover, *The United States in Central America, 1860–1911* (1991); Ralph L. Woodward, *Central America* (1985). See also "Caribbean," "Latin America," and individual countries.

Chad: Thomas Collelo, ed., *Chad* (1990); Samuel Decalo, *Historical Dictionary of Chad* (1987) (E). See also "Africa."

Chile: Michael Francis, *The Limits of Hegemony* (1977); Rex A. Hudson, ed., *Chile* (1990); Michael Monteon, *Chile in the Nitrate Era* (1982); Heraldo Munoz and Carlos Portales, *Elusive Friendship* (1991); Fredrick B. Pike, *Chile and the United States, 1880–1962* (1963); William F. Sater, *Chile and the United States* (1990); Paul E. Sigmund, *The United States and Democracy in Chile* (1993). See also "Latin America" and Whitaker in "Argentina."

China (and Taiwan): Gordon Chang, *Friends and Enemies* (1990); Warren I. Cohen, *America's Response to China* (1990); John K. Fairbank, *China Perceived* (1974) and *The United States and China* (1983); Rosemary Foot, *The Practice of Power* (1995); John Gittings, *The World and China, 1922–1972* (1974); Jonathan Goldstein et al., eds., *America Views China* (1991); Harry Harding, *A Fragile Relationship* (1992); Michael H. Hunt, *The Making of a Special Relationship* (1983); Arnold Xiangze Jiang, *The United States and China* (1988); Wei-cin Lee, *Taiwan* (1990) (B); Ernest R. May and John K. Fairbank, eds., *America's China Trade in Historical Perspective* (1986); Stuart C. Miller, *The Unwelcome Immigrant: The American Image of the Chinese, 1785–1882* (1969); Robert S. Ross, *Negotiating Cooperation* (1995); Michael Schaller, *The United States and China in the Twentieth Century* (1990); David Shambaugh, *Beautiful Imperialist* (1991); Henry Shih-Shan Tsai, *The Chinese Experience in America* (1986); Nancy B. Tucker, *Taiwan, Hong Kong, and the United States* (1994); Shu Guang Zhang, *Deterrence and Strategic Culture* (1992). See also "Asia and Pacific Islands."

Colombia: David Bushnell, *The Making of Modern Colombia* (1993); Robert H. Davis, *Colombia* (1990) (B); Dennis M. Hanratty and Sandra W. Meditz, eds., *Colombia* (1990); Harvey F. Kline, *Colombia* (1995); Richard L. Lael, *Arrogant Diplomacy* (1987); Stephen J. Randall, *Colombia and the United States* (1992) and *The Diplomacy of Modernization* (1977). See also "Latin America" and "Panama (and Panama Canal)."

Comoros: See "Indian Ocean."

Congo (Brazzaville): See "Africa."

Congo (Kinshasa): David N. Gibbs, *The Political Economy of Third World Intervention* (1991); Madeline G. Kalb, *The Congo Cables* (1982); Sean Kelly, *America's Tyrant: The CIA and Mobutu of Zaire* (1993); Dsandra W. Meditz and Tim Merrill, eds., *Zaire* (1994); Michael G. Schatzberg, *Mobutu or Chaos* (1991); Crawford Young and Thomas Turner, *The Rise and Decline of the Zairian State* (1985). See also "Africa" and Helmreich in "Belgium."

Costa Rica: Theodore S. Creedman, *Historical Dictionary of Costa Rica* (1991) (E); Kyle Longley, *The Sparrow and Hawk* (1997); Charles L. Stansifer, *Costa Rica* (1991) (B). See also "Central America" and "Latin America."

Cuba: Jules Benjamin, *The United States and Cuba* (1977); Leslie Bethell, ed., *Cuba* (1992); Ronald H. Chilcote and Sheryl Lutjens, eds., *Cuba, 1953–1978* (1986) (B); Juan del Aguilar, *Cuba* (1988); Jorge Domínguez, *To Make the World Safe for Revolution* (1989); Jesse J. Dossick, ed., *Cuba, Cubans, and Cuban-Americans, 1902–1991* (1992) (B); José M. Hernández, *Cuba and the United States: Intervention and Militarism, 1868–1933* (1993); Donna R. Kaplowitz, *Anatomy of a Failed Embargo* (1998); Morris H. Morley, *Imperial State and Revolution* (1987); Thomas G. Paterson, *Contesting Castro* (1994); Louis A. Pérez, Jr., *Cuba* (1995), *Cuba* (1988) (B), and *Cuba and the United States* (1997); Jaime Suchlicki, *Historical Dictionary of Cuba* (1988) (E). See also "Caribbean," "Latin America," and "Spanish-American-Cuban-Filipino War."

Cyprus: Tozun Bahcheli, *Greek-Turkish Relations Since 1955* (1990); Henry A. Richter, *Greece and Cyprus Since 1920* (1991) (B); Eric Solsten, ed., *Cyprus* (1991). See also Stearns in "Greece."

Czech Republic (and Czechoslovakia): David Short, *Czechoslovakia* (1986) (B); Gordon Skilling, *Czechoslovakia* (1991); Walter Ullmann, *The United States in Prague, 1945–1948* (1978); Betty Miller Unterberger, *The United States, Revolutionary Russia, and the Rise of Czechoslovakia* (1989). See also "Eastern Europe."

Dominican Republic: G. Pope Atkins and Larman C. Wilson, *The Dominican Republic and the United States* (1998) and *The United States and the Trujillo Regime* (1972); Ian Bell, *The Dominican Republic* (1981); Bruce J. Calder, *The Impact of Intervention* (1984); Piero Gleijeses, *The Dominican Crisis* (1978); Richard A. Haggerty, ed., *Dominican Republic and Haiti* (1991); Rayford W. Logan, *Haiti and the Dominican Republic* (1968); Eric P. Roorda, *The Dictator Next Door* (1998); Kai Schoenhals, *Dominican Republic* (1990) (B); Howard J. Wiarda, *The Dominican Republic* (1992). See also "Caribbean" and "Latin America."

Eastern Europe: Robert F. Byrnes, *U.S. Policy Toward Europe and the Soviet Union* (1989); Stephen A. Garrett, *From Potsdam to Poland* (1986); Bennett Kovrig, *Of Walls and Bridges* (1991); Geoffrey Swain and Nigel Swain, *Eastern Europe Since 1945* (1993). Also see "Russia and the Soviet Union," "Europe," and countries.

Ecuador: David Corkill, *Ecuador* (1989) (B); Dennis M. Hanratty, ed., *Ecuador* (1991); David W. Schodt, *Ecuador* (1987). See also "Latin America" and Pike in "Peru."

Egypt: Gregory L. Aftandilian, *Egypt's Bid for Arab Leadership* (1993); Geoffrey Aronson, *From Sideshow to Center Stage* (1986); William J. Burns, *Economic Aid and American Policy Toward Egypt, 1955–1981* (1985); Peter L. Hahn, *The United States, Great Britian, and Egypt, 1945–1956* (1991); Ragai N. Makar, *Egypt* (1988) (B); Helen C. Metz, ed., *Egypt* (1991); Gail E. Meyer, *Egypt and the United States* (1980); William B. Quandt, *The United States and Egypt* (1990). See also "Israel, Palestine, and Arab-Israeli Conflict" and "Middle East."

El Salvador: America's Watch, *El Salvador's Decade of Terror* (1991); Cynthia Arnson, *El Salvador* (1982); Enrique A. Baloyra, *El Salvador in Transition* (1982); Martin Diskin and Kenneth Sharpe, *The Impact of U.S. Policy in El Salvador, 1979–1986* (1986); Richard A. Haggerty, ed., *El Salvador* (1990); T. S. Montgomery, *Revolution in El Salvador* (1982); Ralph Lee Woodward, *El Salvador* (1988) (B). See also "Central America" and "Latin America."

Estonia: Toivo U. Raun, *Estonia and the Estonians* (1991). See also "Baltic States."

Ethiopia: David A. Korn, *Ethiopia, the United States, and the Soviet Union* (1986); Jeffrey S. Lefebvre, *Arms for the Horn* (1991); Harold G. Marcus, *Ethiopia, Great Britain, and the United States, 1941–1974* (1983); Thomas P. Ofcansky, ed., *Ethiopia* (1993); Chris Prouty and Eugene Rosenfeld, *Historical Dictionary of Ethiopia* (1994) (E). Also see "Africa."

Europe: Peter Coffey, *The EC and the United States* (1993); Simon W. Duke and Wolfgang Krieger, eds., *U.S. Military Forces in Europe* (1993); *The Economist Atlas of the New Europe* (1992) (A); Nicholas V. Gianaris, *The European Community and the United States* (1991); John L. Harper, *American Visions of Europe* (1994); Ethan B. Kapstein, *The Insecure Alliance: Energy Crises and Western Politics Since 1914* (1990); Geir Lundestad, *"Empire" by Integration* (1998); Jacques Portes, ed., *Europe and America* (1987); Pascaline Winand, *Eisenhower, Kennedy, and the United States of Europe* (1993). See also "Eastern Europe," "North Atlantic Treaty Organization (NATO)," countries, and wars.

Finland: Jussi M. Hanhimäki, *Containing Coexistence* (1997); Max Jacobson, *Finnish Neutrality* (1969); Robert Rinehart, ed., *Finland and the United States* (1993); Eric Solsten and Sandra W. Meditz, *Finland* (1990). See also "Europe" and "Scandinavia."

France: Henry Blumenthal, *A Reappraisal of Franco-American Relations, 1830–1871* (1959), *France and the United States* (1970), and *Illusion and Reality in Franco-American Diplomacy, 1914–1945* (1986); James A. Carr, ed., *American Foreign Policy During the French Revolution-Napoleonic Period* (1994) (B); Charles Cogan, *Oldest Allies, Guarded Friends* (1994); Frank Costigliola, *The Cold Alliance* (1992); Robert O. Paxton and Nicholas Wahl, eds., *De Gaulle and the United States, 1930–1970* (1994); Irwin M. Wall, *The United States and the Making of Postwar France* (1991); Marvin Zahniser, *Uncertain Friendship* (1975). See also "Europe."

Gabon: David E. Gardinier, *Historical Dictionary of Gabon* (1994) (E). See also "Africa."

Germany and Berlin: David E. Barclay and Elisabeth Glaser-Schmidt, eds., *Transatlantic Image and Perceptions* (1997); Dennis L. Bark and David R. Gross, *A History of West Germany* (1993); Hans W. Gatzke, *Germany and the United States* (1980); Wolfram F. Hanrieder, *Germany, America, Europe* (1989); Manfred Jonas, *The United States and Germany* (1984); Margrit Krewson, *German-American Relations* (1995) (B); Roger P. Morgan, *The United States and West Germany, 1945–1973* (1974); Frank Ninkovich, *Germany and the United States* (1995); Cathal J. Nolan and Carl C. Hodge, eds., *Shepherd of Democracy?* (1992); Hans-Jürgen Schröder, ed., *Confrontation and Cooperation* (1993); Thomas A. Schwartz, *America's Germany* (1991); Eric Solsten, ed., *Germany* (1996); Frank Trommler and Joseph McVeigh, eds., *America and the Germans* (1985); Ian Wallace, *Berlin* (1993) (B); Peter Wyden, *Wall* (1989). See also "Europe," "Holocaust," "War Crimes and Trials," "World War I," and "World War II."

Ghana: LaVerde Berry, ed., *Ghana* (1995); Daniel McFarland, *Historical Dictionary of Ghana* (1985). See also "Africa."

Great Britain: C. J. Bartlett, *"The Special Relationship"* (1992); Kenneth Bourne, *Britain and the Balance of Power in North America, 1815–1908* (1967); Charles S. Campbell, *From Revolution to Rapprochement* (1974); David Dimbleby and David Reynolds, *An Ocean Apart* (1989); Alan P. Dobson, *Anglo-American Relations in the Twentieth Century* (1995); Robert M. Hathaway, *Great Britain and the United States* (1990); David A. Lincove and Gary R. Treadway, eds., *The Anglo-American Relationship* (1988) (B); William Roger Louis and Hedley Bull, eds., *The Special Relationship* (1986); H. G. Nicholas,

The United States and Great Britain (1975); Anne Orde, *The Eclipse of Great Britain* (1996). See also "Canada" and "War of 1812."

Greece: Louis Cassimatis, *American Influence in Greece, 1917–1929* (1988); Theodore A. Couloumbis, *The United States, Greece, and Turkey* (1983); Theodore A. Couloumbis and John O. Iatrides, eds., *Greek-American Relations* (1980); Glenn E. Curtis, ed., *Greece* (1995); John O. Iatrides, ed., *Ambassador MacVeagh Reports: Greece, 1933–1947* (1980); Jon V. Kofas, *Intervention and Underdevelopment: Greece During the Cold War* (1989); Monteagle Stearns, *Entangled Allies* (1991); Lawrence S. Wittner, *American Intervention in Greece, 1943–1949* (1982). See also "Europe" and Richter in "Cyprus."

Grenada: Peter M. Dunn and Bruce W. Watson, eds., *American Intervention in Grenada* (1985); Gordon K. Lewis, *Grenada* (1987); Kai P. Schoenhals and Richard A. Melanson, eds., *Revolution and Intervention in Grenada* (1985). See also "Caribbean."

Guam: Timothy P. Maga, *Defending Paradise* (1988); Earl S. Pomeroy, *Pacific Outpost* (1951); Robert F. Rogers, *Destiny's Landfall* (1995). See also "Asia and Pacific Islands."

Guatemala: Nick Cullather, *Secret History* (1999); Paul J. Dosal, *Doing Business with the Dictators: A Political History of United Fruit in Guatemala, 1899–1944* (1993); Piero Glejeses, *Shattered Hope* (1991); Jim Handy, *Gift of the Devil* (1985); Richard Immerman, *The CIA in Guatemala* (1982); Ralph Lee Woodward, *Guatemala* (1992) (B). See also "Central America" and "Latin America."

Guyana: Tim Merrill, ed., *Guyana and Belize* (1993). See also "Latin America."

Haiti: Frances Chambers, *Haiti* (1983) (B); Rayford W. Logan, *Diplomatic Relations of the United States with Haiti, 1776-1891* (1941); David Nicholls, *From Dessalines to Duvalier* (1979); Brenda Gayle Plummer, *Haiti and the United States* (1992); Robert I. Rotberg, *Haiti* (1971). See also "Caribbean," "Latin America," and Haggerty and Logan in "Dominican Republic."

Hawai'i: Helena G. Allen, *The Betrayal of Queen Lilioukalani* (1982); Ralph S. Kuykendall, *The Hawaiian Kingdom* (1938–1967); Nancy Morris and Love Dean, *Hawai'i* (1992) (B); Merze Tate, *The United States and the Hawaiian Kingdom* (1965). See also "Asia and Pacific Islands."

Honduras: Alison Acker, *Honduras* (1988); Pamela F. Howard-Reguindin, *Honduras* (1992) (B); Harvey Meyer and Jessie Meyer,

Historical Dictionary of Honduras (1994) (E). See also "Central America."

Hong Kong: See Tucker in "China (and Taiwan)."

Hungary: Stephan R. Burant, ed., *Hungary* (1990). See also "Eastern Europe" and "Europe."

Iceland: Donald E. Neuchterlein, *Iceland* (1975). See also "Scandinavia."

India: William J. Barnds, *India, Pakistan, and the Great Powers* (1972); H. W. Brands, *India and the United States* (1990); W. Norman Brown, *The United States and India, Pakistan, and Bangladesh* (1972); Srinivas M. Chary, *The Eagle and the Peacock* (1994); Kenton J. Clymer, *Quest for Freedom* (1995); James Heitzman and Robert L. Worden, eds., *India* (1996); Gary R. Hess, *America Encounters India, 1941–1947* (1971); Harold R. Issacs, *Images of Asia* (1958); Dennis Kux, *India and the United States* (1992); Robert J. McMahon, *The Cold War on the Periphery* (1994); Dennis Merrill, *Bread and the Ballot* (1990); Norman D. Palmer, *The United States and India* (1984); Santosh C. Saha, *Indo-U.S. Relations, 1947–1988* (1990) (B); Stanley Wolpert, *Nehru* (1997). See also "Asia and Pacific Islands" and Wolpert in "Afghanistan."

Indian Ocean: Helen C. Metz, ed., *Indian Ocean: Five Island Countries* (1995). See also "Africa."

Indonesia: Paul F. Gardner, *Shared Hopes, Separate Fears* (1997); Gerald Krausse and Sylvia Krausse, *Indonesia* (1994) (B); Michael Leifer, *Indonesia's Foreign Policy* (1983); Robert J. McMahon, *Colonialism and Cold War* (1981); Robert L. Worden, ed., *Indonesia* (1993). See also "Asia and Pacific Islands."

Iran: James A. Bill, *The Eagle and the Lion* (1988); Richard W. Cottam, *Iran and the United States* (1988); Mark J. Gasiorowski, *U.S. Foreign Policy and the Shah* (1991); Sīrūs Ghanī, *Iran and the West* (1987) (B); James F. Goode, *The United States and Iran, 1946–51* (1989); Nikki R. Keddie and Mark J. Gasiorowski, eds., *Neither East nor West* (1990); Mark H. Lytle, *The Origins of the Iranian-American Alliance, 1941–1953* (1987); Rouhollah K. Ramazani, *The United States and Iran* (1982); Barry Rubin, *Paved with Good Intentions* (1980); Kuross A. Samii, *Involvement by Invitation* (1987); Abraham Yeselson, *United States–Persian Diplomatic Relations, 1883–1921* (1956). See also "Middle East" and "Persian Gulf."

Iraq: Rick Atkinson, *Crusade* (1993); Lawrence Freedman and Efraim Karsh, *The Gulf Conflict, 1990–1991* (1993); Bruce Jentleson,

With Friends like These (1994); Helen C. Metz, ed., *Iraq* (1990); William Stivers, *Supremacy and Oil* (1982). See also "Middle East" and "Persian Gulf."

Ireland: Donald H. Akenson, *The United States and Ireland* (1973); Thomas N. Brown, *Irish-American Nationalism, 1870–1890* (1966); Francis M. Carroll, *American Opinion and the Irish Question, 1910–1923* (1978); Sean Cronin, *Washington's Irish Policy, 1916–1986* (1987); Troy D. Davis, *Dublin's American Policy* (1998); Alan J. Ward, *Ireland and Anglo-American Relations, 1899–1921* (1969). See also "Europe" and "Great Britain."

Israel, Palestine, and Arab-Israeli Conflict: George W. Ball and Douglas B. Ball, *The Passionate Attachment* (1992); Abraham Ben-Zvi, *The United States and Israel* (1994); Ian J. Bickerton and Carla L. Klausner, *A Concise History of the Arab-Israeli Conflict* (1998); Peter Grose, *Israel and the Mind of America* (1983); William Roger Louis and Robert W. Stookey, eds., *The End of the Palestine Mandate* (1986); Camille Mansour, *Beyond Alliance* (1994); Donald Neff, *Fallen Pillars: U.S. Policy Towards Palestine and Israel Since 1945* (1995); Ilan Pappe, *The Israel/Palestine Question* (1999); William B. Quandt, *Peace Process* (1993); John Quigley, *Palestine and Israel* (1990); Bernard Reich, ed., *An Encyclopedia of the Arab-Israeli Conflict* (1996) (E) and *The United States and Israel* (1984); Cheryl Rubenberg, *Israel and the American National Interest* (1986); David Schoenbaum, *The United States and the State of Israel* (1993); Mohammed K. Shadid, *The United States and the Palestinians* (1981); Charles D. Smith, *Palestine and the Arab-Israeli Conflict* (1992); Steven Spiegel, *The Other Arab-Israeli Conflict* (1985); Michael W. Suleiman, ed., *U.S. Policy on Palestine* (1995); Mark Tessler, *A History of the Israeli-Palestinian Conflict* (1994); Edward Tivnan, *The Lobby* (1987). See also "Middle East."

Italy: Frank J. Coppa and William Roberts, *Modern Italian History* (1990) (B); Alexander DeConde, *Half-Bitter, Half-Sweet* (1971); H. Stuart Hughes, *The United States and Italy* (1979); James E. Miller, *The United States and Italy, 1940–1950* (1986); David F. Schmitz, *The United States and Fascist Italy, 1922–1940* (1988); Leo J. Wollemborg, *Stars, Stripes, and Italian Tricolor* (1990). See also "Europe."

Jamaica: See "Caribbean."

Japan: Sadao Asada, *Japan and the World* (1989) (B); Michael A. Barnhart, *Japan and the World Since 1868* (1995); John H. Boyle, *Modern Japan: The American Nexus* (1993); Roger Buckley, *US-Japan Alliance Diplomacy, 1945–1990* (1992); Donald E. Dolan and Robert L. Worden, eds., *Japan* (1992); John K. Emmerson and Harrison M. Holland, *The Eagle and the Rising Sun* (1988); Akira Iriye, *Pacific Estrangement: Japanese and American Expansion, 1897–1911* (1972); Wal-ter LaFeber, *The Clash* (1997); Rita E. Neri, *U.S. and Japan Foreign Trade* (1988) (B); William R. Nester, *Power Across the Pacific* (1996); Charles E. Neu, *The Troubled Encounter* (1975); Michael Schaller, *Altered States* (1997) and *The American Occupation of Japan* (1985). See also "Asia and Pacific Islands," "War Crimes and Trials," and "World War II."

Jordan: Madiha Rashid al-Madfai, *Jordan, the United States, and the Middle East Peace Process* (1993); Helen C. Metz, ed., *Jordan* (1991). See also "Middle East."

Kazakhstan: Glenn E. Curtis, *Kazakhstan, Kyrgyzstan, Tajikistan, Turkmenistan, and Uzbekistan* (1997); Michael Mandelbaum, ed., *Central Asia and the World* (1994).

Kenya: See "Africa" and Lefebvre in "Ethiopia."

Korea and Korean War: Jongsuk Chay, *Diplomacy of Asymmetry* (1990); Bruce Cumings, *Korea's Place in the Sun* (1997) and *The Origins of the Korean War* (1981, 1990); Paul M. Edwards, *The Korean War* (1998) (B); Burton I. Kaufman, *The Korean War* (1997); Yun-Bok Lee and Wayne Patterson, eds., *Korean-American Relations, 1866–1997* (1998); Stewart Lone and Gavan McCormack, *Korea Since 1850* (1993); Donald S. Macdonald, *U.S.-Korean Relations* (1992); James I. Matray, ed., *Historical Dictionary of the Korean War* (1991) (E); Keith McFarland, *The Korean War* (1986) (B); Andrew C. Nahm, *Historical Dictionary of the Republic of Korea* (1993) (E); Don Oberdorfer, *The Two Koreas* (1997); Stanley Sandler, *The Korean War* (1995) (E); Andrea M. Savada, ed., *North Korea* (1994) and *South Korea* (1992); William Stueck, *The Korean War* (1995); Harry G. Summers, Jr., *Korean War Almanac* (1990) (C and E). See also "Asia and Pacific Islands."

Kuwait: Abdul-Reda Assiri, *Kuwaiti Foreign Policy* (1990); Jill Crystal, *Kuwait* (1992) and *Oil and Politics in the Gulf* (1995). See also "Middle East" and "Persian Gulf."

Kyrgyzstan: See "Kazakhstan."

Laos: Timothy N. Castle, *At War in the Shadow of Vietnam* (1993); Helen Cordell, *Laos* (1993) (B); Arthur J. Dommen, *Laos* (1985); Jane Hamilton-Merritt, *Tragic Mountains* (1993); Andrea M. Savada, ed., *Laos* (1995); Charles A. Stevenson, *The End of Nowhere* (1972). See also "Vietnam and Southeast Asia."

Latin America: G. Pope Atkins, *Encyclopedia of the Inter-American System* (1997) (E) and *Latin America in the International System* (1995); John A. Britton, *The United States and Latin America* (1997) (B); Peter

Calvert, *The International Politics of Latin America* (1994); David W. Dent, *U.S.–Latin American Policymaking* (1995) (B); Mark T. Gilderhus, *The Second Century* (2000); Jack W. Hopkins, ed., *Latin America and Caribbean Contemporary Record* (1983–) (AS); John J. Johnson, *A Hemisphere Apart* (1990); Lester D. Langley, *America and the Americas* (1989); Abraham F. Lowenthal, ed., *Exporting Democracy* (1991); Carlos Marichal, *A Century of Debt Crises in Latin America* (1988); John D. Martz, *United States Policy in Latin America* (1995); Michael C. Meyer, ed., *Supplement to a Bibliography of United States–Latin American Relations Since 1810* (1979) (B); James W. Park, *Latin American Underdevelopment* (1995); Fredrick B. Pike, *The United States and Latin America* (1992); Lars Schoultz, *Beneath the United States* (1998); David Shavit, *The United States in Latin America* (1992) (E); Joseph Smith, *Illusions of Conflict: Anglo-American Diplomacy Toward Latin America, 1865–1896* (1979); Peter H. Smith, *Talons of the Eagle* (1996); Barbara Stallings, *Banker to the Third World* (1988); Barbara A. Tenenbaum, ed., *Encyclopedia of Latin American History and Culture* (1995) (E); David F. Trask et al., *A Bibliography of United States–Latin American Relations Since 1810* (1968) (B). See also "Caribbean," "Central America," "Communications," "Monroe Doctrine," "Pan Americanism," and countries.

Latvia: See "Baltic States."

Lebanon: C. H. Bleaney, *Lebanon* (1991) (B); Thomas L. Friedman, *From Beirut to Jerusalem* (1989); Irene Gendzier, *Notes from the Minefield* (1997); Dilip Hiro, *Lebanon* (1993); Itamar Rabinovich, *The War for Lebanon, 1970–1985* (1986). See also "Middle East."

Liberia: D. Elwood Dunn, *The Foreign Policy of Liberia During the Tubman Era, 1944–1971* (1979); Katherine Harris, *The United States and Liberia* (1985); Hassan B. Sisay, *Big Powers and Small Nations* (1985); Charles M. Wilson, *Liberia* (1985). See also "Africa."

Libya: Scott L. Bills, *The Libyan Arena* (1995); Mahmoud G. El-Warfally, *Imagery and Ideology in U.S. Policy Toward Libya, 1969–1982* (1988); P. Edward Haley, *Qaddafi and the United States Since 1969* (1984); Dirk Vanderville, ed., *Qadhafi's Libya* (1995). See also "Africa" and "Middle East."

Lithuania: Saulius Sužiedelis, *Historical Dictionary of Lithuania* (1997) (E). See also "Baltic States."

Madagascar: Hilary Budt, *Madagascar* (1993) (B). See also "Africa" and "Indian Ocean."

Malaysia: James W. Gould, *The United States and Malaysia* (1969). See also "Asia and Pacific Islands."

Maldives: See "Indian Ocean."

Mauritania: Robert E. Handloff, ed., *Mauritania* (1990). See also "Africa."

Mauritius: Larry Bowman, *Mauritius* (1991). See also "Indian Ocean."

Mexico: Leslie Bethel, ed., *Mexico Since Independence* (1991); Lester D. Langley, *Mexico and the United States* (1991); David E. Lorey, ed., *United States–Mexico Border Statistics Since 1900* (1990) (S) and *The U.S.–Mexican Border in the Twentieth Century* (2000); Robert A. Pastor and Jorge G. Castañeda, *Limits to Friendship* (1988); George D. C. Philip, *Mexico* (1993) (B); W. Dirk Raat, *Mexico and the United States* (1997); Karl M. Schmitt, *Mexico and the United States* (1974); Norman E. Tutorow, ed., *The Mexican-American War* (1981) (B); Barbara G. Valk et al., *Borderline* (1988) (B); Josefina Vázquez and Lorenzo Meyer, *The United States and Mexico* (1985); David J. Weber, *The Mexican Frontier, 1821–1846* (1982); Sidney Weintraub, *A Marriage of Convenience* (1990). See also "Latin America."

Micronesia: See "Asia and Pacific Islands."

Middle East: Robert J. Allison, *The Crescent Observed: The United States and the Muslim World, 1776–1815* (1995); H. William Brands, *Into the Labyrinth* (1994); Thomas A. Bryson, *American Diplomatic Relations with the Middle East, 1784–1975* (1977) and *U.S.–Middle East Diplomatic Relations* (1979) (B); Uriel Dann, ed., *The Great Powers in the Middle East, 1919–1939* (1988); John A. DeNovo, *American Interests and Policies in the Middle East, 1900–1939* (1963); James A. Field, *America and the Mediterranean World, 1776–1882* (1969); T. G. Fraser, *The USA and the Middle East Since World War 2* (1989); Martin Gilbert, *Atlas of the Arab-Israeli Conflict* (1993) (A); Burton I. Kaufman, *The Arab Middle East and the United States* (1996); Colin Legum et al., eds., *Middle East Contemporary Survey* (1978–) (AS); George Lenczowski, *American Presidents and the Middle East* (1989); William R. Polk, *The Arab World Today* (1991); David Shavit, *The United States in the Middle East* (1988) (E); Sanford R. Silverburg and Bernard Reich, *U.S. Foreign Policy and the Middle East/North Africa* (1989) (B); Reeva S. Simon et al., eds., *The Encyclopedia of the Modern Middle East* (1996) (E); William Stivers, *America's Confrontation with Revolutionary Change in the Middle East, 1948–83* (1986); Alan R. Taylor, *The Superpowers and the Middle East* (1991). See also "Biological and Chemical Warfare," "Israel, Palestine, and Arab-Israeli Conflict," "Persian Gulf," and countries.

Moldova: See "Belarus."

Mongolia: Robert C. Worden and Andrea M. Savada, eds., *Mongolia* (1991).

Morocco: Leon B. Blair, *Western Window in the Arab World* (1970); Luella J. Hall, *The United States and Morocco, 1776–1956* (1961). See also "Africa" and "North Africa."

Mozambique: Mario Azevedo, *Historical Dictionary of Mozambique* (1991) (E); Maraget Hall and Tom Young, *Confronting Leviathan* (1997); Malyn Newitt, *A History of Mozambique* (1995). See also "Africa."

Myanmar: John F. Cady, *The United States and Burma* (1976); Patricia M. Herbert, *Burma* (1991) (B). See also "Vietnam and Southeast Asia."

Namibia: John J. Grotpeter, *Historical Dictionary of Namibia* (1994) (E). See also "Africa."

Nepal: Andrea M. Savada, ed., *Nepal and Bhutan* (1993).

Netherlands: Doeko Bosscher et al., eds., *American Culture in the Netherlands* (1996); Hans Loeber, ed., *Dutch-American Relations, 1945–1969* (1992); J. W. Schulte Nordholt and Robert P. Swierenga, eds., *A Bilateral Centennial: A History of Dutch-American Relations, 1783–1982* (1982); Gertrude Reichenbach-Consten and Abraham Noordergraaf, eds., *Two Hundred Years of Netherlands-American Interaction* (1985); Cornelis van Minnen, *American Diplomats in the Netherlands, 1815–50* (1993). See also "Europe."

New Zealand: See "Australia."

Nicaragua: Karl Berman, *Under the Big Stick* (1986); E. Bradford Burns, *Patriarch and Folk* (1991); Paul C. Clark, Jr., *The United States and Somoza* (1992); Peter Kornbluh, *Nicaragua* (1987); Tim L. Merrill, ed., *Nicaragua* (1994); Richard Millett, *Guardians of the Dynasty* (1977); Morris H. Morley, *Washington, Somoza, and the Sandinistas* (1994); Neil Narr, *Sandinista Nicaragua* (1990) (B); Robert Pastor, *Condemned to Repetition* (1987); Thomas W. Walker, *Nicaragua* (1991), ed., *Reagan Versus the Sandinistas* (1987), and ed., *Revolution & Counterrevolution in Nicaragua* (1991); Knut Walter, *The Regime of Anastasio Somoza* (1993); Ralph Lee Woodward, *Nicaragua* (1994) (B). See also "Central America" and "Latin America."

Nigeria: Bassey E. Ate, *Decolonization and Dependence* (1987); Helen C. Metz, ed., *Nigeria* (1992); Robert B. Shepard, *Nigeria, Africa, and the United States* (1991); Joseph E. Thompson, *American Policy and African Famine* (1990). See also "Africa."

North Africa: Charles F. Gallagher, *The United States and North Africa* (1963); Richard S. Parker, *North Africa* (1984). See also "Africa."

North Korea: See "Korea and Korean War."

Norway: Mats Berdal, *The United States, Norway, and the Cold War* (1997); Wayne S. Cole, *Norway and the United States* (1989); Ronald C. Popperwell, *Norway* (1972); Sigmund Skard, *The United States in Norwegian History* (1976); Rolf Tamnes, *The United States and the Cold War in the High North* (1991). See also "Europe" and "Scandinavia."

Oceania: See "Asia and Pacific Islands."

Oman: Joseph A. Kechichian, *Oman and the World* (1995). See also "Middle East" and "Persian Gulf."

Pacific Islands: See "Asia and Pacific Islands."

Pacific Rim: See "Asia and Pacific Islands."

Pakistan: Peter R. Blood, ed., *Pakistan* (1995); Iftikhar Malik, *U.S.–South Asian Relations, 1940–1947* (1991); Leo E. Rose and Noor A. Husain, eds., *U.S.–Pakistan Relations* (1985); Shirin Tahirkheli, *The United States and Pakistan* (1982); David D. Taylor, *Pakistan* (1990) (B); M. S. Venkataramani, *The American Role in Pakistan, 1947–1958* (1982). See also Wolpert in "Afghanistan" and Barnds and McMahon in "India."

Palestine: See "Israel, Palestine, and Arab-Israeli Conflict."

Panama (and Panama Canal): Michael L. Conniff, *Panama and the United States* (1992); David N. Farnsworth and James W. McKenney, *U.S.-Panama Relations, 1903–1978* (1983); J. Michael Hogan, *The Panama Canal in American Politics* (1986); Walter LaFeber, *The Panama Canal* (1990); Thomas M. Leonard, *Panama, the Canal, and the United States* (1993) (B); John Major, *Prize Possession* (1993); David McCullough, *The Path Between the Seas* (1977). See also "Latin America."

Paraguay: Anibal Miranda, *United States–Paraguay Relations* (1990); Riordan Roett and Richard S. Sacks, *Paraguay* (1991). See also "Latin America" and Whitaker in "Argentina."

Persian Gulf: Bruce R. Kuniholm, *The Persian Gulf and United States Policy* (1984) (B); Charles A. Kupchan, *The Persian Gulf and the West* (1987); Helen C. Metz, ed., *Persian Gulf States* (1993); Michael

A. Palmer, *Guardians of the Gulf* (1992). See also "Middle East" and Cottam in "Iran."

Peru: James C. Carey, *Peru and the United States, 1900–1962* (1964); Lawrence A. Clayton, *Peru and the United States* (1999); Rex A. Hudson, ed., *Peru* (1993); Fredrick B. Pike, *The United States and the Andean Republics* (1977); Ronald B. St. John, *The Foreign Policy of Peru* (1992). See also "Latin America."

Philippines: Teodoro A. Agoncillo, *A Short History of the Philippines* (1969); David H. Bain, *Sitting in Darkness* (1984); Raymond Bonner, *Waltzing with a Dictator* (1987); H. W. Brands, *Bound to Empire* (1992); Nick Cullather, *Illusions of Influence* (1994); Ronald E. Dolan, ed., *Philippines* (1993); Stanley Karnow, *In Our Image* (1989); Glenn A. May, *Battle for Batangas* (1991); Jim Richardson, *Philippines* (1989) (B); Peter W. Stanley, *A Nation in the Making* (1974). See also "Asia and Pacific Islands" and "Spanish-American-Cuban-Filipino War."

Poland: Glenn E. Curtis, ed., *Poland* (1994); Richard Lukacs, *Bitter Legacy* (1982); Piotr Wandycz, *The United States and Poland* (1980). See also "Eastern Europe" and "Europe."

Portugal: Scott B. MacDonald, *European Destiny, Atlantic Transformations* (1993); Kenneth Maxwell and Michael H. Haltzel, eds., *Portugal* (1990); Eric Solsten, ed., *Portugal* (1994). See also "Europe."

Puerto Rico: Raymond Carr, *Puerto Rico* (1984); Arturo Morales Carrión, *Puerto Rico* (1984); Elena E. Cevallos, *Puerto Rico* (1985) (B); Truman B. Clark, *Puerto Rico and the United States, 1917–1933* (1975); Ronald Fernandez, *The Disenchanted Island* (1996); A. W. Maldonado, *Teodora Moscoso and Puerto Rico's Operation Bootstrap* (1997); José Trías Monge, *Puerto Rico* (1997). See also "Caribbean."

Qatar: See "Persian Gulf."

Romania: Ronald D. Bachman, ed., *Romania* (1990); Joseph F. Harrington and Bruce J. Courtney, *Tweaking the Nose of the Russians* (1991). See also "Eastern Europe."

Russia and the Soviet Union: N. N. Bolkhovitinov and J. Dane Hartgrove, *Russia and the United States* (1987) (B); Peter G. Boyle, *American-Soviet Relations* (1993); Archie Brown et. al., eds, *The Cambridge Encyclopedia of Russia and the Soviet Union* (1994) (E); Glenn E. Curtis, ed., *Russia* (1998); Philip J. Funigiello, *American-Soviet Trade in the Cold War* (1988); John Lewis Gaddis, *Russia, the Soviet Union, and the United States* (1990); Raymond L. Garthoff, *Détente and Confrontation* (1985) and *The Great Transition* (1994); Howard Kushner, *Conflict on the Northwest Coast: American-Russian Rivalry in the Pacific Northwest, 1790–1867* (1975); Walter LaFeber, *America, Russia, and the Cold War* (1997); James K. Libbey, *American-Russian Economic Relations* (1989) (B); J. D. Parks, *Culture, Conflict, and Coexistence: American-Soviet Cultural Relations, 1917–1958* (1983); Norman E. Saul, *Concord and Conflict: The United States and Russia, 1867–1914* (1996) and *The United States and Russia, 1763–1867* (1991); David Shavit, *United States Relations with Russia and the Soviet Union* (1993) (E). See also "Baltic States," "Cold War," "Eastern Europe," and "Europe."

Rwanda: Learthen Dorsey, *Historical Dictionary of Rwanda* (1994) (E). See also "Africa."

Samoa (American): J. A. C. Gray, *Amerika Samoa* (1960); Paul Kennedy, *The Samoan Tangle* (1974); George H. Ryden, *The Foreign Policy of the United States in Relation to Samoa* (1933). See also "Asia and Pacific Islands."

Saudi Arabia: Irvine H. Anderson, *Aramco, the United States, and Saudi Arabia* (1981); Lee Grayson, *Saudi-American Relations* (1982); David E. Long, *The United States and Saudi Arabia* (1989); Helen C. Metz, ed., *Saudia Arabia* (1993); Aaron D. Miller, *Search for Security: Saudi Arabian Oil and American Foreign Policy, 1939–1949* (1980); Nadav Safran, *Saudi Arabia* (1986). See also "Middle East."

Scandinavia: Jussi M. Hanhimäki, *Scandinavia and the United States* (1997); Geir Lundestad, *America, Scandinavia, and the Cold War* (1980); Franklin D. Scott, *Scandinavia* (1975) and *The United States and Scandinavia* (1950). See also "Europe" and countries.

Senegal: R. M. Dilley and J. S. Eades, *Senegal* (1994) (B). See also "Africa."

Serbia: See "Yugoslavia."

Seychelles: See "Indian Ocean."

Singapore: Barbara L. LePoer, ed., *Singapore* (1991).

Slovenia: See "Yugoslavia."

Somalia: John L. Hirsch and Whert B. Oakley, *Somalia and Operation Restore Hope* (1995); Helen C. Metz, ed., *Somalia* (1993). See also "Africa" and Lefebvre in "Ethiopia."

South Africa: James Barber and John Barratt, *South Africa's Foreign Policy* (1990); Thomas Borstelmann, *Apartheid's Reluctant Uncle* (1993); Rita M. Byrnes, ed., *South Africa* (1997); Christopher Coker, *The United States and South Africa, 1968–1985* (1986); Jeffrey V.

Davis, *South Africa* (1994) (B); Terrel D. Hale, *United States Sanctions and South Africa* (1993) (B); Richard W. Hull, *American Enterprise in South Africa* (1990); C. T. Keto, *American–South African Relations, 1784-1980* (1985) (B); Y. G. M. Lulat, *U.S. Relations with South Africa* (1991) (B); Robert K. Massie, *Loosing the Bonds* (1997); William Minter, *King Soloman's Mines Revisited* (1986); Thomas J. Noer, *Briton, Boer, and Yankee* (1978) and *Cold War and Black Liberation* (1985). See also "Africa."

Southeast Asia: See "Vietnam and Southeast Asia."

Spain: James W. Cortada, *Two Nations over Time* (1978), and ed., *Spain in the Twentieth-Century World* (1980); Robert W. Kern, *Historical Dictionary of Modern Spain* (1990) (E); Boris N. Liedtke, *Embracing a Dictatorship* (1998); Eric Solsten and Sandra W. Meditz, eds., *Spain* (1990). See also "Europe" and "Spanish-American-Cuban-Filipino War."

Sri Lanka: Russell R. Ross and Andrea M. Savada, eds., *Sri Lanka* (1990).

Sudan: Carolyn Fkuehr-Lobban et al., *Historical Dictionary of Sudan* (1992) (E); Helen C. Metz, ed., *Sudan* (1992); Peter Woodward, *Sudan* (1989). See also "Africa."

Sweden: Sture Kindmark and Tore Tallroth, eds., *Swedes Looking West* (1983). See also "Europe" and "Scandinavia."

Switzerland: Heinze K. Meier, *Friendship Under Stress: U.S.-Swiss Relations, 1900–1950* (1970) and *The United States and Switzerland in the Nineteenth Century* (1963). See also "Europe."

Syria: David W. Lesch, *Syria and the United States* (1992); Moshe Ma'oz, *Syria and Israel* (1995); Andrew Rathwell, *Secret War in the Middle East* (1995); Bonnie Saunders, *The United States and Arab Nationalism* (1996); Abdul Latif Tibawi, *American Interests in Syria, 1800–1901* (1965). See also "Middle East."

Taiwan (Formosa): See "China (and Taiwan)."

Tajikistan: See "Kazakhstan."

Tanzania: See "Africa."

Thailand: Richard Aldrich, *The Key to the South* (1993); Barbara L. LePoer, ed., *Thailand* (1989); Robert J. Muscat, *Thailand and the United States* (1990). See also "Vietnam and Southeast Asia."

Trieste: Bogdan C. Novak, *Trieste, 1941–1954* (1970); Roberto Rabel, *Between East and West* (1988). See also "Italy."

Trinidad and Tobago: See "Caribbean."

Tunisia: See "North Africa."

Turkey: David J. Alvarez, *Bureaucracy and Cold War Ideology* (1980); George S. Harris, *Troubled Alliance* (1972); Harry H. Howard, *Turkey, the Straits, and U.S. Policy* (1974); Helen C. Metz, ed., *Turkey* (1996). See also "Europe" and Couloumbis and Stearns in "Greece."

Turkmenistan: See "Kazakhstan."

Uganda: Rita M. Byrnes, ed., *Uganda* (1992). See also "Africa."

Ukraine: Lubomyr A. Hajda, ed., *Ukraine in the World* (1998); Steven Woehrel, *Ukraine* (1994). See also "Russia and the Soviet Union."

United Arab Emirates: See "Middle East" and "Persian Gulf."

Uzbekistan: See "Kazakhstan."

Uruguay: Kitty L. Drummond, *Relations Between Uruguay and the United States* (1936); Rex A. Hudson and Sandra W. Meditz, eds., *Uruguay* (1992); Martin Weinstein, *Uruguay* (1987). See "Latin America" and Whitaker in "Argentina."

Venezuela: Judith Ewell, *Venezuela and the United States* (1996); Richard A. Haggerty, ed., *Venezuela* (1993); Sheldon B. Liss, *Diplomacy and Independence* (1978); Stephen G. Rabe, *The Road to OPEC* (1982). See also "Latin America" and "Oil."

Vietnam and Southeast Asia: David L. Anderson, ed., *Shadow on the White House* (1993); John S. Bowman, ed., *The Vietnam War* (1986) (C); Lester H. Brune and Richard Dean Burns, eds., *America and the Indochina Wars, 1945–1990* (1991) (B); William J. Duiker, *Historical Dictionary of Vietnam* (1989) (E); Frances Fitzgerald, *Fire in the Lake* (1972); Lloyd C. Gardner, *Approaching Vietnam* (1988); George C. Herring, *America's Longest War* (1996); Gary R. Hess, *Vietnam and the United States* (1998); George Kahin, *Intervention* (1986); Stanley Karnow, *Vietnam* (1991); Gabriel Kolko, *Anatomy of a War* (1985); Stanley I. Kutler, ed., *Encyclopedia of the Vietnam War* (1995) (E); David G. Marr, *Vietnam* (1992) (B); Robert J. McMahon, *The Limits of Empire* (1999); James S. Olson, *Dictionary of the Vietnam War* (1988) (E) and *The Vietnam War* (1993) (B); Andrew J. Rotter, *The Path to Vietnam* (1987); Robert D. Schulzinger, *A Time for War* (1997); Anthony Short, *The Origins of the Vietnam War* (1989); Harry

G. Summers, Jr., *Vietnam War Almanac* (1985) (C); Marilyn Young, *The Vietnam Wars* (1991). See also "Asia and Pacific Islands," "Military, U.S. Army, and Wars," and "Peace Movements."

Virgin Islands and West Indies: William W. Boyer, *America's Virgin Islands* (1983); Cary Fraser, *Ambivalent Anti-Colonialism: The United States and the Genesis of West Indian Independence, 1940–1964* (1993); Verna P. Moll, *Virgin Islands* (1991) (B). See also "Caribbean."

Yemen: Ahmed Nomen Al-Madhaqi, *Yemen and the USA* (1994); Fred Halliday, *Revolution and Foreign Policy* (1989). See also "Middle East."

Yugoslavia: Phylis Auty, *Yugoslavia* (1965); Leonard Cohen, *Broken Bonds* (1993); John R. Lampe et al., *Yugoslav-American Relations Since World War II* (1991); Lorraine M. Lees, *Keeping Tito Afloat* (1997); Susan Woodward, *Balkan Tragedy* (1995). See also "Eastern Europe."

Zambia: See "Africa."

Zimbabwe: J. D. Omer-Cooper, *A History of Southern Africa* (1994); R. Kent Rasmussen, *Historical Dictionary of Zimbabwe* (1990) (E). See also "Africa."

Overviews of Subjects, Including Atlases (A), Annual Surveys (AS), Bibliographies (B), Biographical Aids (BA), Chronologies (C), Encyclopedias (E), and Statistics (S)

African Americans: Gerald Horne, *Black and Red* (1986); Michael L. Krenn, *Black Diplomacy* (1998); Brenda Gayle Plummer, *Rising Wind* (1996); "Symposium: African Americans and U.S. Foreign Relations," *Diplomatic History*, XX (Fall 1996); Penny von Eschen, *Race Against Empire* (1997). See also "Race and Racism" and Skinner in "Africa."

AIDS Pandemic: J. Mann, Daniel Tarantola, and T. Netter, eds., *AIDS in the World* (1992, 1996); Matthew Smallman-Raynor et al., *Atlas of AIDS* (1992). See also "Health Organizations."

Air Force and Air Power: Charles D. Bright, ed., *Historical Dictionary of the U.S. Air Force* (1992) (E); Alan P. Dobson, *Peaceful Air Warfare* (1991); Richard P. Hallion, *The Literature of Aeronautics, Astronautics, and Air Power* (1984) (B); John B. Rae, *Climb to Greatness* (1968); Michael S. Sherry, *The Rise of American Air Power* (1987); Jeffrey S. Underwood, *The Wings of Democracy* (1991); Bruce W. Watson and Susan W. Watson, *The United States Air Force* (1992) (E). See also "Military, U.S. Army, and Wars" and specific wars.

Alliance for Progress: Jerome Levinson and Juan de Onís, *The Alliance That Lost Its Way* (1970); L. Ronald Scheman, ed., *The Alliance for Progress* (1988). See also "Latin America."

American Revolution: Richard Blanco, ed., *The American Revolution* (1993) (E); Mark M. Boatner III, *Encyclopedia of the American Revolution* (1974) (E); Lester J. Cappon, ed., *Atlas of Early American History: The Revolutionary Era, 1760–1790* (1976) (A); John M. Faragher, ed., *The Encyclopedia of Colonial and Revolutionary America* (1990) (E); Jack P. Greene and J. R. Pole, eds., *The Blackwell Encyclopedia of the American Revolution* (1991) (E); John W. Raimo, ed., *Biographical Directory of American Colonial and Revolutionary Governors, 1607–1789* (1980) (BA).

Anti-Americanism: "Anti-Americanism," *The Annals*, May 1988; Dan Diner, *German Anti-Americanism* (1995); Rob Kroes and Maarten van Rossem, eds., *Anti-Americanism in Europe* (1986); Denis Lacorne et al., eds., *The Rise and Fall of Anti-Americanism* (1990); Richard Pells, *Not Like Us* (1997); Alvin Z. Rubenstein and Donald E. Smith, eds., *Anti-Americanism in the Third World* (1985); David Strauss, *Menace in the West: The Rise of French Anti-Americanism in Modern Times* (1978).

Anticommunism and McCarthyism: Jeff Broadwater, *Eisenhower and the Anti-Communist Crusades* (1992); Peter H. Buckingham, *America Sees Red* (1987) (B); Richard M. Fried, *Nightmare in Red* (1990); Robert Griffith, *The Politics of Fear* (1987); John E. Haynes, *Communism and Anti-Communism in the United States* (1987) (B); Joel Kovel, *Red Hunting in the Promised Land* (1994); Stanley I. Kutler, *The American Inquisition* (1982); Richard G. Powers, *Not Without Honor* (1995); Stephen J. Whitfield, *The Culture of the Cold War* (1991). See also "Cold War."

ANZUS Pact: David W. McIntyre, *Background to the Anzus Pact* (1995). See also "Australia."

Arab-Israeli Conflict: See "Israel, Palestine, and Arab-Israeli Conflict" and "Middle East."

Arms Control: See "Disarmament and Arms Control."

Arms Sales and Trade: Michael Broszka and Thomas Ohlson, *Arms Transfers to the Third World* (1987); Michael T. Klare, *American Arms Supermarket* (1984); Edward J. Laurence, *The International Arms*

Trade (1992); Andrew J. Pierre, *The Global Politics of Arms Sales* (1982). See also "Military, U.S. Army, and Wars."

Assassination: Carl Sifakis, *Encyclopedia of Assassinations* (1991) (E).

Atlantic Charter: Douglas Brinkley and David Facey-Crowther, eds., *The Atlantic Charter* (1994); Theodore A. Wilson, *The First Summit* (1991). See also "World War II."

Biological and Chemical Warfare: G. M. Burck and Charles C. Flowerree, *International Handbook on Chemical Weapons Proliferation* (1991) (E); Anthony H. Cordesman, *Weapons of Mass Destruction in the Middle East* (1991); Stephen Endicott and Edward Hagerman, *The United States and Biological Warfare* (1999); John Norris and Will Fowler, *NBC: Nuclear, Biological, and Chemical Warfare on the Modern Battlefield* (1998) (E); Amy E. Simpson, ed., *The Chemical Weapons Convention Handbook* (1993); Victor A. Utgoff, *The Challenge of Chemical Weapons* (1991).

Bricker Amendment: Duane Tananbaum, *The Bricker Amendment Controversy* (1988). See also "Congress (House and Senate)."

Bureaucracy: Graham Allison, *Essence of Decision* (1971); I. M. Destler, *Presidents, Bureaucrats, and Foreign Policy* (1974); Louis Galambos, ed., *The New American State* (1987); Morton H. Halperin, *Bureaucratic Politics and Foreign Policy* (1974); Irving L. Janis, *Groupthink* (1983); James Q. Wilson, *Bureaucracy* (1989). See also "President (General)."

Business: See "Economic Relations and Business."

Central Intelligence Agency (CIA): See "Intelligence, CIA, and Covert Action."

Chemical Warfare: See "Biological and Chemical Warfare."

Civil War (American): Mark M. Boatner III, *The Civil War Dictionary* (1988) (E); D. P. Crook, *The North, the South, and the Powers* (1974); Richard N. Current, ed., *Encyclopedia of the Confederacy* (1993) (E); John T. Hubbell and James W. Geary, eds., *Biographical Dictionary of the Union* (1995) (BA); Howard Jones, *Union in Peril* (1992); David C. Roller and Robert W. Twyman, eds., *The Encyclopedia of Southern History* (1979) (E); Jon L. Wakelyn, ed., *Biographical Dictionary of the Confederacy* (1977) (BA); Steven E. Woodworth, ed., *The American Civil War* (1996) (B).

Cold War: Stephen Ambrose and David Brinkley, *Rise to Globalism* (1997); Thomas S. Arms, *Encyclopedia of the Cold War* (1994) (E);

Joseph L. Black, *Origins, Evolution, and Nature of the Cold War* (1986) (B); H. W. Brands, *The Devil We Knew* (1993); John Lewis Gaddis, *We Now Know All* (1997); Michael Kort, *The Columbia Guide to the Cold War* (1998) (E); Walter LaFeber, *America, Russia, and the Cold War* (1997); Thomas J. McCormick, *America's Half-Century* (1995); Thomas G. Paterson, *Meeting the Communist Threat* (1988) and *On Every Front* (1992). See also "Disarmament and Arms Control," "Nuclear Arms," "Russia and the Soviet Union," and "Threat Perception and Calculation."

Communications: James L. Baughman, *The Republic of Mass Culture* (1992); David H. Culbert, *News for Everyman* (1976) (radio); Howard H. Frederick, *Global Communications and International Relations* (1992); Julian Hale, *Radio Power* (1975); Daniel R. Headrick, *The Invisible Weapon: Telecommunications and International Politics, 1851–1945* (1991); James G. Savage, *The Politics of International Telecommunications Regulation* (1989); James Schwoch, *The American Radio Industry and Its Latin American Activities* (1990); Anthony Smith, *Geopolitics of Information* (1980); Philip M. Taylor, *Global Communications* (1997). See also "Cultural Relations."

Congress (House and Senate): Betty Austin, *J. William Fulbright* (1995) (B); Stephen G. Christianson, *Facts About the Congress* (1996); Congressional Quarterly, *Biographical Directory of the American Congress* (1997) (BA) and *Congress and the Nation, 1945–1984* (1965–1985) (E); Robert U. Goehlert and John R. Sayre, *The United States Congress* (1981) (B); Barbara Hinckley, *Less Than Meets the Eye* (1994); James M. Lindsey, *Congress and the Politics of U.S. Foreign Policy* (1994); James A. Robinson, *Congress and Foreign Policy-Making* (1967); John Rourke, *Congress and the Presidency in U.S. Foreign Policymaking* (1983); Goran Rystad, ed., *Congress and American Foreign Policy* (1982); John Spanier and Joseph Nogee, eds., *Congress, the Presidency, and Foreign Policy* (1980); U.S. Congress, *Biographical Directory of the United States Congress, 1774–1989* (1989) (BA); Gerald F. Warburg, *Conflict and Consensus* (1989); Stephen R. Weissman, *A Culture of Deference* (1995). See also "Constitution and Constitutional Interpretation," "President (General)," and "War Powers."

Conservation: See "Environment."

Constitution and Constitutional Interpretation: David G. Adler and Larry N. George, eds., *The Constitution and American Foreign Policy* (1996); Henry B. Cox, *War, Foreign Affairs, and Constitutional Power, 1829–1901* (1984); Louis Fischer, *Constitutional Conflicts Between the President and Congress* (1985); Thomas M. Franck and Michael J. Glennon, *Foreign Relations and National Security Law* (1993); Louis Henkin, *Constitutionalism, Democracy, and Foreign Affairs* (1990) and *Foreign Affairs and the Constitution* (1972); Harold Honggju Koh,

The National Security Constitution (1990); Leonard W. Levy et al., eds., *Encyclopedia of the American Constitution* (1986) (E); Gordon Silberstein, *Imbalance of Powers* (1997); Joan E. Smith, *The Constitution and American Foreign Policy* (1989); Abraham Sofaer, *War, Foreign Affairs, and Constitutional Power* (1976). See also "War Powers."

Containment: Terry L. Deibel and John Lewis Gaddis, eds., *Containment* (1986); John Lewis Gaddis, *Strategies of Containment* (1982); Charles Gati, ed., *Caging the Bear* (1974); Deborah Larson, *Origins of Containment* (1985). See also "Cold War."

Counterinsurgency: Benjamin R. Beede, *Intervention and Counterinsurgency* (1984) (B); Douglas S. Blaufarb, *The Counterinsurgency Era* (1977); Larry E. Cable, *Conflict of Myths* (1986); Michael T. Klare and Peter Kornbluh, eds., *Low-Intensity Warfare* (1988); Michael McClintock, *Instruments of Statecraft* (1992); D. Michael Shafer, *Deadly Paradigms* (1988). See also "Intelligence, CIA, and Covert Action."

Credibility: Robert J. McMahon, "Credibility and World Power," *Diplomatic History*, XV (Fall 1991), 455–471; Jonathan Mercer, *Reputation and International Politics* (1996).

Cultural Relations: Paul Braisted, ed., *Cultural Affairs and Foreign Relations* (1968); Jongsuk Chay, ed., *Culture and International Relations* (1990); Morrell Heald and Lawrence S. Kaplan, *Culture and Diplomacy* (1977); Akira Iriye, *Cultural Internationalism and World Order* (1997); Robert D. Johnson, ed., *On Cultural Ground* (1994); Gilbert M. Joseph el al., eds., *Close Encounters of Empire* (1998); Amy Kaplan and Donald E. Pease, eds., *Cultures of United States Imperialism* (1993); Frank Ninkovich, *The Diplomacy of Ideas* (1981); Emily Rosenberg, *Spreading the American Dream* (1982); Anthony Smith, *The Geopolitics of Information* (1980). See also "Communications," "Films, Television, and Cultural Expansion," "Philanthropy and Foundations," and "Propaganda and Public Diplomacy."

Decline Thesis: David P. Calleo, *Beyond American Hegemony* (1987); Paul Kennedy, *The Rise and Fall of the Great Powers* (1987); Henry Nau, *The Myth of America's Decline* (1990); Joseph P. Nye, Jr., *Bound to Lead* (1990).

Decolonization: Franz Ansprenger, *The Dissolution of Colonial Empires* (1989); Prosser Gifford and William Roger Louis, eds., *Decolonization and African Independence* (1988); D. A. Low, *Eclipse of Empire* (1991); Brian Urquhart, *Decolonization and World Peace* (1989).

Defense: See "Military, U.S. Army, and Wars," "Nuclear Arms," and particular wars.

Department of State, Foreign Service, and Diplomatic Practice: W. Wendell Blancke, *The Foreign Service of the United States* (1969); Robert U. Goehlert and Elizabeth Hoffmeister, *The Department of State and American Diplomacy* (1986) (B); Warren F. Ilchman, *Professional Diplomacy in the United States, 1779–1939* (1961); Charles S. Kennedy, *The American Consul* (1990); Henry E. Mattox, *The Twilight of Amateur Diplomacy* (1989); Robert H. Miller et al., *Inside an Embassy* (1992); Cathal Nolan, ed. *Notable U.S. Ambassadors Since 1775* (1998); Elmer Plischke, *United States Diplomats and Their Mission* (1979); Barry Rubin, *Secrets of State* (1985); Robert D. Schulzinger, *The Making of the Diplomatic Mind* (1975); Martin Weil, *A Pretty Good Club* (1978); Richard H. Werking, *The Master Architects* (1977). See also "President (General)."

Dependency: Fernando Henrique Cardoso and Enzo Faletto, *Dependency and Development in Latin America* (1979); Andre Gunder Frank, *Capitalism and Underdevelopment in Latin America* (1967); Vincent A. Mahler, *Dependency Approaches to International Political Economy* (1980); Robert A. Packenham, *The Dependency Movement* (1992). See also "World-System Analysis."

Deterrence: Alexander L. George and Richard Smoke, *Deterrence in American Foreign Policy* (1974); Ted Hopf, *Peripheral Visions* (1994); Robert Jervis et al., *Psychology and Deterrence* (1985). Also see "Cold War" and "Nuclear Arms."

Dictatorships: H. E. Chehabi and Juan J. Linz, *Sultanistic Regimes* (1998); David F. Schmitz, *Thank God They're on Our Side* (1999).

Diplomatic Immunity: Linda S. Frey and Marsha L. Frey, *The History of Diplomatic Immunity* (1999).

Disarmament and Arms Control: Sheikh Rustum Aki, *The Peace and Nuclear War Dictionary* (1989) (E); Stephen E. Atkins, *Arms Control and Disarmament* (1989) (B); Richard Dean Burns, ed., *Encyclopedia of Arms Control and Disarmament* (1993) (E); Jeffrey M. Elliot and Robert Reginald, *The Arms Control, Disarmament, and Military Security Dictionary* (1989) (E); Milton S. Katz, *Ban the Bomb* (1986); Stockholm International Peace Research Institute, *SIPRI Yearbook: International Armaments and Disarmament* (1969–) (AS and S); United Nations, *Disarmament Yearbook* (1976–) (AS); Lawrence S. Wittner, *One World or None* (1993). See also "Cold War," "Nuclear Arms," and "Peace Movements."

Dollar Diplomacy: Emily S. Rosenberg, *Dollar Diplomacy* (1999). See also "Economic Relations and Business."

Domino Theory: Frank Ninkovich, *Modernity and Power* (1994).

Drug Trafficking: Bruce M. Bagley, ed., *Drug Trafficking Research in the Americas* (1997) (B); Donald J. Mabry, ed., *The Latin American Narcotics Trade and U.S. National Security* (1989); Scott B. MacDonald and Bruce Zagaris, eds., *International Handbook on Drug Control* (1992) (E); Arnold H. Taylor, *American Diplomacy and the Narcotics Traffic, 1900–1931* (1969); William O. Walker III, *Drug Control in the Americas* (1981), ed., *Drugs in the Western Hemisphere* (1996), and *Opium and Foreign Policy* (1991).

Economic Relations and Business: William H. Becker and Samuel F. Wells, eds., *Economics and World Power* (1984); David P. Calleo, *The Imperious Economy* (1982); Alfred E. Eckes, Jr., *Opening America's Market* (1995); Michael J. Freeman, *Atlas of World Economy* (1991) (A); Carolyn Gibson, *The McGraw-Hill Dictionary of International Trade* (1994) (E); Judith Goldstein, *Ideas, Interests, and American Trade Policy* (1993); John N. Ingham, *Biographical Dictionary of American Business Leaders* (1983) (BA); John N. Ingham and Lyness B. Feldman, *Contemporary American Business Leaders* (1990) (BA); Edward S. Kaplan and Thomas W. Ryley, *Prelude to Trade Wars: American Trade Policy, 1890–1922* (1994); Diane Kunz, *Butter and Guns* (1997); Thelma Liesner, *One Hundred Years of Economic Statistics* (1989) (S); Wahib Nasrallah, *United States Corporation Histories* (1991) (B); Timothy O'Donnell et al., eds., *World Economic Data* (1991) (S); James S. Olsen, *Dictionary of American Economic History* (1992) (E); Richard Robinson, *United States Business History* (1990) (E); Joan E. Spero and Jeffrey A. Hart, *The Politics of International Economic Relations* (1997); United Nations, *International Trade Statistics Yearbook* (1985–) (AS and S), *World Economic Survey* (1955–) (AS and S), and *Yearbook of International Trade Statistics* (1950–1982) (AS and S); Herman Van Der Wee, *The Search for Prosperity: The World Economy, 1945–1977* (1977); Malcolm Warner, ed., *International Encyclopedia of Business and Management* (1996) (E); Mira Wilkins, *The Emergence of Multinational Enterprise* (1970) and *The Maturing of Multinational Enterprise* (1975); Thomas W. Zeiler, *Free Trade, Free World: The Advent of GATT* (1999). See also "Dollar Diplomacy," "Economic Sanctions and Export Controls," "Export-Import Bank," "Minerals," "North American Free Trade Agreement (NAFTA)," "Tariffs and Protectionism," and Funigiello in "Russia and the Soviet Union."

Economic Sanctions and Export Controls: Margaret P. Doxey, *Economic Sanctions and International Enforcement* (1980); Gary C. Hufbauer and Jeffrey J. Schott, *Economic Sanctions Reconsidered* (1990); William J. Long, *U.S. Export Control Policy* (1989); Donald Losman, *International Economic Sanctions* (1979); Homer E. Moyer, Jr., and Linda L. Mabry, *Export Controls as Instruments of Foreign Policy* (1988); Sidney Weintrub, ed., *Economic Coercion and U.S. Foreign Policy* (1982); Thomas G. Weiss, *Political Gain and Civilian Pain* (1998). See also "Economic Relations and Business" and "Tariffs and Protectionism."

Environment: Robert Broadman, *International Organization and the Conservation of Nature* (1981); Lester R. Brown et al., *State of the World* (1984–) (AS); Lynton K. Caldwell, *International Environmental Policy* (1990); André R. Cooper, Sr., ed., *Cooper's Comprehensive Environmental Desk Reference* (1996) (E); Kurkpatrick Dorsey, *The Dawn of Conservation Diplomacy* (1999); Fridtjof Nansen Institute (Norway), *Green Globe Yearbook* (1992–) (AS); John McCormick, *The Global Environment* (1995) and *Reclaiming Paradise: The Global Environmental Movement* (1989); Organisation for Economic Co-operation and Development, *The State of the Environment* (1991) (E and S); Robert Paehlke, ed., *Conservation and Environmentalism* (1995) (E); Kirkpatrick Sale, *The Green Revolution* (1993); World Resources Institute, *Environmental Almanac* (1992) (E); World Resources Institute (or International Institute for Environment and Development), *World Resources* (1976–). See also "Law of the Sea."

Ethics: Gerald Elfstrom, *Ethics for a Shrinking World* (1990); J. E. Hare and Carey B. Joynt, *Ethics and International Affairs* (1982); Dorothy V. Jones, *Code of Peace* (1991); Kenneth W. Thompson, ed., *Ethics and International Relations* (1985) and *Moral Dimensions of American Foreign Policy* (1984).

Ethnic Conflict: David Callahan, *Unwinnable Wars* (1997); Human Rights Watch, *Slaughter Among Neighbors* (1995); David A. Lake and Donald Rothchild, eds., *The International Spread of Ethnic Conflict* (1998). See also countries.

Ethnic Groups and Immigration: Mohammed E. Ahrari, ed., *Ethnic Groups and U.S. Foreign Policy* (1987); Gerald Chaliand and Jean-Pierre Rageau, *The Penguin Atlas of Diasporas* (1995) (A); Francesco Cordasco, ed., *Dictionary of American Immigration History* (1990) (E); Alexander DeConde, *Ethnicity, Race, and American Foreign Policy* (1992); Robert A. Divine, *American Immigration Policy, 1924–1952* (1963); Louis L. Gerson, *The Hyphenate in Recent American Politics and Diplomacy* (1964); David M. Reimers, *Still the Golden Door: The Third World Comes to America* (1992); Abdul Aziz Said, ed., *Ethnicity and U.S. Foreign Policy* (1977); Stephen Thernstrom, ed., *Harvard Encyclopedia of American Ethnic Groups* (1980) (E); Robert W. Tucker et al., eds., *Immigration and U.S. Foreign Policy* (1990). See also "Refugees."

Exceptionalism: David K. Adams and Cornelis A. van Minnen, eds., *Reflections on American Exceptionalism* (1994). See also "Ideology."

Executive Agreements: Lawrence Margolis, *Executive Agreements and Presidential Power in Foreign Policy* (1986); Wallace M. McClure, *International Executive Agreements* (1941). See also "President (General)."

Export-Import Bank: Frederick C. Adams, *Economic Diplomacy* (1976); Richard E. Feinberg, *Subsidizing Success* (1982); Rita M. Rodriquez, ed., *The Export-Import Bank at Fifty* (1987). See also "Economic Relations and Business."

Extraterritoriality: Wesley R. Fishel, *The End of Extraterritoriality* (1952); Dietr Lange and Gary Born, eds., *The Extraterritorial Application of National Laws* (1987). See also "International Law and Hague Conferences."

Films, Television, and Cultural Expansion: Clayton R. Koppes and Gregory D. Black, *Hollywood Goes to War* (1987); Thomas Doherty, *Projections of War* (1999); James F. Larson, *Global Television and Foreign Policy* (1988); Thomas J. Saunders, *Hollywood in Berlin* (1994); Kristin Thompson, *Exporting Entertainment* (1985). See also "Communications" and "Cultural Relations."

Food Diplomacy and Relief: Nicole Ball, ed., *World Hunger* (1981) (B); Raymond F. Hopkins and Donald J. Puchala, *Global Food Interdependence* (1980); Don Paarlberg, *Toward a Well-Fed World* (1988); Vernon W. Ruttan, ed., *Why Food Aid?* (1993); Hans W. Sinder et al., *Food Aid* (1987); Ross B. Talbott, *The Four World Food Agencies in Rome* (1990). See also "Foreign Aid" and "Humanitarian Relief and Intervention."

Foreign Aid: David Baldwin, *Economic Development and American Foreign Policy, 1943–1962* (1966); Herbert Feis, *Foreign Aid and Foreign Policy* (1964); David H. Lumsdaine, *Moral Vision in International Politics: The Foreign Aid Regime, 1949–1989* (1993); Robert A. Packenham, *Liberal America and the Third World* (1973); Roger Riddell, *Foreign Aid Reconsidered* (1987); Vernon W. Ruttan, *United States Development Assistance Policy* (1995). See also "Food Diplomacy and Relief."

Foreign Investment in the United States: Mira Wilkins, *The History of Foreign Investment in the United States to 1914* (1989). See also "Economic Relations and Business."

Foreign Service: See "Department of State, Foreign Service, and Diplomatic Practice."

French and Indian War: Seymour I. Schwartz, *The French and Indian War, 1854–1763* (1995) (E). See also "Military, U.S. Army, and Wars."

Fulbright Program: Walter Johnson and Francis Collegan, *The Fulbright Program* (1965); Leonard Sussman, *The Culture of Freedom* (1992). See also "Cultural Relations."

Genocide: Israel Charney, ed., *Genocide* (1988) (B); Leo Kuper, *Genocide* (1981); Lawrence J. LeBlanc, *The United States and the Geno-cide Convention* (1991); Ervin Staub, *The Roots of Evil* (1989); Charles B. Stroozier and Michael Flynn, eds., *Genocide, War, and Human Survival* (1996). See also "Holocaust," "Humanitarian Relief and Intervention," and "War Crimes and Trials."

Good Neighbor Policy: David Green, *The Containment of Latin America* (1971); Fredrick B. Pike, *FDR's Good Neighbor Policy* (1995); Bryce Wood, *The Dismantling of the Good Neighbor Policy* (1985) and *The Making of the Good Neighbor Policy* (1961). See also "Latin America."

Guano: Jimmy M. Skaggs, *The Great Guano Rush* (1994).

Health and Medical History of Leaders: Kenneth R. Crispell and Carlos F. Gomez, *Hidden Illness in the White House* (1988); Robert H. Ferrell, *Ill-Advised* (1992); Robert E. Gilbert, *The Mortal Presidency* (1992); Bert E. Park, *Ailing, Aged, Addicted* (1993) and *The Impact of Illness on World Leaders* (1986). See also "President (General)" and "President (By Administration)."

Health Organizations: Javid Siddiqi, *World Health and World Politics* (1994); Paul Weindling, ed., *International Health Organizations and Movements* (1995).

Holocaust: Richard Breitman and Alan M. Kraut, *American Refugee Policy and European Jewry* (1987); Leonard Dinnerstein, *America and the Survivors of the Holocaust* (1982); Henry L. Feingold, *Bearing Witness* (1995); Martin Gilbert, *Auschwitz and the Allies* (1981); Israel Gutman, ed., *Encyclopedia of the Holocaust* (1990) (E); Deborah E. Lipstadt, *Beyond Belief* (1993); Michael R. Marrus, *The Holocaust in History* (1987); David Wyman, *The Abandonment of the Jews* (1984) and *Paper Walls* (1968). See also "Genocide," "Germany and Berlin," "War Crimes and Trials," and "World War II."

Hostage-Taking: Russell D. Buhite, *Lives at Risk* (1995).

Humanitarian Relief and Intervention: Larry Minear and Thomas G. Weiss, *Humanitarian Politics* (1995); Robert I. Rotberg and Thomas G. Weiss, eds., *From Massacres to Genocide* (1996). See also "Ethnic Conflict," "Genocide," "Human Rights," and countries.

Human Rights: America's Watch Staff (periodic reports on Latin American countries); Amnesty International, *The Amnesty International Report* (1977–) (AS); Peter R. Baehr, *The Role of Human Rights in Foreign Policy* (1994); Jack Donnelly and Rhoda E. Howard, eds., *International Handbook of Human Rights* (1987) (E); Charles Humana, *World Human Rights Guide* (1992); Human Rights Watch, *World Report* (1983–) (AS); Natalie Kaufman, *Human Rights Treaties and the Senate* (1990); William Korey, *The Promises We Keep* (1993); Edward Lawson, *Encyclopedia of Human Rights* (1991) (E);

A. Glenn Mower, *Human Rights and American Foreign Policy* (1987) and *The United States, the United Nations, and Human Rights* (1979); A. H. Robertson and J. G. Merrills, *Human Rights in the World* (1997) (B); Lars Schoultz, *Human Rights and United States Policy Toward Latin America* (1981); Kenneth W. Thompson, ed., *The Moral Imperatives of Human Rights* (1980); Sandy Vogelgesang, *American Dream, American Nightmare* (1980). See also "Holocaust," "Humanitarian Relief and Intervention," and "War Crimes and Trials."

Ideology: Richard J. Barnet, *Roots of War* (1972); Edward M. Burns, *The American Idea of Mission* (1957); Arthur A. Ekirch, Jr., *Ideas, Ideals, and American Diplomacy* (1966); Michael H. Hunt, *Ideology and U.S. Foreign Policy* (1987); David M. Potter, *People of Plenty* (1954); E. L. Tuveson, *Redeemer Nation* (1968); William A. Williams, *The Tragedy of American Diplomacy* (1962). See also "Manifest Destiny" and "Race and Racism."

Immigration: See "Ethnic Groups and Immigration."

Imperialism: Michael B. Brown, *The Economics of Imperialism* (1974); Benjamin J. Cohen, *The Question of Imperialism* (1973); Philip Darby, *Three Faces of Imperialism* (1987); Michael Doyle, *Empires* (1986); Gabriel Kolko, *The Roots of American Foreign Policy* (1969); Tony Smith, *The Pattern of Imperialism* (1981); Richard W. Van Alstyne, *The Rising American Empire* (1960). See also "Dependency" and "World-System Analysis."

Indians (Native Americans): Brian W. Dippie, *The Vanishing American* (1982); Michael Green, *The Politics of Indian Removal* (1982); Barry Klein, ed., *Reference Encyclopedia of the American Indian* (1993) (E); Calvin Martin, ed., *The American Indian and the Problem of History* (1986); Francis Paul Prucha, *Atlas of American Indian Affairs* (1990) (A) and *The Indian in American Society* (1985); Michael Rogin, *Fathers and Sons* (1975); Paul Stuart, *Nation Within a Nation* (1987) (S); Carl Waldman, *Atlas of the North American Indian* (1985) (A); Philip Weeks, *Farewell My Nation* (1990).

Intelligence, CIA, and Covert Action: Charles D. Ameringer, *U.S. Foreign Intelligence* (1990); Christopher Andrew, *For the President's Eyes Only* (1995); Paul W. Blackstock and Frank L. Schaf, eds., *Intelligence, Espionage, Counterespionage, and Covert Operations* (1978) (B); Marjorie W. Cline et al., *Scholar's Guide to Intelligence Literature* (1983) (B); George C. Constantinides, *Intelligence & Espionage* (1983) (B); Arthur B. Darling, *The Central Intelligence Agency* (1990); Rhodri Jeffreys-Jones, *The CIA and American Democracy* (1989); Rhodri Jeffreys-Jones and Andrew Lownie, eds., *North American Spies* (1991); Loch K. Johnson, *America's Secret Power* (1989), *A Season of Inquiry* (1985), and *Secret Agencies* (1996); Stephen F. Knott, *Secret and Sanc-* tioned (1996); Mark Lowenthal, *U.S. Intelligence* (1992); Ernest R. May, ed., *Knowing One's Enemies* (1985); Neal H. Petersen, *American Intelligence, 1775–1990* (1992) (B); Walter Pforzheimer, *Bibliography of Intelligence Literature* (1985) (B); John Prados, *The Presidents' Secret Wars* (1986); John Ranelagh, *The Agency* (1986); W. Michael Reisman and James E. Baker, *Regulating Covert Action* (1992); Frank J. Smist, Jr., *Congress Oversees the United States Intelligence Community* (1994); Jeffrey T. Richelson, *A Century of Spies* (1995) and *The U.S. Intelligence Community* (1995); Bradley F. Smith, *The Shadow Warriors* (1983); Gregory F. Treverton, *Covert Action* (1987); Bruce W. Watson et al., eds., *United States Intelligence* (1990) (E); Robin W. Winks, *Clock & Gown* (1987). See also "Assassination."

International Finance: See "International Monetary Fund and System" and "World Bank."

International Law and Hague Conferences: Robert L. Bledsoe and Boleslaw A. Boczek, *The International Law Dictionary* (1987) (E); Calvin D. Davis, *The United States and the First Hague Conference* (1962) and *The United States and the Second Hague Conference* (1976); Ingrid Delupis, ed., *Bibliography of International Law* (1975) (B); Richard Falk et al., eds., *International Law* (1985); James Fox, *Dictionary of International and Comparative Law* (1991) (E); Daniel P. Moynihan, *The Law of Nations* (1990). See also "Law of the Sea."

International Monetary Fund and System: Margaret G. DeVries, *The IMF in a Changing World* (1986); Barry Eichengreen, *Globalizing Capital* (1996); Harold James, *International Monetary Cooperation Since Bretton Woods* (1996); Mary E. Johnson, *The International Monetary Fund* (1993) (B); Robert Soloman, *Money on the Move* (1999); Brian Tew, *The Evolution of the International Monetary Fund, 1945–81* (1982).

International Organizations: Sheikh Ali, *The International Organization and World Order Dictionary* (1992) (E); George W. Baer, ed., *International Organizations, 1918–1945* (1981) (B); Edward J. Osmanczyk, *The Encyclopedia of the United States and International Organizations* (1990) (E); Hans-Albrecht Schraepler, *Directory of International Organizations* (1996); Union of International Associations, *Yearbook of International Organizations* (1948–) (AS). See also specific organizations.

Isolationism: Selig Adler, *The Isolationist Impulse* (1957); Wayne S. Cole, *Roosevelt and the Isolationists* (1983); Justus D. Doenecke, *Anti-Intervention* (1987) (B); Thomas N. Guinsburg, *The Pursuit of Isolationism in the United States Senate* (1982); Manfred Jonas, *Isolationism in America, 1935–1941* (1966).

Journalism and Media: James L. Baughman, *Henry R. Luce and the Rise of the American News Media* (1988); Bernard C. Cohen, *The Press and Foreign Policy* (1963); Joseph P. McKerns, ed., *Biographical Dictionary of American Journalism* (1989) (BA); Brigitte Lebens Nacos, *The Press, Presidents, and Crises* (1990); Johanna Neuman, *Lights, Camera, War* (1995); Michael Schudson, *The Power of News* (1995); Simon Serfaty, *The Media and Foreign Policy* (1990); Ronald Steel, *Walter Lippmann and the American Century* (1980); William H. Taft, ed., *Encyclopedia of Twentieth-Century Journalists* (1986) (BA); John Tebbel and Sarah Miles Watts, *The Press and the Presidency* (1985). See also "Film, Television, and Cultural Expansion" and "Public Opinion."

Korean War: See "Korea and Korean War."

Labor: Philip S. Foner, *U.S. Labor Movement and Latin America* (1988); Ronald Radosh, *American Labor and United States Foreign Policy* (1969); Federico Romero, *The United States and the European Trade Union Movement, 1944–1951* (1992).

Law of the Sea: Jack N. Barkenbus, *Deep Seabed Resources* (1979); Ann L. Hollick, *U.S. Foreign Policy and the Law of the Sea* (1981); D. P. O'Connell, *The International Law of the Sea* (1982); Clyde Sanger, *Ordering the Oceans* (1987); United Nations, *The Law of the Sea* (1991) (B). See also "Environment" and "International Law and Hague Conferences."

League of Nations: Denna F. Fleming, *The United States and the League of Nations* (1932); Warren F. Kuehl, *Seeking World Order* (1969); F. S. Northedge, *The League of Nations* (1986). See also "International Organizations" and "United Nations."

Low Intensity Warfare: See "Counterinsurgency."

Manifest Destiny: Norman A. Graebner, ed., *Manifest Destiny* (1968); Thomas R. Hietala, *Manifest Design* (1985); Reginald Horsman, *Race and Manifest Destiny* (1981); Robert W. Johannsen, ed., *Manifest Destiny* (1998); Anders Stephanson, *Manifest Destiny* (1995); Albert K. Weinberg, *Manifest Destiny* (1935). See also "Ideology."

Marshall Plan: Michael J. Hogan, *The Marshall Plan* (1987); Alan S. Milward, *The Reconstruction of Western Europe, 1945–51* (1984); Imanuel Wexler, *The Marshall Plan Revisited* (1983). See also "Europe" and "Foreign Aid."

Marine Corps: Allan R. Millett, *Semper Fidelis* (1980). See also "Military, U.S. Army, and Wars" and specific wars.

McCarthyism: See "Anticommunism and McCarthyism."

Media: See "Journalism and Media."

Merchant Marine: John A. Butler, *Sailing on Friday* (1997); Rene De La Pedraja, *A Historical Dictionary of the U.S. Merchant Marine and Shipping Industry* (1994) (E).

Military, U.S. Army, and Wars: William M. Arkin et al., *Encyclopedia of the U.S. Military* (1990) (E); Benjamin R. Beede, *Military and Strategic Policy* (1990) (B); Daniel K. Blewett, *American Military History* (1994) (B); John W. Chambers, *To Raise an Army* (1987); Edward M. Coffman, *The Old Army* (1986); E. Ernest Dupuy and Trevor N. Dupuy, *The Harper Encyclopedia of Military History* (1993) (E); John C. Fredriksen, *Shield of the Republic/Sword of Empire* (1990) (B); Kenneth J. Hagan and William R. Roberts, eds., *Against All Enemies* (1986); Robin Higham and Donald J. Mrozek, eds., *A Guide to the Sources of United States Military History* (1975–   ) (B); International Institute for Strategic Studies, *Strategic Survey* (1966–   ) (AS) and *The Military Balance* (1959/1960–   ) (AS); *International Military and Defense Encyclopedia* (1993) (E); John E. Jessup and Louise B. Ketz, eds., *Encyclopedia of the American Military* (1994) (E);   Kenneth Macksey and William Woodhouse, *The Penguin Encyclopedia of Modern Warfare* (1992); Allan R. Millett and Peter Maslowski, *For the Common Defense* (1994); Jay M. Shafritz et al., eds., *Dictionary of Military Science* (1989); Roger J. Spiller and Joseph G. Dawson III, eds., *Dictionary of American Military Biography* (1984) (BA); Jerry K. Sweeney, ed., *A Handbook of American Military History* (1996) (E); Herbert K. Tillema, *International Armed Conflict Since 1945* (1991) (B); Peter G. Tsouras et al., *The United States Army* (1991) (E); U.S. Military Academy, *The West Point Atlas of American Wars, 1689–1953* (1959) (A); Cynthia Watson, *U.S. National Security Policy Groups* (1990) (E); Russell F. Weigley, *The American Way of War* (1973) and *History of the United States Army* (1984). See also "Marine Corps," "Navy and Sea Power," and wars.

Minerals: Alfred E. Eckes, *The United States and the Global Struggle for Minerals* (1979); Jordan E. Helmreich, *Gathering Rare Ores* (1986); Ronnie Lipschutz, *When Nations Clash* (1989). See also "Economic Relations and Business."

Missionaries: Henry Bowden, *Dictionary of American Religious Biography* (1993) (BA); John K. Fairbank, ed., *The Missionary Enterprise in China and America* (1974); Patricia Hill, *The World Their Household* (1985); Jane Hunter, *The Gospel of Gentility* (1984); William R. Hutchison, *Errand to the World* (1987); Paul A. Varg, *Missionaries, Chinese, and Diplomats* (1958). See also "Cultural Relations" and "Ideology."

Monroe Doctrine: Ernest R. May, *The Making of the Monroe Doctrine* (1975); Dexter Perkins, *A History of the Monroe Doctrine* (1963);

Gaddis Smith, *The Last Years of the Monroe Doctrine* (1994). See also "Latin America."

National Security Council: Gerry Andrianopoulos, *Kissinger and Brzezinski* (1991); John Prados, *Keepers of the Keys* (1991); Bromley K. Smith, *Organizational History of the National Security Council During the Kennedy and Johnson Administrations* (1988).

Navy and Sea Power: George W. Baer, *One Hundred Years of Sea Power* (1994); James C. Bradford, *Admirals of the New Steel Navy* (1990), *Captains of the Old Steam Navy* (1986), and *Command Under Sail* (1985); William B. Cogan, *Dictionary of Admirals of the United States Navy* (1989) (BA); Paolo E. Coletta, *A Selected and Annotated Bibliography of American Naval History* (1988) (B); Paolo E. Coletta et al., eds., *American Secretaries of the Navy* (1980) (BA); Michael J. Crawford and Christine F. Hughes, *The Reestablishment of the Navy, 1787–1801* (1995) (B); Kenneth J. Hagan, ed., *In Peace and War* (1984) and *This People's Navy* (1991); John B. Hattendorf and Lynn C. Hattendorf, *A Bibliography of the Works of Alfred Thayer Mahan* (1986) (B); David F. Long, *Gold Braid and Foreign Relations* (1988); Barbara A. Lynch and John E. Vajda, *United States Naval History* (1993) (B); Franklin D. Margiotta, ed., *Brassey's Encyclopedia of Naval Forces and Warfare* (1996) (E); Elmer B. Potter, ed., *Sea Power* (1981); Harold Sprout and Margaret Sprout, *The Rise of American Naval Power* (1966); Jack Sweetman, ed., *American Naval History* (1984) (C); Bruce W. Watson and Susan M. Watson, *The United States Navy* (1991) (E). See also "Military, U.S. Army, and Wars" and wars.

Neutralism and Nonalignment: H. W. Brands, *The Specter of Neutralism* (1989); K. C. Chaudhary, *Non-aligned Summitry* (1988); Steven R. David, *Choosing Sides* (1991); Richard L. Jackson, *The Non-aligned, the UN, and the Superpowers* (1983); Lawrence W. Martin, ed., *Neutralism and Nonalignment* (1962).

Nobel Peace Prize: Irwin Abrams, *The Nobel Peace Prize and the Laureates* (1988); Oaula McGuire, ed., *Nobel Prize Winners Supplement* (1992); Tyler Wasson, ed., *Nobel Prize Winners* (1987). See also "Peace Movements."

Nonproliferation (Nuclear): See "Cold War" and "Nuclear Arms."

North American Free Trade Agreement (NAFTA): Allan Metz, *A NAFTA Bibliography* (1996) (B); Jerry M. Rosenberg, *Encyclopedia of the North American Free Trade Agreement* (1984) (E). See also "Canada" and "Economic Relations and Business."

North Atlantic Treaty Organization (NATO): Timothy Ireland, *Creating the Entangling Alliance* (1981); Robert S. Jordan, Jr., ed., *Generals in International Politics* (1987); Lawrence S. Kaplan, *The Long Entanglement: NATO's First Fifty Years* (1999) and *NATO & the United States* (1994); Augustus R. Norton et al., *NATO* (1985) (B); Joseph Smith, ed., *The Origins of NATO* (1990). See also "Cold War," "Europe," and "Nuclear Arms."

Nuclear Arms: Paul Boyer, *By the Bomb's Early Light* (1985); McGeorge Bundy, *Danger and Survival* (1990); Robert A. Divine, *The Sputnik Challenge* (1993); Lawrence Freedman, *The Evolution of Nuclear Strategy* (1989); Gregg Herken, *Counsels of War* (1985); David Holloway, *The Soviet Union and the Arms Race* (1984); Fred Kaplan, *The Wizards of Armageddon* (1983); Charles R. Morris, *Iron Destinies, Lost Opportunities* (1988); John Newhouse, *War and Peace in the Nuclear Age* (1989); William G. M. Pearson, *The Nuclear Arms Race* (1989) (E); Ronald E. Powaski, *March to Armageddon* (1987); Scott D. Sagan, *The Limits of Safety* (1993); Stephen I. Schwartz, ed., *Atomic Audit* (1998); Richard Smoke, *National Security and the Nuclear Dilemma* (1987); Spencer R. Weart, *Nuclear Fear* (1988); Allan M. Winkler, *Life Under a Cloud* (1993). See also "Cold War," "Disarmament and Arms Control," and "Space and Satellites."

Oil: M. A. Adelman, *The Genie out of the Bottle* (1995); Gerald D. Nash, *United States Oil Policy, 1890–1964* (1968); David S. Painter, *Oil and the American Century* (1986); Stephen J. Randall, *United States Foreign Oil Policy, 1919–1984* (1985); Anthony Sampson, *The Seven Sisters* (1991); Michael B. Stoff, *Oil, War, and American Security* (1980); Fiona Venn, *Oil Diplomacy in the Twentieth Century* (1986); Daniel Yergin, *The Prize* (1991). See also "Mexico," "Middle East," "Minerals," "Organization of Petroleum Exporting Countries (OPEC)," "Venezuela," and Anderson and Miller in "Saudi Arabia."

Olympics: Allen Guttmann, *The Games Must Go On* (1984) and *The Olympics* (1992); Christopher R. Hill, *Olympic Politics* (1996); David Wallechinsky, *The Complete Book of the Summer Olympics* (1996) (E) and *The Complete Book of the Winter Olympics* (1993) (E). See also "Sports."

Organization of American States (OAS): David Sheinin, *The Organization of American States* (1996) (B). See also "Latin America" and "Pan-Americanism."

Organization of Petroleum Exporting Countries (OPEC): M. E. Ahrari, *OPEC* (1986); Albert L. Danielson, *The Evolution of OPEC* (1982); Ian Skeet, *OPEC* (1988). See also "Oil" and Rabe in "Venezuela."

PanAmericanism: J. Floyd Mecham, *The United States and Inter-American Security, 1889–1960* (1961); Arthur P. Whitaker, *The Western Hemisphere Idea* (1954). See also "Latin America."

Peace Corps: Fritz Fischer, *Making Them Like Us* (1998); Elizabeth Cobbs Hoffman, *All You Need Is Love* (1998); T. Zane Reeves, *The Politics of the Peace Corps & Vista* (1988); Gerald T. Rice, *Bold Experiment* (1985); Robert Ridinger, *The Peace Corps* (1989) (B): D. David Searles, *The Peace Corps Experience* (1997). See also "Cultural Relations."

Peacekeeping: Paul F. Diehl, *International Peacekeeping* (1993); William J. Durch, ed., *The Evolution of UN Peacekeeping* (1993); Alan James, *Peacekeeping in International Politics* (1990); Nathan A. Pelcovits, *The Long Armistice* (1993). See also "United Nations."

Peace Movements: Harriet Hyman Alonso, *Peace as a Women's Issue* (1993); Peter Brock, *Pacifism in the United States* (1968); Charles Chatfield, *The American Peace Movement* (1992); Charles DeBenedetti, ed., *Peace Heroes in Twentieth Century America* (1986) and *The Peace Reform in American History* (1980); Catherine Foster, *Women for All Seasons* (1989); Charles F. Howlett, *The American Peace Movement* (1990) (B); Harold Josephson et al., eds., *Biographical Dictionary of Modern Peace Leaders* (1985) (BA); Robert Kleidman, *Organizing for Peace: Neutrality, the Test Ban, and the Freeze* (1993); Elvin Laszlo and Jong Youl Yoo, eds., *World Encyclopedia of Peace* (1986) (E); Robert S. Meyer, *Peace Organizations Past and Present* (1988) (E); David S. Patterson, *Toward a Warless World* (1976); Nancy L. Roberts, *American Peace Writers, Editors, and Periodicals* (1991) (BA); Lawrence S. Wittner, *Rebels Against War* (1984) and *The Struggle Against the Bomb* (1993–   ); Valarie H. Ziegler, *The Advocates of Peace in Antebellum America* (1992). See also specific wars.

Pearl Harbor, 1941: Stanley L. Falk, "Pearl Harbor," *Naval History* (1988) (B); Robert W. Love, Jr., ed., *Pearl Harbor Reexamined* (1990); Martin V. Melosi, *The Shadow of Pearl Harbor* (1977); Frank P. Mintz, *Revisionism and the Origins of Pearl Harbor* (1985); James W. Morley, ed., *The First Confrontation* (1995); Gordon W. Prange, *Pearl Harbor* (1986); Myron J. Smith, Jr., *Pearl Harbor* (1991) (B). Also see "World War II."

Philanthropy and Foundations: Robert Arnove, *Philanthropy and Cultural Imperialism* (1980); Edward H. Berman, *The Influence of the Carnegie, Ford, and Rockefeller Foundations on American Foreign Policy* (1983); Marcos Cueto, ed., *Missionaries of Science: The Rockefeller Foundation and Latin America* (1994); Merle Curti, *American Philanthropy Abroad* (1963); Robert L. Daniel, *American Philanthropy in the Near East, 1820–1960* (1970); Raymond Fosdick, *The Story of the Rockefeller Foundation* (1989). See also "Cultural Relations" and Cobbs in "Brazil."

Population: *The Encyclopedia of Global Population and Demographics* (1998) (E); William Peterson and Renee Peterson, *Dictionary of Demography* (1986) (E).

President (General): James Barber, *The Presidential Character* (1992); E. S. Corwin, *The President* (1957); Robert A. Divine, *Foreign Policy and U.S. Presidential Elections, 1940–1960* (1974); Robert U. Goehlert and Fenton S. Martin, *The Presidency* (1985) (B); George T. Kurian, *A Historical Guide to the U.S. Government* (1997) (E); Leonard W. Levy and Louis Fisher, eds., *Encyclopedia of the American Presidency* (1993) (E); Theodore Lowi, *The Personal President* (1985); John E. Mueller, *War, Presidents, and Public Opinion* (1973); Richard E. Neustadt, *Presidential Power and the Modern Presidents* (1990); Arthur M. Schlesinger, Jr., *The Imperial Presidency* (1973); Robert Sobel, ed., *Biographical Directory of the United States Executive Branch, 1774–1977* (1977) (BA). See also "Bureaucracy," "Congress (House and Senate)," "Constitution and Constitutional Interpretation," "Health and Medical History of Leaders," "Presidents (By Administration)," and "War Powers."

Presidents (By Administration): Harry Ammon, *James Monroe* (1991) (B); Peter H. Buckingham, *Woodrow Wilson* (1989) (B); Richard Dean Burns, *Harry S. Truman* (1984) (B); John Ferling, *John Adams* (1993) (B); James N. Giglio, *John F. Kennedy* (1995) (B); Otis L. Graham, Jr., and Meghan R. Wander, eds., *Franklin D. Roosevelt* (1985) (E); John R. Greene, *Gerald R. Ford* (1994) (B); Richard S. Kirkendall, ed., *The Harry S. Truman Encyclopedia* (1989) (E); Peter B. Levy, *Encyclopedia of the Reagan-Bush Years* (1996) (E); Merrill D. Peterson, *Thomas Jefferson* (1986) (E); Robert A. Rutland, ed., *James Madison and the American Nation* (1994) (E). See also "Health and Medical History of Leaders" and "President (General)."

Privateering: Donald B. Chidsey, *The American Privateers* (1962); Reuben E. Stivers, *Privateers and Volunteers* (1975); Carl E. Swanson, *Predators and Prizes* (1991). See also "Navy and Sea Power."

Propaganda and Public Diplomacy: Leo Bogart, *Premises for Propaganda* (1976) (USIA); Robert Cole, *The Encyclopedia of Propaganda* (1997) (E); Robert E. Elder, *The Information Machine* (1968); Walter Hixson, *Parting the Curtain* (1997); Alexandre Lauien, *The Voice of America* (1988); Gifford Malone, *Political Advocacy and Cultural Communication* (1988); Jarol B. Manheim, *Strategic Public Diplomacy and American Foreign Policy* (1994); Sig Mickelson, *America's Other Voice*

(1983); Michael Nelson, *War of the Black Heavens: The Battles of Western Broadcasting in the Cold War* (1997); Holly C. Shulman, *The Voice of America* (1990); Thomas C. Sorensen, *The Word War* (1968); Allen M. Winkler, *The Politics of Propaganda* (1978). See also "Communications," "Cultural Relations," and "Fulbright Program."

Public Opinion: Richard J. Barnet, *The Rockets' Red Glare* (1990); Bernard C. Cohen, *The Public's Impact on Foreign Policy* (1973); H. Schuyler Foster, *Activism Replaces Isolationism: U.S. Public Attitudes, 1940–1975* (1983); George Gallup, *The Gallup Poll: Public Opinion* (1972–   ) (AS and S); Ole R. Holsti, *Public Opinion and American Foreign Policy* (1996); Ralph B. Levering, *The Public and American Foreign Policy* (1978); David D. Newsom, *The Public Dimension of Foreign Policy* (1996); Melvin Small, *Democracy and Diplomacy* (1996). See also "Journalism and Media" and "President (General)."

Race and Racism: Michael L. Krenn, ed., *Race and U.S. Foreign Policy* (1998); Paul Gordon Lauren, *Power and Prejudice* (1988); Hazel M. McFerson, *The Racial Dimension of American Overseas Colonial Policy* (1997); George E. Shepherd, ed., *Racial Influence on American Foreign Policy* (1971); Jay A. Sigler, ed., *International Handbook on Race and Race Relations* (1987) (E); Rubin F. Weston, *Racism in U.S. Imperialism* (1972). See also "African Americans," "Ethnic Groups and Immigration," "Ideology," and "Manifest Destiny."

Recognition Policy: Thomas M. Franck, *The Power of Legitimacy Among Nations* (1990); L. Thomas Galloway, *Recognizing Foreign Governments* (1978).

Red Cross: Nicholas O. Berry, *War and the Red Cross* (1997); Pierre Bossier, *From Solferino to Tsushima* (1985); John F. Hutchinson, *Champions of Charity* (1996). See also "Humanitarian Relief and Intervention."

Refugees: Anna Bramwell, ed., *Refugees in the Age of Total War* (1988); Gil Loescher, *Beyond Charity* (1993); Gil Loescher and John A. Scalan, *Calculated Kindness* (1986); J. Bruce Nichols, *The Uneasy Alliance: Religion, Refugee Work, and U.S. Foreign Policy* (1988); Michael S. Teitelbaum and Myron Weiner, eds., *Threatened Peoples, Threatened Borders* (1995); U.S. Committee on Refugees, *World Refugee Survey* (1980–   ) (AS). See also "Ethnic Groups and Immigration," "Holocaust," and "Humanitarian Relief and Intervention."

Rivers: *Rand McNally Encyclopedia of World Rivers* (1980) (E).

Scientists and Science: Robert Gilpin and Christopher Wright, eds., *Scientists and National Policy-making* (1964); Greta Jones, *Science, Politics and the Cold War* (1988); Clarence Lasby, *Operation Paperclip*

(1971); Joseph Rotblat, ed., *Scientists, the Arms Race, and Disarmament* (1982); Alice K. Smith, *A Peril and a Hope: The Scientists' Movement in the United States, 1945–47* (1965). See also "Nuclear Arms."

Sectionalism: Peter Trubowitz, *Defining the National Interest* (1998). See also "The South (U.S.)."

Self-Determination: Antonio Cassese, *Self-Determination of Peoples* (1995); David B. Knight and Maureen Davies, *Self-Determination* (1988) (B).

Slave Trade and Slavery: Randall Miller and John Smith, eds., *Dictionary of Afro-American Slavery* (1988) (E); Junius P. Rodriguez, ed., *The Historical Encyclopedia of World Slavery* (1997) (E).

The South (U.S.): Alfred Hero, *The Southerner and World Affairs* (1965); Charles O. Lerche, *The Uncertain South* (1964); Tennant S. McWilliams, *The New South Faces the World* (1988).

Space and Satellites: William E. Burrows, *Deep Black* (1986); Walter A. McDougall, *The Heavens and the Earth* (1985); Jeffrey T. Richelson, *America's Secret Eyes in Space* (1990); Paul B. Stares, *The Militarization of Space* (1985). See also "Nuclear Arms."

Spanish-American-Cuban-Filipino War: Benjamin R. Beede, ed., *The War of 1898 and U.S. Interventions, 1899–1934* (1994) (B); James C. Bradford, ed., *Crucible of Empire* (1993); Louis A. Peréz, Jr., *The War of 1898* (1998); Anne C. Venzon, *The Spanish-American War* (1990) (B). Also see "Cuba," "Military, U.S. Army, and Wars," and "Spain."

Sports: Allen Guttmann, *Games and Empires* (1994). See also "Olympics."

Summit Conferences: Keith Eubank, *The Summit Conference* (1966); Elmer Plischke, *Diplomat in Chief* (1986) and *Summit Diplomacy* (1958); Robert D. Putnam and Nicholas Bayne, *Hanging Together: The Seven-Power Summits* (1984); Gordon R. Weihmiller and Dusko Doder, *U.S.-Soviet Summits* (1986). See also "Cold War."

Tariffs and Protectionism: David A. Lake, *Power, Protection, and Free Trade* (1988); James M. Lutz, *Protectionism* (1988) (B); Robert A. Pastor, *Congress and the Politics of U.S. Foreign Economic Policy, 1929–1976* (1980); Sidney Ratner, *The Tariff in American History* (1972); Frank W. Taussig, *Tariff History of the United States* (1931); Tom E. Terrill, *The Tariff, Politics, and American Foreign Policy, 1874–1901* (1973); Paul Wolman, *Most Favored Nation* (1992); Thomas Zeiler, *American Trade and Power in the 1960s* (1992). See also

"Economic Relations and Business" and "Economic Sanctions and Export Controls."

Telecommunications: See "Communications."

Terrorism: Martha Crenshaw and John Pimlott, eds., *Encyclopedia of World Terrorism* (1996) (E); Christopher Dobson and Ronald Payne, *The Never Ending War* (1987); Lawrence Freedman et al., *Terrorism and International Order* (1986); Robert Kumamoto, *International Terrorism and American Foreign Relations, 1945–1976* (1999); Walter Laqueur, *The Age of Terrorism* (1987); Edward F. Mickolus et al., *International Terrorism in the 1980s* (1989) (C), *Terrorism, 1988–1991* (1993) (C), and *Transnational Terrorism . . . , 1968–1979* (1980) (C); Suzanne R. Ontiveros, *Global Terrorism* (1986) (B); Barry Rubin, ed., *The Politics of Terrorism* (1990); Jeffrey D. Simon, *The Terrorist Trap* (1994); John R. Thackrah, *Encyclopedia of Terrorism and Political Violence* (1987) (E).

Threat Perception and Calculation: Noel E. Firth and James H. Noren, *Soviet Defense Spending: A History of CIA Estimates, 1950–1990* (1998); Robert H. Johnson, *Improbable Dangers* (1994). See also "Cold War."

Think Tanks: Donald E. Abelson, *American Think-Tanks and Their Role in US Foreign Policy, 1976–88* (1996); Peter Grose, *Continuing the Inquiry* (1996); David M. Ricci, *The Transformation of American Politics* (1993); Robert D. Schulzinger, *The Wise Men of Foreign Affairs: The History of the Council on Foreign Relations* (1984); Christopher Simpson, ed., *Universities and Empire: Money and Politics in the Social Sciences During the Cold War* (1999); Bruce L. R. Smith, *The Rand Corporation* (1966); James A. Smith, *The Idea Brokers* (1991); Michael Wala, *The Council on Foreign Relations and American Foreign Policy in the Early Cold War* (1994).

Tourism and Travel: James Clifford, *Routes* (1997); Foster Rhea Dulles, *Americans Abroad* (1964); Cynthia Enloe, *Bananas, Beaches, and Bases* (1990); Maxine Fieffer, *Tourism in History* (1985); Marie-Françoise Lanfant et al., *International Tourism* (1995); Sara Mills, *Discourses of Difference* (1991); David Spurr, *The Rhetoric of Empire* (1993); John Urry, *The Tourist Gaze* (1990).

Trade: See "Economic Relations and Business," "Economic Sanctions and Export Controls," "Tariffs and Protectionism," "United States Trade Representative," and "World Trade Organization (WTO)."

United Nations: Joseph P. Baratta, *Strengthening the United Nations* (1987) (B); Robert A. Divine, *Second Chance* (1967); Seymour M.

Finger, *American Ambassadors at the United Nations* (1987); Thomas M. Frank, *Nation Against Nation* (1985); Max Harrelson, *Fires All Around the Horizon* (1989); Robert C. Hilderbrand, *Dumbarton Oaks* (1990); Evan Luard and Derek Herter, *The United Nations* (1993); Kumiko Matsuura et al., *Chronology and Fact Book of the United Nations, 1941–1991* (1992) (C); Edmund Jan Osmanczyk, *The Encyclopedia of the United Nations and International Relations* (1990) (E); Gary B. Ostrower, *The United States and the United Nations* (1998); William Preston, Jr., et al., *Hope and Folly* (1989) (UNESCO); Caroline Pruden, *Conditional Partners* (1998). See also "International Organizations," "League of Nations," and "Peacekeeping."

United States Trade Representative: Steve Dryden, *Trade Warriors* (1995). See also "Economic Relations and Business."

Vietnam War: See "Vietnam and Southeast Asia."

War Crimes and Trials: Richard L. Lael, *The Yamashita Precedent: War Crimes and Command Responsibility* (1982); John R. Lewis, *Uncertain Judgment* (1979) (B); Philip R. Piccigallo, *The Japanese on Trial* (1979); Telford Taylor, *Nuremberg and Vietnam* (1970); Norman E. Tutorow, ed., *War Crimes, War Criminals, and War Crimes Trials* (1986) (B). See also "Germany and Berlin," "Holocaust," "Human Rights," and "Japan."

War of 1812: John C. Fredriksen, *Free Trade and Sailors' Rights* (1985) (B); Dwight L. Smith, *The War of 1812* (1985) (B). See also "Military, U.S. Army, and Wars."

War Powers: Louis Fischer, *Presidential War Power* (1995); Christopher N. May, *In the Name of War* (1989); Gary M. Stein and Morton H. Halperin, eds., *The U.S. Constitution and the Power to Go to War* (1994); John H. Sullivan, *The War Powers Resolution* (1982); Francis D. Wormuth and Edwin B. Firmage, *To Chain the Dog of War* (1989). See also "Congress (House and Senate)," "Constitution and Constitutional Interpretation," and "President (General)."

West (U.S.) and Frontier: William A. Beck and Ynez D. Haase, *Historical Atlas of the American West* (1989) (A); William Goetzmann and Glyndwr Williams, *The Atlas of North American Exploration* (1992) (A); J. Norman Heard, *Handbook of the American Frontier* (1987) (E); Adrian Johnson, *America Explored* (1974) (E); Howard R. Lamar, ed., *The New Encyclopedia of the American West* (1998) (E); Clyde A. Milner III et al., eds., *The Oxford History of the American West* (1994) (E); Charles Phillips and Alan Axelrod, eds., *Encyclopedia of the American West* (1996) (E); Dan L. Thrapp, *The Encyclopedia of Frontier Biography* (1988–   ) (BA).

Whaling: Daniel Francis, *A History of World Whaling* (1990); Alexander Sarbuck, *History of the American Whale Fishery* (1989). See also "Environment."

World Bank: Devesh Kapur et al., *The World Bank* (1997).

World Cities: Immanuel Ness, *Encyclopedia of World Cities* (1998).

World Health Organization: See "Health Organizations."

World Trade Organization (WTO): Bernard Hoekman and Michel Kostecki, *The Political Economy of the World Trading System* (1996). Also see "Economic Relations and Business."

Women and Gender Issues: Homer L. Calkin, *Women in the Department of State* (1978); Edward P. Crapol, ed., *Women and American Foreign Policy* (1992); John A. Edens, *Eleanor Roosevelt* (1994) (B); Rebecca Grant and Kathleen Newland, eds., *Gender and International Relations* (1991); Human Rights Watch, *Global Report on Women's Human Rights* (1995); Rhodri Jeffreys-Jones, *Changing Differences* (1995); Nancy W. McGlen and Meredith Reid Sarkes, *Women in Foreign Policy* (1993). See also "Peace Movements."

World Court: Michael Dunne, *The United States and the World Court, 1920–1935* (1988); D. F. Fleming, *The United States and the World Court* (1945); Shabtai Rosenne, *The World Court* (1989) (E). See also "International Law and Hague Conferences."

World's Fairs: John E. Findling, ed., *Historical Dictionary of World's Fairs and Expositions* (1990); Robert H. Haddow, *Pavilions of Plenty* (1997); Robert W. Rydell, *All the World's a Fair* (1987) and *World of Fairs* (1993); Robert W. Rydell and Nancy Gwinn, eds, *Fair Representations* (1994). See also "Cultural Relations" and "Propaganda and Public Diplomacy."

World-System Analysis: Thomas J. McCormick, *America's Half-Century* (1995); Immanuel Wallerstein, *Geopolitics and Geoculture* (1991), *The Modern World-System* (1974), *Politics of the World-Economy* (1984), and *World Inequality* (1975). See also "Dependency."

World War I: Arthur Banks, *A Military History Atlas of the First World War* (1975) (A); Martin Gilbert, *Atlas of World War I* (1994) (A); Holger H. Herwig and Neil M. Heyman, *Biographical Dictionary of World War I* (1982) (BA); George T. Kurian, *Encyclopedia of the First World War* (1990) (E); Stephen Pope and Elizabeth-Anne Wheal, *The Dictionary of the First World War* (1995) (E); Anne C. Venzon, ed., *The United States and the First World War* (1995) (B). See also "Military, U.S. Army, and Wars."

World War II: Marcel Baudot et al., eds., *The Historical Encyclopedia of World War II* (1980) (E); David G. Chandler and James Lawton Collins, Jr., eds., *The D-Day Encyclopedia* (1983) (E); I. C. B. Dear and M. R. D. Foot, eds., *The Oxford Companion to World War II* (1995) (E); Robert Goralski, *World War II Almanac* (1981) (C); John Keegan, ed., *The Times Atlas of the Second World War* (1989) (A); Norman Polmar and Thomas B. Allen, *World War II* (1991) (E); John J. Sbrega, *The War Against Japan* (1989) (B); Ronald Spector, "The Scholarship on World War II," *Journal of Military History* (1991) (B); U.S. Military Academy, *Campaign Atlas to the Second World War* (1980) (A); Peter Young, ed., *Atlas of the Second World War* (1973) (A); David T. Zabecki, *World War II in Europe* (1997) (E). See also "Military, U.S. Army, and Wars."

Index